ACCOUNTING
THEORY
TEXT AND READINGS

ACCOUNTING

THEORY

TEXT AND READINGS

Fifth Edition

Richard G. Schroeder
University of North Carolina at Charlotte

Myrtle Clark
University of Kentucky

John Wiley & Sons, Inc.
New York • Chichester • Brisbane • Toronto • Singapore

Cover photo by David Sutherland/Tony Stone Images

Acquisitions Editor	Mike Reynolds
Marketing Manager	Karen Allman
Senior Production Editor	Jennifer Knapp
Design Coordinator	Laura Nicholls
Manufacturing Manager	Susan Stetzer
Illustration Freelance Coordinator	Gene Aiello

This book was set in 9.5 × 27 Meridien by Achorn Graphic Services and printed and bound by Courier Stoughton. The cover was printed by Lehigh Press.

Library of Congress Cataloging-in-Publication Data
Accounting theory : text and readings / [edited by] Richard G.
   Schroeder, Myrtle Clark, Levis D. McCullers. — 5th ed.
        p.   cm.
     Includes bibliographical references and index.
     ISBN 0-471-30532-4
     1. Accounting.   2. Accounting—Problems, exercises, etc.
   I. Schroeder, Richard G.   II. Clark, Myrtle.   III. McCullers, Levis
   D., 1936–   .

   HF5625.A25   1995
   657—dc20   94-3616
                                                         CIP

Printed in the United States of America

10   9   8   7   6   5   4   3   2   1

Preface

The major objective of this fifth edition is to provide accounting students a theoretical background with which to evaluate current accounting practice. This edition represents a major revision from its predecessors and is designed to suit the needs of accounting professionals into the 21st century. Additional material has been added on the historical development of accounting. The approaches to accounting theory, theories on the uses of accounting information and the Conceptual Framework project are presented at the beginning of the text, and serve as the framework for the discussion of various issues throughout the book.

Accounting education has experienced dramatic changes over the life of this accounting theory text. At its inception, much of what was then considered theory was in reality rule memorization. In recent years, external and internal pressures have emerged that are influencing how accounting is taught. Emphasis is now being given to the development of critical thinking skills, the incorporation of ethics into the curriculum, the development of communication skills, and the use of group projects to develop cooperative skills. Among the changes in this edition that were designed to address these new emphases are:

1. Greater emphasis on the relationship of the approaches to theory development with each of the topics discussed throughout the text.

2. Early coverage of theories on the uses of accounting information including: the efficient market hypothesis, agency theory, the capital asset pricing model, human information processing, and critical perspective research.

3. Integration of these theories on the uses of accounting information with various topics throughout the text.

4. Expanded coverage of the FASB's Conceptual Framework project, and a discussion of the relationship of this material to various topics throughout the text.

5. A new section on ethics.

6. Expanded coverage of international accounting.

7. The inclusion of 15 new replacement articles.

8. The inclusion of many cases at the end of each chapter.

As with earlier editions, each chapter contains one or two readings from the ever expanding accounting literature. Each of these readings was selected to provide additional explanation of a particularly complex topic, or to provide a dissenting opinion from existing generally accepted accounting principles. In using these readings we have found it useful to ask the student to answer the following questions:

1. What is the issue the author(s) is addressing?
2. What methodology did the author(s) use to address the issue?
3. Did the author(s) clearly and adequately illustrate the solution?
4. Were you convinced of the author(s)' proposed treatment or solution?

As noted above, each chapter also contains a number of cases. These cases are designed to improve critical thinking skills, and many can be used as group projects to be communicated to the class. In several cases additional research is suggested to assist in solving the cases and specific references are included.

We are indebted to many colleagues whose comments and criticisms contributed to the fifth edition, and we single out for special thanks: Linda Bowen, University of North Carolina at Chapel Hill; Gyan Chandra, Miami University; Don Deis, Louisiana State University; Harry Dickinson; Dan Edwards, Indiana University—Purdue University at Fort Wayne; Ann Gibson, Andrews University; Joseph Hilmy, George Washington University; Anna Lee Meador, Marshall University; Wilda Meixner, Southwest Texas State University; Barbara Shiarappa, Trenton State College; Kevin Stevens, DePaul University; and Ray Thoren, State University of New York at Plattsburgh. We are also indebted to our research assistant Dessa Bergquist; her contributions were invaluable, as was the assistance provided by our typists Elizabeth Brown and Velma Prunner. Appreciation is also extended to our editorial and production team including Mike Reynolds, Tracy Fisher, Jennifer Knapp, Edward Winkleman, and Genevieve Scandone.

Contents

vii

The
Development of
Accounting
Theory

In its simplest form theory may be just a belief, but in order for a theory to be useful it must have wide acceptance. Webster defines theory as: "a systematic statement of principles . . ." and "a formulation of apparent relationships or underlying principles of certain observed phenomena which has been verified to some degree. . . ."[1] The objective of theory is to explain and predict. Consequently, one of the basic goals of the theory of a particular discipline is to have a well-defined body of knowledge that has been systematically accumulated, organized, and verified well enough to provide a frame of reference for future actions.

Theories may be described as normative or positive. Normative theories explain what should be, whereas positive theories explain what is. Ideally, there should be no such distinction because a well-developed and complete theory encompasses both what should be and what is.

The goal of accounting theory is to provide a set of principles and relationships that provide an explanation for observed practices and predict unobserved practices. That is, accounting theory should be able to explain why business organizations elect certain accounting methods over other alternatives and predict the attributes of firms that elect various accounting methods. Accounting theory should also be verifiable through accounting research.

The development of a general theory of accounting is important because of the role accounting plays in our economic society. We live in a capitalistic society, which is characterized by a self-regulated market that operates through the forces of supply and demand. Goods and services are available for purchase in markets, and individuals are free to enter or exit the market

---

[1] *Webster's New Universal Unabridged Dictionary,* 2nd ed. (New York: Simon & Schuster, 1983).

to pursue their economic goals. All societies are constrained by scarce resources that limit the attainment of all individual or group economic goals. The role of accounting in our society is to report how organizations utilize scarce resources and the status of resources and claims to resources.

As discussed in more detail in Chapter 2, there are various "theories of accounting" including: the efficient markets hypothesis, the capital asset pricing model, the human information processing model, positive accounting theory, and the critical perspective model. These various and often competing theories exist because accounting theory is still in its developmental stage.

Accounting research is needed to attain a more general theory of accounting. The various theories of accounting must be subjected to verification. A critical question concerns the usefulness of accounting data to users. That is, does the use of a theory help decision makers make more correct decisions? Various suggestions on the empirical testing of accounting theories have been offered.[2] As theories are tested and either confirmed or discarded, we will move closer to a general theory of accounting.

The Early History of Accounting

Accounting records dating back several thousand years have been found in various parts of the world. These records indicate that at all levels of development people desire information about their efforts and accomplishments. For example, the Zenon papyri, which were discovered in 1915, contain information about the construction projects, agricultural activities, and business operations of the private estate of Apollonius for a period of about 30 years during the third century B.C.

According to Hain, "The Zenon papyri give evidence of a surprisingly elaborate accounting system which had been used in Greece since the fifth century B.C. and which, in the wake of Greek trade or conquest, gradually spread throughout the Eastern Mediterranean and Middle East."[3] The accounting system used by Zenon contained provisions for responsibility accounting, a written record of all transactions, a personal account for wages paid to employees, inventory records, and a record of asset acquisitions and disposals. In addition, there is evidence that all the accounts were audited.[4]

Later, the Romans kept elaborate records, but since they expressed numbers by letters of the alphabet, they were not able to develop any structured system of accounting. It was not until the Renaissance period, approximately 1300–1500, when the Italians were vigorously pursuing trade and commerce, that the need to keep accurate records was felt. Italian merchants borrowed the Arabic numeral system and the basis of arithmetic, and an evolving trend toward the double-entry bookkeeping system we now use developed.

[2] See for example, Robert Sterling, "On Theory Structure and Verification," *The Accounting Review* (July 1970), pp. 444–457.

[3] H. P. Hain, "Accounting Control in the Zenon Papyri," *The Accounting Review* (October 1966), p. 699.

[4] Ibid., pp. 700–701.

In 1494 an Italian monk, Fra Luca Pacioli, wrote a book on arithmetic that included a description of double-entry bookkeeping. Pacioli's work *Summa de Arithmetica Geometria Proportioni et Proportioinalita,* did not fully describe double-entry bookkeeping, but rather formalized the practices and ideas that had been evolving over the years. Double-entry bookkeeping enabled business organizations to keep complete records of transactions and ultimately resulted in the ability to prepare financial statements.

Statements of profit and loss and statements of balances emerged about 1600.[5] Initially, the primary motive for separate financial statements was to obtain information regarding capital. Consequently, balance sheet data were stressed and refined in various ways, while expense and income data were viewed as incidental.[6]

As ongoing business organizations replaced isolated ventures, it became necessary to develop accounting records and reports that reflected a continuing investment of capital employed in various ways and to periodically summarize the results of activities. By the 19th century, bookkeeping expanded into accounting, and the concept that the owner's original contribution, plus or minus profits or losses, indicated net worth emerged. However, profit was considered an increase in assets from any source, as the concepts of cost and income were yet to be developed.

Another factor that influenced the development of accounting during the 19th century was the evolution of joint ventures into business corporations in England. The fact that many individuals, external to the business, needed information about the corporation's activities created the necessity for periodic reports. Additionally, the continuing existence of corporations created the need to distinguish between capital and income.

The statutory establishment of corporations in England in 1845 stimulated the development of accounting standards, and laws were subsequently passed that were designed to safeguard shareholders against improper actions by corporate officers. Dividends were required to be paid from profits, and accounts were required to be kept and audited by persons other than the directors. However, initially anyone could claim to be an accountant, as there were no organized professions or standards of qualifications.

The industrial revolution and the succession of Companies Acts in England also served to increase the need for professional standards and accountants. In the later part of the 19th century, the industrial revolution arrived in the United States, and with it came the need for more formal accounting procedures and standards. This period was also characterized by widespread speculation in the securities markets, watered stocks, and large monopolies that controlled segments of the United States economy.

In the late 1800s the progressive movement was established in the United States, and in 1898 the Industrial Commission was formed to investigate and report on questions relating to immigration, labor, agriculture, manufacturing,

[5] A. C. Littleton, *Accounting Evolution to 1900* (New York: AICPA, 1933).

[6] John L. Cary, *The Rise of the Accounting Profession* (New York: AICPA, 1969), p. 5.

and business. Although no accountants were either on the Commission or used by the Commission, a preliminary report issued in 1900 suggested that an independent public accounting profession should be established in order to curtail observed corporate abuses.

Although most accountants did not necessarily subscribe to the desirability of the progressive reforms, the progressive movement conferred specific social obligations on accountants.[7] As a consequence accountants generally came to accept three general levels of progressiveness: (1) a fundamental faith in democracy, a concern for morality and justice and a broad acceptance of the efficiency of education as a major tool in social amelioration; (2) an increased awareness of the social obligation of all segments of society and introduction of the idea of accountability to the public of business and political leaders; and (3) an acceptance of pragmatism as the most relevant operative philosophy of the day.[8]

The major concern of accounting during the early 1900s was the development of a theory that could cope with corporate abuses that were occurring at that time, and capital maintenance emerged as a concept. This concept evolved from maintaining invested capital intact, to the maintenance of the physical productive capacity of the firm, to the maintenance of real capital. In essence this last view of capital maintenance was an extension of the economic concept of income (see Chapter 3) that there could be no increase in wealth unless the stockholder or the firm were better off at the end of the period than at the beginning.

During the period 1900–1915 the concept of income determination was not well developed. There was, however, a debate over which financial statement should be viewed as most important, the balance sheet or the income statement. Implicit in this debate was the view that either the balance sheet or the income statement must be viewed as fundamental and the other residual, and that relevant values could not be disclosed in both statements.

The 1904 International Congress of Accountants marked the initial development of the organized accounting profession in the United States, although there had been earlier attempts to organize and several states had state societies. At this meeting, the American Association of Public Accountants was formed as the professional organization of accountants in the United States. In 1916, after a decade of bitter interfactional disputes, this group was reorganized into the American Institute of Accountants (AIA).

The American Association of the University Instructors in Accounting was also formed in 1916. Initially this group focused on matters of curriculum development, and it was not until much later that it attempted to become involved in the development of accounting theory.

World War I changed the public's attitude toward the business sector. Many people believed that the successful completion of the war could be,

---

[7] Gary John Previts and Barbara Dubis Merino, *A History of Accounting in America* (New York, Ronald Press, 1979), p. 136.

[8] Richard Hofstadter, *Social Darwinism in American Thought* (Philadelphia, University of Pennsylvania Press, 1944).

at least partially, attributed to the ingenuity of American businesses. As a consequence, the public perceived that business had reformed, and external regulation was no longer necessary. The accountant's role changed from a protector of third parties to the protector of business interests.

Critics of accounting theory during the 1920s suggested that accountants abdicated the stewardship role, placed too much emphasis on the needs of management, and permitted too much flexibility in financial reporting. During this time financial statements were viewed as the representations of management, and accountants did not have the ability to require businesses to use accounting principles they did not wish to employ.

The result of this attitude is well known. In 1929 the stock market crashed and the Great Depression ensued. Although accountants were not initially blamed for these events, the possibility of governmental intervention in the corporate sector loomed.

Accounting in the United States Since 1930

One of the first attempts at improving accounting began shortly after the inception of the Great Depression with a series of meetings between representatives of the New York Stock Exchange (NYSE) and the American Institute of Accountants. The purpose of these meetings was to discuss problems pertaining to the interests of investors, the NYSE, and accountants in the preparation of external financial statements.

Similarly, in 1935 the American Association of University Instructors in Accounting changed its name to the American Accounting Association (AAA) and announced its intention to expand its activities in the research and development of accounting principles and standards. The first result of these expanded activities was the publication, in 1936, of a brief report cautiously titled "A Tentative Statement of Accounting Principles Underlying Corporate Financial Statements." The four-and-one-half-page document summarized the significant concepts underlying financial statements at that time.

The cooperative efforts between the members of the NYSE and the AIA were well received. However, the post-Depression atmosphere in the United States was characterized by regulation. There was even legislation introduced that would have required auditors to be licensed by the federal government after passing a civil service examination.

Two of the most important pieces of legislation passed at this time were the Securities Act of 1933, and the Securities Exchange Act of 1934, that established the Securities and Exchange Commission (SEC). The SEC was created to administer various securities acts. Under powers provided by Congress, the SEC was given the authority to prescribe accounting principles and reporting practices. Although this authority has seldom been used, the SEC has exerted pressure on the accounting profession and has been especially interested in narrowing areas of difference in accounting practice. The role of the SEC is discussed in more detail in Chapter 16.

By 1937 the view was prevalent that if accountants did not come up with answers to issues the SEC would. The profession was also convinced that it did not have the time necessary to develop a theoretical framework of accounting. As a result, the AIA agreed to publish the study by Sanders, Hatfield, and Moore titled *A Statement of Accounting Principles.*

The publication of this work was quite controversial in that it was simply a survey of existing practice that was seen as telling practicing accountants "do what you think is best." The study was also used by some accountants as an authoritative source that justified current practice.

In 1937 the AIA merged with the American Society of Certified Public Accountants and a new, larger organization later named the American Institute of Certified Public Accountants (AICPA) was formed. This organization has had increasing influence over the development of accounting theory.

Over the years, the AICPA established several committees and boards to deal with the need for the further development of accounting principles. First, the Committee on Accounting Procedure (CAP) was established. It was followed by the Accounting Principles Board (APB), which was replaced by the Financial Accounting Standards Board (FASB). Each of these bodies has issued pronouncements on accounting issues. In each case the pronouncements apply to current and future financial statements and are not intended to be applied retroactively unless the pronouncement makes retroactive presentation mandatory.

Committee on Accounting Procedure

Professional accountants became more actively involved in the development of accounting principles following the meetings between members of the New York Stock Exchange and the AICPA and the controversy surrounding the publication of the Sanders, Hatfield, and Moore study. In 1938 the AICPA's Committee on Accounting Procedure was formed. This committee had the authority to issue pronouncements on matters of accounting practice and procedure in order to establish generally accepted practices. The works of the committee were published in the form of *Accounting Research Bulletins* (*ARBs*); however, these pronouncements did not dictate mandatory practice and received authority only from their general acceptance.

The *ARBs* were consolidated in 1953 into *Accounting Terminology Bulletin No. 1*, "Review and Resume"[9] and *ARB No. 43.*[10] From 1953 until 1959 *ARBs No. 44* through *No. 51* were published. The recommendations of these bulletins, which have not been superseded, are contained throughout this text where the specific topics covered by the ARBs are discussed.

Accounting Principles Board

By 1959 the methods of formulating accounting principles were being criticized, and wider representation in the development of accounting principles

---

[9] *Accounting Terminology Bulletin No. 1*, "Review and Resume" (New York: AICPA, 1953).

[10] *Accounting Research Bulletin No. 43*, "Restatement and Revision of Accounting Research Bulletins" (New York: AICPA, 1953).

was sought by accountants and financial statement users. The AICPA reacted by forming the Accounting Principles Board (APB). This body had as its objectives the advancement of the written expression of generally accepted accounting principles, the narrowing of areas of difference in appropriate practice, and the discussion of unsettled and controversial issues. The APB was comprised of between 17 and 21 members who were selected primarily from the accounting profession but also included individuals from industry, government, and academia.

Initially, the pronouncements of the APB that were termed "Opinions" were not mandatory practice; however, the issuance of *APB Opinion No. 2*[11] and subsequent partial retraction contained in *APB Opinion No. 4*[12] highlighted the need for more authority. This controversy was due to differences in accounting for the investment tax credit. In 1961 the investment tax credit was passed by Congress. This legislation provided for a direct tax reduction based on a percentage of the cost of a qualified investment. The APB, after a review of the accounting requirements of this legislation, issued *APB Opinion No. 2*, which stated that this tax reduction amounted to a cost reduction, and the effects of this cost reduction should be amortized over the useful life of the asset acquired. Nevertheless, several large public accounting firms decided to report the results of the investment tax credit only in the period in which it occurred. The APB was thus faced with a serious threat to its authority.

The lack of general acceptance of *APB Opinion No. 2* resulted in the APB partially retreating from its previous position. Though reaffirming the previous decision as being the proper and most appropriate treatment, *APB Opinion No. 4* approved the use of either of the two methods.

The lack of support for some of the APB's pronouncements and concern over the formulation and acceptance of "generally accepted accounting principles" caused the Council of the American Institute of Certified Public Accountants to adopt Rule 203 of the Code of Professional Ethics. This rule requires departures from accounting principles published in *APB Opinions* or *Accounting Research Bulletins* (or subsequently *FASB Statements*) to be disclosed in footnotes to financial statements or in independent auditors' reports when the effects of such departures are material. This action has had the effect of requiring companies and public accountants who deviated from *FASB Statements*, *APB Opinions*, and *Accounting Research Bulletins* to justify such departures.

In addition to the difficulties associated with the passage of *APB Opinions No. 2* and *No. 4*, the Accounting Principles Board encountered other problems. The members of the APB were, in effect, volunteers. These individuals had full-time responsibilities to their employers; therefore, the performance of their duties on the APB became secondary. By the late 1960s criticism of the development of accounting principles again arose. This criticism centered on the following factors.

[11] *Accounting Principles Board Opinion No. 2*, "Accounting for the 'Investment Credit'" (New York: AICPA, 1962).

[12] *Accounting Principles Board Opinion No. 4*, "Accounting for the 'Investment Credit'" (New York: AICPA, 1964).

1. The independence of the members of the APB. The individuals serving on the board had full-time responsibilities elsewhere that might have an impact on their views of certain issues.
2. The structure of the board. The largest eight public accounting firms (at that time) were automatically awarded one member and there were usually five or six other public accountants on the APB.
3. Response time. The emerging accounting problems were not being investigated and solved quickly enough by the part-time members.

The Financial Accounting Standards Board

As a result of the growing criticism of the APB, the board of directors of the AICPA appointed two committees in 1971. The Wheat Committee, named after its chairman, Francis Wheat, was to study how financial accounting principles should be established. The Trueblood Committee, named after its chairman, Robert Trueblood, was to determine the objectives of financial statements.

The Wheat Committee issued its report in 1972 with a recommendation that the APB be abolished and the Financial Accounting Standards Board (FASB) be created. This new board was to be composed of representatives from various organizations, in contrast to the APB, whose members were all from the AICPA. The members of the FASB were also to be paid and were to work full time, unlike the APB members, who served part time and were not paid.

The Trueblood Committee, formally known as the Study Group on Objectives of Financial Statements, issued its report in 1973 after substantial debate and with considerably more tentativeness in its recommendations about objectives than the Wheat Committee had with respect to the establishment of principles. The study group requested that its report be regarded as an initial step in developing objectives and that significant efforts should be made to continue progress on the refinement and improvement of accounting standards and practices. The objectives enumerated by the Trueblood Committee later became the basis for *Statement of Financial Accounting Concepts No. 1* (discussed later in the chapter).

The AICPA quickly adopted the Wheat Committee recommendations, and the FASB became the official body charged with issuing accounting standards. The structure of the FASB is as follows. A panel of electors from nine organizations that support the activities of the FASB is selected. (The nine organizations selecting the electors are representative of the breadth of support for the activities of the FASB in the business community. They are the AICPA, the Financial Executives Institute, the National Association of Accountants, the Financial Analysts Federation, the American Accounting Association, the Security Industry Association, and three not-for-profit organizations.) The electors appoint the board of trustees that govern the Financial Accounting Foundation (FAF). There are 16 trustees of the FAF. Thirteen are formally elected and the remaining 3 are selected by the other trustees. The 13 elected trustees are chosen as follows:

1. Four members are CPAs in public practice, nominated by the AICPA.
2. Two members are financial executives, nominated by the Financial Executives Institute.
3. One member is nominated by the National Association of Accountants.
4. One member is nominated by the Financial Analysts Federation.
5. One member is nominated by the American Accounting Association.
6. One member is nominated by the Security Industry Association.
7. Three members are nominated by various governmental accounting groups.

The FAF appoints the Financial Accounting Standards Advisory Council (FASAC), which advises the FASB on major policy issues, the selection of task forces, and the agenda of topics.

The number of members on the FASAC varies from year to year. The bylaws call for at least 20 members to be appointed. However, the actual number of members has grown to about 30 in recent years to obtain representation from a wider group of interested parties.

The FAF is also responsible for appointing the seven members of the FASB and raising the funds to operate the FASB. The FAF currently collects in excess of $11 million a year to support the activities of the FASB. Figure 1.1 illustrates the current structures of the FASB.

Both the FAF and the FASB have a broader representation of the total profession than did the APB; however, the majority of members are usually CPAs from public practice. This membership structure raises the question of how different the FASB is from the APB. No matter what the answer, however, the FASB is the current body officially designated by the AICPA as having the authority to issue standards for financial accounting. Thus, throughout this book pronouncements of the FASB and APB will be presented as generally accepted accounting principles (GAAP). (One of the first acts of the FASB was to sanction all actions of the APB until such time as they could be reviewed or revised. The APB had done likewise for actions of the Committee on Accounting Procedure. Thus, at this point, the FASB has accepted all currently outstanding pronouncements of both the CAP and the APB.) In this book there will be frequent references to the APB, since much of what will be presented originated with that group. The reader should keep in mind that the FASB has adopted those pronouncements.

Originally the FASB issued two types of pronouncements, *Statements* and *Interpretations*. Subsequently, the Financial Accounting Standards Board established two new series of releases entitled (1) *Statements of Financial Accounting Concepts* (*SFACs*) and (2) *Technical Bulletins*. *SFACs* are intended to establish the objectives and concepts that the FASB will use in developing standards of financial accounting and reporting. To date, the FASB has issued six *Statements of Financial Concepts*, as discussed later in this chapter.

FIGURE 1.1 *Structure of the FASB*

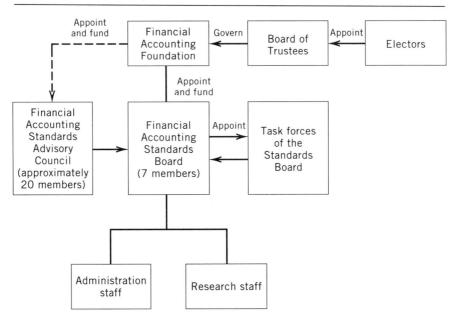

SFACs differ from *Statements of Financial Accounting Standards* in that they do not establish GAAP. Likewise, they are not intended to invoke Rule 203 of the Rules of Conduct of the Code of Professional Ethics. It is anticipated that the major beneficiary of these *SFACs* will be the FASB itself. However, knowledge of the objectives and concepts the board uses should enable financial statement users to better understand the content and limitations of financial accounting information.

Technical Bulletins are strictly interpretive in nature and do not establish new standards or amend existing standards. They are intended to provide guidance on financial accounting and reporting problems on a timely basis.

In summary, the FASB now issues four types of pronouncements.

1. ***Statements of Financial Accounting Concepts***—releases designed to establish the fundamentals upon which financial accounting standards are based. They do not create GAAP and are issued to (1) guide the FASB in setting standards, (2) guide practicing accountants in dealing with unresolved issues, and (3) help educate nonaccountants.

2. ***Statements of Financial Accounting Standards***—releases indicating required accounting methods and procedures for specific accounting issues. SFAS officially create GAAP.

3. ***Interpretations***—modifications or extensions of issues related to previously issued *FASB Statements, APB Opinions,* or *Accounting Research Bulletins.* The

purpose of Interpretations is to clarify, explain, or elaborate on existing *SFASs*, *APB Opinions*, or *ARBs*. They require the support of a majority of the members of the FASB and also create GAAP.

4. **Technical Bulletins**—guidance on accounting and reporting problems issued by the staff of the FASB. *Technical Bulletins* do not officially create GAAP and are used mainly to assist in dealing with implementation problems.

Emerging Issues

The FASB has been criticized for failing to provide timely guidance on emerging implementation and practice problems. During 1984 the FASB responded to this criticism by (1) establishing a task force to assist in identifying issues and problems that might require action, the Emerging Issues Task Force (EITF), and (2) expanding the scope of the *FASB Technical Bulletins* in an effort to offer quicker guidance on a wider variety of issues.

The EITF was formed in response to two conflicting issues. On the one hand, accountants are faced with a variety of issues that are not fully addressed in accounting pronouncements such as interest rate swaps or new financial instruments. These and other new issues need immediate resolution. On the other hand, many accountants maintain that the ever-increasing body of professional pronouncements has created a standards overload problem (discussed in more detail below). The FASB established the EITF in an attempt to simultaneously address both issues. The goal of the EITF is to provide timely guidance on new issues while limiting the number of issues whose resolutions require formal pronouncements by the FASB.

The members of the task force all occupy positions that make them aware of emerging issues. The current members include the directors of accounting and auditing from the largest CPA firms, representatives from smaller CPA firms, and the FASB's Director of Research, who serves as chairman. It is also expected that the chief accountant of the SEC will attend the meetings of the task force and participate in the deliberations.

The EITF discusses current accounting issues that are not specifically addressed by current authoritative pronouncements and advises the FASB staff on whether an issue requires FASB action. Emerging issues arise because of new types of transactions, variations in accounting for existing types of transactions, new types of securities, and new products and services. They frequently involve a company's desire to achieve "off balance sheet" financing or "off income statement" accounting. An issue summary is prepared that defines accounting issues that arise from a given transaction or event, lists pertinent authoritative accounting literature, and discusses any activity to date undertaken by the EITF. Papers may be attached that discuss the issues and the representative views of one or more members of the profession. The EITF may reach a consensus on the treatment of a particular issue from time to time. Consensus on a particular issue is not an authoritative pronouncement— it merely represents the views of the EITF members at that time.

Issues may come to the EITF from a variety of sources. Many are raised by members of the task force themselves; others come from questions asked by auditors. Occasionally an issue may arise because of a question from the SEC or another federal agency.

The task force attempts to arrive at a consensus on each issue. A consensus is defined as 13 of the 15 voting members. A consensus results in the establishment of a GAAP as described in paragraph 5, level (c) of *SAS No. 69* discussed later in the chapter.

Standards Overload

In recent years, the Financial Accounting Standards Board, the Securities and Exchange Commission, and the American Institute of Certified Public Accountants have been criticized for imposing too many accounting standards on the business community. This *standards overload* problem has been particularly burdensome on small businesses that do not have the necessary economic resources to research and apply all the pronouncements issued by these authoritative bodies. Those who contend that there is a standards overload problem base their arguments on two allegations:

1. Not all GAAP requirements are relevant to small business financial reporting needs.
2. Even when they are relevant, they frequently violate the pervasive cost-benefit constraint (discussed later in the chapter).

Critics of the standard-setting process for small businesses also assert that GAAP were developed primarily to serve the needs of the securities market. Many small businesses do not raise capital in these markets; therefore, it is contended that GAAP were not developed with small business needs in mind.

Some of the consequences of the standards overload problem to small business are as follows:

1. If a small business omits a GAAP requirement from audited financial statements, a qualified or adverse opinion may be rendered.
2. The cost of complying with GAAP requirements may cause a small business to forgo the development of other, more relevant information.
3. Small CPA firms that audit smaller companies must keep up to date on all the same requirements as large international firms, but cannot afford the specialists that are available on a centralized basis in the large firms.

Many accountants have argued for differential disclosure standards as a solution to the standards overload problem. That is, standards might be divided into two groups. One group would apply to businesses regardless of size. The second group would apply selectively only to large businesses, small businesses, or particular industries. For example, the disclosure of significant accounting policies would pertain to all businesses, whereas a differential disclosure such as earnings per share would be applicable only to large businesses.

The FASB and various other organizations have been studying this issue for several years, but a complete agreement has not yet been reached. A special committee of the AICPA favored differential measurement.[13] However, the FASB has generally taken the position that financial-statement users might be confused by two measures used to describe or disclose the same economic event. Additionally, bankers (a major source of capital for small businesses) and financial analysts have fairly consistently criticized differential measurement as a solution to the standards overload problem.[14]

Standard Setting as a Political Process

A highly influential academic accountant has stated that accounting standards are as much a product of political action as they are of careful logic or empirical findings.[15] This phenomenon exists because a variety of parties are interested in and affected by the development of accounting standards. Various users of accounting information have found that the best way to influence the formulation of accounting standards is to attempt to influence the standard setters. Consequently, the FASB has come under a great deal of pressure to develop or amend standards so as to benefit a particular user group. In some cases this effort has been successful as in the Business Roundtable's efforts to increase the required consensus for passage of a SFAS from a simple majority to five of the seven members of the FASB.

The growth of these pressures is not surprising considering the fact that many accounting standards have significant economic consequences. *Economic consequences* refers to the impact of accounting reports on various segments of our economic society. Consider the recent release of *FASB Statement No. 106* on Other Post Retirement Benefits. This release requires many companies to change from a pay-as-you-go basis to an accrual basis for health care and other benefits that companies provide to retirees and their dependents. The accrual basis requires companies to measure their obligation to provide future services and accrue these costs during the years employees provide service. The result of *SFAS No. 106* was that many companies simply ceased providing such benefits to their employees, at a large social cost.

The impact on our economic society from *SFAS No. 106* serves to illustrate the need for the FASB to fully consider both the necessity to further develop sound reporting practices and the possible economic consequences of a proposed standard. Accounting standard setting does not exist in a vacuum. It cannot be completely insulated from political pressures nor can it avoid carefully evaluating the possible ramifications of standard setting.

---

[13] Special Committee on Accounting Standards Overload, *Report on the Special Committee on Accounting Standards Overload* (New York: AICPA, 1983).

[14] "The FASB's Second Decade," *Journal of Accountancy* (November 1983), p. 95.

[15] Charles T. Horngren, "The Marketing of Accounting Standards," *Journal of Accountancy* (October 1973), p. 61.

The Evolution of the Phrase Generally Accepted Accounting Principles

One result of the meetings between the AICPA and members of the NYSE discussed earlier was a revision in the wording of the certificate issued by CPAs. The opinion paragraph formerly stated that the financial statements had been examined and were accurate. The terminology was changed to say that the statements are "fairly presented in accordance with generally accepted accounting principles." This expression is now interpreted as encompassing the conventions, rules, and procedures that are necessary to explain accepted accounting practice at a given time. Therefore, financial statements are fair only to the extent that the principles are fair and the statements comply with the principles.

The expression *generally accepted accounting principles* (GAAP) has thus come to play a significant role in the accounting profession. The precise meaning of the term, however, has evolved rather slowly. In addition to official pronouncements promulgated by authoritative organizations, another method of developing GAAP is to determine whether other accountants are using the particular practice in question. These is no need for complete uniformity; rather, when faced with a particular transaction, the accountant is to review the literature and current practice to determine if a treatment similar to the one proposed is being used. For example, if many accountants are using sum-of-year's-digits (SYD) depreciation for assets, this method becomes a GAAP. In the theoretical sense, depreciation may not even be a principle; however, according to current accounting theory formation, if many accountants are using SYD, it becomes a GAAP.

Another example of the historical approach to establishing GAAP is illustrated by the last in, first out (LIFO) inventory method. The use of LIFO inventory was originally sanctioned by the Internal Revenue Service under a particular set of circumstances. Because LIFO inventory will result in lower income taxes during periods of rising prices, more and more companies began searching for those special circumstances in order to use LIFO. Over time many firms began using LIFO, and LIFO acquired the status of a GAAP; therefore, anyone could use LIFO and the CPA could attest that the statements were prepared in accordance with GAAP.

The Accounting Principles Board further refined the definition of GAAP to

> incorporate the consensus at any time as to which economic resources and obligations should be recorded as assets and liabilities, which changes in them should be recorded, when these changes should be recorded, how the recorded assets and liabilities and changes in them should be measured, what information should be disclosed and how it should be disclosed, and which financial statements should be prepared.[16]

---

[16] *Accounting Principles Board Statement No. 4*, "Basic Concepts and Accounting Principles Underlying Financial Statements of Business Enterprises" (New York: AICPA, 1970), par. 27.

This statement did not mean that a GAAP was to be based on what was most appropriate or reasonable in a given situation but that the practice represented consensus; consequently, the APB adopted a positive approach to the development of accounting theory. However, even this definition lacked clarity, since a variety of practices may exist despite a consensus in favor of one or the other. For example, such variation occurs in inventory and depreciation methods.

In 1975 the Auditing Standards Executive Committee of the AICPA issued *Statement on Auditing Standards (SAS) No. 5* with the purpose of explaining more precisely the meaning of the phrase "present fairly . . . in conformity with generally accepted accounting principles" as used in the report of independent auditors. According to the committee, the auditor's opinion on the fairness of an entity's financial statements in conformity with GAAP should be based on the judgment as to whether

> *(a) the accounting principles selected and applied have general acceptance; (b) the accounting principles are appropriate in the circumstances; (c) the financial statements, including the related notes, are informative of matters that may affect their use, understanding, and interpretation; (d) the information presented in the financial statements is classified and summarized in a reasonable manner, that is, neither too detailed nor too condensed; and (e) the financial statements reflect the underlying events and transactions in a manner that presents the financial position, results of operations, and changes in financial position stated within a range of acceptable limits, that is, limits that are reasonable and practicable to attain in financial statements.*[17]

A GAAP thus serves to provide the auditor with a framework for making judgments about the fairness of financial statements on the basis of some uniform standard.

The most precise criterion that has been established for determining whether a practice has gained the stature of a GAAP was originally developed by the AICPA and NYSE committee. Those principles having "substantial authoritative support" were to be classified as GAAP. The meaning of the term was not specifically defined at that time, and no single source exists for all established accounting principles. However, Rule 203 of the AICPA Code of Professional Ethics requires compliance with accounting principles promulgated by the body designated by the Council of the Institute to establish such principles, except in unusual circumstances. (Currently that body is the FASB).

Later, *SAS No. 5* was amended by *SAS No. 43*. This amendment classified the order of priority that an auditor should follow in determining whether an accounting principle is generally accepted. Also, it added to the sources of established accounting principles certain types of pronouncements that did not exist when *SAS No. 5* was issued. This release noted that the determination that a particular accounting principle is generally accepted may be difficult

---

[17] *Statement on Auditing Standards No. 5*, "The Meaning of 'Present Fairly in Conformity with Generally Accepted Accounting Principles' in the Independent Auditor's Report" (New York: AICPA, 1975), par. 4.

because no single source exists for all such principles. The sources of GAAP were identified as

1. Pronouncements of an authoritative body designated by the AICPA Council to establish accounting principles, pursuant to Rule 203 of the AICPA Code of Professional Ethics (*FASB Statements, FASB Interpretations, APB Opinions, Accounting Research Bulletins*).
2. Pronouncements of bodies composed of expert accountants that follow a due process procedure, including broad distribution of proposed accounting principles for public comment, for the intended purpose of establishing accounting principles or describing existing practices that are generally accepted (*AICPA Industry Audit Guides*).
3. Practices or pronouncements that are widely recognized as being generally accepted because they represent prevalent practice in a particular industry or the knowledgeable application to specific circumstances of pronouncements that are generally accepted (*FASB Technical Bulletins*).
4. Other accounting literature.[18]

These recommendations evolved from the sources identified by the APB in 1964 for determining whether an accounting practice had substantial authoritative support. Those sources were

1. Published opinions by committees of the AICPA.
2. Published opinions by committees of the AAA.
3. Affirmative opinions of practicing and academic certified public accountants.
4. Regulations and opinions issued by the Securities and Exchange Commission (SEC).
5. Pronouncements by other regulatory agencies about the accounting to be employed in reporting to the agency.
6. Practices commonly found in business.
7. Writings and opinions of individual accountants found in textbooks and articles.

SAS No. 43 was further amended by *SAS No. 69,* whose stated purpose was to explain the meaning of the phrase "present fairly . . . in conformance with generally accepted accounting principles" in the independent auditor's report.[19] *SAS No. 69* again noted that the determination of the general acceptance of a particular accounting principle is difficult because no single reference

---

[18] *Statement on Auditing Standards No. 43,* "Omnibus Statement on Auditing Standards" (New York: AICPA, 1982), par. 5–7.

[19] *Statement on Auditing Standards No. 69,* "The Meaning of Present Fairly in Conformity With Generally Accepted Accounting Principles in the Independent Auditor's Report (New York, 1993), par. 1.

source exists for all such principles. The release identified the following sources of GAAP:

a. *Accounting principles promulgated by a body designated by the AICPA Council to establish such principles.* This category consists of Statements of Financial Accounting Standards, FASB Interpretations, Accounting Principles Board Opinions *and* AICPA Accounting Research Bulletins.

b. *Pronouncements of bodies, comprised of expert accountants, that deliberate accounting issues in public forums for the purpose of establishing accounting principles or describing existing accounting practices that are generally accepted, provided those pronouncements have been exposed for public comment and have been cleared by a body referred to in category (a).* This category consists of FASB Technical Bulletins, AICPA Industry Audit Guides, *and* AICPA Statements of Position.

c. *Pronouncements of bodies, organized by a body referred to in category (a) and composed of expert accountants, that deliberate accounting issues in public forums for the purpose of interpreting or establishing accounting principles or describing existing accounting practices that are generally accepted, or pronouncements referred to in category (b) that have been cleared by a body referred to in category (a) but have not been exposed for public comment.* This category consists of AICPA Accounting Standards Executive Committee Practice Bulletins and consensus positions of the Emerging Issues Task Force.

d. *Practices or pronouncements that are widely recognized as being generally accepted because they represent prevalent practice in a particular industry, or the knowledgeable application to specific circumstances of pronouncements that are generally accepted.* This category includes AICPA accounting interpretations and implementation guides published by the FASB staff, and practices that are widely recognized and prevalent either generally or in the industry.[20]

SFAS No. 69 went on to indicate that there may be circumstances where there are no established accounting principles for reporting specific transactions. In those instances, it was suggested that it might be possible to report the event or transaction on the basis of its substance by selecting an accounting principle that appears appropriate when applied in a manner similar to the application of an established principle to an analogous transaction or event. In the absence of official pronouncements, other accounting literature may be referenced, including FASB Statements of *Financial Accounting Concepts, APB Statements, AICPA Issues Papers,* Standards of the International Accounting Standards Committee, accounting textbooks, and accounting articles. However, the appropriateness of other literature depends on its relevance to the particular circumstances and the general recognition of the issuer or author as an authority.

[20] Ibid., par. 5.

In this chapter and throughout much of the book, special attention will be given to the pronouncements referred to in Rule 203 of the AICPA Code of Professional Ethics. The reason for this special attention is apparent: Practicing CPAs have an ethical obligation to consider such pronouncements as the primary source of generally accepted accounting principles in their exercise of judgment as to the fairness of financial statements. Opposing views as well as alternative treatments will be considered in the text narrative and in the selected articles; however, the reader should keep in mind that the development of GAAP has been narrowly defined by the AICPA.

Authority

Neither the AICPA nor any of its committees or boards has any legal authority. In order to be a member of the AICPA it is necessary to be a certified public accountant, but it is not necessary to be a member in order to be a CPA. The designation CPA and the license to practice are both granted by the individual states. Therefore, a CPA can become a member of the AICPA if he or she so chooses and, in fact, a majority of practicing CPAs are members.

Under these circumstances, when official statements are issued, those CPAs who are not members of the AICPA can simply choose to ignore the position taken in the statements. Those who are members can also assert that they are following other substantial authoritative support, and the AICPA can do little in the way of penalty. The individual state boards of accountancy, on the other hand, may suspend a CPA's license for a variety of reasons, and that is indeed a significant penalty. The state boards, however, have played virtually no part in developing or establishing accounting principles.

The fact that acceptance and compliance by CPAs with the pronouncements of the APB and the FASB is voluntary, not legally mandatory, is most important to an understanding of the structure of accounting principles that will be presented in this text, since the text draws primarily on those pronouncements. In contrast to the APB and FASB pronouncements, the numerous legal requirements issued by the Securities and Exchange Commission (SEC) *must* be complied with by those companies that report to the SEC.

The Conceptual Framework Project

The Conceptual Framework Project represents an attempt by the FASB to develop concepts useful in guiding the board in establishing standards and in providing a frame of reference for resolving accounting issues. Over the years this project first attempted to develop principles or broad qualitative standards to permit the making of systematic rational choices among alternative methods of financial reporting. Subsequently the project focused on how these overall objectives could be achieved. The FASB has stated that it intends the Conceptual Framework Project to be viewed not as a package of solutions to problems but rather as a common basis for identifying and discussing issues, for asking relevant questions, and for suggesting avenues for research. The Conceptual

Framework Project has resulted in the issuance of six statements of *Financial Accounting Concepts: No. 1:* "Objectives of Financial Reporting by Business Enterprises"; *No. 2:* "Qualitative Characteristics of Accounting Information"; *No. 3:* "Elements of Financial Statements of Business Enterprises"; *No. 4:* "Objectives of Financial Reporting by Nonbusiness Organizations" (because the focus of this text is financial accounting, *SFAC No. 4* will not be discussed here); *No. 5:* "Recognition and Measurement in Financial Statements of Business Enterprises"; and *No. 6:* "Elements of Financial Statements." (*SFAC No. 6* replaced *SFAC No. 3*)

SFAC Nos. 1 and 2 can be described as the goals to guide practice and indicate how these goals are useful in making qualitative decisions about what to report. Specifically, *SFAC No. 1* defines the primary objective of financial reporting as usefulness. *SFAC No. 2* describes how financial statements can be useful in qualitative terms. *SFAC No. 5* explains that *SFAC Nos. 1* and *2* provide the guidelines to be able to recognize and measure accounting information, describes measurability and states that an item must also meet the definition of an element provided in *SFAC No. 6* to be measurable. The Conceptual Framework project is discussed in further detail in the following paragraphs.

Statement of Financial Accounting Concepts No. 1: "Objectives of Financial Reporting by Business Enterprises"

The foundation for *SFAC No. 1* was the work of the Trueblood Committee on the objectives of financial statements; consequently it is an attempt to establish normative accounting theory. *SFAC No. 1* points out that external financial reporting by business enterprises is not an end in itself. That is, it is a source of useful information furnished by management to financial-statement users who can obtain this information in no other way. *SFAC No. 1* established that the overall objective of financial reporting is to give users a basis for choosing among alternative uses of scarce resources. While this objective may seem self-explanatory, it is important because it established that user needs are more important than auditor needs in the development of accounting standards. Consequently effective financial reporting must meet several broad objectives. It must enable current and potential investors, creditors, and other users to

1. Make investment and credit decisions.
2. Assess cash flow prospects.
3. Report enterprise resources, claims to those resources, and changes in them.
4. Report economic resources, obligations, and owners' equity.
5. Report enterprise performance and earnings.
6. Evaluate liquidity, solvency, and flow of funds.
7. Evaluate management stewardship and performance.
8. Explain and interpret financial information.

Following on the basic objective, *SFAC No. 1* went on to state that the FASB intends that these broad objectives will act as guidelines for evaluating the usefulness of new and existing GAAP to users making investment and credit decisions. This goal will help facilitate the efficient use of scarce resources and the operation of capital markets.

Statement of Financial Accounting Concepts No. 2: "Qualitative Characteristics of Accounting Information"

This statement bridges the gap between *Statement of Concepts No. 1* and other statements, issued later, covering the elements of financial statements and their recognition, measurement, and disclosure. It addresses the question: What are the characteristics of accounting information that make it useful? Later statements are then intended to be concerned with how the purposes of financial accounting are to be attained.

SFAC No. 2 notes that accounting choices are made on at least two levels. First, the FASB or other agencies have the power to require businesses to report in some particular way or to prohibit a method that might be considered undesirable. Second, accounting choices between alternatives are made by the reporting enterprise. *SFAC No. 2* attempts to identify and define the qualities that make accounting information useful by developing a number of generalizations or guidelines for making accounting choices on both levels.

The statement indicates that the primary criterion of choice between two alternative accounting methods involves asking which method produces the better, that is, the more useful, information. If the answer to that question is clear, it then becomes necessary to ask whether the value of the better information significantly exceeds that of the inferior information to justify any extra cost (cost–benefit analysis). If a satisfactory answer is given, the choice between alternatives should be clear. The qualities that distinguish better (or more useful) information from inferior (less useful) are primarily the qualities of relevance and reliability (discussed later).

Figure 1.2 illustrates the Hierarchy of Accounting Qualities discussed by *SFAC No. 2* in reviewing the characteristics of accounting information.

From Figure 1.2 we can see that the characteristics of information that make it a desirable commodity are viewed as a hierarchy of qualities, with usefulness for decision making being the most important quality. However, a limitation of the hierarchy is that it does not distinguish between the primary qualities and other qualities, nor does it assign priority among qualities. In the following paragraphs we discuss each of the hierarchical levels in detail.

Decision Makers and Their Characteristics

Each decision maker judges what accounting information is useful, and that judgment is influenced by such factors as the decision to be made, the methods of decision making to be used, the information already possessed or obtained from other sources, and the decision maker's capacity to process the information. These characteristics indicate that generally managers and owners of small or closely held enterprises may find some external financial reporting

FIGURE 1.2 *A Hierarchy of Accounting Qualities*

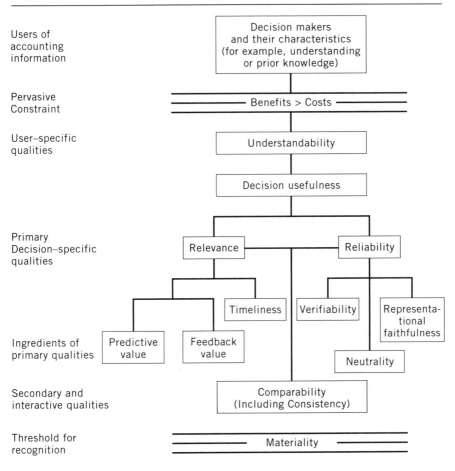

information less useful to them than it is to stockholders of large publicly held enterprises.[21]

Cost–Benefit Constraint
Unless the benefits to be derived from a commodity or service exceed the costs associated with providing it, it will not be sought after. However, financial

[21] This conclusion is expanded on in the FASB's Exposure Draft, "Financial Statements and Other Means of Financial Reporting." This release examines the issues of what information should be provided, who should provide it, and where it should be presented. Additionally, it examines the question: Should GAAP be the same for all companies regardless of size? As noted earlier, the FASB has not issued a final statement that addresses this question.

information differs from other commodities in that the costs of providing financial information fall initially on preparers, whereas the benefits accrue to both preparers and users. Ultimately, a standard-setting body must do its best to meet the needs of society as a whole when it promulgates a standard that sacrifices one of those qualities for the other, and it must constantly be aware of the relationship of costs and benefits.

Understandability

Understandability of information is governed by a combination of user characteristics and characteristics inherent in the information. It serves as a "link" between decision makers and accounting information. To meet the *SFAC No. 1* criterion of usefulness, explicitly the information must be understood by the decision maker. Understandability can be classified as relating to particular decision makers (Does the decision maker speak that language?) or relating to classes of decision makers (Is the disclosure intelligible to the audience for which it is intended?).

Decision Usefulness

According to *SFAC No. 1* financial information is intended to be useful to decision makers. *SFAC No. 1* established that relevance and reliability are the two primary qualities that make accounting information useful for decision making. Subject to constraints imposed by cost and materiality, increased relevance and increased reliability are the characteristics that make information a more desirable commodity—that is, one useful in making decisions. If either of those qualities is completely missing, the information will not be useful. Although, ideally, the choice of an accounting alternative should produce information that is both more reliable and more relevant, it may be necessary to sacrifice some of one quality for a gain in another.

Relevance

Relevant accounting information is capable of making a difference in a decision by helping users to form predictions about the outcomes of past, present, and future events or to confirm or correct prior expectations. Relevant information has predictive value, feedback value, and timeliness.

Predictive Value and Feedback Value

Information can make a difference to decisions by improving decision makers' capacities to predict or by confirming or correcting their earlier expectations. Usually, information does both at once, because knowledge about the outcome of actions already taken will generally improve decision makers' abilities to predict the results of similar future actions.

Timeliness

Having information available to decision makers before it loses its capacity to influence decisions is an ancillary aspect of relevance. If information is not available when it is needed or becomes available so long after the reported events that it has no value for future action, it lacks relevance and is of little or no use. Timeliness alone cannot make information relevant, but a lack of timeliness can rob information of relevance it might otherwise have had.

Reliability
The reliability of a measure rests on the faithfulness with which it represents what it purports to represent, coupled with an assurance for the user that it has that representational quality. To be useful, information must be reliable as well as relevant. Degrees of reliability must be recognized. It is hardly ever a question of black and white, but rather of more reliability or less. Reliability rests on the extent to which the accounting description or measurement is verifiable and representationally faithful. Neutrality of information also interacts with those two components of reliability to affect the usefulness of the information.

Verifiability
Verifiability is a quality that may be demonstrated by securing a high degree of consensus among independent measurers using the same measurement methods. Representational faithfulness, on the other hand, refers to the correspondence or agreement between the accounting numbers and the resources or events those numbers purport to represent. A high degree of correspondence, however, does not guarantee that an accounting measurement will be relevant to the user's needs if the resources or events represented by the measurement are inappropriate to the purpose at hand.

Representational Faithfulness
This quality is the correspondence or agreement between a measure and the phenomenon it purports to represent. Sometimes information may be unreliable because of simple misrepresentation. For example, receivables may misrepresent large sums as collectible that are actually uncollectible. Social scientists have defined this concept as validity.

Neutrality
In formulating or implementing standards, the primary concern should be the relevance and reliability of the information that results, not the effect that the new rule may have on a particular interest. A neutral choice between accounting alternatives is free from bias toward a predetermined result. The objectives of financial reporting serve many different information users, who have diverse interests, and no one, predetermined result is likely to suit all interests.

Comparability and Consistency
Information about a particular enterprise increases greatly in usefulness if it can be compared with similar information about other enterprises and with similar information about the same enterprise for some other period or some other point in time. Comparability between enterprises and consistency in the application of methods over time increases the informational value of comparisons of relative economic opportunities or performance. The significance of information, especially quantitative information, depends to a great extent on the user's ability to relate it to some benchmark.

Materiality Constraint
Materiality is a pervasive concept that relates to the qualitative characteristics, especially relevance and reliability. Materiality and relevance are both defined in terms of what influences or makes a difference to a decision maker, but the

two terms can be distinguished. A decision not to disclose certain information may be made, say, because investors have no need for that kind of information (it is not relevant) or because the amounts involved are too small to make a difference (they are not material). Magnitude by itself, without regard to the nature of the item and the circumstances in which the judgment has to be made, will not generally be a sufficient basis for a materiality judgment. The FASB's present position is that no general standards of materiality can be formulated to take into account all the considerations that enter into an experienced human judgment. Quantitative materiality criteria may be given by the board in specific standards in the future, as in the past, as appropriate. See Chapter 2 for a further discussion of materiality.

Statement of Financial Accounting Concepts No. 5: "Recognition and Measurement in Financial Statements of Business Enterprises"

SFAC No. 5 (discussed in more detail in Chapter 3) sets forth recognition criteria and guidance on what information should be incorporated into financial statements, and when this information should be reported. This release indicates that a full set of financial statements for a period should disclose financial position at the end of a period, earnings for the period, comprehensive income for the period, cash flows during the period, and investments by and distributions to owners during the period. The statement also notes that recognition and measurement in financial statements is subject to a cost–benefit constraint and a materiality threshold.

Although *SFAC No. 5* did not suggest any radical changes in the then current structure and content of financial statements, it did provide the impetus for the change to a statement of cash flows from the statement of changes in financial position that was previously required. Additionally, the scope of the measurement of the operating results of business enterprises was broadened by the definition of comprehensive income.

The future development of accounting theory will use the concepts defined in *SFAC No. 5* as operational guidelines. They should serve as broad boundaries in the development of responses to controversial accounting issues.

Statement of Financial Accounting Concepts No. 6: "The Elements of Financial Statements"

SFAC No. 6 (discussed in more detail in Chapters 2, 3, and 4) defines the ten elements of financial statements that are used to measure the performance and position of economic entities. These ten elements—assets, liabilities, equity, investments by owners, distributions to owners, comprehensive income, revenues, expenses, gains and losses—represent the building blocks with which financial statements are constructed. The definitions of the elements can be used to determine the content of financial statements. That is, if an item does not meet all of the characteristics of an element, it should not be included in the financial statements.

The Role of Ethics in Accounting

Ethics are concerned with the types of behavior society considers right and wrong. Accounting ethics incorporate social standards of behavior as well as behavioral standards that relate specifically to the profession. The environment of public accounting has become ethically complex. The accountants' Code of Professional Ethics developed by the AICPA has been evolving for a number of years, and as business transactions have become more and more complex, ethical issues have also increased in complexity.

The public accountant has a Ralph Nader–type overseer role in our society. This role was described by former Chief Justice of the Supreme Court Warren Burger as follows:

> *Corporate financial statements are one of the primary sources of information available to guide the decisions of the investing public. In an effort to control the accuracy of their financial data available to investors in the securities markets, various provisions of the federal securities laws require publicly held corporations to file their financial statements with the Securities and Exchange Commission. Commission regulations stipulate that these financial reports must be audited by an independent certified public accountant. . . .*
>
> *By certifying the public reports that collectively depict a corporation's financial status, the independent accountant assumes a public responsibility transcending any employment relationship with the client. The independent public accountant performing this special function owes ultimate allegiance to the corporation's creditors and stockholders as well as the investing public. This ''public watchdog'' function demands that the accountant maintain total independence from the client at all times and requires complete fidelity to the public trust.*
>
> *The SEC requires the filing of audited financial statements in order to obviate the fear of loss from reliance on inaccurate information, thereby encouraging public investment in the nation's industries. It is, therefore, not enough that financial statements be accurate; the public must perceive them as being accurate. Public faith in the reliability of a corporation's financial statements depends upon the public perception of an outside auditor as an independent professional.* [22]

Justice Burger has outlined the very important role accountants play in our society. This role requires highly ethical conduct at all times. The role of ethics in accounting will be discussed in more detail in Chapter 16.

Summary

Accounting activities have been conducted for many hundreds of years, but a general theory of accounting that has universal acceptance has not been developed. The factors that have given rise to the need for accounting have included mercantilism, which created the need to account for ventures; the Industrial

---

[22] U. S. vs. Arthur Young and Co. et al., U. S. Supreme Court No. 8206871 U.S.L.W. 4355 (U. S. Mar. 21, 1984) 1.

Revolution, which introduced the need to report to external stockholders; and the Great Depression, which highlighted the need for stricter accounting standards.

The AICPA and its various subgroups continue to be active in the development of accounting principles. In addition, the practices of the accounting profession, the actions of the Securities and Exchange Commission, and the opinions of the academic community influence the development of accounting principles and theory.

The term "generally accepted accounting principles" has become significant in accounting practice. In general, the term refers to a consensus within the profession that a given principle is generally accepted as being appropriate to the circumstances in which it is used. Although there are several possible sources for statements of accounting principles, the most authoritative is the Financial Accounting Standards Board and its predecessors, the Accounting Principles Board and the Committee on Accounting Procedures.

The theoretical framework of accounting has been studied by both the Accounting Principles Board and the Financial Accounting Standards Board. The FASB's conclusions are contained in the conceptual framework project.

In the following readings, the development and current status of the accounting profession is examined further. Stephen Zeff discusses the economic impact of FASB pronouncements. David Koeppen describes a model that can help in understanding the relationships among various *Statements of Financial Accounting Concepts*.

The Rise of "Economic Consequences"

Stephen A. Zeff

Since the 1960s, the American accounting profession has been aware of the increasing influence of "outside forces" in the standard-setting process. Two parallel developments have marked this trend. First, individuals and groups that had rarely shown any interest in the setting of accounting standards began to intervene actively and powerfully in the process. Second, these parties began to invoke arguments other than those that have traditionally been employed in accounting discussions. The term "economic consequences" has been used to describe these novel kinds of arguments.

By "economic consequences" is meant the impact of accounting reports on the decision-making behavior of business, government, unions, investigators, and creditors. It is argued that the resulting behavior of these individuals and groups could be detrimental to the interests of other affected parties. And, the argument goes, accounting standard setters must take into consideration these allegedly detrimental consequences when deciding on accounting questions. The recent debates involving foreign currency translation and the accounting for unsuccessful exploration activity in the petroleum industry have relied heavily on economic consequences arguments, and the Financial Accounting Standards Board and the Securities and Exchange Com-

mission have become extremely sensitive to the issue.[1]

The economic consequences argument represents a veritable revolution in accounting thought. Until recently, accounting policy making was either assumed to be neutral in its effects or, if not neutral, it was not held out to the public as being responsible for those effects. Today, these assumptions are being severely questioned, and the subject of social and economic consequences "has become *the* central contemporary issue in accounting."[2] That the FASB has commissioned research papers on the economic consequences of selected standards and has held a conference devoted entirely to the subject[3] underscores the current importance of this issue.

Accounting policy makers have been aware since at least the 1960s of the

[1] Several articles have been written on "economic consequences." See e.g., Alfred Rappaport, "Economic Impact of Accounting Standards—Implications for the FASB," *JofA*, May77, pp. 89–98; Arthur R. Wyatt, "The Economic Impact of Financial Accounting Standards," *JofA*, Oct.77, pp. 92–94; and Robert J. Swieringa, "Consequences of Financial Accounting Standards," *Accounting Forum*, May 1977, pp. 25–39.

[2] *Report of the Committee on the Social Consequences of Accounting Information* (Sarasota, Fla.: American Accounting Association, 1978), p. 4.

[3] *Conference on the Economic Consequences of Financial Accounting Standards* (Stamford, Conn.: FASB, 1978).

third-party intervention issue,[4] while the issue of economic consequences has surfaced only in the 1970s. Indeed, much of the history of the Accounting Principles Board during the 1960s was one of endeavoring to understand and cope with the third-party forces which were intervening in the standard-setting process. In the end, the inability of the APB to deal effectively with these forces led to its demise and the establishment in 1973 of the FASB.

The true preoccupations of the intervening third parties have not always been made clear. When trying to understand the third-party arguments, one must remember that before the 1970s the accounting model employed by the American Institute of CPAs committee on accounting procedure (CAP) and the APB was, formally at least, confined to technical accounting considerations (sometimes called "accounting principles" or "conceptual questions") such as the measurement of assets, liabilities and income and the "fair presentation" of financial position and operations. The policy makers' sole concern was with the communication of financial information to actual and potential investors, for, indeed, their charter had been "granted" by the SEC, which itself had been charged by Congress to assure

"full and fair disclosure" in reports to investors. Third-party intervenors, therefore, would have had an obvious incentive to appeal to the accounting model used by policy makers rather than raise the specter of an economic consequences model preferred by the third parties.

When corporate management began intervening in the standard-setting process to an increasing degree, therefore, [sic] its true position was probably disguised. An examination of management arguments suggests the following range of tactical rhetoric. Arguments were couched in terms of

1. The traditional accounting model, where management was genuinely concerned about unbiased and "theoretically sound" accounting measurements.

2. The traditional accounting model, where management was really seeking to advance its self-interest in the economic consequences of the contents of published reports.

3. The economic consequences in which management was self-interested.

If one accepts Johnson's dictum that it requires a "lively imagination" to believe that management is genuinely concerned with fair presentation when choosing between alternatives,[5] it could be concluded that the first argument has seldom been employed in third-party interventions. In recent years, particularly since the early 1970s, management has become more candid in its dialogues with the FASB, insistently

---

[4] In this article, I am chiefly concerned with third-party intervention in the standard setting for unregulated industries. Accounting policy makers in this country have been alive for several decades to the accounting implications of the rules and regulations of rate-making in the energy, transportation, and communication industries. See, e.g., George O. May, *Financial Accounting: A Distillation of Experience* (New York: The Macmillan Company, 1943), chs. 7–8, and William A. Paton, "Accounting Policies of the Federal Power Commission—A Critique," *JofA*, June44, pp. 432–460.

[5] Charles E. Johnson, "Management's Role in External Accounting Measurements," in Robert K. Jaedicke, Yuji Ijiri, and Oswald Nielsen (editors), *Research in Accounting Measurement* ([n.p.], AAA, 1966), p. 91.

advancing the third argument and thus bringing economic consequences to the fore.

Two factors tend to explain why economic consequences did not become a substantive issue before the 1970s. First, management and other interested parties predominantly used the second argument cited above, encouraging the standard-setting bodies to confine themselves to the traditional accounting model. Second, the CAP and APB, with few exceptions, were determined to resolve, or appear to resolve, standard-setting controversies in the context of traditional accounting.

Early Uses of Economic Consequences Arguments

Perhaps the first evidence of economic consequences reasoning in the pronouncements of American policy makers occurred as long ago as 1941. In Accounting Research Bulletin No. 11, *Corporate Accounting for Ordinary Stock Dividends,* the CAP, in accordance with "proper accounting and corporate policy," required that fair market value be used to record the issuance of stock dividends where such market value was substantially in excess of book value.[6]

Evidently, both the New York Stock Exchange and a majority of the CAP regarded periodic stock dividends as "objectionable,"[7] and the CAP acted to make it more difficult for corporations to sustain a series of such stock dividends out of their accumulated earnings. As far as this author is aware, the U.S. is still the only country in which an accounting pronouncement requires that stock dividends be capitalized at the fair market value of the issued shares,[8] and this position was originally adopted in this country, at least in part, in order to produce an impact on the stock dividend policies of corporations.

A second evidence of economic consequences' entering into the debates surrounding the establishment of accounting standards, this time involving management representations, occurred in 1947–48. It was the height of the postwar inflation, and several corporations had adopted replacement cost depreciation in their published financial statements.[9] Among the arguments employed in the debate involving the CAP were the possible implications for tax reform, the possible impact on wage bargaining, and the need to counteract criticisms of profiteering by big business. Despite the pressures for accounting reform, the CAP reaffirmed its support of historical cost accounting for depreciation in ARB No. 33, *Depreciation and High Costs,* and in a letter issued in October 1948.

A clear use of the economic consequences argument occurred in 1958, when three subsidiaries of American Electric Power Company sued in the federal courts to enjoin the AICPA from allowing the CAP to issue a letter saying that the deferred tax credit account, as employed in the then-recently issued ARB No. 44 (Revised), *Declining-Balance*

---

[6] Accounting Research Bulletin No. 11, *Corporate Accounting for Ordinary Stock Dividends* (New York: American Institute of Accountants, 1941), pp. 102–103.

[7] George O. May, letter to J. S. Seidman, dated July 14, 1941 (deposited in the national office library of Price Waterhouse & Co. in New York), p. 1.

[8] Price Waterhouse International, *A Survey in 46 Countries: Accounting Principles and Reporting Practices* ([n.p.], PWI, 1975), table 145.

[9] *Depreciation Policy When Price Levels Change* (New York: Controllership Foundation, Inc., 1948), ch. 14.

Depreciation, should be classified as a liability.[10] The three public utility companies were concerned that the SEC, under authority granted by the Public Utility Holding Company Act, would not permit them to issue debt securities in view of the unfavorable debt-to-equity ratios that the proposed reclassification would produce. The case reached the U.S. Supreme Court, where certiorari was denied. In the end, the clarifying letter was issued. Nonetheless, the SEC accommodated the public utility companies by consenting to exclude the deferred tax credit from both liabilities and stockholders' equity for purposes of decisions taken under the Public Utility Holding Company Act.[11]

Shortly after the creation of the APB, the accounting treatment of the investment tax credit exploded on the scene. The three confrontations between the APB and the combined forces of industry and the administrations of Presidents Kennedy, Johnson, and Nixon have already been amply discussed in the literature.[12] The government's argument was not that the accounting deferral of the investment tax credit was bad accounting but that it diluted the incentive effect of an instrument of fiscal policy.

In 1965, the subject of segmental reporting emerged from a hearing of the Senate Subcommittee on Antitrust and Monopoly on the economic effects of conglomerate mergers. The aim of the senatorial inquiry was not to promote better accounting practices for investor use but to provide the subcommittee and other government policy makers with accounting data that would facilitate their assessment of the economic efficacy of conglomerate mergers. Company managements naturally looked on such disclosures as potentially detrimental to their merger ambitions. Pressure applied by this powerful subcommittee eventually forced the hand of the SEC to call for product-line disclosures in published financial reports. The repercussions of this initiative, which had its origin in a Senate hearing room, are still being felt.[13]

In 1967–69, the APB responded to an anguished objection by the startled Investment Bankers Association of America (today known as the Securities Industry Association) to a provision, once thought to be innocuous, in APB Opinion No. 10, *Omnibus Opinion— 1966,* which imputed a debt discount to convertible debt and debt issued with stock warrants. The IBA was concerned about the impact of the accounting procedure on the market for such securities. In Opinion No. 14, *Accounting for*

[10] *The AICPA Injunction Case—Re: ARB [No.] 44 (Revised).* Cases in Public Accounting Practice [No. 1] (Chicago, Ill.: Arthur Andersen & Co., 1960).

[11] *SEC Administrative Policy Re: Balance-Sheet Treatment of Deferred Income-Tax Credits,* Cases in Public Accounting Practice [Nos. 5 and 6] (Chicago, Ill.: Arthur Andersen & Co., 1961), pp. 35–59.

[12] See Maurice Moonitz, "Some Reflections on the Investment Credit Experience," *Journal of Accounting Research,* Spring 1966, pp. 47–61: John L. Carey, *The Rise of the Accounting Profession: To Responsibility and Authority 1937–1969* (New York: AICPA, 1970), pp. 98–104; and Stephen A. Zeff, *Forging Accounting Principles in Five Countries: A History and an Analysis of Trends* (Champaign, Ill.: Stipes Publishing Company, 1972), pp. 178–180, 201–202, 219–221 and 326–327.

[13] Charles W. Plum and Daniel W. Collins, "Business Segment Reporting," in James Don Edwards and Homer A. Black (editors), *The Modern Accountant's Handbook* (Homewood, Ill.: Dow Jones-Irwin, Inc., 1976), pp. 469–511.

Convertible Debt and Debt Issued With Stock Purchase Warrants, the APB rescinded its action in regard to convertible debt while retaining the rest.[14]

From 1968 through 1971, the banking industry opposed the inclusion of bad-debt provisions and losses on the sales of securities in the net income of commercial banks. Bankers believed that the new measure would reflect unfavorably on the performance of banks. Eventually, through a concerted effort by the APB, the SEC, and the bank regulatory agencies, generally accepted accounting principles were made applicable to banks.[15]

From 1968 through 1970, the APB struggled with the accounting for business combinations. It was flanked on the one side by the Federal Trade Commission and the Department of Justice, which favored the elimination of pooling-of-interests accounting in order to produce a slowing effect on the merger movement, and on the other by merger-minded corporations that were fervent supporters of pooling-of-interests accounting. The APB, appearing almost as a pawn in a game of political chess, disenchanted many of its supporters as it abandoned positions of principle in favor of an embarrassing series of pressure-induced compromises.[16]

In 1971, the APB held public hearings on accounting for marketable equity securities, leases, and the explora-

tion and drilling costs of companies in the petroleum industry. In all three areas, powerful industry pressures thwarted the board from acting. The insurance industry was intensely concerned about the possible effects on its companies' stock prices of including the unrealized gains and losses on portfolio holdings in their income statements.[17] The leasing initiative was squelched after senators, representatives, and even the secretary of transportation responded to a letter-writing campaign by making pointed inquiries of the SEC and APB. The letter writers raised the specter of injury that the board's proposed action would supposedly cause to consumers and to the viability of companies in several key industries.[18] The petroleum industry was unable to unite on a solution to the controversy over full costing versus successful efforts costing, as it was alleged that a general imposition of the latter would adversely affect the fortunes of the small, independent exploration companies.[19] Using its considerable political might, the industry succeeded in persuading the board to postpone consideration of the sensitive subject.[20]

On each of the occasions enumerated above, outside parties intervened in the standard-setting process by an appeal

[14] Zeff, pp. 202, 211.

[15] Carey, p. 134; Maurice Moonitz, *Obtaining Agreement on Standards in the Accounting Profession*, Studies in Accounting Research No. 8 (Sarasota, Fla.: AAA, 1974), pp. 38–39; Zeff, pp. 210–211.

[16] Robert Chatov, *Corporate Financial Reporting: Public or Private Control?* (New York: The Free Press, 1975), pp. 212–222; Zeff, pp. 212–216.

[17] Charles T. Horngren, ''The Marketing of Accounting Standards,'' *JofA*, Oct.73, pp. 63–64.

[18] Leonard M. Savoie, ''Accounting Attitudes,'' in Robert R. Sterling (editor), *Institutional Issues in Public Accounting* (Lawrence, Kan.: Scholars Book Co., 1974), p. 326.

[19] See the testimony and submissions in *APB Public Hearing on Accounting and Reporting Practices in the Petroleum Industry*, Cases in Public Accounting Practice [No.] 10 (Chicago, Ill.: Arthur Andersen & Co., 1972).

[20] Savoie, p. 326.

to criteria that transcended the traditional questions of accounting measurement and fair presentation. They were concerned instead with the economic consequences of the accounting pronouncements.

"Economic consequences" have been invoked with even greater intensity in the short life of the FASB. Such questions as accounting for research and development costs, self-insurance and catastrophe reserves, development stage companies, foreign currency fluctuations, leases, the restructuring of troubled debt,[21] domestic inflation and relative price changes, and the exploration and drilling costs of companies in the petroleum industry have provoked widespread debate over their economic consequences.[22] The list is both extensive and impressive, and accounting academics are busily investigating the empirical validity of claims that these and other accounting standards may be linked with the specified economic consequences.

The Standard-Setting Bodies Respond

What have been the reactions of the standard-setting bodies to the intervention by outside parties and the claim that accounting standards should or should not be changed in order to avoid unhealthy economic or social consequences? In the 1940s and 1950s, the CAP enhanced its liaison with interested third parties through a wider circulation of exposure drafts and subcom-

---

[21] At the FASB's public hearing, some bankers warned of the dire economic consequences of requiring banks to write down their receivables following restructurings. Walter Wriston, chairman of Citicorp, asserted that the restructuring of New York City's obligations might just not have occurred if the banks would have been required to write down the carrying value of their receivables. Walter B. Wriston, *Transcript of Public Hearings* on FASB discussion memorandum, *Accounting by Debtors and Creditors When Debt is Restructured* (1977, vol. 1, part 2), pp. 69–70. Yet the FASB, in its lengthy "Basis for Conclusions" in Statement No. 15, *Accounting by Debtors and Creditors for Troubled Debt Restructurings* (in which the feared write-downs were not required), did not refer to bankers' claims about the economic consequences of requiring significant write-downs. Does that omission imply that the FASB paid no attention to those assertions? Did the FASB conduct any empirical research (as it did concerning the economic consequences claims raised in connections with Statement No. 7, *Accounting and Reporting by Development Stage Enterprises*) to determine whether there was adequate ground to sustain such claims?

[22] See, e.g., Joseph M. Burns, *Accounting Standards and International Finance: With Special Reference to Multinationals* (Washington, D.C.: American Enterprise Institute for Public Policy Research, 1976); Committee on the Social Consequences of Accounting Information, pp. 9–12; Rappaport, pp. 90, 92; FASB, *Conference on the Economic Consequences of Financial Accounting Standards*. U.S. Department of Energy, comments before the Securities and Exchange Commission, "Accounting Practices—Oil and Gas Producers—Financial Accounting Standards," unpublished memorandum, dated April 3, 1978.

Evidence attesting to the attention given by the FASB to economic consequences issues may be found in the "Basis for Conclusions" sections of the applicable statements. In addition to companies and industry groups, government departments (such as the Department of Commerce, in Statement No. 7, and the Departments of Energy and Justice, in Statement No. 19, *Financial Accounting and Reporting by Oil and Gas Producing Companies*) were actively involved in the discussion of economic consequences.

mittee reports. From 1958 to 1971, through appointments to key committees, joint discussions and symposiums, mass mailings of exposure drafts, and formal public hearings, the Institute and the APB acted to bring interested organizations more closely into the standard-setting process. The hope was, one supposes, that these organizations would be satisfied that their views were given full consideration before the final issuance of opinions. These accommodations were, however, of a procedural sort, although it is possible that these outside views did have an impact on the substantive content of some of the resulting opinions. It would appear that the APB was at least somewhat influenced by economic consequences in its prolonged deliberations leading to the issuance of Opinions No. 16, *Business Combinations,* and No. 17, *Intangible Assets.*[23] During the public hearings in 1971 on marketable equity securities and the accounting practices of companies in the petroleum industry, management representatives on several occasions asserted economic consequences as relevant considerations. Yet members of the APB's subject-area committees neither asked for proof of those assertions nor, indeed, questioned their relevance to the setting of accounting standards.[24]

Since it was the APB's inability to cope with the pressures brought by outside organizations that hastened its demise, it is worth noting that the FASB includes the Financial Executives Insti-

tute (FEI) among its co-sponsors. In my opinion, the incorporation of the FEI in the formal structure of the Financial Accounting Foundation (FAF, the FASB's parent) is one of the most significant advantages that the FASB possesses in relation to its predecessor.[25]

The procedural machinery established for the FASB is even more elaborate than that which existed in the final years of the APB. The object of these additional procedures has been to expand and intensify the interaction between the board and interested outside parties, notably companies, industry associations, and government departments and agencies. A task force drawn from a broad spectrum of interested groups is appointed prior to the preparation of each discussion memorandum. The DM itself is much bulkier than the modest document the APB had issued before its public hearings; it contains a neutral discussion of the entire gamut of policy issues that bear on the resolution of the controversy before the board. A Financial Accounting Standards Advisory Council (FASAC), composed of representatives of a wide array of interested groups, was appointed to be a sounding board for the FASB. The board itself has been composed of members drawn from accounting practice, the universities, companies, and government—again, so that it would be responsive, and would appear to be responsive, to the concerns of those "constituencies." In an effort to per-

---

[23] Wyatt, pp. 92–93.

[24] *Proceedings* of Hearing on Accounting for Equity Securities. Accounting Principles Board (New York: AICPA, 1971), section A Transcript: and *APB Public Hearing on Accounting and Reporting Practices in the Petroleum Industry.*

[25] The inclusion of the FEI could arguably become the undoing of the FASB. If the FEI were to lose confidence in the board, it is possible that many of the companies that now contribute to the Financial Accounting Foundation might decline to continue doing so, provoking a financial crisis that could threaten the board's viability.

suade skeptics of the merit of its recommendations, the board includes in its statements a lengthy explanation of the criteria, arguments, and empirical considerations it used to fashion the recommended standards.

Following criticism from within the profession of the board's operations and procedures, the FAF conducted a study in 1977 of the entire FASB operation. Among the FAF's many recommendations were proposals that the board expand its formal and informal contacts with interested groups and that it include an economic impact analysis in important exposure drafts. On this latter point the FAF's structure committee concluded: "The Board need not be unduly influenced by the possibility of an economic impact, but it should consider both the possible costs and the expected benefits of a proposal."[26] In addition, the structure committee recommended actions that would strengthen the roles of the task forces and the FASAC.[27] In 1978, under pressure from Congress, the board began to conduct virtually all its formal meetings (including those of the FASAC) "in the sunshine."

The history of the APB and the FASB is one of a succession of procedural steps taken to bring the boards' deliberations into closer proximity to the opinions and concerns of interested third parties. As in the case of the APB, it is possible that an effect of these more elaborate procedures has been a change in the substance of the FASB's conclusions and recommendations.

By the middle 1970s, however, it was decided that the FASB should add economic (and social) consequences to the substantive issues it normally addresses. The inclusion of "probable economic or social impact" among the other "qualities of useful information" in the board's conceptual framework DM,[28] the board's announcement of its interest in empirical studies of economic consequences,[29] and the recommendation of the FAF structure committee that the board inform itself adequately on the "various impacts its pronouncements might have"[30] collectively confirm this new direction. The issue of economic consequences has, therefore, changed from one having only procedural implications for the standard-setting process to one which is now firmly a part of the standard setters' substantive policy framework.

Economic Consequences as a Substantive Issue

Economic consequences have finally become accepted as a valid substantive policy issue for a number of reasons:

- *The tenor of the times.* The decade of the 1970s is clearly one in which American society is holding its institutions responsible for the social, environmental, and economic consequences of their actions, and the crystallized public opinion on this subject eventually became evident

---

[26] Financial Accounting Foundation structure committee, *The Structure of Establishing Financial Accounting Standards* (Stamford, Conn.: FAF, 1977), p. 51.

[27] Ibid., pp. 23–25.

[28] Financial Accounting Standards Board discussion memorandum, *Conceptual Framework for Financial Accounting and Reporting: Elements of Financial Statements and Their Measurement* (Stamford, Conn.: FASB, 1976), par. 367.

[29] Financial Accounting Standards Board, *Status Report*, No. 45, February 7, 1977.

[30] Structure committee, p. 31.

(and relevant) to those interested in the accounting standard-setting activity.

- *The sheer intractability of the accounting problems being addressed.* Since the mid-1960s, the APB and the FASB have been taking up difficult accounting questions on which industry positions have been well entrenched. To some degree, companies that are sensitive to the way their performances are evaluated through the medium of reported earnings have permitted their decision-making behavior to be influenced by their perceptions of how such behavior will be seen through the prism of accounting earnings. Still other such companies have tailored their accounting practices to reflect their economic performances in the best light—and the managers are evidently loathe to change their decision-making behavior in order to accommodate newly imposed accounting standards. This would also be a concern to managers who are being paid under incentive compensation plans.[31]

- *The enormity of the impact.* Several of the issues facing the APB and the FASB in recent years have portended such a high degree of impact on either the volatility or level of earnings and other key financial figures and ratios that the FASB can no longer discuss the proposed accounting treatments without encountering incessant arguments over the probable economic consequences. Particularly apt examples are accounting for foreign exchange fluctuations, domestic inflation and relative price changes, and the exploration and drilling costs of companies in the petroleum industry.

- *The growth in the information economics–social choice, behavioral, income smoothing, and decision usefulness literature in accounting.* Recent writings in the information economics–social choice literature have provided a broad analytical framework within which the problems of economic consequences may be conceptualized. Beginning with Stedry,[32] the literature on the behavioral implications of accounting numbers has grown significantly, drawing the attention of researchers and policy makers to the importance of considering the effects of accounting information. The literature on income smoothing has suggested the presence of a managerial motive for influencing the measurement of earnings trends. Finally, the decision usefulness literature, although it is confined to the direct users of accounting information, has served to lessen the inclination of accountants to argue over the inherent "truth" of different accounting incomes and, instead, to focus on the use of information by those who receive accounting reports.[33]

- *The insufficiency of the procedural reforms adopted by the APB and the FASB.* Despite the succession of

---

[31] Alfred Rappaport, "Executive Incentives vs. Corporate Growth," *Harvard Business Review*, July–August 1978, pp. 81–88.

[32] Andrew C. Stedry, *Budget Control and Cost Behavior* (Englewood Cliffs, N.J.: Prentice-Hall, Inc., 1960).

[33] Committee on concepts and standards for external financial reports, *Statement on Accounting Theory and Theory Acceptance* (Sarasota, Fla.: AAA, 1977), pp. 5–29.

procedural steps which both boards have taken to provide outside parties with a forum for expressing their views, the claims of economic consequences—and the resulting criticisms of the boards' pronouncements—have continued unabated. The conclusion has evidently been reached that procedural remedies alone will not meet the problem.

- *The Moss and Metcalf investigations.* By the middle of 1976, it was known that Congressman John E. Moss (D—Calif.) and the late Senator Lee Metcalf (D—Mont.) were conducting investigations of the performance of the accounting profession, including its standard-setting activities, and it could reasonably have been inferred that the responsiveness of the standard-setting bodies to the economic and social effects of their decisions would be an issue.

- *The increasing importance to corporate managers of the earnings figure in capital-market transactions.* Especially in the 1960s, when capital markets were intensely competitive and the merger movement was fast paced, the earnings figure came to be viewed as an important element of managerial strategy and tactics. This factor is of importance in today's markets, as the pace of merger activity has once again quickened.

- *Accounting figures came to be viewed as an instrument of social control.* The social control of American enterprise has been well known in the rate-regulated energy, transportation, and communications fields, but in recent years the earnings figure has, to an increasing degree, been employed as a control de-

vice on a broader scale.[34] Examples are fiscal incentives (such as the investment tax credit and redefinitions of taxable income that diverge from accounting income) that have an influence on debates surrounding financial reporting,[35] the price-control mechanism of Phase II in 1972–73,[36] and the data base contemplated by the Energy Policy and Conservation Act of 1975.

- *The realization that outsiders could influence the outcome of accounting debates.* Before the 1960s, accounting controversies were rarely reported in the financial press, and it was widely believed that accounting was a constant, if not a fixed, parameter in the management of business operations. With the publicity given to the accounting for the investment credit in 1962–63, to the fractious dialogue within the AICPA in 1963–64 over the authority of the APB, and to other accounting disagreements involving the APB, managers and other outside parties have come

[34] D. R. Scott, though writing in a different context, nonetheless was prophetic in his prediction that accounting would increasingly be used as a means of social control. D. R. Scott, *Cultural Significance of Accounts* (New York: Henry Holt and Co., 1931), esp. ch. 14.

[35] The "required tax conformity" issue of the early 1970s (see Zeff, pp. 218–19) is another instance.

[36] Robert F. Lanzillotti, Mary T. Hamilton, and R. Blaine Roberts, *Phase II in Review: the Price Commission Experience* (Washington, D.C.: Brookings Institution, 1975), pp. 73–77; and C. Jackson Grayson, Jr., and Louis Neeb, *Confessions of a Price Controller* (Homewood, Ill.: Dow Jones-Irwin, Inc., 1974), pp. 71–76.

to realize that accounting may be a variable after all—that the rules of accounting are not unyielding or even unbending.

- *The growing use of the third argument, advanced earlier in the article, in accounting debates.* Mostly for the reasons enumerated above, outside parties began to discard the pretense that their objections to proposed changes in accounting standards were solely, or even primarily, a function of differences over the proper interpretation of accounting principles. True reasons came out into the open, and accounting policy makers could no longer ignore their implications.

It is significant that economic consequences have become an important issue at a time when accounting and finance academics have been arguing that the U.S. capital markets are efficient with respect to publicly available information and, moreover, that the market cannot be "fooled" by the use of different accounting methods to reflect the same economic reality.[37]

The Dilemma Facing the FASB

What are the implications of the economic consequences movement for the FASB? It has become clear that political agencies (such as government departments and congressional committees) expect accounting standard setters to take explicitly into consideration the possible adverse consequences of proposed accounting standards. This expectation appears to be strongest where

the consequences are thought to be significant and widespread—and especially where they might impinge on economic and social policies being pursued by the government. In these instances, the FASB must show that it has studied the possible consequences but that the benefits from implementing the standards outweigh the possible adverse consequences. Where the claimed consequences have implications for economic or social policies of national importance, the FASB should not be surprised if a political resolution is imposed by outside forces.

To what degree should the FASB have regard for economic consequences? To say that any significant economic consequences should be studied by the board does not imply that accounting principles and fair presentation should be dismissed as the principal guiding factor in the board's determination. The FASB is respected as a body of accounting experts, and it should focus its attention where its expertise will be acknowledged. While some observers might opt for determining accounting standards only with regard to their consequences for economic and social welfare, the FASB would surely preside over its own demise if it were to adopt this course and make decisions primarily on other than accounting grounds.

The board is thus faced with a dilemma which requires a delicate balancing of accounting and nonaccounting variables. Although its decisions should rest—and be seen to rest—chiefly on accounting considerations, it must also study—and be seen to study—the possible adverse economic and social consequences of its proposed actions. In order to deal adequately with this latter function, the board may

---

[37] See, e.g., William H. Beaver, "What Should Be the FASB's Objectives?" *JofA*, Aug.73, pp. 49–56.

find it convenient to develop a staff of competent analysts from allied disciplines, notably economics.

Economic consequences bid fair to be the most challenging accounting issue of the 1970s. What is abundantly clear is that we have entered an era in which economic and social conse- quences may no longer be ignored as a substantive issue in the setting of accounting standards. The profession must respond to the changing tenor of the times while continuing to perform its essential role in the areas in which it possesses undoubted expertise.

Using the FASB's Conceptual Framework: Fitting the Pieces Together

David R. Koeppen

Introduction

The conceptual framework adopted by the Financial Accounting Standards Board (FASB) offers the accounting profession an opportunity to develop a new, more consistent, and logical accounting model. A model is described here that can help accountants to understand the relationships between the individual concepts statements presented by the FASB. This model suggests that the framework, as currently conceived, is sufficiently complete to be applied to situations where accounting choices must be made. Developing an understanding of how the individual parts of the conceptual framework interrelate is a first step in learning how the framework might be applied in practice and, correspondingly, learning how to use it effectively.

A Model for Evaluating the Logical Consistency of a Conceptual Framework for Financial Reporting

To further understand the FASB's conceptual framework and how it might be used in practice, a model that describes the relationships between the individual FASB Statements of Financial Accounting Concepts (SFAC) is needed. One such model, which has been used to represent the conceptual process involved in the selection of accounting concepts and procedures, is presented by the American Accounting Association's Committee on External Reporting.[1] The report of the Committee

[1] American Accounting Association, Committee on External Reporting, "An Evaluation of External Reporting Practices: A Report of the 1966–68 Committee on External Reporting," *Supplement to the Accounting Review* (1969), pp. 79–123. A similar model is presented by C. William Emory, *Business Research Methods* (Homewood, Ill.: Richard D. Irwin, Inc., 1980), pp. 135–39.

presents a four-tier model consisting of:

1. Variables and relationships,
2. Object or activity inputs,
3. Attributes, and
4. Measurement procedures.

The latter three tiers represent the essence of measurement theory. For example, objects represent things that we would like to describe through measurement; attributes are the observable properties of objects (such as size, weight, or color); and measurement procedures describe how the measurement shall be taken.[2] A description of each of the four tiers follows.

Variables and Relationships

The essential variables and their relationships must be defined by the users of financial reports. This tier is represented by the decision model(s) of the user. That is, the decision model specifies a dependent variable which the user is interested in predicting, a set of independent variables useful in predicting the dependent variable, and the relationships of the independent variables to that dependent variable. For example, the dependent variable could be the investor's expected return. The independent variables might include the enterprise's net resources and the flow of goods and services to and from the enterprise. The relationships would specify how the flow of goods and services

[2] For further discussions of measurement theory see, for example, Emory, *Business Research Methods*, p. 118; J. Pfanzagl, *Theory of Measurement* (New York: John Wiley & Sons, Inc., 1968), pp. 15–16; and Warren S. Torgerson, *Theory and Methods of Scaling* (New York: John Wiley & Sons, Inc., 1958), pp. 9–10.

to and from the enterprise, as well as its stock of resources, might be utilized to measure and/or predict the return on investment.

Object or Activity Inputs

Object or activity inputs are used to represent the independent variables that may be useful in measuring the dependent variable. If the dependent variable is the investor's expected return, and the relationships define how the flow of goods and services and the enterprise's net resources may be used to measure expected return, then inputs that represent the flow of goods and services and the net resources are needed. Traditionally, revenues and expenses have been used to represent the flow of goods and services, and assets and liabilities have been used to represent the net resources of the enterprise. For example, inventory represents a resource (an asset) of the enterprise. Correspondingly, cost of goods sold represents an outflow of resources (an expense) from the enterprise to others.

Attributes

An attribute is a property of an object or activity input which is to be measured. An attribute incorporates both a measurement concept and a time dimension.

There are two basic measurement concepts for financial attributes: (1) nominal dollars and (2) real, or constant, dollars. At present, financial reporting requires measurement in nominal dollars. No adjustment is made to these nominal dollar measurements to reflect the impact of changing price levels. For example, under the historical cost principle, inventories are recorded in nominal dollars. When the financial statements are prepared, the inventory is included at the recorded amount. An alternative would be to restate the inventory cost to real dollars by indexing for changes in the price level.

Three time dimensions are available for financial attributes: (1) past, (2) present, and (3) future. For example, an attribute of inventory might be its historical cost to acquire. This attribute embraces a time dimension, the cost to acquire the inventory in the *past.* An alternative attribute might be the current cost to acquire the inventory. This would incorporate a different time dimension, the cost to purchase the inventory at the *present* time.

Measurement Procedures

The measurement procedures are the rules for measuring an attribute. For example, the procedures for measuring the historical cost attribute of inventories would have to specify how inventory records will be maintained—either periodic or perpetual—and which cost flow assumption will be used—LIFO, FIFO, weighted-average, or some alternative cost flow. In addition, procedures for applying the lower of cost or market rule would have to be specified.

Connecting the Four Tiers

An important aspect of the four-tier model that should not be overlooked is the need to develop logical connections between each set of the tiers.[3] This requires that criteria for choosing between accounting alternatives be specified (either explicitly or implicitly). These decision criteria form the logical connections between the tiers.

For example, the decision to adopt either LIFO or FIFO for valuing inventory and cost of goods sold requires criteria for making this choice. Since both LIFO and FIFO provide reliable data, some alternative decision criterion must be used.

Ignoring income tax effects, the proponents of LIFO most frequently argue that this cost-flow assumption matches more recent costs against current revenues, providing a better measure of current earnings. Alternatively, proponents of FIFO argue that this cost-flow assumption provides a better valuation of the inventory, enhancing the evaluation of working capital. Implicitly, the LIFO proponents are suggesting that the statement of earnings is more useful to users of financial reports than the statement of financial position. Conversely, the FIFO proponents are suggesting that the statement of financial position is more useful than the earnings statement. Obviously, each group has a different perception of the *relevance* of the statements of earnings and financial position to users of financial reports.

Using the Model to Develop a Conceptual Framework

A well conceived and fully developed conceptual framework should consider each of the four tiers as well as the logical connections between tiers. The FASB's conceptual framework, in conjunction with existing accounting standards, does consider each of the four tiers and the logical connections between them.

In addition, each tier in the model should be considered sequentially in developing new reporting standards or

---

[3] Robert R. Sterling suggests that logical connections have been absent in past attempts to develop conceptual frameworks. Their absence, he notes, has resulted in concepts that are useless and thus ignored by the accounting profession. Sterling, "The Conceptual Framework: An Assessment," *Journal of Accountancy* (November 1982), pp. 103–8.

EXHIBIT 1 *The Four-Tier Model Illustrated*

Model Tiers and Logical Connections	Illustrative Example
First Tier	
Variables and relationships	Variables = Investor's expected return; the net resources of the entity; the flow of resources to and from the entity.
	Relationships define how the net resources and the flow of those resources can predict the investor's expected return.
Decision criteria for selecting the object or activity inputs	Information useful for assessing the investor's expected return.
Second Tier	
Object or activity inputs	Assets, liabilities, revenues, expenses, etc. For example, inventory would be an asset and cost of goods sold would be an expense.
Decision criteria for selecting an attribute to be measured	Select a relevant attribute measurable with sufficient reliability.
Third Tier	
Attributes (properties) —Measurement concept —Time dimension	Historical cost to acquire —Nominal dollars —Past
Decision criteria for establishing the measurement procedures	Criteria for selecting a system, a cost flow assumption, and any other recognition or disclosure issues.
Fourth Tier	
Measurement procedures	Perpetual vs. periodic: LIFO vs. FIFO, etc.; lower of cost or market.

practices and in evaluating existing standards and practices. That sequential process should help to logically direct the development of accounting standards and practices by assisting in selecting a dependent variable, identifying object or activity inputs and their related attributes, and establishing appropriate measurement procedures. The four tiers, and the examples used in describing each tier, are depicted in Exhibit 1.[4]

[4]A model similar to that depicted in Exhibit 1 was also presented by the AAA Committee

The FASB's Conceptual Framework Project

At the present time, the FASB has issued Statements of Financial Accounting Concepts (SFAC) concerning the objectives of financial reporting by business and nonbusiness entities, the qualitative characteristics of accounting in-

on External Reporting as a flowchart incorporating the standards proposed by *A Statement of Basic Accounting Theory* [AAA, 1966]. These standards are omitted in Exhibit 1, but they would be analogous to the connections between each of the four tiers.

EXHIBIT 2 *The Four-Tier Model and the Conceptual Framework*

Model Tiers and Logical Connections	Conceptual Framework
First Tier	
Variables and relationships	Unspecified
Decision criteria for selecting the object or activity inputs	Objectives of financial reporting (Statement Nos. 1 and 4)
Second Tier	
Object or activity inputs	Elements of financial statements (Statement Nos. 3 and 6)
Decision criteria for selecting an attribute to be measured	Qualitative characteristics and recognition criteria (Statement Nos. 2 and 5)
Third Tier	
Attributes (properties)	Attributes (Statement No. 5). Also discussed in FASB Discussion Memorandum (1976)
Decision criteria for establishing the measurement procedures	Qualitative characteristics and recognition criteria (Statement Nos. 2 and 5)
Fourth Tier	
Measurement procedures	Generally accepted accounting principles

formation, the elements of financial statements, and recognition and measurement in financial statements.[5] Those statements constitute the FASB's conceptual framework. The following discussion illustrates how each of those statements (or portions of the statements) relates to the four-tier model. The relationship of existing accounting principles to the four-tier model is also illustrated. Those relationships are depicted in Exhibit 2.

Variables and Relationships

SFAC No. 1 states that the purpose of financial reporting is "to provide information that is useful to those who make economic decisions about business enterprises and about investments in or loans to business enterprises."[6] The diversity of potential users of financial information who make economic decisions about business enterprises requires that the objectives of financial reporting be "those of general purpose external financial reporting. . . ."[7] Thus, it is impossible to state for which spe-

---

[5] Financial Accounting Standards Board, "Objectives of Financial Reporting by Business Enterprises," *Statement of Financial Accounting Concepts No. 1* (New York: FASB, 1978); "Objectives of Financial Reporting by Nonbusiness Organizations," *SFAC No. 4* (New York: FASB, 1980); "Qualitative Characteristics of Accounting Information," *SFAC No. 2* (New York: FASB, 1980); "Elements of Financial Statements," *SFAC No. 6* (New York: FASB, 1985); "Elements of Financial Statements of Business Enterprises," *SFAC No. 3* (New York: FASB, 1980); "Recognition and Measurement in Financial Statements of Business Enterprises," *SFAC No. 5* (New York: FASB, 1984).

[6] FASB, *SFAC No. 1*, par. 16.

[7] Ibid., par. 28.

cific user decision models financial reporting should attempt to provide data. This means that the variables and relationships of the first tier *cannot* be specified as part of the conceptual framework.

Accordingly, the objectives of financial reporting presented by the FASB are very general and emphasize the preparation of *useful* information. Because of the lack of specific user decision models, the usefulness of the data contained in the financial statements cannot be determined—rather, usefulness is a relative concept and accountants must attempt to discern *more* useful information from *less* useful information.

This can be rather discomforting. If the FASB were to select a specific user decision model, then it would be much easier to determine what data would be the most useful. But that would also make the framework unworkable since it is unlikely that the decision model selected would meet the needs of all users (or even a majority of users). Thus, the first tier must, of necessity, remain unspecified.

Instead, the objectives operate as the logical connections between the object or activity inputs and the unspecified user-decision models. And even though *SFAC No. 1* does not specify a particular user decision model, it does suggest that the users of financial information are generally interested in the ability of the business enterprise to generate favorable cash flows to them.[8] The objectives reflect this emphasis on assessing cash flows:

Financial reporting should provide information to help present and potential investors and creditors and other users in assessing the amounts, timing, and un-

certainty of prospective cash receipts from dividends or interest and the proceeds from the sale, redemption, or maturity of securities or loans . . . Thus, financial reporting should provide information to help investors, creditors, and others assess the amounts, timing, and uncertainty of prospective net cash inflows to the related enterprise.[9]

Thus, more useful financial reports can be differentiated from less useful financial reports based upon the degree to which the reports assist users in assessing their future cash returns.

SFAC No. 1 also states that ''[t]he primary focus of financial reporting is information about an enterprise's performance provided by measures of earnings and its components.''[10] This focus on earnings provides the rationale for using accrual accounting instead of cash-basis accounting. It also implies that users of financial statements consider the earnings statement to be the primary financial statement. This suggests that those accounting principles that provide better measures of current earnings, such as LIFO, are more useful and should be preferred over alternative accounting principles.

In summary, *SFAC No. 1* suggests that the object and activity inputs that should be included in the financial reports are those that provide either direct or indirect measures of cash flow potential. Users of the financial reports should be able to use this information to assess the enterprise's future cash flows and its ability to generate positive cash flows to the user.

Object or Activity Inputs
SFAC No. 6 defines ten elements of financial statements which represent the

---

[8] Ibid., pars. 25 and 30.

[9] Ibid., par. 37.

[10] Ibid., par. 43.

object or activity inputs needed to measure the performance and status of an entity. Those ten elements—assets, liabilities, equity, investments by owners, distributions to owners, comprehensive income, revenues, expenses, gains, and losses—are the "building blocks with which financial statements are constructed. . . ."[11] The elements represent the independent variables desired by users for assessing future cash flows.

The definitions of the elements can be used as a "significant first screen in determining the content of financial statements."[12] That is, if an item does not meet *all* of the essential characteristics of an element, then it should *not* be included in the financial statements. Alternatively, if an item does meet all of the essential characteristics of an element, then it *may* be considered for inclusion in the financial statements.

For example, assets are defined as "probable future economic benefits obtained or controlled by a particular entity as a result of past transactions or events."[13] More specifically, *SFAC No. 6* provides three essential characteristics of an asset:

(a) it embodies a probable future benefit that involves a capacity, . . . , to contribute directly or indirectly to future net cash inflows, (b) a particular entity can obtain the benefit and control others' access to it, and (c) the transaction or other event giving rise to the entity's right to or control of the benefit has already occurred.[14]

Goods held in inventory meet the definition of an asset: The inventory has a probable future benefit through resale that will be evidenced by future net cash flows; the entity will obtain this benefit and can control the access of other entities to it; and the transaction (purchase of the goods) that provided the entity with control over this benefit has occurred.

Once an asset has been acquired, it continues to exist until the essential characteristics of the definition are no longer met. That is, either (a) the future benefit of the asset is impaired or destroyed, or (b) the entity can no longer obtain or control that benefit. For example, when goods included in inventory are sold, the entity loses its ability to control others' access to the future benefits of those goods. This would result in an *expense*. If, however, the goods were destroyed in a warehouse fire, the loss of future benefits would be a nonoperating *loss*. If, instead, the future benefits of the goods are impaired because of obsolescence, this impairment would be an operating *loss*.[15]

The existence of a loss due to the impairment of future benefits suggests that a gain might also exist if the future benefits are enhanced. That is in fact the case. The definition of a gain and of comprehensive income are sufficiently broad to include increases in value caused by an increase in the future benefits of the asset. However, it must be remembered that meeting the definitions is only the first screen—meaning that those gains *may* be considered for inclusion in the financial statements—not that they either must be or will be. *SFAC No. 6* states:

---

[11] FASB, *SFAC No. 6*, par. 5.

[12] Ibid., par. 23.

[13] Ibid., par. 25.

[14] Ibid., par. 26.

[15] The distinction between expenses and losses (and between revenues and gains) as parts of comprehensive income is primarily one of display. The primary purpose of making this distinction is to make the financial statements more useful (ibid., pars. 88–89).

Particular items that qualify as assets or liabilities under the definitions may need to be excluded from formal incorporation in financial statements for reasons relating to measurement, uncertainty, or unreliability, but they are not excluded by the definitions.[16]

Consider research and development costs, for example. Those costs meet the three essential characteristics of the definition of an asset—they provide future benefits, the entity can control access to those benefits, and the transaction giving rise to the entity's right to those benefits has occurred. However, the uncertainty of those future benefits and the difficulty of their measurement are so great that no asset is recognized and those costs are expensed as incurred.

Recognition Criteria

SFAC No. 5 provides four recognition criteria that must be met to incorporate an item into the financial statements. Those criteria include (1) definitions of elements, (2) measurability, (3) relevance, and (4) reliability.[17] The definitions have already been discussed. The remaining three recognition criteria introduce attributes, the third tier in the model, and the qualitative characteristics (such as relevance and reliability).

Attributes

The five attributes currently used in financial reporting are discussed briefly in *SFAC No. 5*.[18] These are (a) historical cost, (b) current (replacement) cost, (c) current market value, (d) net realizable value, and (e) present value of future cash flows. Each of these five attributes is used in current practice.

As noted earlier, these attributes differ with respect to the time dimension incorporated in each. Historical costs are based on the *past;* current costs, current market values, and net realizable values are based on the *present;* and the present value of future cash flows is based on the *future.*

The monetary unit or measurement scale suggested by *SFAC No. 5* is nominal dollars. And unless inflation escalates dramatically, nominal dollars will continue to be used for accounting measures.[19]

As an example, inventory is initially recorded at its historical cost—the amount paid to acquire the asset. However, when lower of cost or market is applied in preparing the financial reports, current replacement cost or net realizable value may be used instead of historical cost. Each of these three attributes, however, would be measured in nominal dollars, with no adjustment for changes in price levels.

Selecting an Attribute

More important than the basic attributes, however, is the decision to select one or another of the attributes. How does one choose the most useful attribute in the circumstances?

This decision must be based on the qualities, or qualitative characteristics,

---

[16] Ibid., par. 47.

[17] *SFAC No. 5,* par. 63. The Statement notes that recognition is also subject to a cost–benefit constraint and a materiality threshold.

[18] Ibid., par. 67. These five concepts are presented in more detail in FASB, "Conceptual Framework for Financial Accounting and Reporting: Elements of Financial Statements and Their Measurement," *FASB Discussion Memorandum* (New York: FASB, 1976). The reader is referred to this document for additional discussion of the concepts.

[19] Ibid., pars. 71–72.

of the data.[20] Those "qualities of useful accounting information should provide guidance in choosing between alternative ways of representing economic events."[21] That is, the qualitative characteristics should assist accountants in distinguishing information which is more useful from that which is less useful.

The two primary qualities of accounting information presented in *SFAC No. 2* are summarized in the third and fourth recognition criteria—those qualities are relevance and reliability. If either of those qualities is completely absent, the resulting financial reports will not be useful. If information lacks the ability to make a difference in user decisions, it is irrelevant and thus useless. Alternatively, if information is not reliable, then it cannot be trusted or relied on and is also useless.

Individuals are likely to have different opinions on the importance of each of the two primary qualities in any set of circumstances. The overriding concern, however, should be to provide the most useful information for decision making.

Relevant Information. In order to be relevant, information must have either predictive ability or feedback value and it must be communicated in a timely manner.

Essentially, information has predictive ability or feedback value if it can assist users in reducing uncertainty. Thus, information which aids users in more accurately assessing the amounts, timing, and uncertainty of future cash flows would be preferred.

This information must also be received in a timely manner. Timeliness explains why the use of estimates is so pervasive in financial reporting. Estimates are used to provide information to users about the effects of uncertain events and transactions in a timely manner. Thus, estimates are a response to uncertainty, aiding users in assessing the amounts, timing, and uncertainty of future cash flows.

Assessing the amounts, timing, and uncertainty of future cash flows related to inventory suggests that historical costs would probably not be the most relevant attribute (especially in periods of changing prices). Rather, current costs would probably be more relevant to users. However, because of reliability issues, a current cost system for inventory is unlikely to be adopted.

Reliability Information. To be reliable, information must be representationally faithful, verifiable, and neutral. These characteristics help assure that the information in financial reports can be relied on for decision-making purposes.

Representational faithfulness means that there is a correspondence between what measures appear in the financial statements and what those measures purport to represent. For example, the inventory on the balance sheet should correspond with an existing inventory. If the inventory does not exist, or

---

[20] The qualitative characteristics are pervasive—they can be utilized as decision criteria, or logical connections, in going between any two of the four tiers. Their primary applications, however, are as the connections between the object or activity inputs and the attributes to be measured, and between the attributes and the measurement rules. Correspondingly, the recognition criteria, which are derived largely from the qualitative characteristics, are most useful between these same sets of tiers.

[21] *SFAC No. 2,* par. 11.

if its value has been impaired, then the measure is not representationally faithful.

Obtaining verifiable information helps to minimize bias on the part of the measurer. Verifiable information implies that a consensus or agreement can be reached by different measurers in taking the same measurement. For inventory, the historical cost attribute is the most verifiable; that is, different measurers are likely to agree on the historical cost of the inventory. In cases where the inventory's value has been impaired (such as through obsolescence), the market value of the inventory can usually be verified. However, in cases where the inventory's value has been enhanced, the market value of the inventory is much less likely to be verifiable. (It is easier to obtain agreement on the amount of an unrealized loss than it is the amount of an unrealized gain.)

Reliable information must also be neutral. That is, the information should not be presented so as to influence behavior in a particular direction—it should be concerned primarily with providing useful information.

Selecting the most useful attribute is a difficult decision, but one which must be made. Both relevance and reliability must be considered, and it may be necessary to make trade-offs between these two primary characteristics. For inventory, it would appear that market values are more relevant than historical costs for assessing future cash flows. However, historical costs are more reliable than market values. Market values that reflect a loss in the utility of the inventory appear to be adequately reliable, however, and either the current cost or net realizable value attribute should be used. In general, market values that reflect a gain in the utility of the inventory

are not sufficiently reliable to warrant the use of a market value based attribute.

Measurement Procedures

The final step in the four-tier model is the establishment of the measurement procedures. Establishing the measurement procedures must reflect the information needs of users, the elements involved, the attributes to be measured—in short, all of the previous tiers and decisions which had to be considered—as well as any further recognition and display issues. These procedures make up the content of generally accepted accounting principles (GAAP).

SFAC No. 5 provides general guidance for establishing these measurement procedures or GAAP. In addition to the recognition criteria discussed earlier, *SFAC No. 5* discusses what a full set of financial statements should include, as well as the need for classification and aggregation of the information to be included in the financial statements.[22] The Statement also provides more detailed guidance for the recognition of revenues and expenses.[23]

In general, revenues should not be recognized unless they have been earned and have either been realized or are realizable. This means that the entity must have performed substantially all that is required of it to be entitled to the benefits of the revenues, and the related assets have been exchanged for cash or claims to cash. For inventories, this generally means that no revenue will be recognized until the point of sale—the point at which substantial accomplishment occurs and the revenue

---

[22] *SFAC No. 5,* pars. 13–57.

[23] Ibid., pars. 83–87.

is earned. Point of sale would also correspond with the exchange of the inventory for cash or claims to cash. For certain items, such as precious metals and long-term construction contracts, production may be the point of substantial accomplishment. If the asset is readily convertible to cash or claims to cash, recognition may be appropriate.

Expenses should be recognized when it is apparent that the future benefits to be derived from the asset no longer exist or have been impaired. Recognition may be accomplished by matching the expense with related revenues, by expensing costs in the period benefited, or by a systematic and rational allocation of cost to expense over the periods benefited by the related asset. The method of expense recognition chosen is closely related to the costs—benefits and the materiality of the amounts involved.

Finally, given all else is equal, *SFAC No. 2* suggests that an alternative is preferred if it enhances comparability.[24] This would also encompass consistency of accounting methods and procedures from period to period as well as for similar items within a single accounting period. For example, current accounting standards require that lower of cost or market in the aggregate be applied to current marketable equity securities at year-end. This accounting treatment need not be applied, however, to current marketable debt securities. Consistency suggests that debt securities should be accounted for in the same manner as equity securities. Thus, lower

of cost or market would be the preferred accounting method for current marketable debt securities.

Conclusions

The concepts and interrelationships of the six Concepts Statements have been examined in the context of the four-tier model. This suggests that the provision of useful information requires careful consideration of the needs of users of financial reports, the definitions of the elements of financial statements, the attributes of the elements to be measured, and the rules for taking those measurements. In addition, decision criteria which could be used to logically connect each of the four tiers were essential. The most fundamental of those criteria are the qualitative characteristics. Those characteristics, such as relevance and reliability, assist in making accounting choices.

The FASB's conceptual framework offers the accounting profession an opportunity to develop greater consistency in accounting standards and practices. In terms of the model presented, the FASB's conceptual framework appears to be relatively complete and should be usable in practice. This is not to suggest, however, that its use will be simple or that the framework can be easily applied. Rather, accountants must continue to improve their understanding of the conceptual framework. Only then will they be able to use the conceptual framework to more effectively and efficiently resolve accounting practice problems.

---

[24] *SFAC No. 2*, pars. 111–122.

Cases

- ## Case 1-1

Rule 203 of the AICPA Code of Professional Ethics requires compliance with accounting principles, and Statement of Auditing Standards No. 43 classified the order of priority an auditor should follow in determining whether an accounting principle is generally accepted.

Required:
List and discuss the sources of generally accepted accounting principles.

- ## Case 1-2

The Financial Accounting Standards Board (FASB) has been working on a conceptual framework for financial accounting and reporting. The FASB has issued six *Statements of Financial Accounting Concepts.* These statements are intended to set forth objectives and fundamentals that will be the basis for developing financial accounting and reporting standards. The objectives identify the goals and purposes of financial reporting. The fundamentals are the underlying concepts of financial accounting—concepts that guide the selection of transactions, events, and circumstances to be accounted for; their recognition and measurement; and the means of summarizing and communicating them to interested parties.

The purpose of *Statement of Financial Accounting Concepts No. 2,* "Qualitative Characteristics of Accounting Information," is to examine the characteristics that make accounting information useful. The characteristics or qualities of information discussed in *SFAC No. 2* are the ingredients that make information useful and the qualities to be sought when accounting choices are made.

Instructions
a. Identify and discuss the benefits that can be expected to be derived from the FASB's conceptual framework study.
b. What is the most important quality for accounting information as identified in *Statement of Financial Accounting Concepts No. 2?* Explain why it is the most important.
c. *Statement of Financial Accounting Concepts No. 2* describes a number of key characteristics or qualities for accounting information. Briefly discuss the importance of any three of these qualities for financial reporting purposes.

(CMA adapted)

- ## Case 1-3

When the FASB issues new standards, the implementation date is usually 12 months from date of issuance, with early implementation encouraged. Becky Hoger, controller, discusses with her financial vice-president the need for early implementation of a standard that would result in a fairer presentation of the company's financial condition and earnings. When the financial vice-president determines that early implementation of the standard will adversely affect the reported net income for the year, he discourages Becky from implementing the standard until it is required.

Instructions
a. What, if any, is the ethical issue involved in this case?
b. Is the financial vice-president acting improperly or immorally?
c. What does Hoger have to gain by advocacy of early implementation?
d. Who might be affected by the decision against early implementation?

(CMA adapted)

• Case 1-4

Some accountants have said that politicalization in the development and acceptance of generally accepted accounting principles (i.e., standard setting) is taking place. Some use the term "politicalization" in a narrow sense to mean the influence by governmental agencies, particularly the Securities and Exchange Commission, on the development of generally accepted accounting principles. Others use it more broadly to mean the compromising that takes place in bodies responsible for developing these principles because of the influence and pressure of interested groups (SEC, American Accounting Association, businesses through their various organizations, Institute of Management Accountants, financial analysts, bankers, lawyers, etc.).

Instructions
a. The Committee on Accounting Procedure of the AICPA was established in the mid to late 1930s and functioned until 1959, at which time the Accounting Principles Board came into existence. In 1973, the Financial Accounting Standards Board was formed and the APB went out of existence. Do the reasons these groups were formed, their methods of operation while in existence, and the reasons for the demise of the first two indicate an increasing politicalization (as the term is used in the broad sense) of accounting standard setting? Explain your answer by indicating how the CAP, the APB, and the FASB operated or operate. Cite specific developments that tend to support your answer.
b. What arguments can be raised to support the "politicalization" of accounting standard setting?
c. What arguments can be raised against the "politicalization" of accounting standard setting?

(CMA adapted)

• Case 1-5

The Financial Accounting Standards Board (FASB) is the official body charged with issuing accounting standards.

Required:
a. Discuss the structure of the FASB.
b. How are the Financial Accounting Foundation members nominated?
c. Discuss the types of pronouncements issued by the FASB.

• Case 1-6

During the past several years, The Financial Accounting Standards Board has attempted to strengthen the theoretical foundation for the development of accounting principles. Two of the most important results of this attempt are the Conceptual Framework Project and the Emerging Issues Task Force. During this same period the FASB has been criticized for imposing too many standards on the financial reporting process, the so-called standards overload problem.

Required:
a. Discuss the goals and objectives of
   (i) The Conceptual Framework Project
   (ii) The Emerging Issues Task Force
b. Discuss the standards overload problem.

• Case 1-7

At the completion of the Darby Department Store audit, the president asks about the meaning of the phrase "in conformity with generally accepted accounting principles" that appears in your audit report on the management's financial statements. He observes that the meaning of the phrase must include more than what he thinks of as "principles."

a. Explain the meaning of the term "accounting principles" as used in the audit report. (Do not discuss in this part the significance of "generally accepted.")
b. The president wants to know how you determine whether or not an accounting principle is generally accepted. Discuss the sources of evidence for determining whether an accounting principle has substantial authoritative support. Do not merely list the titles of publications.
c. The president believes that diversity in accounting practice will always exist among independent entities despite continual improvements in comparability. Discuss the arguments that support his belief.

Recommended Additional Readings

Agrawal, Surenda P. "On the Conceptual Framework of Accounting," *Journal of Accounting Literature* (1987), pp. 165–175.

Beresford, Dennis R. "The Balancing Act in Setting Accounting Standards," *Accounting Horizons* (March 1988), pp. 1–7.

Daley, Lane A., and Terry Tranter. "Limitations on the Value of the Conceptual Framework in Evaluating Extant Accounting Standards," *Accounting Horizons* (March 1990), pp. 15–24.

Depree, Chauncey M., Jr. "Testing and Evaluating a Conceptual Framework of Accounting," *Abacus* (1989), pp. 61–73.

Gerborth, Dale L. "The Conceptual Framework: Not Definitions, But Professional Values," *Accounting Horizons* (September 1987), pp. 1–8.

Miller, Paul B. W. "The Conceptual Framework: Myths and Realities," *Journal of Accountancy* (March 1985), pp. 62–71.

Solomons, David. "The FASBs Conceptual Framework: An Evaluation," *Journal of Accountancy* (June 1986), pp. 114–125.

Solomons, David. "The Politicization of Accounting," *Journal of Accountancy* (January 1978), pp. 65–72.

Bibliography

American Accounting Association Committee to Prepare a Statement of Basic Accounting Theory. *A Statement of Basic Accounting Theory.* Sarasota, Fla.: American Accounting Association, 1966.

American Accounting Association, Committee on Concepts and Standards for External Financial Reports. *Statements on Accounting Theory and Theory Acceptance,* 1977.

Barlev, Benzion. "On the Measurement of Materiality." *Accounting and Business Research* (Summer 1972), pp. 194–197.

Beaver, William H. "What Should be the FASB's Objectives?" *Journal of Accountancy* (August 1963), pp. 49–56.

Beresford, Dennis R. "What Is the FASB's Role, and How Is it Performing?" *Financial Executive* (September/October 1988), pp. 20–26.

Bernstein, Leopold A. "The Concept of Materiality." *The Accounting Review,* Vol. 42 (January 1967), pp. 86–95.

Carey, John L. *The Rise of the Accounting Profession,* Vol. 1. New York: American Institute of Certified Public Accountants, 1969.

Carey, John L. *The Rise of the Accounting Profession,* Vol. 2. New York: American Institute of Certified Public Accountants, 1970.

Chambers, Raymond J. "Accounting Principles or Accounting Policies?" *Journal of Accountancy* (May 1973), pp. 48–53.

Chatfield, Michael. *A History of Accounting Thought,* rev. ed. Huntington, N.Y.: Robert E. Krieger Publishing Co., Inc., 1977.

Defliese, Philip L. "The Search for a New Conceptual Framework of Accounting." *Journal of Accountancy* (July 1977), pp. 59–67.

Deinzer, Harvey T. *Development of Accounting Thought.* New York: Holt, Rinehart and Winston, Inc. 1965, Chapters 8 and 9.

Frishkoff, Paul. "An Empirical Investigation of the Concept of Materiality in Accounting." *Empirical Research in Accounting: Selected Studies* (1970), pp. 116–129.

Gellein, Oscar S. "Good Financial Reporting." *The CPA Journal* (November 1983), pp. 39–45.

Glazer, Alan S., and Henry R. Jaenicke. "The Conceptual Framework, Museum Collections, and User Oriented Financial Statements," *Accounting Horizons* (December 1991), pp. 28–43.

Hatfield, Henry Rand. "An Historical Defense of Bookkeeping." *Journal of Accountancy* (April 1924), pp. 241–253.

Hertz, Ronald S. "Standards Overload—a Euphemism." *The CPA Journal* (October 1983), pp. 24–33.

Hines, Ruth D. "The FASBs Conceptual Framework, Financial Accounting and the Maintenance of the Social World." *Accounting, Organizations and Society* (1991), pp. 313–332.

Holder, William, and Kimberly Eudy. "A Framework for Building an Accounting Constitution." *Journal of Accounting Auditing and Finance* (Winter 1982), pp. 111–125.

Horngren, Charles T. "Accounting Principles: Private or Public Sector?" *Journal of Accountancy* (May 1972), pp. 37–41.

Ijiri, Yugi. *Theory of Accounting Measurement.* Sarasota, Fla.: American Accounting Association, 1975.

Larson, Rholan E., and Thomas P. Kelley. "Differential Measurement in Accounting Standards: The Concept Makes Sense." *Journal of Accountancy* (November 1984), pp. 78–86.

Lee, Bernard Z., Rholan E. Larson, and Philip B. Chenok. "Issues Confronting the Accounting Profession." *Journal of Accountancy* (November 1983), pp. 78–85.

Littleton, A. C. *Accounting Evolution to 1900.* New York: AICPA, 1933.

May, Robert G., and Gary L. Sundem. "Research for Accounting Policy: An Overview." *The Accounting Review* (October 1976), pp. 747–763.

Meyer, Philip E. "A Framework for Understanding 'Substance Over Form' in Accounting." *The Accounting Review* (January 1976), pp. 80–89.

Miller, Paul B. W. "A New View of Comparability." *Journal of Accountancy* (August 1978), pp. 70–78.

Murray, Dennis, and Raymond Johnson. "Differential GAAP and the FASB's Conceptual Framework." *Journal of Accounting Auditing and Finance* (Fall 1983), pp. 4–15.

Mosso, David. "Standards Overload—No Simple Solution." *The CPA Journal* (October 1983), pp. 12–22.

Paton, William Andrew. *Accounting Theory*. Houston: Scholars Book Co., 1972 (originally published, New York: The Ronald Press Company, 1922).

Paton, W. A., and A. C. Littleton. *An Introduction to Corporate Accounting Standards*. Sarasota, Fla.: American Accounting Association, 1940.

Pattillo, James W. *The Concept of Materiality in Financial Reporting*. New York: Financial Executives Research Foundation, 1976.

Previts, Gary John. "The SEC and Its Chief Accountants: Historical Impressions." *Journal of Accountancy* (August 1978), pp. 83–91.

Previts, Gary John, and Barbara Dubis Merino. *A History of Accounting in America*. New York: Ronald Press, 1979.

Richardson, Frederick M. "Standards Overload: A Case for Accountant Judgment." *The CPA Journal* (October 1986), pp. 44–52.

Ronen, Joshua, and Michael Schiff. "The Setting of Financial Accounting Standards—Private or Public? *Journal of Accountancy* (January 1978), pp. 66–73.

Snavely, H. Jim. "Needed: An Accounting Constitution." *Management Accounting* (May 1987), pp. 43–47.

Sorter, George H., and Martin S. Gans. "Opportunities and Implications of the Report on Objectives of Financial Statements." *Studies on Financial Accounting Objectives: 1974*. Supplement to Vol. 12 of the *Journal of Accounting Research*, pp. 1–12.

Sprouse, Robert T. "The Importance of Earnings in the Conceptual Framework." *Journal of Accountancy* (January 1978), pp. 64–71.

Sprouse, Robert T. "Prospects for Progress in Financial Reporting." *Financial Analysts Journal* (September–October 1979), pp. 56–60.

Stanga, Keith G., and Jan R. Williams. "The FASB's Objectives of Financial Reporting." *The CPA Journal* (May 1979), pp. 30–34.

Sterling, Robert R. "Conservatism: The Fundamental Principle of Valuation in Traditional Accounting." *Abacus* (December 1967), pp. 109–132.

Sterling, Robert R. "Decision Oriented Financial Accounting." *Accounting and Business Research* (Summer 1972), pp. 198–208.

Sterling, Robert R. "The Going Concern: An Examination." *The Accounting Review* (July 1968), pp. 481–502.

Sterling, Robert R. "A Test of the Uniformity Hypothesis." *Abacus* (September 1969), pp. 37–47.

Tippet, M. "The Axioms of Accounting Measurement." *Accounting and Business Research* (Autumn 1978), pp. 266–278.

Zeff, Stephen A. "Some Junctures in the Evolution of the Process of Establishing Accounting Principles in the U.S.A.: 1917–1972." *The Accounting Review* (July 1984), pp. 447–468.

Zell, Gary A. "The Relationship Between the SEC and the FASB." *The Ohio CPA Journal* (Spring 1982), pp. 81–83.

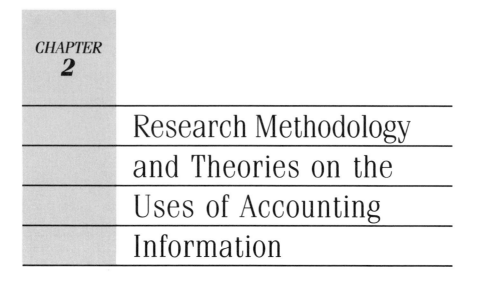

Research Methodology and Theories on the Uses of Accounting Information

To have a science is to have recognized a domain and a set of phenomena in that domain, and next to have defined a theory whose inputs and outputs are descriptions of phenomena (the first are observations, the second are predictions), whose terms describe the underlying reality of the domain.[1] In Chapter 1, the FASB's Conceptual Framework Project was introduced as the state of the art theory of accounting. However, this theory does not explain how accounting information is used because very little predictive behavior is explained by existing accounting theory. Over the years, there has been a great deal of theorizing by accountants that has provided new insights and various ways of looking at accounting and its outcomes. There is a distinction between theorizing and theory construction. Theorizing is the first step to theory construction, but it is frequently lacking because its results are untested or untestable value judgments.[2]

In the following pages we will first introduce several research methods that might be used to develop theories of accounting and its uses. Next a number of theories on the outcomes of accounting are discussed, including the efficient market hypothesis, the capital asset pricing model, agency theory, and critical perspective research. It should be noted that none of these theories is completely accepted; consequently, each of them is somewhere along the path between theorizing and theory.

[1] Peter Caws, "Accounting Research—Science or Methodology," in Robert R. Sterling (ed.) *Research Methodology in Accounting* (Scholars Book Company, 1972), p. 71.

[2] Edwin H. Caplan, "Accounting Research as an Information Source for Theory Construction," in Robert R. Sterling (ed.) *Research Methodology in Accounting* (Scholars Book Company, 1972), p. 46.

Research Methodology

Accounting theory can be developed by using several research methodologies. Among the more commonly identified methodologies are (1) the deductive approach, (2) the inductive approach, (3) the pragmatic approach, (4) the ethical approach, and (5) the behavioral approach. In this section we will briefly describe each of these research approaches. In addition, the scientific method of inquiry, which is essentially a combination of deductive and inductive reasoning, will be presented as a guide to research in accounting theory development.

Deductive Approach

The deductive approach to the development of theory begins with the establishment of objectives. Once the objectives have been identified, certain key definitions and assumptions must be stated. The researcher must then develop a logical structure for accomplishing the objectives, based on the definitions and assumptions. This methodology is often described as "going from the general to the specific." If accounting theory is to be developed using the deductive approach, the researcher must develop a structure that includes the objectives of accounting, the environment in which accounting is operating, the definitions and assumptions of the system, and the procedures and practices, all of which follow a logical pattern.

The deductive approach is essentially a mental or "armchair" type of research. The validity of any accounting theory developed through this process is highly dependent on the ability of the researcher to identify correctly and relate the various components of the accounting process in a logical manner. To the extent that the researcher is in error as to the objectives, the environment, or the ability of the procedures to accomplish the objectives, the conclusions reached will also be in error.

Inductive Approach

The inductive approach to research emphasizes making observations and drawing conclusions from those observations. Thus, this method is described as "going from the specific to the general," because the researcher generalizes about the universe on the basis of limited observations of specific situations.

Accounting Principles Board Statement No. 4 is an example of inductive research. It stated that the "generally accepted accounting principles" that were described in the statement were based primarily on observation of current practice. In addition, the APB acknowledged that the then current principles had not been derived from the environment, objectives, and basic features of financial accounting. Thus, the study was essentially inductive in approach.

Pragmatic Approach

The pragmatic approach to theory development is based on the concept of utility or usefulness. Once the problem has been identified, the researcher attempts to find a utilitarian solution, that is, one that will resolve the problem. This does not suggest that the optimum solution has been found, or that the solution will accomplish some stated objective. (Actually, the only objective may be to find a "workable" solution to a problem.) Thus, any answers obtained through the pragmatic approach should be viewed as tentative solutions to problems.

Unfortunately in accounting, most of the current principles and practices have resulted from the pragmatic approach, and the solutions have been adopted as "generally accepted accounting principles," rather than as an expedient resolution to a problem. As noted in Chapter 1, the Sanders, Hatfield, and Moore study, *A Statement of Accounting Principles,* was a pragmatic approach to theory construction. Unfortunately much subsequent theory development also used this approach. As a result, the accounting profession must frequently admit that a certain practice is followed merely because "that is the way we have always done it," a most unsatisfactory reason, particularly when such questions arise in legal suits.

Scientific Method of Inquiry

The scientific method of inquiry, as the name suggests, was developed for the natural and physical sciences and not specifically for social sciences such as accounting. There are some clear limitations on the application of this research methodology to accounting; for example, the influence of people and the economic environment makes it impossible to hold the variables constant. Nevertheless, an understanding of the scientific method can provide useful insights as to how research should be conducted.

Conducting research by the scientific method involves five major steps, which may also have several substeps.

1. Identify and state the problem to be studied.
2. State the hypotheses to be tested.
3. Collect the data that seem necessary for testing the hypotheses.
4. Analyze and evaluate the data in relation to the hypotheses.
5. Draw a tentative conclusion.

Although the steps are listed sequentially, there is considerable back-and-forth movement between the steps. For example, at the point of stating the hypotheses, it may be necessary to go back to step 1 and state the problem more precisely. Again, when collecting data, it may be necessary to clarify the problem or the hypotheses, or both. This back-and-forth motion continues all through the process and is a major factor in the strength of the scientific method.

The back-and-forth movement involved in the scientific method also suggests why it is difficult to do purely deductive or inductive research. Once the problem has been identified, the statement of hypotheses is primarily a deductive process, but the researcher must have previously made some observations in order to formulate expectations. The collection of data is primarily an inductive process, but determining what to observe and which data to collect will be influenced by the hypotheses. Thus, the researcher may, at any given moment, emphasize induction or deduction, but each is influenced by the other and the emphasis is continually shifting so that the two approaches are coordinate aspects of one method.

Unfortunately, the scientific method of inquiry has received only limited attention in accounting research. Those procedures found to have "utility" have become generally accepted irrespective of whether they were tested for any relevance to a particular hypothesis.

Other Research Approaches

Various writers have also discussed the ethical and behavioral approaches to research as being applicable to the development of accounting theory. Others view these approaches as supportive rather than as specific methods for research; that is, they can, and should, influence the attitude of the researcher but cannot by themselves lead to tightly reasoned conclusions.

The ethical approach, which is attributed to DR Scott,[3] places emphasis on the concepts of truth, justice, and fairness. No one would argue with these concepts as guides to actions by the researcher, but there is always the question of fair to whom, for what purpose, and under what circumstances? Because of questions such as these, this approach may be difficult to use in the development of accounting theory, but it has gained renewed stature by the emergence of a new school of accounting theory development termed "critical perspective" research discussed in the next section of this chapter.

Accounting is recognized as being a practice whose consequences are mediated by the human and social contexts in which it operates and the ways in which it intersects with other organizational and social phenomena. As a consequence, both the behavioral and the economic functioning of accounting are now of interest, and questions are being asked about how accounting information is actually used and how it sometimes seems to generate seemingly undesirable and often unanticipated consequences.[4] From this realization has come a new school of accounting research and theory development termed behavioral accounting research (BAR). BAR is the study of the behavior of accountants or the behavior of nonaccountants as they are influenced by accounting functions and reports[5] and is based on research activities in the behavioral sciences. Since the purpose of accounting is to provide information for decision makers, it seems appropriate to be concerned with how preparers and users react to information. BAR has been seen as studying relevant issues

---

[3]DR Scott, "The Basis for Accounting Principles," *The Accounting Review* (December 1941), pp. 341–349.

[4]Anthony M. Hopwood, "Behavioral Accounting in Retrospect and Prospect," *Behavioral Research in Accounting* (1989), p. 2.

[5]Thomas R. Hofstedt and James C. Kinnard, "A Strategy for Behavioral Accounting Research," *The Accounting Review* (January 1970), p. 43.

but as not having the impact on practice that it should, given the importance of these issues.[6]

The Outcomes of Providing Accounting Information

The development of a theory of accounting will not solve all of the needs of the users of accounting information. Theories must also be developed that predict market reactions to accounting information and how users react to accounting data. In the following section several such theories are presented.

The Efficient Market Hypothesis

Economists have argued for many years that in a free market economy with perfect competition, price is determined by (1) the availability of the product (supply) and (2) the desire to possess that product (demand). According to this theory, the price of the particular product is then determined by a consensus in the marketplace. This process is generally represented by the diagram below.

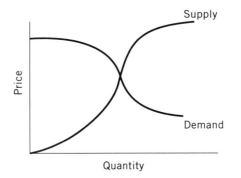

It is also argued that this model is not completely operational in the marketplace because the following assumptions about the perfectly competitive market are routinely violated by the nature of our economic system.

1. All economic units possess complete knowledge of the economy.
2. All goods and services in the economy are completely mobile and can be easily shifted within the economy.
3. Each buyer and seller must be so small in relation to the total supply and demand that neither has an influence on the price or demand in total.
4. There are no artificial restrictions placed on demand, supply, or prices of goods and services.

[6]Edwin H. Caplan, "Behavioral Accounting—A Personal View," *Behavioral Research in Accounting* (1989), p. 115.

The best example of the supply and demand model may be in the securities market, particularly when we consider that stock exchanges provide a relatively efficient distribution system and that information concerning securities is available through many different outlets. Examples of these information sources are

1. Published financial statements from the companies.
2. Quarterly earnings reports released by the corporation through the news media.
3. Reports of management changes released through the news media.
4. Competitor financial information released through financial reports or the news media.
5. Contract awardings announced by the government or private firms.
6. Information disseminated to stockholders at annual stockholders' meetings.

According to the supply and demand model, price is determined by the purchaser's knowledge of relevant information about the product. This model has been refined in the securities market to become known as the efficient market hypothesis (EMH). The issues addressed by the EMH are (1) what information about a company is of value to investors and (2) does the form of the disclosure of various types of corporate information have impact on the understandability of that information?

According to the EMH, the market for securities can be described as efficient if it reflects all available information and reacts instantaneously to new information. Discussions of the EMH in academic literature have varied in the definition of all available information and have resulted in three separate forms of the efficient market hypothesis: the *weak form*, the *semistrong form*, and the *strong form*. The efficient market hypothesis holds that an investor cannot make an *excess return* (a return above what should be expected for a group of securities, given market conditions and the risk associated with the securities) by knowledge of particular pieces of information. The three forms of the EMH differ with respect to their definitions of available information.

Weak Form

The weak form of the EMH is essentially an extension of the random walk theory expressed in the financial management literature. According to this theory, the historical price of a stock provides an unbiased estimate of the future price of that stock, and several studies have supported this argument.[7] However, the argument that stock prices are random does not mean that fluctuation takes place without cause or reason. On the contrary, it suggests that price changes take place because of investor knowledge about perceived earnings potential or alternative investment opportunities.

---

[7] See, for example, E. Fama, "The Behavior of Stock Market Prices," *Journal of Business* (January 1965), pp. 285–299.

According to the weak form of the EMH, an investor cannot make excess returns by simple knowledge of past prices. For example, suppose a certain group of securities with a known risk yields an average return on investment of 10 percent (this average is composed of returns above and below that figure). According to the weak form of the EMH, the stock market incorporates all information on past prices into the determination of the current price. Therefore, the charting of the trends of security prices adds no additional information to the investor. If this form of the EMH is correct, an investor could do just as well by randomly selecting a portfolio of securities as he or she could by charting the past prices of securities and selecting the portfolio on that basis. (It is important to note here that the EMH is based on a portfolio of securities and average returns on investments, not on individual purchases of securities.) The implication of this form of the EMH is that some of the information provided by security analysts is useless. That is, security analysts have correctly maintained that trends in prices are good indicators of future prices. However, knowledge of this information will not aid an investor, because it has already been incorporated into the price determination process in the marketplace.

Semistrong Form
The difference between the weak, semistrong, and strong forms of the EMH lies in the amount of information assumed to be incorporated into the determination of security prices. Under the semistrong form of the EMH, all publicly available information including past stock prices is assumed to be important in determining security prices. In other words, if this form of the EMH is correct, no investor can make an excess return by use of publicly available information because this information has already been considered by the marketplace in establishing security prices. The implication of this form of the EMH for accountants is that footnote disclosure is just as relevant as information in the body of financial statements. Additionally, it suggests that the accounting procedures adopted by a particular organization will have no effect if an investor can convert to the desired method. The results of studies on this form of the EMH have been generally supportive.

Strong Form
According to the strong form of the EMH, all information, including security price trends, publicly available information, and insider information, is impounded into security prices in such a way as to leave no opportunity for excess returns. The implications of this form of the EMH for accountants is that all information available, whether external or internal, will be considered by the marketplace. That is, as soon as a piece of information is known by anyone in a corporation, that information is immediately incorporated into the determination of a security's price in the market. This form, in effect, says that published accounting information is no more valuable than any other type of available information, whether publicly available or not.

Most of the evidence testing this form of the EMH suggests that it is not valid. However, one study of mutual funds, whose managers are more likely to have insider information, indicated that such funds did no better than an individual investor could expect to do if he had purchased a diversified portfolio with similar risk, and, in fact, many did worse than randomly selected portfolios would have done.[8] This study tends to support the strong form of the EMH.

The efficient market hypothesis presents an interesting research challenge for accountants. Research strategies must continue to be designed to test each of the EMH forms so that more solid conclusions can be drawn. The EMH is important to accountants because it provides evidence on the manner in which information about business enterprises is incorporated into the price of corporate securities, and research of this nature will allow investor-oriented accounting principles to be developed.

The Implications of Efficient Market Research

The efficient market hypothesis has implications for the development of accounting theory. Some critics of accounting have argued that the lack of uniformity in accounting principles has allowed corporate managers to manipulate earnings and mislead investors.[9] This argument is based on the assumption that accounting reports are the only source of information on a business organization. The results of EMH research suggest that stock prices are not solely determined by accounting reports. This conclusion has led researchers into investigating how accounting earnings are related to stock prices.

The results of this research imply that accounting earnings are correlated with security returns. Other accounting research has relied on research findings that support the EMH to test market perceptions of accounting numbers and financial disclosures. This research is based on the premise that an efficient market implies that the market price of a firm's shares reflect the consensus of investors regarding the value of the firm. Thus, if accounting information or other financial disclosures reflect items that affect firm value, then they should be reflected in the firms's security price.[10]

The Capital Asset Pricing Model

Investors wish to use accounting information to minimize risk and to maximize returns. The capital asset pricing model (CAPM) is an attempt to deal with both risks and returns. The rate of return to an investor from buying a

---

[8] See, for example, J. Williamson, "Measuring Mutual Fund Performance," *Financial Analyst's Journal* (November–December 1972), pp. 78–84.

[9] Raymond J. Ball and Philip R. Brown, "An Empirical Evaluation of Accounting Income Numbers," *Journal of Accounting Research* (Autumn 1968), pp. 159–178.

[10] Examples of this type of research include G. Peter Wilson, "The Incremental Information Content of the Accrual and Funds Components of Earnings After Controlling for Earnings," *The Accounting Review* (April 1987), pp. 293–321, Thomas L. Stober, "The Incremental Information Content of Financial Statement Disclosures: The Case of LIFO Inventory Liquidations," *Journal of Accounting Research* (Supplement 1986), pp. 138–160, and Bruce Bublitz and Michael Ettredge, "The Information in Discretionary Outlays: Advertising, Research, and Development," *The Accounting Review* (January 1989), pp. 108–124.

common stock and holding it for a period of time is calculated by adding the dividends to the increase (or decrease) in value of the security during the holding period and dividing this amount by the purchase price of the security or

$$\frac{\text{dividends} + \text{increase (or} - \text{decrease) in value}}{\text{purchase price}}$$

Since stock prices fluctuate in response to changes in investor expectations about the firm's future cash flows, common stocks are considered risky investments. In contrast, U.S. Treasury bills are not considered risky investments because the expected and stated rates of return are equal. Risk is defined as the possibility that actual returns will deviate from expected returns, and the amount of potential fluctuation determines the degree of risk.

A basic assumption of the CAPM is that risky stocks can be combined into a portfolio that is less risky than any of the individual common stocks that make up that portfolio. This diversification attempts to match the common stocks of companies in such a manner that environmental forces causing a poor performance by one will simultaneously cause a good performance by another; for example, purchasing the common stock of a beach resort and an umbrella company. Although such negative relationships are rare in our society, diversification will always reduce risk.

Types of Risk
Some risk is peculiar to the common stock of a particular company. For example, a company's stock may decline in value because of the loss of a major customer such as the loss of Hertz as a purchaser of rental cars by the Ford Motor Company. On the other hand, overall environmental forces cause fluctuations in the stock market that have impact on all stock prices, such as the oil crisis in 1974.

These two types of risk are termed unsystematic risk and systematic risk. *Unsystematic risk* is that portion of risk peculiar to a company that can be diversified away. *Systematic risk* is the nondiversifiable portion that is related to overall movements in the stock market and is consequently unavoidable.

As securities are added to a portfolio, unsystematic risk is reduced. Empirical research has demonstrated that unsystematic risk is virtually eliminated in portfolios of 30–40 randomly selected stocks. However, if a portfolio contains many common stocks in the same or related industries, a much larger number of stocks must be acquired.

An additional assumption of the CAPM is that investors are risk aversive; consequently, investors will demand additional returns for taking additional risks. As a result, high-risk securities must be priced to yield higher expected returns than lower risk securities in the marketplace.

A simple equation can be illustrated to express the relationship between risk and return. This equation uses the risk-free return (the Treasury Bill rate) as its foundation and is stated

$$R_s = R_f + R_p$$

where

R_s = the expected return on a given risky security

R_f = the risk-free rate

R_p = the risk premium

Since investors can eliminate the risk associated with acquiring a particular company's common stock by acquiring diversified portfolios, they are not compensated for bearing unsystematic risk. And since well diversified investors are exposed only to systematic risk, investors using the CAPM as the basis for acquiring their portfolios will be subject only to systematic risk. Consequently, the only relevant risk is systematic risk and investors will be rewarded with higher expected returns for bearing market-related risk that will not be affected by company-specific risk.

The measure of the parallel relationship of a particular common stock with the overall trend in the stock market is termed beta (β). β may be viewed as a gauge of a particular stock's volatility to the volatility of the total stock market.

A stock with a β of 1.00 has a perfect relationship to the performance of the overall market as measured by a market index such as Dow-Jones Industrials or the Standard and Poor's 500-stock index. Stocks with a β of greater than 1.00 tend to rise and fall by a greater percentage than the market, whereas stocks with a β of less than 1.00 are less likely to rise and fall than is the general market index. Therefore β can be viewed as a particular stock's sensitivity to market changes, and as a measure of systematic risk.

The previously stated equation can be restated to incorporate β. Recall that we stated the risk-return equation as

$$R_s = R_f + R_p$$

Restating this equation to incorporate β results in

$$R_s = R_f + P_s(R_m - R_f)$$

where

R_s = the stock's expected return

R_f = the risk-free rate

R_m = the expected return on the stock market as a whole

P_s = the stock's beta, which is calculated

The final component of the CAPM is how the risk-expected return relationship and securities prices are related. As was indicated above, the expected return on a security equals the risk-free rate plus a risk premium. In the competitive financial markets assumed by the CAPM, no security will be able to sell at low prices to yield more than its appropriate return, nor will a security be able to sell at higher than market price and offer a low return. Consequently, the CAPM holds that a security's price will not be impacted by unsystematic risk and securities offering relatively higher risk (higher βs) will be priced relatively lower than securities offering relatively lower risk.

A major concern over the use of the CAPM is the relationship of past and future βs. That is, can past βs be used to predict future risk and return relationships? However, much of this concern has been alleviated because empirical research has supported the contention that past βs are good predictors of future stock prices.

The CAPM has also come under the criticism that it contributes to the United States' competitiveness problem. According to critics, United States corporate managers using the CAPM are forced into making safe investments with predictable short-term returns instead of investing for the long term. This is particularly true when companies with higher βs attempt to invest in new ventures. Since a high β is seen as evidence of a risky investment, these companies are forced to accept only new projects that promise high rates of return. As a result researchers have been attempting to develop new models that view the markets as complex and evolving systems to enable business managers to adopt a more long-range viewpoint.

The CAPM is relevant for accounting theory development because it has been used by researchers to test hypotheses that rely on the efficient market hypothesis described earlier. For example, researchers have estimated the expected returns of firms using CAPM to discern whether the release of accounting information has information content. The expected returns are compared to actual returns and the residuals (differences between expected and actual returns) are examined to see if there is a market reaction to the information release. This approach could be used to see if a new FASB pronouncement provides information that was not previously reflected in security prices.

Normative Theory

Financial accounting theory attempts to specify which events to record, how the recorded data should be manipulated, and the manner in which the data should be presented. As discussed earlier, accounting theory has developed pragmatically. That is, if a practice or method has been used to satisfy a particular reporting need in the past by a large number of accountants, its continued use is acceptable. As noted in Chapter 1 few attempts to develop a comprehensive theory of accouning were made prior to World War II. Since that time there has been an increasing demand for a theory of accounting. In the last two decades the efforts to satisfy this demand have permeated accounting literature. These efforts rely heavily on theories developed in mathematics, economics, and finance.

Recall from Chapter 1 there are two basic types of theory: positive and normative. Positive theories attempt to explain observed phenomena. The extreme diversity of accounting practices and application has made development of a comprehensive description of accounting difficult. Concurrently, to become a theory, description must have explanatory value. For example, not only must the use of historical cost be observed, but that use must also be explained.

Normative theories are based on sets of goals, but there is no set of goals that is universally accepted by accountants. Normative accounting theories are usually acceptable only to those individuals who agree with the assumptions on which they are based. Nevertheless, most accounting theories are normative because they are based on some particular objectives of financial reporting.

Agency Theory

Attempts to describe financial statements and the accounting theories from which they originate, and to explain their development based on the economic theories of prices, agency, public choice, and economic regulation, have been grouped under the title *agency theory.* Agency theory attempts to offer a consistent and relatively complete explanation for accounting theories and standards. This research takes the EMH as given and views accounting as the supplier of information to the capital markets.

The basic assumption of agency theory is that individuals maximize their own expected utilities and are resourceful and innovative in doing so. Therefore, the issue raised by agency theory is, What is a particular individual's expected benefit from a particular course of action? That is, how might a manager or stockholder benefit from a corporate decision?

An *agency* is defined as a relationship by consent between two parties, whereby one party (agent) agrees to act on behalf of the other party (principal). For example, the relationship between shareholders and managers of a corporation is an agency relationship, as is the relationship between managers and auditors and, to a greater or lesser degree, that between auditors and shareholders.

Inherent in this theory is the assumption that there is a conflict of interest between the owners of a firm (shareholders) and the managers. This conflict of interest arises from the belief that managers are maximizing their own utility. Similarly, shareholders desire to maximize their own profits. The conflict arises when decisions made by managers to maximize their own utility do not maximize shareholder wealth. For example, a manager may choose accounting alternatives that increase accounting earnings when a management compensation scheme is tied to those earnings.

Agency relationships involve costs to the principals. The costs of an agency relationship have been defined as the sum of (1) monitoring expenditures by the principal, (2) bonding expenditures by the agent, and (3) the residual loss.[11] Watts explains these concepts as follows.

> *Monitoring expenditures are expenditures by the principal to ''control'' the agent's behavior (e.g., costs of measuring and observing the agent's behaviour, costs of establishing compensation policies, etc.). The agent has incentives to make expenditures to guarantee that he will not take certain actions to harm the principal's interest or that he will compensate the principal if he does. These are bonding costs. Finally, even with monitoring and bonding expenditures, the actions taken by the agent will differ from the actions the principal would take*

---

[11] M. Jensen and W. H. Meckling, ''Theory of the Firm: Managerial Behavior, Agency Costs and Ownership Structures,'' *Journal of Financial Economics* (October 1976), p. 308.

himself. . . . the wealth effect of this divergence in actions [is defined] as "residual loss."[12]

Since agency theory holds that all individuals will act to maximize their own utility, managers and shareholders would be expected to incur bonding and monitoring costs as long as those costs were less than the reduction in the residual loss. For instance, a management compensation plan that ties management wealth to shareholder wealth would reduce the agency cost of equity, or a bond covenant that restricts dividend payments would reduce the agency costs of debt. Examples of this last type of costs were included in corporate charters as early as the 1600s. According to agency theory, in an unregulated economy, the preparation of financial statements will be determined by the effect of such statements on agency costs. That is, financial statements would tend to be presented more often by companies with many bond covenants (e.g., restrictions on dividends or relatively more outside debt). Similarly, the greater the value of a company's fixed assets, the more likely a charge for maintenance, repair, or depreciation will be included in the financial statements. The conclusion drawn by agency theory is that multiple methods of accounting for similar circumstances have developed from the desires of various individuals, such as managers, shareholders, and bondholders, to minimize agency costs.

Since private-sector regulations and federal legislation help to determine the items disclosed in financial statements, the effects of regulation and the political process must be added to the results of agency relationships. However, the regulation process is affected by external pressures. Groups of individuals may have incentives to band together to cause the government to transfer wealth, as in farm subsidies. The justification for these transfers is that they are "in the public interest." Additionally, elected officials and special interest groups may use the so-called high profits of corporations to create crises, which are solved by wealth transfers "in the public interest." A prime example is the "windfall profits" tax enacted at the time of the 1974 oil crisis.

The larger a corporation is, the more susceptible it is to political scrutiny and subsequent wealth transfers. Therefore, the larger a company is, the more likely it is to choose accounting alternatives that minimize net income. Conversely, small companies often have incentives to show greater net income in order to increase borrowing potential and available capital. Agency theory holds that these varying desires are a reason for the diversity of acceptable accounting practices.

Agency theory also attributes the preponderance of normative theories of accounting to impact on the political processes. When a crisis develops, elected officials base their positions on "public interest" arguments. These positions are frequently grounded in the notion that the problem is caused by an inefficiency in the market that can only be remedied by government intervention. Elected officials then seek justification of their position in the form of normative theories supporting that position. They also tend to look for theories pre-

---

[12] L. Watts, "Corporate Financial Statements, a Product of the Market and Political Processes," *Australian Journal of Management* (September 1977), p. 131.

scribing accounting procedures that should be used to increase the information available to investors or make the market more efficient.

The advocates of agency theory maintain that it helps to explain financial statements and the absence of a comprehensive theory of accounting. However, the basic assumption that everyone acts to maximize his or her own expected utility causes this theory to be politically and socially unacceptable. Agency theory advocates maintain that this is true regardless of how logically sound the theory may be, or even how well it may stand up to empirical testing. For example, if an elected official supported a theory that explained her or his actions as those that maximize her or his own utility, rather than the public good, the official would not be maximizing her or his own utility.

Agency theory may help to explain the lack of existence of a comprehensive accounting theory. It implies that a framework of accounting theory cannot be developed because of the diverse interests involved in financial reporting. However, there is an even more basic reason why agency theory will have limited direct impact on financial accounting. Agency theory is a descriptive theory in that it helps to explain why a diversity of accounting practices exists. Therefore, even if subsequent testing supports this theory, it will *not* identify the correct accounting procedures to be used in various circumstances, and thus accounting practice will not be changed.

Human Information Processing

The annual reports of large corporations provide investors with vast amounts of information. These reports may include a balance sheet, an income statement, a statement of cash flows, numerous footnotes to the financial statements, a five-year summary of operations, a description of the various activities of the corporation, a message to the stockholders from the top management of the corporation, a discussion and analysis by management of the annual operations, and the report of the company's independent certified public accountant.

The disclosure of all this information is intended to aid investors and potential investors in making buy–hold–sell decisions about the company's securities. Studies attempting to assess an individual's ability to use information have been broadly classified under the title *human information processing* (HIP) research. The issue addressed by these studies is, How do individuals utilize available information?

In general, HIP research has indicated that individuals have a very limited ability to process large amounts of information.[13] There are three main consequences of this finding.

1. An individual's perception of information is quite selective. That is, since individuals are capable of comprehending only a small part of their envi-

---

[13] See, for example, R. Libby and B. Lewis. "Human Information Processing Research in Accounting: The State of the Art." *Accounting Organizations and Society*, Vol. 2, No. 3 (1977), pp. 245–268.

ronment, their anticipation of what they expect to perceive about a particular situation will determine to a large extent what they do perceive.

2. Since individuals make decisions on the basis of a small part of the total information available, they do not have the capacity to make optimal decisions.

3. Since individuals are incapable of integrating a great deal of information, they process information in a sequential fashion.

In summary, individuals use a selective, stepwise information processing system. This system has limited capacity, and uncertainty is frequently ignored.[14]

These findings may have far-reaching disclosure implications for accountants. The current trend of the FASB and SEC is to require the disclosure of more and more information. But if the tentative conclusions of the human information processing research are correct, these additional disclosures may have an effect opposite to what was intended. That is, the goal of the FASB and SEC is to provide all relevant information so that individuals may make informed decisions about the company. However, the annual reports may already contain more information than can be adequately and efficiently processed by individuals.

Research is needed to determine the most relevant information to include in corporate annual reports. Once this goal has been accomplished, accountants will have taken a large step in determining what information to disclose about accounting entities.

Critical Perspective Research

The discussion of the EMH, the CAPM, agency theory, and HIP included references to research studies that attempted to test the hypotheses on which these theories were built. Such testing carries an assumption that knowledge of facts can be gained by observation, and accounting research is completely objective. Critical perspective research rejects the view that knowledge of accounting is grounded in objective principles. Rather researchers adopting this viewpoint share a belief in the indeterminacy of knowledge claims. This indeterminacy view rejects the notion that knowledge is externally grounded and is only revealed through systems of rules that are superior over other ways of understanding phenomena. These researchers attempt to interpret the history of accounting as a complex web of economic, political, and accidental co-occurrences.[15] They have also argued that accountants have been unduly influenced by one particular viewpoint in economics (utility based, marginalist economics). This economic viewpoint holds that business organizations trade in markets that form a part of a society's economy. Profit is the result of these

---

[14] For a more thorough discussion, see R. M. Hogarth, "Process Tracing in Clinical Judgments," *Behavioral Science* (September 1974), pp. 298–313.

[15] C. Edward Arrington and Jere R. Francis, "Letting The Chat Out of the Bag: Deconstruction, Privilege and Accounting Research," *Accounting, Organizations and Society* (1989), p. 1.

activities and is indicative of the organization's efficiency in using society's scarce resources. In addition, these researchers maintain that accountants have also taken as given the current institutional framework of government, markets, prices, and organizational forms,[16] with the result that accounting serves to aid certain interest groups in society to the detriment of other interest groups.[17]

Critical perspective research views mainstream accounting research as being based on the view that there is a world of objective reality that exists independently of human beings that has a determinable nature that can be observed and known through research. Consequently, individuals are not seen as makers of their social reality; instead they are viewed as possessing attributes that can be objectively described (i.e., leadership styles or personalities). The critical perspectivists maintain that mainstream accounting research equates normative and positive theory. That is, what is and what ought to be are the same. It is also maintained that mainstream accounting research theories are put forth as attempts to discover an objective reality, and there is an expressed or implied belief that the observed phenomena are not impacted by the research methodology. In summary, mainstream accounting research is based on a belief in empirical testability.

In contrast, critical perspective research is concerned with the ways societies, and the institutions that make them up, have emerged and can be understood.[18] Research from this viewpoint has been claimed to be based on three assumptions:

1. Society has the potential to be what it is not.
2. Conscious human action is capable of molding the social world to be something different or better.
3. No. 2 can be promoted by using critical theory.[19]

Using these assumptions, critical theory attempts to view organizations in both an historic and a societal context. Its concern is with detecting any hidden meanings that reside in these contexts. Critical theory is concerned with the power of multinational corporations and the resultant distributions of benefits and costs to societies. Critical theory also does not accept the belief of mainstream accounting theories that organizations survive because they are maximally efficient and maintains the methods of research are biased in favor of achieving that conclusion.[20]

[16] Wai Fong Chau, "Radical Development in Accounting Thought," *The Accounting Review* (October 1986), p. 610.

[17] Anthony M. Tinker, Barbara D. Merino, and Marilyn D. Neimark, "The Normative Origins of Positive Theories, Ideology and Accounting Thought," *Accounting Organizations and Society* (1982), p. 167.

[18] Richard C. Laughlin, "Accounting Systems in Organizational Contexts: A Case for Critical Theory," *Accounting, Organizations and Society* (1987), p. 482.

[19] Ibid. p. 483.

[20] Walter R. Nord, "Toward an Optimal Dialectical Perspective: Comments and Extensions on Neimark and Tinker," *Accounting, Organizations and Society* (1986), p. 398.

Critical perspective accounting researchers have been criticized as wanting to change society and only using accounting as incidental to that desire. The contrasting viewpoints of the mainstream and critical perspective schools of accounting research are further illustrated in the readings at the end of the chapter.

The Relationship Between Research, Education, and Practice

Research is necessary for effective theory development. In most professional disciplines, when research indicates that a preferable method has been found to handle a particular situation, the new method is taught to students, who then implement the method as they enter their profession. That is, research results in education that influences practice. For example, physicians once believed that patients undergoing major surgery needed long periods of bed-rest for effective recovery. However, subsequent research indicated that immediate activity and exercise improved recovery rates. Consequently, it is now common practice for doctors to encourage their surgery patients to begin walking and exercising as soon as it is feasible.

The accounting profession has been criticized for not following this model.[21] In fact, prior to the development of the Conceptual Framework by the FASB, research and normative theory had little impact on accounting education. During this period, students were taught current accounting practice as the desired state of affairs, and theoretically preferred methods were almost never discussed in accounting classrooms. As a result, the use of historical cost accounting received little criticism from accounting educators since it was the accepted method of practice, despite the fact that it has little relevance to current decision making. Think about where the medical profession might be today if it had adopted a similar policy—doctors might still be using the practice of bloodletting to cure diseases.

The development of the Conceptual Framework and the refinements of the various theories on the outcomes of accounting are serving to move the relationship of research, education, and practice to a more desirable state. For example, historical cost accounting is now being openly referred to in a disparaging manner as "once upon a time accounting";[22] *SFAS No. 115* now requires certain marketable securities to be valued at their market values (see Chapters 6 and 7); and new schools of thought, such as the critical perspective theorists, are forcing both educators and practitioners to rethink previously unquestioned practices. However, additional progress is still needed. Traditions are difficult to overcome and accountants as a group are not known to advocate a great deal of rapid change.

---

[21] See for example, Robert R. Sterling, "Accounting Research, Education and Practice," *Journal of Accountancy* (September 1973), pp. 44–52.

[22] Richard C. Breeden, Chairman of the SEC, in testimony before the United States Senate Committee on Banking, Housing and Urban Affairs, September 1990.

Summary

Several research approaches are available to assist in developing theories of accounting and its uses. The deductive approach requires the establishment of objectives and then proceeding to specific practices. The inductive approach involves making observation and drawing conclusions from those observations. The pragmatic approach identifies problems and reaches utilitarian solutions. The scientific approach involves testing hypotheses and proposed solutions. The ethical approach emphasizes the concepts of truth, justice, and fairness. Finally, behavioral accounting research studies how individuals are influenced by accounting functions and reports.

Several theories on the outcomes of accounting issues were presented. Efficient market research studies what information is of value to investors and the impact forms of disclosure have on the value of information. Agency theory studies how individuals benefit from particular courses of action. The capital asset pricing model attempts to explain how investors can minimize risk and maximize returns. Human information processing research studies how individuals use and process information. Finally, critical perspective research questions some of the assumptions about economics that accountants have taken as given.

In the following readings David Solomons and Tony Tinker debate the accountant's role as a provider of information and J. Edward Ketz and Arthur Wyatt explore the goals of FASB in light of efficient market research.

Accounting and Social Change: A Neutralist View*

David Solomons

With social change in the broadest sense accounting has little to do. One of the most significant social changes that has occurred in this century is the dramatic improvement in the position of women. Like most social changes, this one has been accompanied by economic changes, such as changes in the pattern of consumption and the distribution of income. Another great social change during the last fifty years is the disappearance of colonialism. That too has brought economic changes in its wake. To suggest any direct connection between those broad developments and accounting would be farfetched indeed.

But on a smaller stage, accounting does have a part to play. It has been asserted, for example, that an accounting standard that requires research and development expenditure to be written off as incurred, in spite of the probable future benefits that are expected to flow from it, depresses the earnings of small immature high-technology companies and thereby discourages technological

Reprinted with permission from *Accounting, Organizations and Society*, Vol. 16, 1991, Elsevier Science Ltd., Pergamon Imprint, Oxford, England.

* Earlier versions of my paper were presented as a Lee Kuan Yew Lecture in the National University of Singapore in December 1986 and to the European Accounting Association at the annual meeting in Stuttgart in April 1989. My thanks are due to the late Steven B. Johnson, formerly of Columbia University, for his help in formulating my ideas on the subject of this paper.

innovation. Without regard, for the moment, to the truth or falsity of that assertion, it well exemplifies the part that accounting may play in encouraging or inhibiting social and economic change.

The question to be addressed here is this. Should accountants see themselves and their discipline as agents to promote (or sometimes to retard) social and economic change? Or should they see themselves as providers of unbiased information, to facilitate social and economic activity by others? By "others" I mean, of course, to include accountants themselves in their capacity as citizens, not as accountants.

A Radical View of Accounting

I want to leave no doubt as to where I stand on this issue. I believe that accountants are like journalists. They should report the news, not make it. This is the view that I shall explore more fully in what follows. But in case it is thought that the opposite view is merely a straw man, I propose to bring into court an outspoken proponent of that other view, and, so far as possible, I shall allow him to speak for himself. I am referring to Dr. Tony Tinker, of Baruch College, CUNY. His views are set out at length in a book, published in 1985, entitled *Paper Prophets: A Social Critique of Accounting*. Tinker and others who think like him use the term "radical accounting" as a label for their views, and it will be convenient if I follow their example.

Let me warn you, before I set out on this examination of radical accounting, that it is not easy to come to grips with it. It is fairly easy to see what radical accountants find to criticize in traditional accounting; and it would not be difficult to suggest modifications of traditional accounting that would go some way to meet those criticisms. But modifications are not what this argument is about. The argument, in fact, is more about the nature of capitalist society and the marginalist theory of value that economists use to explain the working of capitalist economies. This is what Tinker has to say about the dependence of accounting on the marginal theory of value.

Most accounting practice has achieved a harmony with marginalist value theory without much conscious deliberation. This is mainly because marginalism is the only value theory with which most accountants are familiar; thus they reduce all economics to marginalism. . . . Marginalism has virtually monopolized all accounting reflection about value theory, notwithstanding the fact that in order to resolve technical problems of concept operationalization and measurement, accountants have deviated from the marginalist model. These deviations and compromises have all been in terms of the fine print, however; even the much vaunted area of ''social accounting'' is nothing more than marginalism with externalities. The obliviousness of accounting to all other theories of value is sufficient reason for concluding that accounting is unabashedly marginalist in its intellectual affiliations (Tinker, 1985, p. 111).

Tinker then goes on to attribute what he regards as accounting's antisocial bias to this ''intellectual affiliation'' with marginalism. For him, theories are ''weapons of social conflict,'' and accounting theory is no exception. Here is what he has to say on that subject.

Accounting theory, like any social belief, is not merely a passive representation of reality, it is an agent in changing (or perpetuating) a reality. Marginalism provides accounting with a slanted picture of reality that affects both how the latter misperceives, and how it acts on, reality. This slant is ideological insofar as it misconstrues circumstances and events in order to promote certain partisan interests (Tinker, 1985, p. 28).

In a related passage, Tinker has this to say about the social role of accounting.

In addition to reflecting economic exchanges—albeit partially—accounting practice also helps effect economic exchanges. Accounting statements are used in making decisions about the purchase of a company's securities, in assessing a firm's tax liability, in determining the rates a public utility can charge its customers, in deciding whether an employer can afford to pay a wage increase, and so forth. This is not a passive and representational role for accounting; ultimately accounting is part of that exchange process itself—as an informational commodity that promotes exchange. If accounting practice did not participate in exchange in this way, then presumably, competitive pressures would eradicate it as an unnecessary cost of production (Tinker, 1985, pp. 83–84).

I do not understand the distinction that Tinker draws here between accounting's ''passive and representational role'' and its role as an ''informational commodity that promotes exchange.'' A telephone is an informational commodity that promotes exchange; but surely it does this by being passive and ''representing'' the speaker's thoughts to the listener. One could conjure up a bizarre picture of a telephone that not only conveyed one party's thoughts to the other but became itself an actor in the exchange. Tinker's book leaves me with a strong suspicion that this is what he would like accounting to do.

Another source of confusion in trying to interpret Tinker's views stems from the fact that most of the sins of capitalism, as he sees them, are visited on the heads of accountants. Accounting, it seems, has much responsibility for pollution, monopolies, and fraud, as well as other shortcomings of our economic system. We have already noted his view that accounting plays an active role in effecting exchanges and in arbitrating conflicts (a phrase that he uses more than once, by the way). Slaying the messenger that brings bad news, as they did in ancient times, is a custom that Tinker seems to approve of. Accounting reports on an economic system of which Tinker disapproves. Therefore, accounting is to be condemned.

Radical Accounting and Value Theory

But there is more to it than that. The malign influence of accounting on society, as Tinker sees it, stems from the values that are attached to goods and services and resources by the marginalist theory of value in accordance with which our capitalist economy is regulated or self-regulated. I am at a total loss to understand what other values accountants could use. Tinker espouses a Marxist-Labor Theory of Value, which presumably he thinks would give relative values that would be more to his taste. I myself would be happy if teachers and nurses were better paid and business executives, film stars and baseball players were less well paid. But it is obvious that it is society that would have to be changed, not accounting, to bring about such a result. It makes no sense at all to blame accountants for using values determined in the market when they are accounting for market transactions.

There are, it is true, some transactions in which accountants play an active part in determining values. One is the case of regulated industries, such as public utilities, where accounting calculations of cost are used in determining utility rates. Another case is when a value has to be placed on a whole enterprise or a large block of shares in an enterprise that is changing hands. But here, too, there are limits to the values that accountants can determine, and there are other factors at work as well. The most important limit is set by the need for a business to be profitable if it is to survive. A corporation that changes hands at an inflated value will soon flounder if it cannot earn an acceptable rate of return on its investment; and public utility rates that are kept artificially low to benefit consumers will create a demand for state subsidies or will leave the utility unable to raise capital or to replace equipment when it wears out.

The Radical View of Accounting Education

Accounting education does not emerge in a good light from Tinker's criticism of accounting. Here is a passage from his book that reinforces my view that it is society that is really the focus of his attack, not accounting.

Accounting education cannot escape unscathed from this discussion. . . . The accounting education system . . . elevates monetary values as ends in themselves; the surrogate role of money as a mere token expression of human and social needs is ignored. Marx distinguished between the surface appearances of market phenomenon and the underlying social structure that generates the appearances. . . .

Accounting education appears to have outstripped Marx's worst fears in this regard: students are not merely taught to conflate appearance with reality; they learn to reify deceitful appearances and ignore the structure of social reality. . . . Ignorance of this kind multiplies when an accounting education system elevates profit and wealth as ends in themselves and fails to articulate the social purpose of profit and its tenuous connections to social welfare (Tinker, 1985, p. 28).

The idea that accountants should take on the task of looking beyond "market appearances" to the "underlying social reality" is, to say the least, farfetched. It is difficult enough to get consensus as to what constitutes "economic reality", a concept derived from the fabric of *market* phenomena. What hope could there possibly be of finding a consensus as to the nature of "social reality" that is somehow different from market realities?

Positive Elements in Radical Accounting: Neglected Constituencies

There are, to be sure, some elements in radical accounting that should be taken seriously. One is the charge against what Tinker calls "mainline" accounting that it is biased in favor of one or two of the constituencies that it should serve, namely, investors and, to a lesser extent, creditors, while other constituencies are neglected. At least this bias is recognized by the accounting rule-making body in the United States, the Financial Accounting Standards Board. The board has defended the bias,

as regards general purpose financial statements, on pragmatic grounds, as follows:

To identify investors' and creditors' needs as the focal point of financial statement information greatly narrows the range of economic decisions and varied needs for specialized information that general purpose financial statements must try to satisfy, thereby increasing the possibility that the statements can reasonably satisfy the narrower range of needs (FASB, 1976).

That defense is not implausible, so far as *general purpose* financial statements are concerned. But there are other forms of financial reporting that could have been developed to serve the information needs of other constituencies, notably labor and the consumers of the goods and services supplied by business enterprises. Accountants have shown little interest in meeting those informational needs.

It is somewhat difficult to generalize about what might be done to fill these gaps, for more information is already being provided in some countries than in others—the gaps are not the same everywhere. American companies probably make more information available to investors and prospective investors than companies in most other countries. But even there, little thought is given to the needs of labor. Many of these needs were listed in a working paper prepared by the Trade Union Advisory Committee of the Organization for Economic Cooperation and Development (OECD) for a conference on harmonization of accounting standards convened by the OECD in Paris in April 1985 (OECD, 1986). They include:

- statistics of employee turnover, by categories of employee;

- information bearing on job security, such as company plans for expansion and shutdowns;
- shares held by insiders, e.g., management, family proprietors, etc.

This is only a small selection from a longer list of needs that the trade unions presented.

Positive Elements in Radical Accounting: Externalities

A second charge leveled by radical accounting theorists against traditional accounting that needs to be taken seriously is its neglect of externalities. Accounting records transactions that an enterprise enters into, and it therefore takes account of costs for which the enterprise is known to be legally liable. But there may be other costs that it imposes on society for which, under present laws, it is not legally liable. These are not recognized in a company's records and therefore are not included in its financial statements. Examples of these social costs that may be cited are environmental pollution, the impact of plant closings on unemployment in a local community, the effect on health of producing noxious but not illegal substances such as tobacco, and the effect on the environment of erecting unsightly billboards on hitherto unspoiled roads. A particularly clear example of a private cost being transferred to the public arises when a producer of beer or soft drinks switches from using returnable containers to nonreturnables. The cost to society of disposing of the nonreturnable containers strictly should be a deduction in arriving at the producer's social value added; but of course the social cost will not appear in the company's financial statements.

There are positive externalities that go unrecorded also. Thus a company will record the cost of taking down a billboard but will not take credit in its accounts for the improvement in the environment that follows. The same is true for other acts of beautification, e.g. landscaping the area around corporate offices. The multiplier effect of increasing employment by opening a new plant may go far beyond the benefits directly accruing to the employer himself.

Not all externalities are the responsibility of business. As Robert Jensen puts it:

The well-known quotation from Pogo that "the enemy is us" implies that the public-at-large is a source of external diseconomies as well as being the damaged party. Responsibilities for automobile air pollutants, for instance, are difficult to pin solely on the manufacturers, because the drivers themselves are also partly to blame in terms of the condition in which they keep their cars, the way they drive, when they drive, etc. The beer can thrown on my front lawn was not thrown there by the Budweiser Company (Jensen, 1976).

Financial statements capture only those costs and revenues that are internal to an enterprise. This omission of external economies and diseconomies is significant for two reasons. One is that the contribution that an enterprise makes to society, its social value added, may be more or less than the value added that is reported in its statements. Thus its *social* performance is under- or overreported. The second reason why ignoring social costs that are not recognized as private costs is significant is that they may make an enterprise liable for compensation to persons who suffer as a result of its activities. There have been four notable examples in the United States in recent years. The Johns Manville Corporation has had to pay out huge sums to workers and others whose health was impaired by inhaling the company's asbestos. The A. H. Robins company was made bankrupt by claims from women whose health had suffered from the use of a contraceptive device, the Dalkon shield, made by the company. More dramatically, there has been the Bhopal disaster in India. It is too early to say whether Union Carbide has finally settled that matter. In none of these cases did the company's balance sheet show a liability for the compensation payable to the injured parties. The Union Carbide case is different from the other two, because the disaster was sudden and unforeseeable. But in the other two cases, costs were being imposed on society well before the matter came into court. More recently there has been the Alaska oil spill.

Although radical accountants are justified in calling attention to the problems caused by externalities, these problems have been under discussion for many years. The radicals have nothing new to tell us about how to measure the effects of externalities; and unless and until we learn how to solve these measurement problems, this accounting failure is not likely to be remedied.

I have now said all I can say by way of approval of radical accounting. As I have said, what the radicals really want to change is our present form of society and its values. Their attempts to change accounting are almost incidental to their main purpose. How you view radical accounting will therefore depend largely on how you view our present social and economic arrangements.

Supplementary Disclosure as a Means of Changing Corporate Behavior

A desire to use accounting to effect or to inhibit social and economic change is not a monopoly of the radicals. Other accountants who would like to see accounting play an active part as a change agent can be divided into two camps. There are those who are content to encourage or to require supplementary disclosure by corporations about their social behavior, with the expectation that market forces or political pressures will reward good behavior and penalize bad (Colantoni et al. 1974). And there are others who argue that accounting regulators should look to the economic consequences of accounting standards when formulating them, with a view to securing some allegedly desirable objective, e.g. to promote investment in a particular direction, or perhaps to inhibit some wealth transfers that might otherwise take place. The first group wants to influence corporate behavior by encouragement, the second by active involvement in the standard setting process. I shall call this second group accounting activists.

Most people will welcome improved reporting by companies on their social behavior so long as it comes about voluntarily. Presumably the companies will have addressed the costs of the disclosure and will have decided that it brings more than equivalent benefits. Mandated disclosures, on the other hand, must raise a question whether the costs are justified by the benefits *to society*. The fact that the disclosure was not made voluntarily is not conclusive. The benefits to individual companies may fall short of their costs and yet for society as a whole the costs may be justified. In any case, supplementary disclosures of this kind for the purpose of modifying corporate social behavior, whether they are voluntary or mandated, do not impair the integrity of the financial reporting system. They may even improve it.

Accounting Activism and Economic Behavior

Accounting activists are not content to rely on disclosure to bring about changes in corporate behavior. They want to influence behavior more directly, but yet draw back from invoking direct interference by the government. In a country like the United States where accounting rules and standards are spelled out with considerable precision, and where they are numerous and extensive as to their coverage, the activists see accounting standards, which are set by a private sector agency, the Financial Accounting Standards Board, as a ready means of influencing economic activity that suits their particular ends. More often than not, as it happens, influence is brought to bear to *prevent* a change, to maintain the status quo, by trying to block an improvement in financial reporting that the standard setting body is trying to introduce.

There is some controversy among academics as to the magnitude and direction of the economic consequences of accounting standards, but there is no doubt that business executives take the alleged consequences very seriously. I am referring here principally to standards that change accounting measurements, not those that simply call for some change in the information that the preparers of financial statements have to disclose. Most standards do both. Two of the most important such standards worked on recently by the FASB

are *Statement of Financial Accounting Standards No. 87,* "Employers' Accounting for Pensions" (December 1985), and a proposed Statement, "Employers' Accounting for Postretirement Benefits Other Than Pensions," an exposure draft of which was issued in February 1989. The most important postretirement benefit other than pensions is health care coverage, but such benefits may also include legal services, tuition benefits, and others. The amount of controversy generated by these standards can be judged by the fact that the subjects were put on the FASB's agenda way back in 1974. It took 11 years to get the pensions standard out. The controversy over Other Postretirement Benefits is still raging. Both of these standards have brought out the obstructionists, the opponents of change in financial reporting, in force.

These standards are controversial for two reasons. They both involve much looking into the future and many assumptions about what future experience will be with respect to such matters as retirement age, employee mortality, levels of pay, future health care costs, rates of interest, and the value of assets (usually securities) set aside to fund pension and health plans. Actual experience is bound to turn out to be different in some respects from the assumptions on which pensions and health care costs are accrued, with a resulting over- or underaccrual of those costs. Moreover, changes in the assumptions can greatly affect the present value of the benefit obligations disclosed in an enterprise's financial statements. The many uncertainties surrounding the accounting for these benefits have made the whole subject an irritant in the eyes of many American preparers.

The second ground for controversy,

which is even livelier in connection with "other benefits" than with pensions, arises because many enterprises have been content to deal with such benefits on a pay-as-you-go basis, treating benefits as an expense when they are paid out and making no provision for them during employees' working lives, as the proposed new standard will require them to do. The recognition of these obligations, even allowing for the gradual phasing in required by the proposed standard, will have a major impact on financial statements and is decidedly unpopular with American industry.

The gap that separates what is conceptually pure and what is politically feasible for standard setters was vividly illustrated by the FASB in its 1985 standard on pensions, when it admitted with disarming frankness (in paragraph 107) that the gradual amortization of actuarial gains and losses (which the standard requires) rather than their immediate recognition was not ideal. "The Board," it says,

believes that it would be conceptually appropriate and preferable to recognize a net pension liability or asset measured as the difference between the projected benefit obligation and plan assets, either with no delay in recognition of gains and losses, or perhaps with gains and losses reported currently in comprehensive income but not in earnings. However, it concluded that those approaches would be too great a change from past practice to be adopted at the present time.

The reason for the delayed recognition of gains and losses in the Board's standard is the opposition among many of its constituents to the volatility that would be introduced into financial statements if the gains and losses were fully recognized as they occurred. No matter that volatility is a fact of life. It does not belong, it seems, in financial statements, whatever the representation of economic reality might require.

An Extreme Activist View

This example of the FASB's bending to political pressure is a mild one. The result, it seems to me, is to subordinate faithful reporting of financial information to what is politically acceptable to the Board's constituents in industry. If, one day, that constituency becomes more enlightened, it may be that faithful representation will prevail. But one can find more striking examples where the Board has been urged quite openly to subordinate sound accounting to the alleged economic effects that might follow from a new accounting rule or a change in an old one. Some rich examples of this point of view will be found in an Emanuel Saxe lecture by David Hawkins, delivered at Baruch College in New York City in 1973. Hawkins argued there that ". . . because the [Financial Accounting] Standards Board has the power to influence economic behavior it has an obligation to support the government's economic plans" (Hawkins, 1975, p. 11). His lecture is studded with examples of how this might be done. The Board at that time was considering a new standard on leasing, and it was expected to require that long-term leases, which at the time were noted in financial reports but were not required to be included as assets and liabilities in the balance sheet, should be so included. Hawkins argued that putting leases on the balance sheet might raise the cost of financing for certain industries and therefore the board should go slow in pressing for lease capitalization in a period of economic recession. The Board did not take

Hawkins's advice. On the subject of accounting for research and development, he argued that because a requirement to expense such costs might make it more difficult for small high-technology companies to raise capital for growth, the Board should not outlaw the capitalization of R&D altogether. On this matter, too, the Board declined to follow Hawkins's advice.

Another example from Hawkins demonstrates to what absurdities an "activist" approach can lead. After reviewing some earlier advice he had given to the Accounting Principles Board in 1962 urging them to reject the "flow through" treatment of the investment tax credit at that time because he "assumed it was unsound behavior to adopt an accounting method that encouraged corporations to earn material profits immediately by purchasing assets," he explains why he later changed his mind.

Such an approach may have been acceptable and tolerated by the economic planners if the economy was strong and untroubled. But the economy was weak and troubled. . . . Under these conditions I believe now it was irresponsible for me to urge the [APB] to deliberately take action which would lessen the effectiveness of the tax credit in a situation where sound accounting arguments could be made for both the deferral and flow through approaches (Hawkins, 1975, p. 16).

In other words, what is sound accounting when the economy is strong is unsound when the economy is weak. One can conjure up a picture of a standard setting body wetting its collective finger and holding it up to the wind to see if it is blowing hot or cold, and then formulating a standard accordingly.

GAAP vs. RAP

The recent debate about GAAP vs. RAP (Regulatory Accounting Practices) in connection with the savings and loan association (SLA) fiasco has provided another striking example of the subversion of accounting to supposedly serve social ends. Generally accepted accounting principles clearly require that if a financial institution is insolvent, its financial statements should show it as being insolvent. But various regulatory accounting devices have been used to hide the fact of insolvency. One device was to disguise the negative net worth of insolvent SLAs taken over by sound institutions as goodwill in the balance sheets of the acquirers. Another device was legalized in the Competitive Equality Banking Act of 1987.

Under this Act, agricultural banks may be permitted for regulatory purposes to defer and amortize loan losses over a period of up to 7 years, rather than recognize such losses immediately. In addition, regulators may permit an agricultural bank to reappraise real estate or other property acquired as a result of a default on an agricultural loan and defer such losses, if any, and amortize over a period of 7 years.[1]

The statements prepared for use by regulators that incorporated these devices did not purport to comply with GAAP. Their only purpose was to preserve an appearance that the SLA or bank that was in trouble was complying

[1] *Proceedings of the October 8, 1987 Roundtable Discussion on Generally Accepted Accounting Principles and Regulatory Accounting Practices,* ed. Jerry Arnold (Los Angeles: SEC and Financial Reporting Institute, School of Accounting, University of Southern California), p. 59.

with regulatory requirements that, if breached, would require the institution to be closed down. Thus, in the long run, they may have contributed to the magnitude of the insolvencies. Of course, it would have been just as easy, and certainly more honest, for the regulators to waive or relax the regulatory requirements, but that would have made the fact of insolvency, or at least losses, apparent.

A Plea for Neutrality

There should by now be no doubt as to how I view the accounting radicals and accounting activists. I believe they are both misguided, though for different reasons. The radicals really want to change society, and accounting is merely incidental to that desire. The activists want to use accounting to change society, usually in quite small ways, or they want to preserve the status quo by obstructing change. Accountants, as *citizens*, should be as much concerned to bring about desirable changes in society or to prevent undesirable changes as anyone else. But as accountants that is not their job, and they have no special expertise in that direction. Their job is to portray certain aspects of society, not to change it. There are other and better ways to do that.

If accounting is to retain any credibility—and without credibility it is worthless—its guiding light must be neutrality in financial reporting. The FASB has defined neutrality as the "absence in reported information of bias intended to attain a predetermined result or to induce a particular mode of behavior." This is a guidepost that all standard setting bodies should follow, and the FASB's record in this respect has been good. Dennis Beresford, the chairman

of the Board, reaffirmed the importance that the Board attaches to this concept in an address on 1 November, 1988, to a gathering of financial executives. "Neutrality," he said, "is written into our Mission Statement as a primary consideration. And the neutrality concept dominates every Board meeting discussion, every informal conversation, and every memorandum that is written at the FASB."

In a May 1986 address by Arthur Wyatt, then a member of the FASB, there is a clear recognition that neutrality is not always easy to achieve.

The Board believes that its conclusions should be as neutral as they can be when considering the various competing interests within our society. . . . Being neutral in this activity does not mean being unaware of potential consequences, but it does mean focusing on the accounting and economic issues and submerging other biases that might influence the conclusions reached. . . . As private sector standard setters . . . our mission is to establish and improve standards of financial accounting and reporting so that decision makers have available credible, concise, and understandable financial information. That mission precludes placing any particular interest above the interests of the many who rely on financial information (Wyatt, 1986).

I draw attention to Wyatt's recognition that neutrality means "submerging other biases that might influence the conclusions reached." Radicals like Tinker question whether reported information can ever be neutral, because the preparer will always have some biases that will creep in. The bias may be due to a desire to avoid taxation, or to increase managerial bonuses, or to keep reported profits down to avoid public censure for overcharging, or, for those who see accounting as an instrument of the class struggle, to benefit capital at the expense of labor. It is perhaps true that perfect neutrality of information can never be achieved. But it would be as foolish to stop *seeking* it on that account as it would be to stop trying to reduce air and water pollution because completely pure air and pure water can never be attained, or to stop seeking fair-minded judges on the ground that no human being is entirely free from bias, or (to return to an analogy that I used earlier) to stop esteeming journalists who know the difference between reporting and editorializing. We know how much credibility newspapers have in totalitarian countries. If those responsible for regulating accounting ever abandon neutrality as a guiding light, accounting will have lost all value as a provider of useful information. It would then be no more than an exercise in futility.

Bibliography

Colantoni, C., Cooper, W. W., & Dietzer, R., Accounting and Social Reporting, in *Objec-* *tives of Financial Statements*, Vol. 2 (New York: American Institute of Certified Public Accountants, 1974).

Financial Accounting Standards Board. Tentative Conclusions on Objectives of Financial Statements of Business Enterprises (Stamford, Conn.: FASB, 2 December, 1976).

Financial Accounting Standards Board, *SFAS No. 87,* "Employers' Accounting for Pensions" (Stamford, Conn.: FASB, December 1985).

Hawkins, D., Financial Accounting, The Standards Board and Economic Development, *Emanuel Saxe Distinguished Lectures in Accounting 1973–74* (The Bernard M. Baruch College, City University of New York).

Jensen, R. E., *Phantasmagoric Accounting: Research and Analysis of Economic, Social and Environmental Impact of Corporate Business* (American Accounting Association, Studies in Accounting Research, No. 14, 1976).

Organisation for Economic Cooperation and Development, *Harmonization of Accounting Standards: Achievements and Prospects* (Paris: OECD, 1986).

Tinker, T., *Paper Prophets* (New York: Praeger Publishers, 1985).

Wyatt, A. R., "Standard Setting: Process and Politics," *FASB Status Report No. 179* (Stamford, Conn.: FASB 1986).

The Accountant as Partisan

Tony Tinker

David Solomons is an evangelist, not a positivist. He does not say that accounting *is* neutral; only that it should be. We might agree on this point, provided his

Reprinted with permission from *Accounting, Organizations and Society*, Vol. 16, 1991, Elsevier Science Ltd., Pergamon Imprint, Oxford, England.

"neutrality" was tempered and informed by a notion of social justice that acknowledged the diversity of conflicting social interests invested in accounting situations, and that accounting inevitably takes sides in such conflicts. A candid admission by David Solomons of accounting's partisanship in social conflicts would then open up for investigation how we might make the accountant's choice of sides a deliberate and systematic one: a choice that is socially reflective and critically self-conscious.

Unfortunately, Solomons never undertakes this kind of analysis. Instead, he relies on spurious analogies about cartography, speedometers, and journalism in an attempt to legitimatize the neutrality of the FASB and the status quo. Below I question the validity of these analogies and the fallacious notion of financial cartography that springs from them.

Remembering Jim Jones, and Jim and Tammy Bakker, we must be mindful that evangelists have a checkered history. In David Solomons' case, I will argue that his failure to appreciate the radical accounting literature leaves him closer to Canute than to Moses in his call to reverse the tide of radical accounting thought.

The Assumptions of Financial Cartography

The essence of Solomons' financial cartography is that accounting should confine itself to accurately measuring and reporting the monetary values associated with market transactions (Solomons, 1978, 1986, 1991). Financial symbols are the ultimate data for Solomons because, for him, they "faithfully represent" economic reality. Accordingly, he opposes those who question the integrity of financial symbols by trespassing beyond the market realm to their political and social underpinnings. These are areas in which, he argues, accountants have "no special expertise" (Solomons, 1991).

Solomons believes that economic reality exists, independent of our apprehension of it, and that this is the ultimate touchstone of truthfulness and accuracy for accounting symbols (Solo-

mons, 1991). While bias, distortion, and "noise" may interfere in short-term reporting, economic reality eventually prevails in business performance and survival. Thus, for Solomons, accounting *should* report on this underlying economic reality (Solomons, 1986, p. 245).

Solomons makes two implicit assumptions in asserting a tractable correspondence between financial symbols and their reality-referent: First, an epistemological assumption (Philosophical Realism) and second, an economic and social assumption ("The Completeness of the Economic Realm"). Consideration of the first dominates this paper; the second is reviewed only briefly and tangentially.

Philosophical Realism rests on the premise that Reality exists—"out there"—and is unambiguously and faithfully expressed in a system of signs or symbols (Tinker et al., 1982; Lehman & Tinker, 1987; Chua, 1986; Hines, 1988, 1989; Solomons, 1978). Solomons uses several analogies to underscore this point: He argues that accounting should emulate a well-calibrated speedometer in clocking the real economic "roadspeed" of a business entity (Solomons, 1978, p. 37); that it should adopt journalistic standards and report—not make—the news (Solomons, 1991); that it should convey thoughts impartially like a telephone system (Solomons, 1991) and finally, that it should strive for the standards of cartography by devising neutral accounting maps of economic reality (Solomons, 1978, p. 35). Figure 1 summarizes Solomons' notion of Representational Faithfulness or Philosophical Realism.

Representational faithfulness (Philosophical Realism) indicates a correspondence between the levels in Figure 1.

FIGURE 1. *Representational faithfulness.*

Epistemic Level	Metamethodological criteria (Representational faithfulness) ↓
Scientific Level	Accounting theory and practice ↓ ↑
Reality	Economic reality

Thus Solomons appeals to accountants to effect a correspondence between, on one hand, the scientific level of accounting theory and measurement and, on the other hand, the "events" in economic reality. Accounting is held to be akin to journalism, cartography, and speedometry in that we are presumed able to find and extract pure, uncorrupted, neutral "facts" from Economic Reality.[1] The criterion selected by Solomons for instigating this correspondence is shown at the highest (Epistemic) level in the figure: Representational Faithfulness.[2]

[1] The assumption (examined later) is that these levels are independent of each other. Indeed, this independence is a precondition of a correspondence theory of knowledge if vicious circularity is to be avoided (Quine, 1980; Chisholm, 1965). If the levels are not independent—if one level were partially included in the other—then one could no longer serve as an epistemological point of reference for the other; it would be a tautological appeal of validation to an image of itself (Gunn, 1989; Quine, 1980; Tinker, 1988).

[2] This epistemic choice is parachuted in from "outside" the framework. Criteria for endorsing this preference are largely unexamined. True, Solomons does consider a few alternatives to Representational Faithfulness (e.g., market efficiency, Beaver & Dukes,

Solomons' second premise, the "completeness" of the economic realm, actually encompasses a nest of assumptions: First, an economic version of the Realist Assumption, that accounting data is complete in that it can faithfully represent the underlying economic reality.[3] Second, that the accounting symbols of business "survivability" are complete in that they sum up all relevant interests of members of a community, and do so in an expeditious manner (Solomons, 1991).[4] Third, the economic realm is complete in that it can be resolved sepa-

_____

1972, p. 321; the economic capture view, Stigler, 1971; Peltzman, 1976; Watts & Zimmerman, 1978, 1979); but he rejects them using a range of *ad hoc* and often contradictory criteria (Solomons, 1978, pp. 36–39; Johnson, pp. 147–150). Moreover, meta-level criteria themselves require a justification that Solomons does not provide; hence we will see subsequently that while his choice of Representational Faithfulness resolves one problem (vicious circularity) it raises another: of infinite regress (Quine, 1980; Gunn, 1989).

[3] As Hall notes, "reflective" is a better word than "representational" to characterize Solomons' kind of viewpoint because "re"-presentational implies the very notion that Solomons rejects: that the symbol itself may be formative in reconstituting the meaning of the message (Gurevitch et al., 1982; Hall et al., 1978; Hall, 1980, 1983a, b, c, 1985).

[4] This assumption has several components: it refers to the market's level of informational efficiency (semi-strong or strong form); the absence of any delayed, second-to-nth-order effects, and the absence of any serious distributional problems not reflected in market aggregates. The assumption allows Solomons to confine himself to the financial statements as the products of accounting and not concern himself with the second- and third-order "economic consequences" of accounting disclosure (Solomons, 1991; Zeff, 1978.)

rately from the political realm, and that it is possible to "do accounting" in an apolitical manner (Solomons, 1991). If these assumptions do not hold, Solomons' case for financial cartography begins to unravel.[5]

Critique of (Tele)phonocentricity

Consider the commonsense examples Solomons offers to bolster his case for financial cartography: journalism, map-making, speedometry, and telephone communications. Does the telephone really, "convey one parties thoughts to the other"? (Solomons, 1991). Surely, the telephone doesn't convey "thoughts" but what people say. Thoughts and words may be made to differ, intentionally or otherwise. Even if words are like those of Lavinia in Shakespeare's *Titus Andronicus*—"the pure engine of thought"—there is no

guarantee that they will conform to "what is understood".[6] The telephone is selective, and inevitably reflects intended and unintended biases (Ryan, 1982; Arrington & Francis, 1987, 1989).[7]

Solomons' automobile speedometer analogy poorly reflects financial reporting situations. The example would be more appropriate if the speedometer

---

[5] Solomons never addresses the widespread scepticism about market completeness and market efficiency. His response to Zeff, who was one of the first to underscore the politicization and capture of the FASB, completely misses the point (Solomons, 1986, p. 236). While Zeff might agree that, "The FASB would surely preside over its own demise if it were to . . . make decisions primarily on other than accounting grounds" this assumes that Zeff, and critical academics, are dedicated to the preservation of the FASB. This was certainly not a premise of *Paper Prophets*. Charles Lindblom, past president of the American Political Science Association, speaking at an AAA meeting, typified the scepticism surrounding Solomons' market completeness assumption in noting that, in an age when the sales turnover of many conglomerates exceed the GNP of many UN members, it is absurd to accept "voting-with-dollars" as an adequate substitute for a democratic form of regulation of monopoly institutions (Lindblom, 1982, 1984).

[6] Solomons admits that "selectivity" in communication exists, but "the need to be selective . . . does not normally rob [it] of neutrality" (Solomons, 1977, p. 35). Bias, in contrast, occurs when measurements are "selected with particular political ends in mind" (ibid.). This distinction is meaningless because it boils down to the "intent" of the individual. It means that provided the thoughts of the greatest Machiavellian bigot were free of political intrigue and machinations, she could only enunciate neutral statements, according to Solomons.

[7] In his much celebrated critique of reflective approaches, Derrida demonstrates how writing is not reducible to speaking but is an independent form of re-presentation. He shows that writing (the signifier) may affect what is said (the signified) and instances this by when we are "put on our guard" by committing words to paper (Derrida, 1973, 1978). E. P. Thompson provides an earlier example of the irreducibility of different forms of representation (reading and writing) when he describes the wrath of an orthodox Wesleyan minister in discovering working children being taught to write on Sunday in eighteenth century Sheffield. Learning to read and thus absorb God's word was a "spiritual good", whereas writing was "an awful abuse of the Sabbath" and a "secular art" from which "temporal advantage" might accrue (Thompson, 1966, pp. 353–354). For Derrida, there is no transcendental and invariant meaning (and thus perfect reflection) because meaning may change with the speaker, the situation, and "traces" of previous articulations ("the history of discourses").

was wired to the local police station to monitor the driver's speed. Drivers would then be tempted to tamper with speedometer readings to avoid detection and prosecution, and thus would be subject to the same "incentives-to-cheat" as managers who produce financial reports. Such a rewiring would dramatically increase the incidence of tampering, as rental car companies have found when they base their charges on odometer readings. The scale of the multimillion dollar radar detection business indicates the pressures on drivers to cheat, and the irrelevance of Solomons' "Robinson Crusoe type" speedometer example.

Do we really, "judge a map by how well it represents the facts . . . not . . . by the behavioral effects it produces"? (Solomons, 1978, p. 35). Color and size "distortions" to the Manhattan and London subway maps actually facilitate "the behavioral effect of" reaching a destination. Moreover, maps have frequently been political tools in struggles to secure behavioral compliance. European colonial powers "enlarged" their own vicinities and diminished those of others. These "errors" have prompted a flurry of "corrections" in recent years. Maps are never mere miniatures of the original; they are shaped by jingoistic, political, recreational, religious, economic, technical, and other interests—consciously intended, and otherwise. As the semanticist Alfred Korzybski noted, "The map is not the territory" (Korzybski, 1950).

Consider an Australasian map of the world that "inverts" centuries of Eurocentric cartography. Eurocentrics will no doubt argue that this inversion is inconsequential, provided the globe is eventually restored to its "normal" position.

The 1989 CIA map of Israel no longer shows the West Bank as part of Jordan, as did the official 1978 version. The new map sets standards for all U.S. government map-making agencies, and thus has important political, economic, and social distributional effects (*The Jewish Week,* May 5, 1989, p. 4).

Recalling David Solomons' observation that journalists "should report the news, not make it" (Solomons, 1991), we note that the CIA map conforms to a new journalistic code. In June 1989, Israel Broadcasting adopted the biblical names of Judea and Samaria for all future references to the Occupied Territories, banned all references to the Intifada and Chairman Arafat's speeches, designated Arabs who collaborate with the occupation forces as "peaceseekers", and prohibited all positive references to Christianity at Christmas time. The director of Israel Broadcasting was also fired for failing to comply with these reporting standards.[8]

Solomons' Political Lacunae

David Solomons does not say that journalists actually "do" report the news, only that "they should." Similarly, he recognizes that bad cartography does occur, and that "the need to be selective . . . does not normally (although it could) rob the map of its neutrality" (Solomons, 1978, pp. 35, 39).[9] Further,

[8]Tom Wolff's *Bonfire of the Vanities* provides dramatic examples of the way journalists "make" the news in New York. The appearance of a TV news-team at a demonstration guarantees a boom in curious onlookers who then (for news purposes) become part of the demonstration. Journalism is part of the phenomenon being reported on; its own actions reconstitute the reality it is supposedly meant to describe (Wolff, 1987).

[9]Even the late Steven Johnson's sympathetic review of Solomons' 1986 *Making*

he catalogues a range of real and potential violations of Representational Faithfulness in accounting: Hawkins's proposals to exclude leases from balance sheets and his sanction of the "flow through" of the investment tax credit; the amortization of actuarial pension fund gains and losses; the FASB's adherence to historical cost rather than current cost accounting—something he regards as "the primary threat to the credibility of accounting standard setting" (Solomons, 1986, 1991; Johnson, 1988, p. 150).

How does Solomons account for the variegations in interpretation of Representational Faithfulness in accounting, journalism, and cartography? In the main, he doesn't. He gives scant attention to analyzing transgressions. Like Edmund Burke, he seems resigned to the presence of a "swinish multitude", but refuses to dignify its presence with any systematic theoretical interrogation.[10]

Research that investigates accounting errors and distortions by exploring their political and social structural underpinnings is curtly dismissed by Solomons. He rejects the Stigler–Peltzman notion that regulatory bodies, such as the FASB, are captive of the industry they purport to regulate (Stigler, 1961,

1964a, b, 1971; Peltzman, 1976; Tinker, 1984). Likewise, he dismisses Watts and Zimmerman's derivative contention that accounting theories are "Excuses", produced in response to effective demand (Watts & Zimmerman, 1978, 1979; Solomons, 1986, p. 240). Regarding *Paper Prophets,* he refuses to acknowledge that capitalism, based on the asymmetrical relationship of wage labor (requiring personal participation in production) and competitive private property accumulation (which does not) is particularly susceptible to biases and distortions in financial reporting.[11]

Accounting as "Negating of the Negation"

By his own admission, Solomons acknowledges that political forces intrude in the fabrication of accounting signs, yet he fails to theorize the character of this intrusion in any comprehensive way. Figure 2 unveils the radical (critical) accounting alternative that provides an opportunity for interrogating what Solomons takes as unproblematic.

Figure 2 contrasts with Figure 1 because it shows epistemological and accounting considerations as embedded in social reality. Epistemological standards like representational faithfulness, and accounting practices like current and historical cost approaches, are neither inexplicably pre-given nor simple

---

Accounting Policy notes the contradiction between Solomons' commitment to Representational Faithfulness and his trenchant support of current cost against historical cost accounting (Johnson, 1988).

[10] Solomons attributes the FASB's 11-year delay in dealing with pensions (and the even longer delay for postretirement benefits) to controversial and political factors, but he fails to theorize the source of the opposition (or more pertinently, the beneficial interests that profit from nondisclosure), preferring instead to blame "obstructionists."

[11] Examples of such accounting accommodations are legion in *Paper Prophets*: the "cost savings" (and concomitant contingent liabilities) related to toxic dumping; the overvaluation of bank receivables, representing loans "secured" by bribes to corrupt indigenous elites and dictators in the Third World; the mirage of financial viability of savings and loans. Solomons ignores these and other examples cited on pp. 3–78 and 179–207 of the book.

FIGURE 2. *Negation of the negation practical reflexivity in accounting*

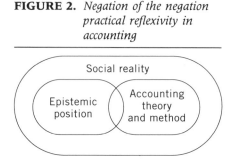

mirror-images of social reality; they are both socially constructed and socially enactive. Thus, ideas and theories (epistemological and accounting) are creatures of their times; this contrasts to Solomons' view that takes the genesis of epistemological ideals and accounting reports as socially "innocent."[12]

More abstractly, the two figures may be contrasted in terms of the relationships between their elements. Figure 1's elements are hierarchically and analytically related; Figure 2's elements are interdependent, forming part of a totalizing schema where no one element is dominant. It follows that Figure 1 envisages final equilibrium solutions, whereas Figure 2 posits resolutions that are temporary and unstable—a permanent state of flux—that requires continual adaptation to new developments and dialectical movements (Dews, 1979, 1986; Ryan, 1982; Horkheimer & Adorno, 1972; Adorno, 1983; Tinker et al., 1982, p. 185; Tinker & Lowe, 1984; Tinker, 1985, p. 113; Neimark & Tinker, 1986). No one element has final

[12] The approach summarized in Fig. 2 has been described in the literature as "negation of the negation" (Cooper, 1983; Tinker et al., 1982; Tinker, 1985; Lehman & Tinker, 1987; Tinker & Neimark, 1988; Neimark & Tinker, 1986; Knights & Willmott, 1983, 1985; Gunn, 1989; Hopper et al., 1987).

priority in the mutual determination of Figure 2.

Representational Faithfulness (Fig. 1) and Practical Reflexivity (Fig. 2) differ in several important respects. First, over the Politicization of the Accounting Sign; second, in relation to "Immaculate Conception" of Representational Faithfulness (to paraphrase Boulding); third, concerning Solomons' Extradition of the Accounting Citizen; and lastly, in the understanding of David Solomons: Partisan or Evangelist? Each of these differences is expanded below.

Politicizing the Accounting Sign

Solomons acknowledges the actuality of political compromise, and, "the subordination of faithful reporting to . . . what is politically acceptable." His response to this deleterious state of affairs is curiously Utopian, however. He offers only a "hope" that, "If, one day that constituency becomes more enlightened . . . faithful representation will prevail" (Solomons, 1991). What social and political conditions constitute this lack of enlightenment, and what would be necessary to bring "obstructionists", "activists", and "radicals" out of the cave into the light, are never articulated by Solomons. He never theorizes their social presence in any systematic fashion, rather he retreats into wishful thinking.

Insofar as Solomons contemplates "the political", it is in terms of crude stereotypes, personified by Big Brother (the government, *à la* David Hawkins) and lunatic fringe radicals who "really want to change our present form of society" (Solomons, 1991). He sirens unrelentingly, "the subversion of accounting to supposedly serve social ends", notwithstanding the parade of "sleeze" and influence-peddling in Washington, perpetrated by representatives of business interests. Does it require "special expertise" to note that HUD corruption, Pentagon "consulting-kickbacks", Wedteck bribes, and a $40 billion fraud component of the savings and loans debacle, were perpetrated by Reagan appointees with the auditor's blessing?

Solomons' political "analysis" does not examine the power wielded by business-financed PAC's over publicly elected officials and by industries over their "regulators." He omits to mention that the influence on Capitol Hill of the savings and loans lobby group is legendary. They deserve full credit for the "sea of goodwill" into which Briloff warned the industry would sink; a warning delivered back in 1982 that was ignored by a congressional committee and the FASB (Briloff, 1990).

Solomons' crude stereotyping diverts our critical attention from the political influence of large corporations who have become enmeshed into the FASB's bureaucratization and institutionalization (Zeff, 1978, 1986; Seligman, 1982, 1983; Merino & Neimark, 1982; Watts & Zimmerman, 1978, 1979; Tinker, 1984; Parker, 1986; Merino, 1989).

While Solomons (through Fig. 1) makes no mention of the part corporations play in shaping FASB disclosure policy, Figure 2's situation of "accounting theory and method" as an interacting element in social reality, enables us to theorize their pervasive influence. Examples of corporate (as well as government) political pressure are legion: we need only to remind ourselves of the political machinations over the investment tax credit (Moonitz, 1966) and the totally inadequate provisions for troubled debt restructuring, now manifest in the third world debt debacle and the savings and loans crisis. The latter is the legacy of the pressure applied by New York banks to the FASB, to protect the banks from the risks of New York City's financial crisis (Wriston, 1977, Vol. 1, Part 2, pp. 69–70; Zeff, 1978, p. 60).

These examples underscore the discretionary power of large corporations, including the discretion they exercise over accounting numbers to "make the world mean" to their own political advantage (Simon, 1959, 1964; Williamson, 1963; Machlup, 1967; Chatov, 1975, 1977; Briloff, 1970, 1972, 1976, 1981, 1984). There is an authoritative semiotic case for recognizing quasi-independent (discretionary) status of accounting "signs": Saussure's Principle of "the arbitrariness of signs" (Saussure, 1960).[13] Saussure's principle highlights the independence (autonomy) of signification from economic reality; that the meaning of signs may change with the speaker, situation, and "traces" of previous articulations ("the history of discourses") (Ravetz, 1984; Derrida, 1976, 1978; Lehman & Tinker, 1987; Arrington & Francis, 1987; 1989).[14]

---

[13] While language represents the most obvious system of signification, semiotic studies extend to all systems of symbolic representation, including accounting signs. Thus, for instance, studies conducted within the semiotic tradition include kinship systems and taboos (Levi-Strauss, 1967), myths (Barthes, 1972), dreams (Ellis, 1980), television and newspaper media (Blumler & Gurevitch, 1983), advertising (Weedon et al., 1980), James Bond films (Eco, 1973) and accounting signification (Lehman, 1985; Lehman & Tinker, 1989, Neimark, 1983, Arrington & Francis, 1987, 1989; Power, 1989; Hines, 1988, 1989; Robson, 1989).

[14] Derrida's critique of Saussure shows the ideological vent created by the arbitrariness of signs. His work reinforces Levi-Strauss's view that, "the world has to be made to mean" (Levi-Strauss, 1977). This has been

Saussure demonstrates that there is no natural connection between the signifier (sound) and the signified (concept). Therefore, the search for Representational Faithfulness is futile because there is nothing to seek! (Hall, 1980, pp. 29–32).[15] In Adorno's terms, there is "no archimedean point of origin" for representations to be faithful to. Ironically, Solomons himself provides one of the most convincing cases against representational faithfulness and confirming the arbitrariness of accounting signs, in his advocacy of current cost over historical cost accounting. Historical cost is clearly a more accurate record of "what actually happened." Current cost methods, in contrast, introduce arbitrariness: in choosing the base period, the commodity basket composing the index, and when to periodically update the in-

dex. Solomons' persuasive case for current cost accounting is not based on representational faithfulness, but its "relevance" to informing present decisions (Johnson, 1988; Solomons, 1986).

Nor does modern semiology support the philosophy of representational faithfulness. Semiology attempts to explain, in socio-politico-psychoanalytic terms, how the social subject (and therefore social practices) are constituted (Barthes, 1972; Coward & Ellis, 1977; Hall, 1978, 1980, 1982, 1983a, b, c). This formulation accords with Figure 2, where signs are not dictated by a faithfulness to a mythical objective reality, but are constituted (and constitute) a conflictual social world. They invest life (practices) with an imaginary relation; the processes by which this "imaginary relation" is produced is central to semiotic research.

Solomons remarks that, in relation to radical (critical) work, he is "at a total loss to understand what other values accountants could use" (Solomons, 1991). Notwithstanding the fact that many valuation alternatives have been proposed (see, for example, Tinker, 1985, pp. 181–203), critical theorists and Solomons differ in the extent to which they regard money values as the quintessence of accounting. Solomons fails to acknowledge the importance of the larger picture: the broad diversity of practices in the accounting milieu, including its pedagogic, literary, ethical, philosophical, political, economic, and aesthetic forms of signification, all of which are interpolated by critical researchers.[16] They investigate what Solo-

---

underscored in numerous semiotic studies, such as Hall's research into the media constructed panic over mugging in the U.K., and Eco's analysis of the underlying ideological structure of the James Bond novel (Hall et al., 1978; Eco, 1973). *Paper Prophets* provides analogous lessons: how theories of value envehicle some social interests at the expense of others (merchants against artisans, capitalist against wage laborer, creditor country against debtor country, polluter against local community, etc.).

[15] Saussure and Derrida's work echoes that work of earlier writers, such as Hegel, Marx, and Gramsci, that has inspired research in the critical accounting tradition (Gramsci, 1971; Lehman, 1985; Lehman & Tinker, 1987). Thus, for instance, Hegel observed in his *Phenomenology of Mind* that, ". . . it is the nature of the fact, the notion, which causes the movement and development, yet this same movement is equally the action of cognition" (Hegel, 1966, para. 577). Marx also stressed that the materialist role of ideas (science) was "not to describe society but to change it."

[16] Forms of signification, envisaged in Fig. 2, that have been the subject of critical accounting research include: concepts of value (Tinker et al., 1982; Tinker, 1985); ideological

mons takes as nonproblematic: the socio-political constitution and effects of accounting signs.

The Immaculate Conception of Representational Faithfulness

Representational Faithfulness can only be justified by a process of infinite regression to ever-higher criteria for validation. In this sense, it has no final authority and is based on an arbitrary assumption. Figure 1 illustrates this: When considering alternatives to Representational Faithfulness—Reliability, Relevance, Timeliness—Solomons rejects them because they do not satisfy a meta-criterion of "usefulness" (Solomons, 1978).

But what meta-meta-criterion legitimates the meta-criterion of usefulness; especially one that doesn't entertain conflicts between classes of people about "usefulness"? Even if we were to answer this question satisfactorily, it only invites another about what criterion to employ at the next higher level,

---

trends and accounting research (Lehman, 1985; Okcabol & Tinker, 1989; Lehman & Tinker, 1987; Tinker et al., 1988a, b, 1989); social themes in GM's annual reports over 60 years (Neimark, 1983, Neimark & Tinker, 1986; Tinker & Neimark, 1987) the rise of professionalism (Armstrong, 1985, 1987; Loft, 1986) and the emergence of the value-added concept (Burchell et al., 1985). Attention has also focused on the manipulation of numerical signification, such as the investment tax credit (Moonitz, 1966; Zeff, 1978), takeover and merger rules (Briloff, 1964, 1970, 1972, 1976, 1981, 1984), pension accounting (Ghicas & Tinker, 1989a, b), Third World debt, and other such relations (Tinker, 1980; Cooper, 1980; Tinker & Lehman, 1989). In each case, signs are not assumed to be "faithful" but problematic; this research inquires into the social constitution of the numerical sign.

and the next, ad infinitum. This is infinite regress; Solomons' criterion of Representational Faithfulness is ultimately founded on an unexamined (arbitrary) premise (Gunn, 1989; Quine, 1980; Chisholm, 1985).

Figure 2 eschews the problem of infinite regress by not appealing to an absolute criterion like Representational Faithfulness. Instead, it shows epistemological criteria emerging from a dialectical interplay with contemporary social and scientific practices (Allen, 1975; Ollman, 1978; Gunn, 1989; Tinker & Neimark, 1988). This socially relative character of epistemological criteria is evident in the turmoil of scientific revolutions at times of social upheaval and crises: Edmund Burke's theoretical appeal for democratization came in response to growing social discontent; Adam Smith provided a theoretical justification for breaking feudal covenants and advancing a laissez-faire ideology, Marx offered an explanation of the disturbing social consequences of capitalism, Marginalism was a counterblast to Marxism by asserting the productivity of private property (Capital) (Allen, 1975; Tinker & Lowe, 1984, p. 45).

There has been a wealth of critical accounting research that affirms the dialectical origins of accounting theory and epistemology and thereby rejects the Immaculate Conception of Representational Faithfulness (see for instance, Tinker et al., 1982; Williams, 1987; Chua, 1986; Hines, 1988, 1989; Sikka et al., 1989; Hopper et al., 1987; Willmott, 1986, 1989; Puxty & Laughlin, 1988; Jackson & Willmott, 1987; Knights & Willmott, 1987; Knights, 1989).

Deportation of the Accounting Citizen

In ominous tones, David Solomons sirens the dark side of *Paper Prophets*: that "radicals" really want to change society, and accounting is merely incidental to that desire" (Solomons, 1991). He concludes that, accountants "have no special expertise" in changing society (ibid.).

Elsewhere, David Solomons states that, "accounting theory has no other purpose than to contribute to social welfare by providing society with useful information" (Solomons, 1986, p. 245). How would he have accountants contribute to "social" welfare without the capacity to envisage the various forms of "social" that are possible? It would seem that, against Solomons' advice, accountants must acquire social "expertise" in order to accomplish what he urges.

Solomons' polemic against "radicals" eventually recedes into hyperbole. Seeking an honorable and responsible social role for accounting does not imply that critical theorists believe that "most of the sins of capitalism . . . are visited on the heads of accountants" (Solomons, 1991) or that violent overthrow is desirable ("changing society as we know it"). Rather, it involves acknowledging responsibility for actions that reverberate beyond the confines of Solomons' restrictive conception of "economic welfare."

Figure 2 and the critical accounting literature offers Solomons some relief in showing how "accounting theory . . . [might] . . . contribute to social welfare." It points to superior tools of analysis because: First, it admits social—not just economic—reality into the picture (Tinker et al., 1988a, b, 1989; Hopper et al., 1987); second, it does not assume that "social welfare" is a monolith, but admits the possibility of there being conflicting social welfares, and that accounting — inevitably — preferences

some, and not others (Tinker, 1980; Cooper, 1980, 1983; Cooper et al., 1981; Berry et al., 1985a, b; Tinker et al., 1982; Knights & Collinson, 1987); third, it rejects Solomons' dualism of accounting versus citizenship—leading to his "Extradition of the accounting Citizen"—by showing that accounting is integral to social change.

Solomons' claim that accountants "have no special expertise" in social analysis is something of a self-fulfilling prophecy. Social illiteracy among accountants is attributable to the disabling, technocratic, asocial education, endorsed by Solomons' own restrictive conception of the subject. Indeed, when confronted with calls for educational reform in *Paper Prophets,* he dismisses them with the remark that they reinforce "my view that it is society that is really the focus of his attack, not accounting" (Solomons, 1991).

Implications: Evangelist or Partisan?

Like the dualisms encountered in David Solomons' paper (accounting and citizenship, accounting and society, accounting and politics), the dichotomy between evangelizing and partisanship is also false.

Solomons himself underscores the fallacies of Representational Faithfulness (Fig. 1) and confirms the validity of Practical Reflexivity or Negation of the Negation (Fig. 2). His writings instance how accounting reports depart from the underlying economic reality—in pensions accounting, in postretirement benefits, in current cost versus historical cost accounting, etc. Yet, while admitting to these discrepancies, he fails to faithfully represent to us the social conditions that reproduce them;

he is silent about political constitution of accounting signs.

This lacuna is not surprising, however, because "the world has to be made to mean," even for David Solomons, and this objective even transcends that of faithfully representing the political underpinnings of accounting signs. The meaning "made" by Solomons, in censoring the political underpinnings of FASB sign-making, is to promote a market vision of economic regulation that masks the role of large corporate bureaucracies in shaping accounting disclosure. Far from being Representationally Faithful, his posture is both evangelical and partisan—albeit unintended—in advancing specific economic interests and beneficiaries.

Solomons advises accountants to behave like schizophrenics and develop multiple (and independent) personalities—as citizen, as family person, as philanthropist, as political actor, as ethical agent, as advocate, and as accountant. These personalities must be kept in different psychic cages, making the accountant akin to the Robinson Crusoe nomad of neoclassical economics.

Figure 2 presents the counter view: that of a social world where roles are inextricably intertwined and conflicting, and where the individual needs to develop a social self-consciousness for transcending conflicts. The same accounting individual often appears on several sides in the same dispute, and without a self-awareness about her role interdependencies, may ultimately contribute to her own repression and exploitation! An auditor who sanctions exhorbitant consulting fees for ex-federal employees officials (so that a client can gain sales orders) may devalue the integrity of the public institutions on which he depends. A financial advisor who assists investors to profit from a low-cost technology may be helping to pollute her own community environment. A controller who encourages his firm to relocate production abroad to save labor costs may diminish U.S. employment and thus aggregate demand for U.S. products—including his own firm's. A tax consultant who successfully lobbies against child care funding may arouse the hostility of a housebound spouse. An accounting academic who devises better methods of management control may ultimately contribute to her own surveillance at work (Lehman & Tinker, 1989).

The successful individual is not a schizophrenic, but one who apprehends and mediates the dialectical interplay of contradictory roles. This is the philosophy of practical reflexivity, negation of the negation, or praxis. As Antonio Gramsci puts it: "The philosophy of praxis is consciousness full of contradictions in which the philosopher himself, understood both individually and as an entire social group, not merely grasps the contradictions, but posits himself as an element of the contradictions and elevates this element to a principle of knowledge and therefore of action" (Gramsci, 1971, pp. 243).

History cautions us with many tales about the fate of messengers who betray their trust. In the 1700s, two French priests who doubled as emissaries, Father Le Vacher and Father Montmesson, were cannonballed over the Mediterranean by irate Turks as a response to a French diplomatic initiative, delivered from the fleet waiting offshore. This salutary variant on "shooting the messenger" should serve as a warning to the profession: its social self-awareness of the contradictions that beset it is woefully inadequate; unless it acts expeditiously it may also suffer a spectacular martyrdom.

Bibliography

Adorno, T., *Negative Dialectics*, translated by Ashton, B. (New York: Seabury Press, 1973).

Allen, V., *Social Analysis: A Marxist Critique and Alternative* (Harmondsworth: Longman, 1975).

Armstrong, P., Changing Management Control Strategies: The Role of Competition Between Accountancy and Other Organisational Professions, *Accounting, Organizations and Society* (1985), pp. 129–148.

Armstrong, P., The Rise of Accounting Controls in British Capitalist Enterprises, *Accounting, Organizations and Society* (1987), pp. 415–436.

Arrington, C. E., & Francis, J. R., Letting the Chat Out of the Bag: Deconstruction, Privilege and Accounting Research, *Accounting, Organizations and Society* (1989), pp. 1–29.

Arrington, E., & Francis, J., Accounting and the Labor of Text Production: Some Thoughts on the Hermeneutics of Paul Riceur, University of Iowa Conference on Accounting and the Humanities (September 1989).

Barthes, R., *Mythologies* (London: Jonathan Cape, 1972).

Beaver, W., The Information Content of Annual Earnings Announcements, *Journal of Accounting Research, Selected Studies—Empirical Research in Accounting* (1968), pp. 67–92.

Beaver, W., *Financial Reporting: An Accounting Revolution* (Prentice-Hall, 1981).

Beaver, W. H., and Dukes, R. E., Interperiod Tax allocation. Earnings Expectations and the Behavior of Security Prices, *Accounting Review* (April 1972).

Berry, A. J., Capps, D., Cooper, D., Ferguson, P., Hopper, T., & Lowe, E. A., Commentary: NCB accounts—a mine of misinformation? *Accountancy* (January 1985a), p. 11–12.

Berry, A. J., Capps, D., Cooper, D., Ferguson, P., Hopper, R., & Lowe, E. A., Management Control in an Area of the NCB: Rationales of Accounting Practices in a Public Enterprise, *Accounting, Organizations and Society* (1985b), pp. 3–28.

Blumler, J., & Gurevitch, M., The Political Effects of Mass Communication, in M. Gurevitch, T. Bennett, J. Curren, and J. Woollacott, (eds), *Culture, Society and Media*, pp. 236–267 (London: Methuen, 1982).

Briloff, A. J., Needed: A Revolution in the Determination and Application of Accounting Principles, *The Accounting Review* (1964), pp. 12–14.

Briloff, A. J., Accounting Practices and the Merger Movement, Testimony to the U.S. Senate Subcommittee on Antitrust and Monopoly of the Committee of the Judiciary (February 1970).

Briloff, A. J., *Unaccountable Accounting* (New York: Harper & Row, 1972).

Briloff, A. J., *More Debits Than Credits* (New York: Harper & Row, 1976).

Briloff, A. J., *The Truth About Corporate Accounting* (New York: Harper & Row, 1981).

Briloff, A. J., Double Entry: Double Think: Double Speak, in Tinker, T. (ed.), *Social Accounting for Corporations: Private Enterprise versus the Public Interest* (New York: Markus Wiener, 1984).

Briloff, A. J., Testimony to the Subcommittee on Oversight and Investigations of the U.S. House of Representative Committee on Energy and Commerce (November 1985).

Briloff, A. J., Accounting and Society: The Broken Covenant, *Critical Perspectives in Accounting* (1990).

Coward, R., & Ellis, J., *Language and Materialism* (London, 1977).

Chatov, R., *Corporate Financial Reporting: Public or Private Control?* (New York: The Free Press, 1975).

Chatov, R., Hearings before the Subcommittee on Reports, Accounting and Management, of the Committee on Governmental Affairs, U.S. Senate, 95th Congress, first session, pp. 20–96 (Washington: U.S. Govt. Printing Office, 1977).

Chisholm, R., The Problem of Empiricism, in Schwartz, R. J. (ed.), *Perceiving, Sensing, and Knowing* (Garden City, N.Y.: Doubleday, 1965).

Chua, W. F., Radical Developments in Accounting Thought, *Accounting Review,* Vol. LXI, No. 4 (October 1986).

Cooper, D., Discussion of Towards a Political Economy of Accounting, *Accounting, Organizations and Society* (1980), pp. 161–166.

Cooper, D., Tidiness, Muddle and Things: Commonalities and Divergencies in Two Approaches to Management Accounting Research, *Accounting Organizations and Society* (1983), pp. 269–286.

Cooper, D., Hayes, D., & Wolf, F., Accounting in Organized Anarchies: Understanding and Designing Accounting Systems in Ambiguous Situations, *Accounting, Organizations and Society* (1981), pp. 119–132.

Derrida, Jacques, *Speech and Phenomena,* translated by Allison, D. (Evanston, 1973).

Derrida, J., *Of Grammatology,* translated by Chakravorty Spivak, G. (Baltimore, 1976).

Derrida, J., *Writing and Difference,* translated by Bass, A. (Chicago, 1978).

Dews, P., The Nouvelle Philosphie and Foucault, *Economy and Society* (1979), Vol. 8, pp. 127–171.

Dews, P., Adorno, Post-Structuralism and the Critique of Identity, *New Left Review* (May–June 1986), pp. 28–44.

Eco, U., Social Life as a sign, in Rovey, D. (ed.), *Structuralism: An Introduction* (Oxford: Clarendon Press, 1973).

Ellis, J., Ideology and Subjectivity, in Hall, S., Hobson, D., Lowe, A., & Willis, P. (eds), *Culture, Media and Language,* pp. 186–194 (London: Hutchinson, 1980).

Foucault, M., *The Archaeology of Knowledge* (London: Tavistock, 1972).

Ghicas, D., & Tinker, T., Pension Terminations, Free Cash Flow, and the Efficiency of Takeover Activity, Baruch College Working Paper (1989a).

Ghicas, D., & Tinker, T., Dishonored Contracts: Accounting and the Expropriation of Employee Pension Wealth, Baruch College Working Paper (1989b).

Gramsci, A., *Selection from the Prison Notebooks* (London: Lawrence & Wishart, 1971).

Gunn, R., Marxism and Philosophy, *Capital & Class* (Spring, 1989), pp. 87–116.

Hall, S., Critcher, C., Jefferson, T., Clarke, J., & Roberts, B., *Policing the Crisis: Mugging, the State, and Law and Order* (London: Macmillan, 1978).

Hall, S., Popular Democratic versus Authoritarian Popularism, in Hunt, A. (ed.) *Marxism and Democracy* (London: Lawrence & Wishart, 1980).

Hall, S., The Rediscovery of Ideology: Return of the Repressed in Media Studies, in Gurevitch, M., Bennett, T., Curren, J. & Woollacott, J. (eds), *Culture, Society and Media* pp. 56–90 (London: Methuen, 1982).

Hall, S., The Great Moving Right Show, in Hall, S., & Jacques, M. (eds), *The Politics of Thatcherism* pp. 19–40 (London: Lawrence & Wishart, 1983a).

Hall, S., The Little Caesars of Social Democracy, in Hall, S., & Jacques, M. (eds), *The Politics of Thatcherism* (London: Lawrence & Wishart, 1983b).

Hall, S., Thatcherism: Rolling Back the Welfare State, pp. 6–19, *Thesis Eleven* (1983c).

Hegel, G. W. F., The Phenomenology of Mind, translated by Baillie, J. B. (London: Allen & Unwin, 1966).

Hines, R., Popper's Methodology of Falsification and Accounting Research, *Accounting Review* (October, 1988), pp. 657–662.

Hines, R., Financial Accounting Knowledge, Conceptual Framework Projects and the Social Construction of the Accounting Profession, *Accounting, Auditing & Accountability Journal* (1989).

Hopper, T., Storey, J., & Wilmott, H., Accounting for Accounting: Towards the Development of a Dialectical View. *Accounting, Organizations and Society* (1987), pp. 437–465.

Horkheimer, M., & Adorno, T., *Dialectic of Enlightenment* (Herder & Herder, New York, 1972).

Jackson, N., & Wilmott, H., Beyond Epistemology and Reflective Conversation: Towards Human Relations, *Human Relations* (1987), pp. 361–380.

Johnson, S. B., A Perspective on Solomons'

Quest for Credibility in Financial Reporting, *Journal of Accounting and Public Policy* (1988), pp. 137–154.

Knights, D., Risk, Financial Self-discipline, and Commodity Relations: An Analysis of Growth and Development of Life Insurance in Capitalism, *Advances in Public Interest Accounting* (1989), pp. 47–69.

Knights, D., & Collinson, D., Disciplining the Shop Floor: A Comparison of the Disciplinary Effects of Managerial Psychology and Financial Accounting, *Accounting, Organizations and Society* (1987), pp. 457–478.

Knights, D., & Willmott, H, Dualism and Domination: An Analysis of Marxian, Weberian and Existenitalist Perspectives, *The Australian and New Zealand Journal of Sociology* (March 1983) pp. 33–49.

Knights, D., Willmott, H., Power and Identity in Theory and Practice, *The Sociological Review* (1985), pp. 22–46.

Korzybski, A. Science and Sanity (London, 1950).

Lehman, C., Discourse, Analysis and Accounting Literature: A Transformation of State Hegemony 1960–1973, Unpublished doctoral dissertation, New York University (1985).

Lehman, C., & Tinker, T., The "Real" Cultural Significance of Accounts, *Accounting Organizations and Society* (1987), pp. 503–522.

Lehman, C., & Tinker, T., Adam Smith and the Subversion of Self, The Sixth Tom Robertson Memorial Lecture, Edinburgh University (1989).

Levi-Strauss, C., *The Scope of Anthropology* (London: Jonathan Cape, 1967).

Lindblom, C. E., *Politics and Markets: The World's Political–Economic Systems* (New York: Basic Books, 1982).

Lindblom, C., Social Accounting for Corporations, in Tinker, T. (ed.), *Social Accounting for Corporations: Private Enterprise versus the Public Interest* (New York: Markus Wiener, 1984).

Loft, A., Toward a Critical Understanding of Accounting: The Case of Cost Accounting in the UK: 1914–1925, *Accounting, Organizations and Society* (1986), pp. 137–169.

Machlup, F., Theories of the Firm: Marginalist, Behavioral, Managerial, *The American Economic Review* (March 1967), pp. 1–33.

Merino, B., An Analysis of the Development of Accounting Knowledge: A Pragmatic Approach, University of Iowa Conference on Accounting and the Humanities (September 1989).

Merino, B., & Neimark, M., Disclosure Regulation and Public Policy: A Sociohistorical Reappraisal, *Journal of Accounting and Public Policy* (1982), pp. 33–57.

Moonitz, M., Some Reflections on the Investment Credit Experience, *Journal of Accounting Research* (Spring 1966), pp. 47–61.

Neimark, M., *The Social Construction of Annual Reports: A Radical Approach to Corporate Control*, Unpublished doctoral dissertation, New York University (1983).

Neimark, M., & Tinker, T., The Social Construction of Management Control Systems, *Accounting, Organizations and Society* (1986), pp. 369–396.

Ollman, B., *Alienation: Marx's Concept of Man in Capitalist Society*, 2nd ed. (Cambridge: Cambridge University Press, 1976).

Okcabol, F., & Tinker, T., The Market for Positive Theory: Deconstructing the Theory for Excuses, *Advances in Public Interest Accounting* (1990), pp. 71–95.

Parker, L. D., Polemical Themes in Social Accounting: A Scenario for Standard Setting, in Neimark, M. (ed.), *Advances in Public Interest Accounting*, pp. 67–93 (Greenwich, Conn. JAI Press, 1986).

Peltzman, S., Toward a More General Theory of Regulation, *The Journal of Law and Economics* (August 1976), pp. 211–248.

Power, M., The Emergence of Audit Evidence, Paper presented at the 12th Annual Congress of the EAA, Stuttgart, West Germany (5–7 April 1989).

Puxty, A. G., & Laughlin, R. C., A Rational Reconstruction of the Decision-Usefulness Criterion, *Journal of Business Finance & Accounting* (1983), pp. 543–559.

Proceedings of the October 8, 1987 Roundtable Discussion on Generally Accepted Accounting Principles and Regulatory Accounting Practices, Jerry Arnold (ed.) (Los Angeles: SEC and Financial Reporting Institute, School of Accounting, University of Southern California).

Quine, W. V., Two Dogmas of Empiricism, in Morick, H. (ed.), *Challenges to Empiricism* (London: Methuen, 1980).

Ravetz, J., Ideological Commitments in the Philosophy of Science, *Radical Philosophy* (Summer, 1984), pp. 5–10.

Robson, K., Accounting Numbers and 'Metaphor': Action at a Distance and the Development of Knowledge, UMIST Working Paper (June 1989).

Ryan, M., *Marxism and Deconstruction: A Critical Articulation* (Baltimore: Johns Hopkins University Press, 1982).

Saussure, F. de., *A Course in General Linguistics* (London: P. Owen, 1960).

Seligman, J., *The Transformation of Wall Street* (1982).

Seligman, J., The Historical Need for a Mandatory Corporate Disclosure System, *The Journal of Corporation Law* (Autumn 1983), pp. 1–61.

Sikka, P., Wilmott, H., & Lowe, T., Guardians of Knowledge and Public Interest: Evidence and Issues of Accountability in the UK Accountancy Profession, *Accounting, Auditing & Accountability Journal* (1989).

Simon, H. A., Theories of Decision Making in Economics and Behavioral Sciences, *The American Economic Review* (June 1959), pp. 253–283.

Simon, H. A., On the Concept of Organizational Goal, *Administrative Science Quarterly* (June 1964), pp. 1–27.

Solomons, D., The Politicization of Accounting, *Journal of Accountancy* (November 1978), pp. 65–72.

Solomons, D., Making Accounting Policy (New York: Oxford University Press, 1986).

Solomons, D., Accounting and Social Change: A Neutralist View, *Accounting Organizations and Society* (1991), pp. 287–295.

Stigler, G. J., The Economics of Information, *Journal of Political Economy* (June 1961), pp. 213–225.

Stigler, G. J., Public Regulation of the Securities Markets, *The Journal of Business* (April 1964a), pp. 112–133.

Stigler, G. J., Comment, *The Journal of Business* (October 1964b), pp. 414–422.

Stigler, G. J., The Theory of Economic Regulation, *The Bell Journal of Economics and Management Science* (Spring 1971), pp. 3–21.

Thompson, E. P., *The Making of the English Working Class* (New York: Vintage Books, 1966).

Tinker, A. M., Towards a Political Economy of Accounting: An Empirical Illustration of the Cambridge Controversies, *Accounting, Organizations and Society* (1980), pp. 147–160.

Tinker, A., Theories of the State and the State of Accounting: Economic Reductionism and Political Voluntarism in Accounting Regulation, *Journal of Accounting and Public Policy* (1984), pp. 55–77.

Tinker, T., *Paper Prophets* (New York: Praeger Publishers, 1985).

Tinker, A. M., Panglossian Accounting Theories: The Science of Apologizing in Style, *Accounting, Organizations and Society* (1988).

Tinker, A. M., Merino, B., & Neimark, M. D., The Normative Origins of Positive Theories: Ideology and Accounting Thought, *Accounting, Organizations and Society* (1982), pp. 167–200.

Tinker, T., & Lowe, E. A., One Dimensional Management Science: Towards a Technocratic Consciousness, *Interfaces* (March–April 1984).

Tinker, T., & Neimark, M., The Role of Annual Reports in Gender and Class Contradictions at General Motors: 1917–1976, *Accounting, Organizations and Society* (1987), pp. 71–88.

Tinker, T., & Neimark, M., The Struggle Over Meaning in Accounting and Corporate Research: A Comparative Evaluation of Conservative and Critical Historiography, *Accounting, Auditing & Accountability Journal* (1988), pp. 55–74.

Tinker, T., Lehman, C., & Neimark, M., Marginalizing the Public Interest: A Critical Look at Recent Social Accounting History, in Ferris, K. (ed.), *Behavioral Accounting Re-*

search: A Critical Analysis (Columbus, Ohio: Century VII, 1988a).

Tinker, T., Lehman, C., & Neimark, M., Bookkeeping for Capitalism: The Mystery of Unequal Exchange, in Mosco V. (ed.), *The Political Economy of Information* (Wisconsin: University of Wisconsin Press, 1988b).

Tinker, T., Lehman, C., & Neimark, M., Falling Down the Hole in "Middle-of-the Road" Theorizing: Political Quietism in Liberal Corporate Social Reporting, Baruch College Working Paper (1989).

Watts, R. I., & Zimmerman, J. L. Towards a Positive Theory of Determination of Accounting Standards, *The Accounting Review* (January 1978), pp. 112–134.

Watts, R. I., & Zimmerman, J. L., The Demand for and the Supply of Accounting Theories: The Market for Excuses, *The Accounting Review* (April 1979), pp. 273–305.

Weedon, C., Tolson, A., & Mort, F., Theories of Language and Subjectivity, in Hall, S., Hobson, D., Lowe, A., & Willis, P. (eds), *Culture, Media and Language,* pp. 195–216 (London: Hutchinson, 1980).

Williams, P. F., The Legitimate Concern With Fairness, *Accounting, Organizations and Society* (1987), pp. 169–189.

Williamson, O. E., Managerial Discretion and Business Behavior, *The Economic Review* (1963), pp. 1032–1057.

Wilmott, H., Organising the Profession: A Theoretical and Historical Examination of the Development of the Major Accountancy Bodies in the UK, *Accounting, Organizations and Society* (1986), Vol. 11, pp. 555–580.

Wilmott, H. C., Serving the Public Interest? A Critical Analysis of a Professional Claim, in Cooper, D. J., & Hopper, T. M. (eds), *Critical Accounts* (London: Macmillan, 1989).

Wolff, T., *Bonfire of the Vanities* (New York: Pantheon Books, 1987).

Wriston, W. B., Transcript of Public Hearings on FASB Discussion Memorandum. Accounting by Debtors and Creditors When Debt is Restructured (1977, Vol. 1).

Zeff, S. A., The Rise of Economic Consequences, *The Journal of Accountancy* (December 1978), pp. 56–63.

Zeff, S. A., Big Eight Firms and the Accounting Literature: the Falloff in Advocacy Writing, *Journal of Accounting, Auditing and Finance* (New Series) (Spring 1986).

A Rejoinder

David Solomons

Reprinted with permission from *Accounting, Organizations and Society,* Vol. 16, 1991, Elsevier Science Ltd., Pergamon Imprint, Oxford, England.

Tinker's reply to my paper is so full of misrepresentations of my position and of philosophical obfuscation that a full reply would have to be longer than any editor would tolerate. I shall try to keep this rejoinder short and (with difficulty) free from the kind of epithets that pepper his paper—"spurious", "fallacious", "sirens unrelentingly", "crude stereotypes", "polemic", "hyperbole", and the like. I shall also ignore quibbles, such as whether the telephone communicates words or thoughts. There are more important matters to debate.

First to establish the fact of misrepresentation, I need only quote passages like the following from Tinker's paper: "When considering alternatives to Representational Faithfulness—Reliability, Relevance, Timeliness—Solomons rejects them because they do not satisfy a meta-criterion of 'usefulness,'" This is plain nonsense. The relationships among these qualitative characteristics of accounting information are carefully discussed in the FASB's *Concepts Statement No. 2,* most of which I wrote, and in Chapter 5 of my *Making Accounting Policy.* If Tinker can read that as rejection, he is beyond my help. Nor am I aware that I have ever "curtly dismissed" research "that investigates accounting errors and distortions," though of course he and I may not always agree about what is an error or distortion or about what constitutes research. There are other misrepresentations of my position in his paper, but further examples would waste valuable space.

At the end of this debate, we are as far apart as ever. Tinker and I simply have different notions of what accounting is about. I think its function is to convey unbiased information on which users can base their own decisions. I acknowledged in my paper that, accountants being human, the avoidance of all bias may not always be achieved; but that should be the aim. For Tinker, accounting is "capitalism's prime adjudicator in social conflict" (*Paper Prophets,* p. 205). An adjudication is a decision. Tinker wants accountants to make the decisions that I think should be left to the *users* of financial reports.

Tinker's discussion of professional "schizophrenia" is illuminating. He seems to think it is unethical for a controller to "encourage his firm to relocate production abroad to save labour costs." But that is not the issue I thought we were debating. The issue is whether the controller should feel free to prepare figures of the comparative cost of producing at home and abroad. I would argue that he would be remiss not to do so, assuming, of course, that all the costs of relocation were included in his computations. The decision about relocation would then be taken by the management, possibly including himself as a member of it. What Tinker calls schizophrenia I call professional integrity. Should doctors not attend to victims of gang warfare or AIDS because they disapprove of the behavior of these patients? Should lawyers never defend unpopular clients? If doing business in South Africa is more profitable than doing business in Nicaragua, should an accountant not report accordingly? Note that I say "report", not "advise."

Representational faithfulness is at the root of our differences. I think it is central to accounting's mission. Tinker simply dismisses it. ". . . [T]he search for Representational Faithfulness is futile because there is nothing to seek!" He then states: "Ironically, Solomons himself provides one of the most convincing cases against representational faithfulness and confirming the arbitrariness of accounting signs, in his advocacy of current cost over historical cost accounting. Historical cost is clearly a more accurate record of 'what actually happened.'" If there is indeed "nothing to seek," we are really in bad shape, unless we are all willing to become solipsists, and dismiss the external world as fantasy. If signs are "arbitrary" and the "independent" of what is being signified, then we are all beating the air, *including the philosopher who makes such a statement, for his signs are also independent of the reality that he is vainly trying to depict.*

As for historical cost accounting, it does indeed give an accurate record of *some* of the things that happened in the past, but it fails to record other relevant events (e.g., relative value changes, price level changes) that may supervene between the date of a transaction and the accounting date. It therefore does not result in faithful representation.

Tinker evades my statement that "I am at a total loss to understand what other values [besides market values] accountants could use" in financial reporting. He asserts that "many valuation alternatives have been proposed," and he refers the reader to pp. 181–203 of *Paper Prophets.* I re-read those pages carefully. I found much about the seamy side of business—pollution, bank failures, the mounting burden of LDC debts—but not a word about valuation alternatives to market values. The emperor simply has no clothes.

It is unnecessary for Tinker to assert that accounting measures are "socially constructed and socially enactive." Of course they are. That is why it is important to make them, to the best of our ability, representationally faithful. The

same is true of other socially important measures such as the census, price indices, measures of GNP, or statistics of road deaths following a change in the speed limit. It is irresponsible to argue that these should *seek* to do anything but represent what they purport to represent. If Tinker were concerned to identify representational *failures,* the difference between us would largely disappear. I do not deny the existence of such failures. But to pin onto accounting failures blame for "influence peddling in Washington, . . . HUD corruption, Pentagon consulting kickbacks, Wedtech bribes . . ." etc., whether perpetrated by Reagan appointees or anyone else, is to exhibit a woeful lack of a sense of proportion. It only draws attention away from accounting shortcomings that it should be our concern to rectify.

The FASB in a World with Partially Efficient Markets

J. Edward Ketz
Arthur R. Wyatt

During the past 20 years or so, accounting argumentation has increasingly dealt with the issue of stock market efficiency. Finance and accounting literature contains a plethora of articles on stock market efficiency, many of which indicate that the stock market is an efficient processor of information. Since

Reprinted with permission from *Journal of Accounting, Auditing & Finance,* Fall 1983, Vol. 7, No. 1, Copyright © 1983 Wanen, Gorham & Lamont, Inc., 210 South St. Boston MA 02111. All Rights Reserved.

the evidence for stock market efficiency seems abundant, some accounts have argued that controversial topics should be adjudicated in terms of efficient market theory.

While the evidence of stock market efficiency is quite convincing and while the concept can be helpful in standards setting, it is doubtful that it can or should become the major vehicle for resolving accounting issues. Accounting theorists and accounting standards-setting bodies have always been concerned with more than just how financial markets obtain, interpret, assimilate, and use accounting information. Stock markets are important, but they are not the alpha and omega of accounting.

The purpose of this article is to explore the goals and the objectives of the Financial Accounting Standards Board (FASB) in a world characterized by partially efficient markets. The next section of the article reviews the concept of stock market efficiency and the FASB's objectives in a world of efficient markets. In the third section the focus is on institutions other than stock markets. We note that in the real world there are institutions other than stock markets, such as credit markets, labor markets, and government agencies, for which the concept of stock market efficiency is irrelevant. The fourth part of this article contains our arguments that in the real world stock markets are not completely efficient and that the objectives for the FASB will differ in a world of partially efficient markets from a world characterized by completely efficient markets. The fifth section examines some of the welfare implications of stock market efficiency. We conclude the article with a discussion of implications for the FASB.

Stock Market Efficiency

A stock market is said to be efficient if the stock market prices fully reflect the available information at any time. In other words, the investor is not playing a game of chance. Rather, stock market returns are a function of the underlying risk of the firm. In pricing assets, the market utilizes whatever information is available, including accounting information. Thus, investors cannot earn abnormally high returns because stock prices are reflective of the risk of the firm.

Fama depicts three levels of efficient markets.[1] The weak form of the efficient markets hypothesis states that the equilibrium expected prices fully reflect the sequence of historical prices. This means that historical price data and volume data for securities cannot be used to earn abnormal returns. For example, technical analysts and chartists can do no better than a simple buy and hold strategy. The semistrong form of the efficient markets hypothesis states that the equilibrium expected prices fully reflect all publicly available information. This means that information about stock splits, stock dividends, secondary offerings of common stock, new issues of stocks, changes in interest rates, etc., cannot be used to earn abnormal information. The semistrong form of the hypothesis implies that information contained in annual reports also cannot be used to earn abnormal returns. The strong form of the efficient markets hypothesis states that the equilibrium expected prices fully reflect all information, public and private. In other words, no trading rule based on inside information can be used to earn abnormal returns.

The evidence is compelling that the stock market is indeed efficient in the weak form. Much evidence also supports the notion of efficient markets in the semistrong form, although a number of anomalies exist.[2] The strong

[1] Eugene F. Fama, "Efficient Capital Markets: A Review of Theory and Empirical Work," *Journal of Finance* (May 1970), pp. 383–417. For a review and a refinement of Fama's definitions, see William H. Beaver, "Market Efficiency," *The Accounting Review* (Jan. 1981), pp. 23–37.

[2] For example, see Thomas R. Dyckman, David H. Downes, and Robert P. Magee, *Efficient Capital Markets: A Critical Analysis* (Prentice-Hall, 1975), Ch. 3.

form, however, may not be a realistic hypothesis since management insiders and exchange specialists appear able to earn excess returns.

Two aspects of the efficient markets hypothesis are important. First, capital assets prices adjust rapidly to new information. Second, capital asset prices adjust to new information in an unbiased manner. This means that capital markets will react to published accounting reports very quickly and quite accurately, assuming accounting reports convey relevant information for assessing share value.

What should be the FASB's objectives given an efficient stock market? Beaver has stated four implications for the FASB given an efficient stock market [1]. First, many reporting issues are trivial. Firms should report using one method and provide sufficient disclosure to permit adjustment to other methods. Second, the role of financial reports is to prevent individuals from earning abnormal returns from inside information. All items should be disclosed if there are no additional costs. Third, naive investors can get hurt by presuming they can trade on published accounting data and earn abnormal returns. The FASB should discourage these beliefs. Fourth, the FASB should realize that accounting reports are not the only suppliers of information. Other sources of information may be more appropriate for disseminating firm information if they involve less cost.

The implications for FASB objectives detailed by Beaver are open to serious question for three reasons. First, stock market agents are not the only users of accounting information. Other consumers have financial information needs that should concern the FASB. Second, we feel that the efficient markets hypothesis is overstated. We present argu-

ments against the efficient markets hypothesis and argue instead for what is termed the partially efficient markets hypothesis. Third, even if stock markets were completely efficient in the informational sense, various reasons suggest that stock markets are not efficient in the allocative sense. These reasons are explained below.

The Stock Market Is Not the Universe

Without a doubt, financial reporting is important for investors. Accounting reports are not the source of information leading to investment decisions; the data are obviously too old. But the discipline of the financial report has a controlling effect on other financial information, which makes the FASB decisions important. Buying and selling shares of stock is not, however, the only economic activity of concern to the FASB. The FASB has a broader mandate than to provide technical guidance related to financial data of interest to stock market agents.

Numerous accounting theorists have based their propositions in part on users other than investors in equity securities, and standards setters have also recognized interests of others than investors in equity securities. The following discussion will demonstrate that often accountants are interested in broad economic effects of accounting, not just the effects in the stock market.

In developing their monograph on corporate accounting, Paton and Littleton do not ignore the effects of accounting numbers [2]. They state, "Investors are not the only parties at interest" [2:2]. Others include employees, customers, governments, and the general public. They also say, "Capital should flow into those industries which serve the public interest, and within an industry into those enterprises in which the management is capable of using capital effectively" [2:3].

Edwards and Bell also were very interested in allocational efficiency [3]. "The essential decision-making function of management is the allocation of resources" [3:3]. "Real realized profit would in many respects be useful as a basis for tax payment. It has the advantages of its money counterpart and also excludes fictional gains from the tax base" [3:128].

Bedford develops his theory on income determination in part because of the role of income in society. Using previous work of May and Alexander, Bedford points out that income may be used as a basis for fiscal policy, as an aid to government supervision, as a basis for price or rate regulation, and as a basis for taxation. Bedford goes on to assert that economists are interested in the concept of income because:

(1) The income objective tends to cause resources to be allocated to their most productive use, provided that competition is free; (2) measured past income may be used either by itself or in combination with other factors as a basis for computing the return on investment to evaluate the effectiveness of management, assuming that income is the primary objective of management; (3) "real" income may be used to evaluate the growth of a nation and the effectiveness, in an economic sense, of the political system under which the nation operates [4:14].

Chambers bases his theory on the importance of accounting, with respect to law, producers and consumers of goods, and taxes [5]. In Chapter 3, Chambers discusses ends, preferences, and valuations and continues by describing the interaction between income and pro-

duction, consumption, and savings. In Chapter 14, Chambers argues that the role of accounting is related to the theory of economic behavior in organized systems and that accountants need a better understanding of these relationships.

In establishing a defense of historical cost accounting, Ijiri focuses in part on the potential controversy concerning performance measurement.

A conflict may arise between past and present shareholders after some shareholders sell their shares based on a poor earnings report. When there is a dispute over the maximum amount the corporation can distribute as dividends, the conflict may be between shareholders and creditors. Perhaps consumers will disagree with shareholders of a regulated corporation on a "fair" return on shareholders' investment, or the corporation may vie with the Internal Revenue Service over taxable income, or divisions may challenge headquarters about incentive compensations that managers are entitled to receive based on divisional profit [6:35].

These excerpts are only a few of those that could have been cited. They are not comprehensive, nor are they intended to be. They do, however, present mosaic that accountants are concerned about economic effects in addition to stock market effects. While these views do not address the efficient markets hypothesis, they support a contention that the focus of accounting is not solely on stock market agents.

Standards-setting bodies have also maintained a perspective on the economic effects of accounting that is broader than stock market effects. This perspective is demonstrated for the Accounting Principles Board (APB) and for the FASB.

The APB issued *APB Statement No. 4* in 1970 [7]. While the primary purpose of the Statement is to delineate and explain the basic concepts and elements of financial accounting, it is interesting that the report begins with a discussion about the uses and users of accounting reports. Admittedly, the APB began with a description of financial information and owners and creditors. The APB extended this list of users to include taxing authorities, employees, customers, lawyers, regulatory or registration authorities, trade associations, and labor unions. These users might make the following decisions for which they would use financial accounting information.

- *Taxing Authorities* Evaluate tax returns; assess taxes or penalties; make investigations and audits.

- *Employees* Negotiate wages; terminate employment; or, for prospective employees, apply for employment.

- *Customers* Anticipate price changes; seek alternative sources or broader bases of supply.

- *Lawyers* Determine whether covenants and contractual provisions are fulfilled; advise on legality of dividends and profit sharing and deferred compensation agreements; draft pension plan terms.

- *Regulatory or Registration Authorities* Assess reasonableness of rate of return; allow or require increases or decreases in prices or rates; require or recommend changes in accounting or disclosure practices; issue cease-and-desist or stock-trading-suspension orders.

- *Trade Associations* Compile industry statistics and make comparisons; analyze industry results.

- *Labor Unions* Formulate wage and contract demands; assess enterprise and industry prospects and strengths.

The APB also discussed the organization of economic activity in society. Societies typically engage in the following economic activities; production, income distribution, exchange, consumption, saving, and investment. Financial accounting may impact each of these economic activities. Indeed, generally accepted accounting principles can be evaluated by relating the financial accounting information to the economic activities impacted.

The FASB is also concerned about the economic effects of promulgated standards and has articulated such concern in *Concepts Statement No. 1* on the objectives of accounting [8].

Financial reporting is not an end in itself but is intended to provide information that is useful in making business and economic decisions—for making reasoned choices among alternative uses of scarce resources in the conduct of business and economic activities. . . . Accordingly, the objectives in this Statement are affected by the economic, legal, political, and social environment in the United States [8 : ¶9].

Potential users identified by the FASB include owners, lenders, suppliers, potential investors and creditors, employees, management, directors, customers, financial analysts and advisers, brokers, underwriters, stock exchanges, lawyers, economists, taxing authorities, regulatory authorities, legislators, financial press and reporting agencies, labor unions, trade associations, business researchers, teachers and students, and the public. While the FASB is principally interested in owners and lenders, it is still very much concerned with other users.

The FASB naturally is concerned about information efficiency. This is seen, for example, in paragraph 34 of *Concepts Statement No. 1*: "Financial reporting should provide information that is useful to present and potential investors and creditors and other users in making rational investment, credit, and similar decisions." Yet the FASB's objectives are broader than information efficiency. Allocational efficiency is also an issue before the FASB.

> *To the extent that financial reporting provides information that helps identify relatively efficient and inefficient users of resources, aids in assessing relative returns and risks of investment opportunities, or otherwise assists in promoting efficient functioning of capital and other markets, it helps to create a favorable environment for capital formation decisions [8 : ¶33].*

The scope of the FASB's standards setting is broad. The FASB needs to investigate, ponder, and decide how accounting numbers induce or hinder or have no effect on the total economy and the actors and institutions thereof. Since the FASB's objectives are broader than those involving only information efficiency of stock markets, the FASB should not necessarily be constrained by implications of the efficient markets hypothesis.

A classic example of this issue is the savings and loan industry. The concept of efficient capital markets is essentially irrelevant for this industry because the vast majority of savings and loan associations are mutual corporations, not stock corporations. Mutual associations do not have common stock, so they obviously do not issue and reacquire shares of stock, nor do investors buy and sell shares of mutual savings associations. There simply is not a stock market price for mutual associations. How can the concept of stock market efficiency apply if a market does not exist?

Accounting issues are nevertheless important for the savings and loan industry. Not too long ago, the Federal Home Loan Bank Board proposed allowing associations to retire mortgage receivables and delay the reporting of the losses. This proposal was not adopted. Specifically, any loss on such a transaction would be set up as an asset account which would be amortized over 10 years. The FASB has objected to such a convoluted rule, and we concur with the FASB. More important for our concern in this article, we agree with the FASB that it should get involved in this area. The FASB has a role to play: It needs to argue for improvement in financial reporting and protest any waywardness such as distorting the definition of an asset and covering up the fact that losses exist.

We also note with interest that the Federal Home Loan Bank Board is considering a proposal to change to current value accounting [9]. A preliminary report by a task force recommends that since high and fluctuating interest rates have grossly distorted financial reports of savings associations, current value reports should supplant conventional statements. We recommend that the FASB study this proposal and provide guidance to the Federal Home Loan Bank Board.

Stock Markets Are Not Completely Efficient

A second limitation on the value of applying stock market efficiency to policy issues in accounting is that the concept of stock market efficiency probably is not fairly descriptive of the real world.[3] Stock markets are not necessarily inefficient; stock markets are only partially efficient. The degree to which markets are efficient is a function of a variety of factors, including the costs of information, the costs of stock market transactions, the quality of information, and the degree of market completeness. We argue that these and other factors tend to impair market efficiency. For simplicity, we focus only on one factor: costs of information.

Stocks are an economic commodity. Accordingly, equilibrium stock prices are determined by supply and demand. At equilibrium supply equals demand. The role of information in such an environment is to lead actors and institutions to change the supply and demand curves. New information leads to new equilibrium prices because demand curves shift on the basis of the new information.

Suppose now that there are two classes of investors, those who are informed and those who are uninformed. Assume that the stock in question has supply S and demand D such that its equilibrium price is P. This relationship is depicted in Figure 1. Assume that new information becomes available such that the correct demand curve is D' and the correct price is P'.

Initially let us assume that information is costless. What happens? The informed investors would immediately recognize that profits can be attained by purchasing the stock at P and selling at P'. They would purchase the stock at P. But the increased demand for the security by the informed investors would drive up the price. As long as an informed investor can purchase the stock at a price below P', that individual would do so. But this would continually drive up the price. This process would continue until the demand curve is shifted to the correct demand curve D' and the price would continually increase until it reached P', the correct price. This phenomenon is termed "arbitrage." Note that the capital asset prices would adjust very rapidly to the new information and that they would do so in an accurate manner.

[3]There is a rich literature primarily in the economics journals that has challenged the efficient markets hypothesis. See Sanford J. Grossman and Joseph E. Stiglitz, "Information and Competitive Price Systems," *American Economic Review* (May 1976), pp. 246–253; Steve Salop, "Information and Monopolistic Competition," *American Economic Review* (May 1976), pp. 240–245; Sanford Grossman," On the Efficiency of Competitive Stock Markets Where Trades Have Diverse Information," *Journal of Finance* (May 1976), pp. 573–585; Sanford Grossman, "Further Results on the Informational Efficiency of Competitive Stock Markets," *Journal of Economic Theory* (June 1978), pp. 81–101; Sanford J. Grossman and Joseph E. Stiglitz, "On the Impossibility of Informationally Efficient Markets," *American Economic Review* (June 1980), pp. 393–408; Stephen Figlewski, "Information Diversity and Market Behavior," *Journal of Finance* (March 1982), pp. 85–102.

FIGURE 1. *Stock prices in a world of costless information.*

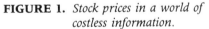

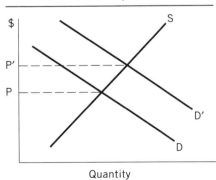

When the adjustment is complete, the price of the security conveys the effects of all the information from the informed investors to the uninformed investors. The uninformed individuals may not know the precise details of the new information, but they know the implications. In other words, when the uninformed investors observe the price of the security change from P to P', they know that new information has been generated and that the new information implies that the correct new equilibrium price is P'. This characterization is the essence of the efficient markets hypothesis; that is, markets are efficient if the price system conveys all of the information from the informed individuals to the uninformed.

Now assume a more realistic world where information is costly. Information costs include education costs, search costs, and costs of analysis. Education costs are the costs of learning and understanding what information is and what it means and how to search for and analyze information. Search costs are the costs for gathering information. These costs include time and effort expended as well as out-of-pocket costs to acquire the information. Costs of analysis are the costs of analyzing information about a security to make a decision about it. These costs are primarily the time and effort expended to process the data. The form of these costs may be transferred; for example, an individual might hire a financial analyst to perform the task rather than do it himself.

Costly information changes the model in a fundamental way. An individual who chooses to be informed and incurs costs to be informed will expect a reasonable return not only on the risky asset being invested in but also on the information costs. This is depicted in Figure 2. As before, we assume that the

FIGURE 2. *Stock prices in a world of costly information.*

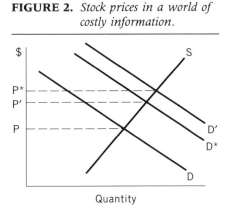

Quantity

initial supply is S and the initial demand is D so that the equilibrium price is P. New information emanates such that it implies that the "correct" price is P'. Informed investors will buy the security at price P and the increased demand will again drive up the price. Unlike the previous example, though, the equilibrium price will never move to the "correct" price P'. Instead the price of the security will be driven up to some price, say P*. It will go no further because the informed investors would be unable to earn a return on their information costs. Indeed, if the price were to move to P', the informed individuals would earn less than the uninformed individuals because the informed investors pay the information costs while the uninformed do not. In this more realistic model, prices do not fully reflect the information. The price system conveys some but not all information. We refer to this concept as the "partially efficient markets hypothesis." This, it should be noted, is not the same thing as the semistrong form described earlier.

The role of the FASB is somewhat different in a world of partially efficient markets than it is in a world of completely efficient markets. Reporting issues might not be trivial. It is not necessarily sufficient to allow firms to choose one method and provide disclosure to permit adjustments to other methods. Adjustments involve costs: education costs in knowing when and how to adjust and costs of analyzing and interpreting the data. If these costs are significant, the related reporting issue is certainly not trivial. Second, the role of financial reports may be broader than simply preventing individuals from earning abnormal returns from inside information. The FASB might perceive that its role is to reduce the noise in accounting numbers so that the resulting capital asset prices are more informative than they otherwise might be. Another possibility is that the FASB might perceive that its role is to reduce or reallocate society's cost of information by requiring disclosure of items that are otherwise searched for and analyzed by some individuals at great cost. The point is that the FASB's role seems to be broader than if the markets were completely efficient.

Informational Efficiency and Allocational Efficiency

Even if stock markets were completely efficient, another issue would have to be raised. The efficient markets hypothesis refers essentially to the results of informational efficiency. Even if stock markets are highly competitive, prices react quickly to new information, and prices accurately reflect new information, do these imply an efficient allocation of scarce resources in the U.S. economy? Unfortunately, the answer appears to be no.

It should be pointed out that economists define efficiency as an allocation of resources such that no alternative feasible allocation can make at least one

person better off without making any person worse off. Economists call this Pareto optimality. Notice that the term "efficiency" in the finance and accounting literature means something very different from that in the economics literature. Stock market efficiency necessarily leads to Pareto optimality if complete risk markets exist. "Complete markets" means that markets exist for all commodities or claims. In such a case, market prices are observable for each commodity or claim. Such a requirement is obviously not met in the real world. Stiglitz has examined a variety of other scenarios, and in each one stock market efficiency does not lead to allocational efficiency.[4]

Stiglitz depicts three levels at which one may analyze the efficiency of the market: exchange efficiency; production efficiency; and information efficiency. Exchange efficiency is a market state where, given the available assets and available information, in a trade or trades of assets no person can be made better off without making someone worse off. Production efficiency is a market wherein assets are produced at such a level that no person can be made better off without making someone worse off, given the available technology, resources, and information. Information efficiency is a market state where information is gathered and utilized so that no person can be made better off without making someone worse off, given the existing assets and beliefs of investors. Note that stock market efficiency examines only information efficiency; it says nothing about exchange or production efficiency.

[4]The arguments of this section are based on Joseph E. Stiglitz, "Pareto Optimality and Competition," *Journal of Finance* (May 1981), pp. 235–251.

That stock market efficiency does not in general lead to Pareto optimality is fundamentally important to accounting. If accounting numbers have an impact on the allocation of scarce resources in the United States, accounting theorists and accounting standards setters should focus on that impact. The question of the relationships between accounting and efficient stock markets takes on a secondary position to the critical question of the impact of accounting on the allocational efficiency of the U.S. society. Many accounting theorists and accounting standards setters have been interested in allocational efficiency at least in a general sense, but this issue has been obscured somewhat recently by those who apparently believe that informational efficiency implies allocational efficiency. Since it does not, accounting theorists and accounting standards setters must address the problems facing the profession with a scope broader than the efficient markets viewpoint.

To cement the arguments made thus far, a specific accounting issue will be examined: inflation accounting. Basically, the stock market may not be affected either by the requirements to disclose inflation accounting numbers or by the numbers themselves. Such a state of affairs does not imply that inflation accounting is useless, for the numbers may have an impact on other users.

For the purposes of this article, let us suppose that empirical tests prove beyond a shadow of doubt that constant dollar accounting and current cost accounting do not enhance the decision-making processes of investors and creditors. Does this supposition lead us to the conclusion that inflation accounting is an exercise in futility? If we consider the needs of labor, the federal govern-ment, internal management, and others, then inflation accounting may not prove to be useless and irrelevant, but it may become a basis for providing better economic decisions in U.S. society [10].

One facet involving inflation accounting deals with labor–management. When labor discusses its percentage increase in wages, it almost always adjusts wages for the inflation rate so that it can report the increase or decrease in real wages. That is certainly a sound approach to follow. United States businesses, however, report profits that are not adjusted for changing prices. These firms are reporting money profits, not real profits. Given that money profits are inevitably greater than real profits during an inflationary period, labor might use the corporate entity's own reported earnings data to support the ability of the entity to raise wages. Rates of profit growth are asserted to exceed rates of wage growth. The fact that the growth rates lack comparability is often overlooked. Would not all interested parties be better served if comparisons such as these were based on data that were comparable?

A second aspect of inflation accounting lies in the tax implications when earnings provide the tax base. Taxes are based primarily on income reported under the historical cost model. Congress often makes some attempts, however, to adjust for inflation, to encourage economic growth, or to achieve some other economic goal. No basis exists, however, to evaluate whether adjustments made to counter inflation have achieved that objective. If earnings were adjusted for the effects of price changes, aggregate income taxes might be different from taxes generated even when inflation adjustments have been attempted. Even if aggregate income taxes were unchanged, taxing on the basis of inflation accounting would produce different effects on different segments of the economy.

Inflation accounting is by no means the only accounting issue that demonstrates possible economic effects outside the stock markets. Other issues include:

- Does *SFAS No. 2*, "Accounting for Research and Development Costs," affect the level of research and development activity in the United States?

- Does *SFAS No. 5*, "Accounting for Contingencies," affect the exchange efficiency of risky assets?

- Does *SFAS No. 7*, "Accounting and Reporting by Development Stage Enterprises," affect the formation of new business in the United States?

- Does *SFAS No. 13*, "Accounting for Leases," affect debt covenants? Does it affect the exchange of capital assets?

- Does *SFAS No. 15*, "Accounting by Debtors and Creditors for Troubled Debt Restructurings," affect the regulation of the banking industry?

- Does *SFAS No. 21*, "Suspension of the Reporting of Earnings per Share and Segment Information," affect the small business segment of society?

- Does *SFAS No. 30*, "Disclosure of Information About Major Customers," affect other customers and suppliers?

- Does *SFAS No. 34*, "Capitalization of Interest Cost," affect the trading of capital assets?

- Do *SFAS No. 35*, "Accounting and Reporting by Defined Benefit Pension Plans," and *No. 36*, "Disclosure of Pension Information," affect employees and labor unions?

- Does *SFAS No. 52*, "Foreign Currency Translation," affect international trading?

These questions all deal with possible economic effects other than stock market effects. Researchers should not be limited to the efficient markets paradigm. Many other economic factors are at work and need to be explored. Accounting researchers are encouraged to expand their horizons and investigate all the economic implications of accounting.

Implications for the FASB

One of the strengths of the FASB relative to its predecessors is extensive research before issuing a major statement of financial accounting standards. Much of the funded research has focused on stock market reactions to certain events. We caution the FASB not to place undue emphasis on these studies. First, a variety of institutions are affected by accounting rules in addition to the stock markets. The FASB should also examine the effects, real or alleged, on these other institutions. Second, the efficient markets hypothesis does not seem to be descriptive of the real world with costly information. We find it difficult to interpret some of the results of capital market research because of the unrealistic assumptions employed, and so we are not sure what policy implications they have. Third, markets might be efficient informationally but not in an allocational sense. The FASB's purpose should, in our opinion, relate to issues of allocational efficiency and not simply to informational efficiency. Essentially, we feel that the world is far more complex and far more diverse than is captured by the efficient markets paradigm. While the concept is helpful in some respects, it would definitely be a mistake to formulate accounting policy on the basis that we live in a world of efficient markets. The FASB is constrained to operate in the real world: It needs to formulate policy given the fact that partially efficient markets characterizes the real world.

References

1. William H. Beaver, "What Should Be the FASB's Objectives?" *The Journal of Accountancy* (Aug. 1973), pp. 49–56.
2. W. A. Paton and A. C. Littleton, *An Introduction to Corporate Accounting Standards* (American Accounting Association. 1940).
3. Edgar O. Edwards and Philip W. Bell, *The Theory and Measurement of Business Income* (University of California Press, 1961).
4. Norton M. Bedford, *Income Determination Theory: An Accounting Framework* (Addison-Wesley, 1965).
5. Raymond J. Chambers, *Accounting, Evaluation and Economic Behavior* (Prentice-Hall, 1966).
6. Yuji Ijiri, *Theory of Accounting Measurement* (American Accounting Association, 1975).
7. *APB Statement No. 4*, "Basic Concepts and Accounting Principles Underlying Financial Statements of Business Enterprises" (1970), especially Ch. 3.
8. *Statement of Financial Accounting Concepts No. 1*, "Objectives of Financial Reporting by Business Enterprises" (FASB, Nov. 1978).
9. *Preliminary Report of the Interoffice Task Force on Market Value Accounting* (Federal Home Loan Bank Board, Aug. 27, 1982).
10. Daryl N. Winn, "The Potential Effect of Alternative Measures on Public Policy and Resource Allocation," in *Economic Consequences of Financial Accounting Standards* (FASB, 1978), pp. 3–37.

Cases

• Case 2-1

Capital Asset Pricing Model

Choose three companies on the New York stock exchange. Compute a beta for the three companies by comparing the movement in their stock with the movement of Standard and Poor's 500 for two years. (For simplicity track the stock prices and the index on the first day of each month for the two-year period.) Compare the betas of the three companies. What do these betas tell you about the relative volatility of the three stocks? If the managers of these three companies are using the capital asset pricing model as the basis for accepting new projects, rank the companies, from lowest to highest, in terms of the rate of return required for new projects.

• Case 2-2

Behavioral Accounting Research

One of the goals of behavioral accounting research is to assess the effect of accounting numbers and presentations on decision making. Design a case with alternate presentations of the same material or alternate numbers to be used to assess the impact of information on decision making. (*Hint*: You may wish to consult Robert Ashton "Integrating Research and Teaching in Auditing: Fifteen Cases on Audit Judgement and Decision Making," *The Accounting Review* (January 1984), pp. 78–97, to assist you in developing a case.)

- ## Case 2-3

Contrasting Views of Profit

Critical perspective theorists maintain that accountants have almost uniformly adopted the marginal economics viewpoint of income and have not considered other views of income. Another view of the nature of income is termed the classical political economy. Compare and contrast these two views of income. Can accounting adopt a different view as to income and maintain its important role in our society? (*Hint*: In addition to the articles by Solomons and Tinker contained in this chapter, a good starting point is contained in Anthony M. Tinker's "Toward a Political Economy of Accounting: An Illustration of the Cambridge Controversies," *Accounting, Organizations and Society,* Vol. 5, No. 1 (1980), pp. 147–160.)

- ## Case 2-4

Discuss the capital asset pricing model including systematic and unsystematic risk, beta, the relationship between risk and return, how to avoid risk and the relationship of beta to stock prices.

- ## Case 2-5

Discuss the assumptions of the supply and demand model inherent in the efficient market hypothesis. Why is the securities market viewed as a good example of the supply and demand model? Discuss the three forms of the efficient market hypothesis.

- ## Case 2-6

Discuss the deductive, inductive, and pragmatic research methods. Include in your discussion examples of accounting research that used each method.

- ## Case 2-7

Discuss agency theory including its basic assumptions, agency relationships, why the political process has impact on agency relationships and why it does or does not explain accounting theory.

- ## Case 2-8

Discuss human information processing research. What is the general finding of this research? What are the consequences of this finding? What impact do these consequences have on accounting?

- ## Case 2-9

What is critical perspective research? How does it differ from traditional accounting research? What are the three assumptions of critical perspective research?

Recommended Additional Readings

Chau, Wai Fong. "Radical Development in Accounting Thought." *The Accounting Review* (October 1986), pp. 601–629.

Hopwood, Anthony M. "Behavioral Accounting in Retrospect and Prospect." *Behavioral Research in Accounting* (1989), pp. 1–22.

Libby, Robert, and Barry L. Lewis. "Human Information Processing Research in Accounting: The State of the Art." *Accounting, Organizations and Society*, Vol. 2. No. 3 (1977), pp. 246–268.

Sterling, Robert R. "Accounting Research, Education and Practice." *Journal of Accountancy* (September 1973), pp. 44–52.

Sterling, Robert R. "On Theory Construction and Verification." *The Accounting Review* (July 1970), pp. 444–457.

Wyatt, Arthur R. "Efficient Market Theory: Its Impact on Accounting." *Journal of Accountancy* (February 1983), pp. 56–65.

Bibliography

Abdel-Khalik, A. Rashad. "The Efficient Market Hypothesis and Accounting Data: A Point of View." *The Accounting Review* (October 1972), pp. 791–793.

American Accounting Association. "Report of the 1976–77 Committee on Human Information Processing." *Committee Reports*, Vol. 1978–2 (August 1977).

Ashton, Robert. *Human Information Processing in Accounting.* Sarasota, Fla.: American Accounting Association, 1982.

Arrington, C. Edward, and Jere R. Francis. "Letting The Chat Out of the Bag: Deconstruction, Privilege and Accounting Research." *Accounting, Organizations and Society* (1989), pp. 1–28.

Ball, Raymond J., and Philip R. Brown. "An Empirical Evaluation of Accounting Income Numbers." *Journal of Accounting Research* (Autumn 1968), pp. 159–178.

Beaver, William. "The Information Content of Annual Earnings Announcements." *Journal of Accounting Research, Selected Studies—Empirical Research in Accounting* (1968), pp. 67–92.

Bierman, Harold, Jr. "The Implications to Accounting of Efficient Markets and the Capital Asset Pricing Model." *The Accounting Review* (July 1974), pp. 557–562.

Caplan, Edwin H. "Behavioral Accounting—A Personal View." *Behavioral Research in Accounting* (1989), pp. 109–123.

Chambers, Anne E., and Stephen H. Penman. "Timeliness of Reporting and the Stock Price Reaction to Earnings Announcements." *Journal of Accounting Research* (Spring 1984), pp. 21–47.

Chambers, R. J. "Stock Market Prices and Accounting Research." *Abacus* (June 1974), pp. 39–54.

Christenson, Charles. "The Methodology of Positive Accounting." *The Accounting Review* (January 1983), pp. 1–22.

Demski, Joel S. "The General Impossibility of Normative Accounting Standards." *The Accounting Review* (October 1973), pp. 718–723.

Downers, David, and Thomas Dyckman. "A Critical Look at the Efficient Market Empirical Research Literature as it Relates to Accounting Information." *The Accounting Review* (April 1973), pp. 300–317.

Dyckman, Thomas R., David H. Downes, and Robert P. Magee. *Efficient Capital Markets and Accounting: A Critical Analysis.* Englewood Cliffs, N.J.: Prentice-Hall, Inc., 1975.

Evans, John, and Stephen H. Archer. "Diversification and the Reduction of Dispersion: An Empirical Analysis." *Journal of Finance* (December 1968), pp. 761–767.

Frankfurter, George M., and Allan Young. "Financial Theory: Its Message to the Accountant." *Journal of Accounting, Auditing and Finance* (1983), pp. 314–324.

Friend, Irwin, and Marshall E. Blume. "Measurement of Portfolio Performance under Uncertainty." *American Economic Review* (September 1970), pp. 561–575.

Friend, Irwin, Randolph Westerfield, and Michael Granito. "New Evidence on the Capital Asset Pricing Model." *Journal of Finance* (June 1978), pp. 903–920.

Gonedes, Nicholas J. "Efficient Capital Market and External Accounting." *The Accounting Review* (January 1972), pp. 11–21.

Hines, Ruth. "Popper's Method of Falsification and Accounting Research." *The Accounting Review* (October 1988), pp. 657–662.

Hofstedt, Thomas R., and James C. Kinnard. "A Strategy for Behavioral Accounting Research." *The Accounting Review* (January 1970), pp. 38–54.

Hopper, Trevor, John Storey, and Hugh Willmott. "Accounting for Accounting: Toward the Development of the Dialectical View." *Accounting, Organizations and Society* (1987), pp. 437–456.

Laughlin, Richard C. "Accounting Systems in Organizational Contexts: A Case for Critical Theory." *Accounting, Organizations and Society* (1987), pp. 479–502.

Lehman, Cheryl, and Anthony Tinker. "The Real Cultural Significance of Accounts." *Accounting, Organizations and Society* (1989), pp. 503–522.

Libby, Robert. *Accounting and Human Information Processing Theory and Applications.* Englewood Cliffs: Prentice-Hall, 1981.

Mattessich, Richard. "Methodological Preconditions and Problems of a General Theory of Accounting." *The Accounting Review* (July 1972), pp. 469–487.

Mayer-Sommer, Alan P. "Understanding and Acceptance of the Efficient Market Hypothesis and Its Accounting Implications." *The Accounting Review* (January 1979), pp. 88–106.

Modigliani, Franco, and Gerald A. Pogue. "An Introduction to Risk and Return." *Financial Analysts Journal* (March–April 1974), pp. 68–80.

Nord, Walter R. "Toward an Optimal Dialectical Perspective: Comments and Extensions on Neimark and Tinker." *Accounting, Organizations and Society* (1986), pp. 398–402.

Roll, Richard. "A Critique of the Asset Pricing Theory's Tests." *Journal of Financial Economics* (March 1977), pp. 129–176.

Sharpe, William. "Capital Asset Prices: A Theory of Market Equilibrium under Conditions of Risk." *Journal of Finance* (September 1964), pp. 425–442.

Sterling, Robert R. (ed.). *Research Methodology in Accounting.* Lawrence, Kan.: Scholars Book Company, 1972.

Tinker, Anthony M. *Paper Profits,* New York: Praeger Publishers, 1985.

Tinker, Anthony M. "Toward a Political Economy of Accounting: An Empirical Illustration of the Cambridge Controversies." *Accounting, Organizations and Society* (1980), pp. 147–160.

Tinker, Anthony M., Barbara D. Merino, and Marilyn D. Neimark. "The Normative Origins of Positive Theories, Ideology and Accounting Thought." *Accounting Organizations and Society* (1982), pp. 167–200.

Tinker, Anthony M., and Marilyn Neimark. "The Struggle Over Meaning in Accounting and Corporate Research: Comparative Evaluation of Conservative and Critical Historiography." *Accounting, Auditing and Accountability* (1988), pp. 55–74.

Tippet, Mark. "The Axioms of Accounting Measurement." *Accounting and Business Research* (Autumn 1978), pp. 266–278.

Watts, Ross, and Jerold L. Zimmerman. "Toward a Positive Theory of Determination of Accounting Standards." *The Accounting Review* (January 1978), pp. 112–134.

Watts, Ross, and Jerold L. Zimmerman. "The Demand for and the Supply of Accounting Theories: The Market for Excuses." *The Accounting Review* (April 1979), pp. 273–305.

Watts, Ross, and Jerold L. Zimmerman. *Positive Accounting Theory.* Englewood Cliffs: Prentice-Hall, 1986.

Watts, Ross, and Jerold L. Zimmerman. "Positive Accounting Theory: A Ten Year Perspective." *The Accounting Review* (January 1990), pp. 131–156.

Williamson, Paul. "The Logic of Positive Accounting Research." *Accounting, Organizations and Society* (1989), pp. 455–468.

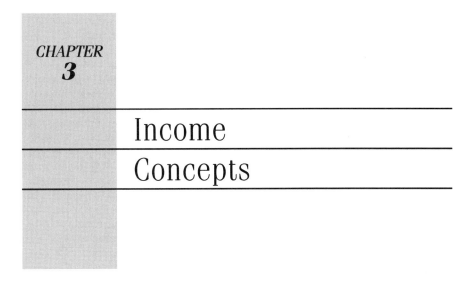

CHAPTER 3

Income
Concepts

The objective of financial accounting is to provide information useful to investors in making predictions about enterprise performance. The emergence of income reporting as the primary source for investor decision making has been well documented,[1] and income reporting aids economic society in a variety of ways. For example, the Study Group on Business Income documented the need for the income concept in society, and Alexander noted the following uses of income in this work.

1. Income is used as the basis of one of the principal forms of taxation.

2. Income is used in public reports as a measure of the success of a corporation's operations.

3. Income is used as a criterion for the determination of the availability of dividends.

4. Income is used by rate-regulating authorities for investigating whether those rates are fair and reasonable.

5. Income is used as a guide to trustees charged with distributing income to a life tenant while preserving the principal for a remainderman.

6. Income is used as a guide to management of an enterprise in the conduct of its affairs.[2]

---

[1] Clifford D. Brown, "The Emergence of Income Reporting: An Historical Study," M.S.U. Business Studies (East Lansing, Mich.: Division of Research, Graduate School of Business Administration, Michigan State University, 1971).

[2] Sidney S. Alexander, "Income Measurement in a Dynamic Economy," *Five Monographs on Business Income,* report by Study Group on Business Income (New York, 1950), p. 6.

115

Despite the wide use of the income concept, there is a general lack of agreement as to the proper definition of income. This disagreement is most noticeable when the prevailing definitions used in the disciplines of economics and accounting are analyzed. Although there is a general consensus that economics and accounting are related sciences and that both are concerned with the activities of business firms and deal with similar variables, there has been a lack of agreement between the two disciplines regarding the proper timing and measurement of income. As a consequence, there has been a good deal of debate over the relative importance of the balance sheet and the income statement in determining income. Those adopting the balance sheet viewpoint see income as the increase in net worth that has occurred during a period—the economic approach. Those favoring the income statement approach view income as the result of certain activities that have taken place during a period. They also view the balance sheet as a list of items remaining after income has been determined by matching costs and revenues—the transactions approach. In order to attempt to reconcile these two viewpoints the following questions will be addressed:

1. What is the nature of income?
2. When should income be reported?
3. Who are the recipients of income?

The Nature of Income

Income may take various forms; for example, Bedford noted that three basic concepts of income are usually discussed in the literature.

1. *Psychic income,* which refers to the satisfaction of human wants.
2. *Real income,* which refers to increases in economic wealth.
3. *Money income,* which refers to increases in the monetary valuation of resources.[3]

These three concepts are all important yet there are advantages and disadvantages associated with each. The measurement of psychic income is difficult because human wants are not quantifiable and are satisfied on various levels as an individual gains real income.[4] Money income is easily measured, but does not take into consideration changes in the value of the monetary unit. Economists generally agree that the objective of measuring income is to determine how much better off an entity has become during some period of time. Consequently economists have focused on the determination of real income. The definition of the economic concept of income is usually credited to the economist J. R. Hicks, who stated:

---

[3] Norton M. Bedford, *Income Determination Theory: An Accounting Framework* (Reading, Mass.: Addison-Wesley Publishing Co., 1965), p. 20.

[4] See, for example, Abraham H. Maslow, *Motivation and Personality* (New York: Harper & Brothers, 1954), Chapter 5.

The purpose of income calculation in practical affairs is to give people an indica-
tion of the amount which they can consume without impoverishing themselves.
Following out this idea it would seem that we ought to define a man's income
as the maximum value which he can consume during a week, and still expect
to be as well off at the end of the week as he was at the beginning.[5]

The preceding Hicksian definition places emphasis on individual income; however, the concept can also be used as the basis for determining business income by changing the word *consume* to *distribute*. A business entity using this concept of income would be required to measure its net assets (assets minus liabilities) at the beginning of a period and at the end of the same period, exclusive of capital and dividend transactions. Business income would be the change in the net asset values over the measurement period. This method of income determination is termed the *capital maintenance* concept by accountants and holds that no income should be recognized until capital has been retained and costs recovered. Initially, the application of the capital maintenance concept may appear to be a simple measurement of the change in net worth exclusive of capital and dividend transactions; however, strict adherence to it entails a much more complex measure of "well-offness" and net worth than usually envisioned by accountants.

Specifically, it would be necessary to measure the *net present values* of enterprise assets and liabilities at the beginning and the end of a particular period and report the difference. Income would be comprised of two components.

1. Increases or decreases in net assets that were the result of operations.

2. Increases or decreases in net assets that were caused by changes in their expected future values.

Although there can be little argument on the theoretical merit of the Hicksian definition, economic income is not generally observable in actual reporting situations.[6] The critics of the use of economic income do not believe that it has practical applicability because of two operational constraints. First, it is subjective because future inflows from assets and outflows from liabilities are not known with certainty. For example, how much cash will be received in the future because an enterprise holds land? Second, the appropriate discount factor is unknown and subject to future conditions. For these reasons accountants have generally not attempted to use the economic concept of real income and have delayed the timing of income reporting until more substantial evidence exists that income has been earned.

Income Recognition

In an attempt to overcome the subjective difficulties associated with using the economic concept of income, accountants have traditionally taken the position

[5] J. R. Hicks, *Value and Capital* (Oxford: Clarendon Press, 1946), p. 172.

[6] William Beaver and Joel Demski, "The Nature of Income Measurement," *The Accounting Review* (January 1979), pp. 38–46.

that income should be reported when there is evidence of an outside exchange (or an "arm's length transaction"). This *transactions* approach generally requires that reported income be the result of dealings with firms and individuals external to the reporting unit and gives rise to the realization principle. The realization principle holds that income should be recognized when the earnings process is complete, or virtually complete, and an exchange has taken place. The exchange transaction is the basis of accountability and determines both the time of revenue recognition and the amount of revenue to be recorded.

Income in an accounting sense contrasts with income in the economic sense in that accounting income is determined by measuring only the *recorded* changes in net asset values, exclusive of capital and dividend transactions, during a period. The accounting concept of income does not attempt to place an expected value on the firm or report on changes in the expected values of assets or liabilities.

Although empirical research has indicated that accounting income is related to market based measures of income such as stock returns,[7] the transactions approach to income determination has been criticized for not reporting all relevant information about business entities. Those who favor a more liberal interpretation of the income concept argue that income should include all gains and losses in assets or liabilities held by an entity during a particular period. This broader measure of income was given its initial impetus by Edwards and Bell in their *Theory and Measurement of Business Income*[8] and Sprouse and Moonitz in *Accounting Research Study No. 3*, "A Tentative Set of Broad Accounting Principles for Business Enterprises."[9]

Edwards and Bell suggested that with only slight changes in present accounting procedures four types of income can be isolated. These income measures are defined as (1) current operating profit—the excess of sales revenues over the current cost of inputs used in production and sold; (2) realizable cost savings—the increases in the prices of assets held during the period; (3) realized cost savings—the difference between historical costs and the current purchase price of goods sold; and (4) realized capital gains—the excess of sales proceeds over historical costs on the disposal of long-term assets. Edwards and Bell contended that these measures are a better indication of well-offness and allow users more information in analyzing enterprise results.[10]

Sprouse, in elaborating on the findings of *Accounting Research Study No. 3*, discussed the concept somewhat more narrowly:

> *Because ownership interests are constantly changing hands, we must strive for timely recognition of measurable changes, and in so doing we must identify the*

---

[7] Robert Ball and Philip Brown, "An Empirical Evaluation of Accounting Income Numbers," *Journal of Accounting Research* (Autumn 1968), pp. 159–178.

[8] Edgar O. Edwards and Philip W. Bell, *The Theory and Measurement of Business Income* (Berkeley and Los Angeles: University of California Press, 1961).

[9] Robert T. Sprouse and Maurice Moonitz, "A Tentative Set of Broad Accounting Principles for Business Enterprises," *Accounting Research Study No. 3* (New York: AICPA, 1962).

[10] Edwards and Bell, op. cit., p. 111.

nature of the changes. As currently reported, income may well be composed of three elements, each of which has considerably different economic significance. Is the gross margin truly the result of operations—the difference between current selling prices of products and current costs of producing products, both measured in today's dollars? How much of the company's income is not the result of its operations but is the result of changes in the value of a significant asset, for example, a large supply of raw material, perhaps a warehouse full of sugar? Such changes are apt to be fortuitous and unpredictable and therefore need to be segregated, if financial statements are to be interpreted meaningfully and if rational investment decisions are to be based on income measurements. And how much of what is now reported as income is not income at all but is merely the spurious result of using a current unit of measurement for revenues and an obsolete unit of measurement for costs—particularly depreciation?[11]

The major change advocated by both Edwards and Bell and *Accounting Research Study No. 3* is the reporting of gains or losses in the net assets of the entity during a period. These changes are termed *holding gains and losses,* and proponents claim that the reporting of holding gains and losses would increase the information content of published financial statements. This argument focuses on two points: (1) windfall gains and losses from holding specific assets and liabilities should be reported as they occur, and (2) changes in the measuring unit should be eliminated from the reporting process. (The discussion of the second point involves dealing with the effects of inflation and will be deferred until Chapter 15.)

The effect on income of the failure to record holding gains is illustrated by the following example. Suppose two individuals, A and B, purchase adjoining 100-acre plots of land for $10,000 on December 31, 1990. Assume that the appraisal value of these plots of land rises to $20,000 on December 31, 1996, and that A sells his land on this date while B retains hers. Traditional accounting practice allows A to recognize a gain of $10,000, whereas B cannot record her gain. This difference occurs even though the economic substance of both events is essentially the same. This example illustrates the effect of the transactions approach to income determination.

Measurement

The reporting of business income assumes that all items of revenue and expense are capable of being measured. One requirement of measurement is that the object or event is capable of being ordered or ranked in respect to some property. Measurement is the assigning of numbers to objects or events according to rules. It is also a process of comparison in order to obtain more precise information to distinguish one alternative from another in a decision situation.

The accounting measuring unit in the United States is the dollar; however, the instability of the measuring unit causes a major problem. For example,

---

[11] Robert T. Sprouse, "The Radically Different Principles of Accounting Research Study No. 3," *Journal of Accountancy* (May 1964), p. 66.

consider the room you are now in. If you were to measure its width in feet and inches today, next week, and next year, accurate measurements would give the same result each time. In contrast, the accounting measurement of sales revenue will undoubtedly differ each year even if exactly the same number of units are sold. Much of this difference will be the result of changes in the value of the dollar.

Another factor that complicates accounting measurement is that arbitrary decisions must be made for periodic reporting purposes. Depreciation, depletion, and amortization are all examples of arbitrary and inexact measurement techniques that complicate the measurement process. Although changes in the measurement unit and arbitrary measurements caused by the necessity of periodic presentation are not likely to disappear in the near future, the users of accounting information should recognize the inherent limitations in the use of measurement techniques in accounting.

Revenue Recognition and Realization

There has been a great deal of confusion in accounting literature over the precise meaning of the terms recognition and realization. Recognition is the formal process of recording a transaction or event, whereas realization is the process of converting noncash assets to cash or claims to cash. However, there have been arguments over the proper timing of revenue recognition. Critics of the accounting process favor the economic concept of real income, whereby revenue is earned continuously over time. For accountants, however, it would not be practical to record revenues on a continuous basis. Rather, the accountant must choose an appropriate point in time on which to record the occurrence of revenues.

In 1964, the American Accounting Association Committee on Realization recommended that the concept of realization could be improved if the following criteria were applied: (1) revenue must be capable of measurement, (2) the measurement must be verified by an external market transaction, and (3) the crucial event must have occurred.[12] The key element in these recommendations is the third criterion. The crucial-event test states that revenue should be realized on the completion of the most crucial task in the earning process. This test results in the recognition of revenue at various times for different business organizations.

The use of the crucial-event test and the transactions approach has resulted in accounting income that measures the difference between sales of the company's product (revenue) and costs incurred in the production and sale of that product (expenses). Revenue has been defined by the Financial Accounting Standards Board as "inflows or other enhancements of assets of an entity or settlements of its liabilities (or a combination of both) during a period

---

[12] American Accounting Association 1964 Concepts and Standards Research Study Committee: The Matching Concept. "The Matching Concept," *The Accounting Review*, Vol. 40 (April 1965), p. 318.

from delivering or producing goods, rendering services or other activities that constitute the entity's ongoing operations."[13]

The use of the realization convention usually results in revenue being recognized at the point of sale; however, the timing of recognition may be advanced or delayed by the nature of the specific transaction. Generally, departures from the point of sale occur due to varying degrees of certainty. When there is a high degree of certainty associated with realization, revenue recognition may precede the point of sale. Conversely, the greater the level of uncertainty associated with realization, the greater is the tendency to delay revenue recognition.

Revenue Recognized During the Production Process
When production of the company's product carries over into two or more periods, the allocation of revenue to the various accounting periods is considered essential for proper reporting. In such cases a method of revenue recognition termed *percentage of completion* may be used. This method allocates revenue on the basis of the percentage of the expected total costs that were incurred in a particular accounting period. The percentage of completion method requires a known selling price and the ability to estimate reasonably the total costs of the product. It is used in accounting for long-term construction contracts such as roads, shipbuilding, and dams. Because the percentage of completion method recognizes income as it is earned, rather than waiting until the transaction has been completed, the concept of revenue recognition provides income measurements that are closer to the economic concept of income espoused by Hicks.

Revenue Recognized at the Completion of Production
When the company's product is to be sold at a determinable price on an organized market, revenue may be realized when the goods are ready for sale. The gold market formerly was an example of this method, in that all gold mined was required to be sold to the government at a fixed price. Some farm products and commodities also meet these conditions. Revenue recognition at the completion of production is defended on the grounds that the event critical to the earnings process has occurred.

Revenue Recognized as Services Are Performed
There are three steps involved in service contracts: (1) order taking, (2) performance of services, and (3) collection of cash. These steps may all be performed in one accounting period or divided between periods. In service contracts, realization should generally be connected with the performance of services, and revenue should be recorded in relation to the degree of services performed. Realization should be tied to services performed because it is the most crucial decision. The signing of the contract results in a partially executory contract, and the collection of cash may precede or follow the performance of services.

---

[13] *Statement of Financial Accounting Concepts No. 6,* "Elements of Financial Statements of Business Enterprises" (Stamford, Conn., 1985) par. 79.

Revenue Recognized as Cash Is Received

In certain circumstances, where the ultimate collectibility of the revenue is in doubt, recognition is delayed until cash payment is received. The installment method and the cash recovery method are examples of delaying revenue recognition until the receipt of cash. However, the Accounting Principles Board stated that revenue recognition should not be delayed unless ultimate collectibility is so seriously doubted that an appropriate allowance for the uncollectible amount cannot be estimated.

Revenue Recognized on the Occurrence of Some Event

In some instances, where binding contracts do not exist or rights to cancel are in evidence, the level of uncertainty may dictate that revenue recognition be delayed until the point of ratification or the passage of time. For example, some states have passed laws that allow door-to-door sales contracts to be voided within certain periods of time. In such cases recognition should be delayed until that period has passed.

Special Recognition Circumstances

Some events do not fall into any of the above categories. Consequently, it may be necessary to establish new GAAP to account for specific types of transactions. For example, the FASB specifically addressed revenue recognition criteria for franchisors and in situations where the right of return exists. In *SFAS No. 45*, "Accounting for Franchise Fee Revenue," the Board stated that franchise fee revenue (net of an appropriate provision for uncollectible accounts) should be recognized when all material services have been substantially performed by the franchisor. In most cases the earliest point at which revenue may be recognized by franchisors will be the start of operations by the franchisee. Additionally, the installment method may be used only when revenue is collected over an extended period of time and there is no reasonable basis for estimating its ultimate collectibility.

In *SFAS No. 48*, "Revenue Recognition When Right of Return Exists," the FASB stated that a seller should recognize revenue at the point of sale when a return privilege exists only when all the following conditions are met.

1. The selling price is fixed or determinable at the date of sale.

2. The buyer has paid or is obligated to pay the seller.

3. The buyer bears the risk of loss from theft or damage.

4. The buyer has economic substance apart from the seller.

5. The seller has no major obligations for future performance involving the resale of the product.

6. Future returns are reasonably estimable.

In the event these conditions are not met and revenue recognition is deferred, revenue should be recognized at the first point at which the return privilege has expired or any conditions are satisfied.

The preceding discussion illustrates that the timing of revenue recognition may differ substantially. The underlying rationale for this diversity is the existence of varying levels of certainty and thus the occurrence of critical events or activities in the earnings process. Unfortunately, there is no specific criterion by which accountants can make judgments as to the most appropriate moments of recognition. Thus, over the years, various precedents and conventions have provided support for the recognition of revenues at different times; the revenue recognition convention has taken on the meaning of a set of criteria to be used when certain circumstances are in evidence.

Matching

In addition to the realization principle, the matching concept is of primary importance in the determination of accounting income because of periodic reporting and the theoretical basis underlying the accrual concept of income. Normal accounting procedures are based on the premise that the business enterprise is a going concern and, as such, must provide periodic reports to investors in order for them to assess their investments. To be relevant, these reports are intended to apprise investors of the earnings that have accrued during the period. Because accounting earnings comprise revenues and expenses, accounting principles have evolved to establish when to recognize revenue and how to match revenues with costs. The process of associating revenues with cost is termed the *matching concept.*

Paton and Littleton described the matching concept as the association of effort and accomplishment.[14] Similarly, an American Accounting Association Committee investigating the matching concept recommended that costs should be related to revenues realized within a specific period on the basis of some correlation of these costs with the recognized revenues.[15]

The determination of when costs are of no future benefit and should therefore be charged against revenue depends on the definitions of the terms *cost, expense,* and *loss.* These terms are defined as follows:

> *Cost—the amount given in consideration of goods received or to be received. Costs can be classified as unexpired (assets), which are applicable to the production of future revenues, and expired, those not applicable to the production of future revenues and thus deducted from revenues or retained earnings in the current period.*[16]
>
> *Expense—outflows or other using up of assets or incurrences of liabilities (or a combination of both) during a period from delivering or producing goods, rendering services, or carrying out other activities that constitute the entity's ongoing major or central operations.*[17]

---

[14] W. A. Paton and A. C. Littleton, *An Introduction to Corporate Accounting Standards,* American Accounting Association Monograph No. 3 (AAA, 1940).

[15] American Accounting Association 1964 Concepts and Standards Research Study Committee, op. cit., pp. 368–372.

[16] Committee on Terminology, AICPA, *Accounting Terminology Bulletin No. 4,* "Review and Resume" (New York, 1953).

[17] *FASB Statement of Concepts No. 6,* op. cit., par. 80.

Loss—decreases in equity (net assets) from peripheral or incidental transactions of an entity and from all other transactions and other events and circumstances affecting the entity during a period except those that result from expenses or distributions to owners.[18]

In other words, expenses are revenue-producing cost expirations whereas losses are non-revenue-producing cost expirations.

These definitions are illustrated as follows:

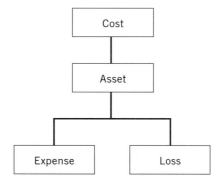

Thus, the accountant must determine the costs that have expired during the current period and whether or not these costs are revenue-producing or non-revenue-producing cost expirations. This determination is aided by separating expenses into product costs and period costs. Product costs are those cost expirations that can be directly associated with the company's product, such as direct material, direct labor, and direct factory overhead. Additionally, it is common practice arbitrarily to assign some costs, such as indirect overhead, to the product even though a direct measure of association may be lacking. *Product costs* are charged to expense on the basis of the number of products sold. Period costs are those cost expirations that are more closely related to a period of time than to a product, such as administrative salaries. *Period costs* are charged to expense on the basis of the period of benefit. All losses are written off in the period in which their lack of future benefit is determined.

In summary it can be seen that the recognition of accounting income is the result of the ability to measure inflows (revenues) and associated outflows (expenses). Where inflows or outflows are not measurable, the timing of income recognition is deferred. Consequently, accounting income is closely tied to past and present operations, and the traditional income statement indicates little in the way of future expectations. Accountants have generally taken the position that the best indicator of the future is past performance and that reporting anticipated gains involves an element of subjectivity in the calculation that could impair the usefulness of financial statements. Additionally, the concepts of conservatism and materiality have played an important role in the determination of accounting income.

[18] Ibid., par. 81.

Conservatism

Sterling called *conservatism* the most influential principle of valuation in accounting.[19] Simply stated, conservatism holds: when in doubt choose the accounting alternative that will be least likely to overstate assets and income.

The principle of conservatism originally gained prominence as a partial offset to the eternal optimism of management and the tendency to overstate financial statements that characterized the first three decades of the 20th century. Conservatism was also seen as overriding the holding gains argument because many accountants believed that by placing the least favorable alternative valuation on the firm, the users of financial accounting information were less likely to be misled. In recent years the pressures for more reliable and relevant information have reduced the influence of this concept. Conservative financial statements are usually unfair to present stockholders and biased in favor of prospective stockholders because the net valuation of the firm does not include future expectations. As a consequence, the company's common stock will be priced at a relatively lower value in the marketplace.

Materiality

The concept of *materiality* has had a pervasive influence on all accounting activities despite the fact that no all-encompassing definition of the concept exists. Although materiality affects the measurement and disclosure of all information presented on the financial statements, it has its greatest impact on items of revenue and expense.

The concept has both qualitative and quantitative aspects. For example, the private sector organizations empowered to develop GAAP have defined materiality both qualitatively and quantitatively. *Accounting Research Study No. 7* provided the following qualitative definition:

> *A statement, fact or item is material, if giving full consideration to the surrounding circumstances, as they exist at the time, it is of such a nature that its disclosure, or the method of treating it, would be likely to influence or to "make a difference" in the judgment and conduct of a reasonable person.*[20]

These organizations have also furnished quantitative definitions of materiality. For example, as quantitative requirements were established in *Accounting Principles Board Opinion No. 18,* an investment of 20 percent or more in the voting stock of an investee is considered material. In *APB Opinion No. 15,* a reduction of less than 3 percent in the aggregate of earnings per share is not considered material. Additionally, the FASB defined a reportable segment as one that constitutes 10 percent of revenues, operating profits, or assets. And

---

[19] Robert R. Sterling, *Theory of the Measurement of Enterprise Income* (Lawrence, Kan.: University of Kansas Press, 1970), p. 256.

[20] Paul Grady, *Accounting Research Study No. 7,* "Inventory of Generally Accepted Accounting Principles for Business Enterprises" (New York: AICPA, 1965), p. 40.

most SFASs contain the following: "The provisions of this Statement need not be applied to immaterial items."[21]

In *Statement of Financial Accounting Concepts No. 2*, the FASB made the following statement regarding materiality.

> *Those who make accounting decisions and those who make judgments as auditors continually confront the need to make judgments about materiality. Materiality judgments are primarily quantitative in nature. They pose the question: Is this item large enough for users of the information to be influenced by it? However, the answer to that question will usually be affected by the nature of the item; items too small to be thought material if they result from routine transactions may be considered material if they arise in abnormal circumstances.[22]*

SFAC No. 2 went on to define materiality judgments as "screens" or thresholds. That is, is an item (error or omission) large enough to pass through the threshold that separates material from immaterial items? The more important the item, the finer is the screen that will exist.

The following items are cited as examples:

1. An accounting change in circumstances that puts an enterprise in danger of being in breach of covenant regarding its financial condition may justify a lower materiality threshold than if its position were stronger.

2. A failure to disclose separately a nonrecurrent item of revenue may be material at a lower threshold than would be the case if the revenue turns a loss into a profit or reverses the trend of earnings from a downward to an upward trend.

3. A misclassification of assets that would not be material in amount if it affected two categories of plant or equipment might be material if it changed the classification between a noncurrent and a current asset category.

4. Amounts too small to warrant disclosure or correction in normal circumstances may be considered material if they arise from abnormal or unusual transactions or events.[23]

Other organizations have also attempted to define materiality. The American Accounting Association contributed both quantitative and qualitative guidelines.

> *Materiality, as used in accounting, may be described as a state of relative importance. Materiality is not, however, entirely dependent upon relative size. Importance may depend on either quantitative or qualitative characteristics, often upon*

---

[21] See, for example, *Statement of Financial Accounting Standards No. 42*, "Determining Materiality for Capitalization of Interest Cost" (Stamford, Conn.: FASB, November 1980), p. 3.

[22] *Statement of Financial Accounting Concepts No. 2*, "Qualitative Characteristics of Accounting Information" (Stamford, Conn.: FASB, May 1980), par. 123.

[23] Ibid., par. 128.

a combination of both. Factors indicative of materiality may be classified as follows:

1. *Characteristics having primarily quantitative significance:*
   a. *the magnitude of the item (either smaller or larger) relative to normal expectation*
   b. *the magnitude of the item relative to similar or related items (relative to total of its class, earnings for the period, etc.)*
2. *Characteristics having primarily qualitative significance:*
   a. *the inherent importance of the action, activity, or condition reflected (unusual, unexpected, improper, in violation of contract or statute, etc.)*
   b. *the inherent importance of the item as an indicator of the probable course of future events (suggestive of a change in business practices, etc.)*[24]

The Securities and Exchange Commission (SEC) used a qualitative definition in Rule 1.02 of Regulation S-X,

The term ''material'' when used to qualify a requirement for the furnishing of information as to any subject limits the information required to those matters about which an average prudent investor ought reasonably to be informed.[25]

In addition, the SEC provides many quantitative guidelines as to how revenues and expenses should be reported and has introduced percentage guidelines. Although the specific guidelines are too numerous to present, 10 percent is a popular figure in the SEC literature.

The Cost Accounting Standards Board (CASB) considered materiality at some length. In its *Statement of Operating Policies, Procedures, and Objectives,* the CASB said,

The Board believes that the administration of its rules, regulations, and Cost Accounting Standards should be reasonable and not seek to deal with insignificant amounts of cost.[26]

Furthermore, the statement goes on to list the following criteria for determining materiality.

1. *The absolute dollar amount involved. . . .*
2. *The amount of the total contract cost compared with the amount under consideration. . . .*
3. *The relationship between a cost item and cost objective. . . .*

---

[24] American Accounting Association, Committee on Concepts and Standards Underlying Corporate Financial Statements, *Accounting and Reporting Standards for Corporate Financial Statements and Preceding Statements and Supplements,* "Standards of Disclosure for Published Financial Reports: Supplementary Statement No. 8" (Columbus, Ohio: American Accounting Association, 1957), p. 49.

[25] Securities and Exchange Commission Regulation S-X Rule 1.02.

[26] *Cost Accounting Standards Board Statement of Operating Policies, Procedures, and Objectives* (Washington, D.C.: Cost Accounting Standards Board, 1973), p. 4.

4. *The impact on government funding.* . . .

5. *The relationship to price.* . . .

6. *The cumulative effect of individually immaterial items.* . . .

The criteria should be considered together; no one criterion is wholly determinative of immateriality. In particular Standards, the Board will give consideration to defining materiality in specific dollar amounts and/or specific percentages of impact on operations covered by the entire Standard or any provision thereof whenever it appears feasible and desirable to do so.[27]

The CASB was progressive in its approach for determining materiality. Note, for instance, the CASB's delineation of criteria and also its statement that in certain instances specific dollars or percentages will be specified.

Finally, significant judicial decisions have concerned themselves with materiality. In the Bar Chris case, the judge stated,

The average prudent investor is not concerned with minor inaccuracies or with errors as to matters which are of no interest to him. The facts which tend to deter him from purchasing a security are facts which have an important bearing upon the nature or conditions of the issuing corporation or its business.[28]

The concept of materiality was expanded in the case of *SEC* v. *Texas Gulf Sulphur Company,* where the decision stated,

Material facts include not only information disclosing the earnings and distributions of a company but also those facts which affect the probable future of the company and those which may affect the desire of investors to buy, sell, or hold the company's securities.[29]

In *Hertzfeld* v. *Laventhal, Krekstein, Horwath and Horwath* the judicial concept of materiality takes somewhat the same form as the current accounting definition, as can be seen from Judge MacMahon's statement referring to an earlier decision.

In this context, material facts are those which a reasonable investor would deem important in making his decision to buy . . . securities. . . . Materiality, therefore, depends on whether a reasonable man . . . ''might well have acted otherwise than to purchase'' if informed of the crucial facts.[30]

These definitions leave much to be desired, and the elusiveness of the concept of materiality is a topic of continuing interest to the Financial Account-

---

[27] Ibid., pp. 4–5.

[28] *Escott et al.* v. *Bar Chris Construction Corporation et al.,* 283 Fed. Supp. (District Court S.D., New York), p. 681.

[29] *Securities and Exchange Commission* v. *Texas Gulf Sulphur Company.* 401 Fed. 2d (2d Cir. 1968), p. 848.

[30] *Hertzfeld* v. *Laventhal, Krekstein, Horwath and Horwath,* Fed. See Law Reports (District Court S.D., New York, 1974), pp. 995–998.

ing Standards Board. Hopefully, new guidelines will be established that narrow the concept and render it operational.

Earnings Quality

Recall from Chapter 1 that the FASB has concluded that relevant information about an entity should provide predictive ability. A major purpose of income reporting is to allow investors to predict future cash flows. Despite the evidence that accounting earnings are good indicators of stock returns, the use of the transactions approach to income determination along with the principle of conservatism, and the materiality constraint, have led security analysts to the conclusion that economic income, rather than accounting income, is a better predictor of future cash flows. Consequently, these individuals have suggested assessing the quality of earnings to predict future cash flows. *Earnings quality* is defined as the degree of correlation between a company's accounting income and its economic income. Several techniques have been developed to use in assessing earnings quality including:

1. Compare the accounting principles employed by the company with those generally used in the industry and by competitions. Do the principles used by the company inflate earnings?
2. Review recent changes in accounting principles and changes in estimates to determine if they inflate earnings.
3. Determine if discretionary expenditures, such as advertising, have been postponed by comparing them to previous periods.
4. Attempt to assess whether some expenses, such as warranty expense, are not reflected on the income statement.
5. Determine the replacement cost of inventories and other assets. Is the company generating sufficient cash flow to replace their assets?
6. Review the notes to financial statements to determine if loss contingencies exist that might reduce future earnings and cash flows.
7. Review the relationship between sales and receivables to determine if receivables are increasing more rapidly than sales.
8. Review the management discussion and analysis section of the annual report and the auditor's opinion to determine management's opinion of the company's future and to identify any major accounting issues.

These techniques can assist in determining whether a company's financial statements have not adequately captured the economic substance of the company's operations. Subsequently, an attempt should be made to adjust the financial statements to reflect economic reality.

Another aspect of the quality of earnings issue is earnings management. *Earnings management* is the attempt by corporate officers to influence short-term reported income. It is believed that managers may attempt to manage earnings because they believe investors are influenced by reported earnings.

The methods of earnings management include the use of production and investment decisions, and the strategic choice of accounting techniques (including the early adoption of new accounting standards). In most cases, earnings management techniques are designed to improve reported income effects; however, such is not always the case. An alternative explanation is the "Big Bath," theory which suggests that management may take the opportunity to report more bad news in periods when performance is low to increase future profits. An argument has also been made that management may choose to take large write-offs in periods when their performance is otherwise extremely positive.

The effort to manage earnings may be irrelevant in light of efficient market research. The general findings of this research indicate that the market is not deceived by the manipulation of accounting numbers. Alternately, if compensation is tied to earnings, there may be utility maximization reasons why managers attempt to manage earnings. Such explanations are tied to agency theory (Discussed in Chapter 2).

Statement of Financial Accounting Concepts No. 5

In 1984 the FASB released its *Statement of Financial Accounting Concepts No. 5*, "Recognition and Measurement in Financial Statements of Business Enterprises." In this document the FASB attempted to broaden the scope of the measurements of the operating results of business enterprises by introducing the definition of comprehensive income as follows:

> *Comprehensive income is the change in equity (net assets) of an entity during a period from transactions and events and circumstances from non-owner sources. It includes all changes in equity during a period except those resulting from investments by owners and distributions to owners.*[31]

This approach represents an attempt by the FASB to tie together the Hicksian capital maintenance approach and the traditional accounting transactions approach to income measurement. Net income is defined as the maximum amount of a firm's resources that can be distributed to owners during a given period of time (exclusive of new owner investments) and still leave the business enterprise as well off at the end of that period as it was in the beginning. However, the FASB attempted to allay fears that the concept of comprehensive income was a radical shift toward using current value measurements by stating that the measurement of most assets and liabilities would not differ under the concept of comprehensive income. Yet it is evident from recent FASB pronouncements such as FASB *Statement of Financial Accounting Standards No. 115*, which requires the use of market values to measure investments in common stock, that the FASB may be making a gradual shift toward current value accounting.

---

[31] *Statement of Financial Accounting Concepts No. 5*, "Recognition and Measurement in Financial Statements of Business Enterprises" (Stamford, Conn.: Financial Accounting Standards Board, 1984), par. 39.

SFAC No. 5 did not suggest major changes in the current structure and content of financial statements. However, it did suggest that a statement of cash flows should replace the previously required statement of changes in financial position and provided the impetus for this statement (discussed in Chapter 4). *SFAC No. 5* attempted to set forth recognition criteria and guidance on what information should be incorporated into financial statements, and when this information should be reported. According to *SFAC No. 5*, a full set of financial statements for a period should show

1. Financial position at the end of the period.
2. Earnings for the period.
3. Comprehensive income for the period.
4. Cash flows during the period.
5. Investments by and distributions to owners during the period.

The statement of financial position should provide information about an entity's assets, liabilities, and equity and their relationship to each other at a moment in time. It should also delineate the entity's resource structure—major classes and amounts of assets—and its financing structure—major classes and amounts of liabilities and equity. The statement of financial position is not intended to show the value of a business, but it should provide information to users wishing to make their own estimates of the enterprise's value.

Earnings is a measure of entity performance during a period. It measures the extent to which asset inflows (revenues and gains) exceed asset outflows. The concept of earnings provided in *SFAC No. 5* is similar to net income for a period determined under the transactions approach. It is expected that the concept of earnings will continue to be subject to the process of gradual change that has characterized its development.

Comprehensive income is defined as a broad measure of the effects of transactions and other events on an entity. It comprises all recognized changes in equity of the entity during a period from transactions except those resulting from investments by owners and distributions to owners.

The relationship between earnings and comprehensive income is illustrated as follows.

Revenues	Earnings
Less: Expenses	Plus or minus cumulative accounting adjustments
Plus: Gains	Plus or minus other nonowner changes in equity
Less: Losses	
= Earnings	= Comprehensive income

The statement of cash flows should directly or indirectly reflect an entity's cash receipts classified by major source and its cash payments classified by major uses during a period. The statement should include cash flow information about its operating, financing, and investing activities.

A statement of investments by and distributions to owners reflects an entity's capital transactions during a period, that is, the extent to which and in what ways the equity of the entity increased or decreased from transactions with owners.

The scope of *SFAC No. 5* and its relationship to other methods of reporting is illustrated in Figure 3.1.

SFAC No. 5 also addresses certain measurement issues that are closely related to recognition. That is, an item and information about it should meet four recognition criteria and should be recognized at the time these criteria are met (subject to the cost-benefit and materiality constraints).

1. **Definitions.**   The item meets the definition of an element contained in *SFAC No. 6* (Discussed in Chapter 4).

FIGURE 3.1   *Relationship of* SFAC No. 5 *to other methods of reporting. (Source: Statement of* Financial Accounting Concepts No. 5, *''Recognition and Measurement in Financial Statements of Business Enterprises'' (Stamford Conn.: FASB, 1985), par. 8.)*

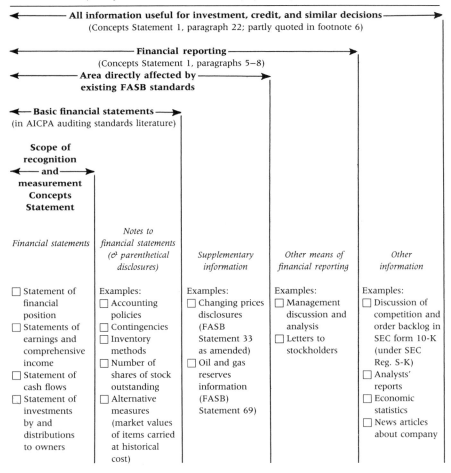

2. *Measurability.*   It has a relevant attribute, measurable with sufficient reliability.

3. *Relevance.*   The information about the item is capable of making a difference in user decisions.

4. *Reliability.*   The information is representationally faithful, verifiable, and neutral.

These recognition criteria are consistent with and in fact drawn from *SFAC Nos. 1, 2,* and *6. SFAC No. 5* goes on to provide guidance in applying the recognition criteria when enterprise earnings are affected by the recognition decision. This guidance is consistent with the doctrine of conservatism. That is, recognition of revenues and gains is based on the additional tests of their (1) being realized or realizable and (2) being earned before recognized as income. Guidance for recognizing expenses and losses is dependent on either consumption of benefit or loss of future benefit.

One of the major gaps in *SFAC No. 5* is its failure to define the term earnings,[32] and it also does not resolve the current value/historical cost debate. This failure is apparently due to the board's position of accepting *decision usefulness* as the overriding objective of financial reporting.

This document is disappointing to those who had hoped it would provide a formula or set of formulas from which solutions to specific accounting problems could be derived. That is, some accountants and financial-statement users would prefer a document that provides answers to questions about when, if at all, a specific event should be recognized and what amount best measures that event.

Income Recipients

In addition to the questions concerning the nature and reporting of income, there is the corollary query: Who are the recipients of income? This question involves determining the proper recipients of income and the proper reporting procedures to incorporate under each of the various alternatives. Hendriksen has suggested that net income may be presented under the following concepts: value added, enterprise net income, net income to investors, net income to stockholders, and net income to residual equity holders.[33] The determination of the net income figure to be reported in each instance turns on the question of whether deductions from revenue are to be viewed as expenses or as income distributions. The question of income determination can, therefore, also turn on whether a particular distribution is termed a distribution of earnings or an external expense.

---

[32] David Solomons, "The Twilight of Income Measurement: Twenty-Five Years On," The Accounting Historians Journal (Spring 1987), p. 5.

[33] Eldon S. Hendriksen, *Accounting Theory,* 4th ed. (Homewood, Ill.: Richard D. Irwin, 1982), pp. 163–167.

Value-Added Concept of Income

The economic concept views income as the current market price (including holding gains) of the company's product less the external cost of goods and services associated with acquiring the product. If the enterprise is thus viewed in the broad social sense, individuals other than owners or creditors may have claims against this income. For example, employees and the government may also be viewed as the recipients of income.

The value-added concept of income may be defined as the net amount of the increase in the market price of a product attributable to each enterprise. It indicates the total amount of income that can be divided among the various interested parties. In recent years this income concept has attained additional attention because of an alternative method of taxation termed the value-added tax.

Enterprise Net Income

The modern corporation generally has two main activities: operations and financing. Enterprise net income is determined from the operations aspect only, and all financing activities and other payments necessitated by operations are regarded as return on investment rather than as expenses. Enterprise net income is consistent with the entity concept, which views the company as independent of and unaffected by the source of capital financing (see Chapter 13 for a further discussion of the entity theory). Moreover, income tax paid by the company is based on enterprise net income and is viewed as a distribution of income to the government. Thus stockholders, bondholders, and the government are viewed as the recipients of income. Under this concept, revenue less all expenses, exclusive of interest and income taxes, provides the net income figure. A major criticism of this concept is the inclusion of the government as an income recipient while excluding employees.

Net Income to Investors

The concept of net income to investors is also consistent with the entity theory. It is based on the view of the accounting equation, which states that assets equal equities. According to this concept, both long-term debtholders and stockholders are viewed as investors in the firm, and income would be reported as revenue less all expenses except interest. The difference between the enterprise net income and net income to investors concepts is the treatment of taxes. Under the net income to investors concept, the government is not viewed as an income recipient and taxes are treated as expenses. The major premise of this concept of income is that the method of obtaining investment funds should not have an impact on income determination.

Net Income to Shareholders

The owners of the enterprise are usually viewed as the proper recipients of income. Accordingly, the net income to shareholders concept is based on the proprietary view of the accounting equation that states assets minus liabilities equals proprietorship (see Chapter 13 for a discussion of the proprietary theory). This view sees income as accruing to both preferred and common stockholders and net income as determined by subtracting all expenses from revenue.

Net Income to Residual Equity Holders

The recent emphasis on earnings per share computations is an outgrowth of the concept of net income to residual equity holders. The income available to common stockholders is viewed as the single most important figure under this concept and, in addition to all expenses, preferred dividends are deducted from revenue in arriving at a net income figure. This concept of income is consistent with recent finance theory, which models earnings in terms of its effect on firm value and common stock. These models are based on the fact that earnings to stockholders are a function of how well firm resources are managed, while other capital sources such as bonds are generally riskless because the income stream is guaranteed for a going concern and not dependent upon the success of the enterprise. Figure 3.2 summarizes the nature of income under each of the preceding assumptions.

Although net income to shareholders is the income concept used in published financial reports, it should be noted that each of these income figures has usefulness in certain circumstances. The value-added concept is used in determining the gross national product; the enterprise net income and net income to investors concepts are useful in determining the profitability of a firm exclusive of financing activities; and the residual equity concept forms the basis of earnings per share computations. The income concept that is most useful will be determined by the goals of the various groups of users.

Summary

Economic income is the result of two factors: (1) the sale of the company's product (*realized income*) and (2) increases or decreases in retained net assets

FIGURE 3.2 *Summary of Various Net Income Concepts*

Current market price of the product
Less: Cost of goods produced and other external expenses
                     = *Value-added Income*
                     Less: Unrealized holding gains and payments to employees
                     = *Enterprise net income*
                     Less: Income taxes
                     = *Net income to investors*
                     Less: Interest charges
                     = *Net income to shareholders*
                     Less: Preferred dividends
                     = *Net income to residual equity holders*

(*realizable income,* that is, holding gains). Complete reporting of income would require including both of these factors; however, limitations in techniques and objective evidence constrain the income reporting process. The timing of income reporting has been constrained by the accounting convention of *realization.* This convention requires that a transaction with an outsider take place, or that there be evidence that such a transaction will soon take place, before revenue is recognized. The timing of revenue recognition may vary with different types of transactions. Accountants have also placed emphasis on the proper matching of cost expiration with the revenue recognized during a particular accounting period in the determination of periodic income.

Another variation in the income concept is that different groups can be viewed as income recipients. The expenses deducted from revenue in reporting income vary with these different assumptions as to the income recipients. There is no one "correct" view of income recipients. Rather, various income recipient assumptions are used by different segments of the economy for different purposes.

The readings for this chapter explore some of these concepts more thoroughly. In "A Comparison of Accounting and Economic Concepts of Business Income," Bert Mitchell focuses on how differences in the concept of income as defined by economists and accountants are affected by several accounting principles, and, in "Concepts of Capital Maintenance," George Gamble examines the concepts of capital maintenance in further detail.

A Comparison of Accounting and Economic Concepts of Business Income

Bert N. Mitchell

The determination of annual business income is, for accountants, a major area of research, study and discussion. Economists, too, are intrigued with this determination. However, the concept of income held by the two groups, broadly, is radically different, as will be evident from the ensuing exposition.

Accountants and economists have been unable to come to terms in developing a uniform concept of income. Indeed, there exists within each profession many different concepts of income. Both professions have agreed that income determination is one of their most important concerns. Irving Fisher, a celebrated American economist, pointed out the prominent role of the income concept to the economists when he stated that:

I believe that the concept of income is, without exception, the most vital concept in economic science . . .[1]

The accountant too, has placed paramount importance on the income statement—it is the most important accounting report in today's business world.

So it is that both accountants and economists have ascribed a most important role to the income concept. But further examination shows that the two

[1] Morton Backer, American Economic, XIV. *Modern Accounting Theory* (Englewood Cliffs, N.J.: Prentice-Hall, Inc., 1966), p. 72.

disciplines have different objectives in their conceptual approach to it.

The economist is concerned primarily with the income of persons, groups of persons, and of society as a whole. The accountant, on the other hand, is concerned primarily with income as it arises in transactions of business enterprises.

The economist's approach to income is therefore much broader than that of the accountant; but the domain of the accountant is also covered by the economist. Since the economist is concerned with income of society as a whole, then of necessity he must be concerned with income of business enterprises that is an integral part of total income. Therefore, income concepts as they apply to business enterprises are common grounds to both economists and accountants. Despite the common interest, each discipline views business income from a different vantage point and consequently sees it in a different light—which is the point of this article.

What Is Business Income?

In accounting, business income is generally conceived as the residual from matching revenue realized against costs consumed.

The economist uses different concepts of income. The Hicksian concept is probably the most generally accepted by economists. Hicks stated that:

It would seem that we ought to define a man's income as the maximum value which he can consume during a week and still expect to be as well off at the end of the week as he was at the beginning.[2]

This approach to being as "well off" at the end of a period as the beginning has been used by the economist to determine business income. Consequently, the economic income of a business for a given period, may be described as:

> . . . *the amount of wealth that can be distributed to the owner during the period without diminishing the entity's future prospects below those that prevailed at the start of the period.*[3]

If a business has residual value of its revenue over its related costs, then it has earned income and consequently increased its net worth. Similarly, if the business is better off at the end of a period than it was at the beginning, then it has also increased its net worth. Consequently, we see that both the economist and the accountant agree that income is an increase in net worth, but each has a different concept of net worth; and therein lies the major difference between the concepts of business income by the accountant and the economist.

The accountant determines net worth on an historical cost basis by the formula of "assets − liabilities = net worth": whereas the economist's determination is "current value of tangible assets + discounted value of future net receipts − liabilities." The following oversimplified example will serve to illustrate the accounting as well as the economic method of computing net

[2] John R. Hicks, *Value and Capital* (Oxford, England: The Clarendon Press, 1946), p. 172.

[3] Backer, op. cit., p. 100.

worth and consequently the determination of income.

This computation reflects some of the basic differences between the accountants' and the economists' concepts of income determination. The accountant does not consider the price level changes or the holding gains resulting from the appreciation of fixed assets.

The differences between these two concepts of increase in net worth, economic income, and accounting income may be reconciled by starting with accounting income and arriving at economic income as follows:

Accounting Income
= Unrealized changes in the value of tangible assets which took place during the period, over and above value changes recognized as depreciation of fixed assets and inventory markdowns.
− amounts realized this period in respect of value changes in tangible assets which took place in previous periods and were not recognized in these periods.
+ changes in the value of intangible assets during the period (which may be considered as changes in the value of goodwill)
= economic income.

Illustration of Net Worth Determination

On January 1, 1967, a corporation was organized with a capital of $100,000 with which it purchased a new building. The building is on land leased for a period of 40 years, at the end of which time, it is assumed, the building will have no value. The corporation then leased the building for a period of 40 years at an annual rental of $20,000. The expected operating cost, including depreciation, would be $15,000 per annum, leaving a net profit of $5,000, disregarding income tax. The determination of the corporation's net worth as of January 1, 1967, and December 31, 1967, computed by the accountant and economist would be as follows: Assume the appropriate rate of interest to be 5 percent.

	Jan. 1 1967	Dec. 31 1967
Net Worth—per CPA		
Assets	$100,000	$105,000
Liabilities	0	0
Net Worth	$100,000	$105,000
Net Worth— per Economist		
Tangible assets	$100,000	$105,000[a]
Goodwill[b]	85,795	85,085
Net Worth	$185,795	$190,085

[a]No change in market value of building.

[b]Represents the discounted value of future net receipts, present value of $5,000 per annum at 5 percent, for 40 and 39 years, respectively.

Illustration of Income Determination

In order to arrive at net income for the year 1967, the accountant would merely determine the excess of revenue realized over cost consumed or $20,000 − $15,000 = $5,000. The same result would be arrived at by obtaining the difference between the net worth at the beginning and end of the period, giving the appropriate recognition to capital additions or withdrawals and dividend distribution, if any. The economist uses only the change-in-net-worth method in arriving at net income. His net income would thus be $4,290 ($190,085 − $185,795).

Variation in Conditions at End of Year

An extension of the economist's concept of income determination is illustrated by the introduction of two factors, both ignored by the accountant but meaningful to the economist. These factors are (1) a rise in the general price index at the end of 1967 to 110 percent of the base period (January 1, 1967), and (2) an increase in the market value of the building, which then had a depreciated basis of $97,500, to $120,000.

Under the above conditions the accounting income would remain at $5,000, as computed earlier, but the economic income would be $7,464, computed as shown in the following table.

Net Worth—Dec. 31, 1967	
Building, at market	$120,000
Other assets	7,500
Discounted value of future receipt	$ 85,085
Less, losses due to price level changes	19,326[a]
	65,759
Net Worth	193,259
Net Worth—Jan. 1, 1967	
Per prior computation	185,795
Net income for the year	$ 7,464

[a]Computed at 110 percent of base at Jan. 1, 1967.

The Underlying Assumption of the Income Concepts

- The going concern.
- Objectivity.
- Realization of revenues.
- Stable monetary unit.

In the succeeding paragraphs, an attempt will be made to bring out the economist's view of the above concepts.

The Going Concern Concept

Accountants have accepted the presumption that:

> . . . in the absence of evidence to the contrary, the productive life of the enterprise may be deemed to be indefinitely long.[4]

As a result of this postulate, all costs of the enterprise are deferred until such time as they have been consumed by a revenue producing process or have expired because of the passing of time.

When fixed assets are purchased they are recorded at cost, which generally represents market price at the time of acquisition. Later change in market value is not recorded, except in the case of a reorganization, appreciation as the asset is a deferred cost chargeable against future revenues in a rational and systematic manner. This line of reasoning is justified by the accountant on the assumption that the life of the entity is indefinitely long and the cost of the asset will eventually be completely written off.

Another case in point is the valuation of accounts receivable. From an accounting standpoint, accounts receivable at any given time are valued at the full expected amount to be collected in future periods, on the presumption that on a going concern basis, there is no need to decrease the asset to its present value. However, the economist, in order to arrive at his current net worth, would consider accounts receivable only at the discounted present value.

The economist rejects the thesis of the going concern as a basis for income determination for the reason that he "values" the company annually. Since he must first determine net worth to compute net income, then each year's balance sheet is equivalent to a terminal determination, except for no provision for liquidation.

Objectivity

The accountant, because of his intention to utilize accuracy in accounting procedures, has come to regard objectivity as a major guidepost. Thus, the accountant endeavors to measure the effects of business transaction on verifiable evidence, whereas the economist generally makes his measurements on the basis of expectations.

Professor Moonitz, in outlining "The Basic Postulates of Accounting," wrote:

> Changes in assets and liabilities and related effects (if any) on revenues, expenses, and retained earnings and the like, should not be given formal recognition in the accounts earlier than the point of time at which they can be measured in objective terms.[5]

The accountant's concept of income, therefore, is well supported by his reliance on objectivity. The process of matching cost against current revenue could not be properly carried out without the full employment and the objective approach. Paton and Little stated that:

> The fundamental problem of accounting . . . is the division of the stream of cost incurred between the present and the future in the process of measuring periodic income.[6]

---

[4] The Study Group on Business Income, "The Changing Concept of Business Income" (New York: The Macmillan Company, 1952), p. 19.

[5] Maurice Moonitz, "The Basic Postulates of Accounting" (New York: American Institute of CPAs, 1961), p. 50.

[6] W. A. Paton and A. C. Littleton, "Introduction to Corporate Accounting Standards"

However, the economist does not adhere to the principle of objectivity in developing his concept of income. There is heavy reliance on subjectivity and individual judgment by the economist in his determination of income. This is so because the economist, before he can arrive at current net income, must first determine the ability of the enterprise to earn future income. He must estimate that the total future income might be (by computing its discounted value), and then arrive at the current net worth of the enterprise. Therefore, since the economist is called upon to predict the future events of the enterprise, in order to arrive at current net worth and net income, then his net income is based upon less objectively verifiable evidence than that of the accountant. Of course, the accountant also estimates future events of the enterprise, such as the useful life of depreciable assets, but in this respect he merely reviews management's determinations. But by and large, the accountant is concerned with what has been, or what is, rather than what might be.

Realization of Revenues

Accountants take the conservative view in determining the point at which income should be recognized. It has become the general practice to record income at the point of realization, indeed at the point of sale. W. A. Paton said:

The process of exchanging product for cash or definite claim to cash, constitutes realization and justifies the description of revenue measured by sale as realized revenues.[7]

(American Accounting Association, 1960), p. 67.

[7] W. A. Paton and W. A. Paton, Jr. *Corporation Accounts and Statements* (New York: The Macmillan Company, 1955), p. 278.

The point of sale is chosen as the time of realization because it offers an objective measurement of the value of the product being exchanged. Further, the disposal of the product is the final fulfillment of the contribution such product can ultimately make to the enterprise. Finally, this position is a conservative one, which is a popular and creditable stance.

If the contribution to be made to the well-being of an enterprise by the assets it owns is anticipated before the actual realization of such contribution, then the entire income for the life of the enterprise could be determined at the time the enterprise is capitalized. But this would be inconsistent with other accounting concepts because

- accounting presumes the business to be a going concern, and
- such measurement could not be made objectively.

On the other hand, the economist conceives that the enterprise at any given time should recognize the income it expects its assets will ultimately contribute in the future. This is done by making an estimate of the value of such future income, and capitalizing it as goodwill (as was done with the expected rental income from the leased building in our prior discussion). If the estimate made by the economist is correct, then all the income of an enterprise would be recognized at the time of its inception except for interest to be earned, if any, since it represents the difference between the future and present values.

In addition, the economist will currently reflect income representing holding gains and monetary fluctuations. In the holding gains, he includes increases in the current market value of assets. For example, appreciation in real estate is recognized as income is determined. The accountant, however, in accordance with generally accepted accounting principles which rest on the realization concept, will not recognize this appreciation until it has actually been realized.

Stable Monetary Unit[8]

The accountant still adheres to the concept of the stable monetary unit. One of the postulates of accounting states:

Fluctuation in value of the monetary unit which is the accounting symbol may properly be ignored.[9]

The economist is diametrically opposed to this presumption and takes an adamant position that all changes in price levels must be reflected in income during the period of such changes. By so doing, the economist adjusts for variable monetary values from one period to another in order to reflect a constant base and thus maintain the "real" monetary value.

The accountant's approach to price-level changes in income determination is to completely ignore the effects of such changes. Here again, the reasoning is based on the interlocking of other basic concepts in accounting. Firstly, income should be reported only when realized and a mere change in the purchasing power of the monetary unit is not a realization of income or loss. Secondly, the life of the enterprise is deemed to be indefinitely long, and therefore, barring a liquidation of the

[8] For a comprehensive treatment of Price-Level Changes, see *Accounting Research Study No. 6.*

[9] "The Changing Concept of Business Income." op. cit., p. 19.

enterprise, the effects of the money fluctuation might never be realized.

Conclusion

The economist and the accountant have different objectives in the determination of income, as well as different concepts of income. The accountant measures income independently, and the balance sheet, in effect, is the residue of prepaid and deferred items. The economist, on the other hand, uses successive balance sheets as real value determinants and the annual increases or decreases represent real economic income. The accountant, on the whole, is interested in what is or what has been, whereas the economist is interested in what might be. Income of an enterprise from the accountants' point of view must be realized and objectively quantified. But the economist's point of view is that income can accrue only after proper provision has been made to keep capital intact. This is done by capitalizing all expected future net receipts as goodwill. Therefore, economic income is the sum of the future net receipts plus interest earned on capital plus other unexpected gains such as appreciation of fixed assets and monetary fluctuations. The economist deals with certainties and uncertainties. If his estimate of the uncertainties turns out to be accurate, then in the long run he would have arrived at the same point of cumulative income as the accountant.

The underlying assumptions on which the economic concepts of income are based bear heavily on subjective judgments, while the accounting assumptions are objective in nature. Nevertheless, there is a great deal of interrelationship of the framework of the two disciplines. As Professor K. E. Boulding wrote in his article, "Economics and Accounting, the Uncongenial Twins":[10]

. . . many of the basic concepts of economics are, in fact, derived from accounting

[10] Boulding, K. E. "Economics and Accounting: The Uncongenial Twins." In W. T. Baxter and Sidney Davidson, eds., *Studies in Accounting Theory* (Homewood, Ill.: Richard D. Irwin, Inc., 1962), p. 44.

practice and many accounting practices have been devised in an attempt to answer what are essentially economic questions.

Notwithstanding whatever degree of interrelationship there is between the development of the theories of accounting and economics, there remain some differences in the conceptual view of business income between the two disciplines.

Concepts of Capital Maintenance

George O. Gamble

Capital maintenance appears to have been elevated in recent accounting literature almost to the status of an accounting basic concept. This is a review of the various forms advocated for measuring capital maintenance.

The FASB, in its conceptual framework discussion memorandum [1], suggests strongly that in conjunction with reaching agreement on the objectives of financial statements it will be necessary to resolve the issue of capital maintenance. If so, this raises capital maintenance to the level of a basic concept of accounting principles, a level it probably has not occupied heretofore. This is a reflection of the growing dissatisfaction with historical cost as the dominant measurable attribute of accounting, exemplified by the monograph of the

AICPA Study Group on the Objectives of Financial Statements [2].

It is in order, therefore, to identify the five capital maintenance concepts that have been developed; to explain in detail their underlying theory, salient characteristics, and the particular basis used to assign a value to the capital each seeks to maintain; and to discuss the major strengths and weaknesses of each concept presented. That will be the objective of this article. Additionally, when appropriate, weaknesses will be evaluated to determine whether they are inherent in the model or whether they result from criticism that the model fails to do what, in fact, it does not purport to do.

Financial Capital Maintenance

The financial capital concept, which is identified with the monetary values of assets contributed by the owners at the time they were contributed, presently appears to be the traditional and dominant view on capital maintenance. The major emphasis of this concept is on the exchange transactions and events that affect the operations and status of an entity. Consequently, the exchange transaction is the major test for admissibility of data to the accounts. Events that have an impact upon the operations and status of an entity also are recorded and are deemed to be equivalent to exchange transactions. Most of the data for applying the financial capital maintenance concept are derived from actual experiences of an entity, and, accordingly, the model is historical in character.

In order to report timely and relevant information, financial statements are prepared periodically. This, of course, means that accountants must exercise their judgment in determining which items should appear in financial statements. The matching concept is presently employed by accountants to aid them in making this judgment. The matching concept seeks to match costs and revenues within a well-defined period of time in order to arrive at a measure of periodic net income. Costs are economic goods and services received to produce revenue: revenues are the outflow of economic goods and services.[1] It should be noted, however, that the conventional definition of revenue focuses on what an entity has received in the exchange transaction, that is an asset or a liquidation of a liability or both. The definition of revenue that is employed in this article focuses on what an entity has given in the exchange transaction, that is, the goods and services that are given in exchange for an asset or a liquidation of a liability or

both. Thus, throughout the article, revenue will be defined as the outflow of economic goods and services, because it is the author's opinion that this definition is consistent with the assumption that one objective of an entity is to provide goods and services to consumers.

In the financial capital concept, expired cost is determined by the expense recognition principle,[2] which states that the expenses of a period are (1) costs directly associated with the revenue of the period, (2) costs associated with the period on some basis other than a direct relationship with revenue, and (3) costs that cannot, as a practical matter, be associated with any other period. The matching concept is extensively discussed in a 1964 release of the AAA Concepts and Standards Research Study Committee [3].

Revenue for a period is generally determined by applying the realization principle. The revenue realization rule[3] states that revenue is generally recognized when both of the following conditions are met: (1) the earning process is complete or virtually complete, and (2) an exchange has taken place. There are, however, alternative bases for revenue recognition. For example, on long-term construction contracts, revenue may be recognized as construction progresses. This has been called percentage of completion or the study group's[4] "progress toward completion of incomplete earnings cycles." Sometimes revenue may be recognized at the completion of production and before the sale is made, for example, in the

---

[1] *Accounting Principles Board Statement No. 4* (New York: American Institute of Certified Public Accountants, 1970), par. 54.

[2] Id. at par. 155.

[3] Id. at par. 150.

[4] Study Group on the Objectives of Financial Statements, *Objectives of Financial Statements* (New York: American Institute of Certified Public Accountants, Oct. 1973), p. 29.

case of certain precious metals and farm products with organized markets to absorb the output.

Definition of Capital

The financial capital concept purports to maintain the monetary value of assets contributed by owners at the time they were contributed and the unadjusted monetary value of earnings retained by an entity. Thus, net income is the excess of the value of outflow of goods over the value of the inflow of goods. That is, income is measured only after the investment, measured in monetary units, is recovered. The term "net income" employed in this article is operating income (the difference between inflow and outflow of economic goods and services). Other types of nonoperating income are accounted for in conventional accounting.

The financial capital maintenance concept has the following salient characteristics: (1) the exchange transaction is the major test for admissibility of data to the accounts, and events deemed equivalent to exchanges are also recorded; (2) the dominant measurement basis is historical cost at the date of a transaction; (3) the dollar (assuming a U.S. orientation) is the standard measurement; (4) the matching concept plays an important role with respect to the amounts that appear on the statement of income; (5) the statement of income discloses the inflow and outflow of economic goods and services; the difference between the inflow and the outflow of economic goods and services is operating (or economic) income (loss); and (6) the capital maintained is the unadjusted monetary investment(s) of stockholders.

Strengths

The capital maintenance concept is an obvious consequence of the contemporary financial accounting model that presumes historical money cost to be the most significant measurable attribute of data contained in financial statements. The major strength of this concept is that it is generally understood by users of financial statements who make their own adjustments for changes in general and specific prices. Thus, it is a neutral information set that is normally based on actual experiences of an entity. Another strength of the financial capital maintenance concept is that it is easy to apply in practice. Furthermore, because income is not normally recognized until realized, this capital maintenance concept is also conservative. Finally, because the unadjusted monetary investments of stockholders are emphasized, this concept of capital maintenance is concerned with the notion of stewardship, which plays an important role in conventional accounting.

Weaknesses

Income under the financial capital maintenance concept is measured only after the unadjusted monetary investments of stockholders have been maintained. This approach is criticized because the value of the dollar has not been stable, which, of course, means its purchasing power has been correspondingly unstable. If the purchasing power of the dollar changes significantly over the temporal dimension of an entity, the dollar at different points in time changes its meaning. It becomes misleading as a standard of measurement. Measurements must be made with units that are equivalent or homogeneous if comparisons are to be clear. Therefore, because of the stable monetary unit assumption, historical dollar amounts are matched with current revenues, and the difference between the two amounts is undefined. Because they are nonadditive in nature, the additivity principle has been violated. Furthermore, any type of intertemporal comparison of financial data may result in misleading conclusions.

The financial capital maintenance concept also permits the inclusion of holding gains in income. As a result of such inclusion, those such as Touche Ross who object to this concept maintain that earnings are overstated.[5] Furthermore, as the Australian Accounting Standards Committee has pointed out, an erosion of an entity's operating capacity would occur if those holding gains are distributed to stockholders in the form of dividends.[6]

The criticism that the financial capital maintenance concept includes inventory profits in earnings is invalidated in the special case wherein the contemporary accounting model allows one to assume a last in, first out (LIFO) cost flow. By assuming a LIFO cost flow and an inventory turnover of at least one, the holding gain would be eliminated from earnings. In fact, a LIFO cost flow assumption with a periodic inventory method is very likely to lead to a higher cost of goods sold than the replacement cost of goods sold. The criticism related to the inclusion of holding gains is not valid.

The holding gains criticism is invalid because it criticizes this capital maintenance concept for something it does not purport to do; that is, it does not purport to measure so-called real gains. To do so would require a change in the major emphasis of this capital mainte-

nance concept from historical *transactions* and *events* to *objects,* because the replacement cost of objects such as inventory (the sold and unsold amounts) and fixed assets would have to be reflected in the data base.

Those who favor the time value of capital maintenance concept argue that another major weakness of the financial capital maintenance concept is that it does not consider the cost of equity financing. The omission of the cost of equity financing weakness can be dismissed, however, on the ground that this concept does not consider imputed interest on stockholders' contributions as a cost to equity security holders. The return to equity security holders is treated as a capital transaction.

Von Hayek's disciples, whose views are explained in more detail in the section entitled "Prospective Income Capital Maintenance," would argue that the financial capital maintenance concept does not maintain a source of funds given a level of income. However, the financial capital maintenance concept does not attempt to maintain a source of funds based on a given level of income. It recognizes the fact that an entity's financing comes from more than one source, for example, debt, retained earnings, and the issuance of additional securities. Purchasing power capital maintenance advocates would argue that the impact of inflation is not reflected in the information set; that is, a general purchasing power gain (loss) is not calculated on monetary assets and liabilities. This weakness is inherent in the model because of the standard of measurement employed in this capital maintenance concept.

Purchasing Power Capital Maintenance

With double-digit inflation confronting the United States in recent years, the

[5] Touche Ross & Co., *Economic Reality in Financial Reporting: A Program for Experimentation* (New York: Touche Ross, 1976), p. 3.

[6] Australian Accounting Standards Committee, *Preliminary Exposure Draft: A Method of Current Value Accounting* (Melbourne: AASC, 1975), par. 21.

stable dollar assumption has been under serious attack by concerned practitioners and academicians, such as Cramer [4] and Moonitz [5]. General purchasing power reflecting the capacity of money to command goods and services varies over time. Consequently, a change in the general purchasing power of the dollar is indicated by a change in the general level of prices. Prices of individual goods and services may change more or less than, or in the opposite direction from, a change in the general price level.

The exchange transaction is also the major test for admissibility of data to the accounts under this concept. Events that have an impact on the status and operations of an entity are also recorded and are deemed to be equivalent to exchange transactions. Most of the data for applying the purchasing power capital maintenance concept are also derived from actual experiences of an entity. The matching concept also plays an intricate role in this capital maintenance concept.

Definition of Capital

The purchasing power capital maintenance concept purports to maintain the purchasing power of stockholders' equity as of the beginning of the period plus or minus any changes, such as additional investment and dividends in stockholders' equity during the period. Thus, income is not measured until the purchasing power of those amounts has been maintained. The following simplified example illustrates this capital maintenance concept. The following assumptions will be used in the example: (1) in 19X0, the consumer price index (CPI) was 100; (2) capital was contributed during the month of December 19X0 in the amount of $100,000; (3) the end-of-the-year CPI for 19X1 is 105; (4) no other capital transactions

occurred during 19X1; and (5) earnings for 19X1 amounted to $200,000.

The beginning capital balance, $100,000, is multiplied by 105/100 to restate the beginning capital balance in terms of end-of-the-year purchasing power to $105,000. In order to maintain the purchasing power of beginning capital, $5,000 of current earnings would be used as a purchasing power adjustment and $195,000 would be added to the retained earnings account. The $5,000 represents a provision for maintenance of capital and thus would appear as a capital adjustment on the balance sheet in the stockholders' equity section.

It should be noted that the simplified example presented to illustrate the purchasing power capital maintenance concept is a short-cut procedure. A more elaborate procedure requires one to express or restate items in the balance sheet and statement of income in terms of the current purchasing power of the dollar. A monetary–nonmonetary distinction is crucial to the restatement procedure, because of the need to determine the general purchasing power gain or loss. The general purchasing power gain or loss is calculated on monetary assets and liabilities.

The purchasing power capital maintenance concept has the following salient characteristics: (1) the exchange transaction and events deemed equivalent to exchanges represent the major test for admissibility of data to the accounts; (2) the dominant measurement basis is current purchasing power at the date of a transaction; (3) general purchasing power of the monetary unit at the balance sheet date is the standard of measurement; (4) the matching concept plays an important role with respect to the amounts that appear on the statement of income; (5) the statement of income measures the inflow and outflow of economic goods and services; the difference between these flows is operating (or economic) income (loss); furthermore, the restated income includes the net general purchasing power gain or loss, which has no counterpart in the conventional statement of income; (6) the impact of changes in the general level of prices is separately disclosed if the financial statements are restated by reporting the net purchasing power gain or loss in the statement of income; and (7) the capital maintained is the purchasing power of stockholders' equity during the period, that is, additional contributions made by stockholders and dividend payments.

Strengths

This discussion shows that the only substantive difference between purchasing power capital maintenance and financial capital maintenance is the standard of measurement. One could say, therefore, that the purchasing power capital maintenance concept is not a new accounting model but simply a technique for expressing financial information in terms of the same unit of measurement, units of general purchasing power, the lack of which is a major weakness of the other concepts of capital maintenance in an inflationary or deflationary environment. The purchasing power capital maintenance concept, by restating amounts so that they are expressed in terms of equivalent units of general purchasing power as of a specific point in time, enables intertemporal comparisons of accounting data to become more meaningful. Furthermore, this concept of capital maintenance permits one to determine, in part, the impact of inflation on an entity by the purchasing power gain or loss calculation on monetary assets and liabilities.

Because the restatement process is a technique for expressing financial information in terms of the same unit of measurement, general purchasing power can be used as the standard of measurement for the financial, physical, prospective income, and time value capital maintenance concepts without changing their attributes.

Weaknesses

Because this concept of capital maintenance is, in substance, based on a restatement technique for expressing financial information in terms of equivalent units of general purchasing power, its weakness is a function of the theory that employs it as a standard of measurement. In addition, problems result from the selection of an appropriate price index to be used for making the conversion. The index number problem is also pervasive because the biases, for example, the goods that are selected for the sample and the area of the country that is used for determining the prices of those selected goods associated with the index selected, will be reflected in the converted numbers.

Physical Capital Maintenance

This concept of capital maintenance concentrates on maintaining the productive capacity of an entity. Productive capacity has been defined in a variety of ways. Gress, for example, writes, "The productive capacity of a business firm is defined as the ability of a firm to produce and distribute a given quantity of goods and services during a specific time period."[7] The Sandilands Report also has set forth definitions of produc-

[7] E. J. Gress, "Replacement Costing and the Maintenance of Productive Capacity Concept of Business Income—Theory and Application" (Ph.D. dissertation, University of Arizona, 1970), p. 83.

tive capacity. The Sandilands' definition that has been selected by some professional organizations in accounting is "the physical assets possessed by the company, so that profit would be the amount that could be distributed after making sufficient provision to replace the physical assets held by the company." The selected Sandilands' definition of productive capacity is presumed to be operational if replacement cost accounting is employed in determining the value of operating assets.[8] Edwards and Bell have discussed this idea at length [6].

Exchange transactions and other events that have an impact upon the operations and status of an equity are the major tests for data admissibility. Thus, replacement cost for operating assets and historical cost for nonoperating assets are the measurement bases. Events such as changes in the replacement cost of inventory and fixed assets are recorded in addition to the conventional unfavorable value changes, for example, lower of cost or market of marketable securities.

The matching concept also plays an important role. Under the physical capital maintenance concept, the matching concept seeks to match current and historical costs with revenue in order to arrive at a measure of periodic net income. Furthermore, the periodic net income calculated under this capital maintenance concept is sometimes referred to (by Davidson and Weil,[9] for

example) as "distributable" or "sustainable" income because as a result of calculating depreciation and cost of goods sold based on their replacement cost, net income reflects the amount that can be distributed to stockholders without impairing the productive capacity of an entity.

Definition of Capital

Capital, under the physical capital maintenance concept, is defined as the operating assets of an entity. Thus, income is not recognized until a provision has been made to replace those assets.[10] The provision to replace operating assets is reflected by reporting depreciation and cost of goods at their replacement cost. Furthermore, it should be noted that realized and unrealized holding gains are added to distributable income to determine so-called economic income (conventional income plus unrealized holding gains). The logic associated with defining income in the above manner is based on the notion that most going concerns expect to operate in the future at a rate of physical activity equal to their current level; thus, periodic net income should not be recognized until a provision has been made to replace an entity's productive assets as they wear out, or, stated another way, to maintain an entity's operating assets at a constant physical level.

The physical capital maintenance concept has the following salient characteristics: (1) historical and selected expected transactions are the major tests for admissibility of data to the accounts; (2) the dominant measurement bases are historical costs at the date of a transaction and replacement cost for fixed assets and inventories at the bal-

[8] Inflation Accounting Committee, *Inflation Accounting: Report of the Inflation Accounting Committee* (London: Her Majesty's Stationery Office, 1975), p. 35.

[9] S. Davidson & R. L. Weil, "Inflation Accounting: The SEC Proposal for Replacement Cost Disclosures," *Financial Analysts Journal* (March/April 1976), pp. 58, 60.

[10] Id. at 60.

ance sheet date; (3) the dollar (again assuming a U.S. orientation) is the standard unit of measurement; (4) the matching concept plays a dominant role with respect to income determination; (5) the statement of income discloses the portion of an entity's income that can be distributed without impairing its physical capacity; accordingly, specific price changes of fixed assets and inventory are excluded from income; and (6) the capital maintained is the current market value of operating assets.

Strengths

The major strength of the physical capital maintenance concept centers in the fact that an increase in an entity's wealth as a result of price changes is excluded from income. Thus, this concept recognizes the notion that the long-run survival of an entity is dependent upon its ability to generate enough income to replace the productive capacity of existing assets. Another strength of this capital maintenance concept is that it provides insight with respect to the dividends that may be paid to stockholders without impairing an entity's ability to replace its existing assets. Furthermore, this concept of capital maintenance recognizes the fact that entities attempt to maintain their share prices by maintaining operating flows at their current level. Maintaining operating flows is, for the most part, not truly synonymous with maintaining productive capacity, but the fact that replacement cost is used as the measurement base for fixed assets and total inventory seems to imply that an entity can, in fact, in a static environment maintain operating flows by maintaining productive capacity.

Weaknesses

In order for entities to maintain their operating flows at their current level,

one has to assume that the margin between input and output prices will remain constant, an assumption not universally accepted, not by Bergert [7], for example. However, because that assumption is rarely, if ever, met, the maintenance of share prices via maintaining operating flows at their current level is a fictitious strength.

The physical capital maintenance concept can also be accused of confusing management decision making with the accounting function. The basis for this accusation is brought to light when one critically evaluates what this capital maintenance concept purports to do. This concept purports to report the continuity of an entity's operations, which can only be achieved by replacing the existing operating assets. The decision about the manner in which an entity should achieve continuity of operations is a management decision, a decision based on goals and objectives, current and future market potentialities or products, availability of raw materials and financial resources, and the adaptability of an entity. Instead of focusing on management decision making, perhaps this concept of capital maintenance should focus on the task of an accountant, which is to measure and to report the results of his measurement.

The physical capital maintenance concept is also plagued with the standard-of-measurement problem. This problem appears in the following way: the difference between the historical and replacement costs of operating assets does not represent real holding gains (losses). Real holding gains (losses) can only be determined by reflecting the historical amounts in terms of current purchasing power and subtracting the current purchasing power of those historical amounts from their replacement prices. Finally, this concept can be criticized for not considering the imputed interest on stockholders' contributions and the capital fund of an entity. These criticisms are not valid, because they criticize this capital maintenance concept for something it does not purport to do.

Prospective Income Capital Maintenance

This concept of capital maintenance was developed by Von Hayek [8], whose stated opinion is:

> To ''maintain capital intact'' is not an aim in itself. It is only desired because of certain consequences which are known to follow from a failure to do so. . . . We are not interested in its magnitude because there is any inherent advantage in any particular absolute measurement of capital, but only because, ceteris paribus, *a change in this magnitude would be a cause of a change in the income to be expected from it, and because in consequence every change in its magnitude may be a symptom for such a change in the really relevant magnitude, income.*[11]

Thus, according to Von Hayek, entities do not focus on maintaining physical capital per se; instead, entities are concerned with the maintenance of *prospective income*, given some level of expectation. One could say, therefore, that this concept of capital maintenance is a maxim for reasonable behavior.

> ''[W]e should not only have to say that nobody ever succeeds in maintaining his capital intact—which in a sense of course would be true—but we should also be prevented from using this concept of maintaining capital intact as a description of the actual behavior of the entrepreneurs. . . .''[12]

As implied above, Von Hayek's theory focuses on the alternative behaviors of an entrepreneur in the case of an unexpected decrease or increase in capital. In the case of a capitalist who faces an unexpected decline in capital, according to Von Hayek, the only alternative that does not offend logical reasoning is that or reducing consumption as soon as the decline in income is seen to the level at which it could be permanently maintained. In the case of a capitalist who faces an unexpected increase in capital, that is, the case where future income unexpectedly rises, there are three viable alternatives available. The first is to consume only the same as before the rise, allowing the extra income to accumulate; the sinking fund thus accumulated would return more than before the unexpected gain. The second option is that of consuming only so much of the additional income that a higher constant return would be enjoyed. The third option is to take the same depreciation allowance as before, consuming all the extra income as it occurs.[13]

In short, Von Hayek's theory of capital maintenance focuses on the relationship between capital value and income. He assumes that they are positively correlated. Thus, an unexpected increase or decrease in capital value would correspondingly cause an increase or decrease in prospective income, and how an entity reacts to the unexpected changes in income will be a function of management's expectations.

Exchange transactions and other events such as unforeseeable changes in the value of operating assets are the major tests for admissibility of data to the accounts. Thus, replacement cost and historical cost are also the measurement bases for this capital maintenance concept. A modification of the match-

---

[11] F. A. Von Hayek, ''The Maintenance of Capital,'' *Economica: New Series* (August 1935), p. 248.

[12] Id. at 243.

[13] Id. at 252–256.

ing concept also is employed. Under the prospective income capital maintenance concept, the matching principle is used to match current and historical costs and current revenue within a well-defined period to determine periodic net income.

Definition of Capital

The notion of capital that is employed in the prospective income capital maintenance concept is that of capital value. The amount of capital is always conceived as an absolute value fund; an unexpected change will raise or lower the fund. Thus, when an unforeseeable event occurs, a capital adjustment account is recognized and the dollar impact of the unforeseeable event does not flow through the statement of income. The following example illustrates this capital maintenance concept.

Assume an entity with two assets and no liabilities. It begins its existence with $20,000 cash and a machine with a market value of $50,000. At the beginning of the entity's life, its net assets are $70,000 and its total equities are equivalent. Assume further that the only revenue the entity receives is from renting out the services of the machine for $10,000 cash per year. There are no expenses except depreciation of the machine.

Immediately after the machine is purchased, assume that some unforeseeable event occurs that causes the market value of the machine to rise to $55,000. Furthermore, assume rental revenue will rise to $10,200 per year. According to this capital maintenance concept, the machinery account would be increased by $5,000 as soon as the unforeseen event occurred and a capital adjustment account would be similarly recognized. The capital adjustment account would be credited directly; the increase does

not flow through the statement of income. Therefore, income for the year would be $4,700: $10,200 revenue less the depreciation expense of $5,500 (one-tenth of the adjusted asset balance of $55,000).

The prospective income capital maintenance concept possesses the following salient characteristics: (1) historical and selected exogenous events are the major tests for admissibility of data to the accounts; (2) the dominant measurement bases are historical and current costs; (3) the dollar is the standard of measurement; (4) a modification of the matching concept to reflect value changes plays an intricate role with regard to income determination; (5) the statement of income measures the inflow and outflow of economic goods and services; the difference between the flows is operating (or economic) income (loss); and (6) the capital maintained is a capital fund, that is, that amount of funds required to maintain a certain level of income.

Strengths

The major strengths of this capital maintenance concept are the relationships between capital value and income. The occurrence of an unforeseeable event causing an increase in the market value of an economic commodity will cause current and prospective income to rise. The converse holds true, with respect to current and prospective income, when the unforeseeable event causes a decline in market value. Thus, capital is not viewed as an absolute amount.

Weaknesses

The major weakness of this capital maintenance concept lies in how the amount of capital is conceived. The amount of capital is always conceived as a capital fund, representing contributions made by stockholders. Therefore, the implied assumption underlying this capital maintenance concept is that contributions made by stockholders are the only sources of capital funds. That assumption appears to be unrealistic, however, in that there are a variety of sources for a capital fund (e.g., debt or equity securities). Thus, the prospective income capital maintenance concept is not a complete concept in the sense that it fails to recognize all the sources contributing to an entity's capital fund.

Measuring unforeseeable events is another weakness. In order to measure unforeseeable events, one would have to decompose changes in the market value of economic commodities in terms of their foreseeable and unforeseeable amounts. Presently, that task is humanly impossible because of the lack of complete knowledge and the other complexities involved. This capital maintenance concept also suffers from the standard-of-measurement problem. Finally, it can be criticized for not considering the time value of stockholders' contributions. This criticism is not valid, however, because it criticizes this capital maintenance concept for something it does not purport to do.

It is the author's opinion that if, as appears to be given, this concept of capital maintenance is concerned with the maintenance of income, the unforeseeable change in the value of capital should not be a part of income but should instead be an addition to the fund that is employed by an entity to generate income.

Maintenance of the Time Value of Capital

This concept of capital maintenance has recently been discussed by Keith Shwayder [9]. It emphasizes that the time value of capital should be considered. The logic associated with Shwayder's opinion emerges when one recognizes the fact that a dollar presently available is more valuable than a dollar not available until a year hence. The present dollar has an opportunity to be invested immediately; therefore, in a year, this dollar will have increased in worth by the amount of interest earned on it. Thus, this concept of capital maintenance recognizes the fact that investors invest, either in the form of debt or equity securities, their funds in an entity only because they expect to receive at least as much as the next best alternative disregarding psychic considerations. Consequently, there is an opportunity cost associated with persuading individuals to forego current consumption for future consumption.

Exchange transactions and other events such as the time value of contributions made by shareholders measured by imputing interest at some relevant rate of discount are the major tests for admissibility of data to the accounts. Hence, historical cost and imputed interests on stockholders' contributions are the measurement bases for this capital maintenance concept. A modification of the matching principle is also employed. The matching principle is used to relate historical costs and revenue within a well-defined period to determine periodic income.

Definition of Capital

The definition of capital employed in the maintenance of the time value of capital concept is the interest-adjusted beginning and current year's change in contributions made by stockholders. Thus, income does not result until the interest-adjusted contributions made by

EXHIBIT 1 *Comparative Analysis of Capital Maintenance Concepts*

	Financial	Purchasing Power	Physical	Prospective Income	Time Value
Test for data admissibility	Actual exchange transactions	Actual exchange transactions	Actual and expected transactions	Actual exchange transactions and unforeseeable market-value change(s)	Actual exchange transactions and the time value of contributions made by owners
Standard of measurement	Monetary units	Purchasing power	Monetary units	Monetary units	Monetary units
Measurement base	Historical monetary units	Current purchasing power	Historical and current monetary units[a]	Historical and current monetary units[b]	Historical monetary units and imputed interest on contributions made by owners
Matching concept	Important for income determination	Important for income determination	Important for income determination	Important for income determination	Important for income determination
Gains/losses from changes in the specific prices of operating assets	Earnings	Not recognized	Capital adjustment	Earnings and capital adjustment[c]	Earnings

Gains/losses from changes in the specific prices of other operating assets	Earnings	Earnings	Earnings	Earnings	Earnings
Gains/losses from change in specific prices of monetary assets and liabilities	Not recognized	Not recognized	Not recognized	Not recognized	Not recognized
Purchasing power gain/loss on monetary assets and liabilities	Not recognized	General purchasing power gain/loss	Not recognized	Not recognized	Not recognized
Capital maintained	Unadjusted monetary investment(s) of stockholders	Purchasing power of stockholders' investment(s)	The specific prices of operating assets	That amount of funds required to maintain a certain level of monetary income	Stockholders' monetary investment plus interest on the investment

[a] Current monetary units for operating assets.

[b] Current monetary units is the measurement base for unforeseeable changes.

[c] Earnings with respect to foreseeable market value changes and capital adjustment for unforeseeable market value changes.

stockholders have been maintained. Furthermore, the interest on contributions made by stockholders is reflected in a capital-adjustment account.

Strengths

The major strength of the time value of capital maintenance concept is that it considers an entity's overall cost of funds. Another strength of this capital maintenance concept is its considering the financing cost associated with equity securities as a cost that must be recovered from an entity's economic operations.

Weaknesses

The major weakness of this concept of capital maintenance centers in the standard of measurement employed. In addition, problems result from the selection of an appropriate interest rate. Other capital maintenance advocates would argue that this concept is weak because it does not consider physical and prospective income capital maintenance.

Conclusion

The vast majority of the weaknesses discussed in the foregoing analyses criticize a model for something it does not purport to do. A common weakness of all the concepts, except for general purchasing power capital maintenance, is the standard of measurement employed. That is, the standard of measurement used by the financial, physical, prospective income, and the time value of capital maintenance concepts is not adequate when the value of the dollar is unstable. In addition, we conclude that the general purchasing power capital maintenance concept is not a distinctive concept of capital but

a technique employed for expressing financial information in terms of the same unit of measurement. Therefore, because it is a technique, it could be used as the standard of measurement for the other concepts to eliminate the above common weaknesses.

Even though the physical and prospective income capital maintenance concepts appear, at first glance, to be identical, there are two substantive differences between them: (1) the prospective income capital maintenance concept records unforeseeable market value changes only, and the physical capital maintenance concept records both foreseeable and unforeseeable market value changes; and (2) the prospective income capital maintenance concept does not reflect value changes on the income statement, and the physical capital maintenance concept does.

References

1. *Conceptual Framework for Financial Accounting and Reporting: Elements of Financial Statements and Their Measurement—A Discussion Memorandum* (Stamford, Conn.: FASB), 1976.
2. Study Group on the Objectives of Financial Statements, *Objective of Financial Statements* (New York: American Institute of Certified Public Accountants), Oct. 1973.
3. Concepts and Standards Research Study Committee, "The Matching Concept." *The Accounting Review* (April 1965), pp. 368–372.
4. Cramer, J. J., Jr. "General Price-Level Restatement: The Problem, Anatomy and Selected Issues," presented at an Arthur Andersen & Co. Seminar for Managers and Partners, Baltimore, 1976.
5. Moonitz, M. *Changing Prices and Financial Reporting* (Champaign, Ill.: Stipes Publishing), 1974.
6. Edwards, E. O. and P. W. Bell, *The Theory and Measurement of Business Income* (Los

Angeles: University of California Press), 1964.

7. Bergert, R. "Reservations About 'Replacement Value' Accounting in the Netherlands," *Abacus* (1974), pp. 1–12.

8. Von Hayek, F. A. "The Maintenance of

Capital," *Economica: New Series* (Aug. 1935), pp. 241–276.

9. Shwayder, K. "The Capital Maintenance Rule and the Net Asset Valuation Rule," *The Accounting Review* (1969), pp. 304–316.

Cases

• Case 3-1

One of the reasons accounting earnings may not be a realistic measure of economic income is the incentive and ability of business managers to manipulate reported profits for their own benefit. This may be particularly true when their company has an incentive compensation plan that is linked to reported net income. The manipulation of earnings is termed *earnings management* and frequently involves income smoothing. Income smoothing has been defined as dampening of fluctuations about some level of earnings that is considered normal for the company. Research has indicated that income smoothing occurs because business managers have a preference for a stable rather than a volatile earnings trend.

Required:
a. Why do business managers prefer stable earnings trends?
b. Discuss several methods that might be used to smooth earnings by business managers.

• Case 3-2

Economic income is considered to be a better predictor of future cash flows than accounting income. A technique used by security analysts to determine the degree of correlation between a firm's accounting earnings and its true economic income is quality of earnings assessment.

Required:
a. Discuss measures that may be used to assess the quality of a firm's reported earnings.
b. Obtain an annual report for a large corporation and perform a quality of earnings assessment.

• Case 3-3

The earning of revenue by a business enterprise is recognized for accounting purposes when the transaction is recorded. In some situations, revenue is recognized approximately as it is earned in the economic sense. In other situations, accountants have developed guidelines for recognizing revenue by other criteria, for example, at the point of sale.

Required:

a. Ignore income taxes.
  i. Explain and justify why revenue is often recognized as earned at the time of sale.
  ii. Explain in what situations it would be appropriate to recognize revenue as the productive activity takes place.
  iii. At what times, other than those included in (i) and (ii), may it be appropriate to recognize revenue? Explain.
  iv. Income measurements can be divided into different income concepts classified by income recipients. The income concepts in the following table are tailored to the listed categories of income recipients.

Income Concepts	Income Recipients
1. Net income to residual equity holders	Common stockholders
2. Net income to investors	Stockholders and long-term debt holders
3. Value-added income	All employees, stockholders, governments, and some creditors

b. For each of the concepts listed in the table, explain in separately numbered paragraphs what major categories of revenue, expense, and other items would be included in the determination of income.

• Case 3-4

Bonanza Trading Stamps, Inc., was formed early this year to sell trading stamps throughout the Southwest to retailers who distribute the stamps gratuitously to their customers. Books for accumulating the stamps and catalogs illustrating the merchandise for which the stamps may be exchanged are given free to retailers for distribution to stamp recipients. Centers with inventories of merchandise premiums have been established for redemption of the stamps. Retailers may not return unused stamps to Bonanza.

The following schedule expresses Bonanza's expectations as to the percentages of a normal month's activity that will be attained. For this purpose, a *normal month's activity* is defined as the level of operations expected when expansion of activities ceases or tapers off to a stable rate. The company expects that this level will be attained in the third year and that sales of stamps will average $2,000,000 per month throughout the third year.

Month	Actual Stamp Sales Percentage	Merchandise Premium Purchases Percentage	Stamp Redemptions Percentage
6	30%	40%	10%
12	60	60	45
18	80	80	70
24	90	90	80
30	100	100	95

Required:

a. Discuss the factors to be considered in determining when revenue should be recognized in measuring the income of a business enterprise.

b. Discuss the accounting alternatives that should be considered by Bonanza Trading Stamps, Inc., for the recognition of its revenues and related expenses.

c. For each accounting alternative discussed in (b) above, give balance sheet accounts that should be used and indicate how each should be classified.

● **Case 3-5**

You were requested to deliver your auditor's report personally to the board of directors of Sebal Manufacturing Corporation and answer questions posed about the financial statements. While reading the statements, one director asked, "What are the precise meanings of the terms cost, expense, and loss? These terms sometimes seem to identify similar items and other times seem to identify dissimilar items."

Required:

a. Explain the meanings of the terms (1) *cost*, (2) *expense*, and (3) *loss* as used for financial reporting in conformity with generally accepted accounting principles. In your explanation discuss the distinguishing characteristics of the terms and their similarities and interrelationships.

b. Classify each of the following items as a cost, expense, loss, or other category, and explain how the classification of each item may change:
   i. Cost of goods sold
   ii. Bad debts expense
   iii. Depreciation expense for plant machinery
   iv. Organization costs
   v. Spoiled goods

c. The terms *period cost* and *product cost* are sometimes used to describe certain items in financial statements. Define these terms and distinguish between them. To what types of items does each apply?

● **Case 3-6**

Revenue is usually recognized at the point of sale. Under special circumstances, however, bases other than the point of sale are used for the timing of revenue recognition.

Required:

a. Why is the point of sale usually used as the basis for the timing of revenue recognition?

b. Disregarding the special circumstances when bases other than the point of sale are used, discuss the merits of each of the following objections to the sales basis of revenue recognition:
   i. It is too conservative because revenue is earned throughout the entire process of production.
   ii. It is not conservative enough because accounts receivable do not repre-

sent disposable funds, sales returns and allowances may be made, and collection and bad debt expenses may be incurred in a later period.

c. Revenue may also be recognized (1) during production and (2) when cash is received. For each of these two bases of timing revenue recognition, give an example of the circumstances in which it is properly used and discuss the accounting merits of its use in lieu of the sales basis.

● **Case 3-7**

The Financial Accounting Standards Board issued *Statement of Financial Accounting Concepts No. 5,* "Recognition and Measurement in Financial Statements of Business Enterprises." In general, this Statement attempts to set recognition criteria and guidance on what information should be incorporated into financial statements and when this information should be reported.

Required:
According to *SFAC No. 5,* five general categories of information should be provided by a full set of financial statements. List and discuss these five categories of information.

Suggested Additional Readings

Barlev, Benzion, and Haim Levy. "On the Variability of Accounting Income Numbers." *Journal of Accounting Research* (Autumn 1979), pp. 305–315.

Barton, A. D. "Expectations and Achievements in Income Theory." *The Accounting Review* (October 1974), pp. 664–681.

Beaver, William H., and Joel S. Demski. "The Nature of Income Measurement." *The Accounting Review* (January 1979), pp. 38–46.

Bedford, Norton M. *Income Determination Theory: An Accounting Framework.* Reading, Mass.: Addison-Wesley, 1965.

Boulding, K. E. "Economics and Accounting: The Uncongenial Twins." In W. T. Baxter and Sidney Davidson, eds., *Studies in Accounting Theory.* Homewood, Ill., Richard D. Irwin, Inc., 1962.

Gellein, Oscar S. "Periodic Earnings: Income or Indicator?" *Accounting Horizons* (June 1987), pp. 59–64.

Shwayder, Keith. "A Critique of Economic Income as an Accounting Concept." *Abacus* (August 1967), pp. 23–35.

Solomons, David. "Economic and Accounting Concepts of Income." *The Accounting Review* (July 1961), pp. 374–383.

Sprouse, Robert T. "The Importance of Earnings in the Conceptual Framework." *Journal of Accountancy* (January 1978), pp. 64–71.

Bibliography

Accounting for Extraordinary Gains and Losses. New York: Ronald Press Co., 1967, particularly Chapters 1, 2, and 3, and Appendix B.

Alexander, Sidney S. "Income Measurement in a Dynamic Economy." Revised by David Solomons and reprinted in W. T. Baxter and Sidney Davidson, eds., *Studies in Accounting Theory,* Homewood, Ill.: Richard D. Irwin, Inc., 1962, pp. 126–200.

American Accounting Association, Committee on External Reporting. "An Evaluation of

External Reporting Practices." *The Accounting Review.* Supplement to Vol. 44 (1969), pp. 79–122.

American Accounting Association 1964 Concepts and Standards Research Study Committee. "The Realization Concept." *The Accounting Review* (April 1965), pp. 312–322.

American Accounting Association 1964 Concepts and Standards Research Committee. "The Matching Concept." *The Accounting Review* (April 1965), pp. 368–372.

American Accounting Association 1972–73 Committee on Concepts and Standards—External Reporting. *The Accounting Review.* Supplement to Vol. 49 (1974), pp. 203–222.

Anderson, James A. *A Comparative Analysis of Selected Income Measurement Theories in Financial Accounting.* Sarasota, Fla.: American Accounting Association, 1976.

Bedford, Norton M. "Income Concept Complex: Expansion or Decline." In Robert R. Sterling, *Asset Valuation and Income Determination.* Lawrence, Kan.: Scholars Book Co., 1971, pp. 135–144.

Chambers, R. J. "Edwards and Bell on Income Measurement in Retrospect." *Abacus* (1982), pp. 3–39.

Chambers, Raymond J. *Accounting, Evaluation and Economic Behavior.* Englewood Cliffs, N.J.: Prentice-Hall, Inc., 1966.

Devine, Carl Thomas. "Loss Recognition." In Sidney Davidson, David Green, Jr., Charles T. Horngren, and George H. Sorter, eds., *An Income Approach to Accounting Theory.* Englewood Cliffs, N.J.: Prentice-Hall, Inc., 1964, pp. 162–172 (originally published in *Accounting Research* [October 1955], pp. 310–320.

Edwards, Edgar O., and Phillip W. Bell. *The Theory and Measurement of Business Income.* Berkeley and Los Angeles: University of California Press, 1961.

Fess, Philip E., and William L. Ferrara. "The Period Cost Concept for Income Measurement—Can it be Defended?" *The Accounting Review* (October 1961), pp. 598–602.

Graese, Clifford E., and Joseph R. Demario. "Revenue Recognition for Long Term Contracts." *Journal of Accountancy* (December 1976), pp. 53–59.

Hepworth, Samuel R. "Smoothing Periodic Income." *The Accounting Review* (January 1953), pp. 32–39.

Horngren, Charles T. "How Should We Interpret the Realization Concept?" *The Accounting Review* (April 1965), pp. 323–333.

Hylton, Delmer P. "On Matching Revenue with Expense." *The Accounting Review* (October 1965), pp. 824–828.

Jarrett, Jeffrey F. "Principle of Matching and Realization as Estimation Problems." *Journal of Accounting Research* (Autumn 1971), pp. 378–382.

Mobley, Sybil C. "The Concept of Realization: A Useful Device." *The Accounting Review* (April 1966), pp. 292–296.

Ohlson, James A. "On the Nature of Income Measurement: The Basic Results." *Contemporary Accounting Research* (Fall 1987), pp. 1–15.

Petri, Enrico. "Income Reporting and APB Opinion No. 18." *Management Accounting* (December 1974), pp. 49–52.

Shwayder, Keith. "The Capital Maintenance Rule and the Net Asset Valuation Rule." *The Accounting Review* (April 1969), pp. 304–316.

Spiller, Earl A., Jr. "The Revenue Postulate—Recognition or Realization." *N.A.A. Bulletin* (February 1962), pp. 41–47.

Sterling, Robert R. *Theory of the Measurement of Enterprise Income.* Lawrence, Kan.: The University Press of Kansas, 1970.

Storey, Reed K. "Revenue Realization, Going Concern and Measurement of Income." *The Accounting Review* (April 1959), pp. 232–238.

Thomas, Arthur L. *Revenue Recognition.* Michigan Business Reports No. 49. Ann Arbor: Bureau of Business Research, Graduate School of Business Administration, University of Michigan, 1966.

Tiller, Mikel G., and Jan R. Williams. "Revenue Recognition Under New FASB Statements." *The CPA Journal* (January 1982), pp. 43–47.

Tucker, Marvin W. "Probabilistic Aspects of Revenue Recognition, Conventional and Innovational." *Australian Accountant* (May 1973), pp. 198–202.

Walker, Lauren M., Gerhard G. Mueller, and Fauzi G. Dimian. "Significant Events in the Development of the Realization Concept in the U.S." *Accountants Magazine* [Scotland] (August 1970), pp. 357–360.

Windal, Floyd W. "The Accounting Concept of Realization." *The Accounting Review* (April 1961), pp. 249–258.

Financial
Statements I:
The Income
Statement

The current financial reporting environment consists of various groups who are affected by and have a stake in the financial reporting requirements of the FASB and the SEC. These groups include investors, creditors, security analysts, regulators, management, and auditors.

Investors in equity securities are the central focus of the financial reporting environment. Investment involves forgoing current uses of resources for ownership interests in companies. These ownership interests are claims to uncertain future cash flows. Consequently, investment involves giving up current resources for future, uncertain resources; and investors require information that will assist in assessing future cash flows from securities.

The Economic Consequences of Financial Reporting

In Chapter 1, we introduced the concept of economic consequences. Income measurement and financial reporting also involve economic consequences including:

1. Financial information can affect the distribution of wealth among investors. More informed investors, or investors employing security analysts, may be able to increase their wealth at the expense of less informed investors.

2. Financial information can affect the level of risk accepted by a firm. As discussed earlier, focusing on short-term, less risky, projects may have long-term detrimental effects.

3. Financial information can affect the rate of capital formation in the econ-

omy and result in a reallocation of wealth between consumption and investment within the economy.

4. Financial information can affect how investment is allocated among firms.

Since these economic consequences may affect different users of information differently, the selection of financial reporting methods by the FASB and the SEC involves trade-offs. Future deliberations of accounting standards must consider these economic consequences.

Income Statement Elements

FASB *Statement of Financial Accounting Concepts (SFAC) No. 1* indicates that the primary focus of financial reporting is to provide information about a company's performance provided by measures of earnings. The income statement is of primary importance in this endeavor because of its predictive value, a qualitative characteristic defined in *SFAC No. 2*. Income reporting also has value as a measure of future cash flows, as a measure of management efficiency, and as a guide to the accomplishment of managerial objectives.

The emphasis on corporate income reporting as the vehicle for relaying performance assessments to investors has caused a continuing dialogue among accountants about the proper identification of revenues, gains, expenses, and losses. These financial statement elements are defined in *SFAC No. 6* as follows:

Revenues.   *Inflows or other enhancements of assets of an entity or settlement of its liabilities (or a combination of both) during a period from delivering or producing goods, rendering services, or other activities that constitute the entity's ongoing major or central operations.*

Gains.   *Increases in net assets from peripheral or incidental transactions of an entity and from all other transactions and other events and circumstances affecting the entity during a period except those that result from revenues or investments by owners.*

Expenses.   *Outflows or other using up of assets or incurrences of liabilities (or a combination or both) during a period from delivering or producing goods, rendering services, or carrying out other activities that constitute the entity's ongoing major or central operations.*

Losses.   *Decreases in net assets from peripheral or incidental transactions of an entity and from all other transactions and other events and circumstances affecting the entity during a period except from expenses or distributions to owners.*[1]

Notice that each of these terms is defined as changes in assets and/or liabilities. This represents a change in emphasis by the FASB from previous definitions provided by the Accounting Principles Board that stressed inflows and outflows. Consequently, current recognition and measurement criteria for revenues, expenses, gains, and losses are more closely associated with asset

---

[1] *Statement of Financial Accounting Concepts No. 6,* "Elements of Financial Statements" (Stamford Conn.: FASB, 1985) pars. 79–88.

and liability valuation issues, and the balance sheet is becoming more than a place to store residual values in the income determination process. As we shall see in subsequent chapters, this changing emphasis is apparent in the accounting treatment specified by the FASB for a variety of issues.

Differences between the changes in assets and/or liabilities, and inflows and outflows definitions of income include:

1. *The changes in assets and or liabilities method determines earnings as a measure of change in net economic resources for a period, whereas the inflows and outflows definition views income as a measure of effectiveness.*

2. *The changes in assets and/or liabilities method depends on the definition of assets and liabilities to define earnings, whereas the inflows and outflows method depends on definitions of revenues and expenses and matching them to determine income.*

3. *The inflow and outflow method results in the creation of deferred charges, deferred credits, and reserves when measuring periodic income; the changes in assets and or liabilities method recognizes deferred items only when they are economic resources or obligations.*

4. *Both methods agree that because investors look to financial statements to provide information from which they can extrapolate future resource flows, the income statement is more useful to investors than is the balance sheet.*

5. *The changes in assets and/or liabilities method limits the population from which the elements of financial statements can be selected to net economic resources and to the transactions and events that change measurable attributes of those net resources. Under the inflow and outflow method, revenues and expenses may include items necessary to match costs with revenues, even if they do not represent changes in net resources.* [2]

An important distinction between revenues and gains and expenses and losses is whether or not they are associated with ongoing operations. Over the years, this distinction has generated questions concerning the nature of income reporting desired by various financial-statement users. Historically, two viewpoints have dominated this dialogue and have been termed the *current operating performance concept* and the *all-inclusive concept* of income reporting. These viewpoints are summarized in the following paragraphs.

Statement Format

The proponents of the *current operating performance* concept of income base their arguments on the belief that only changes and events controllable by management that result from current period decisions should be included in income; consequently, normal and recurring items should constitute the principal measure of enterprise performance. That is, net income should reflect

---

[2] L. E. Robinson, "The Time Has Come to Report Comprehensive Income." *Accounting Horizons* (June 1991), p. 110.

the day-to-day, profit-directed activities of the enterprise, and the inclusion of other items of profit or loss distorts the meaning of the term *net income.*

On the other hand, the advocates of the *all-inclusive* concept of income hold that net income should reflect all items that affected the net increase or decrease in stockholders' equity during the period, with the exception of capital transactions. Specifically, these individuals believe that the total net income for the life of an enterprise should be determinable by summing the periodic net income figures.

The underlying assumption behind this controversy is that the method of presentation of financial information is important. That is, both viewpoints agree on the information to be presented but disagree on where to disclose types of revenue, expenses, gains, and losses. As discussed in Chapters 2 and 3, research has tended to indicate that investors are not influenced by the format of financial statements if the statements disclose the same information. So, perhaps, the concern over statement format is unwarranted.

APB Opinion No. 9

One of the first problems the Accounting Principles Board studied was the question of the financial statement elements to include under the term *net income.* An APB study revealed that business managers were exercising a great deal of discretion in determining which revenues and expenses, and gains and losses, to include on the income statement or on the retained earnings statement. The lack of formal guidelines concerning adjustments to retained earnings resulted in the placement of most items of revenue or gain on the income statement, whereas many expense and loss items that were only remotely related to previous periods were treated as adjustments to retained earnings.

The APB's study of these reporting abuses and its general review of the overall nature of income resulted in the release of *APB Opinion No. 9,* "Reporting the Results of Operations." This opinion took a middle position between the current operating performance and all-inclusive concepts by stating that net income should reflect all items of profit and loss recognized during the period, with the exception of prior period adjustments. Additionally, the prescribed statement format included two income figures: net income from operations and net income from operations plus extraordinary items. This pronouncement required business managers and accountants to determine whether revenues and expenses, and gains and losses, were properly classified as normal recurring items, extraordinary items, or prior period adjustments according to established criteria. In general, the provisions of *APB Opinion No. 9* specified that all items were to be considered normal and recurring unless they met the stated requirements for classification as either extraordinary items or prior period adjustments.

The separation of the income statement into net income from operations and net income after extraordinary items allowed for the disclosure of most items of revenue and expense, or gains and losses, on the income statement during any period. Additionally, it allowed financial-statement users to evaluate the results of normal operations or total income according to their needs.

In later opinions and statements the APB and FASB provided additional guidance on the preparation of the income statement.

Figure 4.1 (on page 180) illustrates an income statement for a company that discloses all the components of income defined by the APB and FASB in various Opinions and Statements. The components of the income statement are discussed in the following paragraphs.

Extraordinary Items

Extraordinary items were originally defined in *APB Opinion No. 9* as events and transactions of material effect that would not be expected to recur frequently and that would not be considered as recurring factors in any evaluation of the ordinary operating processes of the business.[3] This release also provided the following examples of these events and transactions: gains or losses from the sale or abandonment of a plant or a significant segment of the business; gains or losses from the sale of an investment not held for resale, the write-off of goodwill owing to unusual events during the period, the condemnation or expropriation of properties, and major devaluations of currencies in a foreign country in which the company was operating.

The usefulness of the then prevailing definition of extraordinary items came under review in 1973, and the APB concluded that similar items of revenues and expenses were not being classified in the same manner across the spectrum of business enterprises. The board also concluded that business enterprises were not interpreting *APB Opinion No. 9* in a similar manner and decided that more specific criteria were needed to ensure a more uniform interpretation of its provisions. In *APB Opinion No. 30*, "Reporting the Results of Operations," extraordinary items were defined as events and transactions that are distinguished by both their unusual nature and infrequency of occurrence. These characteristics were described as follows.

Unusual nature—the event or transaction should possess a high degree of abnormality and be unrelated or only incidentally related to ordinary activities.

Infrequency of occurrence—the event or transaction would not reasonably be expected to recur in the foreseeable future.[4]

In *APB Opinion No. 30* several types of transactions were defined as not meeting these criteria. These included write-downs and write-offs of receivables, inventories, equipment leased to others, deferred research and development costs, or other intangible assets; gains or losses in foreign currency transactions or devaluations; gains or losses on disposals of segments of a business; other gains or losses on the sale or abandonment of property, plant, and equipment used in business; effects of strikes; and adjustments of accruals on long-term contracts. The position expressed by the Accounting Principles Board in *APB Opinion No. 30* was, therefore, somewhat of a reversal in philoso-

[3] *Accounting Principles Board Opinion No. 9*, "Reporting the Results of Operations" (New York: American Institute of Certified Public Accountants, 1966).

[4] *Accounting Principles Board Opinion No. 30*, "Reporting the Results of Operations" (New York: American Institute of Certified Public Accountants, 1973), par. 20.

phy; some items previously defined as extraordinary in *APB Opinion No. 9* were now specifically excluded from that classification. The result of *APB Opinion No. 30* was the retention of the extraordinary item classification on the income statement; however, the number of revenue and expense items allowed to be reported as extraordinary was significantly reduced.

In the latter years of its existence, the Accounting Principles Board was particularly concerned with the number of alternative methods available to account for similar transactions. Where evidence existed that several alternatives were available, the Board was apparently more concerned with narrowing alternatives than with developing an overall theory of accounting or income reporting. The issuance of *APB Opinion No. 30* may have accomplished this objective, but whether or not it better satisfies user needs is subject to question.

Later the FASB noted in *SFAC No. 5* that the all-inclusive income statement is intended to avoid discretionary omissions from the income statement even though "inclusion of unusual or non-recurring gains or losses might reduce the usefulness of an income statement for one year for predictive purposes."[5] The FASB has also stated that because the effects of an entity's activities vary in terms of stability, risks, and predictability, there is a need for information about the various components of income. However, the FASB has not yet determined how to provide such information.

The separation of extraordinary items from other items on the income statement does not result in a separation of recurring from nonrecurring items. That is, an item that is infrequent but not unusual is classified as operating income. Research has indicated that this requirement is not consistent with the FASB's predictive ability criterion. The classification of nonrecurring items tends to increase the variability of earnings per share before extraordinary items and to decrease the predictive ability of earnings.[6] If this evidence is proven correct, the FASB should consider revising income statement reporting practices so that they provide increased predictive ability when nonrecurring items are in evidence. One possible method of achieving this result might be to require footnote disclosure of the effect of the item on income and earnings per share.

Prior Period Adjustments

The test for the classification of an item as a prior period adjustment (adjustment to retained earnings) was made quite rigid in *APB Opinion No. 9*. In order for events and transactions to be classified as prior period adjustments, they must have been

> *(a) specifically identified and directly related to the business activities of particular prior periods, (b) not attributable to economic events occurring subsequent to the*

---

[5] *Statement of Financial Accounting Concepts No. 5,* "Recognition and Measurement in Financial Statements of Business Enterprises" (Stamford, Conn.: Financial Accounting Standards Board, 1984), par. 35.

[6] A. B. Cameron and L. Stephens, "The Treatment of Non-Recurring Items in the Income Statement and their Consistency with the FASB Concept Statements." *Abacus* (September 1991), pp. 81–96.

date of the financial statements for the prior period, (c) dependent primarily on determination by persons other than management, (d) not susceptible of reasonable estimation prior to such determination.[7]

At the time *Opinion No. 9* was issued, the APB took the position that prior period adjustments that are disclosed as increases or decreases in the beginning retained earnings balance should have been related to events of previous periods that were not susceptible to reasonable estimation at the time they occurred. Additionally, since these amounts were material by definition, it would be expected that the auditor's opinion would be at least qualified on the financial statements issued when the event or transaction took place. Examples of prior period adjustments under *APB Opinion No. 9* were settlements of income tax cases or other litigations. The category of errors was later added to this classification. Errors would, of course, not result in an opinion qualification because they would not be known to the auditors when the financial statements were released.

On June 8, 1976, the Securities and Exchange Commission released *Staff Accounting Bulletin No. 8,* which concluded that litigation is inevitably an economic event and that settlements of litigation constitute economic events of the period in which they occur. This conclusion created a discrepancy between generally accepted accounting principles and the reporting requirements for companies registered with the SEC. Prior to the release of *Staff Accounting Bulletin No. 8,* the FASB had undertaken a study of prior period adjustment reporting of 600 companies and also concluded that a clarification of the criteria outlined in *APB Opinion No. 9* was required.

Subsequently, the FASB issued *SFAS No. 16,* "Prior Period Adjustments," that indicated the only items of profit and loss that should be reported as prior period adjustments are

a. *Correction of an error in the financial statements of a prior period.*

b. *Adjustments that result from the realization of income tax benefits of preacquisition operating loss carry-forwards of purchased subsidiaries.*[8]

This release put the FASB on the side of the all-inclusive concept of income, and when considered in conjunction with *APB Opinion No. 30,* ensures that almost all items of profit and loss are reported as a part of normal recurring operations.

Earnings per Share
The use of the income statement as the primary source of information by decision makers has resulted in a need to disclose the amount of earnings that accrue to different classes of investors. The amount of earnings accruing to holders of debt and preferred stock (termed senior securities) is generally fixed. Common stockholders are considered residual owners. Their claim to corporate profits is dependent on the levels of revenues and associated expenses.

---

[7] *APB Opinion No. 9,* op. cit., par. 23.

[8] *Statement of Financial Accounting Standards No. 16,* "Prior Period Adjustments" (Stamford, Conn.: Financial Accounting Standards Board, 1977), par. 11.

The income remaining after the distribution of interest and preferred dividends is available to common stockholders; it is the focus of accounting income determination. The amount of corporate income accruing to common stockholders is reported on the income statement on a per-share basis.

The basic calculation of earnings per share (EPS) is relatively easy. The net income available to common stockholders, after deducting required payments to senior security holders, is divided by the weighted average number of common shares outstanding during the accounting period. However, this simple method of calculating earnings per share is frequently inappropriate because of the wide variety of securities now being issued by corporations. Many companies have issued stock options, stock warrants, and convertible securities that can be converted into common stock at the option of the holders of the securities. In the event these types of securities are exchanged for common stock, they have the effect of reducing (diluting) the earnings accruing to previous stockholders. Increases in reported earnings may result in the holders of options, warrants, or convertibles exchanging their securities for common stock. Consequently, the effect of increases in earnings could be a decrease in reported earnings per share, that is, the increase in common shares outstanding might be proportionately greater than the increase in net income.

The Accounting Principles Board first discussed the ramifications of these issues in *APB Opinion No. 9* and developed the residual security and senior security concepts. This release stated

> *When more than one class of common stock is outstanding, or when an outstanding security has participation dividend rights, or when an outstanding security clearly derives a major portion of its value from its conversion rights or its common stock characteristics, such securities should be considered "residual securities" and not "senior securities" for purposes of computing earnings per share.*[9]

This provision of *APB Opinion No. 9* was only "strongly recommended" and not made mandatory, but the development of the concept formed the framework for *APB Opinion No. 15*, "Earnings Per Share."[10] The latter opinion noted the importance placed on per-share information by investors and the marketplace and concluded that a consistent method of computation was needed to make EPS amounts comparable across all segments of the business environment.

APB Opinion No. 15 made mandatory the presentation of figures for net income before extraordinary items and total net income and also recommended that per-share amounts for extraordinary items be disclosed when they were reported.[11]

---

[9] *APB Opinion No. 9*, op. cit., par. 23.

[10] *Accounting Principles Board Opinion No. 15*, "Earnings Per Share" (New York: AICPA, 1969).

[11] In *Statement of Financial Accounting Standards No. 21*, the FASB suspended the reporting requirements of *APB No. 15* for nonpublic companies. Nevertheless, if nonpublic companies choose to report earnings per share, they must comply with the provisions of *APB No. 15*.

When common stock is the only residual security, the company is said to have a *simple capital structure* and only one set of earnings per share amounts is presented. A company that has convertible securities, options, warrants, or other rights that on conversion or exercise could (in the aggregate) dilute earnings per share by 3 percent or more was defined as having a *complex capital structure*.

Two earnings per share computations are required for a company with a complex capital structure: (1) primary earnings per share and (2) fully diluted earnings per share. The numerator to use in computing primary earnings per share is determined by summing net income and the net of tax earnings accruing to securities properly classified as common stock equivalents. The denominator consists of the weighted average number of common shares outstanding during the period plus the weighted average number of shares that would be issued if all securities classified as common stock equivalents were assumed to have been exchanged at the beginning of the period or when they became exchangeable during the period. The fully diluted computation adds all contingent issuances of shares available during the period to the denominator and adds the earnings (net of tax) that accrue to these additional securities to the numerator. These computations are

$$\text{Primary earnings per share} = \frac{\begin{array}{l}\text{net income after taxes} - \text{preferred dividends (if declared or on cumulative preferred if not declared for nonconvertible preferred stock or convertible preferred stock that is not a common stock equivalent)} + \text{interest (net of tax effect) and dividends on securities considered to be common stock equivalents}\end{array}}{\begin{array}{l}\text{weighted average number of common shares outstanding} + \text{shares issuable from dilutive common stock equivalents}\end{array}}$$

$$\text{Fully diluted earnings per share} = \frac{\begin{array}{l}\text{the numerator for primary EPS} + \text{interest (net of tax effect) and dividends on securities assumed converted for fully diluted purposes}\end{array}}{\begin{array}{l}\text{the denominator for primary EPS} + \text{all other dilutive contingently issuable shares}\end{array}}$$

The calculation of the primary and fully diluted earnings per share denominator amounts is influenced by the concept of common stock equivalents. *Common stock equivalents* are defined as securities that are not in form common stock but that contain provisions that enable the holders of such securities to become common stockholders and to participate in any value appreciation of the common stock. Examples of common stock equivalents are stock warrants and options, participating securities, and convertible securities subject to the 66⅔ percent Aa bond rating test.[12]

Stock options and stock warrants are always assumed to be common stock equivalents. However, they are included in the calculation of EPS only if their effect is dilutive. Most stock options and warrants require that their exchange for common stock be accompanied by the payment of a sum of money. Thus, if these securities are actually exchanged for common stock, the business entity will have an additional amount of money available. Consequently, the APB faced the problems of how to disclose the effects of this assumed exchange of cash, and how to accrue an earnings rate on the additional assets created by an assumed conversion when calculating EPS. The Board settled on what was termed the *treasury stock method.*

When determining the primary earnings per share effect for options and warrants, two calculations must be made. First, find the number of shares that might be issued if all options and warrants were exercised. Second, find the number of shares that could be purchased on the open market at the average market price of the common stock with the proceeds obtained from the exchange. The positive difference between the shares that could be issued in exchange for options and warrants and the shares assumed repurchased as treasury shares is added to the denominator. (If the difference is negative, it is antidilutive and not included in the calculation of EPS.) When calculating fully diluted EPS, the average market price of the common stock is also used unless the end-of-the-year price is greater than the average price. The average price is used because primary EPS is intended to display the most likely proforma effects of dilution on EPS. If the closing price is greater than the average price then it may indicate a recent price trend, which would result in an even greater dilutive effect.

The application of the treasury stock method is subject to the limitation that the number of common shares deemed repurchased cannot exceed 20 percent of the common shares outstanding at the end of the period. Any excess in the amount of cash assumed available from the exercise of options and warrants is applied first to reduce any short-term or long-term borrowings, and second as if assumed invested in U.S. government securities or commercial paper with the appropriate income tax effects. (As a practical matter the APB recommended that the assumption of exercise of options and warrants should not be reflected in earnings per share data until the market price exceeds the exercise price for substantially all of three consecutive months ending with the last month of the fiscal period.) Because the treasury stock method relies on market price, the repurchase of a large number of treasury shares may affect market price. The 20 percent limitation is intended to provide an alternative to

---

[12] *APB Opinion No. 15* originally specified the prime interest rate for this test. Due to the volatility of the prime rate, the FASB substituted the interest rate on Aa bonds for the prime rate for this test. Later, in 1985, the FASB amended this test from cash yield to effective yield to maturity. This amendment was largely due to the emergence of zero coupon bonds (discussed in Chapter 9).

the repurchase of a material number of shares and still presume a use for the proceeds received upon exercise.

The following steps illustrate the calculation of the shares to be added to the EPS denominator for outstanding options and warrants primary to calculate earnings per share.

Step 1. Determine the number of shares that would be issued if all options and warrants were redeemed.

Step 2. Determine the proceeds accompanying conversion.

Step 3. Determine the average market price of the common stock.

Step 4. Determine the number of treasury shares that could be repurchased with the proceeds for redemption (the results of step 2 divided by the results of step 3).

Step 5. Determine the number of shares to be added to the earnings per share denominator for primary purposes (the results of step 1 minus the results of step 4). *Note that this number is added only if it is positive.*

An Example Assume Company C has 100,000 shares of common stock outstanding and 25,000 options outstanding that allow the holders of these securities to purchase 25,000 common shares at $20 per share. During the year the average market price of the common stock was $25 and the end-of-year price was $23 per share. The steps listed above would be carried out as follows.

Step 1. Number of shares to be issued	25,000
Step 2. Proceeds (25,000 × $20)	$500,000
Step 3. Average market price	$25.00
Step 4. Treasury shares ($500,000 ÷ $25)	20,000
Step 5. Additional shares (25,000 − 20,000)	5,000

In this example, the denominator for both primary and fully diluted earnings per share purposes is 105,000 shares since the end-of-the-year market price of the common stock is less than the average price.

In contrast to the Aa bond rating test for convertible securities (discussed below), which is made only at the time of issuance of convertible securities, the treasury stock computation must be made each period. This annual computation is necessary because the average market price of its common stock will be different each year for most companies.

The original establishment of the 66⅔ percent interest rate test for including convertible securities as common stock equivalents was apparently the result of some disagreement among the board members. Whenever convertible securities are issued, there is always the question of the effect of the conversion feature on the securities' marketability. In some cases, investors may be purchasing these securities for their dividends or interest, while in others, investors may be purchasing them mainly for their conversion rights. The 66⅔ percent test was apparently the result of a compromise and now sets the point of major emphasis on convertibility at 66⅔ percent of the Aa bond yield rate.

That is, when a convertible security has an effective yield to maturity of less than 66⅔ percent of the Aa bond effective interest rate at the date of issuance, it is assumed to be purchased for its conversion feature and, therefore, defined as a common stock equivalent. All other convertible securities that fail the 66⅔ test are assumed to be purchased for their return on investment and are included only in the fully diluted earnings per share computation. The determination of whether a convertible security is currently a common stock equivalent based on the relationship between effective yield and the Aa rate at issuance may not be relevant. Investors in convertible securities are likely to convert based on current market conditions, not the market conditions that were in effect when the securities were issued.

The dilutive effect of convertible securities must be determined prior to including them in the calculation of earnings per share. This calculation is made as follows: (1) calculate simple earnings per share, (2) determine whether the inclusion of the convertible security increases or decreases simple earnings per share. Only convertible securities that decrease simple earnings per share are included in the calculation. Convertible securities that increase EPS are antidilutive and not included.

If more than one type of potentially dilutive securities is present, each calculation is made separately from the most to least dilutive. Those that have an antidilutive effect are excluded from the computation of earnings per share. Antidilution in effect means an increase in earnings per share or a decrease in the loss per share.

Once the number of shares to be included in calculating primary earnings per share is determined, it is necessary to consider whether other contingent issuances may be possible in order to calculate fully diluted earnings per share. The fully diluted figure is intended to show the maximum possible dilution of earnings that could occur if all contingent issuances of common stock had taken place at the beginning of the period or at the time they became issuable during the period. Examples of securities to be included in the computation of fully diluted earnings per share are convertible securities that did not meet the common stock equivalent test and shares that are issuable on the occurrence of some event. These shares are also included only if they have a dilutive effect on earnings per share (fully diluted earnings per share must be less than or equal to primary earnings per share).

After all dilutive securities have been included in the calculation of earnings per share, a materiality test is undertaken. *APB Opinion No. 15* provides that any reduction in earnings per share due to dilutive convertible securities may be ignored if it is less than 3 percent in the aggregate. This materiality test may be expressed as follows. If the total dilution from all dilutive securities is less than 3 percent, the company need only disclose simple earnings per share. If fully diluted earnings per share is less than or equal to 97 percent of basic earnings per share, both primary and fully diluted earnings per share must be disclosed.

The overall objective of earnings per share data is to provide investors with an indication of (1) the value of the firm and (2) expected future dividends. A major theoretical issue surrounding the presentation of earnings per share data is whether this information should be based on historical or forecasted information. Authoritative accounting bodies have generally taken the position that financial information should be based only on historical data, and the views expressed by the *APB Opinion No. 15* followed this trend. However, investors' needs might be better satisfied with measures that predict future cash flows (such as current or pro-forma dividends per share).

Usefulness of Earnings per Share   Earnings per share has been termed a *summary indicator*, that is, a single item that communicates considerable information about an enterprise's performance or financial position. The continuing trend toward complexity in financial reporting has caused many financial statement users to utilize summary indicators. EPS is particularly popular because it is thought to contain information useful in making predictions about future dividends and stock prices, and as a measure of management efficiency. However, as discussed in Chapter 5, cash flow data may provide more relevant information to investors. The use of *summary indicators* such as EPS is discouraged by many accountants. These individuals maintain that an understanding of a company's performance requires a more comprehensive analysis than is provided by a single ratio. This issue is discussed further in the readings that accompany this chapter.

Accounting Changes

The accounting standard of consistency indicates that similar transactions should be recorded and reported in the same manner each year. That is, management should choose the set of accounting practices that best satisfies the needs of the reporting unit and continue to use those practices each year. However, individual entities may occasionally find that reporting is improved by changing the methods and procedures previously used or changes in reporting may be dictated by the FASB or the SEC. Even though the results of efficient market research indicate that changes in income due to changed accounting methods do not affect stock prices, when changes in reporting practices occur, the comparability of financial statements between periods is impaired. The accounting standard of disclosure dictates that the effect of these changes should be reported. The major question surrounding changes in accounting practices is the proper method to use in disclosing them. That is, should previously issued financial statements be changed to reflect the new method or procedure?

The Accounting Principles Board studied this problem and issued its findings in *APB Opinion No. 20*, "Accounting Changes." This release identified three types of accounting changes, discussed the general question of errors in the preparation of financial statements, and defined these changes and errors as follows.

1. **Change in an accounting principle.**   *This type of change occurs when an entity adopts a generally accepted accounting principle that differs from one previously used for reporting purposes. Examples of such changes are a*

change from Lifo to Fifo inventory pricing or a change in depreciation methods.

2. **Change in an accounting estimate.** *These changes result from the necessary consequences of periodic presentation. That is, financial statement presentation requires estimation of future events, and such estimates are subject to periodic review. Examples of such changes are the life of depreciable assets and the estimated collectibility of receivables.*

3. **Change in a reporting entity.** *Changes of this type are caused by changes in reporting units, which may be the result of consolidations, changes in specific subsidiaries, or a change in the number of companies consolidated.*

4. **Errors.** *Errors are not viewed as accounting changes: rather they are the result of mistakes or oversights such as the use of incorrect accounting methods or mathematical miscalculations.*[13]

The board then went on to specify the accounting treatment required to satisfy disclosure requirements in each instance. The basic question was the advisability of retroactive presentation. The following paragraphs summarize the board's recommendations.

Change in an Accounting Principle

When an accounting principle is changed, it should be treated currently. That is, the corporation should present its previously issued financial statements as they were before the change occurred, with the cumulative prior effects of the change shown as a component of net income for the period in which the change occurred. This requirement necessitates determining the yearly changes in net income of all prior periods attributable to changing from one GAAP to another. For example, if a company changed from straight line to sum-of-the-year's-digits depreciation, the cumulative effect of this change on all years prior to the change must be calculated. This total amount of change in income (net of tax) is then disclosed as a separate figure between extraordinary items and net income. In addition, per-share data for all comparative statements should include the results of the change as if the change had been consistently applied. This requirement results in the disclosure of additional pro-forma per-share figures for each period presented in which the change affected net income. The general conclusion of *APB Opinion No. 20* was that previously issued financial statements need not be revised for changes in accounting principles. However, exceptions were noted for situations deemed to be of such importance that they required retroactive presentation in the financial statements of all prior periods presented. Specifically, retroactive presentation is required for (1) a change from LIFO inventory valuation to any other method, (2) any change in the method of accounting for long-term construction contracts, and (3) a change to or from the full-cost method in the extractive industries. In each of these cases the previous income statements must be

---

[13] *Accounting Principles Board Opinion No. 20,* "Accounting Changes" (New York: AICPA, 1971).

recast to reflect the adoption of the new principle, and no additional pro-forma figures need to be disclosed.

Additionally, since it is typically not practicable to compute the cumulative effect of a change to LIFO, changes to LIFO from any other inventory method should be treated prospectively. That is, no restatement of previous financial statements is made and no cumulative effect is reported. In these cases, the ending inventory costed under the old method becomes the beginning LIFO inventory.

Cumulative effect type treatment, with accompanying pro formas and retroactively recasting prior financial statements to reflect the use of a new method is intended to fulfill the qualitative characteristic of comparability. These provisions allow users to compare company performance from one period to the next to detect trends so that projections of future cash flows can be made and firm value thereby determined. The one exception, a change in LIFO, requires additional disclosure of the effect of this accounting change on current period earnings. The user can then adjust current period earnings so that comparisons with prior periods can be made.

Change in Estimates

Estimate changes are handled prospectively. They require no adjustments to previously issued financial statements. These changes are accounted for in the period of the change, or in the period of the change and in the future if more than one period is affected. For example, assume that a company originally estimated an asset to have a useful service life of 10 years, and after 3 years of service the total service life of the asset was estimated to be only 8 years. The remaining book value of the asset will be depreciated over the remaining useful life of 5 years. The effects of changes in estimates on operating income, extraordinary items, and the related per-share amounts must be disclosed in the year they occur. As with accounting changes to LIFO, the added disclosures should aid users in their judgments regarding comparability.

Change in Reporting Entities

Changes in reporting entities must be disclosed retroactively by restating all financial statements presented as if the new reporting unit had been in existence at the time the statements were first prepared. That is, previously issued statements are recast to reflect the results of a change in reporting entity. The financial statements should also indicate the nature of the change and the reason for the change. Additionally, the effect of the change on operating income, net income, and the related per-share amounts must be disclosed for all comparative statements presented. A change in reporting entity may materially alter financial statements. For example, if a previously unconsolidated subsidiary is consolidated, the investment account is removed and the assets and liabilities of the subsidiary are added to those of the parent company. When this occurs, total assets, debt, and most financial ratios are typically affected. Without retroactive restatement for an accounting change in reporting entity, the investor would find it difficult, if not impossible, to compare company performance before and after the accounting change.

Errors

Errors are defined as prior period adjustments in *SFAS No. 16*. In the period the error is discovered, the nature of the error and its effect on operating income, net income, and the related per-share amounts must be disclosed. In the event the prior period affected is reported for comparative purposes, the corrected information must be disclosed for the period in which it occurred. This requirement is a logical extension of retroactive treatment. To continue to report information, known to be incorrect, would be purposely misleading investors. By providing retroactive corrections, users can better assess the actual performance of the company over time.

The following are examples of errors:

1. A change from an accounting practice that is not generally acceptable to a practice that is generally acceptable.

2. Mathematical mistakes.

3. The failure to accrue or defer revenues and expenses at the end of any accounting period.

4. The incorrect classification of costs and expenses.

Special Problems in Income Statement Presentation

Disposal of a Segment of a Business

As indicated earlier, the study of the results of the application of *APB Opinion No. 9* by various entities disclosed some reporting abuses. For example, some companies were reporting the results of the disposal of segment assets as extraordinary while including the revenue from these segments during the disposal period as ordinary income. In its *Opinion No. 30*, the APB concluded that additional criteria were necessary to identify disposed segments of a business. *APB Opinion No. 30* requires the separate presentation of (1) the results of operations prior to the measurement date, and (2) gain or loss on the sale of assets for disposed segments including any operating gains or losses during the disposal period. This information was seen as necessary to users in order to evaluate the past and expected future operations of a particular business entity. The total gain or loss is determined by *summing any gains or losses on disposal of segment assets, and gains or losses incurred by the operations of the disposed segment* during the period of disposal. The following definitions were provided by the APB to aid in determining when and how to report a disposal of a segment of a business.

Segment of a Business A component of an entity whose activities represent a separate major line of business or class of customers. A segment may be a division, department, or joint venture providing its operations can be clearly distinguished physically and operationally. If the component is truly a segment, it should be possible to recast the financial statements to segregate its operations. If its operations cannot be segregated, the presumption is that the component is not a segment.

Measurement Date The date on which management commits itself to a formal plan of disposal. This plan should include identification of the assets, the method of disposal, the period of disposal, the estimated results of operations from the measurement date to the disposal date, and the estimated proceeds from disposal.

Disposal Date The date of sale or the date operations cease.

The accounting treatment for the disposal of a segment of a business is influenced by whether a gain or a loss is anticipated on the measurement date. The expected total gain or loss is determined by comparing the expected net realizable value of the segment assets to the book value of those same assets, less the expenses connected with disposal. Any expected gains or losses on operations of the segment during the period of disposal are then added or subtracted to arrive at the expected total gain or loss. If a loss is expected, the loss is recorded on the measurement date, whereas gains are recognized when realized (ordinarily this will be the disposal date). This accounting treatment is in accordance with the general principle of conservatism discussed earlier in Chapter 2.

Figure 4.1 is a comparative income statement for Company X for 1996 and 1995. It discloses the required presentation for a company with normal, extraordinary, and discontinued operations, and a cumulative effect change in accounting principle for 1996 and normal recurring operations for 1995.

Interim Financial Statements

Many companies issue financial statements for periods of less than a year and also release information on their periodic performance through various news media. These statements' major value is their timeliness. That is, investors need to be aware of any changes in the financial position of the company as soon as possible. In addition, much of the information disclosed in interim financial statements enters into the analytical data used by the government to develop information on the state of the economy, the need for monetary controls, or the need for modifications in the tax laws. Moreover, there is also evidence that interim reporting has an impact on stock prices, indicating that investors do use interim financial information. It is therefore important that interim information be as reliable as possible.

A wide variety of practices have existed with regard to the methods of reporting in these so-called interim periods. Thus such things as seasonal fluctuations in revenues and the application of fixed costs to the various periods have a significant impact on the reported results for interim periods.

In 1973 the APB studied this problem and issued its conclusions in *APB Opinion No. 28*, ''Interim Financial Reporting.'' In reviewing the general question, the board noted that two views existed as to the principal objective of interim financial reporting.

1. *One view held that each interim period was a separate accounting period and that income should be determined in the same manner as for the annual period, thus revenues and expenses should be reported as they occur.*

FIGURE 4.1

COMPANY X
STATEMENT OF INCOME
FOR THE YEARS ENDED DECEMBER 31

			1996	1995
Net sales			$900,000	$840,000
Cost of goods sold			(300,000)	270,000
Gross profit			$600,000	$570,000
Operating expenses			(200,000)	180,000
Operating income			$400,000	$390,000
Other revenue and expense				
Gain on sale of equipment		$ 5,000		
Interest expense		(30,000)	(25,000)	25,000
Pretax income from continu-				
ing operations			$375,000	$365,000
Income tax expense			(75,000)	70,000
Income from continuing oper-				
ations			$300,000	$295,000
Discontinued operations				
(Note 1)				
Gain on disposal of division				
assets	$ 25,000			
Less applicable taxes	12,000	$13,000		
Loss from discontinued				
Division A	$(20,000)			
Less applicable tax re-				
duction	9,000	(11,000)	2,000	
Extraordinary items net of tax				
effect of $10,000 (Note 2)			31,000	
Cumulative effect of change				
in accounting principle net				
of tax effect of $1,800 (SYD				
depreciation to SL)			5,000	
Net income			$338,000	$295,000

1996 Earnings Per Share (Note 3)

	Primary	Fully Diluted
Income from continuing operations	1.76	1.70
Discontinued operations	.02	.02
Extraordinary items	.36	.35
Cumulative effect of accounting change	.06	.06
Net Income	2.20	2.13

Note 1. During 1996 the company disposed of one of its divisions at a net gain of $13,000 after an applicable income tax reduction of $12,000. Net operating losses of the plant prior to the disposal period amounted to $11,000 after an applicable tax reduction of $9,000.

Note 2. In 1996 X sold its 2% investment in Company ABC at a gain of $41,000 less applicable taxes of $10,000.

Note 3. Assuming the appropriate conditions for primary and fully diluted earnings per share calculations, and full compliance with FASB requirements and recommendations for full disclosure.

2. *The other view held that interim periods were an integral part of the annual period, thus revenues and expenses might be allocated to various interim periods even though they occurred only in one period.*[14]

In *APB Opinion No. 28* the Board noted that interim financial information was essential to provide timely data on the progress of the enterprise, and that the usefulness of the data rests on its relationship to annual reports. Accordingly, it was determined that interim periods should be viewed as integral parts of the annual period and that the principles and practices followed in the annual period should be followed in the interim period. However, certain modifications were deemed necessary in order to provide a better relationship to the annual period. That is, the following modifications will assist users of interim financial statements to tie the interim period results into the annual report and allow for more informative disclosure.

1. *Revenue should be recognized on the same basis as in the annual period.*

2. *Costs directly associated with products should be recognized as the revenue from those products is recognized.*

3. *Inventories should be costed on the same flow assumptions as in the annual period except that:*
   a. *The gross profit method is acceptable for an interim period but must be disclosed.*
   b. *The liquidation of base period inventories under the Lifo method may not be appropriate if they are expected to be replaced; in such cases the replacement value of the liquidated base may be used.*
   c. *Losses from the application of the lower of cost or market rule should be recognized during the interim period in which they occur and recoveries of such losses should also be recognized when they occur. However, temporary losses need not be recorded.*
   d. *If standard costs are used, variances not expected to reverse in subsequent periods should be expensed.*

4. *All other costs should be expensed on the basis of direct expenditures made, accruals for estimated expenditures, or amortization of multiperiod expenses. Costs not associated with products should be expensed as incurred or allocated on the basis of the expiration of time or period of benefit.*

5. *Businesses with material seasonal variations should disclose this fact so that interim reports are not misleading.*

6. *Income tax allocation should be based on the tax rate expected to be applicable to the sum of interim periods' net income.*

7. *Extraordinary items and gains or losses from the disposal of a segment of a business should be reported as they occur and not prorated over the year.*

8. *Changes in accounting principles from comparable or previous interim periods*

---

[14] *Accounting Principles Board Opinion No. 28*, "Interim Financial Reporting" (New York: American Institute of Certified Public Accountants, 1973), par. 5.

or a prior annual period should be reported according to the provisions of APB No. 20.[15]

Additionally, it was stated that the publicly traded companies that provide summary information for financial analysis should provide, at minimum, certain information for the interim period in question and the same interim period for the previous year. These guidelines were intended to offset partially the reduction in detail from interim reports.

1. Sales or gross revenues, extraordinary items, the cumulative effect of a change in accounting principle or practice, and net income.
2. Primary and fully diluted earnings per share.
3. Seasonal revenue.
4. Significant changes in income tax provisions or estimates.
5. Disposal of a segment of a business and extraordinary items.
6. Contingencies.
7. Changes in accounting principles.
8. Significant changes in financial position.

Subsequent to the issuance of *APB Opinion No. 28* problems in reporting certain types of events became evident. These problems were mainly concerned with the reporting of the cumulative effect of an accounting change for changes in accounting principles during interim periods, and the reporting of accounting changes during the fourth quarter of a fiscal year by a company whose securities are publicly traded.

With respect to the cumulative adjustments required for interim changes in accounting principles, *APB Opinion No. 28* stated,

> *A change in accounting principle or practice adopted in an interim period that requires an adjustment for the cumulative effect of the change to the beginning of the current fiscal year should be reported in the interim period in a manner similar to that found in the annual report. . . . The effect of the change from the beginning of the annual period to the period of change should be reported as a determinant of net income in the interim period in which the change is made.*[16]

Because of this requirement, the cumulative effect of the change on retained earnings at the beginning of the fiscal year was presented as a component of net income in the interim period in which the change was adopted. However, problems arose because reissued interim period balance sheets did not reflect the cumulative effect of the change on retained earnings, whereas reissued interim period income statements did reflect this effect.

On becoming aware of this inconsistency, the FASB reviewed the provisions of *APB Opinion No. 28* and issued *SFAS No. 3*, "Reporting Accounting

[15] Ibid., pars. 11–15.
[16] Ibid., par. 27.

Changes in Interim Financial Statements.''[17] The provisions of this statement were to apply separately to changes other than changes to the LIFO inventory pricing method and fourth quarter accounting changes made by publicly traded companies.

For all cumulative effect changes other than changes to LIFO, an accounting change made during the first interim period of the fiscal year should reflect the cumulative effect of the change on retained earnings in the net income of the first interim period. For changes in other than the first interim period, no cumulative effect of the change should be included in net income in the period of change. Rather, the new principle should be retroactively applied to all prior interim periods, and the cumulative effect of the change on retained earnings at the beginning of the year should be included in the net income for the first interim period. The statement also specifies certain disclosures as to the nature and justification for the change and its effect on continuing operations, net income, and per-share amounts.

Where changes to the LIFO method of inventory pricing have occurred, the cumulative effect of the change cannot ordinarily be calculated. Therefore, *SFAS No. 3* requires a paragraph explaining the reasons for omitting accounting for a cumulative effect and disclosure of the pro-forma amounts for prior years.

With respect to fourth quarter changes by publicly held companies, some of these organizations are required by the provisions of *APB Opinion No. 28* to disclose certain fourth quarter information in footnotes. Information concerning the effects of an accounting change made during the fourth quarter was not explicitly identified as a part of this requirement. *SFAS No. 3* amended *APB Opinion No. 28* to require such disclosures.

Summary

There has been a great deal of discussion among accountants about the proper concept of income to use and the need for comparability among entities because various financial-statement users have relied on the corporate net income figure. Since 1966 several pronouncements have had a major impact on the preparation of the income statement. These pronouncements affect the presentation of income from normal operations and other sources, earnings per share computations, changes in methods of presenting information, disposal of parts of the entity, and interim financial reports. In each case the number of alternatives is narrowed in an attempt to improve comparability.

The extent to which these pronouncements have improved the understandability of corporate financial reports is not readily determinable. Only the most sophisticated users of financial statements are likely to be able to understand the differences between normal and abnormal events, the effects of accounting changes, or the relative merits of any number of earnings per share figures. Accounting is often criticized as being too simplistic in the estab-

---

[17] *Statement of Financial Accounting Standards No. 3*, ''Reporting Accounting Changes in Interim Financial Statements'' (Stamford, Conn.: Financial Accounting Standards Board, 1974).

lishment of its assumptions about the behavior of revenue and costs; however, attempting to provide comparability while still maintaining some degree of flexibility to accommodate the reporting needs of various entities may lead to more confusion.

In the following readings, R. David Mautz and Thomas Hogan criticize the usefulness of current earnings per share disclosures, and Gordon May and Douglas Schneider report the results of a study of companies reporting accounting changes and conclude that stricter guidelines are needed to help preserve credibility in financial reporting.

Earnings Per Share Reporting: Time for an Overhaul?

R. David Mautz, Jr., and Thomas Jeffery Hogan

Introduction

The preparation of earnings per share (EPS) disclosures for public companies with complex capital structures is much more complicated than dividing income by outstanding common shares.[1] Much of this complexity results from the efforts of standard setters to make EPS disclosures reflect the effects of potentially dilutive securities. A critical evaluation of current EPS disclosures suggests that they are of questionable usefulness. This paper concludes that EPS reporting standards are deficient and sets forth a proposal to modify those standards. The proposed changes are intended to improve the usefulness of EPS reporting without increasing the burden placed on preparers of financial statements.

A prominent feature of the proposal is the recommendation that primary EPS be replaced by an undiluted measure of EPS, which we call basic EPS.[2] The following section focuses on issues surrounding the computation of diluted EPS, such as common stock equivalency, the treasury stock method, and the three percent materiality standard. The next section details the proposed changes in EPS reporting requirements and provides an illustration and explanation of the recommended disclosure format. It is followed by a brief summary and conclusions.

Convertible Securities, Potential Dilution, and EPS Reporting

Finance theory suggests that investors attempt to maximize expected utility. With respect to investments in debt securities, utility can be assumed to be a function of the expected future cash flows associated with those investments and the uncertainty surrounding those cash flows. Market participants evaluate debt characteristics and determine the effective return they are willing to accept. Debt issues which incorporate conversion features complicate this evaluation, since the market must also consider the potential increased returns available if the issuing company performs better than expected.

Conversion features also complicate external financial reporting since they represent a potential dilution of EPS. Just as the default risk associated with a pure debt security is unobservable to investors, debtholders' intentions with respect to exercising conversion features are unobservable to preparers of

[1] The principal authoritative guidance for EPS reporting is: Accounting Principles Board. *Accounting Principles Board Opinion No. 15*, "Earnings Per Share" (New York: May 1969).

[2] Henceforth in this paper, the term "basic EPS" is used to describe the statistic obtained by dividing historical earnings available to common shareholders by weighted average common shares outstanding.

financial statements. Accounting standard setters have sought a linkage between investors' intentions and an observable phenomenon. Lambert terms such linkages "bridge assumptions."[3] The linkage currently made involves the comparison of a security's yield upon issuance with a market-based standard. This benchmark, the average Aa corporate bond yield, is intended to surrogate for the risk-adjusted rate of return that the security would yield absent the conversion feature. When a security's yield rate is significantly lower than this benchmark, accountants assume that investors value the conversion feature highly and are more likely to exercise it.

Current reporting standards for public companies with complex capital structures require presentation of two pro-forma EPS numbers on the face of the income statement when potential dilution is material. The first number, commonly referred to as primary EPS, is prepared assuming that those dilutive securities most likely to be converted are converted on the first day of the fiscal year. The second pro-forma disclosure, fully diluted EPS, is computed assuming that *all* dilutive securities are converted to common stock on the first day of the fiscal year.

This paper focuses on three major concerns related to the usefulness of EPS as currently reported. First, under current standards, historical EPS numbers may be completely supplanted by pro-forma disclosures designed to illustrate possible future effects of conversions to common stock.[4] The impor-

tance of information about potential dilution is apparent.[5] However, that acknowledgment does not necessarily lead to the conclusion that historically based EPS data are of no use to readers.

Second, current standards require the presentation of only two discrete EPS numbers. The possible levels of EPS actually span a range from no dilution to maximum possible dilution. Thus, financial statements currently present a severely truncated disclosure of EPS. Furthermore, the two EPS numbers presented do not represent the endpoints of the range of possible dilution levels.

Third, authoritative standards for EPS reporting incorporate three bridge assumptions which are either untested or unsupported in the empirical literature. These are (1) the assumption that common stock equivalency tests are accurate indicators of conversion likelihood, (2) the assumption that option and warrant proceeds are used to acquire treasury shares (the so-called "treasury stock method"), and (3) the assumption that potential dilution of less than three percent is immaterial.

Lambert points out that bridge assumptions may be established in light of empirical evidence, or they may result from arbitrary stipulation.[6] The cash yield test for common stock equivalency established by *Accounting Principles Board Opinion No. 15 (APB No. 15)* has repeatedly been tested for its predictive power and found to be lacking. Amendments to the *APB No. 15* test and a handful of rival tests have, likewise,

---

[3] Samuel Joseph Lambert, III, "Basic Assumptions in Accounting Theory Construction," *The Journal of Accountancy* (February 1974), p. 43.

[4] This is the Case whenever potential dilution exceeds three percent.

[5] For an empirical study of market reaction to potential dilution, see Lerner, Eugene M., and Rolf Auster, "Does the Market Discount Potential Dilution," *Financial Analysts Journal* (July–August 1969), pp. 118–121.

[6] Lambert, p. 44.

proven poor predictors of conversion.[7] These conclusions suggest that the designation "common stock equivalent" is not meaningful as it is currently defined. That being the case, the adjustment of basic EPS for the assumed conversion of common stock equivalents produces a statistic that is, at best, difficult to interpret. The usefulness of primary EPS is considered in greater detail in the following section.

Both the treasury stock method and the three percent dilution test appear to fall into the category of unverified bridge assumptions. The authors are not aware of any direct evidence that either assumption contributes to the usefulness of EPS disclosures. Yet both practices have important effects on reported EPS. Use of the treasury stock method minimizes the dilutive effect of the assumed exercise of options and warrants. The result is that EPS numbers do not reflect the maximum possible dilution. The three percent materiality standard permits the presentation of a single, undiluted EPS statistic when the difference between basic and fully

[7] See for example: Arnold, Donald F., and Thomas E. Humann, "Earnings Per Share: An Empirical Test of the Market Parity and the Investment Value Methods," *The Accounting Review* (January 1973), pp. 23–33; Frank, Werner G., and Jerry J. Weygandt, "A Prediction Model for Convertible Debentures," *Journal of Accounting Research* (Spring 1971), pp. 116–126; Fulmer, Jr., John G., and James E. Moon, "Tests for Common Stock Equivalency," *Journal of Accounting, Auditing, and Finance* (Fall 1984), pp. 5–14; Givoly, Dan, and Dan Palmon, "Classification of Convertible Debt and Common Stock Equivalents: Some Empirical Evidence on the Effects of APB Opinion 15," *Journal of Accounting Research* (Autumn 1981), pp. 530–543; Hofstedt, Thomas R., and Richard R. West, "The APB, Yield Indices, and Predictive Ability," *The Accounting Review* (April 1971), pp. 329–337.

diluted EPS is less than three percent. The effect of this assumption on users' decisions is not known. The following section outlines a proposal to modify EPS reporting. The issues of common stock equivalency, the treasury stock method, and the three percent materiality standard are discussed in greater detail in that section.

Policy Recommendation

The introduction to this paper calls into question the usefulness of the complex EPS disclosures that are currently mandated for public companies. The previous section focused on some individual problem areas within those disclosures. In this section, we recommend four specific amendments to the accounting standards governing EPS. We believe that each is a step toward meeting our stated objective of improving the usefulness of EPS disclosures without materially increasing the computational burden associated with their presentation. The proposed amendments are:

1. Discontinue presentation of primary EPS in favor of basic EPS;

2. Modify the computation of fully diluted EPS to eliminate the treasury stock method;

3. Eliminate the three percent materiality standard for dual presentation; and,

4. Require the presentation of supplementary information about all potential diluters to assist financial statement readers in assessing the impact on EPS of assumed conversion.

The balance of this section considers the benefits of each proposed change.

Replacing Primary EPS with Basic EPS

As discussed previously, the importance of anticipating future dilution is evident. It is the authors' belief that the merits of presenting historical EPS data are equally apparent. The issue, then, is why primary EPS ought to be discarded rather than reported as part of a three level disclosure (i.e., basic, primary, and fully diluted EPS).

Research findings have repeatedly demonstrated that common stock equivalency testing, a critical element of the primary EPS computation, does not produce interpretable results. This leads to the conclusion that the primary EPS statistic conveys a noisy signal. Performing such a garbled transformation of the basic EPS statistic is unlikely to yield incremental information. Thus, the cost of preparing primary EPS must almost certainly exceed any benefit.

The usefulness of primary EPS can also be examined analytically. Ijiri and Jaedicke provide a mathematical definition of reliability, one of the principal characteristics of useful information.[8] Employing their definition of reliability and assuming that dividend policy is a direct function of earnings, it can be demonstrated that, in the circumstances described, basic EPS is a more reliable measure than primary EPS. Put another way, a financial statement reader attempting to determine a relationship between EPS and dividends will be more successful employing basic EPS.

Actual dividends probably change only in response to long-run changes in income levels. Even under this "sticky" dividend policy, it seems likely that a lagged model employing basic EPS would outperform primary EPS. In a more complex dividend generating scheme, potential dilution might also be an important factor. When the basic EPS statistic does not incorporate information about dilution potential, the supplementary disclosures recommended in point four of this proposal do. Comprehensive raw data of that type are almost certainly more useful than limited disclosures prepared using questionable assumptions.

Finally, the usefulness of primary EPS can be considered in light of empirical findings. A recent study by Millar, Nunthirapakorn, and Courtenay examines the correlations between five per-share measures and stock returns.[9] The measures examined are primary EPS, fully diluted EPS, simple (basic) EPS, and two forms of cash flow per share. The results indicate, "... that, for explaining stock returns, primary and fully diluted EPS are the least informative of the earnings numbers studied. Simple and cash flow forms of earnings are significantly more closely related to stock returns than those earnings reported according to APB 15."[10] Considered collectively, these arguments make a strong case for replacing primary EPS with basic EPS.

Discarding the Treasury Stock Method
The issuance of stock in exchange for options and warrants produces cash inflows for the issuing company, but has no direct effect on income. In terms of calculating diluted EPS, an assumed issuance of stock yields an increase in the denominator and no change in the numerator. The result is a reduction in reported EPS. The treasury stock method

---

[8] Ijiri, Yuji, and Robert K. Jaedicke, "Reliability and Objectivity of Accounting Measurements," *The Accounting Review* (July 1966), pp. 474–483.

[9] Millar, James A., Thakol Nunthirapakorn, and Steve Courtenay, "A Note on the Information Content of Primary and Fully Diluted Earnings Per Share," *Financial Analysts Journal* (September–October 1987), pp. 77–79.

[10] Ibid., p. 79.

dampens this effect by assuming that cash proceeds are used to acquire the company's own shares. Thus, only the net issuance is reflected in the denominator of the EPS calculation. When the shares obtainable under the treasury stock assumption exceed 20 percent of the common shares outstanding, *APB No. 15* recommends the modified treasury stock method. The modification involves the additional assumption that funds in excess of those used to acquire 20 percent of the common shares outstanding are applied to reduce debt or purchase government securities. This, of course, generates additional income in the numerator of the EPS calculation.

The purchase of treasury shares and government securities is not the only investment strategy available to management. While these are reasonable choices in given circumstances, expanding plant facilities, building up inventories, and funding pension obligations are also potentially worthwhile uses for option and warrant proceeds. Selecting a use for cash inflows is the prerogative of management and is likely to involve the consideration of numerous factors.

Eliminating the treasury stock method from the calculation of fully diluted EPS has the same effect as assuming the most conservative investment choice, holding a cash balance. Two principal advantages are evident in this treatment. One is that no speculation about management choices is involved in the preparation of the financial statements. The second is that fully diluted EPS then represents the maximum dilution scenario. Presentation of basic and fully diluted EPS is, thus, a disclosure of both endpoints of the range of dilution possibilities.

The distortive effects peculiar to the modified treasury stock method are ex-

plored in detail by Barley.[11] These include the assumption that, ". . . funds obtained through the exercise of options and warrants are invested in projects which yield returns lower than the cost of equity capital."[12] Barley also cites the influences of market and economic conditions on EPS and the potential for management manipulation as shortcomings of the modified treasury stock method. Shank, too, points out the potential problems resulting from the use of market prices in calculating EPS.[13]

In summary, the treasury stock method and its modified form are predicated on a series of unsupported assumptions. Their use introduces elements of speculation into the calculation of EPS and restricts the range of EPS numbers presented in the financial statements. Eliminating the treasury stock method and presenting supplementary information about potentially dilutive securities should permit financial statement readers to adjust EPS to incorporate their own judgments about the use of option and warrant proceeds.

Abandoning the Three Percent Materiality Standard
SFAC No. 2 discusses materiality guidance, and points out that, "The more important a judgment item is, the finer the screen should be that will be used to determine whether it is material."[14]

[11] Barley, Bennon, "Contingent Equity and the Dilutive Effect on EPS," *The Accounting Review* (April 1983), pp. 385–393.

[12] Ibid., p. 392.

[13] Shank, John K., "Earnings per Share, Stock Prices, and APB Opinion No. 15," *The Journal of Accounting Research* (Spring 1971), pp. 165–170.

[14] Financial Accounting Standards Board, *Statement of Financial Accounting Concepts*

The importance of the EPS statistic and its potential dilution suggest that the screen for materiality ought to be very fine. Whether three percent dilution is an appropriate threshold is an empirical question that can only be answered with reference to decision makers. Research efforts have not established universally appropriate levels of materiality. Given that the fully diluted EPS calculation must be made before a materiality test can be performed, the only saving apparent in permitting a single, undiluted presentation is in printing costs. Requiring dual presentation by all companies with complex capital structures places all the facts in the hands of those who ultimately define materiality, the financial statement readers, at minimal or no cost. It also lessens the urgency associated with attempts to develop quantitative materiality standards.

Presenting Supplementary Information about Potential Diluters

The presentation of detailed information about potentially dilutive securities makes the proposed EPS reporting format a comprehensive disclosure of historical earnings per share and the full range of future dilution possibilities. The principal additional information envisioned in the supplementary disclosures consists of the dilutive effects of individual securities on basic EPS. Ready access to such information facilitates the calculation of all points in the range of potential dilution and permits analysts to make their own assumptions about conversion timing and likelihood. This disclosure is possible at a relatively small marginal cost, because this infor-

mation is needed to calculate fully diluted EPS. Additionally, our proposal concentrates currently required capital structure disclosures in the EPS footnote.[15]

Summary

Exhibit 1 illustrates the presentation of EPS disclosures incorporating the suggested amendments to current practice. The background information and calculations necessary to prepare Exhibit 1 are available from the authors.

While the proposed changes in EPS reporting standards would result in an expansion of printed material, they would not require accounting practitioners to employ sophisticated financial modeling techniques or gather large amounts of additional data.[16] Nor would they necessitate speculation about management's reactions to possible future exercises of convertibles. *SFAC No. 1* states that, "The role of financial reporting in the economy is to provide information that is useful in making business and economic decisions. . . ."[17] In contrast, as Beaver states, "The analyst community is an industry whose product is information,

---

No. 2, "Qualitative Characteristics of Accounting Information" (Stamford, CT: May 1980), par. 128.

[15] See *APB No. 15*, paragraph 19.

[16] At least two proposals have been advanced which recommend the use of more sophisticated procedures for predicting conversion. These are Gaumnitz, Bruce R., and Joel E. Thompson, "Establishing the Common Stock Equivalence of Convertible Bonds," *The Accounting Review* (July 1987), pp. 601–622; and Vigeland, Robert L., "Dilution of Earnings per Share in an Option Pricing Framework," *The Accounting Review* (April 1982), pp. 348–357.

[17] Financial Accounting Standards Board, *Statement of Financial Accounting Concepts No. 1*, "Objectives of Financial Reporting" (Stamford, CT: November 1978), par. 33.

EXHIBIT 1

(on the face of the income statement)
Earnings per share (see Note X)

Without dilution, basic EPS	($8,140,000/900,000)	$9.04
Assuming maximum dilution, fully diluted EPS	($9,280,060/1,580,000)	$5.87

(among the notes to the financial statements)
Note X:

Both basic and fully diluted EPS were calculated based upon 900,000 weighted average shares outstanding. This estimate reflects the stock split as though it had occurred on January 1. Basic EPS is calculated using historical data about earnings and equity. Fully diluted EPS is a pro-forma disclosure presented to illustrate the minimum earnings that would have been available to common shareholders had the holders of other securities exercised their rights to obtain common stock. Management makes no assertions about the likelihood, timing, or amounts of future conversions to common stock. The following table presents information to assist in assessing the dilution potential of individual convertible securities.

Convertible Security	Other Information Available	Income (Numerator) Effect on Basic EPS (in dollars)	Equity (Denominator) Effect on Basic EPS (in common shares)	Assumed Converted in Fully Diluted EPS?
Stock Options	Note A	$0	30,000[a]	Yes
Convertible Bonds	Note B	$840,060	500,000	Yes
Convertible Preferred Stock	Note C	$300,000	150,000	Yes
Contingent Issuance	Note D	$560,000	75,000	No

[a]The actual shares available under options totaled 30,000. Had all options been exercised, Example Company would have received cash totaling $1,350,000. A common assumption regarding the assumed exercise of options is that the company uses the cash proceeds to acquire treasury shares. Had that assumption been applied in this case, the net issuance of shares would have been 4,038 if treasury shares were purchased at the 1987 average price of $52; 5,893 shares would have been assumed issued had the treasury stock purchases been made at $56, the 1987 ending market price.

analysis and interpretation."[18] It is the authors' belief that the proposals set forth in this section would move preparers of EPS disclosures away from the role of financial analysts and toward the role of financial reporters without increasing the already considerable burden of EPS reporting.[19]

Conclusions

APB No. 15 was issued nearly 20 years ago. Since that time, researchers have devoted considerable attention to the calculation and presentation of EPS. This literature suggests widespread concern over the extent to which current reporting standards result in useful disclosures. For example, Boyer and Gibson cite a survey of the readers of *Financial Executive* in which almost three-fourths of the respondents indicated disagreement with the residual security concept. The preferred presentation among that majority was a basic EPS number supplemented by pro-forma disclosures incorporating potential dilution. Perhaps more discon-

certing are their findings that substantial minorities of practitioners and academics are unable to correctly answer questions about the calculation of EPS under current standards.[20]

Numerous specific changes to the *APB No. 15* format have been proposed, and a few have been incorporated into accounting standards. However, the basic structure and assumptions of *APB No. 15* remain intact. The authors believe that, when considered as a whole, the literature examining EPS suggests the need for a comprehensive evaluation and overhaul of EPS reporting standards. This paper details a proposal to modify EPS reporting to improve its usefulness without significantly increasing the related computational burden. The specific changes proposed include the elimination of primary EPS, the treasury stock method, and the three percent materiality standard for dual presentation. Restoration of basic EPS to the face of the income statement and the supplementary disclosure of the effects of individual dilutive securities are also important features of this proposal. While the format proposed and illustrated in this paper is only one of the many possible, the authors strongly believe that EPS reporting should move from selective, pro-forma disclosure to comprehensive historical disclosure supplemented by information to assist in anticipating possible future dilution.

---

[18] Beaver, William, "Current Trends in Corporate Disclosure," *The Journal of Accountancy* (January 1978), p. 48.

[19] The magnitude of this burden is evidenced by the fact that nonpublic companies are exempted from the requirements of *APB No. 15*. See Financial Accounting Standards Board, *Statement of Financial Accounting Standards No. 21*, "Suspension of the Reporting of Earnings Per Share and Segment Information by Nonpublic Enterprises" (Stamford, CT: April 1978).

[20] Boyer, Patricia A., and Charles H. Gibson, "How About Earnings Per Share?," *CPA Journal* (February 1969).

Reporting Accounting Changes: Are Stricter Guidelines Needed?

Gordon S. May and Douglas K. Schneider

The issue of when to permit and how to account for changes in accounting principles involves one of the most basic of all concepts in accounting—that of consistency.[1] The Financial Accounting Standards Board has stated that interperiod consistency in the application of accounting methods helps users better understand and interpret financial accounting data and therefore makes the data more useful.[2]

However, consistent application of accounting methods is desirable only if the pattern of economic flows the ac-

counting methods are designed to reflect is consistent, or the methods can also reflect any changed pattern faithfully. As economic conditions and events change, it may be necessary to change accounting methods to preserve comparability. This is what the FASB had in mind when it stated that consistency in application of accounting methods is a necessary condition for comparability to exist, but consistent application of accounting principles cannot alone produce comparability. Rather, "it is the representational faithfulness of the measurements used, rather than simply the unchanging nature of the measurement rules or classification rules, that results in true comparability over time."[3]

Thus, the preferred choice among alternative methods is the one that possesses the highest degree of representational faithfulness in than it most faithfully depicts the effects of the transaction or event it is used to measure. In practice, the application of representational faithfulness is often not an easy task. Where representational faithfulness cannot be determined, however, a discretionary change in accounting method violates the concept of consistency. From a financial reporting perspective, an accounting change is justified only if the nature of the

[1] There is little empirical evidence to suggest that discretionary changes in accounting principles affect stock prices significantly. [See, for example, R. W. Holthausen, "Evidence on the Effect of Bond Covenants and Management Compensation Contracts on the Choice of Accounting Techniques: The Case of the Depreciation Switch-Back," *Journal of Accounting and Economics 3* (March 1981), pp. 73–109. However, the prevailing view of standard-setting bodies continues to be that stated in *Accounting Principles Board Opinion No. 20*; once adopted, an accounting principle should not be changed unless events or transactions change ["Accounting Changes," *Opinion of the Accounting Principles Board No. 20* (New York: AICPA, 1971), par. 15].

[2] Ibid., par. 15, and "Qualitative Characteristics of Accounting Information," *Statements of Financial Accounting Concepts No. 2* (Stamford, Conn.: FASB, 1980), par. 120.

[3] "Qualitative Characteristics of Accounting Information," *Statements of Financial Accounting Concepts No. 2* (Stamford, Conn.: FASB, 1980), par. 121.

transactions or events changes so that it becomes necessary to change the accounting method applied to maintain representational faithfulness. With sufficient disclosure, an accounting change made under these circumstances will preserve comparability of accounting data.

Have practices relating to accounting changes improved since Cushing's study 12 years ago examined the early impact of *Opinion No. 20,* which placed limits on discretionary accounting changes, and reported significant noncompliance?[4] A study we recently completed shows that there has been some improvement in technical compliance with standards, but there is very strong evidence suggesting that management's primary motivation in making accounting changes is not to achieve representational faithfulness, but rather to manage reported earnings. New evidence suggests a firm is more likely to undertake a discretionary accounting change having a material positive earnings effect than one having a material negative earnings effect. In addition, current disclosure practices raise more questions about management's motivation than they answer and therefore detract from the credibility of the financial reporting process. Additional guidelines concerning accounting changes are needed to help preserve credibility in financial reporting.

Our Recent Data

Using the LEXIS/NAARS data base, we examined all annual reports available in that system for fiscal years ending July 1, 1980, to June 30, 1985. This time

[4] Barry E. Cushing, "Accounting Changes: The Impact of APB No. 20," *Journal of Accountancy* (New York: AICPA, November 1974), pp. 54–62.

period conformed to the earliest available annual reports on the LEXIS/NAARS data base (1980/1981) and the latest fiscal year for which there was a complete file (1984/1985). We established five fiscal years, or five separate files, for the 12 months beginning July 1 and ending June 30 as follows: 1980/1981, 1981/1982, 1982/1983, 1983/1984, and 1984/1985.

Initially we screened each file for annual reports of Fortune 500 companies and their subsidiaries and found a total of 3,831 financial reports during the five-year period, as shown in Exhibit 1. We then further screened these 3,831 reports using accompanying auditors' reports and found a total of 639 with current or prior period consistency exceptions over the five-year period. From these 639 financial reports, a random sample of 60 reports was taken in each of the four fiscal years 1980/1981, 1981/1982, 1982/1983, and 1983/1984. These samples represented approximately one half to one third of the reports with current or prior period consistency exceptions in each fiscal year. Because we found only 47 reports with consistency exceptions in the 1984/1985 fiscal year, we included all of them in our sample for that year. Thus, our overall sample covering the five-year time span totaled 287 annual reports.

We then eliminated all reports with prior period consistency exceptions, which left 156 reports with current consistency exceptions. These 156 reports included as many as 41 reports during the 1980/1981 period and as few as 18 during the 1984/1985 period. They contained a total of 174 individual current year accounting changes, of which 78, or an average of 45 percent, were discretionary. The percentage of total changes that were discretionary ranged

EXHIBIT 1 *Accounting Changes Reported by Fortune 500 Companies and Subsidiaries*

	Fiscal Year Ends Between July and June					
	80/81	81/82	82/83	83/84	84/85	Total
Total number of annual reports found for Fortune 500 companies and their subsidiaries	708	691	734	852	846	3,831
Number of Fortune 500 companies and subsidiaries with current or prior year consistency qualifications						
Sample size	123	158	182	129	47	639
Number of companies found in sample with	60	60	60	60	47	287
current year changes	41	40	35	22	18	156
Discretionary	21 (51%)	14 (35%)	11 (31%)	11 (50%)	13 (72%)	70 (45%)
Nondiscretionary	20 (49%)	26 (65%)	24 (69%)	11 (50%)	5 (28%)	86 (55%)
Number of individual *current* year changes	50	45	36	25	18	174
Discretionary	26 (52%)	15 (33%)	12 (33%)	12 (48%)	13 (72%)	78 (45%)
Nondiscretionary	24 (48%)	30 (67%)	24 (67%)	13 (52%)	5 (28%)	96 (55%)

from a high of 72 percent in 1984/1985 to a low of 33 percent in each of the years 1981/1982 and 1982/1983.

Comparisons with Cushing's Early Results

Exhibit 2 shows comparisons of data from our study with some of Cushing's results ten years earlier. Cushing found that discretionary accounting changes accounted for 61 percent (43 of 70) of all changes made.[5] Our study ten years later found 45 percent (78 of 174) changes were discretionary. Thus, we found a decrease (from 61 percent to 45 percent) in the relative incidence of reported discretionary accounting changes.[6]

Exhibit 3 shows that the largest number of discretionary accounting changes in the early 1980s was attributable to inventory valuation. Overall, such changes accounted for about 46 percent (36 of 78) of all discretionary accounting changes during the five-year period.

Notice the large number of changes in inventory valuation methods in the high inflation years of 1980/1981 and 1981/1982. In the 1980/1981 fiscal year alone, over 58 percent of all changes in inventory valuation methods made during the five-year period occurred. All inventory valuation changes in 1980/1981 (a total of 21) were changes to LIFO, 16 of which (76 percent) decreased earnings. As inflation tapered off in subsequent years, the frequency of changes in inventory valuation methods decreased dramatically as did the percentage that decreased

earnings. If we look at only the last four years of our study, during the lower inflation years, we find only about 29 percent (15 of 52) were inventory valuation changes and only 53 percent (8 of 15) decreased earnings.

As Exhibit 2 shows, changes in inventory valuation methods were also the most frequent type of discretionary accounting change that Cushing reported in the early 1970s, accounting for approximately 28 percent of the total discretionary accounting changes in his sample.[7]

We found other differences in relative frequency of types of accounting changes. Cushing's results indicated that about 14 percent of discretionary accounting changes were caused by changes in depreciation methods;[8] 12 years later we found that such changes accounted for only about eight percent of discretionary changes. Changes in accounting for the investment tax credit accounted for about 19 percent of the discretionary accounting changes we found but were not a factor in Cushing's study.

One very disturbing observation Cushing made was that in 10 percent of the cases where an accounting change was nondiscretionary and in 16 percent of the cases where an accounting change was discretionary, no approval of or exception to the change was made by the auditor even though it was required.[9] We found much improvement in this area, as shown in Exhibit 2. In only five percent of the nondiscretionary changes and four percent of the discretionary changes was the required au-

---

[5] Ibid. Calculated from Exhibit 4, p. 57.

[6] Cushing treated the early application of an accounting standard before it is required as a nondiscretionary change. We followed the same procedure in our study.

[7] Ibid. Calculated from Exhibits 3 and 4, pp. 56–57.

[8] Ibid. Calculated from Exhibit 2, p. 56.

[9] Ibid., p. 57.

EXHIBIT 2 *Results from Our Study Compared with Cushing's*

	Cushing		May & Schneider	
	%	n	%	n
Percentage of Changes That Were[a]				
Discretionary	61	43	45	78
Nondiscretionary	39	27	55	96
Percentage of Discretionary Changes That Were[a]				
Inventory valuation	28	12	46	36
Depreciation methods	14	6	8	6
Pension cost	5	2	9	7
Consolidation policy	9	4	1	1
Valuing subsidiary investments	7	3	1	1
Investment tax credit	0	0	19	15
Other	37	16	16	12
Percentage of Reports Containing Accounting Changes Without Approval or Exception Comment by Auditors[b]				
Discretionary	16	4	4	3
Nondiscretionary	10	5	5	5
Percentage of All Accounting Changes for Which No Justification Was Given[b]	17	13	7	12
Percentage of All Accounting Changes Increasing Earnings[a]	54	38	59	102

[a]To examine trends, Cushing drew a random sample of 100 Fortune 500 firms for a four-year period and found a total of 70 individual changes made. Percentages for Cushing's work were calculated from Exhibits 1, 2, and 4 in his article, from his comments on page 55, and from a review of *APB Opinions*, AICPA industry accounting guides, etc., for the periods involved.

[b]To examine the impact of *APB Opinion No. 20* Cushing examined all Fortune 500 firms for 1972, which resulted in 77 current accounting changes (25 discretionary and 52 nondiscretionary).

ditor approval of or exception to the change missing.

We also found great improvement overall in compliance with the requirement to give justification for the change. In the early 1970s Cushing found that if both discretionary and nondiscretionary accounting changes were considered, about 17 percent of the time no reason for the accounting change was given.[10] In our recent study we found

[10]Ibid., p. 58.

that justification was missing only seven percent of the time. This finding shows substantial improvement if both discretionary and nondiscretionary accounting changes are considered; if only discretionary changes are considered, however, justification is lacking about 13 percent of the time.

Effects on Reported Earnings

Exhibit 4 shows that the effect of most changes was to increase reported earnings. Over the five-year period about 59

EXHIBIT 3 *Types of Discretionary Accounting Changes for Fortune 500 Companies and Subsidiaries*

	Fiscal Year Ends Between July and June						
	80/81	81/82	82/83	83/84	84/85	Total	%
Inventory valuation	21	9	3		3	36	46.2
Depreciation	2			3	1	6	7.7
Pension cost	1		1	2	3	7	8.9
Investment tax credit		6	4	1	4	15	19.2
Fiscal year	1					1	1.3
Accruals and deferrals			2	1	2	5	6.4
Capitalization vs. expensing			2	2		4	5.1
Consolidation policy				1		1	1.3
Valuing subsidiary investments				1		1	1.3
Expensing vs. inventorying	1			1		2	2.6
Total	26	15	12	12	13	78	100.0

percent of all discretionary accounting changes increased reported earnings and the rate during the last four years is even higher. Ninety-two percent (22 of 24) of all discretionary changes that decreased income in 1980/1981 and 1981/1982 are the result of changes in inventory valuation methods. Aside from these changes in the first two years, which were mostly attributable to changing to LIFO, the remainder of the discretionary changes during the five-year period were dominated by those changes that increased income. In fact, 86 percent of the discretionary changes with a material effect reported during the last three years of the study increased reported earnings.

Of perhaps even greater significance than the direction of the effect on earnings is the materiality of the changes as measured by their relative magnitude. To examine materiality, we calculated the percentage impact on earnings in the year of the accounting change (the percentage increase or decrease in earnings) for all the discretionary changes that had a determinable impact, 75 in all. The results are summarized in Exhibit 5. Note that as the percentage effect on earnings increases, the percentage of total accounting changes which are positive increases from 53 percent in the lower quartile to 86 percent in the top quartile. Statistical tests indicate that this pattern of positive and negative effects of accounting changes is extremely unlikely to be the result of chance.[11]

The results suggest that Fortune 500 firms as a whole are more likely to undertake accounting changes having material positive earnings effects than ac-

---

[11] We used the Van Der Waerden nonparametric test to compare the population distributions of positive and negative earnings effects of the accounting changes. Our results suggested that the two populations have statistically different distributions. These results were significant at the .0103 level. To confirm the results of the Van Der Waerden test we also conducted a Wilcoxon rank sum test. Again the results indicated that the two populations do not have the same distributions. This time the results were significant at the .0114 level.

EXHIBIT 4 *Earnings Effect of Discretionary Accounting Changes for Fortune 500 Companies and Subsidiaries*

Direction of Change Effect on Income for Current Year	Fiscal Year Ends Between July and June					
	80/81	81/82	82/83	83/84	84/85	Total
Increase	7 (26.9%)	9 (60.0%)	10 (83.3%)	10 (83.3%)	10 (76.9%)	46 (59.0%)
Decrease	18 (69.2%)	6 (40.0%)	2 (16.7%)		3 (23.1%)	29 (37.2%)
No effect, immaterial or not properly disclosed[a]	1 (3.8%)			2 (16.7%)		3 (3.8%)
Total	26	15	12	12	13	78

[a]Either there was no effect, the effect was immaterial, or the magnitude was either omitted entirely or not clearly stated.

EXHIBIT 5 *Relative Positive and Negative Effect on Earnings of Discretionary Accounting Changes*

Percentage Effect on Earnings	Positive Changes		Negative Changes		Total Changes
	No.	% Total Changes	No.	% Total Changes	
0–25%	28	53	25	47	53
26%–50%	8	80	2	20	10
51%–75%	4	80	1	20	5
75% and greater	6	86	1	14	7
	46		29		75

counting changes having material negative earnings effects.

Credibility Problems

If management clearly follows GAAP and changes accounting procedures only because the new method provides more representationally faithful results, we should expect a more nearly equal occurrence of positive and negative effects on net income. Perhaps the lack of such a finding would not be a big concern if the justification for changes given by management were more complete and more convincing. Yet, when justification is given, it is usually phrased in such vague or general terms as to raise suspicion rather than assuage it.

As indicated in Exhibit 6, by far the most prevalent justifications are typified by statements such as "to better conform to the matching process" or "to conform to industry practice." Neither of these statements is sufficiently informative. While each may technically conform to the disclosure requirement, of GAAP, it is hard to defend either as conforming to the spirit of that requirement.

Indeed, an accounting change, if made to represent transactions and events more faithfully, will probably do a better job of matching. However, without more substantive disclosure of the nature of change in the transactions or events, a vaguely worded claim that better matching will result, as is evident in almost 53 percent of all discretionary changes in our sample, may raise suspicion about management's real motivation. This is particularly true if the accounting change results in higher reported earnings.

Conformance to industry practice has become a major justification for making accounting changes. It was the reason given in 19 percent of all discretionary cases we looked at.

An accounting change made to "conform to industry practice" is particularly bothersome because the justification suggests that no change in transactions or events has taken place but that the change has been made because other similar companies use the new method. Indeed, there is not even a pretense that the new method more faithfully represents transactions and events, for if that were the case, we could expect a better justification to be given; at the very least, we could expect a claim that better matches results. Seemingly, we must conclude that the change was made without regard to the representational faithfulness criteria in order to achieve

EXHIBIT 6 *Managerial Justification for Discretionary Accounting Changes*

	Fiscal Year Ends Between July and June					
	80/81	81/82	82/83	83/84	84/85	Total
Matching principle	16	7	6	6	6	41 (52.3%)
Conformity to industry practice	3	5	3		4	15 (19.2%)
More accurate reflections of operations and capital investments	2			2		4 (5.1%)
More accurate and consistent valuing of inventory	2			1		3 (3.8%)
More appropriate depreciation method	1			1		2 (2.6%)
Change in foreign tax laws		2				2 (2.6%)
Due to a seasonal product line's increased importance					1	1 (1.3%)
No justification given	2	1	3	2	2	10 (12.8%)
Total	26	15	12	12	13	78 (99.7%)[a]

[a] 0.3 percent rounding error.

other ends, and that perhaps only coincidentally does better matching or more representational faithfulness occur.

Often a statement is included that such a change to conform to industry practice makes comparisons with other companies in the industry more valid. Comparability may be improved, but only if the change is to a method that is judged to be at least equal to the old method in representational faithfulness. Otherwise, the additional "comparability" gained is perhaps imaginary. And why hasn't management used the more commonly used method before? Again, without more substantive disclosure of justification for the change, the evidence concerning timing of implementation and effect on earnings of accounting changes only increases suspicion about management's intent.

Changes made to conform to industry practice may at times be truly justified on the basis of comparability, but the manner and circumstances under which such justification is given in practice certainly does very little to foster credibility.

Conclusion

Evidence suggests that management's primary motivation in making discretionary accounting changes is not to reflect economic flows more accurately, but rather to manage reported earnings. It is probably true that the evidence does not tell the whole story—that in many instances there may be a difference between fact and appearance. But the accounting profession is no stranger to the fact versus appearance argument—that debate has been the concern of auditors for years when assessing the issue of independence. We as a profession recognize that credibility depends upon appearances more than fact.

Credibility must be the overriding issue in financial reporting as well as in auditing. Without credibility the reporting process is ineffectual. Regardless of whether the apparent problems with accounting changes are fact or mere appearance, to preserve credibility we need to change practice. If the problem is one only of appearance, better disclosure is called for. At a minimum, more convincing justification of discretionary accounting changes should be required; general claims of better matching or representational faithfulness should not be allowed without further convincing explanation. If the problem is one of fact, we need to find a mechanism to ensure that the concepts upon which generally accepted accounting principles are based are followed—that financial reporting alternatives are indeed chosen with representational faithfulness in mind. More specific disclosure requirements may be sufficient to provide this mechanism. If such disclosure requirements are not sufficient, it may be desirable to require some specific criteria to be met before an accounting change is allowed. In either case, the accounting profession should provide additional guidelines for practice.

Cases

• Case 4-1

The Borak Company has $4,200,000 of income prior to selecting its methods of calculating cost of goods sold, bad debts, and depreciation. Three generally accepted alternatives exist by which to account for each of these expenses as follows:

Cost of goods sold

FIFO	$1,600,000
Average	$1,700,000
LIFO	$1,800,000

Depreciation

SL	$ 200,000
SYD	$ 300,000
DDB	$ 400,000

Bad Debts

Direct write-off	$ 100,000
% Sales	$ 150,000
% AR	$ 200,000

Required:
a. Make a selection from each of the above expenses and calculate net income for Borak. (*Note:* Ignore income tax considerations and any auditor constraints that might arise from changing accounting principles.)

b. Address the following question.
   i. Was your selection based on achieving the highest net income figure?
   ii. Justify the use of each of the three practices you selected.
   iii. All companies must make choices similar to these for a variety of transactions. How can the investing public compare firms that use different accounting practices?
   iv. Is it likely that the selection of alternative practices you selected will have the same results on income in the future? Discuss.
   v. Does the existence of these and other alternatives allow management to mislead the securities market?
   vi. Should accounting treatment alternatives continue to exist?

● **Case 4-2**

The motion picture industry has undergone a significant change during the past four decades. Originally, companies such as Paramount Pictures had to rely solely on domestic and foreign screenings of their movies for their revenues. The birth of the television industry in the 1950s resulted in opportunities for broadcasting rights to networks and individual stations. Moreover, the introduction of cable television in the 1970s opened up substantial new sources of revenue. Additionally, the unsaturated demand for new films resulted in a market for "made for television" films. Finally, the invention of the video recorder opened another revenue source for these companies.

The production of a film involves four phases.

1. The acquisition of the story rights.
2. Preproduction including script development, set design, cost selection, costume design, and selection of a filming location.
3. The actual filming.
4. Postproduction including film editing, adding the musical score and special effects.

Warmen Brothers Production Company has just finished the production of "Absence of Forethought," a movie expected to be successfully distributed to all available markets.

Required:
a. What markets are available to Warmen Brothers for this film?
b. In what order would you suggest Warmen Brothers attempt to enter each market? Why?
c. How should revenues be recognized from each market?
d. How should costs be matched against these revenues?
e. What effect will your decisions have on Warmen Brothers income statements for the years revenue is recognized?

Note: You may wish to consult *FASB Statement No. 53*, "Financial Reporting by Producers and Distributors of Motion Picture Films."

• **Case 4-3**

Goods Company is a major manufacturer of foodstuffs whose products are sold in grocery and convenience stores throughout the United States. The company's name is well known and respected because its products have been marketed nationally for over 50 years.

In April 1996 the company was forced to recall one of its major products. A total of 35 persons in Chicago were treated for severe intestinal pain, and eventually 3 people died from complications. All of the people had consumed Goods' product.

The product causing the problem was traced to one specific lot. Goods keeps samples from all lots of foodstuffs. After thorough testing, Goods and the legal authorities confirmed that the product had been tampered with after it had left the company's plant and was no longer under the company's control.

All of the product was recalled from the market—the only time a Goods product has been recalled nationally and the only time for tampering. Persons who still had the product in their homes, even though it was not from the affected lot, were encouraged to return the product for credit or refund. A media campaign was designed and implemented by the company to explain what had happened and what the company was doing to minimize any chance of recurrence. Goods decided to continue the product with the same trade name and same wholesale price. However, the packaging was redesigned completely to be tamper resistant and safety sealed. This required the purchase and installation of new equipment.

The corporate accounting staff recommended that the costs associated with the tampered product be treated as an extraordinary charge on the 1996 financial statements. Corporate accounting was asked to identify the various costs that could be associated with the tampered product and related recall. These costs ($000 omitted) are as follows.

1. Credits and refunds to stores and consumers	$30,000
2. Insurance to cover lost sales and idle plant costs for possible future recalls	5,000
3. Transportation costs and off-site warehousing of returned product	1,000
4. Future security measures for other products	4,000
5. Testing of returned product and inventory	700
6. Destroying returned product and inventory	2,400
7. Public relations program to reestablish brand credibility	4,200
8. Communication program to inform customers, answer inquiries, prepare press releases, etc.	1,600
9. Higher cost arising from new packaging	700
10. Investigation of possible involvement of employees, former employees, competitors, etc.	500
11. Packaging redesign and testing	2,000
12. Purchase and installation of new packaging equipment	6,000

| 13. Legal costs for defense against liability suits | 600 |
| 14. Lost sales revenue due to recall | 32,000 |

Goods' estimated earnings before income taxes and before consideration of any of the above items for the year ending December 31, 1996, are $230 million.

Required

a. Goods Company plans to recognize the costs associated with the product tampering and recall as an extraordinary charge.
   i. Explain why Goods could classify this occurrence as an extraordinary charge.
   ii. Describe the placement and terminology used to present the extraordinary charge in the 1996 income statement.
b. Refer to the 14 cost items identified by the corporate accounting staff of Goods Company.
   i. Identify the cost items by number that should be included in the extraordinary charge for 1996.
   ii. For any item that is not included in the extraordinary charge, explain why it would not be included in the extraordinary charge.

(CMA adapted)

• Case 4-4

Over the years, two types of income statements based on differing views of the concept of income have been advocated by accountants. These types have been termed the *current operating performance* and *all-inclusive* concepts of income.

Required:

a. Discuss the general nature of these two concepts of income.
b. How would the following items be handled under each concept?
   i. Cost of goods sold
   ii. Selling expenses
   iii. Extraordinary items
   iv. Prior period adjustments

• Case 4-5

It is important in accounting theory to be able to distinguish the types of accounting changes.

Required:

a. If a public company desires to change from the sum-of-the-years'-digits depreciation method to the straight-line method for its fixed assets, what type of accounting change would this be? How would it be treated? Discuss the permissibility of this change.
b. When pro-forma disclosure is required for an accounting change, how are these pro-forma amounts determined?
c. If a public company obtained additional information about the service lives of some of its fixed assets that showed that the service lives previously

used should be shortened, what type of accounting change would this be? Include in your discussion how the change should be reported in the income statement of the year of the change, and what disclosures should be made in the financial statements or notes.

d. Changing specific subsidiaries comprising the group of companies for which consolidated financial statements are presented is an example of what type of accounting change, and what effect does it have on the consolidated income statements?

• Case 4-6

Progresso Corporation, a new audit client of yours, has not reported earnings per share data in its annual reports to stockholders in the past. The president requested that you furnish information about the reporting of earnings per share data in the current year's annual report in accordance with generally accepted accounting principles.

Required:

a. Define the term *earnings per share* as it applies to a corporation with a capitalization structure composed of only one class of common stock and explain how earnings per share should be computed and how the information should be disclosed in the corporation's financial statements.

b. Explain the meanings of the terms *senior securities* and *residual securities,* which are often used in discussing earnings per share, and give examples of the types of items that each term includes.

c. Discuss the treatment, if any, that should be given to each of the following items in computing earnings per share of common stock for financial statement reporting.

   i. The declaration of current dividends on cumulative preferred stock.

   ii. The acquisition of some of the corporation's outstanding common stock during the current fiscal year. The stock was classified as treasury stock.

   iii. A two-for-one stock split of common stock during the current fiscal year.

   iv. A provision created out of retained earnings for a contingent liability from a possible lawsuit.

   v. Outstanding preferred stock issued at a premium with a par value liquidation right.

   vi. The exercise at a price below market value but above book value of a common stock option issued during the current fiscal year to officers of the corporation.

   vii. The replacement of a machine immediately before the close of the current fiscal year at a cost 20 percent above the original cost of the replaced machine. The new machine will perform the same function as the old machine, which was sold for its book value.

• Case 4-7

The unaudited quarterly statements of income issued by many corporations to their stockholders are usually prepared on the same basis as annual statements, the statement for each quarter reflecting the transactions of that quarter.

Required:
a. Why do problems arise in using such quarterly statements to predict the income (before extraordinary items) for the year? Explain.
b. Discuss the ways in which quarterly income can be affected by the behavior of the costs recorded in a *repairs and maintenance of factory machinery* account.
c. Do such quarterly statements give management opportunities to manipulate the results of operations for a quarter? If so, explain or give an example.

● **Case 4-8**

The controller of Navar Corporation wants to issue to stockholders quarterly income statements that will be predictive of expected annual results. He proposes to allocate all fixed costs for the year among quarters in proportion to the number of units expected to be sold in each quarter, stating that the annual income can then be predicted through use of the following equation:

annual income =

$$\text{quarterly income} \times \frac{100\%}{\text{percentage of unit sales applicable to quarter}}$$

Navar expects the following activity for the year.

	Units	Average per Unit	Total (in $1,000s)
Sales revenue:			
First quarter	500,000	$2.00	$1,000
Second quarter	100,000	1.50	150
Third quarter	200,000	2.00	400
Fourth quarter	200,000	2.00	400
	1,000,000		
Costs to be incurred:			
Variable:			
Manufacturing		$0.70	700
Selling and administrative		0.25	250
		$0.95	950
Fixed:			
Manufacturing			380
Selling and administrative			220
			600
Income before income taxes			$ 400

Required:
Ignore income taxes in answering the following questions.
a. Assuming that Navar's activities do not vary from expectations, will the controller's plan achieve his objective? If not, how can it be modified to do so? Explain and give illustrative computations.
b. How should the effect of variations of actual activity from expected activity be treated in Navar's quarterly income statements?
c. What assumption has the controller made in regard to inventories? Discuss.

• Case 4-9

Accounting Principles Board Opinion No. 20 is concerned with accounting changes.

Required:
a. Define, discuss, and illustrate each of the following in such a way that one can be distinguished from the other:
   i. An accounting change
   ii. A correction of an error in previously issued financial statements
b. Discuss the justification for a change in accounting principle.
c. Discuss the reporting (as required by *Accounting Principles Board Opinion No. 20*) of a change from the LIFO method to another method of inventory pricing.

• Case 4-10

Sometimes a business entity may change its method of accounting for certain items. The change may be classified as a change in accounting principle, a change in accounting estimate, or a change in reporting entity. Listed below are three independent, unrelated sets of facts relating to accounting changes.

Situation 1
A company determined that the depreciable lives of its fixed assets are presently too long to fairly match the cost of the fixed assets with the revenue produced. The company decided at the beginning of the current year to reduce the depreciable lives of all its existing fixed assets by five years.

Situation 2
On December 31, 1995, Gary Company owned 51 percent of Allen Company, at which time Gary reported its investment using the cost method due to political uncertainties in the country in which Allen was located. On January 2, 1996, the management of Gary Company was satisfied that the political uncertainties were resolved and the assets of the company were in no danger of nationalization. Accordingly, Gary will prepare consolidated financial statements for Gary and Allen for the year ended December 31, 1996.

Situation 3
A company decides in January 1995 to adopt the straight-line method of depreciation for plant equipment. The straight-line method will be used for new acquisitions as well as for previously acquired plant equipment for which depreciation had been provided on an accelerated basis.

Required:
For each of the preceding situations, provide the information indicated below. Complete your discussion of each situation before going on to the next situation.
a. Type of accounting change
b. Manner of reporting the change under current generally accepted accounting principles, including a discussion, where applicable, of how amounts are computed
c. Effects of the change on the statement of financial position and earnings statement
d. Footnote disclosures that would be necessary

• Case 4-11

Morgan Company grows various crops and then processes them for sale to retailers. Morgan has changed its depreciation method for its processing equipment from the double-declining balance method to the straight-line method effective January 1 of this year. This method has been determined to be preferable.

In the latter part of this year, Morgan had a large portion of its crops destroyed by a hailstorm. Morgan has incurred substantial costs in raising the crops destroyed by the hailstorm. Severe damage from hailstorms in the locality where the crops are grown is rare.

Required:
a. How should Morgan report and calculate the effect of this change in accounting principle relative to the depreciation method in this year's income statement? Do not discuss earnings per share requirements.
b. Where should Morgan report the effects of the hailstorm in its income statement? Why?
c. How does the classification in the income statement of an extraordinary item differ from that of an operating item? Why? Do not discuss earnings per share requirements.

• Case 4-12

David Company's statements of income for the year ended December 31, 1996 and December 31, 1995, are presented below. Additional facts are as follows:

DAVID COMPANY
STATEMENTS OF INCOME

	Year Ended December 31	
	1996	1995
	(000 omitted)	
Net sales	$900,000	$750,000
Costs and expenses:		
Cost of goods sold	720,000	600,000
Selling, general and administrative expenses	112,000	90,000
Other, net	11,000	9,000
Total costs and expenses	843,000	699,000
Income from continuing operations before income taxes	57,000	51,000
Income taxes	23,000	24,000
Income from continuing operations	34,000	27,000
Loss on disposal of Dex Division, including provision of $1,500,000 for operating losses during phase-out period, less applicable income taxes of $8,000,000	8,000	—
Cumulative effect on prior years of change in depreciation method, less applicable income taxes of $1,500,000	—	3,000
Net income	$ 26,000	$ 30,000
Earnings per share of common stock:		
Income before cumulative effect of change in depreciation method	$ 2.60	$ 2.70
Cumulative effect on prior years of change in depreciation method, less applicable income taxes	—	.30
Net income	$ 2.60	$ 3.00

- On January 1, 1995 David Company changed its depreciation method for previously recorded plant machinery from the double-declining-balance method to the straight-line method. The effect of applying the straight-line method for the year of and the year after the change is included in David Company's statements of income for the year ended December 31, 1996, and December 31, 1995 in "cost of goods sold."

- The loss from operations of the discontinued Dex Division from January 1, 1996, to September 30, 1996 (the portion of the year prior to the measurement date), and from January 1, 1995, to December 31, 1995, is included in David Company's statements of income for the year ended December 31, 1996, and December 31, 1995, respectively, in "other, net."

- David Company has a simple capital structure with only common stock outstanding, and the net income per share of common stock was based on the weighted average number of common shares outstanding during each year.
- David Company common stock is listed on the New York Stock Exchange and closed at $13 per share on December 31, 1996, and $15 per share on December 31, 1995.

Required:
Determine from the preceding additional facts whether the presentation of those facts in David Company's statements of income is appropriate. If the presentation is appropriate, discuss the theoretical rationale for the presentation. If the presentation is not appropriate, specify the appropriate presentation and discuss its theoretical rationale.

Do not discuss disclosure requirements for the notes to the financial statements.

Recommended Additional Readings

Bernstein, Leopold A. "Extraordinary Gains and Losses—Their Significance to the Financial Analyst." *Financial Analysts Journal* (November–December 1972), pp. 49–52, 88–90.

Boyer, Patricia A., and Charles H. Gibson. "How About Earnings Per Share?" *The CPA Journal* (February 1979), pp. 36–41.

Coughlan, John W. "Anomalies in Calculating Earnings Per Share." *Accounting Horizons* (December 1988), pp. 80–88.

Cushing, Barry E. "Accounting Changes: The Impact of APB Opinion No. 20." *Journal of Accountancy* (November 1974), pp. 54–62.

Dudley, Lola Woodard. "A Critical Look at EPS." *Journal of Accountancy* (August 1985), pp. 102–111.

Jaenicke, Henry R., and Joseph Rascoff. "Segment Disposition: Implementing APB Opinion No. 30." *Journal of Accountancy* (April 1974), pp. 63–69.

Nurnberg, Hugo. "Annual and Interim Financial Reporting of Changes in Accounting Estimates." *Accounting Horizons* (September 1988), pp. 15–25.

Rapaccioli, Donna, and Allen Schiff. "Reporting Sales of Segments Under APB Opinion No. 30." *Accounting Horizons* (December 1991), pp. 53–68.

Bibliography

Barton, M. Frank, William B. Carper, and Thomas S. O'Conner. "Chartered Financial Analysts Speak Out in the Need and Information Content of Interim Financial Reports." *The Ohio CPA* (Winter 1979), pp. 28–32.

Beresford, Dennis R. "Understanding the New Rules for Interim Financial Reporting." *The Ohio CPA* (Winter 1975), pp. 27–35.

Beresford, Dennis R., and Earl J. Elbert. "Reporting Discontinued Operations." *The Ohio CPA* (Spring 1974), pp. 56–65.

Berstein, Leopold A. "Reporting the Results of Operations—A Reassessment of APB Opinion No. 9." *Journal of Accountancy* (July 1970), pp. 57–61.

Bows, Albert J., Jr., and Arthur R. Wyatt. "Improving Interim Financial Reporting." *Journal of Accountancy* (October 1973), pp. 54–59.

Brown, Lawrence D. "Accounting Changes and the Accuracy of Analysts' Earnings Forecasts." *Journal of Accounting Research* (Autumn 1983), pp. 432–443.

Curry, Dudley W. "Opinion 15 vs. a Comprehensive Financial Reporting Method for Convertible Debt." *The Accounting Review* (July 1971), pp. 495–503.

Deming, John R. "New Guidelines for Extraordinary Items." *The CPA Journal* (February 1974), pp. 21–26.

Eisenman, Seymour, Murray S. Akresh, and Charles Snow. "Reporting Unusual Events in Income Statements." *The CPA Journal* (June 1979), pp. 23–27.

Gibson, Charles H., and John Daniel Williams. "Should Common Stock Equivalents Be Considered in Earnings per Share?" *The CPA Journal* (March 1973), pp. 209–213.

Greipel, Rudolph C. "Review of APB Opinion No. 20—Accounting Changes." *The CPA Journal* (January 1972), pp. 17–24.

Hopwood, William S., and James C. McKeown. "The Incremental Informational Content of Interim Expenses over Interim Sales." *Journal of Accounting Research* (Spring 1985), pp. 161–174.

Kahn, Nathan, and Allen Schiff. "Tangible Equity Changes and the Evolution of the FASB's Definition of Income." *Journal of Accounting Auditing and Finance* (Fall 1985), pp. 40–49.

Knutson, Peter H. "Income Distribution: The Key to Earnings per Share." *The Accounting Review* (January 1970), pp. 55–58.

Koons, Robert L. "Changes in Interim Reports Are Coming." *Financial Executive* (July 1978), pp. 48–54.

Lambert, Richard A. "Income Smoothing as Rational Equilibrium Behavior." *The Accounting Review* (October 1984), pp. 604–618.

Matulich, Serge, Loren A. Nikolai, and Steven K. Olson. "Earnings Per Share: A Flowchart Approach to Teaching Concepts and Procedures." *The Accounting Review* (January 1977), pp. 233–247.

Miller, Jerry D. "Accounting for Warrants and Convertible Bonds." *Management Accounting* (January 1973), pp. 26–28.

Miller, Rene A. "Interim Financial Accounting and Reporting—Review of APB Opinion No. 28." *The CPA Journal* (September 1973), pp. 755–761.

Nichols, Donald R. "The Never-to-Recur Unusual Item—A Critique of APB Opinion No. 30." *The CPA Journal* (March 1974), pp. 45–48.

Pacter, Paul A. "APB Opinion No. 15: Some Basic Examples." *The New York Certified Public Accountant* (August 1970), pp. 638–646.

Rhodes, Lola, and H. J. Snavely. "Convertible Bonds and Earnings Per Share." *The CPA Journal* (December 1973), pp. 1116–1119.

Ricks, William E., and John S. Hughes. "Market Reactions to a Non-Discretionary Accounting Change: The Case of Long-Term Investments." *The Accounting Review* (January 1985), pp. 33–52.

Savage, Linda, and Joel Siegel. "Disposal of a Segment of a Business." *The CPA Journal* (September 1978), pp. 32–37.

Schiff, Michael. "Accounting Reporting Problems—Interim Financial Statement." New York: Financial Executives Research Foundation, 1978.

Werner, G. Frank, and Jerry J. Weygandt. "Convertible Debt and Earnings Per Share: Pragmatism vs. Good Theory." *The Accounting Review* (April 1970), pp. 280–289.

Financial Statements II: The Balance Sheet and the Statement of Cash Flows

Financial reports can be divided into two categories. The first category discloses the results of the flow of resources over time and includes the income statement, the statement of retained earnings, and the statement of cash flows. The second category summarizes the status of resources at a particular point in time.

These two categories suggest an important distinction in measurement emphasis between *flows* and *stocks*. Flows are productive services that must be measured over some period of time, whereas stocks are resources that are measured at a particular point in time. The emphasis on the income statement in recent years is frequently based on the assumption that flows are more important than stocks. This assumption has resulted in the measurement of stocks at residual values. A measurement technique that emphasized the balance sheet would be based on the assumption that flows should be measured only when the characteristics of specific assets and liabilities have changed, and the FASB's recent embracement of the asset-liability approach indicates that changes in asset and liability valuations are becoming more important in income determination.

Accounting is the means by which management reports to various users of financial information. The evaluation of the financial position of a business enterprise is an important factor for satisfying the needs of creditors, stockholders, management, the government, and other interested parties. Management attempts to satisfy these needs by presenting information on resources, obligations, and equities of the company at periodic intervals.

213

In this chapter we will first discuss the balance sheet and the measurement techniques currently used to disclose assets, liabilities, and equity. In so doing, there is no presumption on our part that current stock measurement techniques provide enough relevant information to the users of financial statements; rather, we believe a thorough examination of these techniques will disclose their inherent limitations. Later in the chapter, we will discuss the evolution of the third major financial statement from the statement of changes in financial position to the statement of cash flows.

The Balance Sheet

The balance sheet should disclose the wealth of a company at a point in time. *Wealth* is defined as the present value of all resources less the present value of all obligations. However, as noted earlier, the use of present value measurement techniques in accounting is limited; and a variety of methods are currently used to measure changes in the individual components of the elements of the balance sheet. These measurement techniques can be summarized as past oriented—historical; current oriented—replacement amounts; and future oriented—expected amounts.

Over the years, accounting theorists have debated the merits of using each of these measurement techniques. Those favoring historical cost base their argument on the premise that cost is objective and verifiable. Historical cost is not based on subjective estimations; rather it is the result of the value buyers and sellers have agreed to in an ''arm's length'' transaction. Some accounting theorists have even suggested that historical cost actually represents the present value of expected future cash flows at the time the exchange takes place. It is also argued that accountants serve a stewardship role, and because cost measures actual resources exchanged, it is relevant to readers of financial statements. Opponents of historical cost maintain that values may change over time and, consequently, that historical cost can loose its relevance as a valuation base.

Those favoring current cost measurement hold that this value reflects current conditions, and, therefore, represents the current value to the firm. Opponents point out that current values may not be available for all balance sheet elements, and that recording current values on the balance sheet would result in recording unrealized gain and losses on the income statement.

Those favoring expected future values maintain that this valuation procedure approximates the economic concept of income and is, therefore, the most relevant value to the users of financial statements. Critics of expected future value point out (as noted in Chapter 3) that the future cash flows associated with the elements of the balance sheet are difficult to estimate, the timing of these cash flows is uncertain, and an appropriate discount rate is difficult to ascertain.

In the following paragraphs we will look more closely at the measurement techniques actually used to value the balance sheet elements. This review will reveal that no single measurement basis is used for all of the elements; rather a variety of measurement techniques are currently acceptable depending on the circumstances and available information.

Balance Sheet Elements

The *Financial Accounting Standards Board Statement of Concepts No. 6* defined the elements of the balance sheet as:

> **Assets**   *Assets are probable future economic benefits obtained or controlled by a particular entity as a result of past transactions or events. An asset has three essential characteristics: (1) it embodies a probable future benefit that involves a capacity, singly or in combination with other assets, to contribute directly or indirectly to future net cash inflows; (2) a particular enterprise can obtain the benefit and control others' access to it; and (3) the transaction or other event giving rise to the enterprise's right to or control of the benefit has already occurred.*

> **Liabilities**   *Liabilities are probable future sacrifices of economic benefits arising from present obligations of a particular entity to transfer assets or provide services to other entities in the future as a result of past transactions or events. A liability has three essential characteristics: (1) it embodies a present duty or responsibility to one or more other entities that entails settlement by probable future transfer or use of assets at a specified or determinable date, on occurrence of a specified event, or on demand; (2) the duty or responsibility obligates a particular enterprise, leaving it little or no discretion to avoid the future sacrifice; and (3) the transaction or other event obligating the enterprise has already happened.*

> **Equity**   *Equity is the residual interest in the assets of an entity that remains after deducting its liabilities. In a business enterprise, the equity is the ownership interest. Equity in a business enterprise stems from ownership rights (or the equivalent). It involves a relation between an enterprise and its owners as owners rather than as employees, suppliers, customers, lenders, or in some other nonowner role.*[1]

These definitions form the basis of the FASB's asset–liability approach that is prevalent in many subsequent standards. They represent a departure from previous definitions that viewed the balance sheet as a statement of residual amounts whose values were frequently arrived at through income determination. For example, consider the definitions of assets and liabilities presented by the Accounting Principles Board in *Statement No. 4*:

> *(assets are) economic resources of an enterprise that are recognized and measured in conformity with generally accepted accounting principles including certain deferred charges that are not resources.*[2]

[1] *Financial Accounting Standards Board Statement of Concepts No. 6*, "Elements of Financial Statements of Business Enterprises" (Stamford, Conn.: FASB, 1985), pars. 25, 26, 35, 36, and 49.

[2] *Accounting Principles Board Statement No. 4*, "Basic Concepts and Accounting Principles Underlying Financial Statements of Business Enterprises" (AICPA, 1970), par. 132.

> *(liabilities are) economic obligations of an enterprise that are recognized and measured in conformity with generally accepted accounting principles.*[3]

That is, deferred charges, which result from unexpired costs not charged to expense, are assets; and liabilities are created because of the necessity to record debits.

Even with their limitations, the APB definitions were believed to be significant improvements over previous definitions when they were released. Prior to that time assets had been defined as debit balances carried forward when the books were closed, and liabilities were defined as credit balances carried forward, except those representing owners' equity.[4]

The preceding *SFAC No. 6* definitions should be carefully examined. They assert that assets are economic resources of an enterprise and that liabilities are economic obligations of an enterprise. These statements probably correspond to most users' understanding of the terms *assets* and *liabilities* and, therefore, they are not likely to be misunderstood. However, in order to properly understand the numbers presented on a balance sheet, the user must be aware of the recognition and measurement procedures associated with generally accepted accounting principles. These procedures are a combination of past, present, and future measurement techniques.

In addition, it has been considered more informative to provide subclassifications for each of these balance sheet elements. This classification scheme makes information more easily attainable to the various interested user groups and allows for more rapid identification of specific types of information for decision making. In general, the following classification scheme may be viewed as representative of the typical balance sheet presentation.

Assets
Current assets
Investments
Property, plant, and equipment
Intangible assets
Other assets

Liabilities
Current liabilities
Long-term liabilities
Other liabilities

Stockholders' Equity
Capital stock
Additional paid-in capital
Retained earnings

In the following paragraphs we examine each of the components of the balance sheet and discuss the accounting principles currently being used in measuring these components.

---

[3] Ibid., par. 132.

[4] *Accounting Terminology Bulletin No. 1*, "Review and Resume" (AICPA, 1953), pars. 26–27.

Assets

Current Assets

The most commonly encountered definition of current assets was supplied by the Committee on Accounting Procedure. This definition may be summarized as follows: current assets are those assets that may *reasonably be expected* to be realized in cash or sold or consumed during the normal operating cycle of the business or one year, whichever is longer. The operating cycle is defined as the average time it takes to acquire materials, produce the product, sell the product, and collect the proceeds from customers.[5]

Current assets are presented on the balance sheet in order of their liquidity and generally include the following items: cash, cash equivalents, temporary investments, receivables, inventories, and prepaid expenses. Nevertheless, special problems are connected with the valuation procedure for most of these items.

Companies are now required to determine whether temporary investment in debt and equity securities have a readily determinable fair value. If they do not, they are accounted for under the cost method. For those securities that have readily determinable fair values, companies must classify them as trading securities, available-for-sale securities, or in the case of debt, held-to-maturity securities. Trading securities and available-for-sale securities are reported at fair value. Unrealized gains and losses for trading securities are reported in earnings, while unrealized gains and losses for available-for-sale securities are reported as a separate component in stockholders' equity. Debt securities for which management has a positive intent to hold-to-maturity, which are currently classified as temporary, are carried in the balance sheet at amortized cost. Amortized cost implies that premiums or discounts, which arose when the purchase price of the debt security differed from face value, are being amortized over the remaining life of the security. For those debt securities having short terms, for example U.S. treasuries, amortization of premiums and discounts are generally ignored for materiality reasons.

Receivables are generally recorded at amounts that approximate the expected present value of those items, since they are to be consumed in a short period of time. Generally accepted accounting principles dictate that items should not be valued at an amount in excess of their current value. It is considered appropriate to value receivables at their recorded amount less an amount deemed to be uncollectible, or their *expected net realizable value.*

Inventories and prepaid expenses present some additional valuation issues. With the emphasis on net income reporting, the inventory valuation process has become secondary to the matching of expired inventory costs to sales. The use of any of the acceptable inventory flow assumption techniques (e.g., LIFO, FIFO, weighted average discussed in Chapter 6) prescribes the amount that remains on the balance sheet, and it is likely that each of these flow assumptions will result in different inventory valuations in fluctuating

---

[5] *Accounting Research Bulletin No. 43,* "Restatement and Revision of Accounting Research Bulletins" (AICPA, 1953), Chapter 3, par. 5.

market conditions. Additionally, the accounting convention of conservatism requires that a lower of cost or market valuation be used for inventories. In any case, the financial-statement user should interpret the inventory figure as being less than its estimated selling price.

Prepaid items are valued at historical cost with an appropriate amount being charged to expense each year until they are consumed. Prepaid expenses are included under the current asset section because it is argued that if these items had not been paid in advance, they would require the use of current funds. However, the same argument might be made for other assets, and the fact that the lives of many prepaid items encompass several accounting periods does not add to the logic of the argument. It should be noted that prepaid items are not usually material, and perhaps that is where the argument loses its significance.

As can be seen from the previous discussion, two problems arise in attempting to classify an asset as current: (1) the period of time over which it is to be consumed and (2) the proper valuation technique. In many cases historical precedent rather than accounting theory has dictated the inclusion of items as current assets. The valuation procedures associated with each of the items may in themselves be appropriate, but when all items are summed to arrive at a figure termed total current assets, it is difficult to interpret the result. This total approximates the minimum amount of cash that could be collected during the next fiscal period, but leaves to the imagination of the user the actual amount expected to be realized. The issues associated with the valuation of current assets and current liabilities (i.e., working capital) are explored more fully in the next chapter.

Investments

Investments may be divided into three categories.

1. Securities acquired for specific purposes, such as the use of idle funds for long periods or to exercise influence on operations of another company.
2. Assets not currently in use by the business organization, such as land held for a future building site.
3. Special funds to be used for special purposes in the future, such as sinking funds.

The primary factor used in deciding which items to include under the investments caption is *managerial intent*. That is, an organization may own two identical blocks of common stock in another company, but one block may be classified as a current asset because it is anticipated that these shares will be disposed of in the current period, whereas the other block may be classified as an investment because the intention is to retain it for a longer period.

Equity securities acquired to influence the operations of other companies are required to be accounted for by the equity method. This treatment adjusts historical cost for income of the investee and dividends received. As with temporary investments, all other investments in equity securities are accounted for under the cost method when there is no readily determinable fair value for these securities. Those equity securities that have readily determinable fair values and debt securities that are not classified as held-to-maturity, are considered available-for-sale. Long-term available-for-sale securities are treated in the same manner as temporary securities similarly classified. That is, these securities are reported at fair value and unrealized gains and losses are recognized as a separate component of stockholders' equity. Debt securities classified as held-to-maturity—that is, those debt securities that management has positive intent to hold to maturity—are reported at amortized cost.

Property, Plant, and Equipment and Intangibles

Although property, plant, and equipment and intangibles are physically dissimilar assets, the valuation procedures associated with them are similar. Except for land, the cost of these assets is allocated to the various accounting periods benefiting from their use. In the case of property, plant, and equipment, the carrying value is disclosed as the difference between cost and accumulated depreciation. However, intangible assets are generally disclosed at the net amount of their cost less amortization.

These valuation procedures are again the result of the emphasis on income reporting. Various methods of depreciation and amortization are available, but there is no attempt to disclose the current value of long-term assets or the expected future cash flows from holding these assets on the financial statements. The emphasis rather is on a proper matching of revenues and expenses, with asset valuation being the residual effect of this process.

Other Assets

The preceding asset category captions usually will allow for the disclosure of all assets, but some corporations include a final category termed "other assets." Items such as fixed assets held for resale or long-term receivables may be included under this category. The valuation of these items is generally their carrying value on the balance sheet at the time they were originally recorded in the other assets category. Since the amounts associated with these items are usually immaterial, it is unlikely that any alternative valuation procedure would result in a significantly different carrying value.

Asset Valuation

From the preceding discussion it can be seen that many different measurement techniques are used when valuing assets on the typical balance sheet. Under almost any measurement scheme devised, it is common practice to add and subtract only like items measured in the same manner. However, the measurement of assets on the balance sheet takes an unusual form when we consider that sums are derived for subclassifications as well as total assets.

Consider the following measurement bases that are included in a typical balance sheet presentation of assets:

Asset	Measurement Basis
Cash	Current value
Accounts receivable	Expected future value
Marketable securities	Fair value or amortized cost
Inventory	Current or past value
Investments	Fair value or amortized cost
Property, plant, and equipment	Past value adjusted for depreciation

Summing these items is much like adding apples and oranges. If assets are truly economic resources of the firm, it seems plausible to conclude that the totals on the statements should reflect somewhat more than values arrived at by convention. Presentation of information on the expected future benefits to be derived from holding these items would better satisfy user needs.

Liabilities

Current Liabilities

Current liabilities have been defined as "obligations whose liquidation is reasonably expected to require the use of existing resources properly classified as current assets or the creation of other current liabilities."[6] Notice that, although the operating cycle is not explicitly discussed in this definition, it is implied because the definition of current liabilities depends on the definition of current assets. Examples of current liabilities are short-term payables, the currently maturing portion of long-term debt, and accrued liabilities.

Current liabilities are usually measured at liquidation value because their period of existence is relatively short and the satisfaction of these obligations generally involves the payment of cash. Since current liabilities usually require the use of current funds, it might be considered justifiable to offset them against current assets. However, the principle of disclosure requires that they be shown separately unless a specific right of offset exists. *APB Opinion No. 10* emphasized this point in stating: "It is a general principle of accounting that offsetting of assets and liabilities in the balance sheet is improper except where a right of offset exists."[7]

Long-Term and Other Liabilities

Long-term liabilities are those obligations that will not require the use of current assets within the current year or operating cycle. In general, these obligations take the form of bonds, notes, and mortgages and are originally valued at the amount of consideration received by the entity incurring the obligation. A problem exists, however, when this consideration is different from the amount to be repaid. Generally accepted accounting principles dictate that premiums or discounts on long-term obligations should be written off over the life of the obligation to properly reflect the effective interest rate on the debt. In such cases the conventions of realization and matching dictate the balance sheet presentation of long-term liabilities. This is an example of the use of discounted cash flow techniques to measure a balance sheet element.

The long-term liability section also may include long-term prepayments on contracts, deferred income taxes, minority interests in consolidations, and, in some cases, contingent liabilities, each of which has an associated measurement problem. Deferred revenues are measured at their historical cost and retained at that amount until the situation that caused them to be recorded

---

[6] Ibid., Chapter 3, par. 7.

[7] *Accounting Principles Board Opinion No. 10,* "Omnibus Opinion—1966" (New York: AICPA, 1966).

has reversed. Those reversals are dictated by the conventions of realization and matching. Minority interests are recorded at the unowned percentage of equity in a specific subsidiary and are adjusted according to the realization convention. Contingent liabilities, when they are actually recorded on the books, are measured as the best approximation of a future loss that the entity believes is forthcoming on the basis of the convention of conservatism.

Liability Valuation

As with assets, liabilities are measured by a number of different procedures. Most current liabilities are measured by the amount of resources that it will ultimately take to cancel the obligation and ignore the time value of money. Long-term liabilities, on the other hand, are frequently measured by the present value of future payments discounted at the yield rate at the date of issue. In all cases, liability valuations are not changed to reflect current changes in the market rates of interest. The failure to consider the current market interest rates may cause the financial statements to be biased in favor of current creditors, particularly when many obligations are of a long-term nature.

Equity

State laws and corporate articles of incorporation make generalizations about the equity section of the balance sheet somewhat difficult. However, certain practices have become widespread enough to discuss several standards of reporting.

Common Stock

Common stock is measured at historical cost. Initially, most corporations designate a par or stated value for their stock, and as each share of common stock is sold, an amount equal to the par or stated value is reported in the common stock section of the balance sheet. Any differences between selling price and par value are then reported under the caption "additional paid-in capital." These captions have no particular accounting significance except perhaps to determine an average issue price of common stock if such a computation seems meaningful.

Preferred Stock

Many companies also issue other classes of stock termed "preferred." These shares generally have preference as to dividends and a stated amount of dividends must be paid to preferred shareholders before any dividends can be paid to the common stockholders. The measurement basis of preferred stock is similar to that of common stock, with amounts divided between the par value of the shares and additional paid-in capital. Thus, the reported balance sheet amounts also represent historical cost.

Retained Earnings

Ownership interest in a corporation may be defined as the residual interest in the company's assets after the liabilities have been deducted. The recorded amount of retained earnings is clearly associated with the measurement techniques used in recording specific assets and liabilities; however, this amount should not be confused with any attempt to measure the owners' current value interest in the firm. Consequently, the measurement of retained earnings is dependent on the measurement of revenues and cost expirations over the life of the firm.

Most states require that dividends not exceed the balance of retained earnings, and stockholders may wish to have extra dividends distributed when the retained earnings balance becomes relatively large. However, individual entities may have various long-range plans and commitments that do not allow for current distribution of dividends, and firms may provide for the dissemination of this information through an appropriation of retained earnings. This appropriation is termed a *reserve* and is measured by the sum of retained earnings set aside for the stated purpose. It should be emphasized that this appropriation does not provide the cash to finance such projects and is only presented to show managerial intent. This intent might just as easily be disclosed through a footnote.

The measurement of equity can be said to be based primarily on the measurement of specific assets and liabilities. The transfer of assets to expense and the cancellation of liabilities determines the measurement of changes in equity. As such, equity does not have a measurement criterion other than a residual valuation.

Evolution of the Statement of Cash Flows

Prior to 1971, the income statement and the balance sheet were the only financial statements required under generally accepted accounting principles. However, many large firms were including additional financial statements to disclose relevant information needed to make economic decisions. These disclosures were in response to investors, creditors, and others who voiced the desire to receive information on the financing and investing activities of business organizations. One of the additional financial statements that was prepared in response to this need was termed the *funds statement.* This statement reported on the resources provided and the uses to which these resources were put during the reporting period.

Funds statements were not uniformly prepared initially and the method of reporting sources and application of resources depended on the concept of funds preferred by the reporting entity. In general, the concepts of funds used can be categorized as (1) cash, (2) working capital, and (3) all financial resources, although other concepts of funds such as quick assets or net monetary assets may also have been encountered.

Statements using the cash concept of funds summarize all material changes in the cash balance. Therefore, the funds statement becomes, in effect, a statement of cash receipts and disbursements, and the impact of these receipts and disbursements on all other accounts is reported.

Under the working capital definition of funds, all material transactions that result in a change in working capital are reported (working capital being defined as current assets minus current liabilities). When using this concept, *funds* is defined as the amount of increases or decreases in cash, receivables, inventories, payables, and other current items.

Finally, if the all-financial-resources concept is used, the entity reports on the effect of all transactions with outsiders. This concept of funds must be used in conjunction with another concept of funds (e.g., cash, working capital) and includes all items that affect the financing and investing activities of the enterprise. An example of an all-financial-resources transaction that would not appear on a traditional statement prepared using the cash or working capital concepts is the purchase of assets by issuing stock. The advantage of the all-financial-resources concept is its inclusion of all transactions that are important items in the financial administration of the entity.

APB Opinions No. 3 and No. 19

In 1963 the Accounting Principles Board noted the increased attention that had been given to flow of funds analysis and issued *APB Opinion No. 3*. This release suggested that funds statements should be presented as supplemental information in financial reports but did not make such disclosures mandatory.[8] In *APB Opinion No. 3* the board also suggested that the title of the statement be as descriptive as possible.

By 1971 the Accounting Principles Board had noted that regulatory agencies were requiring the preparation of funds statements and that a number of companies were voluntarily disclosing funds statements in their annual reports. As a result, the Board issued *APB Opinion No. 19*, which stated that information usually contained on the funds statement was essential to financial-statement users and that such a statement should be presented each time a balance sheet and an income statement were prepared. Additionally, the Board stated that the funds statement should be prepared in accordance with the all-financial-resources concept and that the statement should be titled "Statement of Changes in Financial Position."[9]

The Board went on to prescribe the format of the statement as follows.

1. *The statement may be prepared in such a manner as to express the financial position in terms of cash, cash and temporary assets, quick assets, or working capital so long as it utilizes the all-financial-resources concept and gives the most useful portrayal of the financing and investing activities of the entity.*

2. *In each case the statement should disclose the net change in the cash, cash and temporary investments, quick assets or working capital, depending on the form of presentation.*

3. *The statement should disclose outlays for long-term assets, net proceeds from the sale of long-term assets, conversion of long-term debt or preferred stock*

---

[8] *Accounting Principles Board Opinion No. 3*, "The Statement of Source and Application of Funds" (New York: AICPA, 1963).

[9] *Accounting Principles Board Opinion No. 19*, "Reporting Changes in Financial Position" (New York: AICPA, 1971).

to common stocks, issuances and repayments of debts, issuances or repurchases
of capital stock and dividends.[10]

The statement of changes in financial position was designed to enable
financial statement users to answer such questions as

1. Where did the profits go?
2. Why weren't dividends larger?
3. How was it possible to distribute dividends in the presence of a loss?
4. Why are current assets down when there was a profit?
5. Why is extra financing required?
6. How was the expansion financed?
7. Where did the funds from the sale of securities go?
8. How was the debt retirement accomplished?
9. How was the increase in working capital financed?

Although definitive answers to these questions are not readily obtainable
from a casual inspection of the statement, usual practice was to elaborate on
the presentation in the footnotes. Additionally, comparative analyses covering
several years of operations enable the user to obtain useful information on
past methods and practices and the contribution of funds derived from operations to the growth of the company.

The statement of changes in financial position was designed to report on
the financial operations of the company and to disclose the results of the
company's financial management policies. It was also designed to improve
the predictive decision-making ability of users.

Cash Flow Information

The cash inflows and outflows of a business are of primary importance to
investors and creditors. The presentation of cash flow information by a business enterprise should enable investors to (1) predict the amount of cash that
is likely to be distributed as dividends or interest in the future and (2) evaluate
the potential risk of a given investment.

The FASB has emphasized the importance of cash flow information in its
deliberations. *Statement of Financial Accounting Concepts No. 1* states that effective financial reporting must enable investors, creditors, and other users to (1)
assess cash flow prospects and (2) evaluate liquidity, solvency, and flow of
funds.

The presentation of cash flow data is necessary to evaluate a firm's liquidity, solvency, and financial flexibility. *Liquidity* is the firm's ability to convert
an asset to cash or to pay a current liability. It is referred to as the "nearness
to cash" of an entity's economic resources and obligations. Liquidity informa-

---

[10] Ibid.

tion is important to users in evaluating the timing of future cash flows; it is also necessary to evaluate solvency and financial flexibility.

Solvency refers to a firm's ability to obtain cash for business operations. Specifically, it refers to a firm's ability to pay its debts as they become due. Solvency is necessary for a firm to be considered a "going concern." Insolvency may result in liquidation and losses to owners and creditors. Additionally, the threat of insolvency may cause the capital markets to react by increasing the cost of capital in the future; that is, the amount of risk is increased.

Financial flexibility is the ability of a firm to use its financial resources to adapt to change. It is the ability of a firm to take advantage of new investment opportunities or to react quickly to a "crisis" situation. Financial flexibility comes in part from quick access to the company's liquid assets. However, liquidity is only one part of financial flexibility. Financial flexibility also stems from a firm's ability to generate cash from its operations, contributed capital, or the sale of economic resources without disrupting continuing operations.

The presentation of cash flow data is intended to enable investors to make rational decisions by providing them with useful information. The FASB, in *Statement of Financial Concepts No. 2*, identified *relevance* and *reliability* as the primary ingredients that make accounting information useful. A statement of cash flows undoubtedly allows for the presentation of more useful information to investors and creditors because it enables users to be able to predict the probability of future returns and evaluate risk.

In 1987 the Financial Accounting Standards Board issued *Statement of Financial Accounting Standards No. 95*, "Statement of Cash Flows." This Statement established standards for cash flow reporting and superseded *APB Opinion No. 19*, "Reporting Changes in Financial Position." As a result, all business enterprises are now required to present a statement of cash flows in place of the statement of changes in financial position as a part of the full set of financial statements.

Historical Perspective

The format required by *SFAS No. 95* for the presentation of the statement of cash flows evolved over a number of years. In 1980 the FASB issued a discussion memorandum entitled *Reporting Funds Flows, Liquidity and Financial Flexibility* as a part of the conceptual framework project. The major questions raised in this Discussion Memorandum included:

1. Which concept of funds should be adopted?
2. How should transactions not having a direct impact on funds be reported?
3. Which of the various approaches should be used for presenting funds flow information?
4. How should information about funds flow from operations be presented?
5. Should funds flow information be separated into outflows for (a) maintenance of operating capacity, (b) expansion of operating capacity, and (c) nonoperating purposes?

Later in 1981, an exposure draft entitled *Reporting Income, Cash Flows, and Financial Position of Business Enterprises* was issued by the FASB. This exposure draft concluded that funds flow reporting should focus on cash rather than working capital. However, a final statement was not issued during this time and the FASB decided to consider the subject of cash flow reporting in connection with a study of recognition and measurement concepts.

In 1984 the FASB issued *Statement of Financial Accounting Concepts No. 5,* ''Recognition and Measurement in Financial Statements of Business Enterprises.'' Included in this statement is the conclusion that a cash flow statement should be part of a full set of financial statements. Concurrently, the Financial Executives Institute was reviewing the issue of cash flow reporting. In 1984 this organization published *The Funds Statement: Structure and Use.* This study pointed out several areas of diversity inherent in the Statement of Changes in Financial Position. For example, *APB Opinion No. 19* allowed different definitions of funds, different definitions of cash and cash flow from operations, and different forms of presentation of the statement of changes in financial position.

During 1985 and 1986, the FASB organized a task force on cash flow reporting, and issued an exposure draft that proposed standards for cash flow reporting. The FASB was concerned that the divergence in practice affected the understandability and usefulness of the information presented to investors, creditors, and other users of financial statements. Additionally, some financial statement users were contending that accrual accounting had resulted in net income not reflecting the underlying cash flows of business enterprises. That is, too many arbitrary allocation procedures, such as deferred taxes and depreciation, resulted in a net income figure that was not necessarily related to the earning power of an enterprise.

Purposes of the Statement of Cash Flows

The primary purpose of the statement of cash flows is to provide relevant information about cash receipts and cash payments of an enterprise during a period. This purpose is consistent with the objectives and concepts delineated in *Statements of Financial Accounting Concepts Nos. 1* and *5.*

SFAC No. 1 stressed that financial reporting should provide information to help present and potential investors assess the amount, timing, and uncertainty of prospective cash receipts from interest, dividends, the sale of securities, and the proceeds from loans. These cash flows are seen as important because they may affect an enterprise's liquidity and solvency.

SFAC No. 5 indicated that a full set of financial statements should show cash flows for the period. *SFAC No. 5* also described the usefulness of cash flow reporting in assessing an entity's liquidity, financial flexibility, profitability, and risk.

These objectives and concepts delineated in *SFAC Nos. 1* and *5* led the FASB to conclude that the statement of cash flows should replace the statement of changes in financial position as a required financial statement. The statement of cash flows is intended to help investors, creditors, and others assess future cash flows, provide feedback about actual cash flows, evaluate the availability of cash for dividends and investments and the enterprise's ability to finance growth from internal sources, and identify the reasons for differences between net income and net cash flows. An additional reason for the focus on cash rather than working capital is the questionable usefulness of working capital in evaluating liquidity. That is, a positive working capital balance does not necessarily indicate liquidity and a negative working capital balance may not indicate a lack of liquidity. More information is needed on receivable and inventory financing to evaluate the overall liquidity of a business enterprise.

Statement Format

The statement of cash flows reports changes during an accounting period in cash and cash equivalents from the following activities:

1. Net cash flows from operations.
2. Investing transactions.
3. Financing transactions.

   Cash equivalents are defined as highly liquid investments that are both readily convertible to known amounts of cash and so near to maturity that they present insignificant risk changes in value because of changes in interest rates. In general, only investments with original maturities of three months from the date of purchase will qualify as cash equivalents.

Cash Flows from Operating Activities

Cash flows from operating activities are generally the cash effect from transactions that enter into the determination of net income exclusive of financing and investing activities. Among the cash inflows from operations are the following:

1. Receipts from sales of goods and services and collections on accounts or notes from customers.
2. Receipts of interest and dividends.
3. All the receipts that are not the result of transactions defined as investing or financing activities. Examples of such transactions are amounts received to settle lawsuits or insurance settlements.

   Cash outflows from operations include:

1. Cash payments to acquire materials for manufacture or goods for resale, and cash payments to reduce payables and notes to creditors.
2. Cash payments to other suppliers and employees.
3. Cash payments to governments for taxes, duties, fines, and fees or penalties.
4. Cash payments to lenders and creditors for interest.
5. All other payments that are not the result of transactions defined as in-

vesting or financing activities. Examples of such transactions are payments to settle lawsuits and cash contributions to charities.

SFAS No. 95 encouraged companies to report operating activities by reporting major classes of gross cash receipts, major classes of gross cash payments, and the difference between them—the net cash flow from operating activities. Reporting gross cash receipts and payments is termed the *direct method,* and includes reporting the following classes of operating cash receipts and payments:

1. Cash collected from customers.
2. Interest and dividends received.
3. Other operating cash receipts.
4. Cash paid to employees and other suppliers of goods and services.
5. Interest paid.
6. Income taxes paid.
7. Other operating cash payments.

A company that chooses not to use the direct method for reporting operating cash flow information must report the same amount of operating cash flow by adjusting net income to reconcile it with operating cash flow. This method of reporting is termed the *indirect method.* The required adjustments include the effect of past deferrals of operating cash receipts and payments; accruals of expected operating cash receipts and payments; and the effect of items related to investing and financing activities such as depreciation, amortization of goodwill, and gains or losses on the sale of property, plant, and equipment.

A company that uses the direct method must reconcile net income to net cash flow from operating activities in a separate schedule. If the indirect method is used, the reconciliation is reported within the statement of cash flows. Consequently it is sometimes referred to as the *reconciliation method.*

Cash Flow from Investing Activities

Investing activities include making and collecting loans, acquiring and disposing of debt or equity securities of other companies, and acquiring and disposing of property, plant, and equipment and other productive resources. Examples of cash inflows from investing activities are

1. Receipts from the collection or sales of loans made to other entities.
2. Receipts from the collection or sale of other companies' debt instruments.
3. Receipts from the sales of other companies' equity instruments.
4. Receipts from the sales of property, plant, and equipment and other productive assets.

Examples of cash outflows from investing activities are

1. Disbursement for loans made by the enterprise to other entities.
2. Payments to acquire other companies' debt instruments.

3. Payments to acquire other companies' equity instruments.

4. Payments to acquire property, plant, and equipment and other productive assets.

Cash Flows from Financing Activities

Financing activities result from obtaining resources from owners, providing owners with a return of and a return on their investment, borrowing money and repaying the amount borrowed, and obtaining and paying for other resources from long-term creditors. Cash inflows from financing activities include

1. Proceeds from issuing equity instruments.

2. Proceeds from issuing debt instruments or other short- or long-term borrowings.

    Cash outflows from financing activities include

1. Payments of dividends or other distributions to owners.

2. Repayments of amounts borrowed.

It should be noted that although loans to or investments in other companies are classified as investing activities and repayments of amounts borrowed is classified as a financing activity, cash receipts from dividends and interest and cash payments for interest are classified as operating activities.

Foreign Currency Cash Flow

A statement of cash flows of an enterprise engaging in foreign currency transactions or having foreign operations must report foreign currency cash flows using the exchange rate in effect at the time of the cash flow. The statement must report the effect of exchange rate changes on cash balances held in foreign currencies as a separate part of the reconciliation of the change in cash and cash equivalents during the period. (See Chapter 17 for a further discussion of foreign currency translation.)

The following additional disclosures are required by *SFAS No. 95:*

1. An accounting policy that describes the method of determining cash equivalents.

2. Information about other investing and financing activities that result in recognized assets or liabilities but do not result in cash receipts or payments (e.g., acquisition of property, plant, and equipment from the exchange of the company's common stock).

Illustrative Statements of Cash Flows

Exhibit 5-1 illustrates a statement of cash flows prepared using the direct method and Exhibit 5-2 illustrates a statement of cash flows prepared using the indirect method.

Uses of Cash Flow Information

A major objective of accounting is to present data that allows investors and creditors to predict the amount of cash that will be distributed in the form of

EXHIBIT 5.1 *Direct Method*

STATEMENT OF CASH FLOWS
For the Year Ended December 31, 1996
Increase (Decrease) in Cash and Cash Equivalents

Cash flows from operating activities		
Cash received from customers	$12,370	
Cash paid to suppliers and employees	(11,460)	
Interest received	140	
Interest paid	(120)	
Income taxes paid	(180)	
Cash paid to settle lawsuit	(30)	
Net cash provided by operating activities		$ 720
Cash flows from investing activities		
Proceeds from sale of facilities	$ 450	
Payment received on note for sale of facilities	75	
Capital expenditures	(800)	
Net cash used in investing activities		(275)
Cash flows from financing activities		
Net borrowings under line of credit agreement	$ 275	
Principal payments under capital lease obligation	(120)	
Proceeds from issuing long-term debt	300	
Proceeds from issuing common stock	150	
Dividends paid	(125)	
Net cash provided by financing activities		480
Net increase in cash and cash equivalents		$ 925
Cash and cash equivalents at beginning of year		500
Cash and cash equivalents at end of year		$1,425

dividends and interest, and to allow an evaluation of risk. Net income is the result of changes in assets and liabilities, some cash, some current, and some noncurrent; consequently, it cannot be equated with a change in cash. The statement of cash flows discloses the effects of earnings activities on cash resources, how assets were acquired, and how they were financed. The ability of an enterprise to generate cash from operations is an important indicator of its financial health and the degree of risk associated with investing in the firm.

The investors and creditors of a firm anticipate a return that is, at least, equal to the market rate of interest for investments with equal risk. Or, stated differently, investors expect to receive a discounted present value of future cash flows that is equal to or greater than their original investment. The past cash flows from a firm are the best available basis for forecasting future cash flows.

The FASB stressed the importance of cash flows to investors when it stated:

EXHIBIT 5.2 *Indirect Method*

STATEMENT OF CASH FLOWS
For the Year Ended December 31, 1996
Increase (Decrease) in Cash and Cash Equivalents

Cash flows from operating activities		
Net income		$ 540
Adjustments to reconcile Net Income to Cash provided by operating activities		
Depreciation and Amortization	$ 315	
Provisions for losses on Accounts Receivable	110	
Gain on sale of Property, Plant, & Equipment	(50)	
Payment received on Installment Note Receivable	25	
Increase in Accounts Receivable	(175)	
Decrease in Inventory	50	
Increase in Prepaid Rent Expense	(30)	
Decrease in Accounts Payable	(115)	
Increase in Income Taxes Payable	35	
Increase in Other Liabilities	15	
Total Adjustments		180
Net Cash Provided by Operating Activities		$ 720
Cash flows from investing activities		
Proceeds from sale of facilities	$ 450	
Payment received on note for sale of facilities	75	
Capital expenditures	(800)	
Net cash used in investing activities		(275)
Cash flows from financing activities		
Net borrowings under line of credit agreement	$ 275	
Principal payments under capital lease obligation	(120)	
Proceeds from issuing long-term debt	300	
Proceeds from issuing common stock	150	
Dividends paid	(125)	
Net cash provided by financing activities		480
Net increase in cash and cash equivalents		$ 925
Cash and cash equivalents at beginning of year		500
Cash and cash equivalents at end of year		$1,425

. . . *financial reporting should provide information to help investors, creditors, and others assess the amounts, timing and uncertainty of prospective cash inflow to the related enterprise.*[11]

[11] *Statement of Financial Accounting Concepts No. 1,* "Objectives of Financial Reporting by Business Enterprises." (New York: FASB, 1978), par. 37.

The ability to predict returns to investors and creditors is somewhat complex because management may decide to use cash in a variety of manners, and the uses of cash are interrelated. For example, available cash may be reinvested in assets, used to expand facilities and markets, used to retire debt and equity, or used to pay dividends. Accounting researchers are interested in determining the relationship between accounting information and decision making. Empirical research has indicated that cash flow data has incremental information content over accrual earnings data, and that cash flow data is superior to changes in working capital information.[12] These findings support the FASB's position on the disclosure of cash flow data because they provide evidence that such information may result in better decisions. They also indicate that even given the uncertainties surrounding the alternate uses of available cash by firms, knowledge of past cash flow information allows investors and creditors to make better predictions of future cash flows and assessments of risk.

Development Stage Enterprises

A company in the development stage is a new organization attempting to become a going concern. Consequently, some of the expenditures made by the company may be considered investments in the future, and some of the reporting principles may be altered during the development period. Many companies in the development stage are faced with financing problems, and the use of generally accepted accounting principles may in themselves compound these financing problems. That is, reporting all start-up costs as expenses during the first years of operations will cause reported income to be reduced and thereby make it more difficult for the company to obtain investment funds.

The proper reporting procedures to use in accounting for development stage enterprises have been discussed for many years. The basic question in these discussions has been: Should generally accepted accounting principles differ for an organization just beginning operations? In 1975 the Financial Accounting Standards Board undertook a study of this question and issued its *Statement No. 7*, "Accounting and Reporting by Development Stage Enterprises."[13] This release specifies guidelines for the identification of a development stage enterprise and for the procedures to be used to record and report on the activities of these types of organizations.

The Board noted that the activities of a development stage enterprise typically would be devoted to financial planning, raising capital, exploring for natural resources, developing natural resources, research and development,

---

[12] Robert M. Bowen, David Burgstahler, and Lane A. Daley, "The Incremental Information Content of Accruals Versus Cash Flows," *The Accounting Review* (October, 1987), pp. 723–747.

[13] *Statement of Financial Accounting Standards No. 7*, "Accounting and Reporting by Development Stage Enterprises" (Stamford, Conn.: Financial Accounting Standards Board, 1975).

acquiring assets, recruiting and training personnel, developing markets, and beginning production. Thus, the FASB defined development stage enterprises as those devoting substantially all their efforts to establishing a new business, and required that either of the following conditions be met:

1. Planned principal operations have not commenced.
2. Planned principal operations have commenced, but no significant revenue has been received.[14]

The FASB reached the conclusion that generally accepted accounting principles should apply to development stage enterprises, and that GAAP should govern the recognition of revenue and the determination of whether a cost should be charged to expense or capitalized. That is, reporting on the activities of a development stage enterprise should not differ from any other type of organization. However, the FASB did state that certain additional information should be disclosed for development stage enterprises:

a. *A balance sheet, including any cumulative net losses reported with a descriptive caption such as "deficit accumulated during the development stage" in the stockholders' equity section.*

b. *An income statement, showing amounts of revenue and expenses for each period covered by the income statement and, in addition, cumulative amounts from the enterprise's inception.*

c. *A statement of . . . (cash flows), showing the sources and uses of . . . (cash) for each period for which an income statement is presented and, in addition, cumulative amounts from the enterprise's inception.*

d. *A statement of stockholders' equity showing from the enterprise's inception:*
   1. *For each instance, the date and number of shares of stock, warrants, rights or other equity securities issued for cash and for other consideration.*
   2. *For each issuance, the dollar amounts (per share or other equity unit in total) assigned to the consideration received for shares of stock, warrants, rights, or other equity securities. Dollar amounts shall be assigned to any noncash consideration received.*
   3. *For each issuance involving noncash consideration, the nature of the noncash consideration and the basis for assigning amounts.*[15]

The conclusions reached in *SFAS No. 7* indicate that the board believed that additional standards of disclosure for development stage enterprises would alleviate the accounting and reporting problems faced by these companies. This belief indicated that the FASB was retaining the emphasis on interfirm comparability initiated by the APB. That is, similar situations should be reported in a similar manner by all companies. It also provided additional evidence that the FASB believed that GAAP should be the same for all business organizations regardless of their special needs or particular environment.

---

[14] Ibid., par. 8.

[15] Ibid., par. 11.

Summary

The measurement techniques currently being used for assigning values to balance sheet items have been criticized for failing to give enough relevant information to financial statement users. A review of balance sheet disclosure procedures indicates that most valuations are the result of the residual effect of the emphasis on net income reporting. Consequently, they make little contribution to the users' ability to predict the future.

Partially in response to a need, the statement, now titled the statement of cash flows, has become the third major financial statement. This requirement has evolved over time from an original emphasis on changes in working capital to the current emphasis on cash flows.

Standards of accounting and reporting for development stage enterprises are also discussed in this chapter. In its *Statement No. 7*, the FASB set out guidelines for defining development stage enterprises and for reporting on their activities. The FASB retained the view that GAAP should be the same for all organizations, but did allow the reporting of additional information for development stage organizations.

In the readings for this chapter, George Sorter and Monroe Ingberman attempt to develop an understanding of the objectives of accounting, and Hugo Nurnberg discusses some inconsistencies and ambiguities created by *SFAS No. 95*.

The Implicit Criteria for the Recognition, Quantification, and Reporting of Accounting Events

George H. Sorter and Monroe Ingberman

Introduction

The great predominance of theoretical accounting literature has concerned itself with the development of normative theories that have had little impact on, or relation to, prevalent accounting practice. On the other hand, the great predominance of authoritative pronouncements by the CAP, APB, or FASB have concerned themselves with narrowly defined practice areas without explicit consideration of how these pronouncements fitted into a consistent structure suitable for achieving the defined objectives of accounting. We presently have almost 90 FASB standards and approximately 50 previous pronouncements that have not been superseded, and yet we have no criteria that define what is to be recognized as an accounting event, or how the event to be recognized should be quantified and reported.

In the first section of this paper, we attempt to rationally reconstruct the implicit criteria that govern the recognition, quantification, and reporting process of accounting. In the second section, we present a discussion of some problem areas as well as an analysis of the consistency, utility, and implications of the criteria. The criteria represent an abstraction and summarization of the myriad individual pronouncements and practical applications that constitute generally accepted accounting principles (GAAP) and are in no way normative. We believe such a descriptive analysis to be both useful and necessary.

Identifying the explicit criteria governing existing practice should be the first essential step before attempting an integrated analysis of the logic and utility of the existing framework of accounting. What many perceive to be the failure of the FASB's conceptual framework project may well be due to the normative approach the Board has adopted, blessing the apparent status quo without, however, attempting to describe and understand what the status quo actually consists of. Since we have meager knowledge of how the stated objectives of accounting can be achieved, a clear understanding of "what is" appears a necessary first step toward determining "what should be." This paper is an attempt at taking this first step.

The Basic Data Base of Accounting

The basic data base of accounting consists of reporting performance having monetary consequences by an accounting unit and reporting subsequent events that alter the previously recorded consequences of performance. Usually, the performance that is recorded is part of an exchange transaction, which would generally consist of three stages: The first stage is an agreement between two parties that results in each party's receiving a right to receive goods, services, money, or a claim to money in exchange for assuming an obligation to provide goods, services, money, or a claim to money. The second and third stages of the exchange transaction consist of the performance by each party pursuant to such agreements. Accounting's recognition criteria are such that the agreement phase of an exchange transaction is never recognized, whereas performance by either party is always recognized as an accounting event by both parties. In double entry accounting, each accounting event is assumed to produce a two-fold impact on the assets and equities of an entity. The assets of an entity are best thought of as the rights to beneficially utilize economic resources. A resource is beneficially utilized when a net incremental benefit is expected to result from utilization. The equities of an entity are an obligation to provide economic resources to others or to permit the utilization of resources by others. (These definitions are not those stated in authorized pronouncements, for reasons discussed in a following section.) The two impacts of an event on assets and equities are quantified in terms of past, present, highly probable future, or hypothetical cash flows as determined by the quantification criteria provided below.

Criteria for Recognizing Accounting Events

We define an accounting event as any event that results in an entry on the books or records of a firm. The recogni-

tion criteria that follow provide the necessary and sufficient conditions for recognizing all accounting events in the sense that every accounting event satisfies at least one of the criteria and all events satisfying one of the criteria are recognized as accounting events. The criteria, however, do contain some redundancy because an event may be recognizable by more than one of the criteria. No attempt has been made to eliminate this redundancy in order to state explicitly what otherwise might have been only subtly implied.

Recognition Criteria Relating to Performance

The following criteria assure that performance pursuant to an agreement by either party to the agreement is recognized as an accounting event by both parties to the agreement.

1. ***All cash receipts and disbursements are accounting events.*** Cash receipt or cash disbursement usually represents performance by one party or another pursuant to an agreement. In some cases, donations and similar events represent unilateral performance by the accounting unit. Since the main objective of financial statements is to facilitate the assessment of cash flows, a rule requiring the recognition of cash flows is self-explanatory.

2. ***Acquisitions of economic resources are accounting events.*** An economic resource is said to be acquired when any entity obtains the right to utilize for its benefit all or nearly all of the services available from that economic resource. Under this criterion, the purchase of goods as well as the transfer of negotiable instruments is recognized as an accounting event. This criterion also requires the capitalization of a lease by the lessee

if the conditions of FASB Statement No. 13 are met. This standard provides that a lease is capitalized when substantially all of the risks and rewards of ownership—and thus, the right to utilize nearly all of the services from the leased asset—are transferred. Usually when an economic resource is acquired, the selling party to an agreement has performed, and it is this performance by the seller that is recognized by the buyer under this criterion. Also encompassed by the criterion is the receipt of an economic resource not pursuant to an agreement, as in the receipt of a gift.

3. *The provision of an economic resource is an accounting event.* An economic resource is provided when an entity relinquishes the right to utilize all, or nearly all, of the services available from that resource. This criterion provides for the recognition by the seller of his performance to provide goods in a sales transaction as well as unilateral performance not pursuant to an agreement. To the extent that the economic resource disposed of or acquired is cash (criterion 1), criteria 2 and 3 are redundant. All three of these recognition criteria, however, relate to the recognition of performance under an agreement. The next two criteria are mixed in that they may either require recognition of performance or recognize changes in a previously recorded event.

Criteria Relating to Either Performance or Changes in Consequences

4. *The extinguishment of the right to utilize an economic resource is an accounting event.* Extinguishment

consists of a reduction either in the duration or in the quantity of a right to utilize resources. A reduction in the *quantity* of rights occurs when raw materials are transformed into finished goods or finished goods are sold, whereas depreciation of plant and equipment or the amortization of lease facilities or of insurance policies represents a reduction in the *duration* of a right. This criterion demands recognition of an extinguishment of an entity's right to utilize economic resources whether or not that right has previously been recognized as an accounting asset. When cost of goods sold is recognized, clearly the extinguishment represents a decrease in an accounting asset. Similarly, if a right to a service has been prepaid and a prepaid asset results, then the decrease in the duration of that right as time passes represents a reduction in an accounting asset. On the other hand, if a right to utilize a resource is acquired without a prepayment or without the acquisition of goods, no accounting asset is recognized since no performance has yet occurred. Nevertheless, when that right is extinguished, an accounting event results. Rent expense (the extinguishment of a right to utilize the rented space) is recognized whether or not a prepaid rent asset had previously been set up. In either case, a right to utilize the rented facility has been extinguished.

In an analogous fashion, labor expense, tax expense, and legal expenses all represent extinguishments of rights to labor services, government services, and legal services and are recognized as an accounting event whether or not an accounting asset has previously been recognized. When the right being extinguished has been recognized as an accounting asset, the event alters the previously recorded consequences of a prior accounting event. On the other hand, when the right being extinguished has not been recognized as an accounting asset, then the extinguishment represents the buyer's recognition of performance by the supplier of the service.

5. *The extinguishment of an obligation to permit utilization of an entity's resource for the benefit of another entity is an accounting event.* Again, an extinguishment occurs when either the duration or the quantity dimension of an obligation is reduced. Such an extinguishment of an obligation is an accounting event whether or not the obligation had previously been recognized as an accounting liability. The situation is analogous to that described in relation to criterion 4 above. When an agreement is reached to provide services, an obligation to permit the utilization of an economic resource for the benefit of others is assumed by the seller of the service. However, this obligation to provide the service and to permit another to utilize the economic resource is recognized as an accounting liability only if payment has already been received, in which case a deferred credit account is set up. Whether or not payment has been received, however, the extinguishment of the obligation to permit the utilization of an economic resource is an accounting event. When rent revenue is recognized, it represents recognition by the seller of his performance in having permitted someone else to utilize an economic resource, thereby reducing the duration of the remaining

obligation, whether or not the rent has been prepaid. Similarly, interest revenue (and, in general, all revenue) is recognized as an event reducing the duration of an obligation to provide service. Criteria 3 and 5 are redundant in some respects since, obviously, criterion 3 is a special case of having permitted the utilization of a resource through the surrender of the resource.

6. *An event that establishes that it is probable and measurable that the net benefit to be derived from utilization of an economic resource is less than the accounting description of the right to utilize that economic resource or that the sacrifice needed to discharge an obligation is greater than the accounting description of that obligation is an accounting event.* This criterion sanctions the recognition of events such as the write-down to market of inventory and marketable securities. The recognition of losses on long-term construction contracts, disposals of segments of a business, and an imminent expropriation of assets by foreign governments all represent examples of the force of this criterion.

The various loss contingencies included in FASB Statement No. 5, where *probable* and *measurable* are defined terms, represent additional examples of the application of this criterion. The application of this criterion does not require an existing asset or liability. The accounting quantification of an asset may be zero and events may establish that the net benefit derived from that asset is negative. This occurs, for instance, when the market price declines below the contract price for merchandise that a firm is committed to purchase. The purchase commitment is not a recognizable accounting event; therefore, the net accounting description of the economic resource to be acquired is zero. However, when the market decline occurs, it is probable and measurable that the net benefit (benefit less sacrifice to be incurred) of acquiring and utilizing this asset will be negative and, thus, the loss on the purchase commitment is recognized.

Net benefit, as encompassed by this criterion, is the arithmetic rather than the present value of the difference between the benefits and sacrifices. Thus, a net restructuring of debt that alters the amount of timing of future interest payments so that the present value of the receipts is reduced and is less than the accounting description does not meet the test of this criterion unless the money to be received is less than the accounting description of the right.

7. *An event other than an agreement that creates or changes the right to receive or the obligation to provide money or the functional-currency equivalent of money to be received or provided is an accounting event.* Under this criterion, such diverse events as a tax refund, a favorable or unfavorable judgment in a law suit, and the impact of currency fluctuation on monetary items denominated in a currency other than the functional currency all are recognizable. A quite different type of event, but one that also falls into the provision of this criterion, is a dividend declaration.

8. *Descriptive changes are accounting events.* A change from a record description to a description considered preferable that does not describe a change in the underlying rights or

obligations is a descriptive change. Descriptive changes may be recognized because the previously recorded description is no longer appropriate. Examples of this are when work in process is reclassified as finished goods or long-term debt is reclassified as a current liability in the period preceding maturity, or when an estimated uncollectible is reclassified as an actual uncollectible without a bankruptcy finding. These types of events are called reclassifications.

Other descriptive events are the adoption of a different method of accounting such as a "change in accounting principle" and error corrections. Some descriptive changes are mandatory, such as error corrections and changes in accounting principles required by authoritative pronouncements; others are customary, such as closing entries and the reclassification entries cited above. Some changes, however, are optional, such as changing from FIFO to LIFO or any change in accounting principles not due to a new authoritative pronouncement. These optional changes must be justified by showing that the new description is more accurate, more reliable, or more useful.

Criteria for Quantifying Accounting Events

The previously stated recognition criteria determine which events are recorded. The quantification criteria below determine how effects of each event on assets and equities are quantified.

1. *Current cash flows are quantified by the amount of cash that changes hands.*

2. *The acquisition of an economic re-*

source is quantified by the cash outflow associated with the acquisition of the resource. The cash outflow associated with an acquisition is the cash that has been paid for the resource, the cash (or present value of the cash if materially different) that is required to be paid for the resource, or, in case of a barter transaction, the cash that would have been paid in an analogous transaction.

3. *The provision of an economic resource pursuant to an exchange agreement is quantified by the cash inflow associated with the provision.* The cash inflow associated with a provision of a resource is the cash that has been received, the cash (or present value of the cash if materially different) that is legally entitled and is expected to be received, or, in a barter transaction, the cash that would have been received in an analogous cash transaction.

3a. *The unilateral provision of an economic resource not pursuant to an agreement is quantified by the accounting description of the economic resource provided.*

4. *The extinguishment of the right to utilize an economic resource is quantified by the accounting description of the right or the cash sacrifice required by the acquisition of the right times the fraction of the right utilized.* If the right being extinguished has previously been recorded as an accounting asset, an accounting quantification exists. If the right being extinguished is one that has not been recognized as an accounting asset, then the cash sacrifice required for the acquisition of the right is the cash that is required to be paid (present value if materi-

ally different) or, in a barter transaction, the cash that would have been paid in an analogous cash transaction. If cash has already been paid, then an accounting description of the right and an accounting asset will exist. The accounting description of the right being extinguished if it exists was originally quantified, however, in terms of the cash outflow or sacrifice associated with the acquisition of that asset. Thus directly or indirectly, the extinguishments of rights are always quantified in terms of the cash outflow associated with the acquisition of the right.

5. *The extinguishment of an obligation to permit the utilization of an entity's economic resource for the benefit of another entity is quantified by the accounting description of that obligation or the cash benefit that results from the assumption of the obligation times the fraction of the obligation extinguished.* The cash benefit resulting from the assumption of the obligation is the cash that is entitled to be and is expected to be received (present value if materially different) or, in a barter transaction, the cash that would have been received in an analogous cash transaction.

6. *An event recognizing that the net benefit to be derived from utilizing an economic resource is less than the accounting description of the right to utilize that economic resource or that the sacrifice needed to discharge an obligation is greater than the accounting description of that obligation is quantified by the arithmetic but not present-value difference between the accounting description and the amount of expected benefit or sacrifice.*

7. *An event other than an agreement that creates or changes the right to receive or the obligation to provide money or the functional-currency equivalent of money is quantified by the amount of or change in the money or functional-currency equivalent that is to be received or provided.*

8. *All nonmandatory descriptive changes are quantified in terms of the previously existing quantifications. Mandatory descriptive changes are quantified as required by authoritative pronouncements.*

The above quantification criteria require that every accounting quantification describe either an actual, required future, or hypothetical cash flow associated with the acquisition and disposition of rights and obligations. With the exception of barter transactions, which occur rarely, these quantification criteria could be summarized in terms of a concept of "a preferred quantification." A preferred quantification consists of (1) an actual increase or decrease in cash; (2) in the absence of an actual increase or decrease in cash, a highly probable and legally required future increase or decrease in cash; and (3) a measurable decrease in an existing accounting quantification. If we accept the concept of a preferred quantification, the quantification criteria are as follows:

1. For any event that contains one preferred quantification, quantify both effects of the event in terms of that preferred quantification.

2. For any event containing two preferred quantifications, quantify the effects of the event by utilizing both preferred quantifications. Usually this is accomplished by expressing

the event as the sum of two events, each quantified by one of the preferred quantifications, as is the case of the sale event which is split into a sales inflow of revenue and a cost of goods sold event.

3. If an event does not produce any preferred quantification, quantify both effects of the event by the cash increase or decrease that would have occurred in the most likely analogous transaction. These shortcut rules seem to correctly describe all events with the exception of descriptive changes and barter transactions. As a consequence of these rules, assets (or the right to utilize economic resources) are quantified in terms of the cash sacrifice that was necessary to acquire these rights, whereas equities or obligations are quantified in terms of the cash benefit resulting from the assumption of the obligation.[1]

A cash sacrifice would not have been incurred to acquire an asset unless the benefit expected from utilizing that asset was greater than the sacrifice, and a liability or obligation would not have been assumed unless the burden of that obligation was expected to be less than the benefit that was received in exchange. The difference between assets and liabilities, therefore, can in the first instance be interpreted to be the minimum expected net benefit of utilizing

---

[1] How can accounts payable, for example, be thought of as quantified in terms of a cash benefit? When goods are received but not presently paid for, a cash benefit results. Had the goods been acquired for cash, a cash outflow would have resulted. Thus by assuming the obligation represented by accounts payable, a cash outflow that did not need to be made resulted.

existing rights and discharging existing liabilities. When assets and liabilities are first acquired, this relationship holds because of quantification rules 1, 2, and 4. Subsequent to acquisition this relationship continues to hold or should continue to hold because of recognition and quantification rules 6 and 7. In general we would expect book value to be less than economic value since book value represents minimum expected benefits whereas economic value represents expected benefits. To the extent that this relationship does not always hold, it is the function of some of the ambiguities and inconsistencies encountered in the application of the measurement rules, particularly due to the inconsistent treatment of present values discussed below.

Reporting Criteria[2]

All events recognized as accounting events are reported in the balance sheet in terms of the effects these events had on the assets and equities of the unit. For some events considered especially important, accounting reports not only the consequences of the event in the balance sheet, but also the occurrence of the event in an events statement such as the income statement or the statement of cash flows (fund statements).

Reporting Criterion 1. *The occurrence of all cash receipts and disbursements is reported directly or indirectly in the statement of cash flows.* A direct reporting exists when the cash flows are labeled as cash receipts or disbursements; an indirect reporting results when the cash receipts and disbursements are reported in terms of the related changes on assets and equities.

Reporting Criterion 2. *The acquisition of a noncurrent economic resource is reported in the statement of cash flows.* The acquisition of a noncurrent economic resource is considered an investment event and must be recorded either in the body of the cash flow statement or in a separate schedule attached to that statement.

Reporting Criterion 3. *The provision of an economic resource pursuant to an exchange agreement is reported in the income statement if and only if there are no unresolved monetary consequences of the agreement.* The monetary consequences of an agreement are said to be resolved when the entity is legally entitled to all inflows, when these inflows are measurable and probable, and when any outflow required to effectuate the agreement either has already occurred or is probable and measurable.

Reporting Criterion 4. *The extinguishment of the right to utilize an economic resource is reported in the income statement as an expense or loss unless the utilization is associated with manufacturing a tangible, salable product.*[3]

Reporting Criterion 5. *The extinguishment of an obligation to permit the utilization of an entity's economic resource for the benefit of another entity is reported in the income statement as revenue if the entity is legally entitled to a probable and measurable cash inflow.*

Reporting Criterion 6. *Events that reduce an accounting description of an economic resource to a net benefit or*

---

[2] Reporting criteria assume that the FASB Exposure Draft on cash flow statements will be adopted essentially unchanged.

[3] The reporting criteria as defined here do not distinguish between expenses and losses and gains and revenue. This distinction is solely a semantic one and has no operational significance.

increase the accounting description of a liability to a net sacrifice are recorded in the income statement as losses unless the resource affected is a noncurrent marketable security. Thus, the write-down of current marketable securities to market is reported in the income statement; the write-down of noncurrent securities is not.

Reporting Criterion 7. *Events other than agreements that create or change the right to receive or the obligation to provide money or the functional currency equivalent of money are reported in the income statement as gains or losses.*

Reporting Criterion 8. *Descriptive changes are reported in the income statement only if required by an authoritative pronouncement.*

Implications of the Reporting Criteria

Events considered especially important are reported not only through their effects on assets and equities in the balance sheet but also more directly by reporting their occurrence in the cash flows and income statements. As the name implies, cash events plus significant investment and financing events that are not cash events are required to be reported in the cash flows statement. The events required to be reported in the income statement are basically the extinguishment of obligations resulting from the provision of goods and services when there are no unresolved future monetary consequences and the extinguishment of rights to utilize resources that do not create future unresolved monetary consequences. Thus, for instance, the extinguishment of a right to utilize goods in the manufacturing process creates an unresolved future monetary consequence—the amount of money for which the inventory being manufactured can be sold. That utiliza-

tion is not reported in the income statement. The income statement reports those provisions and utilizations of rights and obligations whose monetary consequences have already been resolved. On the other hand, the balance sheet, in addition to these events, reports events with unresolved future monetary consequences.

Problem Areas

The above criteria of recognition, quantification, and reporting appear to explain all, or at least most, of observed GAAP relating to financial statements. Not included in these criteria are those governing supplementary statements, additional information, and footnote disclosures. In deriving these criteria, obviously many events proved troublesome to classify and analyze and, as may well be imagined, no sooner was a criterion structured to encompass one recalcitrant event than another event no longer fit. We believe that as presently stated, the criteria accommodate most of present practice, but we're sure one area or another has been overlooked. Some of the most interesting and difficult problems and issues that were encountered are discussed below.

A most difficult area was the infrequently occurring barter transaction. It was very difficult to structure the criteria so that a barter transaction of unlike goods results in revenue, but a barter of like goods does not. The solution that prevailed, if somewhat strained, was that under the quantification criteria a barter transaction provision is quantified in terms of the cash flows in an analogous cash transaction. When one object is exchanged for a like object, the analogous cash transaction can be assumed to be the cash flows in acquiring the original asset. If that interpretation is valid, then the provision of the asset is quantified by the same amount as the cost of the assets surrendered, and thus no revenue results.

"Bad debt expense" also was interesting to analyze under these criteria. Analysis showed that the bad debt problem is not really a recognition problem, but rather a quantification problem. Bad debt expense is not an expense in the sense that expenses are the extinguishments of rights to utilize a resource. Rather, the bad debt expense represents a quantification of the sales inflow in terms of the amount of inflow that is probable and measurable. Under this view, bad debt expense should properly be treated as a reduction or contra to sales revenue rather than as an expense.

An interesting issue revolved about the accounting treatment of borrowing money versus borrowing other assets. When a loan is made, two events occur, one of which is recognized as an accounting event. Cash is transferred from one party to another, and since all cash flows are recognized as accounting events, this transfer is recorded. The second event that occurs is an agreement to permit the use of cash for a limited period by another party in exchange for the interest specified. This latter event is an executory contract and is not recognized as an accounting event. The utilization of the right to use the cash by the borrower is an interest expense, and the extinguishment of the obligation to allow the borrower to use the cash for his benefit represents a revenue event for the lender. These events are recognized only when and to the extent that the right and obligation are extinguished. When a physical asset is borrowed and the transfer of the asset from one party to another occurs, no analogous accounting event is recognized or recognizable. In neither case is

the right to use the asset for a limited time or the obligation to permit the use of the asset for a limited time recognized as an accounting asset and liability.

Foreign currency translation posed several problems. Looking at an advanced textbook would make it appear that a forward exchange contract is a recognizable accounting event. This would be troublesome since it represents an executory contract that normally would not be recognizable. In looking at existing practice and in querying the Financial Accounting Standards Board staff concerned with the foreign currency translation project, it became clear that actually no authoritative pronouncement demands the recognition of a forward exchange contract when it is entered into, and it is generally not recorded. The translation from a functional currency to a reporting currency is not encompassed by these rules because it occurs only in consolidation and thus does not require an accounting entry. The gain or loss due to changes in exchange rate for a forward exchange contract and the gain or loss in the right to receive the functional-currency equivalent of money, however, are recognizable accounting events. These events are analogous to the recognized loss due to the market decline of inventory for which a purchase commitment exists. In both cases, a loss (and in one case, a gain) is recognized even though the underlying asset and liability may not be recognized as accounting assets and liabilities.

Finally, the criteria provide interesting insight into the use of the percentage-of-completion method of recognizing revenue. Whether the percentage-of-completion method or the completed-contract method should be used would seem to depend on whether the performance by the seller-producer under the contract is to construct or to deliver the facility. If the obligation is to construct, then as construction proceeds the obligation to construct is reduced and a recognizable event should result. Under this circumstance, percentage-of-completion would seem to be appropriate. On the other hand, if the obligation is to deliver a finished product, then no reduction in the obligation occurs as construction takes place and the completed-contract method would seem to be more appropriate.

All of these problems proved interesting and tractable. The one problem that was incapable of resolution, however, was the one of deferred taxes. Even the criteria cannot seem to make a rational case for deferred taxes.

Assessment of the Criteria

If the criteria presented are valid, then it is quite clear that accounting as it exists today is misperceived as basically an economic discipline. According to the operational criteria, it seems to be primarily a legal discipline in that it deals with a universe of events giving rise to the acquisition and disposition of some, but not all, of an entity's legal rights and legal obligations. These legal rights and obligations are quantified in terms of the cash exchanged or required and expected to be exchanged in acquiring the rights and obligations.

If this characterization of the accounting process is correct, then the definitions of the elements of financial statements presented by the Financial Accounting Standards Board in Concepts Statement No. 6 are not appropriate. Concepts Statement No. 6 defines assets as "probable future economic benefits obtained or controlled by a particular entity as a result of past transactions or events" (par. 25). An obvious but minor deficiency of the definition is, of course, that a future benefit cannot exist today—only an expectation of a benefit can exist—and thus under the definition no asset can presently exist. A more serious deficiency of the definition, however, is that the definition is not compatible with what accounting does and how it quantifies. If an asset is a future benefit, it should clearly be quantified in terms of that future benefit, and changes in future benefits should be recognized as accounting events. As we have seen, however, assets are not quantified in terms of the future benefits, and changes in future benefits are generally not recognized as accounting events.

On the other hand, characterizing assets in terms of rights appears to be consistent with the recognition and quantification rules. To quantify a future benefit in terms of a past cost is an absurdity, but to quantify a right in terms of the event creating that right is not. Changes in recorded rights, be they changes in either quantity or duration, are inevitably recognized as accounting events. Thus, depreciation—the change in the duration of a right—is an accounting event regardless of whether the resource for which the right exists increases or decreases in value.

Even the write-down of assets recognized under recognition criterion 5 is consistent with the definition presented of an asset as a right to utilize an economic resource with the expectation of incremental future benefit. The quantification criteria provide that an asset is quantified in terms of the cash outflows associated with the acquisition of the right to utilize that asset. To the extent that the expected benefit from utilization is less than the accounting quantification, or sacrifice of acquiring the right, no incremental future benefit (excess of benefit over sacrifice) is expected and, thus, no asset exists.

An analogous argument can be made for preferring a definition of equities in terms of obligations rather than future sacrifices. First, the obligation definition encompasses both liabilities and stockholders' equity, whereas the definition presented in Concepts Statement No. 6 requires a residual definition of equities. Liabilities and stockholders' equity represent an obligation to transfer or permit the utilization of economic resources. For liabilities, this obligation is defined as to amount, time, and duration; for stockholders' equity, the obligation is open-ended and its duration is limitless.

Inconsistencies Observed

Two major inconsistencies of the recognition and quantification rules were observed. The first is that the recognition rules, while dealing with legal rights and obligations, result in the omission of an extremely important segment of rights and obligations. Contractual rights and obligations are not recorded as assets and liabilities, and the assumption of those rights and obligations is not an accounting event. At a time when contractual rights and obligations are assuming an ever-increasing importance, it is hard to rationalize this omission from the accounting universe. It results in essentially equivalent rights and obligations being disclosed and quantified in a variety of ways. The right to utilize an economic resource that has not yet been received is shown as an asset only if a deposit has been made. But whether or not a deposit has been made does not impact the right to uti-

lize that resource. Further, the quantification of the right depends on the size or the amount of the deposit. Thus, we have the paradoxical situation that a right or an obligation may be quantified in varying amounts including zero when the fundamental legal right or obligation is identical.

The second major inconsistency is accounting's ambivalent attitude toward present value. When an activity is to be quantified in terms of future cash flows, sometimes the required quantification is in present-value terms and sometimes it's in absolute terms. There does not appear to be any logical reasoning for how this incongruity arose or why it is allowed to persist.

Conclusion

What the above analysis demonstrates is that accounting is primarily concerned with the cash consequences of the assumption of legal rights and obligations, and that accounting provides an archival history of those cash consequences. If we accept the fact that the objective of financial statements is to facilitate the assessment of cash flows, then it is clearly evident that such an archival history of the cash consequences of legal rights and obligations is useful; but it is equally evident that it is not sufficient to allow an assessment of the cash consequences. The question remains how a history of the cash consequences of rights and obligations can be modified and what additional information can be and should be presented in order to more satisfactorily accomplish the agreed-on objectives.

EXHIBIT 1

I. Criteria for Recognizing Accounting Events
   1. All cash receipts and disbursements are accounting events.
   2. Acquisitions of economic resources are accounting events.
   3. The provision of an economic resource is an accounting event.
   4. The extinguishment of the right to utilize an economic resource is an accounting event.
   5. The extinguishment of an obligation to permit utilization of an entity's resource for the benefit of another entity is an accounting event.
   6. An event that establishes that it is probable and measurable that the net benefit to be derived from utilization of an economic resource is less than the accounting description of the right to utilize that economic resource or that the sacrifice needed to discharge an obligation is greater than the accounting description of that obligation is an accounting event.
   7. An event other than an agreement that creates or changes the right to receive or the obligation to provide money or the functional-currency equivalent of money to be received or provided is an accounting event.
   8. Descriptive changes are accounting events.
II. Criteria for Quantifying Accounting Events
   1. Current cash flows are quantified by the amount of cash that changes hands.
   2. The acquisition of an economic resource is quantified by the cash outflow associated with the acquisition of the resource.
   3. The provision of an economic resource pursuant to an exchange agreement is quantified by the cash inflow associated with the provision.
   3a. The unilateral provision of an economic resource not pursuant to an agreement is quantified by the accounting description of the economic resource provided.
   4. The extinguishment of the right to utilize an economic resource is quantified by the accounting description of the right or the cash sacrifice required by the acquisition of the right times the fraction of the right utilized.
   5. The extinguishment of an obligation to permit the utilization of an entity's economic resource for the benefit of another entity is quantified by the accounting description of that obligation or the cash benefit that results from the assumption of the obligation times the fraction of the obligation extinguished.
   6. An event recognizing that the net benefit to be derived from utilizing an economic resource is less than the accounting description of the right to utilize that economic resource or that the sacrifice needed to discharge an obligation is greater than the accounting description of that obligation is quantified by the arithmetic but not present-value difference between the accounting description and the amount of expected benefit or sacrifice.
   7. An event other than an agreement that creates or changes the right to receive or the obligation to provide money or the functional-currency equivalent of money is quantified by the amount of or change in the money or functional-currency equivalent that is to be received or provided.
   8. All nonmandatory descriptive changes are quantified in terms of the previously existing quantifications. Mandatory descriptive changes are quantified as required by authoritative pronouncements.
III. Criteria for Reporting Accounting Events
   1. The occurrence of all cash receipts and disbursements is reported directly or indirectly in the statement of cash flows.

EXHIBIT 1 *(Continued)*

2. The acquisition of a noncurrent economic resource is reported in the statement of cash flows.
3. The provision of an economic resource pursuant to an exchange agreement is reported in the income statement if and only if there are no unresolved monetary consequences of the agreement.
4. The extinguishment of the right to utilize an economic resource is reported in the income statement as an expense or loss unless the utilization is associated with manufacturing a tangible, salable product.
5. The extinguishment of an obligation to permit the utilization of an entity's economic resource for the benefit of another entity is reported in the income statement as revenue if the entity is legally entitled to a probable and measurable cash inflow.
6. Events that reduce an accounting description of an economic resource to a net benefit or increase the accounting description of a liability to a net sacrifice are recorded in the income statement as losses unless the resource affected is a noncurrent marketable security.
7. Events other than agreements that create or change the right to receive or the obligation to provide money or the functional equivalent of money are reported in the income statement as gains or losses.
8. Descriptive changes are reported in the income statement only if required by an authoritative pronouncement.

Inconsistencies and Ambiguities in Cash Flow Statements Under FASB Statement No. 95

Hugo Nurnberg

FASB Statement No. 95 (SFAS-95) requires firms to provide a cash flow

© 1993 American Accounting Association, *Accounting Horizons*, Vol. 7, No. 2, June 1993, pp. 60–75. Reprinted with permission.

The author appreciates the helpful comments of Leopold Bernstein (Baruch College), Steven Lustgarten (Baruch College), Carl L. Nelson (University of California—Santa Barbara), John L. O'Donnell (Michigan State University), Joyce Strawser (Baruch College), and two anonymous reviewers. Any errors, of course, are the responsibility of the author alone.

statement for each period for which results of operations are provided. The cash flow statement explains the change during the period in cash and cash equivalents, and classifies cash receipts and cash payments as resulting from investing, financing, or operating activities (SFAS-95, paras. 7, 14). This latter requirement represents a major change from APB Opinion No. 19 (APBO-19), which permitted but did not require a three-way classification of funds flows in the old statement of changes in financial position.

Although the three-way classification of SFAS-95 is loosely based on the finance literature, certain modifications result in inconsistent or ambiguous classifications of certain cash flows. Accordingly, reported cash flow from operating activities under SFAS-95 frequently includes cash flows from investing and financing activities. Similarly, reported cash flows from investing activities and financing activities frequently exclude certain cash flows properly attributable to them.

Many of these classification issues applied to the old statement of changes in financial position under APBO-19, and were extensively documented in the literature (see, e.g., Nurnberg 1983; Drtina and Largay 1985; Ketz and Largay 1987). Although SFAS-95 substantially enhances uniformity in funds concept and statement presentation relative to APBO-19, the fact that some of these classification issues remain unresolved under SFAS-95 is not widely recognized and understood by report users.

Purpose of Paper

This paper examines the distinctions among operating, investing, and financing activities made in SFAS-95, and compares them with similar distinctions in the finance literature. It identifies several inconsistencies and ambiguities in this three-way classification and in the disclosure requirements of SFAS-95, and demonstrates the following:

1. The required three-way classification under SFAS-95 results in reporting similar cash flows differently and different cash flows similarly, just the opposite of the desired characteristic of financial reporting to report similar things similarly and different things differently.

2. The classification of interest and div-

idend receipts and interest payments as operating cash flows under SFAS-95 results in contaminating reported cash flow from operating activities with the interest and dividend effects of investing and financing activities. It also produces a peculiar if not counterintuitive presentation in the cash flow statement of the retirement of bonded debt originally issued at a discount.

3. The classification of income taxes as operating cash flows under SFAS-95 contaminates reported cash flow from operating activities with the tax effects of gains and losses relating to investing and financing activities.

4. The requirement to disclose noncash investing and financing transactions under SFAS-95 is ambiguous.

5. The required presentation of third-party financing transactions under SFAS-95 is also ambiguous and results in reporting similar cash flows differently and different cash flows similarly.

Trichotomy in Finance Literature

The finance literature notes that investing and financing decisions are interrelated (see, e.g., Brealey and Myers 1984, 443–61; Solomon and Pringle 1980, 441–42), and that both are related to operating decisions (see, e.g., Brealey and Myers 1984, 229, 701; Solomon and Pringle 1980, 142, 315). Nevertheless, the finance literature posits that, for many purposes, it is useful to distinguish between investing decisions and financing decisions (see, e.g., Brealey and Myers 1984, 101, 279; Solomon and Pringle 1980, 362, 435–41), and to separate investing and financing decisions from operating decisions (see, e.g., Solomon and Pringle 1980, 315).

Operating decisions address questions such as which goods and services to sell, which goods and services to purchase, which employees to hire and at what compensation levels, which facilities to rent, and so forth.

Investing decisions address such questions as how much a firm should invest and what specific assets a firm should invest in. From the finance perspective, all asset acquisition decisions are investing decisions and are fundamentally alike, whether involving long-term assets such as plant and equipment, or short-term assets such as inventories and trade receivables. For analytical purposes, however, long-term asset acquisition decisions are usually viewed as investing decisions, whereas short-term acquisition decisions are usually viewed as working capital management decisions.

Financing decisions deal with the volume and structure of a firm's financing, including whether the cash required for investment should be generated by internal or external sources and, if the latter, whether by debt or equity securities. From the finance perspective, all borrowing decisions are fundamentally alike, whether involving long-term liabilities such as mortgage and bonded debt or short-term liabilities such as bank loans and trade payables. For analytical purposes, however, long-term borrowing decisions are usually viewed as financing decisions, whereas short-term borrowing decisions are usually viewed as working capital management decisions.

Comparing the three-way classification of SFAS-95 to the finance literature emanates from the decision usefulness orientation of financial reporting. Because the objective of financial reporting is to provide information that is useful in credit and investment decisions (see SFAC-1, 1978, paras. 30–

32), cash flow statements should provide information needed for credit and investment decision models. Many of these decision models are specified in the finance literature and use financial ratios. For example, Weston and Copeland (1992, 205) suggest certain financial ratios which use operating cash flow in either the numerator or denominator. The usefulness of these ratios as well as cash flow information generally should be enhanced by classifying cash flows in the cash flow statement as they are classified in the finance literature.

Trichotomy Under SFAS-95

Under SFAS-95, cash flows are classified as relating to operating, investing, or financing activities.

Operating Activities

In SFAS-95, the FASB defines (para. 21) operating activities as a residual category to include all transactions and events other than investing and financing activities. It notes that operating activities generally relate to producing and delivering goods and providing services, and that the cash flows from operating activities are generally the cash effects of transactions and other events that enter into the determination of net income.

Under SFAS-95, operating cash inflows include interest and dividend collections on debt and equity securities of other entities, customer collections from the sale of goods and services, and all other receipts not defined as investing or financing inflows, such as supplier refunds, collections on lawsuits, and most insurance proceeds. Operating cash outflows include interest payments (unless capitalized), payments for inventories, payments to employees, payments to suppliers of other goods and services, payments to governments for taxes, duties, fines, and other fees, and all other payments not defined as investing or financing outflows, such as customer refunds, payments under lawsuits, and charitable contributions.

Investing Activities

SFAS-95 defines (para. 15) investing activities to include (1) making and collecting loans and (2) acquiring and disposing of debt or equity instruments and plant assets. Thus, investing cash outflows include payments to make or acquire loans, payments to acquire debt or equity securities of other entities, and payments to acquire plant assets. Investing cash inflows include receipts from collecting or disposing of loans, receipts from sales of debt or equity securities of other entities, and receipts from sales of plant assets.[1] Note that under SFAS-95, interest and dividend collections are classified as operating inflows, not investing inflows.

Financing Activities

SFAS-95 defines (para. 15) financing activities to include (1) obtaining resources from owners and providing them with a return on, and a return of, their investment; (2) borrowing money and repaying amounts borrowed, or

otherwise settling the obligation; and (3) obtaining and repaying other resources obtained from creditors on long-term credit. Under SFAS-95, financing cash inflows include proceeds from issuing debt or equity securities, and proceeds from other short- or long-term borrowings. Financing cash outflows include dividend payments, outlays to reacquire or retire equity securities, and repayments of amounts borrowed. Note that under SFAS-95, interest payments are classified as operating outflows, not financing outflows.

Evaluation of SFAS-95 Trichotomy

The rationale offered in SFAS-95 (paras. 55, 81) for the three-way distinction among operating, investing, and financing cash flows is that investors and creditors consider the relationships among certain cash flows to be important to their analysis of financial performance, and that classifying cash flows as operating, investing, and financing facilitates the evaluation of significant relationships within and among these basic activities. This classification, the FASB notes (SFAS-95, para. 84) ". . . links cash flows that are often perceived to be related, such as cash proceeds from borrowing transactions and cash repayments of borrowings . . . [and results in a cash flow] . . . statement which reflects the cash flow impact of each of the major activities of the enterprise."

There are several inconsistencies and ambiguities in this three-way classification, however, relating to the following: (1) arbitrariness of classifications; (2) interest earnings and interest cost; (3) retirement of bonded debt; and (4) income taxes.

---

[1] Classification depends on the nature of the firm's operations. It is presumed that investing activities include lending activities as well as acquisition and sale of securities, but that presumption may be overcome. For example, acquisitions and dispositions of securities held in trading accounts of broker dealers and loans originally acquired for resale by certain financial institutions are comparable to acquisition and disposition of inventories by merchandising and manufacturing companies, hence are classified (SFAS-102 1989, paras. 8–9) as operating activities, not investing activities.

Arbitrariness of Classifications

Most classification systems are somewhat arbitrary. Classification involves weighing the relative significance of similarities and differences. Under SFAS-95, the unavoidable arbitrariness of the three-way classification sometimes results in classifying similar cash flows differently and different cash flows similarly. Additionally, although the three-way classification of cash flows under SFAS-95 links certain related cash flows, it does *not* link other cash flows that are either functionally or legally related.

Operating versus investing activities. In a research monograph which influenced the FASB deliberations on cash flow reporting, Heath notes (1978, 129) that the purchase and sale of inventories is in one sense fundamentally the same as the purchase and sale of plant assets; both are usually considered part of a firm's normal *operating* activities. The case for treating the purchase and sale of plant assets differently from the purchase and sale of inventories must be based, Heath argues (ibid., 130), on the grounds that they are of different significance to those interested in the cash inflows and cash outflows of a business enterprise. According to Heath (ibid.), the purchase and sale of plant assets are of special significance because they are of relatively infrequent occurrence, because they are often relatively large in amount, and because management is likely to have more control over their timing than it does over the purchase and sale of inventories. Nonetheless, Heath notes (ibid.) that distinguishing between operating and investing activities is likely to be troublesome.

In its 1980 Discussion Memorandum, the FASB also recognizes (1980, 43) the similarity of purchases of inventory and purchases of plant assets. Unlike Heath, however, the FASB notes (ibid.) that one might argue that both represent *investing* activities. Nevertheless, the FASB (ibid., 44) classifies the former as operating activities and the latter as investing activities, largely because ". . . payments to suppliers for inventories are regarded normally as part of operating activities and payments for property, plant, and equipment as part of investing activities."

Thus, to the extent that payments for inventories and plant assets are fundamentally alike, the distinction between operating and investing activities is flawed or unnecessary. This notwithstanding, a consensus has developed that payments for inventories should be classified as operating outflows whereas payments for plant assets should be classified as investing outflows, consistent with the finance literature.

Operating versus financing activities. A similar ambiguity arises in classifying payments of amounts borrowed. Cash outflows to suppliers and lenders are fundamentally alike, yet the former are classified as operating whereas the latter are classified as financing under SFAS-95.

Heath notes (1978, 130–32) that some activities with a financing dimension, such as inventory purchases on account, should be excluded from financing activities because their spontaneous financing components are incidental to an enterprise's operations and do not affect its capital structure. According to Heath, only negotiated financing activities should be reported as financing activities. In its 1980 Discussion Memorandum, the FASB also notes (ibid., 43) this ambiguity in the three-way classification. Nevertheless, both Heath and the FASB favor classifying cash outflows to suppliers as operating and cash outflows to lenders as financing.

There are at least two inconsistencies in the reasoning underlying this classification. First, it assumes that inventory purchases on account always involve current liabilities. Second, it assumes that report users are interested principally in the capital structure which, by definition, excludes current liabilities. What about those admittedly less common situations where inventory purchases on account involve long-term liabilities? What about those report users interested in the financial structure which, by definition, includes all liabilities, not just long-term liabilities?[2]

Because cash outflows to suppliers and lenders are fundamentally alike, the distinction between operating and financing activities based on payee is ambiguous. This ambiguity has been resolved by classifying outflows to suppliers as operating and outflows to lenders as financing, consistent with the finance literature.

Investing versus financing activities. Finally, a similar ambiguity arises in distinguishing between investing and financing activities. SFAS-95 classifies cash flows according to the transactions that cause them. Cash inflows are not classified according to uses and, similarly, cash outflows are not classified according to sources.[3] To illustrate this ambiguity,

cash receipts from the sale of plant assets are investing inflows even when the proceeds are used to retire debt, and cash receipts from issuing debt are financing inflows even when the proceeds are used to purchase plant assets. Such cash inflows and outflows might be viewed as functionally related, but are not necessarily "linked" and are not reported in the same section of the cash flow statement under SFAS-95.

Interest Collections and Interest Payments

For merchandising and manufacturing firms, most commentators (see, e.g., Smith and Skousen 1981, 107–108; Welsch et al. 1982, 87–88) suggest that interest earnings and interest cost relate to peripheral or incidental operating activities or to investing and financing activities, not to central operating activities, at least for income reporting purposes. The FASB appears to concur with this classification (FASB 1979a), for income reporting at the aggregate firm level.

For cash flow reporting, however, the FASB states that interest and dividend collections are operating inflows and interest payments are operating outflows unless capitalized (see SFAS-95, paras. 17, 22–23). This prescribed classification contradicts the finance literature. Clearly, interest and dividend collections result from making loans or investments in debt and equity securities and, therefore, relate to investment activities. Similarly, interest payments result from incurring debt and, therefore,

---

[2] Some authors distinguish between financial structure and capital structure. For example, Weston and Copeland note (1992, p. 565) that financial structure refers to a firm's total financing, and includes current liabilities, deferred tax liabilities, long-term debt, preferred stock, and common stock (including retained earnings), whereas capital structure refers to its permanent financing, and includes just the latter three items.

[3] An exception is that cash flows from futures

contracts, forward contracts, option contracts, or swap contracts accounted for as hedges of identifiable transactions or events may be classified in the same category as the items being hedged. See SFAS-104, para. 7(b).

relate to financing activities. Indeed, the finance literature emphasizes the similarity of interest and dividend payments—interest is paid for the use of debt capital, whereas dividends are paid for the use of equity capital. It follows, therefore, that interest and dividend receipts are *not* operating inflows and interest payments are *not* operating outflows, notwithstanding SFAS-95.

The FASB acknowledges (ibid., paras. 86, 89) that a reasonable case could be made for classifying interest payments as financing outflows and interest and dividend collections as investing inflows. But the FASB notes (ibid., para. 90) that under prior practice, almost all published funds statements implicitly classified interest collections and interest payments as operating flows. Additionally, it perceives widespread support (ibid.) for what might be referred to as the *inclusion concept,* whereby ". . . operating cash flow should, insofar as possible, include items whose effects are included in determining net income to facilitate an understanding of the reasons for the differences between net income and net cash flow from operating activities." Because of this inclusion concept, the FASB concludes (ibid.) that it ". . . was not convinced that changing the prevalent [prior] practice . . . would necessarily result in a more meaningful presentation of cash flows." Rather, the FASB favors evolutionary changes in cash flow reporting (see ibid., para. 120) and, for the present, classifies interest payments and interest and dividend collections as operating cash flows.[4]

[4]Interestingly, the Governmental Accounting Standards Board (GASB) classifies interest and dividends receipts on loans (except program loans), debt instruments of other entities, equity securities, and cash manage-

It is inconsistent, however, for the FASB to cite the inclusion concept and prior practice to decide that cash flow from operating activities should include interest payments and interest and dividend collections but exclude cash flows relating to gains and losses from plant asset disposals. Like interest payments and interest and dividend collections, gains and losses on plant asset disposals are included in net income, and the cash flows relating to these gains and losses were frequently included in operating funds flow under prior practice.[5] Consistent citation of the inclusion concept and prior practice might have led the FASB to classify all of these cash flows as operating, a ridiculous result. Instead, the FASB should have ignored the inclusion concept and prior practice and classified interest and dividend collections as investing inflows and interest payments as financing outflows, because they relate to investing and financing activities, as noted earlier.

ment and investment pools as investing inflows, interest payments for purposes unrelated to capital assets as noncapital financing outflows, and interest payments directly related to capital assets as capital and related financing outflows; all other interest receipts and interest payments are classified as operating cash flows.

On the other hand, the International Accounting Standards Committee (IASC) proposes (1991, paras. 34–35) to classify interest and dividend receipts as either operating or investing inflows and interest payments as either operating or financing outflows.

[5]Under prior practice, most companies used the indirect method to calculate funds flow from operations, and income was not adjusted for nonoperating gains and losses. Accordingly, disposals of plant and equipment were reported at net book value, and nonoperating gains and losses were implicitly included in operating funds flow. See Nurnberg 1983, 810.

More important, because interest and dividend collections and interest payments are classified as operating cash flows under SFAS-95, reported cash flow from operating activities includes cash flows relating to investing and financing activities. Similarly, reported cash flows from investing and financing activities exclude cash flows relating to these activities. It follows that the effectiveness of the cash flow statement to distinguish among operating, investing, and financing activities is impaired. Indeed, three of the seven FASB members dissented to the issuance of SFAS-95 in part for this reason.[6]

This impairment may be material. An extreme example of the impact of interest *payments* on cash flow from operating activities is found in the 1991 cash flow statement of Westinghouse. For 1991, consolidated operating cash flow is $703,000,000 net of $1,006,000,000 of interest payments. If these interest payments had been classified as financing outflows, consolidated operating cash flow would have increased by 243 percent to $1,709,000,000.[7] An extreme example

of the impact of interest *collections* on operating cash flow is illustrated in the 1991 cash flow statement of the Financial Accounting Foundation. For 1991, operating cash flow is a positive $655,000, including $876,000 of interest collections, or 134 percent of the net amount. If these interest collections had been classified as investing inflows, operating cash flow would have been a negative $221,000.

By classifying interest and dividend collections and interest payments as operating cash flows, the FASB has forgone the opportunity to more substantially improve the quality of financial reporting by sharpening the distinction among operating, investing, and financing cash flows.[8] It should reconsider the issue.

___

[6] The FASB wavered in its deliberations with respect to classifying these items in the cash flow statement. Interest and dividend collections and interest payments were classified as operating in the July 1986 Exposure Draft. In March 1987, however, the FASB tentatively concluded to classify interest and dividend receipts as investing inflows and interest payments as financing outflows (see Action Alert, No. 87-11, 18 March 1987). But in April 1987, the FASB reverted to the original operating classification of the Exposure Draft (see Action Alert, No. 87-16, 22 April 1987).

[7] This and several additional examples from published financial reports illustrate the effect on cash flow from operating activities of including interest payments and collections,

dividend collections, and the income tax effects of gains and losses relating to investing and financing activities. Of course, cash flow from operating activities should be adjusted to exclude all of these items, not just one item at a time as is illustrated in this paper. Space limitations preclude this more complete analysis.

[8] Mitigating this contaminating effect is the requirement of SFAS-95 to disclose the amount of interest payments (net of amounts capitalized), either as a separate line item under the direct method, or as a supplemental disclosure under the indirect method. The FASB reasons (SFAS-95, para. 90) that this disclosure will enable report users who wish to consider interest payments as financing outflows to do so for their own analytical purposes. Unfortunately, SFAS-95 has no comparable requirement to disclose the amount of interest collections as a supplemental item under the indirect method for report users who wish to consider interest collections as investing inflows for their own analytical purposes; it does require disclosure of interest and dividend collections as a separate line item under the direct method.

Bonded Debt

SFAS-95 states that "repayments of amounts borrowed" are financing outflows (para. 20(b)), whereas "payments to lenders and other creditors for interest" are operating outflows (para. 23(d)). Unofficially, the FASB staff indicates that the intent of SFAS-95 is to classify repayments of *original* amounts borrowed as financing outflows. It follows that SFAS-95 requires the debtor to report an excess of maturity value over issuance price, or issuance discount, as an operating outflow, because it represents the additional interest cost paid in one lump sum (see also Stewart et al., 7). For zero coupon debt, all the interest cost is paid at maturity, and frequently exceeds the original amount borrowed.

This treatment produces a peculiar if not counterintuitive presentation: Operating cash flow decreases due to the retirement of debt when the debt was issued at a discount, although the debt retirement itself is a financing activity (see Nurnberg 1990, 50–54).[9] The dollar amounts may be material. For example, in its 1990 annual report, Turner Broadcasting System discloses (fn. 4) the repayment in 1989 of $292,000,000 of accreted value of zero coupon senior notes. In its three-year comparative cash flow statement, Turner correctly deducts $206,102,000 of payments of accreted amounts and discount expensed upon retirement of related secu-

rities[10] from the subtotal $410,286,000 operating cash flow *before* interest payments to calculate the $25,792,000 operating cash flow for 1989. Operating cash flow would have been $231,900,000, or 899.1 percent more than the $25,792,000 reported amount, if this $206,102,000 payment was reported as a financing outflow.[11]

The peculiar presentation of cash outflows to retire debt originally issued at a discount results under SFAS-95 because of the classification of interest payments as operating outflows and debt repayments as financing outflows. A much more understandable and objective presentation classifies all payments to creditors as financing out-

---

[9] An analogously peculiar presentation in the cash flow statement of the bondholder results from applying SFAS-95 rules to the maturation of bond investments acquired at a discount: Operating cash flow increases by the accumulated discount, which represents interest collections, although the collection at maturity itself is an investing activity.

[10] It is not possible from the published disclosures to determine the portion of this $206,102,000 payment that represents accreted interest on the zero coupon notes and the portion that represents discount expensed upon the retirement of related securities.

[11] An alternative practice has developed of reporting the entire payment of debt at retirement as a financing outflow. This practice is illogical and contrary to the spirit of SFAS-95, however, as it understates the operating outflow for accreted interest cost and overstates cash flow from operating activities. The amount of the understatement of the operating outflow for interest cost and the overstatement of cash flow from operating activities increases the larger the issuance discount and the longer the maturity term of the debt. For zero coupon debt, this practice results in reporting no operating outflow for interest cost. For example, in its 1991 comparative cash flow statement, Imcera Group reports a $217,400,000 financing outflow for the partial redemption of zero coupon debt, including accreted interest, and $165,100,000 of operating cash flow for 1991. Unfortunately, the precise amount of accreted interest is not determinable from the published disclosures.

flows, whether for interest or principal, consistent with the finance literature. This presentation also avoids the need to allocate payments to creditors between operating and financing activities.

Income Taxes

Because income tax payments and refunds are operating cash flows under SFAS-95, cash flow from operating activities includes the income tax effects of gains and losses relating to investing or financing activities, such as gains and losses on plant asset disposals and similar items.[12]

Similarly, under SFAS-95, cash flow from operating activities includes the income tax effects of certain noncash investing or financing activities. For example, exchanges of personalty for realty are nonmonetary transactions involving dissimilar assets under APB Opinion No. 29 (1973, paras. 18–21) and taxable exchanges under federal tax law. For both book and tax purposes, gain or loss is recognized for the difference between the fair value of the consideration received and the basis of the consideration given. Book gain or loss differs from tax gain or loss by any difference between book and tax basis.

Under prior practice, there were three acceptable methods of reporting the tax

[12] A comparable situation arises for the tax effects of investing or financing transactions that involve no gain or loss for book purposes but gain or loss for tax purposes due to a difference between book and tax basis. For example, the sale of plant assets at book value generates no gain or loss for book purposes but results in gain or loss for tax purposes equal to the difference between book and tax basis. Under SFAS-95, cash flow from operating activities includes the income tax effects of these gains or losses for tax purposes.

effects of gains and losses on plant asset disposals in the funds statement (see Nurnberg 1983, 808–811). Most firms did not allocate income taxes in the funds statement and reported as proceeds from plant asset disposals the book value, not the cash receipt. Under this *book value* method, funds flow from operations was overstated by the after-tax gain or understated by the after-tax loss, and neither the before- nor after-tax proceeds from the disposal were reported as a single figure anywhere in the funds statement. A few firms allocated income taxes in the funds statement and reported plant asset disposals on an *after-tax* basis. This *intraperiod tax allocation* method resulted in reporting funds flow from operations uncontaminated by the tax effects of the gain or loss on the disposal. Finally, some firms did not allocate income taxes in the funds statement and reported the cash proceeds from plant asset disposals on a *before-tax* basis. Under this *flow-through* method, funds flow from operations was reduced by any tax paid on the gain and increased by any tax savings on the loss. Although not documented, presumably there was a comparable variation in reporting the tax effects of other gains and losses in published funds statements under prior practice.

Under SFAS-95, however, only the flow-through method is permitted in the cash flow statement. SFAS-95 is an improvement over prior practice because it prohibits the book value method for plant asset disposals. But SFAS-95 is not as great an improvement as possible because it also prohibits intraperiod tax allocation in the cash flow statement. The FASB reasons (SFAS-95, para. 92) that tax allocation in the cash flow statement ''. . . would be so complex and arbitrary that the benefits, if any, would not justify the costs involved." Many years ago, the same type of criticism was directed at intraperiod tax allocation in the income statement (see SEC 1945, 142–55; Greer 1945, 98–99), but the procedure has long since become a generally accepted accounting principle (see Patten 1964, 876–79; APBO-11 1967, paras. 51–52; SFAS-96 1987c, paras. 137–41; SFAS-109 1992, paras. 35–38). Both the APB and the FASB concluded that intraperiod tax allocation in the income statement is *not* so complex and arbitrary and that the benefits more than justify the costs.

Income taxes should be allocated in the cash flow statement in order to more accurately distinguish among cash flows from operating, investing, and financing activities. Although intraperiod tax allocation for cash flow reporting requires estimates of tax payments attributable to individual investing and financing activities, these estimates may be made using intraperiod tax allocation methods already developed for income reporting. Moreover, although any estimate may be complex and/or arbitrary, some estimate is better than no estimate at all. Without intraperiod tax allocation, cash flow from operations is understated by the tax on gains and overstated by the tax savings on losses relating to investing and financing activities. Perhaps the FASB will ultimately conclude that intraperiod tax allocation in the cash flow statement is no more complex and arbitrary than its income statement counterpart, and that the benefits more than justify the costs.

Under the current rules of SFAS-95, when the amounts are material, it is recommended (see Ernst and Whinney 1988, 23) that firms disclose the income tax effects of gains and losses relating to investing and financing activities, to

alert report users that the reported cash flow from operating activities is contaminated by the tax effects of these gains and losses. For example, Alexander & Baldwin Inc. discloses in its 1990 annual report that the $97,368,000 operating cash flow for 1989 has been reduced by $36,890,000 of income taxes paid on gains from disposals of property and investments, although the proceeds from those disposals were included in cash flows from investing activities. Cash flow from operating activities uncontaminated by the taxes paid on these investing transactions is $134,258,000, or 37.89 percent more than the reported amount. Another example is American Bankers Insurance Group, Inc., which discloses in its 1990 annual report (fn. 5) that approximately $2,000,000 of tax payments in 1988 on the gain on the sale of an affiliate are reported under operating activities, although the proceeds from the sale are reported under investing activities. Accordingly, the $77,186,000 operating cash flow for 1988 is 2.5 percent less than the $79,186,000 amount that would have been reported if the $2,000,000 of tax payments were reported as an investing outflow.

Still more interesting is that some firms allocate income taxes in cash flow statements despite the prohibition of SFAS-95, presumably because the amounts reported for cash flow from operating activities would otherwise be considered to be misleading. For example, the 1990 comparative cash flow statement of Mead Corporation reports $42,600,000 of income taxes on gains from sales of businesses and properties added back to net income to calculate the $497,300,000 operating cash flow for 1988, and a $42,600,000 outflow immediately after the $333,800,000 inflow from sales of businesses and properties among investing activities; without this addback, cash flow from operating activities for 1988 would have been reported as $454,700,000, or 9 percent less than the reported amount. Two much more dramatic examples are Fairchild Corporation and Capital Southwest Corporation. The fiscal 1991 comparative cash flow statement of Fairchild Corporation reports a $69,500,000 outflow for income taxes paid on assets sold as an investing outflow in fiscal 1990; consistent with SFAS-95, cash flow from operating activities for fiscal 1990 would have been a negative $231,630,000 rather than the negative $162,130,000 amount reported, or 42 percent more. Similarly, the 1991 comparative cash flow statement of Capital Southwest Corporation reports a $3,981,812 outflow for income taxes paid on realized investment gains as an investing outflow for fiscal 1989; under SFAS-95, cash flow from operating activities for fiscal 1989 would have been a negative $2,581,540, 284 percent less than the positive $1,400,272 actually reported.

Noncash Transactions

In the Exposure Draft to SFAS-95 (1986, para. 4), the FASB proposed that the primary purpose of the cash flow statement is to provide information about the cash receipts and cash payments of a firm during a period, and that a secondary purpose is to provide information about the investing and financing activities of the firm during the period. Consistent with these two purposes, the Exposure Draft required disclosure of noncash investing and financing transactions either in the cash flow statement or in a separate schedule. Examples of noncash investing and financing transactions include (1) con-

verting debt to equity, (2) acquiring assets by assuming directly related liabilities, such as purchasing a building by incurring a mortgage to the seller, (3) obtaining an asset by entering into a capital lease, and (4) exchanging noncash assets or liabilities for other noncash assets or liabilities. Formerly, such transactions were reported as nonfund investing and financing activities in the statement of changes in financial position. By permitting disclosure of these noncash investing and financing transactions in the cash flow statement, the Exposure Draft held open the possibility that a comparative cash flow statement for a series of years, like the predecessor comparative statement of changes in financial position, would report all the investing and financing activities of a firm.

Unlike the Exposure Draft, however, SFAS-95 (para. 4) retains the primary purpose but deletes the secondary purpose of the cash flow statement. The FASB concluded that the effectiveness of the cash flow statement would be enhanced if its purpose was restricted to reporting only cash flows, and therefore prohibits reporting noncash transactions in the cash flow statement. Nevertheless, SFAS-95 requires (para. 32) disclosure of all noncash investing and financing transactions that affect recognized assets or liabilities but that do not result in cash inflows or outflows. The FASB reasons (SFAS-95, para. 70) that although these noncash transactions result in no cash inflows or outflows in the periods in which they occur, they generally have a significant effect on cash flows in subsequent periods. SFAS-95 makes more uniform the reporting of noncash investing and financing transactions by prescribing supplemental disclosure outside the cash flow statement and prohibiting their disclosure in the cash flow statement. Unfortunately, the result of this narrower focus is that a comparative cash flow statement, unlike a comparative statement of changes in financial position, does not report all of a firm's investing and financing transactions.

For example, if a firm acquires equipment under capitalized leases, the inception of the lease is a noncash investing and financing transaction to be disclosed outside the cash flow statement, whereas the subsequent lease payments are allocated between interest and principal and reported in the cash flow statement as operating and financing outflows, respectively. Accordingly, a comparative cash flow statement for a series of years does not report all investing and financing transactions relating to this lease. Neither the original investment outflow nor the original borrowing inflow is reported in the cash flow statement, but the repayment is reported later as a financing outflow. From a cash flow statement perspective, the firm appears to be paying off a phantom loan, although the loan itself is reported in the balance sheet. A similar result occurs when a firm acquires real estate by assuming an existing mortgage or by giving a mortgage or installment note to the seller. Only the downpayment is reported as an investing outflow; all subsequent principal payments are reported as financing outflows.

Still another example of the incomplete reporting of financing activities in the cash flow statement under SFAS-95 is the conversion or exchange of debt for equity. A comparative cash flow statement reports the original borrowing as a financing inflow, but settlement of the debt by conversion or exchange is not reported as a financing change is not reported as a financing outflow because it does not involve cash.

Installment Purchases and Sales of Plant Assets

Under SFAS-95, there are certain inconsistencies in reporting installment purchases and sales of plant assets. For installment *purchases* of plant assets, only *early* payments of principal, such as advance payments and down payments, are investing cash outflows (SFAS-95, para. 17(c), fn. 6); subsequent installment payments of principal are financing outflows.[13] For installment *sales* of plant assets, however, *all* installment receipts of principal are investing inflows (SFAS-95, para. 16(c))—not just the early receipts of principal.[14] The inconsistency results from classifying *all* installment receipts of principal on sales of plant assets as investing inflows but only *some* installment payments of principal on purchases of plant assets as investing

---

[13] The FASB concluded (1987, para. 96) that it would be unduly burdensome to separate installment payments to sellers of plant assets, which otherwise would be investing outflows, from installment payments to third-party creditors, which are financing outflows. Rather, SFAS-95 classifies both types of installment payments as financing outflows.

[14] SFAS-95 does not explicitly consider the ease or difficulty of separating receipts of principal from installment sales of plant assets from other installment receipts. Presumably, it concluded that it would *not* be unduly burdensome to separate installment receipts from buyers of plant assets, which are investing inflows, from installment receipts from creditors for serialized borrowings such as reverse equity realty loans, which are financing inflows.

outflows. Moreover, because most installment payments of principal on purchases of plant assets are classified as financing outflows, a comparative cash flow statement for a series of years does not report all the investing and financing activities of a firm.[15]

Additionally, SFAS-95 provides little guidance in defining advance payments and down payments. This is a particular concern for equipment acquired under capitalized leases. Conceptually, the early lease payments are analogous to down payments in purchase-borrow transactions, and should be classified as investing outflows. In Appendix A of SFAS-95, however, the illustrative lease transaction is treated in its entirety as a noncash investing and financing transaction, and none of the lease payments are classified as investing outflows. SFAS-95 implies, therefore, that all payments under a capital lease are for interest and principal on a loan and should be classified as operating and financing outflows, respectively, and that no payments are down payments classified as investing outflows. One author (see Mosich 1989, 1183) explicitly concurs with this view, even for leases in which the first annual payment occurs at the inception of the lease and clearly functions as a down payment.

[15] There is another inconsistency in the classification of payments of installment debt under SFAS-95 (paras. 17(c), fn. 6, and 95–96): As noted earlier, installment payments for plant asset purchases are financing outflows, not investing outflows, although they result from plant asset purchases, which are classified as investing activities. On the other hand, installment payments for inventories are operating outflows, even though they could be viewed as financing outflows.

Unclear Disclosure Requirements

Although SFAS-95 requires supplemental disclosure of noncash investing and financing transactions, it is not clear which noncash transactions require disclosure and which do not. For the most part, the noncash investing and financing transactions for which separate disclosure is explicitly required by SFAS-95 involve external parties and were formerly reported in the statement of changes in financial position as separate nonfund resources provided and applied.

Under prior practice, each of these noncash transactions was typically viewed as equivalent to two hypothetical transactions, a cash inflow and a cash outflow of equal amount. For example, because acquisitions of equipment under capitalized leases were viewed as equivalent to a long-term borrowing followed by immediate payment to acquire equipment, such external noncash transactions were reported in the statement of changes in financial position. As noted earlier, they must also be disclosed under SFAS-95, but *not* in the cash flow statement.

Although the rationale of two hypothetical cash transactions is satisfactory for some purposes, it opens the way for other hypothetical interpretations which are not so acceptable. As Moonitz noted long ago (1956, 380), it is preferable to emphasize that funds flow as a result of external transactions, rather than postulate hypothetical cash transactions. Thus, stock dividends were not usually reported in the statement of changes in financial position, even though stock dividends could be viewed as equivalent to two hypothetical transactions—payment of a cash dividend followed immediately by issuance of stock to the same stockholders for cash. Besides, stock dividends were adequately reported in the statement of changes in stockholders' equity. For similar reasons, stock dividends do not represent noncash financing transactions requiring disclosure under SFAS-95, presumably because they are not external transactions and also because they are adequately disclosed elsewhere in financial reports. Nevertheless, stock dividends are occasionally disclosed among noncash financing activities. As an example, Commerce Clearing House reports (1991, 17, 25) a $17,418,000 common stock dividend among the supplementary disclosures of noncash financing activities as well as in the statement of changes in stockholders' equity.

Several authors (see, e.g., Mosich 1989, 1187; Seiler 1991, 8–22; Williams et al. 1989, 1185–86) conclude, however, that *cash* dividend declarations per se *are* noncash financing transactions requiring disclosure under SFAS-95 when the amounts declared differ from the amounts paid during the year. This issue is not addressed explicitly in SFAS-95. In practice, a few firms (see, e.g., Cash America Investments; Farmland Industries; Larrizza Industries) disclose dividend declarations with the disclosures of noncash investing and financing activities. Presumably, most firms conclude that any differences between dividends declared and dividends paid are adequately disclosed by comparing amounts reported in the cash flow and retained earnings statements.

Under prior practice, reclassifications of noncurrent liabilities as current liabilities often were reported as nonfund resources applied and provided in the funds statement because ". . . the pool of net disposable money-assets or of net working capital . . . [was] diminished . . . [by] an event giving rise to a decline in funds" (Moonitz 1956, 382). Although not explicitly considered in APBO-19, some authors (see, e.g., Kieso and Weygandt 1983, 1087; Miller et al. 1982, 767) interpreted that pronouncement to require disclosure of debt reclassifications as nonfund resources provided and applied, whereas other authors (see, e.g., Davidson et al. 1985; Danos and Imhoff 1986) did not address the issue.

SFAS-95 does not explicitly consider whether debt reclassification should be disclosed as significant noncash financing activities. Some authors (see, e.g., Mosich 1989, 1183) interpret SFAS-95 to require disclosure of debt reclassifications as noncash financing activities, whereas other authors (see, e.g., Chasteen et al. 1989; Kieso and Weygandt 1989; Nikolai and Bazley 1991; Seiler 1989; Smith and Skousen 1990; Welsch and Zlatkovich 1989; Williams et al. 1989) do not address the issue. In practice, few firms (see, e.g., DST Systems Inc.; Mechanical Technology Incorporated; Pacific Enterprises; Rent-A-Wreck of America, Inc.; and Simetco Inc.) disclose debt reclassifications along with disclosures of noncash investing and financing activities. Most such disclosures involve reclassifications from current to noncurrent, not noncurrent to current.

Third-Party Financing Transactions

Although the cash flow statement reports only cash flows, SFAS-95 does not provide adequate guidance as to whether cash actually flows in some third-party financing transactions. Cash inflows occur as checks are received and deposited, and cash outflows occur as checks are issued, but some third-party financing transactions do not involve deposits and issuances of checks.

For example, assume a firm obtains third-party financing for equipment purchases. The third-party creditor issues a check payable to the firm, which the firm immediately endorses over to the equipment dealer rather than depositing it and issuing its own check. Does receipt of the third-party check constitute a cash inflow? Does endorsement of the check constitute a cash outflow? SFAS-95 does not provide definitive guidance. Some firms report such transactions gross, as both financing inflows and investing outflows, whereas other firms report such transactions net in the cash flow statement with supplemental disclosure among noncash financing and investing activities, but the variations cannot be documented from published cash flow statements. Does the reporting change if the check is payable to the equipment dealer but given to the firm which in turn gives it to the dealer? Does the reporting change if the third-party creditor mails the checks directly to the equipment dealer? Again, SFAS-95 does not provide definitive guidance.[16]

Limited guidance is provided for third-party financing provided by banks. Here the FASB reasons (SFAS-95, para. 7, fn. 1) that because cash includes demand deposits, charges and credits to a demand deposit account are cash receipts and cash payments

to both the firm owning the account and the bank holding it. Accordingly, for third-party financing provided by banks, the transaction is reported gross if the firm's demand deposit account is increased for the loan and decreased for the payment, regardless of whether the firm endorses or conveys a bank check to the equipment dealer. The transaction is reported net, however, if the firm's demand deposit account is *not* affected by the loan and subsequent payment. Thus, the cash flow statement presentation of the transaction by the borrower depends on the internal accounting for the transaction by the lender![17] This is contrary to the usual situation where the financial reporting of a transaction by one firm is unaffected by the financial reporting by the other party to the transaction.

Summary and Conclusions

This paper compared the distinctions in SFAS-95 among operating, investing, and financing activities with similar distinctions in the finance literature. It identified several inconsistencies and ambiguities in the three-way classification of cash flows under SFAS-95, and demonstrated how the effectiveness of the cash flow statement and related disclosures to distinguish among operat-

---

[16] These issues were considered by the FASB at a meeting on 26 October 1988. The FASB promised some additional guidance, but in the form of a journal article by a FASB staffperson rather than a question and answer implementation guide. Unfortunately, the staffperson left the FASB before completing the journal article.

[17] Similarly, when a firm rolls over a certificate of deposit upon maturity, the bank may or may not increase and decrease the firm's demand deposit account, yet the FASB reasons (SFAS-104, 1989, para. 20) that one procedure results in a cash inflow and a cash outflow, whereas the other results in neither. Thus, the firm whose bank increases and decreases its demand deposit account when a loan or certificate of deposit is renewed reports higher cash flows relative to another firm whose bank does not adjust its demand deposit account for such renewals.

ing, financing, and investing activities is impaired.

More specifically, this paper demonstrated that the three-way classification under SFAS-95 and the ambiguous presentation of third-party financing transactions result in reporting similar cash flows differently and different cash flows similarly, just the opposite of the desired characteristic of financial reporting to report similar things similarly and different things differently. The paper also demonstrated that the classification of interest, income taxes, and dividend collections as operating cash flows results in contaminating cash flow from operating activities with the interest and dividend effects of investing and financing activities as well as with the tax effects of gains and losses relating to investing and financing activities, and produces a peculiar if not counterintuitive cash flow statement presentation of the retirement of bonded debt originally issued at a discount. Finally, this paper demonstrated that the requirements to report third-party financing transactions and disclose noncash investing and financing transactions are ambiguous.

Thus, this paper demonstrated that SFAS-95 is internally inconsistent and ambiguous in some important respects. Because the FASB has so far been unable to more substantially sharpen the distinction among operating, financing, and investing cash flows, it has forgone the opportunity to further enhance the comparability of cash flow statements.

By highlighting these inconsistencies and ambiguities, it is hoped that readers will be more aware of certain limitations of cash flow statements prepared under SFAS-95. More specifically, it is hoped that readers have been made aware that the amount reported as cash flow from operating activities does not reflect all of the cash flow consequences of operating activities and, similarly, that the amounts reported as cash flow from investing and financing activities do not reflect all of the cash flow consequences of investing and financing activities, respectively. Accordingly, these amounts should not be incorporated into operating, investing and financing decision models without adjustment.

References

Accounting Principles Board. 1967. Accounting for Income Taxes. *Opinion No. 11.* New York: AICPA.

———. 1973. Accounting for Nonmonetary Transactions. *Opinion No. 29.* New York: AICPA.

Alexander & Baldwin, Inc. 1990. *Annual Report.*

American Bankers Insurance Group, Inc. 1990. *Annual Report.*

Brealey, R. A., and S. C. Myers. 1988. *Principles of Corporate Finance.* 3rd ed. New York: McGraw-Hill Book Company.

Cash America Investments Inc. 1990. *Annual Report.*

Chasteen, L. G., R. E. Flaherty, and M. C. O'Connor. 1989. *Intermediate Accounting.* 3rd ed. New York: Random House.

Commerce Clearing House. 1991. *Annual Report.*

Cushing, B. E. 1977. On the Possibility of Optimal Accounting Principles. *The Accounting Review* 52 (April): 308–21.

Danos, P., and E. A. Imhoff, Jr. 1986. *Intermediate Accounting.* 5th ed. Englewood Cliffs, N.J.: Prentice-Hall.

Davidson, S., L. J. Hanouille, C. P. Stickney, and R. L. Weil. 1985. *Intermediate Accounting Concepts, Methods, and Uses.* 4th ed. Hinsdale, Illinois: The Dryden Press.

Drtina, R. E., and J. A. Largay III. 1985. Pitfalls in Calculating Cash Flow from Operations. *The Accounting Review* 60 (April): 314–26.

DST Systems Inc. 1989. *Annual Report.*

Ernst & Whinney. 1988. *Statement of Cash Flows: Understanding and Implementing FASB Statement No. 95.* Cleveland: E&W.

Fairchild Corporation. 1991. *Annual Report.*
Farmland Industries, Inc. 1990. *Annual Report.*
Financial Accounting Foundation. 1991. *Annual Report.*
Financial Accounting Standards Board. 1978. Objectives of Financial Reporting by Business Enterprises. *Concepts Statement No. 1.* Stamford, Conn.: FASB.
———. 1979a. Capitalization of Interest Cost. *Statement No. 34.* Stamford, Conn.: FASB.
———. 1979b. Reporting Earnings. *Discussion Memorandum.* Stamford, Conn.: FASB.
———. 1980a. Reporting Funds Flows, Liquidity, and Financial Flexibility. *Discussion Memorandum.* Stamford, Conn.: FASB.
———. 1980b. Elements of Financial Statements of Business Enterprises. *Concepts Statement No. 3.* Stamford, Conn.: FASB.
———. 1981. Reporting Income, Cash Flows, and Financial Position of Business Enterprises. *Exposure Draft.* Stamford, Conn.: FASB.
———. 1985. Recognition and Measurement in Financial Statements of Business Enterprises. *Concepts Statement No. 5.* Stamford, Conn.: FASB.
———. 1985. Elements of Financial Statements. *Concepts Statement No. 6.* Stamford, Conn.: FASB.
———. 1987a. *Action Alerts,* No. 87-11 (March 18) and No. 87-16 (April 22).
———. 1987b. Statement of Cash Flows. *Statement No. 95.* Stamford, Conn.: FASB.
———. 1987c. Accounting for Income Taxes. *Statement No. 96.* Stamford, Conn.: FASB.
———. 1989. Statement of Cash Flows— Exemption of Certain Enterprises and Classification of Cash Flows from Certain Securities Acquired for Resale. *Statement No. 102.* Norwalk, Conn.: FASB.
———. 1989. Statement of Cash Flows— Net Reporting of Certain Cash Receipts and Cash Payments and Classification of Cash Flows from Hedging Transactions. *Statement No. 104.* Norwalk, Conn.: FASB.
General Motors Corporation. 1991. *Annual Report.*
Government Accounting Standards Board. 1989. Reporting Cash Flows of Proprietary and Nonexpendable Trust Funds and Governmental Entities That Use Proprietary Fund Accounting. *Statement No. 9.* Norwalk, Conn.: FASB.
Greer, H. C. 1945. Treatment of Income Taxes in Corporate Financial Statements. *The Accounting Review* 20 (January): 96–101.
Heath, L. C. 1978. *Financial Reporting and the Evaluation of Solvency.* New York: AICPA.
———. 1988. Cash Flow Statement in Intermediate Accounting Textbooks. *Accounting Horizons* 2 (December): 107–16.
International Accounting Standards Committee. 1991. Statement of Cash Flows. *Exposure Draft.* London: IASC.
Ketz, J. E., and J. A. Largay III. 1987. Reporting Income and Cash Flow from Operations. *Accounting Horizons* 1 (June): 9–18.
Kieso, D. E., and J. J. Weygandt. 1983. *Intermediate Accounting.* 4th ed. New York: John Wiley & Sons.
———, and ———. 1989. *Intermediate Accounting.* 6th ed. New York: John Wiley & Sons.
Larrizza Industries Inc. 1990. *Annual Report.*
Mead Corporation. 1990. *Annual Report.*
Mechanical Technology Incorporated. 1989. *Annual Report.*
Moonitz, M. 1956. Reporting on the Flow of Funds. *The Accounting Review* 31 (July): 375–85.
Mosich, A. N. 1989. *Intermediate Accounting.* 6th ed. New York: McGraw-Hill Book Company.
Nikolai, L. A., and J. D. Bazley. 1991. *Intermediate Accounting.* 5th ed. Boston: Kent Publishing Co.
Nurnberg, H. 1983. Issues in Funds Statement Presentation. *The Accounting Review* 63 (October): 799–812.
———. 1990. Interest and Long-term Bonds in the Cash Flow Statement Under FASB Statement No. 95. *CPA Journal* (January): 50–54.
Pacific Enterprises. 1988. *Annual Report.*
Patten, R. J. 1964. Interperiod Income Tax Allocation—A Practical Concept. *The Accounting Review* 39 (October): 876–79.

Rent-A-Wreck of America, Inc. 1988 *Annual Report.*

Seiler, M. E. 1991. Statement of Cash Flows. *Accountants' Handbook.* eds. D. R. Carmichael, S. B. Lilien, and M. Mellman. New York: John Wiley & Sons.

Simetco Inc. 1988. *Annual Report.*

Smith, J. M., and K. F. Skousen. 1987. *Intermediate Accounting.* Comprehensive Volume. 9th ed. Cincinnati: South-Western Publishing Co.

Solomon, E., and J. J. Pringle. 1980. *An Introduction to Financial Management.* 2nd ed. Santa Monica, California: Goodyear Publishing Company.

Stewart, J. E., P. R. Ogorzelec, D. L. Baskin, Jr., and T. J. Duffy. 1988. Implementing the New Statement of Cash Flows for Banks. *Bank Accounting and Finance* (Spring): 3–19.

Thorn Apple Valley, Inc. 1991. *Annual Report.*

U.S., Securities and Exchange Commission.

1945. In the Matter of "Charges in Lieu of Taxes"—Statement of the Commission's Opinion Regarding "Charges in Lieu of Taxes" in the Profit and Loss Statement. *Accounting Series Release No. 53.* Washington: SEC.

Weston, J. F., and T. E. Copeland. 1992. *Managerial Finance.* 9th ed. Hinsdale, Illinois: The Dryden Press.

Welsch, G. A., C. T. Zlatkovich, and W. T. Harrison. 1982. *Intermediate Accounting.* 6th ed. Homewood, Illinois: Richard D. Irwin.

———, and ———. 1989. *Intermediate Accounting.* 8th ed. Homewood, Illinois: Richard D. Irwin.

Westinghouse Electric Corporation. 1991. *Annual Report.*

Williams, J. R., K. G. Stanga, and W. W. Holder. 1989. *Intermediate Accounting.* 3rd ed. San Diego: Harcourt Brace Jovanovich, Publishers.

Cases

• Case 5-1

The financial statement on the next page was prepared by employees of your client, Linus Construction Company. The statement is unaccompanied by footnotes, but you have discovered the following:

a. The average completion period for the company's jobs is 18 months. The company's method of journalizing contract transactions is summarized in the following pro-forma entries:

1. Materials, supplies, labor, and overhead $xxx,xxx
charged to construction
Cash, various other assets, payables, de- $xxx,xxx
preciation, and other accounts
To record actual costs incurred on jobs

2. Materials, supplies, labor, and overhead $xxx,xxx
charged to construction
Unearned revenue on work in progress $xxx,xxx
To accrue but defer estimated profit earned on work in progress.

3. Accounts receivable $xxx,xxx
Unearned revenue on work in progress $xxx,xxx
To charge customers for costs incurred to date.
(Most contracts provide that customers

LINUS CONSTRUCTION COMPANY
Statement of Financial Position
October 31, 1990

Current assets:

Cash		$ 182,200	
Accounts receivable (less allowance of $15,000 for doubtful accounts)		220,700	
Materials, supplies, labor, and overhead charged to construction		2,026,000	
Materials and supplies not charged to construction		288,000	
Deposits made to secure performance of contracts		360,000	$3,076,900

Less Current Liabilities:

Accounts payable to subcontractors		$ 141,100	
Payable for materials and supplies		65,300	
Accrued payroll		8,260	
Accrued interest on mortgage note		12,000	
Estimated taxes payable		66,000	292,660
Net working capital			$2,784,240

Property Plant and Equipment (at cost):

	Cost	Depreciation	Value	
Land and buildings	$ 983,300	$310,000	$ 673,300	
Machinery and equipment	905,000	338,000	567,000	
Payments made on leased equipment	230,700	230,699	1	
	$2,119,000	$878,699	$1,240,301	

Deferred charges:

Prepaid taxes and other expenses		$ 11,700	
Points charged on mortgage note		10,800	22,500
Total net working capital and noncurrent assets			4,047,041

Less Deferred Liabilities:

Mortgage note payable		$ 300,000	
Unearned revenue on work in progress		1,898,000	2,198,000
Total Net Assets			$1,849,041

Stockholders' Equity:

6% preferred stock at par value		$ 400,000	
Common stock at par value		800,000	
Paid-in surplus		210,000	
Retained earnings		483,641	
Treasury stock at cost (370 shares)		(44,600)	
Total Stockholders' Equity			$1,849,041

> are in progress 95 percent of amounts billed shall be remitted within 15 days of billing. On job completion, the remainder of the contract price is billed and recorded in an entry [s] in which the profit or loss realized on the job is also recognized.)

4. Cash	$xxx,xxx	
Accounts receivable		$xxx,xxx
To record collections.		
5. Accounts receivable	$xxx,xxx	
Unearned revenue on work in progress		$xxx,xxx
(Loss) Profit realized on completed jobs	$xxx,xxx or	$xx,xxx
Materials, supplies, labor, and overhead charged to construction		$xxx,xxx
To record completion of job number.		

b. Linus both owns and leases equipment used on construction jobs. Typically, its equipment lease contracts provide that Linus may return the equipment on completion of a job or may apply all rentals in full toward purchase of the equipment. About 70 percent of lease rental payments made in the past have been applied to the purchase of equipment. While leased equipment is in use, rents are charged to the account *payments made on leased equipment* (except for $1 balance) and are charged to jobs on which the equipment has been used. In the event of purchase the balance in the *payments made on leased equipment* account is transferred to the *machinery and equipment* account and the depreciation and other related accounts are corrected.

c. Management is unable to develop dependable estimates of costs to complete contracts in progress.

Required:

a. Identify the weaknesses in the financial statement.

b. For each item identified in part (a), indicate the preferable treatment and explain why the treatment is preferable.

• Case 5-2

The argument among accountants and financial statement users over the proper valuation procedures for assets and liabilities has resulted in the release of *SFAS No. 115*. The statement requires current value disclosures for all investments. Recently, the chairman of the Securities and Exchange Commission termed historical cost valuations "once upon a time accounting." Historical cost accounting also has been criticized as contributing to the Savings and Loan crisis in the 1980s. During that period these financial institutions continued to value assets at historical cost when they were billions of dollars overvalued. Critics of current value accounting point out that objective market values for many assets are not available, current values cannot be used for tax purposes, using current values can cause earnings volatility and management could use current value to "manage earnings."

Required:
a. Determine how current values might be determined for investments, land, buildings, equipment, patents, copyrights, trademarks, and franchises.
b. How might the use of current values in the accounting records cause earnings volatility?
c. Discuss how management might manage earnings using current cost data.

● Case 5-3

Obtain a copy of a large corporation's annual report and refer to the statement of cash flows.

Required:
a. Did the company use the direct method or the indirect method of disclosing cash flows?
b. Comment on the relationship between cash flows from operations and net income for the year of the statement and the previous year.
c. What were the most significant sources of cash from operating activities during the period covered by the statement? What percent of total cash inflows do these sources represent? Answer the same question for the previous period.
d. Was the cash from operations more than or less than dividends during the period covered by the statement and the previous period?
e. What were the firm's major investing activities during the period covered by the statement and the previous period? Were cash flows from operations more or less than cash flows from investing activities for the company in question?
f. What were the most significant cash flows from financing activities during the year of the statement and the previous year?
g. Review the management discussion and analysis sections of the financial statements to determine if any additional information is available concerning the company's investment or financing strategy.

● Case 5-4

The measurement of assets and liabilities on the balance sheet is frequently a secondary goal to income determination. As a result, various measurement techniques are used to disclose assets and liabilities.

Required:
Discuss the various measurement techniques used on the balance sheet to disclose assets and liabilities.

● Case 5-5

Presenting information on cash flows has become an important part of financial reporting.

Required:

a. What goals are attempted to be accomplished by the presentation of cash flow information to investors?

b. Discuss the following terms as they relate to the presentation of cash flow information.
   i. Liquidity.
   ii. Solvency.
   iii. Financial flexibility.

Recommended Additional Readings

Bierman, Harold Jr. "Measurement and Accounting." *The Accounting Review* (July 1963), pp. 501–507.

Ijiri, Yuri. "Cash-Flow Accounting and Its Structure." *Journal of Accounting, Auditing and Finance* (Summer 1978), pp. 331–348.

Ketz, J. Edward, and James A. Largay III. "Reporting Income and Cash Flows from Operations." *Accounting Horizons* (June 1987), pp. 9–17.

Kirk, Donald J. "On Future Events: When Incorporated into Today's Measurements?" *Accounting Horizons* (June 1990), pp. 86–92.

Lee, T. A. "A Note on Users and Uses of Cash Flow Information." *Accounting and Business Research* (Spring 1983), pp. 103–106.

Lee, T. A. "Cash Flow Accounting, Profit and Performance Measurement: A Response to a Challenge." *Accounting and Business Research* (Spring 1985), pp. 93–97.

Salamon, Gerald L. "Cash Recovery Rates and Measures of Firm Profitability." *The Accounting Review* (April 1982), pp. 292–302.

Stabus, George J. "Measurement of Assets and Liabilities." *Accounting and Business Research* (Autumn 1963), pp. 243–262.

Trenholm, Barbara, and Francisco Arcelus. "Accounting Valuation Methods: Structuring An Unstructured Problem." *Accounting Horizons* (September 1989), pp. 82–89.

Bibliography

American Accounting Association Committee on Accounting Valuation Bases. "Report of the Committee on Accounting Valuation Bases." *The Accounting Review,* Supplement to Vol. 47 (1972), pp. 535–573.

American Accounting Association. "Report of the Committee on Foundations of Accounting Measurement." *The Accounting Review.* Supplement to Vol. 46 (1979), pp. 36–45.

Ashton, Robert H. "Objectivity of Accounting Measures: A Multirule-Multimeasurer Approach." *The Accounting Review* (July 1977), pp. 567–575.

Braiotta, Louis, Jr. "Cash Basis Statement of Changes." *The CPA Journal* (August 1984), pp. 34–40.

Crooch, G. Michael, and Bruce E. Collier. "Reporting Guidelines for Companies in a State of Development." *The CPA Journal* (July 1973), pp. 579–584.

Fadel, Hisham, and John M. Parkinson. "Liquidity Evaluation by Means of Ratio Analysis." *Accounting and Business Research* (Spring 1978), pp. 101–107.

Heath, Loyd C. "Financial Reporting and the Evaluation of Solvency." New York: American Institute of Certified Public Accountants, 1978.

Heath, Loyd C. "Financial Reporting and the Evaluation of Solvency." Accounting Research Monograph No. 3. AICPA, 1978.

Heath, Loyd C. "Is Working Capital Really Working?" *Journal of Accountancy* (August 1980), pp. 55–62.

Heath, Loyd C. "Let's Scrap the 'Funds' Statement." *Journal of Accountancy* (October 1978), pp. 94–103.

Heath, Loyd C., and Paul Rosenfield. "Solvency: The Forgotten Half of Financial Reporting." *Journal of Accountancy* (January 1979), pp. 48–54.

Jaedicke, Robert K., and Robert T. Sprouse. *Accounting Flows: Income, Funds, and Cash.* Englewood Cliffs, N.J.: Prentice-Hall, Inc., 1965.

Largay, James A., III, Edward P. Swanson, and Max Block. "The 'Funds' Statement: Should It Be Scrapped, Retained or Revitalized?" *Journal of Accountancy* (December 1979), pp. 88–97.

Lemke, Kenneth W. "The Evaluation of Liquidity: An Analytical Study." *Journal of Accounting Research* (Spring 1970), pp. 47–77.

Mason, Perry. *Cash Flow Analysis and the Funds Statement.* New York: American Institute of Certified Public Accountants, 1961.

Moonitz, Maurice. "Reporting on the Flow of Funds." *The Accounting Review* (July 1956), pp. 378–385.

Nurnberg, Hugo. "APB Opinion No. 19—Pro and Con." *Financial Executive* (December 1972), pp. 58–60, 62, 64, 66, 68, 70.

"Report of the Committee on Accounting Valuation Bases." *The Accounting Review.* Supplement to Vol. 47 (1972), esp. pp. 556–568.

"Report of the Committee on Foundations of Accounting Measurements." *The Accounting Review,* Supplement to Vol. 46 (1971), pp. 3–48.

Spiller, Earl A., and Robert L. Virgil. "Effectiveness of APB #19 in Improving Funds Reporting." *Journal of Accounting Research* (Spring 1974), pp. 112–133.

Sprouse, Robert T. "Balance Sheet—Embodiment of the Most Fundamental Elements of Accounting Theory." *Foundations of Accounting Theory.* Gainesville, Fla.: University of Florida Press, 1971, pp. 90–104.

Staubus, George J. "An Induced Theory of Accounting Measurement." *The Accounting Review* (January 1985), pp. 53–75.

Staubus, George J. "The Market Stimulation Theory of Accounting Measurement." *Accounting and Business Research* (Spring 1986), pp. 117–132.

Swanson, Edward P., and Richard Vangermeersch. "Statement of Financing and Investing Activities." *The CPA Journal* (November 1981), pp. 32, 34–36, 38–40.

Tippett, Mark. "The Axioms of Accounting Measurement." *Accounting and Business Research* (Autumn 1978), pp. 266–278.

Walker, R. G. "Asset Classification and Asset Valuation." *Accounting and Business Research* (Autumn 1974), pp. 286–296.

CHAPTER 6

Working Capital

A company's *working capital* is the net short-term investment needed to carry on day-to-day activities. The measurement and disclosure of working capital on financial statements has been considered an appropriate accounting function for decades and the usefulness of this concept for financial analysis is accepted almost without question. However, there are some serious problems with the concept such as (1) inconsistencies in the measurements of the various components of working capital, (2) differences of opinion over what should be included as the elements of working capital, and (3) a lack of precision in the meaning of certain key terms involved in defining the elements of working capital, such as *liquidity* and *current*. This chapter (1) examines the foundation of the working capital concept, (2) reviews the concept and its components as currently understood, and (3) discusses how the concept might be modified to add to its usefulness.

Development of the Working Capital Concept

The concept of working capital originated with the distinction between fixed and circulating capital at the beginning of the 20th century. As noted in Chapter 1, at that time accounting was in its adolescent stage and such concepts as asset, liability, income, and expense were not clearly understood.[1] The impetus for the fixed and circulating capital definitions came from court decisions on the legality of dividends in Great Britain. As first defined, fixed capital was money expended that was sunk once and for all, while circulating capital

[1] For a complete documentation of the history of the working capital concept, see William Huizingh, *Working Capital Classification* (Ann Arbor: Bureau of Business Research, Graduate School of Business Administration, University of Michigan, 1967).

was defined as items of stock in trade, which are parted with and replaced by similar items in the ordinary course of business.

These definitions were not readily accepted by members of the accounting profession, some of whom feared that the general public would misinterpret the distinction. Soon thereafter British and American accountants began to examine the valuation bases of various assets, and gave increased attention to a method of accounting termed the *double-account system*. The double-account system divided the balance sheet horizontally into two sections. The upper portion contained all the long-lived assets, the capital, the debt, and a balancing figure that represented the difference between capital and long-term liabilities, and long-lived assets. The lower section contained all other assets, current liabilities, and the balancing figure from the top section.

During this same period the notion of *liquidity* was becoming established as a basis for the classification of assets on the financial statements. Liquidity classification schemes were intended to report on the short-run solvency of the enterprise; however, criticisms arose which suggested that such schemes were in conflict with the going-concern concept. Nevertheless, the liquidity concept continued to gain acceptance among accountants and financial statement users and was included by Paton in his distinction between fixed and current assets.[2] Paton noted that length of life, rate of use, and method of consumption were important factors in distinguishing between fixed and current assets. He elaborated on these factors as follows: A fixed asset will remain in the enterprise two or more periods, whereas current assets will be used more rapidly; fixed assets may be charged to expense over many periods, whereas current assets are used more quickly; and fixed assets are used entirely to furnish a series of similar services, whereas current assets are consumed.[3]

During the first three decades of the 20th century, the balance sheet was viewed as the principal financial statement by most users in the United States. During this period, financial statements were prepared on the basis of their usefulness to creditors, and investors were left to make their decisions on whatever basis they felt applicable. In 1936 the American Institute of Certified Public Accountants attempted to modify this viewpoint when it acknowledged the different points of view of the creditor and the investor as follows.

> *As a rule a creditor is more particularly interested in the liquidity of a business enterprise and the nature and adequacy of its working capital; hence the details of the current assets and current liabilities are to him of relatively more importance than details of long-term assets and liabilities. He also has a real interest in the earnings, because the ability to repay a loan may be dependent upon the profits of the enterprise. From an investor's point of view, it is generally recognized that earning capacity is of vital importance and that the income account is at least as important as the balance sheet.*[4]

[2] William A. Paton, *Accounting Theory* (New York: Ronald Press, 1922).

[3] Ibid., pp. 215–216.

[4] *Examination of Financial Statements by Independent Public Accountants* (New York: AICPA, 1936), p. 4.

By the 1940s the concept of working capital as a basis for determining liquidity had become well established, even though there was some disagreement as to its exact meaning. The confusion centered on how to identify current assets and whether the classification should be based on those items that *will be* converted into cash in the short run or those that *could be* converted into cash. At this time the one-year rule as the basis for classifying assets as current or noncurrent was fairly well established. But Anson Herrick, who was an active member of the American Institute of Certified Public Accountants, began to point out some of the fallacies of the one-year rule.

Herrick focused on the differences in preparing statements for credit and investment purposes and noted some inconsistencies in current practice, such as including inventories under the current classification when their turnover might take more than a year while excluding trade receivables due more than a year after the balance sheet date.[5] His thoughts are summarized in the following statement.

> *It is not logical to adopt a practice which may result in substantial difference between the reported amount of net current assets . . . and the amount which would be shown if the statement were to be prepared a few days earlier or later.*[6]

In lieu of the one-year rule, Herrick proposed the *operating cycle* as the basis for classifying assets as current. This distinction was based on the contrast of the assets' economic substance as either *fixed* or *circulating* capital.[7]

In 1947, while Herrick was a committee member, the Committee on Accounting Procedure issued *Accounting Research Bulletin No. 30*. This release defined current assets as "cash or other resources commonly identified as those which are reasonably expected to be realized in cash or sold or consumed during the normal operating cycle of the business." Current liabilities were defined as "debts or obligations, the liquidation or payment of which is reasonably expected to require the use of existing resources properly classifiable as current assets or the creation of other current liabilities."[8] The operating cycle was then defined as "the average time intervening between the acquisition of materials or services . . . and the final cash realization." The committee also established one year as the basis for classification when the operating cycle was shorter than one year.[9] Although this distinction was slightly modified by *Accounting Research Bulletin No. 43*, it has stood essentially intact since that time, and was recently reaffirmed in *SFAS No. 115* as discussed later in the chapter.

---

[5] Anson Herrick, "Current Assets and Current Liabilities," *Journal of Accountancy* (January 1944), pp. 48–55.

[6] Ibid., p. 49.

[7] Ibid., p. 50.

[8] *Accounting Research Bulletin No. 30*, pp. 248–249.

[9] Ibid., pp. 247, 249.

Current Usage

It is usually argued that the working capital concept provides useful information by giving an indication of an entity's liquidity and the degree of protection given to short-term creditors. The concept gained increased prominence after the issuance of *Accounting Principles Board Opinion No. 19,* which made the presentation of a statement of changes in financial position mandatory. Specifically, the presentation of working capital can be said to add to the flow of information to financial statement users by (1) indicating the amount of margin or buffer available to meet current obligations, (2) presenting the flow of current assets and current liabilities from past periods, and (3) presenting information on which to base predictions of future inflows and outflows. In the following sections we examine the measurement of the items included under working capital.

Components of Working Capital

The *Accounting Research Bulletin No. 43* definitions of current assets and current liabilities include examples of each classification as follows:

Current Assets

a. *cash available for current operations and items which are the equivalent of cash*

b. *inventories of merchandise, raw materials, goods in process, finished goods, operating supplies, and ordinary maintenance materials and parts*

c. *trade accounts, notes, and acceptances receivable*

d. *receivables from officers, employees, affiliates, and others if collectible in the ordinary course of business within a year*

e. *installment or deferred accounts and notes receivable if they conform generally to normal trade practices and terms within the business*

f. *marketable securities representing the investment of cash available for current operations*

g. *prepaid expenses, such as insurance, interest, rents, taxes, unused royalties, current paid advertising service not yet received and operating supplies*[10]

Current Liabilities

a. *obligations for items which have entered into the operating cycle, such as payables incurred in the acquisition of materials and supplies to be used in the production of goods or in providing services to be offered for sale*

b. *collections received in advance of the delivery of goods or performance of services*

c. *debts which arise from operations directly related to the operating cycle, such*

---

[10] *Accounting Research Bulletin No. 43,* "Restatement and Revision of Accounting Research Bulletins" (New York: AICPA, 1953), pars. 6010–11.

as accruals for wages, salaries and commission, rentals, royalties, and income and other taxes

d. other liabilities whose regular and ordinary liquidation is expected to occur within a relatively short period of time, usually twelve months, are also intended for inclusion, such as short-term debts arising from the acquisition of capital assets, serial maturities of long-term obligations, amounts required to be expended within one year under sinking fund provisions and agency obligations arising from the collection or acceptance of cash or other assets for the account of third persons[11]

These items will now be examined in more detail.

Current Assets

Cash

The accurate measurement of cash is important not only because cash represents the amount of resources available to meet emergency situations, but also because most accounting measurements are based on actual or expected cash inflows and outflows. The prediction of future cash flows is essential to investors, creditors, and management to enable these groups to determine (1) the availability of cash to meet maturing obligations, (2) the availability of cash to pay dividends, and (3) the amount of idle cash that can safely be invested for future use. Measuring cash normally includes counting not only the cash on hand and in banks but also formal negotiable paper, such as personal checks, cashier's checks, and bank drafts.

The amount of cash disclosed as a current asset must be available for current use and not subject to any restrictions. For example, sinking fund cash should not be reported as a current asset because it is intended to be used to purchase long-term investments, or to repay long-term debt.

It has also become commonplace for banks to require a portion of amounts borrowed to remain on deposit during the period of the loan. These deposits are called *compensating balances*. This type of agreement has two main effects: (1) It reduces the amount of cash available for current use and (2) it increases the effective interest rate on the loan. In 1973, the SEC issued *Accounting Series Release No. 148*, which recommended that compensating balances against short-term loans be shown separately in the current assets section of the balance sheet. Compensating balances on long-term loans may be classified as either investments or other assets.[12]

Cash Equivalents

Firms frequently invest cash in excess of immediate needs in short-term, highly liquid investments. Whether cash is on hand, on deposit, or invested in a

---

[11] Ibid., par. 6011.

[12] "Amendments to Regulation S-X and Related Interpretations and Guidelines Regarding the Disclosure of Compensating Balances and Short-Term Borrowing Agreements." *Accounting Series Release No. 148* (Washington D.C.: SEC, November 13, 1973).

short-term investment that is readily convertible to cash is irrelevant to financial statement users' assessments of liquidity and future cash flows. The investment of idle funds in cash equivalents to earn interest is a part of the firm's cash management policy. This policy is in contrast to investing capital in the hope of benefiting from favorable price changes that may result from changes in interest rates or other factors. In order to distinguish between cash management and investment policies, *Statement of Financial Accounting Standards No. 95* defines cash equivalents as short-term investments that satisfy the following two criteria:

1. Readily convertible into a known amount of cash.
2. Sufficiently close to its maturity date so that its market value is relatively insensitive to interest rate changes.

Generally, only investments purchased within three months of their maturity value will satisfy these criteria. Examples of cash equivalents are short-term investments in U. S. treasury bills, commercial paper, and money market funds. The purchase and sale of these investments are viewed as a part of the firm's cash management activities rather than a part of its operating, financing, and investing activities. Additionally, the FASB noted that different types of firms in different industries might pursue different cash management and investing strategies. Consequently, each firm must disclose its policy for treating items as cash equivalents, and any change in that policy must be treated as a change in accounting principle that requires the restatement of prior years' financial statements.

Temporary Investments

In the event that the cash and cash equivalent balances are larger than necessary to provide for current operations, it is advisable to invest idle funds until their use becomes necessary. Investments classified as current assets must be readily marketable and intended to be converted into cash within the operating cycle or a year, whichever is longer. Short-term investments are generally distinguished from cash equivalents by relatively longer investment perspectives, at relatively higher rates of return.

In theory, the procedures used to report the value of temporary investments on the balance sheet should provide investors with an indication of the resources that will be available for future use; that is, the amount of cash that could be generated from the disposal of these securities. Most temporary investments are unlike other assets in that an objectively determined measurement of their value is available in the securities market on a day-to-day basis. Therefore, accountants have been divided over the proper methods to use to value temporary investments. Three alternative methods for reporting temporary investments have been debated: **historical cost, fair value,** and the **lower of cost or market.**

The *historical cost* method reports temporary investments at their acquisition cost until disposal. The advocates of historical cost believe an objectively verified purchase price provides the most relevant information about investments to decision makers. They also argue that current market prices do not provide any better information on future prices than does original cost, and that only realized gains and losses should be reported on the income statement.

Investments reported at *fair value* are adjusted to reflect both upward and downward changes in value, and these changes are reported as either gains or losses on the income statement. Advocates of the fair value method state that current amounts represent the current resources that would be needed to acquire the same securities now and also the amount that would be received from the sale of the securities. Additionally, they note that fair value is as objectively determined as historical cost for most investments, and it also presents more timely information on the effect of holding investments.

The *lower of cost or market* method, as originally defined, reports only downward adjustments in the value of temporary investments. The proponents of this method believe that it provides users with more conservative balance sheet and income statement valuations. They argue that conservative valuations are necessary in order not to mislead investors.

Accounting for temporary investments when their value falls below cost was studied by the Financial Accounting Standards Board in response to stock market conditions in 1973 and 1974. During this period the stock market declined substantially from previous levels and then made a partial recovery. The general movement in stock prices during this period had two main effects on financial reporting for investments:

1. Some companies used the historical cost method and did not write their investments down to reflect market prices and were therefore carrying their portfolios of investments at amounts above current market prices.

2. Some companies used the lower of cost or market method, valued their investments at market values, and wrote their investments down to current prices when the stock market reached its lowest level. The partial recovery experienced by the stock market then could not be reflected on these companies' financial statements, which resulted in the companies carrying their investments at an amount below both cost and current market.

Subsequently, the FASB issued *SFAS No. 12*, "Accounting for Certain Marketable Securities," which attempted to alleviate this problem.[13]

According to the provisions of *SFAS No. 12*, marketable equity securities classified as current assets were to be valued at their aggregate cost or market value, whichever is lower on each balance sheet date. This determination was to be made by comparing the total cost of the entire portfolio of temporary investments in equity securities against its total market value. Losses in market value were to be accounted for as charges against income and reported on the balance sheet by way of a valuation account offset against the temporary investment account.

These were requirements not substantially different from previous practice. However, the FASB did provide for one major difference. If losses had

---

[13] Financial Accounting Standards Board, *Statement of Financial Accounting Standards No. 12*, "Accounting for Certain Marketable Securities" (Stamford, Conn.: FASB, 1975).

previously been recorded, and a valuation account was in existence, a subsequent recovery of market value was to be reported as income to the extent of previously recorded losses. The following example illustrates the provisions of this statement.

	Date	Portfolio Cost	Portfolio Market Value	Reported Increase/ (Decrease) of Income	Reported Increase/ (Decrease) of Valuation Account
Initial purchase	1/1/91	$18,000	$18,000	$0	$0
Balance sheet date	12/31/92	18,000	20,000	0	0
Balance sheet date	12/31/93	18,000	15,000	(3,000)	3,000
Balance sheet date	12/31/94	18,000	17,000	2,000	(2,000)
Balance sheet date	12/31/95	18,000	21,000	1,000	(1,000)

If all or any part of the portfolio was sold, a gain or loss was recognized on the sale by comparing the original cost of the securities sold with the proceeds from the sale. The valuation account was not affected by the sale of securities. Changes in the valuation account were recorded on the balance sheet date by comparing the cost of the remaining securities with their market value to determine the required balance in the valuation account. If no securities remained, the entire valuation account was eliminated.

The provisions of *SFAS No. 12* were anticipated to have the impact of allowing investors to evaluate the management of the temporary investment portfolio. For example, it might be possible to compare the yearly change in the market value of the portfolio to the overall trend in the stock market to assess the effect of management's temporary investment strategy.

SFAS No. 12 referred only to marketable equity securities and did not alter the accounting treatment required for other types of temporary investments. Under traditional GAAP, other temporary investments would have been reported by using either the cost or the lower of cost or market methods. However, if the lower of cost or market method was used, losses were recorded only when there had been a permanent impairment in value. Subsequent recoveries in market value were not recorded.

Later, concerns began to be expressed about the different accounting treatments allowed for investments in equity versus debt securities. Specifically, questions were raised about using the lower of cost or market method where diminished values were reported, whereas value appreciations were not reported. Additionally, the issue of gains trading was raised. *Gains trading* is the practice of selling securities that appreciated in value in order to recognize a gain, while holding securities with unrealized losses. This practice is generally confined to trading in debt securities where the historical cost method of accounting is used.

As a result, the FASB undertook a project to address accounting for both equity and debt securities. This project was limited in scope because not all financial assets were included (e.g., receivables), and current accounting requirements for financial liabilities were not changed. The result of this project was the release of *Statement of Financial Standards No. 115,* "Accounting for Certain Investments in Debt and Equity Securities." The provisions of this statement became effective for fiscal periods beginning after December 15, 1993.

SFAS No. 115 requires companies to classify equity and debt securities into one of the following three categories:

Trading securities   Securities held for resale.

Securities available for sale   Securities not classified as trading securities or held-to-maturity securities.

Securities held to maturity   Securities for which the reporting enterprise has both the positive intent and ability to hold those securities to maturity.

Trading securities are reported at fair value, and all unrealized holding gains and losses are also reported at fair value and recognized in earnings. Available-for-sale securities are reported at fair value; however, unrealized holding gains and losses for these securities are not included in periodic net income; rather they are reported as a separate component of stockholders' equity until realized. Held-to-maturity securities are accounted for by the historical cost method and any premium or discount, reflected as a difference between the acquisition price and the security's maturity value, is amortized over the remaining life of the security.

Trading securities are reported as current assets on the balance sheet. Individual held-to-maturity and available-for-sale securities are reported as either current assets or investments as appropriate. The appropriate classification is to be based on the definitions provided in *ARB No. 43,* discussed earlier.

The transfer of a security between investment categories is accounted for at fair value. At the date of the transfer, the security's unrealized holding gain or loss shall be accounted for as follows:

1. For a security transferred from the trading category, the unrealized holding gain or loss will already have been recognized in earnings, so no additional recognition is required.

2. For a security transferred into the trading category, the unrealized holding gain or loss at the date of the transfer shall be recognized immediately.

3. For a debt security transferred into the available-for-sale category from the held-to-maturity category, the unrealized holding gain or loss shall be recognized in a separate component of stockholders' equity.

4. For a debt security transferred into the held-to-maturity category from the available-for-sale category, the unrealized holding gain or loss shall continue to be reported in a separate component of stockholders' equity, but shall be amortized over the remaining life of the security as an adjustment to interest in a manner similar to the amortization of a premium or discount.

These requirements were adopted to further deter gains trading. If all transfers could be made at fair value and all holding gains and losses recognized immediately in earnings, the possibility of discretionary transfers to recognize earnings would be left open. The approach adopted is similar to recognizing holding gains and losses in a manner consistent with the category into which the security is being transferred.

Receivables

The term *receivables* encompasses a wide variety of claims held against others. Receivables are classified into two categories for financial statement presentation: (1) trade receivables and (2) nontrade receivables.

The outstanding receivables balance constitutes a major source of cash inflows to meet maturing obligations; therefore, the composition of this balance must be carefully evaluated so that financial statement users are not misled. In order for an item to be classified as a receivable, both the amount to be received and the expected due date must be subject to reasonable estimation.

Ideally, each enterprise would make only cash sales; however, given the nature of our economic society, most firms must extend various types of credit. Businesses sell on credit to increase sales, but when credit is extended, losses from nonpayments invariably occur. Once a business decides to sell on credit, it may record bad debts by one of the following procedures:

1. Bad debts are recorded as the loss is discovered (the direct write-off method).
2. Bad debts are estimated in the year of the sale (the estimation method).

Under the *direct write-off* method, a loss is recorded when a specific customer account is determined to be uncollectible. Frequently this determination may not be made until a subsequent accounting period and, therefore, results in an improper matching of revenues and expenses. Additionally, *SFAS No. 5* requires estimated losses to be accrued when it is probable that an asset has been impaired or a liability incurred, and the amount of the loss can be estimated. Since these conditions are usually satisfied for uncollectible accounts, most companies estimate bad debts.

Two methods may be used to estimate expected losses from nonpayment of outstanding accounts receivable: (1) the estimated loss is based on annual sales and (2) the estimated loss is based on the outstanding accounts receivable balance. When the estimated loss is based on annual sales, the matching process is enhanced because expenses are directly related to the revenues that caused the expenses. On the other hand, a more precise measure of anticipated losses can usually be made by reviewing the age and characteristics of the various accounts receivable. When the amount of loss is based on the outstanding accounts receivable, the net balance of the asset account closely resembles the expected amount to be collected in the future (*net realizable value*). With the increased emphasis on the income statement as the primary financial statement, most accountants now recommend estimating losses on the basis of sales; however, where sales and credit policies are relatively stable, it is unlikely that the use of either method of estimation will materially affect reported expenses.

Some accountants have also suggested that receivables should be carried at their present value by applying a discount factor. But others argued that this treatment is not usually considered necessary due to the relatively short collection (or discount) period involved for most accounts receivable. The FASB's recent embracement of the asset and liability approach has also had implications for this issue. Under the provisions of *SFAS No. 114*, "Accounting by Creditors for the Impairment of a Loan," creditors must now evaluate the probability that receivables will be collected. In the event that it is probable that all amounts will not be collected, the present value of the expected future cash payments must be calculated. When this present value is less than the recorded value of the loan, a loss is recognized and charged to bad debt expense, and the receivable is reduced through a valuation allowance. Alternatively, loss impairment may be measured based on the fair market value of the receivable, or if collateralized, the fair market value of the collateral. The definition of a probable loss is that a future event is likely to occur, which is consistent with the definition provided in *SFAS No. 5*, "Accounting for Contingencies." (See Chapter 9 for a discussion of accounting for contingencies).

Inventories

The term *inventory:*

> . . . designate[s] the aggregate of those items of tangible personal property which: (1) are held for sale in the ordinary course of business, (2) are in process of production for such sale, or (3) are to be currently consumed in the production of goods or services to be available for sale.[14]

The valuation of inventories is of major importance for two reasons. First, inventories generally constitute a major portion of current assets; consequently, they have a significant impact on determining working capital and current position. Second, inventory valuation has a major and immediate impact on the reported amount of net profit.

Inventory valuation procedures differ from the valuation procedures associated with cash, cash equivalents, temporary investments, and receivables. The amounts disclosed for cash, cash equivalents, temporary investments, and receivables approximate the amount of funds expected to be received from these assets. The amount of inventory disclosed on the financial statements does not represent the future cash receipts expected to be generated. Rather, it represents the acquisition value of a cost expected to generate future revenues.

The proper valuation of inventories rests on answers to the following questions.

1. What amount of goods are on hand?
2. What cost flow assumption is most reasonable for the enterprise?
3. Has the market value of the inventory declined since its acquisition?

---

[14] "Restatement and Revision of Accounting Research Bulletins." *Accounting Research and Terminology Bulletins, No. 43* (New York: AICPA, 1953).

Inventory Quantity   The inventory quantity question posed above involves determining the amount of goods on hand by (1) an actual count, (2) perpetual records, or (3) estimating procedures.

Business enterprises that issue audited financial statements are usually required to *actually count* all items of inventory at least once a year unless other methods provide reasonable assurance that the inventory figure is correct. When the inventory count is used to determine ending inventory, as in a *periodic inventory system,* the expectation is that all goods not on hand were sold. However, other factors, such as spoilage and pilferage, must be taken into consideration.

When inventory quantity is determined by the *perpetual records method,* all items of an inventory are tabulated as purchases and sales occur, and the amount of inventory on hand and the amount contained in the accounting records should be equal. However, it is usually necessary to verify the perpetual record by an actual count of inventory at least once a year. Accounting control over inventories is increased by the use of a perpetual system. But a perpetual system should be used only when the benefits derived from maintaining the records are greater than the cost of keeping the records.

Estimation methods are used when it is impossible or impractical to count or keep perpetual records for the inventory. Two methods may be used to estimate inventories: (1) the gross profit method and (2) the retail method. The *gross profit* method computes the ending inventory on a dollar basis by subtracting the estimated cost of sales from the cost of goods available. This method is especially useful in estimating inventories for interim financial statements or in computing losses from casualties, such as fire or theft.

The *retail method* is used most frequently where merchandise is available for sale directly to customers, such as in department or discount stores. When using this method, the retail value of inventory is computed by subtracting the retail price of goods sold from the retail price of goods available. Inventory at cost is then computed by applying the average markup percentage to the ending inventory at retail.

Both the gross profit and retail methods, although approximating balance sheet values, fail to provide management with all available information concerning the quantity and unit prices of specific items of inventory. For this reason an actual count of goods on hand should be made annually.

Flow Assumptions   Historically the matching of costs with associated revenues has been the primary objective in inventory valuation. That is, balance sheet valuation was viewed as secondary to income determination. Each of the flow assumptions discussed below necessarily requires a trade-off between asset valuation and income determination. Four methods are available to account for the flow of goods from purchase to sale: (1) specific identification, (2) first in, first out, (3) last in, first out, and (4) averaging.

If an exact matching of expenses and revenues is the primary objective of inventory valuation, then *specific identification* of each item of merchandise sold may be the most appropriate method. However, even this method has low informational content to balance sheet readers because the valuation of inventories at original cost generally has little relation to future expectations. When using the specific identification method, the inventory cost is determined by keeping a separate record for each item acquired and totaling the cost of the inventory items on hand at the end of each accounting period. Most companies find that the cost of the required record keeping associated with the procedure outweighs any expected benefits and turn to other methods. Specific identification is most feasible where the volume of sales is low and the cost of individual items is high, for example, jewelry, automobiles, and yachts.

The *first in, first out* (FIFO) *method* is based on assumptions about the actual flow of merchandise throughout the enterprise; in effect, it is an approximation of specific identification. In most cases this assumption conforms to reality because the oldest items in the inventory are the items management wishes to sell first, and where perishables are involved, the oldest items must be sold quickly or they will spoil.

The FIFO flow assumption satisfies the historical cost and matching principles since the recorded amount for cost of goods sold is similar to the amount that would have been recorded under specific identification if the actual flow of goods is on a FIFO basis. Additionally, the valuation of inventory more closely resembles the replacement cost of the items on hand, and thereby allows financial statement users to evaluate future working capital flows more accurately. During the last decade, rising inflation rates have caused accountants to question the desirability of using FIFO. Using older and lower unit costs during a period of inflation causes an inflated net profit figure that may mislead financial statement users. This inflated profit figure could also result in the payment of additional income taxes.

The *last in, first out* (LIFO) *method* of inventory valuation is based on the assumption that current costs should be matched against current revenues. Most advocates of LIFO cite the matching principle as the basis for their stand and argue that the past five decades of almost uninterrupted inflation require that LIFO be used to more closely approximate actual net income. These arguments are also based on the belief that price level changes should be eliminated from the statements, and LIFO is in effect a partial price level adjustment. (See Chapter 15 for a further discussion of price level adjustments.)

An added impetus to the use of LIFO in external financial reports is the Internal Revenue Service's requirement that this method must be used for reporting purposes when it is used for income tax purposes. (This requirement was amended to allow footnote or other supplemental information using FIFO or some other method. However, care must be exercised so as not to imply that another method might be a better measure of income.) Since LIFO can result in substantial tax savings, many companies that might not otherwise use it for reporting purposes do so because of income tax considerations. This situation is an unfortunate example of tax accounting dictating financial reporting.

In addition to the LIFO advantage of matching current costs and current revenues, this flow assumption may also eliminate inventory holding gains when the amount of inventory remains stable from year to year. On the other hand, inventory valuations under LIFO are almost meaningless when attempting to assess the working capital position of the firm. And if inventory is depleted beyond normal levels, the cost of goods sold associated with these items may be very low and out of date and may result in additional tax payments when prices are rising.

The computation of inventory valuation under LIFO requires a great deal of bookkeeping because the physical quantity of each item of inventory must be recorded. Additionally, as technology changes, the raw materials necessary to manufacture a product may change. Strict application of LIFO would require a new LIFO inventory base for each item of inventory. Dollar-value LIFO overcomes these disadvantages by using current costs and inventory pools. The general assumption of dollar-value LIFO is that the real increase or decrease in inventory can be estimated by eliminating the price change from the physical quantity of the ending inventory. This real increase or decrease is determined by comparing the beginning and ending inventory valuations at base-year costs.

The calculation of inventory under the dollar value LIFO method requires the use of index numbers (discussed later) measured at base-year prices and can be summarized as follows:

Step 1. Price the ending inventory at current cost.

Step 2. Restate the ending inventory by applying the base-year index to the current cost (year-end index/base-year index).

Step 3. Restate the beginning inventory by applying the base-year index to its current cost (beginning-of-the-year index/base-year index).

Step 4. Compare the ending inventory at base-year prices with the beginning inventory at base-year prices to determine if there was an increase or decrease in inventory at base year prices.

Step 5. (a) Increases—price the beginning inventory at the previous year's cost and add the additional inventory at current prices. (b) Decreases—subtract the decrease at the base-year price from the latest items acquired at the base-year price. Price the remaining inventory items at the cost in existence when they were acquired.

The computation of dollar value LIFO requires the use of an index, and either a price index or a cost index may be used. A *price index* is a general index prepared by an external organization such as the U.S. Bureau of Labor Statistics. The Economic Recovery Act of 1981 made price indices more acceptable when it authorized their use for tax purposes. A *cost index* is internally generated and more specific to a company's inventory. Cost indices are generally prepared by using a sample of the total inventory. Two methods may be used to compute a cost index: (1) the double extension method and (2) the link-chain method.

Under the *double extension* method, the ending inventory sample is priced at current-year costs and divided by the ending inventory at base-year costs to arrive at the cost index. Under the *link-chain* method, the cost index is found by computing the ratio of the current cost of the ending inventory to the beginning-of-the-year current cost of the ending inventory, and multiplying this ratio by the cost index for the previous year.

The major argument in favor of the use of dollar-value LIFO is expediency, and the procedure has little theoretical foundation. In addition to the disadvantages of LIFO discussed previously, dollar-value LIFO may create an additional problem if the index number is based on an economy-wide average. When an economy-wide average index number is applied against a particular inventory item, it is an approximation of the change in the price associated with the inventory item. Consequently, the use of an index could further distort the amount disclosed on the financial statements.

Averaging techniques are, in effect, a compromise position between first in, first out and last in, first out. When averaging is used, each purchase affects both inventory valuation and cost of goods sold. Therefore, averaging does not result in either a good match of costs with revenues or a proper valuation of inventories in fluctuating market conditions. Proponents of averaging base their arguments on the necessity of periodic presentation. That is, all the transactions during a particular period are viewed as reflective of the period as a whole rather than as individual transactions. The advocates of averaging maintain that financial statements should reflect the operations of the entire period as a whole rather than as a series of transactions.

When the averaging method used is a weighted or moving weighted average, a claim can be made that the cost of goods sold is reflective of the total period's operations; however, the resulting inventory valuation is not representative of expected future cash flows. If the simple average method is used, the resulting valuations can result in completely distorted unit prices when lot sizes and prices are changing.

Market Fluctuations   Many accountants have advocated valuing inventories at market because they believe that current assets should reflect current values. This might add to the information content of the working capital computation, but to date the doctrine of conservatism has been seen as overriding the advantages claimed by current valuation advocates. Nevertheless, when inventories have declined in value, traditional accounting thought is that the future selling price will move in the same direction and anticipated future losses should be recorded in the same period as the inventory decline.

The AICPA has provided the following definitions to use in applying the lower of cost or market rule to inventories.

> *As used in the phrase* lower of cost or market *the term* market *means current replacement cost (by purchase or reproduction, as the case may be) except that:*
>
> 1. *market should not exceed the net realizable value (i.e., estimated selling price in the ordinary course of business less reasonably predictable costs of completion and disposal), and*
>
> 2. *market should not be less than net realizable value reduced by an allowance for an approximately normal profit margin.*[15]

It should be noted that the application of the lower of cost or market rule results in inventory being recorded at an *expected utility* value and in the record-

---

[15] Ibid., Chap. 4, para. 7.

ing of a "normal profit" when the inventory is sold. Therefore, expenses are understated in the period of sale that may give rise to misinterpretations by external users.

The use of the lower of cost or market rule for inventories is consistent with the qualitative characteristics of accounting information contained in *Statement of Financial Accounting Concepts No. 2,* and the definitions of assets and losses contained in *Statement of Financial Accounting Concepts No. 6.* That is, when the cost of inventory exceeds its expected benefit, a reduction of the inventory to its market value is a better measure of its expected future benefit.

The major criticism of the lower of cost or market rule is that it is applied only for downward adjustments. Therefore, holding losses are recognized while holding gains are ignored. As noted earlier, this criticism has not been viewed as important as maintaining conservative financial statements, and the importance of the concept of conservatism was reaffirmed by the FASB in *Statement of Financial Accounting Concepts No. 5.*

Prepaids

Prepaid items result from recording expected future benefits from services to be rendered. They do not represent current assets in the sense that they will be converted into cash, but rather in the sense that they will require the use of current assets during the operating cycle if they were not in existence.

The measurement of prepaids is generally the residual result of the attempt to charge their expiration to expense, and little attention is given to balance sheet valuations. Two main cost expiration methods are used in the measurement of prepaids: (1) specific identification and (2) time. Specific identification is used where the items are consumed, as with office supplies, and time is used where no tangible asset is in existence and rights are in evidence over a certain period, such as with unexpired insurance or prepaid rent.

In most cases, the amortization method will be of little consequence because of the relative unimportance of these items. However, where substantial prepayments occur, care should be exercised to ensure that the allocation method is reasonable under the circumstances.

Current Liabilities

Payables

The measurement of payables presents no particular difficulty, since the amount of the obligation is usually fixed by a transaction and involves a promise to pay at a subsequent date. As with receivables, recording discounts from face value is not considered necessary because the period of debt is generally short. However, where interest is not specifically stated on notes payable, *Accounting Principles Board Opinion No. 21,* "Interest on Receivables and Payables," requires that interest be calculated for certain types of notes.[16]

---

[16] *Accounting Principles Board Opinion No. 21,* "Interest on Receivables and Payables" (New York: AICPA, 1971).

(See Chapter 9.) In addition to notes and accounts payable, dividends and taxes represent payables that require the use of current funds.

It should be noted that liability recognition frequently results from the necessity to recognize an asset or an expense where the focus of attention is not on the liability. However, the recognition of short-term liabilities may have significant impact on the working position of the enterprise.

Deferrals

Generally, deferrals are a special type of liability whose settlement requires the performance of services rather than the payment of money. Examples of deferrals include such items as subscriptions collected in advance or unearned rent. They are similar to prepaid expenses in that they are generally the residual result of the attempt to measure another amount. In this case the amount attempted to be measured is revenue, whereas it was an expense in the case of prepaids.

The placement of deferrals in the current liability section of the balance sheet has been criticized because they are not really liabilities in the general sense of the term in that there is no claimant. However, unless they are unusually large, it is unlikely that recording deferrals as liabilities will have much impact on financial statement presentation. Care should be taken to ensure that the company is not being overly cautious in reporting income as a deferral, and to determine that the deferral accounts are not being used as an additional allowance for uncollectible accounts.

Current Maturities

Unlike most assets, liabilities may be transferred from the long-term to the current classification due to the passage of time. Where the payment of long-term debt in the current period requires the use of current funds, proper accounting dictates that this amount be classified as current. Not all current maturities are classified as current liabilities. When the long-term liability is to be retired out of a special fund or by issuing additional long-term debt, the obligation should not be classified as current.

The proper classification of current maturities is of great importance because of the significance it can have on the working capital presentation. When adequate provision has not previously been made to retire current maturities, a company may find itself in a weak working capital position and future capital sources may evaporate.

Modification of the Working Capital Concept

Earlier it was suggested that the working capital concept was useful to investors, creditors, and management to indicate the amount of buffer available to meet current obligations, present information about cash flows, and predict future cash flows. However, current usage suggests that much of the foundation for the working capital concept is based on an evolution of long-established customs and conventions. That is, the historical examination of the development and current status of the working capital concept suggests that it is more closely associated with the notion of circulating capital than the fulfillment of various user needs concerning liquidity and cash flows.

Current practice is based on the assumption that the items classified as current assets will be used to retire existing current liabilities and that the measurement procedures used in valuing these items provide a valid indicator of the amount of cash expected to be realized or paid. Closer examination of these assumptions discloses two fallacies: (1) all the items are not measured in terms of their expected cash equivalent and (2) some of the items will never be received or paid in cash.

On the current asset side only cash, which is actual, and receivables, which are measured at expected net realizable value, show a high degree of correlation with the cash that will become available. In cases where the market price is lower than cost, temporary investments may also indicate the current cash equivalent; but where market is higher than cost, this relationship does not exist. Inventories are measured at cost, but the expectation is that they will be exchanged for amounts substantially above cost. Prepaid expenses have been included as current assets because if they had not been acquired, they would require the use of current assets in the normal operations of the business. However, prepaids will be used rather than exchanged for cash and, therefore, do not aid in predicting future cash flows. An enumeration of the valuation procedure associated with current liabilities exposes similar problems. Payables and the current portion of long-term debt represent the amounts to be paid in cash to retire these obligations during the coming period, but deferred credits will be retired by the performance of services rather than the payment of monies.

If the working capital concept is to become truly operational, it would seem necessary to modify it in such a manner as to show the amount of actual buffer between maturing obligations and the resources expected to be used in retiring these obligations. Such presentation should include only the current cash equivalent of the assets to be used to pay the existing debts. It would therefore seem more reasonable to base the working capital presentation on the monetary–nonmonetary dichotomy used in price level accounting. (See Chapter 15.) To review this concept briefly, monetary items are claims to or against specific amounts of money; all other assets and liabilities are nonmonetary.

The monetary working capital presentation would list as assets cash, cash equivalents, temporary investments, and receivables and would list as liabilities current payables. Additionally, it is suggested that more meaningful information could be provided if all temporary investments were measured by their current market price including securities held to maturity. This presentation would have the following advantages: (1) it would be a more representative measure of liquidity and buffer because it would be more closely associated with future cash flows, (2) it would provide more information about actual flows because only items expected to be realized or retired by cash transactions would be included, and (3) it would allow greater predictive ability because actual cash flows could be traced.

The concept of working capital is a valid and useful device for presenting information to financial statement users, and yet its usefulness is impaired because much of the concept's foundation is based on tradition rather than user needs. The implementation of new ideas into accounting theory is always a slow and tedious process, but the adoption of this new concept of working capital should more completely satisfy users' needs.

Summary

A review of the concept and components of working capital from a historical point of view shows that the concept has its foundation in an earlier period, when the focus was on the balance sheet and the ability to repay debts. Because of these factors, the presentation of working capital has not evolved fast enough to accommodate user needs.

An examination of the various measurement bases of current assets and current liabilities indicates that the measurement bases and methods of reporting the various accounts are dissimilar. We believe that user needs would be better satisfied if the working capital concept were modified to include only monetary items.

In the following reading, Loyd Heath suggests an alternative method of disclosing assets and liabilities.

Is Working Capital Really Working?

Loyd C. Heath

Accounting practices that have developed under conditions existing at one point in time may become so firmly embedded in our thought processes that they will come to be regarded as natural or inevitable. As a result, these practices may not be reexamined and reevaluated in the light of changed circumstances and conditions. The practice of classifying assets and liabilities as current or noncurrent to determine the difference between them—an amount commonly known as working capital—is one such practice. It began early in this century in response to the perceived needs of commercial bankers and today is a vestige of a bygone era. I believe this practice is misleading and should be abandoned.[1]

My reasons are set forth in this article, which explains why the present practice is not useful in evaluating a company's solvency and recommends an alternative that would be neither a radical departure from present disclosure practices nor costly to implement.

Author's note: I would like to thank Thomas W. McRae, CPA, and Paul Rosenfield, CPA, manager and director of the American Institute of CPAs accounting standards division, respectively, for their invaluable comments and suggestions during the preparation of this article.

[1] The analysis and recommendations that follow are based on my monograph, *Financial Reporting and the Evaluation of Solvency,* Accounting Research Monograph no. 3 (New York: AICPA, 1978).

Misconceptions of Classification

Many accountants view the practice of classifying assets and liabilities as current or noncurrent as one of identifying the "actual" or the "true" amount of a company's working capital. For example, Anson Herrick, who was a member of the committee on accounting procedure of a predecessor organization of the American Institute of CPAs at the time the current bulletin on working capital[2] was issued and who claimed to be the person responsible for developing the bulletin's definitions of current assets and current liabilities,[3] later described the work of that committee as follows:

As the bulletin . . . indicates, it was believed that the existing procedures for the determination of working capital were arbitrary, inconsistent, and frequently did not result in the development of a true *amount of working capital and, accordingly, it would be desirable for procedures to be provided which would do so. There was no thought that the committee was doing anything other than developing a more logical concept of working capital which, because* more accu-

[2] Chapter 3A, "Current Assets and Current Liabilities," Accounting Research Bulletin no. 43, *Restatement and Revision of Accounting Research Bulletins* (New York: American Institute of Accountants, 1953).

[3] Anson Herrick, "A Review of the Work of the Accounting Procedure Committee," JofA, Nov. 54, p. 627.

rate, *would be more useful. (Emphasis added.)*[4]

Contrary to Herrick's assumption, current–noncurrent classification, like all classification, is not a search for the truth; it is a purposive human activity. How we classify things or whether we classify them at all depends on the objectives we wish to achieve by classification:

> *What we call things and where we draw the line between one class of things and another depend upon the interests we have and the purposes of the classification.*
>
> *Classification is not a matter of identifying "essences" as is widely believed. It is simply a reflection of social convenience and necessity—and different necessities are always producing different classifications.*[5]

The terms current assets and current liabilities have no "true" meaning independent of the purposes to be served in defining them. They can be defined for financial reporting in many different ways. A search for the "true" definitions of current assets and current liabilities or definitions that identify the "essence," the "substance" or the "fundamental characteristic" of current assets, current liabilities or working capital can only result in confusion and, ultimately, in failure.

Present Practice Not Useful

The primary objective of classifying assets and liabilities as current or noncurrent is to provide information useful in evaluating a company's solvency. Chapter 3A, "Current Assets and Current Liabilities," of Accounting Research Bulletin no. 43, *Restatement and Revision of Accounting Research Bulletins,* begins with the statement "The working capital of a borrower has always been of prime interest to grantors of credit," and Leopold A. Bernstein noted that "the popularity of working capital as a measure of liquidity and of short-term financial health is so widespread that it hardly needs documentation."[6]

There are at least three ways in which the current–noncurrent classification might be useful in evaluating a company's solvency:

1. As a means of disclosing important attributes of assets and liabilities.

2. As a tool in predicting financial failure.

3. As a convenience to users who wish to calculate ratios.

Failure to Disclose Attributes

A prerequisite to the effective communication of attributes through classification is that all items classified the same way have some attribute in common. That attribute is the criterion used to partition the items into classes. A user of classified data then knows that, if an item is classified in a certain way, it possesses a certain attribute. Communication of attributes is one of the principal functions of nearly all forms of classification.

Present balance sheet classification has been described in accounting literature as "inconsistent," "illogical" and "irrational" because the items classified

---

[4] Anson Herrick, "Comments by Anson Herrick," JofA, Nov. 60, p. 52.

[5] S. I. Hayakawa, *Language in Thought and Action,* 2d ed. (New York: Harcourt Brace Jovanovich, 1964), pp. 215 and 217.

[6] Leopold A. Bernstein, *Financial Statement Analysis: Theory, Application and Interpretation,* rev. ed. (Homewood, Ill.: Richard D. Irwin, Inc., 1978), p. 447.

as current have no meaningful attribute in common. There is no identifiable attribute that all assets classified as current have that all assets classified as noncurrent do not have.

For example, Philip E. Fess said it was inconsistent to classify a three-year prepaid insurance premium as current while machinery with a three-year life is classified as noncurrent,[7] Arthur Andersen & Co. questioned the "logic" of classifying crude oil inventories in tanks as current while similar underground reserves are classified as noncurrent;[8] and Huizingh labeled "irrational" and "inconsistent" the practice of classifying as current the materials and supplies that will be used to maintain fixed assets while the fixed assets themselves are classified as noncurrent.[9] In all three cases, the basic problem is that the assets classified as current and other assets classified as current have no common attribute that distinguishes them from assets classified as noncurrent.

Because of these questionable asset classifications, describing an asset as current or as noncurrent communicates no useful information about it. Assets classified as current cannot be described as "those that will normally be converted into cash within a year" because many that will not be so converted are classified as current while others that will are classified as noncurrent; they cannot be described as assets "reason-

ably expected to be realized in cash or sold or consumed during the normal operating cycle" because many that will be so realized during the next operating cycle (whatever its length)—such as a portion of plant and equipment and wasting assets—are excluded; they cannot be described as those resources that will be used to pay liabilities classified as current because cash generated from the use of all assets is used to pay liabilities (both current and noncurrent).

The only attribute that all assets classified as current have in common is that they are the assets that, under present accepted practice, are classified as current—an attribute that has no informational content whatever to a user of financial statements concerned with evaluating the solvency of a business enterprise. This same criticism also applies to present practice in classifying liabilities; a current liability can only be described as a liability that is classified as current.

Misleading Disclosure of Attributes

Many classification rules followed in practice not only fail to communicate information but they also mislead the user who believes that accountants classify assets and liabilities on the basis of one attribute when they actually use an entirely different criterion. For example, the user who believes that current assets are "cash and other assets that are reasonably expected to be realized in cash or sold or consumed during the normal operating cycle of the business or within one year if the operating cycle is shorter than one year"[10] is misled by the common practice of classifying a three-year

[7] Philip E. Fess, "The Working Capital Concept," *Accounting Review,* April 1966, p. 267.

[8] Arthur Andersen & Co., *Accounting and Reporting Problems of the Accounting Profession.* 4th ed. (Chicago, Ill.: Arthur Andersen & Co., 1973), pp. 169 and 173–74.

[9] William Huizingh, *Working Capital Classification* (Ann Arbor, Mich.: University of Michigan, 1967), p. 107.

[10] Accounting Principles Board Statement no. 4, *Basic Concepts and Accounting Principles Underlying Financial Statements of Business Enterprises* (New York: AICPA, 1970), par. 198.

prepaid insurance premium as a current asset even though the operating cycle of the insured is less than one year. The user is also misled by the classification of underground oil reserves that are "reasonably expected to be . . . sold . . . within one year" as noncurrent assets.

Poor Prediction of Financial Failure

One approach to evaluating the usefulness of financial information is to measure its ability to predict the outcome of future events.[11] This approach has been used by several researchers in recent years to evaluate the usefulness of financial ratios in predicting financial failure.[12] One of William H. Beaver's studies is of particular interest here because it was concerned with the relative predictive power of different types of ratios[13] rather than with the more general question of the predictive power of a group of ratios.

Beaver found ratios based on current–noncurrent classification to be mediocre predictors of financial failure. None of them predicted nearly as well in any of the five years before failure as the ratios of cash flow to total debt, net income to total assets or total debt to total assets. In four of the five years before failure, the current ratio did not even predict as well as the ratio of just plain cash to total assets.

[11] For a discussion of this approach, see William H. Beaver, John W. Kennelly and William H. Voss, "Predictive Ability as a Criterion for the Evaluation of Accounting Data," *Accounting Review*, October 1968, pp. 675–83.

[12] For discussion and citations of these studies, see Baruch Lev, *Financial Statement Analysis: A New Approach* (Englewood Cliffs, N.J.: Prentice-Hall, Inc., 1974), ch. 9.

[13] William H. Beaver, "Alternative Accounting Measures as Predictors of Failure," *Accounting Review*, January 1968, pp. 113–22.

Calculation Convenience—a Disservice to Users

It might be argued that accountants should continue to classify assets and liabilities as a convenience to users who wish to examine the current and other working capital ratios to spare them the need to do their own classification. That argument is not convincing, however, because many users ignore the accountant's classification and classify in their own ways. For example, after pointing out that the definition of current assets in chapter 3A of ARB no. 43 begins with the phrase "for accounting purposes," Roy A. Foulke comments: "This definition as indicated by its first three words is not for credit purposes, management purposes, or analysis purpose; it is solely 'for accounting purposes.'"[14]

He then lists those assets that he believes should be classified as current and adds: "In this volume, operating supplies and ordinary maintenance material and parts, receivables from officers and employees, no matter how they arose, and prepaid expenses are excluded from current assets."[15]

[14] Roy A. Foulke, *Practical Financial Statement Analysis*, 6th ed. (New York: McGraw-Hill, Inc. 1968), p. 71n. See also Morton Backer, *Financial Reporting for Security Investment and Credit Decisions*, NAA Research Studies in Management Reporting no. 3 (New York: National Association of Accountants, 1970, pp. 47–48.) Graham, Dodd and Cottle note: "From the analyst's viewpoint it is best to include in the current assets all cash items that are within the company's control, including those which it does not show as current but *could show* if it so elected." (Benjamin Graham, David L. Dodd and Sidney Cottle, *Security Analysis: Principles and Technique*, 4th ed. [New York: McGraw-Hill, Inc., 1962], p. 203.)

[15] Foulke, p. 72n.

Modern Solvency Evaluation

A simplistic solution to the problems of current–noncurrent classification, such as adopting a one-year classification rule, will not work because it deals with the symptoms and not with the cause of the problem. Current–noncurrent classification was originally adopted in the belief that it would provide information helpful to users who wanted to see how much protection they would have if the enterprise should become insolvent and be forced to liquidate. A two-to-one current ratio supposedly meant that, if current assets fell by 50 percent, current creditors would still come out whole. But the entire approach by financial statement users to the evaluation of solvency has changed since then.[16] Today, users of financial statements realize that they virtually never come out whole or anywhere near it after a bankruptcy. Their primary need is for information that helps them evaluate whether the enterprise will remain solvent. The current–noncurrent distinction is of little use for that. Modern solvency evaluation is based on users' estimates of the company's prospective cash receipts and payments and evaluation of its financial flexibility.[17]

There are two basic reasons why a simple current–noncurrent classification system is an ineffective way to communicate the information users need to estimate prospective cash receipts and payments and to evaluate

financial flexibility. First, two classes are inadequate to disclose all the information that needs to be disclosed about some assets and liabilities. Receivables and payables, for example, must be broken down by maturity dates into more than two classes for users to be able to estimate a company's cash receipts and required payments. Second, the same classification criteria cannot be applied to all assets and liabilities. Inventories, for example, cannot be broken down on the same basis as receivables because it is not known when they will be sold. Classifying them as either current or noncurrent may provide a misleading indicator of prospective cash movements. An increasing current ratio may conceal slow collections and slow-moving inventories.

Recommended Alternative to Present Practice

What is needed is a new approach to providing balance sheet information that is useful in modern solvency evaluation. I recommend the following alternative to the current–noncurrent classification:

1. Disclosure of supplemental information about the attributes of specific assets and liabilities.

2. Classification of liabilities on the basis of the different types of credit sources available to business enterprises.

3. Arranging assets in the conventional order now used but discontinuing the practice of classifying them as current or noncurrent.

Disclose Supplemental Information

In addition to the information now disclosed in the notes to the financial statements, users concerned about evaluat-

---

[16] See chapter 2 of the monograph described in footnote 1.

[17] The term "financial flexibility" refers to a company's capacity to control its cash receipts and payments to survive a period of financial adversity. The concept is discussed more fully in the monograph described in footnote 1.

ing a company's solvency should have information about the amounts and timing of cash receipts and payments from receivables and payables. Such information would help them estimate a company's cash receipts and required cash payments. A lengthening of the age of a company's receivables, for example, may portend reduced cash receipts in the following period.

Disclosing the amounts and timing of receivables and payables cannot be accomplished by simply showing when the balance sheet amounts of those accounts are due. Many receivables and payables are carried at their present values rather than at the amounts of cash to be received or paid in future periods.[18] A company that issues $1 million of 10-year 10 percent bonds at par, for example, would show a $1 million liability on its balance sheet even though it is obligated to pay a total of $2 million—$100,000 per year for 10 years plus an additional $1 million at the end of the tenth year. The amounts and timing of cash flows from receivables and payables should be disclosed in a separate schedule rather than in the balance sheet itself.

Classify Liabilities Based on Sources of Credit

Hunt, Williams and Donaldson distinguished between two basic sources of credit available to a company: spontaneous and negotiated.[19] They described

spontaneous or self-generating sources as those that "grow out of normal patterns of profitable operation without especial effort or conscious decision on the part of owners or managers,"[20] such as normal trade credit, accrued expenses and accrued taxes. Negotiated sources are those requiring conscious effort or specific negotiation by owners or managers such as bank loans, sales of commercial paper, sales of bonds, installment purchases and financing leases.

The distinction between spontaneous and negotiated sources of credit is relevant to the evaluation of both a company's financial flexibility and its future case requirements. It is relevant to evaluating financial flexibility because different underlying considerations determine the amount of credit available from each of them. The amount available from spontaneous sources depends on considerations such as the volume of purchases of inventories and supplies, normal credit terms of a company's suppliers and conventional practices such as the frequency of salary and wage payments. Credit available from spontaneous sources tends to increase as sales rise and to fall as sales decline.

Credit available from negotiated sources, on the other hand, depends more on lenders' evaluations of a company's ability to repay a loan when it is

---

[18] See APB Opinion no. 21, *Interest on Receivables and Payables* (New York: AICPA, 1971).

[19] Pearson Hunt, Charles M. Williams and Gordon Donaldson, *Basic Business Finance,* rev. ed. (Homewood, Ill.: Richard D. Irwin, Inc., 1961), pp. 116 and 169. R. K. Mautz made a similar distinction in sources of financing. Referring to "primary financing interests" and "incidental financing interests,"

he argued that incidental financing interests including, for example, trade creditors and employees, "provide financing, but this is neither the primary intent of the particular interest nor the basic reason for the transaction." (R. K. Mautz, *An Accounting Technique for Reporting Financial Transactions,* Special Bulletin no. 7 [Urbana, Ill.: University of Illinois Bureau of Economic and Business Research, 1951], pp. 21–22.)

[20] Hunt, Williams and Donaldson, p. 116.

due. The total amount of credit available to a company through spontaneous sources tends to be limited to a rather narrow range. It is inexpensive or even cost free up to a certain point; beyond that, it becomes very costly as cash discounts are lost, suppliers refuse to ship goods and so forth. The amount of credit available from negotiated sources varies widely, depending on creditors' evaluations of the overall credit worthiness of a company.

The distinction between spontaneous and negotiated sources of credit is also relevant in estimating a company's future cash requirements. Liabilities that arise from spontaneous sources tend to "roll over" more or less automatically; debts that are paid are more or less constantly being replaced by new debts. Consequently, it is not necessary to consider a company's spontaneous liabilities when estimating its forthcoming need for cash unless there is reason to expect that, because of a decline in sales or a change in business practices, the amount of those liabilities will change. Negotiated liabilities on the other hand, whether short term or long term, are expected to be paid off, and they must therefore be considered in estimating a company's cash needs. Some of them may be rolled over or refinanced, but that is different from the rolling over of spontaneous liabilities. It does not occur automatically in the normal course of purchasing goods and paying wages and taxes but requires arm's-length negotiation with a creditor who will once again evaluate the company's overall credit worthiness.

Keep Asset Order Without Classification

For most industries other than regulated utilities, assets are presented in the order of cash, marketable securities,

trade receivables, inventories and so forth. That order has no particular significance,[21] but both accountants and financial statement users are familiar with it. Assets should continue to be arranged in the conventional order because changing it would confuse users in much the same way that changing the order of the keys on a typewriter would confuse typists.

Illustration and Discussion of Recommended Changes

The balance sheet in Exhibit 1 and the supporting schedule of receivables and financing liabilities in Exhibit 2 for Example, Inc., illustrate the recommended balance sheet format and the recommended types of additional disclosures. Liabilities are classified as operating, tax and financing. Operating and tax liabilities are provided from spontaneous sources of credit; financing liabilities are provided from negotiated sources. The term "financing liabilities" is used rather than negotiated liabilities because it is more likely to be readily understood.

Information on when receivables and payables are due is included in the ma-

---

[21] Trying to list assets in order of liquidity is a waste of time because the term "liquidity" has no agreed-upon meaning. Some accountants view it in terms of the number of steps an asset must pass through before it is converted into cash (receivables are more liquid than inventory because inventory must be converted into receivables before being converted into cash); some view it in terms of the amount of time that will normally pass before an asset is converted into cash (some inventory will be converted into cash before some receivables); and still others view it in terms of how quickly an asset can be converted into cash (some plant and equipment *can* be converted into cash faster than some inventory).

EXHIBIT 1 *Example, Inc., Balance Sheet*

	12/31/79	12/31/78
Assets		
Cash	$ 21,968	$ 15,666
Marketable securities (current market value		
$23,608 and $29,198)	18,459	21,521
Trade accounts and notes receivable	70,143	66,276
Allowance for uncollectibles	(973)	(906)
Net receivables	69,170	65,370
Inventories		
Finished goods	73,610	62,102
Goods in process	22,109	16,998
Raw materials and supplies	13,167	10,605
Total inventories	108,886	89,705
Prepayments	8,164	5,222
Properties		
Land, buildings and equipment at cost	349,615	319,101
Accumulated depreciation	(136,171)	(125,591)
Net properties	213,444	193,510
Other assets	1,609	3,873
Total assets	$441,700	$394,867
Liabilities and stockholders' equity		
Operating liabilities (due within one year)		
Trade accounts and notes payable	$ 47,662	$ 49,518
Accrued expenses	29,601	26,401
Total	77,263	75,919
Tax liabilities		
On reported taxable income	13,061	11,996
Withheld from employees and miscellaneous	3,906	4,111
Deferred as a result of timing differences in		
depreciation	39,664	37,605
Total tax liabilities	56,631	53,712
Financing liabilities		
Notes payable to banks	48,605	15,513
Mortgage payable	26,000	28,000
7% debentures payable, due December 31, 1995	25,000	25,000
Total financing liabilities	99,605	68,513
Total liabilities	233,499	198,144
Stockholders' equity		
5% convertible preferred stock $100 par value	40,000	70,000
Common stock $10 par value	90,000	70,000
Capital in excess of par	41,609	24,114
Retained earnings	36,592	32,609
Total stockholders' equity	208,201	196,723
Total liabilities and stockholders' equity	$441,700	$394,867

EXHIBIT 2 *Example, Inc., Maturity Schedule of Receivables and Financing Liabilities*

	12/31/79	12/31/78
Trade accounts and notes receivable		
Overdue	$ 1,398	$ 1,206
Due within one year	37,111	36,692
Due one–two years	24,906	21,605
Due two–three years	9,205	10,331
Due after three years	4,915	4,034
Total	77,535	73,868
Less: amount representing interest	7,392	7,592
Per balance sheet	$ 70,143	$ 66,276
Financing liabilities		
Due within one year	$ 28,435	$ 23,054
Due one–two years	15,670	5,830
Due two–three years	15,510	5,670
Due three–four years	15,350	5,510
Due four–five years	15,190	5,350
Due five–ten years	23,550	24,350
Due ten–fifteen years	17,710	20,350
Due after fifteen years	33,750	35,500
Total	165,165	125,614
Less: amount representing interest	65,560	57,101
Per balance sheet	$ 99,605	$ 68,513

turity schedule (Exhibit 2). The total amounts to be received or paid differ from the related balance sheet figures by amounts that represent interest. The amount of overdue receivables is identified because it provides an objective indication of the quality of a company's receivables.

For many years there has been a clear trend toward disclosing more information about the attributes of specific assets and liabilities in the notes to the financial statements. Much of that information is clearly relevant in evaluating a company's financial flexibility and in estimating its future cash receipts and payments. Disclosure of credit commit-ments, compensating balance requirements, and minimum amounts due under long-term leases are examples. Other disclosures will undoubtedly be proposed in the future. When they are, the guiding consideration should be whether the proposed disclosure can reasonably be expected to be useful in evaluating a company's financial flexibility and in estimating its future cash receipts and payments.

A Modest Proposal

This is a proposal that additional information about the attributes of individual assets and liabilities be disclosed as an alternative to classifying assets and liabilities as current or noncurrent. It is a modest proposal. It would not require a radical departure from present disclosure practices nor be costly to implement. The rationale underlying it is that the recommended approach would provide more useful information for evaluating a company's solvency than present practice based on current–noncurrent classification. That practice is directed toward the calculation of the current ratio and other measures based on the concept of working capital as a measure of solvency; the recommended alternative emphasizes the disclosure of additional data that can be combined and used in various ways related to the solvency dimension of financial statement analysis.

Cases

• Case 6-1

The Walton Company purchases its merchandise at the current market price and prices its product for sale annually. The company uses a periodic inventory system. Data on inventory and sales for 1996 are as follows:

Beginning inventory	2,000 units @ $2.00 per unit
3/31 Purchased	4,000 units @ $2.10 per unit
6/30 Purchased	5,000 units @ $2.20 per unit
9/30 Purchased	3,000 units @ $2.30 per unit
12/31 Purchased	4,000 units @ $2.40 per unit
Sales	15,000 units @ $2.50 per unit

Required:
a. Calculate the after-tax profit if other expenses are $20,000 and the tax rate is 30% using FIFO, LIFO, and weighted average.

   Assume the company had an opening cash balance of $10,000, inventory was its only other asset, it had no liabilities at the beginning of the year, its net worth was comprised entirely of common stock with a $1 par value and all purchases were made for cash.
b. Prepare an end of year balance sheet for Walton using each of the three inventory valuation methods.
c. Comment on the company's financial picture as portrayed under each inventory valuation procedure. What has caused these results?
d. Would your answer have been different if 1996 had been a year in which the inventory purchased by Walton declined in price?

• Case 6-2

Rivera Company
The Rivera Company, a small retail store, has been in business for a few years. The company's current policy is that all sales are made for cash, and all cash sales are deposited in the company's bank account. The bank account does

not pay interest and the company does not have any temporary investments. Rivera's sales average $90,000 a month, its gross profit is 40 percent, and the average checking account balance is $50,000.

Juan Rivera, the owner, recently hired a consultant to review the company's short-term liquid asset policy. The consultant recommended that Rivera invest its idle cash in temporary investments and accept credit sales. Juan Rivera is investigating the following alternatives.

Temporary Investments

1. Invest in three-month certificates yielding 8.5 percent interest. Early withdrawals from this account will result in the loss of all interest earned.

2. Open an investment account earning 7.5 percent. The minimum amount that can be invested in this account is $25,000, and the bank must be notified seven days in advance for all withdrawals.

3. Open a NOW checking account paying 5.5 percent interest. No notification is required for withdrawals.

Credit Sales

1. Accept credit sales from customers holding a national credit card. One credit card company has offered Rivera a 5 percent service charge rate and will sustain all bad debts losses. If this offer is accepted, it is expected that monthly sales will increase by 15 percent, but 50 percent of the current cash customers will become credit customers.

2. Establish its own credit department. This alternative will require hiring an additional employee at an annual salary of $24,000. Monthly sales are expected to increase by 40 percent, and it is expected that 20 percent of the existing cash customers will become credit customers. It is estimated that bad debts will be 5 percent of credit sales.

Required:
a. Which short-term investment policy should Rivera adopt? Why?
b. Which credit policy should Rivera adopt? Why?

● **Case 6-3**

SFAS No. 115 requires companies to assign their portfolio of investment securities into (1) trading securities, (2) securities available for sale, and (3) held-to-maturity securities.

Required:
a. Define each of these categories of securities and discuss the accounting treatment for each category.
b. Discuss how companies are required to assign each category of securities into its current and noncurrent portions.
c. Some individuals maintain that the only proper accounting treatment for all marketable securities is current value. Others maintain that this treatment might allow companies to "manage earnings." Discuss the arguments for each position.

● **Case 6-4**

Cost for inventory purposes should be determined by the inventory cost flow method most clearly reflecting periodic income.

Required:
a. Describe the fundamental cost flow assumptions of the average cost, FIFO, and LIFO inventory cost flow methods.
b. Discuss the reasons for using LIFO in an inflationary economy.
c. Where there is evidence that the utility of goods, in their disposal in the ordinary course of business, will be less than cost, what is the proper accounting treatment and under what concept is that treatment justified?

● **Case 6-5**

Steel Company, a wholesaler that has been in business for two years, purchases its inventories from various suppliers. During the two years, each purchase has been at a lower price than the previous purchase.

Steel uses the lower of FIFO cost or market method to value inventories. The original cost of the inventories is above replacement cost and below the net realizable value. The net realizable value less the normal profit margin is below the replacement cost.

Required:
a. In general, what criteria should be used to determine which costs should be included in inventory?
b. In general, why is the lower of cost or market rule used to report inventory?
c. At what amount should Steel's inventories be reported on the balance sheet? Explain the application of the lower of cost or market rule in this situation.
d. What would have been the effect on ending inventories and net income for the second year had Steel used the lower of average cost or market inventory method instead of the lower of FIFO cost or market inventory method? Why?

● **Case 6-6**

Anth Company has significant amounts of trade accounts receivable. Anth uses the allowance method to estimate bad debts instead of the specific write-off method. During the year, some specific accounts were written off as uncollectible, and some that were previously written off as uncollectible were collected.

Anth also has some interest-bearing notes receivable for which the face amount plus interest at the prevailing rate of interest is due at maturity. The notes were received on July 1, 1995, and are due on June 30, 1997.

Required:
a. What are the deficiencies of the specific write-off method?

b. What are the two basic allowance methods used to estimate bad debts, and what is the theoretical justification for each?
c. How should Anth account for the collection of the specific accounts previously written off as uncollectible?
d. How should Anth report the effects of the interest-bearing notes receivable on its December 31, 1996, balance sheet and its income statement for the year ended December 31, 1996? Why?

● Case 6-7

Accountants generally follow the lower cost or market basis of inventory valuations.

Required:
a. Define *cost* as applied to the valuation of inventories.
b. Define *market* as applied to the valuation of inventories.
c. Why are inventories valued at the lower of cost or market? Discuss.
d. List the arguments against the use of the lower of cost or market method of valuing inventories.

● Case 6-8

On December 31, 1995, Carme Company had significant amounts of accounts receivables as a result of credit sales to its customers. Carme Company uses the allowance method based on credit sales to estimate bad debts. Based on past experience, 1 percent of credit sales normally will not be collected. This pattern is expected to continue.

Required:
a. Discuss the rationale for using the allowance method based on credit sales to estimate bad debts. Contrast this method with the allowance method based on the balance in the trade receivables accounts.
b. How should Carme Company report the allowance for bad debts account on its balance sheet at December 31, 1995? Also, describe the alternatives, if any, for presentation of bad debt expense in Carme Company's 1995 income statement.

● Case 6-9

At the end of the first year of operations, Key Company had a current equity securities portfolio classified as available for sale securities with a cost of $500,000 and a fair value of $550,000. At the end of its second year of operations, Key Company had a current equity securities portfolio classified as available for sale securities with a cost of $525,000 and a fair value of $475,000. No securities were sold during the first year. One security with a cost of $80,000 and a fair value of $70,000 at the end of the first year was sold for $100,000 during the second year.

Required:

a. How should Key Company report the preceding facts in its balance sheets and income statements for both years? Discuss the rationale for your answer.

b. How would your answer have differed if the security had been classified as trading securities?

• Case 6-10

Specific identification is sometimes said to be the ideal method for assigning cost to inventory and to cost of goods sold.

Required:

a. List the arguments for and against the foregoing statement.

b. First in, first-out; weighted average; and last-in, first-out methods are often used instead of specific identification. Compare each of these methods with the specific identification method. Include in your discussion analysis of the theoretical propriety of each method in the determination of income and asset valuation. (Do not define the methods or describe their technical accounting procedures.)

• Case 6-11

In order to effect an approximate matching of current costs with related sales revenue, the last-in, first-out (LIFO) method of pricing inventories has been developed.

Required:

a. Describe the establishment of and subsequent pricing procedures for each of the following LIFO inventory methods:

  i. LIFO applied to units of product when the periodic inventory system is used

  ii. Application of the dollar-value method to a retail LIFO inventory or to LIFO units of product (these applications are similar)

b. Discuss the specific advantages and disadvantages of using the dollar-value LIFO applications. Ignore income tax considerations.

Recommended Additional Readings

Bohan, Michael P., and Steven Rubin. "LIFO: What Should Be Disclosed?" *Journal of Accountancy* (February 1985), pp. 72–77.

Fess, Philip. "The Working Capital Concept." *The Accounting Review* (April 1966), pp. 266–270.

Gosman, Martin L., and Philip E. Meyer. "SFAS 94's Effect on Liquidity Disclosure." *Accounting Horizons* (March 1992), pp. 88–100.

Reeve, James, and Keith Stanga. "Balance Sheet Impact of Using LIFO: An Empirical Study." *Accounting Horizons* (September 1987), pp. 9–16.

Schuetze, Walter P. "What Is an Asset?" *Accounting Horizons* (September 1993), pp. 66–70.

Strobel, Caroline D., and Ollie S. Powers. "Accounting for Inventories: Where We Stand." *The CPA Journal* (May 1981), pp. 41–46.

Wyatt, Arthur. "The SEC Says: Mark to Market." *Accounting Horizons* (March 1991), pp. 80–84.

Bibliography

Barden, Horace G. *The Accounting Basis of Inventories.* New York: American Institute of Certified Public Accountants, 1973.

Bastable, C. W., and Jacob D. Merriwether. "FIFO in an Inflationary Environment." *Journal of Accountancy* (March 1976), pp. 49–55.

Beresford, Dennis R., and Michael H. Sietta. "Short-Term Debt Agreements—Classification Issues." *The CPA Journal* (August 1983), pp. 32–37.

Buckley, John W., and James R. Goode. "Inventory Valuation and Income Measurement: An Improved System." *Abacus* (June 1976), pp. 34–48.

Copeland, Ronald M., Joseph F. Wojdak, and John K. Shank. "Use Lifo to Offset Inflation." *Harvard Business Review* (May–June 1971), pp. 91–100.

Cramer, Joe J. "Incompatibility of Bad Debt 'Expense' with Contemporary Accounting Theory." *The Accounting Review* (July 1972), pp. 596–598.

Dun, L. C. "Working Capital—A Logical Concept." *Australian Accountant* (October 1969), pp. 461–464.

Fox, Harold F. "Exploring the Facts of Lifo." *National Public Accountant* (October 1971), pp. 22–25.

Gambling, Trevor E. "Lifo vs. Fifo under Conditions of 'Certainty.'" *The Accounting Review* (April 1968), pp. 387–389.

Haried, Andrew A., and Ralph E. Smith. "Accounting for Marketable Equity Securities." *The Journal of Accountancy* (February 1977), pp. 54–62.

Hirschman, Robert W. "A Look at 'Current' Classifications." *Journal of Accountancy* (November 1967), pp. 54–58.

Hoffman, Raymond A., and Henry Gunders. *Inventories: Control, Costing and Effect upon Income and Taxes,* 2d ed. New York: Ronald Press, 1970.

Holmes, William. "Market Value of Inventories—Perils and Pitfalls." *Journal of Commercial Bank Lending* (April 1973), pp. 30–35.

Huizingh, William. *Working Capital Classification.* Ann Arbor: Bureau of Business Research, Graduate School of Business Administration, University of Michigan, 1967.

Hunter, Robert D. "Concept of Working Capital." *Journal of Commercial Bank Lending* (March 1972), pp. 24–30.

Johnson, Charles E. "Inventory Valuation—The Accountant's Achilles Heel." *The Accounting Review* (April 1954), pp. 15–26.

Lemke, Kenneth W. "The Evaluation of Liquidity: An Analytical Study." *Journal of Accounting Research* (Spring 1970), pp. 47–77.

McAnly, Herbert T. "How LIFO Began." *Management Accounting* (May 1975), pp. 24–26.

Moonitz, Maurice. "The Case against Lifo as an Inventory-Pricing Formula." *Journal of Accountancy* (June 1953), pp. 682–690.

Moonitz, Maurice. "Accounting for Investments in Debt Securities." In *Essays in Honor of William A. Paton,* Stephen A. Zeff, Joel Demski, and Nicholas Dopuch, eds., Ann Arbor, Mich.: The University of Michigan Graduate School of Business Administration Division of Research, 1979, pp. 57–72.

Morse, Dale, and Gordon Richardson. "The LIFO/FIFO Decision." *Journal of Accounting Research* (Spring 1983), pp. 106–127.

Munter, Paul, and Tommy Morse. "Transfers of Receivables with Recourse." *The CPA Journal* (July 1984), pp. 52–60.

O'Connor, Stephen J. "LIFO: Still a Valid Management Tool?" *Financial Executive* (September 1978), pp. 26–30.

Pantiack, Wayne G. "Last-In First-Out Accounting for Inventories." *The CPA Journal* (July 1985), pp. 42–48.

Skinner, R. C. "Combining LIFO and FIFO." *International Journal of Accounting, Education and Research* (Spring 1975), pp. 127–134.

Staubus, George J. "Testing Inventory Accounting." *The Accounting Review* (July 1968), pp. 413–424.

Storey, Reed K., and Maurice Moonitz. *Market Value Methods for Intercorporate Investments in Stock.* New York: American Institute of Certified Public Accountants, 1976.

Sunder, Shyam. "Optional Choice between FIFO and LIFO." *Journal of Accounting Research* (Autumn 1976), pp. 277–300.

Long-Term
Assets I:
Property, Plant,
and Equipment

The evolution of the circulating and noncirculating capital distinction into the working capital concept has been accompanied by the separate classification and disclosure of long-term assets. In this chapter we shall examine one of the categories of long-term assets—property, plant, and equipment. Long-term investments and intangibles are discussed in Chapter 8.

Property, Plant, and Equipment

The items of property, plant, and equipment generally represent a major source of future service potential to the enterprise. The valuation of property, plant, and equipment assets is of interest to financial-statement users because it indicates the physical resources available to the firm and perhaps may also give some indication of future liquidity and cash flows. These valuations are particularly important in capital-intensive industries such as automobile manufacturing because property, plant, and equipment constitutes a major component of the company's total assets. The objectives of plant and equipment accounting are

1. Accounting and reporting to investors on stewardship.
2. Accounting for the use and deterioration of plant and equipment.
3. Planning for new acquisitions, through budgeting.
4. Supplying information for taxing authorities.
5. Supplying rate-making information for regulated industries.

Accounting for Cost

Many business enterprises commit substantial corporate resources to acquire property, plant, and equipment. Investors, creditors, and other users rely on accountants to report the extent of corporate investment in these assets. The initial investment, or cost to the enterprise, represents the sacrifice of resources given up now to accomplish future objectives. Traditionally, accountants have placed a great deal of emphasis on the principle of objective evidence to determine the initial valuation of long-term assets. Cost is the preferred valuation method used to account for the acquisition of property, plant, and equipment because cost is more easily identified and verified than any other valuation method. There is also a presumption that the agreed-on purchase price represents the future service potential of the asset to the buyer in an arm's-length transaction.

The theoretically preferable measurement technique for items of property, plant, and equipment is the discounted present value of all future earnings of these assets. That is, the amount and timing of all future earnings attributable to an asset are calculated and the appropriate discount factor for the firm is applied to those earnings. The resulting measurement indicates the value of the asset to the enterprise at a particular point in time—that is, the current measurement of its future service potential to the enterprise.

If the purchase price does, in fact, reflect the future service potential of the asset, as measured by the present value of future earnings at acquisition, then cost is not only objective and verifiable; it is also the theoretically correct value of the asset when it is acquired. Whether or not the management of a firm actually goes through a formal process of discounting future earnings in arriving at a purchase price of an asset, there seems to be tacit agreement that, at least intuitively, the process does occur. But for subsequent financial reporting purposes, accountants generally take the position that cost should be viewed as objective and verifiable evidence of what was paid and not as a representation of future service potential. They argue, as discussed in Chapter 3, that it is difficult, if not impossible, to measure future service potential because (1) neither the amount nor timing of future earnings may be subject to reasonable estimation, and (2) there is no generally accepted method of determining the appropriate discount factor to be used in the calculation.

Despite the objectivity and verifiability of the purchase price as the basis for initially recording property, plant, and equipment, the assignment of cost to individual assets is not always as uncomplicated as might be expected. When assets are acquired in groups, when they are self-constructed, when they are acquired in nonmonetary exchanges, or when property contains assets that are to be removed, certain accounting problems arise. These issues are discussed in the following sections.

Group Purchases

When a group of assets is acquired for a lump-sum purchase price, such as the purchase of land, buildings, and equipment for a single purchase price, an accounting problem arises. That is, the total acquisition cost must be allocated to the individual assets so that this cost can be charged to expense as the service potential of the individual assets expires.

The most frequent, though arbitrary, solution to this allocation problem has been to assign the acquisition cost to the various assets on the basis of the weighted average of their respective appraisal values. Where appraisal values are not available, the cost assignment may be based on the relative carrying values on the seller's books. Since no evidence exists that either of these values is the relative value to the purchaser, assignment by either of these procedures would seem to be a violation of the objectivity principle, but the use of these methods is usually justified on the basis of expediency and the lack of acceptable alternative methods.

Self-Constructed Assets

Self-constructed assets give rise to questions about the proper components of cost. While it is generally agreed that all expenses directly associated with the construction process should be included in the recorded cost of the asset (material, direct labor, etc.), there are controversial issues regarding the assignment of fixed overhead and the capitalization of interest. The fixed-overhead issue has two aspects: (1) Should any fixed overhead be allocated? and, (2) If so, how much fixed overhead should be allocated? This problem has further ramifications. If a plant is operating at less than full capacity and fixed overhead is assigned to a self-constructed asset project, charging the project with a portion of the fixed overhead will cause the profit margin on all other products to increase during the period of construction. Three approaches are available to resolve this issue:

1. Allocate no fixed overhead to the self-construction project.

2. Allocate only incremental fixed overhead to the project.

3. Allocate fixed overhead to the project on the same basis as it is allocated to other products.

Some accountants favor the first approach. They argue that the allocation of fixed overhead is arbitrary and therefore only direct costs should be considered. Nevertheless, the prevailing opinion is that the construction of the asset required the use of some amount of fixed overhead, and fixed overhead is a proper component of cost. Closer examination also reveals some additional issues.

When the production of other products has been discontinued to produce a self-constructed asset, allocation of the entire amount of fixed overhead to the remaining products will cause reported profits on these products to decrease. (The same amount of overhead is allocated to fewer products.) Under these circumstances the third approach seems most appropriate. On the other hand, it seems unlikely that an enterprise would discontinue operations of a profitable product to construct productive facilities except in unusual circumstances.

When operations are at less than full capacity, the second approach is the most logical. The decision to build the asset was probably connected with the availability of idle facilities. Increasing the profit margin on existing products by allocating a portion of the fixed overhead to the self-construction project will distort reported profits.

A corollary to the fixed overhead allocation question is the issue of the capitalization of interest charges during the period of the construction of the asset. During the construction period, extra financing for materials and supplies will undoubtedly be required, and these funds will frequently be obtained from external sources. The central question is the advisability of capitalizing the cost associated with the use of these funds. Some accountants have argued that interest is a financing rather than an operating charge and should not be charged against the asset. Others have noted that if the asset was acquired from outsiders, interest charges would undoubtedly be part of the cost basis to the seller and would be included in the sales price. Additionally, public utilities normally capitalize both actual and implicit interest (when their own funds are used) on construction projects because future rates are based on the costs of services. Charging existing products for the expenses associated with a separate decision results in an improper matching of costs and revenues. Therefore, a more logical approach is to capitalize incremental interest charges during the construction period. Once the new asset is placed in service, interest is charged against operations.

The misapplication of this theory resulted in abuses during the first part of the 1970s when many companies adopted the policy of capitalizing all interest costs. However, in 1974 the SEC established a rule preventing this practice.[1] Later, in 1979, the FASB issued *SFAS No. 34*, "Capitalization of Interest Costs."[2] In this release, the FASB took the position that interest should be capitalized only when an asset requires a period of time to be prepared for its intended use.

The primary objective of *SFAS No. 34* was to recognize interest cost as a significant part of the historical cost of acquiring an asset. The criteria for determining if an asset qualifies for interest capitalization are that the asset must not yet be ready for its intended purpose and must be undergoing activities necessary to get it ready. Qualified assets are defined as (1) assets that are constructed or otherwise produced for an enterprise's own use and (2) assets intended for sale or lease that are constructed or otherwise produced as discrete projects. Additionally, *SFAS No. 34* excluded interest capitalization for inventories that are routinely manufactured or otherwise produced in large quantities on a repetitive basis. Assets that are currently in use or are not undergoing the activities necessary to get them ready for use are also excluded.

An additional issue addressed by *SFAS No. 34* was the determination of the proper amount of interest to capitalize. The FASB decided that the amount of interest to be capitalized is the amount that could have been avoided if the

---

[1] "Capitalization of Interest by Companies Other than Public Utilities," *SEC Accounting Series Release No. 163* (Washington, D.C.: SEC, 1974).

[2] Financial Accounting Standards Board, *Statement of Financial Accounting Standards No. 34*, "Capitalization of Interest Costs" (Stamford, Conn.: FASB, 1979), par. 9.

asset has not been constructed. The interest rate to be used is either the weighted average rate of interest charges during the period or the interest charge on a specific debt instrument issued to finance the project. The amount of avoidable interest is determined by applying the appropriate interest rate to the average amount of accumulated expenditures for the asset during the construction period. The capitalized amount is the lesser of the calculated "avoidable" interest and the actual interest incurred. Additionally, only actual interest costs on present obligations may be capitalized, not imputed interest on equity funds.

Removal of Existing Assets

When a firm acquires property containing existing structures that are to be removed, a question arises concerning the proper treatment of the cost of removing these structures. Current practice is to assign removal costs less any proceeds received from the sale of the assets to the land, since these costs are necessary to put the site in a state of readiness for construction.

Assets Acquired in Noncash Transactions

Assets may also be acquired by trading equity securities, or one asset may be exchanged in partial payment for another (trade-in). When equity securities are exchanged for assets, the cost principle dictates that the recorded value of the asset is the amount of consideration given. This amount is usually the market value of the securities exchanged. If the market value of the securities is not determinable, it is necessary to assign cost to the property on the basis of its fair market value. This procedure is a departure from the cost principle and can be viewed as an example of the use of replacement cost in current practice.

When assets are exchanged, for example, in trade-ins, additional complications arise. Accountants have long argued the relative merits of using the fair market value versus the book value of the exchanged asset. In 1973 the Accounting Principles Board released its *Opinion No. 29,* "Accounting for Nonmonetary Transactions," which concluded that fair value should (*generally*) be used as the basis of accountability.[3] Therefore, the cost of an asset acquired in a straight exchange for another asset is the fair market value of the surrendered asset.

This general rule is subject to one exception. In *Opinion No. 29* the APB stated that exchanges should be recorded at the book value of the asset given up when the exchange is not the culmination of the earning process. Two examples of exchanges that do not result in the culmination of the earning process are

1. Exchange of a *product or property held for sale* in the ordinary course of business (inventory) for a product or property to be sold in the same line of business to facilitate sales to customers other than parties to the exchange.

2. Exchange of a *productive asset* not held for sale in the ordinary course of

---

[3]*Accounting Principles Board Opinion No. 29,* "Accounting for Nonmonetary Transactions" (New York: AICPA, 1973).

business for a *similar* productive asset or an equivalent interest in the same or similar productive asset.[4]

If the exchanged assets are dissimilar, the presumption is that the earning process is complete, and the acquired asset is recorded at the fair value of the asset exchanged including any gain or loss. This requirement exists for straight exchanges and for exchanges accompanied by cash payments (*boot*). For example, if Company G exchanges cash of $2,000, and an asset with a book value of $10,000 and a fair market value of $13,000, for a dissimilar asset, a gain of $3,000 should be recognized [$13,000 − $10,000], and the new asset is recorded at $15,000.

On the other hand, accounting for the exchange of *similar productive assets* takes a somewhat different form. According to the provisions of *APB Opinion No. 29*, losses on the exchange of similar productive assets are always recognized in their entirety whether or not boot (cash) is involved. However, gains are never recognized unless boot is present, and only the recipient of boot may recognize a gain. The recipient of boot recognizes a gain in the ratio of the boot to the total consideration received. In effect, the receiver of boot is recognizing a proportionate sale and proportionate trade-in. For example, assume Company S acquires an asset with a fair market value of $10,000 and $5,000 cash in exchange for an asset with a book value of $12,000 and a fair market value of $15,000. A gain of $1,000 is recognized. The recognized gain is calculated as follows.

$$\text{recorded gain} = \frac{\text{boot}}{\text{boot} + \text{fair market value of asset acquired}} \times \text{total gain*}$$

$$\frac{\$5,000}{\$5,000 + \$10,000} \times \$3,000* = \$1,000$$

*($15,000 − 12,000) The new asset is recorded at $8,000 ($10,000 − $2,000 gain not recognized).

Donated and Discovery Values

Assets are sometimes acquired by corporations as gifts from municipalities, local citizens groups, or stockholders as inducements to locate facilities in certain areas. The FASB has defined such contributions as transfers ". . . of cash or other assets to an entity or settlement or cancellation of its liability from a voluntary nonreciprocal transfer by another entity acting other than as an owner."[5] The cost principle holds that the recorded values of assets should be the consideration given in return, but since donations are nonreciprocal transfers, strict adherence to this principle would result in a failure to record donated assets at all. On the other hand, failure to report values for

---

[4] Ibid., par. 21.

[5] Financial Accounting Standards Board, *Statement of Financial Accounting Standards No. 116,* "Accounting for Contributions Received and Contributions Made" (Stamford, Conn., FASB, 1993), par. 5.

these assets on the balance sheet is inconsistent with the full disclosure principle.

Previous practice required donated assets to be recorded at their fair market values. A similar amount was recorded in an equity account termed *donated capital.* Thereafter, as the service potential of the donated assets declines, depreciation is charged to operations, as discussed later in the chapter. Recording donated assets at fair market values is defended on the grounds that if the donation had been in cash, the amount received would have been recorded as donated capital, and the cash could have been used to purchase the asset at its fair market value.

SFAS No. 116 requires that the inflow of assets from a donation be considered revenue.[6] If so, the fair market value of the assets received represents the appropriate measurement. However, this argument may be flawed. According to *SFAC No. 6,* revenues arise from the delivery or production of goods and the rendering of services. If the contribution is a nonreciprocal transfer, then it is difficult to see how a revenue has been earned. Alternately, it may be argued that the inflow represents a gain. This later argument is consistent with the Conceptual Framework's definition of a gain, as resulting from peripheral or incidental transactions and with the definition of comprehensive income as the change in net assets resulting from nonowner transactions. Under this approach, the asset and gain would be recorded at the fair market value of the asset received, thereby allowing full disclosure of the asset in the balance sheet.

Similarly, valuable natural resources may be discovered on property subsequent to its acquisition, and the original cost may not provide all relevant information about the nature of the property. In such cases, the cost principle is modified to account for the appraisal increase in the property. A corresponding increase is recorded as an unrealized gain in stockholders' equity. An alternative practice consistent with the Conceptual Framework's definition of comprehensive income would be to recognize the appraisal increase as a gain.

Cost Allocation

Capitalizing the cost of an asset implies that the asset has future service potential. Future service potential indicates that the asset is expected to generate or be associated with future resource flows. As those flows materialize, the matching concept (discussed in Chapter 3) dictates that certain costs no longer have future service potential and should be charged to expense during the period the associated revenues are earned. Because the cost of property, plant, and equipment is incurred to benefit future periods, it must be spread, or allocated, to the periods benefited. The process of recognizing, or spreading, cost over multiple periods is termed *cost allocation.* For items of property, plant, and equipment, cost allocation is referred to as *depreciation.* As the asset is depreciated, the cost is said to expire—that is, it is expensed. (See Chapter 3 for a discussion of the process of cost expiration.)

[6] Ibid., par. 8.

As discussed earlier, balance sheet measurements should theoretically reflect the future service potential of assets at any moment in time. Accountants generally agree that cost reflects future service potential at acquisition. However, in subsequent periods expectations about future resource flows may change. Also, the discount rate used to measure the present value of the future service potential may change. As a result, the asset may still be useful, but due to technological changes, its future service potential at the end of any given period may differ from what was originally anticipated. Systematic cost allocation methods do not attempt to measure changes in expectations or discount rates; consequently, no systematic cost allocation method can provide balance sheet measures that consistently reflect future service potential.

The historical cost accounting model presently dominant in accounting practice requires that the costs incurred be allocated in a systematic and rational manner. Thomas extensively studied the topic of cost allocation and concluded that all allocation is based on arbitrary assumptions and that no one method of cost allocation is superior to another.[7] At the same time, it cannot be concluded that the present accounting model provides information that is not useful for investor decision making. A number of studies document an association between accounting income numbers and stock returns. This evidence implies that historical cost based accounting income, which employs cost allocation methods, has information content. (See Chapter 3 for a further discussion of this issue.)

Depreciation

Once the appropriate cost of an asset has been determined, certain decisions must be made as to the expiration of that cost. At the extremes, the entire cost of the asset could be expensed when the asset is acquired; or, alternately, cost could be retained in the accounting records until disposal of the asset when the entire cost is expensed. However, neither of these approaches provides for a satisfactory measure of periodic income. Thus, the concept of depreciation was devised in an effort to allocate the cost of property, plant, and equipment over the periods that receive benefit from the use of long-term assets.

Financial statement users' desire for periodic presentation of information on the result of operations necessitated allocating asset cost to the periods receiving benefit from the use of the asset. Because depreciation is a form of cost allocation, all depreciation concepts are related to some view of income measurement. A strict interpretation of the FASB's comprehensive income concept would require that changes in service potential be recorded in income. Economic depreciation has been defined as the change in the discounted present value of the items of property, plant, and equipment during a period. If the discounted present value measures the service potential of the asset at a

---

[7]Arthur L. Thomas, "The Allocation Program in Financial Accounting Theory," *Studies in Accounting Research No. 3* (American Accounting Association, 1969).

point in time, the change in service potential interpretation is consistent with the economic concept of income.

As discussed in Chapter 3, recording cost expirations by the change in service potential is a difficult concept to operationalize. Consequently, accountants have adopted a transactions view of income determination, and view income as the end result of revenue recognition according to certain criteria, coupled with the appropriate matching of expenses with those revenues. Thus, most depreciation methods emphasize the matching concept and little attention is directed to balance sheet valuation. Depreciation is typically described as a process of systematic and rational cost allocation that is not intended to result in the presentation of asset fair value on the balance sheet. This point was first emphasized by the Committee on Terminology of the American Institute of Certified Public Accountants as follows:

> *Depreciation accounting is a system of accounting which aims to distribute the cost or other basic value of tangible capital assets, less salvage value (if any), over the estimated useful life of the unit (which may be a group of assets) in a systematic and rational manner. It is a process of allocation, not valuation.*[8]

The AICPA's view of depreciation is particularly important to an understanding of the difference between accounting and economic concepts of income and also provides insight into many misunderstandings about accounting depreciation. Economists see depreciation as the decline in real value of assets. Other individuals believe that depreciation charges, and the resulting accumulated depreciation, provide the source of funds for future replacement of assets. Still others have suggested that business investment decisions are influenced by the portion of the original asset cost that has been previously allocated. That is, new investments cannot be made because the old asset has not been fully depreciated. These views are not consistent with the stated objective of depreciation for accounting purposes. In the following section we examine the accounting concept of depreciation more closely.

The Depreciation Process

The depreciation process for long-term assets comprises three separate factors:

1. Establishing the proper depreciation base.
2. Estimating the useful service life.
3. Choosing a cost apportionment method.

Depreciation Base

The depreciation base is that portion of the cost of the asset that should be charged to expense over its expected useful life. Because cost represents the future service potential of the asset embodied in future resource flows, the theoretical depreciation base is the present value of all resource flows over the

---

[8] *Accounting Terminology Bulletin No. 1,* "Review and Resume" (New York: AICPA, 1953), p. 9513.

life of the asset, until disposition of the asset. Hence, it should be cost minus the present value of the salvage value. In practice, salvage value is not discounted, and as a practical matter, it is typically ignored. Proper accounting treatment requires that salvage value be taken into consideration. For example, rental car agencies normally use automobiles for only a short period and the expected value of these automobiles at the time they are retired from service would be material and should be considered in establishing the depreciation base.

Useful Service Life

The useful service life of an asset is the period of time the asset is expected to function efficiently. Consequently, an asset's useful service life may be less than its physical life, and factors other than wear and tear should be examined to establish the useful service life.

Various authors have suggested possible obsolescence, inadequacy, supersession, and changes in the social environment as factors to be considered in establishing the expected service life. For example, jet airplanes have replaced most of the propeller-driven planes on the airlines, and ecological factors have caused changes in manufacturing processes in the steel industry. Estimating such factors requires a certain amount of clairvoyance—a quality difficult to acquire.

Depreciation Methods

Most of the controversy in depreciation accounting revolves around the question of the proper method to use in allocating the depreciation base over its estimated service life. Theoretically, the expired cost of the asset should be related to the value received from the asset in each period; however, these measurements are extremely difficult. Accountants have, therefore, attempted to estimate expired costs by other methods. These methods may be categorized as follows:

1. Straight line.
2. Accelerated.
3. Units of activity.
4. Group and composite.
5. Retirement and replacement.
6. Compound interest.

Straight Line The straight-line method allocates an equal portion of the depreciable cost of an asset to each period the asset is used. Straight-line depreciation is often justified on the basis of the lack of evidence to support other methods. Since it is difficult to establish evidence that links the value received from an asset to any particular period, the advocates of straight-line depreciation accounting argue that other methods are arbitrary and therefore inappropriate. The use of the straight-line method implies that the asset is declining in service potential in equal amounts over its estimated service life.

Accelerated Depreciation The-sum-of-the-year's-digits and fixed-percentage-of-declining-base are the most frequently encountered methods of acclerated depreciation.[9] These methods result in larger charges to expense in the earlier years of asset use, although little evidence supports the notion that assets actually decline in service potential in the manner suggested by these methods. Advocates contend that accelerated depreciation is preferred to straight-line because as the asset ages, the smaller depreciation charges are associated with higher maintenance charges. The resulting combined expense pattern provides a better matching against the associated revenue stream. Accelerated depreciation methods probably give balance sheet valuations that are closer to the actual value of the assets in question than straight-line, since most assets depreciate in value more rapidly in their earlier years of use. But since depreciation accounting is not intended to be a method of asset valuation, this factor should not be viewed as an advantage of using accelerated depreciation methods.

Units of Activity   Where assets, such as machinery, are used in the actual production process, it is sometimes possible to determine the total expected output to be obtained from these assets. Depreciation may then be based on the number of units of output during an accounting period. The activity measures of depreciation assume that each product produced during the asset's existence receives the same amount of benefit from the asset, an assumption that may or may not be realistic. Additionally, care must be exercised in establishing a direct relationship between the measurement unit and the asset. For example, when direct labor hours are used as a measure of the units of output, a decline in productive efficiency in later years of the asset's use may cause the addition of more direct labor hours per product, which would result in charging more cost per unit.

Group and Composite Depreciation   Group and composite depreciation are similar methods that apply depreciation to more than one asset during each accounting period. The advantage claimed for both methods is that they simplify record keeping; however, they may also obscure gains and losses on the disposal of individual assets. Group depreciation is used for homogeneous assets that are expected to have similar service lives and residual values. Composite depreciation is used for dissimilar assets with varying service lives and residual values.

In either case, the total cost of the assets is capitalized in a single account and treated as if it were a single asset for depreciation purposes. The depreciation rate is based on the average life of the assets, and periodic depreciation is calculated by multiplying the balance in the asset account by this rate. In the event an individual asset is taken out of service, no gain or loss is recognized, because the entire asset has not been retired. In an individual retirement, accumulated depreciation is charged for the difference between the original cost and the proceeds received. Any gain or loss is recorded when the entire group of assets has been taken out of service.

---

[9] Since 1981 the Internal Revenue Code has specified various accelerated depreciation methods to be used to determine taxable income. The method to use depends upon the year of acquisition of the asset and the type of asset.

Retirement and Replacement Methods   Retirement and replacement methods have been advocated by some accountants as expedient alternatives to the other methods of depreciation. Although retirement and replacement methods have not gained wide acceptance, they are used by public utilities. These methods recognize depreciation only at the time an asset reaches the end of its service life. Under the retirement method, depreciation is charged only when the asset is taken out of service, whereas the replacement method charges to depreciation the cost of new assets while retaining the original cost of plant and equipment acquired as an asset. Where the number of assets in use is large and a similar number of replacements is occurring each year, these methods might be justified, but in general they completely distort the matching process. Another disadvantage inherent in the use of the retirement and replacement methods is that the computation of net income may be significantly influenced and manipulated by management through advancing or postponing the replacement period.

Compound Interest Methods   Compound interest methods of depreciation have received attention because they focus on cost recovery and rate of return on investments. As discussed previously, assets may be viewed as future services to be received over their service lives, and the cost of the asset may then be viewed as the present value of the periodic services discounted at a rate of interest that takes into consideration the risk of the investment. The two compound interest depreciation methods most often encountered are the annuity method and the sinking fund method.

Under the *annuity method,* depreciation is based on the theory that production should be charged not only with the depreciable cost of the property, but also with the unrecovered income that might have been earned if the funds had been invested in some other manner.

The major criticism voiced against the use of the annuity method is including interest in the periodic depreciation charge. Including interest as an element of the cost of the asset may be theoretically correct, but it is not a generally accepted accounting procedure.

The *sinking fund method* is based on the assumption that an asset replacement fund is being established to replace the assets retired.

The sinking fund method takes into consideration the time value of money and results in a constant rate of return on book value. This method has been criticized, however, because it yields an increasing charge to depreciation in each year of asset life, while accountants generally agree that the service potential of the asset actually decreases each year.

An important point to note about all the depreciation methods is that no matter how simple or complex the calculations involved, the end result is an arbitrary cost allocation. The asset value disclosed on the balance sheet may not even approximate the current value of the asset. Therefore, since the avowed purpose of depreciation methods is to allocate cost, not determine value, the depreciation method selected should provide the most appropriate allocation of cost to the periods of benefit.

Accounting for Oil and Gas Properties

The assignment of cost to oil and gas properties has been a controversial subject for a number of years. These assets are unlike other long-term assets in that relatively large expenditures are required to find them, and for every successful discovery there are frequently many "dry holes."

For a number of years there have been two major methods of accounting advocated for recording and expensing the costs incurred in the development and production of oil and gas properties. These methods are termed the successful-efforts and the full-cost methods.

Under the *successful-efforts* method, costs that are directly identifiable with successful projects are capitalized and the costs of nonproducing efforts are expensed. The *full-cost* method capitalizes all the costs (whether they result in successful or unsuccessful projects) incurred for exploration and drilling within a large geographic area or cost center. Under both methods, the capitalized costs are subsequently allocated to expense as depletion by the units of activity method, as discussed earlier in the chapter. These alternatives can yield significantly different periodic asset valuations and net income figures.

The proponents of full costing maintain that oil companies undertake exploration and drilling activities knowing that only a small proportion of that activity will be fruitful. Therefore, unsuccessful activities must be viewed in the overall context of the entire exploration effort and all costs related to the overall effort must be matched with the production from the few successful wells. Opponents to full costing argue that exploration efforts in one geographical area often bear little resemblance or relationship to exploration efforts in another dissimilar geographical area and therefore it is theoretically incorrect to match the costs of unsuccessful wells with the revenue of successful wells discovered in other locations.

A second area of controversy concerns the relative financial effects of the full-cost and successful-efforts methods. One argument centers on the relative valuation of assets and measurement of net income under each method. Proponents of the full-cost method contend that the capitalization of all drilling costs results in a measurement of assets that is closer to the present value of proved reserves and further results in a higher net income. The larger assets and higher income enable small producers to attract the capital necessary to continue operations.

The proponents of the successful-efforts method counter by saying that there will not be a significant restriction on the inflow of capital to smaller producers solely due to the accounting method utilized. The evidence in the accounting literature from the efficient market research (discussed in Chapter 2) indicates that the stock market does not respond to changes in income that are caused by using alternative accounting principles.[10]

The Financial Accounting Standards Board undertook a study of these

---

[10] For a further discussion of these issues, see Steven M. Flory and Steven D. Grossman, "New Oil and Gas Accounting Requirements," *The CPA Journal* (May 1978), pp. 39–43.

arguments and, in December 1977, issued *SFAS No. 19*, ''Financial Accounting and Reporting by Oil and Gas Companies.'' In this release the board accepted the viewpoints advanced by the proponents of the successful-efforts method. The following is a summary of the rationale given for this decision.

1. Costs should be capitalized if they are expected to provide identifiable future benefits; otherwise they are considered to be an expense. Successful efforts is consistent with this concept while full cost is not.

2. Accounting focuses on individual assets. Aggregation (e.g., average cost methods for inventories) is considered acceptable only when its use is not expected to give results materially different from accounting for individual assets. With full cost, all acquisition, exploration, and development costs incurred in the broad cost centers (countries or continents) are aggregated and capitalized even if they relate to unsuccessful activities. Under successful efforts, only those costs relating directly to specific oil and gas reserves are capitalized.

3. Financial statements should report on the results of economic influences as they occur. If a firm's operations yield widely fluctuating earnings or only minor fluctuations, the financial statements should report them. If the statements do not show these differences that are perceived by investors and lenders as representing differences in risk, or if differences are shown that really do not exist, then capital may not be allocated equitably in the market. Full cost tends to obscure failure and risk by capitalizing both successful and unsuccessful activities; the successful-efforts method clearly depicts the risk involved by expensing unsuccessful operations.

4. Proponents of full cost argue that unsuccessful activities are unavoidable in the search for oil and gas, but there has been no direct cause-and-effect relationship demonstrated at the company level between total costs and reserves discovered. As with research-and-development costs, the absence of discernible future benefits at the time the costs are incurred indicates that these costs should not be capitalized.

5. Small companies argued that their ability to raise capital will be impaired if successful effort is required to be used because their income statements would more likely report net losses and their balance sheets could report cumulative deficits in stockholders' equity. Studies on the effect of accounting methods on securities prices are not conclusive. The claim that successful efforts would inhibit a company's ability to obtain capital has not been demonstrated or refuted conclusively. In addition, accounting standards should not be designed to foster national economic goals, but instead should objectively report the results of operations.

Soon after the release of *SFAS No. 19*, many small oil and gas producers voiced objections and asked the U.S. Congress for relief from its provisions. This pressure ultimately resulted in three SEC Accounting Series Releases on oil and gas accounting. The result of these pronouncements was a posture of support for the overall efforts of the FASB but a rejection of the provisions of *SFAS No. 19*.

In reaction to *SFAS No. 19,* the SEC asserted that both the full-cost and successful-efforts methods were so inadequate that it did not matter which was employed. As a substitute the SEC recommended a method termed *reserve recognition accounting* (RRA). This method is a current-value approach that is based on the net present values of a company's oil and gas reserves.

The SEC's justification for RRA was based on the contention that neither the full-cost nor the successful-efforts method discloses the most important event for oil and gas properties—the discovery of oil and gas reserves. Additionally, it argued that the earnings process for these companies is different from other companies in other industries. That is, the marketability of the product is relatively assured; therefore, a departure from point-of-sale revenue recognition is justified. RRA received considerable criticism from the oil and gas industry. The relevance of RRA to investor decision-making was questioned. Because RRA considers only proven reserves, significant reserves might be ignored, resulting in understated asset values. Additionally, the SEC recommended a 10 percent discount rate, but this rate was criticized as arbitrary and not taking into consideration any firm-specific factors such as risk, or general economic factors such as inflationary pressures, that might affect the firm's cost of capital. Finally, studies indicated that RRA lacked the precision needed to be used as a basis for audited figures in annual reports. Taken together, the criticisms of opponents and empirical evidence indicated that RRA may not satisfy either of the primary qualitative characteristics of financial information—relevance and reliability. As a result of these criticisms, in 1981 the SEC abandoned its support of RRA and returned jurisdiction of the issue to the FASB. To date no further action has been taken by the FASB.

Later, *SFAS Nos. 33* and *39* were issued by the FASB. These releases required large publicly held oil and gas companies to report the effects of changing prices on certain types of assets (see Chapter 14 for a further discussion of *SFAS No. 33*). At this time the board recognized that the accumulation of all the required information was placing a significant burden on oil- and gas-producing companies. The usefulness of the required data was also questioned, as was the failure to disclose other, seemingly more relevant information.

Thereafter, a task force comprised of individuals from the oil and gas industry and the financial and accounting community was formed to aid in the development of reporting standards for the oil and gas industry. The result of this review was the publication of Statement of *Financial Accounting Standards No. 69,* "Disclosures about Oil and Gas Producing Activities."

According to this release, publicly traded companies with significant oil and gas activities are required to disclose the following as supplementary information to their published financial statements.

1. Proven oil and gas reserve quantities.

2. Capitalized costs relating to oil- and gas-producing activities.

3. Costs incurred in oil and gas property acquisition, exploration, and development activities.

4. Results of operations for oil- and gas-producing activities.
5. A standardized measure of discounted future net cash flows relating to proven oil and gas reserve quantities.

Capital and Revenue Expenditures

The purchase and installation of plant and equipment does not eliminate expenditures associated with these assets. Almost all productive facilities require periodic maintenance that should be charged to current expense. The cost of the asset to the enterprise includes the initial cost plus all costs associated with keeping the asset in working order. However, if additional expenditures give rise to an increase in future service potential, these expenditures should not be charged to current operations. Expenditures that increase future service potential should be added to the remaining unexpired cost of the asset and be charged to expense over the estimated remaining period of benefit.

In most cases the decision to expense or capitalize expenditures is fairly simple and is based on whether the cost incurred is "ordinary and necessary" or "prolongs future life." But frequently this decision becomes more complicated and additional rules have been formulated that assist in determining whether an expenditure should be recorded as a capital improvement. If the asset's life is increased, the efficiency provided is increased, or if output is increased, the cost of an expenditure should be capitalized and written off over the expected period of benefit. All other expenditures made subsequent to acquisition should be expensed as incurred.

Recognition and Measurement Issues

Accounting depreciation methods are objective because they use historical cost. Moreover, once selected, the resulting depreciation charges are generally reliable. Nevertheless, all accounting depreciation methods have similar recognition and measurement problems. Given that fixed assets are intended to provide service potential over multiple future years, each cost allocation method requires estimates of salvage value and useful life, and given the rapidly changing competitive environment, revisions of these estimates may be required each accounting period.

It can also be argued that accounting depreciation methods do not provide relevant information for users. Users desire information that is useful in predicting future cash flows. Users are also aware that management makes a decision each period to either reinvest in available long-term assets or to replace existing long-term assets with new ones. Consequently, a current value approach to depreciation may be more consistent with investor needs.

Recording depreciation using a current value balance sheet approach would require knowledge of the reinvestment value of each long-term asset at the end of each accounting period. Such a determination may be impracticable or even impossible. The assets in question may be old, or they may be so specialized that there is no readily determinable market value. Alternative discounted present value techniques require estimates of future cash flows that may be unreliable. And appraisal values may not be realistic. Therefore, there is no simple answer to the determination of the most appropriate approach to depreciation. This determination is dependent, to a large extent, on an individual's perception of the necessary trade-off between relevance and reliability.

Summary

Property, plant, and equipment are usually the major long-term assets of a company. The overall objectives in accounting for these assets are to give management, investors, and government authorities useful information about these assets and to plan for a new acquisition through realistic budgeting.

A number of problems arise in choosing methods for assigning costs for these assets. Generally accepted accounting principles have been developed to handle most of these troublesome areas.

Assigning asset cost to the period of benefit remains the major problem in accounting for property, plant, and equipment. There are a number of views as to the nature of depreciation as well as a number of alternative methods of calculating and assigning these costs.

In the readings for this chapter Kathryn Means and Paul Kazenski analyze the internal consistency of *SFAS No. 34*, and the rationale for the various methods of depreciation are discussed in greater detail by John Pick in "Concepts of Depreciation."

SFAS 34: A Recipe for Diversity

Kathryn M. Means and Paul M. Kazenski

While preparers of financial statements are required to comply with Generally Accepted Accounting Principles, adherence to GAAP, *per se*, is no guarantee that financial statements will fairly represent either the financial position or the results of operations of an enterprise. Preparers of financial statements *must* take into account the qualitative characteristics of the information being presented.

Applying promulgated GAAP should provide like results in like circumstances. To properly serve the users of financial information, standards should both limit diversity in practice, and, at least in part, insure the quality of the information presented. When a standard lacks sufficient internal consistency to meet these expectations, it fails the user and becomes a prime candidate for examination in light of the recently completed Conceptual Framework project.

SFAS No. 34, "Capitalization of Interest Cost," is such a standard. It lacks sufficient internal consistency to insure that the results of its application will be verifiable and representationally faithful. Consequently, the financial information may lack comparability.

The FASB noted in SFAC No. 2 that ". . . in seeking comparability, accountants must not disguise real differences, nor create false differences" [par. 119]. This article will show that SFAS No. 34 is structured so as to allow the preparer

of financial statements the opportunity to create or disguise differences, intentionally or unintentionally.

The Purpose and Application of the Standard

SFAS No. 34 was issued in 1979 in response to an SEC moratorium on the capitalization of interest by nonutility firms. Prior to the issuance of the Standard, utility companies routinely capitalized interest costs associated with "self-constructed" assets. The SEC became concerned about the growing lack of comparability as nonutility enterprises also began to adopt the practice.

This Standard settled the issue by requiring all enterprises to capitalize interest on assets which are (1) constructed for the enterprise's own use, or (2) produced as discrete projects which are intended for sale or lease to others [par. 9]. The Standard refers to these as "qualifying assets."

One objective of requiring that interest be capitalized is "to obtain a measure of acquisition cost that more closely reflects the enterprise's total investment in the asset . . ." [par. 7]. Traditionally, the historical cost of an asset has included all expenditures required to bring the asset to condition and location necessary for use. The Board took the position that interest is an acquisition cost, and should be included as a part of the asset's historical cost [par. 6].

The amount of interest included in the asset's cost is a portion of the enterprise's total interest cost incurred during the "capitalization period." The capitalization period begins when expenditures have been made, activities are in progress, and interest cost is being incurred. It continues until the asset is ready for its intended use [par. 17].

The intent of the Standard is to capitalize the amount of interest that theoretically could have been avoided if expenditures for the asset had not been made. The Standard refers to this as "avoidable interest" [par. 12]. This theoretically avoidable interest is not limited to the cost associated with new debt used to finance the project. It includes other interest cost that theoretically could have been avoided had the funds expended on the project been used, instead, to extinguish debt.

To determine the amount of avoidable interest, the Standard requires the use of a "capitalization rate." This rate may be a "specific borrowing rate" (e.g., the rate associated with a construction loan), or a weighted average of the rates associated with the firm's outstanding debt [par. 13]. The capitalization rate is then applied to the "weighted average accumulated expenditures"—the expenditures weighted for the time they are outstanding during the period.

ferent computational approaches are being presented.[1] Apparently, depending on one's interpretation, there is more than one "correct" method which can be used to determine the amount of interest to be capitalized.

In attempting to reconcile the different approaches, we noted that difficulties in applying the Standard arise when three conditions are present: (1) the enterprise has both specific and other (general) debt outstanding; (2) the interest rates associated with the general and specific debts differ; and (3) the amounts and/or timing of the specific borrowing are not coincident with the amounts or timing of the expenditures. These alternatives involve the application of a specific borrowing rate and a weighted average rate to the total of qualifying expenditures.

Given a problem in which these three conditions are present, the alternative solutions presented in accounting texts each appear consistent with some interpretation of the Standard. The balance of this article will demonstrate the internal inconsistencies within the Standard which allow each of these alternatives to be justified. We will accomplish this by the use of the illustration which follows.

Identifying the Problem

We were alerted to the difficulties in applying this Standard by the change in the computational methods presented in the fourth and fifth editions of Kieso and Wygandt's *Intermediate Accounting*. This change was especially interesting in that essentially the same numerical example was used, but the illustrated solutions had significantly different results.

A review of other intermediate accounting texts revealed that several dif-

A Numerical Illustration

Assume that a company begins construction of a qualifying asset on April 1 with an expenditure of $600,000. Two additional expenditures of $300,000 each were made on July 1 and October 1.

---

[1] Examples of three approaches may be found in the following intermediate accounting texts: Kieso and Weygandt, fourth edition (1983); Kieso and Weygandt, fifth edition (1986); Welsch, Newman, Zlatkovich, seventh edition (1986).

The project was considered complete and ready for use on December 31.

The firm obtained a 15 percent construction loan for $600,000 on July 1 (the specific debt). During the year the firm also had outstanding additional debt of $1,200,000 at 9 percent (the general debt).

Given these facts, the weighted average accumulated expenditures can be calculated as follows:

The calculations given above are generic in nature, that is, they are independent of the approach which will ultimately be used to compute the amount of interest to be capitalized. The difficulties with the Standard arise when one attempts to compute "avoidable interest."

Calculation of Weighted Average Accumulated Expenditures

Date	Expenditures	×	Capitalization Period	=	Wtd. Average Accumulated Expenditures
4/1	$ 600,000		9/12		$450,000
7/1	300,000		6/12		150,000
10/1	300,000		3/12		75,000
Total	$1,200,000				$675,000

The amount of interest to be capitalized on the project is limited to the actual interest cost incurred by the firm during the accounting period [par. 15]. It is necessary, then, to determine the actual interest cost incurred by this firm as shown below.

Calculation of Actual Interest

Construction note	$ 600,000 ×
Five year note	15% × 6/12 =
Actual interest	$45,000
	1,200,000 ×
	9% × 12/12 =
	108,000
	$153,000

Given the facts, this firm will capitalize an amount less than or equal to its total interest cost of $153,000.

Calculating Avoidable Interest: A Technical Problem

As mentioned previously, the computation of avoidable interest may involve the application of either (1) a specific borrowing rate, (2) a weighted average rate, to the total of qualifying expenditures, (3) or both. These alternatives, when applied to the illustration, produce significantly different results.

As we will show, the first alternative would be to capitalize an amount equal to $96,750 while the second would be to capitalize $74,250. Consequently, we are faced with an unfortunate situation where identical assets constructed under identical circumstances may carry different acquisition values.

This situation results from a conflict between the intent of the Standard as given in paragraph 12, and the computational guidance offered in paragraph 13. For convenience, these two paragraphs are reproduced in their entirety in the appendix to this paper.

Applying the Specific Borrowing Rate: The First Alternative

To apply the guidance in paragraph 13 to the illustration, the following computations could be made:[2]

Calculation of Avoidable Interest

Wtd. Average Accumulated Expenditures	×	Interest Rate	=	Avoidable Interest
$600,000		15%		$90,000
75,000		9%		6,750
$675,000				$96,750

This computation complies literally with paragraph 13. First, the specific borrowing rate of 15 percent is applied to the amount of accumulated expenditures which do not exceed the specific borrowing ($600,000). Then the rate on other debt (nine percent) is applied to the amount of accumulated expenditures which exceed the specific borrowing ($75,000).

However, the result fails to comply with the intent of the Standard. By applying the 15 percent specific borrowing rate to the average accumulated expenditures equal to the loan proceeds, this alternative capitalizes *more* interest than could have actually been avoided with respect to the specific debt. In fact, the amount calculated above is twice the interest cost actually incurred on this debt during the capital-

---

[2] An example of this method can be found in Kieso and Weygandt, *Intermediate Accounting*, fourth edition, pp. 482–484.

ization period. Certainly, this kind of result could not have been intended by the Board, since it so clearly fails to reflect the economic realities.

The overstatement of avoidable interest is a direct result of the Standard's definition of excess accumulated expenditures as the difference between the weighted average accumulated expenditures and the gross (unweighted) specific loan proceeds [par. 13]. This definition results in a matching of weighted and unweighted amounts, which is difficult to justify theoretically.

The specific debt in this illustration could have provided *no more than* $300,000 of the average accumulated expenditures, since it is outstanding for only six months. In the calculation of avoidable interest, above, the loan proceeds are not weighted for the amount of time the funds are available. Thus the loan is treated as though it provided a full $600,000 of the average accumulated expenditures.

The overstatement of avoidable interest related to the specific debt occurs whenever the (1) capitalization period begins subsequent to the beginning of the period and (2) the average accumulated expenditures exceed the specific loan amount. In those cases, the results obtained from applying this alternative are identical to capitalizing interest *prior* to the beginning of the capitalization period.

Applying the Weighted Average Rate: The Second Alternative

The Standard states that an enterprise *may* use the specific borrowing rate as the capitalization rate. The Board's use of the word ''may'' rather than ''shall'' necessarily implies that an enterprise may choose *not* to consider the specific borrowing rate explicitly in its calculation of avoidable interest. In this case, the firm would calculate a weighted average of the rates associated with its outstanding debt. This would than be used as the capitalization rate to be applied to the total of average accumulated expenditures.

Given the facts in the illustration, the weighted average rate would be 11 percent. This rate would then be applied to the total average accumulated expenditures as follows:[3]

Calculation of Avoidable Interest

Average Accumulated Expenditures	×	Interest Rate	=	Avoidable Interest
$675,000		11%		$74,250

Given the simplicity of the computation, its conformity with the Standard's computational guidance is clear. However, given a case where a specific borrowing exists, this alternative will neither fully adhere to the Standard's intent, nor reflect the economic realities.

The interest cost associated with the specific debt clearly could have been avoided if the construction project had not been undertaken. The weighted average approach, however, ignores the incremental nature of this debt. Instead, it views all borrowed funds as being commingled within a single pool from which expenditures are drawn.

Consequently, when a specific debt exists, this method disguises the fact that a portion of the firm's debt, and its interest cost, are directly associated with the project. This alternative offers an

enterprise the opportunity to select a rate with which to capitalize interest on a basis unrelated to the facts. The representational faithfulness of the results, then, are questionable.

A Solution Based on Economic Facts

The Board's objective was that interest be capitalized "to obtain a measure of acquisition cost that more closely reflects the enterprise's total investment in the asset . . ." [par. 7]. Incremental interest costs associated with the acquisition of an asset are considered to be a part of this total investment.

Difficulty in applying the Standard as a whole results from the fact that one cannot both adhere to the intent of the Standard, and comply with its computational guidelines, simultaneously. This is compounded by the fact that the computational guidelines provide for more than one "correct" method of application.

One approach to eliminating the conflict between the intent of the Standard and its computational guidelines would be to:

1. Prescribe that the interest cost incurred on a specific borrowing during the capitalization period be included as part of the asset's cost. This could be accomplished quite simply by changing "may" to "shall" in sentence three of paragraph 13.

2. Eliminate the matching of weighted and unweighted amounts by redefining excess accumulated expenditures as the difference between the weighted average accumulated expenditures and the *weighted average* loan amount.

Applying these changes to the illustration, we would calculate the following amounts:

---

[3] An example of this approach can be found in Welsch, Newman, Zlatkovich, *Intermediate Accounting,* seventh edition, pp. 611–615.

Weighted average accumulated expenditures	$675,000
Weighted average loan amount ($600,000 × 6/12)	300,000
Excess average accumulated expenditures	$375,000
Interest to be capitalized:	
Specific borrowing (actual cost incurred)[a]	$ 45,000
Excess expenditures ($375,000 × 9%)	33,750
Avoidable interest	$ 78,750

[a]During the capitalization period:
$600,000 × 15% × 6/12

These changes would provide computational guidelines which, when applied to a single set of facts and circumstances, yield consistent results which adhere to the intent of the Standard, and are representationally faithful, as well.

When a debt is specifically associated with the acquisition of an asset, it is theoretically correct to capitalize all *interest cost* incurred on this debt during the capitalization period. The proposed solution would capitalize $45,000—the actual amount of interest cost incurred, and therefore, clearly avoidable.

Additional funds expended beyond those obtained from the specific borrowing could theoretically have been used to repay other outstanding debt of the enterprise. The interest cost incurred as a result of *not* extinguishing this other debt is properly considered "avoidable," as well. In the proposed solution, the $33,750 represents interest on the excess expenditures of $375,000 which could have been used to eliminate a portion of the firm's nine percent debt.

In the case where an enterprise has no specific debt related to the project, all expenditures would be considered to be "excess expenditures" to which a weighted average interest rate would be applied. This would be consistent with the view that all funds invested in the project could theoretically have been used to repay outstanding debt.

Defining Avoidable Interest: A Conceptual Problem

A solution to the technical problems discussed above could be accomplished by amending the Standard's computational guidelines. However, a conceptual problem still remains which cannot be solved simply by altering these guidelines.

This conceptual problem results from a lack of clarity with respect to the definition of avoidable interest. The interest capitalized is intended to be that which could have been avoided by ". . . avoiding additional borrowings *or* by using the funds expended for the assets to repay existing borrowings" [par. 12, emphasis added]. The Board's use of the word "or" leaves open the question as to whether the avoidance of additional borrowings or the use of funds invested in the asset for the theoretical repayment of existing debt is to receive preference.

Depending upon where one places emphasis, two solutions emerge. These can be demonstrated by altering the original illustration as follows. The date of the specific loan is changed to January 1, and an additional expenditure of $100,000 is also made on that date. The dates and amounts of subsequent expenditures remain unchanged. This results in weighted average accumulated expenditures of $775,000.

A solution which emphasizes the use of invested funds to repay existing debt is shown on page 330.[4]

[4]An example of this approach can be found in Kieso and Weygandt, *Intermediate Accounting*, fifth edition, pp. 417–418.

Invested Funds Used to Repay Existing Borrowings			Weighted Avg. Accumulated Expenditures		Interest Rate		Avoidable Interest
$ 100,000	×	12/12 =	$100,000	×	15%	=	$15,000
500,000	×	9/12 =	375,000	×	15%	=	56,250
100,000	×	9/12 =	75,000	×	9%	=	6,750
300,000	×	6/12 =	150,000	×	9%	=	13,500
300,000	×	3/12 =	75,000	×	9%	=	6,750
$1,300,000			$775,000				$98,250

A second solution, which emphasizes the avoidance of additional borrowings is given below:

Weighted average accumulated expenditures	$775,000
Weighted average loan amount ($600,000 × 12/12)	600,000
Excess average accumulated expenditures	$175,000
Interest to be capitalized:	
Specific borrowing (actual cost incurred)[a]	$ 90,000
Excess expenditures ($175,000 × 9%)	15,750
Avoidable interest	$105,750

[a]During the capitalization period.

This dilemma will arise whenever, at the date of the specific loan, the accumulated expenditures are less than the loan proceeds. It is the treatment of this difference which causes the results to differ.

The first solution assumes that avoidable interest accrues only on the funds invested in the asset. The second solution views the entire specific debt as avoidable and, therefore, the entire interest cost associated with it as avoidable.

The Standard, as currently written, provides insufficient guidance to determine which interpretation the Board intended. Again, the application of SFAS No. 34 to this set of circumstances may give results which are questionable

in terms of their comparability and representational faithfulness.

Should SFAS No. 34 Be Revisited?

Users of accounting information properly expect that statements prepared in good faith will properly reflect the enterprise's activities and financial position. Unfortunately, the guidelines for implementation which were provided in the Standard are subject to alternative interpretations. Some of these interpretations may, as we have shown, produce results which conflict with the intent of the Standard. Consequently, the Standard is deficient in the sense that equally competent preparers dealing with identical circumstances may arrive at substantially different results.

Statements of Financial Accounting Standards should both limit diversity in practice, and, at least in part, insure the quality of the information presented. The Board, itself, noted in SFAC No. 2 that "Information about an enterprise gains greatly in usefulness if it can be compared with similar information about other enterprises . . ." [par. 111]. SFAS No. 34 does not provide assurance with respect to the qualitative characteristics of verifiability and representational faithfulness.

As a result, this Standard may have done little to enhance comparability. There is a diversity of interpretation evident in the variety of presentations in accounting texts. This may be indicative of a diversity in practice, as well.

Due to the inability of this Standard to insure the qualitative aspects of the financial information being reported, and the potential for diversity of application in practice, we believe that an examination of SFAS No. 34 by the Board is warranted.

Appendix

Paragraph 12: The Intent of the Standard

The amount of interest cost to be capitalized for qualifying assets is intended to be that portion of the interest cost incurred during the assets' acquisition periods that theoretically could have been avoided (for example, by avoiding additional borrowings or by using the funds expended for the assets to repay existing borrowings) if expenditures for the assets had not been made.

Paragraph 13: The Computational Guidelines

The amount capitalized in an accounting period shall be determined by applying an interest rate(s) ("the capitalization rate") to the average amount of accumulated expenditures for the asset during the period. The capitalization rates used in an accounting period shall be based on the rates applicable to borrowings outstanding during the period. If an enterprise's financing plans associate a specific new borrowing with a qualifying asset, the enterprise may use the rate on that borrowing as the capitalization rate to be applied to that portion of the average accumulated expenditures for the asset that does not exceed the amount of that borrowing. If average accumulated expenditures for the asset exceed the amounts of specific new borrowings associated with the asset, the capitalization rate to be applied to such excess shall be a weighted average of the rates applicable to other borrowings of the enterprise.

Concepts of Depreciation—
Business Enterprises

John Pick

American accounting theory began to deal with depreciation in the nineteenth century and, at the century's end, treated it mainly as an acknowledgment of the deterioration of business assets due to wear and tear.[1] In that early concept, the recognition of depreciation was at times an alternative to that of repair and maintenance expenses. Today, the depreciation charge has the independent status of an accounting principle.

Unfortunately, the financial community sometimes seems inclined to treat depreciation as something "unreal"[2] and to give primary consideration to income without depreciation, the so-called "cash-flow." That is due to several factors, such as the insufficiency of information furnished in public financial reports with respect to depreciation, the ambiguity of the concept itself, and the multiplicity of procedures. One source of ambiguity is the indiscriminate, simultaneous listing of financial and managerial accounting aspects of depreciation in the professional literature. This article will deal only with ex-ternal reporting aspects, unless a phase of managerial accounting evidently bears upon the problem at hand. Depreciation for internal reporting can vary widely.

Terminology

Kohler defines the term "concept" as "any abstract idea serving a systematizing function."[3] In Webster, a concept is ". . . a theoretical construct. . . ."[4] Accordingly, the nature of depreciation should be obtained inductively from accounting practices and/or deductively from accounting theory. Either procedure is impeded by the involvement of terms each of which has several meanings. These terms are: value, asset, capital, and income.

Value

"Value" in the popular sense denotes value in use or value in exchange. The former is the value to the owner, the latter is the market value. Value is also used in the sense of serviceability. However, that engineering term indicates only one of the factors influencing the value to the owner and/or the market value. A fourth meaning of value appears in the accountancy's book value.

[1] P. D. Woodward, "Depreciation—Development of an Accounting Concept," *Accounting Review*, Vol. 31 (January 1956), pp. 71–76.

[2] Benjamin Graham, David L. Dodd, and Sidney Cottle, *Security Analysis* (4th ed., New York: McGraw-Hill Book Co., 1962), p. 151.

[3] Eric L. Kohler, *A Dictionary for Accountants* (3rd ed.: Englewood Cliffs, N.J.: Prentice-Hall, 1963), p. 114.

[4] *Webster's Third International Dictionary* (Springfield, Mass.: G. & C. Merriam Company, 1961).

Here the word is used in a neutral sense.[5]

Asset

In present accounting practice, the book value of a fixed asset denotes an unexpired prepayment for service benefits. The prepayment and the service potentials embodied in an asset are not necessarily equivalent monetarily and often are differently emphasized conceptually. Two quotations illustrate the conceptual divergence. The American Institute of Certified Public Accountants (AICPA) stresses the prepayment view: "[an asset may be defined as] something represented by a debit balance . . . on the basis that it represents . . . an expenditure made which . . . is properly applicable to the future."[6] The American Accounting Association (AAA) emphasizes the economic utility aspect: "assets are . . . aggregates of service potentials available for or beneficial to expected operations."[7]

Capital

Both net assets and the equity in them are frequently referred to as capital. Accordingly, capital may mean the monetary amounts appearing as balances in proprietorship accounts, or real capital in the sense of the actual service potentials of the business, its purchase and/or earning power.

Income

Definitions of assets and capital naturally influence those of income. Business income may signify either the residuum remaining after offsetting credits and debits representing revenue and costs or expenses according to accounting rules, or it may identify the amount "which is available for distribution outside the firm without contraction of the level of its operating capacity,"[8] or it may express the increase of service potentials, i.e., of the capitalized value of future expectations.[9]

Practical Concepts of Depreciation

The variations in underlying terminology make a detailed evaluation of existing definitions of depreciation an expansive undertaking. Those definitions are classified by Coughlan and Strand as indicating (1) a decrease in value with the lapse of time, (2) impaired serviceability, (3) the value difference from an appraisal standard, and (4) amortized cost.[10]

That roughly corresponds with Goldberg's listing of (1) fall in market price, (2) physical deterioration, (3) fall in value, and (4) allocation of cost.[11]

[5] Joseph D. Coughlan and William K. Strand, *Depreciation Accounting, Taxes and Business Decisions* (New York: Ronald Press Company, 1969), p. 17.

[6] AICPA, Accounting Terminology Bulletin No. 1, "Review and Resume" (*AICPA*, 1953), p. 13.

[7] American Accounting Association (AAA), "Accounting and Reporting Standards for Corporate Financial Statements and Preceding Statements and Supplements, 1957 Revision," (Madison, Wis.: AAA, School of Commerce, University of Wisconsin, 1957), p. 3.

[8] AAA, Committee on Concepts and Standards—Long-Lived Assets, "Accounting for Land, Buildings, and Equipment," Supplementary Statement No. 1, *Accounting Review*, Vol. 39 (July 1964), p. 696.

[9] Study Group on Business Income, *Changing Concepts of Business Income* (New York: Macmillan Co., 1952), pp. 8–10.

[10] Coughlan and Strand, op. cit., p. 12.

[11] Louis Goldberg, *Concepts of Depreciation* (Sydney: The Law Book Company of Australasia, Pty., Ltd., 1969), p. 4.

Singer finds that depreciation has been referred to as meaning (1) the systematic amortization of cost without regard to value during life; (2) the exhaustion of service-units embodied in fixed assets; (3) the loss in value due to wear and tear, deterioration, and obsolescence; (4) physical deterioration and consequent loss in value; and (5) a means to keep real capital intact.[12]

The Significance of the Definitions

The definitions indicate five thoughts on what the depreciation provision represents. These concepts are influenced by whether they lean in an operational or financial direction.

Apart from the five concepts is a sixth one that adopts for reporting purposes the income-tax-motivated amount, however unrealistic. This aspect is here ignored.

The prevailing concepts are:

Operational-oriented:
   recognition of wear and tear, inadequacy, and obsolescence
Financial-oriented:
   provision for replacement

   a means of income determination

   a measure of asset valuation

   a measure of the maintenance of capital

The following discussion, accordingly, deals with the concept of depreciation by reference to the operational causes of the depreciation charge and its four financial purposes and functions.

Causal Concept—Impact of Repairs and Maintenance

The reference of depreciation to its causes is a favorite of textbooks. These

list physical causes consisting of wear, tear, and the action of elements, and functional causes consisting of gradual obsolescence, inadequacy, and all other causes. Obsolescence, as considered here, is that which is the gradual type and which is expected where improvement is constant. Sudden obsolescence requires accounting treatment only when it occurs.

The aspect of deterioration has been historically important in gaining depreciation the recognition as a legitimate business expense[13] and is still part of its definition in the 1936 uniform system of accounts for electric and gas utilities. However, physical and economic serviceableness may influence the choice of a fixed asset's rate of depreciation, but they do not identify the concept. An asset is depreciated on books even if, for a certain length of time, it becomes more effective with use. Besides, the causes of deterioration usually are difficult to separate and to measure, as they may comprise use, and abuse.

As a result, repairs and maintenance do not enter the depreciation concept. A firm's standard of maintenance affects an asset's efficiency and life; but depreciation in accounting may differ from engineering figures; using an asset does not necessarily mean using it up. Although many companies coordinate depreciation and maintenance accounting by aligning depreciation methods with estimated future maintenance and repairs, it seems better—where possible—to budget repairs and maintenance, accrue them annually, and to let depreciation follow its own rules.[14]

---

[12] Frank A. Singer, "'Depreciation'—Better Left Unsaid," *Accounting Review*, Vol. 32 (July 1957), p. 406.

[13] Woodward, op. cit.

[14] Rufus Wixon, ed., *Accountants' Handbook* (4th ed., New York: Ronald Press, 1956), pp. 17, 21; George L. Battista and Gerald R. Crowningshield, "Accounting for Deprecia-

Replacement Concept

External reporting of depreciation has been ascribed mainly two purposes: the economic purpose of providing for the replacement of capital goods consumed in operations, and the accounting purpose of income determination.

"Replacement" may mean physical replacement, replacement of output capacity, and replacement of value, although the concern sometimes is to restore to current assets, through the depreciation provision, the amounts diverted earlier to noncurrent assets. The first two meanings usually are implied in depreciation's replacement concept. That term must not be confused with depreciation using current replacement costs as periodic charges. Such charges may be chosen for reasons unconnected with asset replacement, such as the desire to match current dollar revenue with current dollar costs. Thus restricted, replacement depreciation may mean either (1) that depreciation is taken in order to reserve funds for asset replacement, or (2) that depreciation itself reserves funds by designating them for replacement purchases, or (3) that depreciation provides funds.

A study published by the National Association of Accountants in 1958 reveals that generally management is concerned with the effect of depreciation policy on the flow of cash to fixed assets and back, but that for various reasons it has not adopted a policy of using special depreciation procedures in order to reserve replacement funds.[15] Exceptions to the general rule are found with utilities. In some states utilities must set up sinking funds for asset replacement and use the sinking fund method of depreciation.

By itself, depreciation does not earmark funds for replacement purposes, though it is an amortization of the investment in fixed assets. Depreciation is taken on irreplaceable assets too. The funds equaling a period's depreciation are not segregated but put to many uses. Once replacement is made, it is impossible to trace the funds used for it to recovered capital, profits, or investors' contributions.

Finally, the idea that depreciation actually provides funds was found to be a fallacy long ago.[16] It is revenue that provides funds. Tax savings by depreciation do not provide funds in the industry where depreciation counts really, namely the utilities. Those tax savings generally have to be passed on to customers.[17] Where tax savings stay with the firm, depreciation does not generate funds but—like any other cost—saves them from pay-out to the government. Anyhow, funds saved by depreciation are not, in many instances, too important for asset replacement. Even total accelerated depreciation often has not come near to the amounts needed to keep modern plants well equipped.[18]

Input Concept

The objective of depreciation, to determine net income by the assignment of plant cost as input to operations, is generally accepted today. The classical definition of this concept is that of the AICPA: "Depreciation accounting is a system of accounting which aims to dis-

tion and Repair Costs," *National Association of Accountants (NAA) Bulletin,* Vol. 45 (December 1963), p. 30.

[15] NAA, "Current Practice in Accounting for Depreciation," Research Report No. 33 (April 1958), pp. 10–13.

[16] Rufus Wixon, ed., op. cit., pp. 17, 49f.

[17] William A. Paton, *Corporate Profits* (Homewood, Ill.: Richard D. Irwin, 1965), p. 33.

[18] Graham, Dodd, and Cottle, op. cit., p. 157.

tribute the cost . . . over the estimated life of the unit . . . in a systematic and rational manner. It is a process of allocation, not of valuation. . . ."[19] This definition conceives depreciation as the expiration of prepayments in the course of business operations and as the corresponding write-off on books. Changes of the price of service potentials (assets) already paid for are considered irrelevant. The asset cost is a historical fact; the capital, of which it forms a part, is an aggregate of various historical dollars. The cost write-offs are not meant as economic measurements of wear and tear: the remaining asset values are mere residuals on a balance sheet which is just a tabular statement of balances, functioning as footnote to the income statement.[20] The method of calculating the write-offs is "of minor importance"[21] so long as it is rational and systematic.

That leaves the choice of amortization methods wide open. Obviously, not every rational method is acceptable; it has to be reasonable in the light of surrounding circumstances. As reasonableness is judgmental, guidelines become necessary.

Hendriksen discusses four: (1) the decline in the service value of the asset, (2) the cost of services used, (3) the net service contribution, and (4) the output value of the services.[22] Item one, the decline in service value, leads right back to the valuation question, which the AICPA definition abhors.

Problems of Input Concept

The input concept does not only fail to provide guidance for the selection of amortization methods but also may lead to the matching of revenue measured in current dollars with expense expressed in historical dollars. Two remedies have been proposed, namely the application of price-level indexes and the use of current cost, i.e., mainly replacement costs.

A recent statement of the AICPA recommends price-level translations only for supplementary statements and declares as undesirable the restriction of translations to single items like depreciation.[23] The AAA Committee on Concepts and Standards—Long-Lived Assets recommends the recognition of holding gains and losses due to price changes.[24] Defining assets and income differently from the AICPA, the committee believes that where the economic value of service potential—i.e., the discounted value of the corresponding future cash flows—cannot be measured in ways "that meet the test of verifiable evidence," reference should be made to the current cost of securing the same or equivalent value. The committee still is primarily concerned with income determination.

However, the committee recognizes asset valuation and depreciation expense determination as interdependent; the determination of one reflects that of the other. Moonitz and Sprouse take a similar position as the AAA committee but in addition recommend periodic

---

[19] AICPA, op. cit., p. 25.

[20] Herman W. Bevis, *Corporate Financial Reporting in a Competitive Economy* (New York: Macmillan Co., 1965), pp. 129–130.

[21] W. A. Paton and A. C. Littleton, *An Introduction to Corporate Accounting Standards* (Urbana, Ill.: AAA. College of Commerce and Business Administration, University of Illinois, 1954), p. 17.

[22] Eldon S. Hendiksen, *Accounting Theory* (Homewood, Ill.: Richard D. Irwin, 1965), p. 311.

[23] AICPA, Statement of the Account Principles Board No. 3 (1969), p. 19.

[24] AAA, Committee on Concepts and Standards—Long-Lived Assets, loc. cit., p. 695.

fixed asset revaluations.[25] To go still one step further, Edwards and Bell stress current costs as such and not only as clues, and develop a system that integrates both historical and current costs. These writers see the difference between historical and current cost as a *holding gain* of which a part is realized by depreciation.[26]

Somewhat differently, the AAA Committee to Prepare a Statement of Basic Accounting Theory recommends the showing of historical and current costs parallel in multicolumn statements, and the reporting of both realized and unrealized holding gains.[27]

The diversity of proposals indicates the need for a concept that narrows down the choice of procedures. Even if depreciation serves primarily as an income determinant, its actual effects on asset valuation and capital maintenance determination have to be considered; those functions might furnish the needed fruitful concept.

Valuation Concept

Viewed as asset valuation, depreciation conceivably may work with: (1) present values of future cash flows attributable to the asset, or (2) with market prices, appraisals, price-level index applications, or replacement costs as indicators of those present values, or (3) with the last four as such in their own right.

Appraisal depreciation as an independent system is not used for going concerns any more and would not present systematic, but erratic, patterns. Price-level index applications do not produce independent values but only translate given ones. The use of market prices in their own right is most prominently presented by Professor Chambers as part of an accounting system that is based on the theory of cash equivalents and which has to be accepted or refuted in total.[28] Replacement costs or current costs have been mentioned above as input measurements, not primarily concerned with asset valuation. That leaves present values for discussion.

Sinking Fund Method

Mathematically, present values are applications of compound interest. One extension of compound interest, the sinking fund method, was mentioned previously. This method, the application of which does not have to coincide with the establishment of an actual fund, results in increasing periodic charges due to the interest on the increasing hypothetical fund balance. Only few assets justify such charges; however, the method still is sometimes recommended for more general use.[29]

Present Value Methods

A related procedure is the annuity method, which arrives at equal annual charges by adding to the sinking fund depreciation the periodic interest on the unamortized asset balance. The annuity method requires the recording of imputed interest, and its total depreciation

[25] Robert T. Sprouse and Maurice Moonitz, "A Tentative Set of Broad Accounting Principles for Business Enterprises," Accounting Research Study No. 3 (AICPA, 1962), p. 34.

[26] Edgar D. Edwards and Philip W. Bell, *The Theory and Measurement of Business Income* (Berkeley and Los Angeles: University of California Press, 1961), pp. 162ff.

[27] AAA, Committee to Prepare a Statement of Basic Accounting Theory (Evanston, Ill.: AAA, 1966), pp. 29.35.

[28] Raymond J. Chambers, *Accounting, Evaluation and Economic Behavior* (Englewood Cliffs, N.J.: Prentice-Hall, 1966), pp. 208–209.218.

[29] David Solomons, *Divisional Performance: Measurement and Control* (New York: Financial Executives Research Foundation, 1965), p. 135.

charges exceed the asset cost. It also presumes constancy of future revenue and charges other than depreciation, and assumes constant reinvestment of the cash inflow equaling the amortizations. The method is rarely used. Recording imputed interest does not appeal to most financial accountants, nor is the equality of periodic charges always realistic. Many fixed assets decline in service value much faster in the first years of use than in the later years.

It is possible, however, to modify the annuity method so as to avoid the recording of imputed interest and to obtain accelerated depreciation. This is achieved by discounting each of the annuities as of the date of asset acquisition and by using the discounted amounts as depreciation charges. The farther a charge is removed, the less will be its present value (present-value-of-annual-cash-flows method).

nowadays.[30] It logically represents the valuation concept of depreciation. Useful results therefore would validate the concept.

Exhibit 1 illustrates both (A) the present - value - of - annual - cash - flows method and (B) the balance-of-present-value method. Given is a depreciable asset producing a net cash flow with a present value of $12,000 equally spread over three years.

In this case an interest rate of 6% is assumed. The capital recovery factor at 6% for 3 years of 0.31411 and is easily found in tables labeled correspondingly. This factor applied to $12,000 gives $4,489. The present value factors are equally easily found in tables labeled "present value of $1." Their application to $4,489 gives the amounts in column (A). The expiration of service potentials, shown in column (B), can be computed as shown in Exhibit 2 (cents omitted).

An alternative computation is somewhat faster (cents omitted):

Year	1/1 Investment	Cash Flow	6% Interest	Depreciation
1	$12,000	$4,489	$720	$3,769
2	8,231	4,489	493	3,996
3	4,235	4,489	254	4,235

Present Value—Expired Service Potential Method

Another procedure in the same direction compares the present values of the services embodied in the asset as of the beginning and as of the end of a report period and uses the difference, the expired service potential, as depreciation (balance-of-present-value method). That is the method most often discussed

[30] W. A. Paton and W. A. Paton, Jr., *Asset Accounting: An Intermediate Course* (New York: Macmillan Co., 1952), p. 272. Harold Bierman, Jr., "Depreciable Assets—Timing of Expense Recognition," *Accounting Review*, Vol. 36 (October 1961), pp. 613–618; T. N. Young and C. G. Peirson, "Depreciation-Future Services Basis," *Accounting Review*, Vol. 42 (April 1967), pp. 338–341; Hugo Nurnberg, "Present Value Depreciation and Income Tax Allocation," *Accounting Review*, Vol. 43 (October 1968), p. 719; AAA, "Report of Committee on Managerial Decision

EXHIBIT 1

Year	Equivalent Annual Cash Flow	Present Factor Value at 6%	(A) Annual Cash Flow Discounted at 6%	(B) Diminution of Total Present Value
1	$4,489	0.943396	$ 4,235	$ 3,769
2	4,489	0.889996	3,996	3,996
3	4,489	0.839619	3,769	4,235
			$12,000	$12,000

EXHIBIT 2

	First Year	Second Year	Third Year
Service potential at beginning	$12,000	$8,231	$4,235
Present value of 2nd year's annuity	$ 4,235[a]		
Present value of 3rd year's annuity	3,996[b]	4,235[c]	
Service potential left	$ 8,231	$4,235	0
Service potential expired	$ 3,769	$3,996	$4,235

[a] 4489 × .943396

[b] 4489 × .889996

[c] 4489 × .943396

The interest amounts are not recorded on books but appear as profits on the income statement. Each year's opening asset balance equals the total of the remaining service potentials.

In this case, the balance-of-present-value method results in increasing charges, whereas the present-value-of-annual-cash-flows method naturally has the opposite result. However, the former method also can lead to equal and to decreasing depreciation charges—depending on the size of the individual amount representing the asset's periodic net service contributions. In such cases, both the interest rate and the annual net cash inflows have to be found. The cost of capital usually serves as interest rate. That cost can be computed by dividing the market value of a firm's common share into the firm's annual income expected by investors. The estimated service contributions may represent the prospective asset or the production of "real revenue . . . less all operating costs other than depreciation . . ." attributable to it.[31]

The previous example's result of the balance-of-present-value method, a decelerated depreciation, is usually unrealistic. As the example's assumption of

Models," *Accounting Review,* Supplement to Vol. 44 (1969), p. 76.

[31] Isaac N. Reynolds, "Selecting the Proper Depreciation Method," *Accounting Review,* Vol. 36 (April 1961), p. 240.

equal annual service contributions is not uncommon, the method must be judged as failing to provide the valuation concept of depreciation with the necessary support of overall usefulness. That does not mean, however, that present value procedures cannot be meaningfully related to the fourth depreciation concept, that of capital maintenance. Whereas asset valuation and input measurement are functionally integrated, capital maintenance rules are independent of net asset valuation rules.[32]

Maintenance of Capital Concept

Depreciation has been defined "as a means of measuring whether capital is retained intact for further use."[33] This definition calls for three comments. First, depreciation cost is not different from other costs as *cause* of the retention of capital, both with respect to dividend policy and otherwise.[34] Retaining capital intact is the role of revenue, i.e., recovering costs and expenses. The *measurement* of the retention is the function of the income statement, including depreciation. Second, capital and costs must be stated in the same dollars as revenue in order to make the measurement of capital maintenance meaningful, and capital must signify not merely an aggregate of historical money amounts but the purchase and/or earnings power of the business. Third, as-

suming absence of price-level changes, a period's plant cost consumption is fully recovered by revenue if the period shows a profit, and is partly recouped in case of a loss. In the latter situation, depreciation may measure how far (and not whether) capital has been maintained; special computations will be needed.

Accordingly, under present accounting conditions, the function of depreciation as a measure of capital maintenance presents a concept rather weak by itself. However, it is exactly this concept that provides accounting guidance. It recommends that the present value of the net cash flow of a future year attributable to a specific asset shall be the asset's depreciation in that year. Barring price changes, such depreciation will indicate, in the case of profits, what part of the revenue must be reinvested to maintain the firm's earning power in the pattern of the original budget. The difference between the present value and the budgeted amount of each annual net cash flow would represent a return on capital, earned during the period from the acquisition of the service potential to the year of its consumption and realized in that year.

An example illustrates some mathematical details. Given is an asset cost of $10,000, a 6% cost of capital, and a net service (utility) contribution of $12,000 distributed over three years in the sum-of-the-year's-digits method (cents omitted).

The present value factors are the same as in the first example. The equivalent differential is computed with the equation:

$$899 = \frac{X}{2(1.06)} + \frac{X}{3(1.06)^2} + \frac{X}{6(1.06)^3}$$

$$= X\left[\frac{0.9434}{2} + \frac{0.89}{3} + \frac{0.8396}{6}\right];$$

$$X = 990$$

---

[32] Keith Shwayder, "The Capital Maintenance Rule and the Net Asset Valuation Rule," *Accounting Review*, Vol. 44 (April 1969), pp. 304–316.

[33] Coughlan and Strand, op. cit., pp. 1.9f.

[34] Paton and Paton, op. cit., p. 262; but William A. Paton, "Depreciation—Concept and Measurement," *Journal of Accounting* (October 1959), p. 39, stresses the understatement of depreciation as cause of impairment of capital resources.

Year	Cash Flow	Present Value at 6%	Equivalent Differential	Present Value at 6%	Total Present Value
1	$ 6,000	$ 5,660	$495	$467	$ 5,193
2	4,000	3,560	330	294	3,266
3	2,000	1,679	165	138	1,541
	$12,000	$10,899	$990	$899	$10,000

The excess of the total of present values over the asset cost—$899 in this case—is either recorded and then amortized[35] or is initially deducted from the present values. The last procedure is followed above.

Arguments Against Capital Maintenance Method

The following arguments have been advanced against such use of present values:

1. Estimates of the asset's net service contributions are necessary.

2. The cost of capital, too, may involve judgment.

3. Complications may arise due to subsequent changes in expectations.

4. The asset purchase is influenced by demand and supply. The buyer has no guarantee for the fulfillment of his expectations.[36]

5. The variety of fixed assets makes computations of present values difficult.[37]

6. The method is not applicable to non-revenue-producing items, such as personnel recreation facilities.[38]

7. The earnings power of assets is collective. The cash flow is attributable to the aggregate of assets.[39]

8. Cash savings, net service contributions, and time-adjusted accrued revenues and expenses are often discounted from the end of the year of their occurrence, whereas they occur throughout the year.[40]

The first two objections do not carry weight. Accountants are used to making judgments. Moreover, the judgment involved here is that of the decision-making and presumably well-informed management. The third objection should not be overrated. Expectations are usually capitalized only once, namely when the decision to acquire an asset is made; that decision entails the proper depreciation charges.[41] The fourth objection scarcely needs a rebuttal. Future does not hold any guarantees whatsoever. Regardless of supply and demand, no businessman buys

[35] Wendell P. Trumbull, op. cit., p. 465.

[36] Paton and Paton, op. cit., p. 272.

[37] Rufus Wixon, ed., op. cit., pp. 17.24f.

[38] Bierman, op. cit.

[39] Eugene L. Grant and Paul T. Norton, Jr., *Depreciation* (Rev. ptg.: New York: Ronald Press, 1955), p. 38.

[40] Harold Bierman, Jr., "Further Study of Depreciation," *Accounting Review*, Vol. 41 (April 1966), pp. 271–274, proposes that sales and purchases on account be time-adjusted by discounting them back to the date they are made, and then be considered part of the cash stream of that date.

[41] Bierman, "Depreciable Assets. . . ." op. cit., p. 613.

without expecting a return of and on capital. The fifth and sixth objections have limited merit only. (Depreciation in a non-profit organization is not included in this paper's discussion.) As to the seventh objection, that the earnings power of assets is collective, the rebuttal has been offered that businessmen make individual asset projections daily.[42] The last objection, finally, is taken care of by present value tables constructed on the assumption of the uniformity of cash flows during the year.

Favorable Aspects of Capital Maintenance Method

Favorable to the use of present values is that

1. Interest is a factor in the cost of any fixed asset.

2. The time value of money is finding increasing accounting recognition, e.g., in AICPA Accounting Principles Board Opinions No. 5 and No. 8.

3. People place a higher value on services to be rendered soon than on those of later delivery.

4. With present value methods, depreciation can be applied on the basis of activities instead of time intervals.

5. Present value computations are used by management in asset acquisition decisions. Usually, management will buy a plant asset if the present value of the expected net cash inflows exceeds the cost (net present value method), or if the internal rate (yield) is satisfactory. The internal rate is the rate that equates the cost of the assets with the present value of the annuity of net cash inflows attributable to the asset. The internal

rate method commonly is less favored than the net present value method.

The above argument is decisive for upholding the conclusion drawn from the capital maintenance concept. According to the AAA "the use by investors of published financial statements . . . should be considered of primary importance."[43] The opportunity to appraise management's ability to realize expectations is crucial for an investor's decision to hold, buy, or sell. However, perusal of a corporation's president's report with its forecasts and declarations of intentions—if those are furnished as they should be—is useless to the investor if he is not given financial statements that incorporate the thought processes underlying managerial decisions and thereby offer the opportunity to compare past expectations with present realizations. Generally speaking, financial reports contain the results of managerial decisions, should reflect the format of the decision-making process, and [should] be consistent with its models. Compliance therewith is said to be in the interest of the company itself, because otherwise managers may be tempted to make dysfunctional decisions.[44]

Exceptions to Capital Maintenance Method

The capital maintenance concept with its present-value-of-the-annual-cash-flows method has been found here as superior with respect to the other con-

---

[42] Trumbull, op. cit., p. 462, n. 4.

[43] AAA, 1957 Revision. . . . op. cit., p. 7.

[44] Michael Schiff, "Effect of Variations in Accounting Methods on Capital Budgeting," *NAA Bulletin*, Vol. 46 (July 1965), p. 58; AAA, "Report of the Committee on Managerial Decision Models," loc. cit., p. 58.

cepts. However, it is not a panacea either but subject to exceptions. These concern mainly three situations: the existence of industry-wide depreciation practices; a firm's lack of sophisticated accounting staff; and the multitude and variety of fixed assets in a company.

While the capital maintenance method draws support from offering investors an opportunity to judge corporate managerial efficiency, it contributes little to financial analysis through intercompany comparisons. Although such comparisons usually are difficult where depreciation is a material item, industry-wide depreciation practices may help, if the respective plants' ages and historical costs are similar. In that case sound uniform practices may prevail over the capital maintenance method.

That may be especially true for smaller companies having limited fixed asset investments. Besides, those companies will look to trade practices in depreciation for other reasons. They often will lack an accounting staff sophisticated enough to handle the maintenance of capital method. In the absence of trade practices, they will use then the conventional method best suited for them.

Even in large, well-staffed companies the capital maintenance method—though otherwise applicable—may not always be practical. If the fixed assets are numerous, they often are depreciated jointly by group depreciation for similar items and composite depreciation for dissimilar ones; both commonly use a constant annual rate. Whether such depreciations are theoretically justifiable (e.g., with the previously mentioned reasoning that the earnings power of assets is collective), does not merit a discussion here. More than one firm using group or composite depreciation has experienced an unrealistic balance in its accumulated depreciation account. Any underlying theory, therefore, will not be persuasive, and the case for joint depreciations rests on expediency.

Summary

In this paper five concepts of depreciation were set forth:

1. Recognition of the physical or functional deterioration of a fixed asset (causal concept).

2. Provisions for replacement of depreciable assets (replacement concept).

3. A means of income determination, at present usually through measuring operational plant input by amortization of the prepayment representing plant cost (input concept).

4. A measure of asset valuation, essentially by specifying the expiration of service potentials (valuation concept).

5. A measure of the maintenance of capital, mainly in case of profitable operations and price-level stability (maintenance of capital concept).

In spite of some interdependence, the concepts do not have equal import. The causal concept does not typify accounting practice. The replacement concept has long been considered irrelevant for external reports. The input concept is presently dominant; however, it gives little guidance to the practice of depreciation accounting. The valuation concept provides more guidance. Nevertheless the concept fails because its logical extension, the balance-of-present-value method, often yields unreasonable results. The capital maintenance concept is not quite realistic, considering the present state of accountancy. However, it provides better guidance than the valuation and input concepts; as a rule, the present value of an asset's service in a future year will be that year's depreciation expense. Acceptance of price-level adjustments will strengthen this concept.

The five concepts were discussed mainly as to their plausibility and fruitfulness. The different meanings of their components such as asset, income, and capital were mentioned but not evaluated themselves. It behooves us therefore to trace the relevant depreciation concepts directly to basic accounting theory as anchorage.

The valuation concept represents the proprietary theory. That theory focuses accounting on the changes in the business wealth of the owners of a firm, is balance sheet oriented, and prevailed during the last century. The input concept represents the entity theory. This theory dominates today, stresses the business entity instead of its owners as accounting matter, and is income statement oriented. The average corporation has investors whose main interest is the earnings-per-share figure, and it is run by managers whose efficiency usually is judged by the periodic income produced. The yearly amortization of a low historical cost of fixed assets serves those managers well. The maintenance of capital concept can be aligned with the relatively recent enterprise theory. This theory sees in the large corporation an institution that is financially self-supporting, has diversified activities, and allows its stockholders in effect only the right to conventional dividends.[45] Concern about these enterprises exceeds that about their stockholders[46] and relates strongly to the maintenance of real capital. Such maintenance does not only mean security for investors, employees, and customers but also contributes stability to society as a whole.

[45] Waino W. Suojanen, "Enterprise Theory and Corporate Balance Sheets." *Accounting Review*, Vol. 33 (January 1958), pp. 56–65.

[46] Bevis, op. cit., p. 9.

Cases

• Case 7-1

The City of Martinsville donated land to Essex Company. The fair value of the land was $100,000. The land had cost the city $45,000.

Required:

a. Describe the current accounting treatment for the land. Include in your answer the amount at which the land would be valued by Essex Company and any other income statement or balance sheet effect.

b. Under the recommendations outlined in *SFAS No. 116* the FASB required that donated assets be recorded at fair value and that revenue be recognized equivalent to the amount recorded for a donation.
   i. Defend the FASB's position. In your answer refer to the Conceptual Framework.
   ii. Criticize the FASB's position. In your answer refer to the Conceptual Framework.

c. Assume that immediately before the donation, Essex had assets totaling $800,000 and liabilities totaling $350,000. Compare the financial statement effects of the FASB requirement with previous practice. For example, how would EPS be affected or ratios such as debt-to-equity?

• Case 7-2

On October 10, 1994, Mason Engineering Company completed negotiations on a contract for the purchase of new equipment. Under the terms of the agreement the equipment may be purchased now or Mason may wait until January 10, 1995, to make the purchase. The cost of the equipment is $400,000. It will be financed by a note bearing interest at the market rate of interest. Straight-line depreciation over a 10-year life will be used for book purposes. Double declining balance over seven years will be used for tax purposes (½ year's depreciation will be taken in the year of purchase regardless of the date of purchase).

Required:
a. Discuss the financial statement impacts of postponing the purchase of the equipment. Would the market price of the firm's common stock be affected by any or all of these impacts? Do not assume in your discussion that the postponement will have impact on revenues or any operating costs, other than depreciation.
b. Discuss any cash flow impacts related to postponing the purchase of the equipment.
c. Efficient markets assume that stockholder wealth is affected by the amount and timing of cash flows. Which alternative is more favorable to them: purchasing before year-end, or waiting until January? Explain your answer.

• Case 7-3

During 1994 (its first year of operations) the Jerry Oil and Gas Rigging Company drilled 10 oil wells. One is producing. It cost $700,000 to drill. Seven are dry holes, costing $500,000 each. Jerry is still drilling the other well. So far, Jerry has sunk $220,000 into this well.

The producing well is expected to provide 5 million barrels of oil.

Required:
a. Assume production and sale of 2,000 barrels in 1994. What will be the cost of sales under the successful efforts method and the full cost method? What other expense(s), if any, related to drilling will be recognized under each case?
b. Which alternative will allow Jerry to present more favorable-looking financial statements? Explain.
c. Which method is more representationally faithful? Explain.
d. Discuss whether drilling the dry holes qualifies as an asset under the Conceptual Framework's definition of assets. Give pros and cons.

● Case 7-4

Depreciation continues to be one of the most controversial, difficult, and important problem areas in accounting.

Required:
a. Explain the conventional accounting concept of depreciation accounting.
b. Discuss its conceptual merit with respect to
   i. The value of the asset.
   ii. The charge(s) to expense.
   iii. The discretion of management in selecting the method.
c. Explain the factors that should be considered when applying the conventional concept of depreciation to the determination of how the value of a newly acquired computer system should be assigned to expense for financial reporting purposes (income tax considerations should be ignored).
d. What depreciation methods might be used for the computer system? Describe the advantages and disadvantages of each.

● Case 7-5

Jay Manufacturing, Inc. began operations five years ago producing probos, a new type of instrument it hoped to sell to doctors, dentists, and hospitals. The demand for probos far exceeded initial expectations, and the company was unable to produce enough probos to meet demand.

The company was manufacturing probos on equipment it built at the start of its operations, but to meet demand more efficient equipment was needed. Company management decided to design and build the equipment since equipment that was currently available on the market was unsuitable for producing probos.

In 1995 a section of the plant was devoted to development of the new equipment and a special staff of personnel was hired. Within six months a machine was developed at a cost of $170,000 that successfully increased production and reduced labor cost substantially. Sparked by the success of the new machine, the company built three more machines of the same type at a cost of $80,000 each.

Required:
a. In addition to satisfying a need that outsiders cannot meet within the desired time, what other reasons might cause a firm to construct fixed assets for its own use?
b. In general, what costs should be capitalized for a self-constructed asset?
c. Discuss the proprietary (give pros and cons) of including in the capitalized cost of self-constructed assets:
   i. The increase in overhead caused by the self-construction of fixed assets.
   ii. A proportionate share of overhead on the same basis as that applied to goods manufactured for sale. Take into consideration whether the company is at full capacity or not.
d. Discuss the proper accounting treatment of the $90,000 ($170,000 −

$80,000) by which the cost of the first machine exceeded the cost of the subsequent machines.

● **Case 7-6**

Your client found three suitable sites, each having certain unique advantages, for a new plant facility. In order to investigate thoroughly the advantages and disadvantages of each site, one-year options were purchased for an amount equal to 5 percent of the contract price of each site. The costs of the options cannot be applied against the contracts. Before the options expire, one of the sites was purchased at the contract price of $60,000. The option on this site had cost $3,000. The two options not exercised had cost $3,500 each.

Required:
Present arguments in support of recording the cost of the land at each of the following amounts:
a. $60,000
b. $63,000
c. $70,000

● **Case 7-7**

Property, plant, and equipment (plant assets) generally represent a material portion of the total assets of most companies. Accounting for the acquisition and usage of such assets is, therefore, an important part of the financial reporting process.

Required:
a. Distinguish between revenue and capital expenditures and explain why this distinction is important.
b. Briefly define depreciation as used in accounting.
c. Identify the factors that are relevant in determining the annual depreciation and explain whether these factors are determined objectively or whether they are based on judgment.
d. Explain why depreciation is shown as an adjustment to cash in the operations section on the statement of cash flows.

● **Case 7-8**

A company may acquire plant assets (among other ways) for cash, on a deferred payment plan, by exchanging other assets, or by a combination of these ways.

Required:
a. Identify six costs that should be capitalized as the cost of the land. For your answer, assume that land with an existing building is acquired for cash and that the existing building is to be removed in the immediate future so that a new building can be constructed on the site.

b. At what amount should a company record a plant asset acquired on a deferred payment plan?

c. In general, at what amount should plant assets received in exchange for other nonmonetary assets be recorded? Specifically, at what amount should a company record a new machine acquired by exchanging an older similar machine and paying cash? Would your answer be the same if cash were received?

● **Case 7-9**

George Company purchased land for use as its corporate headquarters. A small factory that was on the land when it was purchased was torn down before construction of the office building began. Furthermore, a substantial amount of rock blasting and removal had to be done to the site before construction of the building foundation began. Because the office building was set back on the land far from the public road, George Company had the contractor construct a paved road that led from the public road to the parking lot of the office building.

Three years after the office building was occupied, George Company added four stories to the office building. The four stories had an estimated useful life of five years more than the remaining estimated life of the original building.

Ten years later the land and buildings were sold at an amount more than their net book value and George Company had a new office building constructed in another state for use as its new corporate headquarters.

Required:
a. Which of the preceding expenditures should be capitalized? How should each be depreciated or amortized? Discuss the rationale for your answers.
b. How would the sale of the land and building be accounted for? Include in your answer how to determine the net book value at the date of sale. Discuss the rationale for your answer.

● **Case 7-10**

Among the principal topics related to the accounting for the property, plant, and equipment of a company are acquisitions and retirements.

Required:
a. What expenditures should be capitalized when equipment is acquired for cash?
b. Assume the market value of equipment is not determinable by reference to a similar purchase for cash. Describe how the acquiring company should determine the capitalized cost of equipment purchased by exchanging it for each of the following:
  i. Bonds having an established market price.
  ii. Common stock not having an established market price.
  iii. Similar equipment not having a determinable market price.

c. Describe the factors that determine whether expenditures relating to property, plant, and equipment already in use should be capitalized.
d. Describe how to account for the gain or loss on the sale of property, plant, or equipment.

● Case 7-11

A certified public accountant is frequently called on by management for advice regarding methods of computing depreciation. Although the question arises less frequently, of comparable importance is whether the depreciation method should be based on the consideration of assets as units, or as a group, or as having a composite life.

Required:
a. Briefly describe the depreciation methods based on treating assets as
   i. Units.
   ii. A group or having a composite life.
b. Present arguments for and against the use of each of the two methods.
c. Describe how retirements are recorded under each of the two methods. Give the rationale for each case.

Recommended Additional Readings

Barefield, Russel M., and Eugene Comiskey. "Depreciation Policy and the Behavior of Corporate Profits." *Journal of Accounting Research* (Autumn 1971), pp. 351–58.

Bennett, Anthony H. "Depreciation and Business Decision Making." *Accounting and Business Research* (Winter 1972), pp. 3–28.

Burt, Oscar R. "Unified Theory of Depreciation." *Journal of Accounting Research* (Spring 1970), pp. 28–57.

Grinyer, J. R. "A New Approach to Depreciation." *Abacus* (March 1987), pp. 43–54.

Johnson, Orace. "Two General Concepts of Depreciation." *Journal of Accounting Research* (Spring 1968), pp. 29–37.

Kim, M., and G. Moore. "Economic Vs. Accounting Depreciation." *Journal of Accounting and Economics* (April 1988), pp. 111–126.

Lowe, Howard. "The Essential of a General Theory of Depreciation." *The Accounting Review* (April 1963), pp. 293–301.

McKeown, James C. "Comparative Application of Market and Cost Based Accounting Models." *Journal of Accounting Research* (Spring 1973), pp. 65–78.

Snavely, Howard J. "Current Cost for Long-Lived Assets: A Critical View." *The Accounting Review* (April 1969), pp. 344–353.

Wright, F. K. "Toward A General Theory of Depreciation." *Journal of Accounting Research* (Spring 1964), pp. 80–90.

Bibliography

Alciatore, Mimi L. "The Reliability and Relevance of Reserve Value Accounting Data: A Review of the Empirical Research." *Journal of Accounting Literature* (1990), pp. 1–38.

Anthony, Rober N. *Accounting for the Cost of Interest.* Lexington, Mass.: Lexington Books, 1975.

Arcady, Alex T., and Charles E. Baker. "Capitalization of Interest Cost—Implementing FASB Statement No. 34." *The Ohio CPA* (Autumn 1980), pp. 137–141.

Arnett, Harold E. "APB Opinion No. 29: Accounting for Nonmonetary Transactions—Some New Perspectives." *Management Accounting* (October 1978), pp. 41–48.

Barnea, Amir. "Note on the Cash-flow Approach to Valuation and Depreciation of Productive Assets." *Journal of Financial and Quantitative Analysis* (June 1972), pp. 1841–1846.

Baxter, W. T. "Depreciating Assets: The Forward Looking Approach to Value." *Abacus* (December 1970), pp. 120–131.

Beidelman, Carl R. "Valuation of Used Capital Assets." *Studies in Accounting Research No. 7.* American Accounting Association, 1973.

Bierman, Harold, Jr., and Thomas R. Dyckman, "Accounting for Interest During Construction." *Accounting and Business Research* (Autumn 1979), pp. 267–272.

Cappettini, Robert, and Thomas E. King. "Exchanges of Nonmonetary Assets: Some Changes." *The Accounting Review* (January 1976), pp. 142–147.

Castellano, Joseph F., Clarence E. Campbell, and Harper A. Roehm. "An Application of APB Opinion 29." *The Ohio CPA* (Winter 1976), pp. 17–19.

Chambers, Raymond J. "Asset Measurement and Valuation." *Cost and Management* (March–April 1971), pp. 30–35.

Cotteleer, Thomas F. "Depreciation, an Accounting Enigma." *Management Accounting* (February 1971), pp. 23–24, 27.

Coughlan, Joseph D., and William K. Strand. *Depreciation: Accounting, Taxes, and Business Decisions.* New York: Ronald Press, 1969.

Dixon, Robert L. "Decreasing Charge Depreciation—A Search for Logic." *The Accounting Review* (October 1960), pp. 590–597.

Flory, Steven M., and Steven D. Grossman. "New Oil and Gas Accounting." *The CPA Journal* (May 1978), pp. 39–43.

Goldberg, L. "Concepts of Depreciation." In *Studies in Accounting Theory,* W. T. Baxter and Sidney Davidson, eds. Homewood, Ill.: Richard D. Irwin, Inc., 1962, pp. 236–258.

Gray, O. Ronald. "Implementation of FASB Statement No. 34: Capitalization of Interest Cost." *The National Public Accountant* (April 1980), pp. 23–25.

Greipel, Rudolph C. "Accounting for Nonmonetary Transactions—A Review of APB Opinion No. 29." *The CPA Journal* (January 1974), pp. 34–39.

Grossman, Steven D., Alan G. Mayper, and Robert B. Welker. "Oil and Gas Disclosures—The FASB Reacts." *The CPA Journal* (May 1983), pp. 24–29.

Harris, Trevor S., and James A. Ohlson. "Accounting Disclosures and the Market's Valuation of Oil and Gas Properties: Evaluation of Market Efficiency and Functional Fixation." *The Accounting Review* (October 1990), pp. 764–780.

Imhoff, Eugene A., and Paul A. Janell. "Opinion No. 29: A New Valuation Method." *Management Accounting* (March 1979), pp. 50–53.

Lambert, S. J., and Joyce C. Lambert. "Concepts and Applications in APB Opinion No. 29." *Journal of Accountancy* (March 1977), pp. 60–68.

Lamden, Charles W., Dale L. Gerboth, and Thomas W. McRae. *Accounting for Depreciable Assets.* New York: American Institute of Certified Public Accountants, 1975.

Lev, Baruch, and Henri Theil. "A Maximum Entropy Approach to the Choice of Asset Depreciation." *Journal of Accounting Research* (Autumn 1978), pp. 286–293.

McIntyre, Edward V. "Present Value Depreciation and the Disaggregation Problem." *The Accounting Review* (January 1977), pp. 261–271.

Most, Kenneth S. "Depreciation in Economic and Accounting Theories." *Accountant* (February 25, 1971), pp. 237–240.

Mullen, Louis E. "Spotlight on Estimated Economic Life of Depreciable Assets." *The CPA Journal* (August 1973), pp. 662–666.

NAA Management Accounting Practices Committee. "Fixed Asset Accounting: The Allocation of Costs." *Management Accounting* (January 1974), pp. 43–49.

NAA Management Accounting Practices Committee. "Fixed Asset Accounting: The Capitalization of Costs." *The CPA Journal* (March 1973), pp. 193–207.

Nikolai, Loren A. "Simplifying Nonmonetary Exchanges." *The CPA Journal* (January 1977), pp. 69–71.

Paton, William A. "Depreciation—Concept and Measurement." *Journal of Accountancy* (October 1959), pp. 38–43.

Peasnell, K. V. "The CCA Depreciation Problem—An Analysis and Proposal." *Abacus* (December 1977), pp. 123–140.

Pidock, Wayne L. "Accounting for Net Salvage." *Management Accounting* (December 1970), pp. 49–52.

Thomas, Arthur L. *Studies in Accounting Research No. 9,* "The Allocation Problem: Part Two." Sarasota, Fla.: American Accounting Association, 1974.

Warrell, C. J. "The Enterprise Value Concept of Asset Valuation." *Accounting and Business Research* (Summer 1974), pp. 220–226.

Young, T. N., and C. G. Peirson. "Depreciation—Future Services Basis." *The Accounting Review* (April 1967), pp. 338–341.

Long-Term
Assets II:
Investments
and Intangibles

Investments in the securities of other corporations are made for a variety of reasons such as obtaining additional income, creating desirable relationships with suppliers, obtaining partial or full control over related companies, or adding new products. The decision to classify these investments as long-term rather than as current assets is based on the concept of *managerial intent*. When management intends to use the securities for long-term purposes, they are separately classified on the balance sheet as long-term investments rather than as temporary investments.

As discussed in Chapter 5, the balance sheet category, investments, includes investments in equity and debt securities of other enterprises, assets not currently in use, and special funds. This chapter discusses investments in equity and debt securities. Detailed discussion of equity investments will be limited to those that do not result in consolidated financial statements. In addition, the topic of intangible assets will also be addressed.

Investments in Equity Securities

The term *equity securities* is defined in *Statement of Financial Accounting Standards* (*SFAS*) *No. 115* as:

> *Any security representing an ownership interest in an enterprise (for example, common, preferred, or other capital stock) or the right to acquire (for example, warrants, rights, and call options) or dispose of (for example, put options) an ownership interest in an enterprise at fixed or determinable prices.*[1]

---

[1] Financial Accounting Standards Board, *Statement of Financial Accounting Standards No. 115,* "Accounting for Certain Investments in Debt and Equity Securities" (Stamford, Conn.: FASB, 1993), par. 137.

Equity securities do not include redeemable preferred stock or convertible bonds.

Equity securities may be acquired on an organized stock exchange, over the counter, or by direct sale. In addition, warrants, rights, and options may be attached to other securities (bonds or preferred stock), or they may be received from the issuer, cost free, to enable the enterprise to maintain its present proportionate share of ownership.[2] The recorded cost of investments in equity securities includes the purchase price of the securities plus any brokerage fees, transfer costs, or taxes on transfer. When equity securities are obtained in a nonmonetary transaction, the recorded cost is based on fair market value of the consideration given, or, if fair market value is unavailable, the fair market value of the marketable equity security received.

Subsequent to acquisition, there are five methods of accounting and financial statement presentation that are utilized under current GAAP for the various types of equity securities: (1) consolidation, (2) the equity method, (3) the cost method, (4) the fair value method, and (5) the market value method. These methods are not alternatives for recording investments in equity securities. They are applied on the basis of the investee's percentage of ownership or surrounding circumstances. Each method and the circumstances under which it is applicable are described in the following paragraphs. In addition, the theoretical merits of another method that has been advocated, lower of cost or market, will also be discussed.

Consolidation

Consolidated financial statements are required when an investor owns enough common stock to obtain control over the investee. *Control* is defined in *SFAS No. 94* as ownership of a majority voting interest (over 50 percent) unless the parent company is precluded from exercising control or unless control is temporary.[3] *Consolidation* requires that at the balance sheet date the investment account (accounted for during the year under the equity method described below) be replaced by the assets and liabilities of the investee company. In the consolidation process the investee assets and liabilities are consolidated with (added to) those of the controlling parent company. Consolidated financial statements are discussed in detail in Chapter 13.

Equity Method

Under the *equity method*, adjustments are made to the recorded cost of the investment to account for profits and losses of the investee. These adjustments are based on the investor's percentage of ownership of the investee. For exam-

---

[2] Allowing investors to maintain their proportionate share of ownership is one of the basic rights of common stock ownership. This right is referred to as the preemptive right.

[3] Financial Accounting Standards Board, *Statement of Financial Accounting Standards No. 94,* "Consolidation of all Majority-Owned Subsidiaries" (Stamford, Conn.: FASB, 1988), par. 13.

ple, if the investee reports a profit, the investor will report as income its pro-rata ownership share of the investee profit and increase the carrying value of the investment account by the same amount. On the other hand, dividends received are recorded as a decrease in the carrying value of the investment account for the amount of the dividend received. Dividends are not recorded as income since the income of the investee is recorded by the investor as it is earned by the investee. In other words, under the equity method, dividends are viewed as distributions of accumulated earnings. Because the accumulation of earnings increases the investment account, the distribution of earnings decreases the investment account. Consequently, the investment account represents the investee's equity in the investment.

In *Accounting Research Bulletin No. 51*, the Committee on Accounting Procedure described the equity method[4] and stated that it is the preferred method of accounting for unconsolidated subsidiaries.[5] In 1971, the Accounting Principles Board (APB) reported its conclusions on a study of the accounting for long-term investments in stocks by issuing *APB Opinion No. 18*, "The Equity Method of Accounting for Investments in Common Stock."[6] *APB Opinion No. 18* clarified the applicability of the equity method to investments of common stock in subsidiaries; however, it was noted that the equity method was not a valid substitute for consolidation.[7]

The Board went on to say that the equity method is most appropriate when an investor has the ability to significantly influence financing and operating decisions even though it holds less than 50 percent of the voting stock. Ability to exercise significant influence can be determined in a number of ways, including

1. Representation on the board of directors.
2. Participation in policy-making processes.
3. Material intercompany transactions.
4. Interchange of managerial personnel.
5. Technological dependency.
6. The percent of ownership the investor has in relation to other holdings.[8]

Nevertheless, the Board noted that determining the ability to influence is not always clear and "in order to achieve a reasonable degree of uniformity in application"[9] an investment of 20 percent or more of the voting stock of

---

[4] *ARB No. 51* did not refer to the equity method by name.

[5] Committee on Accounting Procedure, *Accounting Research Bulletin No. 51*, "Consolidated Financial Statements" (New York: AICPA, 1959), par. 19. The APB reiterated this position in *APB Opinion No. 10*, "Omnibus Opinion of 1966" (par. 3), and referred to the procedure described in *ARB No. 51* as the equity method.

[6] Accounting Principles Board, *Opinion No. 18*, "The Equity Method of Accounting for Investments in Common Stock" (New York: AICPA, 1971).

[7] Ibid., par. 14.

[8] Ibid., par. 17.

[9] Ibid.

the investee is deemed to constitute evidence of a presumption of the ability to exercise significant influence. Conversely, ownership of less than 20 percent of the voting stock leads to the presumption that the investor does not have significant influence unless an ability to exercise significant influence can be demonstrated.[10] Consequently, it was concluded that significant influence is normally attained when an investor holds 20 percent or more of the voting stock of an investee unless the surrounding circumstances indicate a lack of ability to influence.

Circumstances arise when an investor holds 20 percent or more of the outstanding common stock of an investee but does not have the ability to exercise significant influence. FASB *Interpretation No. 35* suggests that the following facts and circumstances might preclude an investor from using the equity method even if an investment of 20 percent or more is held:

1. *Opposition by the investee, such as litigation or complaints to governmental regulatory authorities, challenges the investor's ability to exercise significant influence.*

2. *The investor and investee sign an agreement under which the investor surrenders significant rights as a shareholder.*

3. *Majority ownership of the investee is concentrated among a small group of shareholders who operate the investee without regard to the views of the investor.*

4. *The investor needs or wants more financial information to apply the equity method than is available to the investee's other shareholders (e.g., the investor wants quarterly financial information from an investee that publicly reports only annually), tries to obtain that information, and fails.*

5. *The investor tries and fails to obtain representation on the investee's board of directors.*[11]

The APB's decision to embrace the equity method was based on the objectives of accrual accounting; that is, the reporting of transactions when they occur rather than as cash is collected. When the investor can exercise significant influence over the investee, the results of operating decisions better reflect the periodic outcomes resulting from making the investment, rather than distributions of the investor's share of accumulated profits, which in and of themselves may be unrelated to performance. The Board apparently believed that the cash flow needs of investors can be satisfied by the significant influence test and that reporting needs are of primary importance.

The Cost Method

When there is a lack of significant influence or control, investments in common stocks are accounted for under either the cost method or the market

---

[10] Ibid.

[11] Financial Accounting Standards Board, *Interpretation No. 35*, "Criteria for Applying the Equity Method of Accounting for Investments in Common Stock" (Stamford, Conn.: FASB, 1981), par. 4.

value method. These methods also apply to all other equity securities. When there is no readily determinable market price for equity securities, the cost method must be used. Use of a fair value approach is currently required under *SFAS No. 115* for all equity securities for which fair value is readily determinable and for which neither consolidation nor the equity method is required.

Under the cost method an investment in equity securities is carried at its historical cost. Revenue is recorded and reported as dividends are received.

The cost method may be criticized because it does not measure current fair value. Historical cost provides information relevant for determining recovery when the securities are acquired. Current fair market value would provide a similar measure for the current accounting period. If the purpose of financial statements is to provide investors, creditors, and other users with information useful in assessing future cash flows, the current assessment of recoverable amounts, current market values, would be relevant. Even for those equity securities that are not actively traded, an estimate of current fair value may be more relevant than cost.

Despite some speculation at the time *APB Opinion No. 18* was issued that fair market value might be embraced by the APB, *APB Opinion No. 18* did little to add to its acceptability. The use of fair value is a departure from the historical cost principle. The APB apparently was not prepared to take the radical step of endorsing a departure from historical cost despite the fact that the information needed to determine the fair values for most investments is readily available. However, the FASB reversed this position in *SFAS No. 115*. Fair value accounting is now required in several circumstances, as discussed later in the chapter.

The Lower of Cost or Market Method

As discussed earlier in Chapter 6, in 1975 the FASB issued *SFAS No. 12*. This release required that equity securities having readily determinable market values that were not accounted for under the equity method or consolidation be accounted for by applying lower of cost or market (LCM). Under the LCM method as prescribed by *SFAS No. 12*, marketable equity securities were separated into current and long-term portfolios. Each portfolio was carried on the balance sheet at the lower of that portfolio's aggregate cost or market value. This process was accomplished by the use of a valuation allowance for each portfolio, which measured the amount by which the aggregate cost of the investment portfolio exceeded aggregate market value at the balance sheet date. For temporary investments in marketable equity securities, the unrealized losses and subsequent recoveries were recognized in the income statement. In contrast, for long-term investments in marketable equity securities, the cumulative effect of unrealized losses and recoveries was reported as negative stockholders' equity.

The FASB's advocacy of the LCM method in *SFAS No. 12* was not a strict departure from historical cost. Rather, it was simply further evidence of the overriding concern for conservatism discussed earlier in Chapter 3. LCM for marketable securities can be defended on the grounds that the recording of cost implies recovery of that cost. It is reasonable to assume that management would not invest in assets that are not recoverable. By the same token, when recovery has declined temporarily through decline in market value, it is reasonable to reduce the book value of assets to the lower market value.

The LCM method was criticized because it did not result in consistent treatment of all marketable equity securities. Gains were treated differently from losses, and temporary investments were treated differently from long-term investments without a rational explanation. Furthermore, it is inconsistent to recognize market value increases up to cost, but not to market. Opponents of *SFAS No. 12* argued that the consequent recognition of unrealized gains is so arbitrary that no recognition of these gains would be preferable.

Finally, the determination of LCM on an aggregate basis may be deceptive. Unrealized losses are offset against unrealized gains. In a subsequent period when a security is sold, prior cumulative unrecognized gains and losses will be recognized causing a mismatching of gain and loss recognition within the period in which it occurred.

The Fair Value Method

SFAS No. 115, "Accounting for Certain Investments in Debt and Equity Securities,"[12] describes the current GAAP for equity securities that have readily determinable fair values and that are not subject to the equity method under *APB Opinion No. 18* or to consolidation. According to *SFAS No. 115*, the fair value of an equity security is readily determinable if:

1. *The sales prices or bid-and-ask quotations are currently available on a securities exchange registered with the Securities and Exchange Commission (SEC) or in the over-the-counter market when they are publicly reported by the National Association of Securities Dealers Automated Quotations systems or by the National Quotation Bureau.*

2. *The security is traded only in foreign markets and if the foreign market is of a breadth and scope comparable to one of the U. S. markets referred to above.*

3. *The investment is in a mutual fund that has a fair value per share (unit) that is published and is the basis for current transactions.*[13]

Under the fair value method, at acquisition, equity securities are to be classified as either **trading** or **available-for-sale**. As discussed earlier in Chapter 6, *trading securities* are defined as "securities that are bought and held principally for the purpose of selling them in the near term (thus held for only a short period of time."[14] Trading securities are actively and frequently bought and sold, generally with the objective of generating profits from short-term price movements. *Available-for-sale securities* are those equity securities having

---

[12] Financial Accounting Standards Board, *Statement of Financial Accounting Standards No. 115,* "Accounting for Certain Investments in Debt and Equity Securities" (Stamford, Conn.: FASB, 1993).

[13] Ibid., par. 3.

[14] Ibid., par. 12.

readily determinable market prices that are not considered trading securities.[15] All trading securities are to be classified as current assets. Available-for-sale securities are to be classified as current or long-term depending on whether they meet the *ARB No. 43* definition of current assets, described in Chapters 5 and 6. Accordingly, these securities will be classified as current if they are reasonably expected to be realized in cash or sold or consumed during the normal operating cycle of the business or one year, whichever is longer. All other available-for-sale securities will be classified as long-term investments.

At each balance sheet date, long-term equity securities subject to the *SFAS No. 115* provisions are to be reported at fair value. Unrealized holding gains and losses for available-for-sale securities (current and long-term) will be excluded from earnings. The cumulative unrealized holding gains and losses for these securities will be reported as a net amount as a separate component of stockholders' equity. Dividend income for available-for-sale securities will continue to be included in earnings.

When an equity security is transferred from the trading category to the available-for-sale category or vice versa, the transfer is to be accounted for at fair value at the date of transfer. The treatment of unrealized holding gains shall be as follows:

1. *For a transfer from the trading category to the available-for-sale category, the unrealized holding gain or loss is recognized in income up to the date of transfer. It is not reversed.*

2. *For a transfer from the available-for-sale category to the trading category, the unrecognized holding gain or loss at the date of transfer is recognized immediately in earnings.*[16]

The FASB's primary impetus for requiring fair value accounting for investments in equity securities is relevance. The advocates of fair value accounting for investments in securities believe that fair value is useful in assisting investors, creditors, and other users in evaluating the performance of enterprise investing strategies. According to *SFAC No. 1* users of financial information are interested in assessing the amount, timing, and risk associated with expected net cash inflows to the enterprise. These assessments aid in evaluating the potential outcome of their own personal investing strategies because the expected cash flows to the enterprise are the main source of expected cash flows from the enterprise to them. Fair value is market determined. It reflects the market consensus regarding the expected resource flows of a security discounted by the current interest rate adjusted for the risk associated with that security.

In addition, the fair value method partially eliminates the uneven-handed treatment that *SFAS No. 12* afforded to gains and losses. All unrealized gains and unrealized losses will be treated the same for asset valuation purposes. For trading securities, the gains and losses will be recognized in those periods

---

[15] Ibid.

[16] Ibid., par. 15.

in which they occur; thus, for these assets the method is consistent with other accrual accounting requirements. It is also consistent with the *SFAC No. 6* definition of comprehensive income, because comprehensive income is based on changes in net assets and would include changes in the market values of assets. For trading securities, there will be no further masking of gains against losses that occurred under the aggregate valuation approach of *SFAS No. 12.*

However, inconsistent income statement treatment for equity securities will continue. Unrealized gains and losses for available-for-sale securities will not be recognized until they are reclassified as trading securities and sold. Thus, for these securities there will be no accrual accounting based matching of market gains and losses in the period in which they are incurred. The result will be a distortion of reported earnings.

Finally, the readily determinable criteria precludes fair value accounting for those securities that are not actively traded. Some advocates of fair value would argue that other estimates of fair value would be more meaningful than historical cost. Nevertheless, the FASB decided to limit the scope of fair value accounting for investments in securities to those which are readily determinable in the market. These measures are reliable and do not rely on imprecise measures that subjective judgments regarding market values would entail.

Market Value Method

Under the market value method, investment income is recorded for dividends received and unrealized gains and losses are recognized in earnings; none are carried directly to stockholders equity. All upward and downward changes in market value of the investment shares are recorded as income or losses. Changes in the market value of the investment require adjustment to the carrying value of the investment account. Thus, the market value method is analogous to the fair value method for trading securities described above. It has become accepted industry practice for certain industries, such as mutual funds, where it has attained the status of GAAP.

Exhibit 8.1 summarizes the approaches that are considered current GAAP for equity securities. Exhibit 8.2 summarizes the effects of various events on the investment account and the reported income of the investor under each of these methods. Consolidation is omitted from Exhibit 8.2 because it is a reporting method and not a method for recording transactions and events.

Investments in Debt Securities

Investments in debt securities, such as bonds or government securities, are initially recorded at cost and it is not unusual for the purchase price of a debt instrument to differ from its face value. This difference reflects the fluctuations in market interest rates that have occurred since the time the debt instrument was initially offered for sale to the present. Thus, debt instruments are often sold at a premium or discount. For a detailed discussion of how the amount of a bond premium or discount is determined and their effects on interest see Chapter 9.

EXHIBIT 8.1 *Accounting for Investments in Equity Securities*

	For Common Stock			
Percentage of ownership	0	20	50	100
Accounting method	Fair Value Method (if fair value is readily determinable)	Equity Method	Consolidation	
	Cost Method (if fair value is not readily determinable)			
	Market Value Method (for certain companies)			

The provisions of *SFAS No. 115* also apply to investments in debt securities, when the fair value of these securities is readily determinable. Prior to the issuance of *SFAS No. 115,* all debt securities that were classified as long-term were accounted for by amortizing the premium or discount over the term of the bond, regardless of the intent or ability of the investing entity to hold the investment to maturity or whether the investment had a readily determinable fair value. Regulators and others expressed concerns that the recognition and measurement of investments in debt securities, particularly those held by financial institutions, should better reflect the intent of the investor to hold, make available to sell, or trade these securities. Moreover, the provisions of *SFAS No. 12* did not apply to investments in debt securities. Some enterprises applied LCM to these securities; others accounted for them under the cost method. The result was that the accounting treatment for these securities was inconsistent from one entity to the next; therefore, it was difficult to compare the performance of these investments across companies.

SFAS No. 115 requires that at acquisition individual investments in debt securities be classified as trading, available-for-sale, or held-to-maturity. Those debt securities that are classified as trading or available-for-sale are to be treated in the same manner as equity securities that are similarly classified. That is, the fair value method described above will apply to these securities. Thus, the discussion that follows will be limited to those debt securities that are classified as held-to-maturity.

Debt instruments are to be classified as *held-to-maturity* "only if the reporting enterprise has the positive intent and ability to hold those securities to maturity."[17] A debt security may continue to be classified as held-to-

---

[17] Ibid., par. 7.

EXHIBIT 8.2 *Effects of the Cost, Fair Value, Equity, and Market Value Methods on Investment and Income*

Event	Cost	Fair Value		Equity	Market Value
		Trading Securities	Available-for-Sale Securities		
Acquire 25% of common stock of S Company for $100,000	Investment increased $100,000	Investment increased $100,000	Investment increased $100,000	Investment increased $100,000	Investment increased $100,000
Investee reports net income of $10,000	No effect on investment or income	No effect on investment or income	No effect on investment or income	Investment increased $2,500; income increased $2,500	No effect on investment or income
Investee pays dividends of $5,000 (25% investor)	No effect on investment; income increased $1,250	No effect on investment; income increased $1,250	No effect on investment; income increased $1,250	Investment decreased $1,250; no effect on income	No effect on investment; income increased $1,250
Investor's shares increased in value by 5% of original cost	No effect on investment or income	Investment increased $5,000; income increased $5,000	Investment increased $5,000; no effect on income	No effect on investment or income	Investment increased $5,000; income increased $5,000
Investor's shares decreased in value by 10% of original cost	No effect on investment or income	Investment decreased $10,000; income decreased $10,000	Investment decreased $10,000; no effect on income	No effect on investment or income	Investment decreased $10,000; income decreased $10,000

maturity even if sold or called prior to maturity if (a) the sale date (or call date if exercise of the call is probable) occurs so near to the maturity date that interest rate risk has no substantial effect on fair value or (b) the sale occurs after the enterprise has already collected a substantial portion (85 percent or more) of the principal outstanding at acquisition.[18]

Debt securities that are classified as held-to-maturity are to be measured at *amortized cost*. When these debt securities are sold at a premium or discount, the total interest income to the investing enterprise over the life of the debt instrument from acquisition to maturity is affected by the amount of the premium or discount. Measurement at amortized cost means that the premium or discount is amortized each period to calculate interest income. (Chapter 9 illustrates how a premium or discount affects interest over the life of a bond.) Amortization of the premium or discount is treated as an adjustment to interest income and to the investment account.

Two methods of debt premium or discount amortization are available: straight-line and effective interest. Under the *straight-line* method, the premium or discount is divided by the number of periods remaining in the life of the debt issue. In each subsequent period, an equal amount of premium or discount is written off as an interest income adjustment. The rationale underlying the use of the straight-line method is its ease of computation and the belief that premium or discount amortization are relatively minor changes. Therefore, the use of other methods would result in only minor differences.

When the effective interest method is used, the actual rate of return on the debt instrument must be computed at the time the investment is acquired. This interest rate is then applied to the carrying value of the investment in each interest period to determine the interest income. Using the effective interest method results in a uniform rate of return over the life of the investment. The use of this method is based on the belief that the investment was acquired at a certain yield and that the financial statements issued in subsequent periods should reflect the effects of that decision.

When it is evident that the investor has changed intent to hold a debt security to maturity, the security is transferred to either the trading or the available-for-sale category. The transfer is accounted for at fair value. If the security is transferred to the trading category, the unrealized gain or loss at the date of transfer is recognized in income. If the security is transferred to the available-for-sale category, the unrealized gain or loss at the date of transfer is recognized in a separate component of shareholders' equity. When a change from the available-for-sale category to the held-to-maturity category occurs, the amount of accumulated unrealized holding gains and losses that exists at the date of transfer will continue to be reported as a separate component of stockholders' equity, but will be amortized over the remaining life of the debt security as an adjustment to interest income. The effect of this treatment is that interest income each period will be what it would have been under the amortized cost method, but the carrying value of the debt security on the

---

[18] Ibid., par. 11.

balance sheet in subsequent periods will reflect the amortized market value at the date of transfer, rather than amortized cost.

A change in circumstances may result in the change of intent to hold a debt security to maturity, but may not call into question the classification of other debt as held-to-maturity if the change in circumstances is due to one or more of the following:

1. Evidence of significant deterioration in the issuer's credit worthiness.
2. A tax law change that eliminates or reduces the tax-exempt status of interest on the debt security.
3. A major business combination or disposition (such as sale of a segment of the business) that necessitates the sale or transfer of the debt security in order to maintain the enterprise's existing interest rate risk position or credit risk policy.
4. A change in statutory or regulatory requirements that significantly modifies either what constitutes a permissible investment or the maximum level of investment that the enterprise can hold in certain kinds of securities.
5. A change in regulatory requirements that significantly increases the enterprise's industry capital requirements that causes the enterprise to downsize.
6. A significant increase in the risk weights of debt securities used for regulatory risk-based capital purposes.

A debt security will not be classified as held-to-maturity if the enterprise intends to hold the security for an indefinite period. An indefinite holding period is presumed if for example, the debt security would be available to be sold in response to:

1. Changes in market interest rates and related changes in the security's prepayment risk.
2. Needs for liquidity. Examples indicating a need for liquidity include: for financial institutions, the withdrawal of deposits or the increased demand for loans and for insurance companies, the surrender of insurance policies, or the payment of insurance claims.
3. Changes in the availability and yield on alternative investments.
4. Changes in funding sources and terms.
5. Changes in foreign currency risk.[19]

SFAS No. 115 addresses issues concerning the relevance of fair value to investors, creditors, and other users. However, in allowing the continued use of amortized cost for debt securities that are intended to be held to maturity, it does not address concerns that the use of the amortized cost method permits the recognition of holding gains through the selective sale of appreciated debt instruments recorded at amortized cost at the date of sale. This affords management the opportunity to engage in gains trading and to selectively manage

[19] Ibid., par. 9.

reported earnings. Moreover, it does not address the criticism that accounting for debt securities is based on management's plan for holding or disposing of the investment, rather than on the characteristics of the asset itself. In allowing three distinct categories, the same company could give three different accounting treatments to three otherwise identical debt securities. Critics argue that these issues can be resolved only by reporting all debt and equity securities that have determinable fair values at fair value and by including all unrealized gains and losses in earnings as they occur.

The FASB countered that the procedures outlined in *SFAS No. 115* reflect the economic consequences of events and transactions. The reporting requirements better reflect the manner in which enterprises manage their investments and the impact of economic events on the overall enterprise. Moreover, the following disclosure requirements should provide fair value information that should prove useful to investor decision making in addition to the reporting requirements outlined above. For securities classified as available-for-sale and separately for securities classified as held-to-maturity, the enterprise is to report

1. Aggregate fair value.
2. Gross unrealized holding gains.
3. Gross unrealized holding losses.
4. The amortized cost basis by major security type.

Permanent Decline in Fair Value

When a decline in the fair value of a long-term investment that is classified as available-for-sale is determined to be other than temporary, an *other-than-temporary impairment* will be considered to have occurred. In this case the investment account balance for this security is written down to fair value, a loss is included in earnings, and a new cost basis is established. The new cost basis for recognition of gain or loss on reclassification or sale will not be adjusted for subsequent recoveries of the recognized loss. All subsequent increases in fair value will be recorded as adjustments to the separate component in stockholders' equity, in the same manner as subsequent unrealized losses.[20] Similar treatment will be given for other-than-permanent declines in investments in debt securities that are classified as held-to-maturity.

Impairment of Investments in Unsecuritized Debt

Investments in unsecuritized debt, principally accounts and notes receivable, are subject to the provisions of *SFAS No. 114*, "Accounting by Creditors for Impairment of Loans."[21] Recall from Chapter 6 that these loans are "impaired

---

[20] Ibid., par. 16.

[21] Financial Accounting Standards Board, *Statement of Financial Accounting Standards No. 114*, "Accounting by Creditors for Impairment of a Loan" (Stamford, Conn.: FASB, 1993).

when, based on current information and events, it is probable that a creditor will be unable to collect all amounts due according to the contractual terms of the loan agreement,"[22] including interest. To reiterate, in these cases, impairment is measured based on the present value of expected future cash flows discounted at the loan's effective interest rate as determined at the origin or acquisition of the loan. Alternatively, impairment may be measured using the market price for the loan or, if the loan is collateralized, the fair value of the collateral. If the resulting measurement of impairment is less than the carrying value of the loan (including interest and unamortized loan fees, premium or discount), the impairment is recognized by creating a valuation allowance and making a corresponding charge to bad debt expense.[23]

In subsequent accounting periods, for those impairments that were calculated by discounting cash flows, impairment is remeasured to reflect any significant changes (positive or negative) in the cash flow expectations used to calculate the original loan impairment. For those impairments that were measured using fair values, similar remeasurements are made to reflect subsequent significant changes in fair value. However, the loan carrying value may not be written up to a value that exceeds the recorded investment in the loan. For balance sheet purposes, the changes are reflected in the valuation allowance account.[24]

For income statement purposes, changes in the present value of the expected future cash flows of an impaired loan may be treated in one of two ways:

1. Increases that are attributable to the passage of time are reported as interest income; the balance of the change in present value is an adjustment to bad debt expense.

2. The entire change in present value is reported as an adjustment to bad debt expense.[25]

All changes in the measurement of impairment that are based on changes in fair value are reflected in earnings as adjustments to bad debt expense.[26]

At each balance sheet date, the following disclosures are required:

1. The recorded investment in the impaired loans.

2. The beginning and ending balance in the allowance account and the activity occurring during the period in that account.

3. The income recognition policy, including the amount of interest income recognized due to changes in the present value of the impaired loan.[27]

---

[22] Ibid., par. 8.

[23] Ibid., pars. 13 and 14.

[24] Ibid., par. 16.

[25] Ibid., par. 17.

[26] Ibid., par. 18.

[27] Ibid., par. 20.

SFAS No. 114 is intended to address whether present value measures should be used to measure loan impairment. The pronouncement clarifies present GAAP for loan impairments by specifying that both principal and interest receivable should be considered when calculating loan impairment. The prescribed measurement methods should reflect the amount that is expected to be recovered by the creditor so that investors, creditors, and other users can better assess the amount and timing of future cash flows. the initial present value recorded for the loan reflected the expectations at that time regarding expected future cash flows. Because the loan was originally recorded at a discounted amount, ongoing assessment for impairment should be treated in a similar manner. The added uncertainty associated with expectations regarding the future cash flows from impaired loans should not preclude the use of discounted cash flows. The impairment represents a deterioration in quality as reflected in the change in cash flow expectations. Thus, the impairment itself does not indicate that a new loan has replaced the old one. Rather, the old loan is continuing, but expectations about future cash flows have changed; hence, the contractual interest rate is the appropriate rate to discount those cash flows.

Critics argue that the effect of impairment is a change in the character of the loan that should be measured directly. If so, the contractual interest rate is no longer relevant. The most desirable direct measure of an impaired loan is fair value. If no market value exists, the creditor should discount the expected future cash flows utilizing an interest rate that is commensurate with the risk involved. Moreover, allowing the use of a fair value alternative is inconsistent with requiring the original loan interest rate to be used when the discounting alternative is selected. To be consistent in approach, the discounting should require an interest rate commensurate with the risk associated with the current status of the loan; such a rate is implicit in the fair value of the loan. In addition, the pronouncement allows three alternative measures of loan impairment with no guidance on when to use one method over the other. Allowing alternatives in this manner enables enterprises to utilize the provisions of this pronouncement to manage their financial statements.

Intangibles

It is difficult to define the term *intangibles* adequately. Kohler defined it as capital assets having no physical existence and whose value depends on the rights and benefits that possession confers to the owner.[28] However, Paton had previously noted that the lack of physical existence test was not particularly helpful and suggested that intangibles are assets more closely related to the enterprise as a whole than to any components.[29] It should also be noted that many intangibles convey a sort of monopolistic right to their owners.

---

[28] Eric L. Kohler, *A Dictionary for Accountants,* 3rd ed. (Englewood Cliffs, N.J.: Prentice-Hall, 1963), p. 269.

[29] William A. Paton and William A. Paton, Jr., *Asset Accounting* (New York: Macmillan Co., 1952), pp. 485–490.

Examples of intangibles are patents, copyrights, franchises, leaseholds, and goodwill.

Intangible assets derive their value from the special rights and privileges that they convey, and accounting for these assets involves the same problems as accounting for other long-term assets. Specifically, an initial carrying amount must be determined; this initial carrying value must be systematically and rationally allocated to the periods that receive benefit; and if the asset's value declines substantially and permanently, the unamortized carrying value must be written down. These problems are magnified in the case of intangibles because their very nature makes evidence elusive. Both the value and the useful lives of intangibles are difficult to determine.

In reviewing the topic of intangibles, the Accounting Principles Board noted that these assets might be classified on several different bases.

Identifiability—separately identifiable or lacking specific identification.

Manner of acquisition—acquired singularly, in groups, or in business combinations, or developed internally.

Expected period of benefit—limited by law or contract, related to human or economic factors, or having indefinite or indeterminate duration.

Separability from an entire enterprise—rights transferable without title, salable, or inseparable from the enterprise or a substantial part of it.[30]

The foregoing definitions suggest that intangibles may be classified according to whether they are *externally acquired* (purchased from outsiders) or *internally developed*. Additionally, they may be classified as *identifiable* or *unidentifiable*. These last two classifications relate to the Type (a) and Type (b) classifications contained in *ARB No. 43* and discussed later in the chapter.

Accounting for Cost

The initial valuation process for intangible assets generally follows the same standards employed for other long-lived assets. Cost includes all expenditures necessary to acquire an individual asset and make it ready for use. When intangibles are purchased from outsiders, assigning cost is fairly easy, and the methods used in allocating cost to groups of assets and by exchanges of other assets are similar to those discussed for tangible fixed assets.

However, companies frequently develop intangible assets internally. The Accounting Principles Board addressed the problems inherent in accounting for internally developed intangibles in *Opinion No. 17*. The Board's conclusions are based on the identifiability characteristic defined earlier.

> *A company should record as assets the costs of intangible assets acquired from other enterprises or individuals. Costs of developing, maintaining, or restoring intangible assets which are not specifically identifiable, have indeterminate lives, or are inherent in a continuing business and related to the enterprise as a whole—such as goodwill—should be deducted from income when incurred.*[31]

[30] *Accounting Principles Board Opinion No. 17*, "Intangible Assets" (New York: AICPA, 1970).

[31] Ibid., par. 24.

The identifiability criterion alleviated much of the problem in accounting for the cost of intangible assets and is yet another example of the APB's attempts to narrow alternatives. Where a specific cost can be assigned to a specific asset, intangibles are carried forward at recorded values. Where either a specific asset or specific amount is indeterminable, no attempt should be made to carry values forward.

Amortization

The matching principle dictates that the cost of intangible assets be apportioned to the expected periods of benefit. In *Accounting Research Bulletin No. 43* it was noted that this process involved two separate types of intangibles.

> a. *those having a term of existence limited by law, regulation, or agreement, or by their nature (such as patents, copyrights, leases, licenses, franchises for a fixed term and goodwill as to which there is evidence of limited duration).*
>
> b. *those having no such term of existence and as to which there is, at the time of acquisition, no indication of limited life (such as goodwill generally, going value, trade names, secret processes, subscription lists, perpetual franchises, and organization costs).*[32]

This release resulted in the adoption of a classification scheme that identified intangibles as either Type (a) or Type (b), and these terms became widely used in discussing the issues associated with recording and amortizing intangible assets. In *APB Opinion No. 17*, the terms *Type (a)* and *Type (b)* were not specifically used and the terms *identifiable* and *unidentifiable* were substituted. In this release, the APB noted that then-current practices allowed for the following variations in treatment of unidentifiable intangibles: (1) retention of cost until a reduction of value was apparent, (2) amortization over an arbitrary period, (3) amortization over estimated useful life with specified minimum and maximum periods, and (4) deduction from equity as acquired.[33]

In *Opinion No. 17* the APB concluded that intangible assets should be amortized by systematic charges to income over the estimated period to be benefited. The Board also suggested that the following factors should be considered in estimating the useful lives of intangibles:

1. Legal, regulatory, or contractual provisions may limit the maximum useful life.

2. Provisions for renewal or extension may alter a specific limit on useful life.

3. Effects of obsolescence, demand, competition, and other economic factors may reduce a useful life.

4. A useful life may parallel the service life expectancies of individuals or groups of employees.

---

[32] *Accounting Research Bulletin No. 43*, "Restatement and Revision of Accounting Research Bulletins" (New York: AICPA, 1953), p. 6019.

[33] *APB Opinion No. 17*, op. cit.

5. Expected actions of competitors and others may restrict present competitive advantages.

6. An apparently unlimited useful life may in fact be indefinite and benefits cannot be reasonably projected.

7. An intangible asset may be a composite of many individual factors with varying effective lives.[34]

The period of amortization should be determined from a review of the foregoing factors, but should not exceed 40 years. The straight-line method of amortization was required to be used unless another method could be demonstrated to be more appropriate.

As noted earlier, the release of *APB Opinion No. 17* narrowed the accounting treatment available for similar transactions; however, whether or not it created the desired result is subject to question. *APB Opinion No. 17* is criticized by some because it places values on the balance sheet that relate to future expectations (for example, purchased goodwill), and others disagree with the Board's conclusions because it assigns costs to arbitrary periods where there is no evidence that costs have expired (for example, perpetual franchises). Further evidence of the lack of acceptability of this pronouncement lies in the fact that originally it was part of *APB Opinion No. 16*, ''Business Combinations''; however, since enough members of the APB objected to various provisions of both Opinions, it was necessary to separate them to obtain the required majority for passage.

Goodwill

The topic of goodwill has been of interest for many years. As initially conceived, it was viewed as good relations with customers. Such factors as a convenient location and habits of customers were viewed as adding to the value of the business. Yang described it as everything that might contribute to the advantage an established business possessed over a business to be started anew.[35] Since that time, the concept of goodwill has evolved into an earning power concept in which the value of goodwill is determined by subtracting the book value of a firm's net assets from the total value of the enterprise.

Catlett and Olson summarized the characteristics of goodwill that distinguish it from other elements of value as follows:

1. *The value of goodwill has no reliable or predictable relationship to costs that may have been incurred in its creation.*

2. *Individual intangible factors that may contribute to goodwill cannot be valued.*

3. *Goodwill attaches only to a business as a whole.*

4. *The value of goodwill may, and does, fluctuate suddenly and widely because of the innumerable factors that influence that value.*

[34] Ibid., par. 27.

[35] J. M. Yang, *Goodwill and Other Intangibles* (Ronald Press, 1927), p. 29.

5. *Goodwill is not utilized or consumed in the production of earnings.*

6. *Goodwill appears to be an element of value that runs directly to the investor or owner in a business enterprise.*[36]

In assigning a value to goodwill, current practice attempts to discount the present value of expected superior earnings (expected future earnings less normal earnings for the industry). This process involves forecasting future earnings and choosing an appropriate discount rate.

The forecasting of future earnings is a risky proposition. Since the best indication of the future is the past, current revenue and expense figures should be used. However, the following points are relevant to this process:

1. The use of too few or too many years may distort projections.

2. Trends in earnings should be considered.

3. Industry trends are important.

4. Overall economic conditions can be significant.

In choosing the discount rate to be used in making goodwill calculations, the objective is to approximate the existing cost of capital for the company. This approximation must take into consideration existing and expected risk conditions as well as earnings potential.

Although goodwill may exist at any point in time, in practice, it is recognized for accounting purposes only when it is acquired through purchase of an existing business.[37] Only then is the value of goodwill readily determinable, because the purchase embodies an arm's length transaction wherein assets, often cash or marketable securities, are exchanged. The value of the assets exchanged indicates a total fair value for the business entity acquired. The excess of total fair value over the fair value of identifiable net assets is considered goodwill. This practice fulfills the stewardship function of accounting and facilitates the accountability for managers to stockholders. However, it can be argued that when a company acquires stock so that it can exercise significant influence or control, part of the purchase price represents an influence or control premium and is not a payment for goodwill. In this case, two intangible assets are purchased and should be given separate accounting treatment.

When goodwill is recorded it is considered an intangible asset and as such is subject to the *APB Opinion No. 17* requirements for amortization of cost over useful life or 40 years, whichever comes first.[38] The case for amortization is based on accrual accounting. The company has paid for the goodwill. The goodwill will presumably generate future earnings and thus its cost should be

---

[36] George R. Catlett and Norman O. Olson, *Accounting for Goodwill* (New York: AICPA, 1968), pp. 20–21.

[37] In certain cases, goodwill is recognized when a new partner is admitted to a partnership or when a partner leaves a partnership.

[38] The *Revenue Reconciliation Act of 1993* allows goodwill to be written off over a 15-year period for income tax purposes. Consequently, a new income tax timing difference has been created by this legislation, and the previous permanent difference has been eliminated.

matched against those future earnings as they arise. However, in the case of goodwill, it is difficult, if not impossible, to estimate what that useful life will be. If goodwill measures excess earning power, how long can it be expected to last? An economist would say that it would not last very long because competition would drive it away. If so, it should be written off over a relatively short period of time. On the other hand, if the goodwill is attributable to some ability associated with the enterprise, its employees, or management, that would be difficult for others to duplicate, then it may have an indefinite useful life, in which case it may be inappropriate to amortize goodwill at all.

Some accountants argue that goodwill should be written off when it is acquired because it would then receive the same treatment as inherent goodwill (goodwill that exists but is not paid for). There are costs associated with developing inherent goodwill. These costs are written off as they are incurred. Moreover, when goodwill is acquired, further cost will be incurred to continue excess earnings ability. Hence, to amortize the cost of goodwill acquired over future periods represents a double counting of cost. The immediate write-off of purchased goodwill could be treated as an extraordinary item because it represents a transaction outside the normal trading activity of the acquiring or investee enterprise.

Opponents of immediate write-off of goodwill contend that the purchase of goodwill implies future profitability; thus, it is inconsistent and perhaps misleading to investors to write off the cost of goodwill because it represents an asset having future service potential. This is particularly true for investments in people intensive companies, for example, in service industries. For these investments, the amount of goodwill acquired relative to other assets is high; thus, the immediate write-off would be material and would have a major and misleading impact on financial ratios, particularly debt to equity and return on investment. Moreover, future profits would be inflated because they would not be matched against the cost of the investment.

The FASB is currently addressing measurement and reporting issues associated with goodwill as a part of its project on consolidations. These issues will be discussed in Chapter 14.

Brand Recognition Accounting

Brand recognition, embodied, for example, in tradenames and trademarks or as the result of advertising efforts, is similar to goodwill. It too may result in future profits that otherwise would not accrue; thus brand recognition has future service potential and may be considered an asset. If so, investors interested in evaluating a company may take this asset into consideration even though it may not appear on the corporate balance sheet.

In current practice, trademarks and tradenames are recognized only if purchased. Research and development costs and the cost of advertising that eventually result in brand recognition are expensed as incurred. Hence, brand recognition rarely appears in published financial statements. When it is recorded, the asset is considered an intangible asset and is amortized in accordance with *APB Opinion No. 17*. Like goodwill, determination of useful life is questionable and useful life could even be indefinite. Unlike goodwill, brand recognition is not likely to be driven away by competition. Thus, the write-off under the rules for intangible assets may be questionable.

When an enterprise invests in a business that has brand recognition, that part of the purchase price that is normally considered goodwill may actually be due, at least in part, to brand recognition. Some accountants argue that the excess of cost over the fair value of identifiable net assets should be allocated between goodwill and brand recognition and that due to differences in anticipated useful lives should be subjected to different amortization periods or rules. Perhaps the purchase price attributable to goodwill should be amortized and the cost attributable to brand recognition should not.

There are obvious measurement problems associated with such an allocation. Because the current value of goodwill and brand recognition is a function of the future profits that each will generate, the separation of cost into goodwill and brand recognition components would require the separate measurement and discounting of cash flow expected to be derived from each component. At a minimum, it would be necessary to derive a fair value for one component and presume that the rest of the cost paid applies to the other component. But how would the acquiring firm identify which cash flows will result from which asset? Excess earnings would be provided by both assets, but it would be difficult to determine how much of the excess earnings will be derived from each asset. Such a measurement would be complicated further when it is felt that some of the purchase price of the investment was paid for an influence or control premium. In this case, an allocation should be made to three separate intangible assets.

Research and Development Costs

Large corporations are continually attempting to improve their product lines, develop new products, improve manufacturing methods, and develop improved manufacturing facilities. Accounting for the cost of the activities of the research department is a complicated process because some costs may never result in future benefits. For those costs that will provide future benefit, an asset exists, but due to the uncertainty surrounding the present determination of which costs will result in future benefits, and over what periods those future benefits will be realized, many accountants view such determinations as too subjective and unreliable. In the past, many corporations recognized the importance of developing accounting procedures to allow such costs to be capitalized and amortized on a reasonable basis. For example, one study suggested that such costs might be classified as follows:

1. *Basic research.* Experimentation with no specific commercial objective.
2. *New product development.* Experimental effort toward previously untried products.
3. *Product improvement.* Effort toward improving quality or functional performance of current product lines.

4. *Cost and/or capacity improvement.* Development of new and improved processes, manufacturing equipment, etc., to reduce operations costs or expand capacity.

5. *Safety, health, and convenience.* Improvement of working conditions generally for purposes of employee welfare, community relations, etc.[39]

This classification scheme would make it easier to identify the costs that should be deferred and those that should be expensed. The authors of this study suggested that categories 1, 2, and 3 should generally be deferred and amortized, whereas 4 and 5 should be charged to expense because of the difficulty in determining the future periods expected to receive benefit.[39]

APB Opinion No. 17 requires the immediate expensing of intangible assets that are not specifically identifiable because these costs do not specifically generate revenue and have dubious future service potential. This provision was adopted to discourage the manipulation of research and development expenses. (Many companies were capitalizing research and development costs in low-profit years and writing them off in a lump sum in high-profit years.)

Later the FASB restudied the issue of research and development costs and issued *SFAS No. 2*. This release requires all research and development costs to be charged to expense as incurred. To distinguish research and development costs from other costs, the FASB provided the following definitions.

Research *is planned search or critical investigation aimed at discovery of new knowledge with the hope that such knowledge will be useful in developing a new product or service or new process or technique or in bringing about a significant improvement to an existing product or process.*

Development *is the translation of research findings or other knowledge into a plan or design for a new product or process or for a significant improvement to an existing product or process whether intended for sale or use. It includes the conceptual formulation, design and testing of product alternatives, construction of prototypes, and operation of pilot plants. It does not include routine or periodic alterations to existing products, production lines, manufacturing processes and other ongoing operations even though these alterations may represent improvements and it does not include market research or market testing activities.*[40]

Since many costs may have characteristics similar to research and development costs, the FASB also listed activities that would and would not be included in the category of research and development costs as follows:

[39] Donald L. Madden, Lewis D. McCullers, and Relmond P. Van Daniker, "Classification of Research and Development Expenditures: A Guide to Better Accounting." *The CPA Journal* (February 1972), pp. 139–142.

[40] Financial Accounting Standards Board, *Statement of Financial Accounting Standards No. 2,* "Accounting for Research and Development Costs" (Stamford, Conn.: FASB, October 1974), par. 8.

Research and Development Activities	*Activities Not Considered Research and Development*
Laboratory research aimed at discovery of a new knowledge	Engineering follow-through in an early phase of commercial production
Searching for applications of new research findings	Quality control during commercial production including routine testing
Conceptual formulation and design of possible product or process alternatives	Troubleshooting breakdowns during production
Testing in search for or evaluation of product or process alternatives	Routine, ongoing efforts to refine, enrich, or improve the qualities of an existing product
Modification of the design of a product or process	Adaptation of an existing capability to a particular requirement or customer's need
Design, construction, and testing of preproduction prototypes and models	Periodic design changes to existing products
Design of tools, jigs, molds, and dies involving new technology	Routine design of tools, jigs, molds, and dies
Design, construction, and operation of a pilot plant not useful for commercial production	Activity, including design and construction engineering, related to the construction, relocation, rearrangement, or start-up of facilities or equipment.
Engineering activity required to advance the design of a product to the manufacturing stage	Legal work on patent applications, sale, licensing, or litigation[41]

Summary

A number of measurement problems arise in accounting for investments in equity and debt securities and for intangibles. Less than majority investments in common stock are accounted for by the cost method, the fair value method, the equity method, or the market value method, according to the percentage of ownership in the investee held by the investor or the surrounding circumstances. The equity method satisfies the requirements of accrual accounting for those investments wherein the investor has the ability to exercise significant influence over the investee. The fair value method provides information relevant to investor decision making for investments in debt and equity securities that have readily determinable fair values. Dividend and interest income for these securities are recognized as received or receivable.

Investments in debt securities that management intends to hold to maturity are carried at amortized cost. Income from debt is recognized as interest is paid and is adjusted at year-end for amounts that have accrued since the

---

[41] Ibid., pars. 9 and 10.

last interest payment date. The interest income is adjusted for the amortization of discounts and premiums to reflect the total interest earned over the life of the debt instrument from the purchase date to the maturity date. The straight-line or effective interest methods can be used to amortize discounts or premiums.

Intangible assets are identified as either *identifiable* or *unidentifiable*. Identifiable intangible assets are written off over their period of benefit. Unidentifiable intangible assets, purchased from outsiders, are written off over their period of benefit, not to exceed 40 years.

In the articles that follow, Lawrence Ponemon and K. Ragunandan discuss *SFAS No. 115*, and J. Ron Colley and Ara G. Volkan analyze the goodwill issue within the framework of FASB pronouncements.

Accounting for Investments in Debt and Equity Securities

Lawrence A. Ponemon and K. Raghunandan

Concerns have been expressed by regulators and others about the recognition and measurement of investments in debt securities by financial institutions. Such criticism intensified following the recent difficulties experienced by savings and loan institutions and banks. The criticisms specifically expressed were—

- the unacceptable diversity in practice in accounting for investments in debt securities;

- fair value information about debt securities is more relevant than historical cost information; and

- using historical cost information permitted the practice of "gains trading."

It was contended that using fair or market value of debt securities would be more relevant to assess the solvency of financial institutions.

In response to such concerns, the Financial Accounting Standards Board recently devoted considerable attention to its project on financial instruments. The first step in the process was the issuance of Statement of Financial Accounting Standards (SFAS) No. 107 *Disclosures about Fair Value of Financial Instruments.* FASB's next step was the issuance of SFAS No. 115 titled *Accounting for Certain Investments in Debt and Equity Securities.* This standard will supersede SFAS No. 12, *Accounting for Certain Marketable Equity Securities.*

Equity and Debt Securities

Even though regulatory criticism was primarily targeted at accounting for debt securities, fair value is equally relevant to debt and equity securities. Therefore, the FASB decided to include in the current standard accounting for investments in equity securities, but only those having readily determinable fair values. Equity investments in closely held companies and partnerships are excluded from the scope of the standard because they would not constitute equity securities with readily determinable market values.

For debt securities, even if there are no quoted market prices, a reasonable estimate of fair value can be calculated by using a variety of pricing techniques such as discounted cash flow analysis, matrix pricing, option-adjusted spread models, and fundamental analysis.

Scope of the Statement

The FASB decided to limit the scope of the project in order to expedite the resolution of some problems with current accounting practice. Since the Board was not able to identify a workable approach for including liabilities, SFAS No. 115 addresses only issues related to accounting for certain financial assets without changing the accounting for related liabilities. One consequence of a limited scope, however, was the Board's decision not to require all investments in debt securities to be reported at fair value, with changes in fair value included in earnings. Thus, the

FASB's approach can be viewed as a compromise.

The new standard will not change accounting for (1) investments in equity securities accounted for under the equity method or investments in consolidated subsidiaries, and (2) entities such as brokers and dealers in securities, defined benefit pension plans, and investment companies because the specialized accounting practices of such entities include accounting for substantially all investments in securities at market or fair value.

While the new standard would be equally applicable to public and nonpublic entities, not-for-profit organizations are exempted. The FASB decided to address the issue of investments by not-for-profit organizations in a separate project related to financial display by such organizations.

Three Categories

SFAS No. 115 requires that investments in securities be classified into one of the following three categories:

- Held to maturity;
- Trading; or
- Available for sale.

For all three categories realized gains and losses, which arise when securities are disposed of, are included in the determination of earnings. Further, dividend and interest income including amortization of premium and discount is included in earnings for all three categories. The differences in accounting treatment between the categories of securities arise only with respect to unrealized gains and losses. Each security must be classified into one of the three categories at the time of the acquisition. Further, at each reporting date the appropriateness of the classification must be reviewed.

Held-to-Maturity

The first category, held to maturity, consists of debt securities that the entity has "positive intent and ability" to hold to maturity. For securities held to maturity, fair values may not be appropriate, since, absent default, amortized cost will be realized and any interim unrealized gains and losses will reverse. The FASB decided that such securities are appropriately carried at amortized cost in the financial statements. Therefore, for debt securities classified as held to maturity, no unrealized gains and losses will be recognized in financial statements.

The FASB deliberately decided to make the held-to-maturity category restrictive. If the intent of management is to hold a security only for an "indefinite period," that would not constitute a security which can be classified as held-to-maturity. Therefore, debt securities cannot be classified as held-to-maturity if they might be sold in response to changes in—

- market interest rates and related prepayment risk of the security;
- liquidity needs;
- availability and yield of alternative investments;
- funding sources and terms; and
- foreign currency risk.

Clearly, managerial intent plays a crucial role in classifying a debt security as held-to-maturity. In establishing such intent, relevant factors to examine include past experience of sales or transfers of such securities. Certain dispositions of securities which are classified as held-to-maturity would not be inconsistent with the intent to hold the securities to maturity, if they meet either of the following two criteria:

1. The date of sale is so near the maturity date (within three months) that changes in market interest rates would not have a significant impact on the value of the security; or

2. The sale occurs after a substantial portion (85%) of the principal outstanding at acquisition has been collected.

In some situations, significant unforeseeable circumstances could cause a change in intent with respect to some securities without affecting the entity's intent to hold other debt securities to maturity. Selling a security prior to maturity because of—

• A significant increase in credit risk of the security;

• A change in tax law eliminating the tax exempt status of the interest on a security; or

• A major business combination or disposition that necessitates the sale or transfer of securities to maintain existing interest rate risk position or credit risk policy would not be inconsistent with classification in the held-to-maturity category.

It is important to emphasize that the first of the three situations requires considerable judgement. There are three other circumstances in which changes with respect to some held-to-maturity securities would not call into question the intent with respect to other securities currently classified as held-to-maturity. These relate primarily to situations faced by regulated financial institutions: changes in statutory or regulatory requirements about permissible investments, significant increases in

capital requirements, or significant increase in the risk weights used for risk-based capital purposes.

Trading Securities and Securities Available for Sale

All other debt securities and all equity securities are classified either as trading securities or as securities available for sale. For such securities, the FASB decided that changes in fair value are relevant to assess managerial decisions and actions in maximizing profitable use of resources. Hence, the new standard requires that such changes in fair value be reflected in the financial statements. However, there are crucial differences in the accounting for trading securities and securities classified as available for sale.

Trading securities reflect active and frequent buying and selling, and are held for short periods of time with the objective of generating profits from short-term differences in price. For trading securities, unrealized holding gains and losses are both recognized by including them in earnings. Unrealized holding gains and losses measure the total change in fair value—consisting of unpaid interest income earned or unpaid accrued dividend and the remaining change in fair value from holding the security.

All other securities are classified as available for sale. Thus, all marketable equity securities—except those categorized as trading securities—which are now covered by SFAS No. 12, are classified as available for sale. This category also includes debt securities which might be sold prior to maturity to meet liquidity needs or as part of a risk management program.

For securities classified as available for sale, the new standard requires that unrealized gains and losses be excluded

TABLE 1 *Portfolio of XYZ Co.*

Security	Type of Security	Cost	No. of Securities	Market Price
A	Equity	10	1,000	6
B	Debt	10	1,000	9
C	Debt	10	1,000	8

from the determination of earnings, but reported separately and accumulated net of an income tax effect in a separate component of shareholders' equity. This represents a significant change from present practice for marketable equity securities classified as current assets. Under SFAS No. 12, unrealized losses for such securities and recoveries of such losses have to be recognized in the income statement for the period.

Another important change relates to unrealized holding gains. SFAS No. 12 used the lower of cost or market approach on a portfolio-wide basis, and prevented the recognition of unrealized holding gains except to the extent they represented recoveries of past unrealized holding losses. Under the new standard unrealized holding gains can be recognized as a net adjustment of shareholders' equity.

Cash flows from purchases and disposition of held-to-maturity and available-for-sale securities must be classified as cash flows from investing activities. Cash flows from transactions of trading securities must be classified as cash flows from operating activities.

The impact of the new proposals on the income statement and balance sheet are illustrated in greater detail using two examples.

XYZ Company

Assume that the portfolio of XYZ Co. consists of the marketable securities at the end of an accounting period as shown in Table 1.

At the end of the period, accounting for the portfolio of securities would be as follows:

Current Accounting Practice

Assume equity security A is a current asset. For this security, as per SFAS No. 12, the lower of cost or market rule would apply. The market value is $6,000. Since this is less than the cost of $10,000, an unrealized loss of $4,000 would be recognized in the income statement for the period. For debt securities, under present practice, no unrealized loss need be recognized.

Thus, for the entire portfolio the effect would be as follows:

- Income statement effect: A loss of $4,000 would be recognized.

- Balance sheet effect: Assuming a 34% marginal tax rate, shareholders' equity would be reduced by $2,640 (0.66 × $4,000).

Under SFAS 115

Assume that debt security C is classified as "held to maturity." Thus, the reduction in value of that security will not be recognized. Assume further that debt security B is classified as "available for sale." In other words, none of the securities is classified as "trading securities."

For equity security A, the unrealized holding loss is as before, $4,000. For debt security B, the net unrealized holding loss is $1,000.

Thus, for the entire portfolio the effect would be as follows:

- Income statement effect: There would be no impact on the income statement.

- Balance sheet effect: Assuming a 34% marginal tax rate as before, the reduction in shareholders' equity would now be $3,300 (0.66 × [4,000 + 1,000]).

Thus, while the new standard would eliminate the losses to be recognized on the income statement and thus lead to a higher net income (or lower net loss) than would currently be reported, the impact on the shareholders' equity is more negative than is currently the case.

KLM Company

Assume the portfolio of KLM Co. consists of the marketable securities at the end of an accounting period as shown in Table 2.

At the end of the period, accounting for the portfolio of securities would be as follows:

Current Accounting Practice

Assume equity security D is a current asset. For this security, as per SFAS No. 12, the lower of cost or market rule would apply. The market value is $12,000. Since this is more than the

cost of $10,000, there would not be an adjustment in the reported value of the portfolio. For debt securities, under current practice, no unrealized loss need be recognized.

Thus, for the entire portfolio the effect would be as follows:

- Income statement effect: No unrealized holding gain or loss is recognized.

- Balance sheet effect: No impact.

Under SFAS 115

Assume that debt security F is classified as "held to maturity." Thus, the reduction in value of that security will not be recognized. As before, assume further that all the other securities are classified as "available for sale." In other words, none of the securities is classified as "trading securities."

For equity security D, the unrealized holding gain is $2,000. For debt security E, the unrealized holding loss is $1,000. Thus, for the entire portfolio of securities available for sale, the net holding gain is $1,000.

For the entire portfolio, the effects would be as follows:

- Income statement effect: None of the unrealized losses or gains would flow through the income statement.

- Balance sheet effect: Assuming a 34% marginal tax rate as before, there would now be a net increase of $660 (0.66 × $1,000) in shareholders' equity.

TABLE 2 *Portfolio of KLM Co.*

Security	Type of Security	Cost	No. of Securities	Market Price
D	Equity	10	1,000	12
E	Debt	10	1,000	9
F	Debt	10	1,000	8

Thus, the standard would lead to a higher value of reported shareholders' equity being shown on the balance sheet than under current accounting practice.

Transfer Among Categories

Transfers among the three categories are accounted for at fair value. If a security is transferred into or from the trading category, any unrealized holding gains and losses must be recognized in earnings. If a debt security is transferred from the held-to-maturity category to the available for sale category, unrealized holding gains and losses must be recognized in a separate component of shareholders' equity. For a transfer from the available-for-sale category to the held-to-maturity category, unrealized holding gains and losses will continue to be reported as a separate component of shareholders' equity, but should be amortized over the remaining life of the security (similar to the amortization of premium or discount).

In all such situations, details about such transfers must be disclosed in the footnotes to the financial statements. Given the definitions of held-to-maturity and trading securities, transfers from the held-to-maturity category and transfers into or out of the trading category are expected to be rare.

Impairment of Securities

While temporary declines in market value for securities classified as available-for-sale or held-to-maturity are not recognized in the income statement of the period, the new standard requires other-than-temporary declines to be recognized in earnings for the period. The written down cost basis cannot be changed for subsequent recoveries in fair value.

Subsequent increases and decreases in fair value should be included in the separate component of equity.

Disclosures

Trading securities must be reported as current assets in classified balance sheets. Individual securities held-to-maturity or available-for-sale should be reported as current or noncurrent, as appropriate under the requirements of ARB No. 43. The individual amounts for the three categories of securities need not be presented in the statement of financial position, as long as the information is provided in the notes.

The notes should include information about aggregate fair value, gross unrealized holding gains, gross unrealized holding losses, and amortized cost basis by major security types as of each reporting date. The standard specifies that for financial institutions, the following would constitute major security types:

- Equity securities;
- Debt securities issued by the U.S. Treasury and other U.S. government corporations;
- Debt securities issued by states of the U.S. and political subdivisions of the states;
- Debt securities issued by foreign governments;
- Corporate securities;
- Mortgage-backed securities; and
- Other debt securities.

In addition, all reporting entities are required to disclose information about the contractual maturities of securities classified as held-to-maturity or available-for-sale, for the most recent date for which financial position is presented. The maturity groupings for financial institutions are specified as follows:

- Within one year;
- After 1 year through 5 years;
- After 5 years through 10 years; and
- After 10 years.

Securities not due at a single maturity date can be disclosed separately rather than be allocated over several maturity groupings.

The notes should also disclose revenues, gross realized gains, and gross realized losses from the sale of securities available for sale; gross gains and gross losses included in earnings from transfers of securities; the change in net unrealized holding gain or loss that has been included in earnings or in the separate component of shareholders' equity. Further, if there are any sales of or transfers from securities classified as held-to-maturity details including the circumstances leading to the decision to sell or transfer must be provided in the notes.

Transition

The new statement is effective for fiscal years beginning after December 15, 1993. Earlier application as of the beginning of the fiscal year is permitted for fiscal years beginning after the statement was issued. For fiscal years beginning prior to December 16, 1993, initial adoption as of the end of the fiscal year is permitted. Retroactive application of the statement is prohibited since the classification of securities at any point in time is dependent on managerial intent. The initial effect of applying this statement should be reported as the effect of a change in accounting principle (cumulative effect approach). However, the unrealized holding gain or loss, net of tax effect, for securities available for sale should be reported as an adjustment of the balance of the separate component of shareholders' equity.

Issue of Volatility

Why did the FASB require recognition of fair value in the balance sheet but exclude the effect of changes in fair value in the income statement for the period? Many have noted that requiring changes only in the accounting for assets without a corresponding change in the accounting for liabilities would have the potential for significant volatility in reported earnings. Such volatility would be unrepresentative of the way institutions manage their business and would have significant impact on the economy. For instance, it has been suggested that one consequence of such a move would be that financial institutions will be reluctant to engage in long-term lending or invest in long-term instruments such as long-term U.S. Treasury securities. This could seriously weaken the economy by raising the cost of capital for the Treasury, curtailing consumer lending, and raising home mortgage rates.

In response to such concerns, the FASB chose a compromise option of requiring the recognition and measurement of changes in fair value but not requiring that such changes be recognized in the income statement for the period. This may not eliminate the problem completely, however, since changes in fair value can still have an adverse impact on the net worth of financial institutions and lead to potential problems with capital adequacy requirements.

The Future

The FASB noted that this standard is only an interim solution, since the standard does not address all criticisms related to accounting for investments in securities. For example, the significant use of managerial intent as a criterion to distinguish among the three categories of securities can lead to comparability problems. In addition, the standard will not reduce the opportunities for selectively managing earnings by engaging in "gains trading"—the practice of selling those securities whose values have appreciated and thereby including realized gains in earnings and selectively excluding unrealized losses from earnings. Further, the standard's requirement that unrealized gains and losses be recognized in earnings when they are transferred between categories provides yet another opportunity to manage earnings.

The FASB is currently engaged in a detailed project on the recognition and measurement of financial instruments.

That project addresses assets as well as liabilities. Further, companies are required to disclose market values of financial instruments under SFAS No. 107.

Disclosures about Fair Value of Financial Instruments

Some have suggested that the FASB ought to have waited and examined the results of applying SFAS No. 107 in practice before addressing the issue of financial statement recognition and measurement of securities. The FASB has stated that the new standard is an interim solution given the current diversity in accounting practice. The FASB expects that the use of fair value accounting for financial instruments will be reassessed at an appropriate future time, taking into consideration the experiences from applying SFAS Nos. 107 and 115.

Accounting for Goodwill

J. Ron Colley and Ara G. Volkan

Introduction

The Financial Accounting Standards Board (FASB) has placed accounting for business combinations and goodwill in its list of current issues. Thus, the profession will once more debate this century-old controversy, and reexamine the accounting principles and procedures mandated by the various Opinions of the Accounting Principles

Board. Whether the final standards resulting from the review of this subject area will contain any changes in the present accounting rules remains to be seen. If the past is a good predictor of the future, the capitalization of goodwill issue will be at the center of intense discussions since major revisions of the accounting rules for business combinations cannot occur without a change in the profession's view of goodwill.

The purpose of this paper is to analyze the goodwill issue within the framework established by the pronouncements of the FASB. First, the two basic views of goodwill are presented. This discussion is followed by an examination of the factors underlying goodwill. The feasibility of using these factors to eliminate the goodwill account is examined next. We conclude that complete elimination of goodwill will not occur since the interaction of its components results in synergism. This section is followed by an argument for not capitalizing goodwill based on the measurability criterion advocated by the FASB. Finally, the financial consequences of this accounting alternative for goodwill on the risk and return ratios of a sample of firms are examined.

Two Views of Goodwill

Excess Earnings View

Two basic views of goodwill can be distinguished from a review of the literature. The first view holds that goodwill represents an above normal earnings capacity.[1] A price is paid in excess of the market value of net assets acquired (excess or goodwill hereafter) because profits in excess of a normal return on these net assets are anticipated. Thus, goodwill can be viewed as the present value of the anticipated excess earnings discounted over a certain number of years. The discount period will reflect the estimated life or duration of the reason(s) underlying the excess returns.

For example, a firm may decide to acquire the net assets of another in order to add certain production capabilities to its existing product lines. An alternative would have been to develop these products internally. If the firm can estimate the dollar amounts of the expenditures over the time period necessary to develop these production and sale capabilities, and the income lost due to waiting for the sales to start, then the amount of goodwill paid will, ideally, be equal to the difference between the present value of these amounts computed using the project time horizon, the internal rate of return of the acquiring firm, and the anticipated return on the market value of the identifiable net assets of the acquired firm.

Therefore, determination of goodwill will depend on the estimates of future earnings or cash flows, normal rate of return, value of identifiable net assets, and the discount period. Under this approach a proper assessment of the judgments used in the determination of the excess price paid over the value of the identifiable net assets of a company is not possible if one disagrees with any of the estimates used by the purchaser. Both the transaction itself and the excess payment which is a part of it are unique in the sense that one is dealing with imperfect markets where, generally, there is only one buyer and one seller.

Hidden Assets View

The second view states that goodwill represents various assets of the acquired firm which are not currently disclosed in its balance sheet. Tearney[2] offers excellent arguments in support of this view when he suggests that goodwill consists of many intangible assets which are separately identifiable and that such identification would enable the amortization of each asset over its useful life eliminating the need for the term "goodwill." If this view can be operationalized, a proper assessment of man-

---

[1] George R. Catlett and Norman O. Olson, *Accounting Research Study No. 10* (New York: AICPA, 1968).

[2] M. G. Tearney, "Accounting for Goodwill: A Realistic Approach," *The Journal of Accountancy* (July 1973), pp. 41–45.

agement's judgment in arriving at the excess payment amount can be made since the assumed values of the assets underlying the excess can be compared to values recorded in instances when these assets are bought and sold individually.

Factors Underlying Goodwill

In order to examine the feasibility of implementing either of these two views, a list of the components of goodwill would be most helpful. Such lists have been proposed in various studies that employ either the survey or deductive/normative methodologies, with or without empirical analysis.

Survey and Deductive Studies

An example of a list of factors supporting the first view of goodwill is a study by Mace and Montgomery[3] that identified five major factors affecting a firm's decision to purchase another firm. The most important reasons for business acquisitions were found to be "market factors." Firms purchase other businesses in order to acquire their "market share" or their excess earnings and cash flow capacity that derive from marketing success. Mace and Montgomery cite the following reasons for acquisitions:

1. Accomplishing market objectives (9.8 percent);

2. Saving time in expanding into a new area (4.3 percent);

3. Acquiring management skills (5.6 percent);

4. Achieving product diversification (40.1 percent); and

5. Achieving integration (33.2 percent).

[3]M. L. Mace, and G. E. Montgomery, *Management Problems of Corporate Acquisitions* (Boston: Harvard University Press, 1962).

On the other hand, Nelson,[4] supporting a middle ground between the first and the second views, argues that goodwill generally consists of the following "elements":

1. Customer lists;

2. Organization costs;

3. Developmental costs;

4. Trademarks, trade names, and brands;

5. Secret processes and formulas;

6. Patents;

7. Copyrights;

8. Licenses;

9. Franchises; and

10. Superior earnings power.

A comparison of the above two lists may suggest a lack of agreement as to the identity of the components of goodwill. But the differences mainly lie in the level of aggregation of these components. While the first list contains general factors underlying goodwill, the second list specifies individual items, which, taken together, may underlie these general factors. Thus, it is entirely possible that the reality is in between these two views and an accounting procedure common to all business acquisitions involving goodwill can be established.

An Empirical Study

A study conducted by Falk and Gordon[5] (hereafter F&G) contains the most comprehensive list of empirically identifi-

[4]R. H. Nelson, "The Momentum Theory of Goodwill," *Accounting Review* (October 1953), pp. 491–499.

[5]Haim Falk and L. A. Gordon, "Imperfect Markets and the Nature of Goodwill," *Journal of Business Finance and Accounting* (April 1977), pp. 443–463.

TABLE 1 *Factors Underlying Goodwill*

Factor A:	Increasing Short-Run Cash Flows
	Production economies
	Raise more funds
	Cash reserves
	Low cost of funds
	Reducing inventory holding cost
	Avoiding transaction cost
	Tax benefit
Factor B:	Stability
	Assurance of supply
	Reducing fluctuations
	Good government relations
Factor C:	Human Factor
	Managerial talent
	Good labor relations
	Good training programs
	Organizational structure
	Good public relations
Factor D:	Exclusiveness
	Access to technology
	Brand name

able factors as well as elements (characteristics) of goodwill we have encountered in the literature. F&G conducted in-depth interviews with top executives to select 17 characteristics for use in a questionnaire sent to a sample of financial executives. These 17 characteristics were expressed in four groups (factor categories) established through the use of cluster analysis. This methodology first identifies the many elements of goodwill and then mathematically determines the interrelationships of these elements to form a set of factors (clusters). The four factors thus identified are labeled as: (a) Increasing short-run cash flow; (b) Stability; (c) Human factor; and (d) Exclusiveness. The characteristics within each cluster are presented in Table 1.[6] A recent arti-

[6] Ibid., p. 453.

cle by Anderson[7] lists some of the items in Table 1 as the focal points of the acquisition strategy of Johnson & Johnson. In the next section an attempt will be made to employ these factors and characteristics as a means of eliminating the need for the goodwill account.

Attributes of Goodwill and Synergism

The F&G study can be used as a means of implementing both views of goodwill if the useful life and dollar value of each factor can be determined for amortization purposes. However, the useful life of a factor can only be determined if its individual characteristics are examined. For example, the "exclusiveness" factor has "brand name" and "access to technology" as individual characteristics. But a purchased brand name will likely have a different useful life than purchased technology.

An a priori classification of factors also has similar problems. For example, to say that a major objective of many acquisitions is "achieving integration" is not enough. An acquisition which "achieves integration" can have characteristics which are included in all four of the F&G clusters. The benefits of integration may include reducing inventory holding costs, assurance of supply, and access to technology and managerial talent (among others).

Moreover, the characteristics must not only be identified, but also must be assigned meaningful dollar values. For acquisitions in which the excess consists of only one or two characteristics this may be feasible. However, it is likely that most acquisitions will involve an excess consisting of a multitude of char-

[7] C. M. Anderson, "1 × 1 = 3," *Management Accounting* (April 1987), pp. 28–31.

acteristics and the problem of assigning meaningful dollar values to interrelated characteristics will render the exercise hopeless.

For example, characteristics such as organizational structure, good training programs, and good labor relations may be correlated resulting in a purchase price that is based upon the interaction of these characteristics rather than a separate consideration of each characteristic. The F&G study[8] resulted in the following correlation matrix for these three variables which shows some degree of interdependence:

	OS	TP	LR
Organizational Structure (OS)	1	.45	.40
Training Programs (TP)		1	.49
Labor Relations (LR)			1

Thus, in most cases, the assignment of individual dollar values to a group of purchased intangibles may not be meaningful. Rather, the purchased entity can be evaluated only as a whole because the value of the entity is based on the proper functioning of the interrelated parts to achieve some objective. Furthermore, the value of an acquired firm as a separate entity may be less than its value to an acquiring firm for which there is a particularly good fit. That is, the combination of the two firms may result in synergism.[9,10] Viewing an acquisition as synergistic is illustrated by the 1984 annual report of Black & Decker[11] which states:

We are proceeding to integrate the acquired operations . . . in order to capitalize on synergistic possibilities including lower costs, increased brand awareness and an even greater number of new product opportunities.

Therefore, it is quite possible that the goodwill that is recorded in acquisitions consists of many identifiable elements. However, such identification is not likely to result in the clear assignment of the entire purchase price to all identified assets (tangible and intangible). Some residual and the problem of how to account for this residual will remain. Thus, neither of the two views of goodwill can be used to obtain an independently verifiable measure of the entire excess payment since the nature of the residual included in it defies such verification.

An Argument for not Capitalizing Goodwill

Should the unidentified portion of the excess payment (hereafter "goodwill" means the unidentified portion of the excess or the residual) be capitalized? This question has been debated for several decades. The decision of whether to capitalize goodwill is usually supported by a theoretical discussion of whether goodwill is an asset.

However, the discussion of whether goodwill is an asset is a moot point if the amount of goodwill cannot be measured for capitalization purposes. Guidance in the issue of capitalization of goodwill can be found in past pronouncements of the FASB.

The Measurability Criterion

In 1974, the FASB decided against capitalization of R&D expenditures because of the uncertainty of future benefits. The decision of the FASB to expense all

[8] Haim Falk and L. A. Gordon, p. 459.

[9] Malcolm C. Miller, "Goodwill—An Aggregation Issue," *Accounting Review* (April 1973), pp. 280–291.

[10] C. M. Anderson, p. 28.

[11] Black & Decker, 1984 *Annual Report*, p. 3.

R&D costs was not in conflict with the idea that, theoretically, some R&D expenditures did have future benefit and should have been capitalized. Rather, the Board stated that "not all of the economic resources of an enterprise are recognized as assets for financial accounting purposes."[12]

One of the reasons used by the Board as the basis for the decision not to capitalize R&D expenditures was the "measurability" criterion. The future benefit of R&D expenditures is so difficult to measure that expensing R&D costs was viewed as more appropriate than even partial capitalization of these expenditures.

The criterion of measurability was given further support in Statement of Financial Accounting Concepts No. 5. The Statement required that four fundamental criteria should be met in order for an item to be recognized in the financial statements. One of these criteria is measurability. To be recognized, an item must be ". . . measurable with sufficient reliability."[13] Thus, in order to be capitalized, goodwill must meet the measurability criterion established by the FASB, which requires that a verifiable (reliable) estimate of the dollar value of the asset be known.

Moreover, a decision to capitalize goodwill will require an estimate of its useful life for amortization purposes. (Nonamortization is a possibility, but this still requires an estimate of a useful life into perpetuity.) As mentioned earlier, goodwill appears to consist of many factors and elements and each transaction creating goodwill may involve a unique mix of these. Therefore, the determination of the useful life of goodwill requires that the dollar value and useful lives of these factors and elements be identified.

Post-Acquisition Problems

The failure to identify and measure the value of the elements underlying the residual creates problems with capitalizing goodwill both at the acquisition date and after the date of acquisition. As an example of the latter, assume that a premium is paid for a firm partly because of contracts the firm possesses which give exclusive access to a customer base. The acquiring firm has purchased the contracts for the exclusive rights they provide. If the contracts are expected to remain in effect for 20 years, then they should be separately capitalized and amortized over a 20-year period. If for some reason the contracts are unexpectedly terminated and their value lost, the unamortized cost of the contracts should immediately be written off.

However, if the contracts are not separately identified and thus are included as a part of goodwill, it is unlikely that a portion of goodwill will be written off upon the termination of the contracts. This is one of the major problems with the current method of accounting for goodwill. A periodic determination of whether the current market value of the goodwill asset is lower than its unamortized cost is not likely to occur. Thus, the impairment of the asset is next to impossible to determine.

Even if one assumes that the factors and elements underlying goodwill can be identified and objective measures of their useful lives are available, their continued existence is subject to serious reservations. For example, in a competitive environment, any advantage that

---

[12] Financial Accounting Standards Board, *Statement of Financial Accounting Standards No. 2* (Stamford: FASB, 1974), par. 43.

[13] Financial Accounting Standards Board, *Statement of Accounting Concepts No. 5* (Stamford: FASB, 1984), par. 63.

a business has because of its reputation and relations with its customers must be regenerated by new efforts and expenditures. If the customers are left unattended, it will not take long for them to go elsewhere. Thus, within a short time after the purchase of goodwill, the meaning of its recorded value (whether amortized or not) is subject to serious doubts. When does the purchased goodwill expire and the internally generated goodwill come into effect?

Problems at the Date of Acquisition

There are also problems with measurement at the acquisition date. It is not uncommon for firms to be acquired at a market price per share that is far in excess of the price per share before information of the impending acquisition was available. If the markets are efficient, the market price per share prior to the release of information concerning the takeover attempt should be a valid representation of the value of the stand-alone firm. If investors are willing to pay a substantially higher price for the firm than was determined by market forces, they must expect the value of the acquired firm to be greater to their company than its value as a stand-alone firm.

Thus, a premium is being paid for synergism based upon the judgment of the management of the acquiring firm. In most instances, the transaction is at arm's length and independent observers (e.g., auditors) can easily verify the purchase price. However, the verification of the value of the premium included in this purchase price is not possible since the only source of goodwill measurement is management representations. That is, the estimates used in the computation of the price paid are the only evidential matter available and an independent appraiser engaged by the auditor will probably arrive at a different amount for the excess payment.

Accounting Alternatives

The discussion presented so far leads to the conclusion that goodwill cannot be capitalized because the auditor cannot attest to its measured amount. If this argument is supported by the FASB, then accounting for the unidentified portion of the excess (goodwill or residual) must reflect the substance of this transaction by debiting equity. In this manner management will have to prove the validity of its assumptions, and amounts that do not belong in a balance sheet will be disposed of.

However, the FASB may decide that, in the case of business acquisitions, the measurement process is sufficiently objective and the measured amount itself is verifiable and reliable. It may also be argued that the management would not have paid for the excess if it did not have future benefit, especially when the amount is determined through negotiations between a willing buyer and a willing seller. Therefore, regardless of the nature of the excess, the FASB may decide to capitalize the residual under the caption of goodwill arguing that the management intent and the price paid for the investment indicate the existence of some future benefit. Moreover, one can argue in favor of using management intent as evidence by indicating that management would not voluntarily try to allocate any portion of the excess to goodwill since its amortization is not tax deductible.

If the residual is capitalized as goodwill, then an amortization period or useful life must be determined. Since the nature of the residual under consideration is analogous to the first view of goodwill, a logical choice would be the time period selected by management to compute the present value of the excess earnings or cash flows. Thus, management's estimates may be used in the amortization process as it was done when the decision was made to capitalize goodwill.

As previously stated, the reasons for the excess payment, specifically the acquisition of market share or market factors, have relatively short useful lives as they relate to projects that can be accomplished within, for example, a five-year period.[14] Thus, the 40-year amortization period used in current practice is too long and cannot be supported on either theoretical or technical grounds. Consequently, a rapid amortization (specifically if the use of the present value amortization method is permitted by the FASB) of capitalized goodwill over a relatively short period of time should occur and the reported financial indicators of companies with material amounts of capitalized goodwill will be affected.

Financial Consequences of Noncapitalization

If the FASB agrees with the contention that the amounts presently capitalized and reported on the balance sheets under the caption of "goodwill" need to be amortized quite rapidly and/or written off immediately, there will be an impact on the total assets (decrease), total equity (decrease), and net income (increase slightly) reported in the financial statements. The impact will even be greater if we assume the worst and the entire amount of goodwill currently present on the balance sheet is written off immediately. Since the FASB is generally concerned with the financial consequences of its standards, it is worthwhile to examine the magnitude of the impact of such an accounting policy change on the risk (debt-to-equity) and performance (return-on-investment) ratios. These ratios are extensively used by financial analysts to determine the credit ratings and stock prices of companies.

To accomplish this objective we first obtained from the COMPUSTAT tapes a list of all firms with total assets of $100 million or more for the years 1980 through 1984, a period of high merger activity. We assumed that large asset bases indicated well diversified and mature firms that may have gone through a number of mergers and accumulated substantial amounts of goodwill.[15] Thus, we biased the sample selection in order to obtain the maximum possible impact of the accounting policy change. This step yielded 359 firms that had sufficient data for the time period chosen.

Second, we obtained the goodwill amount reported on the annual and/or 10-K report balance sheets of the firms in our sample. After eliminating all firms with insufficient data (for many firms the amount was immaterial or zero), our final sample sizes ranged from 59 (1980) to 65 (1984). In some cases the goodwill amount was incorporated in "other assets" or "other intangibles" and could not be separately

---

[14] See, for example: A. H. Rosenbloom, "How to Determine the Value of a Business: A Case Study," *The Practical Accountant* (March 1983), pp. 28–34; and P. Anthony, "Goodbye Goodwill—Hello Share of the Market," *Management Accounting* (June 1977), pp. 31–40.

[15] Including all the firms in the COMPUSTAT tapes in our sample resulted in a ratio of goodwill (or other assets) to total assets of .018 compared to a ratio of .034 if only "large" firms are included in the sample. Thus, we tried to obtain the largest possible impact.

identified. In such instances the amount representing these general categories was used. Thus, a positive error in the measured financial consequences may exist. (A list of companies is available from the authors.)

Next, we computed the debt-to-equity (DTE) and net income-to-total assets (ROA) ratios of the firms in our sample for each of the five years. Finally, we repeated this step assuming that the goodwill (or other assets) amount was deducted from total assets and total equity and its amortization was added back to net income (NEWROA and NEWDTE, respectively).

It is important to note that the distributions of the ROA and DTE ratios are not symmetrical about their means (i.e., these two distributions are not normal). Therefore, it is necessary to have another measure in addition to the mean and standard deviation in order to adequately describe these two distributions. The coefficient of skewness (CS) provides a measure of the direction and extent of skewness or lack of symmetry. A positive CS means that most observations forming the distribution are to the left of the mean, indicating a long tail to the right. The larger the numerical value of the CS, the more skewed is the distribution.

The results of our observations show (see Table 2) that:

1. Average ROA is .0804 while average NEWROA is .0844 indicating an increase of .4 percentage points with a range of 0 to 1.7 percentage points;

2. Average DTE is .9481 while average NEWDTE is 1.0310 indicating an increase of 8 percentage points with a range of .2 to 110.0 percentage points;

3. The average ratio of goodwill (or other assets) to total assets is .034;

4. The average ratio of goodwill (or other assets) to retained earnings is only .089; and

5. All of the coefficients of skewness in Table 2 are positive numbers, indicating that the bulk of each distribution is to the left of the mean. Therefore, most of the observed differences between the DTE and NEWDTE and ROA and NEWROA ratios are smaller than the mean. Alternatively, very few differences between the two ratios are substantially larger than the mean.

It follows that the average impact of the suggested change in accounting policy on ROA may be viewed as immaterial (according to a 5 percent materiality criterion) while the impact is modest on DTE, indicating an increase in these ratios of 4.9 percent versus 8.7 percent, respectively. This is not a surprising result, since goodwill is much larger in proportion to equity than it is to total assets.

Conclusions

The measurability criterion has been clearly established as one of the main principles of asset recognition by the FASB and should be given primary consideration in the selection of a method of accounting for goodwill. There is a problem of uncertainty of future benefits when acquisitions involve purchase prices based upon management's judgment regarding synergistic possibilities. Extensive efforts to identify the elements of the purchased intangibles may reduce the amount of the unidentified portion that has commonly been labeled as goodwill, but will not eliminate it. Application of the measurability criterion to business combinations suggests that this residual amount must not be capitalized.

TABLE 2

Year	Number of Firms	ROA	New ROA	Difference Amount	Difference Percent	Standard Deviation	Coefficient of Skewness	Goodwill to Asset Ratio
1980	59	.0840	.0878	.0038	4.5	.0039	2.7	.0318
1981	60	.0838	.0875	.0038	4.5	.0037	2.2	.0320
1982	62	.0749	.0790	.0041	5.5	.0041	2.2	.0373
1983	64	.0762	.0800	.0038	5.0	.0036	2.2	.0350
1984	65	.0833	.0875	.0042	5.0	.0036	2.2	.0359

Year	Number of Firms	DTE	New DTE	Difference Amount	Difference Percent	Standard Deviation	Coefficient of Skewness	Goodwill to R/E Ratio
1980	59	.9090	.9811	.0721	7.9	.1096	3.1	.0807
1981	60	.9277	.9943	.0666	7.2	.1217	2.2	.0785
1982	62	.9817	1.0837	.1020	10.4	.2358	6.7	.0913
1983	64	.9298	1.0117	.0819	8.8	.1460	5.6	.0960
1984	65	.9924	1.0843	.0919	9.3	.1424	5.9	.0988

We, therefore, proposed a two-step approach to accounting for goodwill. First, all intangible and tangible assets that form the basis for the excess payment over fair values of net assets acquired must be identified, capitalized, and amortized over their useful lives. Second, any remaining unidentifiable portion of the excess must be written off against equity on date of acquisition.

Direct write-off of goodwill against equity produces minimal impact on the ROA and a modest impact on the DTE ratios of the companies included in our sample. However, one must note that even this modest impact is overstated. For approximately 40 percent of the observations, goodwill is not separately identified but is included with other intangibles in the other assets category. Therefore, the amount of time and effort spent by the profession to resolve the debate on whether or not to capitalize goodwill must be in proportion to the relatively small economic consequence of this problem.

Cases

• Case 8-1

On June 30, 1996, your client, the Vandiver Corporation, was granted patents covering plastic cartons that it has been producing and marketing profitably for the past three years. One patent covers the manufacturing process and the other covers the related products.

Vandiver executives tell you that these patents represent the most significant breakthrough in the industry in the past 30 years. The products have been marketed under the registered trademarks Safetainer, Duratainer, and Sealrite. Licenses under the patents have already been granted by your client to other manufacturers in the United States and abroad and are producing substantial royalties.

On July 1, 1996, Vandiver commenced patent infringement actions against several companies whose names you recognize as those of substantial and prominent competitors. Vandiver's management is optimistic that these suits will result in a permanent injunction against the manufacture and sale of the infringing products and collection of damages for loss of profits caused by the alleged infringements.

The financial executive has suggested that the patents be recorded at the discounted value of expected net royalty receipts.

Required:
a. What is an intangible asset? Explain.
b. Discuss whether the patents, in this case, fit the *SFAC No. 6* definition of assets. Would your answer be the same if Vandiver is expected to lose the lawsuit? Explain.
c. i. What is the meaning of "discounted value of expected net royalty receipts"? Explain.
   ii. How would such a value be calculated for net royalty receipts?
d. What basis of valuation for Vandiver's patents would be generally accepted in accounting? Give supporting reasons for this basis.

e. i. Assuming no practical problems of implementation and ignoring generally accepted accounting principles, what is the preferable basis of valuation for patents? Explain.

ii. What would be the preferable theoretical basis of amortization? Explain.

f. What recognition, if any, should be made of the infringement litigation in
the financial statements and in the notes to the financial statements for the
year ended September 30, 1996? Discuss.

• Case 8-2

Xavier Co. purchased $1,000,000 face amount of Yodel Corp., 16 percent
bonds on December 31, 1986, for $881,000. Two years later Zandale Co.
purchased $1,000,000 face amount of Yodel Corp. bonds for $1,164,000. Each
purchasing company plans to hold the bonds until maturity, 12/31/94.

Under current GAAP, Xavier and Zandale will recognize the following
amounts in their financial statements.

	Xavier		Zandale	
12/31	Asset	Income	Asset	Income
1986	$881,000	$ 0		
1987	889,000	168,000		
1988	898,000	169,000	$1,164,000	$ 0
1989	908,000	170,000	1,144,000	140,000
1990	921,000	173,000	1,122,000	138,000
1991	936,000	175,000	1,096,000	132,000
1992	954,000	178,000	1,068,000	132,000
1993	975,000	181,000	1,036,000	128,000
1994	0	185,000	0	124,000
		$1,399,000		$796,000

During this time period, the market price of the Yodel bonds varied
widely. At the end of each year, the closing price and related market interest
rates were as follows:

12/31	*Closing Price*	*Yield*
1986	88.1	19%
1987	104.2	15
1988	116.4	12
1989	122.8	10
1990	115.5	11
1991	97.8	17
1992	98.4	17
1993	97.4	19

Required:

a. Even though Xavier and Zandale have purchased the same par value bonds, their financial statements reflect different amounts each year. How are they accounting for the bonds, and why do their financial statements differ?

b. Assume that Xavier had classified their investment in Yodel bonds as available-for-sale, but long-term. How would their assets and income differ, if any, over the above time period? Discuss this accounting treatment. In your answer, construct a table similar to the one above and show the amounts that would appear in assets and income. Show a separate column for interest income and unrealized gains, if any, that would be reflected in earnings.

c. Would your answer to (b) be different if Xavier had classified the investment as available-for-sale, but short-term? Explain.

d. Assume that Zandale had classified their investment in Yodel bonds as trading. How would their assets and income differ, if any, over the above time period? Discuss this accounting treatment. In your answer, construct a table similar to the one above and show the amounts that would appear in assets and income. Show a separate column for interest income and unrealized gains, if any, that would be reflected in earnings?

e. Discuss the FASB's rationale for the three different classifications.

f. Which approach to classification do you think is more relevant to investors? Why?

- ## Case 8-3

Qtip Corp. owns stock in Maxey Corp. The investment represents a 10 percent interest, and Qtip is unable to exercise significant influence over Maxey.

The Maxey stock was purchased by Qtip on January 1, 1993, for $23,000. The stock consistently pays an annual dividend to Qtip of $2,000. Qtip classifies the stock as available-for-sale. Its fair value at 12/31/93 was $21,600. This amount was properly reported as an asset in the balance sheet. Due to the development of a new Maxey product line, the market value of Qtip's investment rose to $27,000 at 12/31/94.

The Qtip management team is aware of the provisions of *SFAS No. 115*. The possibility of changing the classification from available-for-sale to trading is discussed. This change is justified, management says, because they intend to sell the security at some point in 1995 so that they can realize the gain.

Required:

a. Discuss the role that managerial intention plays in the accounting treatment of equity securities that have a readily determinable fair value.

b. What income statement effect, if any, would the change in classification have for Qtip?

c. Discuss the ethical considerations of this case.

d. Opponents of *SFAS No. 115* contend that allowing a change in classification masks effects of unrealized losses and results in improper matching of market value changes with accounting periods. Describe how the accounting treatment and the proposed change in classification would result in this sort of mismatching.

• Case 8-4

Victoria Company has both current and noncurrent equity securities portfolios. All of the equity securities have readily determinable fair values. Those equity securities in the current portfolio are considered trading securities. At the beginning of the year, the market value of each security exceeded cost.

During the year, some of the securities increased in value. These securities (some in the current portfolio and some in the long-term portfolio) were sold. At the end of the year, the market value of each of the remaining securities was less than original cost.

Victoria also has investments in long-term bonds, which the company intends to hold to maturity. All of the bonds were purchased at face value. During the year some of these bonds were called by the issuer prior to maturity. In each case the call price was in excess of par value. Three months before the end of the year, additional similar bonds were purchased for face value plus two months' accrued interest.

Required:
a. How should Victoria account for the sale of the securities from each portfolio? Why?
b. How should Victoria account for the marketable equity securities portfolios at year-end? Why?
c. How should Victoria account for the disposition prior to their maturity of the long-term bonds called by their issuer? Why?
d. How should Victoria report the purchase of the additional similar bonds at the date of acquisition? Why?

• Case 8-5

On July 1, 1994, Dynamic Company purchased for cash 40 percent of the outstanding capital stock of Cart Company. Both Dynamic Company and Cart Company have a December 31 year-end. Cart Company, whose common stock is actively traded in the over-the-counter market, reported its total net income for the year to Dynamic Company, and also paid cash dividends on November 15, 1994, to Dynamic and its other stockholders.

Required:
How should Dynamic Company report the foregoing facts in its December 31, 1994, balance sheet and its income statement for the year then ended? Discuss the rationale for your answer.

● Case 8-6

The Thomas Company is in the process of developing a revolutionary new product. A new division of the company was formed to develop, manufacture, and market this new product. As of year-end (December 31, 1994) the new product has not been manufactured for resale; however, a prototype unit was built and is in operation.

Throughout 1994 the new division incurred certain costs. These costs include design and engineering studies, prototype manufacturing costs, administrative expenses (including salaries of administrative personnel), and market research costs. In addition, approximately $500,000 in equipment (estimated useful life, 10 years) was purchased for use in developing and manufacturing the preproduction prototype and will be used to manufacture the new product. Approximately $200,000 of this equipment was built specifically for the design development of the new product; the remaining $300,000 of equipment was used to manufacture the new product once it is in commercial production.

Required:
a. What is the definition of *research* and *development* as defined in *Statement of Financial Accounting Standards No. 2?*
b. Briefly indicate the practical and conceptual reasons for the conclusion reached by the Financial Accounting Standards Board on accounting and reporting practices for research and development costs.
c. In accordance with *Statement of Financial Accounting Standards No. 2,* how should the various costs of Thomas just described be recorded in the financial statements for the year ended December 31, 1994?

● Case 8-7

The Financial Accounting Standards Board issued *Statement of Financial Standards No. 115* to describe the accounting treatment that should be afforded to equity securities that have readily determinable market values that are not accounted for under the equity method or consolidation. An important part of the statement concerns the distinction between trading securities and available-for-sale securities.

Required:
a. Compare and contrast trading securities and available-for-sale securities.
b. How are the trading securities and available-for-sale securities classified in the balance sheet? In your answer, discuss the factors that should be considered in determining whether a security is classified as trading or available-for-sale and as current or noncurrent.
c. How do the above classifications affect the accounting treatment for unrealized losses?
d. Why does a company maintain an investment portfolio containing current and noncurrent securities?

• Case 8-8

Presented below are four unrelated situations involving equity securities that have readily determinable fair values.

Situation 1

A noncurrent portfolio with an aggregate market value in excess of cost includes one particular security whose market value has declined to less than one-half of the original cost. The decline in value is considered to be other than temporary.

Situation 2

The balance sheet of a company does not classify assets and liabilities as current and noncurrent. The portfolio of marketable equity securities includes securities normally considered to be trading securities that have a net cost in excess of market value of $2,000. The remainder of the portfolio is considered noncurrent and has a net market value in excess of cost of $5,000.

Situation 3

A marketable equity security, whose market value is currently less than cost, is classified as a noncurrent security that is available-for-sale but is to be reclassified as a trading security.

Situation 4

A company's noncurrent portfolio of marketable equity securities consists of the common stock of one company. At the end of the prior year the market value of the security was 50 percent of original cost, and the effect was properly reflected in the balance sheet. However, at the end of the current year the market value of the security had appreciated to twice the original cost. The security is still considered noncurrent at year-end.

Required:

Determine the effect on classification, carrying value, and earnings for each of the preceding situations. Complete your response to each situation before proceeding to the next situation.

Recommended Additional Readings

Bierman, Harold Jr., and Roland E. Dukes. "Accounting for Research and Development Costs." *Journal of Accountancy* (April 1975), pp. 44–55.

Davis, Michael. "Goodwill Accounting: Time for an Overhaul." *Journal of Accountancy* (June 1992), pp. 75–78, 80, 82, 83.

Duval, Linda, Ross Jennings, John Robinson, and Robert B. Thompson II. "Can Investors Unravel the Effects of Goodwill Accounting?" *Accounting Horizons* (June 1992), pp. 1–14.

Nix, Paul E., and David E. Nix. "A Historical Review of the Accounting Treatment of Research and Development Costs." *The Accounting Historians' Journal* (June 1992), pp. 51–78.

Pactor, Paul A. "Applying APB Opinion No. 18—Equity Method." *Journal of Accountancy* (September 1971), pp. 54–62.

Parks, James T. "The Portfolio Accounting Controversy." *Journal of Accountancy* (November 1989), pp. 81–84, 86.

Pizzy, Alan. "Accounting for Goodwill and Brands." *Management Accounting* (September 1991), pp. 22, 23, 26.

Swieringa, Robert J. "Recognition and Measurement Issues in Accounting for Secured Assets." *Journal of Accounting Auditing and Finance* (Spring 1989), pp. 169–186.

Wines, Grueme, and Colin Ferguson. "An Empirical Investigation of Accounting Methods for Goodwill and Intangible Assets." *Abacus* (March 1993), pp. 90–105.

Bibliography

Abdel-khalik, A. Rashad. "Advertising Effectiveness and Accounting Policy." *The Accounting Review* (October 1975), pp. 657–670.

Barrett, M. Edgar. "Accounting for Intercorporate Investments: A Behavioral Field Experiment." *Journal of Accounting Research. Empirical Research in Accounting* (1971), pp. 50–65.

Barrett, M. Edgar. "APB Opinion No. 18: A Move Toward Preferences of Users." *Financial Analysts Journal* (July–August 1972), pp. 47–50, 52–55.

Catlett, George R., and Norman O. Olson. "Accounting for Goodwill." *Accounting Research Study No. 10.* New York: AICPA, 1968.

Clinch, Greg, and Joseph Magliolo. "Market Perceptions of Reserve Disclosures Under SFAS No. 69." *The Accounting Review* (October 1992), pp. 843–861.

Copeland, Ronald M., Robert Strawser, and John G. Binns. "Accounting for Investments in Common Stock." *Financial Executive* (February 1972), pp. 36–38ff.

Dukes, Roland E. "An Investigation of the Effects of Expensing Research and Development Costs on Security Prices." In *Proceedings in the Conference on Tropical Research in Accounting,* Michael Schiff and George Sorter, eds. New York: New York University, 1976, pp. 147–193.

Elliot, John, Gordon Richardson, Thomas Dyckman, and Roland Dukes. "The Impact of SFAS No. 2 on Firm Expenditures on Research and Development: Replications and Extensions." *Journal of Accounting Research* (Spring 1984), pp. 85–102.

Falk, Haim, and Joseph C. Miller. "Amortization of Advertising Expenditures." *Journal of Accounting Research* (Spring 1977), pp. 12–22.

Gellein, Oscar S., and Maurice S. Newman. "Accounting for Research and Development Expenditures." *Accounting Research Study No. 14.* New York: AICPA, 1973.

Gridley, F. W. "Accounting for R&D Costs." *Financial Executive* (April 1974), pp. 18–22.

Gynther, Reg S. "Some Conceptualizing on Goodwill." *The Accounting Review* (April 1969), pp. 247–255.

Johnson, Orace. "A Consequential Approach to Accounting for R&D." *Journal of Accounting Research* (Autumn 1967), pp. 164–172.

Lall, R. M. "Conceptual Veracity of Goodwill." *Accountancy* (October 1968), pp. 728–732.

Lee, T. A. "Goodwill: An Example of Will-o'-the-Wisp Accounting." *Accounting and Business Research* (Autumn 1971), pp. 318–328.

Lynch, Thomas Edward. "Accounting for Investments in Equity Securities by the Equity and Market Value Methods." *Financial Analysts' Journal* (January–February 1975), pp. 62–69.

MacIntosh, J. C. C. "Problem of Accounting for Goodwill." *Accountancy* (November 1974), pp. 30–32.

Miller, Malcolm C. "Goodwill—An Aggregation Issue." *The Accounting Review* (April 1973), pp. 280–291.

Munter, Paul, and Thomas A. Ratcliff. "Accounting for Research and Development Activities." *The CPA Journal* (April 1983), pp. 54–65.

Newman, Maurice S. "Accounting for Research and Development Expenditures." *The CPA Journal* (April 1974), pp. 55–58.

O'Connor, Melvin C., and James C. Hamre. "Alternative Methods of Accounting for Long-Term Nonsubsidiary Intercorporate Investments in Common Stock." *The Accounting Review* (April 1972), pp. 308–319.

Picconi, Mario J. "A Reconsideration of the Recognition of Advertising Assets on Financial Statements." *Journal of Accounting Research* (Autumn 1977), pp. 317–326.

Sands, John E. *Wealth, Income and Intangibles.* Toronto: Toronto University Press, 1963.

Tearney, Michael G. "Accounting for Goodwill: A Realistic Approach." *Journal of Accountancy* (July 1973), pp. 41–45.

Tearney, Michael G. "Compliance with the AICPA Pronouncements on Accounting for Goodwill." *The CPA Journal* (February 1973), pp. 121–125.

Weinwurm, Ernest H. "Modernizing the Goodwill Concept." *Management Accounting* (December 1971), pp. 31–34.

Wesley, Charles E., and Thomas J. Linsmeier. "A Further Examination of the Economic Consequences of SFAS No. 2." *Journal of Accounting Research* (Spring 1992), pp. 156–164.

Zucca, Linda J., and David R. Campbell. "A Closer Look at Discretionary Writedowns of Impaired Assets." *Accounting Horizons* (September 1992), pp. 30–41.

Long-Term
Liabilities

The importance of short-term liabilities as an element of working capital was discussed in Chapter 6. In this chapter we examine the nature of long-term liabilities. The emphasis will be on the recognition and measurement of transactions and events as liabilities, with specific attention to some of the more troublesome aspects.

Investors, creditors, and other users view the separation of liabilities into their current and noncurrent elements as important because their decision models utilize the working capital concept, current ratios, and projections of expected future cash flows to analyze and compare the performance of firms. Moreover, the amount of long-term debt relative to equity is also relevant because the debt-to-equity ratio is directly related to the risk associated with investing in the firm's stock.[1] As the debt-to-equity ratio of a firm increases, the market's perception of the riskiness of investing in the firm's stock also rises. Thus, it is important that accountants have criteria to appropriately classify liabilities as short-term or long-term so that decision makers can reliably evaluate the firm's ability to meet current needs and to determine the level of riskiness inherent in projections of future cash flows over time.

The Definition of Liabilities

Statement of Financial Accounting Concepts (*SFAC*) *No. 6* describes the elements comprising the balance sheet as assets, liabilities, and equity. Assets have fu-

---

[1] See Robert S. Hamada, "The Effect of the Firm's Capital Structure on the Systematic Risk of Common Stocks," *The Journal of Finance* (March 1969), pp. 13–31, and Mark E. Rubinstein, "A Mean-Variance Synthesis of Corporate Financial Theory," *The Journal of Finance* (May 1973), pp. 167–181.

401

ture economic benefit. Liabilities and equity provide resources (capital) for the acquisition of assets. The amount of liabilities a firm has relative to equity is termed the firm's capital structure.

In current accounting practice, liabilities and equity are treated as two separate and distinct elements of the firm's capital structure. This distinction is apparent in the fundamental accounting equation

$$\text{assets} = \text{liabilities} + \text{equity}$$

Accordingly, liabilities and equity are both claimants to enterprise assets; but equity represents an ownership interest, whereas liabilities are creditor claims. These interests are different and their separate disclosure is relevant to decision makers who rely on published financial information.[2]

Theories of equity postulate how the balance sheet elements are related and have implications for the definitions of both liabilities and equity. The two prominent theories of equity—entity theory and proprietary theory—imply unique relationships between assets, liabilities, and equity.

The *entity theory* depicts the accounting equation as

$$\text{assets} = \text{equities}$$

According to the entity theory, there is no fundamental difference between liabilities and owners' equity.[3] They both provide capital to the business entity and receive income in return in the form of interest and dividends. Under entity theory, liabilities and equity would require separate line disclosure in the balance sheet, but there would be no subtotals for total liabilities or total equity, and no need for separate or distinct definitions for each.

The *proprietary theory* views the net assets of the firm as belonging to the owners.[4] Under this theory, equity is equal to the net worth of the owners. The proprietary theory relationship is articulated as

$$\text{assets} - \text{liabilities} = \text{equity}$$

Although the AICPA, APB, and FASB have not formally described this relationship as the theory underlying the elements of financial statements, the APB defined liabilities and owners' equity in *Statement No. 4* and stated that the approach implicit in their definitions is that assets minus liabilities equals owners' equity.[5]

[2] See Myrtle W. Clark, "Entity Theory, Modern Capital Structure Theory, and the Distinction between Debt and Equity," *Accounting Horizons* (September 1993).

[3] William A. Paton, *Accounting Theory* (New York: Ronald Press Co., 1922), p. 73.

[4] Henry Rand Hatfield, *Accounting, Its Principles and Problems* (New York: D. Appleton & Co., 1927) pp. 171, 221.

[5] Accounting Principles Board, *Statement No. 4*, "Basic Concepts and Accounting Principles Underlying Financial Statements of Business Enterprises" (New York: AICPA, 1970), par. 132.

In addition, *SFAC No. 6* has defined liabilities and equities in a manner that is also consistent with proprietary theory as follows.

Liabilities—probable future sacrifices of economic benefits arising from present obligations of a particular entity to transfer assets or provide services to other entities in the future as a result of past transactions or events.

Equities—the residual interest in the assets of an entity that remains after deducting its liabilities. In a business enterprise the equity is the ownership.[6]

Recognition and Measurement of Liabilities

According to *SFAC No. 5*, to recognize an item as a liability in financial statements, it must meet the definition of liabilities found in *SFAC No. 6*, and it must be measurable. Accountants take a transactions approach to measuring liabilities.[7] Liabilities are measured at the amount established in an exchange. Theoretically, liabilities should be measured at the present value of the future cash flows, discounted at the market rate of interest. The discounted present value measures the fair market value of the liability at issuance. For example, as described in detail in a later section, the issue price of a bond represents the present value of the interest payments and the maturity value, discounted at the market rate of interest. Discounting is generally ignored for current liabilities because the undiscounted value is not materially different from the discounted present value.

The classification and measurement of items as liabilities is not always straightforward. For example, the FASB has recently issued a pronouncement requiring the recognition as liabilities of the present value of postretirement benefits, such as health-care for retired employees, even though the benefits may not be paid for many years in the future and there is a great deal of uncertainty surrounding projections of future cash flows. The FASB supports this kind of recognition by referring to the *SFAC No. 6* definition of liabilities. Postretirement benefits represent sacrifices of future resources resulting from employees having earned those future benefits during present and prior accounting periods.

Unfortunately, the definitions in *SFAC No. 6*, like those in *APB Statement No. 4*, leave many unresolved questions. In the following section we will examine some of these questions and attempt to develop more specific criteria for the proper classification of items as liabilities.

Debt Versus Equity

The preceding definitions require the classification of all items on the right-hand side of the balance sheet into their liability or equity components. This requirement presumes that all financial interests in the enterprise are liability

---

[6] Financial Accounting Standards Board, *Statement of Financial Accounting Concepts No. 6*, "Elements of Financial Statements" (Stamford, Conn.: FASB, 1985), pars. 35 and 49.

[7] Ibid., par. 67, and APB, op. cit., par. 181.

or equity interests, and further assumes that these distinctions are readily apparent to whoever is preparing financial statements. There are at least two fallacies in these assumptions: (1) the wide variety of securities issued by the modern complex corporation does not readily lend itself to classification schemes, and (2) there are no authoritative guidelines to use in applying the classification schemes. What one individual may view as debt another may view as equity.

The FASB has recognized that these problems exist in their recent discussion memorandum titled "Distinguishing between Liability and Equity Instruments and Accounting for Instruments with Characteristics of Both."[8] The impetus for the discussion memorandum is the increasing use of *complex financial instruments,* which have both debt and equity characteristics.

An example of a security presenting this type of dilemma is redeemable preferred stock. Under current GAAP, redeemable preferred stock is considered equity even though it must be repaid. Nevertheless the SEC has ruled that future cash obligations attached to preferred stock that is subject to mandatory redemption or whose redemption is outside the control of the issuer should be highlighted so as to distinguish it from permanent capital.[9] These securities must not be included under the heading, stockholders' equity. Moreover, they may not be included in total liabilities. The SEC has in effect created a separate *"temporary" equity* balance sheet category. Such a category is not recognized as an element of financial statements in *SFAC No. 6.*

So long as accountants feel that the present sharp distinction between debt and equity should be continued, such examples point to the need for accountants to develop additional criteria to aid in classifying items on the right-hand side of the accounting equation as either debt or equity. A discussion of some of the decision factors that may be used is contained in the following section.

Consolidated Set of Decision Factors

The following set of 13 factors is presented as a guide to assist in determining the classification of items on the right-hand side of the accounting equation as either debt or equity. The sequence in which the factors are presented is not intended to reflect any judgment about their relative importance.

Maturity Date

Debt instruments typically have a fixed maturity date, whereas equity instruments do not mature. Because they do mature, debt instruments set forth the redemption requirements, and one of the requirements may be the establish-

---

[8] FASB Discussion Memorandum, "Distinguishing between Liability and Equity Instruments and Accounting for Instruments with Characteristics of Both" (Stamford, Conn.: FASB, August 20, 1990).

[9] U. S. Securities and Exchange Commission, Accounting Series Release No. 268, *Presentation in Financial Statements of "Redeemable Preferred Stocks."* In *SEC Accounting Rules* (Chicago: Commerce Clearing House, Inc., 1983).

ment of a sinking fund in order to ensure that funds will be available for the redemption.

Claim on Assets
In the event the business is liquidated, creditors' claims take precedence over those of the owners. There are two possible interpretations of this factor. The first is that all claims other than the first priority are equity claims. The second is that all claims other than the last are creditor claims. The problem area involves all claims between these two interpretations: Those claims that are subordinated to the first claim but take precedence over the last claim.

Claim on Income
A fixed dividend or interest rate has a preference over other dividend or interest payments; that it is cumulative in the event it is not paid for a particular period is considered to indicate a debt security. On the other hand, a security that does not provide for a fixed rate, one that gives the holder the right to participate with common stockholders in any income distribution, or one whose claim is subordinate to other claims may indicate an ownership interest.

Market Valuations
Market valuations of liabilities are not affected by company performance so long as the company is solvent. Conversely, the market price of equity securities is affected by the earnings of the company and investor expectations regarding future dividend payments.

Voice in Management
The most frequent evidence of a voice in the management of a corporation is a voting right. This right is normally limited to common stockholders, but it may be extended to other investors if the company defaults on some predetermined conditions. For example, if interest is not paid when due or profits fall below a certain level, voting rights may be granted to other security holders, thus suggesting that the security in question has ownership characteristics.

Maturity Value
A liability has a fixed maturity value that does not change throughout the life of the liability. An ownership interest does not mature, except in the event of liquidation; consequently, there is no maturity value.

Intent of Parties
The courts have determined that the intent of the parties is one factor to be evaluated in ruling on the debt or equity nature of a particular security. Investor attitude and investment character are two subfactors that help in making this determination. Investors may be divided into those who want safety and those who want capital growth, and the investments may be divided into those that provide either safety or an opportunity for capital gains or losses. If the investor was motivated to make a particular investment on the basis of safety and if the corporation included in the issue those features normally equated with safety, then there is an indication that the security is debt rather than equity. However, if the investor was motivated to acquire the security

by the possibility of capital growth and if the security offered the opportunity of capital growth, the security will be viewed as equity rather than debt.

Preemptive Right
A security that is included in the preemptive right of common stockholders (the right to purchase common shares in a new stock offering by the corporation) may be considered to have an equity characteristic. Securities not carrying this right may be considered debt.

Conversion Features
A security that may be converted into common stock has at least the potential to become equity if it is not currently considered equity. A historical study of eventual conversion or liquidation may be useful in evaluating this particular factor.

Potential Dilution of Earnings per Share
This factor might be considered as a subfactor of *conversion* because the conversion feature of a security is the most likely cause of dilution of earnings per share, other than a new issue of common stock. In any event, a security that has the potential to dilute earnings per share is assumed to have equity characteristics.

Right to Enforce Payments
From a legal point of view, creditors have the right to receive periodic interest at the agreed-upon date and to have the maturity value paid at the maturity date. The enforcement of this right may result in the corporation being placed in receivership. Owners have no such legal right; therefore, the existence of the right to enforce payment is an indication of a debt instrument.

Good Business Reasons for Issuing
Determining what constitutes good business reasons for issuing a security with certain features rather than one with different features presents a difficult problem. Two relevant subfactors are the alternatives available and the amount of capitalization. Securities issued by a company in financial difficulty or with a low level of capitalization may be considered equity on the grounds that only those with an ownership interest would be willing to accept the risk, whereas securities issued by a company with a high level of capitalization may be viewed as debt.

Identity of Interest Between Creditors and Owners
When the individuals who invest in debt securities are the same individuals, or family members, who hold the common stock, an ownership interest is indicated.

Long-Term Debt Classification

Once a particular security has been classified as a liability, it may be recorded as either a current liability or a long-term liability. The classification of an item as a long-term liability is based on the one-year or current-operating-cycle rule. If the settlement of an existing obligation is not expected to use an asset properly classified as current or be replaced by another current liability, it is classified as a long-term liability. The most frequently encountered long-term liabilities are bonds payable, long-term notes payable, lease obligations, pension obligations, deferred taxes, other long-term deferrals, and, occasionally, contingent liabilities. Leases, pensions, and taxes are discussed separately in the following chapters. In this section we examine the recording and reporting requirements for bonds, notes, deferrals, and contingencies.

Bonds Payable

When additional funds are needed to expand the business or for current operations, a corporation has the choice of issuing debt or equity securities. There are four basic reasons why a corporation may wish to issue debt rather than equity securities.

1. *Bonds may be the only available source of funds.*   Many small and medium-size companies may appear too risky for investors to make a permanent investment.

2. *Debt financing has a lower cost.*   Since bonds have a lower investment risk than stock, they traditionally have paid relatively low rates of interest. Investors acquiring equity securities generally expect a greater return. In recent years, however, market conditions have changed, and the cost of debt financing has been more volatile.

3. *Debt financing offers a tax advantage.*   Payments to debt holders in the form of interest are deductible for income tax purposes, whereas dividends on equity securities are not.

4. *The voting privilege is not shared.*   If a stockholder wishes to maintain his or her present percentage ownership in a corporation, he or she must purchase the current ownership portion of each new common stock issue. Debt issues do not carry ownership or voting rights; consequently they do not dilute voting power. Where the portion of ownership is small and holdings widespread, this consideration is probably not very important.

The use of borrowed funds is known as *trading on the equity.* The customary reason for using borrowed funds is the expectation of investing them in a capital project that will provide a return in excess of the cost of the acquired funds. The stockholders' investment serves as protection for the bondholders' principal and income, and the strength of current earnings and the debt–equity relationship both influence the rate of interest required by the debt holder. When using debt financing it should be recognized that trading on the equity increases the rate of return to common stockholders only when the return on the project is greater than the cost of the borrowed funds. Earnings (less their related tax effect) in excess of interest payments will increase earnings per share. However, if the return on the investment project falls below the stipulated bond interest rate, earnings per share will decline.

Bond Classifications

Bonds frequently are classified by the nature of the protection offered by the company. Bonds that are secured by a lien against specific assets of the corporation are known as *mortgage bonds*. In the event the corporation becomes bankrupt and is liquidated, the holders of mortgage bonds have first claim against the proceeds from the sale of the assets that secured their debt. If the proceeds from the sale of secured assets are not sufficient to repay the debt, mortgage bondholders become general creditors for the remainder of the unpaid debt.

Debenture bonds are not secured by any property or assets, and their marketability is based on the general credit of the corporation. A long period of earnings and continued favorable predictions are necessary for a company to sell debenture bonds. Debenture bondholders become general creditors of the corporation in the event of liquidation.

Bond Selling Prices

Bonds are generally sold in $1,000 denominations and carry a stated amount of interest. The *stated interest rate* is printed on the *bond indenture* (contract). It determines the amount of interest that will be paid to the investor at the end of each interest period. The stated rate will approximate the rate management believes necessary to sell the bonds given the current state of the economy and the perceived risk associated with the bonds. A bond issued with a relatively low amount of perceived risk will offer a lower interest rate than a bond issue with a relatively higher amount of risk.

The decision to issue bonds and their subsequent sale may take place over a relatively long period of time. From the time the bonds are authorized until they are issued, economic conditions affecting interest rates may change. As a result, at issuance the stated interest rate may differ from the *market rate* for bonds of similar perceived risk. The investor will be unwilling to invest in a bond yielding interest at a rate less than the market rate. Similarly, the issuing company will be unwilling to issue a bond yielding an interest rate that is higher than the market rate. Because the stated rate is predetermined and cannot be changed, the market price is adjusted so that the *effective rate* of interest is equal to the market rate.

The rate of interest necessary to sell a bond issue is known as the *yield rate* on the bonds. The amount investors are willing to invest is the amount that will yield the market rate of interest, given the amount and timing of the stated interest payments and the *maturity value* of the bonds. Thus, the issue price of the bond is equal to the sum of the present value of the principal and interest payments, discounted at the yield rate. If investors are willing to accept the interest rate stated on the bonds, they will be sold at their *face value*, or *par*, and the yield rate will equal the stated interest rate. When the market rate of interest exceeds the stated interest rate, the bonds will sell below face value (at a *discount*), thereby increasing the effective interest rate. Alternatively, when the market rate of interest is less than the stated interest rate, the bonds will sell above face value (at a *premium*), thereby lowering the effective interest rate.

To illustrate, assume that the XYZ Corporation issued $100,000 of 10 percent, 10-year bonds on January 1, 1996. Interest on these bonds is to be paid annually each December 31. If these bonds are actually sold to yield 9 percent, the bond selling price will be calculated as follows.

Present value of maturity value	
$100,000 × 0.422411[a]	$ 42,241.10
Present value of interest payments	
$10,000 × 6.417658[b]	64,176.58
	$106,417.68

[a] Present value of $1 : $i = 0.09$, $n = 10$.
[b] Present value of an ordinary annuity of $1 : $i = 0.09$, $n = 10$.

Since investors must accept an interest rate lower than the rate stated on the bonds, the bond selling price will be higher than the face value of the bonds. The increased selling price has the effect of lowering the yield rate. That is, the amount of interest stipulated on the bonds will be the amount paid to investors each interest payment date, but the actual cash amount invested has increased. The result is that total interest expense over the life of the bonds will be less than the stated amount of interest by the amount of the premium.

Total interest paid		
$10,000 × 10	$100,000.00	$100,000.00
Principal payment at maturity	100,000.00	
Total paid by the borrower	$200,000.00	
Issue price	106,417.68	
Total Interest expense	$ 93,582.32	93,582.32
Premium on the bonds		$ 6,417.68

On the other hand, assume that the rate of interest required by investors is 12 percent. The bond selling price will be reduced to achieve a higher yield rate as follows.

Present value of maturity value	
$100,000 × 0.321973[a]	$32,197.30
Present value of interest payments	
$10,000 × 5.650223[b]	56,502.23
	$88,699.53

[a] Present value of $1 : $i = 12$, $n = 10$.
[b] Present value of an ordinary annuity of $1 : $i = 12$, $n = 10$.

In this case the yield rate is higher than the stated rate because the cash payment to investors remains the same while the amount borrowed has decreased. The total interest expense over the life of the bonds will exceed the total interest payments by the amount of the discount, $11,300.47 ($100,000 − 88,699.53).

When bonds are issued between interest payment dates, because interest payments are fixed by the bond indenture, investors will receive the full amount of the interest payment on the interest payment date even though the bonds have not been held for the entire interest period. To compensate the issuer, the investor pays interest accrued from the contract date to the date of issuance. The *accrued interest* will be repaid to the investor on the next interest payment date and therefore is a current liability to the issuing corporation. The issue price is determined by discounting the maturity value and interest payments from the contract date to maturity plus the return on the bond from the contract date to the date of issuance minus the amount of accrued interest paid.

Bond Issue Costs

The costs to issue bonds may be substantial. The issuing corporation incurs attorney's fees, costs to print the bonds, the cost of preparing the bond prospectus, and sales brokerage commissions. Under *APB Opinion No. 21, bond issue costs* are treated as a deferred charge and shown on the balance sheet as an asset. The asset is amortized from the date of issue to the maturity date of the bonds. The rationale for this treatment is that the costs were incurred to derive benefit from the issuance of the bonds because the debt proceeds contribute to the earnings process. Consequently, they represent future service potential and are assets.

In contrast, debt issue costs were cited by *SFAC No. 6* as an expenditure that does not meet the definition of an asset.[10] The FASB argued that these costs reduce the proceeds of borrowing, resulting in a higher effective interest rate. Consequently, they have no future benefit. This argument provides a basis for adding the discount to the carrying value of the debt and allowing it to affect the calculation of periodic interest expense. Alternatively, the FASB stated that because they provide no future benefit, debt issue costs may be treated as an expense of the period of borrowing.[11]

Bond Interest Expense

Interest is the cost of borrowing, and because debt is borrowed over a period of time, it should be allocated over the period benefited. As shown above, the total interest over the life of the bond issue is affected by the presence of a

---

[10] Financial Accounting Standards Board, *Statements of Financial Accounting Concepts No. 6,* "Elements of Financial Statements" (Stamford, Conn.: FASB, 1985), par. 237.

[11] Ibid.

premium or discount. In these cases, the calculation of *interest expense* involves amortization of the premium or discount. There are two methods of allocating interest expense and the associated premium or discount over the life of the bond issue: (1) the straight-line method and (2) the effective interest method. Under the *straight-line method*, the total discount or premium is divided by the total number of interest periods to arrive at the amount to be amortized each period. This method gives an equal allocation per period and results in a stable interest cost per period.

However, the assumption of a stable interest cost per interest period is not realistic when a premium or discount is involved. The original selling price of the bonds was set to yield the market rate of interest. Therefore, the more valid assumption is that the yield rate should be reflected over the life of the bond issue. The *effective interest method* satisfies this objective by applying the yield rate to the varying value of the bonds in each successive period to determine the amount of interest expense to record. When using the effective interest method, the premium or discount amortization is determined by finding the difference between the stated interest payment and the amount of interest expense recorded for the period.

The effective interest method is theoretically preferable because it results in a stable interest rate per period and discloses a liability balance on the balance sheet equivalent to the present value of the future cash flows at the original market rate of interest. Additionally, *APB Opinion No. 21* requires the use of the effective interest method unless the results obtained from the use of the straight-line method are not materially different. Some companies use the straight-line method because it is easy to calculate, and because the difference between income statement and balance sheet values reported under the two methods from period to period are relatively minor.

Zero Coupon Bonds

A *zero coupon* or *deep discount bond* is a bond sold at considerably less than its face value that does not provide periodic interest payments or carry a stated rate of interest. The interest cost to the issuer is determined by the effective interest method and allocates the total discount over the life of the bond issue. For example, if $100,000 of zero coupon bonds with a life of 10 years are issued to yield 12 percent, the issue price will be $32,197 and the unamortized discount will be $67,803.

Many accountants have questioned the logic of purchasing zero coupon bonds because of the Internal Revenue Code regulation that requires investors to include the yearly discount amortization as income prior to the time the cash interest is actually received. However, zero coupon bonds became popular with pension funds because (1) they usually do not contain a call provision and therefore the stated return is guaranteed until maturity and (2) they offer *reinvestment return*, which means that all the interest is reinvested at the same rate of return over the life of the issue. In addition, the income from pension investments is tax deferred. No tax is paid until distributions are made during retirement.

Call Provisions

Long-term debt is issued under the prevailing market conditions at the time it is issued. In unfavorable market conditions it may be necessary to pay unusually high interest rates or to include promises in the *bond indenture* (the agreement between the issuing corporation and the bondholders) that inhibit the financial operation of the company. For example, the indenture may include restrictions on dividends, a promise to maintain a certain working capital position, or the maintenance of a certain debt–equity relationship.

Most companies protect themselves from the inability to take advantage of future favorable changes in market conditions by including a call provision in the bond indenture. This provision allows the company to recall debt at a prestated percentage of the issue price.

The recall, or *early extinguishment*, of debt may take two forms: (1) the borrowed funds may no longer be needed and the debt is therefore canceled, which is termed *debt retirement*; or (2) the existing debt may be replaced with another debt issue, termed *debt refunding*.

The cancellation of existing debt poses no particular accounting problem. Any gain or loss resulting from the difference between the carrying value and the call price is treated as a gain or loss in the year the cancellation takes place. The theory behind this treatment is that the recall of the debt was a current decision and should therefore be reflected in current income.

The argument is not quite so convincing in the case of refunding transactions. In *ARB No. 43,* three methods of accounting for the gain or loss from a refunding transaction were discussed.

1. Make a direct write-off of the gain or loss in the year of the transaction.

2. Amortize the gain or loss over the remaining life of the original issue.

3. Amortize the gain or loss over the life of the new issue.[12]

Recognizing the gain or loss over the remaining life of the old issue is favored by some accountants because they view this as the period of benefit—that is, a higher interest cost would have been incurred during this period if the old issue had not been refunded. Those who favor recognizing the gain or loss over the life of the new issue base their argument on the matching concept, that is, the lower interest rates obtained by the refunding should be adjusted to reflect any refunding gain or loss. Finally, those accountants favoring immediate write-off argue that this method is the most logical because the value of the debt has changed over time, and paying the call price is the most favorable method of eliminating the debt.

ARB No. 43 stated a preference for the first method and allowed the second. Later, *APB Opinion No. 6* allowed the use of the third method under

---

[12] *Accounting Research Bulletin No. 43,* "Restatement and Revision of Accounting Research Bulletins" (New York: AICPA, 1953).

certain circumstances.[13] In effect, these two releases frequently permitted a company to use any one of three available methods.

After a subsequent reexamination of the topic, the APB issued *Opinion No. 26*, "Early Extinguishment of Debt."[14] In this release the Board took the position that all early extinguishments were fundamentally alike (whether retirements or refundings) and that they should be accounted for in the same manner. Since the accounting treatment of retirements was to reflect any gain or loss in the period of recall, it was concluded that any gains or losses from refunding should also be reflected currently in income. Thus, options two and three are no longer considered acceptable under generally accepted accounting principles.

A short time later, the FASB undertook a study of the reporting requirements for gains and losses arising from early extinguishment of debt. This review was undertaken because of pressure from the SEC. Prevailing market conditions in 1973 and 1974 allowed several companies to reacquire long-term debt at prices well below face value. For example, in 1973 United Brands was able to realize a $37.5 million gain by exchanging $12.5 million in cash and $75 million in 9⅛ percent debentures for $125 million of 5½ percent convertible subordinated debentures. This entire gain was reported as ordinary income.

Upon completion of its study, *SFAS No. 4*, "Reporting Gains and Losses from Extinguishment of Debt,"[15] was issued. This release requires gains and losses on all extinguishments, whether early or at scheduled maturity, to be classified as extraordinary items without regard to the criteria of "unusual nature" or "infrequency of occurrence." Additionally, the following disclosures are required.

1. *A description of the extinguishment transactions, including the sources of any funds used to extinguish debt if it is practicable to identify the sources.*

2. *The income tax effect in the period of extinguishment.*

3. *The per share amount of the aggregate gain or loss net of related tax effect.*[16]

Subsequently, *APB Opinion No. 26* was amended by *Statement of Financial Accounting Standards No. 76*, "Extinguishment of Debt." This release made the provisions of *APB Opinion No. 26* applicable to all debt extinguishments, whether early or not, except those specifically exempted by other pronouncements (e.g., debt restructurings). Debt was considered to be extinguished in the following circumstances.

---

[13] *Accounting Principles Board Opinion No. 6*, "Status of Accounting Research Bulletins" (New York: AICPA, 1965).

[14] *Accounting Principles Board Opinion No. 26*, "Early Extinguishment of Debt" (New York: AICPA, 1972).

[15] Financial Accounting Standards Board, *Statement of Financial Accounting Standards No. 4*, "Reporting Gains or Losses from Extinguishment of Debt" (Stamford, Conn.: FASB, 1975).

[16] Ibid., par. 9.

1. The debtor has paid the creditor and is relieved of all obligations regardless of whether the securities are canceled or held as treasury bonds by the debtor.

2. The debtor is legally released from being the primary obligor by the creditor, and it is probable that no future payment will be required (*legal defeasance*).

3. The debtor places cash or other essentially risk-free securities (such as government securities) in a trust used solely for satisfying both the scheduled interest payments and principal of a specific obligation, with the possibility of future payments being remote (*in substance defeasance*).

Under the third situation, known as in substance defeasance, the debt is considered extinguished even though the debtor is not legally released from being the primary obligor of the debt. The principles of in substance defeasance are as follows.

1. Government securities are purchased that have face values, maturity dates, and interest rates nearly identical to those of the debt being retired.

2. The purchased government securities and the debt being retired are placed in an irrevocable trust. The purpose of this trust is to satisfy the principal and interest obligations of the debt issue.

This treatment created a controversy among some accountants, who claimed it could allow management to manipulate income—that is, a gain on extinguishment could be recorded when the debtor has not been legally released from the obligation.

This criticism resulted in a review of the provisions of *SFAS No. 76* as they related to instantaneous in substance defeasance transactions (where the interest rate on the purchased securities is higher than that on the debt). This review resulted in release of *FASB Technical Bulletin 84-4*. It requires a company involved in an in substance defeasance transaction to report separately the assets and debt and the interest revenue and expense.

Convertible Debt

Senior securities (bonds or preferred stock) that are convertible into common stock at the election of the bondholder play a frequent role in corporate financing. There is rather widespread agreement that firms sell convertible securities for one of two primary reasons. Either the firm wants to increase equity capital and decides that convertible securities are the most advantageous way, or the firm wants to increase its debt or preferred stock and discovers that the conversion feature is necessary to make the security sufficiently marketable at a reasonable interest or dividend rate. Additionally, there are several other factors that, at one time or another, may motivate corporate management to decide to issue convertible debt. Among these are to

1. Avoid the downward price pressures on the firm's stock that placing a large new issue of common stock on the market would cause.

2. Avoid dilution of earnings and increased dividend requirements while an expansion program is getting under way.

3. Avoid the direct sale of common stock when the corporation believes that its stock is currently undervalued in the market.

4. Penetrate that segment of the capital market that is unwilling or unable to participate in a direct common stock issue.

5. Minimize the flotation cost (costs associated with selling securities).

The remainder of this section will concentrate on convertible debt. Convertible preferred stock is discussed in Chapter 13.

Accounting for *convertible debt* has been the subject of controversy for a number of years. Convertible debt is a *complex financial instrument.* Complex financial instruments combine two or more fundamental financial instruments. Convertible debt combines debt with the option to convert. This combination raises questions regarding the nature of convertible debt and as a result raises questions regarding the appropriate accounting treatment.

There is no question regarding the nature of straight-debt issues. These bonds are liabilities and nothing more. Convertible debt, however, can be viewed in a number of ways. One possibility is to ignore the conversion feature and treat convertible debt like a straight-debt issue. This is the current required treatment under *APB Opinion No. 14.* This approach is defended on the basis that the bond and conversion option are not separable. Thus, the conversion feature itself, regardless of its nature, has no marketable valuation. Opponents of the current requirement argue that it results in an understatement of interest expense and an overstatement of bond indebtedness.

A second view holds that the conversion feature is equity, and as such, its value should be separated from the bond and included in stockholders' equity as additional paid-in capital. Proponents of this view argue that the conversion feature has value that is a function of the price of the stock, not the bond. Investors are willing to pay for the option to convert. Moreover, due to the flexibility to convert or hold the bond, they may also accept a lower interest rate on the debt than would otherwise be obtainable. Therefore, the valuation of the equity component would be the difference between the price at which the bonds might have been sold and the price at which they were sold. This position was initially embraced by the APB in *Opinion No. 10,*[17] but shortly after, due to widespread opposition by corporate management, it was superseded by *APB Opinion No. 12.*[18]

A third view is that convertible debt should be classified according to its governing characteristic.[19] The governing characteristic is based on whether the instrument satisfies the definition of a liability or equity at the date of

[17] Accounting Principles Board, *Opinion No. 10,* "Omnibus Opinion—1966" (New York: AICPA, 1966).

[18] Accounting Principles Board, *Opinion No. 12,* "Omnibus Opinion—1967" (New York: AICPA, 1967).

[19] Financial Accounting Standards Board, Discussion Memorandum, "Distinguishing between Liability and Equity Instruments and Accounting for Instruments with Characteristics of Both" (Stamford, Conn.: 1990), par. 287.

issuance. The FASB has described four alternative approaches by which the governing characteristic might be determined. The first three would classify convertible debt as a liability. The approaches are

1. Classify based on the contractual terms in effect at issuance. Without conversion, interest and maturity payments must be made; therefore convertible debt should be classified as a liability.
2. Classify as a liability if the instrument embodies an obligation to transfer financial instruments to the holder if the option were exercised.
3. Classify in accordance with the fundamental financial instrument having the highest value.
4. Classify based on the most probable outcome. A convertible bond would be classified as an equity security if conversion is deemed to be the more probable outcome.[20]

A fourth view is based on alternative 2 above. This view considers the bond and the option to be two distinct liabilities that warrant separate disclosure.[21] Because the option obligates the corporation to transfer stock to the bondholder upon conversion, the option itself may be considered a liability. The corporation may satisfy the obligation at any time before exercise by buying the bonds in the open market or by exercising a call. At exercise, because the corporation could have sold the stock at market value, the securities exchanged represent compensation. That is, common stock is used in lieu of cash. An exercise would typically occur when the market price of the stock is high enough to motivate conversion. Thus, at exercise the corporation would receive less than it would have received had the stock transaction occurred at market price. Consequently, the decision to allow the bonds to be exercised causes the corporation to suffer a loss. Since equity transactions are between the corporation and stockholders acting as owners, such a loss is inconsistent with the definition of equity. Finally, if the options are never exercised, the initial value received for the conversion feature cannot be equity because the bondholders never acted in an ownership capacity.

Long-Term Notes Payable

Long-term notes payable are similar to debenture bonds in that they represent future obligations to repay debt. The promise to pay is generally accompanied by a provision for interest on the borrowed funds. The amount of interest charged will depend on such factors as the credit standing of the borrower, the amount of current debt, and usual business customs.

During the early 1970s, the Accounting Principles Board studied the notes receivable and payable phenomenon. This study disclosed a rather unusual occurrence in that some note transactions were being conducted without an accompanying interest charge. These transactions were apparently being car-

[20] Ibid., par. 289, 290.

[21] Clark, op. cit.

ried out for such purposes as maintaining favorable customer relations, maintaining current suppliers, or ensuring future services. After this study, the APB issued *Opinion No. 21*, "Interest on Receivables and Payables,"[22] which provided guidelines for cases in which no rate of interest was stipulated on notes or the rate stipulated was clearly inappropriate.

The provisions of *APB Opinion No. 21*, in summary form, are as follows.

1. Notes exchanged solely for cash are assumed to have a present value equal to the cash exchanged.

2. Notes exchanged for property, goods, and services are presumed to have a proper rate of interest.

3. If no interest is stated or the amount of interest is clearly inappropriate on notes exchanged for property, goods, and services, the present value of the note should be determined by (whichever is more clearly determinable):
   a. Determining the fair market value of the property, goods, and services exchanged.
   b. Determining the market value of the note at the time of the transaction.

4. If neither 3a nor 3b is determinable, the present value of the note should be determined by discounting all future payments to the present at an imputed rate of interest. This imputed rate should approximate the rate of similar independent borrowers and lenders in arm's-length transactions.[23]

When the face value of the note differs from its present value, the difference is shown as premium or discount on the face value of the note and is amortized over the life of the note by the *effective interest method* in such a manner as to reflect a constant rate of interest. This amortization will be deducted from the premium or discount each year, as discussed earlier for bond discount and premiums, in such a manner that at the time of repayment the face value and carrying value are equal.

Although *APB Opinion No. 21* was designed to require the recording of interest on most notes receivable and payable, it specifically *exempted* the following types of transactions.

1. Normal trade transactions not exceeding a year.

2. Amounts that will be applied to the purchase of property, goods, and services.

3. Security deposits.

4. Customary activities of financial institutions.

5. Transactions where the rate is affected by the regulations of government agencies.

6. Transactions between parent and subsidiaries and between subsidiaries of a common parent.

---

[22] *Accounting Principles Board Opinion No. 21*, "Interest on Receivables and Payables" (New York: AICPA, 1971).

[23] Ibid., pars. 11–13.

The following example illustrates the application of *APB Opinion No. 21.*
The Elliott Company sold the Kelliher Company an asset on January 1, 1996, with a book value of $5,000, accepting a noninterest-bearing $10,000 five-year note in exchange. (Assume a prevailing interest rate of 8 percent. The present value of $1 in five years at 8 percent is $0.681.) The entries to record the acquisition of the asset by Kelliher, the receipt of the note by Elliott, and the recording of interest at the end of the first two years are

	Elliott			Kelliher		
Jan. 1, 1996	Note receivable	$10,000		Asset	$6,810	
	Asset		$5,000	Discount on notes payable	3,190	
	Discount on notes receivable		3,190	Note payable		$10,000
	Gain		1,810			
Dec. 31, 1996	Discount on notes receivable	545		Interest expense	545	
	Interest income		545	Discount on notes payable		545
	(8% of $6,810)			(8% of $6,810)		
Dec. 31, 1997	Discount on notes receivable	588		Interest expense	588	
	Interest income		588	Discount on notes payable		588
	(8% of $7,355)			(8% of $7,355)		

Short-Term Debt Expected to Be Refinanced

Some corporations have attempted to improve their liquidity position by excluding that portion of short-term debt from current liabilities that was expected to be refinanced on a long-term basis. This treatment resulted in disclosure variations between companies and led to the issuance of *SFAS No. 6,* "Classification of Short Term Obligations Expected to Be Refinanced." In this release, the FASB took the position that short-term obligations cannot be disclosed as long-term liabilities unless the following conditions exist: (1) there is an intention to refinance current liabilities on a long-term basis and (2) the corporation demonstrates the ability to refinance such liabilities. The intent of the company to refinance current obligations means that working capital will not be reduced by the satisfaction of the obligation. The ability to refinance means that the company has an agreement to refinance the obligations on a long-term basis with a qualified creditor.

A company may refinance short-term debt on a long-term basis by replacing a current liability with long-term debt or ownership securities. Additionally, refinancing may be demonstrated if the current liability is extended, renewed, or replaced by other short-term debt.

A short-term obligation that is excluded from the current liability section of the balance sheet requires disclosure in the financial-statement footnotes. This disclosure must include a general description of the financing agreement and the terms of any new obligation incurred or expected to be incurred or equity securities issued or expected to be issued as a result of the refinancing.

Deferred Credits

Deferred credits are not liabilities in the usual sense of the word, in that they will not normally be satisfied by the payment of funds but rather by the performance of services. They result from the double-entry accounting system, which requires a credit for every debit. The most frequently encountered deferred credits are

1. Income received in advance.
2. Deferred taxes.
3. Unrealized gross profit on installment sales (usually no longer appropriate).

These items are either anticipated future revenues (unearned income) or foreseen future expense payments (deferred taxes). But there is no assurance that all deferrals will ultimately be included in income determination.

Although unearned revenues fit the definition of liabilities found in *SFAC No. 6*, deferred gross profit on installment sales does not.[24] Unearned revenues reflect liabilities to perform future services resulting from transactions for which the company was compensated in advance. Deferred gross profits arise from prior performance of services, the compensation for which has not yet been received and the future receipt of which is in doubt. The corporation has no further obligation to the customer or client; rather it is the customer or client who is obligated to the corporation. Because the deferred gross profit resulted from the recognition of a receivable that continues to reflect unrecovered cost, the deferred gross profit is conceptually an asset valuation and should be shown as a contra to the receivable on the balance sheet.[25]

The deferral section of the balance sheet is grounded in the principle of conservatism. As discussed in Chapter 3, this principle requires that revenue recognition be postponed until there is assurance that it is earned, but expenses are to be recorded as incurred.

Contingencies

A contingency is a possible future event that will have some impact on the firm. Although *Accounting Principles Board Statement No. 4* required the disclosure of contingencies,[26] it made no effort to define or give examples of them. Among the most frequently encountered contingencies are

---

[24] *SFAC No. 6*, op. cit., par. 233.

[25] Ibid., par. 234.

[26] *APB Statement No. 4*, op cit.

1. Pending lawsuits.
2. Income tax disputes.
3. Notes receivable discounted.
4. Accommodation endorsements.

The decision to record contingencies should be based on the principle of disclosure. That is, when the disclosure of an event adds to the information content of financial statements, it should be reported. Some authors have argued for basing this decision on expected value criteria. That is, if a potential obligation has a high probability of occurrence, it should be recorded as a liability, whereas potential obligations with low probabilities are reported in footnotes.

On the other hand, the reporting of some types of contingencies may result in a self-fulfilling prophecy. For example, a frequently encountered contingency problem is the question of including the possible loss from a lawsuit in the liability section of the balance sheet. The dollar value of the loss can generally be determined by applying expected value criteria, but placing the item on the balance sheet may supply the plaintiff with additional evidence of the company's guilt. The corporation here is faced with the dilemma of conflicting responsibilities to its financial-statement users to disclose all pertinent information while at the same time minimizing losses.

The FASB reviewed the nature of contingencies in *SFAS No. 5,* "Accounting for Contingencies."[27] This release defines two types of contingencies—gain contingencies (expected future gains) and loss contingencies (expected future losses).

With respect to gain contingencies, the board took the position that these events should not usually be reflected currently in the financial statement because to do so might result in revenue recognition before realization. However, adequate disclosure should be made of all gain contingencies while exercising due care to avoid misleading implications as to the likelihood of realization.[28]

The criteria established for recording loss contingencies require that the likelihood of loss be determined as follows.

Probable.   The future event is likely to occur.
Reasonably possible.   The chance of occurrence is more than remote but less than likely.
Remote.   The chance of occurrence is slight.

Once the likelihood of a loss is determined, contingencies are charged against income and a liability recorded if both of the following conditions are met.

---

[27] Financial Accounting Standards Board, *Statement of Financial Accounting Standards No. 5,* "Accounting for Contingencies" (Stamford, Conn.: FASB, 1975).

[28] Ibid.

1. Information available prior to the issuance of the financial statements indicates that it is probable that an asset had been impaired or a liability had been incurred at the date of the financial statements.
2. The amount of the loss can be reasonably estimated.[29]

If a loss is not accrued because one or both of these conditions has not been met, footnote disclosure of the contingency should be made when there is at least a reasonable possibility that a loss may have been incurred.

SFAS No. 5 is evidence of the FASB's preference for the conservatism convention. However, this statement resulted in the application of separate standards for the reporting of revenues and expenses. The provisions of *SFAS No. 5* might cause one company to record a liability without a corresponding asset being recorded by the claimant company. These procedures are not conducive to the development of a general theory of accounting and are further evidence of the need to establish a broad framework within which to establish consistent accounting principles.

Other Liability Measurement Issues

During the past several years, some additional measurement issues relating to liabilities have arisen. Among the most important of these are accrued liabilities for compensated absences and the disclosure of "off–balance sheet" financing arrangements.

Compensated absences occur due to paid vacations, paid holidays, and sick leaves. An accrued liability for compensated absences must be recorded when:

1. The right to receive compensation is attributable to services previously rendered.
2. The right vests or accumulates.
3. The payment of the compensation is probable.
4. The amount of the payment can be reasonably estimated.

The proportion of debt in a firm's capital structure is often perceived as an indicator of the level of risk associated with investing in that company. Recently, some innovative financing arrangements have been structured by corporations in such a manner that they do not satisfy liability recognition criteria. These arrangements are termed *off–balance sheet* financing. The principal goal of these arrangements is to keep debt off the balance sheet. For example, several oil companies may form a joint venture to drill for offshore oil, and agree to make payments to support the venture over time. In such cases, neither their share of the assets nor the future liability will appear on the balance sheet.

The FASB currently has an off–balance sheet financing project on its agenda. The objective of this project is to develop broad standards of financial accounting and reporting about financial instruments and related transactions.

---

[29] Ibid., par. 8.

Due to the complexity of these issues, the FASB has decided to give the widest possible exposure to proposed statements prior to their release. As an interim step, the Board determined that improved disclosure of certain information is necessary. Subsequently, the FASB completed two disclosure phases, which resulted in the issuance of *SFAS No. 105*, "Disclosure of Information about Financial Instruments with Off–Balance Sheet Risk and Financial Instruments with Concentrations of Credit Risk" in 1990, and the issuance of *SFAS No. 107*, "Disclosures about Fair Value of Financial Instruments," in 1991.

SFAS No. 105 defines a financial instrument as cash, evidence of an owner-ship interest in an entity, or a contract that both

1. Imposes on one entity a contractual obligation to (a) deliver cash or another financial instrument to a second entity, or (b) to exchange financial instru-ments on potentially unfavorable terms with the second entity.

2. Conveys to the second entity a contractual right to (a) receive cash or another financial instrument from the first entity, or (b) to exchange other financial instruments on potentially favorable terms with the first entity.

Examples of financial instruments with off–balance sheet risk are out-standing loan commitments, outstanding commercial letters of credit, financial guarantees, recourse obligations on receivables sold, obligations to repurchase securities sold, outstanding commitments to purchase or sell financial instru-ments at predetermined prices, and future contracts. The risk of loss from financial instruments includes the possibility that a loss may occur due to the failure of another party to perform according to the terms of the contract (*credit risk*) and the possibility that future changes in market price may make a financial instrument less valuable (*market risk*).

Some financial instruments are recognized as assets, and the amount rec-ognized reflects the risk of loss to the entity. Some financial instruments that are recognized as liabilities expose the entity to the possibility of loss because the ultimate obligation may be greater than the amount of the recorded liabil-ity. Finally, other financial instruments not recognized as either assets or liabil-ities may ultimately expose the entity to a risk of loss.

SFAS No. 105 requires entities recording financial instruments with off–balance sheet risk to disclose

1. The face or contractual amount.

2. The nature and terms, including a discussion of (a) the credit and market risk of those instruments, (b) the cash requirements of those instruments, and (c) the related accounting policy disclosures as required by *APB Opinion No. 22* (see Chapter 16).

Entities recording financial instruments with off–balance sheet credit risk must disclose

1. The amount of loss that would be incurred if any party failed to comply with the terms of the contract.

2. The entity's policy of requiring collateral to support instruments subject to

credit risk, information about the entity's access to that collateral, and a description of any collateral supporting the financial instrument.

Additionally, entities are required to disclose all significant concentrations of credit risk arising from all financial instruments, whether from individual counterparties or groups of counterparties. Group concentrations of credit risk exist if a number of counterparties are engaged in similar activities having similar economic characteristics that would cause their ability to meet contractual obligations to be similarly affected by changes in economic or other conditions. The following is to be disclosed for each significant concentration:

1. Information about the activity, region, or economic characteristic that identifies the concentration.

2. The amount of loss due to credit risk that the entity would incur if the parties to the concentration failed to perform the contract.

3. The entity's policy of requiring collateral to support financial instruments subject to credit risk, information about the entity's access to that collateral, and the nature and description of the collateral supporting the financial instruments.

SFAS No. 107 requires the disclosure of fair value of financial instruments for which an estimate of fair value is practicable. The methods and assumptions used to estimate fair value also must be disclosed. The fair value of a financial instrument is defined as ''. . . the amount at which the instrument could be exchanged in a current transaction between willing parties, other than in a forced or liquidation sale.''[30] A quoted market price is cited as the best evidence of fair value.

These disclosure requirements apply to financial instruments regardless of whether they are assets or liabilities or whether they are reported or not reported in the balance sheet. The following are exempt from the *SFAS No. 107* requirements. Many of them already have extensive disclosure requirements.

1. Deferred compensation arrangements such as, pensions, postretirement benefits, and employee stock option and purchase plans.

2. Debt extinguished and the related assets removed from the balance in cases of in substance defeasance.

3. Insurance contracts, other than financial guarantees and investment contracts.

4. Leases.

5. Warranty obligations and rights.

6. Unconditional purchase obligations.

7. Investments accounted for under the equity method.

8. Minority interest.

---

[30] Financial Accounting Standards Board, *Statement of Financial Accounting Standards No. 107,* ''Disclosures about Fair Value of Financial Instruments'' (Stamford, Conn.: FASB, 1991), par. 5.

9. Equity investments in consolidated subsidiaries.
10. Equity instruments classified in stockholders' equity.[31]

In addition, fair value disclosure is not required for trade receivables whose carrying amount approximates fair value.[32]

Troubled Debt Restructurings

Occasionally corporations experience difficulty repaying their long-term debt obligations. These difficulties frequently result in arrangements between the debtor and the creditor that allow the debtor to avoid bankruptcy. For example, in 1976, Continental Investment Corporation satisfied $34 million of the $61 million debt owed to the First National Bank of Boston by transferring all its stock in Investors Mortgage Group, Inc. (a subsidiary) to the bank. Accountants and financial-statement users became concerned over the lack of GAAP by which to account for these agreements. Consequently, the Financial Accounting Standards Board began a study of agreements of this type, termed *troubled debt restructurings.* This study focused on three questions: (1) Do certain kinds of troubled debt restructurings require reductions in the carrying amounts of debt? (2) If they do, should the effect of the reduction be reported as current income, deferred to a future period, or reported as contributed capital? (3) Should contingently payable interest on the restructured debt be recognized before it becomes payable?

The underlying issues in each of these questions relate to the recognition of liabilities and holding gains. A liability should be recorded at the amount of probable future sacrifice of economic benefits arising from present obligations. A holding gain occurs when the value of the liability decreases. The result of the review of these questions was the release of *SFAS No. 15,* "Accounting by Debtors and Creditors for Troubled Debt Restructurings."[33]

According to *SFAS No. 15,* a troubled debt restructuring occurs when "the creditor for economic or legal reasons related to the debtor's financial difficulties grants a concession to the debtor that it would not otherwise consider."[34] A troubled debt restructuring may include, but is not limited to, one or any combination of the following.

1. *Modification of terms of a debt such as one or a combination of:*
   a. *Reduction . . . of the stated interest rate for the remaining original life of the debt.*
   b. *Extension of the maturity date or dates at a stated interest rate lower than the current market rate for new debt with similar risk.*

---

[31] Ibid., par. 8.

[32] Ibid., par. 13.

[33] Financial Accounting Standards Board, *Statements of Financial Accounting Standards No. 15,* "Accounting by Debtors and Creditors for Troubled Debt Restructurings" (Stamford, Conn.: FASB, 1977), par. 2.

[34] Ibid.

c. Reduction . . . of the face amount or maturity amount of the debt as
stated in the instrument or other agreement.
d. Reduction . . . of accrued interest.

2. *Issuance or other granting of an equity interest to the creditor by the debtor
to satisfy fully or partially a debt unless the equity interest is granted pursuant
to existing terms for converting the debt into an equity interest.*

3. *A transfer from the debtor to the creditor of receivables from third parties,
real estate, or other assets to satisfy fully or partially a debt.*[35]

Modification of Terms

A restructuring agreement involving only a modification of terms is accounted
for on a prospective basis and results in one of the two following situations.

1. The amount of principal and interest to be repaid is greater than the current
carrying value of the liability; therefore, no gain is recognized by the debtor.

2. The amount of principal and interest to be repaid is less than the current
carrying value of the liability; therefore, a gain is recognized by the debtor.

In the event it is determined that the total amount to be repaid exceeds
the carrying value of the debt on the date of the restructuring agreement, no
adjustment is made to the original carrying value of the liability. However, it
is necessary to determine the effective interest rate that equates the total future
payments with the current carrying value. This rate is then applied to the
carrying value of the obligation each year to determine the amount of interest
expense. The difference between the recorded amount of interest expense and
any cash payment reduces the carrying value of the liability.

If the total future cash payments are determined to be less than the carrying value of the obligation, the amount of the liability is reduced to the total
amount of the cash to be repaid. The debtor then recognizes an extraordinary
gain for the amount of this adjustment and all future payments are recorded
as reductions in the amount of the liability. That is, the debt is treated as
though there is no interest rate.

Under *SFAS No. 15*, a creditor treated a troubled debt restructuring resulting in a modification of terms in a manner similar to the debtor. No loss
was recognized when the total amount receivable from the debtor under the
modified arrangement was greater than the current carrying value of the receivable. Similarly, when the total future cash flows under the modified terms
were less than the current carrying value, a loss was recognized for the difference.

This practice was criticized because the creditor would recognize a loss
only when the total future cash flows were less than the current carrying value
of the loan. The loss recognized would result in a carrying value of the impaired loan equal to the total future cash flows. Consequently, no interest
income could be recorded over the term of the new agreement. In the case

---

[35] Ibid., par. 5.

where no loss is recognized, the current loan amount was presumed to be the amount borrowed, forcing the interest rate on the modified loan arrangement to be unrealistically low. These results were inconsistent with other reporting requirements for similar financial instruments. The restructured financial instruments were not recorded initially at fair value, nor is interest calculated using the market rate implied in the loan agreement.

As a part of its financial instruments project, the FASB addressed the issue of whether a creditor should measure an impaired loan based on the present value of the future cash flows related to the loan. The Board concluded that it would be inappropriate to continue to ignore the time value of money and issued *SFAS No. 114*, "Accounting by Creditors for Impairment of a Loan."[36]

SFAS No. 114 requires creditors to measure receivables that result from a troubled debt restructure involving a modification of terms at the present value of expected future cash flows discounted at the loan's effective interest rate.[37] A bad debt loss is recognized and a valuation allowance is credited for the difference between the restructured measurement and the current carrying value of the loan. The effective interest rate used to discount the expected future cash flows is to be the rate on the original contractual agreement, rather than the rate specified in the restructuring agreement.[38] The rationale for use of the original loan rate is that the restructure represents continuing efforts to recover the original loan.

As a practical expedient, the creditor may alternatively value the receivable based on the loan's observable market price. If the receivable is collateralized, it may be valued at the fair value of the collateral.[39]

Income over the life of the restructured loan may be recognized in one of two ways.

1. Changes in the present value of expected future cash flows that are due to the passage of time are reported as interest income, while those changes attributable to changes in expectations regarding future cash flows are reported as bad debt expense.

2. All changes in the present value of expected future cash flows are treated as adjustments to bad debt expense.[40]

SFAS No. 114 may be criticized on the basis that its requirements are inconsistent with the intent of the pronouncement. The resulting restructured loan measurements will not provide the fair value of the restructured loan, because the interest rate used was based on prior conditions and probably

---

[36] Financial Accounting Standards Board, *Statement of Financial Accounting Standards No. 114*, "Accounting by Creditors for Impairment of a Loan" (Stamford, Conn.: FASB, 1993).

[37] Ibid., par. 13.

[38] Ibid., par. 14.

[39] Ibid., par. 13.

[40] Ibid., par. 17.

does not reflect current conditions or the risk inherent in the restructured cash flows.

SFAS No. 114 does not mention the debtor. Therefore, the debtor will continue to record the restructure in accordance with *SFAS No. 15*. This results in a lack of symmetry between debtor and creditor treatment of the same financial instrument.

Satisfaction of the Debt Through an Asset or Equity Swap

When a debtor exchanges an asset or an equity interest in satisfaction of a liability, the transfer is recorded on the basis of the fair market value of the asset or equity interest transferred. Market value is determined at the time of the exchange by the fair market value of the asset or equity exchanged, unless the fair market value of the debt satisfied is more clearly evident. An extraordinary gain is recognized for the excess of the recorded liability over the fair market value of the asset transferred. The creditor records a corresponding bad debt loss (not an extraordinary item). In the case of asset exchanges, it is also necessary to record a gain or loss on disposition of the assets to the extent of any difference between the asset's fair market value and its carrying value.

Equity for debt swaps can increase reported income by the amount of the extraordinary gain on debt restructure and by reduced interest expense. Also, debt is removed from the balance sheet and replaced by equity, thereby improving the financial position of the company and its debt-to-equity ratios. For example, in 1990, Financial Corp. of Santa Barbara swapped $50 million of equity for debt and recognized an extraordinary gain of $36.5 million.[41] The common shares issued replaced preferred stock, subordinated debentures, and notes.

Disclosure of Restructuring Agreements

SFAS No. 15 requires the following disclosures by debtors entering into restructuring agreements.

1. A description of the principal changes in terms and/or the major features of settlement for each restructuring agreement.
2. The aggregate gain on debt restructures and the related income tax effect.
3. The per share amount of the aggregate gain on restructuring net of the related income tax effect.
4. The aggregate gain or loss recognized during the period on transfers of assets.

[41] "Financial Corp. of Santa Barbara's Net Jumps Sevenfold," *Wall Street Journal* (April 24, 1990), Sec. C, p. 22.

For creditors subject to the provisions of *SFAS No. 114,* the *SFAS No. 15* requirement that the amount of any commitments to lend additional funds to the debtor still applies. Under *SFAS No. 114,* these creditors are required to disclose

1. The recorded investment balance at the balance sheet date as well as the related total allowance for credit losses.
2. The beginning balance in the allowance account and the changes in it during the period.
3. The creditor's income recognition policy.[42]

Summary

In the readings that follow, Halsey G. Bullen, Robert C. Wilkins, and Clifford C. Woods III describe in detail the nature of fundamental financial instruments and their associated measurement and recognition problems. Although this article predates the issuance of subsequent pronouncements that affect creditor accounting for impaired debt and accounting for investments in debt and equity securities, the fundamental financial instruments approach is relevant to both *SFAS No. 114* and *SFAS No. 115* and to other issues currently being addressed by the FASB. In the subsequent article, Thomas E. King, Alan K. Ortegren, and Robin M. King analyze the appropriateness of allocating the proceeds of convertible debt between debt and equity and the implications of such allocations for other securities that have debt and equity components.

---

[42] Financial Accounting Standards Board, *Statement of Financial Accounting Standards No. 114,* "Accounting by Creditors for Impairment of a Loan" (Stamford, Conn.: FASB), 1993, par. 20.

The Fundamental Financial Instrument Approach

Halsey G. Bullen, Robert C. Wilkins, and Clifford C. Woods III

Because of the seemingly endless complexity and diversity of innovative financial instruments, the Financial Accounting Standards Board is taking the approach of breaking down these instruments to resolve the numerous recognition and measurement issues associated with them.

The approach is based on the premise that all financial instruments are made up of a few different "building blocks"—fundamental financial instruments—and that determining how to recognize and measure those fundamental instruments is the key to reaching consistent solutions for the accounting issues raised by other, more complex instruments and by various relationships between instruments.

Identifying Fundamental Financial Instruments

To identify which instruments are fundamental, the FASB turned first to its definition of a financial instrument (see Exhibit 1). The definition the FASB has established distinguishes between instruments that entail one party's right to receive and another party's obliga-

tion to deliver and those that entail rights and obligations to exchange.

If a financial instrument obligates one party to deliver cash or other instruments, that party has a liability—a payable in the broadest sense—and the other party has an asset—a receivable. A right to receive or an obligation to deliver entails a one-way transfer; this transfer would involve no further quid pro quo.

In contrast, a financial instrument that entails a right or obligation to exchange looks to a further transaction that will, if it occurs, consist of a two-way flow of cash and other financial instruments—an exchange. Whether a contract to exchange gives rise to an asset, a liability, or perhaps both is determined by the potential for a favorable or unfavorable result. To be an asset, such a contract must entitle a party to exchange on terms that are at least potentially favorable. (For example, a call option to buy a bond next month for $1,000 has the potential to become favorable to its holder—the market price of the bond could rise above $1,000 by then.) Likewise, to be a liability, such a contract must obligate a party to exchange on terms that are at least potentially unfavorable.

Conditionality of rights and obligations is another characteristic that distinguishes between fundamental financial instruments. A right to receive or an obligation to deliver cash or another instrument—a one-way transfer—may be either unconditional or conditional on some event. The same is true for a right or obligation to ex-

Expressions of individual views by the members of the FASB and its staff are encouraged. The views expressed in this article are those of Messrs. Bullen, Wilkins, and Woods. Official positions of the FASB are determined only after extensive due process and deliberation.

EXHIBIT 1 *What's a Financial Instrument?*

The FASB's July 1989 revised exposure draft, *Disclosure of Information about Financial Instruments with Off-Balance-Sheet Risk and Financial Instruments with Concentrations of Credit Risk,* defines a financial instrument as cash, evidence of an ownership interest in an equity, or a contract that is both

- A (recognized or unrecognized) contractual right of one entity to (1) receive cash or another financial instrument from another entity or (2) exchange other financial instruments on potentially favorable terms with another entity.

- A (recognized or unrecognized) contractual obligation of another entity to (1) deliver cash or another financial instrument to another entity or (2) exchange financial instruments on potentially unfavorable terms with another entity.

That definition includes traditional instruments such as receivables, payables, debt securities, and common stock, as well as more innovative financial instruments such as financial futures and forward contracts, interest rate swaps and caps, collateralized mortgage obligations, and financial guarantees. It excludes contracts for the purchase or sale of commodities or other goods, services, inventories, property, plant and equipment, as well as tax obligations.

change cash and other financial instruments—a two-way exchange.

Conditional exchanges can be further subdivided into

- Instruments whose rights and obligations are conditional on events

within the control of one party to the contract (for example, in an option contract, the conditional event is generally the option holder's decision to exercise).

- Instruments whose rights and obligations are conditional on events beyond the control of either party to the contract (for example, in a financial guarantee, the conditional event that could take place might be default on some other contract by a third party).

How important that subdivision of conditionality may end up being for accounting recognition and measurement will have to remain to be seen.

Those contractual distinctions between financial instruments helped lead to FASB to its current list of six tentatively identified fundamental financial instruments, which are defined in Exhibit 2.

Recognition and Measurement

Recognition and measurement questions to be answered for each fundamental instrument fall into four categories:

Recognition. Whether and when an asset or liability should initially be recorded in the statement of financial position.

Initial measurement. At what amount an asset or liability should initially be recorded.

Subsequent measurement. At what amount an asset or liability should be reported after recognition and initial measurement; in particular, whether gain or loss should be recognized as a result of some or all changes in market value.

Derecognition. Whether and when an asset or liability should be re-

EXHIBIT 2 *Six Tentatively Identified Fundamental Financial Instruments*

Unconditional receivable (payable). An unqualified right (obligation) to receive (deliver) cash or another financial asset on or before a specified date or on demand. These contracts entail a future one-way transfer of one or more financial assets. Examples are trade accounts, notes, loans, and bonds receivable (payable).

Conditional receivable (payable). A right (obligation) to receive (deliver) cash or another financial asset dependent on the occurrence of an event beyond the control of either party to the contract. These contracts entail a potential one-way transfer of one or more assets. Examples include interest rate caps and floors, insurance contracts without subrogation rights, and compensation promised to a third party if a transaction or other event occurs.

Forward contract. An unconditional right and obligation to exchange financial instruments. Examples include forward purchase and sale contracts, futures contracts, and repurchase agreements that obligate both parties to a future exchange of financial instruments. (Forward and futures contracts for the purchase or sale of metals, grain, or other goods do not qualify as financial instruments because the items to be exchanged are not both financial instruments.)

Option. A right (obligation) to exchange other financial instruments on potentially favorable (unfavorable) terms that is conditional on the occurrence of an event within the control of one party to the contract. Most commonly, the conditional event is an option holder's decision to exercise the right to demand the exchange. Examples include warrants, loan commitments, and exchange-traded and other put or call options. Bonds or stocks with attached warrants, mortgages that allow the borrower to prepay, and convertible bonds are examples of compound financial instruments containing options.

Guarantee or other conditional exchange. A right (obligation) to exchange financial instruments on potentially favorable (unfavorable) terms that is conditional on the occurrence of an event outside the control of either party. Examples include performance bonds, letters of credit, and all other contracts for which the obligor, on occurrence of a specified event, would receive the subrogation or other rights to another financial instrument in exchange for its delivery of a financial instrument.

Equity instrument. An ownership interest in an equity. It typically entitles its holder to a pro rata share of any distributions made to that class of holders but only entails a right (obligation) to receive (deliver) cash or other financial instrument assets on the entity's liquidation. Examples include common stock and partnership interests.

This set of fundamental instruments is being reexamined as the recognition and measurement phase proceeds. Some categories might be combined if analysis shows they should be accounted for similarly, while others might have to be divided.

EXHIBIT 3 *Mortgages and Mortgage-Backed Securities*

A typical fixed-rate residential mortgage is a combination of a series of required cash flows—each an unconditional receivable (payable)—and the privilege of prepaying the remaining principal balance at any time—an option written (held). The prepayment option is favorable to the homeowner. If interest rates decline, the borrower can refinance at a lower rate without penalty. And it's that possibility that makes prepayment options unfavorable for banks, thrifts, and other mortgage investors; the prepayment option embedded in everyday residential mortgages is the wild card that makes investing in mortgages (and mortgage-backed securities) so much riskier than it might at first seem to be.

Mortgage-backed securities are created by bundling mortgages into a pool and offering (often through a trust) different interests in that pool to different investors. Mortgage-backed securities take several forms. In some, "senior" investors might be entitled to all cash collected from the pool until they recoup their entire investment plus, say, 9% interest; "subordinated" investors might be entitled to whatever remaining cash is collected.

Alternatively, a pool of mortgages might be split into several classes (or "tranches") of securities, each of which entitles investors to different seniority and rates of return—or split into securities entitling investors to only the interest payments or only the principal payments. Often, financial guarantees are an important part of these securities.

In terms of fundamental instruments, mortgage-backed securities combine unconditional receivables (payables), conditional receivables (payables), guarantees, options, and perhaps equity instruments (representing interests in the residual value of a trust). Examining these components to determine which have been transferred to investors or others and which have been retained by the security's sponsor may help in resolving the troublesome "sale or financing" derecognition question that is raised on many occasions when these securities are first created.

---

moved from the statement of financial position—and whether gain or loss should be recognized.

While the recognition and initial measurement of financial instruments are not necessarily easy to resolve, the more difficult issues are in subsequent measurement and derecognition.

Compound Financial Instruments

Financial instruments that do not meet the definition of one of the fundamental financial instruments can be analyzed as made up of fundamentals in various combinations. Some of these compound instruments may combine only a few fundamental instruments; for example, a callable zero-coupon bond combines (from the issuer's perspective) an unconditional payable and a call option held.

Other compound instruments are more complex. They may contractually link several fundamental instruments. Exhibits 3 and 4 show how two kinds of compound instruments—mortgages

EXHIBIT 4 *Interest Rate Swaps*

The interest rate swap was invented in the early 1980s to aid companies able to borrow cheaply at floating interest rates but seeking fixed rates and vice versa. It has become an essential tool of finance since its creation.

A straightforward interest rate swap might require one party—the "fixed-rate payer"—to pay a fixed interest rate times a notional principal amount at the end of each of the next five years; the counterparty would be required to pay the floating London interbank offered rate times the same notional principal amount at the same intervals. There are no principal payments and the fixed rate is typically negotiated to eliminate any need for a cash payment at the outset. For convenience, the parties usually agree that a single net payment be made at each due date.

Interest rate swaps typically are entered into a connection with a borrowing, although the swap counterparty usually is not the lender. Some have described the economic position of a floating-rate borrower/fixed-rate payer in a swap as being the same as

that of a fixed-rate borrower, but there is a difference. In an interest rate swap, the borrower is exposed to a credit risk since the swap counterparty might default.

The interest rate swap can be analyzed into fundamental financial instruments in at least two ways:

- As a series of forward contracts (to exchange a floating-rate cash receipt for a fixed payment).

- As a series of variable-rate receivables and a series of fixed-rate unconditional payables to be settled by net payments after setoff.

Which of these analyses is more appropriate for swaps, whether the choice affects the accounting result, and whether the relationship between an interest rate swap and a debt incurred at the same time should affect the accounting for either or both instruments are among the questions the financial instruments project is expected to deal with in resolving the diversity in current accounting practice for swaps.

---

and mortgage-backed securities and interest rate swaps—can be broken down into fundamental instruments.

The FASB anticipates that the recognition and measurement of various compound instruments can be approached by analyzing them in terms of their fundamental financial instrument components. Determining the accounting for each fundamental instrument should point the way to the accounting for any compound financial instrument. While that may sound challenging, it mirrors the current business practices of

many buyers and sellers of mortgages, corporate bonds, and other compound financial instruments.

Relationships Between Financial Instruments

At the same time, the FASB will consider whether some of the contractual and other relationships between financial instruments—whether fundamental or compound—should affect the accounting for one or more of the related instruments. Relationships that raise accounting issues include those between hedging and hedged instruments, assets and liabilities that can be set off against each other, secured debt and securing assets (either with or without recourse to other assets of the borrower), options that are "covered" by particular assets and in-substance defeasances, and other dedications of specific assets to the settlement of specific liabilities.

The Goal: Accounting Standards for Financial Instruments

Breaking down complex financial instruments into their fundamental components is not a new idea. On the contrary, it often is acknowledged by many investment bankers, financial managers, economists, and finance academics

EXHIBIT 5 *Authoritative Literature That May Be Affected by the Recognition and Measurement Phase of the Financial Instruments Project*

Document	Title	Area that may be affected
Accounting Principles Board Opinion no. 21	*Interest on Receivables and Payables*	Accounting and scope restrictions.
FASB Statement no. 12	*Accounting for Certain Marketable Securities*	Entire statement (both debt and equity securities are financial instruments).
FASB Statement no. 15	*Accounting by Debtors and Creditors for Troubled Debt Restructurings*	Entire statement.
FASB Statement no. 52	*Foreign Currency Translation*	Forward exchange contract and hedging provisions.
FASB Statement no. 65	*Accounting for Certain Mortgage Banking Activities*	Mortgage loans, mortgage-backed securities, and the sale of loans with servicing retained.
FASB Statement no. 76	*Extinguishment of Debt*	Entire statement.
FASB Statement no. 77	*Reporting by Transferors for Transfers of Receivables with Recourse*	Entire statement.
FASB Statement no. 80	*Accounting for Futures Contracts*	Entire statement.
FASB Statement no. 91	*Accounting for Nonrefundable Fees and Costs Associated with Originating or Acquiring Loans and Initial Direct Costs of Leases*	Initial and subsequent measurement issues.
Various AICPA accounting and audit guides, especially those for banks, savings and loan associations, finance companies, investment companies, and brokers and dealers in securities.		Some specialized accounting principles will be reexamined. Areas that may be affected include the distinction between trading and investment accounts, allowances for loan losses, and valuing repossessed collateral.

(usually in the context of how best to manage financial risks) as the way in which complex financial instruments are created and valued in the marketplace. Similarly, the FASB's approach is intended to break down complex financial instruments to determine their economic substance and thereby develop consistent accounting standards.

As the FASB's financial instruments project proceeds, numerous generally accepted accounting principles will be reconsidered and some surely will have to change. Exhibit 5 indicates some of the authoritative accounting literature subject to reconsideration in the project. Another indication of the potential for change in current practice may be the FASB's tentative conclusions on fundamental instruments, which include the tentative decision to measure certain options held or written at their current market values or at estimates of those values based on option pricing models or other techniques, if this is feasible.

The FASB plans to issue an initial discussion document on the recognition and measurement of financial instruments in 1990. As planned, it would present the fundamental financial instrument approach and the issues the project aims to resolve, expressed in terms of accounting for fundamental instruments, compound instruments and hedging, and other relationships between financial instruments. The document also is expected to provide the FASB's preliminary views on some of those issues. Ultimately, after considering written comments on the discussion document, a public hearing planned for late 1990, and further deliberations and exposure drafts, the project's goal is to issue accounting standards that resolve the accounting issues of financial instruments on a consistent conceptual basis.

The fundamental financial instrument approach is a tool intended to help resolve the recognition and measurement issues of new as well as traditional financial instruments. The approach should help the FASB resolve today's issues and help practicing accountants answer tomorrow's inevitable accounting questions about innovative financial instruments and off-balance-sheet financing. The approach is still being developed and the FASB welcomes suggestions and supportive or critical comments from all of its constituents.

A Reassessment of the Allocation of Convertible Debt Proceeds and the Implications for Other Hybrid Financial Instruments

Thomas E. King, Alan K. Ortegren, and Robin M. King

As the use of convertible bonds increased dramatically in the 1960s, a

Copyright © American Accounting Association, *Accounting Horizons* (September 1990). Reprinted with permission.

question arose as to how to account for the issuance of such securities. Many argued that a convertible bond consists of two bundled securities, a straight bond and an option to acquire stock.

Acceptance of this view implies that the issuer's accounting treatment recognize both features of the security and allocate the issue proceeds partially to debt and partially to equity. The Accounting Principles Board (APB), however, chose to require, in *APBO 14,*[1] that no portion of the proceeds of convertible debt be attributed to the equity or conversion feature of the debt. At the time considerable controversy surrounded the issue, and, in retrospect, the arguments presented by the APB to support its position seem less than convincing.

This concern again has come to the forefront as new types of hybrid securities have appeared in recent years. With many of these securities, the question is whether the proceeds of issuance are associated with debt, equity, or a combination of the two. When related to both debt and equity, the question is how the issue amount is to be allocated between the two. The Financial Accounting Standards Board's (FASB) financial instruments project is intended to address accounting and reporting issues created by these nontraditional securities. New attention to hybrid securities is needed because the approach taken by the APB more than 20 years ago seems unable to capture the substance of these securities.

This article reexamines accounting for the proceeds of convertible bond issues and assesses the practicality of estimating price differentials attributed to different features of a hybrid instrument in a real trade setting. The results of this study are relevant to accounting for traditional convertible bonds, normally issued at prices significantly in excess of their straight debt values (i.e., at lower coupon rates and yields than straight debt), and the newer hybrid securities. Evidence provided by this study bears directly on the practicality of making the kinds of estimates needed to apply the FASB's stated approach to dealing with hybrid financial instruments.

The Importance of Hybrid Financial Instruments

Financial reporting issues related to company financing are among the most important facing the accounting profession today. The accounting literature and the popular financial press contain many articles about off–balance sheet financing, hidden debt, dilution of earnings, and other problems associated with new approaches to financing. Keeping abreast of the new financial instruments and understanding their nature have become increasingly difficult.[2] Examples of new financial instruments include asset-backed securities (such as those collateralized by mortgages or credit card receivables), traditional bonds split so that interest and principal sell separately (e.g., STRIPS, CATS), and puttable stock. King and Ortegren[3] discuss one type of hybrid security, the adjustable rate convertible note, and demonstrate some of the difficulties in

---

[1] Accounting Principles Board Opinion No. 14, "Accounting for Convertible Debt and Debt Issued with Stock Purchase Warrants" (AICPA, March 1969).

[2] For a description of some new financial instruments, see R. Sanborn and M. Atchison, "A CPA's Field Guide to New Financial Instruments," *Journal of Accountancy* (October 1985), pp. 165–172; and T. Rollins, D. Stout, and D. O'Mara, "The New Financial Instruments," *Management Accounting* (March 1990), pp. 35–41.

[3] T. King and A. Ortegren, "Accounting for Hybrid Securities: The Case of Adjustable Rate Convertible Notes," *The Accounting Review* (July 1988), pp. 522–535.

accounting for this and similar securities using currently acceptable procedures.

Interestingly, an unintended result of *APBO 14* is the creation of new hybrid securities specifically designed around the opinion's requirements; i.e., they are designed to comply in form with *APBO 14* while avoiding the spirit of its requirements. One example is the adjustable rate convertible note. Another is the "synthetic" convertible, discussed in a later section. *APBO 14* therefore bears partial responsibility for the explosion in number and diversity of financial instruments.

One indication of the magnitude of the problems related to financial instruments is that the FASB's Emerging Issues Task Force has focused on issues concerning financial instruments, financial institutions, or off–balance sheet financing in almost half of the more than 200 items it has considered since its formation in 1984.[4] Thus, the FASB's project dealing with financial instruments is quite timely and is viewed in the profession as one of far-reaching importance.

The FASB's Financial Instruments Project

The FASB's financial instruments project is divided into three related phases:

- Disclosure
- Recognition and measurement
- Distinguishing between liabilities and equity

The FASB undertook phase three of the project largely in response to problems of applying *APBO 14* to new financial instruments that cloud the distinction between debt and equity. These innovative financial instruments and relatively recent changes in the financial markets also ". . . have raised fundamental questions about the adequacy of current accounting standards for *traditional* instruments."[5]

In attempting to resolve issues associated with accounting for both traditional and new hybrid financial instruments in phases two and three of the project, the FASB adopted a "fundamental financial instrument approach."

The approach is based on the premise that all financial instruments are made up from a few "building blocks"— fundamental financial instruments— and that resolving the accounting issues related to those building block instruments will help resolve the accounting issues related to the other instruments. . . .[6]

In applying this building block approach, the FASB intends to deal with such questions as:

How should a compound financial instrument (such as convertible debt) with both liability and equity fundamental components be accounted for? Should the entire instrument be accounted for in the aggregate as either a liability or equity or should the instrument be broken into its fundamental components for financial reporting purposes?[7]

Consistent with the direction of the FASB's project, this study follows a building block approach and deals spe-

---

[4] C. Woods III and H. Bullen, "An Overview of the FASB's Financial Instruments Project," *Journal of Accountancy* (November 1989), p. 43.

[5] Ibid.

[6] Financial Accounting Standards Board, Financial Accounting Series, *Status Report* (January 8, 1990), p. 5.

[7] Woods and Bullen, op. cit., p. 47.

cifically with the feasibility of dividing hybrid financial instruments into their component fundamental instruments. Further, as recognized by the FASB, this approach applies to both new and traditional financial instruments. Although the focus in this study is on traditional convertible bonds, the fundamental financial instrument approach leads to identification of certain basic instruments that can be combined and configured in different ways to form hybrid financial instruments. This approach, therefore, is a general approach to dealing with all types of financial instruments.

The Stance of the APB

APBO 10 required that, upon issuance of convertible bonds or bonds with stock warrants, ". . . the portion of the proceeds attributable to the conversion feature or the warrants should be accounted for as paid-in capital. . . ."[8] In determining the amount of proceeds attributable to the conversion feature or warrants, *APBO 10* indicated that the amount assigned to equity would be the difference between the issue price of the debt and the estimated price at which the debt would have been issued without the equity feature.

A short time later, the APB issued *APBO 12*, suspending the accounting treatment for convertible debt required by *APBO 10*. The APB noted that, based on their observations and comments received, convertible securities ". . . raise difficult estimation and other problems. . . ."[9] After further study the APB

issued *APBO 14*, stipulating that no portion of the proceeds from the issuance of convertible debt should be assigned to the conversion feature of the securities. Five of the 18 members of the APB dissented from this requirement.

Interestingly, *APBO 14* gave a conceptual reason for abandoning the debt/equity allocation requirement of *APBO 10* in addition to the practical estimation problems. The principal rationale identified in *APBO 14* for treating all proceeds from the issuance of convertible debt as attributable to the debt was the "inseparability of the debt and conversion option." Practical estimation difficulties were identified only as a secondary consideration.

The Inseparability Argument

The validity of the "inseparability argument" has been questioned from the beginning. Within *APBO 14* itself, the dissenting views included examples of generally accepted accounting treatments of ". . . separate accounting recognition for disparate features of single instruments. . . ."[10] The literature includes additional arguments and examples indicating the inappropriateness of ignoring the value associated with the conversion feature simply because the debt and conversion feature could not be separately traded.[11] Casting further doubt on the viability of the inseparabil-

---

[8] Accounting Principles Board Opinion No. 10, "Omnibus Opinion—1966" (AICPA, December 1966), par. 8.

[9] Accounting Principles Board Opinion No. 12, "Omnibus Opinion—1967" (AICPA, December 1967), par. 11.

[10] APB Opinion No. 14, par. 9.

[11] See, for example, A. Ford, "Should Cost be Assigned to Conversion Value?" *The Accounting Review* (October 1969), pp. 818–822; A. Ford, "Why Cost Should be Assigned to Conversion Value—A Critique of APB Opinion No. 14," *The New York Certified Public Accountant* (October 1970), pp. 826–829; and L. Imdieke and J. Weygandt, "Classification of Convertible Debt," *The Accounting Review* (October 1969), pp. 798–805.

ity argument, *APBO 14* itself concluded that ". . . when convertible debt is issued at a substantial premium, there is a presumption that such premium represents paid-in capital."[12] This provision suggests that the failure to separately recognize conversion features was not a matter of inseparability but rather one of materiality. This, in turn, implies that the major reason for the APB's position in *APBO 14* was its original concern over measuring the value of the conversion feature.

An additional flaw in the approach of *APBO 14* is the failure to differentiate between two possible causes of a substantial premium. A substantial premium when a convertible debt security is issued could be due to a conversion feature with a significant value unto itself, a nominal interest rate set significantly above the prevailing market rate for the instrument, or some combination of the two. By not distinguishing between these two sources of a substantial premium, *APBO 14* allows for a significant premium caused by a high nominal interest rate to be assigned to equity.

Practical Problems of Allocation

The traditional argument against accounting for any issue proceeds attributable to the conversion feature as equity flows from the practical problems of assigning a subjective value to the conversion feature. Brigham[13] provides a theoretical model for determining the portion of the proceeds from convertible bonds associated with the debt, with the residual value assignable to the

conversion feature. Brigham's model identifies the present value of a pure debt instrument through the use of a ". . . market rate of interest on equivalent risk, pure debt issues." The difference between this value of a pure debt instrument and the total issue proceeds is residually assigned to the conversion feature, precisely the approach required in the superseded *APBO 10*.

Imdieke and Weygandt[14] discuss the problems of actually measuring conversion value in practice. After pointing out the existence of models to estimate the value of the conversion feature and noting the lack of consistency between these models, Imdieke and Weygandt call for further research on whether assessments of conversion value can be made with reasonable accuracy.

Allocations of convertible bond issue amounts should be possible by estimating the straight-debt value (the price at which the securities would sell without the conversion feature) of convertible securities. Discussions with professional bond traders and underwriters indicate that they regularly make the kinds of valuations needed for an accounting allocation of the issue price of convertible bonds. Moreover, pricing by different bond traders is expected to be relatively homogeneous, otherwise those traders consistently far "off the market" would soon be out of business.

Form Over Substance

The requirements of *APBO 14* seem to emphasize the form of a financial instrument at the expense of substance. As an example, a hybrid security known as a "synthetic" convertible bond enables companies to issue what

[12] APB Opinion No. 14, par. 18.

[13] E. Brigham, "An Analysis of Convertible Debentures: Theory and Some Empirical Evidence," *Journal of Finance* (March 1966), pp. 35–54.

[14] L. Imdieke and J. Weygandt, "Accounting for That Imputed Discount Factor," *Journal of Accountancy* (June 1970), pp. 54–58.

is essentially convertible debt and at the same time skirt the major requirement of *APBO 14*. A synthetic convertible is a nonconvertible bond with detachable stock warrants and certain other characteristics. According to *APBO 14:*

> . . . the portion of the proceeds of debt securities issued with detachable stock purchase warrants which is allocable to the warrants should be accounted for as paid-in-capital . . . The same accounting treatment applies to issues of debt securities (issued with detachable warrants) which may be surrendered in settlement of the exercise price of the warrant.[15]

Therefore, the proceeds from the issuance of synthetic convertibles are appropriately allocated between debt and equity.

The additional features of the nonconvertible bond that make it equivalent to a convertible are that (1) the bond may be tendered at face value as payment for the stock upon exercise of the warrants and (2) the nominal interest rate on the bond is low enough that the value of the bond as straight debt (without the warrants) is well below its face amount. These features virtually assure that, if the warrants are exercised, the bonds will be tendered in payment.

The form of these securities is such that under *APBO 14* the proceeds from issuance must be accounted for partially as debt and partially as equity. In substance, however, these securities are equivalent to convertible bonds; exercise of the warrants, with the accompanying issuance of stock, most assuredly results in the tendering (conversion) of the bonds. *APBO 14*, therefore, effectively requires that securities nearly

identical in substance be accounted for in significantly different ways.[16]

Assessing the Value of Special Debt Features

The research reported next examines two aspects of the practicality of assessing the value of conversion and other features of debt. First, the study considers whether estimates of conversion feature values presently are being made in practice. Second, the study deals with the reliability of such estimates.

Assessing the Value of Conversion Features in Practice

Discussions with 11 bond traders and underwriters indicated that finance professionals currently do estimate price or yield differentials associated with specific features or characteristics of debt securities and assign these differentials to the securities when issuing or trading those securities.[17] The general approach for pricing corporate bonds is to determine the yield for U.S. Treasury securities of similar maturity and then to adjust for differences in risk and other characteristics. Major differences include bond ratings, conversion features, debt seniority and collateral, sinking fund requirements, and call protection.

---

[15] APB Opinion No. 14, par. 16.

[16] While application of *APBO 14* results in different accounting treatments for the two instruments, the guidelines in *APBO 15,* "Earnings Per Share" (AICPA, May 1969), par. 43, specify that, for purposes of computing earnings per share, securities not specifically dealt with in the opinion ". . . should be dealt with in accordance with their substance. . . ." As synthetic convertibles are not mentioned directly in *APBO 15,* they presumably should be treated in the same way as convertible securities when computing earnings per share.

[17] King and Ortegren, pp. 530–531.

The first part of this study provides additional evidence regarding whether finance professionals currently make assessments of the price or yield associated with convertible debt issues as if the issues were nonconvertible. This part of the study involved a mail survey of 29 convertible bond underwriters. Where King and Ortegren focused mainly on bond traders, this survey solicited underwriters (1) to see if they price bonds using the same approach as traders and (2) because they are responsible for pricing the bonds at original issue.

A relatively small sample of underwriters was used for two reasons. First, the results of this portion of the study were meant only to add to the evidence already provided by King and Ortegren. Second, there are relatively few underwriters of convertible securities compared with the number of underwriters in general.

Twelve responses were received. In addition to their yes or no responses, 5 respondents provided clarifying comments. The survey results are reported in Table 1; nearly all respondents answered yes to the three questions asked. The clarifying comments accompanying the one dissenting response to Question

1 indicated that the respondent's firm normally considers straight equity as an alternative to convertible debt, but does estimate a straight-debt rate as a basis for pricing convertibles. The clarifying comments explaining the one "no" response to Question 3 focused on computation of the conversion premium and are not inconsistent with a "yes" response.

These results indicate that convertible bond underwriters currently do estimate the yields or prices associated with convertible debt as if the debt were nonconvertible, and that these estimates are used in making important financing decisions. The results also indicate that these underwriters use a "building block" approach to estimate the price or yield of convertible securities from a benchmark security, with adjustments for differences between the securities, such as convertibility, rating, and seniority.

The Reliability of Estimates of the Value of Conversion Premiums

The fact that convertible bond underwriters and their clients make financing decisions based on estimates of conversion premiums (or yield differences) implies that such an approach could be

TABLE 1 *Results of Survey of Bond Underwriters*

Question	Yes	No
1. Prior to the issuance of convertible debt, do you and your clients normally consider the issuance of nonconvertible debt as an alternative?	11	1
2. When considering the issuance of convertible debt, do you normally estimate the yield (effective interest rate) that would be required to issue the debt if it were nonconvertible?	12	0
3. When establishing an issue price for convertible debt, do you base the price (or yield) on the price (or yield) of other securities (e.g., Treasuries) and adjust for differences in ratings and features (e.g., convertible, call protection, sinking fund requirements)?	11	1

used to assist accountants in accounting for the proceeds of convertible debt issues. The standard for measuring the ability to estimate the value of conversion premiums should be whether agreement exists among those making the estimates. Value at a particular point in time represents a consensus among those in the market and is based on knowledge and expectations at that point in time. For accountants, the relevant question is whether a consensus can be reached as to the value of a conversion premium when a convertible security is issued. Once a security is traded in the market, this consensus on value is evidenced by the market price. Apparently underwriters have been reasonably successful in estimating the value of conversion premiums because nearly all convertible bonds are issued at par value or a price very near to par value.[18]

Evidence Regarding the Ability to Achieve a Consensus as to Value

Although the current successful use of estimates of conversion premiums can be observed in practice, this study provides some additional evidence that a reasonable consensus can be achieved when adjusting bond prices and yields for differences in features and characteristics. An experiment was designed in which traders at firms making a market in a nonconvertible issue of a company with a convertible issue outstanding were asked what price they would

---

[18]Underwriters generally attempt to issue corporate bonds at par (except zero coupon bonds). See F. Fabozzi and F. Zarb, *Handbook of Financial Markets* (Homewood, Illinois: Dow Jones–Irwin, 1981), p. 255; and D. Kieso and J. Weygandt, *Intermediate Accounting*, Sixth Edition (New York: John Wiley & Sons, 1989), p. 627.

quote for the convertible bonds if the bonds were nonconvertible. This was done in a real trade setting by a professional bond trader, although the question was hypothetical. All quotes solicited for the study for an individual bond were obtained within a few minutes of each other.

Bond traders rather than underwriters were used in the study because individual underwriters possess detailed knowledge about securities they underwrite, but not generally about those underwritten by others. Thus, unless underwriters were placed in an artificial situation, only one subject per bond would be available for the study, precluding any assessment of consensus. On the other hand, a number of traders often make a market in a particular security and work with that security on a regular basis, providing a number of subjects for each bond. The evidence provided by King and Ortegren and by the survey of underwriters in this study indicates that bond traders and underwriters employ similar or identical models for pricing convertible debt instruments (excluding convertible bonds trading primarily off the value of the underlying stock).

The experimental design included the following conditions:

1. There had to be both convertible and nonconvertible bonds outstanding for each company used. Different approaches often are used in pricing convertible and nonconvertible bonds in the after-markets, and the same individuals do not normally trade both convertibles and nonconvertibles. In this experiment, nonconvertible traders were asked to price the convertible bonds as if the bonds were nonconvertible.

2. For each security, there had to be at

least five market-makers. Because some market-makers were expected not to participate, a consensus would be hard to establish with a lesser number.

3. The firms selected for the study could not have nonconvertible bonds listed on an exchange. Listed prices might allow traders to make assessments of the value of the hypothetical securities that were biased by the quoted prices of the firms' nonconvertible bonds.

4. The bonds could not be nearing maturity, they had to be trading with interest (i.e., not in default on interest payments), the company could not be in bankruptcy, nor could there be other obvious abnormalities that might significantly affect the company's bond prices.

Only two companies met all of the conditions, partly because there often are only a few market-makers for bonds that are not heavily traded. Those bonds that are heavily traded often are listed on an exchange.

Table 2 shows the price quotes obtained for the two issues in this part of the study; the price variation is less than 5 percent. Even though the evidence generated is limited because of the strict requirements placed on the bond issues that could be included in the study, it does indicate achievement of a reasonable consensus as to the value of the debt and equity portions of convertible debt. Generalizing from a sample of two securities and quotes from seven traders should be done with care; however, the results do conform to the overall pattern established by other evidence.

A Test of Consensus with Respect to Bond Valuation

Difficulties associated with a direct test of whether consensus could be achieved in valuing conversion premiums led to a more indirect approach that focused on a somewhat broader issue. Bond underwriters and traders value a bond by (1) considering all features of the bond and (2) adjusting the price or yield for each of the relevant features or characteristics. A convertible bond trades in a fashion similar to a nonconvertible bond (but with a yield difference) as long as the bond's straight debt value is significantly above the value of the stock into which the bond is convertible. Convertibility is just one of many features considered when valuing the bond. Each relevant feature may cause the underwriter or trader to incremen-

TABLE 2 *Estimates of the Debt Value of Convertible Bonds*

Bond Issuer	Nominal Rate and Maturity	Moody's Bond Rating	Price Estimates	Bid Variation as % of Low Bid	Bid Variation as % of Face Value
MCI Communications	7.75% 2003	BA3	65 64 62, 62	4.8	3.0
Midlantic Banks, Inc.	8.25% 2010	A2	78 77 75.5	3.3	2.5

tally increase or decrease the estimate of the appropriate price or yield for that bond. For example, a trader bidding on a corporate bond might base the bid on the relevant-maturity Treasury security, increase the yield (decrease the price) for the lower rating of the corporate and for a call feature, and decrease the yield (increase the price) for a sinking fund provision.

Existence of a conversion feature is one additional element to be considered along with other features in valuing a bond. *APBO 14* indicates that adjustments for features other than the conversion privilege also may be needed because nonconvertible bonds often have different restrictions and characteristics than convertibles.[19] Thus, the broader question is whether a general consensus among individuals valuing convertible bonds can be reached when valuing various convertibles with different ratings and features. In other words, can finance professionals agree as to the value attributable to the various features and characteristics that are found in convertible bonds?

To test this question, an experiment was conducted in which corporate bond market-makers were asked to bid on convertible bonds. The bids of the different traders were compared for each bond to determine the extent to which the traders agreed with one another in their bidding. Because the bonds used in the experiment were selling at prices well in excess of the equivalent stock values—the bonds were not trading off the stock values—the traders were expected to estimate both the debt value of the bonds and the value of the various additional features, including the conversion option, and provide total valuations in the form of bids.

The experiment was conducted by a

professional bond trader in a real trade setting; the market-makers from whom bids were solicited were not aware that an experiment was being conducted. All bids on a particular issue were solicited within a few minutes of one another, as would be done in a real trade situation.

Corporate bonds for the study were selected from those listed in both the National Daily Quotation Service (Bond Section) and Moody's Bond Record. Only bonds with at least eight market-makers were included in the experiment. A higher limit for the minimum number of market-makers was set than in the previous section because bids (a commitment to buy at a particular price) were solicited in this part of the study rather than quotes (general levels with no commitment). Therefore, some market-makers were expected to "pass" rather than bid, passes often having to do with that trader's inventory position. In addition, not all market-makers in a particular issue were asked to bid. Traders often establish working relationships with particular market-makers and may avoid dealing with certain other market-makers for some reason. Bids were solicited from at least five market-makers for each security; the selection of specific market-makers from whom to solicit bids for each security was left to the trader.

Only bonds not listed on an exchange nor included in the NASDAQ (National Association of Securities Dealers Automated Quotation) system for over-the-counter securities and only bonds trading with interest and not nearing maturity were selected. Bond listings and automated quotes were viewed as having the potential for reducing the variability of bids because market-makers would have knowledge of other bids. Unusual situations were excluded because the aim of the study was to fo-

---

[19] APB Opinion No. 14, par. 8.

cus on the valuation of bond features and not upon assessments of the impact of unusual occurrences. Further, the bonds selected had to be trading at prices well in excess of the equivalent stock prices.

A total of six bond issues were found to be suitable for the study. The relatively small number of usable bonds resulted primarily from the need for a sufficient number of bids for each bond issue so that the degree of consensus could be assessed while ensuring that traders were unable to use electronically shared information in the determination of those bids.

As indicated in Table 3, the six bond issues used in the study carried Moody's bond ratings ranging from BAA3 to B3. The issues also reflected a range of relationships between the value of the convertible bonds and the value of the equivalent shares into which those bonds were convertible (see Price of Equivalent Shares in Table 3).

The bids received for each bond issue in the study are shown in Table 3, as is the variation (high bid minus low bid) for each bond, both as a percentage of the low bid and as a percentage of the par value of the bond. The variation of bids as a percentage of the low bid ranges from .8% to 2.3%, and the variation of bids as a percentage of the face value of the bonds ranges from .5% to 2%.[20] While no attempt was made to

define or test for statistical significance of the variability of bids, under virtually any measure of materiality used in accounting, the variations found would be considered not material.

The results of this experiment are not conclusive evidence that finance professionals agree in their estimates of the values of conversion premiums. Given, however, that valuation of the straight-debt component of a convertible security is very mechanistic, little variability would be expected in the valuation of this component of a convertible security.[21] Thus, the small amount of bid variability over the several securities in the study implies a lack of variability in estimates of individual features of the securities.

Summary, Conclusions, and Implications

The results of this study provide insight into (1) the practicality of the fundamental financial instrument approach identified by the FASB as the appropriate means of accounting for new hybrid financial instruments and (2) the question of whether the *APBO 14* guidelines for accounting for traditional convertible debt securities should be restructured to conform with the APB's original position in *APBO 10*.

APBO 14 presented two reasons for requiring that all proceeds of convertible bond issues be accounted for as debt. The first reason given was the inseparability of the constituent components. This argument was not well supported in the opinion or in the literature. Because *APBO 14* requires that when the equity element of a convertible debt issue is significant it should

---

[20] The analysis excludes one bid received for the bonds of Tri-Star Pictures. As can be seen from Table 3, one bid (80) differed from the others by a considerable margin. This bid was provided by a market-maker who stated that the normal trader specializing in that issue was absent that day and he was not very familiar with the issue. In the opinion of the trader soliciting the bids, the substitute market-maker bid well off the market, a method sometimes used by traders to pass.

[21] M. Stephens, ''Inseparability and the Valuation of Convertible Bonds,'' *Journal of Accountancy* (August 1971), p. 57.

TABLE 3 *Bids on Selected Convertible Bonds*

Bond Issuer	Nominal Rate and Maturity	Moody's Bond Rating	Bids	Price of Equivalent Shares*	Bid Variation as % of Low Bid	Bid Variation as % of Face Value
America West Air	7.5% 2011	B2	59.5, 59.5 59.125 59, 59 58.5 Pass	500	1.7	1.0
Convex Computer Corp.	6.0% 2012	B3	63.5, 63.5, 63.5 63 Pass, Pass	339	.8	.5
Costco Wholesale Corp.	7.25% 2011	B3	97 96.25 96 Pass, Pass	792	1.0	1.0
Hechinger Corp.	5.5% 2012	BAA3	90.25 90 89.5 89 Pass, Pass, Pass	638	1.4	1.3
Nortek Inc.	7.5% 2006	B1	64, 64, 64, 64 63	265	1.6	1.0
Tri-Star Pictures, Inc. (Columbia Pictures Entertainment, Inc.)	7.125% 2006	B2	88 87.75 87.5 87 86 80** Pass	672	2.3	2.0

*This column represents the market value of the equivalent shares for a $1000 face value bond on the day bids were solicited for the bonds. A comparison of the value of equivalent shares to the value of a $1000 bond can be accomplished by multiplying the amounts in the Bids column by 10.

**See footnote 20.

be recognized, materiality seems to be the issue, not inseparability. The major reason for not apportioning some amount to the conversion feature of convertible debt seems to relate to the practical problems of making such an allocation.

While the practical difficulties of estimating the value of a conversion option may have been a barrier at the time *APBO 14* was issued, accounting and finance professionals now have had more than 20 years of experience in dealing with convertible securities and, to a lesser extent, other types of hybrid financial instruments. Clearly those estimates are being made currently. Evidence presented in this study supports previous findings and shows that finance professionals do estimate the prices (or yields) of convertible bonds as if they were nonconvertible and then value the conversion feature. These estimates are apparently suitable for decisions involving many millions of dollars and should prove satisfactory for the accounting allocations originally required by *APBO 10*.

This study also provides evidence that different finance professionals assessing the same debt features independently can achieve a consensus as to the value of the debt. Currently, even though there is agreement that a conversion option has value, accountants assign it a value of zero. While there is no way of determining the "true value" of a particular debt feature such as a conversion option, agreement among finance professionals should provide a better estimate than accounting for the feature as if it had no value.

In sum, the study provided several pieces of evidence collectively favoring the feasibility of estimating the portion of the proceeds of convertible debt issues attributable to the conversion feature. This evidence supports the notion of accounting for hybrid financial instruments according to the economic substance of the instruments by dealing with each of the key elements individually instead of classifying an entire instrument as either debt or equity. The approach reported herein may help resolve the issues currently before the FASB involving hybrid financial instruments.

Cases

- ## Case 9-1

On January 1, 1994, Plywood Homes, Inc., issued 20-year, 4 percent bonds having a face value of $1,000,000. The interest on the bonds is payable semi-annually on June 30 and December 31. The proceeds to the company were $975,000 (i.e., on the day they were issued the bonds had a market value of $975,000). On June 30, 1994, the company's fiscal closing date, when the bonds were being traded at 98½, each of the following amounts was suggested as a possible valuation basis for reporting the bond liability on the balance sheet.

1. $975,625 (proceeds, plus six months' straight-line amortization)
2. $1,000,000 (face value)

3. $1,780,000 (face value plus interest payments)

4. $985,000 (fair value)

Required:

a. Distinguish between nominal and effective interest rates.

b. Explain the nature of the $25,000 difference between the face value and the market value of the bonds on January 1, 1994.

c. Between January 1 and June 30, the market value of the company's bonds increased from $975,000 to $985.000. Explain. Discuss the significance of the increase to the company.

d. Evaluate each of the four suggested alternatives for reporting the bond liability on the balance sheet, giving arguments for and against each alternative. Your answer should take the investor and the reporting company into consideration.

• Case 9-2

Whiley Company issued a $100,000, 5-year, 10 percent note to Security Co. on January 2, 1993. Interest was to be paid annually each December 31. The stated rate of interest reflected the market rate of interest on similar notes.

Whiley made the first interest payment on December 31, 1993, but due to financial difficulties was unable to pay any interest on December 31, 1994.

Security agreed to the following terms:

1. The $100,000 principal would be payable in five equal installments, beginning December 31, 1995.

2. The accrued interest at December 31, 1994, would be forgiven.

3. Whiley Company would be required to make no other payments.

Because of the risk associated with the note, it has no determinable fair value. The note is secured by equipment having a fair value of $80,000 at December 31, 1994. The present value of the five equal installments discounted at 10 percent is $75,815.

Required:

a. Under current GAAP, at which amount would Whiley report the restructured liability at December 31, 1994? Explain. How much gain would Whiley recognize in its income statement for 1994? Explain. How much interest expense would Whiley recognize in 1995? Explain.

b. Under current GAAP, what alternatives does Security have for reporting the restructured receivable? Explain. How would each alternative affect the 1994 income statement and future interest revenue? Explain.

c. Discuss the pros and cons of the alternatives in (b) and compare them to the prior GAAP treatment (treatment that was reciprocal to the debtor).

d. If the provisions of *SFAS No. 114* were to be extended to debtors, what would be the incremental effect (difference between what would be reported under *SFAS No. 114* and current GAAP for debtors) on Whiley's financial statements, debt-to-equity ratio, and EPS for 1994 and 1995? Explain.

• Case 9-3

Baker Company needs $1,000,000 to expand its existing plant. Baker management is considering the following two alternative forms of financing.

1. At the beginning of 1994, issue $1,000,000 of convertible, 10-year, 10 percent bonds. Each $1,000 bond can be converted into 20 shares of Baker $10.00 par value common stock. The conversion may take place any time after three years.
2. At the beginning of 1994, issue 10,000 shares of $100 par value, $10, redeemable preferred stock. The preferred is redeemable at $102 10 years from the date of issue.

Baker management is concerned about the effects of the two alternatives on cash flows, their financial statements, and future financing for other planned expansion activities. Also, there are existing debt covenants that restrict the debt-to-equity ratio to 2 : 1; $1,000,000 in new debt would cause the debt-to-equity ratio to be close to 2 : 1. Baker believes that either the bonds or the preferred stock could be sold at par value. Their income tax rate is 34 percent.

The Baker Company common stock is currently selling for $45.00 per share.

Required:
a. Discuss the theoretical and currently generally accepted accounting treatments for convertible bonds.
b. Discuss the SEC and currently generally accepted accounting treatments for redeemable preferred stock.
c. Compare the effects of the two financing alternatives on Baker Company's balance sheet, income statement, and cash flows under current GAAP. Your comparison should consider 1994 and future years, the potential conversion of the bonds, and the debt covenant restrictions.
d. If the FASB were to decide to recognize the value for conversion (conversion feature) as equity, would this have an impact on the decision of Baker Company, and how would Baker Company's financial statements be affected if they chose the convertible bond alternative? Would the decision to select convertible bonds versus redeemable preferred stock be affected, especially in light of the concern regarding the debt covenant restrictions?

• Case 9-4

The appropriate method of amortizing a premium or discount on issuance of bonds is the effective interest method.

Required:
a. What is the effective interest method of amortization and how is it different from or similar to the straight-line method of amortization?
b. How is interest and the amount of discount or premium amortization computed using the effective interest method, and why and how do amounts obtained using the effective interest method differ from amounts computed under the straight-line method?

c. Generally, the effective interest method is defended on the grounds that it provides the appropriate amount of interest expense. Does it also provide an appropriate balance sheet amount for the liability balance? Why, or why not?

• **Case 9-5**

Gains or losses from the early extinguishment of debt that is refunded can theoretically be accounted for in three ways.

1. Amortized over the life of old debt.
2. Amortized over the life of the new debt issue.
3. Recognized in the period of extinguishment.

Required:
a. Discuss the supporting arguments for each of the three theoretical methods of accounting for gains and losses from the early extinguishment of debt.
b. Which of the three methods would provide a balance sheet measure that reflects the present value of the future cash flows discounted at the interest rate that is commensurate with the risk associated with the new debt issue? Why?
c. Which of the three methods is generally accepted and how should the appropriate amount of gain or loss be shown in a company's financial statements?

• **Case 9-6**

Angela Company is a manufacturer of toys. During the year, the following situations arose.

• A safety hazard related to one of its toy products was discovered. It is considered probable that liabilities have been incurred. Based on past experience, a reasonable estimate of the amount of loss can be made.

• One of its small warehouses is located on the bank of a river and could no longer be insured against flood losses. No flood losses have occurred after the date that the insurance became unavailable.

• This year, Angela began promoting a new toy by including a coupon, redeemable for a movie ticket, in each toy's carton. The movie ticket, which cost Angela $2, is purchased in advance and then mailed to the customer when the coupon is received by Angela. Angela estimated, based on past experience, that 60 percent of the coupons would be redeemed. Forty percent of the coupons would be actually redeemed this year, and the remaining 20 percent of the coupons are expected to be redeemed next year.

Required:
a. How should Angela report the safety hazard? Why? Do not discuss deferred tax implications.

b. How should Angela report the uninsured flood risk? Why?

c. How should Angela account for the toy promotion campaign in this year?

• **Case 9-7**

Business transactions often involve the exchange of property, goods, or services for notes on similar instruments that may stipulate no interest rate or an interest rate that varies from prevailing rates.

Required:

a. When a note is exchanged for property, goods, or services, what value should be placed upon the note
   i. If it bears interest at a reasonable rate and is issued in a bargained transaction entered into at arm's length? Explain.
   ii. If it bears no interest and/or is not issued in a bargained transaction entered into at arm's length? Explain.

b. If the recorded value of a note differs from the face value,
   i. How should the difference be accounted for? Explain.
   ii. How should this difference be presented in the financial statements? Explain.

• **Case 9-8**

On April 1, 1993, Janine Corporation sold some of its 5-year, $1,000 face value 12 percent term bonds dated March 1, 1993, at an effective annual interest rate (yield) of 10 percent. Interest is payable semiannually, and the first interest payment date is September 1, 1993. Janine uses the interest method of amortization. Bond issue costs were incurred in preparing and selling the bond issue.

On November 1, 1993, Janine sold directly to underwriters, at lump-sum price, $1,000 face value, 9 percent serial bonds dated November 1, 1993, at an effective interest rate (yield) of 11 percent. A total of 25 percent of these serial bonds are due November 1, 1995, a total of 30 percent on November 1, 1997. The rest are due on November 1, 2000. Interest is payable semiannually and the first interest payment date is May 1, 1994. Janine uses the interest method of amortization. Bond issue costs were incurred in preparing and selling the bond issue.

Required:

a. How would the market price of the term bonds and the serial bonds be determined?

b. i. How would all items related to the term bonds, except for bond issue costs, be presented in a balance sheet prepared immediately after the term bond issue was sold?
   ii. How would all items related to the serial bonds, except for bond issue costs, be presented in a balance sheet prepared immediately after the serial bond issue was sold?

c. What alternative methods could be used to account for the bond issue costs for the term bonds in 1993? Which method(s) is (are) considered current GAAP? Which method(s), if any, would affect the calculation of interest expense? Why?

d. How would the amount of interest expense for the term bonds and the serial bonds be determined for 1993?

• Case 9-9

The two basic requirements for the accrual of a loss contingency are supported by several basic concepts of accounting. Four of these concepts are periodicity (time periods), measurement, objectivity, and relevance.

Required:
Discuss how the two basic requirements for accrual of a loss contingency relate to the four concepts listed above.

• Case 9-10

The following three independent sets of facts relate to (1) the possible accrual or (2) the possible disclosure by other means of a loss contingency.

Situation 1
A company offers a one-way warranty for the product that it manufactures. A history of warranty claims has been compiled and the probable amount of claims related to sales for a given period can be determined.

Situation 2
Subsequent to the date of a set of financial statements, but prior to the issuance of the financial statements, a company enters into a contract that will probably result in a significant loss to the company. The amount of the loss can be reasonably estimated.

Situation 3
A company has adopted a policy of recording self-insurance for any possible losses resulting from injury to others by the company's vehicles. The premium for an insurance policy for the same risk from an independent insurance company would have an annual cost of $2,000. During the period covered by the financial statements, there were no accidents involving the company's vehicles that resulted in injury to others.

Required:
Discuss the accrual of a loss contingency and/or type of disclosure necessary (if any) and the reason(s) why such a disclosure is appropriate for each of the three independent sets of facts above. Complete your response to each situation before proceeding to the next situation.

Recommended Additional Readings

Byington, J. Ralph, and Paul Munter. "Disclosures about Financial Instruments." *CPA Journal* (September 1990), pp. 42–44, 46–48.

Clark, Myrtle W. "Entity Theory, Modern Capital Structure Theory, and the Distinction between Debt and Equity." *Accounting Horizons* (September 1993).

Imdieke, Leroy F., and Jerry J. Weygandt. "Accounting for that Imputed Discount Factor." *Journal of Accountancy* (June 1970), pp. 54–58.

Kulkarni, Deepak. "The Valuation of Liabilities." *Accounting and Business Research* (Summer 1980), pp. 291–297.

Mielke, David E., and James Seifert. "A Survey on the Effects of Defeasing Debt." *Journal of Accounting, Auditing and Finance* (1987), pp. 65–78.

Nair, R. D., Larry E. Rittenberg, and Jerry J. Weygandt. "Accounting for Interest Rate Swaps—A Critical Evaluation." *Accounting Horizons* (September 1990), pp. 20–30.

Pariser, David B. "Financial Reporting Implications of Troubled Debt." *CPA Journal* (February 1989), pp. 33–39.

Stephens, Matthew J. "Inseparability and the Valuation of Convertible Bonds." *Journal of Accountancy* (August 1971), pp. 54–62.

Bibliography

Amble, Joan Lordi. "The FASB's New ED on Disclosures." *Journal of Accountancy* (November 1989), pp. 63, 64, 66–69.

Anton, Hector R. "Accounting for Bond Liabilities." *Journal of Accountancy* (September 1956), pp. 53–56.

Bevis, Herman. "Contingencies and Probabilities in Financial Statements." *Journal of Accountancy* (October 1968), pp. 37–41.

Carpenter, Charles G., and Joseph F. Wojdak. "Capitalizing Executory Contracts: A Perspective." *New York CPA* (January 1971), pp. 40–47.

Castellano, Joseph F., and Gerald E. Keyes. "An Application of APB Opinion No. 21." *The Ohio CPA* (Summer 1972), pp. 86–91.

Clancy, Donald K. "What Is a Convertible Debenture? A Review of the Literature in the U.S.A." *Abacus* (December 1978), pp. 171–179.

Cloud, Douglas, Jack E. Smith, and Edwin Waters. "When Is a Liability Not a Liability?" *National Public Accountant* (December 1986), pp. 42–47.

Collier, Boyd, and Curtis Carnes. "Convertible Bonds and Financial Reality." *Management Accounting* (February 1979), pp. 47, 48, 52.

Cramer, Joe J., Jr. "The Nature and Importance of Discounted Present Value in Financial Accounting and Reporting." *The Arthur Andersen Chronicle* (September 1977), pp. 27–39.

Davis, Larry R., Linda M. Lovata, and Kirk L. Philipich. "The Effect of Debt Defeasance on the Decisions of Loan Officers." *Accounting Horizons* (June 1991), pp. 64–70.

Falk, Haim, and Stephen L. Buzby. "What's Missing in Accounting for Convertible Bonds?" *CA Magazine* (July 1978), pp. 40–45.

Ford, Allen. "Should Cost Be Assigned to Conversion Value?" *The Accounting Review* (October 1969), pp. 818–822.

Gamble, George O., and Joe J. Cramer, Jr. "The Role of Present Value in the Measurement and Recording of Nonmonetary Financial Assets and Liabilities: An Examination." *Accounting Horizons* (December 1992), pp. 32–41.

Henderson, M. S. "Nature of Liabilities." *Australian Accountant* (July 1974), pp. 328–330, 333–334.

Hughes, John S. "Toward a Contract Basis of Valuation in Accounting." *The Accounting Review* (October 1978), pp. 882–894.

Jacobsen, Lyle E. "Liabilities and Quasi Liabilities." In *Modern Accounting Theory*, Morton Backer, ed. Englewood Cliffs, N.J.: Prentice-Hall, Inc., 1966, pp. 232–249.

King, Raymond D. "The Effect of Convertible Bond Equity Values on Dilution and Leverage." *The Accounting Review* (July 1984), pp. 419–431.

Ma, Ronald, and Malcolm C. Miller. "Conceptualizing the Liability." *Accounting and Business Research* (Autumn 1978), pp. 258–265.

McCullers, Levis D. "An Alternative to APB Opinion No. 14." *Journal of Accounting Research* (Spring 1971), pp. 160–164.

Melcher, Beatrice. *Stockholders' Equity*. New York: American Institute of Certified Public Accountants, 1973.

Meyers, Stephen L. "Accounting for Long Term Notes." *Management Accounting* (July 1973), pp. 49–51.

Miller, Jerry D. "Accounting for Warrants and Convertible Bonds." *Management Accounting* (January 1973), pp. 26–28.

Moonitz, Maurice. "The Changing Concept of Liabilities." *Journal of Accountancy* (May 1960), pp. 41–46.

Munter, Paul. "The Financial Instruments Project Marches On." *CPA Journal* (July 1992), pp. 30–32, 34–36.

Pacter, Paul. "A Synopsis of APB Opinion No. 21: An Explanation of the Provisions of the APB Opinion on Interest on Receivables and Payables." *Journal of Accountancy* (March 1972), pp. 57–67.

Roden, Peyton F. "The Financial Implications of In-Substance Defeasance." *Journal of Accounting Auditing and Finance* (1987), pp. 79–89.

Rogers, Richard L., and Krishnagopal Menon. "Accounting for Deferred-Payment Notes." *The Accounting Review* (July 1985), pp. 547–557.

Savage, Charles L. "Review of APB Opinion No. 28—Early Extinguishment of Debt." *The CPA Journal* (April 1973), pp. 283–285.

Shoenthal, Edward R. "Contingent Legal Liabilities." *The CPA Journal* (March 1976), pp. 30–34.

Sprouse, Robert T. "Accounting for What-You-May-Call-Its." *Journal of Accountancy* (October 1966), pp. 45–53.

Swieringa, Robert J., and Dale Morse. "Accounting for Hybrid Convertible Debentures." *The Accounting Review* (January 1985), pp. 127–133.

Waxman, Robert N. "Review of APB Opinion No. 21—Interest on Receivables and Payables." *The CPA Journal* (August 1972), pp. 627–633.

Weil, Roman L. "Role of Time Value of Money in Financial Reporting." *Accounting Horizons* (December 1990), pp. 47–67.

Accounting for
Income Taxes

Most accountants agree that corporate income tax is an expense. Treating income tax as an expense is required under current generally accepted accounting principles (GAAP). This treatment is consistent with proprietary theory because the earnings that accrue to owners are reduced by corporate obligations to the government. Also, because income tax does not result from transactions with owners, expensing corporate income tax is consistent with the *SFAC No. 6* definition of comprehensive income. Thus, on the surface accounting for income taxes would appear to be a nonissue.

However, accounting for income taxes has been a most controversial financial accounting topic for many years. The controversy centers around a number of reporting and measurement issues. This chapter will trace the historical development of GAAP for income taxes. We will examine the theoretical accounting issues as well as the reporting requirements of *Accounting Principles Board (APB) Opinion No. 11, Statement of Financial Accounting Standards (SFAS) No. 96,* and the current authoritative pronouncement, *SFAS No. 109.*

Historical Perspective

Accounting for income taxes became a significant issue in the 1940s when the Internal Revenue Code (IRC) permitted companies to depreciate the cost of emergency facilities considered essential to the war effort over a period of 60 months.[1] For a five-year period, businesses were able to reduce taxable income below what it would have been under the accounting method of depreciation. The total depreciation charge over the life of the asset was the

[1] Frank R. Rayburn, "A Chronological Review of the Authoritative Literature on Interperiod Tax Allocation: 1940–1985," *The Accounting Historians Journal* (Fall 1986), p. 91.

same for financial accounting income and for taxable income, but the allocation of cost to financial accounting income in each accounting period differed significantly from the allocation to taxable income. Prior to this Internal Revenue Service regulation, accounting practitioners expensed income tax as it was incurred per the corporate tax return. Some accountants argued that when accelerated tax depreciation is allowed, expensing the amount of the tax liability incurred in each period results in material distortions of periodic earnings. For example, when pretax financial accounting income is the same in each accounting period, tax expense fluctuates and reported earnings is not normalized.

The Committee on Accounting Procedure responded in 1944 by issuing *Accounting Research Bulletin (ARB) No. 23,* "Accounting for Income Taxes."[2] *ARB No. 23* subsequently became Chapter 10, Section B of the AICPA's consolidated set of accounting procedures, *ARB No. 43.*[3] This release stated,

> Income taxes are an expense that should be allocated, when necessary and practicable, to income and other accounts, as other expenses are allocated. What the income statement should reflect . . . is the expense properly allocable to the income included in the income statement for the year.[4]

It follows that items reported in the income statement have tax consequences. These tax consequences are expenses and should be treated in a manner similar to other expenses reported in the income statement. Accrual accounting requires the recognition of revenues and expenses in the period incurred, without regard to the timing of cash receipts and payments. Consequently, the tax effects of business transactions should be recorded in a similar manner. That is, income tax should be allocated to periods so that the items reported on the income statement are matched with their respective tax consequences. The allocation of income taxes to accounting periods is termed *interperiod tax allocation.*

ARB No. 23 did not apply to those cases where "differences between the tax return and the income statement will recur regularly over a comparatively long period of time."[5] A debate ensued as to whether the tax consequences of all items resulting in tax treatment that differs from accounting treatment should be allocated. In addition, *ARB No. 23* did not provide clear guidance on how to measure specific tax consequences. The nature of income taxes was subsequently studied by the APB, which issued *APB Opinion No. 11,* "Accounting for Income Taxes."[6] *APB Opinion No. 11* extended interperiod tax allocation

---

[2]American Institute of Accountants, Committee on Accounting Procedure, *Accounting Research Bulletin No. 23,* "Accounting for Income Taxes" (New York: AIA, 1944).

[3]American Institute of Accountants, Committee on Accounting Procedure, *Accounting Research Bulletin No. 43,* "Restatement and Revision of Accounting Research Bulletins" (New York: AIA, 1953).

[4]Ibid., Section B, par. 4.

[5]Ibid., Section B, par. 1.

[6]Accounting Principles Board, *Opinion No. 11,* "Accounting for Income Taxes" (New York: AICPA, 1967).

to all items resulting in differences in the timing of revenue and expense recognition in the income statement and the tax return. The measurement and reporting procedures required under *APB Opinion No. 11* were consistent with the income statement approach outlined in *ARB No. 43*. Nevertheless, this *Opinion* was widely criticized. Opponents argued that the resulting balance sheet amounts did not reflect the future tax consequences of economic events and transactions. In response the Financial Accounting Standards Board (FASB) issued *SFAS No. 96*, "Accounting for Income Taxes,"[7] which proscribed a balance sheet approach to allocating income taxes among accounting periods. *SFAS No. 96* did not silence the critics of accounting for income taxes, and some of the provisions of *SFAS No. 96* were so controversial that the FASB was compelled to delay the effective date of the pronouncement twice. Subsequently, *SFAS No. 96* was superseded by *SFAS No. 109*, "Accounting for Income Taxes."[8]

The Income Tax Allocation Issue

According to *Statement of Financial Accounting Concepts (SFAC) No. 1*, the objective of financial reporting is to provide information that is useful in predicting the amounts and timing of future cash flows.[9] GAAP guide the reporting and measurement of economic events and transactions to meet this goal.

Most economic events and transactions have tax cash flow consequences. These consequences are reported on tax returns in accordance with the IRC. The IRC is enacted by Congress. The goal of the IRC is to provide revenue, in an equitable manner, to operate the Federal Government, and on occasion the IRC may also be used to regulate the economy. These same economic events and transactions are also reported in published financial statements by following GAAP. In many instances, the reporting requirements of the IRC differ from the reporting requirements for financial accounting as defined by GAAP. As a result, the taxes paid in a given year may not reflect the tax consequences of events and transactions that are reported in the income statement for that same year.

When the IRC requires that revenues and expenses be recognized in different accounting periods from GAAP, taxable income is temporarily different from pretax financial accounting income. This temporary difference is termed an *originating difference*. In a subsequent period the event that caused the originating difference will reverse itself. The reversal is termed a *reversing difference*. Originating and reversing temporary differences cause an accounting problem that is termed the *income tax allocation issue*.

[7] Financial Accounting Standards Board, *Statement of Financial Accounting Standards No. 96*, "Accounting for Income Taxes" (Stamford, Conn.: FASB, 1987).

[8] Financial Accounting Standards Board, *Statement of Financial Accounting Standards No. 109*, "Accounting for Income Taxes" (Stamford, Conn.: FASB, 1992).

[9] Financial Accounting Standards Board, *Statement of Financial Accounting Concepts No. 1*, "Objectives of Financial Reporting by Business Enterprises" (Stamford, Conn.: FASB, 1978), par. 37.

The objectives of accounting for income taxes are to recognize the amount of taxes payable or refundable for the current year and to recognize the future tax consequences of temporary differences as well as net operating losses (NOLs) and unused tax credits.[10] To facilitate discussion of the issues raised by the concept of interperiod tax allocation, we will first examine the nature of differences among pretax financial income, taxable income, and NOLs.

Permanent and Temporary Differences

Differences between pretax financial accounting income and taxable income are either **permanent differences** or **temporary differences.** Temporary differences between pretax financial accounting income and taxable income affect two or more accounting periods and, thus, are the focus of the income tax allocation issue. Permanent differences do not have income tax allocation consequences.

Permanent Differences

Most *permanent differences* between pretax financial accounting income and taxable income occur when specific provisions of the IRC exempt certain types of revenue from taxation or prohibit the deduction of certain types of expenses. Others occur when the IRC allows tax deductions that are not expenses under GAAP. Permanent differences arise because of federal economic policy or because Congress may wish to alleviate a provision of the IRC that falls too heavily on one segment of the economy. There are three types of permanent differences:

1. *Revenue recognized for financial accounting reporting purposes that is never taxable.* Examples include interest on municipal bonds and life insurance proceeds payable to a corporation for an insured employee.

2. *Expenses recognized for financial accounting reporting purposes that are never deductible for income tax purposes.* An example is life insurance premiums on employees. (Until 1994 the amortization of goodwill was a permanent difference but the *Revenue Reconciliation Act of 1993* allows goodwill to be amortized over a 15-year period).

3. *Income tax deductions that do not qualify as expenses under GAAP.* Examples include percentage depletion in excess of cost depletion and the special dividend exclusion.

Permanent differences affect pretax financial accounting income or taxable income, but not both. A corporation that has nontaxable revenue or additional deductions for income tax reporting purposes will report a relatively lower taxable income as compared to pretax financial accounting income than it would have if these items were not present, whereas a corporation with

---

[10] Financial Accounting Standards Board, *Statements of Financial Accounting Standards No. 109,* "Accounting for Income Taxes" (Stamford, Conn.: FASB, 1992), pars. 3 and 6.

expenses that are not tax deductible will report a relatively higher taxable income.

Temporary Differences

Temporary differences between pretax financial accounting income and taxable income arise because the timing of revenues, gains, expenses, or losses in financial accounting income occurs in a different period from taxable income. These timing differences result in assets and liabilities having different bases for financial accounting purposes than for income tax purposes at the end of a given accounting period. Additional temporary differences occur because specific provisions of the IRC create different bases for depreciation or for gain or loss recognition for income taxes purposes than are used for financial accounting purposes. Since many of these additional temporary differences relate to more complex provisions of the tax laws, only timing differences will be discussed in detail.

Reversals of originating differences that cause current taxable income to be less than current financial accounting income cause future taxable income to exceed future financial accounting income. The difference is taxable in future accounting periods. In this case, the amount of the reversal is termed a *taxable amount.* The opposite occurs for originating differences that cause current taxable income to exceed current financial accounting income. These temporary differences result in future *deductible amounts.* The existence of future taxable or deductible amounts implies that temporary differences have future tax consequences. The future tax consequences argument rests on the inherent GAAP assumption that reported amounts of assets and liabilities will be recovered or settled, respectively. For example, GAAP requires lower-of-cost-or-market for assets when full recovery of cost is not expected. This assumption implies that reversals of temporary differences occur when reported amounts of assets are recovered or reported amounts of liabilities are settled.[11]

APB Opinion No. 11 limited the scope of temporary differences to timing differences. *Timing differences* occur when taxable revenues or gains, or tax deductible expenses or losses, are recognized in one accounting period for financial accounting reporting purposes and in a different accounting period for income tax purposes. The resulting tax consequences affect current and future accounting periods.

Timing differences may be classified into two broad categories:

Current Financial Accounting Income Exceeds Current Taxable Income[12]

1. ***Revenues or gains are included in financial accounting income prior to the time they are included in taxable income.*** For example, gross profit on installment sales is included in financial accounting income at the point of sale but is generally reported for tax purposes as the cash is collected.

---

[11] Ibid., par. 11.

[12] *SFAS No. 109* describes these temporary differences in paragraph 11.

2. *Expenses or losses are deducted to compute taxable income prior to the time they are deducted to compute financial accounting income.* For example, a fixed asset may be depreciated by MACRS depreciation for income tax purposes and by the straight-line method for financial accounting purposes.[13]

Current Financial Accounting Income Is Less Than Current Taxable Income

1. *Revenues or gains are included in taxable income prior to the time they are included in financial accounting income.* For example, rent received in advance is taxable when it is received but is recorded for financial accounting purposes under the accrual method as it is earned.

2. *Expenses or losses are deducted to compute financial accounting income prior to the time they are deducted to determine taxable income.* For example, product warranty costs are estimated and recorded as expenses at the time of sale of the product for financial accounting purposes, but deducted as actually incurred in later years to determine taxable income.

SFASs No. 96 and *No. 109* broadened the scope of temporary differences by including all "events that create differences between the tax bases of assets and liabilities and their amounts for financial reporting."[14] For example, an asset donated to a business has a zero basis for tax purposes, but is recorded at its fair market value for financial accounting purposes. This creates a temporary difference that will reverse either through depreciation or the sale of the asset; thus, these additional temporary differences also result in tax consequences that affect two or more accounting periods.

Additional Temporary Differences[15]

1. *A reduction in the tax basis of depreciable assets because of tax credits.* The amounts received on future recovery of the amount of the asset for financial accounting purposes will be taxable when the asset is recovered. For example, the IRC allows taxpayers to reduce the depreciation basis of assets by half of the amount of the investment tax credit (ITC) taken for the asset. As a result, future taxable incomes will exceed future pretax financial accounting income by the amount of the tax basis reduction. Hence, the basis reduction is a temporary difference that creates a future taxable amount. The future taxable amount is equivalent to the amount needed to recover the additional financial accounting asset cost basis.

2. *The ITC accounted for by the deferred method.* Recall that the preferred treatment of accounting for the ITC is to reduce the cost of the related asset by the amount of the ITC. If this method is used, the amounts received on

---

[13] MACRS depreciation frequently results in relatively higher depreciation amounts than straight-line depreciation in the early years of an asset's life.

[14] Ibid., par. 3.

[15] These temporary differences are also described in *SFAS No. 109*, par. 11.

future recovery of the reduced cost of the asset for financial accounting purposes will be less than the tax basis of the asset. The difference will be tax deductible when the asset is recovered.

3. *Foreign operations for which the reporting currency is the functional currency.* The provisions of *SFAS No. 52*, "Foreign Currency Translation,"[16] require certain assets to be remeasured from the foreign currency to U. S. dollars using historical exchange rates when the reporting currency is the functional currency.[17] If exchange rates subsequently change, there will be a difference between the foreign tax basis and the U. S. dollar historical cost of assets and liabilities. That difference will be taxable or deductible for foreign tax purposes when the reported amounts of the assets and liabilities are recovered and settled, respectively.

4. *An increase in the tax basis of assets because of indexing for inflation.* The tax law may require adjustment of the tax basis of a depreciable asset for effects of inflation. The inflation-adjusted basis of the asset will then be used to compute future tax deductions for depreciation, or the gain or loss on the sale of the asset. Amounts received on future recovery of the remaining cost of the asset recorded for financial accounting purposes will then be less than the remaining tax basis of the asset, and the difference will be tax deductible when the asset is recovered.

5. *Business combinations accounted for by the purchase method.* There may be differences between the assigned value and the tax basis of the assets and liabilities recognized in a business combination accounted for as a purchase.[18] These differences will result in taxable or deductible amounts when the recorded amounts of the assets are recovered or the recorded amounts of the liabilities are settled.

Under current GAAP, published financial statements should reflect the tax consequences of economic events and transactions reported in those financial statements. Because temporary differences affect current and future tax payments, the current period income tax expense comprises the *current provision for taxes* (taxes payable in the tax return) and the results of interperiod tax allocation (*deferred income taxes*). The deferred tax component of tax expense reflects the tax consequences of current period originating and reversing differences. The expected cash flows of future tax consequences resulting from temporary differences between pretax financial accounting income and taxable income reflect anticipated future tax benefits (*deferred tax assets*) or payables (*deferred tax liabilities*).

[16] Financial Accounting Standards Board, *Statement of Financial Accounting Standards No. 52,* "Foreign Currency Translation" (Stamford, Conn.: FASB, 1981).

[17] *SFAS No. 52* defines the functional currency as the currency of the primary economic environment in which an entity operates. See Chapter 16 for a discussion of foreign currency translation.

[18] Under the purchase method of accounting for business combinations, the assets and liabilities acquired are recorded at their fair market values, not their previous book values. See Chapter 14 for a discussion of business combinations.

Net Operating Losses

A NOL occurs when the amount of total tax deductions and losses is greater than the amount of total taxable revenues and gains during an accounting period. The IRC allows corporations reporting NOLs to carry these losses back and forward to offset other reported taxable income (currently back three years and forward 15 years).

A NOL carryback is applied to the taxable income of the three preceding years in reverse order beginning with the earliest year and moving forward to the most recent year. If unused NOLs are still available, they are carried forward for up to 15 years to offset any future taxable income. NOL carrybacks result in the refund of prior taxes paid. Thus, the tax benefits of NOL carrybacks are currently realizable and are recorded for financial accounting purposes as reductions in the current period loss. A receivable is recognized on the balance sheet and the associated benefit is shown on the current year's income.

Whether to recognize the potential benefit of a NOL carryforward has added additional controversy to the income tax accounting debate. The APB argued that the benefit of a NOL carryforward is generally not assured in the loss period.[19] Nevertheless, *APB Opinion No. 11* allowed the recognition of anticipated benefit to be realized from a NOL carryforward in the unusual circumstances when realization is assured beyond any reasonable doubt.[20] *SFAS No. 96* did not allow potential tax benefits of NOL carryforwards to be treated as assets. The FASB position is based on the following argument:

> *Incurring losses or generating profits in future years are future events that are not recognized in financial statements for the current year and are not inherently assumed in financial statements for the current year. Those future events shall not be anticipated, regardless of probability, for purposes of recognizing or measuring . . . [income taxes] . . . in the current year.*[21]

SFAS No. 109 liberalizes the policies for recognizing tax assets (as discussed later) and, thus, for the financial accounting treatment of NOL carryforwards.

Conceptual Issues

The questions raised by the income tax allocation issue involve whether and how to account for the tax effects of the differences between taxable income, as determined by the IRC, and pretax financial accounting income determined under GAAP. Some accountants believe that it is inappropriate to give any accounting recognition to the tax effects of these differences. Others believe that recognition is appropriate but disagree on the method to use. There is

---

[19] Accounting Principles Board, *Opinion No. 11*, "Accounting for Income Taxes" (New York: AICPA, 1967), par. 43.

[20] Ibid.

[21] Ibid., par. 15.

also disagreement on the appropriate tax rate to use and whether reported future tax effects should be discounted to their present values. Finally, there is a lack of consensus over whether interperiod tax allocation should be applied comprehensively to all differences or only to those expected to reverse in the future. Each of these conceptual issues will be examined in more detail in the following paragraphs.

Allocation Versus Nonallocation

Although authoritative pronouncements have consistently required inter-period tax allocation, some individuals maintain that the amount of income tax expense reported on a company's income statement should be the same as the income taxes payable for the accounting period as determined by the income tax return. Under this approach no interperiod allocation of income taxes is necessary.

Advocates of nonallocation argue as follows:

1. Income taxes result only from taxable income. Whether the company has accounting income or not is irrelevant. Hence, attempts to match income taxes with accounting income provide no relevant information for users of published financial statements.

2. Income taxes are different from other expenses; therefore, allocation in a manner similar to other expenses is not relevant. Expense is a measure of the cost of generating revenue; income taxes generate no revenues. They are not incurred in anticipation of future benefits, nor are they expirations of cost to provide facilities to generate revenues.

3. Income taxes are levied on total taxable income, not on individual items of revenue and expense. Therefore, there can be no temporary differences related to these items.

4. Interperiod tax allocation hides an economic difference between a company that employs tax strategies that reduce current tax payments (and is there-fore economically better off) and one that does not.

5. Reporting a company's income tax expense at the amount paid or currently payable is a better predictor of future cash outflows of the company because many of the deferred taxes will never be paid, or will be paid only in the distant future.

6. Income tax allocation entails an implicit forecasting of future profits. To incorporate such forecasting into the preparation of financial information is inconsistent with the long-standing principle of conservatism.

7. There is no present obligation for the potential or future tax consequences of present or prior transactions because there is no legal liability to pay taxes until an actual future tax return is prepared.

8. The accounting record keeping and procedures involving interperiod tax allocation are too costly for the purported benefits.

On the other hand, the advocates of interperiod tax allocation cite the following reasons to counter the preceding arguments or to criticize nonallocation:

1. Income taxes result from the incurrence of transactions and events. As a result, income tax expense should be based on the results of the transactions or events that are included in financial accounting income.

2. Income taxes are an expense of doing business, and should involve the same accrual, deferral, and estimation concepts that are applied to other expenses.

3. Differences between the timing of revenues and expenses do result in temporary differences that will reverse in the future. Expanding, growing businesses experience increasing asset and liability balances. Old assets are collected, old liabilities are paid, and new ones take their place. Deferred tax balances grow in a similar manner.

4. Interperiod tax allocation makes a company's net income a more useful measure of its long-term earning power and avoids periodic income distortions resulting from income tax regulations.

5. Nonallocation of a company's income tax expense hinders the prediction of its future cash flows. For instance, a company's future cash inflows from installment sales collection would usually be offset by related cash outflows for taxes.

6. A company is a going concern, and income taxes that are currently deferred will eventually be paid. The validity of other assets and liabilities reported in the balance sheet depends on the presumption of a viable company and hence the incurrence of future net income.

7. Temporary differences are associated with future tax consequences. For example, reversals of originating differences that provide present tax savings are associated with higher future taxable incomes and therefore higher future tax payments. In this sense, deferred tax liabilities are similar to other contingent liabilities that are currently reported under GAAP.

Comprehensive Versus Partial Allocation

If the arguments in favor of the interperiod allocation of income taxes are accepted, the next issue to address is whether allocation should be applied on a comprehensive or partial basis. Under *comprehensive allocation,* the income tax expense reported in an accounting period is affected by all transactions and events entering into the determination of pretax financial accounting income for that period. Comprehensive allocation results in including the tax consequences of all temporary differences in deferred tax assets and liabilities, regardless of how significant or recurrent. Proponents of comprehensive allocation view all transactions and events that create temporary differences as affecting cash flows in the accounting periods when the originating differences reverse. Under this view, an originating temporary difference is analogous to an unpaid accounts receivable or accounts payable invoice; when a temporary difference reverses, it is collected or paid.

In contrast, under *partial allocation,* the income tax expense reported in an accounting period would not be affected by those temporary differences that are not expected to reverse in the future. That is, proponents of partial allocation argue that, in certain cases, groups of similar transactions or events may continually create originating differences in the future that will offset any reversing differences, resulting in an indefinite postponement of deferred tax consequences. In effect, these types of temporary differences are more like permanent differences. Examples of these types of differences include depreciation for manufacturing companies with large amounts of depreciable assets and installment sales for merchandising companies.

Advocates of comprehensive allocation raise the following arguments:

1. Individual temporary differences do reverse. By definition a temporary difference cannot be permanent; the offsetting effect of future events should not be assumed. It is inappropriate to look at the effect of a group of temporary differences on income taxes; the focus should be on the individual items comprising the group. Temporary differences should be viewed in the same manner as accounts payable. That is, although the total balance of accounts payable may not change, many individual credit and payment transactions affect the total.

2. Accounting is primarily historical. It is inappropriate to offset the income tax effects of possible future transactions against the tax effects of transactions that have already occurred.

3. The income tax effects of temporary differences should be reported in the same period as the related transactions and events in pretax financial accounting income.

4. Accounting results should not be subject to manipulation by management. That is, a company's management should not be able to alter the company's results of operations and ending financial position by arbitrarily deciding what temporary differences will and will not reverse in the future.

In contrast, advocates of partial income tax allocation argue that

1. All groups of income tax temporary differences are not similar to certain other groups of accounting items, such as accounts payable. Accounts payable "roll over" as a result of actual individual credit and payment transactions. Income taxes, however, are based on total taxable income and not on the individual items constituting that income. Therefore, consideration of the impact of the *group* of temporary differences on income taxes is the appropriate viewpoint.

2. Comprehensive income tax allocation distorts economic reality. The income tax regulations that cause the temporary differences will continue to exist in the future. For instance, Congress is not likely to reduce investment incentives with respect to depreciation. Consequently, future investments

are virtually certain to result in originating depreciation differences of an amount to at least offset reversing differences. Thus, consideration should be given to the impact of future, as well as historical, transactions.

3. Assessment of a company's future cash flows is enhanced by using the partial allocation approach. That is, the deferred income taxes (if any) reported on a company's balance sheet under partial allocation would be more reflective of the future cash flows.

4. Accounting results should not be distorted by the use of a rigid, mechanical approach, such as comprehensive tax allocation. Furthermore, an objective of the audit function is to identify and deter any management manipulation.

Discounting Deferred Taxes

Current GAAP requires comprehensive interperiod income tax allocation. Reported deferred tax assets and liabilities reflect anticipated future tax consequences resulting from temporary differences between pretax financial accounting income and taxable income. Specific measurement issues, such as the appropriate method and tax rate to use to calculate deferred tax balances, will be discussed in the following sections. This section addresses the issue of whether deferred taxes, regardless of the measurement method used, should be discounted.

Proponents of reporting deferred taxes at their discounted amounts argue that the company that reduces tax payments is economically better off. It is their belief that by discounting deferred taxes, a company best reflects the operational advantages in its financial statements. Furthermore, proponents feel that discounting deferred taxes is consistent with the accounting principles established for such items as notes receivable and notes payable, pension costs, and leases. They argue that discounted amounts are considered to be the most appropriate indicators of future cash flows.

Critics of discounting counter, stating that discounting deferred taxes mismatches taxable transactions and the related tax effects. That is, the taxable transaction would be reported in one period and the related tax effects over several periods. They also argue that discounting would conceal a company's actual tax burden by reporting as interest expense the discount factor that would otherwise be reported as part of income tax expense. Furthermore, deferred taxes may be considered as interest-free loans from the government that do not require discounting because the effective interest rate is zero.

Alternative Interperiod Tax Allocation Methods

Three methods of income tax allocation, which may be used in conjunction with either the comprehensive or partial allocation approach, have been advocated. These are (1) the deferred method, (2) the asset/liability method, and (3) the net-of-tax method. Each method is described below.

The Deferred Method

The *deferred method* of income tax allocation is an income statement approach. It is based on the concept that income tax expense is related to the period in which income is recognized. The deferred method measures income tax expense as though the current period pretax financial accounting income is reported on the current year's income tax return. The tax effect of a temporary difference is the difference between income taxes computed with and without inclusion of the temporary difference. The resulting difference between income tax expense and income taxes currently payable is a debit or credit to the deferred income tax account.

The deferred tax account balance is reported in the balance sheet as deferred tax credit or deferred tax charge. *Under the deferred method, the deferred tax amount reported on the balance sheets is the effect of temporary differences that will reverse in the future and that are measured using the income tax rates and laws in effect when the differences originated.* No adjustments are made to deferred taxes for changes in the income tax rates or tax laws that occur after the period of origination. When the deferrals reverse, the tax effects are recorded at the rates in existence *when the temporary differences originated.*

APB Opinion No. 11 required comprehensive interperiod income tax allocation using the deferred method.[22] Like its predecessor, *ARB No. 43, APB Opinion No. 11* concluded that "income tax expense should include the tax effects of revenue and expense transactions included in the determination of pretax accounting income."[23] The use of the deferred method caused considerable controversy. The primary criticism was that neither deferred tax charges nor deferred tax credits have the essential characteristics of assets or liabilities. Because the deferred method does not use tax rates that will be in effect when temporary differences reverse, they do not measure probable future benefits or sacrifices; hence, the resulting deferred taxes do not meet the definition of assets or liabilities in *SFAC No. 6.* The deferred tax balances simply represent the cumulative effects of temporary differences waiting to be adjusted in the matching process of some future accounting period.

Arguments in favor of the deferred method of interperiod tax allocation include the following:

1. The income statement is the most important financial statement, and matching is a critical aspect of the accounting process. Thus, it is of little consequence that deferred taxes are not true assets or liabilities in the conceptual sense.

2. Deferred taxes are the result of historical transactions or events that created the temporary differences. Since accounting reports most economic events on an historical cost basis, deferred taxes should be reported in a similar manner.

---

[22] APB, op. cit., pars. 34 and 35.

[23] Ibid., par. 34.

3. Historical income tax rates are verifiable. Reporting deferred taxes based on historical rates increases the reliability of accounting information.

The Asset/Liability Method

The *asset/liability method* of income tax allocation is balance sheet oriented. The intent is to accrue and report the total tax benefit or taxes payable that will actually be realized or assessed on temporary differences when they reverse. A temporary difference is viewed as giving rise to either a tax benefit that will result in a decrease in future tax payments or a tax liability that will be paid in the future at the then-current tax rates. Theoretically, the future tax rates used should be estimated, based on expectations regarding future tax law changes. However, current GAAP requires that the future tax rates used to determine current period deferred tax asset and liability balances be based on currently enacted tax law.[24] *Under the asset/liability method, as defined by current GAAP, the deferred tax amount reported on the balance sheet is the effect of temporary differences that will reverse in the future and that are measured using the currently enacted tax rates and laws that will be in effect when the temporary differences reverse.* Adjustments, however, are made to deferred tax asset and liability accounts for any changes in the income tax rates or laws when these changes are enacted.

When using the asset/liability method, income tax expense is the sum of (or difference between) the changes in deferred tax asset and liability balances[25] and the current provision for income taxes per the tax return. According to the FASB, deferred taxes under the asset/liability method meet the conceptual definitions of assets and liabilities established in *SFAC No. 6.*[26] For instance, the resulting deferred tax credit balances of an entity can be viewed as probable future sacrifices (i.e., tax payments based on future tax rates) arising from present obligations (taxes owed) as a result of past transactions (originating differences). That is, deferred taxes measure future resource flows that result from transactions or events already recognized for financial accounting purposes.

Arguments in favor of the asset/liability method of interperiod tax allocation include the following:

1. The balance sheet is becoming a more important financial statement. Reporting deferred taxes based on the expected tax rates when the temporary differences reverse increases the predictive value of future cash flows, liquidity, and financial flexibility.

2. As discussed earlier, reporting deferred taxes based on the expected tax rates is conceptually more sound because the reported amount represents

---

[24] FASB, op. cit., par. 8.

[25] Under *SFAS No. 109* there may also be a valuation allowance for deferred tax assets. Changes in the valuation allowance would also affect income tax expense. The valuation allowance is discussed later in the chapter.

[26] Ibid., par. 63.

either the likely future economic sacrifice (future tax payments) or economic benefit (future reduction in taxes).

3. Deferred taxes may be the result of historical transactions; but, by definition, they are taxes that are postponed and will be paid (or will reduce taxes) in the future at the future tax rates.

4. Estimates are used extensively in accounting. The use of estimated future tax rates for deferred taxes poses no more of a problem regarding verifiability and reliability than using, say, estimated lives for depreciation.

5. Because the tax expense results from changes in balance sheet values, its measurement is consistent with the *SFAS No. 6* definition of comprehensive income.

The Net-of-Tax Method

The *net-of-tax method* is more a method of disclosure than a different method of calculating deferred taxes. Under this method, the income tax effects of temporary differences are computed by applying either the deferred method or the asset/liability method. The resulting deferred taxes, however, are not separately disclosed on the balance sheet. Instead, *under the net-of-tax method the deferred charges (tax assets) or deferred credits (tax liabilities) are treated as adjustments of the accounts to which the temporary differences relate.* Generally, the accounts are adjusted through the use of a valuation allowance rather than directly. For instance, if a temporary difference results from additional tax depreciation, the related tax effect would be subtracted (by means of a valuation account) from the cost of the asset (along with accumulated depreciation) to determine the carrying value of the depreciable asset. Likewise, the carrying value of installment accounts receivable would be reduced for the expected increase in income taxes that will occur when the receivable is collected (and taxed). Reversals of temporary differences would reduce the valuation allowance accounts.

Two alternatives exist for disclosing the periodic income tax expense on the income statement under the net-of-tax method. Under the first alternative, the tax effects of temporary differences are included in the total income tax expense. Thus, the income tax expense is reported in a manner similar to the deferred method or the asset/liability method. Under the second alternative, income tax expense is reported at the same amount as current income taxes payable, and the tax effects of temporary differences are combined with the revenue or expense items to which they relate. For instance, the tax effect of additional tax depreciation would be reported as an adjustment to depreciation expense.

The basic argument in favor of the net-of-tax method of interperiod tax allocation centers on the notion that all revenue and expense transactions involve changes in specific asset and liability accounts and are recorded accordingly. Therefore, accounting for the tax effects of temporary differences should be no different. Because temporary differences are the result of events that affect the future taxability and tax deductibility of specific assets and liabilities, they have future economic consequences that should be reflected in the value of the related assets and liabilities. For instance, when tax depreciation exceeds financial accounting depreciation, income tax expense is higher than current income taxes payable because an excess amount of the cost of the depreciable asset has been charged against taxable income. Thus, the excess (temporary difference) has reduced the future tax deductibility of the depreciable asset cost, and the carrying value of the asset should be reduced accordingly.

There are several arguments against the net-of-tax method. The primary argument is that there are many factors that affect the value of assets and liabilities but are not recorded in the accounts. To single out one factor (impact on future taxes) as affecting value is inappropriate. Besides, it is not always possible to determine the related asset or liability account.[27] Furthermore, it is argued that the net-of-tax method is too complex to use and distorts traditional concepts for measuring assets and liabilities.

FASB Dissatisfaction with the Deferred Method

The deferred method was prescribed by *APB Opinion No. 11*. In 1982, the FASB, prompted by criticisms and concerns voiced in the literature and letters to the Board regarding the deferred method, began to reconsider accounting for income taxes. In *SFAC No. 6*, the FASB indicated that deferred income tax amounts reported on the balance sheet did not meet the newly established definitions for assets and liabilities.[28] The application of the deferred method by business enterprises most frequently resulted in reporting a deferred tax credit balance. Under the deferred method, deferred tax credits result when the payment of income tax is deferred to a later period. However, the tax rate used to measure the deferral may not be in effect when the deferred taxes are actually paid. If deferred income tax credit balances are liabilities, then the amounts reported in balance sheets should reflect the future resource outflows that will be required to settle them. Thus, any changes in tax rates and tax law that would change the future impact of temporary differences on income tax payments should be recognized for financial reporting purposes in the period when tax rate and tax law changes are enacted.

Subsequently, the Tax Reform Act of 1986 significantly reduced income tax rates and created additional pressure to consider a change in the method of accounting for temporary differences. After weighing the various arguments in favor of nonallocation and interperiod income tax allocation, the comprehensive and partial income allocation approaches, and the deferred, asset/liability, and net-of-tax methods of applying income tax allocation, in 1987 the FASB released *SFAS No. 96*, which concluded that

---

[27] Net operating losses (NOLs) create deferred tax asset balances under current GAAP. NOLs do not result from temporary differences resulting from any single transaction or event. There are no assets or liabilities on the balance sheet for NOLs.

[28] Financial Accounting Standards Board, *Statement of Financial Accounting Concepts No. 6,* "Elements of Financial Statements" (Stamford, Conn.: FASB, 1985), par. 241.

1. Interperiod income tax allocation of temporary differences is appropriate.
2. The comprehensive allocation approach should be applied.
3. The asset/liability method of income tax allocation should be used.

In addition to accepting the arguments presented earlier in favor of the asset/liability method, the FASB amplified on these arguments and provided the following rationale for its conclusions:

1. The income tax consequences of an event should be recognized in the same accounting period as that event is recognized in the financial statements. Although most events affect taxable income and pretax financial accounting income in the same accounting period, the income tax consequences of some events are deferred. Temporary differences result from events that have deferred tax consequences.

2. Recognition of deferred income taxes is consistent with accrual accounting. Under accrual accounting, there is an assumption that there will be future recovery and settlement of reported amounts of assets and liabilities, respectively. That assumption necessitates the recognition of deferred tax consequences of those temporary differences that will become refundable or payable when the reported amounts of assets and liabilities are recovered and settled, respectively. On the other hand, earning future income and incurring future losses are events that are *not* assumed in the current accounting period under accrual accounting; thus, they should not be assumed for income tax accounting.

3. Under the asset/liability method, the deferred tax consequences of temporary differences generally are recognizable liabilities and assets. That is, a deferred tax liability represents the amount of income taxes that will be payable in future years when temporary differences result in taxable income at that time. Likewise, a deferred tax asset represents that amount of income taxes that will be refundable when temporary differences result in tax deductible amounts in future years.

Note that the FASB stressed that temporary differences result in future tax consequences, rather than the allocation of tax among accounting periods. Nonallocation, partial allocation, and the deferred and net-of-tax methods were rejected and are *not* GAAP. Furthermore, reporting deferred taxes using a present value approach was not considered by the FASB and is also *not* acceptable accounting for income taxes. The asset/liability approach presumably measures the future tax consequences for prior events or transactions. The following sections describe the *SFAS No. 96* arguments and conclusions regarding the nature of deferred tax liabilities and deferred tax assets, and how they should be measured and reported.

Deferred Tax Liability

The three essential characteristics of a liability established by *SFAS No. 6* are that (1) it must embody a present responsibility to another entity that involves settlement by probable future transfer or use of assets at a specified or determinable date, on occurrence of a specified event, or on demand; (2) the responsibility obligates the entity, leaving it little or no discretion to avoid the future sacrifice; and (3) the transaction or event obligating the entity has already happened. The deferred tax consequences of temporary differences that will result in net taxable amounts in future years meet these characteristics.[29] The first characteristic is met by a deferred tax liability because (1) the deferred tax consequences stem from the requirements of tax law and hence are a responsibility to the government, (2) settlement will involve a probable future transfer or use of assets when the taxes are paid, and (3) settlement will result from events specified by the tax law. The second characteristic is met because, based on the government's tax rules and regulations, income taxes definitely will be payable when temporary differences result in net taxable amounts in future years. The third characteristic is met because the past events that created the temporary differences are the same past events that result in the deferred tax obligation.

Deferred Tax Asset

The three essential characteristics of an asset are that (1) it must embody a probable future benefit that involves a capacity to contribute to future net cash inflows, (2) the entity must be able to obtain the benefit and control other entities' access to it, and (3) the transaction or other event resulting in the entity's right to or control of the benefit must already have occurred. The deferred tax consequences of temporary differences that will result in net deductible amounts in future years that may be *carried back* as permitted by tax law meet these characteristics.[30] The first characteristic is met because a tax benefit is guaranteed. When the future year actually occurs, one of two events will occur. Either the deductible amount will be used to reduce actual income taxes for that year, or the deductible amount will result in a refund of taxes paid in the current or preceding years. The second characteristic is met because the entity will have an exclusive right to the tax benefit resulting from the carryback. Finally, the third characteristic is met because the entity must have earned taxable income in the current or past years for a carryback to be considered realizable.

On the other hand, a net deductible amount that cannot be carried back to the present or prior periods or an unused NOL carryforward does not have a refund guarantee. These deductions must be carried to future years in order to obtain a tax benefit. Consequently, the entity must have future taxable income for a future tax benefit to occur. Since earning income in future years has not yet occurred and is not inherently assumed in preparing financial statements, the third characteristic is *not* met for net deductible amounts that

---

[29] Financial Accounting Standards Board, *Statement of Financial Accounting Standards No. 96,* "Accounting for Income Taxes" (Stamford, Conn.: FASB, 1997), pars. 83–89.

[30] Ibid., pars. 97–102.

cannot be carried back to obtain a refund of taxes already paid. Nor is it met for NOL carryforwards. In other words, these items represent gain contingencies that may not be realized.

In summary, the deferred tax consequences of temporary differences that result in net deductible amounts in future years that may be carried back to present and prior years are an asset. But *SFAS No. 96* limited the recognition of benefit of all other net deductible amounts to reductions of deferred tax liabilities. Under this pronouncement, they are not recorded as assets—a treatment consistent with the treatment of other gain contingencies.

Business Dissatisfaction with *SFAS No. 96*

After *SFAS No. 96* was issued, and prior to its mandatory implementation date, many businesses expressed concerns regarding the effect the standard would have on their financial statements and the cost that would be incurred in implementing the standard. These objections became so widespread that the implementation date was first postponed from 1988 to 1989,[31] and later from 1989 to 1991.[32]

The major objections to *SFAS No. 96* centered on the cost of scheduling that would be necessary to determine whether a deferred tax asset could be recognized and the loss of some deferred tax assets because of the zero future income assumption. Prior to the effective date of *SFAS No. 96*, the FASB received (1) requests for about 20 different limited-scope amendments to its provisions; (2) many requests to change the criteria for recognition and measurement of deferred tax assets to anticipate, in certain circumstances, the tax consequences of future income; and (3) requests to reduce the complexity of scheduling the future reversals of temporary differences and considering hypothetical tax planning strategies. On June 5, 1991, the Board issued an Exposure Draft proposing a new standard to supersede *SFAS No. 96*. Later, on June 17, 1991, the Board issued another Exposure Draft to delay the effective date for the implementation of *SFAS No. 96* for a third time to December 15, 1992 (effective for 1993 statements) to allow time for interested parties to respond to the June 5, 1991, Exposure Draft. Finally, in early 1992 *SFAS No. 109* was issued.

SFAS No. 109

The FASB was convinced by the critics of *SFAS No. 96* that deferred tax assets should be treated similarly to deferred tax liabilities and that the scheduling

---

[31] Financial Accounting Standards Board, *Statement of Financial Accounting Standards No. 100*, "Accounting for Income Taxes—Deferral of the Effective Date of FASB Statement No. 96" (Stamford, Conn.: FASB, 1988).

[32] Financial Accounting Standards Board, *Statement of Financial Accounting Standards No. 103*, "Accounting for Income Taxes—Deferral of the Effective Date of FASB Statement No. 96" (Stamford, Conn.: 1989).

requirements of *SFAS No. 96* were often too complex and costly. However, the Board did not want to return to the deferred method and remained committed to the asset/liability method. *SFAS No. 109* responded to these concerns by allowing the separate recognition and measurement of deferred tax assets and liabilities without regard to future income considerations[33] using the average enacted tax rates[34] for future years. The deferred tax asset is to be reduced by a *tax valuation allowance* if available evidence indicates that it is *more likely than not (a likelihood of more than 50 percent)* that some portion or all of the deferred tax asset will not be realized.[35]

These requirements result in the following more simplified series of steps for determining deferred tax liability and asset balances:[36]

1. Identify temporary differences, NOL carryforwards, and unused tax credits.
2. Measure the total deferred tax liability by applying the expected tax rate to future taxable amounts.
3. Measure the total deferred tax asset by applying the expected future tax rate to future deductible amounts and NOL carryforwards.
4. Measure deferred tax assets for each type of unused tax credit.
5. Measure the valuation allowance based on the above more likely than not criterion.

The Valuation Allowance

The deferred tax asset measures potential benefits to be received in future years from NOL carryovers, deductible amounts arising from temporary differences, or unused tax credits. Because there may be insufficient future taxable income to actually derive a benefit from a recorded deferred tax asset, *SFAS No. 109* requires a *valuation allowance* sufficient to reduce the deferred tax asset to the amount that is more likely than not to be realized. The *more likely than not* criterion is a new measurement yardstick for the FASB. Previously, in establishing standards for contingent liabilities, the FASB introduced the terms *probable, reasonably probable,* and *remote*. The use of these terms for deferred tax assets would imply *an affirmative judgment approach* wherein recognition would require probable realization; however, no recognition would be given to deferred tax assets when the likelihood of realization is less than probable. The Board decided against the use of this approach to solve the income tax

---

[33] Financial Accounting Standards Board, *Statement of Financial Accounting Standards No. 109,* "Accounting for Income Taxes" (Stamford, Conn.: FASB, 1992), par. 17.

[34] For most companies, the marginal tax rate and the average tax rate are the same. Those companies for which a graduated tax rate is a significant factor are to use the average graduated tax rate applicable to the amount of estimated taxable income for the years when the deferred tax assets or liabilities are expected to be settled. Ibid., par. 18.

[35] Ibid., par. 17.

[36] Ibid., par. 17.

issue because it felt that probable was too stringent a benchmark for the recognition of deferred tax assets.[37]

The FASB also considered an *impairment approach* that would require deferred tax asset recognition unless it is probable that the asset will not be realized. The impairment approach was also deemed problematic because it would result in recognition of a deferred tax asset that is not expected to be realized when the likelihood of its not being realized is less than probable.[38]

The more likely than not criterion was selected because it would eliminate any distinction between the affirmative judgment and impairment approaches. As a practical matter, the use of this criterion would provide both of the following results:

a. Recognition of a deferred tax asset if the likelihood of realizing the future tax benefit is more than 50% (the affirmative judgment approach).

b. Recognition of a deferred tax asset unless the likelihood of not realizing the future tax benefit is more than 50% (the impairment approach).[39]

In other words, the FASB chose a middle ground, which in effect embraced both approaches, *rather than selecting one over the other.* The use of the more likely than not criterion allows practitioners to ignore the zero future income assumption. That is, accountants may assume that there will be sufficient future taxable income to realize deferred tax assets unless evidence indicates that it is more likely than not that it will not be realized.

The Board considered various criteria to determine when impairment might apply but did not come to any definitive conclusions. The realization of future benefit from a deductible temporary difference or carryover ultimately depends on the incurrence of taxable income that is of an appropriate character to utilize the carryover of a NOL or credit, or against which a deductible amount may be applied. *SFAS No. 109* cited the following as possible sources of taxable income (affirmative evidence) that may enable the realization of deferred tax assets:

1. Future reversals of existing taxable temporary differences.

2. Future taxable income exclusive of taxable temporary differences and carryovers.

3. Taxable income in the current or prior years to which deductible amounts resulting from temporary differences could be carried back.

4. In order to prevent a NOL or tax credit carryover from expiring, prudent and feasible tax planning strategies that an enterprise ordinarily might not take may be employed to

   a. Accelerate taxable amounts against which to apply carryforwards.

---

[37] Ibid., par. 95.

[38] Ibid.

[39] Ibid.

b. Change the character of taxable or deductible amounts from ordinary income or loss to capital gain or loss.

c. Switch from tax exempt to taxable investments.[40]

SFAS No. 109 stressed that the exercise of judgment is necessary to determine whether a valuation allowance should be reported and, if so, the level of impairment of the deferred tax asset that is more likely than not to occur. On the downside, negative evidence (potential impairment) might include the following:

1. A history of NOL or tax credit carryforwards expiring unused.

2. Anticipated losses (by a presently profitable enterprise).

3. Unsettled circumstances that may adversely affect future operations and profits.

4. A carryover period that is so brief that it would limit realization of deferred tax benefits if (a) a significant deductible temporary difference is expected to reverse in a single year or (b) the business operating cycle is traditionally cyclical.[41]

This type of negative evidence should be weighed against positive evidence such as

1. Existing contracts or sales backlog.

2. Significant appreciation of an asset's value over its tax basis.

3. A strong earnings history (exclusive of the NOL or deductible temporary differences) coupled with evidence that the loss is an aberration rather than a continuing condition.[42]

By relaxing the future income assumption, the necessity of scheduling that was required under *SFAS No. 96* is greatly reduced. If it is assumed that there will be sufficient taxable income in future years to realize the tax benefit of existing deductible amounts, the carryback and carryforward provisions of *SFAS No. 96* would not be needed. If, on the other hand, it is not possible to assume sufficient future taxable income, then scheduling may be needed to determine the balance in the valuation allowance account. However, scheduling is no longer required to determine the proper classification of the deferred amount between current and noncurrent. The deferred tax balance is to be classified as current or noncurrent in the same manner as the assets and liabilities to which the deferred taxes relate.

The adoption of the *more likely than not* approach led the FASB to conclude that a similar approach should be used for NOLs, unused credits, and deductible amounts resulting from temporary differences. Under *SFAS No. 109* NOLs will now result in deferred tax assets unless it is more likely than not that

---

[40] Ibid., pars. 21 and 22.

[41] Ibid., par. 23.

[42] Ibid., par. 24.

they will not be able to be applied against future taxable income. This is a significant change in that millions of dollars of potential benefit that have heretofore been unreported will be included in the assets of companies.

Shift in Interpretation of Future Tax Consequences

In requiring the separate measurement of deferred tax liabilities and deferred tax assets and the reduction of deferred tax assets by the valuation allowance, the resulting balance sheet amounts would not reflect the effects of netting deductible amounts against taxable amounts or the certain guarantee of realization for deferred tax assets that would have occurred under *SFAS No. 96*. In short, the *SFAS No. 109* provisions introduced different levels of certainty regarding expected future cash flows. As a result, the FASB reexamined whether the resulting deferred tax liabilities and deferred tax assets fit the definitions of liabilities and assets found in *SFAC No. 6*. The Board concluded that they do and that the information provided is useful, understandable, and no more complex than any other approach to accounting for income taxes.[43] These conclusions are based on the following arguments regarding the *SFAS No. 109* deferred tax liability and deferred tax asset.

Deferred Tax Liability

In requiring the separate measurement of deferred tax assets and deferred tax liabilities, deferred tax liabilities will not measure the effects of net taxable amounts. Nevertheless, according to *SFAS No. 109*, the resulting deferred tax liabilities meet all three essential characteristics of liabilities outlined in *SFAC No. 6* (described previously).[44] Again, the first characteristic of a liability is that it embodies a present obligation to the enterprise to settle by probable future transfer or use of assets upon the occurrence of a specified event, or on demand. This characteristic is met because the deferred tax liability measures an obligation to the government resulting from the deferred tax consequences of taxable temporary differences that stem from the requirements of the tax law.

The second characteristic, that the enterprise is obligated and has little or no discretion to avoid future sacrifice, is also met. It may be possible to delay future reversals of temporary differences by postponing events such as recovery or settlement of assets or liabilities; but, eventually, these temporary differences will become taxable. Hence, the only relevant question is when, not whether, the tax consequences will occur. Finally, the future payment of tax is the result of past transactions or events that created the originating temporary differences. This satisfies the third characteristic of a liability, that the transaction or event that obligates the enterprise has already happened.

---

[43] Ibid., par. 63.

[44] Ibid., pars. 75–79.

Deferred Tax Asset

The FASB also concluded that *SFAS No. 109* deferred tax assets, reduced by the valuation allowance, meet the *SFAC No. 6* characteristics of assets.[45] The first characteristic of an asset is that it embodies a capacity to contribute directly or indirectly to enterprise future net cash inflows. There is no question that deductible amounts that may be carried back to offset taxable income that has already been incurred embody a probable future benefit because they contribute directly to future net cash inflows. Other deductible amounts and carryovers under the more likely than not criterion, because they may be used to reduce future taxable amounts, will contribute indirectly to future cash flows.

The second characteristic of an asset is that the enterprise can obtain the benefit and can control others' access to it. To the extent that these benefits will occur, the enterprise has an exclusive right to those benefits as they are realized and therefore can control access to it.

The third characteristic of an asset is that the transaction or event that resulted in the enterprise obtaining the right to control the benefit has already occurred. Because deferred tax asset realization under *SFAS No. 96* was guaranteed, the critical event giving rise to the asset was prior taxable income. However, *SFAS No. 109* allows recognition if the weight of the evidence implies that it is more likely than not that realization will occur. Thus, the existence or absence of future taxable income is critical to deferred tax asset recognition under current GAAP for those deductible amounts and carryforwards that will not result in a refund of prior taxes paid. "The Board concluded that earning taxable income in future years (a) is the event that confirms the existence of recognizable tax benefit at the end of the current year and (b) is not the prerequisite event that must occur before a tax benefit may be recognized as was the case under the requirements of [SFAS No.] 96."[46]

Financial Statement Disclosure

Several disclosure issues arise in connection with the reporting of income taxes on financial statements.

Income Statement Presentation and Related Disclosures

The portrayal of the effects of taxation on major segments of the income statement and on items carried directly to retained earnings is enhanced by allocating the income tax expense for a period among these items. The allocation of income tax within an accounting period is termed *intraperiod tax allocation*. Intraperiod tax allocation is required under current GAAP.[47] Income tax

---

[45] Ibid., pars. 80–86.

[46] Ibid., par. 86.

[47] Ibid., par. 43.

expense (or benefit) is disclosed for net income from continuing operations, gains or losses resulting from the disposal of a segment of a business, extraordinary items, and the cumulative effect of changes in accounting principles. Additionally, the tax effect of any prior period adjustments to Retained Earnings must be disclosed.

In addition, *SFAS No. 109* requires disclosure of the significant components of income tax attributable to income from continuing operations. These components include

1. The current provision (or benefit) for income taxes.
2. Deferred tax expense or benefit (exclusive of items 3–8 listed below).
3. Investment tax credits.
4. Government grants (to the extent that they reduce income tax expense).
5. The benefits of operating loss carryforwards.
6. Tax expense that results from allocations of tax benefits to balance sheets in a business combination.
7. Adjustments to the deferred tax liability or asset for enacted changes in tax laws or a change in the tax status of the reporting entity.
8. Adjustments of the beginning balance of the valuation allowance because of a change in circumstances that causes a change in judgment about the realizability of the related deferred tax asset.

Balance Sheet Presentation and Related Disclosures

The current provision (or benefit) is reported in the balance sheet as a current liability or asset. Deferred tax balances are reported as assets and liabilities. They are classified as (1) the net current amount and (2) the net noncurrent amount. This classification is based on the classification of the related asset or liability that caused the deferred item.[48] That is, a deferred tax asset or liability is related to an asset or liability if a reduction of the asset or liability will cause the temporary difference to reverse. A deferred tax asset or liability that is not related to an asset or liability, including deferred tax assets created by NOL or tax credit carryforwards, is classified as current or noncurrent according to the expected reversal date of the temporary difference. A net noncurrent deferred tax asset is classified as an Other Asset. A noncurrent net deferred tax liability is classified as a Long-term Liability. The valuation allowance (and the net change in it) associated with deferred tax assets that do not meet the *more likely than not to be realized* criterion must be disclosed. Also, companies must disclose the approximate tax effect of each item that gives rise to a significant portion of deferred tax liabilities and assets (exclusive of the valuation allowance).[49]

[48] Ibid., par. 41.
[49] Ibid., par. 43.

SEC Disclosure Requirements

The Securities and Exchange Commission (SEC) has also adopted disclosure requirements for corporations issuing publicly traded securities. The disclosures required include

1. A reconciliation of the difference between income tax expense and the amount of tax expense that would have been reported by applying the normal rate to reported income for the company. This requirement highlights the special provisions of the tax code that benefited the company.

2. The amount of any temporary difference that is due to the deferral of investment tax credits (when and if the ITC is applicable).

These requirements are intended to provide information to investors and others on the effective tax rates of corporations.

Taken together, the SEC and *SFAS No. 109* financial statement disclosure requirements allow investors, creditors, and other users of financial information to make better decisions. Specifically,

1. The quality of earnings can be assessed because special situations that give rise to one-time earnings are highlighted.

2. Future cash flows can be more easily assessed because reversals of deferred tax assets and liabilities are highlighted.

3. Government regulation of the economy is enhanced because it is easier to calculate actual tax rates.

Summary

Interperiod income tax allocation has been a controversial issue for many years. The Committee on Accounting Procedure, the Accounting Principles Board, and the Financial Accounting Standards Board have all examined the topic and issued pronouncements. In *SFAS No. 109*, the FASB recommended the use of an asset/liability approach that allows for the recognition of both assets and liabilities that arise from interperiod tax allocation. Additionally, the potential tax benefit of net operating loss carrybacks and carryforwards can be recognized if it is more likely than not that they will be realized.

In the reading for this chapter, John Kissinger presents a view of deferred income taxes as a summary measurement correction that adjusts the various income statement items to an aggregate net-of-tax valuation.

In Defense of Interperiod
Income Tax Allocation

John N. Kissinger

In January 1982, responding to numerous criticisms of APB Opinion No. 11 [1] and related pronouncements, the FASB added accounting for income taxes to its technical agenda. Some critics of APB Opinion No. 11 contend that interperiod income tax allocation is inconsistent with the current accounting model[1] because it results in deferred charges and credits in the balance sheet that do not fit any traditional balance

[1] This paper contains several references to the "current accounting model." While a complete description of the model is beyond the scope of this paper, some basic elements assumed include articulating financial statements; income calculated through the matching of expenses with their associated revenues; emphasis of substance over form; an income statement comprising revenues, expenses, gains, losses, and related contra and adjunct accounts (e.g., sales discounts, returns, and allowances); and a balance sheet comprising assets, liabilities, permanent owners' equity, and related contra and adjunct accounts (e.g., allowance for uncollectible receivables, accumulated depreciation, premium or discount on bonds payable, etc.). This model is assumed to include FASB Statements of Financial Accounting Concepts (SFACs), official pronouncements of the FASB and its predecessors that are currently in effect (except those pertaining to accounting for income taxes), and other practices generally accepted through custom though not formalized in authoritative pronouncements.

sheet category [2]. Other accountants accept interperiod tax allocation in principle but object to its application when an enterprise uses accelerated depreciation in the tax return but straight-line depreciation in the financial statements. According to these accountants, the resulting timing differences do not reverse in the short run, creating a permanent deferred credit that distorts the representation of financial position [3, 4, 5].

This paper develops a combination method of comprehensive interperiod income tax allocation that answers these criticisms. The discussion addresses two separate issues associated with accounting for income taxes: (1) the amount and nature of the item to be reported in the income statement, and (2) the manner in which any difference between this amount and the amount of taxes currently claimed by the government should be reported in the balance sheet.

Income Taxes in the Income Statement—The Net-of-Tax Theory

The focus of the debate over income taxes in the income statement has been whether the amount reported should follow financial statement pretax accounting income or tax return taxable income. An important issue in the debate has been the nature of income taxes—expense of doing business or distribution of income. If income taxes are an expense, then presumably the matching principle applies and the reported amount should follow pretax accounting income. If, however, income taxes are a distribution of income (e.g., similar to dividends), then the matching principle does not apply and the reported amount should follow taxable income.

The problem is that income taxes do not fit either category particularly well. On the one hand, because they do not arise until after revenue has been earned, they do not fit the theorist's traditional definition of an expense, "the using or consuming of goods or services in the process of obtaining revenues" [6:187]. On the other hand, because they are involuntary, they do not fit the traditional notion of an income distribution. Fortunately, the net-of-tax theory provides a solution to this dilemma.

The basis of the net-of-tax theory is the assumption that every taxable revenue or gain and every deductible expense or loss has an associated tax effect. If income taxes were assessed at a constant rate, measuring such individual tax effects would be a relatively simple matter. Furthermore, in the absence of timing differences, the government's claim for the period would equal the sum of these individual tax effects. Under such circumstances, a separate income statement line for income taxes would not be necessary. Instead, each revenue, expense, gain, and loss could be reported net of its related tax effect in a manner similar to that currently used for extraordinary items.

It seems appropriate that the process of measuring income statement items should incorporate an adjustment for tax effects. In the current accounting model, revenues, expenses, etc., are classified as temporary owners' equity accounts. Ideally, therefore, amounts reported in the income statement should reflect the impact of such items on residual owners' equity—not owners' equity and government treasuries combined.

The problem with this approach, of course, is that income statement items are not subjected to a uniform tax rate. The existence of different tax brackets, coupled with the fact that taxable revenues and deductible expenses are netted in the tax return, makes it impossible to report individual income statement items net of tax without arbitrary incorrigible allocations whose validity can be neither verified nor refuted [7,8]. Thus, even in the absence of timing differences, the tax effect of the various revenues, expenses, etc., can only be measured as a single net amount. The net-of-tax theory suggests, however, that this amount is neither an expense nor a distribution of income but rather a summary measurement correction that adjusts various income statement items to an aggregate net-of-tax valuation; that is, income taxes is a contra-income account.

It follows that tax effects should be reported in the same accounting period as the associated income statement items. Additionally, measurement of the tax effects should reflect, as closely as possible, the government's eventual claim against entity assets. Otherwise, the measurement process is neither complete nor internally consistent and after-tax income will not equate with income to residual equity holders. For this reason, income taxes in the earnings statement should be based on pretax accounting income. The tax rate schedules used, however, should be those in effect (or expected to be in effect) when the various revenues, expenses, etc., will appear in the tax return.

In addition to the above arguments, there are at least two other reasons to base income taxes in the earnings statement on pretax accounting income. First, this approach makes accountants' allocations internally consistent. An entity may not change accounting methods arbitrarily from one period to the next; therefore, it seems inappropriate that for a given asset an entity might use straight-line depreciation for one calculation (depreciation expense) in an income statement while using double-declining-balance depreciation for another calculation (income taxes) in the same income statement. Similarly, it seems inappropriate that an entity might include installment sales revenue in the income statement because collection of the related receivable was reasonably assured while omitting the associated tax effect because collection might not occur. Without interperiod tax allocation, however, such inconsistencies would be common.

The second argument concerns dividends and compensation based on after-tax income. When timing differences arise that cause taxable income to exceed pretax accounting income, failure to use interperiod tax allocation results in a charge against current earnings for taxes actually related to future earnings. In this case, the consequences—delayed dividends or compensation—may not be severe. When timing differences arise that cause pretax accounting income to exceed taxable income, however, failure to recognize the government's full future claim against assets earned in the current period could lead to liquidating dividends and/or unrecoverable excess compensation.

Income Taxes in the Balance Sheet

When, as a result of timing differences, the amount of income taxes currently charged against earnings differs from the amount currently claimed by the government, the difference must be reflected in the balance sheet. One criticism of interperiod tax allocation is that the tax effects of timing differences do not fit any traditional balance sheet category. For this reason, any defense of the practice must demonstrate that such tax effects do have balance sheet interpretations consistent with the current accounting model.

Taxable revenue results in a government claim against entity assets. While deductible expenses may reduce such a claim, however, deductions have no tax effect unless there is some revenue (past, present, or future) against which they may be offset. The reason for this distinction is the absence of a negative income tax. Thus, while revenue tax effects may exist alone, expense tax effects can only exist as offsets to revenue tax effects. Because of this fundamental distinction in economic substance, revenue timing differences require a different balance sheet interpretation than expense timing differences. Other authors have recognized that the tax effects of various types of timing difference are not all identical. These authors, however, have concluded that the distinctions derive from whether a revenue or expense appears earlier in the financial statements or the tax return [9, 10], whether the tax effect has a debit or credit balance [11], and whether the timing differences are long-term or short-term [12].

To demonstrate that the appropriate distinction is between revenue and expense timing differences, the analysis that follows will consider individually the tax effects resulting from

1. Revenue (or gain) reported in the income statement before the tax return.
2. Revenue (or gain) reported in the tax return before the income statement.
3. Expense (or loss) reported in the income statement before the tax return.
4. Expense (or loss) reported in the tax return before the income statement.

Revenue (or Gain) Reported in the Income Statement Before the Tax Return

Common examples of this type of timing difference include

profits on installment sales . . . recorded in the accounts on the date of sale but reported in tax returns when later collected and revenues on long-term contracts . . . recorded in the accounts on a percentage-of-completion basis but reported in tax returns on a completed-contract basis [11:108–109].

According to Statement of Financial Accounting Standards (SFAS) No. 5, "an existing condition involving uncertainty as to possible . . . loss [or expense] . . . that will ultimately be resolved when one or more future events occur or fail to occur" is recognized in the accounts as a liability whenever the following two conditions are met:

Information available prior to issuance of the financial statements indicates that it is probable that . . . a liability had been incurred at the date of the financial statements. It is implicit in this condition that it must be probable that one or more future events will occur confirming the fact . . . [and] [t]he amount . . . can be reasonably estimated [13:par. 8].

An entity may not recognize revenue on the accrual basis until collection of the sales price is reasonably assured [14:Ch. 1A, par. 1]. If, however, collection of the sales price is reasonably assured, then it is probable that a liability for taxes exists. The argument that no such liability arises until an enterprise reports revenue in the tax return confuses absence of a specific settlement date with absence of an obligation. Present tax laws obligate an enterprise to pay taxes on all taxable earnings. Consistency therefore requires that when revenue is recognized, its associated tax effect should be accrued as a liability if the amount is capable of reasonable estimation. Furthermore, the amount reflected should be based on the tax rate expected to apply when the revenue is reported in the tax return since this rate will determine the actual cash flow.

Revenue (or Gain) Reported in the Tax Return Before the Income Statement

Timing differences of this type result, for example, if customer or client advances are taxed when collected but are not reported in the income statement until earned. The FASB defines assets as "probable future economic benefits" [15:par. 19]. Paying income tax on unearned fees relieves an entity of the obligation to pay such tax later. Furthermore, if the entity must return advances because it is unable to provide the contracted merchandise or service, it is entitled to a tax refund. In either case, tax payments on unearned fees clearly create probable future economic benefit and it is consistent with the current accounting model to record such payments as assets.

For timing differences of this type, the current tax rate determines the amount actually claimed by the government.

This rate should, therefore, be used to measure the tax effect.

Expense (or Loss) Reported in the Income Statement Before the Tax Return

This category includes timing differences that arise (1) when expenses or losses are accrued in the financial statements but reported on a cash basis in the tax return, or (2) when expenditures are charged to expense or loss in the financial statements earlier than they are deducted in the tax return. Examples of the first type include timing differences related to product warranties and deferred compensation. Examples of the second type generally involve some past expenditures and include timing differences that would arise if an enterprise used accelerated depreciation in the financial statements but straight-line depreciation in the tax return, or if it expensed organization costs immediately in the financial statements but amortized such costs in the tax return. An exception is the timing difference that occurs when bad debt expense is based on the allowance method in the financial statements but on the direct write-off method in the tax return. In this special case, because the eventual deduction effectively corrects an earlier period's reported taxable revenue, the tax effect of the timing difference is an asset—a refund due for overpaid taxes. Furthermore, because the amount refunded is based on the tax rate in effect when the deduction is claimed, the amount reported should be based on the tax rate expected at that time.

In practice, timing differences of the second type are rare. Ordinarily, when a past expenditure is involved, the charge against reported income will occur after the tax deduction rather than before it.

Whether the charge against income precedes the deduction or follows it, however, the same analysis should apply because, in either case, the expenditure precedes both. For these reasons, the remainder of this section focuses on timing differences of the first type. Examination of the second type is deferred until the next section.

In the balance sheet, the liability for an accrued expense or loss indicates a probable future cash outflow for some existing or contingent obligation. If expenditures to satisfy the obligation are tax deductible, however, any resulting tax savings will reduce the entity's net cash outflow. Therefore, if satisfaction of an obligation is expected to result in tax savings, that obligation should be reported net of the expected tax effect. Otherwise the amount reported will lack representational faithfulness because it will consistently exceed the expected and, ultimately, actual net outflow.

The actual cash flow effect of any deduction depends on its amount and the tax rate applicable when it is claimed. For this reason, when expenses are accrued in the financial statements before they are deducted in the tax return, the estimated tax effect of the timing difference should take expected future tax rates into account. Additionally, the estimate should take into account the likelihood of taxable revenue against which the deduction may be offset. If no such revenue is anticipated (even with carryback and carryforward), the expected tax effect should be zero.

Expense (or Loss) Reported in the Tax Return Before the Income Statement

Timing differences of this type generally involve some past expenditure that is deducted in the tax return earlier or at a faster rate than is expensed in the financial statements. The most common example is the use of accelerated depreciation in the tax return but straight-line depreciation in the financial statements.

In Accounting Research Study No. 9, *Interperiod Allocation of Corporate Income Taxes,* Black argues that the tax effects of such timing differences are liabilities [11:114]. While claiming a deduction currently may foreclose the opportunity of using that deduction in a future period, however, it does not, by itself, create a future tax obligation. Tax obligations only result from taxable revenue or gain. Thus for this type of timing difference, interpretation as a liability is not appropriate. Instead, the proper approach is to treat the tax effect as a valuation adjustment (offset) to the asset giving rise to the timing difference. To understand why net-of-tax accounting is appropriate here, it is necessary to examine the tax effects more closely.

The FASB defines assets as "probable future economic benefits obtained or controlled by a particular entity as a result of past transactions or events" [15: par. 19]. A probable future tax deduction resulting from a past expenditure satisfies all the conditions inherent in this definition. Expected tax benefits, however, are not recognized as a separate asset. Instead, the asset account that reflects expected benefits from some economic resource's use, sale, etc., also reflects any tax benefits associated with the expenditure to obtain that resource. In this case tax effects (benefits) arise when potentially deductible expenditures occur and they continue to exist until the deductions are either claimed or lost. When the deductions are claimed, the resulting tax savings are a recovery of—not an expiration of—asset cost. They should, therefore, be accounted for in the same manner as residual value—excluded from the depreciable base—and, instead, deducted from the asset's carrying amount when realized.

Exhibits 1 and 2 illustrate the effect of such an approach on a fixed asset's book value. The exhibits are based on the following assumptions: asset cost, $11,000; expected useful life, four years; expected residual value, $1,000; marginal tax rate, 40 percent. Exhibit 1 assumes straight-line depreciation in both the financial statements and the tax return. Exhibit 2 assumes straight-line depreciation in the financial state-

EXHIBIT 1 *Financial Statement Depreciation Method: Straight-Line*
Tax Return Depreciation Method: Straight-Line
Tax Savings Treated as a Cost Recovery: Yes
Tax Allocation Procedures: Not Applicable

	Year 1	Year 2	Year 3	Year 4
Book Value at Beginning of Year	$11,000	$8,500	$6,000	$3,500
Less: Depreciation ("Tax Adjusted")[a]	(1,500)	(1,500)	(1,500)	(1,500)
Less: Realized Tax Savings[b]	(1,000)	(1,000)	(1,000)	(1,000)
Book Value at End of Year	$ 8,500	$6,000	$3,500	$1,000

[a] (.25)($11,000 − $1,000 − $4,000).

[b] (.40)(.25)($11,000 − $1,000).

EXHIBIT 2 *Financial Statement Depreciation Method: Straight-Line*
Tax Return Depreciation Method: Sum-of-the-Years'-Digits
Tax Savings Treated as a Cost Recovery: Yes
Tax Allocation Procedures: Not Applicable

	Year 1	Year 2	Year 3	Year 4
Book Value at Beginning of Year	$11,000	$7,900	$5,200	$2,900
Less: Depreciation ("Tax Adjusted")[a]	(1,500)	(1,500)	(1,500)	(1,500)
Less: Realized Tax Savings[b]	(1,000)	(1,200)	(800)	(400)
Book Value at End of Year	$ 7,900	$5,200	$2,900	$1,000

[a] $(.25)(\$11,000 - \$1,000 - \$4,000)$.

[b] Year 1 $(.40)(.40)(\$11,000 - \$1,000)$.
   2 $(.40)(.30)(\$11,000 - \$1,000)$.
   3 $(.40)(.20)(\$11,000 - \$1,000)$.
   4 $(.40)(.10)(\$11,000 - \$1,000)$.

ments but sum-of-the-years'-digits depreciation in the tax return. In both cases, expected tax savings over the asset's useful life amount to $4,000 (40% of the difference between the asset's cost and its expected residual value). The net expected cost of benefits that will expire over the asset's useful life (the tax-adjusted depreciable base), therefore, must be $6,000 (acquisition cost less expected residual value and tax savings). In these illustrations, the asset's book value is reduced each year by straight-line amortization ($1,500) of the tax-adjusted depreciable base and

by the actual cost recovery realized as tax savings.

If an entity uses the same depreciation method in both its financial statements and its tax return, the financial statement depreciation rate will correspond to the actual rate at which tax savings are realized. Therefore, book values over the asset's useful life will be the same whether or not tax savings are separately accounted for. A comparison of the book values in Exhibit 1 with those in Exhibit 3 verifies this point for straight-line depreciation.

If, however, the entity uses a different

EXHIBIT 3 *Financial Statement Depreciation Method: Straight-Line*
Tax Return Depreciation Method: Any
Tax Savings Treated as a Cost Recovery: No
Tax Allocation Procedures: No

	Year 1	Year 2	Year 3	Year 4
Book Value at Beginning of Year	$11,000	$8,500	$6,000	$3,500
Less: Depreciation[a]	(2,500)	(2,500)	(2,500)	(2,500)
Book Value at End of Year	$ 8,500	$6,000	$3,500	$1,000

[a] $(.25)(\$11,000 - \$1,000)$.

EXHIBIT 4   *Financial Statement Depreciation Method: Straight-Line*
Tax Return Depreciation Method: Sum-of-the-Years'-Digits
Tax Savings Treated as a Cost Recovery: No
Tax Allocation Procedures: Yes

	Year 1	Year 2	Year 3	Year 4
Book Value at Beginning of Year	$11,000	$7,900	$5,200	$2,900
Less: Depreciation[a]	(2,500)	(2,500)	(2,500)	(2,500)
Add: Tax Effect of Timing Difference[b]	(600)	(200)	200	600
Book Value at End of Year	$ 7,900	$5,200	$2,900	$1,000

[a] $(.25)($11,000 - $1,000)$.

[b] Straight-Line Depreciation	$2,500	$2,500	$2,500	$2,500
Sum-of-the-Years'-Digits Depreciation	4,000	3,000	2,000	1,000
Difference	($1,500)	($ 500)	$ 500	$1,500
× Tax Rate	.40	.40	.40	.40
Tax Effect of Timing Difference	($ 600)	($ 200)	$ 200	$ 600

depreciation method in the financial statements than it uses in the tax return, the financial statement depreciation rate will not correspond to the rate at which tax savings are realized. In this case, as Exhibits 2 and 3 demonstrate, book values over the asset's useful life will differ depending on whether or not tax savings are separately accounted for. Note that, if tax savings are not separately accounted for, the rate at which they are deducted from the asset's book value is effectively the financial statement depreciation rate and not the (generally faster) rate at which they are actually realized. Therefore, if an entity uses straight-line depreciation in the financial statements but an accelerated depreciation method in the tax return and does not account for tax savings separately, the asset's book value will imply a greater unused tax benefit than actually remains.

Net-of-tax interperiod tax allocation procedures adjust an asset's book value for the tax effect of any associated timing differences. When a fixed asset's

cost is charged to expense at a different rate than it is deducted in the tax return, such an adjustment effectively compensates for differences between the financial statement depreciation rate and the rate at which tax savings are realized. Exhibit 4 illustrates traditional net-of-tax treatment, assuming straight-line depreciation in the financial statements and sum-of-the-years'-digits depreciation in the tax return. As a comparison of this exhibit with Exhibit 2 suggests, net-of-tax procedures give results equivalent to separate treatment of tax savings as a recovery of asset cost. Accounting for tax savings as a recovery of asset cost is consistent with the treatment afforded residual value; therefore, a net-of-tax interpretation here is consistent with the current accounting model.

For timing differences of this type, the tax rate in effect when the expenditure is deducted in the tax return determines the actual amount recovered through tax savings. Thus, if an expenditure is deducted in the tax return before it is

TABLE 1 *Recommended Accounting for the Tax Effects of Timing Differences*

Type of Timing Difference	Example	Balance Sheet Classification	Tax Rate
Revenue (or Gain) Reported in the Income Statement before the Tax Return	Profit on installment sales	Liability	Expected future
Revenue (or Gain) Reported in the Tax Return before the Income Statement	Rent or royalty fees received in advance	Asset	Current
Expense (or Loss) Reported in the Income Statement before the Tax Return			
a. Accrued Expense (or Loss)	Product warranties	Valuation adjustment to the associated liability	Expected future
b. Deferred Expenditure	Accelerated depreciation in the tax return, straight-line depreciation in the financial statements	Valuation adjustment to the associated asset	Expected future
Expense (or Loss) Reported in the Tax Return before the Income Statement	Straight-line depreciation in the tax return, accelerated depreciation in the financial statements	Valuation adjustment to the associated asset	Current

charged to expense, the tax effect of the timing difference should be based on the current tax rate. If, on the other hand, the expenditure is charged to expense before it is deducted on the tax return, the tax effect should be based on the rate expected to apply when the timing difference reverses.

Summary and Conclusions

Critics of current accounting for income taxes have urged the FASB to abandon comprehensive interperiod allocation. It is the specific manner chose to implement tax allocation that is deficient, however, not the concept itself. The combination method of interperiod allocation described in Table 1 is consistent with the current accounting model. Furthermore, its adoption would eliminate the virtually permanent deferred credit that results when a going concern uses accelerated depreciation in the tax return but straight-line depreciation in the financial statements.

Adoption of the accounting recommended in Table 1 would require some change in accounting practice. Perhaps the only significant change, however, would be net-of-tax treatment if timing differences relate to past expenditures. Regarding tax effects as assets or liabilities instead of deferred charges or credits should have no impact on financial statement location. Furthermore, as a practical matter, when future tax rates are prescribed to measure a tax effect, current rates likely would still be used because, in most cases, they will be the best estimator of the relevant future rates.

Comprehensive interperiod income tax allocation makes accountants' financial statement allocations consistent, reduces the likelihood that an enterprise will pay liquidating dividends or unrecoverable excess compensation, and can be implemented in a manner that is entirely consistent with the current accounting model. For these reasons, the FASB should modify interperiod income tax allocation procedures, not abandon them.

References

1. APB Opinion No. 11, *Accounting for Income Taxes* (New York: AICPA, 1967).
2. Paul Rosenfield and William C. Dent. "No More Deferred Taxes." *The Journal of Accountancy* (February 1983), pp. 44–55.
3. Sidney Davidson. "Accelerated Depreciation and the Allocation of Income Taxes." *The Accounting Review* (April 1958), pp. 173–80.
4. Sidney Davidson, Lisa Skelton, and Roman Weil. "A Controversy over the Expected Behavior of Deferred Tax Credits." *The Journal of Accountancy* (April 1977), pp. 53–59.
5. Keith W. Lantz, Andrew G. Snyir, and John J. Williams. "A Second Look at the Expected Behavior of Deferred Tax Credits." *Cost and Management* (March/April 1978), pp. 46–50.
6. Eldon S. Hendriksen. *Accounting Theory*, 4th ed. (Richard D. Irwin, Inc., 1982).
7. Arthur L. Thomas. *The Allocation Problem in Financial Accounting Theory*. Studies in Accounting Research No. 3 (American Accounting Association, 1969).
8. Arthur L. Thomas. *The Allocation Problem: Part Two*. Studies in Accounting Research No. 9 (American Accounting Association, 1974).
9. Raymond E. Perry. "Comprehensive Income Tax Allocation." *The Journal of Accountancy* (February 1966), pp. 23–32.
10. Arthur R. Wyatt, Richard Dieter, and John E. Stewart. "Tax Allocation Revisited." *The CPA Journal* (March 1984), pp. 10–18.
11. Homer A. Black. *Interperiod Allocation of Corporate Income Taxes* (New York: AICPA, 1966).
12. Bill N. Schwartz. "Income Tax Allocation: It Is Time for a Change." *Journal of Accounting, Auditing & Finance* (Spring 1981), pp. 238–247.
13. SFAS No. 5, *Accounting for Contingencies* (Stamford, Conn.: FASB, 1975).
14. ARB No. 43, *Restatement and Revision of Accounting Research Bulletins* (New York, AICPA, 1953).
15. SFAC No. 3, *Elements of Financial Statements of Business Enterprises* (Stamford, Conn.: FASB, 1980).

Cases

- ### Case 10-1

The Whitley Corporation's year-end is December 31. It is now October 1, 1994. The Whitley management team is taking a look at the prior nine months and attempting to make some short-term strategy decisions.

Whitley has experienced steady growth over the five preceding years. The result has been a steadily increasing EPS. Last year Whitley reported an EPS of 1.95.

This year, due to a mild recession, Whitley's sales have fallen off. Management is looking for strategies that may improve the appearance of their financial statements. At the same time there is a need for new equipment in the plant. Despite the recession, Whitley has enough cash to make the purchase.

Based on the year's performance to date and extrapolation of the results to year-end, management feels that the pretax financial accounting income for the year will be $200,000. Transactions from prior years have resulted in a deferred tax asset of $15,000 and a deferred tax liability of $70,000 at the beginning of 1994. The temporary difference of $37,500 that resulted in the deferred tax asset is expected to completely reverse by the end of 1994. The deferred tax liability resulted totally from temporary depreciation differences. There will be a pretax reversal of $42,500 in this temporary difference during 1994.

Based on presently enacted tax law, the purchase of the equipment will result in a future taxable amount of $50,000. Whitley management feels that it can wait four to six months to purchase the machine. Whitley's tax rate is 40 percent.

Required:
a. Determine the projected amount of income tax expense that would be reported if Whitley waits until next year to purchase the equipment.
b. Determine the projected amount of income tax expense that would be reported if Whitley purchases the equipment in 1994.
c. Should Whitley wait to purchase the equipment? Your answer should take into consideration the expected financial statement effects, as well as the effect on EPS. Support your conclusions with pro-forma data. The number of shares that Whitley will use to calculate EPS is 55,500.
d. What are the ethical considerations of this case?

- ### Case 10-2

The FASB has carefully avoided the issue of discounting deferred taxes. *Statement of Financial Accounting Standards No. 109,* "Accounting for Income Taxes" states that

> . . . a deferred tax liability or asset should be recognized for the deferred tax consequences of temporary differences and operating loss or tax credit carryfor-

wards. . . . *Under the requirements of this Statement: . . . Deferred tax liabilities and assets are not discounted.*[1]

Required:

a. Assuming that firm deferred tax liabilities exceed deferred tax assets, select that approach to measurement, discounting or nondiscounting, that is best supported by the qualitative characteristics of *SFAC No. 2* by placing an X in the following evaluation matrix under the measurement approach selected. For example, if you feel that discounting has higher representational faithfulness, put an X under column 2 beside representational faithfulness. Column 3 is provided for those cases for which a given concept is not applicable.

SFAC No. 2 Qualitative Characteristic	Nondiscounting (1)	Discounting (2)	Neither (3)
1. Relevance			
a. Timeliness			
b. Predictive and feedback value			
2. Reliability			
a. Representational faithfulness			
b. Verifiability and neutrality			
3. Understandability			
4. Comparability			

b. Discuss the reasons for your evaluations.

c. Present arguments supporting the discounting of deferred taxes.

d. Present arguments opposing the discounting of deferred taxes.

- **Case 10-3**

One of the main criticisms of *SFAS No. 96* was that most deferred tax assets could not be recognized. *SFAS No. 109* liberalized the recognition of deferred tax assets. Deferred tax assets are now recognized for all deductible amounts and carryovers. However, the amount reported may be reduced or eliminated by a valuation allowance if it is more likely than not that the deferred tax asset will not be realized.

Required:

a. Describe how the more likely than not criterion satisfied both the affirmative judgment approach and the impairment approach to asset recognition. How does this differ from typical asset recognition?

[1] Ibid., pars. 64 and 66.

b. Cite examples that indicate affirmative evidence supporting the recognition of deferred tax assets.
c. Cite examples of potential impairment of deferred tax assets.
d. Given that some of each type of evidence may exist, how might the more likely than not criterion present management with an ethical dilemma? Explain.

• Case 10-4

Income tax allocation is an integral part of generally accepted accounting principles. The applications of intraperiod income tax allocation (within a period) and interperiod tax allocation (among periods) are both required.

Required:
a. Explain the need for intraperiod income tax allocation.
b. Accountants who favor interperiod income tax allocation argue that income taxes are an expense rather than a distribution of earnings. Explain the significance of this argument. Do not explain the definitions of expense or distribution of earnings.
c. Discuss the nature of the deferred income tax accounts and possible classifications in a company's balance sheet.
d. Indicate and explain whether each of the following independent situations should be treated as a temporary difference or a permanent difference.
   i. Estimated warranty costs (covering a three-year period) are expensed for accounting purposes when incurred.
   ii. Depreciation for accounting and income tax purposes differs because of different bases of carrying the related property. The different bases are a result of a business combination treated as a purchase for accounting purposes and as a tax-free exchange for income tax purposes.
   iii. A company properly uses the equity method to account for its 30 percent investment in another company. The investee pays dividends that are about 10 percent of its annual earnings.
e. For each of the above independent situations, determine whether those situations that are treated as temporary differences will result in future taxable amounts or future deductible amounts and whether they will result in deferred tax assets or deferred tax liabilities. Explain.

• Case 10-5

Statement of Financial Accounting Standards No. 109, "Accounting for Income Taxes," requires interperiod income tax allocation for temporary differences.

Required:
a. Define the term *temporary difference.*
b. List the examples of temporary differences contained in *SFAS No. 109.*
c. Defend comprehensive interperiod income tax allocation.

- **Case 10-6**

Statement of Financial Accounting Standards No. 109, "Accounting for Income Taxes," requires companies to use the asset/liability method of interperiod income tax allocation.

Required:

a. Discuss the criteria for recognizing deferred tax assets and deferred tax liabilities under the provisions of *SFAS No. 109*.
b. Compare and contrast the asset/liability method and the deferred method.

Recommended Additional Reading

Smith, Darlene A., and Gary R. Freeman. *SFAS 109*, "Accounting for Income Taxes." *The CPA Journal* (April 1992), pp. 16–25.

Bibliography

Arthur Andersen & Co. *Accounting for Income Taxes.* Chicago: Arthur Andersen & Co., 1961.

Barton, A. U. "Company Income Tax and Interperiod Allocation." *Abacus* (September 1970), pp. 3–24.

Baylis, A. W. "Income Tax Allocation—A Defense." *Abacus* (December 1971), pp. 161–172. See also A. D. Barton. "Reply to Mr. Baylis." *Abacus* (December 1971), pp. 173–175.

Beaver, William, and Roland E. Dukes. "Interperiod Tax Allocation and Delta-Depreciation Methods: Some Empirical Results." *The Accounting Review* (July 1973), pp. 549–595.

Bevis, Donald J., and Raymond E. Perry. *Accounting for Income Taxes.* New York: AICPA, 1969.

Bierman, Harold, Jr. "One More Reason to Revise Statement 96." *Accounting Horizons* (June 1990), pp. 42–46.

Bierman, Harold, and Thomas R. Dyckman. "New Look at Deferred Taxes." *Financial Executive* (January 1974), pp. 40ff.

Black, Homer A. "Interperiod Allocation of Corporate Income Taxes." *Accounting Research Study No. 9.* New York: AICPA, 1966.

Chambers, R. J. "Tax Allocation and Financial Reporting." *Abacus* (December 1968), pp. 99–123.

Chaney, Paul K., and Debra C. Jeter. "Accounting for Deferred Income Taxes: Simplicity? Usefulness?" *Accounting Horizons* (June 1989), pp. 6–13.

Cramer, Joe J., Jr., and William J. Schrader. "Investment Tax Credit." *Business Horizons* (February 1970), pp. 85–89.

Givoly, Dan, and Carla Hayn. "The Valuation of the Deferred Tax Liability: Evidence from the Stock Market." *The Accounting Review* (April 1992), pp. 394–410.

Godlick, Neil B., and Richard P. Miller. "Applying APB Opinions Nos. 23 and 24." *Journal of Accountancy* (November 1973), pp. 55–63.

Hill, Thomas. "Some Arguments Against the Interperiod Allocation of Income Taxes." *The Accounting Review* (July 1957), pp. 528–537.

Laibstain, Samuel. "New Look at Accounting for Operating Loss Carry-Forwards." *The Accounting Review* (April 1971), pp. 342–351.

Meonske, Norman R., and Hans Sprohge. "How to Apply the New Accounting Rules for Deferred Taxes." *The Practical Accountant* (June 1988), pp. 15–50.

Moonitz, Maurice. "Some Reflections on the Investment Credit Experience." *Journal of Accounting Research* (Spring 1966), pp. 47–61.

Moore, Carl L. "Deferred Income Tax—Is It a Liability?" *New York CPA* (February 1970), pp. 130–138.

Norgaard, Corine T. "Financial Implications of Comprehensive Income Tax Allocation." *Financial Analysts Journal* (January–February 1969), pp. 81–85.

Nurnberg, Hugo. "Critique of the Deferred Method of Interperiod Tax Allocation." *New York CPA* (December 1969), pp. 958–961.

Nurnberg, Hugo. "Deferred Tax Assets Under FASB Statement No. 96." *Accounting Horizons* (December 1989), pp. 49–56.

Pointer, Larry Gene. "Disclosing Corporate Tax Policy," *Journal of Accountancy* (July 1973), pp. 56–61.

Price Waterhouse & Co. *Is Generally Accepted Accounting for Income Taxes Possibly Misleading Investors?* New York: Price Waterhouse & Co., 1967.

Raiburn, Michael H., Michael R. Lane, and D. D. Raiburn. "Purchased Loss Carryforwards: An Unresolved Issue." *Journal of Accountancy* (November 1983), pp. 98–108.

Rayburn, Frank R. "A Chronological Review of the Authoritative Literature on Interperiod Tax Allocation: 1945–1985." *The Accounting Historians Journal* (Fall 1986), pp. 89–108.

Read, William J., and Robert A. J. Bartsch. "The FASB's Proposed Rules for Deferred Taxes." *Journal of Accountancy* (August 1991), pp. 44–46, 48, 50–53.

Revsine, Lawrence. "Some Controversy Concerning Controversial Accounting Changes." *The Accounting Review* (April 1969), pp. 354–358.

Rosenfield, Paul, and William C. Dent. "No More Deferred Taxes." *Journal of Accountancy* (February 1983), pp. 44–55.

Smith, Willis A. "Tax Allocation Revisited—Another Viewpoint." *The CPA Journal* (September 1984), pp. 52–56.

Stamp, Edward. "Some Further Reflections on the Investment Credit." *Journal of Accounting Research* (Spring 1967), pp. 124–128.

Throckmorton, Jerry J. "Theoretical Concepts for Interpreting the Investment Credit." *Journal of Accountancy* (April 1970), pp. 45–52.

Voss, William M. "Accelerated Depreciation and Deferred Tax Allocation." *Journal of Accounting Research* (Autumn 1968), pp. 262–269.

Watson, Peter L. "Accounting for Deferred Tax on Depreciable Assets." *Accounting and Business Research* (Autumn 1979), pp. 338–347.

Weber, Richard P. "Misleading Tax Figures: A Problem for Accountants." *The Accounting Review* (January 1977), pp. 172–185.

Wheeler, James E., and Willard H. Galliart. *An Appraisal of Interperiod Income Tax Allocation.* New York: Financial Executives Research Foundation, 1974.

Williams, Edward E., and M. Chapman Findly. "Discounting Deferred Tax Liabilities: Some Clarifying Comments." *Journal of Business Finance and Accounting* (Spring 1975), pp. 121–133.

Wolk, Harry I., Dale R. Martin, and Virginia A. Nichols. "Statement of Financial Accounting Standards No. 96: Some Theoretical Problems." *Accounting Horizons* (June 1989), pp. 1–5.

Wolk, Harry I., and Michael G. Tearney. "Income Tax Allocation and Loss Carry-Forwards: Exploring Uncharted Ground." *The Accounting Review* (April 1973), pp. 292–299.

Wyatt, Arthur R., Richard Dieter, and John E. Stewart. "Tax Allocation Revisited." *The CPA Journal* (1984), pp. 10, 12, 14–16, 18.

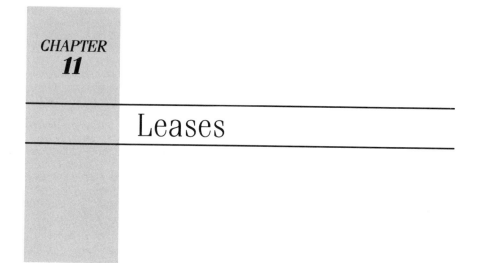

Leases

Business firms generally acquire *property rights* in long-term assets by purchases that are funded either by internal sources or by externally borrowed funds. The accounting issues associated with the purchase of long-term assets were discussed in Chapter 7. Leasing is an alternative means of acquiring long-term assets to be used by business firms. Leases that are not in-substance purchases provide for the *right-to-use* property by lessees in contrast to purchases that transfer property rights to the user of the long-term asset. Lease terms generally obligate lessees to make a series of payments over a future period of time. As such, they are similar to long-term debt; however, if a lease is correctly structured, it enables the lessee to engage in *off–balance sheet financing* (discussed in Chapter 9) because certain leases are not recorded as long-term debt on the balance sheet. Business managers frequently wish to use off–balance sheet financing because of a desire to improve the financial position of their companies. However, as noted earlier in the text, efficient market research indicates that off–balance sheet financing techniques are incorporated into user decision models in determining the value of a company.

Leasing has become a popular method of acquiring property because of the following advantages:

1. It offers 100 percent financing.

2. It offers protection against obsolescence.

3. It is frequently less costly than other forms of financing the cost of the acquisition of fixed assets.

4. It does not add debt to the balance sheet.

Many long-term leases have most of the attributes of long-term debt. That is, they create an obligation for payment under an agreement that is noncancelable. The adverse effects of debt are also present in leases in that an inability to pay may result in insolvency. Consequently, even though there are statutory limitations on lease obligations in bankruptcy proceedings, these limits do not have impact on the probability of the adverse effects of non-payment on asset values and credit standing in the event of nonpayment of lease obligations. The statutory limitations involve only the evaluation of the amount owed after insolvency proceeding have commenced.

Management's choice between purchasing and leasing is a function of strategic investment and capital structure objectives, the comparative costs of purchases of assets versus leasing assets, the availability of tax benefits, and perceived financial reporting advantages. The tax benefit advantage is a major factor in leasing decisions. From a macro-economic standpoint, the tax benefits of owning assets may be maximized by transferring them to the party in the higher marginal tax bracket. Firms with lower effective tax rates may engage in more leasing transactions than firms in higher tax brackets since the tax benefits are passed on to the lessor. El-Gazzar et al.[1] found evidence to support this theory; firms with lower effective tax rates were found to have a higher proportion of leased debt to total assets than did firms with higher effective tax rates.

Some lease agreements are in-substance long-term installment purchases of assets that have been structured to gain tax or other benefits to the parties. Since leases may take different forms, it is necessary to examine the underlying nature of the original transaction to determine the appropriate method of accounting for these agreements. That is, they should be reported in a manner that describes the intent of the lessor and lessee rather than the form of the agreement.

Over the years, two predominant methods for allocating lease revenues and expenses to the periods covered by the lease agreement have emerged in accounting practice. One method, termed a *capital lease,* is based on the view that the lease constitutes an agreement through which the lessor finances the acquisition of assets by the lessee. Consequently, capital leases are in-substance installment purchases of assets. The other method is termed an *operating lease* and is based on the view that the lease constitutes a rental agreement between the lessor and lessee.

The basic accounting questions associated with leases are (1) What characteristics of the lease agreement require a lease to be reported as an in-substance long-term purchase of an asset? (2) Which characteristics allow the lease to be recorded as a long-term rental agreement?

The accounting profession first recognized the problems associated with leases in *Accounting Research Bulletin (ARB) No. 38.* This release recommended that if a lease agreement was in substance an installment purchase of property, it should be recorded as an asset and a liability by the lessee. As with many of the ARBs, the recommendations of this pronouncement were largely ig-

---

[1] El-Gazzar, Shamir M., Steven Lilien, and Victor Pastena, "Accounting for Leases by Lessees," *Journal of Accounting and Economics* (October 1986), pp. 217–237.

nored in practice, and the lease disclosure problem remained an important accounting issue.

Later in 1964, the Accounting Principles Board issued *Opinion No. 5,* "Reporting of Leases in Financial Statements of Lessees." The provisions of *APB Opinion No. 5* (discussed later in the chapter) required leases that were in-substance purchases to be capitalized on the financial statements of lessees. This conclusion was no match for the countervailing forces against the capitalization of leases that were motivated by the ability to present a more favorable financial structure and patterns of income determination. As a result, relatively few leases were capitalized under the provisions of *APB Opinion No. 5.*

The APB also issued three other statements dealing with accounting for leases by lessors and lessees, *APB Opinion No. 7,* "Accounting for Leases in Financial Statement of Lessors," *APB Opinion No. 27,* "Accounting for Lease Transactions by Manufacturers or Dealer Lessors," and *APB Opinion No. 31,* "Disclosure of Lease Transactions by Lessees." Nevertheless, the overall result of these statements was that few leases were being capitalized and that lessor and lessee accounting for leases lacked symmetry. That is, these four *Opinions* allowed differences in recording and reporting the same lease by lessors and lessees.

In November 1976, the FASB issued *SFAS No. 13* "Accounting for Leases" which superseded *APB Opinion Nos. 5, 7, 27,* and *31.* A major purpose of *SFAS No. 13* was to achieve a greater degree of symmetry of accounting between lessees and lessors. In an effort to accomplish this goal, the Statement established standards of financial accounting and reporting for both lessees and lessors. One of the problems associated with the four *Opinions* issued by the APB was that they allowed differences in recording and reporting the same lease by lessors and lessees. Adherence to *SFAS No. 13* substantially reduces (though does not completely eliminate) this possibility.

The conceptual foundation underlying *SFAS No. 13* is based on the view that "a lease that transfers substantially all of the benefits and risks incident to the ownership of property should be accounted for as the acquisition of an asset and the incurrence of an obligation by the lessee and as a sale or financing by the lessor."[2] This viewpoint leads immediately to three basic conclusions: (1) The characteristics that indicate that substantially all the benefits and risks of ownership have been transferred to the lessee must be identified. These leases should be recorded as if they involved the purchase and sale of assets (*capital leases*). (2) The same characteristics should apply to both the lessee and lessor; therefore, the inconsistency in accounting treatment that previously existed should be eliminated. (3) Those leases that do not meet the characteristics identified in (1) should be accounted for simply as rental agreements (*operating leases*).

It has been suggested that the choice of structuring a lease as either an

---

[2]Financial Accounting Standards Board, *Statement of Financial Accounting Standards No. 13,* "Accounting for Leases" (Stamford, Conn.: FASB, 1976), par. 60. This Statement was later amended in 1980 to incorporate several FASB pronouncements that expanded on the principles outlined in the original pronouncement.

operating or capital lease is not independent of the original nature of leasing as opposed to buying the asset. As indicated earlier, companies engaging in lease transactions may attempt to transfer the benefits of owning assets to the lease party in the higher tax bracket. Additionally, Smith and Wakeman[3] identified eight non-tax factors that make leasing more attractive than purchase:

1. The period of use is short relative to the overall life of the asset.
2. The lessor has a comparative advantage over the lessee in reselling the asset.
3. Corporate bond covenants of the lessee contain restrictions relating to financial policies the firm must follow (maximum debt to equity ratios).
4. Management compensation contracts contain provisions expressing compensation as a function of return on invested capital.
5. Lessee ownership is closely held so that risk reduction is important.
6. Lessor (manufacturer) has market power and can thus generate higher profits by leasing the asset (and controlling the terms of the lease) than by selling the asset.
7. The asset is not specialized to the firm.
8. The asset's value is not sensitive to use or abuse (owner takes better care of the asset than does the lessee).

Obviously, some of these reasons are not subject to lessee choice but are motivated by the lessor and/or the type of asset involved. However, short periods of use and the resale factor favor the accounting treatment of a lease as operating, whereas the bond covenant and management compensation incentives favor a structuring of the lease as a capital lease. Additionally, lessors may be more inclined to seek to structure leases as capital leases to allow earlier recognition of revenue and net income. That is, a lease that is reported as an in-substance sale by the lessor frequently allows for revenue recognition at the time of the original transaction rather than over the life of the lease.

Criteria for Classifying Leases

In *SFAS No. 13*, the FASB outlined specific criteria to assist in classifying leases as either capital or operating leases. In the case of the lessee, if at its inception the lease meets any one of the following four criteria, the lease is classified as a capital lease; otherwise, it is classified as an operating lease:

1. The lease transfers ownership of the property to the lessee by the end of the lease term. This includes the fixed noncancelable term of the lease plus various specified renewal options and periods.
2. The lease contains a bargain purchase option. This means that the stated purchase price is sufficiently lower than the expected fair market value of

---

[3] Smith, Clifford, Jr., and L. Macdonald Wakeman, "Determinants of Corporate Leasing Policy," *Journal of Finance* (July 1985), pp. 895–908.

the property at the date the option becomes exercisable and that exercise of the option appears, at the inception of the lease, to be reasonably assured.

3. The lease term is equal to 75 percent or more of the estimated remaining economic life of the leased property, unless the beginning of the lease term falls within the last 25 percent of the total estimated economic life of the leased property.

4. The present value at the beginning of the lease term of the minimum lease payments (the amounts of the payments the lessee is required to make excluding that portion of the payments representing executory costs such as insurance, maintenance, and taxes to be paid by the lessee) equals or exceeds 90 percent of the fair value of the leased property less any related investment tax credit retained by the lessor. (This criterion is also ignored when the lease term falls within the last 25 percent of the total estimated economic life of the leased property).[4]

The criteria for capitalization of leases are based on the assumption that a lease that transfers to the lessee the risks and benefits of using an asset should be recorded as an acquisition of a long-term asset. However, the criteria are seen as arbitrary as no explanation was provided by the FASB for choosing a lease term of 75 percent, or a fair value of 90 percent as the cut-off points. Additionally, the criteria have been viewed as redundant and essentially based on the fourth criterion (see the article by Coughlan accompanying this chapter).

In the case of the lessor (except for leveraged leases, discussed later), if a lease meets any one of the preceding four criteria plus *both* of the following additional criteria, it is classified as a sales type or direct financing lease:

1. Collectibility of the minimum lease payments is reasonably predictable.

2. No important uncertainties surround the amount of unreimbursable costs yet to be incurred by the lessor under the lease.[5]

Accounting and Reporting by Lessees under *SFAS No. 13*

Historically, the primary concern in accounting for lease transactions by lessees has been the appropriate recognition of assets and liabilities on the lessee's balance sheet. This concern has overridden the corollary question of revenue recognition on the part of lessors. Therefore, the usual position of accountants has been that if the lease agreement was in substance an installment purchase, the "leased" property should be accounted for as an asset by the lessee, together with its corresponding liability. Failure to do so results in an understatement of assets and liabilities on the balance sheet. Lease arrangements that are not considered installment purchases constitute *off–balance sheet financing* arrangements (discussed in Chapter 9) and should be properly disclosed in the footnotes to financial statements.

[4] Ibid., par. 7.

[5] Ibid., par. 8.

As early as 1962, the accounting research division of the AICPA recognized that there was little consistency in the disclosure of leases by lessees and that most companies were not capitalizing leases. It therefore authorized a research study on reporting of leases by lessees. Among the recommendations of this study were the following:

> To the extent, then, that leases give rise to property rights, those rights and related liabilities should be measured and incorporated in the balance sheet.
>
> To the extent, then, that the rental payments represent a means of financing the acquisition of property rights which the lessee has in his possession and under his control, the transaction constitutes the acquisition of an asset with a related obligation to pay for it.
>
> To the extent, however, that the rental payments are for services such as maintenance, insurance, property taxes, heat, light, and elevator service, no asset has been acquired, and none should be recorded. . . .
>
> The measurement of the asset value and the related liability involves two steps: (1) the determination of the part of the rentals which constitutes payment for property rights, and (2) the discounting of these rentals at an appropriate rate of interest.[6]

The crucial difference in the conclusion of this study and the existing practice was the emphasis on *property rights* (the right to use property), as opposed to the *rights in property*—ownership of equity interest in the property.

The APB considered the recommendations of this study and agreed that certain lease agreements should result in the lessee recording an asset and liability. The board concluded that the important criterion to be applied was whether the lease was in substance a purchase, that is, rights in property, rather than the existence of property rights. This conclusion indicated that the APB agreed that assets and liabilities should be recorded when the lease transaction was in substance an installment purchase in the same manner as other purchase arrangements. The APB, however, did not agree that the right to use property in exchange for future rental payments gives rise to the recording of assets and liabilities, since no equity in property is created.

In *Opinion No. 5*, the APB asserted that a noncancelable lease, or a lease cancelable only on the occurrence of some remote contingency, was probably in substance a purchase if either of the two following conditions exists:

1. The initial term is materially less than the useful life of the property, and the lessee has the option to renew the lease for the remaining useful life of the property at substantially less than the fair rental value.

2. The lessee has the right, during or at the expiration of the lease, to acquire the property at a price that at the inception of the lease appears to be substantially less than the probable fair value of the property at the time or times of permitted acquisition by the lessee.[7]

---

[6] John H. Myers, *Accounting Research Study No. 4,* "Reporting of Leases in Financial Statements" (New York: AICPA, 1962), pp. 4–5.

[7] *Accounting Principles Board Opinion No. 5,* "Reporting of Leases in Financial Statements of Lessees" (New York: AICPA, 1964), par. 10.

The presence of either of these two conditions was seen as convincing evidence that the lessee was building equity in the property.

The APB went on to say that one or more of the following circumstances tend to indicate that a lease arrangement is in substance a purchase:

1. The property was acquired by the lessor to meet the special needs of the lessee and will probably be usable only for that purpose and only by the lessee.

2. The term of the lease corresponds substantially to the estimated useful life of the property, and the lessee is obligated to pay costs such as taxes, insurance, and maintenance, which are usually considered incidental to ownership.

3. The lessee has guaranteed the obligations of the lessor with respect to the leased property.

4. The lessee has treated the lease as a purchase for tax purposes.[8]

In addition, the lease might be considered a purchase if the lessor and lessee were related even in the absence of the preceding conditions and circumstances. In that case,

> A lease should be recorded as a purchase if a primary purpose of ownership of the property by the lessor is to lease it to the lessee and (1) the lease payments are pledged to secure the debts of the lessor or (2) the lessee is able, directly or indirectly, to control or influence significantly the actions of the lessor with respect to the lease.[9]

These conclusions caused controversy in the financial community because some individuals believed that they resulted in disincentives to leasing. Those holding this view maintained that noncapitalized leases provide the following benefits:

1. Improved accounting rate of return and debt ratios, thereby improving the financial picture of the company.

2. Better debt ratings.

3. Increased availability of capital.

On the other hand, the advocates of lease capitalization hold that these arguments are, in essence, attempts to deceive financial statement users. That is, a company should fully disclose the impact of all its financing and investing activities and not attempt to hide the economic substance of external transactions.

Capital Leases

The views expressed in *APB Opinion No. 5* concerning the capitalization of those leases that are ''in-substance installment purchases'' are significant from

---

[8]Ibid., par. 11.

[9]Ibid., par. 12.

a historical point of view for two reasons. First, in *SFAS No. 13*, the FASB based its conclusion on the concept that a lease that "Transfers substantially all of the benefits and risks of the ownership of property should be accounted for as the acquisition of an asset and the incurrence of an obligation by the lessee, and as a sale or financing by the lessor." Second, to a great extent, the accounting provisions of *SFAS No. 13* applicable to lessees generally follow *APB Opinion No. 5*.

The provisions of *SFAS No. 13* require a lessee entering into a capital lease agreement to record both an asset and a liability at the lower of the following:

1. The sum of the present value of the *minimum lease payments* at the inception of the lease (see following discussion).

2. The fair value of the leased property at the inception of the lease.

The rules for determining minimum lease payments were specifically set forth by the Board. In summary, those payments that the lessee is obligated to make or can be required to make with the exception of executory costs should be included. Consequently, the following items are subject to inclusion in the determination of the minimum lease payments:

1. Minimum rental payments over the life of the lease.

2. Payment called for by a bargain purchase option.

3. Any guarantee by the lessee of the residual value at the expiration of the lease term.

4. Any penalties that the lessee can be required to pay for failure to renew the lease.[10]

Once the minimum lease payments or fair market value is determined, the next step is to compute the present value of the lease payments. The interest rate to be used in this computation is generally the lessee's incremental borrowing rate. This is the rate the lessee would have been charged had he or she borrowed funds to buy the asset with repayments over the same term. If the lessee can readily determine the implicit interest rate used by the lessor and if that rate is lower than his or her incremental borrowing rate, then the lessee is to use the lessor's implicit interest rate for calculating the present value of the minimum lease payments. If the lessee does not know the lessor's interest rate (a likely situation), or if the lessor's implicit interest rate is higher than the lessee's incremental borrowing rate, the lessee and lessor will have different amortization schedules to recognize interest expense and interest revenue, respectively.

Capital lease assets and liabilities are to be separately identified in the lessee's balance sheet or in the accompanying footnotes. The liability should be classified as current and noncurrent on the same basis as all other liabilities, that is, according to when the obligation must be paid.

Unless the lease involves land, the asset recorded under a capital lease is to be amortized by one of two methods. Leases that meet either criterion 1 or

---

[10] *SFAS No. 13*, op. cit., par. 5.

2 on page 499 are to be amortized in a manner consistent with the lessee's normal depreciation policy for owned assets. That is, the asset's economic life to the lessee is used as the amortization period. Leases that do not meet criterion 1 or 2 but meet either criterion 3 or 4 are to be amortized in a manner consistent with the lessee's normal depreciation policy, using the lease term as the period of amortization. In conformity with *APB Opinion No. 21*, "Interest on Receivables and Payables," *SFAS No. 13* requires that each minimum payment under a capital lease be allocated between a reduction of the liability and interest expense. This allocation is to be made in such a manner that the interest expense reflects a constant interest rate on the outstanding balance of the obligation (i.e., the effective interest method). Thus, as with any loan payment schedule, each successive payment allocates a greater amount to the reduction of the principal and a lesser amount to interest expense. This procedure results in the loan being reflected on the balance sheet at the present value of the future cash flows discounted at the effective interest rate.

Disclosure Requirements for Capital Leases

SFAS No. 13 also requires the disclosure of additional information for capital leases. The following information must be disclosed in the lessee's financial statements or in the accompanying footnotes:

1. The gross amount of assets recorded under capital leases as of the date of each balance sheet presented by major classes according to nature or function.
2. Future minimum lease payments as of the date of the latest balance sheet presented, in the aggregate and for each of the five succeeding fiscal years.
3. The total minimum sublease rentals to be received in the future under noncancelable subleases as of the date of the latest balance sheet presented.
4. Total contingent rentals (rentals on which the amounts are dependent on some factor other than the passage of time) actually incurred for each period for which an income statement is presented.[11]

A later section of this chapter provides an illustration of these disclosure requirements together with requirements for lessors.

Operating Leases

All leases that do not meet any of the four criteria for capitalization are to be classified as operating leases by the lessee. Failure to meet any of the criteria means that the lease is simply a rental arrangement and, in essence, should be accounted for in the same manner as any other rental agreement, with certain exceptions. The rent payments made on an operating lease are normally charged to expense as they become payable over the life of the lease. An exception is made if the rental schedule does not result in a straight-line basis of payment. In such cases, the rent expense is to be recognized on a

---

[11] Ibid., par. 16.

straight-line basis, unless the lessee can demonstrate that some other method gives a more systematic and rational periodic charge.

In *Opinion No. 31*, "Disclosure of Lease Commitments by Lessees," the APB observed that many different users of financial statements were dissatisfied with the information being provided about leases. Although there were many criticisms being voiced over accounting for leases, the focus of this opinion was on the information that should be disclosed about noncapitalized leases.

The following disclosures are required for operating leases by lessees:

1. *For operating leases having initial or remaining noncancelable lease terms in excess of one year:*
    a. *Future minimum rental payments required as of the date of the latest balance sheet presented in the aggregate and for each of the five succeeding fiscal years.*
    b. *The total of minimum rentals to be received in the future under noncancelable subleases as of the date of the latest balance sheet presented.*
2. *For all operating leases, rental expense for each period for which an income statement is presented, with separate amounts for minimum rentals, contingent rentals and sublease rentals.*
3. *A general description of the lessee's leasing arrangements including, but not limited to the following:*
    a. *The basis on which contingent rental payments are determined.*
    b. *The existence and terms of renewals or purchase options and escalation clauses.*
    c. *Restrictions imposed by lease agreements, such as those concerning dividends, additional debt, and further leasing.*[12]

It is the FASB's contention that the preceding accounting and disclosure requirements for capital and operating leases by lessees give users information useful in assessing a company's financial position and results of operations. The requirements also provide many specific and detailed rules, which should lead to greater consistency in the presentation of lease information.

Accounting and Reporting by Lessors

The major concern in accounting for leases in the financial statements of lessors is the appropriate allocation of revenues and expenses to the period covered by the lease. This concern contrasts with the lessee's focus on the balance sheet presentation of leases. As a general rule, lease agreements include a specific schedule of the date and amounts of payments to be made by the lessee to the lessor. The fact that the lessor knows the date and amount of payment does not necessarily indicate that revenue should be recorded in the same period the cash is received. Accrual accounting frequently gives rise to situations in which revenue is recognized in a period other than when payment is received, in order to measure more fairly the results of operations.

[12] Ibid., par. 16.

The nature of the lease and the rent schedule may make it necessary for the lessor to recognize revenue that is more or less than the payments received in a given period. Furthermore, the lessor must allocate the acquisition and operating costs of the leased property, together with any costs of negotiating and closing the lease, to the accounting periods receiving benefits in a systematic and rational manner consistent with the timing of revenue recognition. The latter point is consistent with the application of the matching principle in accounting, that is, determining the amount of revenue to be recognized in a period and then ascertaining which costs should be matched with that revenue.

The criterion for choosing between accounting for lease revenue by either the capital or operating methods historically was based on the accounting objective of fairly stating the lessor's periodic net income. Whichever method would best accomplish this objective should be followed. *SFAS No. 13* has now set forth specific criteria for determining the type of lease as well as the reporting and disclosure requirements for each type.

According to *SFAS No. 13*, if at its inception a lease agreement meets the lessor criteria for classification as a capital lease and if the two additional criteria for lessors contained on page 500 are met, the lessor is to classify the lease either as a *sales-type lease* or a *direct financing lease,* whichever is appropriate. All other leases, except leveraged leases (discussed in a separate section), are to be classified as operating leases.

Sales-Type Leases

A capital lease should be recorded as a *sales-type lease* by the lessor when there is a manufacturer's or dealer's profit (or loss). This implies that the leased asset is an item of inventory and the seller is earning a gross profit on the sale. Sales type leases arise when manufacturers or dealers use leasing as a means of marketing their products.

Table 11.1 depicts the major steps involved in accounting for a sales-type lease by a lessor. The amount to be recorded as gross investment (a) is the total amount of the minimum lease payments over the life of the lease, plus any unguaranteed residual value accruing to the benefit of the lessor. Once the gross investment has been determined, it is to be discounted to its present value (b) using an interest rate that causes the aggregate present value at the beginning of the lease term to be equal to the fair value of the leased property. The rate thus determined is referred to as the interest rate implicit in the lease.

The difference between the gross investment (a) and the present value of the gross investment (b) is to be recorded as unearned interest income (c). The unearned interest income is to be amortized as interest income over the life of the lease using the interest method described in *APB Opinion No. 21.* Applying the interest method results in a constant rate of return on the net investment in the lease. The difference between the gross investment (a) and the unearned interest income (c) is the amount of net investment (d), which is equal to the present value of the gross investment (b). This amount is classified as a current or noncurrent asset on the lessor's balance sheet in the

TABLE 11.1 *Accounting Steps for Sales-Type Leases*

Gross investment (a) *minus*	XX
Present value of gross investment (b) *equals*	XX
Unearned income (c)	XX
Gross investment (a) *minus*	XX
Unearned income (c) *equals*	XX
Net investment (d)	XX
Sales (e) *minus*	XX
Cost of goods sold (f) *equals*	XX
Profit or loss (g)	XX

same manner as all other assets. Revenue from sales-type leases is thus reflected by two different amounts: (1) the gross profit (or loss) on the sale in the year of the lease agreement and (2) interest on the remaining net investment over the life of the lease agreement.

For sales-type leases, because the critical event is the sale, the initial direct costs associated with obtaining the lease agreement are written off when the sale is recorded at the inception of the lease. These costs are disclosed as selling expenses on the income statement.

Direct Financing Leases

When no manufacturer's or dealer's profit (or loss) is recorded, a capital lease should be accounted for as a direct financing lease by the lessor. Under the direct financing method, the lessor is essentially viewed as a lending institution for revenue recognition purposes. If a lessor records a capital lease under the direct financing method, each payment must be allocated between interest revenue and investment recovery. In the early periods of the agreement, a significant portion of the payment will be recorded as interest, but each succeeding payment will result in a decreasing amount of interest revenue and an increasing amount of investment recovery due to the fact that the amount of the net investment is decreasing.

For direct financing leases, the FASB adopted the approach of requiring the recording of the total minimum lease payments as a receivable on the date of the transaction and treating the difference between that amount and the asset cost as unearned income. Subsequently, as each rental payment is received, the receivable is reduced by the full amount of the payment, and a portion of the unearned income is transferred to earned income.

TABLE 11.2 *Accounting Steps for Direct Financing Leases*

Gross investment (a)	XX
minus	
Cost (b)	XX
equals	
Unearned income (c)	XX
Gross investment (a)	XX
minus	
Unearned income (c)	XX
equals	
Net investment (d)	XX
Unearned income (c)	XX
minus	
Initial direct costs (e)	XX
equals	
Unearned income to be amortized (f)	XX

Table 11.2 illustrates the accounting steps for direct financing leases. Gross investment (a) is determined in the same way as in sales-type leases, but unearned income (c) is computed as the difference between gross investment and the cost (b) of the leased property. The difference between gross investment (a) and unearned income (c) is net investment (d), which is the same as (b) in the sales type lease.

Initial direct costs (e) in financing leases are treated as an adjustment to the investment in the leased asset. Because financing the lease is the revenue generating activity, *SFAS No. 91* requires that this cost be matched in proportion to the recognition of interest revenue. In each accounting period over the life of the lease, the unearned interest income (c) minus the indirect cost (e) is amortized by the effective interest method. Because the net investment is increased by an amount equal to the initial direct costs, a new effective interest rate must be determined in order to apply the interest method to the declining net investment balance. Under direct financing leases the only revenue recorded by the lessor is disclosed as interest revenue over the lease term. Since initial direct costs increase the amount disclosed as the net investment, the interest income reported represents interest net of the write-off of the initial direct cost.

Disclosure Requirements for Sales-Type and Direct Financing Leases

In addition to the specific procedures required to account for sales-type and direct financing leases, the FASB established certain disclosure requirements. The following information is to be disclosed when leasing constitutes a significant part of the lessor's business activities in terms of revenue, net income, or assets:

1. *The components of the net investment in leases as of the date of each balance sheet presented:*
   a. *Future minimum lease payments to be received with deduction for any executory costs included in payments and allowance for uncollectibles.*
   b. *The unguaranteed residual value.*
   c. *Unearned income.*
2. *Future minimum lease payments to be received for each of the five succeeding fiscal years as of the date of the latest balance sheet presented.*
3. *The amount of unearned income included in income to offset initial direct costs charged against income for each period for which an income statement is presented. (For direct financing leases only.)*
4. *Total contingent rentals included in income for each period for which an income statement is presented.*
5. *A general description of the lessor's leasing arrangements.*[13]

The board indicated its belief that these disclosures by the lessor, as with the disclosures by lessees, would aid the users of financial statements in their assessment of the financial condition and results of operations of lessors. Note also that these requirements make the information disclosed by lessors and lessees more consistent.

Operating Leases

Those leases that do not meet the criteria for classification as sales-type or direct financing leases are accounted for as operating leases by the lessor. As a result the leased property is reported with or near other property, plant, and equipment on the lessor's balance sheet and is depreciated following the lessor's normal depreciation policy.

Rental payments are recognized as revenue when they become receivables unless the payments are not made on a straight-line basis. In that case, as with the lessee, the recognition of revenue is to be on a straight-line basis. Initial direct costs associated with the lease are to be deferred and allocated over the lease term in the same manner as rental revenue (usually on a straight-line basis). However, if these costs are not material, they may be charged to expense as incurred.

If leasing is a significant part of the lessor's business activities, the following information is to be disclosed for operating leases:

1. *The cost and carrying amount, if different, of property on lease or held for leasing by major classes of property according to nature or function, and the amount of accumulated depreciation in total as of the date of the latest balance sheet presented.*

---

[13] Ibid., par. 23.

2. *Minimum future rentals on noncancelable leases as of the date of the latest balance sheet presented, in the aggregate and for each of the five succeeding fiscal years.*

3. *Total contingent rentals included in income for each period for which an income statement is presented.*

4. *A general description of the lessor's leasing arrangements.*[14]

Lessee and Lessor Disclosure Illustration

The following illustration of accounting and disclosure by lessees and lessors is based on Appendixes C and D of *SFAS No. 13*.[15] In the example, the leased property is an automobile.

Lease Terms and Assumptions

The terms and assumptions of the lease are as follows.

Lessor's cost of the leased property (automobile)	$5,000
Fair value of the leased property at inception of the lease	$5,000
Estimated economic life of the leased property	5 years

The lease has a fixed noncancelable term of 30 months, with a rental of $135 payable at the beginning of each month. The lessee guarantees a residual value of $2,000 at the end of the lease and will receive any excess of the sales price over that amount. (A guaranteed residual value by the lessee is treated as an additional payment at the end of the lease term by the lessee to the lessor.) The lessee pays executory costs. The lease is renewable periodically on a decreasing rate, the rentals specified are fair, the estimated residual is reasonable, and no investment tax credit is available. The lessee depreciates the owned automobiles on a straight-line basis. The incremental borrowing rate is 10.5 percent per year. There are no initial direct costs of negotiating and closing the transaction. At the end of the lease term the asset is sold for $2,100.

Computation of Minimum Lease Payments (Lessee and Lessor)

The minimum lease payments are computed as follows:

Minimum rental payments over the lease term ($135 × 30 months)	$4,050
Lessee guarantee of the residual value at the end of the lease term	2,000
Total minimum lease payments	$6,050

[14] Ibid., par. 23.

[15] Ibid., pars. 121–122.

The lessor's implicit interest rate in this lease is 12.036 percent, which is the rate implicit in the recovery of the fair value of the property at the inception of the lease ($5,000) through the minimum lease payments (30 monthly payments of $135 and the lessee's guarantee of the $2,000 residual value).

Classification of the Lease

The lease can be classified by examining it in relation to the four criteria discussed earlier on pages 499 and 500.

Criterion 1 is not met because the lease does not transfer ownership of the property to the lessee by the end of the lease term.

Criterion 2 is not met because the lease does not contain a bargain purchase option.

Criterion 3 is not met because the lease term is not equal to 75 percent or more of the estimated economic life of the property.

Criterion 4 is met in the lessee's case because the present value ($5,120) of the minimum lease payments using the incremental borrowing rate (10.5 percent) exceeds 90 percent of the fair value of the property at the inception of the lease. In the lessor's case, the present value ($5,000) of the minimum lease payments using the implicit rate also exceeds 90 percent of the fair value of the property. As a result of meeting the present-value test, the lessee will classify the lease as a capital lease and, assuming that the two additional lessor criteria are met, the lessor will classify the lease as a direct financing lease because there is no manufacturers' or dealers' profit.

The preceding present values were determined as follows:

	Lessee's Computation Using the Incremental Borrowing Rate of 10.5% Because It Is Lower Than the Implicit Rate	Lessor's Computation Using the Implicit Rate of 12.036%
Minimum lease payments:		
Rental payments	$3,580	$3,517
Residual guarantee by lessee	1,540	1,483
	$5,120	$5,000
Fair value of the property at inception of the lease	$5,000	$5,000

Balance Sheet Presentation

The lessee and lessor will report the lease in their balance sheets as follows:

**LESSEE COMPANY
BALANCE SHEET**

Assets		*Liabilities*	
Leased property under capital leases, less accumulated amortization	XXX	*Current:* Obligations under capital leases	XXX
		Noncurrent: Obligations under capital leases	XXX

The lessee should also explain the various terms and conditions of the lease in a footnote.

**LESSOR COMPANY
BALANCE SHEET**

Assets	
Current assets:	
Net investment in direct financing leases	XXX
Noncurrent assets:	
Net investment in direct financing leases	XXX

The lessor should also describe the lease in a footnote.

Sales and Leasebacks

In a sale and leaseback transaction, the owner of property sells the property and then immediately leases it back from the buyer. These transactions frequently occur when companies have limited cash resources or when they result in tax advantages. Tax advantages occur because the sales price of the asset is usually its current market value and this amount generally exceeds the carrying value of the asset on the seller's books. Therefore, the tax-deductible periodic rental payments are higher than the previously recorded amount of depreciation expense.

Most sales and leaseback transactions are treated as a single economic event according to the lease classification criteria previously discussed on pages 499 and 500. That is, the lessee-seller applies the *SFAS No. 13* criteria to the lease agreement and records the lease as either capital or operating and the gain or loss on the sale is amortized over the lease term. However, in certain circumstances where the lessee retains significantly smaller rights to use the property, any gain or loss may be immediately recognized. In these cases it is argued that two distinctly different transactions have occurred because the rights to use have changed.

Leveraged Leases

A leveraged lease is defined as a special leasing arrangement involving three different parties: (1) the equity holder—the lessor; (2) the asset user—the lessee; and (3) the debt holder—a long-term financer.[16] A leveraged lease may be illustrated as follows:

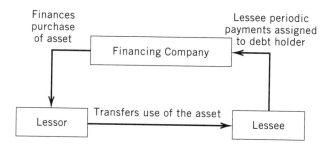

The major issue in accounting for leveraged leases is whether the transaction should be recorded as a single economic event or as separate transactions. All leveraged leases meet the criteria for direct financing leases. However, a leveraged lease might be accounted for as a lease with an additional debt transaction, or as a single transaction. The FASB determined that a leveraged lease should be accounted for as a single transaction, and provided the following guidelines.

The lessee records the lease as a capital lease. The lessor records the lease as a direct financing lease and the investment in capital leases is the net result of several factors:

1. *Rentals receivable, net of that portion of the rental applicable to principal and interest on the nonrecourse debt.*

2. *A receivable for the amount of the investment tax credit to be realized on the transaction.*

3. *The estimated residual value of the leased asset.*

4. *Unearned and deferred income consisting of the estimated pretax lease income (or loss), after deducting initial direct costs remaining to be allocated to income over the lease term and the investment tax credit remaining to be allocated to income over the least term.*[17]

---

[16] A fourth party may also be involved when the owner-lessor initially purchases the property from a manufacturer.

[17] *FASB Statement No. 13*, op. cit., par. 43.

Once the original investment has been determined, the next step is to project cash receipts and disbursements over the term of the lease, then compute a rate of return on the net investment in those years in which it is positive. Annual cash flow is the sum of gross lease rental and residual value (in the final year), less loan interest payments plus or minus income tax credits or charges, less loan principal payments, plus investment tax credit realized. The rate to be used in the computation is that "which when applied to the net investment in the years in which the net investment is positive will distribute the net income to those years." [18]

In a footnote to an illustration of the allocation of annual cash flow to investment and income, *SFAS No. 13* includes the following comment:

> *[The rate used for the allocation] is calculated by a trial and error process. The allocation is calculated based upon an initial estimate of the rate as a starting point. If the total thus allocated to income differs under the estimated rate from the net cash flow the estimated rate is increased or decreased, as appropriate, to devise a revised allocation. This process is repeated until a rate is selected which develops a total amount allocated to income that is precisely equal to the net cash flow. As a practical matter, a computer program is used to calculate [the allocation] under successive iterations until the correct rate is determined.* [19]

This method of accounting for leveraged leases was considered to associate the income with the unrecovered balance of the earning asset in a manner consistent with the investor's view of the transaction. Income is recognized at a level rate on net investment in years in which the net investment is positive and is thus identified as "primary" earnings from the lease.

In recent years there have been efforts by companies to circumvent *SFAS No. 13*. These efforts are mainly used by lessees who do not wish to report increased liabilities or adversely affect their debt-equity ratios. However, unlike lessees, lessors do not wish to avoid recording lease transactions as capital leases. Consequently, the trick is to allow the lessee to record a lease as an operating lease while the lessor records it as either a sales-type or direct financing.

Accounting for Loan Origination Fees and Costs

In 1986, the FASB issued *SFAS No. 91*, "Accounting for Nonrefundable Fees and Costs Associated with Originating or Acquiring Loans and Initial Direct Costs of Leases." This release was issued in response to the controversy surrounding loan fee accounting and has a significant impact on lenders and investors in debt obligations, particularly banks, finance companies, mortgage companies, leasing companies, and insurance companies. The issue involves accounting for front-end, loan-origination fees that are charged for loans or lines of credit. These fees are not generally refundable even if the loan is repaid prior to maturity or if the borrower decides not to exercise the line of credit.

Previously, these origination fees were accounted for by one of the following methods.

[18] Ibid., par. 44.
[19] Ibid., par. 123.

Income Lenders generally view loan origination fees as compensation for the cost of evaluating the creditworthiness of borrowers. Consequently, many recognized these fees as income when the loan was made or the line of credit expired. Additionally, loan origination costs are expensed as incurred. As a result, origination fees and the related expenses were regarded as separate activities from lending.

Discount on the loan Under this method, origination fees are considered a discount on the loan, and the amount of funds received by the borrower is equal to the principal amount less the origination fee. This method views origination fees and costs as an integral part of the lending process; consequently, these fees and costs are deferred and amortized over the life of the loan as a yield adjustment.

SFAS No. 91 requires the second method. That is, all loan fees and costs must be amortized as a yield adjustment using the interest method. Additionally, the unamortized balance of the deferred loan fee/cost must be included as a part of the related loan balance.

The application of *SFAS No. 91* will improve the comparability of the financial statements of lending and leasing companies; however, this improvement will create additional costs. Among these are the cost of changing accounting methods as well as reduced earning over the short term because of the deferral of origination fees. *SFAS No. 91* recommends restating prior years' earnings when preparing comparative statements to minimize the second cost.

Summary

Statement of Financial Accounting Standards No. 13 sets forth clear criteria for identifying leases that are to be capitalized by lessees and treated as sales-type or direct financing leases by lessors. The criteria were designed to achieve symmetry in accounting between lessees and lessors. The achievement of symmetry, however, will depend on such things as whether comparable interest rates are used by the lessee and lessor in calculating the present value of the minimum lease rentals, whether the two certainty criteria applied by the lessor are met, and whether current leasing techniques are continued or new off–balance sheet techniques are found. Thus, the statement may achieve its stated objective, or it may simply cause the demise of current leasing activities and the creation of some different approaches for securing and providing the use of the assets.

The impact of *SFAS No. 13* was to significantly curtail one of the most widely used methods of off–balance sheet financing. However, some corporate managers may still attempt to circumvent the requirements of *SFAS No. 13*, and also attempt to generally understate long-term debt in an effort to improve the financial picture of their companies. A careful reading of the footnotes to the financial statements and management's comments may help to shed light on the possible existence of unrecorded liabilities.

In the article that follows, John Coughlan discusses several problems associated with applying *SFAS No. 13*.

Regulation, Rents, and Residuals

John W. Coughlan

Everybody except the landlord seems to want to regulate rents. Even the Financial Accounting Standards Board has gotten into the act by regulating the manner of accounting for rents. In FASB Statement No. 13, *Accounting for Leases*,[1] the FASB proposes the follow-

[1] Financial Accounting Standards Board Statement No. 13, *Accounting for Leases* (Stamford, Conn.: Financial Accounting Standards Board, November 1976), employs the term "capital lease" from the lessee's perspective only. For the lessor, it divides capital leases into "sales-type leases" and "direct financing leases." Since there is no comment here about the distinction between sales and financing leases, and since both correspond to what from the lessee's perspective is referred to as a capital lease, the term capital lease will be used for both lessee and lessor. The purpose of this article is to probe the basic flaws in the capital vs. operating distinction; therefore, the extension of these flaws to sales, financing, and leveraged leases will not be discussed. Likewise, the concern will be the quilt (Statement No. 13) rather than the patches (FASB Statement Nos. 17, *Accounting for Leases—Initial Direct Costs;* 22, *Changes in the Provisions of Lease Agreements Resulting From Refundings of Tax-Exempt Debt;* 23, *Inception of the Lease;* 26, *Profit Recognition on Sales-Type Leases of Real Estate;* 27, *Classification of Renewals of Extensions of Existing Sales-Type or Direct Financing Leases;* 28, *Accounting for Sales With Lease-backs;* and 29, *Determining Contingent Rentals;* and FASB interpretations Nos. 19, *Lessee Guarantee of the Residual Value of Leased Prop-*

ing "basic concept" in distinguishing between "capital leases" and "operating leases":

> . . . *a lease that transfers substantially all of the benefits and risks . . . should be accounted for as the acquisition of an asset and the incurrence of an obligation by the lessee and as a sale or financing by the lessor. All other leases should be accounted for as operating leases. In a lease that transfers substantially all of the benefits and risks of ownership, the economic effect on the parties is similar, in many respects, to that of an installment purchase . . . [par. 60].*

The distinction is one of common sense: since corporate controllers and accounting practitioners are traditionally blessed with this commodity, there ~~would have~~ been no problem in applying this "rewards and risks" distinction.

Statement No. 13 did not stop here, however. It imposed additional criteria purportedly to assist in applying the basic concept. In doing so, it created a

erty; 21, Accounting for Leases in a Business Combination; 23, Leases of Certain Property Owned by a Governmental Unit or Authority; 24, Leases Involving Only Part of a Building; 26, Accounting for Purchase of a Leased Asset by the Lessee During the Term of the Lease; and 27, Accounting for a Loss on a Sublease). It must be obvious that any quilt which requires 13 patches in three years must be rent beyond repair. In mid-January the FASB announced plans to issue this year a single pronouncement that would integrate Statement No. 13 and all the amendments and interpretations of that statement.

complex[2] document with fundamental flaws that go to the very essence of the distinction:

- It introduces two criteria—(a) and (b)—that are clearly implicit in another criterion—(d)—and are therefore redundant.

- It introduces a rate for discounting purposes—the "incremental borrowing rate"—in circumstances in which it is unlikely the rate can ever be used but expresses faith that it is this rate which will "generally" be used for the lessee's accounting for capital leases.

- Its excessive regulatory zeal leads to arbitrary distinctions capable, for example, of putting two almost identical lessors (say, two "rent a car" companies) in different industrial classifications, one renting machinery (operating leases) and the other making loans (capital leases).

The Lessor's Criteria

The lessor shall treat as a capital lease—that is, shall interpret as a lease involving a sale or financing event—any lease that meets both of the following two requirements (pars. 7 and 8):

- It must meet any one of four criteria, which are designated (a), (b), (c), and (d).

- There must be no important uncertainties about certain future cash flows.

[2] For a good analysis of some of the complexities of Statement No. 13, see Raymond J. Clay, Jr., and William W. Holder, "A Practitioner's Guide to Accounting for Leases," *JofA*, Aug. 77, pp. 62–68. See also J. Kenneth Alderman and C. Wayne Alderman, "Accounting for Leases," *JofA*, June 79, pp. 74–79.

The first requirement is an "or" proposition: it is enough if a lease meets any of the four criteria. However, it can easily be demonstrated that, if criterion (d) belongs on the list, there is no need for (a) or (b).

Criterion (d)

It is no exaggeration to say that everything in the first test turns on criterion (d):

The present value at the beginning of the lease term of the minimum lease payments . . . equals or exceeds 90 percent of . . . the fair value of the leased property . . . to the lessor at the inception of the lease. . . . A lessor shall compute the present value of the minimum lease payments using the interest rate implicit in the lease . . . [par. 7].

Example 1

A lessor leases an automobile with a fair value of $5,000 at $135 per month for 30 months, with the initial payment to occur at inception. At the end of 30 months, the lessee is to return the car, the lessor is to sell it, and the lessee guarantees it will be worth $2,000 at that time. If it sells for less than $2,000, the lessee will make up the difference. The $2,000 is referred to as a "guaranteed residual value." Criterion (d) requires that the minimum lease payments—which include the guaranteed residual—be discounted by use of the "interest rate implicit in the lease," which is 1 percent per month compounded monthly, as shown in Exhibit 1. The example is drawn from Appendix C of Statement No. 13, which points out that the present value of the minimum lease payments is $5,000 and that it is 100 percent of fair value. Is it a coincidence the present value works

EXHIBIT 1 *Illustration of Criterion (d)*

	Minimum Lease Payments	×	Discount Factors	=	Present Values
Month 1	$ 135	×	$1/(1.01)^0$	=	$ 135
Month 2	135	×	$1/(1.01)^1$	=	134
Month 30	135	×	$1/(1.01)^{29}$	=	101
					3,517
Month 31	2,000	×	$1/(1.01)^{30}$	=	1,483
Totals	$6,050				$5,000

out to exactly 100 percent rather than 98 percent or 103 percent?

It is no happenstance: it is no coincidence. It is a consequence of the definition of the interest rate implicit in the lease. This rate discounts the minimum lease payments to the fair value of the property at the inception of the lease. In the example, the interest rate implicit in the lease is *i* in equation 1, as follows:

Equation 1
$$5,000 = 135/(1 + i)^0 + 135/(1 + i)^1$$
$$+ + 135/(1 + i)^{29}$$
$$+ 2000/(1 + i)^{30}$$

In solving this equation for *i*, it will be found that the implicit rate is approximately .01 in decimal form or 1 percent per month.

The present value computed by means of this implicit rate is exactly 100 percent of fair value because we are locked in a circle. The implicit rate is that rate which equates the present value of the minimum lease payments to the fair value at the inception of the lease. If the minimum lease payments are then discounted by this implicit rate, it should be no surprise that their present value is exactly equal to the fair value. What is involved is two applications of the above equation 1: in the first application, the $5,000 is treated as

known and the accountant solves for the unknown *i*, finding it to be 1 percent; in the second, the 1 percent is known and employed to discount the minimum lease payments to the unknown present value, which—surely to nobody's surprise—turns out to be the same $5,000 with which the accountant began!

Were there nothing else than what has been described, all leases without exception would meet criterion (d). O. J. Simpson sprinting through the airport would have to tarry with the complexities of capital leases and Statement No. 13 would be nonsense. However, there is "something else"—the "unguaranteed residual value" (URV), defined as the estimated residual value of the leased property at the end of the lease exclusive of any portion guaranteed by the lessee. Statement No. 13 defines the interest rate implicit in the lease as follows:

The discount rate that, when applied to (i) the minimum lease payments . . . and (ii) the unguaranteed residual value . . . accruing to the benefit of the lessor, causes the aggregate present value at the beginning of the lease term to be equal to the fair value of the leased property . . . to the lessor at the inception of the lease . . . [par. 5(k)].

Example 2

Assume the same lease except that now, while it is reasonable to suppose that the auto will be worth $2,000 after 30 months, the lessee makes no guarantee concerning residual value, which accordingly becomes a URV. From the quotation above, it is apparent that the URV is included in the determination of the implicit interest rate so that it is the same 1 percent per month that solves equation 1, with the discounted values appearing as follows: 5,000 = 3,517 + 1,483.

The term with the asterisk is the present value of the minimum lease payments, and the final term is the present value of the URV. While the URV plays a role in the determination of the implicit rate, it is not included in the present value used in criterion (d). Indeed, it is the presence of the URV in the implicit rate definition and its absence from (d) that saves Statement No. 13 from a vicious circle. Since the present value of the minimum lease payments to be used in (d)—the asterisked 3,517 —is less than 90 percent of the 5,000 fair value, (d) is not met and the lease is an operating lease. The important thing to notice is that the present value is other than 100 percent of fair value. This can only happen within the Statement No. 13 framework if there is a URV. Furthermore, it is only if this URV is substantial in relation to the minimum lease payments that criterion (d) can be failed.

The Redundancy of Criteria (a) and (b)

The redundancy of criteria (a) and (b) can now be seen. Criterion (a) states: "The lease transfers ownership of the property to the lessee by the end of the lease. . . ." While the leased property

may have some residual value at termination, it can have none accruing to the lessor. Any lease meeting (a)—that is, transferring ownership by the end of the lease term—will have no URV to the lessor, and the implicit rate, no matter what the fair value and the minimum lease payments, will always discount minimum lease payments to exactly 100 percent of fair value. A lease that meets (a) must meet (d).

Criterion (b) states: "The lease contains a bargain purchase option." Since the bargain purchase option is included in minimum lease payments and title is assumed to pass, there can be no URV accruing to the lessor, and the lease must have a present value of 100 percent of fair value and thereby meets (d).

If either (a) or (b) is met, by definition alone, there can be no URV to the lessor and (d) must be met. Since requirement 1 is met if one of the four lettered criteria is met, there is no need to check (a) or (b) if (d) is met. A list that includes (d) has no need for (a) or (b).

Criterion (c)

It would be convenient if it could be demonstrated that leases meeting criterion (c)—". . . lease term . . . is equal to 75 percent or more the estimated economic life of the leased property . . ."—automatically meet (d). Unfortunately, it is possible (but difficult) to construct examples to the contrary.

Nevertheless, for the sake of simplicity, (c) should be eliminated for the very good reason that the great majority of leases that meet (c) also meet (d). Bear in mind that that URV for a lease covering 75 percent or more of economic life will, because of the partial obsolescence of the asset and its need for greater maintenance, be small and the present value of that URV will be but a small part of the value at inception. (Indeed, paragraph 75 of Statement No. 13 so states.) Accordingly, it is apparent that, because of the circle previously cited, almost all leases meeting (c) meet (d), and, therefore, (c) may on practical grounds also be considered redundant.

A Simplified Criterion

The first requirement for a capital lease from the lessor's viewpoint—namely, that it meet one or more of the lettered criteria—has now been condensed into the single criterion (d). In so condensing, it is recognized that there are a few leases that meet (c) (just barely) and nevertheless fail (d) (just barely). It is further recognized that there are no leases that meet (a) or (b) that do not meet (d).

Can the retention of (a) to (b) be justified because a lack of knowledge might make it impossible to apply (d)? Suppose, for example, the lessor could not determine fair value and could not, therefore, apply (d). But any assistance that (a), (b), or (c) would provide in such a case would be nugatory. Statement No. 13's prescribed lessor accounting for capital leases requires a knowledge of the implicit rate, which in turn requires a knowledge of the same fair value and cash flow information that is required to apply (d). If the criterion (d) information is not available, there is no point using (a) to (c) to determine the operating or capital character of a lease since the information needed to account for a capital lease is also not available.

The Statement No. 13 requirements for a capital lease may accordingly be simplified by dropping (a), (b), and (c) and by using only (d) or its shadow, the URV, so that the lessor's two requirements may be stated as follows:

- The URV must be small or nominal.[3]
- There must be no important uncertainties about certain future cash flows.

In a quest for an even more concise statement of the capital lease requirement, return to the URV and ask why it should make a difference. Consider any lease, such as the one in example 2, with a sufficiently large URV to fail criterion (d) and be classified as an operating lease. Now let the lessee guarantee the residual value as in example 1; recalling the circle, the present value will be 100 percent of fair value and the lease will meet (d) and will be classified as a capital lease. While the total to be received is identical—at least on an expected value basis—more of it is guaranteed. A guarantee of residual value is sufficient to convert all operating leases to capital leases.

Apparently the Statement No. 13 view is that there is no problem accounting for the lease payments as a long-term receivable with appropriate recognition of interest income if there is little uncertainty about cash flows and some assurance that the lessor will recover his investment and earn a positive interest rate, whereas important elements of uncertainty pertaining to the future cash flows—particularly if there is some doubt about the ability to fully recover the fair value of the leased asset—should lead to the operating classification. Seen from this perspective, it is risk and uncertainty—the nat-

---

[3]This approach is similar to that in a statement of position issued by the accounting standards division of The American Institute of CPAs, which did not specify an exact percentage but, instead, suggested capitalization when the residual value was expected to be "nominal" (*JofA*, Oct. 75, p. 14 and Dec. 75, p. 26).

ural human tendency to fear the dark—that is the enemy of the capital lease. The simplified two-point criterion suggested above might be further condensed since both points deal with uncertainties about future cash flows. One could replace the two-point test with a one-point test relating to the subjective probability of recovering the fair value of the leased property and (possibly) some positive amount of interest:

- Capital leases are those for which there is at least an X probability of recovering the fair value of the leased asset.

One hopes that the practitioner would be permitted to rely on his judgment to pick the probability (it might be stated in terms of a reasonable expectation), but the FASB could (and undoubtedly would) prescribe a probability. Such a simplified test (if passed) would in all likelihood lead to the same leases being classified as capital leases as those using the Statement No. 13 criteria and (if failed) would lead to the same leases being classified as operating leases as those using the statement's criteria. Where the classifications of particular leases differed, the difference would generally result from arbitrary consequences of the overly complex criteria in Statement No. 13 rather than from differences in the underlying purposes.

The Incremental Borrowing Rate

Turning to the lessee, a curious aspect of Statement No. 13 is the introduction of a new interest rate "the incremental borrowing rate"—which may play some role in the classification scheme but cannot play any role (despite the statement's suggestions to the contrary) in the accounting.

The lessee's incremental borrowing

rate is defined as the "rate that, at the inception of the lease, the lessee would have incurred to borrow over a similar term the funds necessary to purchase the leased asset" (par. 5 (1)). Following is another version of criterion (d) that includes certain wording omitted in the excerpt printed on page 517.

The present value at the beginning of the lease term of the minimum lease payments . . . equals or exceeds 90 percent of . . . the fair value of the leased property . . . to the lessor . . . A lessee shall compute the present value of the minimum lease payments using his incremental borrowing rate . . . unless (i) it is practicable for him to learn the implicit rate computed by the lessor and (ii) the implicit rate computed by the lessor is less than the lessee's incremental borrowing rate. If both of those conditions are met, the lessee shall use the implicit rate [par. 7 (d)].

Assuming the lessee knows the implicit rate,[4] it can be demonstrated that

---

[4] Surely a reasonable assumption despite Statement No. 13's suggestion to the contrary in the above excerpt of (d). All that is needed to infer the implicit rate are three items of information: the minimum lease payments, the URV, and the fair value of the leased property to the lessor at the inception of the lease. Since the minimum lease payments are the principle subject matter of the lease agreement, presumably the lessee knows as much about them as the lessor.

Possibly the lessor knows more about URV than the lessee. Recall from the previous analysis, however, that the URV cannot be too great if the lease is classified as a capital lease. Given that the lessee is correct in classifying a lease as a capital lease, it follows that the URV will not be too substantial and it is therefore unlikely that the lessee's estimate can be sufficiently erroneous to make a material difference to his computation of the implicit rate.

the implicit rate will always be employed in the accounting whether it is higher or lower than the incremental borrowing rate. Suppose first the implicit rate is less than the incremental borrowing rate[5] so that, following the

This leaves the fair value of the leased property to the lessor at the inception of the lease. Much of the personality (office equipment, computers, fleets of trucks, etc.) to which Statement No. 13 is currently being applied has a well-established purchase price that is readily available to the lessee: to the extent it is not, antitrust efforts at the federal level are increasingly making it available. Accordingly, it may be concluded that, for most of the leased property to which Statement No. 13 is currently applied, the lessee may make almost as good an estimate of the implicit rate as the lessor. The FASB also appears to believe that the lessee can infer within limits that implicit rate; since the first draft of this article was written, the FASB has issued an exposure draft of a proposed statement requiring the lessee in certain circumstances to make a "reasonable estimate" of the implicit rate.

Even in those rare cases in which no reasonable estimate of the implicit rate can be made, the conclusion in this article—that the incremental borrowing rate will never be used—still stands. Admittedly, with regard to certain personality and some reality, usually with perpetual life, the lessor may have better information with regard to fair value. But it still cannot be inferred that the incremental borrowing rate will play a role because the lessee's ignorance of fair value will prevent application of the all-important criterion (d), the 90-percent-of-fair-value test! Such leases rarely meet criterion (a) or (b) and usually cannot meet (c). The ignorance of fair value prevents the lessee not only from knowing the implicit rate but also from classifying the lease as a capital lease and having an opportunity to use the incremental borrowing rate.

[5]There are good reasons to think the implicit rate will be less. Statement No. 13 treats cap-

above quotation, the implicit rate is used for classification purposes in criterion (d). The implicit rate will also be used for the accounting. *The incremental borrowing rate plays no role.*

Now suppose the incremental borrowing rate is lower. From the above quotation, it is apparent this incremental rate will be employed to test criterion (d): if the test is met, one might assume, other things being equal, that the incremental borrowing rate would play a role in the accounting. But here is a key passage:

> *The lessee shall record a capital lease as an asset and an obligation at an amount equal to the present value at the beginning of the lease term of minimum lease payments. . . .* However, if the amount so determined exceeds the fair value of the leased property at the inception of the lease, the amount recorded as the asset and obligation shall be the fair value. . . . *The discount rate to be used in determining present value of the minimum lease payments shall be that prescribed for the lessee in paragraph 7(d) [par. 10, emphasis supplied].*

If there is no URV, the present value as discounted by the implicit rate is exactly 100 percent of fair value. Since it is now hypothesized that the incremental borrowing rate is less than the implicit rate, it is apparent that the similar present value using the lower incremental borrowing rate will exceed 100 percent of fair value. Observing the italicized limitation to fair value in the above

ital transactions as being, in part at least, credit transactions, and the mere fact that the lessee in effect "borrows" from the lessor rather than from his next best source of credit (the incremental borrowing rate) would suggest the lessor's interest rate—the implicit rate—is lower.

quotation, it seems obvious that the lessee will capitalize the fair value, which is based on the implicit rate, not the incremental rate: the other prescriptions in Statement No. 13 (particularly paragraph 12) make it apparent that it is the implicit rate which will be used in all subsequent accounting. *The incremental borrowing rate still plays no role in the accounting.*

The best illustration is example 1, but this time regarded from the lessee's viewpoint. This example is straight from Statement No. 13, which specifies that while the implicit rate is 1 percent per month the incremental borrowing rate is only .875 percent per month. The present value using this lower incremental borrowing rate is $5,120 which, as observed in Statement No. 13, exceeds the fair value of $5,000. The illustration of lessee accounting in the statement accordingly involves a capitalization of the fair value of $5,000 (which implies use of the implicit rate, not the incremental borrowing rate), and the subsequent entries are based throughout on the implicit rate. When there is no URV or only a small one, the present value using the lower incremental borrowing rate will exceed fair value and *the incremental borrowing rate cannot play a role.*

Even if there is a substantial URV (see the appendix, page 525, for a detailed analysis), the conclusion still stands, *the incremental borrowing rate can play no role in the accounting.*

Unfortunately, this analysis cannot be reconciled with the explicit assumption in Statement No. 13 that the lessee will "generally" use the incremental borrowing rate:

"With respect to the rate of interest to be used in determining the present value of the minimum lease payments for recording the asset and obligation under a capital lease, the Board concluded the rate should generally be that which the lessee would have incurred to borrow for a similar term the funds necessary to purchase the leased asset (the lessee's incremental borrowing rate)" (par. 93).

May one conclude that the architects of the labyrinth also get lost in its corridors?

Third-Party Guarantors

It has been demonstrated that there is only one interest rate in Statement No. 13, the implicit rate, and it was previously demonstrated that, using this implicit rate, only (d) of the lettered criteria need be tested. Recalling that criterion (d) is always met and that all leases are capital leases unless there is a URV, it is to be hoped that no excess of regulatory zeal, and no desire to specify everything, has led the FASB to make any mistakes in the concept or definition of this central concept of URV.

Example 3A

Hurts Rent-A-Car leases automobiles on a daily basis. The rental fee for a day, net of certain executory costs (such as maintenance), is $51. Hurts does not insure these cars since it serves as its own insurance company. An auto has a fair value of $5,000 when rented, and Hurts anticipates it will be worth $5,000 when returned 24 hours later. The lessee pays the $51 when he returns the auto. By solving the following equation for i

$$5,000 = 5,051/(1 + i)$$

it will be found that the implicit rate is approximately 1 percent per day compounded daily. The minimum lease payment is $51; if this amount is discounted one day at 1 percent, it will have a present value of $50, which is far below 90 percent of the fair value, or $4,500. Accordingly, (d) is not met, the lease will be classified as an operating one, the auto will remain on Hurts's books (where it will be depreciated) and the $51 will be recognized as rental revenues.

Example 3B

Mavis Rent-A-Car owns title to autos, hands keys to its customers, and employs maintenance mechanics, but these peripherals are simply a clever "cover" for its real business, which is making one-day loans at usurious interest rates. Mavis keeps only $50 of each daily rental fee and requires the lessee to use the other $1 to buy a contract with an independent insurance company, which guarantees the auto will be worth $5,000 when returned. Since the cash flow expectations are approximately the same as for Hurts, Mavis will compute the implicit rate in the same fashion and will discover the implicit rate to be 1 percent per day. But, since the definition of URV states that it is the estimated residual value of the leased property "exclusive of any portion guaranteed by the lessee *or by a third party unrelated to the lessor*" (par. 5(i), emphasis supplied), the Mavis $5,000 is a guaranteed residual; as such it is an integral part of the minimum lease payments since such payments include "any guarantee of the residual value . . . by a third party unrelated to either the lessee or the lessor, provided the third party is financially capable of discharging the obligations that may arise from the guarantee" (par. 5 (j) ii). Now test criterion (d) by discounting the minimum lease payments—the full $5,050—at the implicit rate of 1 percent:

$$5,050/1.01 = 5,000$$

Since there is no URV, it is not surprising that the present value is exactly 100 percent of fair value but, since (d) is met, it may come as a considerable shock to Mavis to find it is in the short-term loan business rather than in auto leasing. Lapses in logic and obfuscating complexities aside, can there be merit to a pronouncement that puts Hurts in car renting and Mavis in loan sharking?

Accounting and Authority

The tale of two leases, the operating lease and the capital lease, is neither the best nor the worst of FASB statements. Surely its emphasis on future cash flows and on present values, while foreshadowed to some extent in prior pronouncements (notably Accounting Principles Board Opinion Nos. 21, *Interest on Receivables and Payables*; 5, *Reporting of Leases in Financial Statements of Lessee*; 7, *Accounting for Leases in Financial Statements of Lessors*; 27, *Accounting for Lease Transactions by Manufacturer or Dealer Lessor*; and 31, *Disclosure of Lease Commitments by Lessees*), must be counted among its more positive and forward-looking developments.[6] Just as surely, its implicit belief that accounting requires authority, and authority of a complex and stifling character, must constitute its most negative and backward-looking features.

In matters of social interaction, where differences of opinion must be resolved in some manner, authority in the form

---

[6] Also see a research study that has had much to do with the development of thought regarding leases: John H. Myers, Accounting Research Study No. 4, *Reporting of Leases in Financial Statements* (New York: AICPA, 1962).

of laws, legislatures, judges, and juries may be necessary. If accounting falls in this arena—and there is a growing opinion that it does as witness the existence of the FASB and the Cost Accounting Standard Board—the path ahead is clear. There will be an increasing amount of regulation, and it will be imposed with the muscle of the federal government. The official pronouncements will have the full force of law but will follow the model so carefully set since 1935 by the committee on accounting procedure of the American Institute of Accountants (a predecessor of the AICPA), the APB, and the FASB. These official pronouncements will differ in no important respect from their predecessors except that they may be more voluminous and more costly. One hopes that there is a better road.

Usefulness—not authority—is the final arbiter of accounting. If its "economic consequence" is a better allocation of scarce resources, then it needs no authority. If it does not perform a useful function in that sense, then no authority will help.[7]

Appendix

If there is no URV, or only a small one, then the incremental borrowing rate is completely irrelevant to the accounting. It will be demonstrated in this appendix that, even with a substantial URV, there is little possibility that the incremental borrowing rate can play any role in the accounting.

Observe first that a substantial URV

[7]See also John W. Coughlan, *Guide to Contemporary Theory of Accounts* (Englewood Cliffs, N.J.: Prentice-Hall, 1965), p. 1, and Accounting Principles Board Statement No. 4, *Basic Concepts and Accounting Principles Underlying Financial Statements of Business Enterprises* (New York: AICPA, 1970), par. 21.

usually leads to the lease's being classified as an operating lease and therefore provides no opportunity to employ the incremental borrowing rate (see example 2, page 519).

What is required is a URV that is small enough to permit the lease to meet criterion (d) but, at the same time, large enough so that, using the lower incremental borrowing rate, the present value will be less than fair value. (Otherwise fair value and the implicit interest rate will be employed.) Whether such a small-enough, large-enough URV is even possible depends on the meaning of "fair value."

Example 4

The lessee acquires the use of an asset with a five-year life by making rental payments of $1,000 per year at the beginning of each of the first three years. At the beginning of the fourth, with two years of life to go, the asset reverts to the lessor, at which date it is expected to be worth $471, its URV. The lessee's incremental borrowing rate is 10 percent and, assuming the asset has a fair value to the lessor at the inception of the lease of $2,800, the implicit rate is 20 percent, as shown in Exhibit 2.

Statement No. 13 is unambiguous regarding the application of (d) in this situation. The lessee would use his incremental borrowing rate and the appropriate present value is accordingly $2,736 from the above tabulation. Criterion (d) requires that this present value equal or exceed 90 percent of the "fair value . . . *to the lessor* . . ." (emphasis supplied). That fair value to the lessor would include the present value of the URV and would accordingly be the $2,800 in the tabulation. Clearly the $2,736 using the incremental borrowing rate exceeds 90 percent of fair value, and Statement No. 13 would re-

EXHIBIT 2 *Two Interpretations of ''Fair Value''*

	Present Values	
	at 10%	at 20%
$1,000	$1,000	$1,000
1,000	909	833
1,000	827	694
Minimum lease		
payments	$2,736	2,527 FV B
Unguaranteed residual value ($471)	273	
Total		$2,800 FV A

quire capitalization. So far there's no problem, and the incremental borrowing rate has played a role in the classification scheme.

But now turn to the accounting and consider Statement No. 13's limitation in paragraph 10 (see page 522) of the amount capitalized to the fair value. Two interpretations of fair value are possible, and both lead to problems for Statement No. 13:

• If the fair value limitation refers to fair value to the lessor (the $2,800 labeled ''FV A'' in the tabulation), the same fair value that is used in criterion (d) for classification purposes would be employed in the accounting, and the amount capitalized would be the $2,736 from the tabulation: this is less than FV A of $2,800, and the subsequent accounting would indeed be based on 10 percent, the incremental borrowing rate. But now observe that because the URV must be not great (for fear of failing (d)), the difference in the amount capitalized as between using the two interest rates is trivial. Further, while the interest rates (10 percent vs. 20 percent) differ considerably, an exploration of the net effect on the income state-

ment in the ensuing years should convince the reader that, if both interest expense and depreciation are considered, the net impact on the income statement is negligible. The incremental borrowing rate, if appropriate at all, gives results that cannot differ much from the implicit rate; therefore, the accountant who wants to simplify Statement No. 13 may employ the implicit rate in all cases and, if ever called to account, may simply quote the boldface sentence that appears in all FASB statements, including No. 13: "The provisions of this Statement need not be applied to immaterial items." Even allowing for this interpretation, it may be concluded that *the incremental borrowing rate can play no material role in the accounting.*

But this interpretation is difficult to allow. To arrive at such a result, one must include in fair value the present value of the URV. While URV may be relevant to the lessee's classification of a lease as operating or capital, and criterion (d) so implies, it is hardly conceivable that URV can have any relevance to the subsequent accounting for leases classified as capital leases. In deciding whether a lease is operating or capital, it may make sense for the lessee to inquire whether he acquires the full service potential of the leased asset or whether there is a substantial URV that reverts to the lessor. But in limiting the capitalized present value to fair value, it makes little sense to include in the limitation the present value of the unguaranteed residual, a residual that goes to the lessor and that is surely irrelevant to the lessee except possibly for classification purposes.

- It is far more meaningful to interpret paragraph 10 in terms of the fair value relating to the service potential acquired by the lessee. While Statement No. 13, in defining the implicit rate (paragraph 5 (k)), specifies fair value to the lessor and again, in stating criterion (d), refers to the lessor, its paragraph 10 limitation is in the discussion of lessee accounting and omits the crucial words "to the lessor" even though the term "fair value" is used twice: ". . . if the amount so determined exceeds the fair value of the leased property at the inception of the lease, the amount recorded as the asset and obligation shall be the fair value." To make sense out of this fair value limitation, it must surely be fair value to the lessee.

But this fair value to the lessee is simply the present value of the minimum lease payments discounted by the implicit rate. It is the $2,527 labeled "FV B" in the tabulation. Since it is hypothesized throughout this appendix that the incremental borrowing rate is lower than the implicit rate, the present value using the lower incremental borrowing rate will always be higher than that using the implicit rate; therefore, the fair value limitation must always be binding and that fair value will be capitalized and amortized by use of the implicit rate, not the incremental borrowing rate. *Given that the implicit rate is known, the incremental borrowing rate can never play any role in the accounting.*

Cases

• Case 11-1

On January 2, 1996, two identical companies, Daggar Corp. and Bayshore Company, lease similar assets with the following characteristics:

1. The economic life is eight years.
2. The term of the lease is five years.
3. Lease payment of $20,000 per year is due at the beginning of each year beginning January 2, 1996.
4. The fair market value of the leased property is $96,000.
5. Each firm has an incremental borrowing rate of 8 percent and a tax rate of 40 percent.

Daggar capitalizes the lease whereas Bayshore records the lease as an operating lease. Both firms depreciate assets by the straight-line method, and both treat the lease as an operating lease for federal income tax purposes.

Required:
a. Determine earnings (i) before interest and taxes, and (ii) before taxes for both firms. Identify the source of any differences between the companies.
b. Compute any deferred taxes resulting from the lease for each firm in the first year of the lease.
c. Compute the effect of the lease on the 1996 reported cash from operations for both firms. Explain any differences.
d. Compute the effect of the lease on 1996 reported cash flows from investing activities for both firms. Explain any differences.
e. Compute the effect of the lease on 1996 reported cash flow from financing activities for both firms. Explain any differences.
f. Compute the effect of the lease on total 1996 cash flows for both companies. Explain any differences.
g. Give reasons why Daggar and Bayshore may have wanted to use different methods to report similar transactions.

• Case 11-2

On January 2, 1996, Grant Corporation leases an asset to Pippin corporation under the following conditions:

1. Annual lease payments of $10,000 for 20 years.
2. At the end of the lease term the asset is expected to have a value of $2,750.
3. The fair market value of the asset at the inception of the lease is $92,625.
4. The estimated economic life of the lease is 30 years.
5. Grant's implicit interest rate is 12 percent; Pippin's incremental borrowing rate is 10 percent.
6. The asset is recorded in Grant's inventory at $75,000 just prior to the lease transaction.

Required:
a. What type of a lease is this for Pippin? Why?
b. Assume Grant capitalizes the lease. What financial statement accounts are affected by this lease and what is the amount of each effect?
c. Assume Grant uses straight-line depreciation. What are the income statement, balance sheet, and statement of cash flow effects for 1996?
d. How should Grant record this lease? Why? Would any additional information be helpful in making this decision?
e. Assume that Grant treats the lease as a sales-type lease and the residual value is not guaranteed by Pippin. What financial statement accounts are affected on January 2, 1996?
f. Assume instead that Grant records the lease as an operating lease and uses straight-line depreciation. What are the income statement, balance sheet, and statement of cash flow effects on December 31, 1996?

• Case 11-3

To meet the need for its expanding operations, Johnson Corporation obtained a charter for a separate corporation whose purpose was to buy a land site, build and equip a new building, and lease the entire facility to Johnson Corporation for a period of 20 years. Rental to be paid by Johnson was set at an amount sufficient to cover expenses of operation and debt service on the corporation's 20-year serial mortgage bonds. During the term of the lease, the lessee has the option of purchasing the facilities at a price that will retire the bonds and cover the costs of liquidation of the corporation. Alternatively, at the termination of the lease, the properties will be transferred to Johnson for a small consideration. At the exercise of the option or at the termination of the lease, the lessor corporation will be dissolved.

Required:

a. Under certain conditions, generally accepted accounting principles provide that leased property be included in the balance sheet of a lessee even though legal title remains with the lessor.
  i. Discuss the conditions that would require financial statement recognition of the asset and the related liability by a lessee.
  ii. Describe the accounting treatment that should be employed by a lessee under the conditions you described in your answer to part (i).
b. Unless the conditions referred to in (a) are present, generally accepted accounting principles do not embrace asset recognition of leases in the financial statements of lessees. However, some accountants do advocate recognition by lessees that have acquired *property rights*. Explain what is meant by property rights and discuss the conditions under which these rights might be considered to have been acquired by a lessee.
c. Under the circumstances described in the case, how should the Johnson Corporation account for the lease transactions in its financial statements? Explain your answer.

• Case 11-4

On January 1, 1995, Lani Company entered into a noncancelable lease for a machine to be used in its manufacturing operations. The lease transfers ownership of the machine to Lani by the end of the lease term. The term of the lease is eight years. The minimum lease payment made by Lani on January 1, 1995, was one of eight equal annual payments. At the inception of the lease, the criteria established for classification as a capital lease by the lessee were met.

Required:

a. What is the theoretical basis for the accounting standard that requires certain long-term leases to be capitalized by the lessee? Do not discuss the specific criteria for classifying a specific lease as a capital lease.
b. How should Lani account for this lease at its inception and determine the amount to be recorded?
c. What expenses related to this lease will Lani incur during the first year of the lease, and how will they be determined?
d. How should Lani report the lease transaction on its December 31, 1995, balance sheet?

- ## Case 11-5

Doherty Company leased equipment from Lambert Company. The classification of the lease makes a difference in the amounts reflected on the balance sheet and income statement of both Doherty Company and Lambert Company.

Required:
a. What criteria must be met by the lease in order that Doherty Company classify it as a capital lease?
b. What criteria must be met by the lease in order that Lambert Company classify it as a sales-type or direct financing lease?
c. Contrast a sales-type lease with a direct financing lease.

- ## Case 11-6

On January 1, Borman Company, a lessee, entered into three noncancelable leases for brand-new equipment, Lease J, Lease K, and Lease L. None of the three leases transfers ownership of the equipment to Borman at the end of the lease term. For each of the three leases, the present value at the beginning of the lease term of the minimum lease payments, excluding that portion of the payments representing executory costs such as insurance, maintenance, and taxes to be paid by the lessor, including any profit thereon, is 75 percent of the excess of the fair value of the equipment to the lessor at the inception of the lease over any related investment tax credit retained by the lessor and expected to be realized by the lessor.

The following information is peculiar to each lease:

- Lease J does not contain a bargain purchase option; the lease term is equal to 80 percent of the estimated economic life of the equipment.

- Lease K contains a bargain purchase option; the lease term is equal to 50 percent of the estimated economic life of the equipment.

- Lease L does not contain a bargain purchase option; the lease term is equal to 50 percent of the estimated economic life of the equipment.

Required:
a. How should Borman Company classify each of the three leases and why? Discuss the rationale for your answer.
b. What amount, if any, should Borman record as a liability at the inception of the lease for each of the three leases?
c. Assuming that the minimum lease payments are made on a straight-line basis, how should Borman record each minimum lease payment for each of the three leases?

- ## Case 11-7

1. Capital leases and operating leases are the two classifications of leases described in FASB pronouncements from the standpoint of the lessee.

Required:

    a. Describe how a capital lease would be accounted for by the lessee both at the inception of the lease and during the first year of the lease, assuming the lease transfers ownership of the property to the lessee by the end of the lease.

    b. Describe how an operating lease would be accounted for by the lessee both at the inception of the lease and during the first year of the lease, assuming equal monthly payments are made by the lessee at the beginning of each month of the lease. Describe the change in accounting, if any, when rental payments are not made on a straight-line basis. Do not discuss the criteria for distinguishing between capital leases and operating leases.

2. Sales-type leases and direct financing leases are two of the classifications of leases described in FASB pronouncements, from the standpoint of the lessor.

Required:

Compare and contrast a sales-type lease with a direct financing lease as follows:

a. Gross investment in the lease.

b. Amortization of unearned interest income.

c. Manufacturer's or dealer's profit.

Do not discuss the criteria for distinguishing between the leases described above and operating leases.

• Case 11-8

Milton Corporation entered into a lease arrangement with James Leasing Corporation for a certain machine. James's primary business is leasing and it is not a manufacturer or dealer. Milton will lease the machine for a period of three years, which is 50 percent of the machine's economic life. James will take possession of the machine at the end of the initial three-year lease and lease it to another, smaller company that does not need the most current version of the machine. Milton does not guarantee any residual value for the machine and will not purchase the machine at the end of the lease term.

    Milton's incremental borrowing rate is 10 percent and the implicit rate in the lease is 8½ percent. Milton has no way of knowing the implicit rate used by James. Using either rate, the present value of the minimum lease payment is between 90 percent and 100 percent of the fair value of the machine at the date of the lease agreement.

    James is reasonably certain that Milton will pay all lease payments, and, because Milton has agreed to pay all executory costs, there are no important uncertainties regarding costs to be incurred by James.

Required:

    a. With respect to Milton (the lessee) answer the following.

        i. What type of lease has been entered into? Explain the reason for your answer.

   ii. How should Milton compute the appropriate amount to be recorded for the lease or asset acquired?

   iii. What accounts will be created or affected by this transaction and how will the lease or asset and other costs related to the transaction be matched with earnings?

   iv. What disclosures must Milton make regarding this lease or asset?

b. With respect to James (the lessor) answer the following.

   i. What type of leasing arrangement has been entered into? Explain the reason for your answer.

   ii. How should this lease be recorded by James and how are the appropriate amounts determined?

   iii. How should James determine the appropriate amount of earnings to be recognized from each lease payment?

   iv. What disclosures must James make regarding this lease?

• Case 11-9

On January 1, 1995, Von Company entered into two noncancelable leases for new machines to be used in its manufacturing operations. The first lease does not contain a bargain purchase option; the lease term is equal to 80 percent of the estimated economic life of the machine. The second lease contains a bargain purchase option; the lease term is equal to 50 percent of the estimated economic life of the machine.

Required:

a. What is the theoretical basis for requiring lessees to capitalize certain long-term leases? *Do not discuss the specific criteria for classifying a lease as a capital lease.*

b. How should a lessee account for a capital lease at its inception?

c. How should a lessee record each minimum lease payment for a capital lease?

d. How should Von classify each of the two leases? Why?

Recommended Additional Readings

El-Gazzar, Shamir M., Steven Lilien, and Victor Pastena. "Accounting for Leases by Lessees." *Journal of Accounting and Economics* (October 1986), pp. 217–237.

El-Gazzar, Shamir M., Steven Lilien, and Victor Pastena. "Use of Off–Balance Sheet Financing to Circumvent Financial Covenant Restrictions." *Journal of Accounting Auditing and Finance* (Spring 1989), pp. 217–231.

Hartman, Bart P., and Heibatollah Sami. "Impact of Accounting Treatment of Leasing Contracts on User Decision Making: A Field Experiment." *Advances in Accounting* (1989), pp. 23–35.

Imhoff, Eugene A., and Jacob K. Thomas. "Economic Consequences of Accounting Standards: The Lease Disclosure Rule Change." *Journal of Accounting and Economics* (December 1988), pp. 277–310.

Imhoff, Eugene A., Robert C. Lipe, and David W. Wright. "Operating Leases: Impact of Constructive Capitalization." *Accounting Horizons* (March 1991), pp. 51–63.

Lewis, Craig M., and James Schallheim. "Are Debt and Leases Substitutes?" *Journal of Financial and Quantitative Analysis* (December 1992), pp. 497–511.

Smith, Clifford, Jr., and L. MacDonald Wakeman. "Determinants of Corporate Leasing Policy." *Journal of Finance* (July 1985), pp. 895–908.

Bibliography

Abdel-Khalik, A. Rashad, Robert B. Thompson, and Robert E. Taylor. "The Impact of Reporting Leases Off the Balance Sheet on Bond Risk Premiums: Two Exploratory Studies." *Economic Consequences of Financial Accounting Standards.* FASB, 1978, pp. 103–155.

Anton, Hector R. "Leveraged Leases—A Marriage of Economics, Taxation and Accounting." In *DR Scott Memorial Lectures in Accountancy,* Vol. 6, Alfred R. Roberts, ed. Columbia, Mo.: University of Missouri, 1974, pp. 81–113.

Berger, Peter, and Kenneth Blomster. "Lease Accounting Issues." *The CPA Journal* (December 1988), pp. 76–78.

Bowman, Robert G. "The Debt Equivalence of Leases: An Empirical Investigation." *The Accounting Review* (April 1980), pp. 237–253.

Clay, Raymond J., and William W. Holder. "A Practitioner's Guide to Accounting for Leases." *Journal of Accountancy* (August 1977), pp. 61–68.

Collins, William A. "Accounting for Leases-Flowcharts." *Journal of Accountancy* (September 1978), pp. 60–63.

DeFliese, Philip L. "Accounting for Leases: A Broader Perspective." *Financial Executive* (July 1974), pp. 14–23.

Deming, John R. "An Analysis of FASB No. 13." *Financial Executive* (March 1978), pp. 46–51.

Dieter, Richard. "Is Lessee Accounting Working?" *The CPA Journal* (August 1979), pp. 13–19.

FASB Discussion Memorandum. *Accounting for Leases.* Stamford, Conn.: Financial Accounting Standards Board, 1974.

Elam, Rick. "Effect of Leases Data on the Predictive Ability of Financial Ratios." *The Accounting Review* (January 1975), pp. 25–43.

Finnerty, Joseph F., Rich N. Fitzsimmons, and Thomas W. Oliver. "Lease Capitalization and Systematic Risk." *The Accounting Review* (October 1980), pp. 731–739.

Grinnel, D. Jacque, and Richard F. Kochanek. "The New Accounting Standards for Leases." *The CPA Journal* (October 1977), pp. 15–21.

Hawkins, David. "Objectives, Not Rules for Lease Accounting." *Financial Executive* (November 1970), p. 34.

Hawkins, David F., and Mary M. Wehle. *Accounting for Leases.* New York: Financial Executives Research Foundation, 1973.

Hazard, Albert W., and Raymond E. Perry. "What FASB Statement No. 91 Means for Accountants and Auditors." *Journal of Accountancy* (February 1988), pp. 28, 30, 32–34, 36.

Ingberman, Monroe, Joshua Ronen, and George H. Sorter. "How Lease Capitalization Under FASB Statement No. 13 Will Affect Financial Ratios." *Financial Analysts Journal* (January–February 1979), pp. 28–31.

Kuo, Horng-Ching. "Evaluation of Alternative Approaches to Lessee Accounting in the Context of Risk Assessment." *Review of Business and Economic Research* (Fall 1988), pp. 31–44.

Lander, Gerald, and Alan Reinstein. "Coping with SFAS No. 91." *The CPA Journal* (April 1988), pp. 73–75.

Ma, Ronald. "Accounting for Long-Term Leases." *Abacus* (June 1972), pp. 12–34.

Myers, John H. *Reporting of Leases in Financial Statements.* New York: American Institute of Certified Public Accounts, 1962.

Shachner, Leopold. "The New Accounting for Leases." *Financial Executive* (February 1978), pp. 40–47.

Swieringa, Robert J. "When Current Is Noncurrent and Vice Versa." *The Accounting Review* (January 1984), pp. 123–130.

Wyatt, Arthur R. "Leases Should Be Capitalized." *The CPA Journal* (September 1974), pp. 35–58.

Zises, Alvin. "The Pseudo-Lease—Trap and Time Bomb." *Financial Executive* (August 1973), pp. 20–25.

Pensions and

Other

Postretirement

Benefits

Accounting for the Cost of Pension Plans

For many years, employers have been concerned with providing for the retirement needs of their work force. This concern has resulted in the adoption of pension plans on a massive scale since World War II. Generally, companies provide for pension benefits by making periodic payments to an outside third party, termed a funding agency. This agency then assumes the responsibility for investing the pension funds and making the periodic payments to the recipients of benefits.

The two most frequently encountered types of pension plans are defined contribution plans and defined benefit plans. In a *defined contribution plan*, the employer promises to contribute a certain amount into the plan each period. For example, the employer may promise to contribute 8 percent of the employee's salary each year. However, no promise is made concerning the ultimate benefits to be paid. Benefits are ultimately determined by the return earned on the invested pension funds during the investment period.

In a *defined benefit plan*, the amount of pension benefits to be received in the future is defined by the terms of the plan. For example, the retirement plan of a company may promise that an employee retiring at age 65 will receive 2 percent of the average of the highest 5 years' salary for every year of service. An employee working for this company for 30 years will receive a pension for life equal to 60 percent of the average of his or her highest 5 salary years. When a company establishes a defined benefit pension plan, it is necessary to determine the annual contribution necessary to meet the benefit requirements in the future.

Accounting for defined contribution plans is relatively straightforward. Since the risk for future benefits is borne by the employee, the employer's only expense is the annual promised contribution to the pension plan. This amount of contribution is the periodic pension expense. When a company adopts a defined contribution pension plan, the employer's financial statements should disclose the existence of the plan, the employee groups covered, the basis for determining contributions, and any significant matters affecting comparability from period to period (such as amendments increasing the annual contribution percentage).

On the other hand, accounting for defined benefit plans is much more complex. In these plans, the pension benefits to be received in the future are affected by uncertain variables such as turnover, mortality, length of employee service, compensation levels, and the earnings of the pension fund assets. In defined benefit plans, the risks are borne by employers because they must make large enough contributions to meet the pension benefits promised. As a result, the amount of periodic pension expense incurred may not be equal to the cash contributed to the plan.

Since the future pension benefits are affected by uncertain variables, employers hire actuaries to assist in determining the amount of periodic contributions necessary to satisfy future requirements. The actuary takes into consideration the future benefits promised and the characteristics of the employee group (such as age and sex). He or she then makes assumptions about such factors as employee turnover, future salary levels, and the earnings rate on the funds invested, and arrives at the present value of the expected benefits to be received in the future. The employer then determines the funding pattern necessary to satisfy the future obligation.

The employer's actuarial funding method may be either a cost approach or a benefit approach. A *cost approach* estimates the total retirement benefits to be paid in the future and then determines the equal annual payment that will be necessary to fund those benefits. The annual payment necessary is adjusted for the amount of interest assumed to be earned by funds contributed to the plan.

A *benefit approach* determines the amount of pension benefits earned by employee service to date and then estimates the present value of those benefits. Two benefit approaches may be used: (1) the accumulated benefits approach and (2) the benefits/years of service approach. The major difference between these two methods is that under the *accumulated benefits approach,* the annual pension cost and liability are based on existing salary levels, whereas under the *benefits/years of service approach* (also called the *projected unit credit method*) the annual pension cost and liability are based on the estimated final pay at retirement. The liability for pension benefits under the accumulated benefits approach is termed the *accumulated benefits obligation,* whereas the liability computed under the benefits/years of service approach is termed the *projected benefit obligation.*

Even though the actuarial funding approaches have been defined, accounting for the cost of pension plans has caused a great deal of controversy over the years and several authoritative pronouncements have been issued. In the following sections we will trace the evolution of pension accounting standards.

Historical Perspective

The rapidly increasing number of pension plans adopted by companies just following World War II caused accountants to question the then current treatment of accounting for pension costs. A major concern was the fact that many new pension plans gave employees credit for their years of service before the adoption of the plan. The point at issue was the most appropriate treatment of costs associated with this past service. In *Accounting Research Bulletin No. 47, "Accounting for Costs of Pension Plans,"* the Committee on Accounting Procedure of the AICPA stated its preference that costs based on current and future service be systematically accrued during the expected period of active service of the covered employees, and costs based on past services be charged off over some reasonable period. The allocation of past service cost was to be made later on a systematic and rational basis and not cause distortion of the operating results in any one year.

The APB observed that despite *ARB No. 47,* accounting for the cost of pension plans was inconsistent from year to year, both among companies and within a single company. Sometimes the cost charged to operations was equal to the amount paid into the fund during a given year; at other times no actual funding occurred. Moreover, the amortization of past service cost ranged up to 40 years.

Accounting inconsistencies and the growing importance of pension plan costs prompted the APB to authorize *Accounting Research Study No. 8, "Accounting for the Cost of Pension Plans."* This study was published in 1965 and, after careful examination of its recommendations, the APB issued *Opinion No. 8, "Accounting for the Cost of Pension Plans"* in 1966. Since the conclusions of the APB were generally similar to those of the research study, we shall review only the *Opinion* here.

APB Opinion No. 8 identified the basic problems associated with accounting for the cost of pension plans as (1) measuring the total amount of costs associated with a pension plan, (2) allocating the total pension costs to the proper accounting periods, (3) providing the cash to fund the pension plan, and (4) disclosing the significant aspects of the pension plan on the financial statements.

The conclusions expressed by the APB concerning these questions were based to a large extent on two basic beliefs or assumptions. First, the Board believed that most companies will continue the benefits called for in a pension plan even if the plan is not fully funded on a year-to-year basis. Therefore, the cost should be recognized annually whether or not funded. Second, the Board adopted the view that the cost of all past service should be charged against income after the adoption or amendment of a plan and that no portion of such cost should be charged directly to retained earnings. In *APB Opinion No. 8,* several issues were addressed and various terms were introduced. In the following paragraphs we will examine these issues and terms as originally defined by the APB; however, it should be noted that subsequent pronouncements have modified these definitions or changed the terminology.

Normal Cost

The current expense provision of pension cost was termed normal cost in *APB Opinion No. 8*. This was the amount that was required to be expensed each year based on the current number of employees and the actuarial cost method being used. As noted earlier, the actuarial cost method must take into consideration such factors as employee turnover, mortality, and the treatment of actuarial gains and losses.

Past Service Cost

When a pension plan is adopted, the employees are usually given credit for previous years of service. These benefits are referred to as *past service cost* and should be charged as expense in current and future periods. Past service cost is calculated by determining the present value of the amount of future benefits accruing to the current employee group. Prior to the issuance of *APB Opinion No. 8*, many companies charged past service costs against retained earnings as prior period adjustments. This policy was based on the theory that the benefits of employee service had been obtained in prior periods; therefore, the cost associated with those benefits should be charged to previous periods. *APB Opinion No. 8* eliminated this treatment of past service costs, and later pronouncements concurred.

Prior Service Cost

Prior service costs are pension costs assigned to years prior to the date of a particular actuarial valuation. Prior service cost arises as a result of an amendment to the original pension agreement or changes in the actuarial assumptions of the pension plan. When the pension agreement is amended or the underlying assumptions change, it becomes necessary to recalculate the expected future benefits accruing to the current employee group. This calculation is similar to the determination of past service cost.

Actuarial Gains and Losses

The pension cost for any period is based on several assumptions. These assumptions frequently do not coincide with actual results. It is therefore necessary to make periodic adjustments so that actual experience is recognized in the recorded amount of pension expense. Under *APB Opinion No. 8*, periodic pension expense included normal cost and amortization of past and prior service costs. These costs were estimated based on actuarial assumptions. If in a subsequent period, the actuary would revise his or her assumptions based on new information, a periodic adjustment would be required. *APB Opinion No. 8* termed the deviations between the actuarial assumptions and subsequent changes in assumptions due to actual experience *actuarial gains and losses.*

The amount of any actuarial gain or loss was to be recognized over current and future periods by one of two acceptable methods:

1. *Spreading.*   The net actuarial gains and losses are applied to current and future costs through an adjustment to either normal cost or past service cost each year.

2. ***Averaging.*** An average of the sum of previously expensed annual actuarial gains and losses and expected future actuarial gains and losses is applied to normal cost.

Basic Accounting Method

Prior to the time *APB Opinion No. 8* was issued, the Board could not completely agree on the most appropriate measure of cost to be included in each period. Consequently, it was decided that annual cost should be measured by an acceptable actuarial cost method, consistently applied, that produces an amount between a specified minimum and maximum. (In this context, an acceptable actuarial cost method should be rational and systematic and should be consistently applied so that the cost is reasonably stable from year to year.)

The minimum annual provision (see Fig. 12.1) for pension cost could not be less than the total of

FIGURE 12.1 *Minimum and Maximum Provision for Annual Pension Cost Under* APB Opinion No. 8.

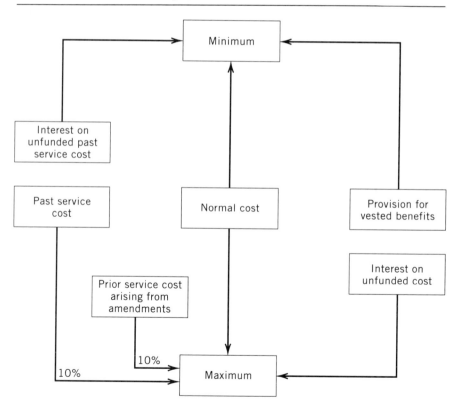

1. Normal cost (cost associated with the years after the date of adoption or amendment of the plan).
2. An amount equivalent to interest on any unfunded past or prior service cost.
3. If indicated, a provision for vested benefits (benefits that are not contingent on the employee continuing in the service of the company).

The maximum annual provision (see Fig. 12.1) for pension cost could not be more than the total of

1. Normal cost.
2. Ten percent of the past service cost (until fully amortized).
3. Ten percent of the amounts of any increase or decrease in prior service cost arising from amendments of the plan (until fully amortized).
4. Interest equivalents on the difference between provisions, that is, pension costs and amounts funded.

The Board's disagreement revolved around two differing viewpoints regarding the nature of pension cost. One view held that pensions are a means of promoting efficiency by (1) providing for the systematic retirement of older people and (2) fulfilling a social obligation expected of a business enterprise. Accordingly, pension costs are associated with the plan itself rather than specific employees, and the amount of pension expense is the amount that must be contributed annually in order to keep the plan in existence indefinitely. The alternate view was that pensions are a form of supplement benefit to the current employee group, so that the amount of pension expense in any period is related to specific employees. This view is rooted in labor economics and is based on the theory that employees contract for wages based on their marginal revenue product. Thus, a pension represents payments during retirement of deferred wages that were earned during each year of employment, and the amount of pension expense is established by determining the benefits expected to become payable to specific employees in the future. Under either view annual pension expense would include normal costs. However, only the second view would include past and prior service costs in the determination of annual pension cost.

By requiring the specified minimum and maximum provisions, *APB Opinion No. 8* did narrow the range of practices previously employed in determining the annual provision of pension cost. However, it should be noted that these minimum and maximum provisions were arbitrarily determined. Thus, the only theoretical justification for their use was a higher degree of uniformity. In addition, the Board decided that only the difference between the amount charged against income and the amount funded should be shown in the balance sheet as accrued or prepaid pension cost. The unamortized and unfunded past and prior service cost was not considered to be a liability by the Board and was not required to be disclosed on the balance sheet. This decision caused a great deal of controversy and resulted in many debates among accountants over the proper amount of future pension costs to be disclosed on financial statements.

Disclosure Requirements

A subsequent review by the FASB of the information disclosed by companies offering pension plans indicated that more informative disclosures were necessary. *SFAS No. 36,* "Disclosure of Pension Information," was the result of this review. According to this release, the following information must be disclosed for a company's pension agreement:

1. *A statement that such plans exist, identifying or describing the employee groups covered.*

2. *A statement of the company's accounting and funding policies.*

3. *The provision for pension cost for the period.*

4. *The actuarial present values of accumulated vested plan benefits and plan net assets available for benefits.*

5. *The nature and effect of significant matters affecting comparability for all periods presented, such as changes in accounting methods (actuarial cost method, amortization of past and prior service cost, treatment of actuarial gains and losses, etc.), changes in circumstances (actuarial assumptions, etc.) or adoption or amendment of a plan.*

6. *Description of significant actuarial assumptions and the methods used to determine fair value of assets and actuarial value of accumulated benefits.*

7. *Other postretirement benefits, accounting policy followed, and recorded cost.*[1]

The following information must also be disclosed and prepared in accordance with the provisions of *SFAS No. 35* (discussed later in the chapter): (1) the actuarial present value of vested and nonvested accumulated plan benefits, (2) the plan's net assets available for benefits, (3) the assumed rates of return used in determining the present values of vested and nonvested plan benefits, and (4) the date as of which the benefit information was determined.

The Pension Liability Issue

In 1981, the FASB proposed a significant change in the method to account for pension cost. The board enumerated several reasons for this proposed change. First, the number of pension plans had grown enormously since the issuance of *APB Opinion No. 8* in 1966. A research study performed by Coopers & Lybrand indicated there were approximately 500,000 private pension plans in the United States in 1979, with total plan assets in excess of $320 billion. There had also been significant changes in laws, regulations, and economic factors affecting pension plans, not the least of which was double-digit inflation.

---

[1] Financial Accounting Standards Board, *FASB Statement No. 36,* "Disclosure of Pension Information" (Stamford, Conn.: FASB, 1980), par. 8.

A second reason cited by the FASB for studying pension accounting was the Board's contention that pension information was inadequate, despite the increased disclosures mandated by *SFAS No. 36*. Finally, the flexibility of permitted actuarial methods resulted in a lack of comparability among reporting companies, according to some financial statement users.

The basic issues involved in the FASB's proposal entitled "Preliminary Views" were

1. What is the period over which the cost of pensions should be recognized? In 1981, pension costs could be recognized over 30–40 years, which is generally longer than the current work force is expected to continue working.

2. How should pension costs be spread or allocated to the individual periods? The basic question here was whether the practice of choosing among a variety of acceptable costs and funding methods met the needs of financial statement users.

3. Should information about the status of pensions be included in the statement of changes in financial position? This was undoubtedly the most controversial of the issues considered.

The positions taken in the FASB's "Preliminary Views" would have required an employer that sponsors a defined benefit pension plan to recognize a net pension liability (or asset) on its balance sheet. This disclosure would have been composed of the following three components: *the pension benefit obligation* less *the plan's net assets available for benefits* plus or minus *a measurement valuation allowance*. This calculation of pension cost coincides with the view that pension expense should be recognized in the period in which the employees render their services. This view is consistent with the matching principle.

One of the organizations that opposed the position of the "Preliminary View" was the AICPA task force on pension plans and pension costs. This group's opposition was expressed in several general areas:

1. The amounts involved do not meet the definition of assets or liabilities under *SFAC No. 3* (now *SFAC No. 6*).

2. A pension arrangement is essentially an executory contract that under existing generally accepted accounting principles is accounted for only as the covered services are performed.

3. Too much subjectivity is involved in determining the amount of the net pension liability—that is, the number is too "soft" to be reported in basic financial statements.

4. Finally, the FASB had not demonstrated the need to amend *APB Opinion No. 8* extensively.

Despite this opposition, the FASB remained steadfast in its determination to change previous pension accounting methods. Under the method originally advocated in "Preliminary Views," the pension benefit obligation would have comprised an accrual for benefits earned by the employees but not yet paid, including prior service credits granted when a plan is initiated or amended. The obligation would include both vested and nonvested benefits and would be measured based on estimates of future compensation levels.

The measure of the pension benefit obligation proposed was called the *actuarial present value of accumulated benefits with salary progression*. It is consistent with the measurement method required under *SFAS No. 36*, with one key difference. The liability disclosed under *SFAS No. 36* pertains to accumulated benefits and did *not* take into account any future salary increases, whereas the proposed method would have required a forecast of salary growth for pension plans that define benefits in terms of an employee's future salary. Since most sponsors utilize financial pay plans, the salary growth assumption would result in pension benefit obligations larger than those previously being reported.

On the other hand, if plan assets exceeded the benefit obligation, a company would report a net pension asset on its balance sheet. The plan's investment assets available for benefits would be measured at fair value, consistent with *SFAS No. 35*, "Accounting and Reporting for Defined Benefit Pension Plans" (discussed later in this chapter).

The third component of the net pension liability was to be the measurement valuation allowance. This component was intended to reduce the volatility of the net pension liability inherent in the prediction of future events, such as changes in the pension benefit obligation and the plan assets, due to experience gains and losses or changes in actuarial assumptions.

Under "Preliminary Views," the amount of annual pension expense that an employer would recognize was the sum of

1. The increase in the pension benefit obligation attributable to employee service during the period (conceptually similar to "normal cost").

2. The increase in the pension benefit obligation attributable to the accrual of interest on the obligation (resulting from the fact that the obligation is the discounted present value of estimated future payments).

3. The increase in plan assets resulting from earnings on the assets at the assumed rate (reducing the periodic pension expense).

4. The amortization of the measurement valuation allowance, which may either increase or decrease the pension expense. Actuarial gains or losses would be included in the measurement of valuation allowance.

Statement of Financial Accounting Standards No. 87

After deliberating the issues addressed in "Preliminary Views" for several years, the FASB reached a consensus in 1985 and issued *SFAS No. 87*, "Employers' Accounting for Pensions." This release was the result of compromises and resulted in several differences from the original position of the FASB expressed in "Preliminary Views." *SFAS No. 87* took the position that pension information should be prepared on the accrual basis and retained three fundamental aspects of past pension accounting: (1) delaying recognition of certain events, (2) reporting net cost, and (3) offsetting assets and liabilities.

The delayed-recognition feature results in systematic recognition of changes in the pension obligation (such as plan amendments). It also results in changes in the values of assets set aside to meet those obligations.

The net cost feature results in reporting as a single amount the recognized consequences of the events that affected the pension plan. Three items are aggregated to arrive at this amount: (1) the annual cost of the benefits promised, (2) the interest cost resulting from the deferred payment of those benefits, and (3) the result of investing the pension assets.

Offsetting means that the value of the assets contributed to a pension plan and the liabilities recognized as pension cost in previous periods are disclosed as a single net amount in the employer's financial statements.

The members of the FASB expressed the view that understandability, comparability, and the usefulness of pension information will be improved by narrowing the range of methods available for allocating the cost of an employee's pension to individual periods of service. The Board also expressed the view that the pension plan's benefit formula provides the most relevant and reliable indicator to how pension costs and pension benefits are incurred. Therefore, three changes in previous pension accounting were required by *SFAS No. 87:*

1. A standardized method of measuring net pension cost. The Board indicated that requiring all companies with defined benefit plans to measure net period pension cost taking into consideration the plan formula and the service period would improve comparability and understandability.

2. Immediate recognition of a pension liability when the accumulated benefit obligation exceeds the fair value of the pension assets. The accumulated benefit obligation is calculated using present salary levels. Because salary levels generally rise, the amount of the unfunded accumulated benefit obligation represents a conservative floor for the present obligation for future benefits already earned by the employees.

3. Expanded disclosures intended to provide more complete and current information than can be practically incorporated into the financial statements at this time.

Pension Cost

Under the provisions of *SFAS No. 87,* net pension cost is comprised of several components reflecting different aspects of the benefits earned by employees and the method of financing those benefits by the employer. The following components are required to be included in the net pension cost recognized by an employer sponsoring a defined benefit pension plan:

1. Service cost.
2. Interest cost.
3. Return on plan assets.
4. Amortization of unrecognized prior service cost.
5. Amortization of gains and losses.
6. Amortization of the unrecognized net obligation or unrecognized net asset at the date of the initial application of *SFAS No. 87* (the transition amount).

The *service cost* component is determined as the actuarial present value of the benefits attributed by the pension formula to employee service for that period. This requirement means that one of the benefit approaches discussed earlier must be used as the basis for assigning pension cost to an accounting period. It also means that the benefits/years of service approach should be used to calculate pension cost for all plans that use this benefit approach in calculating earned pension benefits. The FASB's position is that the terms of the agreement should form the basis for recording the expense and obligation, and the plan's benefit formula is the best measure of the amount of cost incurred each period. The discount rate to be used in the calculation of service cost is the rate at which the pension benefits could be settled, such as by purchasing annuity contracts from an insurance company. This rate is termed the *settlement-basis discount rate.*

The *interest cost* component is determined as the increase in the projected benefit obligation due to the passage of time. Recall that the pension liability is calculated on a discounted basis and accrues interest each year. The interest cost component is determined by accruing interest on the previous year's pension liability at the settlement-basis discount rate.

The *return on plan assets* component is the difference between the fair value of these assets from the beginning to the end of the period, adjusted for contributions, benefits, and payments. That is, the interest and dividends earned on the funds actually contributed to the pension fund combined with changes in the market value of invested assets will reduce the amount of net pension cost for the period. *SFAS No. 87* allows the use of either the actual return or the expected return on plan assets when calculating this component of pension expense.

Prior service cost is the total cost of retroactive benefits at the date the pension plan is initiated or amended. Prior service cost is assigned to the expected remaining service period of each employee expected to receive benefits. (As a practical matter, the FASB allows for a simplified method of assigning this cost to future periods; the company may assign this cost on a straight-line basis over the average remaining service life of its active employees.)

Gains and losses include *actuarial* gains and losses or *experience* gains and losses. Actuarial gains and losses occur when the actuary changes assumptions, resulting in a change in the projected benefit obligation. For example, if the actuary increases the discount rate, the beginning projected benefit obligation is reduced. This means that prior expense recognition for interest, service cost, and prior service cost was overstated. Thus, the amount of the change in the beginning projected benefit obligation is an actuarial gain. Experience gains and losses occur when net pension cost includes the expected, rather than the actual, return on plan assets. The expected return presumes that plan assets will grow to a particular amount by the end of the period. If for example, the actual return is greater than expected, future pension costs will be defrayed further and there is an experience gain. *SFAS No. 87* contains a minimum requirement for the recognition of these gains and losses. At a minimum, the amount of gain or loss to be amortized in a given period is the amount by which the cumulative unamortized gains and losses exceed what the pronouncement termed the *corridor*. The corridor is defined as 10 percent of the greater of the projected benefit obligation or market value of the plan assets. The excess, if any, is divided by the average remaining service period of employees expected to receive benefits. The rationale for the use of the corridor approach is that typically these gains and losses are random errors and should have an expected value of zero. That is, over time, actuarial gains and losses should offset each other. Only extreme values should be recognized. The corridor procedure is similar to statistical procedures that are designed to identify outliers.

SFAS No. 87 requires significant changes in pension accounting from what was previously required in *APB Opinion No. 8*. As a result, the board decided to allow for a relatively long transition period. Most companies were not required to follow the provisions of *SFAS No. 87* until the 1987 calendar year. Additionally, the minimum liability provision (discussed in the next section) was not required to be reported until calendar year 1989. Since these changes were so significant, an *unrecognized net obligation* or *unrecognized net asset* frequently resulted when changing to the new reporting requirements. Therefore, the provisions of *SFAS No. 87* required companies to determine, on the date the provisions of this statement were first applied, the amount of (1) the projected benefit obligation and (2) the amount of the fair value of the plan assets. This resulted in either an unrecognized net obligation or unrecognized net asset. This amount, termed the *transition amount*, was to be amortized on a straight-line basis over the average remaining service period of employees expecting to receive benefits.

Minimum Liability Recognition
Unlike other expenses that are recognized in the income statement, periodic pension cost is not tied to changes in balance sheet accounts. *SFAS No. 87* requires amortization of prior service cost, gains and losses, and the transition amount, but the unamortized amounts for these items are not recorded. Hence, the *funded status* of the plan (the difference between the projected benefit obligation and the fair value of plan assets) is not recognized in the accounting records. Recall that the FASB's original position on this issue, expressed in "Preliminary Views," was that a liability exists when the projected benefit obligation exceeds the plan assets (i.e., the plan is underfunded) or that an asset exists when the reverse is true. Since agreement on this issue could not be reached, the Board developed a compromise position that requires recognition of a liability, termed *the minimum liability*, when the accumulated benefit obligation exceeds the fair value of the plan assets. Thus, even though future salary levels are used to calculate pension expense, the liability reported on the balance sheet need only take into consideration present salary levels.

The portion of the underfunded pension obligation that is not already recognized in the accounting records occurs because the company has unamortized prior service cost or unamortized gains and losses. Because the minimum liability is based on current salary levels and is therefore likely to be less than the underfunded projected benefit obligation, total unamortized prior service cost and unamortized gains and losses are likely to exceed the amount needed to increase the pension liability to the minimum required. *SFAS No. 87* requires that when an additional liability is recognized to meet the minimum liability requirement, the offsetting debit is to be allocated first to an intangible asset for the unamortized prior service cost. The remainder, if any, is due to unamortized net losses and is reported as an element of stockholders' equity. The minimum liability is reassessed at the end of each accounting period, and necessary adjustments are made directly to the intangible asset or stockholders' equity. The following example illustrates the application of the provisions of *SFAS No. 87*.

The Stevens Company has a defined benefit pension plan covering all its 100 full-time employees. Prior to January 1, 1987, the cumulative pension expense recognized equaled its contributions. On January 1, 1987, Stevens adopted *SFAS No. 87*. On the date of transition the projected benefit obligation and plan assets were

Projected benefit obligation	$3,000,000
Fair value of plan assets	1,700,000
Unrecognized net obligation	$1,300,000

Additional Information

1. The benefits per years of service approach indicates that the actuarial present value of the benefits earned during 1987 were	$ 180,000
2. The settlement basis discount rate is	9%
3. The expected rate of return is	9%
4. The actual return on plan assets during 1987 was	$ 120,000
5. The employees' average remaining service period at January 1, 1987, was	10 years
6. Accumulated benefit obligation 12/31/87	$2,800,000

Components of Pension Cost

Service cost (given)	$ 180,000
Interest cost (9% × $3,000,000)	$ 270,000
Actual return on plan assets	($ 120,000)
Prior service cost	0
Return adjustment [($1,700,000 × .09) − 120,000]	($ 33,000)
Prior service cost	0
Gain or loss [no element (B) gain or loss is recognized since the unrealized gain or loss at the beginning of the period is 0.]	0
Transition amount (net underfunding at transition— that is, the projected benefit obligation is less than the fair value of plan assets, or $3,000,000 − 1,700,000 = $1,300,000. This amount is amortized over the average employee service life of 10 years)	130,000
Pension expense	$ 427,000

Funding Status

According to *SFAS No. 87*, the projected benefit obligation measures Stevens Company's present obligation to its employees to provide future pension benefits. A part of that obligation has been satisfied through funding. Any remaining obligation would satisfy the definition of a liability. For Stevens Company the funded status at December 31, 1987, would be determined as follows (assuming no changes in actuarial assumptions and funding at 12/31/87 of $400,000):

Projected benefit obligation at 1/1/87	$3,000,000
Interest during 1987	270,000
Service cost for 1987	180,000
Projected benefit obligation at 12/31/87	$3,450,000
Plan assets at 1/1/87	$1,700,000
Actual return in 1987	120,000
Funding at 12/31/87	400,000
Plan assets at 12/31/87	2,220,000
Underfunded projected benefit obligation	$1,230,000

Because prior cumulative pension expense equaled contributions, there is no beginning accrued pension asset or liability balance; hence, the accounting records for Stevens Company include only the following at December 31, 1987:

Pension expense	$427,000
Accrued pension liability (427,000 − 400,000)	27,000

The recorded liability differs from the underfunded status of the plan by $1,203,000 ($1,230,000 − 27,000). Why? Stevens Company had a transition amount of $1,300,000 at January 1, 1987. This amount comprised unamortized prior service cost and any unamortized actuarial gains and losses when the transition was made to *SFAS No. 87*. Of this amount $130,000 was recognized in the 1987 pension expense. The remainder, $1,170,000, is not on the books. In addition, pension expense included the expected return of $153,000 ($120,000 + 33,000). The actual return was $120,000. the difference, $33,000, is an experience loss. None of this loss has been recognized in pension expense. Thus the unrecorded liability includes:

Unamortized transition amount	$1,170,000
Unamortized experience gain	33,000
Unrecognized net obligation	$1,203,000

Calculation of the Minimum Liability

Under *SFAS No. 87*, Stevens Company is not required to report the foregoing unrecognized net obligation in its balance sheet. Instead, at a minimum it is required to report the amount by which the accumulated benefit obligation exceeds the fair value of plan assets, or $580,000 ($2,800,000 − 2,220,000). Stevens Company already has a liability for $27,000 on its books. To meet the minimum requirement $553,000 ($580,000 − 27,000) additional liability must be added. If we assume that most of the transition amount was unamortized prior service cost, all of the $553,000 will be considered an intangible asset, even though some of the unrecognized underfunding is due to unrecorded losses.

Disclosures

SFAS No. 87 requires employers to disclose information beyond that previously required. Perhaps the most significant of these new disclosures are the components of net pension cost and the funding status of the plan. Specifically, employers sponsoring defined benefit plans must disclose the following information:

1. A description of the plan including employee groups covered, type of benefit formula, funding policy, types of assets held, significant nonbenefit liabilities if any, and the nature and effect of significant matters affecting comparability of information for all periods presented.

2. The amount of net periodic pension cost for the period showing separately the service cost component, the interest cost component, the actual return on assets for the period, and the net total of other components.

3. A schedule reconciling the funded status of the plan with amounts reported in the employer's statement of financial position, showing separately
   a. The fair value of plan assets.
   b. The projected benefit obligation identifying the accumulated benefit obligation and the vested benefit obligation.
   c. The amount of unrecognized prior service cost.
   d. The amount of unrecognized prior net gain or loss.
   e. The amount of any remaining unrecognized net obligation or net asset existing at the date of initial application of *SFAS No. 87.*
   f. The amount of any additional liability recognized.
   g. The amount of net pension asset or liability recognized in the statement of financial positions (this is the net result of combining the preceding six items).
   h. The weighted average assumed discount rate and the weighted average expected long-term rate of return on plan assets.

The annual pension cost reported by corporations under *SFAS No. 87* will usually be different than disclosed under the provisions of *APB Opinion No. 8.* The magnitude of these differences will depend on such factors as the pension plan's benefit formula, employees' remaining service periods, investment returns, and prior accounting and funding policies. Companies that have underfunded pension plans with a relatively short future employee service period may be required to report significantly higher pension expense.

   In releasing *SFAS No. 87*, the Board stated that this pronouncement was a continuation of its evolutionary search for more meaningful and more useful pension accounting information. The Board also stated that while it believes that the conclusions it reached are a worthwhile and significant step in that direction, these conclusions are not likely to be the final step in the evolution. Table 12.1 compares the evolution of these standards from *APB Opinion No. 8* through "Preliminary Views" to *SFAS No. 87.*

TABLE 12.1 *Comparison of Previous Accounting Practice With FASB's "Preliminary Views" and* Statement of Financial Accounting Standards No. 87

Issue	Previous Accounting	Preliminary Views	SFAS No. 87
Recognition of a liability.	A liability recognized equal to accumulated expense based on an acceptable actuarial method less amounts funded.	Recognizes a net pension liability (or asset) based on services rendered by the employees, using an actuarial method the FASB concludes is most appropriate for accounting purposes.	Recognition of a liability if periodic cost exceeds contributions to the plan. Additional "minimum liability" recognized when the accumulated benefit obligation exceeds the fair value of the plan assets.
Recognition of plan assets as employer's assets.	Not recognized as employer's assets.	Recognizes plan assets as an offset against the pension obligation. Could result in a net asset.	Not recognized as employer's assets.
Measurement of pension liability and expense.	Based on a number of actuarial cost methods that achieve systematic and rational allocation of pension cost.	Proposes one method as most appropriate for accounting purposes; the projected-unit-credit method for final pay and career-average pay plans, and the accumulated benefits method for flat benefit plans.	Based on the terms of the pension agreement. Uses the accumulated benefits approach for plans based on existing salary levels and the benefits per years of service approach for plans based on future salary levels.
Accounting for changes in the plan, including a new one that gives credit for past service.	No immediate recognition of an accounting liability.	Recognizes the increased pension benefit obligation (liability) and records an intangible asset representing expected future economic benefits.	No immediate recognition of the liability.

	Pension expense and the related actuarial liabilities are recognized over a number of future periods.	Pension expense would include amortization of prior service cost over the average remaining service period of active plan participants.	Recognizes increased pension expense over the expected remaining service period of employees expected to receive benefit. No immediate recognition of the liability.
Accounting for actuarial gains or losses (measurement changes).	Included in pension expense in a systematic and rational manner (i.e., spread or averaged over a period of 10 to 20 years).	Establishes a measurement valuation allowance consisting of realized and unrealized experience gains and losses and effects of changes in actuarial assumptions, which would be a component of the net pension liability. Recognizes measurement changes prospectively through amortization of the measurement valuation allowance based on the average remaining service period of active plan participants.	Corridor approach adopted. Ten percent of the excess of any annual gain or loss in excess of the greater of the projected benefit obligation or the market value of the plan assets is recognized over the average service period of employees expected to receive benefits.

Source: Adapted from Coopers & Lybrand, *Executive Alert Newsletter*, Dec.–Jan. 1985, p. 14.

551

SFAS No. 87—Theoretical Issues

The issuance of *SFAS No. 87* may have created as many issues as it resolved. Criticism of the pronouncement has been directed at the projected benefits approach, the use of the settlement rate to discount projected benefits, allowing alternative measures of return, and the minimum liability requirement.

Projected Benefits Approach   When the benefit formula utilizes future salary levels, *SFAS No. 87* requires that the measurement of service cost and the employer's present obligation for future benefits earned to date be calculated utilizing projected future salary levels. This measurement can be defended on the basis that employees contract for retirement benefits. These benefits are earned while the employee works; thus, matching would dictate that they are an accrued expense. Also, the projected benefit obligation represents a present obligation to pay the future benefits. Thus, the projected benefit obligation qualifies as a liability under *SFAS No. 6.*

However, critics contend that the projected obligation implies that the benefits earned to date will be paid. This is true only for those employees who have vested benefits or who will remain employees until the benefits do vest. Some feel that only vested benefits should be considered a present liability because vested benefits are the only portion that the company has a present legal obligation to pay if the plan were terminated. Others feel that the accumulated benefits approach provides the more appropriate measure because it is a conservative estimate of the present obligation for future benefits and would be the amount that the employer would set aside if the plan were terminated and the employer wanted to provide for all employees who are vested and may vest in the future. Moreover, the accumulated benefits approach does not require subjective projections of future salary levels. At the other extreme, some feel that the projected benefits approach understates the present liability because it does not take into consideration projected years of service.

The Settlement Rate   *SFAS No. 87* requires that the actuarially determined projected benefit obligation be calculated utilizing a discount rate at which the plan could be effectively settled. For example, the rate at which the company could currently obtain an annuity contract to provide the projected future benefits would be an appropriate settlement rate. The FASB felt that the actuary's rate should not be affected by the return expected on funded assets. The projected benefit obligation is a liability. The discount rate selected is chosen to measure the liability, and has nothing to do with how the assets that are set aside to satisfy that liability are invested.

Opponents argue that the settlement rate is a short-term current rate and that the pension obligation is not going to be settled currently; rather, it is a long-term phenomenon. The settlement rates fluctuate from period to period resulting in volatile measures of the projected benefit obligation, service cost, and interest. Some agree with the FASB that the discount rate used need not be the expected return on plan assets, but argue that it should be based on a more long-run measure of typical pension fund asset returns over time. Others argue that the fund provides the means by which the company will settle the pension obligation, and thus the return on the plan assets is the relevant rate at which to discount projected benefits.

Return on Plan Assets   *SFAS No. 87* requires that net pension cost include the actual return or that the actual return be adjusted to the expected return. Allowing these two alternatives represents a compromise. The FASB favors including the actual return. For the most part the actual return is a realized return. Furthermore, recognition of the actual return is consistent with the comprehensive income concept. Nevertheless, the Board's preference for measuring the return component was criticized because it would produce volatile measures of pension expense from period to period. The FASB conceded by allowing the expected return to be included instead utilizing the expected rate of return on plan assets applied to the market-related asset value of the plan assets. The market-related asset value is a long-term measure of asset value. Hence, the expected return should allow the smoothing of net period pension cost. At the same time, allowing the minimum amortization of actuarial and experience gains and losses should provide further assurance of a smoother, less volatile periodic pension expense.

Reporting the Minimum Liability   One aim of *SFAS No. 87* was to report the net pension obligation on the balance sheet. However, for many companies, reporting the net obligation measured using projected benefits would have a dramatic effect on total liabilities and debt-to-equity ratios. Moreover, there were some who contended that the projected benefit obligation overstates the pension liability because it does not represent the legal liability or the most likely settlement amount. The Board acquiesced to the concerns and opted for a minimum liability measurement based on the more conservative accumulated benefit obligation.

If the projected benefit obligation provides the more appropriate measure, then reporting the minimum liability understates liabilities. Furthermore, it is inconsistent with the measurement of periodic pension expense, which is measured utilizing projected benefits. Such an inconsistency perpetuates the criticism regarding pension reporting under *APB Opinion No. 8*, that pension accounting is contrary to the fundamental notion that the financial statements should be articulated. Empirical research has demonstrated that pension obligations are considered liabilities,[2] but to date there is no conclusive evidence that one method of measuring the obligation or pension expense is perceived by the market as better than another.

Accounting for the Pension Fund

Until 1980, accounting practice often relied on the actuary's funding and cash flow considerations for measuring pension costs and accumulated pension

---

[2] See, for example, W. Landsman, "An Empirical Investigation of Pension Fund Property Rights," *The Accounting Review* (October 1986), pp. 662–691, and D. S. Dhaliwal, "Measurement of Financial Leverage in the Presence of Unfunded Pension Obligations," *The Accounting Review* (October 1986), pp. 651–61.

benefits. At that time, *Accounting Principles Board Opinion No. 8*, "Accounting for the Costs of Pension Plans," stated that accounting for pension expense and related liabilities were separate and distinct from actuarial costing for funding purposes. However, according to *SFAS No. 35*, "Accounting and Reporting by Defined Benefit Pension Plans," the status of plans for financial reporting purposes is to be determined by actuarial methodology designed not for funding purposes but, rather, for financial reporting purposes.

Neither the FASB nor its predecessors had issued authoritative accounting standards specifically applicable to pension plans. Therefore, the financial reporting by those plans varied widely. *SFAS No. 35* establishes accounting and reporting standards designed to correct this shortcoming.

The primary objective of *SFAS No. 35* is to provide financial information that is useful in assessing a pension plan's current and future ability to pay benefits when due. In attempting to accomplish this objective, *SFAS No. 35* requires that pension plan financial statements include four basic categories of information:

1. Net assets available for benefits.
2. Changes in net assets during the reporting period.
3. The actuarial present value of accumulated plan benefits.
4. The significant effects of factors such as plan amendments and changes in actuarial assumptions on the year-to-year change in the actuarial present value of accumulated plan benefits.

Information about net assets must be available for plan benefits at the end of the plan year and must be prepared using the accrual basis of accounting.

The statement also sets standards for information regarding participants' accumulated plan benefits. Accumulated plan benefits are defined as those future benefit payments attributable under the plan's provisions to employees' service rendered to date. Information about these accumulated benefits may be presented either at the beginning or at the end of the plan year. Accumulated plan benefits are to be measured at their actuarial present value, based primarily on history of pay and service and other appropriate factors.

The Employee Retirement Income Security Act

In 1974, Congress passed the Employee Retirement Income Security Act (ERISA), also known as the Pension Reform Act of 1974. The basic goals of this legislation were to create standards for the operation of pension funds and to correct abuses in the handling of pension funds.

ERISA establishes guidelines for employee participation in pension plans, vesting provisions, minimum funding requirements, financial statement disclosure of pension plans, and the administration of the pension plan. Shortly thereafter, the FASB undertook a study of the impact of ERISA on *APB Opinion No. 8*. The conclusions of this study are contained in *FASB Interpretation No. 3*:

> *1. The Pension Reform Act of 1974 is concerned with pension cost funding requirements. The fundamental concept of APB Opinion No. 8, that the*

amount of pension cost expense is not necessarily determined by funding policies, is not affected by ERISA.

2. *No change in the computation of the required minimum and maximum provisions is required by ERISA.*

3. *Compliance with ERISA's participation vesting or funding requirements may change the amount of expense that might otherwise have been incurred.*

4. *Any additional expenses incurred because of compliance with the provisions of ERISA shall be charged to current and future periods subsequent to the date the pension plan became subject to ERISA's provisions.*[3]

In essence, *FASB Interpretation No. 3* states that the provisions of *APB Opinion No. 8* were not affected by ERISA. However, compliance with the act's requirements can increase the amount of pension cost charged to expense in current and future periods over what it would have been prior to the enactment of ERISA. The provisions of *SFAS No. 87* are also not affected by ERISA. The pronouncements of the APB and FASB are concerned with periodic expense and liability recognition. The provisions of ERISA are mainly concerned with the funding policies of pension plans.

Other Postretirement Benefits

In December 1990, the FASB issued *SFAS No. 106*, "Employers' Accounting for Postretirement Benefits Other Than Pensions."[4] This pronouncement deals with the accounting for all benefits, other than pension benefits, offered to retired employees, commonly referred to as OPEB. Although its provisions apply to a wide variety of postretirement benefits, such as tuition assistance, day care, legal services, and housing subsidies, the most significant OPEBs are retiree health care benefits and life insurance. Based on the notion that management promises OPEBs in exchange for current services, the Board felt that OPEBs are similar to defined benefit pension plans and as such deserve similar treatment. Consequently, *SFAS No. 106* requires that the cost of OPEBs be accrued over the working lives of the employees expected to receive them. However, due to the controversial nature surrounding measurement and reporting issues related to the employer's obligation for OPEBs, the Board decided not to require minimum liability balance sheet disclosure.

Prior to the issuance of *SFAS No. 106*, employers accounted for OPEBs on a pay-as-you-go basis, postponing any recognition of expense until the postretirement period. Due to the magnitude of these expenditures, particularly in light of rising health care costs, to require firms to change from a cash basis to an accrual basis would have had a major impact on financial reporting.

---

[3] *FASB Interpretation No. 3*, "Accounting for the Cost of Pension Plans Subject to the Employee Retirement Income Security Act of 1974" (Stamford, Conn.: FASB, 1974).

[4] Financial Accounting Standards Board, *Statement of Financial Accounting Standards No. 106*, "Employers' Accounting for Postretirement Benefits Other Than Pensions" (Stamford, Conn.: FASB, 1990).

A recent *Wall Street Journal* article described *SFAS No. 106* as "one of the most significant changes in accounting ever . . . that could cut corporate profits by hundreds of billions of dollars."[5] Due to the expected impact of the pronouncement, some have argued that its provisions may cause management to curtail or even eliminate OPEBs, and as a result *SFAS No. 106* may eventually have adverse economic consequences for employees. The reduction or elimination of OPEBs could have a significant impact on an individual's ability to finance future health and life insurance costs. It could also ultimately result in additional costs to the federal government, and therefore to the taxpayer, through increased Medicare payments.

Although on the surface OPEBs are similar to defined benefit pension plans, they have characteristics that necessitate different accounting considerations and that have been the source of considerable controversy:

1. Defined benefit pension payments are determined by formula, whereas the future cash outlays for OPEBs depend on the amount of services, such as medical care, that the employees will eventually receive. Unlike pension plan payments, there is no "cap" on the amount of benefits to be paid to participants. Hence, the future cash flows associated with OPEBs are much more difficult to predict.

2. Unlike defined pension benefits, employees do not accumulate additional OPEB benefits with each year of service.

3. OPEBs do not vest. That is, employees who leave have no further claim to future benefits. Employees have no statutory right to vested health care benefits. Defined benefits are covered by stringent minimum vesting, participation, and funding standards, and are insured by the Pension Benefit Guaranty Corporation under ERISA. Health and other OPEBs are explicitly excluded from ERISA.

SFAS No. 106 requires that the periodic postretirement benefit expense comprise the same six components as pension expense. Nevertheless, there are measurement differences owing to the foregoing differences between the characteristics of OPEBs and those of defined benefit pension plans. The determination of the return on assets and the amortization of gains and losses for OPEBs and defined benefit pension plans is the same. We will concentrate on those components that are treated differently.

Service Cost

The service cost component of net periodic pension cost is that portion of the ending projected benefit obligation attributable to employee service during the current period. The basis for computing OPEB *service cost* is the *expected postretirement benefit obligation* (EPBO), which is defined as the actuarial present value of the total benefits expected to be paid assuming full eligibility is

---

[5] "FASB Issues Rule Change on Benefits," *The Wall Street Journal,* December 29, 1990, p. A3.

achieved.[6] Measurements included in the calculation of the EPBO include estimated effects of medical cost, inflation, and the impact of technological advancements and future delivery patterns. The service cost component for OPEBs is the ratable portion of the EPBO attributable to employee service in the current period.

Interest

Interest is calculated by applying the discount rate by the *accumulated postretirement benefit obligation* (APBO). The APBO is that portion of the EPBO attributable to employee service rendered to the measurement date. Once the employee is fully eligible to receive OPEB benefits, the APBO and the EPBO are equivalent.[7]

Amortization of Prior Service Costs

For OPEBs *prior service cost* is the increase in the APBO attributed to an increase in benefits to employee service rendered in prior periods. *SFAS No. 106* requires that prior service cost be recognized over the life expectancy of the employees when most participants are fully eligible to receive benefits. If employees are not fully eligible, prior service cost is amortized to the date of full eligibility. OPEB gains on decreases in benefits are required to be offset against both unrecognized prior service cost and unrecognized transition obligations.

Amortization of the Transition Obligation

The transition obligation under *SFAS No. 106* is the difference between the APBO and the fair value of funded OPEB assets. The transition amount may be recognized immediately, or amortized over the average remaining service lives of active participants. The employer may elect a minimum amortization period of 20 years. The amount of amortization allowed is constrained. The cumulative expense recognized as a result of electing to defer recognition of the transition amount may not exceed the cumulative expense that would occur on a pay-as-you-go basis.

Disclosure

Like *SFAS No. 87*, *SFAS No. 106* requires the disclosure of plan details, including the funding policy and amounts and types of funded assets, the components of net periodic cost, and a reconciliation of the funded status of the plan with amounts reported in the statement of financial position. Recognizing the

---

[6] Ibid., par. 20.

[7] Ibid., pars. 20 and 21.

sensitivity of the assumptions used to measure OPEB costs, *SFAS No. 106* also requires disclosure of

1. The assumed health care cost trend rates used to measure the EPBO.
2. The effects of a one-percentage-point increase in the assumed health care cost trend rates.

Postemployment Benefits

In addition to postretirement benefits, employers often provide benefits to employees who are inactive due to, for example, a lay-off or disability, but not retired. In *SFAS No. 112*, "Employer's Accounting for Postemployment Benefits,"[8] the FASB determined that these benefits are compensation for services rendered and as such the provisions of *SFAS No. 5*, "Accounting for Contingencies," and *SFAS No. 43*, "Accounting for Compensated Absenses," provide the appropriate accounting treatment. Hence, a loss contingency should be accrued when the payment of postemployment benefits is probable, the amount of the loss contingency can be reasonably estimated, the employer's obligation is attributable to employee services already rendered, and the employee's rights to postemployment benefits vest or accumulate.

Summary

Accounting for the cost of pension plans continues to be a controversial issue. Although both the Accounting Principles Board and the Financial Accounting Standards Board have addressed this issue, a complete consensus has not been achieved. There still are a variety of views on what constitutes a company's liability and periodic expense for a pension plan. There are also differing views on how to measure and disclose pension assets and liabilities on financial statements. Finally, the SFAS on accounting for other postretirement benefits has created a great deal of controversy.

In the articles that follow, Joseph Rue and David Tosh discuss some continuing unresolved issues associated with accounting for pensions and other postretirement benefits; and Robert McLendon, Alex Arcady, and James Johnson describe *SFAS No. 106* and discuss implementation issues as well as potential impacts the pronouncement may have on financial reporting and management strategies.

---

[8] Financial Accounting Standards Board, *Statement of Financial Accounting Standards No. 112*, "Employers' Accounting for Postemployment Benefits" (Stamford, Conn.: FASB, 1992).

Continuing Unresolved Issues of Pension Accounting

Joseph C. Rue and David E. Tosh

Introduction

In December 1985, the Financial Accounting Standards Board (FASB) finished the second phase of the pension reporting project by issuing *Statement of Financial Accounting Standards No. 87 (SFAS No. 87)*. The project was begun in 1974. The time required for its completion attests to the complexity and controversy associated with the issues confronting the Board. The pronouncement's issuance lends credibility to the Board's ability to shape a policy position from a set of conflicting perspectives on a number of fundamental accounting questions. While this accomplishment is laudable, the compromises necessary to achieve policy closure in the pension area have resulted in some reporting requirements which are difficult to defend on either strict theoretical or practical grounds. While a number of issues can be raised concerning the requirements of *SFAS No. 87*, in this paper we have chosen to focus primarily on the balance sheet effects. In particular, we question the proposed measurement and recognition of both the pension obligation and the related intangible asset.

Beyond the focus on the specific aspects of the pension pronouncement, we believe it worthwhile to explore some possible reasons for the conflicting perspectives which ultimately gave form to *SFAS No. 87*. Insights into the origins of the conflicting perspective facilitate and strengthen our proposed solutions to the specific problems identified. Moreover, such inquiry may suggest areas where improvements are possible in the conceptual structure underlying the standards-setting process.

In the discussion which follows we will: provide some background on these pension reporting issues; examine some potential sources of the reporting problems; and propose solutions which will address the problems we raise.

Background

Employers' reporting of defined benefit pension plans has evolved over a number of years. Early attempts at setting accounting standards for pensions are found in *Accounting Research Bulletins No. 34 and No. 47*. Prior to the issuance of *SFAS No. 87*, employer accounting for pensions was based on *APBO No. 8*. The reporting under *APBO No. 8* was directed primarily at periodic expense measurement. The accounting rules prescribed by the opinion resulted in a balance sheet liability for the sponsor only if cumulative plan funding was less than cumulative pension expense. Since periodic pension expense under *APBO No. 8* was determinable by any of a number of acceptable actuarial techniques, and since the inclusion in periodic pension expense of a component representing benefits granted for prior years of service (past and/or prior service cost) was at the discretion of the sponsor, many observers believed that the liability disclosure was inadequate. In particular, many were concerned that the failure to recognize a liability for past and prior service cost distorted the portrayal of the firm's financial position by ignoring what was, in many cases, a significant obligation of the firm.

The counter arguments to this view took one of two perspectives.[1] First, some argued that the liability for past and prior service is executory only. Although these benefits are granted retroactively (based upon prior service), the conventional view is that they will induce greater work force productivity in the future. Accordingly, it was argued that the firm's liability for these benefits does not accrue until the enhanced productivity is delivered in the future. The second argument relied heavily on the going concern assumption. Under the assumption that the firm, its pension plan, and work force will continue intact indefinitely into the future, a more or less permanent deferral of the past and prior service obligation can exist. While the specific composition of the obligation will change with the work force, the magnitude may remain relatively stable. Given this view, some argued that accounting recognition of this amount was unnecessary since it was not payable in the foreseeable future.

In 1974 the Employee Retirement Income Security Act (ERISA) became law. This legislation clarified many of the sponsors' duties and obligations associated with the operation of a pension plan. ERISA imposed a contingent liability upon employers for accrued, unfunded pension benefits (including past and prior service costs). The legislative extension of the employer's legal liability was a catalyst for the pension project begun by the FASB in 1974.

Statement No. 36

SFAS No. 36 was promulgated in 1980 as an interim reporting measure pending the completion of the project. The thrust of this statement was to require footnote disclosure of the sponsor's unfunded accumulated benefit obligation. The accumulated benefit obligation is the actuarial present value of benefits (both vested and nonvested) attributed by the pension benefit formula to service before the reporting date and based upon employee service and compensation prior to that date. The procedure contemplated by *SFAS No. 36* for measuring the obligation adopted a comparatively uniform actuarial technique for identifying periodic pension cost (the accumulated benefit method) and included past and prior service costs in the computation.

The issuance of *SFAS No. 36*, while establishing a tentative position on the measurement of the pension obligation, also produced some controversy. Several observers expressed the view that any measure of the pension obligation should exclude nonvested benefits. This same concern was expressed often as the pension project progressed.[2] Those holding this view argued that nonvested benefits do not meet the definition of a liability because they are contingent on

---

[1] AICPA, "Accounting for Pension Costs," *AICPA Professional Standards* (New York: American Institute of Certified Public Accountants, 1980), pp. 8525–26.

[2] Leonard Lorensen and Paul Rosenfield, "Vested Benefits—A Company's Only Pension Liability," *Journal of Accountancy* (October 1983), pp. 64–76.

future events. The event necessary to cause the vesting of these benefits is the employee's continuing affiliation with the firm, clearly a future occurrence.

Preliminary Views and Exposure Draft

The FASB's *Preliminary Views* proposed that sponsors report a liability equal to the unfunded project benefit obligation. This measure is conceptually similar to the accumulated benefit obligation in that it incorporates past and prior service cost and reflects a benefit approach to periodic cost attribution, but it explicitly considers expected future employee compensation levels if the plan is pay-related (i.e., career-average or final-pay plans). A strong argument was made for the inclusion of salary progression in the liability measure since, ultimately, future cash outflows for pension benefits would be a function of salary levels at that time. Opposing viewpoints took the position that included expected future salaries in the computation was tantamount to recording an executory liability since the level of the future compensation depends upon uncertain future events.[3]

An additional feature associated with the liability measurement and recognition question was how to treat the debit which would arise when the liability was booked. Under *APBO No. 8*, the liability recognized was equal to normal cost plus interest and, in some cases, amortization of past and prior service cost. The related debit was treated as an expense. As the pension project progressed, however, several proposals were made to include all past and prior

service costs in the recognized liability. The proposed recognition of this additional liability (unamortized past and prior service costs) was not only controversial in itself (as discussed above), but also resulted in different views on how to treat the related debit.

The debit could be thought of as measuring the cost of retroactive pension benefits granted for service prior to plan adoption or amendment. While most would agree with this conceptual interpretation of the debit, there was some disagreement regarding its financial statement disposition. Various respondents to the FASB *Exposure Draft* and *Preliminary Views* suggested alternative treatments for the debit ranging from recognizing the amount as an expense in the current period to offsetting it against the liability.

The rationales for their various positions are, to some extent, related to the arguments discussed in connection with the liability question. The argument for recognizing the debit as an asset is derived from the notion that retroactive benefits are granted with the expectation that improved employee services will be received in the future. Some view these expected benefits as future economic resources accruing to the firm as the result of past events and accordingly perceive them as assets. Others question the degree of control which the firm has over these benefits. The benefits occur only as an employee delivers services in the future.[4] From this perspective, they are viewed as uncertain future benefits (contingent assets) which do not satisfy the concept of an asset. Thus, the Board was also con-

---

[3] Donald Kirk, "Pension Accounting: A Major Theme of the 1980s," *Journal of Accountancy* (October 1981), pp. 92–100.

[4] FASB, "Employers' Accounting for Pensions," *Exposure Draft* (Stamford, Conn.: Financial Accounting Standards Board, 1985), p. 43.

fronted with a variety of viewpoints concerning the treatment of the pension "asset."

The discussion above highlights several of the major points of contention which arose during the debate over, and the development of, balance sheet reporting principles for pension costs. A general theme running through these controversial issues is the degree of certainty or uncertainty with which future services can be expected from employees. In a later section of the paper we will consider the way in which disagreement over the probability of future service delivery impacted both the debate and the pronouncement (*SFAS No. 87*) on pension accounting. First, however, we explore a possible reason for the disagreement.

Sources of the Disagreement— The Unit Problem

What we observe with respect to both the liability and asset questions is a wide range of views concerning the accounting nature of the phenomena. Although lacking evidence, we suspect that most observers would agree upon the intrinsic nature of these phenomena (i.e., the retirement benefits represent some form of obligation to the firm; by granting retroactive benefits there will likely be improved work force morale and, therefore, productivity). Given this agreement and the existence of accepted theoretical constructs for assets and liabilities, it may, at first, seem surprising that the financial reporting constituency could hold such a diversity of views. Moreover, since the FASB appears to consider this range of views in structuring acceptable pronouncements, the level of diversity will set operational parameters for the standard-setting process. The interpretation of accounting constructs as well as the consistency with which the interpretations are made will likely be influenced by the level of disagreement within the constituent group. Accordingly, we believe an inquiry into the underlying causes of such diversity of opinion on pension accounting may provide valuable insights to the profession in examining other controversial subjects.

Devine puts these problems into perspective when he discusses "the unit problem." The unit problem revolves around the selection of the scope or perspective from which to apply measurement and recognition conventions. This choice is critical and will affect the outcome of the application. Devine states:

We begin with the old, but important, procedural problem: whether to select small units and aggregate them so long as they prove to be useful or to select a large unit and use imputation devices until interest wanes. . . . Many of the arguments and controversies in accounting result from undisclosed differences in points of view with regard to the accountability units selected.[5]

The problem is one of selecting appropriate attributes for characterizing the event for which one wishes to account. The accounting process involves the identification, grouping, and measurement of what are believed to be relatively homogeneous events. If the events are not strictly homogeneous, however, a problem can arise in selecting the attributes of the group or class to be portrayed by the accounting process. Some may take a specific or individual perspective which examines the attri-

[5] Carl Thomas Devine, "The Unit Problem," *Essays in Accounting Theory* (Sarasota, Fla.: American Accounting Association, 1985), p. 2.

butes of one member of the group and assumes that those attributes may be generalized to the other members. Others may take an aggregate perspective which attempts to identify attributes relevant to the accounting process by examining the behavior of the group taken as a whole rather than focusing on individual members. Given some nontrivial degree of heterogeneity within the group, an observer adopting an individual perspective will most likely identify a different set of accounting attributes for the class of events than someone who takes the aggregate perspective. Thus, supportable alternative perspectives (individual versus aggregate) can emerge which will lead to different positions on the relevant attributes of an accounting phenomenon and to different conclusions concerning its accounting disposition.

An example of this is found in *SFAS No. 5, Accounting for Contingencies.* The statement recommends accounting recognition for those contingent obligations (i.e., liabilities which do not yet exist with certainty) which are both probable and measurable. The statement specifically cites warranty obligations as a contingent liability which will be given accounting recognition if the warranties satisfy the above conditions. Judging from current practice it appears that most warranty obligations qualify for recognition. Yet it is unlikely that a warranty obligation will arise from a given sales transaction. The probability that a particular product will be defective is small. The basis for recognizing warranties as an accounting liability must, therefore, be grounded in an aggregate perspective of the nature of the obligation: a perspective which evaluates the probability of a liability, not the attributes of an individual sales event. Experience with aggregate sales and re-

lated warranties provides the rationale. Thus, the perspective from which the evaluation is made will affect the conclusion concerning the existence of a warranty obligation.

Accounting Perspective

The choice of perspective from which to evaluate a class of accounting phenomena should be based upon our understanding of their underlying nature. If the phenomena are seen as members of a group where each member's range of potential behavior has impact only to the extent that it contributes to the behavior of the group, then an aggregate perspective is suggested. Alternatively, if this range of potential is fully realizable for each phenomenon under normal conditions, then an individual perspective is suggested.

This argument is supported in portfolio theory. If an investor decides to invest money in a group of securities, the price behavior of an individual security is relevant to his assessment of the profitability of the investment only to the extent that it contributes to the portfolio's return. Alternatively, if the money is invested in only one security, the full range of that security's price behavior is relevant to the profitability assessment. In the first case, the identification of security price behavior relevant to investment profitability should be made from an aggregate perspective. In the second case, the individual perspective is appropriate.

The perspective issue becomes a problem when the standard-setting process moves forward without achieving some consensus on the appropriate level from which to address the accounting question. Failure to resolve this issue can lead to accounting pronouncements which are internally inconsistent from a perspective standpoint. We believe that such is the case with the pension pronouncement. Secondly, given the resolution of perspective in one area of accounting, consistency in standard setting would suggest that such resolution be relied upon, where appropriate, as a precedent. However, judging from conflicting standard-setting efforts regarding oil and gas exploration costs and computer software development costs, consistency in perspective across pronouncements is not occurring.[6]

We believe that much of the controversy over the reporting of the pension obligation and related asset arises from conflicting perspectives on the phenomena in question. As was noted earlier, we take as given a consensus on the general nature of the phenomena. There appear, however, to be a number of different interpretations concerning whether or not these phenomena satisfy the criteria for asset and liability recognition. We submit that the perspective from which they are viewed affects the interpretation process.

Inconsistent Perspective in the Pension Debate and Pronouncement

Much of the debate over the various issues in the pension area results from the adoption of different perspectives in identifying the relevant accounting attributes of the employee group. Many

[6] Computer software development costs are viewed as assets only at the point where the commercial viability of the individual project is established (the individual perspective), whereas the full costing approach to exploration cost accounting treats the cost of drilling a dry hole as an asset since they further the overall exploration effort (an aggregate perspective).

of the arguments made can be traced to an individual perspective where the characteristics of an individual employee's working life are used in conceiving the phenomenon to be portrayed by the accounting. Other positions are more directly linked to an aggregate perspective which evaluates the properties of the entire employee group.

These different perspectives identify different attributes of the work force as being useful in resolving pension accounting questions. Many of the accounting issues hinge on the probability of the employees remaining with and rendering services to the employer in the future. For those adopting the individual perspective, the prospect of future service delivery is not viewed as sufficiently probable to warrant accounting recognition since a particular employee may not remain with the firm throughout his or her career. Those working from an aggregate perspective, however, will probably come to a different conclusion. While the delivery of future services from an individual employee is not particularly certain, there is a much higher probability that the employee group as a whole will render such services. Thus, the different perspectives will give rise to different assessments. This can lead to different conclusions concerning the disposition of the various pension accounting issues.

Salary Progression

On the question of salary progression, most observers would agree that the future obligation for benefits payable from a pay-related plan will reflect future salary levels if the employee in question remains with the firm until retirement. Those arguing against recognition of the salary progression effect are making the evaluation from an individual employee perspective.

If an employee with vested benefits did not render future services, the employer's obligation would be limited to amounts based on compensation to date.[7]

Similar to the warranty liability example discussed earlier, the obligation to a particular employee for future pay-related benefits may not be sufficiently probable to merit recognition. However, if the question is viewed from the perspective of the entire work force, a different conclusion would be reached because the uncertainty associated with individual cases is diversified away.

Parts of *SFAS No. 87* suggest that the FASB looks at the salary progression problem from an individual employee point of view. But actually, the FASB, in the pronouncement, straddles the salary progression issue. Salary progression is reflected in the measurement of periodic pension expense. However, where an additional liability is recognized for unamortized past and prior service costs (i.e., the minimum liability discussed), expected future salary levels are not reflected.

Nonvested Benefits and Past Service Costs

Differing views on the likelihood of future service delivery can also be linked with the debate over recognition of nonvested benefits and past and prior service costs. Both of these potential obligations are frequently viewed as executory liabilities which will not accrue until services are rendered in the future. If, however, they represent probable future sacrifices of cash, an argument can

[7] FASB, *SFAS No. 87, Employers' Accounting for Pensions* (Stamford, Conn.: Financial Accounting Standards Board, 1985), p. 44.

be made for their immediate recognition. Those arguing in favor of recognition most likely base their beliefs on an aggregate perspective (i.e., the probability of future service delivery and related future cash outflow is high). Those opposing such treatment probably base their evaluation on the individual perspective.

The balance sheet liability required by *SFAS No. 87* is the larger of the minimum liability or unfunded accrued pension expense. The minimum liability is the unfunded accumulated benefit obligation which reflects past and prior service costs and nonvested benefits, but includes no provision for salary progression (as noted above). The alternative measure (i.e., unfunded accrued pension expense) results from the failure to fund accrued periodic pension expense and incorporates nonvested benefits and salary progression for normal service but not unamortized past and prior service costs. The lack of a consistent perspective in defining these alternative measures is evidenced by the pronoucement's differential treatment of past and prior service costs. Since the minimum liability includes unamortized past and prior service cost, this implies that an aggregate perspective was taken. The exclusion of past and prior service costs from the alternative measure suggests an individual perspective.

Pension Asset

The above discussion also bears directly on the pension asset recognition issue. The pension asset recognized pursuant to *SFAS No. 87* will most often be associated with unamortized past and prior service costs and will reflect, therefore, the expected future services discussed above. The evaluation of whether or not these services are probable and under the control of the employer (i.e., qualify for asset recognition) depends upon which of the above perspectives is adopted. By recognizing a pension asset the FASB appears to be adopting an aggregate perspective. The asset could be thought of as representing the employee group's acceptance of the pension plan and their promise to deliver future services. But the statement requires the recognition of an intangible asset only in those years when a minimum liability is recorded. Thus, the factors which influence when and to what extent the minimum liability is booked will similarly determine the existence of the intangible asset. Consequently, the intangible has the unusual property of existing in some years and disappearing in others. The reporting perspective can shift significantly from year to year: when the minimum liability is recognized, an aggregate view of the sponsor's control over the benefits of future employee service is in operation; when the minimum liability is not recognized, an individual view must be assumed.

The variable perspective observed to be at work in the case of the intangible asset was probably neither intended nor the result of compromise on the asset question. Rather, we suspect that its treatment follows from concessions made to competing perspectives on the liability issue and an unwillingness on the Board's part to expense the resulting debit. We are not aware of any other asset which would react in such a way. Thus, we observe that this "debit" may not be an asset, but merely a necessity to give balance sheet recognition to the liability.

Recommendation—Need for Consensus on Perspective

Our primary suggestion is that a consistent perspective should have been adopted in identifying accounting procedures in this area. While we believe that an aggregate perspective would be more appropriate in the pension context (discussed below), having a consistent perspective underpinning the final pronouncement is fundamental. In addition to providing a conceptual handle to grasp for those who are responsible for the pronouncement's implementation, a consistent perspective should improve the user's ability to understand the various pension disclosures which will result. Secondly, allowing the diversity of perspective observed in the debate to carry over to the pronouncement can have adverse consequences for the standard-setting process. On the one hand such a result is a basis for challenging the FASB's ability to establish generally accepted accounting principles in controversial areas. Moreover, such a result sets a confusing precedent not only for purposes of future standard-setting but also for the exercising of professional judgment.

Diversity of opinion is probably vital to the standard-setting process, but when the debate is ended, some consensus on the relevant accounting attributes of the phenomenon in question must be achieved. The exact steps to be taken in achieving consensus are not clear. We suspect, as a preliminary step, that sensitizing the profession to the need for consensus on perspective will help. This awareness should stimulate a dialogue involving members of both the practitioner and academic communities which we hope will lead to an acceptable resolution.

With respect to the pension accounting questions, our belief is that an aggregate perspective should have been adopted. Any serious attempt at identifying a meaningful measure of the employer's pension obligation depends upon the attributes of the employee group. The attributes of individual employees are relevant to this process, but only to the extent that they are revealed through the group. Since the nature of measurement in this area relies so heavily upon the aggregate actuarial attributes of the phenomenon, we feel that the accounting measures should have been grounded in the same perspective. Thus, salary progression, nonvested benefits, and past and prior costs should be taken into consideration in both asset and liability recognition in determining pension expense. The pension asset should be shown in all years.

Unfortunately, the new pension pronouncement does not result in accounting measures which consistently represent what they purport to represent. As a result of this, financial statement users may have to adjust reported financial statement pension liabilities for past and prior service cost and for salary progressions as they have previously done before *SFAS No. 87.*[8]

Conclusion

The purpose of this paper has been to explore some of the theoretical and reporting problems associated with the pension accounting arising under *SFAS No. 87.* A potential source of the conflict concerning accounting treatment for pensions and other related areas is "the unit problem." This problem revolves around the selection of a perspective from which to apply measurement and

recognition conventions. Viewing the pension issues from different perspectives can produce different interpretations regarding the satisfaction of the requirements for asset and liability recognition.

If not mediated, these differences can result in the promulgation of a variety of conflicting and inconsistent accounting principles as evidenced by the above observations. Some level of controversy is probably a prerequisite to the development of accounting principles which have general application. The determination of representative accounting rules and their acceptance by the accounting constituency is more likely to follow from a process which encourages a variety of opinions, if it also provides a mechanism to achieve consensus among them. Unfortunately, the existing mechanism of due process seems only to be able to achieve compromise among various positions. The distinction between consensus and compromise is that the former implies agreement over matters of opinion while the latter does not.

The problem of unmediated conflicts in perspective, we believe, ultimately stems from the lack of a well-articulated and operational framework by which accounting perspectives may be evaluated and criticized. This is not so much a criticism of the conceptual framework as it currently exists as it is a call for ongoing attempts to clarify the theoretical constructs and linkages that are found there. These efforts to bring resolution to the elements of the framework may render some of the controversy and debate groundless, thereby improving the efficiency of the standards-setting process.

[8] Feldstein and Seligman, "Pension Funding, Share Prices and National Savings," *Journal of Finance* (September 1981), p. 801.

OPEBs: FASB Prescribes Strong Medicine

Robert G. McLendon, Alex T. Arcady, and James S. Johnson

Providing benefits such as health care and life insurance to retirees have long been a way of life for many companies. Under traditional accounting practices, companies have been able to satisfy employee demands by promising benefit payments far in the future while accounting for those promises on a pay-as-you-go or cash basis. The FASB's SFAS 106, *Employers' Accounting for Postretirement Benefits Other Than Pensions,* will change those accounting practices dramatically. This statement will require businesses to recognize the estimated future cost of providing other postretirement benefits (OPEBs) as an expense as employees render service, instead of when benefits are paid.

The new OPEB accounting model will cause reported OPEB expense for most companies to increase from the amounts presently reported on a cash basis. For mature companies with relatively large numbers of retirees, studies indicate that the annual OPEB expense could be anywhere from two to seven times the amount currently expensed on a cash basis. For companies with few retirees and a relatively young work force, the multiple of expense could be much higher.

The FASB's project on OPEBs has focused significant attention on the implications of providing postretirement benefits, including the spiraling cost of health care. In 1990, the U.S. spent more than $650 billion on health care, more than 12% of the Gross National

Product. Despite concentrated efforts to contain employee health care costs, medical spending during 1990 increased at an alarming rate and the prospects for the future are not encouraging.

Understanding the new accounting rules for OPEBs will provide companies with the opportunity to plan for implementation and evaluate how cost containment strategies and funding alternatives can be integrated with overall corporate objectives relating to employee benefit programs.

The OPEB Accounting Model

A prominent feature of the OPEB accounting model is how it "ties together" or reconciles a plan's funded status with amounts reported in the balance sheet and income statement. The reconciliation illustrated in Exhibit 1 also can be useful in analyzing the changes that occur as a result of plan amendments or other significant events, such as a plan curtailment or settlement. Because the accounting model provides for the deferred recognition of certain items—such as the transition obligation, gains and losses, and prior service costs—the reconciliation also provides insights into the cumulative amount of benefit costs that have yet to be recognized in the financial statements.

In the example, the company's cash basis OPEB expense equals the amount of benefits paid during the year, or $800. However, application of the provisions of SFAS 106 on a prospective basis increases the annual OPEB ex-

EXHIBIT 1 *The OPEB Accounting Model*

		Analysis of OPEB Activity ($000s) Debit (Credit)				
	Accumulated Postretirement Benefit Obligation	Unrecognized Transition Obligation	Unrecognized Net (Gain) or Loss	Unrecognized Prior Service Cost	Accrued OPEB Cost	Net Annual OPEB Cost
Balances—						
Beginning of year	$(10,000)	$ 10,000				
Plan activity:						
Service cost	(900)					$ 900
Interest cost	(1,100)					1,100
Benefit payments	800				$ 800	
Plan amendments	(1,500)			$1,500		
Liability gains and losses:						
Changes in assumptions	(300)		$ 300			
Experience gains/losses	200		(200)			
Amortization:						
Unrecognized prior service cost from plan amendments				(100)		$ 100
Unrecognized obligation existing at transition (straight-line over 20 years)		(500)				500
Net annual OPEB cost					(2,600)	$2,600
Balances—						
End of year	$(12,800)	$ 9,500	100	$1,400	$(1,800)	
		OPEB expense if adopted by cumulative effect accounting change				$2,100
		Cash basis OPEB expense				$ 800

Note: Plan is not pre-funded.

pense to $2,600—more than three times the pay-as-you-go cost. As an alternative, if the company were to recognize the $10,000 transition obligation immediately as the cumulative effect of an accounting change, the annual OPEB expense for the year would be $2,100 ($2,600 minus $500 representing amortization of the transition obligation). However, income (before tax) would be reduced by the $10,000 transition amount.

The example spreadsheet also illustrates the interaction of the various components of OPEB cost defined in SFAS 106.

The Components of OPEB Cost

Service Cost Service cost represents the actuarial present value of the portion of the OPEB obligation considered to be "earned" during the period. The FASB concluded the estimated total cost of providing the future benefits—referred to as the expected postretirement benefit obligation (EPBO)—generally should be allocated on a straight-line basis over the employee service period. The employee service period begins with the employee's date of hire (or the date that credited service begins, if later) and ends at the date the employee is fully eligible for benefits, even if the full eligibility date precedes the expected retirement date.

The allocation period was extremely controversial because many believe the period that best reflects the nature of the exchange—benefits in exchange for service—would end at the expected retirement date. However, the FASB concluded the total cost of providing promised benefits should be recognized by the time they are earned. If employees do not "earn" incremental benefits during additional years of service, no cost should attribute to those years.

Interest Cost Interest cost reflects the imputed growth during the period in the portion of the EPBO that has been "earned" by employee services provided as of a particular date—referred to as the accumulated postretirement benefit obligation (APBO)—using the assumed discount rate. Since the APBO is recognized on a present value basis, imputed interest compounds on benefits associated with prior employee service.

Return on Plan Assets Actual return on plan assets represents the investment return on any plan assets set aside to fund the benefits promised. Since few OPEB plans have been pre-funded, this will not be a significant component for most companies. In the example, the return on plan assets is considered to be zero.

Gains and Losses Gains and losses arise when the actual experience of the plan is different from initial estimates or if the expected return on assets, if any, differs from the actual return. Because gains and losses can fluctuate significantly from year to year, and losses in one period might be offset by gains in another period, recognition of such amounts may be deferred. However, if the cumulative net amount of previously unrecognized gains or losses exceeds 10% of the APBO, that excess portion must be amortized into income over the average remaining service period through the expected retirement date of active plan participants. Alternative recognition methods are allowed if they result in equal or greater amortization.

Prior Service Costs Prior service costs result from plan amendments that change benefits and are attributed to employee services rendered before the date of the amendment. A company may amend its OPEB plan to increase benefits promised during retirement, to enhance productivity, reduce turnover, or improve employee morale, thereby increasing the APBO. An increase in the APBO due to a plan amendment is recognized on a prospective basis by assigning equal amounts to the remaining future service periods through the date of full eligibility for active plan participants.

If a plan amendment reduces benefits, referred to as a negative plan amendment, then a reduction in the APBO results. A reduction in the APBO for a negative plan amendment would be accounted for by first reducing any unrecognized prior service cost and any unrecognized transition obligation. Any remaining reduction in the APBO is recognized over future service periods. This is consistent with the method used to recognize plan amendments that increase benefits.

Transition Obligation The transition obligation represents the unfunded OPEB obligation at the date SFAS 106 is initially adopted. The transition obligation is calculated as the difference between the APBO and plan assets (if any), minus any OPEB liabilities that previously have been recognized on the balance sheet. Companies can recognize the transition obligation as the cumulative effect of an accounting change (included as a charge against net income in the year SFAS 106 is adopted), or over future periods as a component of annual OPEB expense. Prospective recognition will be phased in over the average remaining employee service period through expected date of retirement. If the remaining service period is less than 20 years, an optional 20-year period may be used.

Effective Date

For public companies and companies that sponsor plans which have more than 500 participants in the aggregate, the provisions of SFAS 106 are effective for fiscal years beginning after December 15, 1992. For non-U.S. plans, and for defined benefit OPEB plans of non-public companies with no more than 500 participants in the aggregate, adoption is not required until fiscal years beginning after December 15, 1994. Early adoption is encouraged; but restating previously issued annual financial statements is prohibited.

Planning for Implementation

Companies can benefit now by identifying the extent of their OPEB obligation and by considering steps to contain the rising costs of satisfying their commitments to retirees—particularly the cost of providing health care.

Determine Benefits Promised

The new accounting rules are based heavily on what the FASB refers to as the "substantive plan." As a result, companies should first evaluate summary plan descriptions and other benefit communications to determine the extent of their OPEB obligation. In many cases, assessing the benefits that have been promised will require a coordinated effort by different disciplines. In recent litigation involving attempts to reduce benefits, courts have looked not only to plan documents, but also to employee newsletters, past practices and, even verbal promises in employee meetings and exit interviews, to determine what benefits the employer has promised. In evaluating those promises, it is important to consult with legal, human resources, and other appropriate departments within an organization.

Gather Data Needed for OPEB Calculations

Next, companies will need to accumulate the information needed to measure the OPEB obligation. Demographic information about active and retired plan participants and dependents will have to be gathered (e.g., sex and date of birth for all plan participants and eligible dependents, plus date of hire, turnover rate, full eligibility date, and assumed age at retirement for active plan participants). In addition, historical per capita claims cost data by participant age will be needed.

Few companies presently have adequate information about claims cost readily accessible. Some companies will find that information about retiree medical costs are combined with information about active employees or that the required per capita cost information has not been categorized by age groups. Other companies will find much of the needed information is just not available. In those cases, outside parties—such as insurance carriers, consulting actuaries, or claims processors—might be able to develop the information needed.

Although companies may not be able to avoid the difficulties of the initial information gathering process, they should consider ways to make the process easier going forward. In some cases, modifying existing information systems will provide the ongoing means of accumulating the required information.

Prepare Actuarial Estimates

Once companies have obtained the necessary information, the next step will be to measure the OPEB obligation. Measuring the OPEB liability will require actuarial techniques and the use of assumptions about a myriad of future events. Some of these events include employees' continued active service with the company, retirement date, life expectancies, medical costs by age group, and future increases in the costs of providing the promised benefits. The rate of expected increases in future health care costs—determined using a health care cost trend rate—includes highly subjective assumptions about future medical inflation, delivery methods, intensity of services, and the impact of technological advances in the health care industry. This assumption will be the most difficult to determine under the SFAS 106 model, not only because limited historical data exists, but also because historical cost patterns might not indicate future trends.

From a financial statement perspective, the use of an appropriate trend rate is critical because of its impact on the estimate of total costs that will be incurred. To the extent that the trend rate assumption is reflective of future costs, the OPEB accounting model will produce financial statement results that are representative of the costs necessary to satisfy the OPEB commitment. Admittedly, no one can predict with any certainty what health care costs will do in the future. However, most actuaries do agree that the unprecedented increases in health care costs cannot continue indefinitely. While many agree that increases of the magnitude experienced during the last few years are likely to continue in the near term, the long-range outlook is that the trend rate will be approximately 6% to 8%, annually.

Because the EPBO represents a measure of future benefit payment streams, it will be discounted to today's dollars using present value techniques. The discount rate is to be based on the current rate of return on high-quality, fixed-income investments currently available, and expected to be available during the period over which the benefits are expected to be paid. Because the discount rate will fluctuate based on market changes, the requirement to equate the discount rate to current rates will result in some volatility in the calculated amounts.

For purposes of measuring the EPBO, companies can, in certain circumstances, anticipate future plan changes that are designed to shift future cost increase to plan participants. To the extent that a company can demonstrate, either through past practices of maintaining a consistent level of cost sharing or through communications of its intent to institute future plan changes regarding cost sharing provisions, those changes can be anticipated in the measurement process. In the FASB's view, changes of this nature constitute a part of the "substantive plan," which should be the basis for accounting.

To facilitate long-term benefit planning, information about a company's OPEB obligations should be segregated by plan, by participants and dependents, by early and normal retirees, and by current and future retirees. With this type of information, companies can determine the various characteristics of their OPEB obligations and analyze the expected effects of proposed plan changes and cost containment alternatives.

Determine the Accounting Impact

Using actuarial estimates, companies can determine the effect of the estimated obligation and benefit cost on their financial statements. Determining the accounting consequences of promised benefits can also help companies begin planning how to minimize the financial statement impact of the new accounting rules. In addition to the annual expense increases that most companies will experience, companies should consider whether recording OPEB liabilities could result in violations of financial covenants of loan agreements.

In considering when and how to adopt SFAS 106, companies should consider the impact of the FASB's new rules on accounting for income taxes. Under SFAS 109, *Accounting for Income Taxes,* the potential future tax benefit is recognized, but subject to a "more likely than not" realizability test. Under SFAS 109's predecessor, SFAS 96, the tests for recognition of the deferred tax asset were more stringent. Many companies postponed early recognition of the OPEB liability until SFAS 109 was issued in February 1992.

To minimize the negative impact on future operating results, some companies are considering recording the accumulated postretirement benefit obligation immediately as the cumulative effect of an accounting change. While this approach would result in an immediate reduction in equity and increase in liabilities, future operating results would improve because future periods would not reflect amortization charges relating to the transition obligation (i.e., the unfunded accumulated benefit obligation). Thus, the return on equity would improve—in some cases, dramatically.

Cost Containment Strategies

In coming to grips with the skyrocketing costs of health care, many companies are challenging the nature and extents of the promises made and are considering various plan design modifications and funding alternatives.

Changes in Delivery Systems and Practices

Before reducing employee benefits, companies should consider changes designed to reduce the cost of health care, without sacrificing quality. Changes in delivery systems and increased emphasis on preventive health practices can reduce current benefit costs for active employees and, ultimately, can result in lower costs for retirees. Changes of this type include:

- *Alternative Delivery Systems.* Use of a restricted network of health care providers; for example, HMOs (health maintenance organizations) and PPOs (preferred provider organizations);

- *Administrative Efficiencies.* Eliminate duplication and inefficiencies in claims processing;

- *Patient Care Management.* Offer alternative forms of care to patients (e.g., home care as well as hospitalization);

- *Wellness Programs.* Promote healthy practices among the workforce to reduce utilization of costly medical services.

These approaches can significantly reduce the annual cost increases from those of an indemnity type plan, which typically has exceeded 20% per year for the last several years.

Plan Design Modifications

Some companies are considering benefit reductions or cost-shifting measures to control their share of costs. When reviewing plan modifications, it is important to consider the impact on employees and employee relations. Companies should evaluate potential adverse legal consequences from changing existing plans. In some cases, the courts have ruled against employer actions to reduce or terminate benefits unilaterally. This especially is true if a company, through various communications to employees, has promised benefits beyond those provided in the written plan document.

Among broad types of plan design changes, some companies have considered replacing their existing OPEB plan with other forms of benefit programs. For example, substituting a defined contribution plan for a defined benefit plan would have the immediate effect of placing a ceiling on the costs for which a company ultimately would be responsible. Replacement also could involve providing additional employee benefits through a new or enhanced profit-sharing or pension plan. The objective is to have retirees look to those other arrangements to provide the funds for the payment of their medical expenses, while achieving current tax deductibility for the company.

Other plan changes should be considered. The level of employee contribution could be based on the type of coverage provided. Employee contributions for spousal coverage could be increased. Varying employee contributions based on the amount of deductibles elected by the employee is another option that can be considered. Cost ceilings, lifetime maximums, and Medicare integration also can be useful cost-management tools.

Companies also are contemplating changes to eligibility requirements for full benefits. As companies focus on how OPEB plans fit into their employee benefit packages, some companies have concluded that it is not equitable to provide the same level of benefits to retirees with only 10 years of service as is provided to retirees with 30 years of service. Instead, the level of benefits or employee contributions provided can be based on the years of service provided. For example, as the years of service increase, the required level of co-insurance or employee contribution decreases. Because the plan's eligibility requirements are such that an employee would not be eligible for full benefits until retirement, the attribution period would be extended to the retirement date—reducing the annual cost charged against income under the new accounting rules.

Consider Funding Alternatives

Future cash flow requirements and funding alternatives also should be explored. To date, funding OPEB plans generally has been unattractive because only limited tax incentives are available under existing law. While there appears to be some interest in Congress for providing additional tax incentives for funding, no substantial legislation appears close to enactment, particularly considering the current emphasis on reducing the budget deficit. Two funding options that presently offer attractive tax advantages are Voluntary Employee Beneficiary Association (VEBA) trusts and Sec. 401(h) pension trusts.

Required Disclosures— 1991 and Beyond

Extensive disclosures, similar in many respects to those for pensions, will be required for OPEBs. Disclosures required by SFAS 106 include:

- Description of the plan, employee groups covered and funding policies;
- Components of net periodic postretirement benefit cost for each year presented;
- Key actuarial assumptions used in the measurement; and
- Reconciliation of the funded status of the plan to the amounts presented in the balance sheet.

The composite health care cost trend rate assumed for the first year after the financial statement date also must be disclosed. A general description of the expected direction and pattern of change in the trend rate for subsequent years, as well as the anticipated long-term rate, must be presented.

A sensitivity analysis is required that discloses the effect of a 1% increase in the health care cost trend rate assumption on the APBO and on the aggregate of the service and interest cost components of net periodic OPEB cost. This disclosure is intended to highlight the degree to which the critical health care cost trend rate assumption can affect the required measurements.

In accordance with SEC Staff Accounting Bulletin 74, *Disclosure of the Impact that Recently Issued Accounting Standards Will Have on the Financial Statements of the Registrant When Adopted in a Future Period,* public companies are required to disclose the expected financial statement effects of adopting the new standard. If the financial statement effects are not known, companies should disclose that fact. For 1990 annual reports, many companies disclosed only that the complex analysis required to estimate the impact of the new statement had not been completed and that decisions had not been made regarding accounting alternatives. The SEC has stated it expects more quantitative disclosures in 1991 reports than those provided in 1990.

Companies are required by APBO 22, *Disclosure of Accounting Policies,* to disclose which accounting principle is being followed when alternative policies exist. SFAS 106 creates an alternative accounting policy until it is required to be adopted. Until companies adopt SFAS 106, SFAS 81, *Disclosure of Postretirement Health Care and Life Insurance*

Benefits, requires disclosure of the accounting and funding policies being followed for postretirement benefit programs. In satisfying those disclosure requirements, nonpublic companies also should disclose that the FASB's recent standard on OPEBs will require the use of the accrual method of accounting. The disclosures could be included in the footnote describing the company's accounting policies.

Anticipate the Unexpected

SFAS 106 involves many complexities and represents a major challenge to the business community. Although the new rules are not effective until 1993, expected problems in gathering data and making estimates, and the need to manage the skyrocketing costs, make it imperative for companies to begin evaluating their situations now.

Cases

• Case 12-1

Michaels Corporation has a defined benefit pension plan. In 1987, Michaels adopted the provisions of *SFAS No. 87.* At January 1, 1987, the projected benefit obligation (PBO) was $400,000. Cumulative funding and cumulative pension expense under *APB Opinion No. 8* were equal. Plan assets were heavily invested in the stock market, and due to a bear market, the market value of plan assets at January 1, 1987, was $590,000. Michaels Corporation elected to write off the transition amount over a 15-year period.

For the year 1993, net periodic pension cost was negative.

Required:
a. Is the transition amount considered an asset or a liability? Explain.
b. Discuss how the transition amount in this case would affect net periodic pension expense.
c. Discuss why net periodic pension expense would be negative. In your answer list and describe any and all factors that may cause net periodic pension expense to be negative.
d. Would the pension expense for Michaels have been negative prior to the adoption of *SFAS No. 87?* Why the difference, if any?

• Case 12-2

Goodson Novelty Company has the opportunity to adopt both *SFAS No. 106,* "Employers' Accounting for Postretirement Benefits," and *SFAS No. 109,* "Accounting for Income Taxes" in the same year. The election of *SFAS No. 109* would result in the creation of a deferred tax asset for $250,000. There is currently a deferred tax liability for $50,000. This account is not expected to change. Both deferred tax accounts are considered long-term. The amount by which the postretirement expense would exceed the pay-as-you-go amount is $195,000.

Required:
a. Describe the impact of the simultaneous adoption of both standards to the financial statements of Goodson Novelty Company.

b. If you were Goodson Novelty management, would you elect to adopt both standards in the same year? Why or why not? What would investors think? Would there be an effect on the market price of Goodson Novelty shares?

- ## Case 12-3

Pension accounting has become more closely associated with the method of determining pension benefits.

Required:
a. Discuss the following methods of determining pension benefits.
    i. Defined contribution plan
    ii. Defined benefit plan
b. Discuss the following actuarial funding methods.
    i. Cost approach
    ii. Benefit approach.

- ## Case 12-4

Statement of Financial Accounting Standards No. 87, "Employers Accounting for Pensions," requires a new method of accounting for pension cost.

Required:
a. Discuss the following components of annual pension cost
    i. Service cost
    ii. Interest cost
    iii. Actual return on plan assets
    iv. Amortization of unrecognized prior service cost
    v. Amortization of the transition amount
b. Discuss the composition and treatment of the minimum liability provision.

- ## Case 12-5

Carson Company sponsors a single-employer defined benefit pension plan. The plan provides that pension benefits are determined by age, years of service, and compensation. Among the components that should be included in the net pension cost recognized for a period are service cost, interest cost, and actual return on plan assets.

Required:
a. What two accounting problems result from the nature of the defined benefit pension plan? Why do these problems arise?
b. How should Carson determine the service cost component of the net pension cost?
c. How should Carson determine the interest cost component of the net pension cost?
d. How should Carson determine the actual return on plan assets component of the net pension cost?

- ### Case 12-6

Postretirement benefits other than pensions (OPEBs) are similar to defined benefit pension plans in some respects and different in others.

Required:

a. Discuss the characteristics of OPEBs that make them different from defined benefit pension plans.
b. Discuss how the accounting for OPEBs differs from the accounting for defined benefit pension plans.
c. In what respects are OPEBs similar to defined benefit pension plans? Explain.
d. In what respects is the accounting for OPEBs similar to, or the same as, the accounting for defined benefit pension plans? Explain.

Recommended Additional Readings

Harper, Robert M., Jr., William G. Mister, and Jerry R. Strawser. "The Effect of Recognition versus Disclosure of Unfunded Postretirement Benefits on Lenders' Perceptions of Debt." *Accounting Horizons* (September 1991), pp. 50–56.

Langer, Russell, and Baruch Lev. "The FASB's Policy of Extended Adoption for New Standards: An Examination of FAS No. 87." *The Accounting Review* (July 1993), pp. 515–533.

Lucas, Timothy S., and Betsy Ann Hollowell. "Pension Accounting: The Liability Question." *Journal of Accountancy* (October 1981), pp. 57–67.

Mills, Robert H. "SFAS 87: An Improvement in Pension Reporting?" *CPA Journal* (July 1989), pp. 37, 38, 40–42.

Revsine, Lawrence. "Understanding Financial Accounting Standard 87." *Financial Analysts Journal* (January–February 1989), pp. 61–68.

Thomas, Paula B., and Larry E. Farmer. "OPEB: Improved Reporting or the Last Straw?" *Journal of Accountancy* (November 1990), pp. 102–104, 107, 109, 110, 112.

Wilbert, James R., and Kenneth E. Dakdduk. "The New FASB 106: How to Account for Postretirement Benefits." *Journal of Accountancy* (August 1991), pp. 36–41.

Wyatt, Arthur. "OPEB Costs: The FASB Establishes Accountability." *Accounting Horizons* (March 1990), pp. 108–110.

Bibliography

Abrams, Reuben W. "Accounting for the Cost of Pension Plans and Deferred Compensation Contracts." *New York CPA* (April 1970), pp. 300–307.

Brownler, E. Richard, and S. David Young. "Pension Accounting: A New Proposal." *The CPA Journal* (July 1985), pp. 28–34.

Cassell, Jules M., and Diana W. Kahn. "FASB Statement No. 35: Not Enough About the Future?" *Financial Executive* (December 1980), pp. 44–51.

Deaton, William C., and Jerry J. Weygandt. "Disclosures Related to Pension Plans." *Journal of Accountancy* (January 1975), pp. 44–51.

Deitrick, James W., and C. Wayne Alderman. "Pension Plans: What Companies Do—and Do Not—Disclose." *Management Accounting* (April 1980), pp. 24–29.

Dewhirst, John F. "A Conceptual Approach to Pension Accounting." *The Accounting Review* (April 1971), pp. 365–373.

Doley, Lane Alan. "The Valuations of Reported Pension Measures for Firms Sponsoring Defined Benefit Plans." *The Accounting Review* (April 1984), pp. 177–198.

Goldberg, Seymour. "Pension Planning and the CPA." *Journal of Accountancy* (May 1984), pp. 68–72.

Goldstein, Leo. "Unfunded Pension Liabilities May Be Dangerous to Corporate Health." *Management Accounting* (April 1980), pp. 20–22.

Grant, Edward B., and Thomas R. Weirich. "Current Developments in Pension Accounting." *The National Public Accountant* (July 1980), pp. 11–15.

Hicks, Ernest L. "Accounting for the Cost of Pension Plans," *Accounting Research Study No. 8.* New York: AICPA, 1965.

Kirk, Donald J. "Pension Accounting: Where the FASB Now Stands." *Journal of Accountancy* (June 1980), pp. 82–88.

Langenderfer, Harold Q. "Accrued Past-Service Pension Costs Should Be Capitalized." *New York CPA* (February 1971), pp. 137–143.

Lorensen, Leonard, and Paul Rosenfield. "Vested Benefits—A Company's Only Pension Liability." *Journal of Accountancy* (October 1983), pp. 64–76.

Ostuw, Richard. "How to Deal with Retiree Needs Under OPEP." *Financial Executive* (January/February 1989), pp. 37–40.

Philips, G. Edward. "Pension Liabilities and Assets. *The Accounting Review* (January 1968), pp. 10–17.

Schuchart, J. A., and W. L. Sanders, Jr. "Pension Fund Considerations." *Management Accounting* (March 1972), pp. 49–52.

Smith, Jack L. "Actuarial Cost Methods—Basics for CPA." *Journal of Accountancy* (February 1977), pp. 62–66.

Smith, Jack L. "Needed: Improved Pension Accounting and Reporting." *Management Accounting* (May 1978), pp. 43–46.

Stone, Mary C. "The Changing Picture for Pension Accounting." *The CPA Journal* (April 1983), pp. 32–42.

Stone, Mary, and Robert Ingram. "The Effect of Statement No. 87 on the Financial Reports of Early Adopters." *Accounting Horizons* (September 1988), pp. 48–61.

Walken, David M. "Accounting for Reversions from Pension Plans." *Journal of Accountancy* (February 1985), pp. 64–70.

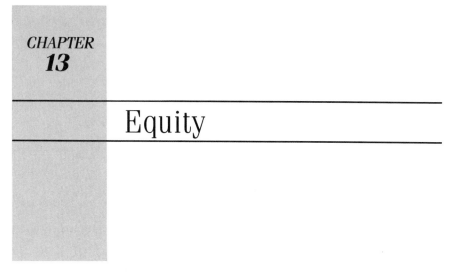

Equity

Equity is the basic risk capital of an enterprise. Equity capital has no guaranteed return and no timetable for the repayment of the capital investment. From the standpoint of enterprise stability and exposure to risk of insolvency, a basic characteristic of equity capital is that it is permanent and can be counted on to remain invested in good times as well as bad times. Consequently, equity funds can be most confidently invested in long-term assets and be exposed to the greatest risks.

The investor in the common stock of an enterprise must balance the existence of debt, which represents a risk of loss of investment, against the potential of high profits from financial leverage. The mix of debt and equity investments in a company is termed its *capital structure.* There has been considerable debate over the years over whether the cost of capital for an enterprise varies with different capital structures, that is, with different mixtures of debt and equity. Modigliani and Miller[1] found that the cost of capital of an enterprise is, except for the tax deductibility of interest, not affected by the mix of debt and equity. This is true, they asserted, because each individual stockholder can inject his or her own blend of risk into the total investment position.

In this chapter we take the position that the degree of risk of an enterprise as perceived by a potential investor is a given. In the following paragraphs we will review some theories of equity, and discuss the theoretical issues associated with recording the various components of equity.

---

[1] F. Modigliani and M. Miller, "Cost of Capital, Corporation Finance and the Theory of Investment," *American Economic Review* (June 1958), pp. 261–297.

Theories of Equity

In Chapter 9, two theories of equity, the proprietary theory and the entity theory, were introduced. These and several other theories may provide a frame of reference for the presentation of financial statements. When viewing the applicability of the various theories of equity, it is important to keep in mind that the purpose of a theory is to provide a rationale or explanation for some action. The proprietary theory gained prominence because the interests of the owner(s) were seen as the guiding force in the preparation of financial statements. However, as the interests of other users became more significant, accountants made changes in financial report formats without adopting a particular equity theory.

In the following discussion, the student should keep in mind that the adoption of a particular theory could influence a number of accounting and reporting procedures. Also note that the theories represent a point of view toward the firm for accounting purposes that is not necessarily the same as the legal view of the firm.

Proprietary Theory

According to the proprietary theory, the firm is owned by some specified person or group. The ownership interest may be represented by a sole proprietor, a partnership, or by a number of stockholders. The assets of the firm belong to these owners and any liabilities of the firm are also the owners' liabilities. Revenues received by the firm immediately increase the owner's net interest in the firm and, likewise, all expenses incurred by the firm immediately decrease the net proprietary interest in the firm. This theory holds that all profits or losses immediately become the property of the owners, and not the firm, whether or not they are distributed. Therefore, the firm exists simply to provide the means to carry on transactions for the owners and the net worth or equity section of the balance sheet should be viewed as

$$\text{assets} - \text{liabilities} = \text{proprietorship}$$

Additionally, under the proprietary theory, financial reporting is based on the premise that the owner is the primary focus of the financial statements. The proprietary theory is particularly applicable to sole proprietorships where the owner is the decision maker. When the form of the enterprise becomes more complex, and the ownership and management become separated, this theory becomes less acceptable. An attempt has been made to retain the concepts of the proprietary theory in the corporate situation; however, many accountants have asserted that it cannot meet the requirements of the corporate form of organization.[2] Nevertheless, we still find significant accounting policies that can be justified only through the acceptance of the proprietary theory. For example, the calculation and presentation of earnings-per-share

---

[2] See, for example, William J. Vatter, "Corporate Stock Equities," Part 1, in *Modern Accounting Theory*, Morton Backer, ed. (Englewood Cliffs, N.J.: Prentice-Hall, 1966), p. 251.

figures is relevant only if we assume that those earnings belong to the share-holders prior to the declaration of dividends.

Entity Theory

The rise of the corporate form of organization, which was (1) accompanied by the separation of ownership and management, (2) limited the liability of owners, and (3) resulted in the legal definition of a corporation as a person, encouraged the evolution of new theories of ownership. Among the first of these theories was the entity theory, which is expressed as

$$\text{assets} = \text{equities}$$

The entity theory, like the proprietary theory, is a point of view toward the firm and the people concerned with its operation. This viewpoint places the firm, and not the owners, at the center of interest for accounting and financial reporting purposes. The essence of the entity theory is that creditors as well as stockholders contribute resources to the firm, and the firm exists as a separate and distinct entity apart from these groups. The assets and liabilities belong to the firm and not the owners. As revenue is received, it becomes the property of the entity, and expenses incurred are obligations of the entity. Any profits are the property of the entity and accrue to the stockholders only when a dividend is declared. Under this theory all the items on the right-hand side of the balance sheet, except retained earnings that belong to the firm, are viewed as claims against the assets of the firm, and individual items are distinguished by the nature of their claims. Some items are identified as creditor claims and others as owner claims; but, nevertheless, they are claims against the firm as a separate entity.

Goldberg has illustrated the difference between the proprietary and entity theories by way of an example involving a small child in possession of his or her first unit of monetary exchange.

> *Suppose that a small child is given, say £1, with which he can do whatever he likes. If (as is most likely) he is not familiar with the idea of ownership, he will think (i) "Here is £1"; and (ii) "This £1 is mine." These thoughts comprise the essence of the proprietary viewpoint and of double entry, for if the child were a born accountant, he would express the same thoughts as (i) "There exists an asset," and (ii) "I have a proprietary interest in that asset." That is to say, the £1 is regarded from two aspects: (1) as something that exists—an asset; and (ii) as belonging to somebody—my asset. Suppose further that, until the child can decide what he will do with the £1 he puts it in a money box. The entity theory can be introduced here by personalizing the money box—it involves adopting the point of view that the money box now has the £1 and owes £1 to the child.*[3]

---

[3] Louis Goldberg, *An Inquiry into the Nature of Accounting* (American Accounting Association, Monograph No. 7, 1963), p. 126.

Imbedded in this illustration is the fundamental distinction between the proprietary and entity theories—perceptions of the right-hand side of the balance sheet. Individuals who view net income as accruing only to owners will favor the proprietary approach, whereas those taking a broader view of the nature of the beneficiaries of income will favor the entity approach.

Entity theory makes no distinction between debt and equity. Both are considered sources of capital, and the operations of the firm are not affected by the amount of debt relative to equity.[4] Thus, under entity theory debt-to-equity ratios would not provide relevant information for investor decision making.[5] Yet present accounting practice makes a sharp distinction between debt and equity. Moreover, the amount of debt relative to equity is generally considered an important indicator of risk.[6] Such a distinction implies that accountants must separately identify and classify liabilities from equities. Nevertheless, complex financial instruments such as convertible bonds may comprise debt and equity components. Due to the problems associated with identifying and measuring the fundamental components of these financial instruments, the FASB was prompted to issue a discussion memorandum (DM), "Distinguishing between Liability and Equity Instruments and Accounting for Instruments with the Characteristics of Both."[7] The DM asks whether the sharp distinction should be continued. In other words, should accounting follow entity theory or should accounting attempt to identify and separately report the elements of debt and equity? If the distinction is to continue, decisions must be made regarding the nature of fundamental financial instruments and how to appropriately measure them.

Other Theoretical Approaches

Several authors have noted inadequacies in the entity and proprietary approaches and have developed additional viewpoints or perspectives from which to rationalize the recording and reporting of accounting information. The most notable of these new viewpoints are the fund theory, the commander theory, the enterprise theory, and the residual equity theory. Each of these theories will be considered separately.

Fund Theory
Vatter attacks the proprietary theory as too simplistic for modern corporate reporting.[8] He sees no logical basis for viewing the corporation as a person in the legal sense and argues that the corporation is the people it represents.

---

[4] W. A. Paton, *Accounting Theory* (New York: The Roland Press, 1922).

[5] M. W. Clark, "Entity Theory, Modern Capital Structure Theory, and the Distinction Between Debt and Equity," *Accounting Horizons* (September 1993), pp. 14–31.

[6] Ibid.

[7] Financial Accounting Standards Board, *Discussion Memorandum: Distinguishing between Liability and Equity Instruments and Accounting for Instruments with Characteristics of Both* (Stamford, Conn.: FASB, 1990).

[8] William J. Vatter, *The Fund Theory of Accounting and Its Implications for Financial Reports* (Chicago, Ill.: University of Chicago Press, 1947).

The fund theory attempts to abandon the personal relationship advocated by the proprietary theory and the personalization of the firm advocated by the entity theory. Under the fund approach, the measurement of net income plays a role secondary to satisfying the special interests of management, social control agencies (e.g., government agencies), and the overall process of credit extension and investment. The fund theory is expressed by the following equation:

$$\text{assets} = \text{restrictions on assets}$$

This theory explains the financial recording of an organization in terms of three features, as follows:

1. *Fund*   An area of attention defined by the activities and operations surrounding any one set of accounting records, and for which a self-balancing set of accounts is created.
2. *Assets*   Economic services and potentials.
3. *Restrictions*   Limitations on the use of assets.

These features are applied to each homogeneous set of activities and functions within the organization, thus providing a separate accounting for each area of economic concern.

The fund theory has not gained general acceptance in financial accounting; it is more suitable to governmental accounting. The fund theory is a somewhat radical change from current practices and the added volume of bookkeeping it would require has inhibited its adoption. The use of the fund approach in government accounting is principally attributed to the legal restrictions typically imposed on each fund, thus requiring a separate accounting for each.

Commander Theory

The entity theory adopts the point of view of the business entity, whereas the proprietary theory takes the viewpoint of the proprietor. But, asks Goldberg, "What of the point of view of the managers, that is, of the activity force in a . . . company?"[9] Goldberg argues that this question is of major importance because of the divergent self-interested viewpoints of owners and managers in large-scale corporations. In fact, so relevant is this divergence, "that in recent years a whole new field of study, going under the name of 'management accounting' and an ancillary literature have grown up, in which the emphasis is laid upon accountants for information to enable them (the managers) to carry out their function of control of property with a view to its increase."[10]

The commander approach is offered as a replacement for the proprietary and entity theories because it is argued that the goals of the manager (commander) are at least equally important to those of the proprietor or entity.

[9] Goldberg, op. cit., p. 152.

[10] Ibid., p. 152.

The proprietary, entity, and fund approaches emphasize persons, personalization, and funds, respectively, but the commander theory emphasizes control. Everyone who has resources to deploy is viewed as a commander.

The commander theory, unlike the proprietary, entity, and fund approaches, has applicability to all organizational forms (i.e., sole proprietorship, partnership, and corporation). The form of organization does not negate the applicability of the commander view because the commander can take on more than one identity in any organization. In sole proprietorships or partnerships, the proprietors or partners are both owners and commanders. Under the corporate form, both the managers and stockholders are commanders in that they each maintain some control over resources (i.e., managers control the enterprise resources and stockholders control returns on investment emerging from the enterprise).

The commander theory argues that the notion of control is broad enough to encompass all relevant parties to the exclusion of none. The function of accounting, then, takes on an element of stewardship, and the question of to whom resource increments flow is not relevant. Rather, the relevant factor is how the commander allocates resources to the benefit of all parties. Responsibility accounting is consistent with the commander theory. Responsibility accounting identifies the revenues and costs that are under the control of various "commanders" within the organization, and financial statements are organized to highlight the contributions of each level of control to enterprise profits. The commander theory is not on the surface a radical move from current accounting practices, and it has generated little reaction in accounting circles.

Enterprise Theory

Under the enterprise theory, the business unit, most notably those listed on national or regional stock exchanges, is viewed as a social institution, composed of capital contributors having "a common purpose or purposes and, to a certain extent, roles of common action."[11] Management within this framework essentially maintains an arm's-length relationship with owners and has as its primary responsibilities (1) the distribution of adequate dividends and (2) the maintenance of friendly terms with employees, consumers, and government units. Because this theory applies only to large nationally or regionally traded issues, it is generally considered to have only minor impact on accounting theory, or the development of accounting principles and practices.

Residual Equity Theory

Residual equity is defined by Staubus as "the equitable interest in organization assets which will absorb the effect upon those assets of any economic event that no interested party has specifically agreed to."[12] Here, the common share-

[11] Waino Soujanen, "Enterprise Theory and Corporate Balance Sheets," *The Accounting Review* (January 1958), p. 56.

[12] George J. Staubus, "The Residual Equity Point of View in Accounting," *The Accounting Review* (January 1959), p. 3.

holders hold the residual equity in the enterprise by virtue of having the final claim on income, yet they are the first to be charged for losses. The residual equity holders are vital to the firm's existence in that they are clearly the highest risk takers and provide a substantial volume of capital during the firm's developmental stage.

The residual equity theory is formulated as

$$\text{assets} - \text{specific equities} = \text{residual equities}$$

Under this approach, the residual of assets, net of the claim of specific equity holders (creditors and preferred stockholders), accrue to residual owners. In this framework, the role of financial reporting is to provide prospective and current residual owners with information regarding enterprise resource flows so that they can assess the value of their residual claim. Management is in effect a trustee responsible for maximizing the wealth of residual equity holders. Income accrues to the residual owners after the claims of specific equity holders are met. Thus, the income to specific equity holders, including interest on debt and dividends to preferred stockholders, would be deducted in arriving at residual net income. This theory is consistent with models that are formulated in the finance literature,[13] with current financial statement presentation of earnings per share, and with the conceptual framework's emphasis on the relevance of projecting cash flows. Again, as with the fund, commander, and enterprise theories, the residual equity approach has gained little attention in financial accounting.

Definition of Equity

Statement of Financial Accounting Concepts (SFAC) No. 6 defines equity as a residual interest. However, the residual interest described therein is not equivalent to residual equity defined above. Rather, it is the difference between assets and liabilities.[14] Hence, under *SFAC No. 6*, the definition and characteristics of equity hinge on the definitions and characteristics of assets and liabilities. *SFAC No. 6* defines equity in total, but does not define the attributes of the elements of equity. It does note that enterprises may have more than one class of equity, such as common stock and preferred stock. Equity is defined as the difference between assets and liabilities, and liabilities are described as embodying an obligation to transfer assets or provide services to another entity in the future as the result of some prior transaction or event. Consequently, the distinguishing feature between liabilities and equities is that equities do not obligate the entity to transfer future resources or provide services. There is no obligation to distribute resources to equity holders until declared by the board of directors or unless the entity is liquidated.

---

[13] Clark, op. cit.

[14] Financial Accounting Standards Board, *Statement of Financial Accounting Concepts No. 6,* "Elements of Financial Statements" (Stamford, Conn.: FASB, 1985), par. 60.

Under the *SFAC No. 6* definition, if a financial instrument issued by the enterprise does not fit the definition of a liability, then it must be an equity instrument. The DM questions whether the definition of equity should continue to be governed by the definition of liabilities or whether it should be separately defined. If equity were independently defined, then the liabilities might be the residual outcome of identifying assets and equity. In this case, the equation describing the relationship between financial statement elements could be stated as

$$\text{assets} - \text{equity} = \text{liabilities}$$

Alternatively, equity might be defined as an absolute residual, as under the residual equity theory, and a third category added to the balance sheet—"quasi-equity." The quasi-equity category might include items such as preferred stock or minority interest. This category would allow accountants to retain the definition of liabilities and treat the quasi-equity category as a residual. If this form of financial statement presentation should emerge, then other issues would have to be addressed, such as the definition of earnings. For example, as stated before, a residual equity definition of equity would imply that preferred dividends would be subtracted in the determination of net income.

Recording Equity

The American economy is characterized by three forms of business organization: sole proprietorships, partnerships, and corporations. Although the number of sole proprietorships greatly exceeds the number of partnerships and corporations in the United States, the greatest amount of economic activity is carried out by corporations. This is due to the efficiency of corporate production and distribution systems. Several advantages accrue to the corporate form and help to explain its emergence. Among these are

1. *Limited liability*   Stockholders are liable only for the amount of their original investment (unless that investment is less than the par value of the shares). Creditors may not look to the assets of individual owners for debt repayments in the event of a liquidation as is possible in the case of sole proprietorships and partnerships.
2. *Continuity*   The corporation's life is not affected by the death or resignation of owners.
3. *Investment liquidity*   Corporate shares may be freely exchanged on the open market. Many shares are listed on national security exchanges, which improves their marketability.
4. *Variety of ownership interest*   Shares of corporate stock usually contain four basic rights: the right to vote for members of the board of directors of the corporation and thereby participate in management, the right to receive dividends, the right to receive assets on the liquidation of the corporation,

and the preemptive right to purchase additional shares in the same proportion to current ownership interest if new issues of stock are marketed. Any
or all of these rights may be sacrificed by shareholders in return for special
privileges. This results in an additional class of stock termed *preferred stock,*
which may have either or both of the following features:

a. Preference as to dividends.
b. Preference as to assets in liquidation.

The corporate form of business organization allows management specialists to be employed. The owners thereby gain an expertise not normally available in sole proprietorships or partnerships. Evidence of the extent of this
advantage can be found in the growth of business schools in the major universities. A large percentage of the students in these programs are in training to
obtain employment in a large corporation.

As noted earlier, two major types of stock may be found in any corporation, preferred stock and common stock. Preferred stockholders give up one
or more of the rights usually accruing to stockholders for preference as to
dividends or to assets in liquidation. Common stockholders retain these rights
and have a residual claim on both the earnings and assets in liquidation. A
corporation's capital section usually is subdivided into several components. In
addition to disclosing the legal claims ownership groups have against the assets
of the corporation, the separation of the components of capital gives information on the sources of capital, dividend requirements, and priorities in liquidation.

The components of the capital section are classified by source in the following manner:

I. Paid-in capital (contributed capital)
   A. Legal capital-par, stated value, or entire proceeds if no par or stated
      value accompanies the stock issue
   B. Additional paid-in capital—amounts received in excess of par or stated
      value
II. Unrealized capital
III. Earned capital
   A. Appropriated
   B. Unappropriated

Each of these components is discussed in further detail in the following
sections.

Paid-in Capital

The limited liability advantage of the corporate form of business organization
provides that creditors may look only to the assets of the corporation to satisfy
their claims. This factor has caused various states to enact laws that attempt
to protect creditors and inform them of the true nature of the assets and
liabilities of individual corporations. Additionally, state laws generally protect
creditors by establishing the concept of *legal capital*—the amount of net assets

that cannot be distributed to stockholders. These laws vary from state to state, but the par or stated value of the outstanding shares generally constitutes a corporation's legal capital. State laws generally require legal capital to be reported separately from the total amount invested. As a result, ownership interests are classified as capital stock or additional paid-in capital in excess of par value. The classification *additional paid-in capital* includes all amounts originally received for shares of stock in excess of par or stated value. In unusual cases, stock may be sold for less than par value. In the event the corporation is liquidated, the holders of securities acquired for less than their par value could be required to pay the corporation the amount of the difference between the original investment and par value in order to protect creditors.

Stock Subscriptions

Large corporations frequently sell entire issues of stock to a group of investment advisors, or *underwriters*, who then attempt to resell the shares to the public. The corporation is thereby relieved of the responsibility of selling and recording the individual share transactions over long periods of time. The underwriters keep a record of the new shareholders and incur the selling costs. However, when the corporation is unable or unwilling to sell stock through underwriters, records must be kept of each transaction with the new shareholders.

When shares of stock are sold by a corporation directly to individuals, it is a common occurrence for individuals to contract to purchase shares on an installment basis. These individuals, termed *subscribers*, usually receive the rights of ownership when they contract to purchase the shares on subscription but do not actually receive any shares until payment for all subscribed shares has been received. That is, each installment received is viewed as a percentage payment on each contracted share, and no shares are issued until all are paid in full. In some states, capital stock subscribed is viewed as a part of legal capital even though the shares are not outstanding. In other states, the subscribed shares are included in legal capital only after they have been fully paid and issued.

When a stock subscription takes place, the corporation has a legally enforceable claim against the subscribers for the balance due on the subscriptions. Therefore, receivables resulting from stock subscriptions embody probable future economic benefits and fit the definition of assets. However, present practice typically follows SEC Regulation S-X, which requires stock subscriptions receivable to be disclosed in stockholders' equity. Proponents of this treatment argue that the enterprise's recourse if the receivable is not collected is not to issue the stock. Moreover, the enterprise may not pursue collection and therefore these receivables are sufficiently uncertain to qualify them as recognizable assets. Also, it is argued that stock subscriptions receivable are different from other receivables because they do not result from transferring assets or providing services.

Special Features

Securities other than common stock may contain features that allow (1) the holders of these securities to become common stockholders, (2) the corporation to reacquire these securities, or (3) the rate of return on the securities to fluctuate. Among these features are convertible provisions, call provisions, cumulative provisions, participating provisions, and redemption provisions. These provisions are found most frequently on preferred stock, but some of them may also be found on long-term debt, as discussed in Chapter 9.

Conversion   A convertible feature is included on a preferred stock issue to make it more attractive to potential investors. Usually, a conversion feature is attached to allow the corporation to sell its preferred shares at a relatively lower dividend rate than is found on other securities with the same degree of risk. The conversion rate is normally set above the current relationship of the market value of the common share to the market value of the preferred convertible shares. For example, if the corporation's common stock is selling at $10 per share and the preferred stock has a selling price of $100 per share, the conversion rate might be set at eight shares of common for one preferred. All other things being equal, it would appear to be profitable for the preferred shareholders to convert to common when the value of the common shares rises above $12.50 per share. However, it is normal for the market price of the preferred shares to fluctuate in proportion to the market price of the common; therefore, an individual would not be able to make a profit by simply converting one type of security to another. Convertible stock is attractive to investors because the exchange ratio tends to tie the market price of the preferred stock to the market price of the common stock.

When preferred stock is converted to common stock, the proper accounting treatment is to transfer the par value of the preferred, plus a proportionate share of any additional paid-in capital on the preferred stock, to common stock. If this amount differs from the par or stated value of common stock, it is apportioned between par or stated value and additional paid-in capital on common stock.

If a residual equity approach were adopted to define the components of equity, then a determination would need to be made regarding the conversion feature. The recognition and measurement problems associated with separate recognition of the conversion feature of preferred stock would be similar to those that are associated with convertible bonds (see Chapter 9 for a discussion of these recognition and measurement issues). However, even if current practice is retained and preferred stock continues to be disclosed as an element of stockholders' equity, separate disclosure of the conversion feature may have information content.[15]

Call Provisions   Call provisions allow the corporation to reacquire preferred stock at some predetermined amount. Call provisions are included on securities by corporations because of uncertain future conditions. Current conditions dictate the return on investment that will be attractive to potential investors, but conditions may change so that a lower return on investment may be offered by the corporation in the future. Additionally, market conditions may make it necessary to promise a certain debt-equity relationship at the time of

---

[15] Clark, op. cit.

issue. Call provisions allow the corporation to take advantage of future favorable conditions and indicate how the securities may be retired. The existence of a call price tends to set an upward limit on the market price of nonconvertible securities, since investors will not normally be inclined to purchase shares that could be recalled momentarily at a lower price.

Cumulative Provisions   Preferred shareholders normally have a preference as to dividends. That is, no common dividends may be paid in any one year until all required preferred dividends for that year are paid. Corporations usually also include added protection for preferred shareholders in the form of a cumulative provision. This provision states that if all or any part of the stated preferred dividend is not paid in any one year, the unpaid portion accumulates and must be paid in subsequent years before any dividend can be paid on common stock. Any unpaid dividend on cumulative preferred stock constitutes a dividend in arrears and should be disclosed on the financial statements even though it is not a liability until actually declared by the board of directors of the corporation. Dividends in arrears are important in predicting future cash flows and as an indicator of financial flexibility and liquidity.

Participating Provisions   Participating provisions allow preferred stockholders to share dividends in excess of normal returns with common shareholders. For example, a participating provision might indicate that preferred shares are to participate in dividends on a 1:1 basis with common stock on all dividends in excess of $5 per share. This provision requires that any payments of more than $5 per share to the common stockholder also be made on a dollar-for-dollar basis to each share of preferred.

Redemption Provision   A redemption provision indicates that the preferred stock may be exchanged by the shareholder for cash in the future. The redemption provision may include a mandatory maturity date or specify a redemption price. Redeemable preferred stock has several of the debt characteristics discussed earlier, in Chapter 9. In fact, the Securities and Exchange Commission requires separate disclosure of such shares in its reports because of their special nature. At present the FASB does not require similar treatment, although footnote disclosure is required.

Stock Options and Warrants

Many corporations have agreements with employees and security holders termed stock options and stock warrants that may result in the issuance of additional shares of common stock. Stock option and stock warrant agreements can significantly affect the amount of common stock outstanding, and the method of accounting for them should be carefully evaluated.

Stock Options   Executive stock option plans have become an important element of the compensation package for corporate officers over the years. These plans allow corporate officials to purchase a stated number of shares of stock at an established price for some predetermined period. In the past, stock option plans were especially advantageous because of income tax regulations that taxed proceeds at the capital gains rate when the securities purchased under stock option plans were sold. Current tax laws have substantially reduced the tax advantage of stock options; nevertheless, they are still used by many corporations as a part of the total compensation package.

Stock option plans are most valuable when the option price is lower than the market price. For this reason, stock option plans are viewed as an incentive that influences the holders of options to try to increase corporate profits, and thereby increase the value of the company's common shares on the stock market. These plans have a potentially dilutive effect on other shareholders, since exercising options results in additional stockholder claims against the same amount of income. The relative effects of this potential dilution versus the effect of management's incentive to increase profits should be examined by current and potential shareholders. Such measurements are, of course, quite difficult.

In 1972 the Accounting Principles Board reviewed the issue of accounting for stock options and issued *APB Opinion No. 25,* "Accounting for Stock Issued to Employees." [16] Two types of plans were defined, noncompensatory and compensatory.

A *noncompensatory stock option plan* was defined as one not primarily designed as a method of compensation, but rather as a source of additional capital or of more widespread ownership among employees. Four essential characteristics of noncompensatory plans were defined: (1) the participation of all full-time employees, (2) the offering of stock on an equal basis or as a uniform percentage of salary to all employees, (3) a limited time for exercise of the option, and (4) a discount from market price that would not differ from a reasonable offer to stockholders. When these conditions are met, the plan does not discriminate in favor of company employees; thus, the corporation is not required to record any compensation expense.

Compensatory stock option plans, on the other hand, give employees an option that is not offered to all employees or to stockholders. These plans involve the recording of an expense, and the timing of the measurement of this expense can greatly affect its impact on financial reports. The six possible measurement dates to determine the amount of compensation expense associated with a stock option plan originally discussed in *ARB No. 43* were reviewed in Appendix B to *APB Opinion No. 25.* These dates are

1. The date of the adoption of an option plan.
2. The date on which an option is granted to a specific individual.
3. The date on which the grantee has performed any conditions precedent to exercise of the option.
4. The date on which the grantee may first exercise the option.
5. The date on which the option is exercised by the grantee.
6. The date on which the grantee disposes of the stock acquired. [17]

---

[16] *Accounting Principles Board Opinion No. 25,* "Accounting for Stock Issued to Employees" (New York: AICPA, 1972).

[17] Ibid., par. 6.

The APB concluded that compensation expense should be measured on the first date on which both the number of shares to be received by a particular individual and the option price are known. In most cases, this will be the date on which the option is granted to a specific individual. The compensation expense is equal to the difference between the market price of the stock on the measurement date and the price the employee is required to pay.

The determination of the measurement date is of primary importance for compensatory stock option plans. In some plans, the date of the grant is the measurement date and, therefore, the amount of compensation is known. In other plans the measurement date is later than the date of the grant and the annual compensation expense must be estimated.

If the date of the grant and the measurement date are the same, deferred compensation and common stock options are established for the total amount of compensation cost. The deferred compensation cost is offset against the common stock options in the stockholders' equity section and amortized to expense over the period of benefit. In the event the measurement date is later than the date of the grant, total compensation cost cannot be measured on the date of the grant. Therefore, annual compensation expense is estimated and common stock options are recorded during each period until the measurement date is reached.

Occasionally, available stock options may not be exercised. In the event an option is not exercised prior to the expiration date, previously recognized compensation expense is not affected; however, on the expiration date, the value of any previously recorded common stock options is transferred to additional paid-in capital.

The rationale for the use of the *APB Opinion No. 25* measurement date is that it coincides with the date that the corporation commits to a specified number of shares, and because the shares could have been sold in the market rather than set aside for the employees, the difference between market value of those shares and the option price on the date committed represents the opportunity cost associated with the options and thus the total compensation. An alternative argument, in favor of the *APB Opinion No. 25* measurement date, relies on labor economic theory. From the employee's perspective, the employees contract for services based on the amount of marginal revenue product they provide. Accordingly, the employee accepts the options in lieu of current wages. Consequently, the difference between the current market price and the option of the shares represents employee compensation.

Many accountants believe that the established procedures for recognizing common stock options result in understated income statement and balance sheet valuations. It should be noted that employees accepting stock options are accepting an investment in the firm in lieu of additional cash compensation. The ultimate value of this investment lies somewhere between zero— when the market price never exceeds the option price—and a very large return—when the market price rises substantially above the option price. Some accountants have advocated recording the value of the option at the expected value that lies between these two extremes; however, this procedure would result in a more subjective valuation. The recording and measurement of common stock option plans will undoubtedly continue to be a controversial issue in the near future. In addition, recent innovations utilizing leverage and preferred stock have added to the complexity of employee stock option plans. The article at the end of this chapter by Deming and Wise reviews these issues in greater detail.

Stock Warrants   Stock warrants are certificates that allow holders to acquire shares of stock at certain prices within stated periods. These certificates are generally issued under one of two conditions:

1. As evidence of the *preemptive right* of current shareholders to purchase additional shares of common stock from new stock issues in proportion to their current ownership percentage.

2. As an inducement originally attached to debt or preferred shares to increase the marketability of these securities.

Under current practice, the accounting for the preemptive right of existing shareholders creates no particular problem. These warrants are not recorded except as memoranda in the formal accounting records. In the event warrants of this type are exercised, the value of the shares of stock issued is measured at the amount of cash exchanged.

Detachable warrants attached to other securities require a separate valuation because they may be traded on the open market. The amount to be attributed to these types of warrants depends on their value in the securities market. Their value is measured by determining the percentage relationship of the price of the warrant to the total market price of the security and warrant, and applying this percentage to the proceeds of the security issue. This procedure should be followed whether the warrants are associated with bonds or preferred stock.

In *APB Opinion No. 14,* the Accounting Principles Board supported this approach when it stated,

> The Board is of the opinion that the portion of the proceeds of debt securities issued with detachable stock purchase warrants which is applicable to the warrants should be accounted for as paid-in capital. The allocation should be based on the relative fair value of the two securities at the time of issuance.[18]

If the warrants are exercised, their value will be added to the cash received to arrive at the carrying value of the common stock. In the event the warrants are not exercised within the designated period, the portion of the cost of the security allocated to the warrants will remain on the books as paid-in capital.

The Equity/Liability Question

The DM on distinguishing between debt and equity questions whether financial option contracts that obligate the enterprise to issue its own stock are liabilities or equity. In present practice, these contracts are treated as equity.

---

[18]*Accounting Principles Board Opinion No. 14,* "Accounting for Convertible Debt and Debt Issued with Stock Purchase Warrants" (New York: AICPA, 1969), par. 16.

This practice implies that exercise of an option involves a nonreciprocal transfer wherein the issuing enterprise receives something of value (e.g., employee services), but gives up nothing of value in return. Therefore, financial option contracts that do not result in the eventual payment of assets or the performance of services do not qualify as liabilities. Moreover, unlike debt securities, the value of options written on an enterprise's own stock is a function of the market price of the underlying common stock.

Alternatively, financial option contracts can be viewed as obligations to issue stock conditional upon exercise of the holder. They give the holder the right to exchange financial instruments on specified terms. The shares issued represent compensation for the cash received. Because the shares could have been sold at market value, they are issued to the option holder in lieu of cash. The obligation to make the exchange may be satisfied at any time by buying the option at the current market price. Financial option contracts entail a contractual obligation of the issuing corporation to deliver financial instruments upon exercise on potentially unfavorable terms to preexisting common stockholders. At exercise the corporation receives less cash than it would if the stock issues were sold at the current market price. Consequently, the decision of the issuer to allow exercise to occur results in a loss. The loss is an opportunity cost, which "is financed by diluting the preexisting stockholders' wealth."[19] That is, the option holders profit at the expense of preexisting stockholders. Therefore, they are not acting in the role of owners.

Unrealized Capital

Unrealized capital arises from events not connected with the issuance of stock or the normal profit-directed operations of the company. Unrealized capital results from the need to recognize assets or changes in value of other balance sheet items that have been excluded from the components of income by an authoritative body. The recognition issues for these items are discussed elsewhere in the text. The major examples of unrealized capital are (1) unrealized gains and losses on investments in debt and equity securities classified as available for sale securities (discussed in Chapter 8) and (2) unrealized gains and losses resulting from the translation of certain investments in foreign subsidiaries (discussed in Chapter 17). Although these items are not included in earnings under current GAAP, they are defined in *SFAC No. 6* as components of comprehensive income.

Retained Earnings

Legal restrictions in most states allow corporations to pay dividends only when there are accumulated, undistributed earnings. These restrictions have resulted in the division of owners' equity into the paid-in capital and earned capital sections. Although some states allow dividends from paid-in capital in the

---

[19] FASB, op. cit., par. 134.

event of deficits, corporate managements generally do not wish to deplete capital, and distributions of this type are rare.

Retained earnings represent the accumulated net profits of a corporation that have not been distributed as dividends. It also should be noted that accumulated retained earnings do not necessarily mean that a corporation has the cash available with which to pay dividends. Accumulated earnings allow corporations to distribute dividends; the actual cash funds to pay these dividends must be available or acquired from other sources.

In many cases the retained earnings balance disclosed on the financial statements is divided into appropriated and unappropriated sections. Appropriated retained earnings comprise that portion of retained earnings that are not available to distribute as earnings. Appropriations may arise from legal restrictions, contractual restrictions, or internal decisions. However, an appropriation does not provide the funds with which to accomplish stated objectives, and it can be argued that these disclosures might be just as effective as footnotes.

Stock Dividends

As noted previously, corporations may have accumulated earnings but not have the funds available to distribute these earnings as cash dividends to stockholders. In such cases, the company may elect to distribute some of its own shares of stock as dividends to current stockholders. Distributions of this type are termed *stock dividends.* When stock dividends are minor, relative to the total number of shares outstanding, retained earnings is reduced by the market value of the shares distributed. Capital stock and additional paid-in capital are increased by the par value of the shares and any excess, respectively. In theory, a relatively small stock dividend will not adversely affect the previously established market value of the stock. The rationale behind stock dividend distributions is that the stockholders will receive additional shares with the same value per share as those previously held. Nevertheless, stock dividends are not income to the recipients. They represent no distribution of corporate assets to the owners and are simply a reclassification of ownership interests.

Stock Splits

A procedure somewhat similar to stock dividends, but with a different purpose, is a *stock split.* The most economical method of purchasing and selling stock in the stock market is in blocks of 100 shares, and this practice affects the marketability of the stock. The higher the price of an individual share of stock, the fewer are the number of people able to purchase the stock in blocks of 100. For this reason many corporations wish to maintain the price of their stock within certain ranges. When the price climbs above that range, the firm may decide to issue additional shares to all existing stockholders (or split the stock). In a stock split each stockholder receives a stated multiple of the number of shares currently held (usually 2 or 3 for 1), which lowers the market price per share. In theory, this lower price should be calculated by dividing the current price by the multiple of shares in the split, but intervening variables in the marketplace frequently affect prices simultaneously. A stock split does not cause any change in the stockholder's equity section except to increase the number of actual shares outstanding and reduce the par or stated value per share. No additional values are assigned to the shares of stock issued in a stock split because no distribution of assets or reclassification of ownership interests occurs.

A question sometimes arises as to whether a stock dividend is in actuality a stock split and should be treated accordingly. In a stock dividend, no material change in the market price of the shares is anticipated, whereas stock splits are undertaken specifically to change the market price of the shares. A large stock dividend can cause market prices to decline regardless of the terminology attached to the distribution. A rule of thumb is that if a stock dividend is at least 20 to 25 percent of the outstanding shares, the distribution should be recorded in a manner similar to a stock split. Stock distributions of this magnitude are termed *large stock dividends.* When large stock dividends are declared, standard practice is to capitalize an amount of retained earnings equal to the par value of the shares issued.

Treasury Stock

Capital may be reduced by formally repurchasing and canceling outstanding shares of stock; however, the corporation may informally reduce capital by acquiring shares on the open market without canceling them. These reacquired shares are termed *treasury stock.* Reacquisition of a company's own stock reduces both assets and stockholder equity and results in a legal restriction on retained earnings.

Two methods of accounting for treasury stock are found in current practice, the cost method and the par-value method. Under the *cost method,* the presumption is that the shares acquired will be resold and two events are assumed: (1) the purchase of the shares by the corporation and (2) the reissuance to a new stockholder. The reacquired shares are recorded at cost and this amount is disclosed as negative stockholders' equity by deducting it from total capital until the shares are resold. Because treasury stock transactions are transactions with owners, any difference between the acquisition price and the sales price is generally treated as an adjustment to paid-in capital (unless sufficient additional paid-in capital is not available to offset any "loss"; in such cases retained earnings is charged).

Under the *par-value method,* it is assumed that the corporation's relationship with the original stockholder is ended. The transaction is in-substance a retirement; hence, the shares are considered constructively retired. Therefore, legal capital and additional paid-in capital are reduced for the original issue price of the reacquired shares. Any difference between the original issue price and the reacquisition price is treated as an adjustment to additional paid-in capital (unless a sufficient balance is not available to offset a "loss" and retained earnings is charged). The par value of the reacquired shares is disclosed as a deduction from capital stock until the treasury shares are reissued.

The disclosure requirements for treasury stock in financial statements are not clearly defined by generally accepted accounting principles. For example, *APB Opinion No. 6* states:

> When a corporation's stock is acquired for purposes other than retirement (formal or constructive), or when ultimate disposition has not yet been decided, the cost of acquired stock may be shown separately, as a deduction from the total capital stock, capital surplus, and retained earnings, or may be accorded the accounting treatment appropriate for retired stock, or in some circumstances may be shown as an asset.[20]

This *Opinion*, in effect, allows for virtually any presentation of treasury stock desired by a corporation and disregards the reasons for the acquisition of the shares. Treasury stock is clearly not an asset because a company cannot own itself, and dividends are not paid on treasury shares. Similarly "gains" and "losses" on treasury stock transactions are not to be reported on the income statement becuase of the possibility of income manipulation, and because gains and losses cannot result from investments by owners or distributions to owners. The presentation of treasury shares on the financial statements should be reviewed by the FASB, and a presentation that more closely resembles the purpose of the acquisition of treasury shares should be required.

Quasi-Reorganizations

A corporation that suffers losses over an extended period of time may find it difficult to attract new capital. That is, debt holders and stockholders wish to receive a return on their investments, but a period of unprofitable operations may restrict the corporation's ability to offer interest and dividend payments. This is particularly true for stockholders who cannot receive dividends unless there is a positive retained earnings balance.

In some cases a corporate reorganization allowed under the provisions of state law may be attempted as an alternative to bankruptcy. These situations are termed *quasi-reorganizations*, and the company is given a fresh start by eliminating the deficit balance in retained earnings and writing down any overvalued assets. If a quasi-reorganization is undertaken, the corporation must clearly disclose its plan to the stockholders and receive their formal approval.

Modigliani and Miller[21] found that the actual payment of dividends did not affect the market value of an enterprise, whereas the ability to pay dividends did affect a firm's market value. A quasi-reorganization gives a firm the ability to pay dividends sooner than it would have been able to without a quasi-reorganization, and can positively affect the market value of a reorganized enterprise. Therefore, a firm that is unable to pay dividends because of

---

[20] *Accounting Principles Board Opinion No. 6*, "Status of Accounting Research Bulletins" (New York: AICPA, 1965), par. 12.

[21] F. Modigliani and M. Miller, "Cost of Capital, Corporation Finance and the Theory of Investment," *American Economic Review* (June 1958), pp. 261–297.

negative retained earnings will be able to raise new capital more economically if it first engages in a quasi-reorganization.

The steps involved in a quasi-reorganization are

1. Assets are written down to their fair market value against retained earnings or additional paid-in capital.

2. The retained earnings deficit is eliminated against additional paid-in capital or legal capital.

3. The zero retained earnings balance is dated and this date is retained until it loses its significance (typically 5 to 10 years).

Summary

There are a number of theoretical approaches to the recording and reporting of ownership equity. The proprietary and entity theories are the two major approaches, but accounting theorists have developed other viewpoints. These include the fund, commander, enterprise, and residual equity theories.

In addition to an understanding of the theoretical bases of equity reporting, it is important to understand the generally accepted accounting principles associated with the recording and reporting of equity. Preferred stock, common stock, additional paid-in capital, subscriptions, options, and warrants all require somewhat different accounting treatments.

Another aspect of equity reporting is the valuation of retained earnings. Although retained earnings exist in an accounting sense and allow the distribution of cash dividends, the actual funds for such distribution may not be available. In addition, stock dividends, stock splits, treasury stock, and quasi-reorganization all affect the reporting of equity securities, and each of these has its own reporting requirements.

In the following readings, Arthur Lorig reviews the theories of equity and examines the conflicts between the proprietary and entity theories in detail. In the second article, John Deming and Bret Wise discuss innovations in employee stock option plans and some recognition and measurement issues related to them.

Some Basic Concepts of Accounting and Their Implications

Arthur N. Lorig

Part I

There are certain basic over-all concepts regarding the fundamental nature of business and other organizations from which one reasons to arrive at some accounting decisions, including aspects of classification, measurement, and reporting. These concepts are variously termed theories, schools of thought, viewpoints, conventions, approaches, methods of viewing, and even doctrines. They are so different from one another that they lead to different conclusions or accounting decisions. This often results in controversy and sometimes confusion and misunderstanding.

Two of the concepts are widely held—the proprietary and the entity concepts. Other concepts or theories have been proposed as being improvements upon or more realistic than the two mentioned. These include the fund theory, the enterprise theory, and the residual equity theory. However, thus far they have so little recognition or support in accounting literature and practice that they will receive only slight consideration here.

Although the proprietary and entity theories are used widely, they often are not recognized as basic concepts. Many practicing accountants seem never to have even heard of them. In arriving at

conclusions in some areas of accounting, these accountants have not sought to establish a premise from which to reason, but instead have merely assumed one or the other of the two concepts without being aware of the assumptions. Furthermore, not being conscious of their assumptions, they sometimes unknowingly shift from one to the other in treating different problems of even the same business organization. Some of their conclusions and decisions as a result may be inconsistent and even incongruous, and at odds with decisions made by other accountants on the same problems.

There is a possibility that, if practicing accountants understood the concepts and could agree on one as being the more acceptable and therefore the one which should be adopted, the differences resulting from the use of divergent concepts might be eliminated. Perhaps pointing out the areas of conflicting thought which have resulted will generate enough interest on the part of the accountants to induce them to take some action to select one concept and adhere to it. It is that hope which initially prompted the study.

This paper is divided into two parts. Definitions and a somewhat general discussion of the concepts were found to be necessary and are taken up in Part I. The areas of conflict arising out of the existence of the differing concepts are disclosed in Part II. Readers who tend to be impatient with theoretical discussions may wish to turn to Part II first to see if the disclosures are of interest to them.

Should One Concept Suffice?

There is, of course, the question of whether it is possible to have one basic concept apply to all accounting entities, or whether the different types of such entities naturally require different concepts. For example, is the corporate structure so unlike that of a sole proprietorship that a different basic theory should be used? Do governments and other nonprofit organizations have unique characteristics which call for a basic concept different from one suited to a profit-making enterprise? Should a corporate family, a parent and subsidiary companies, adopt a special viewpoint for its accounting different from that of a single corporation?

First, let it be pointed out that a legal entity, such as a corporation, is not identical with an accounting entity. The latter is not in any way limited by legal provisions. An accounting entity is one for which a self-balancing group of accountants is provided (assuming double-entry accounting, which is generally considered essential to complete accounting). It may go well beyond corporate limits to include many related corporations. At the other extreme, it may involve only a small fund of a municipality with very few accounts, such as a special revenue or agency fund. To reason basically about an accounting entity from a legal limitation standpoint would be a mistake.

Disregarding, then, any legal differences, are there other factors which might necessitate different accounting approaches for various types of accounting entities? Writers on this subject think not. Even two writers with

views directly adverse in their preferences of a basis theory agree that one should suffice.[1] That also seems to be the belief of the chief advocate of the fund theory.[2] It was an assumption made at the start of this study, and no reasons were found later to abandon it.

Equities

It will be apparent as the discussion proceeds that the theories are concerned directly only with items which appear on the credit side of the balance sheet. These items are referred to collectively as equities. They are claims against, or equitable rights in, the assets (or the values reflected in the assets) reported on the debit side. Of necessity, consideration will be given to the two major types of equities—outside and inside, or creditors and proprietors—with their several subclassifications; and to the possibility of a third type, the equity of the accounting entity itself. While this last may not seem sensible at this point, the need for considering such a possibility will be shown later.

The equities are sometimes thought of as sources of capital, which in effect they are, with a few possible exceptions such as taxes payable and claims for damages. The sources are divided into short-term (current liabilities) and long-

[1] See George Husband, "The Corporate-Entity Fiction and Accounting Theory," *The Accounting Review,* September 1938, p. 242; and Walter G. Kell, *The Equities Concept and Its Application to Accounting Theory* (unpublished doctoral thesis), Graduate College of the University of Illinois, Urbana, Ill., 1952, p. 2.

[2] William J. Vatter, *The Fund Theory of Accounting and Its Implication for Financial Reports* (Chicago: The University of Chicago Press, 1947).

term (bonds, stocks, and retained earnings), the long-term group being of particular importance in the entity theory.

Before taking up the main subject of this study—a disclosure of the conflicting thoughts arising out of adhering to differing basic concepts—it seems desirable to define the concepts themselves. This is not an easy task because of the considerable confusion existing in accounting literature regarding the two main theories, the entity and proprietary theories. But that very confusion points to the need for defining the terms.

The Proprietary Concept

According to the proprietary theory, the business or other organization being accounted for belongs to one or more persons thought of as proprietors or owners, and their viewpoint is reflected in the accounting. The assets are regarded as their assets and the liabilities as their liabilities. The business is merely a segregated portion of their financial interests, accounted for separately because it is convenient or necessary for various reasons to do so. The balance sheet equation expressing this viewpoint is "Assets − Liabilities = Proprietorship."

For accounting purposes, a corporation is looked upon as not different fundamentally from a sole proprietorship, the stockholders simply being an association of individuals joined together in owning the one business. The corporation as a legal entity is nothing more than "a device of a representative nature by means of which the associations' business affairs may be conveniently administered with certain legal privileges and within certain legal limitations."[3]

The emphasis in accounting is upon the proprietors' equity, and a major purpose of the accounting is to determine the proprietors' net income or the changes in the proprietorship. The undistributed or retained earnings are assumed to belong to the proprietors.

Just who constitutes the proprietors in a business corporation is not entirely clear. Certainly the common stockholders are included. The preferred stockholders also are generally considered in that category, though normally they have no voice in operating the business. In practice, the financial return to them is always considered a distribution and is chargeable only to net profits current or accumulated, and payable only when declared in the form of a dividend. Both classes of stockholders, therefore, are distinctly different from the creditor group, and this distinction is basic in the proprietary concept. Hence, for purposes of this study, the proprietors in a business corporation will be assumed to include all stockholders.

Some Criticisms of the Proprietary Concept

Y. C. Chow raises the question whether perhaps all long-term investors—stockholders and bond or mortgage—may not be assumed to be proprietors.[4] This appears to be the view of some entity theorists in claiming there is too little difference between the two groups to justify basing a general accounting theory on the distinction. Nevertheless, an overwhelming majority of accountants consider only shareholders as owners.

The proper answer to the question who are the proprietors is most readily

[3] Robert T. Sprouse, "The Significance of the Concept of the Corporation in Accounting Analyses," *The Accounting Review,* July 1957, p. 370.

[4] Y. C. Chow, "The Doctrine of Proprietorship," *The Accounting Review,* April 1942, pp. 162–163.

seen in a case of a small business enterprise. Assume a situation where a very few individual entrepreneurs seek to conduct business for profit. They have available the several forms of business organization from which to choose— individual proprietorships for each, a partnership, or corporation. Presumably they will select the form which best meets their balanced desires of high profit (including minimizing taxes), little risk, continued existence, ease of sale of interests, etc. Whichever form they select could permit them to obtain additional funds through long-term borrowing without giving up any of their effective control over the business operations. The basic accounting theory could be the same regardless of the form of organization selected, and the distinction between creditors and owners need not vary because of the form of organization.

Another objection raised against the proprietary viewpoint is that it is impossible to determine the profits of individual common stockholders of a corporation, some and possibly most of whom acquire their shares by purchase on the market at various prices. The simple notion of corporate profit being a personal gain of the proprietors, as called for in the proprietary concept, is said not to be applicable.[5] The reasoning in this objection is not clear. Even if the profit to an individual shareholder takes into account factors external to the business which are not shown on the books of the accounting entity, this should not argue against the proprietary concept. The stockholder's share of the increase in the proprietorship (the residual equity) of the business is easily calculated. What further calculation must be made to determine his net gain or loss is his

personal affair. It is not a concern of the other members of the associated individuals, the stockholders, represented in the proprietorship.[6]

Husband answers the objection differently. He calls attention to

the usual accounting assumption that new stockholders always step into the shoes of original stockholders. From this point of view the book values are their values. More realistically, however, only the placing of accounting on an economic basis can actually solve this problem. The accountant's problem here is one of convention, not of reality.[7]

Other characteristics said to raise questions as to the applicability of the proprietary concept are that the stockholders' control through voting is passive and of doubtful significance: that the invested capital cannot be withdrawn at will; that the managers are responsive to the wishes of other equity interests, too; and that these other equities also assume risks and have a claim on income. There is truth in each of these. But why they negate the proprietary viewpoint is not at all clear. Basically the stockholders are the owners with control and bear the greatest risk and their rights constitute the residual equity. The managers may be removed

---

[5] Vatter, op cit., p. 4.

[6] The problem is not greatly different from that of determining the current profits on the sale of an item unrealistically carried in inventory at a value far below its current market cost because of using the LIFO method of valuation. We accept the book profit on the sale, knowing it is unrealistic when judged by the current purchase cost of the item. If we wish to know the margin of current profit, we make a separate determination.

[7] George Husband, "The Equity Concept in Accounting," *The Accounting Review,* October 1954, p. 558.

by the stockholders and hence tend to serve stockholders' interests above other interests.

Furthermore, recent developments have resulted in some merging of executives' economic interests with those of stockholders. A very high percentage of large businesses have stock option plans for their executives. Executive incentive bonus plans also are now being used by the majority of large industrial companies. Both have resulted in increased managements' interest in enhancing profits and have done much to identify their interests with those of the proprietors.[8]

The Entity Concept

According to the entity concept, the business or other unit being accounted for must be considered as entirely apart from the shareholders or other owners. Not only is there a complete self-balancing set of accounts for the entity: the entity is conceived of as having a separate existence—an arms'-length relationship with its owners. The relation to the owners is regarded as not particularly different from that to the long-term creditors. The balance sheet equation does not distinguish between creditors and proprietors but is simply "Assets = Equities." The accounting and reporting are for the entity itself as entirely separate from the owners.

Beyond this simple statement of what the entity concept is lies uncertainty and even confusion. The nature of the equities side of the equation is not clear. Decided differences of opinion on this point are expressed in accounting literature. Some writers seem to want to maintain the distinction between credi-

tors and owners yet treat them similarly in the accounting.[9] Others regard proprietors as creditors,[10] and the widespread use of "Liabilities" as a heading for the whole credit side of the balance sheet indicates this is a commonly held opinion.[11]

Among the recent writers on the entity concept, there seems to be universal agreement that the income of a corporation is not income of the stockholders—that it becomes their income only when and to the extent that dividends are declared.[12] This means that the retained earnings belong to the corporation itself and measure its equity in itself,[13] as meaningless as that concept

---

[8] William H. White, *The Changing Criteria in Investment Planning* (Washington, D.C.: The Brookings Institution, 1962), pp. 21–23.

[9] Walter Kell claims that, although stockholders are considered to be "outsiders" under this theory, this does not indicate a stockholder is a creditor. Op. cit., p. 84.

[10] See Stephen Gilman, *Accounting Concepts of Profit* (New York: The Ronald Press Company, 1939), pp. 25, 26, 51. Also see Husband (1938), op. cit., p. 244.

[11] Of the 600 corporate balance sheets studied by the staff of the American Institute of Certified Public Accounts for the year 1962, about 49% used the single word "Liabilities" to head the credit side. The trend seems to be away from using it, however. Kell reports that in 1950 the ratio was 286/477 or 60%, and that a study by Field in 1936 showed the ratio as 86%. See Kell, op. cit., pp. 94–95.

[12] A. C. Littleton states that in early concepts of the entity theory, "profit was but an additional 'indebtedness' to the sources of the property in use." See his *Accounting Evaluation to 1900* (New York: American Institute Publishing Company, Inc., 1933), p. 194.

[13] Some writers favoring the entity theory seem reluctant to accept this inevitable conclusion, claiming that the retained earnings are rightfully part of the stockholders' equity even though the income is not theirs. See Gilman, op. cit., p. 61, and Kell, op. cit., pp. 85 and 162.

might be. One writer suggests that even the "business capital supplied by stockholders to the corporation does not represent the equity of the former, but rather that of the latter."[14]

Much emphasis is given by entity theorists to the following views and facts regarding an incorporated business:

> The stockholders have practically the same relation to the corporation as the bondholders.
>
> They do not own the profit made by the company.
>
> They are mere investors in the corporation with practically no say in its operation.
>
> The properties are owned by the corporation itself, not the stockholders.
>
> The accounting and financial reporting are for all interested parties, including the entity's administration. They are not intended specifically for the stockholders.

These indicate the stockholders are closer to a creditor status than the creditors are to an owners' status. And since under the entity concept the stockholders and long-term creditors are to be treated similarly, it is logical that both classes should be regarded as creditors. As stated earlier, this is acknowledged by some of the entity theorists and it will be the assumption in this study.[15]

[14] David H. Li, "The Nature of Corporate Residual Equity under the Entity Concept," *The Accounting Review,* April 1960, p. 261.

[15] The entity theorists who do not regard stockholders as creditors prefer to consider long-term creditors as somewhat equivalent to stockholders. To them, interest on borrowings is a distribution of income, not an expense. But their position is less tenable, and certainly less consistent with the idea of a separate entity, than the one maintained here.

Hence, it will be accepted herein that, under the entity theory, the credit side of the balance sheet consists of liabilities except for undistributed earnings which belong to the entity itself. Furthermore, inasmuch as the theory extends to all accounting entities, partners and sole proprietors also hold such a creditor relationship to their respective business enterprises under that theory.

Criticisms of the Entity Concept

Perhaps the chief criticisms of the entity concept will arise from the unusual accounting decisions or principles which logically must follow from adopting it in dealing with accounting problems. These decisions will be discussed later. Here it is intended to point out other objections.

A major criticism is that the creditor relationship between the accounting entity and the owners is unrealistic and hence an improper basis upon which to build a theoretical accounting structure. The common stockholders of a corporation cannot be creditors because if they were it should be possible to determine the amounts owed and to ultimately pay them off. And even if it were possible to pay them off, it could only be by liquidating the corporation and paying them not only their recorded investment but the accumulated earnings—an acknowledgment that those earnings did belong to them all along. This is not in conformity with the entity theory.

A main reason why Sprague considered the entity theory unsatisfactory is that the rights of the proprietor are so very different from the rights of creditors. Proprietors' rights involve dominion over the assets and the power to use them as they choose or even sell them—the creditors' not being able to interfere except under extraordinary circumstances. The rights of the creditors are limited to definite sums which do not shrink when assets shrink, while the proprietors' rights are elastic, they suffering losses, expenses, and shrinkage and benefiting from profits, revenues, and increases of value.[16] Canning objected to the use of the term "liabilities" to head the right-hand side of the balance sheet because it is "seriously confusing and misleading."[17]

Another basis for criticism is disclosed in a simple comparison. A corporation is not a person but merely a device, created to benefit the originators. It is, in a sense, a machine. As viewed under the entity concept, it may be likened to a machine that has become personified and has declared a form of independence from its creator and owner, denying any closer relation or greater responsibility to him than to one who lent money used in building it. In the case of the machine, it clearly is an unacceptable viewpoint: in the case of the corporation, it should be also.

In a similar manner it is possible to compare a business entity, as viewed under the entity theory, with a government created by men to serve their interests. The individuals given the responsibilities of seeing that the government's functions are carried out often assume it has a separate existence. They tend to forget it is merely a useful device or servant of its creators and begin to regard it as having a will of its own with a right to determine its own functions and even to expect service of its citizens. "Ask not what your country can do for you but what you can do for your country" is the admonition of one well-known public administrator. In like manner a corporation may mistakenly be regarded as entitled, through its management, to act independently of the stockholders' wishes and to expect them to allow the use of their money with little to say as to how it should be used. The concept of an independent entity with its own motivations and interests seems unjustified in both cases and even dangerous to the long-run welfare of the originators.

When the entity theory is applied to noncorporate situations, its flaws become more apparent. Partners and sole proprietors have difficulty conceiving of themselves as of the same general nature as their long-term creditors and recognizing that the profits are not theirs until withdrawn. When approached with the concept, they are perplexed and, if inclined to be courteous, change the subject hurriedly because of danger of getting angry.

Carried to an extreme situation, the entity concept would dictate that an individual's personal possessions be accounted for as a separate entity, distinct from himself. Then those possessions owe him for their worth, and the income from his investments does not really become his until he consumes it. The concept appears somewhat ludicrous when applied to such a situation.

Other Theories

An "enterprise theory" has been proposed as being more realistic than the entity theory for those corporations with common stock listed on stock exchanges and hence subject to considerable control by governments.[18] A corporation is viewed as concerned with its

[16] Charles E. Sprague, *The Philosophy of Accounts* (New York: The Ronald Press Company, 1912), p. 47.

[17] John B. Canning, *The Economics of Accountancy* (New York: The Ronald Press Company, 1929), p. 55.

[18] Waino W. Suojanen, "Enterprise Theory and Corporate Balance Sheets," *The Accounting Review*, January 1958, pp. 56–65.

place in society and having as its main objectives survival and growth. Its management feels no great responsibility to the owners and attempts to satisfy them only to the extent of "conventionally adequate dividends." This responsibility is considered somewhat on a par with that of paying high wages to employees or maintaining friendly relations with governments, the public, and consumers.

This theory could have only very limited application[19] and is therefore not useful as a general over-all theory. Furthermore, it does not seem to accord with observable attempts of management to withstand labor unions' demands and to seek lower interest costs in order to improve profits. Nor can it be said that survival and growth are incompatible with stockholders' desires; many of them prefer the resultant capital gains in preference to high cash dividends.

Eugene V. Rostow wrote of the seeming ineffective stockholders' control of management and of the latter's responsibility to other groups. And yet he concluded that the objectives of the corporation should be, and are, to provide profits and operate according to economic laws.[20] He believes the rule of long-term profit maximization is more in accord with public expectancy than any other alternatives.[21]

Another proposal is one made by William Vatter, which he calls the fund theory.[22] In this theory he avoids personalizing the entity. Rather, he divides the entity into various areas of interest devoid of direct relationship to any group of persons, each area to have its own self-balancing set of accounts. Those individuals concerned with the equity would be expected to use the accounting reports for the areas in which their interests lie.

This proposal appears to have been scientifically conceived but it has demerits, too. One writer critically points out that Vatter's "statement of operations" is not an income statement but contains additional data, such as appear in a source and application of funds statement, and items usually relegated to footnotes, such as unrealized gains. The reader of the financial reports is expected to calculate net income according to his own concept of what that calculation should include.[23] This writer knows of no adoption of the fund theory during the fifteen years which have passed since the proposal was published. Hence it will not be considered further here.

One other proposal will be mentioned—that the basic theory in accounting be from the point of view of the residual equity.[24] The residual equity in a corporation is that of common stockholders who have the final claim on income and who are the first to be charged with a loss. Under this concept, all prior claims to income would be re-

---

[19] This theory could apply to only a few thousand out of close to a million corporations existent in the United States.

[20] Eugene V. Rostow, "To Whom and For What Ends is Corporate Management Responsible," Chapter 3 in Edward S. Mason (ed.), *The Corporation in Modern Society* (Cambridge: Harvard University Press, 1959), p. 67.

[21] Ibid., p. 70.

[22] Vatter, op. cit.

[23] Loyd C. Heath, "A Critical Review of the Fund Theory of Accounting and its Implications for Financial Reports," an unpublished paper.

[24] This is described in George J. Staubus, "The Residual Equity Point of View in Accounting," *The Accounting Review,* January 1959, pp. 3–31. Kell also discusses it, op. cit., pp. 116–118.

garded as cost, including dividends to preferred stockholders and even Class A common dividends.[25] Again this writer knows of no case where this view is adhered to and will not consider it further in this treatise.

Part II

Conflicts in Principles and Practice Arising out of the Proprietary and Entity Concepts

Thus far, explanations have been given of the important proprietary and entity concepts now generally used by accountants (often unknowingly) as the

[25]Y. C. Chow, op. cit., p. 162.

bases for accounting principles and decisions. It is now intended to take up the main objective of this study—to disclose and briefly discuss the conflicts in accounting thought and action that have arisen out of the use of the two concepts. Hopefully, this might make accountants aware of the suspect nature of some of their decisions. It also should point out the seriousness of using two very different concepts somewhat indiscriminately.

The conflicts to be examined will be introduced in the form of questions, with "yes" and "no" answers given for the proprietary and entity concepts. Brief discussions of explanations will follow when considered desirable.

	Proprietary Concept	*Entity Concept*
1. *Are the net earnings of a business to be considered income of the stockholders (or other owners)?* Under the entity concept, the income is that of the business enterprise itself until dividends are declared or distribution otherwise made.	Yes	No
2. *Should earnings per share be reported?* The earnings per share has real significance to stockholders under the proprietary theory. Under the entity concept the earnings do not belong to the stockholders and the amount per share would carry misleading inferences.	Yes	No
3. *Are corporate retained earnings, or earned surplus, part of the stockholders' equity?* According to the entity theory, the retained earnings must be regarded as belonging to the entity itself. Some entity theorists hesitate to admit this, but there can be no alternative if the stockholders are not to receive income until distribution is made. Certain types of capital surplus, such as donated surplus, appreciation surplus, and surplus arising through reorganizations, also belong to the entity. However, capital surplus arising out of sale of capital stock at a premium is regarded as part of the stockholders' equity under both concepts.	Yes	No

4. *Do the two taxes, corporate income tax and per-*

	Proprietary Concept	*Entity Concept*
sonal income tax on corporate cash dividends, result in double taxation? Under the proprietary concept, the income of the corporation is the income of the stockholders and hence tax is levied twice on the same income. However, there is a probability that some companies are able to pass along part of the burden of the corporate income tax to their customers through their sale prices. In such cases the tax burden on the stockholders would not truly be double.	Yes	No
5. ***May the income of corporations be taxed justifiably to the stockholders at the time it is earned by the corporation, prior to its distribution as dividends?*** In this respect stockholders, under the proprietary theory, are comparable to members of a partnership and are properly subject to tax on undistributed corporate income. It appears, then, that theoretically a choice develops between the alternatives of accepting as justified either double taxation or a personal tax on proportional shares or undistributed profits.[26] In the latter case, the government might tax the corporate profits tentatively and, when dividends are received by shareholders and included in their taxable income, allow their share of the corporate tax as a credit on their personal tax.	Yes	No
6. ***Should cash dividends be regarded as an expense to the corporation?*** Herein lies an injustice in the federal income tax. The entity theory is adhered to by the government in levying a corporate income tax, but the proprietary theory must be the basis used in denying the corporation a deduction of the dividends as an expense.	No	Yes
7. ***May a parent and subsidiary companies be accounted for as one economic unit through use of consolidated statements?*** When, as under the entity theory, the relationship is debtor and creditor, a consolidated picture is not proper. Under the proprietary theory, the subsidiaries' income belongs to the stockholders, including a parent	Yes	No

[26] Actually, such a choice already is available to certain small business corporations through Subchapter S of the Internal Revenue Code. Under carefully defined conditions, corporate income is permitted as if they were members of a partnership.

	Proprietary Concept	*Entity Concept*
company, at the time it is earned and hence may be included with the parents' own earnings through consolidation. To prepare consolidated statements is to espouse the proprietary concept.		
8. *Should a parent company take up on its books its proportionate share of its subsidiaries' profits and losses?*	Yes	No
9. *Are consolidated corporate income tax returns justified?*	Yes	No
10. *Is a dividend declared out of retained earnings and payable in capital stock (a stock dividend) to be regarded as income to the recipients?* Under the entity concept, inasmuch as the stock dividend would entail a transfer from retained earnings (representing the corporation's equity in itself) to capital stock (representing a liability to the stockholders), it must be regarded as an income to the stockholders. However, a premium on capital stock is a part of the stockholders' equity and a dividend, cash or stock, charged against such a premium account would not be income to the stockholders.	No	Yes
11. *Should a cash dividend declared immediately after stock is purchased be considered as income to the new stockholder?* According to the entity theory, no corporate earnings are income to the stockholder until received as a dividend. Hence, unless the amount is regarded as stockholder income at this time, it never would be. Under the proprietary theory, the former stockholder received income when the corporation earned it. Being undistributed, it is assumed logically to be included in the price of the stock and its receipt now would be merely a return of capital to the new owner.	No	Yes
12. *Should preferred stock dividends in arrears be recorded as a corporate expense, and a liability for it set up?* The answer under the entity concept is difficult to determine. The stockholder does not own corporation income until a dividend is declared. And yet a preferred stockholder has a preferred claim which is practically certain to be met if corporation income is ample. And since a dividend is expense under this concept,	No	Possibly

	Proprietary Concept	*Entity Concept*

it would seem highly irregular not to recognize such an accrual of probable expense.

13. *May a corporate deficit be shown on the debit side of the balance sheet?* As long as the business is a going concern, it could be expected that the deficit might be offset by future earnings which are now owned by the stockholders. Hence it seems improper under the entity concept to show a reduced liability to the stockholders to the amount of the deficit. In case liquidation is anticipated, the deficit is expected to be used later to reduce the liability to stockholders. In this respect it is similar to a sinking fund which normally is shown on the debit side of the balance sheet. However, liquidation is a very limited experience for a firm and the location of the deficit under those conditions is of little importance so long as it is carefully identified.

| | No | Yes |

14. *May discount on capital stock with reason be charged to retained earnings?* The retained earnings do not belong to the stockholders under the entity concept, and the discount is an offset to the liability shown in the capital stock account. To wipe out the discount against retained earnings would result in an increase in the liability to the stockholders. Under the proprietary theory, the retained earnings do belong to the stockholders, and the charge-off of discount would not affect the position of that group.

| | Yes | No |

15. *May gain on the acquisition of treasury stock be credited to retained earnings?* The gain on the treasury stock transaction is a net gain to the entity under the entity concept, for the liability to stockholders is reduced in an amount greater than that paid out. Furthermore, the transaction with the former stockholder is completed and the gain is realized, just as a gain in paying off a liability is realized. Under the proprietary theory opinion is divided on this question but the majority opinion favors recording the treasury stock at cost and reporting it as a deduction from the total of capital stock and related surplus items.

| | No | Yes |

16. *Is cost the best basis of asset value to use in financial reports?* Since under the entity concept the stockholders are regarded as creditors, it

| | Probably not | Yes |

	Proprietary Concept	Entity Concept

would be inaccurate to show as liabilities more or less than the amounts invested. And to reflect any gain or loss in asset values, resulting from price changes, in the entity's equity in itself would be rather meaningless.[27] On the other hand, under the proprietary concept where accounting is for the owners, there is real doubt whether adhering to cost is as satisfactory as reporting the more realistic current values, especially for inventories and investments.

17. ***Should the calculated book value per share of common stock include a proportionate part of retained earnings?*** The retained earnings do not belong to the stockholders under the entity concept. Hence the book value cannot properly include any part of those earnings. This can lead to absurd results as in the case of a certain closely held corporation with capital stock of $2,000 and retained earnings in excess of $500,000.

	Yes	No

18. ***Is the common account form of balance sheet (debits on the one side, credits on the other) the clearest form for presenting the financial position?*** The equation for the entity concept is "Assets = Equities (or Liabilities)" and this corresponds to the account form. The equation for the proprietary concept is "Assets − Liabilities = proprietorship" and the report form of statement of financial position expresses that relationship most clearly.

	No	Yes

19. ***Do stock market values provide a logical basis for valuing common capital stock held as investments?*** Stock market values do assume that both past and future earnings of a corporation belong to the stockholders and therefore reflect the proprietary point of view.

	Yes	No

[27] Gilman states, "The entity, as such, is not concerned with economic measures of valuation but rather symbolizes in terms of money various transactions reflecting a charge and discharge relationship between entity and proprietor. . . . From the entity viewpoint valuation at cost is natural." Op. cit., p. 55.

Conclusion

The above questions are those which occurred to the writer or were found in the course of this study. While undoubtedly not presenting a complete list of the problems arising out of the selection of one or the other of the two basic concepts, they are thought to be inclusive enough to reveal how important to accounting practice and theory the selection of proper concept is.

An examination of the answers indicates that the proprietary concept is adhered to by accountants in a large majority of their decisions regarding the questions. In this writer's opinion, in only three questions (numbers 5, 16, and 18) is the entity viewpoint the one generally favored. In all of the other sixteen questions, the proprietary viewpoint seems to be the one generally held.

Is there a way to determine if one concept can be found to be entirely correct and the other wrong? This writer knows of none. The law does not provide a way, and lawyers appear to be just as inconsistent or as uncertain in their views on the corporate entity as the accountants.[28]

Can we possibly conduct accounting without personal points of view—i.e., thoroughly objectively? Vatter suggested his fund theory as a means of doing this, but it has not taken hold. Raby stated that the entity concept can be maintained objectively,[29] but to this writer he was not convincing. His argument that management's responsibilities are to the entity, not to the stockholders or creditors or employees or society,[30] means that the responsibilities

are to animate creation, and that seems inconceivable. One does not feel responsible to a machine.

Accounting is a tool, and requires a classification in the form of accounts and groupings or accounts for summarizing transactions. In setting up such a classification, we must have points of view. It may be the long-term investors, or all the equities, or the common stockholders, or perhaps the government's (as to when a separate set of accounts is prepared for a utility to satisfy governmental demand for information). And one of those interests must be a dominant one, and it naturally would be the one which created the business entity.

The thought occurs that possibly we could allow individual selection of a basic concept out of the several possibilities, as we do between cash and accrual accounting. For some the entity theory might seem the best selection, as for a very large corporation. For smaller corporations and partnerships and sole proprietorships the proprietary theory would seem more appropriate. Were this permitted, it should be expected that whatever the selection in a given instance, it be adhered to consistently.

However, there would be less confusion to the users of financial statements if one of the two main concepts were selected for all accounting entities, and used consistently by each entity. From his study, the writer concluded that the proprietary concept is the more realistic and theoretically accurate and practical, and more in conformity with actual practice. Its adoption as the basic concept to be used for all accounting entities would be a boon to improved clarity in accounting.

---

[28] See Robert T. Sprouse, "Legal Concepts of the Corporation," *The Accounting Review,* January 1958, pp. 37–49.

[29] William L. Raby, "The Two Faces of Accounting," *The Accounting Review,* July 1959, p. 461.

[30] Ibid., p. 455.

ESOP Accounting: Past, Present and Future

John R. Deming and Bret W. Wise

The past two years have seen a wave of leveraged employee stock ownership plans (ESOPs) sweep through the corporate community. Although ESOPs have long been a popular and versatile financing tool for closely held businesses, recently there has been a significant trend to establish ESOPs by major public companies (see Exhibit 1).

In response to the growing interest in ESOPs, Wall Street has developed innovative financing techniques and new forms of ESOP securities providing sponsors with greater flexibility as well as significant cash flow benefits. In many cases, these new ESOP structures also produce a favorable effect on net income and earnings per share (EPS). The FASB and the SEC have taken an interest in the accounting issues raised by the more complex ESOP arrangements. Among the possible accounting changes being considered that would dramatically affect sponsors' accounting for ESOPs in the future are:

- Measuring expense by the fair value of shares allocated;
- Charging dividends on unallocated shares to expense;
- Consolidation of ESOPs; and
- Changes in the way shares are reflected in EPS calculations.

Reasons for the ESOP Movement

The increased interest in ESOPs is founded on several attractive features. Favorable tax treatment given ESOP lenders in certain circumstances has allowed ESOPs, and their sponsors through the ESOP, to borrow at reduced interest rates. Other provisions in the tax law allow a deduction for dividends paid on ESOP shares, which has been a particularly attractive feature to public companies. Although Congress has recently taken steps to limit some tax-related ESOP benefits, the growth of ESOPs has continued into 1990.

Many employers believe that employee productivity may be enhanced by giving employees a share in the company ownership. Others in the corporate community believe that unfriendly takeovers may be thwarted when a large share of the company ownership is in the hands of employees. A landmark court decision in January 1989 (*Shamrock Holdings v. Polaroid*) greatly strengthened companies' ability to use ESOPs as a defensive tactic against hostile takeovers.

Several companies have used ESOPs to finance leveraged buyout (LBO) transactions. One of the largest ESOP financings ($1.75 billion) was put together by the Avis Corporation in its 1987 LBO in which Avis became 100% employee-owned. And in a vivid example of East meeting West, some economists believe that ESOPs are a viable vehicle for transferring ownership of

EXHIBIT 1 *Recent ESOPs*

Sponsor	Security Purchased	Amount
Boise Cascade Corporation	Convertible Preferred	$300 million
Chevron Corporation	Common	$1 billion
Delta Air Lines, Inc.	Convertible Preferred	$500 million
ITT Corporation	Convertible Preferred	$700 million
J. C. Penney Company, Inc.	Convertible Preferred	$700 million
Lockheed Corporation	Common	$500 million
McDonald's Corporation	Convertible Preferred	$300 million
The Proctor & Gamble Company	Convertible Preferred	$1 billion
Ralston Purina Company	Convertible Preferred	$500 million
Sara Lee Corporation	Convertible Preferred	$350 million
Texaco, Inc.	Convertible Preferred	$500 million
U. S. West, Inc.	Common	$500 million
Whitman Corporation	Convertible Preferred	$500 million
Xerox Corporation	Convertible Preferred	$785 million

state-owned businesses in Eastern Europe to private hands.

Many companies are redesigning employee benefit plans to contain the cost of pension and other postretirement benefits, such as retiree medical insurance. Incorporating benefit plans into an ESOP ties employees' retirement benefits more closely to the market performance of the company's stock. For example, Ralston Purina, Boise Cascade, and Whitman have recently begun to utilize ESOPs to fund postretirement medical benefits for current employees.

Although there are many reasons for the popularity of ESOPs, companies have discovered that the recently developed technique of issuing convertible preferred stock to the ESOP, rather than common stock, can produce a positive impact on net income and EPS. Existing accounting standards, issued in 1976, do not address some of the newer ESOP funding arrangements. As a result, the FASB's Emerging Issues Task Force (EITF) has addressed many ESOP-related questions (see Exhibit 2) and the Accounting Standards Executive Committee (AcSEC) of the AICPA has added

a project to its agenda to explore the fundamental accounting issues underlying ESOP arrangements.

Existing Accounting for ESOPs

ESOPs were conceived in the 1950s. Until recently, however, ESOP structures were relatively simple, typically involving only common stock of the employer and often leveraged with mortgage-type (level payment) debt with terms of 10 years or less. As the popularity of ESOPs increased in the late 1980s, the nature of ESOP arrangements became more complex. The increased complexity generated differing interpretations of the accounting literature, which was written in simpler times.

In 1976, the AICPA issued Statement of Position (SOP) 76-3, *"Accounting Practices for Certain Employee Stock Ownership Plans,"* to address certain accounting issues relating to leveraged ESOPs. The primary recommendations of the SOP are:

- An obligation of an ESOP should be recognized as a liability by the sponsoring company when the sponsor

EXHIBIT 2 *ESOP Issues Addressed by the EITF*

Issue No.	Topic
85-10	Employee Stock Ownership Plan Contribution Funded by a Pension Plan Termination (Rescinded by FASB Statement 88)
85-11	Use of an Employee Stock Ownership Plan in a Leveraged Buyout
86-4	Income Statement Treatment of Income Tax Benefit for Employee Stock Ownership Plan Dividends
86-27	Measurement of Excess Contributions to a Defined Contribution Plan or Employee Stock Ownership Plan
87-23	Book Value Stock Purchase Plans
88-27	Effect of Unallocated Shares in an Employee Stock Ownership Plan on Accounting for Business Combinations
89-8	Expense Recognition for Employee Stock Ownership Plans
89-10	Sponsor's Recognition of Employee Stock Ownership Plan Debt
89-11	Sponsor's Balance Sheet Classification of Capital Stock with a Put Option Held by an Employee Stock Ownership Plan
89-12	Earnings-per-Share Issues Related to Convertible Preferred Stock Held by an Employee Stock Ownership Plan
90-4	Earnings-per-Share Treatment of Tax Benefits for Dividends on Stock Held by an Employee Stock Ownership Plan

guarantees the obligation or commits to make future contributions sufficient to service the ESOP debt. This liability is offset by a corresponding reduction in equity; both the liability and the offsetting debit to equity are reduced as the ESOP debt is paid.

- Contributions or commitments to make contributions to the ESOP are recognized as compensation expense and interest expense by the sponsor.

- All of the sponsor's shares held by the ESOP are treated as outstanding in the sponsor's calculation of EPS, regardless of whether those shares have been allocated to participants' accounts.

- Dividends paid on shares held by the ESOP are charged directly to retained earnings by the sponsor.

The ESOP structure has evolved since 1976. Sponsors now are issuing equity securities to ESOPs with complex conversion, redemption, and dividend features and are financing ESOPs with other than mortgage-type debt. Some of these features were not anticipated in the SOP. For example, in a leveraged ESOP arrangement:

- The sponsor may issue convertible preferred stock to the ESOP and use dividends to service the ESOP's debt, reducing the sponsor's required contributions.

- The ESOP loan may provide for variable payments rather than level payments.

- The sponsor may not guarantee the ESOP debt.

- The terms of convertible preferred stock issued to an ESOP may be structured to avoid classification as a common stock equivalent for purposes of EPS calculations.

- The plan may provide ESOP participants with a guaranteed value for the convertible preferred stock upon their retirement or termination.

These arrangements raise a number of accounting issues, many of which have been addressed by the EITF (see Exhibit 2). Three controversial issues addressed by the EITF in 1989 are: expense recognition for leveraged ESOPs, treatment of ESOP debt by the sponsor, and ESOP issues affecting the calculation of EPS.

Expense Recognition

The SOP recommends that contributions or commitments to make contributions to an ESOP should be recognized as compensation and interest expense by the sponsor. Many companies have interpreted this to allow an employer to expense contributions made to the ESOP on a cash basis.

At the time the SOP was issued, borrowings of ESOPs were primarily in the form of mortgage-type debt or debt with level principal payments. In addition, the tax law at that time required that ESOP shares be allocated to participant accounts based on principal payments on the related ESOP debt. As a result, the sponsor recognized compensation expense equal to the cost of the shares allocated to participants as ESOP debt principal payments were made.

In recent years, the financing of ESOPs has evolved to include nonlevel debt, such as increasing debt service payments over the term of the debt. In addition, current tax law requires that ESOPs with debt terms in excess of 10 years allocate shares based on both principal and interest payments. As a result, ESOP shares purchased using borrowings in excess of 10 years are now allocated in part based on interest payments.

For example, assume that an ESOP borrows $100 million at 9% to be repaid over 15 years with level annual principal and interest payments. In the first year, the trustee makes the annual debt service payment of $12.4 million, consisting of $3.4 million principal and $9 million interest. Because the ESOP has repaid one-fifteenth of its total debt service (principal and interest), the trustee is required to allocate shares with a cost of $6.7 million (one-fifteenth of the shares) to participants. However, the ESOP has only paid for shares with a cost of $3.4 million, as represented by the principal payment on the ESOP debt. The difference of $3.3 million represents the cost of ESOP shares that have been allocated to participants before the debt used to purchase the shares has been paid.

Some companies have interpreted the SOP to allow expense recognition on a cash basis. In the example above, recognizing expense on a cash basis results in $12.4 million of expense in the first year, essentially deferring compensation expense on $3.3 million of shares allocated, for which principal payments have not been made. This perceived deferral of expense was the primary factor that prompted the EITF to address expense recognition by leveraged ESOPs. The EITF interpreted the SOP to require a sponsor to:

- Account for the financing and compensation elements of a leveraged ESOP separately;

- Recognize interest expense as incurred by the ESOP;

- Recognize compensation expense equal to the cost of shares allocated for the period; and

- Recognize dividends used to service ESOP debt as a direct reduction of retained earnings.

This approach is commonly referred to as *the shares allocated method*. In simple terms, the consensus requires a sponsor to recognize interest expense as incurred and to recognize the cost of the shares (compensation expense) when the shares are allocated to participants. In the example above, the sponsor would recognize expense of $15.7 million in the first year consisting of $9 million interest and $6.7 million compensation for the cost of shares allocated. The shares allocated method results in $3.3 million additional expense in the first year of the ESOP as compared to expense recognized on a cash basis. A more complex example of the shares allocated method, including the effects of dividends, is included as Exhibit 3.

Recognition of ESOP Debt
The SOP provides that the obligation of an ESOP should be recognized as a liability by the sponsor when the sponsor guarantees the obligation or commits to make future contributions sufficient to service the ESOP debt.

Questions have arisen in practice as to whether the ESOP's debt should be recognized in the sponsor's balance sheet when the sponsor does not guarantee the debt. In June 1989, the EITF concluded that the debt of an ESOP should be recorded as a liability of the sponsor in all circumstances except when the ESOP has the ability and intent to satisfy the debt from sources other than dividends on the sponsor's stock, contributions from the sponsor, or the sale or exchange of the sponsor's securities. Considering the structure of most ESOP arrangements, this consensus effectively requires all ESOP debt to be recorded as a liability in the sponsor's balance sheet.

Earnings Per Share Issues
The recent trend of issuing other than "plain vanilla" common shares to ESOPs has created several EPS issues.

A security frequently used in ESOP arrangements today is high-yield convertible preferred stock (see Exhibit 1). The use of this security is advantageous to companies because dividends are charged to retained earnings, effectively reducing the expense the company must recognize in its income statement. However, for EPS purposes the preferred dividends reduce income available to common shareholders.

Convertible preferred stock held by an ESOP usually carries a dividend rate in excess of the common dividend rate and is typically convertible into a fixed number of shares of common stock. The sponsor may, however, guarantee that upon termination or retirement the employee will receive common stock, cash, or a combination of stock and cash, with a value equal to a specified minimum value for the convertible preferred stock. The provision is commonly referred to as a *guaranteed floor feature*.

Questions have arisen regarding the treatment of the convertible preferred stock held by an ESOP in EPS computations, including:

- Should convertible preferred shares be considered common stock equivalents in the calculation of primary EPS?

- How does the assumed conversion of the convertible preferred shares impact fully diluted EPS?

- What effect does the guaranteed floor feature have on EPS?

The EITF addressed these issues in the fall of 1989. On the first issue, the EITF concluded that the convertible preferred

EXHIBIT 3 *ESOP Expense Recognition*

Assumptions:

- ESOP borrows $100 million at 9% for 15 years.
- ESOP purchases $100 million (1 million shares at $100 per share) of sponsor's 8% convertible preferred stock.
- Dividends on unallocated preferred shares are used for ESOP debt service.
- Shares are allocated at the end of the period.
- Preferred stock is convertible into common stock at a 1 to 1 ratio.
- ESOP debt service payments increase 5% per year.

The following illustration shows expense recognition by the sponsor under the shares allocated method. All amounts shown are in thousands except the number of shares allocated.

	ESOP Debt Service			Dividends on Unallocated Shares	Cash Contribution Required	Number of Shares Allocated	Shares Allocated Method	
Year	Principal	Interest	Total				Compensation Expense[1]	Net Expense
		(A)	(B)	(C)	(B) − (C)	(D)	(E)	(A) + (E) − (C)
1	$ 319	$ 9,000	$ 9,319	$ 8,000	$ 1,319	46,347	$ 4,635	$ 5,635
2	814	8,971	9,785	7,629	2,156	48,665	4,867	6,209
3	1,376	8,898	10,274	7,240	3,034	51,097	5,110	6,768
4	2,014	8,774	10,788	6,831	3,957	53,653	5,365	7,308
5	2,734	8,593	11,327	6,402	4,925	56,334	5,633	7,824
6	3,547	8,347	11,894	5,951	5,943	59,153	5,915	8,311
7	4,461	8,028	12,489	5,478	7,011	62,113	6,211	8,761
8	5,487	7,626	13,113	4,981	8,132	65,216	6,522	9,167
9	6,636	7,132	13,768	4,460	9,308	68,474	6,847	9,519
10	7,922	6,535	14,457	3,912	10,545	71,900	7,190	9,813
11	9,357	5,822	15,179	3,337	11,842	75,491	7,549	10,034
12	10,959	4,980	15,939	2,733	13,206	79,271	7,927	10,174
13	12,742	3,994	16,736	2,099	14,637	83,235	8,324	10,219
14	14,725	2,847	17,572	1,433	16,139	87,392	8,739	10,153
15	16,907	1,523	18,430	734	17,696	91,659	9,166	9,955
Total	$100,000	$101,070	$201,070	$71,220	$129,850	1,000,000	$100,000	$129,850

[1]The compensation expense element under the shares allocated method is measured by the cost of the shares allocated in the period ($100 per share).

should not be considered a common stock equivalent unless the yield of the preferred stock at the date of issuance is less than 66⅔% of the corporate Aa bond rate (the yield test in FASB Statement 85).

The second issue arises when the dividend rate on the convertible preferred stock exceeds the dividend rate on the common stock. Thus, if the convertible preferred stock held by the ESOP were converted to common stock, the sponsor would be required to make additional contributions to meet the ESOP's debt service requirements. These additional contributions would be charged to expense instead of retained earnings.

The EITF concluded that, in calculating fully diluted EPS under the if-converted method, net income should be reduced by the excess of the preferred dividends over common dividends assuming conversion of the preferred shares. For example, assume that the ESOP holds 100,000 shares of convertible preferred stock which has an $8 per share annual dividend. The preferred stock is convertible into 100,000 shares of the sponsor's common stock, which paid a dividend of $3 per share. In calculating fully diluted EPS, the sponsor would be required to assume conversion of the preferred shares into common shares and to reduce net income available to common shareholders by $500,000 (100,000 shares × $5) for the difference between the preferred and common dividend rates.

The existence of a guaranteed floor feature further complicates the application of the if-converted method in calculating fully diluted EPS. If the market price of the common stock is less than the guaranteed value of the convertible preferred stock, the employer has a contingent obligation to issue additional

shares of stock or to pay the shortfall in cash (depending on the provisions of the ESOP) when the employee retires or otherwise leaves the company. Many ESOPs allow the company to choose whether it will satisfy the guaranteed floor feature in cash or stock.

A question arises as to how a sponsor should reflect the guaranteed floor feature in its fully diluted EPS calculations. Specifically, if the market price of the common stock is less than the guaranteed floor price, should the company include the additional shares that would be required to satisfy the floor feature in the number of shares outstanding for fully diluted EPS calculations?

The EITF concluded that fully diluted EPS calculations should include the number of common shares based on the stated conversion rate for unallocated shares and the number of common shares equivalent to the guaranteed value for the preferred shares allocated to participants (but not less than the number of shares based on the stated conversion rate). EPS amounts for prior periods should be restated if the number of shares issued, or contingently issuable, subsequently changes because of market price fluctuations. The EITF reached this consensus in part because only participants can exercise the guaranteed floor feature (i.e., the guaranteed floor feature does not attach to the convertible preferred shares until allocated to participants).

The EITF also concluded that if the sponsor is either required to, or has the ability and expressed intent to satisfy the guaranteed floor feature in cash, the stated conversion rate should be used for all shares and no additional issuance of shares related to the guaranteed floor feature need to be assumed.

Exhibit 4 provides an example of the impact of convertible preferred stock,

EXHIBIT 4 *Earnings Per Share*

Assumptions are the same as Exhibit 3, plus the following:

- The preferred stock is not a common stock equivalent.
- There are 10 million common shares outstanding.
- Common dividends are $3 per share annually.
- At the end of year five, 256,096 preferred shares have been allocated.
- Sponsor guarantees that participants will receive common stock with a value of at least $100 upon termination or retirement.
- At the end of year five, the common stock is trading at $70 per share.

Earnings per common share for year 5, ignoring income taxes, would be computed as follows (all amounts in thousands except earnings per share amounts):

	Primary	Fully Diluted
Net Income	$100,000	$100,000
Preferred Dividends	(8,000)	
Additional Contribution Required for Dividend Shortfall If Converted	—	4,001[1]
Income Available to Common Shareholders	$ 92,000	$ 95,999
Common Shares Outstanding	10,000	10,000
If Converted:		
Unallocated Shares at Stated Rate	—	744[2]
Allocated Shares at Guaranteed Value	—	366[3]
Common Equivalent Shares Outstanding	10,000	11,110
Earnings Per Share	$ 9.20	$ 8.64

[1] Dividend shortfall is equal to the difference between the preferred dividends on shares unallocated during the year of $6,401,904 (800,238 shares at $8 per share), less dividends of $2,400,714 on the common shares ($3 per share) under the if-converted method.

[2] Unallocated preferred shares at the end of the year of 743,904 converted at the stated ratio of 1 to 1.

[3] Allocated shares convert at the guaranteed rate of $100 per share as follows: 256,096 preferred shares allocated at the end of the year at $100 per share, divided by the common stock price of $70 per share.

including the existence of a guaranteed floor feature, on EPS computations.

The guidance of the EITF has provided a level of consistency in practice on a short-term basis. However, as ESOP structures change and become more complex there is a growing need to reconsider the fundamental accounting model for ESOPs.

The Future of ESOP Accounting

AcSEC initiated a project in 1989 to reconsider the SOP and other accounting issues related to ESOPs, including those addressed by the EITF. Some contentious issues which may be addressed by AcSEC are:

- Measurement of compensation expense;
- The treatment of dividends on unallocated ESOP shares;
- Consolidation of ESOPs in the financial statements of the sponsor; and
- The treatment of ESOP shares in the computation of EPS.

Measuring Expense: Cost or Fair Value?

The SOP (as interpreted in EITF Issue 89-8) provides that the cost of shares held by an ESOP should be charged to expense in the period allocated to participants. The cost basis was considered the appropriate measurement principle when the SOP was written because ESOPs were viewed as similar to defined contribution pension plans, where the risks and rewards of ownership of the assets rest with the employee, not with the employer.

Under the cost approach, an employer that sets aside shares today in a leveraged ESOP will recognize expense in future years (when the shares are allocated to participants) at today's cost basis. Some accountants believe that the employer retains the risks and rewards of ownership related to the unallocated shares and, thus, the employer should recognize compensation expense equal to the fair value of the shares in the period allocated to participants. This argument rests on the premise that the fair value of the shares allocated represents a more meaningful measure of the economic benefit provided to the employee and the sacrifice made by the employer.

To illustrate, assume the facts as in Exhibit 3, except that the shares appreciate in value at a rate of 10% per year. In year 5, the per share value would be $161 versus $100 at the in-

ception of the ESOP. Under the cost basis approach, the compensation component of ESOP expense in year 5 would be measured by the cost of the shares allocated of $5.6 million (56,334 shares at $100 per share). On the other hand, if expense is measured based on the fair value of the shares allocated, the compensation element would be $9.1 million (56,334 shares at $161 per share).

This same example may be used to demonstrate how the risks and rewards of ownership with respect to unallocated shares may rest with the sponsor. Assume that the ESOP has been formed to provide for a portion of the employer's match for employee 401(k) savings plan contributions. Further assume that in year 5 the employer is required to provide $10 million in benefits under the 401(k) match arrangement. In these circumstances (where the market price of the ESOP shares has increased to $161 per share), the sponsor would provide $9.1 million of the benefits through the ESOP and make an additional contribution to the 401(k) savings plan of $900,000. If instead the share value had dropped to $50 per share in year 5, the allocation of shares in the ESOP would satisfy only $2.8 million (56,334 shares at $50 per share) of the obligation, requiring an additional contribution by the sponsor of $7.2 million. Clearly in these circumstances the risks and rewards of ownership of the unallocated shares rests with the sponsor.

Fair value expense measurement would have a dramatic impact on the expense recognized by many sponsors of ESOPs. To demonstrate the effect of fair value expense treatment refer again to Exhibit 3 and assume appreciation in the value of the stock of 10% per year. The following table provides the expense recognition on a cash basis, using the shares allocated method, and using the shares allocated method but measuring compensation expense by the fair value of shares allocated (amounts in thousands).

too much volatility into reported earnings. This would be especially true for high-tech and rapidly growing compa-

		Compensation Expense		
			Shares Allocated Method	
Year	Market Price Per Share	Cash Basis	Cost	Fair Value
1	$110	$1,319	$5,635	$6,098
5	$161	$4,925	$7,824	$11,261
10	$259	$10,545	$9,813	$21,245
15	$417	$17,696	$9,955	$39,011

A decrease in value of the sponsor's shares would likewise decrease the expense recognized under the fair value approach as compared to the cost basis approach.

ESOPs are analogous to variable stock compensation plans for which sponsors measure compensation expense based on the fair value of shares issued in accordance with APB Opinion 25, *"Accounting for Stock Issued to Employees."* The measurement of expense for stock or stock options issued to employees has been controversial for some time and, as a result, the FASB added a project to its agenda in 1984 to readdress the accounting for employee stock compensation plans. The FASB has tentatively agreed that Opinion 25 should not be retained, but has been unable to agree on a new measurement approach. FASB decided in 1988 to consider stock compensation issues in conjunction with its broader project on accounting for financial instruments. This project will not be completed for several years.

It is likely that a change to fair value expense recognition would be strongly opposed by the business community. Many public companies believe that a fair value approach would introduce

nies that experience significant share value growth. Critics believe that a fair value method of measuring ESOP expense is inappropriate because the cash flow consequences to the company are determined when shares are issued to the ESOP. These companies argue that ESOPs are similar to restricted stock compensation plans in which the number of shares to be granted to employees is fixed when the ESOP is established; thus, the sponsor's expense measurement should be based on the original cost of the shares.

Currently there is substantial disagreement as to the appropriate measure of expense for ESOP shares. Many who favor a cost approach believe that the effect of changes in fair value can be adequately dealt with through disclosure. They also believe that financial statement users will not understand the earnings fluctuations produced by fair value and question whether this approach provides useful new information. Because of the need to educate users, they believe that ESOP accounting should not move to fair value until the FASB has made more progress on its financial instruments project. However, because of the evolution of ESOP structures, others believe that the cost approach disguises the economic differences among ESOPs and feel that the time has come for fair value expense measurement.

Treatment of Dividends

One of the more controversial issues in ESOP accounting has been the treatment of dividends on shares held by an ESOP. The SOP requires that dividends on all shares held by an ESOP should be charged to retained earnings. In a leveraged ESOP arrangement, this results in a portion of the cost of benefits provided to employees being charged to retained earnings rather than as an expense. Assume that Company A and Company B provide identical benefits to their employees and that Company A funds the benefits from working capital while Company B funds the benefits through an ESOP. In this situation, Company B would report higher net income because the portion of the benefits funded via dividends on ESOP shares would be charged directly to retained earnings.

To illustrate this concept, refer to year 5 in Exhibit 3. In year 5, the sponsor would recognize expense under the shares allocated method of $7.8 million (consisting of the compensation element of $5.6 million, interest of $8.6 million, less dividends on unallocated shares of $6.4 million). By contrast, if dividends on unallocated shares used for ESOP debt service were charged to expense, the sponsor would recognize expense of $14.2 million (consisting of compensation of $5.6 million and interest of $8.6 million).

One unique feature of ESOPs is that the tax law allows a deduction for dividends paid on ESOP shares. The tax benefit from dividends on shares held by the ESOP is credited directly to retained earnings under APB Opinion 11 and is treated as a reduction of income tax expense under FASB Statement 96. Thus, under Statement 96, a sponsor excludes from its income statement that portion of its ESOP contribution made in the form of dividends, but is able to recognize the tax benefit of the dividends in net income. Some accountants believe that dividends on ESOP shares should be charged to expense consistent with the treatment under the tax law and the treatment of the related tax benefit under Statement 96.

Irrespective of the inconsistent tax treatment, some believe that dividends on unallocated ESOP shares are more analogous to compensation expense than to a distribution to shareholders. Those in this camp would point to EITF Issue 86-27, in which the EITF concluded that dividends on unallocated shares should be charged to expense. Further, in the case of preferred stock with a stated dividend rate held by an ESOP, an argument has been made that the dividends on the preferred stock are simply a contractual payment to fund the ESOP debt and not a distribution to shareholders. Lastly, proponents of the consolidation concept, discussed below, contend that expense treatment of dividends on unallocated ESOP shares is consistent with the consolidation approach.

Consolidation of ESOPs

In some respects, current ESOP accounting represents a quasi-consolidation approach. The sponsor is required to record a liability for the ESOP debt with a corresponding reduction in shareholders' equity, frequently referred to as *deferred compensation* or *guarantee of ESOP debt*. The effect of this treatment is consistent with consolidation of the ESOP, in which case the sponsor would record the ESOP debt and a reduction of equity for unallocated shares held by the ESOP (i.e., treasury shares) in the consolidated financials.

On the other hand, the present ESOP accounting model treats all shares held by the ESOP as outstanding for EPS calculations. Many believe that the treatment of all ESOP shares, including unallocated shares, as outstanding creates excessive dilution of EPS. Further, under existing accounting, dividends on all shares are charged to retained earnings. Some believe that charging dividends on unallocated shares to retained earnings is not appropriate because the IRS now permits dividends on all shares to be used by the sponsor to service ESOP debt.

Thus, the present ESOP accounting model is internally inconsistent. The model requires the debt of the ESOP to be recorded by the sponsor, with a corresponding reduction in equity, consistent with the view that the ESOP is a nonindependent entity, similar to a subsidiary or grantor trust. However, the model requires all shares to be treated as outstanding for EPS and dividend purposes, consistent with the view that the ESOP is an unrelated, independent entity.

The FASB has been at work on a major project involving consolidations since 1982. FASB Statement 94, issued in 1987, requires consolidation of all majority-owned subsidiaries, except in certain limited circumstances. The FASB expects to issue a discussion document later in 1990 in which the Board will set forth its preliminary views on the concept of a reporting entity. Many believe that consolidation of ESOPs is a logical step that would provide a more consistent framework for addressing the ESOP accounting issues that have arisen in recent years.

Earnings Per Share Issues

One question that will be reconsidered by AcSEC is whether unallocated shares should be treated as outstanding for EPS purposes. As noted, the SOP requires all ESOP shares to be considered outstanding for EPS computations. If AcSEC concludes that consolidation of ESOPs in the financial statements of the sponsor is appropriate or that dividends on unallocated shares should be charged to expense, it would be consistent to treat only allocated shares as outstanding in EPS calculations. Interestingly, a minority of the AcSEC members in 1976 favored such treatment. The EITF consensus on Issue 86-27 also requires this treatment when an employer terminates a defined benefit pension plan and rolls the proceeds into an ESOP.

Some sponsors believe that treating all shares as outstanding does not recognize the economics of ESOP arrangements. Further, they believe that including all shares in EPS calculations produces less-meaningful and potentially misleading EPS amounts. In particular, many public companies opposed the EITF conclusions on EPS issues. Some financial analysts agree with these views and have ignored the adjustments made to reported EPS of companies with large ESOPs.

Under existing accounting, the cost of ESOP shares is charged to expense when the shares are allocated to participants. Inherent in this concept is an assumption that the risks and rewards of unallocated shares have not passed from the sponsor to the employee. To those who believe that the sponsor effectively controls the ESOP, it seems inconsistent to treat these same shares as outstanding for EPS purposes.

Consideration of only allocated shares as outstanding in EPS calculations could have a positive impact on reported EPS. Assume that a sponsor of a common stock ESOP has net earnings of $100 million per year and 10 million common shares outstanding. Assume further that the sponsor issues one million common shares to the ESOP which will be allocated over 15 years using the share allocation schedule in Exhibit 3. The sponsor would report the following EPS, assuming that (1) all ESOP shares are outstanding and (2) only allocated ESOP shares are outstanding:

Year	All Shares Outstanding	Only Allocated Shares Outstanding
1	$9.09	$10.00
5	$9.09	$9.80
10	$9.09	$9.51
15	$9.09	$9.17

In year 16, EPS would be the same under either method because all ESOP shares would be allocated and considered outstanding. Treating only allocated ESOP shares as outstanding removes the excessive EPS dilution in the early years of the ESOP. As the shares are allocated to employees, the shares are reflected as outstanding, consistent with the economics of the ESOP arrangement.

A New ESOP Accounting Model

A variety of ESOP issues continue to develop in practice. These issues, along with diverse views on the appropriate approaches to use in accounting for them, have prompted AcSEC to reconsider the way businesses report ESOP arrangements. It seems likely that AcSEC will conclude that the current ESOP accounting model requires a major overhaul. One possible approach would be to:

- Measure compensation expense based on the fair value of shares allocated;
- Expense interest as incurred on ESOP debt;
- Change dividends on unallocated shares to expense instead of retained earnings; and
- Treat only allocated shares as outstanding for EPS purposes.

This model is essentially a consolidation approach based on the premise that the risks and rewards of unallocated ESOP shares rests with the sponsor. The model is internally consistent with respect to the treatment of ESOP shares for expense measurement, recognition of dividends, and EPS calculations. Further, this model would result in consistent treatment for different types of plans, such as non-leveraged ESOPs, leveraged ESOPs, and 401(k) savings plans.

A change in practice of this magnitude would have a material effect on the financial statements of many companies. Many ESOP sponsors and others are certain to consider fair value expense measurement too revolutionary a change from present practice. A worthwhile alternative would be to adopt the above model but retain cost basis expense measurement and require disclosure of the fair value of shares allocated. This approach would be more acceptable to the corporate community and, thus, could be implemented in a relatively short time frame. This compromise would improve financial reporting of ESOPs by providing a more conceptually sound and consistent model in the short term while the FASB continues its work on the financial instruments project.

Cases

- **Case 13-1**

Raun Company had the following account titles on its December 31, 1995, trial balance:

Six percent cumulative convertible preferred stock, $100 par value
Premium on preferred stock
Common stock, $1 stated value
Premium on common stock
Retained earnings

The following additional information about the Raun Company was available for the year ended December 31, 1995.

1. There were 2,000,000 shares of preferred stock authorized, of which 1,000,000 were outstanding. All 1,000,000 shares outstanding were issued on January 2, 1985, for $120 a share. The Aa Corporate bond interest rate was 8.5 percent on January 2, 1985, and 10 percent on December 31, 1995. The preferred stock is convertible into common stock on a one-for-one basis until December 31, 1996; thereafter, the preferred stock ceases to be convertible and is callable at par value by the company. No preferred stock has been converted into common stock, and there were no dividends in arrears at December 31, 1995.

2. The common stock has been issued at amounts above stated value per share since incorporation in 1955. Of the 5,000,000 shares authorized, there were 3,500,000 shares outstanding at January 1, 1995. The market price of the outstanding common stock has increased slowly, but consistently, for the last five years.

3. The company has an employee stock option plan where certain key employees and officers may purchase shares of common stock at 100 percent of the market price at the date of the option grant. All options are exercisable in installments of one-third each year, commencing one year after the date of the grant, and expire if not exercised within four years of the grant date. On January 1, 1995, options for 70,000 shares were outstanding at prices ranging from $47 to $83 a share. Options for 20,000 shares were exercised at $47 to $79 a share during 1995. No options expired during 1995, and additional options for 15,000 shares were granted at $86 a share. Of these, 30,000 were exercisable at that date at prices ranging from $54 to $79 a share.

4. The company also has an employee stock purchase plan through which the company pays one-half and the employee pays one-half of the market price of the stock at the date of the subscription. During 1995 employees subscribed to 60,000 shares at an average price of $87 a share. All 60,000 shares were paid for and issued late in September 1995.

5. On December 31, 1995, there was a total of 355,000 shares of common stock set aside for the granting of future stock options and for future purchases under the employee stock purchase plan. The only changes in the stockholders' equity for 1995 were those described previously, 1995 net income, and cash dividends paid.

Required:

a. Prepare a stockholders' equity section of the balance sheet of Raun Company at December 31, 1995; substitute, where appropriate, Xs for unknown dollar amounts. Use good form and provide full disclosure. Write appropriate footnotes as they should appear in the published financial statements.

b. Provide theoretical justification for your treatment of the employee stock option plan. In your discussion, explain why your treatment fits the definition of equity or liabilities, whichever is appropriate.

c. Explain how the amount of the denominator should be determined to compute primary earnings per share for presentation in the financial statements. Be specific as to the handling of each item. If additional information is needed to determine whether an item should be included or excluded or the extent to which an item should be included, identify the information needed and the way the item would be handled if the information were known. Assume Raun Company had substantial net income for the year ended December 31, 1995.

• Case 13-2

Arts Corp. offers a generous employee compensation package that includes employee stock options. The exercise price has always been equal to the market price of the stock at the date of grant. The corporate controller, John Jones, believes that employee stock options, like all obligations to issue the corporation's own stock, are equity. The new staff accountant, Marcy Means, disagrees. Marcy argues that when a company issues stock for less than current value, the value of preexisting stockholders' shares is diluted.

Required:

a. Under existing generally accepted accounting principles, describe how Arts Corp. should account for its employee stock option plan.

b. Pretend you are hired to debate the issue of the proper treatment of options written on a company's own stock. Formulate your argument, citing concepts and definitions to buttress your case assuming
   1. You are siding with John.
   2. You are siding with Marcy.

• Case 13-3

Drake Company reported the following for 1995:

Current Assets	$ 37,000
Current Liabilities	19,000
Revenues	450,000

Cost of Goods Sold	220,000
Noncurrent Assets	186,000
Bonds Payable (10%, issued at par)	100,000
Preferred Stock, $5, $100 Par	20,000
Common Stock, $10 Par	50,000
Paid-in-Capital in Excess of Par	48,000
Operating Expenses	64,000
Retained Earnings	36,000

Common stockholders received a $2 dividend during the year. The preferred stock is noncumulative and nonparticipating.

Required:
a. Ignoring income taxes, prepare an income statement and balance sheet for Drake Company at December 31, 1995, that is consistent with each of the following theories of equity:
   1. Entity theory
   2. Proprietary theory
   3. Residual equity theory
b. For each theory cited above, compute the December 31, 1995, debt-to-equity ratio. If none would be computed, discuss why.

● **Case 13-4**

For numerous reasons a corporation may reacquire shares of its own capital stock. When a company purchases treasury stock, it has two options as to how to account for the shares: the cost method and the par-value method.

Required:
Compare and contrast the cost method and the par value method for each of the following.
a. Purchase of shares at a price less than par value
b. Purchase of shares at a price greater than par value
c. Subsequent resale of treasury shares at a price less than purchase price, but more than par value
d. Subsequent resale of treasury shares at a price greater than both purchase price and par value
e. Effect on net income

● **Case 13-5**

Carrol, Inc., accomplished a quasi-reorganization effective December 31, 1995. Immediately prior to the quasi-reorganization, the stockholders' equity was as follows:

Common stock, par value $10 per share authorized issued and outstanding 400,000 shares	$4,000,000

Additional paid-in capital   600,000
Retained earnings (deficit)   (900,000)

Under the terms of the quasi-reorganization, the par value of the common stock was reduced from $10 per share to $5 per share and equipment was written down by $1,200,000.

Required:
Discuss the accounting treatment necessary to accomplish this quasi-reorganization.

• Case 13-6

Stock options are widely used as a form of compensation for corporate executives.

a. Identify five methods that have been proposed for determining the value of executive stock options.
b. Discuss the conceptual merits of each of these proposed methods.

• Case 13-7

On January 1, 1995, as an incentive to improved performance of duties, Recycling Corporation adopted a qualified stock option plan to grant corporate executives nontransferable stock options to 500,000 shares of its unissued $1 par value common stock. The options were granted on May 1, 1995, at $25 per share, the market price on that date. All the options were exercisable one year later and for four years thereafter providing that the grantee was employed by the corporation at the date of exercise.

The market price of this stock was $40 per share on May 1, 1996. All options were exercised before December 31, 1996, at times when the market price varied between $40 and $50 per share.

Required:
a. What information on this option plan should be presented in the financial statements of Recycling Corporation at (1) December 31, 1995, and (2) December 31, 1996? Explain.
b. It has been said that the exercise of such a stock option would dilute the equity of existing stockholders in the corporation.
    i. How could this happen? Discuss.
    ii. What conditions could prevent a dilution of existing equities from taking place in this transaction? Discuss.

• Case 13-8

The proprietary theory, the entity theory, and the funds theory are three approaches to accounting for equities.

Required:
a. Describe briefly each of these theories.
b. State your reasons for emphasizing the application of one of these theories to each of the following.
   i. Single proprietorship
   ii. Partnership
   iii. Financial institutions (banks)
   iv. Consolidated statements
   v. Estate accounting

• Case 13-9

The total owners' equity (excess of assets over liabilities) is usually shown under a number of subcaptions on the balance sheet of a corporation.

Required:
a. List the major subdivisions of the stockholders' equity section of a corporate balance sheet and describe briefly the nature of the amounts that will appear in each section.
b. Explain fully the reasons for subdividing the amount of stockholders' equity, including legal, accounting, and other considerations.
c. Describe four different kinds of transactions that will result in paid-in or permanent capital in excess of legal or stated capital.
d. Various accounting authorities have recommended that the terms *paid-in surplus* and *earned surplus* not be used in published financial statements. Explain briefly the reason for this suggestion and indicate acceptable substitutes for the terms.

• Case 13-10

The directors of Lenox Corporation are considering issuing a stock dividend. They have asked you to discuss the proposed action by answering the following questions.

a. What is a stock dividend? How is a stock dividend distinguished from a stock split from a legal standpoint? From an accounting standpoint?
b. For what reasons does a corporation usually declare a stock dividend? A stock split?
c. Discuss the amount, if any, of retained earnings to be capitalized in connection with a stock dividend.

• Case 13-11

A corporation's capital (stockholders' equity) is a very important part of its statement of financial position.

Required:
Identify and discuss the general categories of capital (stockholders' equity) for a corporation. Be sure to enumerate specific sources included in each general category.

• Case 13-12

Stock splits and stock dividends may be used by a corporation to change the number of shares of its stock outstanding.

Required:
a. What is meant by a stock split effected in the form of a dividend?
b. From an accounting viewpoint, explain how the stock split effected in the form of a dividend differs from an ordinary stock dividend.
c. How should a stock dividend which has been declared but not yet issued be classified in a statement of financial position? Why?

• Case 13-13

Jones Company has adopted a traditional stock option for its officers and other employees. This plan is properly considered a compensatory plan.

Required:
Discuss how accounting for this plan will affect net earnings and earnings per share. (Ignore income tax considerations and accounting for income tax benefits.)

Recommended Additional Readings

Clark, Myrtle W. "Entity Theory, Modern Capital Structure Theory, and the Distinction Between Debt and Equity." *Accounting Horizons* (September 1993), pp. 14–31.

Haley, Brian W., and Thomas A. Ratcliff. "Accounting for Incentive Stock Options." *The CPA Journal* (1982), pp. 32–39.

Kimmel, Paul, and Terry D. Warfield. "Variation in Attributes of Redeemable Preferred Stock: Implications for Accounting Standards." *Accounting Horizons* (June 1993), pp. 30–40.

Nair, R. D., Larru E. Rittenberg, and Jerry J. Weygandt. "Accounting for Redeemable Preferred Stock: Unresolved Issues." *Accounting Horizons* (June 1990), pp. 33–41.

Roberts, Michael L., William D. Samson, and Michael T. Dugan. "The Stockholders' Equity Section: Form Without Substance." *Accounting Horizons* (December 1990), pp. 35–46.

Bibliography

Alvin, Gerald. "Accounting for Investment and Stock Rights: The Market Value Method." *The CPA Journal* (February 1973), pp. 126–131.

Bird, Francis A., Lewis F. Davidson, and Charles H. Smith. "Perceptions of External Accounting Transfers under Entity and Proprietary Theory." *The Accounting Review* (April 1975), pp. 233–244.

Birnberg, Jacob G. "An Information Oriented Approach to the Presentation of Common Stockholders' Equity." *The Accounting Review* (October 1964), pp. 963–971.

Boudreaux, Kenneth J., and Stephen A. Zeff. "A Note on the Measure of Compensation Implicit in Employee Stock Options." *Journal of Accounting Research* (Spring 1976), pp. 158–162.

Chang, Emily C. "Accounting for Stock Splits." *Financial Executive* (March 1969), pp. 79–80, 82–84.

Committee on Tax and Financial Entity Theory. "Report of the Committee on Tax and Financial Entity Theory." *The Accounting Review,* supplement to Vol. 48 (1973), pp. 187–192.

Foster, Taylor W., III, and Don Vickrey. "The Information Content of Stock Dividend Announcements." *The Accounting Review* (April 1976), pp. 360–370.

Goldberg, Louis. *An Inquiry into the Nature of Accounting.* American Accounting Association, Monograph No. 7, 1963.

Gynther, Reginald S. "Accounting Concepts and Behavioral Hypotheses." *The Accounting Review* (April 1967), pp. 274–290.

Hawkins, David F., and Walter J. Campbell, *Equity Valuation: Models, Analysis and Implications.* New York: Financial Executives Research Foundation, 1978.

Husband, George. "The Corporate-Entity Fiction and Accounting Theory." *The Accounting Review* (September 1938), pp. 241–253.

Li, David H. "The Nature of Corporate Residual Equity under the Entity Concept." *The Accounting Review* (April 1960), pp. 197–201.

Lowe, Howard D. "The Classification of Corporate Stock Equities." *The Accounting Review* (July 1961), pp. 425–433.

Melcher, Beatrice. *Accounting Research Study No. 15,* "Stockholders' Equity." New York: AICPA, 1973.

Millar, James A. "Split or Dividend: Do the Words Really Matter?" *The Accounting Review* (January 1977), pp. 52–55.

Modigliani, F., and M. Miller. "Cost of Capital, Corporation Finance and the Theory of Investment." *American Economic Review* (June 1958), pp. 261–297.

1964 Concepts and Standards Research Committee—The Business Entity. "The Entity Concept." *The Accounting Review* (April 1965), pp. 358–367.

Pusker, Henri C. "Accounting for Capital Stock Distributions (Stock Split-Ups and Dividends)." *New York CPA* (May 1971), pp. 347–352.

Rogers, Donald R., and R. W. Schattke. "Buy-Outs of Stock Options: Compensation or Capital?" *Journal of Accountancy* (August 1972), pp. 55–59.

Scott, Richard A. "Owners' Equity, the Anachronistic Element." *The Accounting Review* (October 1979), pp. 750–763.

Simons, Donald R., and Jerry J. Weygandt. "Stock Options Revisited: Accounting for Option Buy-Outs." *The CPA Journal* (September 1973), pp. 779–783.

Smith, Clifford W., Jr., and Jerold L. Zimmerman. "Valuing Employer Stock Option Plans Using Option Pricing Methods." *Journal of Accounting Research* (Autumn 1976), pp. 357–364.

Smith, Ralph E., and Leroy F. Imdieke. "Accounting for Stock Issued to Employees." *Journal of Accountancy* (November 1974), pp. 68–75.

Soujanen, Waino. "Enterprise Theory and Corporate Balance Sheets." *The Accounting Review* (January 1958), pp. 56–65.

Sprouse, Robert T. "The Significance of the Concept of the Corporation in Accounting Analyses." *The Accounting Review* (July 1957), pp. 369–378.

Staubus, George J. "The Residual Equity Point of View in Accounting." *The Accounting Review* (January 1959), pp. 3–13.

Thomas, Paula Bevels, and Larry E. Farmer. "Accounting for Stock Options and SARs: The Equality Question." *Journal of Accountancy* (June 1984), pp. 92–98.

Vatter, William J. "Corporate Stock Equities." *Modern Accounting Theory*. Morton Backer, ed. Englewood Cliffs, N.J.: Prentice-Hall, 1966.

Vatter, William J. *The Fund Theory of Accounting and Its Implications for Financial Reports*. Chicago, Ill.: University of Chicago Press, 1947.

Weygandt, Jerry J. "Valuation of Stock Option Contracts." *The Accounting Review* (January 1977), pp. 40–51.

CHAPTER 14

Accounting for
Multiple Entities

Since the inception of the corporate form of organization, business enterprises have found it beneficial to combine operations to achieve efficiencies of scale. These combined operations may vary from corporate joint ventures in which two or more corporations join together as a partnership for a particular project, such as drilling an offshore oil well, to the sale of one company to another. Accounting for the acquisition of one company by another is complicated by the fact that various terms may be used to describe these acquisitions. Such terms as *consolidation, combination, merger, pooling of interest,* and *purchase* have all been used interchangeably despite the fact that they are not all the same and some are subclassifications of others. In this chapter we shall focus on four aspects of accounting for multiple entities: (1) the acquisition of one company by another—*combinations,* (2) the reporting of parent and subsidiary relationships—*consolidations* and *segment reporting,* (3) accounting for the acquisition of a company by acquiring stock directly from the stockholders—*tender offers,* and (4) accounting for acquired subsidiaries—*push-down accounting.*

Business Combinations

Combining two or more previously separate business organizations into a single entity has been an observable phenomenon since the late 1800s. Wyatt has categorized this phenomenon as follows:

The classical era   The period from 1890 to 1904, following the passage of the Sherman Act. These combinations were generally accomplished through a holding company whose purpose was vertical integration of all operations from the acquisition of raw materials to the sale of the product.

Second wave The period from the end of World War I to the end of the 1920s. These combinations were generally piecemeal acquisitions whose purpose was to expand the operations of the acquiring company.

Third wave The period from the end of World War II through the 1960s. These again were piecemeal acquisitions designed to strengthen competitive position, diversify into new areas, or keep up with technological changes.[1]

In addition to the foregoing reasons, several other factors may cause a business organization to consider combining with another organization.

Tax consequences The purchasing corporation may accrue the benefits of operating loss carryforwards from acquired corporations.

Growth and diversification The purchasing corporation may wish to acquire a new product or enter a new market.

Financial considerations A larger asset base may make it easier for the corporation to acquire additional funds from capital markets.

Competitive pressure Economies of scale may alleviate a highly competitive market situation.

Profit and retirement The seller may be motivated by a high profit or the desire to retire.[2]

After the Securities and Exchange Commission was established during the 1930s, two methods of accounting for business combinations evolved: *purchase* and *pooling of interests*. These methods are described in more detail in the following comments.

In accounting for business combinations it is essential to recall that fair reporting of the results of economic events for a particular enterprise is the essence of the accounting process. These reports should not be biased in favor of any group and must be based on the underlying substance of the economic events. There are two methods of achieving majority ownership in another corporation: (1) the acquiring corporation purchases the voting stock of the acquired corporation for cash or (2) the acquiring corporation exchanges its voting stock for the voting stock of the acquired corporation. The essential question then becomes: Is the economic substance of these events different enough to warrant different methods of accounting?

As noted earlier, there are two methods of accounting for business combinations: (1) purchase and (2) pooling of interests. Under the *purchase* method, the assets of the acquired company are recorded at their market value in the same manner as was discussed in Chapter 7 for group purchases of assets. That is, the individual *fair market value* of each asset is recorded. Any liabilities assumed by the acquiring company are then deducted from this amount and any excess between the net assets received and the cash paid is recorded as

---

[1] Arthur R. Wyatt, *A Critical Study of Accounting for Business Combinations* (New York: AICPA, 1963), pp. 1–5.

[2] Ibid., pp. 6–8.

goodwill. As discussed in Chapter 8, goodwill is amortized over a period not to exceed 40 years. If the difference between the net assets received and the cash paid is negative, noncurrent assets (other than investments) are reduced. If the balance of the noncurrent assets is reduced to zero, a deferred credit is created and amortized. Additionally, reported income for the new combined company will include the acquiring company's income for the entire year and the acquired company's income since the date of acquisition.

The *pooling of interests* method accounts for the combination as the uniting of ownership interests. That is, it is not accounted for as an acquisition but rather as a fusion of two or more previously separate entities. The recorded amounts of assets and liabilities of the merging companies are added together on the balance sheet of the combined corporation and goodwill is *not* recorded. The par value of the stock of the acquiring company, which was issued to obtain the acquired entity, replaces the stock of the acquired entity. The remaining stockholders' equity amounts for the two entities are then combined. Additionally, income for the new reporting unit includes the income since the last reporting date for each of the previously separate companies. For example, if P Corporation acquired S Corporation on December 15, 1995, and both companies' fiscal year ended on December 31, the combined corporation reports S's net income for the entire year of 1995.

In addressing the question posed earlier on the propriety of using different recording and reporting techniques, it should be noted that two distinctly different economic events may occur in a business combination. When cash is exchanged, only one ownership group remains, even though there may be two separate legal entities, because one controls the other only one entity in essence survives. When voting stock is exchanged, all the previous owners are still present, and the companies have simply united to carry on their previously separate operations. It would therefore seem appropriate to use the purchase method for cash transactions and the pooling of interest method for stock exchanges.

The Accounting Principles Board reviewed this question and in 1970 issued *Opinion No. 16*, "Business Combinations."[3] The Board found merit in the use of both methods and did not propose that one method be used to the exclusion of the other. The APB noted that the two methods were not alternatives for accounting for the same transaction and established specific criteria for determining whether a combination should be accounted for as a purchase or as a pooling of interests. All transactions that involve the exchange of cash are to be recorded as purchases, whereas exchanges of voting stock are to be reported as pooling of interests subject to certain specific criteria. If any of the criteria are violated, the combination must be recorded as a purchase. These criteria are classified as (1) attributes of the combining companies, (2) manner of combining interests, and (3) absence of planned transactions. In essence, they were established to ensure that a combination could not be recorded as

---

[3] *Accounting Principles Board Opinion No. 16*, "Business Combinations" (New York: APB, 1970).

a pooling of interests where one group of stockholders achieved an advantage over another, or where the combined corporation did not plan to carry on the activities of the previously separate companies. These requirements are summarized as follows.

Attributes of the Combining Companies

1. Each of the combining companies is autonomous and has not been a subsidiary or division of another corporation within two years before the plan of combination is initiated.

2. Each of the combining companies is independent of the other combining companies (*independent* means no more than 10 percent investment in the outstanding voting stock of any combining company at the date of acquisition).

These attributes are intended to ensure a true fusion of two previously separate, distinct stockholder interests and assets. Consequently, criterion 1 prohibits fragments of prior entities from being pooled, whereas criterion 2 prohibits prior relationships between the two entities. Prior relationships between the combining entities would mean that the present combination combines only the previously uncombined segment. Additionally, prior relationships between the combined entity and other entities would indicate that only a portion of another entity is combined with the acquiring entity.

Manner of Combining Interests

1. The combination is effected in a single transaction or is completed in accordance with a specific plan within one year after the plan is initiated.

2. A corporation offers and issues only common stock with rights identical to those of the majority of its outstanding voting common stock in exchange for substantially all the voting common stock interest of another company at the date the plan of combination is consummated (*substantially all* means 90 percent or more of the outstanding voting common stock at the date the plan is consummated).

3. None of the combining companies changes the equity interest of the voting common stock in contemplation of effecting the combination within two years before the plan is initiated or between the date the plan is initiated and the date it is consummated. (Such changes might include distribution to stockholders, exchanges, retirements, or additional issuances.)

4. Each of the combining companies reacquires shares of voting common stock only for purposes other than business combinations, and no company reacquires more than a normal number of shares between the date the combination is initiated and consummated (normal reacquisition determined by pattern prior to initiation of the plan).

5. The ratio of the interest of an individual common stockholder to those of other common stockholders in a combining company remains the same as

a result of the exchange of stock to effect the combination. (The proportion of shares received is equal to each individual stockholder's relative proportion of previous ownership.)

6. The voting rights to which the common stock ownership interests in the resulting combined corporation are entitled are exercisable by the stockholders; the stockholders are neither deprived of nor restricted in exercising those rights for a period.

7. The combination is resolved at the date the plan is consummated and no provisions of the plan relating to the issue of securities or other considerations are pending.

The intent of the manner of combining interests attributes is to ensure that the continuation of prior ownership interests of the combining companies occurs in a manner that leaves their interests in the combined assets virtually unchanged. Under these conditions, all stockholders of the acquired entity are treated in an even-handed manner. There are no transactions designed to manipulate and bring about the combination or to favor one group of stockholders over another.

Absence of Planned Transactions

1. The combined corporation does not agree directly or indirectly to retire or reacquire all or part of the common stock issued to effect the combination.

2. The combined corporation does not enter into other financial arrangements for the benefit of former stockholders of a combining company, such as a guaranty of loans secured by stock issued in the combination, which in effect negates the exchange of equity securities.

3. The combined corporation does not intend or plan to dispose of a significant part of the assets of the combining companies within two years after the combination other than disposals in the ordinary course of business of the formerly separate companies and to eliminate duplicate facilities or excess capacity.[4]

Such planned transactions would have counteracted the conditions for a continuation of prior ownership interests. In effect, they would allow a purchase to be disguised as a pooling of interests. The parties to a business combination may prefer that it be recorded as a pooling of interests. Poolings do not change the recorded values of assets combined with the acquiring entity regardless of the value of the stock exchanged. The revenues and expenses (and subsequent cash flows) of the acquired entity would presumably be unaffected by the form of business combination, but, under the purchase method, recorded asset costs tend to be higher than under a pooling of interests. Those additional costs are written off against profits, resulting in lower earnings. Consequently, management may be prompted to structure the terms of a business combination to comply with the pooling criteria.

[4]Ibid., pars. 46–48.

It should be emphasized that pooling of interests is appropriate only when there is an exchange of voting stock and each of the foregoing conditions has been met. Where a combination has been effected by a cash transaction or any *one* of the foregoing conditions has been violated, the purchase method must be used. Additionally, when the purchase method is appropriate for combinations involving the exchange of voting common stock, the fair market value of the securities exchanged is the measure of the acquisition price.

Consolidations

When a business organization acquires control over one or more others through the acquisition of a majority of the outstanding voting stock, stockholders of the acquiring company (the *parent* company) have an interest in the assets of combined parent/*subsidiary* entity. It is logical to presume that financial statements that combine the results of both parent company and subsidiary operations and financial position would be more meaningful, at least to parent company stockholders, than presenting the separate financial statements of the parent company and each individual subsidiary company.[5] For accounting purposes, the entire group is considered a unified whole, and *SFAS No. 94* requires majority-owned subsidiaries to be *consolidated* unless the parent is precluded from exercising control or control is temporary.[6]

The criteria for the preparation of consolidated financial statements were originally described in *Accounting Research Bulletin No. 51* as follows:

1. A parent–subsidiary relationship must exist. (The parent must own at least 51 percent of the subsidiary.)
2. The parent exercises control over the subsidiary. (Where the courts are exercising control as in a bankruptcy, consolidation is not appropriate.)
3. The parent plans to maintain control over the subsidiary during the near future. (Subsidiaries that are to be sold in the near future should not be consolidated.)
4. The parent and subsidiary should operate as an integrated unit and non-homogeneous operations should be excluded.
5. The fiscal years of the units should approximate each other. (Generally, they should fall within 93 days of each other, or appropriate adjustments should be made to reflect similar closing dates.)[7]

The underlying philosophy of both *ARB No. 51* and *SFAS No. 94* is the presentation of a single, though fictional, entity with economic but not legal

---

[5]Committee on Accounting Procedure, *Accounting Research Bulletin No. 51*, "Consolidated Financial Statements," par. 1.

[6]Financial Accounting Standards Board, *Statement of Financial Accounting Standards No. 94*, "Consolidation of All Majority-Owned Subsidiaries" (Stamford, Conn.: FASB, 1987).

[7]*Accounting Research Bulletin No. 51*, "Consolidated Financial Statements" (New York: AICPA, 1959).

substance. In the preparation of consolidated financial statements, two overriding principles prevail. The first is balance sheet oriented while the second is income statement oriented.

1. The entity cannot own or owe itself.
2. The entity cannot make a profit by selling to itself.

The result of the first principle is to eliminate all assets on one company's books that are offset by liabilities on the other, for example, an account receivable on the parent's books relating to a corresponding account payable on the subsidiary's books. In the preparation of consolidated statements, the account receivable of the parent is eliminated against the account payable of the subsidiary. In applying the second principle, all intercompany sales and profits are eliminated. For example, a sale by one company is offset against a purchase by an affiliated company. (A detailed discussion of the preparation of consolidated financial statements is beyond the scope of this text.)

The Concept of Control

The impetus for consolidations is the control of the parent company over the subsidiary. Control is defined as "the power of one entity to direct or cause the direction of the management and operating and financing policies of another entity."[8] Control is normally presumed when the parent owns, either directly or indirectly, a majority of the voting stock of the subsidiary. The following exceptions indicating an inability to control a majority-owned subsidiary are cited by *SFAS No. 94*:

1. The subsidiary is in a legal reorganization or bankruptcy.
2. There are severe governmentally imposed uncertainties.

The issuance of *SFAS No. 94* was prompted by concerns over off–balance sheet financing. *ARB No. 51* allowed majority-owned subsidiaries to be excluded from consolidation (1) when the subsidiary is a foreign subsidiary, (2) when the minority interest in the subsidiary (subsidiary shares not owned by the parent company) is large relative to the equity interest of parent company stockholders in the consolidated net assets, and (3) when the subsidiary has nonhomogeneous operations.[9] The last exception, the *nonhomogeneity exception*, allowed parent companies to create financing subsidiaries or leasing companies and keep debt or capital lease obligations off the parent company balance sheets. *SFAS No. 94* eliminated these three exceptions.

In a 1991 discussion memorandum on consolidation policies and procedures, the FASB addressed the issue of whether control and the level of ownership are synonymous. In other words, the Board posed the question: Should consolidation be extended to situations where the parent company has control,

---

[8] Financial Accounting Standards Board, *Discussion Memorandum: An Analysis of Issues Related to Consolidation Policy and Procedures* (Stamford, Conn.: FASB, 1991), par. 122.

[9] Committee on Accounting Procedure, op. cit., pars. 2 and 3.

but less than majority ownership? Opponents contend that the determination of other than legal control is too subjective for practical implementation. Nevertheless, there is widespread use of the control rather than the majority ownership criterion in other countries, for example, Canada, Australia, and the United Kingdom.

Theories of Consolidation

There are two prominent equity theories of consolidation: *entity theory* and *parent company theory*. Each theory implies a unique philosophy regarding the nature and purpose of consolidated financial statements. Current practice conforms strictly to neither theory. It retains elements of both theories. Beams describes this hybrid of concepts underlying current consolidation practices and theories as *contemporary theory.*[10]

Entity Theory
Entity theory was discussed in Chapter 13. According to the entity theory of equity, the consolidated group (parent company and subsidiaries) is an entity, separate from its owners. Thus, the emphasis is on control of the group of legal entities operating as a single unit. Consolidated assets belong to the consolidated entity, and the income earned by investing in those assets is income to the consolidated entity, rather than to parent company stockholders. Hence, the purpose of consolidated statements is to provide information to all shareholders—parent company stockholders and outside minority stockholders of the subsidiaries.

Parent Company Theory
Parent company theory has evolved from the proprietary theory of equity described in Chapter 13. Under parent company theory, parent company stockholders are viewed as having a proprietary interest in the net assets of the consolidated group. The purpose of consolidated statements is to provide information primarily for parent company stockholders. The resulting financial statements reflect a parent company perspective. The assets and liabilities of the subsidiary are substituted for the parent company's investment in the subsidiary, the parent company stockholders' equity is equal to consolidated stockholders' equity, and the subsidiary revenues, expenses, gains, and losses are substituted for the parent company's investment income in the subsidiary.

Minority Interest

When a portion of the stock of a subsidiary is owned by investors outside the parent company, this ownership interest is referred to as a *minority interest.* The value of this investment results from holding shares in an affiliated company, and the determination of equity, the payment of dividends, and the basis for a claim should a liquidation ensue are all based on a claim against a

[10] Floyd A. Beams, *Advanced Accounting,* 5th edition (Englewood Cliffs: Prentice-Hall, 1991), pp. 437–439.

particular subsidiary. Therefore, the minority interest must gauge its financial status from the subsidiary company, not the parent or the consolidated group. Under current practice the minority interest is calculated as the percentage ownership in the subsidiary's net assets at the date of acquisition, plus the percentage of retained earnings since acquisition.

The classification of minority interest on consolidated balance sheets poses a problem. The prevailing pronouncements on consolidations, *ARB No. 51* and *SFAS No. 94*, neither define what minority interest is nor describe how it should be treated in published financial statements. Moreover, the prevailing consolidation theories imply different interpretations of the very nature of minority interest. In practice, minority interest has been variously (1) disclosed as a liability, (2) separately presented between liabilities and stockholders' equity, and (3) disclosed as a part of stockholders' equity.

The first two alternative treatments are consistent with parent company theory. Under parent company theory, only parent company stockholders play a proprietary role; hence, minority shares are an outside interest and should not be included in stockholders' equity. It is argued that the consolidation process has no impact on the reporting entity and are of no benefit to minority shareholders. Yet minority interest does not fit the definition of liabilities found in *Statement of Financial Accounting Concepts No. 6;* therefore, there is no established theoretical basis for reporting minority interest as debt. At the same time, minority stockholders do not enjoy the ownership privileges of parent company stockholders. Their interest is in only a part of the consolidated entity, a part over which they cannot exercise control, and, thus, they are unable to act as owners in the usual sense. Some proponents of parent company theory argue that the unique nature of minority interest is best portrayed by placing it between liabilities and stockholders' equity.

Entity theory implies that minority interest is an equity interest. The consolidated enterprise is considered one economic unit and minority shareholders contribute resources in the same manner as parent company stockholders. Moreover, like parent company stockholders, their respective interest is enhanced or burdened by changes in net assets from nonowner sources—a prerequisite for equities as described in *SFAC No. 6*, paragraph 62. Although the FASB has not officially defined minority interest, *SFAC No. 6* identified minority interest as an example of an equity interest stating that minority stockholders have ownership or residual interests in the consolidated enterprise.[11]

Proportionate Consolidation

Due to the controversy surrounding the inability to reach a consensus on the nature of minority interest, some accountants advocate an alternative, proportionate consolidation. Proportionate consolidation would ignore minority interest altogether. Under this approach, the parent company would report only its share of the assets and liabilities of the subsidiary entity, and no minor-

---

[11] Financial Accounting Standards Board, *Statement of Financial Accounting Concepts No. 6,* "Elements of Financial Statements" (Stamford, Conn.: FASB, 1985), par. 254.

ity interest need be reported. Rosenfield and Rubin[12] contend that when the parent company acquires the voting stock of the subsidiary, it obtains a right to receive its pro-rata share of dividends of the subsidiary company, implying that only the corresponding pro-rata share of subsidiary net assets is relevant to parent company stockholders. This argument ignores the concept of control that is fundamental to the very nature of consolidations. If the parent company controls the net assets of the subsidiary entity, then it controls 100 percent of those net assets, not only its proportionate share. It follows that if consolidated financial statements are intended to report the results of utilizing the assets controlled, consolidation of 100 percent of subsidiary net assets would be relevant.

A determination of the nature of minority interest is important because its very nature affects the underlying premises of alternative accounting treatments for the recognition and measurement of consolidated assets and earnings. A complete discussion of the issues involved is beyond the scope of this text. In the next section we will describe the implications of consolidation theories and the nature of minority interest recognition and measurement. Similar implications apply to other consolidated net assets.

Goodwill

Goodwill was described in Chapter 8 as an intangible asset. It is recorded when a purchase business combination occurs. In current practice, the measurement of goodwill is consistent with parent company theory. Goodwill is recorded as the difference between the cost of the investment made to acquire the subsidiary shares and the fair value of the parent company's proportionate share of the identifiable net assets of the subsidiary. No goodwill is attributed to minority interest. The result is that the value of minority interest reported on the consolidated financial statements is not affected by the consolidation process; thus, it reflects the minority interest's share of the reported book value of the subsidiary entity.

Under entity theory, because the emphasis is on the entity and not the parent company, goodwill would be valued at its total market value implied by the purchase price paid for the parent company investment. In this case, the equity interest in goodwill would be allocated between the parent company and minority interest. The result would be that the minority interest, like the parent company interest, would be measured at fair value. The balance sheet would then reflect the total fair value of the goodwill under the control of the parent company.

Drawbacks of Consolidation

The growth of business combinations has created companies with diversified operations termed *conglomerates*. The result has been the aggregation of finan-

---

[12] Paul Rosenfield and Steven Rubin, "Minority Interest: Opposing Views," *Journal of Accountancy* (March 1986), pp. 78–80, 82, 84, 86, 88–90.

cial information from various lines of business into one set of financial reports. Each new business combination results in the loss of some information to the investing public because previously reported data is now combined with existing data in consolidating financial reports.

The loss of information may be further exacerbated by the reporting requirements of *SFAS No. 94*. Assets and liabilities of heterogeneous companies are now required to be consolidated. Although empirical research indicates that the liabilities of previously unconsolidated subsidiaries may be perceived by market participants as parent company liabilities,[13] it is expected that there would be a loss of comparability among the financial information provided across companies comprising varying combinations of different types of business entities. In addition, proponents of proportionate consolidation argue that the consolidation process exaggerates reported amounts for assets and liabilities and hence affects the calculation of performance measures, such as debt-to-equity ratios.

Some accountants would prefer that in addition to consolidated financial statements companies also report the separate financial statements of the individual companies that constitute the consolidated group. In this way, users would evaluate the individual as well as the combined performance and financial position of the group and may better be able to assess the incremental addition of each unit to the total combined reporting entity.

Segment Reporting

Current generally accepted accounting principles (GAAP) do not require the reporting of separate financial statements of the companies composing a consolidated group. Nevertheless, *segment reporting,* the reporting of financial information on a less than total enterprise basis, is required under *SFAS No. 14*.

Previous GAAP required or recommended less than total enterprise reporting only in limited areas. For example, *ARB No. 43* recommended certain disclosures about foreign operations, *APB No. 18* required disclosure of certain information about companies accounted for by the equity method of accounting, and *APB No. 30* required the disclosure of information about discontinued segments. However, segmental information became an increasing part of corporate reporting during the 1970s because of two factors:

1. In 1969, the Securities and Exchange Commission required line-of-business reporting in registration statements, and in 1970 these requirements were extended to the 10-K reports.

2. In 1973, the New York Stock Exchange urged that line-of-business reporting, similar to that provided on the 10-K reports, be included in the annual reports to stockholders.

The proponents of segmental reporting base their arguments on two points:

---

[13] E. E. Comiskey, R. A. McEwen, and C. W. Mulford, "A Test of Pro Forma Consolidation of Finance Subsidiaries," *Financial Management* (Autumn 1987), pp. 45–50.

1. Various types of operations may have differing prospects for growth, rates of profitability, and degrees of risk.

2. Since management responsibility is frequently decentralized, the assessment of management ability requires less than total enterprise information.[14]

Subsequent study of the problem resulted in the issuance of *SFAS No. 14* in 1976.[15] This pronouncement requires a corporation issuing a complete set of financial statements to disclose

1. The enterprise's operations in different industries.

2. Its foreign operations and export sales.

3. Its major customers.[16]

In requiring these disclosures, *SFAS No. 14* provided the following definitions:

1. **Industry segment**   Component of an enterprise engaged in providing a product or service or group of related products and services primarily to unaffiliated customers for a profit.

2. **Reportable segment**   An industry segment for which information is required to be reported by this segment.

3. **Revenue**   Sales to unaffiliated customers and intersegment transactions similar to those with unaffiliated customers.

4. **Operating profit or loss**   Revenue minus all operating expenses including the allocation of corporate overhead.

5. **Identifiable assets**   Tangible and intangible enterprise assets that are used by the industry segment.[17]

The major problems associated with these disclosures are (1) the determination of reportable segments, (2) the allocation of joint costs, and (3) transfer pricing. In determining its reportable segments, an enterprise is required to identify the individual products and services from which it derives its revenue, group these products by industry lines and segments, and select those segments that are significant with respect to the industry as a whole. These procedures require a considerable amount of managerial judgment, and the following guidelines are presented:

1. **Existing profit centers**   The smallest units of activity for which revenue and expense information is accumulated for internal planning and control purposes represents a logical starting point for determining industry segments.

---

[14]*An Analysis of Issues Related to Financial Reporting for Segments of a Business Enterprise*, FASB Discussion Memorandum (Stamford, Conn.: FASB, 1974), pp. 6–7.

[15]*Statement of Financial Accounting Standards No. 14*, "Financial Reporting for Segments of a Business Enterprise" (Stamford, Conn.: FASB, 1976).

[16]Ibid.

[17]Ibid., par. 10.

2. *Management organization* The company's internal organizational structure generally corresponds to management's view of the major segments.

3. *Investor expectations* The information provided should coincide with the type of information needed by the public.

4. *Competitive factors* Although the disclosure of all industry segment information might injure a company's competitive position, the required disclosures are not more detailed than those typically provided by an enterprise operating within a single industry.[18]

The problems associated with the allocation of joint costs and transfer pricing also cause some difficulty in reporting segmental information. Joint costs should be allocated to the various segments in the most rational manner possible; however, since the allocation process is frequently quite arbitrary, this process may have a profound effect on reporting segmental income.

The transfer pricing problem arises when products are transferred from division to division, and one division's product becomes another's raw material. In many cases these interdivisional transfers are recorded at cost plus an amount of profit. Most accountants advocate eliminating the profit from interdivisional transfers before they are reported as segmental information.

Once the grouping of products and services by industry lines has been accomplished, *SFAS No. 14* requires companies to provide answers to the following questions:

1. Which of its segments meets the definition of reportable segments?

2. What information should be disclosed for each reportable segment?

3. Where should the required information be disclosed on the financial statements?

Reportable Segments

SFAS No. 14 requires that each industry segment that is significant to the enterprise as a whole be identified as a *reportable segment* and suggests the following separate tests for significance.

1. Its revenue, including unaffiliated customers and intersegment transfers, is 10 percent or more of combined revenue to all unaffiliated customers and intersegment transfers.

2. The absolute amount of profit or operating loss is 10 percent or more of the greater in absolute amount of
   a. The combined operating profit of all industry segments that did not incur an operating loss.
   b. The combined operating loss of all industry segments that incurred an operating loss.

3. Its identifiable assets are 10 percent or more of the combined identifiable assets of all industry segments.[19]

[18] Ibid., par. 13.

[19] Ibid., par. 15.

Additionally, it is required that the combined revenue from sales to all unaffiliated customers of all reportable segments constitutes at least 75 percent of the combined revenue from sales to unaffiliated customers of all industry segments. Furthermore, the disclosure of segmental information is not required where an enterprise is regarded as operating predominantly in a single industry (revenue, profits, and assets each constitute more than 90 percent of related combined totals for all industry segments).

Disclosed Information

SFAS No. 14 requires the following information to be presented for each of the reportable segments:

1. Revenue.
2. Profitability.
3. Identifiable assets.
4. Other disclosures.
    a. Depreciation, depletion, and amortization for each segment.
    b. Capital expenditures for each segment.
    c. Equity method investees that are vertically related and the geographic location of such investees.
    d. Changes in accounting principles (as defined by *APB Opinion No. 20*) that relate to industry segments.[20]

Method of Disclosure

Three alternative methods of disclosure of segmental information are allowed by *SFAS No. 14:*

1. Within the body of the financial statements, with appropriate explanatory disclosures.
2. Entirely in the footnotes to the financial statements.
3. In a separate schedule that is included as an integral part of the financial statements.

In analyzing segmental information, the user should keep in mind that the comparison of a segment from one enterprise with a similar segment from another enterprise has limited usefulness unless both companies use similar disaggregation procedures. The procedures used for the allocation of common costs to various segments are particularly crucial to this process, and unless similar allocation procedures are followed, comparisons may be completely distorted.

Tender Offers

It has been suggested that the period since 1970 constitutes a fourth major merger period. Since 1970, the tender offer has become an increasingly popular

---

[20] Ibid., par. 22.

method of creating a merger. A *tender* offer is an attempt by outsiders to obtain control of a firm by offering to buy the outstanding common stock at a specified price during a specified period of time. A tender offer will occur when the outsiders believe that the target firm's assets can be used more efficiently. This new wave of mergers has been aided by the relaxing of antitrust rules against vertical and horizontal mergers and the deregulation of certain industries. A tender offer differs from the more traditional merger proposal in that it is made directly to the target's stockholders. Consequently, tender offers require neither the approval nor even notification of the target's managers or board of directors. A traditional merger proposal usually must be approved by the target company's board of directors before it is submitted to a vote of shareholders.

Tender offers and mergers are both voluntary exchanges and will be agreed on only if both parties to the exchange expect to benefit. In mergers, not only must the acquiring firm and shareholders of the target firm benefit, so must the managers of the target firm. However, in tender offers, management is not a party to the exchange. In such cases management may not be perceived to benefit from the tender offer and in fact may be harmed. For this reason, tender offers are sometimes hostile (opposed by management) and sometimes friendly, whereas mergers are always friendly.

The noninvolvement of target management in a tender offer has been argued to be a desirable feature of this method of transferring ownership of a company since it may provide the benefit of displacing poorly performing management. Management's major responsibility is to the corporate shareholders. However, because of the difficulty in day-to-day oversight, firms have the incentive to devote part of their resources to enhancing management prerogatives rather than profit maximization. If this occurs, the firm will not be operating efficiently and its stock will be undervalued. It is argued that the market for corporate control can act as an external check on management. Undervalued shares invite takeover attempts as outsiders realized that gains can be made by expelling inefficient, entrenched management. That is, replacing entrenched managers with executives more willing to seek a profit maximization strategy should improve the valuation of the firm's shares in the market.

Tender offers are frequently financed by leveraged buy-outs. In a *leveraged buy-out*, a small group of investors acquires a company. The financing for this buy-out is largely obtained by issuing debt. This debt is frequently called *junk bonds* because of the associated high interest rate and perceived degree of risk. When a tender offer is financed by a leveraged buy-out the debt is ultimately repaid either by selling a part of the acquired company's assets or from operations. Some authors claim that this process results in a pool of costs imposed on society and argue that a socioeconomic impact study should accompany each potential takeover.[21] Others contend that takeovers create economic incentives that are much more compelling, resulting in a greater

---

[21] See for example, A. J. Briloff, "Cannibalizing the Transcendent Margin: Reflections on Conglomeration, LBOs, Recapitalizations and Other Manifestations of Corporate Mania," *Financial Analysts Journal* (May–June 1988), pp. 74–80.

devotion to efficiency and risk-taking by management. The tender offer phenomenon has resulted in the development of a new jargon to describe the behavior of management, the raider, and stockholders in a takeover situation. Some of these terms are:[22]

Crown Jewel   The most valued asset held by a target. Divestiture of this asset by the target is frequently a defense to resist a takeover.

Golden Parachute   The provisions of the employment contracts of top-level management that provide for severance pay or other compensation should they lose their jobs in a takeover.

Greenmail   The premium paid by a targeted company to a raider in exchange for his or her shares of the targeted company.

Lockup Defense   Gives a friendly party the right to purchase assets of the targeted firm, in particular the crown jewel, thus dissuading a takeover attempt.

Poison Pill   Gives stockholders, other than those involved in a hostile takeover, the right to purchase securities at a very favorable price in the event of a takeover.

Raiders   The person(s) or corporation attempting a takeover.

Shark Repellents   Antitakeover corporate charter amendments such as staggered terms for directors, super-majority requirement for approving a merger, or mandate that bidders pay the same price for all shares in a buyout.

Stripper   A successful raider who, once the target is acquired, sells off some of the assets of the target company.

Target   The company at which a takeover attempt is directed.

Two-Tier Offer   A takeover offer that provides a cash price for sufficient shares to obtain control of the corporation, then a lower (noncash securities) price for the remaining shares.

White Knight   A merger partner solicited by management of a target who offers an alternative merger plan to that offered by a raider, which protects the target company from the attempted takeover.

The increased number of tender offers have tested the loyalty of corporate managers to their shareholders. If managers do not resist a takeover, they often lose their jobs, while the defeat of a lucrative offer from a raider can be costly to shareholders. There is even evidence that managers frequently resist the sale of their firms when the bids substantially exceed current market values. This evidence is an example of agency theory (discussed in Chapter 2), and serves as evidence that managers may tend to serve in their own interests at stockholders' expense.

One of the most common examples of a managerial action that is in conflict with shareholders' interest is the payment of greenmail. This practice is also frequently accompanied by a standstill agreement, which prohibits the

---

[22] M. Ott and G. J. Santoni. "Mergers and Takeovers—The Value of Predators' Information," *Bulletin, Federal Reserve Bank of St. Louis* (December 1985), p. 17.

raiders from owning any of the target firm's shares for a specified period. Another antitakeover defense is the use of poison pills that make the target less attractive to the raider.

A management operating in the best interest of its shareholders will attempt to increase the takeover premium if it senses that a takeover is possible. One method of accomplishing this is to encourage a bidding contest, in which uninformed potential acquirers are invited to bid and to provide them with the information necessary to realize a profit from taking over the target.

Push-Down Accounting

Under the purchase method of accounting for consolidations, the parent company values subsidiary assets to reflect market value, but the subsidiary accounting for these asset values is not changed. Push-down accounting is a controversial accounting technique that requires a subsidiary company issuing separate financial statements to restate the reported value of its assets to the carrying amounts reported by the parent on the consolidated financial statements. That is, the subsidiary revalues its assets and liabilities to fair market value and recognizes goodwill in its own statements. Push-down accounting is required for publicly held companies whenever substantially all the common stock is acquired and the company has no outstanding public debt or preferred stock.[23]

In 1979, the AICPA's task force on consolidations examined the issues associated with push-down accounting.[24] Later, the FASB issued a discussion memorandum that contained arguments for and against push-down accounting.[25] The proponents of push-down accounting base their arguments on the following factors:

1. The price paid by the new owners, when there is a substantial change in ownership, is the most relevant basis for the measurement of assets, liabilities, and results of operations of the entity.

2. The substance of transactions resulting in changes in ownership is the same as if the new owners purchased the net assets of an existing business and established a new entity.

3. *APB Opinion No. 16* requires consolidated financial statements to reflect the parent's purchase price. The separate financial statements should also reflect that purchase price for purposes of symmetry.

4. *SFAS No. 14* requires that the separate segment financial information reflect

---

[23] Securities and Exchange Commission Staff Accounting Bulletin No. 54, *Staff Views on the Application of the ''Push Down'' Basis of Accounting in the Separate Financial Statements of Subsidiaries Acquired in Purchase Transactions* (Washington, D.C.: November 3, 1983).

[24] Accounting Standards Executive Committee, Issues Paper, *''Push Down'' Accounting* (New York: AICPA, October 30, 1979).

[25] Financial Accounting Standards Board, Discussion Memorandum, *An Analysis of Issues Related to Accounting For Business Combinations and Purchased Intangibles* (Stamford, Conn.: FASB, 1976), par. 399–405.

the parent's cost basis for each segment. Although every subsidiary is not a segment, issuing financial statements on other than a push-down basis could result in reporting conflicting financial information for the same segment or subsidiary.

5. The parent's purchase of the subsidiary is an exchange that justifies the establishment of a new cost basis.

Others argue that push-down accounting is not appropriate for the following reasons:

1. Transactions of the entity's shareholders are not transactions of the entity and, therefore, should not affect the method of accounting employed by the entity.

2. Consistency is impaired for those who depend on comparable financial statements.

3. Push-down accounting may create problems for the subsidiary in maintaining compliance with previous agreements with outsiders (e.g., debt covenants) because those agreements were based on financial data prepared on the old basis of accounting.

4. *SFAS No. 14* deals with reporting segments of a business and is not relevant to push-down accounting.

5. There is no logical method of determining which owners' transactions should qualify for push-down accounting.

The impact of the use of push-down accounting is illustrated in Exhibit 14.1. Assume a group of investors acquires a company in a leveraged buy-out transaction. The investors use $2,500 of their own funds and borrow $8,000 to acquire 100 percent of an entity's outstanding common stock. The lender required the loan to be recorded on the books of the acquired company because it was secured by the acquired company's assets. The estimated value of the acquired company's property plant and equipment was $12,000. Exhibit 14.1 illustrates the acquired company's balance sheet under historical and push-down accounting.

Under the historical cost treatment the cost of the acquired shares will be disclosed as treasury shares at cost and the company's financial position appears dismal. That is, the company's total equity has a deficit balance and the book value of the property, plant, and equipment is less than the debt they are securing. The push-down treatment paints an entirely different picture. It reflects the equity contribution of the new owners and the debt in light of the more realistic value of the fair market value of the property, plant, and equipment.

Despite these advantages, push-down accounting has been viewed as causing two major complications arising from its implementation—a reduction in reported net income and a violation of consistency. Net income is reduced when push-down accounting is used because the book value of assets is usually increased. The increased carrying value of assets leads to higher depreciation charges resulting in relatively lower reported net income. How-

EXHIBIT 14.1 *Historical Cost v. Push-Down*

	Alternative 1		Alternative 2	
	(1)	(2)	(3)	(4)
		(in thousands)		
	Historical Cost		Push-Down Treatment	
	Before Purchase	After Purchase	Push-Down Entries	Purchase Bases
Cash	$ 1,300	$ 1,300	$ —	$ 1,300
Accounts receivable	3,500	3,500	—	3,500
Inventories	1,400	1,400	—	1,400
Prepaid expenses	200	200	—	200
Total current assets	6,400	6,400		6,400
Property and equipment, net	8,900	8,900	$3,100^1$	12,000
Other assets	400	400	—	400
Excess of cost over book value of net assets acquired	—	—	$1,400^1$	1,400
	$15,700	$15,700	$4,500	$20,200
Accounts payable	$ 2,900	$ 2,900	$ —	$ 2,900
Notes payable	1,200	1,200	—	1,200
Accrued expenses	800	800	—	800
Total current liabilities	4,900	4,900	—	4,900
Long-term debt	4,800	12,800	$8,000^2$	12,800
Deferred income taxes	1,800	1,800	$(1,800)^1$	—
			$2,500^3$	
Common stock	1,000	3,500	$(1,000)^4$	2,500
Retained earnings	3,200	3,200	$(3,200)^4$	
	4,200	6,700	(1,700)	2,500
Treasury stock	—	(10,500)	—	—
Total stockholders' equity (deficit)	4,200	(3,800)	(1,700)	2,500
	$15,700	$15,700	$4,500	$20,200

Push-down entry components applied to column 1:

[1] Purchase accounting adjustments per *APB Opinion No. 16.*

[2] To record borrowed financing for acquisition.

[3] To record equity financing for acquisition.

[4] To record purchase of outstanding shares.

Source: Adapted from Michael E. Cunningham, "Push Down Accounting Pros and Cons," *Journal of Accountancy* (June 1984), p. 75.

ever, this criticism has been seen to conflict with the concept of neutrality articulated in *SFAC No. 2*.[26] That is, accounting standards should be based on the relevance and reliability of the information produced, not on the effect the rules may have on any interest group.

The consistency issue can be resolved if the users of financial statements are provided adequate disclosures that allow them to evaluate the impact of push-down accounting. For example, companies might prepare pro-forma financial statements indicating how the company's financial statements might have appeared if push-down accounting had not been implemented by the company.

An additional issue is raised when the parent acquires less than 100 percent of the subsidiary's common stock. That is, should 100 percent of the assets' book value be revalued for push-down accounting purposes? Or should the assets be revalued only to the extent of the common stock acquired by the parent? This question has not been completely resolved. The SEC requires push-down accounting only when substantially all the company's common stock is acquired. The SEC also allows recording the new basis of a subsidiary's assets only to the extent of the common stock acquired. That is, if 90 percent of the outstanding common stock is acquired, each asset will be recorded at 90 percent of the difference between its book value and market value.

Summary

There are several aspects to consider in accounting for multiple entities: (1) recording the acquisition of one company by another—combinations, (2) recording and reporting parent and subsidiary relations—consolidations and segment accounting, and (3) reporting the separate statements of subsidiaries—push-down accounting.

In accounting for business combinations, two methods of acquisition may be used. A subsidiary may be acquired by a cash exchange or by an exchange of voting stock. Additionally, two methods of accounting—the purchase and pooling of interest methods—may be used to record these acquisitions. These two methods are not alternatives for recording the same transaction. Exchanges of voting stock that satisfy certain criteria are recorded as pooling of interests; all other combinations are recorded as purchases.

Accounting for consolidations involves three major problems: (1) the presentation of consolidated assets, liabilities, and equity; (2) the presentation of consolidated net income; and (3) the presentation of minority interest. Guidelines have been established for handling each of these problems. In addition, *SFAS No. 14* established criteria for the disclosure of segmental information.

In the readings that follow, John Dewhirst discusses some additional issues raised by *APB Opinion No. 16* in accounting for business combinations, and Myrtle Clark discusses conceptual issues related to entity theory, parent company theory, and the nature of minority interest.

---

[26] P. B. Thomas and J. L. Hagler, "Push Down Accounting: A Descriptive Assessment," *Accounting Horizons* (September 1988) pp. 26–31.

Accounting for Business Combinations—The Purchase vs. Pooling of Interests Issue

John F. Dewhirst

In recent years no single accounting controversy has generated as much discussion and conflict in the United States as the struggle of the Accounting Principles Board of the American Institute of Certified Public Accountants (AICPA) to establish principles of accounting for business combinations. The struggle culminated in the issue of *Opinion 16— Business Combinations,* summarized as follows:

> *The Board finds merit in both the purchase and pooling of interests methods of accounting for business combinations and accepts neither method to the exclusion of the other. The arguments in favor of the purchase method of accounting are more persuasive if cash or other assets are distributed or liabilities are incurred to effect a combination, but arguments in favor of the pooling of interests method of accounting are more persuasive if voting common stock is issued to effect a combination of common stock interests.*
>
> *The Board also concludes that the two methods are not alternatives in accounting for the same business combination. A single method should be applied to an entire combination.[1]*

Reprinted with permission from *CA* magazine, published by the Canadian Institute of Chartered Accountants, Toronto, Canada, September 1972.

[1] The Accounting Principles Board, "Business Combinations," *Opinion No. 16* (New York: AICPA, August 1970), p. 294.

In Canada, an empirical study of Canadian experience with business combinations accounting has been published, but no principles of accounting for business combinations have been issued to date by the Canadian Institute of Chartered Accountants (CICA).[2] In view of the present situation in Canada, this article will analyze the purchase vs. pooling controversy and make recommendations on principles of accounting for business combinations.

Business Combinations, and Pooling and Purchase—Some Definitions and Implications

Opinion No. 16 (AICPA) specifies that:

> *A business combination occurs when a corporation and one or more incorporated or unincorporated businesses are brought together into one accounting entity. The single entity carries on the activities of the previously separate, independent entities.[3]*

A business combination is classified as a purchase when:

> *Consideration other than (voting) equity shares is exchanged and one group of*

[2] S. Martin et al., *Business Combinations in the 1960's: A Canadian Profile* (Toronto: CICA, 1969).

[3] *Opinion No. 16,* op cit., p. 281.

shareholders gives up its ownership interest in the assets it formerly controlled.[4]

while a business combination is classified as a pooling of interests when:

Voting equity shares are exchanged and both groups of shareholders continue their ownership interests in the combined companies.[5]

A business combination, therefore, represents the joining together of two formerly separate accounting entities as one entity, and the applicability of purchase or pooling accounting methods to the combination depends primarily on *the consideration exchanged,* i.e., voting common stock to qualify as pooling and nonvoting stock, liabilities, and/or assets to qualify as purchase. In addition, the choice between purchase and pooling hinges further on whether proportionate ownership interests have been maintained. Pooling assumes that the ownership interests of the combining companies are preserved in the combined companies, and purchase accounting assumes that only the purchaser company's ownership interest survives.

The business combinations accounting issue is important because the two proposed methods—purchase and pooling—can result in very different post-combination statements of financial position and results of operations. The pooling accounting method carries forward the net book values of both parties to the combination, along with their retained earnings balances. The

purchase accounting method, on the other hand, carries forward the net book values of the assets of the purchaser company and states the net assets of the purchased company at fair market value. In addition, purchase accounting carries forward the retained earnings of the purchaser company only.

The main problem in resolving the business combination accounting controversy is to differentiate between substance and form, with substance providing the foundation for our choice of accounting. In this process, the overall business combinations accounting controversy can be factored into several subissues. Each subissue can be analyzed separately, and the interaction of the conclusions reached for each subissue, hopefully, will point the way to the appropriate accounting for business combinations.

The Entity Concept, the Corporation, and Its Relation to Shareholders

The entity concept in financial accounting specifies that accounting is done for specific business entities. In Hendriksen's words:

The main reason for the significance of this concept is that it defines the area of interest and thus narrows the possible objects and activities and their attributes that may be selected for inclusion in financial reports.

One approach to the definition of the accounting entity is to determine the economic unit which has control over resources, accepts responsibilities for making and carrying out commitments, and conducts economic activity. Such an accounting entity may be either an individual, a partnership, or a legal corporation, or consolidated group.

An alternative approach is to define the entity in terms of the area of economic

---

[4] R. C. Holsen. "Another Look at Business Combinations," in A. R. Wyatt, *A Critical Study of Accounting for Business Combinations,* Accounting Research Study No. 5 (New York: AICPA, 1963), p. 110.

[5] Ibid.

interest of particular individuals, groups or institutions.[6]

The entity concept and its interpretation underlies much of the controversy over purchase vs. pooling. For example, purchase accounting implies that one of the two parties to a business combination purchases the other party, resulting in the termination of one entity (the purchased company) and the continuation of the other entity (the purchaser). Pooling accounting, on the other hand, implies that both parties to the combination survive as entities in combined form. *The resolution of the "surviving entity" question is important because entity considerations affect post-combination stockholders' equity accounting, and can be used to determine the need for a new basis of accounting (revaluation of assets).*

It is generally accepted in financial accounting that as long as a specific business entity survives as a going concern, no new basis of accounting arises. That is, assets are recorded at fair market value when purchased and they remain on the books at their acquisition cost in accordance with the cost concept. When an entity purchases one asset or the entire bundle of assets that constitute a going concern from another entity, it is generally accepted that the appropriate basis of valuation on the purchaser's books is fair market value (for the asset of going concern) and the basis of accounting on the books of the company being purchased is not relevant.

In the area of stockholders' equity classification, it is generally accepted to carry forward from period to period the retained earnings of an entity that still qualifies as a going concern. In the case

[6] E. S. Hendriksen, *Accounting Theory,* rev. ed. (Homewood, Ill.: R. D. Irwin, 1970), p. 99.

of pooling, if both entities are held to survive in a "federal" form, then it is legitimate to carry forward the retained earnings of both companies. Under purchase accounting, however, it is not appropriate to carry forward the retained earnings of the purchased or dissolved party to the combination because they applied only to that terminated entity. As a result, the retained earnings of the purchaser are carried forward and the retained earnings of the purchased company become "invested capital" of the purchaser.

Given the differences in the potential applicability of generally accepted accounting principles to combination accounting *depending upon the nature of the business entity (entities) that survives a combination,* the determination of the nature of the surviving entity under different conditions is crucial for our analysis.

As in all areas of the business combinations accounting controversy the matter of separating substance from form becomes exceedingly important. Some of the important questions that have to be resolved in determining the nature of the surviving entity (entities) include:

1. Does the legal form of the survivor matter, for example, whether one or both of the combining parties remain as legal corporations, or a new legal corporation is formed and both previous legal entities disappear?

2. Does the maintenance of proportionate owners' interests in the combined companies indicate that both entities survive in a federation?

3. Does the fact that the owners of one of the parties to the combination emerge with "effective control" over the combination because of their superior size and voting strength mean

that the smaller party ceases to exist as an entity, federated or otherwise?

4. Does the fact that the combined companies constitute a new "economic entity" with a very different economic nature than the two precombination companies indicate that a new entity is formed and both prior entities cease to exist?

Questions such as these must be analyzed carefully if the proper accounting is to result.

It is generally accepted that legal entity status, while in many situations an indicator of the boundaries of an accounting entity, is not the chief criterion for distinguishing accounting entities to serve as a focus for accounting. For example, legally separate entities (parents and subsidiaries) are combined in the preparation of consolidated financial statements which purport to show the financial position and results of operations of a *single* accounting entity. As a result, the legal form of the corporate combination should not be the major determinant of the nature of the surviving entity.

The maintenance of proportionate ownership interests is the major justification for the pooling of interests approach to accounting. The assumption under pooling is that "the entity" is synonymous with proportionate ownership of common voting stock, and that when a combination is effected by exchanging voting stock the perpetuation of *both entities* is accomplished. That is, the original corporate entities are not really involved and "the combination is in substance an arrangement among stockholders who exchange mutual risks and benefits."

Several challenges can be hurled against the assumption that the exchange of common voting shares so that proportionate interests are maintained is in substance *solely an arrangement among stockholders* and does not constitute the termination of one or more of the original entities. First, the idea that a "pooling" combination is in substance solely "an arrangement among stockholder groups" is a naive interpretation of contemporary business reality in the great majority of cases. It might be a reasonable interpretation of the facts when a former legally separate subsidiary is merged with its former parent,[7] or possibly when two "closely-held" corporations of similar size join together by exchanging voting stock. In the more common case of a combination involving one or more companies whose common shares are "widely held," however, it is unrealistic to assume that the combination is effected by stockholders. Rather, the action is planned, negotiated, and executed by the "professional" managements of both firms, and the shareholders generally have only token, *ex post facto* involvement.

Second, the relative size or dominance of the two parties to the combination is believed by many observers to far outweigh the significance of the perpetuation of proportionate ownership interest in widely held corporations. Many of these observers would maintain that it is a gross misrepresentation of the facts to imply, as pooling ac-

[7] APB *Opinion No. 16*, op. cit., par. 5, states that "the term business combination in this opinion excludes . . . a transfer of net assets or exchange of shares between companies under common control . . . such as between a parent corporation and its subsidiary. . . ." In my article the joining of a legally separate parent and subsidiary is termed a business combination but not one of substance, only form, and one in which the pooling of interests method should be applied.

counting implies, that *both* entities survive when one party to the combination clearly dominates post-combination business decisions, policy making, dividend declarations, and so forth, through its superior voting power and control of the board of directors and management. In other words, ownership without the powers and control that are associated with ownership is tantamount to a loss of effective proportionate ownership and the relegation to the status of an ordinary investor. And since the great majority of business combinations involve one party who is dominant, and who achieves effective voting control over the combined companies, one entity disappears (the smaller party) and the other entity survives (the dominant party).

Third, changes in the "economic nature" of the combined companies (compared to the sum of the individual predecessor companies) can be interpreted as a signal that *one or both* of the parties to the combination cease to exist as an entity. In the social science of economics, questions of resource combination, resource use, and resource productivity and earning power predominate over questions of resource ownership. From the point of view of economics, therefore, whether or not a new entity arises would appear to hinge on whether the combination leads to expectations of: major changes in cost structure (fixed vs. variable cost, and economies of scale); changes in asset composition and structure; changes in capital structure (debt vs. equity); changes in seasonal, cyclical, and trend cash flow patterns, revenue patterns, expense patterns, and earnings patterns. Changes such as these imply that a new economic entity has emerged and there is no justification for claiming that one or more of the parties to the combination

survives as an economic entity (i.e., their basic economic nature is changed by the combination).

In summary, an analysis of the implications of the entity concept for business combinations accounting suggests that in the vast majority of cases *when common voting shares are exchanged* (i.e., cases in which one party achieves effective control of the combined companies), only a dominant entity survives and one of the original entities ceases to exist. In a similar fashion, when one entity purchases another entity and the *consideration exchanged is cash or any form except proportionate common voting shares,* the purchased entity ceases to exist and the purchaser entity survives. In a third less common situation, *where two entities of similar size combine* so that neither party to the combination dominates the combined companies and where the combination is accompanied by several opportunities for the introduction of economies of scale and synergy *resulting in a significant change in the economic nature of the two entities,* it can be held that neither entity survives and that a new economic entity is created by the combination.

As a consequence, when a dominant entity is combined with a smaller entity, *regardless of the form of the consideration exchanged* and the dominant entity is deemed to be the only one to survive, a new basis of accountability (fair market value) is required for the dissolved entity only, and only the retained earnings of the dominant entity are brought forward. In a situation where the two parties to the combination are of similar size and power, and where there are abundant opportunites for changes in the post-combination economic nature of the parties, a new economic entity is created. Both old entities dissolve, a new basis of accountability for *both* parties is established, and the retained earnings from *neither* party is carried forward.[8]

The Going Concern Concept

Though not mentioned specifically by many observers, the going concern concept is relevant to the resolution of the purchase vs. pooling controversy. Implicit in the arguments of the supporters of pooling accounting, and closely related to the discussion of the entity concept above, is the assumption that no new basis of accounting (revaluation) is called for, and that the retained earnings of both companies involved in the combination can be carried forward, because *no new going concern is created.*

Precedent exists, however, to suggest that when there is a major "rupture" or "discontinuity" in a going concern such as a financial reorganization, a new basis of accountability does arise. For example, when a company is on the brink of bankruptcy and its asset values are overstated on the "books" in relation to any foreseeable estimate of revenues that they might generate, it is generally acceptable to write them down to "reasonable" values in order to make future accounting-determined earnings and

dividends possible. In other words, the expected earning power of the assets determines that assets are overvalued, and the need for a "fresh start" in the basis of accounting is recognized. In Byrd's words:

> A reorganization enables a company to obtain a fresh start without the expense and disruption involved in creating a new corporate entity. Typically a reorganization results in the write-down of overvalued assets and the elimination of a deficit. There is usually an adjustment in the long-term liabilities and a reduction in the par value of share capital. The adjustments clear the way for showing profits and paving dividends in future years. . . . After a reorganization the limited company is considered to be starting fresh—in effect as a new corporate entity.[9]

For related reasons, a significant change in the economic prospects and make-up of a combination over the prospects and make-up of the sum of the separate entities before combination suggests that a discontinuity has occurred in the going concern status of the corporations prior to and after combination, and a "fresh start" or new basis of accounting is required. In this situation, however, since economic prospects are likely to be *enhanced* by the combination, an upward revaluation of assets is suggested.

The Combination as an Exchange Transaction

In *Accounting Research Study No. 5*, Wyatt concluded that a business combina-

---

[8] There is some controversy over whether or not retained earnings should be carried forward when two entities combine and are deemed to form a "new economic entity" [see G. Mulcahy, "Accounting for Business Combinations," *CCA* (July 1972), p. 46]. The position in my article of not carrying forward the retained earnings of either party to the combination when a new entity results is based on accepted accounting practice. Personally, however, I do not have strong feelings one way or another on the issue, and I could accept carrying forward the retained earnings of both parties as long as they were properly labeled and disclosed.

[9] H. A. Finney, H. E. Miller, and K. F. Byrd, *Principles of Accounting: Intermediate*, 6th ed., Canadian ed. (Scarborough, Ont.: Prentice-Hall, 1966), p. 810.

tion ". . . is basically an exchange event in which two economic interests bargain to the consummation of an exchange of assets and/or equities."[10] Also, according to Paton and Littleton:

> The activities of the specific business enterprise, with respects to which the accountant must supply pertinent information, consist largely of exchange transactions with other enterprises. Accounting undertakes to express these exchanges quantitatively. The basic subject matter of accounting is therefore the measured consideration involved in exchange activities, especially those which are related to services acquired (cost, expense) and services rendered (revenue, income).[11]

"Measured consideration," in this case, represents the cash price or cash equivalent price of other consideration exchanged as determined by "unrestricted negotiations between independent parties" in an arm's-length transaction. "In cases in which the consideration employed in acquiring goods or services is in the form of capital stock. . . . The proper measure of actual cost in such circumstances is the amount of money which could have been raised through the issue of the securities."[12]

It goes without saying that the great majority of business combinations constitute significant exchange transactions between independent, arm's-length parties (except possibly the com-

bination of a formerly legally separate parent and subsidiary), and as a consequence it is a signal for the determination of the "measured consideration" exchanged and the recording in the combined companies' books of this consideration. At the same time, to justify the carrying forward of the book of values of both parties to the combination as pooling supporters do, we would have to ignore reality and assume that no exchange transaction took place between independent corporate parties.

Consistency of Results Over Time

One of the major reported drawbacks of purchase accounting, and one of the alleged advantages of pooling, stems from the potential "inconsistency" between pre- and post-combination earnings and earnings per share when purchase accounting methods are applied. Company managements, quite understandably, want post-merger results to be as consistent and comparable as possible with the sum of combining companies' premerger results. The application of purchase accounting in a combination normally results in a change in the valuation of tangible assets and the introduction of purchased goodwill, which can have the effect of reducing post-merger earnings, earnings per share and realign many of the key financial ratios calculable from the balance sheet and income statement.

In addition, assuming unrealistically that there are no *new* economic benefits from combination, post-merger results will generally tend to be poorer when purchase accounting is applied, than the sum of the pre-merger results of the combining companies. Purchase accounting produces poorer results be-

[10] A. R. Wyatt, *A Critical Study of Accounting for Business Combinations*, Accounting Research Study No. 5 (New York: AICPA, 1963), p. 104.

[11] W. A. Paton and A. C. Littleton, *An Introduction to Corporate Accounting Standards* (Madison, Wis.: American Accounting Association, 1962), p. 11.

[12] Ibid., pp. 26–28.

cause of the attendant upward valuation of the purchased company and the resulting higher future expense write-offs. Therefore, regardless of whether purchase, pooling, or some alternative form of accounting is appropriate for business combinations from an accounting theory point of view, company managements will be encouraged to promote pooling accounting because it normally presents their future performance in a more favorable light. The finding of a major Canadian study that the great majority of Canadian business combinations were accounted for as purchases does not change the above tendency, because Canadian accounting principles allow purchase accounting to become "pseudo-purchase accounting" (the opportunity to avoid amortizing goodwill against revenues and not requiring companies to write up tangible assets and identifiable intangibles) and have the same impact on future results as if pooling accounting was actually implemented.[13]

Hendriksen maintains that it is misleading in most combinations to assume that the sum of the prior combination earnings of the two parties is in any way comparable to the after combination earnings when he states:

It has also been recommended that when prior results of operations are presented for comparative purposes, the previous data (of the separate parties) should also be restated on a pooling basis as if the combination had taken place in an earlier period. The apparent objective is to show meaningful trends of income and earnings per share data that can be used for predictive purposes. However, this is a misuse of comparative data, because a discontinuity has occurred. The combined

firm is not the same as a group of separate firms and it is misleading to assume that nothing has happened. Furthermore, the combination generally results in a new capitalization and new relationships among the equity holders. It is misleading to assume that these new capitalization relationships existed in an earlier period under entirely different circumstances.[14]

Research has established that many company managements appear to base investment decisions on the potential impact of these decisions on externally reported financial accounting results, rather than on the basis of the inherent economic merits of each project.[15] As a consequence, pooling accounting, which assumes that the prior-combination results of the two companies are comparable to post-combination results, might encourage managers to use the wrong data for decision making. In addition, some observers believe that much of the impetus for the disastrous history of the conglomerate movement in the United States and the phenomenon of "merger by numbers" can be traced to the availability of the pooling of interests accounting device, and conglomerate managements' practices of basing their merger decisions on projected short-run pooling of interests—determined earnings per share and price-earnings ratios.

Revaluation of Only One Party to the Combination

A major complaint of the supporters of pooling accounting, and a well-founded

[13] S. Martin, et al., op. cit.

[14] Hendriksen, op. cit., p. 547.

[15] E. M. Lerner and A. Rappaport, "Limit DCF in Capital Budgeting," *Harvard Business Review* (September–October 1968), pp. 133–139.

complaint in the opinion of the author *in some circumstances*, is the "inconsistent" practice, when purchase accounting is applied, of stating the purchased company's net assets at fair market value while carrying forward the book value of net assets of the company designated to be the purchaser. Besides claiming that this action results in an inconsistent treatment of both parties to the combination, some supporters of pooling maintain that this practice results in mixing together different valuation bases and making the resulting accounting data less meaningful.

Contrary to the opinions of some supporters of pooling accounting, the use of pooling accounting does not result in consistent valuation bases for both parties to the combination because the historical cost book values of both companies are composed of mixed valuation bases. That is, even though the assets are recorded at historical cost, they were purchased in different time intervals when the current cost levels and purchasing power of the dollar differed. In addition, in the most common combination situation (where one company buys the other company, or where one company is dominant and emerges with effective control after an exchange of shares) one entity continues and the other entity dissolves. In this situation, generally accepted accounting principles dictate that there is no need to establish a new basis of accounting (revaluation) for the continuing entity (the purchaser, or dominant party), while a new basis of accounting is required for the purchased or minor party.

The objection of some pooling supporters does make sense, however, in combinations involving companies of similar size where one cannot claim in any reasonable manner that one company dominates the other company or vice versa. About all one can verify in these situations is that one of the two parties *initiated* the combination proposal; but this, in itself, is not sufficient justification for a new basis of accounting for only one of the parties at the exclusion of the other.

The Consideration Exchanged—Substance or Form

As mentioned above, regardless of all ancillary reasons for distinguishing between the applicability of purchase or pooling accounting in a given business combination, the single operational criterion that has emerged to distinguish the appropriateness of the two alternatives is whether the combination is effected by means of an exchange of common voting stock or some other form of consideration. If common stock is exchanged the combination is viewed as a pooling requiring no revaluation of either of the combining company's assets.

In a "naive" bookkeeping sense, the consideration transferred is important because if one company purchases the assets or stock of another company, the double-entry mechanism requires that debits equal credits after the acquisition. In other words, if cash and/or bonds transferred exceed the historical cost net book value of the assets of the acquired company, a debit "short-fall" is created by the transaction, and the double-entry system requires that the event be recorded as a purchase with the attendant recognition of purchased goodwill.

On the other hand, if common shares are exchanged for net assets or shares of the acquired company, the "recording value" of the acquired company is not determined directly by the act of exchanging consideration, and the accountant faces the additional responsibility of placing a value or dollar assignment to the consideration given up (or received). In this situation, the double-entry mechanism does not force him to record an imbalance between debits and credits. Any imbalance that does arise will be strictly a function of the value he assigns to the consideration exchanged. In a very fundamental sense, therefore, the primary practical reason for the two alternative methods stems from the accountant's opportunity to place a value on the consideration exchanged interacting with the double-entry mechanism.

Aside from the mechanics of the double-entry system and the discretion allowed the accountant in selecting a valuation, are there differences in substance between the several types of consideration that may be exchanged in a business combination? Are these differences in consideration exchanged important enough to justify two radically different methods of accounting for business combinations?

From the point of view of the common shareholders in both companies involved in the combination, all forms of consideration that might be exchanged are equally important. To the shareholders, the combination represents an exchange of resources (cash, or other assets) or potential resources (unissued bonds or common stock), for the resources, earning power, and possibly, the management talent inherent in the other company involved in the combination.

The form of the consideration given is not of critical importance to common shareholders of both companies, *rather it is the resource values given up regardless of any form vs. the resource values received.* The cost or value of any consideration given, on either side of the combination, is ultimately the opportunity cost of the resources (or potential resources in the case of common stock) involved

(i.e., the return forgone by not using those resources in their next most profitable use). The form of the consideration exchanged, therefore, does not appear to justify in itself two different methods of accounting for business combinations. And since differences in the form of consideration exchanged appear to be the major rationalization supporting pooling of interest accounting, one can conclude that pooling accounting is of questionable validity.

Because the value of the consideration given on either side of the combination, regardless of form, is the opportunity cost of the resources exchanged, and because the minimum required rate of return on new investment projects or the cost of capital to the company is the recognized opportunity cost of finance in corporations, the pooling method gives rise to further criticisms. Implicit in the pooling method is the assumption that the cost of capital to the acquiring firm can be equated to the historical cost net book value of the acquired company. This unusual conclusion is justified because the common stock issued by the acquiring company is valued at the net book value of the assets of the acquired company regardless of the fair market value of the shares exchanged.

Related to this unrealistic assumption about the opportunity cost of capital implicit in pooling accounting is the additional charge that the pooling of interests accounting device results in the inappropriate conversion of hidden stockholders' equity values into postcombination net income. This charge is based on the observation that issued stock and net assets received are not valued at fair market value, resulting in future post-combination net income being overstated by an unrealistically low level of expenses as the expired assets are matched with revenues. If the consideration exchanged was valued at fair market value as in the case of *internal* expansion, owners' equity, associated assets, future expenses, and net income would be realistically determined.

The Combination Decision

Reasons for Business Combinations

The reasons for business combinations are many[16] and in a given prospective combination *one or more* of the following objectives normally apply: (1) to obtain an established research capability, (2) to obtain established management and/or employee skills, (3) to obtain economies of scale in production and marketing, (4) to obtain liquid assets or financing capability, (5) to obtain control over sources of raw materials and parts, (6) to diversify into a stable line to help offset seasonal or cyclical unstable markets, (7) to obtain expertise in a new technology, (8) to accomplish vertical integration, (9) to reduce competition, and (10) to improve the position of stockholder-

---

[16]Many "nonquantitative" considerations are also important to business combination decisions, for example, the role that management of the potential acquisition will play in the companies after combination. Nonquantitative factors are especially important in the bargaining strategy stage. See G. E. MacDougal and F. V. Malek, "Master Plan or Merger Negotiations," *Harvard Business Review* (January–February 1970), pp. 77–82; J. S. R. Shad, "The Financial Realities of Mergers," *Harvard Business Review* (November–December 1969), pp. 138–141; R. M. Hexter, "How to Sell Your Company," *Harvard Business Review* (May–June 1968), pp. 71–77; and W. F. Rockwell, Jr., "How to Acquire a Company," *Harvard Business Review* (May–June 1968), pp. 121–132.

owners with respect to income tax law and estate tax law.[17]

In addition, a business combination is often considered to be an alternative to *internal growth or expansion for several reasons:* (1) the time required to enter a new industry or achieve other objectives is often shortened substantially, (2) the desired facilities and trained personnel might be less costly, (3) the large scale financing required might be handled more easily and cheaply through a direct exchange of shares than through the public capital markets, and (4) the risks of combining with an established concern might be less than venturing into a new industry or achieving other objectives by means of internal expansion.[18]

The Combination Decision Process

As discussed above, the reasons for business combinations are many and in a particular combination situation the two parties might have different reasons. Regardless of the reasons, however, the quantitative aspects of the combination decision process are best described as a form of investment or capital budgeting decision. Both parties will undertake the following steps:

1. *Place a present value on their own company as it is now.* The extent of this analysis will differ depending on the nature of the combination and can vary all the way from both parties determining an "intrinsic value" for their own common shares, to valuing the companies as a whole. In valuing the company as a whole the procedure followed includes:

---

[17]J. F. Weston and E. F. Brigham, *Managerial Finance,* 2d ed. (Toronto: Holt, Rinehart and Winston, 1962), pp. 631–638.

[18]Ibid.

(a) forecasting future net *cash* profits (cash revenues minus cash expenses) by year over the expected life of the company; (b) present-valuing the forecasted net cash profits by means of an appropriate discount rate. The appropriate discount rate in the majority of situations is the opportunity cost of capital (the policy-set required minimum rate of return or cut-off rate for new capital investment proposals) to the company.

2. *Place a present value on the other company who is a party to the combination.* The methodology will be the same as described in (1) above.

3. Both companies independently estimate the *incremental* cash profits that will result from the economies, cross-fertilization, and synergy created by the combination. They will then present-value these incremental cash profits to determine the value added by the combination.

4. Both companies estimate *their own* contribution to the incremental cash profits of the combination, discount these at their own cost of capital, and arrive at "their share" of the value added.

5. Each company now adds its estimate of the value of their own company as it is now [(1) above] to their estimate of their share added [(4) above] to arrive at their floor or base positions for negotiation.

6. Room for bargaining exists if each company's floor or base position for negotiation is *below* the value assigned by the other party to the combination. If the reverse holds true, the combination will not take place.

Room for bargaining can exist because both parties to the combination:

(1) make independent (and probably different) estimates of future net cash profits for their company and the other party, (2) both companies probably have different expectations as to the economic results of the combination, and their own and the other party's contribution to these incremental economic results, (3) both parties probably have different cost of capital rates (or minimum required rates of return for new capital investment proposals).

The Point of View of the User of Accounting Information

The American Accounting Association in A Statement of Basic Accounting Theory maintains that:

Accounting information is the chief means of reducing the uncertainty under which external users act as well as a primary means of reporting on stewardship. . . . Most decisions based on accounting information involve some kind of prediction. Common samples include forecasts of future earnings, of probable repayment of debt, and of likely managerial effectiveness.

Those external users who have or contemplate having a direct relationship with an enterprise must decide, on the basis of all available information, whether to affiliate with or to modify an existing relationship with the firm.

It is not the function of the accountant to dictate the decision models for users of accounting data. However, to the extent that there is a consensus with regard to all or part of a specific decision model, the accountant should select, process, and report relevant data.[19]

---

[19] AAA Committee, *A Statement of Basic Accounting Theory* (Evanston, Ill.: American Accounting Association, 1966), pp. 19–22.

Further, when comparing the point of view of economics, which focuses on the decision-making processes of individuals and entities, with the point of view of accounting, Edwards and Bell state:

The overwhelming test of the adequacy of accounting data as developed for any particular period must be their comparability with the expectations originally specified for that period. Where economics deals with a set of expectations and an expected profit which represents a summary of these expectations, accounting attempts to develop a list of actual events and the actual profits which result from them. [20]

Taking the American Accounting Association point of view and combining it with Edwards and Bell's statement, we find that financial accounting information is relevant or useful to external users to the extent that it:

1. Aids them to predict variables that are important in making sound decisions (i.e., provides data specified by their decision models), and

2. Serves to explain the actual results achieved by the firm over time in a manner that is comparable with the expectations originally held by the users.

From the point of view of one important user—the present and prospective common stockholder—what variables about the firm's economic behavior are relevant? First and foremost, the common stock investor is interested in predicting the future timing and rate of growth in dividends per share and mar-

ket price per share. At the same time, in formulating his expectations about the future he is also interested in reports of the actual performance of the company to compare with his original expectations. The future timing and rate of growth in dividends per share and market price per share depend very much on the attained and expected timing and rate of growth of earnings per share; therefore, the investor is interested in an earnings per share calculation that will explain what economic progress has actually been achieved, and how useful the reported earnings per share will be in predicting future economic progress.

In the business combination decision, the common stock investor realizes that company management chose to invest company resources (including those in which he has an equity) into a combination with another company rather than into some alternative use, including the possibility of achieving the same objectives through internal expansion. He also realized that those resources (including the use of potential resources such as unissued common shares) have a cost. At a minimum the cost to the company and the cost to him as a shareholder is the cost of capital to the company or the required minimum rate of return on new capital investments, while at the maximum, the cost to the company is the return forgone by not investing those resources in their next most profitable employment. If the company invests in projects (including combinations) that earn *less* than the cost of capital, the common shareholder is likely to suffer a dilution in the value of his equity in the business.

From the common shareholder's point of view, therefore, his main interest in the combination decision is to assess the values or resources given up by

---

[20] E. O. Edwards and P. W. Bell, *The Theory and Measurement of Business Income* (Berkeley and Los Angeles: University of California Press, 1961), p. 4.

his company against the values or resources contributed by the other party to the combination. If the combination promises to generate a rate of return in excess of the cost of capital of the resources his company devotes to it, the shareholder will expect higher earnings and earnings per share, as well as greater dividends per share and/or a greater increase in market price per share.

From the point of view of relevant information to the common stockholder-user of financial accounting data, therefore, it would appear that the following accounting methods would result in an earnings per share figure that is more consistent with his decision model than an earnings per share figure based on pooling accounting: (1) an accounting method that will report the fair market value of the resources given up or exchanged, and (2) an after-combination earnings per share figure determined by matching combination fair market value costs with the higher revenues that are expected to result from the combination.

The pooling accounting method will not produce results that are consistent with the stockholders' decision model because pooling implies that the consideration exchanged represents a sacrifice equivalent to the net historical cost book value of the acquired company. The net historical cost book value of the acquired company, however, bears no relationship to the fair market value or the cost of capital inherent in the consideration exchanged. Pooling also results in unrealistic future earnings per share figures because the higher future revenues generated by the benefits of combination will be matched with irrelevant costs, to produce in the usual case a gross overstatement of future net earnings attributable to the combination.

When fair market value is assigned to the tangible and intangible assets of the acquired company, future expense matching will be consistent with the revenues that flow from the synergy and economies of the combination, and future predictions of earnings per share based on these earnings figures are likely to be more reliable. In addition, companies that expand by means of mergers and acquisitions will be more directly comparable with companies that choose to expand by internal growth.

Fair market value is also superior to the pooling approach in providing data to shareholders and/or management to measure the success or failure of the company management's combination decision. The discussion above on the combination decision process demonstrates that the managements of both companies *base their combination decision on whether the expected future earnings from the combination* discounted by the cost of capital *will exceed the fair market value of the consideration given in exchange.* To turn around and report the actual future earnings based on anything other than the fair market value of the consideration exchanged will result in financial accounting data which is inconsistent with the specifications of management's original combination decision, and will also tend to make "bad" merger decisions look "good," and "good" merger decisions look "phenomenal."

Summary of the Analyses of Subissues and Recommendations for Business Combinations

The *weight of the preceding analyses* generates considerable doubt about the validity of the concept of pooling of interests accounting, except possibly in situations where nothing of substance has happened, for example, when a parent combines with a "controlled" subsidiary. In all situations where cash or any form of consideration is exchanged other than common shares, one of the previous parties to the combination ceases to exist and purchase accounting is normally appropriate. However, in cases where the combination results in major economic changes to *both* original parties: for example, where two companies of similar size combine and there are several changes in the economic nature of the combined firms, regardless of the form of consideration exchanged, *both companies should be revalued at fair market value to* reflect the fact that a new economic entity emerges with assets of substantially different earning power than *either* predecessor.

Practical Considerations of the Proposed Basis for Business Combinations

Market Value for Fair Market Value Purposes

The selection of fair market value to assign to the purchased company's net assets and both companies' net assets in the case of the creation of a new economic entity can be difficult in practice for many reasons. In the first place, when shares are exchanged, several possible valuation points of view are possible. For example, in the case of a purchase situation (where a dominant firm merges with a smaller firm) the fair market value of the smaller firm's net assets can be based on (a) the dominant firm's estimate of the value of its shares exchanged, (b) the smaller firm's estimate of the value of the dominant firm's shares, and (c) the capital market's estimate of the value of the dominant firm's shares.

Likewise, in the situation where two companies (Company A and B) of similar size and enhanced economic prospects combine to form Company AB, calling for a revaluation of both parties, the fair market value of the combined companies can differ depending upon whether the accountant considers (1) Company A's estimate of the value of Company AB, (2) Company B's estimate of the value of Company AB, (3) Company A's estimate of the value of Company A, (4) Company B's estimate of the value of Company A, (5) Company A's estimate of the value-added to the combination in total and by each of Companies A and B, (6) Company B's estimate of the value-added to the combination in total and by each of Company A and B, and (7) the capital market's estimate of the combination of Company AB's share value.

The discussion demonstrates that the accountant will be faced with an overwhelming array of possible "fair market values," even if he has access to the negotiation working papers of both parties to the combination. In addition, these fair market values can differ significantly from one party to the other, because of the differences in expectations between the parties, and differences in the cost of capital to both parties. As a consequence, *the accountant should select the capital market value of the shares exchanged shortly after combination, as an impartial, market-determined, objective basis for the determination of fair market value and associated combination goodwill for accounting purposes.*

Fair Market Value Where Capital Market Prices Are Unavailable or Unrealistic

In those few situations where the after-combination capital market price of the shares exchanged is not available or is unreliable because, for example, the market for the stock is "thin," or the stock is not listed or traded over the counter, another approach to valuation must be used. A less desirable but reasonable alternative approach would be *to revalue only the tangible assets and identifiable intangible assets at fair market value* (e.g., replacement cost), thereby refraining from computing and recording combination goodwill. This second approach would be less desirable and not as realistic as the first approach mentioned above, and would only be used by the accountant in those situations where market conditions surrounding the stock exchanged were such that any share price chosen would not be objective or reliable enough to qualify as fair market value for accounting purposes.

Determining the Type of Combination and the Appropriate Accounting Methods

According to the analyses presented above, three possible combination situations might arise with three different methods of accounting applicable. In the first situation (and probably an infrequent combination situation), a combination takes place in which nothing of economic substance happens. For example, regardless of the form of consideration exchanged (stock, cash, bonds, etc.) the combination of a former separate legal entity subsidiary with a former separate legal entity parent company, results in no change in economic substance. Because the parent controlled the subsidiary before combination all foreseeable economic advantages have already been exploited, and the combination is one of form and not economic substance. In this situation, no new basis of accounting is called for by the combination and the book values of the former companies are brought forward.

Second, the great majority of combination situations encountered will involve a large, dominant firm with a much smaller firm. In most of these cases the major changes of economic substance that result from the combination (e.g., earnings, revenues, etc.) are attributable to the restructuring and prospects of the smaller firm component. The larger firm component of the combination will likely remain substantially unchanged in an economic sense from its precombination economic make-up. In this situation, *regardless of the form of consideration exchanged,* a new basis of accounting will be applied to the net assets of the smaller party, and no new basis of accounting applied to the dominant party.

Third, a much smaller number of combination situations encountered will involve two entities of similar size, whose joining together will result in material changes in economic results and structure. In essence, a new economic entity is born out of the combination, and material economic changes are expected to occur to both original parties to the combination. In these situations, a new basis of accounting (valuation at fair market value) is required for *both* parties to the combination to reflect the economic substance inherent in the event.[21]

[21] Two alternative methods have been reported by Gertrude Mulcahy to account for a business combination where a "new economic entity" is held to be created and an acquirer cannot be identified to qualify for purchase accounting. One method consists of arbitrarily selecting one of the combining firms as the "acquirer" and applying purchase accounting, and the other alternative would be to arbitrarily designate the combination as a pooling. Both alternatives are inferior to the "new economic entity" ap-

When deciding to which of the three categories a particular combination belongs, the accountant can look to the following for guidance: (1) the precombination relationship of the two parties (e.g., subsidiary and parent), (2) the relative sizes of the two parties (e.g., as indicated by sales, net income, assets, stockholders' equity, and so forth), (3) all available information surrounding the combination event, from the internal documents (e.g., minutes) of the two parties to the information reported by external sources, to assess the degree of expected economic change.

The Related Issue of Accounting for Goodwill

In Canada, there are several options available at present for dealing with combination goodwill: (1) goodwill can be left on the books unamortized, (2) it can be amortized systematically over a reasonable period in the future, and (3) it can be written off immediately against surplus. In the United States, on the other hand, Accounting Principles Board *Opinion No. 17* does not allow the immediate write-off of combination goodwill and requires that goodwill be amortized systematically over a period of not more than forty years from the date of combination. Also, in Canada, while it is recommended in the *CICA Handbook* that *tangible* and *identifiable intangible* assets of purchased companies be revalued at fair market value, in practice virtually no Canadian companies do so. Instead, all of the excess of consideration paid over book value of the acquired company is assigned to

"purchased" goodwill.[22] The effect of these practices and options in goodwill accounting in Canada is to result in virtually all cases of purchase accounting having the *same effect* on postcombination earnings and earnings per share as the outright application of pooling accounting.

The analysis of the issue of accounting for goodwill is beyond the scope of this article; however, the author believes that the issue of business combinations accounting should be decided and principles issued *before* the principles of accounting for combinations goodwill are decided.[23] Otherwise, in Canada we are likely to experience the intense problems faced by the American Institute of Certified Public Accountants when they first attempted to do away with pooling accounting and at the same time forbid the immediate write-off of purchased goodwill against surplus.

Conclusion

The analysis of several subissues in the pooling vs. purchase accounting con-

---

proach recommended in my article because they are not based on the underlying economic conditions inherent in the combination (See G. Mulcahy, op. cit., p. 45.)

[22] S. Martin et al., op. cit.

[23] The issue of accounting for goodwill is a controversial one and can have a major impact on the net result of business combination accounting. For a discussion of some of the positions, see G. Mulcahy, ibid., p. 46, and particularly Catlett and Olsen, *Accounting for Goodwill*, ARS No. 10 (New York: AICPA, 1968), and R. Gynther, "Some Conceptualizing on Goodwill," *Accounting Review* (April 1969), pp. 247–255. In my opinion Catlett's and Olsen's analysis and recommendation to write purchase goodwill off against surplus immediately after combination flies in the face of the economic facts of the situation, and Gynther's analysis and recommendations are closer to my own thinking on the subject.

troversy including the application of relevant accounting concepts and the information needs of stockholder users of accounting information has led to the following recommendations. Pooling accounting lacks theoretical merit and is not consistent with the information needs of stockholder investors and should be virtually abandoned. What is now known as purchase accounting should be retained and applied to the great majority of combinations involving a dominant party with a small party, regardless of the form of consideration exchanged. When two companies of similar size combine with prospects of material economic change arising out of combination, both parties' net assets should be restated at fair market value to give recognition to the birth of a new economic entity.

Evolution of Concepts of Minority Interest

Myrtle W. Clark

The Financial Accounting Standards Board (FASB) is currently evaluating consolidation accounting methods under the agenda project—Consolidations and Related Matters [FASB, Highlights, 1991]. The first phase is completed and resulted in the issuance of *SFAS No. 94, Consolidation of All Majority-owned Subsidiaries.* The second phase is under way; and on September 10, 1991, the FASB issued a discussion memorandum (DM), *An Analysis of Issues Related to Consolidation Policy and Procedures,* which "is intended to cover all aspects of accounting for affiliations between entities . . ." (FASB, 1991, par. 4).

The DM addresses a number of procedural and theoretical issues wherein a parent company has a controlling interest in a subsidiary entity. In those cases

where there is less than 100 percent ownership, the appropriateness of a particular accounting approach (e.g., the measurement of goodwill or the treatment of unrealized profit arising from intercompany transactions) hinges upon the nature of noncontrolling "minority" interest, which in turn relies upon the nature of the reporting entity.[1]

[1] The DM and authors in the literature refer to the two prominent theories of equity—parent company theory and entity theory (discussed later in the paper)—to support positions taken on the nature of minority interest and to relate those positions to various accounting procedures and policies. The following example illustrates the importance of a concept of minority interest to consolidation principles and procedures. When published financial statements are prepared from the perspective of the parent company, minority interest is considered an outside interest. Under this view, when an interest in a subsidiary is purchased, goodwill is equal to cost minus the fair value of the proportion of

Thus, a concept of minority interest is important to the development and implementation of consolidation policies and procedures.

Minority interest has not received a great deal of attention in the accounting literature. The question of the fundamental nature of minority interest has been linked to the question of whether the appropriate basis of accounting should rely upon the entity concept or the parent company concept. That is, the two prominent equity theories of consolidation—entity theory[2] and parent company theory—typically appear as a basis of support for discussions pertaining to minority interest. Under the entity theory, corporate assets are independent of capital structure, and majority and minority stockholders provide alternative sources of corporate resources. Parent company theorists perceive parent company investors as the primary benefactors of the consolidated group, and minority stockholdings as outside interests.

There is little official guidance on how to account for minority interest or how to handle matters which rely upon a concept of minority interest. *"ARB No. 51, Consolidated Financial Statements* and *FASB Statement No. 94 . . .* are the prevailing authoritative literature on accounting and reporting standards for consolidated financial statements"

(FASB, 1991, par. 14). Neither pronouncement offers a definition of minority interest nor prescribes how to treat or measure minority interest in published financial statements.[3] Minority interest has appeared as a liability, between liabilities and stockholders' equity, and in stockholders' equity. Before accountants can determine how to measure and present minority interest, a consensus on the nature of minority interest is needed. Is it debt' or equity, or perhaps neither?

This paper traces the evolution of concepts of minority interest from the early 1900s to the present. The developments are placed in perspective relative to the evolution of the entity and parent company theories. The nature of minority interest, but not its measurement, is discussed. No attempt is made to critically evaluate the theoretical merits of minority interest concepts or related consolidation theories.

Early Views of Minority Interest

Minority interest has been referred to as a liability, equity, or neither. References describing the placement of minority interest in corporate balance sheets began appearing in text books and journal articles in the early 1900s.[4] Differences of

---

identifiable net assets acquired. Conversely, when the business entity is considered to be independent of its capital providers (entity theory), minority stockholders are viewed as having an equity interest. In this case, goodwill would be recorded at its total fair value, imputed from the cost of the acquisition to the parent.

[2] In the DM, the FASB referred to entity theory as the "economic unit" theory.

[3] *ARB No. 51* does not expressly define a concept of reporting entity, a concept of consolidated financial statements, or a concept of minority interest (See for example FASB, 1991, par. 20). According to the DM, *ARB No. 51* expressed some preferences, but set forth few hard and fast rules.

[4] The earliest reference is a presentation made by William M. Lybrand at the annual meeting of the American Association of Public Accountants in October 1908, which was

opinion were evident from the start. Newlowe (1948) examined 150 journal articles and books from 1908 through 1945. He determined that 84 references proposed that minority interest be listed, but either preferred no classification or did not mention where minority interest should be placed. Four authors preferred that minority interest be placed among liabilities, and 28 preferred to classify minority interest as an element of stockholders' equity. The other 34 sources cited did not address the nature of minority interest.

Early references proffered their views of what minority interest is but did not offer theoretical defenses for particular positions taken. Moreover, proponents of one view did not typically refer to alternative accounting treatments. For example, when referring to matters ". . . appertaining to minority shareholders. . . ," Dickinson (1918) stated

> *The proper practice is to take up as a liability the par value of the outstanding stock, together with its relative share of surplus, but when the amount involved is small, the proportion of surplus is not always set aside [1918, p. 183].*

Finney described minority interest as a "capital liability to outsiders," stating

_____

published in two parts in *The Journal of Accountancy* in November 1908 and December 1908. Lybrand depicted "Common Stock of Subsidiary Companies Not Owned by the Holding Corp." under a general heading of "Liabilities," following "Common Stock of the Holding Corp." (November 1908, p. 40). In Part II, Lybrand stated that "Under capital stocks will be included the stock issues of the holding company and separately stated, such part of the stocks of the subsidiary companies as are not owned by the holding company" (December 1908, p. 120).

> *If there is a minority interest, it would be wrong to eliminate the capital stock and surplus or deficit accounts of the subsidiary entirely, because they represent two things: (1) The capital liability to the holding company, which is an intercompany relation and is therefore eliminated; and (2) the capital liability to the minority stockholders, which is an outside relation and must therefore be shown in the consolidated balance sheet [1922, p. 20].*

Newlowe referred to minority interest as "proprietors," noting

> *From the point of view of the majority interests, the algebraic sum of the capital stock, surplus, deficit, and proprietorship reserves belonging to minority interests is a liability. However, the minority stockholders rank as proprietors rather than creditors. The minority interest, therefore should be shown on the consolidated balance sheet as a special net worth account [1926, p. 6].*

And, Rorem wrote

> *In cases where the parent company owns most, but not all, of the stock of the subsidiary, the interest of minority stockholders should be shown separately as a special proprietary item on the consolidated balance sheet [1928, p. 440].*

In all four cases, no more was said about the nature of minority interest.

During the 1940s, authors began to offer theoretical arguments to support a favored position. For example, Sunley and Carter argued

> *This interest of the minority is thus somewhat similar to the interest of a creditor. The creditor hopes for the prosperity of his customer so that he may receive some share in that prosperity; but, on the other hand, the creditor does not wish*

his customer's prosperity to be made at the expense of the creditor's own profits [1944, p. 361].

In addition, the pros and cons of alternative accounting treatments for minority interest began to be compared and contrasted. Childs wrote

It would seem that a minority interest should not be looked upon as a liability unless it represents recalcitrant stockholders whom the majority is trying to buy out or a capital consumed by losses which, nevertheless, has a "nuisance" value. It does not have a lien on any assets; it does have a proprietary equity in certain assets and is a part of the capital of the enterprise. To deny a minority interest co-ordinate status with the majority because it does not represent an equity in the assets of more than one legal entity is no more logical than to deny a liability a co-ordinate position with other consolidated liabilities for the same reason [1949, p. 55].

Minority Interest as a Liability—AAA

The initial position of the American Accounting Association (AAA) was that minority stockholdings are outside interests. Kohler presented a paper at the 1929 annual meeting of the AAA which was later published in *The Accounting Review*. The paper represented "the main opinion" of the Executive Committee regarding the topic of consolidated reports (Kohler, 1938, p. 63). The Committee determined that "outside stockholders" possess attributes of creditors because "their interests do not parallel those of the controlling entity" (Kohler, 1938, p. 67). Consistent with others writing on the topic of minority interest during this period, no theoretical support was given for this statement.

In 1955, the AAA Committee on Concepts and Standards issued *Supplementary Statement No. 7, "Consolidated Financial Statements."* Consistent with the 1929 Executive Committee's position, minority interest was referred to as an "outside financial interest" along with preferred stock and debt instruments (AAA, 1955, p. 194). However, the 1955 Committee did not mention where minority interest should be shown in published financial statements, nor did the Committee offer a definition of what minority interest is.

The thrust of the 1955 Statement was to set forth basic principles of consolidated financial statements. One of those principles was that: "In so far as practicable, the consolidated data should reflect the underlying assumption that they represent the operations, resources, and equities of a single entity" (AAA, 1955, p. 194). A subsequent Statement, *"Accounting and Reporting Standards for Corporate Financial Statements: 1957 Revision,"* expanded and clarified the principle of the consolidated entity, but again was silent on the subject of the nature of minority interest (AAA, 1957).

Proponents of the entity concept argue that classifying minority interest as a liability is inconsistent with the view that consolidated financial statements are prepared for a single entity. Thus, the 1957 AAA Committee's silence on this point may be interpreted as indicating a shift from the 1929 Executive Committee's position as described by Kohler.

Minority Interest as Equity

The view which holds that minority interest is an equity interest is rooted in the development of the entity theory. Paton described the essence of the entity theory. Paton (1922) proposed that the accounting equation is properly depicted as "Assets = Equities." Equities were described as ". . . a marvelous diffusion of all aspects of ownership—control, income, risk, etc.—among a host of investors" (Paton, 1922, p. 73). Accordingly, all types of corporate securities represent equity in corporate assets. Paton argued that a mere change in the source of corporate capital does not affect the cost of factors of production. It follows that the corporate entity is independent of its capital structure. Assets are corporate assets, and income is corporate income until distributed as returns to the various capital providers.[5] Under this scenario, consolidated financial statements would be prepared for the entity, rather than being extensions of the separate financial statements of the parent company.

Moonitz (1942) pointed out that because there was no generally accepted theory of consolidation, a number of confusing alternative and sometimes contradictory practices coexisted. He extended the discussion of the entity theory to consolidated financial statements and argued that the entity concept provides an appropriate theoretical base. Moonitz viewed the consolidated balance sheet as a depiction of assets and liabilities associated with an affiliated group as though they belonged to a single operating unit. Following Paton's argument, Moonitz stated

In accordance with our fundamental premise, a consolidated balance sheet contains a list of the assets and liabilities

[5]In his theory book Paton did not describe minority interest nor did he address any consolidation issues vis-a-vis the entity theory. His ideas were extended to consolidation policies by Moonitz (1942).

assignable to an affiliated group treated as a single operating unit. The net worth or capital is therefore the net worth or capital of the whole group [1942, pp. 241–2].

That is, the minority interest, like the controlling interest, provides net worth which is utilized to carry on the operating activities of the consolidated group. According to Moonitz, "minority interest serves as a reminder that complete community of interest in the affiliated companies does not exist, and the divergence of interest must be recognized" (1942, p. 241). Thus, net worth should be divided between controlling and minority interest in order not to exaggerate the extent of the equity of the controlling interest.

Position of the Committee on Accounting Procedure

Although the AICPA has not taken an official stand on the nature of minority interest, *ARB 43* (1953) does provide support for the entity concept. In Chapter 7, the following statement is made: "The income of the corporation is determined as that of a separate entity without regard to the equity of the respective shareholders in such income" (Section B, par. 6). This statement is consistent with the entity theory position taken by Paton and Littleton in 1940. Specifically, the corporation can be viewed as "an institution separate and distinct from the parties who furnish funds" (Paton and Littleton, 1940, p. 8).

On the other hand, *ARB 51* states

The purpose of consolidated statements is to present, primarily for the benefit of the shareholders and creditors of the parent company, the results of operations and the financial position of a parent company and its subsidiaries essentially as if the group were a single company with one or more branches or divisions *[par. 1].*

No mention is made of where to place outside interests on the balance sheet, but the above statement could provide support for the "parent company" theory of equity which has been utilized to justify placement of minority interest outside of owners' equity. If consolidated financial statements are prepared to benefit parent company capital providers, then the consolidation process merely sets forth the details of parent company investments. From the parent company perspective, consolidations transform parent company financial statements and do not provide information which is relevant for minority interest decision making.

The Origin of Parent Company Theory

The parent company theory has evolved from the proprietary theory of equity, which in the corporate context has been referred to as an association, or representative viewpoint. Husband described the corporation as ". . . a group of individuals associated for the purpose of business enterprise, so organized that its affairs are conducted through representatives" (1938, p. 242). He argued that although stockholders do not have legal title to corporate assets, they are proprietors because their equity changes in response to the incurrence of corporate income. Consequently, stockholders are proprietors. They possess title in equity. In a later paper, Husband expanded his arguments and referred to the corporation as an agency organization which operates for the benefit of the common stockholder entrepreneur (Husband, 1954). Although Husband referred to his theory as an association, or representative viewpoint, it is consistent with the proprietary theory of equity in

which the corporation is seen as an association of entrepreneurs (Li, 1960, p. 258).

Husband did not address the issue of the nature of minority interest. Although he referred to consolidated statements, no attempt was made to link the development of the proprietary theory to the early propositions that minority interest is not appropriately considered a part of owners' equity. As a result, the early concepts of "outside interests" and the proprietary theory were developed independently of each other. Conversely, early concepts of minority interest as owners' equity were linked to the entity concept and arguments of proponents have relied upon the development of and implications inherent in the entity concept.

Positions Taken in the 1960s

Those Based on the Entity Theory

During the 1960s, the entity concept was expanded upon, but little new was said about implications for minority interest. Moonitz continued to defend the entity concept and argued that minority interest clearly reflects proprietary ownership because there is no obligation to pay anything to minority shareholders (1960, p. 46). Sapienza (1960) agreed and proposed that minority interest be presented in the balance sheet as a special class of stockholders.

In 1964, an AAA Committee was charged to explore the depth and significance of the entity concept. The ensuing AAA report concluded that the role of the entity concept should be to serve as a guide for determining what information should be reported to users (AAA, 1965, p. 358). The report stated that consolidated financial statements are prepared primarily for parent company stockholders (a position which is consistent with that taken by the AICPA in *ARB 51*). Those stockholders are interested in information about investments in subsidiary companies. However, because the essence of the reporting entity is that its existence is separable from any view on how to report, "the concept does not dictate solutions to the valuation and disclosure problems arising from business combinations" (AAA, 1965, p. 367).

On the surface, the 1965 AAA report appeared to support the entity concept, but narrowed it from that envisioned by Moonitz and Paton and Littleton. Instead of the economic unit being regarded as the corporation itself, the emphasis that consolidated statements are prepared primarily for the parent company's stockholders appeared to redefine the entity concept in terms of the primary user of published financial statements. In essence, this new definition could be seen as a relabeling of Husband's proprietary theory, and as such could be interpreted as providing support for the 1938 AAA "outside interests" position. However, like its predecessor committees, the 1965 AAA committee report did not specifically address minority interest.

Minority Interest as a Separate and Distinct Equity

Writing prior to the 1965 AAA report, Smolinski (1963) described minority interest as a "unique" interest. He said that it is neither a liability nor an item of owners' equity. Rather, minority interest "is an interest in only one unit of the consolidated entity, and any rights which it has, are rights to the net assets of this unit" (Smolinski, 1963, p. 167). In other words, majority stockholders, not minority stockholders, have a claim to the total consolidated net assets. This view has apparently been shared by a large number of consolidated entities, because historically, a majority of companies have reported minority interest between debt and stockholders' equity. (See for example, Campbell, 1962, p. 99, and FASB, 1991, p. 21.)

Positions Taken in the 1970s

Expansion of the Entity Concept

Hendriksen (1970) favored a return of the entity concept to encompass like consideration of all equity providers as envisioned by Paton and Littleton and Moonitz. He pointed out that the stated objective of *ARB 51* was to view the reporting enterprise as a single economic unit, but at the same time emphasized the interests of the parent company's shareholders. Hendriksen stated

If the entire enterprise is really one economic unit, all interested parties should be given equal consideration, as in the enterprise theory; or the entity theory should be expanded to include the entire economic entity rather than merely the legal entity of the parent corporation [1970, p. 515].

Stated differently, Hendriksen felt that the entity concept as described in official pronouncements was too narrowly defined to encompass the true nature of economic entity. Limiting the reporting entity to the parent company has resulted in treating minority shareholders as outsiders, in the same manner as liabilities. Nevertheless, both majority and minority stockholders provide equity capital to the entire enterprise. Hence, minority interest should be accorded treatment similar to that of the parent company's stockholders.

International Accounting Standards

In 1972, the Accountants International Study Group, which was associated with the AICPA and similar bodies in other countries, reported on the results of a study regarding the nature of consolidated financial statements. The report favored the "parent company" concept which it described as one which views consolidated financial statements as an extension of the parent company statements. As such, the consolidation process simply replaces the parent company's investment account with the individual assets and liabilities underlying that investment. When this occurs, minority shareholders are considered an outside group.

The study group report stated that the predominant practice in the United States, Canada, and the United Kingdom is to show the minority interest as a separate item outside stockholders' equity. The report concluded that this practice is appropriate. It did not state whether minority interest should be reported as a liability or be placed in a separate category between liabilities and stockholders' equity. However, to state that it should be reported as a separate item could be interpreted as supporting the latter position. The subsequent pronouncement *(International Accounting Standard No. 3)* officially affirmed the position taken by the study group. That is, minority interest is not an element of stockholders' equity and should be shown as a separate item.

Minority Interest as a Standing Source of Capital

Scott (1979) was critical of placing minority interest in a separate category. He described placement of items such as minority interest between liabilities and stockholders' equity as "items, seemingly adrift in a 'no man's land'" (Scott, 1979, p. 758).

Instead, Scott proposed that the classification of equities should depend on whether or not they provide permanent sources of capital. He argued that the going concern assumption negates the relevance of dividing equities between liabilities and owners' equity. Accordingly, such a division is based upon legal claims which are not resorted to under normal circumstances (Scott, 1979, p. 759). Scott stated that sources of capital should be divided between transitory sources and standing sources. Because contributions of majority and minority stockholders are relatively permanent, both should be classified as standing sources of capital.

Recent Views

No Reporting of Minority Interest

A recent argument holds that because there is no consensus on the nature of minority interest, parent company stockholders would be better served if no minority interest was reported at all. Rosenfield and Rubin (1985) commented that minority interest does not fit neatly into any balance sheet category. Proportional consolidation, in which the parent company reports only its proportionate share of the items reported by a subsidiary, was described as having appealing characteristics (Rosenfield and Rubin, 1985, p. 95). Although both authors appear to believe that minority interest should not be reported in consolidated financial statements, their 1986 article presented opposing views on how not to do so.

According to Rosenfield, a new view of equity is needed. He argued that consolidated financial statements should continue to reflect the total assets and liabilities of the parent and subsidiary. But the residual represents the combined interest of majority and minority stockholders in the consolidated reporting entity itself and is, therefore, the entity's equity in its own assets. The implication is that consolidated entities should report only one amount—the residual (Rosenfield and Rubin, 1986, p. 84). This view is consistent with Husband's description of the entity concept as providing a rationale for disclosing stockholder claims as equity (1954, p. 556). Another name given to the Rosenfield view is contemporary theory (see Beams below).

Rubin countered, stating that Rosenfield's approach would still include minority interest in stockholders' equity. Hence it would still be disclosed, but camouflaged. He proposed that "the only sound way to exclude amounts that relate to minority stockholdings from the numbers column is to exclude all such amounts, and the only way to do that is through proportional consolidation" (Rosenfield and Rubin, 1986, p. 88). The contention is that when a subsidiary's voting stock is acquired, the parent obtains the right to receive a pro-rata share of dividends, when declared. This pro-rata claim implies that only the parent's pro-rata share of the subsidiary's assets and liabilities is relevant information to parent company stockholders. Hence, proportional consolidation provides relevant information to the primary users of consolidated statements, present and prospective parent company investors.

The FASB's View

Like its predecessors, the Committee on Accounting Procedure and the Accounting Principles Board, the FASB has yet to take an official stand on the nature of minority interest. Nevertheless, the Board has described minority interest as an example of a financial statement item which fits the definition of equities, rather than liabilities. Reflecting the view of Moonitz, *SFAC No. 6* (1985) states

Minority interests in net assets of consolidated subsidiaries do not represent present obligations of the enterprise to pay cash or distribute other assets to minority stockholders. Rather, these stockholders have ownership or residual interests in a consolidated enterprise [par. 254].

In the recent Discussion Memorandum, *Distinguishing between Liability and Equity Instruments and Accounting for Instruments with Characteristics of Both,* the FASB reiterated the position that minority interest does not meet current definitions of liabilities and thus must be an equity interest (FASB, 1990, par. 16). The Board acknowledged that "Advocates of the parent company concept, however, generally take the position that a minority interest is a liability or perhaps that it is neither a liability nor equity" (FASB, 1990, par. 16). The Discussion Memorandum went on to say that the issue of the nature of minority interest is being addressed as a part of the entity project.

SFAS No. 94 determined that, unless control was clearly lacking, all majority owned subsidiaries should be consolidated. The standard amends *ARB 51,* but does not change the stated objective of consolidated financial statements. When discussing the basis for its conclusions, the Board stated that "Those who invest in the parent company of an affiliated group of corporations invest in the whole group, which constitutes the enterprise that is a potential source of cash flows to them as a result of their investment" (*SFAS No. 94,* Appendix B, 1987, par. 34). This means that consolidated financial statements provide relevant information to parent company investors in accordance with the objectives of financial reporting as outlined in *SFAC No. 1* (*SFAS No. 94,* Appendix B, 1987, par. 35). At the same time, the reference to investing in "the whole group" could be interpreted as implying that parent company stockholders provide capital for the economic entity, an entity concept perspective.

The FASB's 1991 consolidation procedures DM presented and discussed the pros and cons of alternative views of consolidation theory and the nature of minority interest. Based on paragraph 1 of *ARB 51*, the Board defined consolidated financial statements as

A set of financial statements that presents, primarily for the benefit of the shareholders and creditors of the parent company, the combined assets, liabilities, revenues, expenses, gains, losses, and cash flows of a parent and those of its subsidiaries that satisfy the criteria established for consolidation [1991, par. 61].

The wording of the definition retains the parent company focus of *ARB 51* while allowing the flexibility to include alternative consolidation criteria. The Board acknowledged that issues being addressed and those to be addressed in subsequent FASB releases may result in redefinitions or even new categories of the elements of financial statements. Hence, it is unclear just what position, if any, will emerge.

Legal Claims

According to *SFAC No. 6*, "liabilities and equities are mutually exclusive claims to or interests in the enterprise's assets by entities other than the enterprise, and liabilities take precedence over ownership interests" (1985, par. 54). This statement implies that the classification of minority interest should be unambiguous. Minority interest is either an equity or a liability interest. Classification between liabilities and stockholders' equity does not qualify as an element of financial statements.

The FASB determined that equity is an "ownership interest" which is "enhanced or burdened by increases and decreases in net assets from nonowner sources as well as investments by owners and distributions to owners" [*SFAC No. 6*, 1985, par. 62). Assets and liabilities can be independently defined and measured (Hendriksen, 1970, p. 495). But the value of equity is affected by operations and the income of the enterprise. Unlike liabilities, "no class of equity carries an unconditional right to receive future transfers of assets from the enterprise except in liquidation, and then only after liabilities have been satisfied" (*SFAC No. 6*, 1985, par. 62).

There is no question that majority stockholdings fit the definition of equity. A strong case can be made that minority stockholdings do also. Minority interest is affected by investments, dividends, and earnings of the subsidiary entity. Their only claim to corporate assets is residual in nature. Like the majority, minority interest does not represent a present obligation to distribute corporate resources. Future receipt of corporate assets is contingent upon the declaration of dividends or liquidation.

Nevertheless, while majority stockholders control and have an ownership interest in the combined entity, the minority interest's residual claim is limited to the net assets of the subsidiary's segment of the combined entity. Moreover, their segment of the consolidated group is controlled by the parent company. They may participate in policy decisions of the subsidiary, but cannot control them. Hence, from the minority stockholders' perspective, a noncontrolling interest in the consolidated entity is unlike that of the majority.

Positions Taken in Recent Textbooks

The inability of official bodies to decide what to do with minority interest is reflected in current advanced accounting textbooks. Like their early counterparts, some textbooks classify minority interest as a liability, some as a part of stockholders' equity, and some as neither. Others present alternative views but express no preference.[6]

Fischer, Taylor, and Leer (1990) stress entity theory. They define and measure minority interest as an equity interest and include it in stockholders' equity. Heufner and Largay concur, stating

We believe that the minority interest problem is one of disclosure of the fact that not all of S's shares are held internally. Since the resources controlled by the consolidated entity relate to both the majority and minority stockholders, in consolidation both sets of interests must be treated consistently. In our view, minority shareholders may be viewed as shareholders in the consolidated entity even though their interest is limited to part of the consolidated entity. Therefore it is our view that the amount assigned to the minority interest should be included as a separate item within consolidated stockholders' equity [1992, p. 181].

Larsen (1991) takes the opposite view. He argues that minority shareholders are a special class of creditors. This position is buttressed by the argument that minority shareholders typically do not exercise ownership control whatsoever.

Pahler and Mori (1991) assert that the consolidation process has no impact

upon the reporting entity. Therefore, ". . . consolidated financial statements are usually of no benefit whatsoever to the minority shareholders" (Pahler and Mori, 1991, p. 212), and minority interest should not be a part of stockholders' equity. At the same time, reporting minority interest as a liability has little or no theoretical support. Rather, minority interest ". . . is an equity interest, but not of the parent company, which is the reporting entity" (Pahler and Mori, 1991, p. 211). Pahler and Mori conclude that reporting minority interest between liabilities and stockholders' equity reflects its unique nature.

Beams (1991) states that neither entity theory nor parent company theory are consistently followed in practice. He describes a third theory which he calls contemporary theory (pp. 437–439). Contemporary theory is described as a merging of the two equity theories. Like parent company theory, contemporary theory identifies the primary user as common stockholders of the parent company. At the same time, the financial statements present the financial position and results of operations of a single business entity. Minority interest is reported as a part of stockholders' equity but is not reported as a separate amount. Contemporary theory is consistent with the position taken by Rosenfield (Rosenfield and Rubin, 1986); with the 1965 AAA Committee's definition of the entity concept; and with the purpose of consolidated financial statements set forth in *ARB 51* (which was reaffirmed in the appendix to *SFAS No. 94*).

Current Accounting Practice

Lack of agreement on a theory of consolidation and a consistent treatment of the nature of minority interest is reflected in current accounting practice.

[6] For example, Hoyle (1991) and Griffin, Williams, Boatsman, and Vickrey (1991) do not express a preference for a particular consolidation approach, nor do they appear to prefer any one method of presenting minority interest in consolidated financial statements.

A sample of 100 industrial companies which reported minority interest in their balance sheets in 1990 was drawn from Compustat. Company balance sheets on Compustat Corporate Text were scanned for the placement of minority interest. Of the 100 companies, only 11 reported minority interest as an element of stockholders' equity. Twenty-one companies added minority interest to liabilities. Twenty-five companies placed minority interest between stockholders' equity and a subtotal for liabilities. The remaining 43 companies listed minority interest above stockholders' equity, but did not subtotal the preceding liabilities. In this context, minority interest appears to be indistinguishable from liabilities. It appears that the preparer is content to allow the user to decide whether to include minority interest with liabilities when conducting financial statement analyses. It is clear that practice has not conformed to the FASB's definition of minority interest in *SFAC No. 6*. However, it is not clear whether practitioners view minority interest as a liability or a separate unclassified item.

Summary

This paper traced the development and discussion of concepts regarding the nature of minority interest from the views which appeared in the literature during the early 1900s through 1991. Current views which have appeared in recent journal articles and textbooks and in current accounting practice were also examined.

Concepts of minority interest are tied directly to the evolution of theories of corporate equity. The review has shown that entity theorists originally perceived corporate reporting as reflecting the legal entity of the corporate enterprise. It follows that all claims to corporate assets should receive the same treatment. Under this concept, minority interests would be treated in a manner similar to majority stockholdings.

As the entity theory evolved, its definition was narrowed to take a user oriented approach which is consistent with the contemporary theory as described by Beams. Accordingly, consolidated financial statements are prepared primarily for the parent company's stockholders, but because they report the consolidated companies as a single economic entity, the residual equity includes both minority and majority interest in the consolidated net assets.

The parent company concept evolved from the representative viewpoint proposed by Husband. The parent company concept is consistent with the proprietary theory of equity which holds that a corporation's primary responsibility is to provide a return to its common stockholders—the corporate entrepreneurs. For the consolidated entity, corporate entrepreneurs are the parent company's common stockholders, not minority stockholders. Hence, minority interest is an outside interest and should not be reported as an element of stockholders' equity. Proponents have used this theory to argue that minority interest is a liability, and that it should be presented in its own special category, even for proportional reporting wherein no minority interest is reported at all.

The evolution has led to no conclusion on the issue of the nature of minority interest. The FASB has taken no stand. Nor is there any consensus in the literature on the appropriateness of any one position.

References

Accountants International Study Group, "Consolidated Financial Statements," *Cur-*

rent *Recommended Practices in Canada, the United Kingdom and the United States* (September 1972).

American Accounting Association, "Accounting and Reporting Standards for Corporate Financial Statements: 1957 Revision," *The Accounting Review* (October 1957): 536–546.

———, Committee on Concepts and Standards, "Consolidated Financial Statements, Supplementary Statement No. 7." *The Accounting Review* (April 1955): 194–197.

———, 1964 Concepts and Standards Research Study Committee—The Business Entity Concept, "The Entity Concept," *The Accounting Review* (April 1965): 358–367.

American Institute of Certified Public Accountants, Inc., "Consolidated Financial Statements," *Accounting Research Bulletin No. 51* (August 1959).

———, "Reinstatement and Revision of Accounting Research Bulletins," *Accounting Research Bulletin No. 43* (June 1953).

Beams, Floyd A., *Advanced Accounting*, 5th ed., Englewood Cliffs: Prentice-Hall (1991).

Campbell, J. D., "Consolidation vs. Combination," *The Accounting Review* (January 1962): 99–102.

Childs, William Herbert, *Consolidated Financial Statements: Principles and Procedures*, Ithaca: Cornell University Press (1949).

Dickinson, Arthur Lowes, *Accounting Practice and Procedures*, New York: The Ronald Press Company (1918).

Financial Accounting Standards Board, "An Analysis of Issues Related to Consolidation Policy and Procedures," *Discussion Memorandum* (September 10, 1991).

———, "Consolidation of All Majority-Owned Subsidiaries," *Statement of Financial Accounting Standards No. 94* (October 1987).

———, "Distinguishing between Liability and Equity Instruments and Accounting for Instruments with Characteristics of Both," *Discussion Memorandum* (August 21, 1990).

———, "Elements of Financial Statements," *Statement of Financial Accounting Concepts No. 6.* (December 1985).

———, "Highlights of First Quarter of 1991," *Status Report No. 219, Financial Accounting Series No. 102* (April 9, 1991).

Finney, H. A., *Consolidated Statements for Holding Companies and Subsidiaries*, New York: Prentice-Hall (1922).

Fischer, Paul M., William James Taylor, and J. Arthur Leer, *Advanced Accounting*, 4th ed., Cincinnati: South-Western (1990).

Griffin, Charles H., Thomas H. Williams, James R. Boatsman, and Don W. Vickrey, *Advanced Accounting*, 6th ed., Homewood: Richard D. Irwin (1991).

Hendriksen, Eldon S., *Accounting Theory*, Homewood: Richard D. Irwin (1970).

Heufner, Ronald J., and James A. Largay III, *Advanced Financial Accounting*, 3rd ed., Fort Worth: The Dryden Press (1992).

Hoyle, Joe B., *Advanced Accounting*, 3rd ed. Homewood: Richard D. Irwin (1991).

Husband, George R., "The Corporate-Entity Fiction and Accounting Theory," *The Accounting Review* (1938): 241–253.

———, "The Entity Concept of Accounting," *The Accounting Review* (October 1954): 552–563.

International Accounting Standards Committee, "Consolidated Financial Statements," *International Accounting Standard No. 3* (1976).

Kohler, E. L., "Some Tentative Propositions Underlying Consolidated Reports," *The Accounting Review* (March 1938): 63–77.

Larsen, E. John, *Modern Advanced Accounting*, 5th ed., New York: McGraw Hill (1991).

Li, David H., "The Nature of Corporate Residual Equity Under the Entity Concept," *The Accounting Review* (April 1960): 258–263.

Lybrand, William M., "The Accounting of Industrial Enterprise," *The Journal of Accountancy* (November 1908): 32–40.

———, "The Accounting of Industrial Enterprise. Part II," *The Journal of Accountancy* (December 1908): 111–121.

Moonitz, Maurice, "The Changing Concept of Liabilities," *The Accounting Review* (May 1960): 41–46.

———, "The Entity Approach to Consolidated Statements," *The Accounting Review* (July 1942): 236–242.

Newlowe, George Hills, *Consolidated Balance Sheet*, New York: The Ronald Press Co. (1926).

————, *Consolidated Statements: Including Mergers and Acquisitions*, Boston: D. C. Heath and Co. (1948).

Pahler, Arnold J., and Joseph E. Mori, *Advanced Accounting: Concepts and Practice*, 4th ed., San Diego: Harcourt Brace Jovanovich, Inc. (1991).

Paton, William Andrew, *Accounting Theory*, New York: The Ronald Press (1922).

———— and A. C. Littleton, *An Introduction to Corporate Accounting Standards*, Chicago: American Accounting Association (1940).

Rorem, Clarence Rufus, *Accounting Methods*, Chicago: The University of Chicago Press (1928).

Rosenfield, Paul, and Steven Rubin, "Contemporary Issues in Consolidation and the Equity Method," *Journal of Accountancy* (June 1985): 94–97.

———— and ————, "Minority Interest: Opposing Views," *Journal of Accountancy* (March 1986): 78–80, 82, 84, 86, 88–90.

Sapienza, S. R., "The Divided House of Consolidations," *The Accounting Review* (July 1960): 503–510.

Scott, Richard A., "Owners' Equity, The Anachronistic Element," *The Accounting Review* (October 1979): 750–763.

Smolinski, Edward J., "The Adjunct Method in Consolidations," *Journal of Accounting Research* (1963): 149–178.

Sunley, William T., and William J. Carter, *Corporation Accounting*, New York: The Ronald Press Co. (1944).

Cases

• Case 14-1

The board of directors of Kessler Corporation, Bar Company, Cohen, Inc., and Mason Corporation are meeting jointly to discuss plans for a business combination. Each of the corporations has one class of common stock outstanding. Bar also has one class of preferred stock outstanding. Although terms have not yet been settled, Kessler will be the acquiring or issuing corporation. Because the directors want to conform to generally accepted accounting principles, they have asked you to attend the meeting as an advisor.

Consider the following questions independently of the others and answer each in accordance with generally accepted accounting principles. Explain your answers.

Required:

a. Assume that the combination will be consummated August 31, 1995. Explain the philosophy underlying the accounting and how the balance sheet accounts of each of the four corporations will appear on Kessler's consolidated balance sheet on September 1, 1995, if the combination is accounted for as a
   i. Pooling of interests
   ii. Purchase

b. Assume that the combination will be consummated August 31, 1995. Explain how the income statement accounts of each of the four corporations will be accounted for in preparing Kessler's consolidated income statement for the year ended December 31, 1995, if the combination is accounted for as a
   i. Pooling of interests
   ii. Purchase

c. Some of the directors believe that the terms of the combination should be agreed on immediately and that the method of accounting to be used (whether pooling of interests, purchase, or a mixture) may be chosen at some later date. Others believe that the terms of the combination and the method to be used are very closely related. Which position is correct?

d. Kessler and Mason are comparable in size; Cohen and Bar are much smaller. How do these facts affect the choice of accounting method?

e. Bar was formerly a subsidiary of Tucker Corporation, which has no other relationship to any of the four companies discussing combination. Eighteen months ago Tucker voluntarily spun off Bar. What effect, if any, do these facts have on the choice of accounting method?

f. Kessler holds 2,000 of Bar's 10,000 outstanding shares of preferred stock and 15,000 of Cohen's 100,000 outstanding shares of common stock. All of Kessler's holdings were acquired during the first three months of 1995. What effect, if any, do these facts have on the choice of accounting method?

g. It is almost certain that Mrs. Victor Mason, Sr., who holds 5 percent of Mason's common stock, will object to the combination. Assume that Kessler is able to acquire only 95 percent (rather than 100 percent) of Mason's stock, issuing Kessler common stock in exchange.

   i. Which accounting method is applicable?

   ii. If Kessler is able to acquire the remaining 5 percent at some future time—in five years, for instance—in exchange for its own common stock, which accounting method will be applicable to this second acquisition.

h. Since the directors feel that one of Mason's major divisions will not be compatible with the operations of the combined company, they anticipate that it will be sold as soon as possible after the combination is consummated. They expect to have no trouble in finding a buyer. What effect, if any, do these facts have on the choice of accounting method?

• Case 14-2

Because of irreconcilable differences of opinion, a dissenting group within the management and board of directors of the Algo Company resigned and formed the Bevo Corporation to purchase a manufacturing division of the Algo Company. After negotiation of the agreement, but just before closing and actual transfer of the property, a minority stockholder of Algo notified Bevo that a prior stockholder's agreement with Algo empowered him to prevent the sale. The minority stockholder's claim was acknowledged by Bevo's board of directors. Bevo's board then organized Casco, Inc., to acquire the minority stockholder's interest in Algo for $75,000, and Bevo advanced the cash to Casco. Bevo exercised control over Casco as a subsidiary corporation with common officers and directors. Casco paid the minority stockholder $75,000 (about twice the market value of the Algo stock) for his interest in Algo. Bevo then purchased the manufacturing division from Algo.

Required:

a. What expenditures are usually includable in the cost of property, plant, and equipment acquired in a purchase?

b. i. What are the criteria for determining whether to consolidate the financial statements of Bevo Corporation and Casco, Inc.?
   ii. Should the financial statements of Bevo Corporation and Casco, Inc., be consolidated? Discuss.
c. Assume that unconsolidated financial statements are prepared. Discuss the propriety of treating the $75,000 expenditure in the financial statements of the Bevo Corporation as
   i. An account receivable from Casco
   ii. An investment in Casco
   iii. Part of the cost of the property, plant, and equipment
   iv. A loss

• **Case 14-3**

The most recently published statement of consolidated earnings of National Industries, Inc., appears as follows:

NATIONAL INDUSTRIES, INC.
Statement of Consolidated Earnings
for the Year Ended March 31, 1996

Net sales	$38,041,200
Other revenue	407,400
Total revenue	38,448,600
Cost of products sold	27,173,300
Selling and administrative expenses	8,687,500
Interest expense	296,900
Total cost and expense	36,157,700
Earnings before income taxes	2,290,900
Provision for income taxes	1,005,200
Net earnings	$ 1,285,700

Charles Norton, a representative of a firm of security analysts, visited the central headquarters of National Industries for the purpose of obtaining more information about the company's operations.

In the annual report, National's president stated that National was engaged in the pharmaceutical, food processing, toy manufacturing, and metal working industries. Mr. Norton complained that the published statement of earnings was of limited utility in his analysis of the firm's operations. He said that National should have disclosed separately the profit earned in each of its component industries. Further, he maintained that several items appearing on the statement of consolidated retained earnings should have been included on the statement of earnings, namely, a gain of $633,400 on the sale of the furniture division in early March of the current year and an assessment for additional income taxes of $164,900 resulting from an examination of the returns covering the years ended March 31, 1995 and 1996.

Required:

a. Discuss the accounting problems involved in measuring net profit by industry segments within a company.

b. With reference to National Industries' statement of consolidated earnings, identify the specific items where difficulty might be encountered in measuring profit by each of its industry segments and explain the nature of the difficulty.

c. i. What criteria should be applied in determining whether a gain or loss should be excluded from the determination of net earnings?

   ii. What criteria should be applied in determining whether a gain or loss that is properly includable in the determination of net earnings should be included in the results of ordinary operations or shown separately as an extraordinary item after all other terms of revenue and expense?

   iii. How should the gain on the sale of the furniture division and the assessment of additional taxes each be presented in National's financial statements?

• Case 14-4

Since the 1970s, the tender offer has become a popular method of creating a merger. Tender offers are frequently financed by leveraged buy-outs.

Required:

a. Discuss how a merger is created when a tender offer is financed by a leveraged buy-out.

b. Discuss the following terms that are associated with tender offers.

   i. Crown jewel
   ii. Golden parachute
   iii. Greenmail
   iv. Poison pill
   v. Raider
   vi. Shark repellent
   vii. Target
   viii. Two-tier offer
   ix. White knight

• Case 14-5

Push-down accounting is now required for reporting the separate subsidiary financial statements for companies acquired and accounted for by the purchase method.

Required:

a. Discuss the accounting treatment required by push-down accounting for a subsidiary acquired and accounted for under the purchase method of accounting.

b. Discuss the arguments for and against push-down accounting.

• Case 14-6

The Whit Company and the Berry Company, a manufacturer and retailer, respectively, entered into a business combination whereby the Whit Company acquired for cash all the outstanding voting common stock of the Berry Company.

Required:
a. The Whit Company is preparing consolidated financial statements immediately after the consummation of the newly formed business combination. How should the Whit Company determine in general the amounts to be reported for the assets and liabilities of Berry Company? Assuming that the business combination resulted in goodwill, indicate how the amount of goodwill is determined.
b. Why and under what circumstances should Berry Company be included in the entity's consolidated financial statements?

• Case 14-7

The Bert Company and the Lyle Company entered into a business combination accounted for as a pooling of interests.

Required:
a. How should the expenses related to effecting the business combination be handled, and why?
b. How should the results of operations for the year in which the business combination occurred be reported? Why is this reporting appropriate?

• Case 14-8

In order properly to understand current generally accepted accounting principles with respect to accounting for and reporting on segments of a business enterprise, as stated by the Financial Accounting Standards Board in its *Statement No. 14,* it is necessary to be familiar with certain unique terminology.

Required:
With respect to segments of a business enterprise, explain the following terms:
a. Industry segment
b. Revenue
c. Operating profit and loss
d. Identifiable assets

• Case 14-9

A central issue in reporting on industry segments of a business enterprise is the determination of which segments are reportable.

Required:
a. What are the tests to determine whether or not an industry segment is reportable?

b. What is the test to determine if enough industry segments have been separately reported on and what is the guideline on the maximum number of industry segments to be shown?

Recommended Additional Readings

Bierman, Harold, Jr. "Proportionate Consolidation and Financial Analysis." *Accounting Horizons* (December 1992), pp. 5–17.

Briloff, Abraham J. "Dirty Pooling." *The Accounting Review* (July 1967), pp. 489–496.

Brownlee, E. Richard II, Norman S. Siegel, and Kurt D. Rasmuss. "Mergers and Acquisitions, New Considerations." *The CPA Journal* (March 1989), pp. 12–14, 16, 18–20.

Hector, Gary. "Are Shareholders Cheated by LBOs?" *Fortune* (January 19, 1987), pp. 98–100.

Knoeber, Charles R. "Golden Parachutes, Shark Repellents, and Hostile Tender Offers." *The American Economic Review* (March 1986), pp. 155–167.

Moore, James. "Push-Down Accounting: FAS 200?" *Management Accounting* (November 1988).

Pactor, Paul. "Revising GAAP for Consolidations: Join the Debate." *The CPA Journal* (July 1992), pp. 38–40, 42, 44, 47.

Rosenfield, Paul, and Steven Rubin. "Minority Interest: Opposing Views." *Journal of Accountancy* (March 1986), pp. 78–80, 82, 84, 86, 88–90.

Bibliography

Backman, Jules. "Economist Looks at Accounting for Business Combinations." *Financial Analysts Journal* (July–August 1970), pp. 39–48.

Baldwin, Bruce A. "Segment Earnings Disclosure and the Ability of Security Analysts to Forecast Earnings Per Share." *The Accounting Review* (July 1984), pp. 376–384.

Bartlett, Thomas M., Jr. "Problems in Accounting for a Business Purchase." *Financial Executive* (April 1973), pp. 52–71.

Baxter, George C., and James C. Spinney. "A Closer Look at Consolidated Financial Statement Theory." *CA Magazine* (January 1975), pp. 31–36.

Bergstein, Sol. "More on Pooling of Interest." *Journal of Accountancy* (March 1972), pp. 83–86.

Brenner, Vincent C. "Empirical Study of Support for APB Opinion No. 16." *Journal of Accounting Research* (Spring 1972), pp. 200–208.

Brown, Frank A., and Philip L. Kintzele. "The Effects of FASB Statement No. 14 on Annual Reports." *The Ohio CPA* (Summer 1979), pp. 98–103.

Burton, John C. *Accounting for Business Combinations: A Practical and Empirical Comment.* New York: Financial Executives Research Foundation, 1970.

Cohen, Stuart. "Segment Reporting by Diversified Corporations," *Massachusetts CPA Review* (March–April 1979), pp. 15–20.

Dewberry, J. Terry. "A New Approach to Business Combinations." *Management Accounting* (November 1979), pp. 44–49.

Eigen, Martin M. "Is Pooling Really Necessary?" *The Accounting Review* (July 1965), pp. 563–570.

Eiteman, Dean S. *Pooling and Purchase Accounting.* Ann Arbor: University of Michigan, 1967.

Foster, William C. "Does Pooling Present Fairly?" *The CPA Journal* (December 1974), pp. 36–41.

Foster, William C. "The Illogic of Pooling." *Financial Executive* (December 1974), pp. 16–21.

Fotenos, James F. "Accounting for Business Combinations: A Critique of APB Opinion Number 16." *Stanford Law Review* (January 1971), pp. 330–346.

Fritzemeyer, Joe R. "Accounting for Business Combinations: The Evolution of an APB Opinion." *Journal of Accountancy* (August 1969), pp. 35–49.

Gagnon, Jean-Marie. "Purchase-Pooling Choice: Some Empirical Evidence." *Journal of Accounting Research* (Spring 1971), pp. 52–72.

Gitres, David L. "Negative Goodwill Paradox." *The CPA Journal* (December 1978), pp. 45–48.

Gosman, Martin L., and Philip E. Meyer. "SFAS 94's Effect on Liquidity Disclosure." *Accounting Horizons* (March 1992), pp. 88–100.

Gunther, Samuel P. "Lingering Pooling Problems." *The CPA Journal* (June 1973), pp. 459–463.

Harmon, David Perry, Jr. "Pooling of Interests: A Case Study." *Financial Analysts Journal* (March–April 1968), pp. 82–88.

Heian, James B., and James B. Thies. "Consolidation of Finance Subsidiaries: $230 Billion in Off–Balance-Sheet Financing Comes Home to Roost." *Accounting Horizons* (March 1989), pp. 1–9.

Lauver, R. C. "The Case for Poolings." *The Accounting Review* (January 1966), pp. 65–74.

Lurie, Adolph. "Segment Reporting—Past, Present, and Future." *The CPA Journal* (August 1979), pp. 27–30.

Lurie, Adolph. "Selecting Segments of a Business." *Financial Executive* (April 1980), pp. 34–44.

Mednick, Robert. "Companies Slice and Serve Up their Financial Results under FASB 14." *Financial Executive* (March 1979), pp. 44–56.

Moonitz, Maurice. *The Entity Theory of Consolidated Statements.* Brooklyn, N.Y.: The Foundation Press, 1951.

Moville, Wig De, and A. George Petrie. "Accounting for a Bargain Purchase in a Business Combination." *Accounting Horizons* (September 1989), pp. 38–43.

Ott, Mack, and G. J. Santoni. "Mergers and Takeovers—The Value of Predators' Information." *Bulletin: Federal Reserve Bank of St. Louis* (December 1985), pp. 16–28.

Rappaport, Alfred, and Eugene M. Lerner. *A Framework for Financial Reporting by Diversified Companies.* New York: National Association of Accountants, 1969.

Rappaport, Alfred, and Eugene M. Lerner. *Segment Reporting for Managers and Investors.* New York: National Association of Accountants, 1972.

Sapienza, Samuel R. "Business Combinations." In *Modern Accounting Theory,* Morton Backer, ed. Englewood Cliffs, N.J.: Prentice-Hall, 1966, pp. 339–365.

Sapienza, Samuel R. "Distinguishing between Purchase and Pooling." *Journal of Accountancy* (June 1961), pp. 35–40.

Sapienza, Samuel R. "Divided House of Consolidations." *The Accounting Review* (July 1960), pp. 503–510.

Savage, Allan H., and B. J. Linder. "Meeting the Requirements of Line of Business Reporting." *Financial Executive* (November 1980), pp. 38–44.

Savage, Linda, and Joel Siegel. "Disposal of a Segment of a Business." *The CPA Journal* (September 1978), pp. 32–37.

Schrader, William J., Robert E. Malcom, and John J. Willingham. "In Support of Pooling." *Financial Executive* (December 1969), pp. 54–63.

Shieifer, Andrei, and Robert Vishny. "Greenmail, White Knights and Shareholders' Interest." *Rand Journal of Economics* (Autumn 1986), pp. 293–309.

Slesinger, Reuben E. "Conglomeration: Growth and Techniques." *Accounting and Business Research* (Spring 1971), pp. 145–154.

Snavely, Howard J. "'Pooling' Is Good Accounting." *Financial Analysis Journal* (November–December 1968), pp. 85–89.

Snavely, Howard J. "Pooling Should Be Mandatory." *The CPA Journal* (December 1975), pp. 23–26, and (April 1976), pp. 5–6.

Solomons, David. *Divisional Performance: Measurement and Control.* Homewood, Ill.: Richard D. Irwin, 1968.

Sprouse, Robert T. "Diversified Views about Diversified Companies." *Journal of Accounting Research* (Spring 1969), pp. 137–159.

Steedle, Lamont F. "Disclosure of Segment Information—SFAS 14." *The CPA Journal* (October 1983), pp. 34–47.

Thomas, Paula B., and J. Larry Hagler. "Push Down Accounting: A Descriptive Assessment." *Accounting Horizons* (September 1988), pp. 26–31.

Weidenbaum, Murry, and Stephen Vogt. "Takeovers and Stockholders: Winners and Losers." *California Management Review* (Summer 1987), pp. 157–168.

Wyatt, Arthur R. *A Critical Study of Accounting for Business Combinations.* New York: American Institute of Certified Public Accountants, 1963.

Wyatt, Arthur R. "Inequities in Accounting for Business Combinations." *Financial Executive* (December 1972), pp. 28–35.

Current Value
and General
Purchasing Power
Accounting

The use of historical-cost information in accounting records and financial statements has been a generally accepted accounting principle over the years. The widespread acceptance of this convention can be attributed to its objectivity and the transactions approach to income determination. Many accountants believe that only external exchanges should be measured and reported. Consequently, events that do not involve transactions are usually ignored. For example, unrealized increases in asset values are rarely recorded, since no external arm's-length transaction has occurred.

Under the historical-cost concept, transactions are measured on the basis of the number of original dollars involved. Such measurements are considered to be "objective," since the amount of cost, or revenue, can be easily verified by referring to invoices, checks, deposit receipts, and other documents. Thus, *verifiability*—which essentially means that two accountants with similar knowledge and experience could review and evaluate a transaction and reach approximately the same conclusion—and *objectivity* are accounting concepts that have been closely related to the historical-cost concept over the years.

The significance of objectivity as a major criterion for the recognition and measurement of accounting information has been questioned by various financial statement user groups for over 50 years. This criticism arises because the use of historical-cost information frequently results in income not being recognized during the period in which it occurs, for example, changes in the value of assets held by a company, and overstated income in periods of inflation. Two accounting problems are created by these factors:

1. *Valuation problem* The value of individual assets changes in relation to all other assets in the economy, irrespective of any changes in the general level of prices.

2. *Measurement unit problem*   The value of the measurement unit changes because prices change in general.

Opposition to historical cost has resulted in the development of two basically different viewpoints on the type of financial information that should be presented to account for the effect of changing values and prices. One viewpoint advocates statements prepared on the basis of current value. Current value is related to the economic concept of well-offness discussed in Chapter 3. This viewpoint addresses the valuation problem. A second viewpoint proposes financial statements that utilize historical cost information and then adjust this information to account for the effect of the overall change in prices (price-level-adjusted financial statements). This viewpoint addresses the measurement unit problem.

There are several alternative methods of determining current value, such as entry price or replacement cost, exit or selling price, and the discounted present value of expected future cash flows. Similarly, price-level financial statements have been referred to under a variety of different names such as stabilized accounting, inflation accounting, financial reporting in units of general purchasing power, and constant dollar accounting. In the following sections we will discuss the general nature of these concepts and review the evolution of the reporting requirements to account for changes in current value and price.

Current Value Accounting

The concept of *capital maintenance,* discussed in Chapter 3, indicates that no income should be recognized until capital has been maintained and costs recovered. This concept requires all assets and liabilities to be stated at their current values, and various methods have been advocated to accomplish this objective.

The most common approaches to current-value measurement are (1) entry price or replacement cost, (2) exit value or selling price, and (3) discounted present value of expected future cash flows. Each of these approaches will be discussed briefly in order to demonstrate their strengths and weaknesses.

Entry Price or Replacement Cost

Experiments using entry price or replacement cost measurements were first attempted in the 1920s. Renewed interest in the concept was generated by the work of Edwards and Bell,[1] first published in 1961. This approach to asset valuation and income determination was also advanced by Sprouse and

---

[1] E. O. Edwards and P. W. Bell, *Theory and Measurement of Business Income* (Berkeley, Calif.: University of California Press, 1961), pp. 33–69.

Moonitz[2] and a committee of the American Accounting Association,[3] among others.

Although the current accounting model relies heavily on historical cost, recent pronouncements and discussion memorandums issued by the FASB indicate a move toward providing more current value information. For example, *SFAS No. 33,* as amended, establishes guidelines for reporting supplementary current cost information for certain nonmonetary assets (these provisions are described later in this chapter); as discussed in Chapter 8, *SFAS Nos. 114* and *115* require the reporting of fair value for investments in certain financial instruments; and companies are required to disclose additional market value for information under *SFAS Nos. 105* and *107.*

When the value of a firm's assets is determined on the basis of entry price, the emphasis is on the cost of replacing the assets with similar assets. That is, what would it cost to purchase other assets similar to the ones the firm is now using? When this approach is used, each asset is valued at the amount it would cost to replace it with a similar asset in a similar condition.

According to Edwards and Bell, current entry prices allow the assessment of managerial decisions to hold assets by segregating current value income (holding gains and losses) from current operating income.[4] Under the assumption that operations will continue, this dichotomy allows the long-run profitability of the enterprise to be assessed. The recurring and relatively controllable profits can be evaluated vis-à-vis those factors that affect operations over time, but are beyond the control of management. Replacement cost provides a measure of the cost of replacing the present productive capacity and, hence, a means of evaluating how much the firm can distribute to stockholders and still maintain its productive capacity.

Nevertheless, there are numerous measurement problems encountered in determining replacement cost values. That is, the firm may be able to determine precisely the replacement cost for inventories and certain other assets; however, for many assets, particularly the physical plant, there may not be a ready market from which to acquire replacement assets. Therefore, it may be impossible to determine precisely the cost of replacement. In such cases the firm may be required to appraise the assets in order to arrive at an approximation of their current replacement value.

An alternative approach to approximate replacement cost is to use a specific purchasing power index. A specific index is designed to measure what has happened to a specific segment of the economy rather than the economy in total. When this approach is used, an index is chosen and applied to the

---

[2] Robert T. Sprouse and Maurice Moonitz, "A Tentative Set of Board Accounting Principles for Business Enterprises," *Accounting Research Study No. 3* (New York: AICPA, 1962).

[3] American Accounting Association, *A Statement of Basic Accounting Theory* (Evanston, Ill., AAA, 1966).

[4] Edwards and Bell, op cit., p. 73.

assets to obtain a measure of their replacement value. Many critics of general purchasing power adjustments assert that the use of a general index is irrelevant because it does not relate to the specific company, or does not relate perfectly to the assets of a given firm. Thus, the use of a specific index may result in valuations of assets that are closer to current value than a general index, but the result is still approximate. The actual value can be determined only when an exchange occurs.

Finally, the relevance of entry values has been questioned. Sterling argued that the entry value of unowned assets is relevant only when asset purchases are contemplated. For owned assets, entry value is irrelevant to what could be realized upon sale of those assets and to their purchase since they are already owned.[5] Moreover, the current replacement cost of a company's assets does not measure the capacity, on the basis of present holdings, to make decisions to buy, hold, or sell in the market place.[6] In short, the contention is that it does not disclose the entity's ability to adapt to present decision alternatives.

Exit Value or Selling Price

A method that may be used to determine current value is exit value or selling price. This valuation approach, which was first advocated by McNeal,[7] in the 1930s and was developed further by Sterling[8] and Chambers,[9] requires an assessment of each asset from a disposal point of view. That is, all assets— inventory, plant, equipment—are valued on the basis of what the selling price would be if the firm chose to dispose of its assets. In determining the cash equivalent exit price, it is presumed that the assets will be sold in an orderly manner, rather than in a forced liquidation.

Because holding gains and losses receive immediate recognition, the exit price approach to valuation completely abandons the realization principle for the recognition of revenues. The critical event for earnings recognition purposes becomes the point of purchase or production rather than the point of sale.

Chambers and Sterling contend that exit prices have decision relevance. Accordingly, each accounting period, management decides whether to hold, sell, or replace the asset. It is argued that exit prices provide users with better information to evaluate liquidity and thus the ability of the enterprise to adapt

[5] Robert R. Sterling, *Toward a Science of Accounting* (Houston, Texas: Scholars Book Co., 1979), p. 124.

[6] Chambers, op cit., p. 92.

[7] Kenneth McNeal, *Truth in Accounting* (Philadelphia: University of Pennsylvania Press, 1939).

[8] Robert R. Sterling, *Theory of Measurement of Enterprise Income* (Lawrence, Kan.: University of Kansas Press, 1970).

[9] Raymond J. Chambers, *Accounting, Evaluation and Economic Behavior* (Englewood Cliffs, N.J.: Prentice-Hall, 1966).

to changing economic stimuli. Because management has the option of selling the asset, exit price provides a means of assessing downside risk. It measures the current sacrifice of holding the asset and thereby provides a guide for evaluating management's stewardship function.

Like entry prices, value also poses measurement problems. First, there is the basic problem of determining a selling price for the assets, such as property, plant, and equipment, for which there is no ready market. Second, there is a question as to which selling price should be used. For example, should the value be based on forced liquidation prices or prices arising from sales in the normal course of business? The latter approach may be feasible for assets such as inventory but may be impracticable, if not impossible, for the physical plant, since it would not be disposed of in the normal course of operation.

One can argue that replacement costs are more relevant measures of the current value of fixed assets, whereas exit values are better measures of the current value of inventory items. Since management intends to use rather than sell fixed assets, their value in use is what it would cost to replace them. On the other hand, inventory is purchased for resale. Consequently, its value is directly related to its selling price to customers.

Discounted Cash Flow

A third approach to the measurement of asset value is discounted cash flow. According to this concept, the present value of the future cash flows expected to be received from the assets and liabilities is the relevant value of the assets and liabilities disclosed on the balance sheet. Income is measured under this method as the difference between the present value of the assets and liabilities at the end of the period and their present value at the beginning of the period. This measurement process is similar to the economic concept of income and is perhaps the closest approximation of the actual value of the assets in use.

A strong argument can be made for the concept of discounted cash flow. All assets are presumed to be acquired for the future service potential they provide to the firm. Furthermore, there is a presumption that the initial purchase price was paid because of a belief that the asset would generate sufficient revenue in the future to make its acquisition worthwhile. Thus, either implicitly or explicitly, the original cost was related to the present value of expected cash flows. This concept, in effect, holds that the same rationale that was applied to the original purchase should be applied at the end of each period to measure current value and periodic income.

There are three major measurement problems associated with the concept of discounted cash flow. First, the concept depends on an estimate of future cash flows by time periods. As a result, both the amount of cash to be generated in the future and the timing of that cash flow must be determined.

The second problem arises once the amount and timing of the cash flow has been estimated. In order to determine the current value of those future flows, they must be discounted to the present, since a dollar received in the future is not as valuable as a dollar received today. A discount factor must, therefore, be selected and applied to the estimates of future cash flows.

A third problem is created by the fact that the assets of a firm are interrelated. Revenues are generated by the combined use of a company's resources. Therefore, even if the company's future cash flows and the appropriate discount rate could be precisely determined, it would not be practicable to determine exactly how much each asset contributed to those cash flows. As a result, the discounted present value of individual firm assets cannot be determined and summed to determine the present value of a company.

Use of present-value techniques to measure current value can be only as valid as the estimates of future cash flows, the timing of those flows, and the appropriateness of the discount factor. To the extent that these estimates are valid, the measurement of the present value of future service potential is probably the most relevant measurement to disclose on the balance sheet. That is, this measurement is relevant in the sense that the balance sheet would provide information about the ability of the assets to produce income in the future.

Financial Reporting in Units of General Purchasing Power

As indicated in Chapter 1, a basic principle of accounting is the measurement of transactions in terms of dollars. There is also an implicit, if not explicit, assumption that the dollar is a stable measuring unit. However, the purchasing power of the dollar changes; therefore, the stable-dollar assumption has never been completely valid. The position of authoritative accounting bodies over the years has been that the amount of change in prices has been relatively insignificant. Although this position may have been accepted in the earlier days of accounting, there has been a growing consensus that the measuring unit must be adjusted to reflect the impact of inflation.

Historical Perspective

The literature on the impact of changes in value of the measuring unit is rather lengthy. The following comments are not intended to be a comprehensive survey of this literature; instead, they are provided to illustrate the development of current thought on the subject.

The most comprehensive of the early efforts to bring about changes in the measuring unit can be attributed to Henry Sweeney. In the early 1930s he published a series of articles on the subject, and his book, *Stabilized Accounting*,[10] published in 1936, set forth the procedures for adjusting financial statements to a common-sized dollar. Sweeney was motivated by the belief that it is impossible to develop meaningful financial statements when elements are measured in different-sized dollars.

---

[10]Henry W. Sweeney, *Stabilized Accounting* (New York: Harper & Bros., 1930).

In 1947,[11] 1948,[12] and 1953,[13] the Committee on Accounting Procedure (CAP) of the American Institute of Certified Public Accountants addressed itself to the accounting problems created by the rather dramatic increase in the general level of prices following World War II. The major concern of the CAP was the amount of depreciation expense being charged against current income. That is, the historical-cost depreciation write-off of the assets was much lower than the current depreciation cost. However, the CAP concluded that depreciation expense should be based on historical cost. In these three ARBs, the Committee gave its full support to the use of supplementary financial schedules, explanations, or footnotes that management might use to explain that enterprise profits sufficient to replace productive facilities at current prices must be retained to remain in business.

In 1963 the AICPA issued a research study on the effects of price level changes. *Accounting Research Study No. 6*[14] suggested that unless financial statements were adjusted for changes in the general purchasing power of the dollar they were likely to be misleading. The study also proposed the methods and procedures for making the necessary adjustments. (The adjustment procedures will be discussed in a later section of this chapter.)

The Accounting Principles Board reacted to *ARS No. 6* and the effect of inflation by issuing *APB Statement No. 3*.[15] In essence, the Board said that it agreed with *ARS No. 6* that price-level-adjusted statements contain much useful information that would not otherwise be available to the users of historical-dollar financial statements. Therefore, it was concluded that general price-level information could be presented as a supplement to the basic historical-dollar financial statements but not as an integral part of the basic statements.

The APB went on to state that the degree of inflation or deflation in an economy might become so great that historical dollar statements would lose their significance, but such was not the case in the United States at that time. In a footnote, the Board observed that it had not determined the degree of inflation or deflation that might cause general price level statements to become more meaningful than historical-cost statements.

In 1974 the Financial Accounting Standards Board decided that inflation had become a significant enough problem to warrant some further action and

---

[11] *Accounting Research Bulletin No. 33*, "Depreciation and High Costs" (New York: AICPA, 1947).

[12] Committee on Accounting Procedure, letter to American Institute of Certified Public Accountants members reaffirming the recommendations of *Accounting Research Bulletin No. 33*, October 1948.

[13] *Accounting Research Bulletin No. 43*, Chapter 9, Section A, "Depreciation and High Costs" (New York: AICPA, 1953).

[14] Staff of the Accounting Research Division, *Accounting Research Study No. 6*, "Reporting the Financial Effects of Price-Level Changes" (New York: AICPA, 1963).

[15] *Accounting Principles Board Statement No. 3*, "Financial Statements Restated for General Price-Level Changes" (New York: AICPA, 1969).

issued a proposed statement entitled "Financial Reporting in Units of General Purchasing Power."[16] This statement, which was rejected in 1976, would have required the following information, at a minimum, to be presented in units of general purchasing power for each period for which an income statement was presented:

1. *Total revenue.*
2. *Depreciation of property, plant and equipment.*
3. *Net general purchasing power gain or loss from holding monetary assets and liabilities. (If a complete or condensed general purchasing power income statement is presented, this amount shall be presented as a separate item.)*
4. *Income from continuing operations (that is, income including net general purchasing power gain or loss from holding monetary assets and liabilities but before discontinued operations, extraordinary items, and the cumulative effect of accounting changes.)*
5. *Net income.*
6. *Net income per common share.*
7. *Cash dividend per common share.*[17]

There was a further requirement that, for each date for which a balance sheet is presented, the following information, at a minimum, should be presented in units of general purchasing power:

1. *Inventories.*
2. *Working capital.*
3. *Total property, plant, and equipment, net of accumulated depreciation.*
4. *Total assets.*
5. *Total common stockholders' equity.*[18]

Despite the FASB's failure to act, in 1976 the SEC decided that inflation had become a serious enough problem to warrant disclosure of some of its effects in financial statements. *Accounting Series Release No. 190* required certain companies to disclose data on the replacement cost of their productive capacity and inventories.

In 1979 the FASB again opened the question of the effects of changing prices on financial reporting. This review resulted in the publication of *SFAS No. 33*, "Financial Reporting and Changing Prices."[19] As a result, most large companies were required to report both constant-dollar and current-cost data as supplemental information.

---

[16] Proposed Statement of Financial Accounting Standards, "Financial Reporting in Units of General Purchasing Power" (Stamford, Conn.: Financial Accounting Standards Board, 1974).

[17] Ibid., p. 17.

[18] Ibid.

[19] *FASB Statement No. 33*, "Financial Reporting and Changing Prices" (Stamford, Conn.: Financial Accounting Standards Board, 1979).

The general requirements of *ASR No. 190* and *SFAS No. 33* are contrasted in Table 15.1 on page 702.

In addition to the historical aspects of this issue, there are several key conceptual issues involved in measuring with units of general purchasing power.

Meaning and Significance of General Purchasing Power Adjustments

The concept of general purchasing power deals with the inflationary or deflationary forces operating in the economy as a whole that have a general impact on the purchasing power of the dollar. (The remainder of this discussion will examine inflation; however, in the event of deflation, the same rationale would apply, only in reverse.) This concept does not refer to a dollar spent on a specific good; rather, it refers to dollars spent in general throughout the economy.

The basic rationale of general purchasing power adjustments is that two items should be measured with the same-size dollar so that they can be properly added together to get a valid result. This total is not intended to reflect what the items are worth, since these purchasing power adjustments are not concerned with value. Rather, the purpose is to measure all items with a common-sized unit so that the impact of changes in the general purchasing power of the dollar can be determined. Consequently, if the desire is to measure some aspect of the economy using dollars, then those dollars should have the same purchasing power significance. Otherwise one might measure X in 1985 dollars and Y in 1995 dollars.

For example, suppose the historical cost of two different items was $10, but one was purchased in 1985 and the other in 1995. Under current accounting practice the two are added together and totaled as $20. However, there is clearly a difference in purchasing power in 1985 and 1995 because of the effect of inflation. Therefore, if changes in purchasing power are to be considered, the $10 from 1985 should be adjusted to the same-size dollars as the $10 from 1995. The adjustment would be as follows, assuming 50 percent inflation from 1985 to 1995.

	Unadjusted	Adjustment Factor (%)	Adjusted
1985	$10	150	$15
1995	10	100	10
	$20		$25

The adjusted number simply means that the two amounts are equal to $25 of 1995 purchasing power, since the $10 in 1985 would have purchased one and one-half times more than the $10 in 1995.

The adjustment could have been in the opposite direction, in which case

TABLE 15.1 *Relationship of SFAS No. 33 to SEC Replacement Cost Rules*

	SFAS No. 33	*ASR No. 190*
Applicability		
Entities	Public companies	Registrants
Size tests	At least: $125 million of inventories and gross properties *or* $1 billion of total assets	Inventories and gross properties at least $100 million *and* 10% of total assets
Reported in	Annual Reports (including Form 10-K)	Form 10-K
Reported for	Consolidated entity	Consolidated entity and each complete set of other statements
Measurement		
Approach	Current cost and constant dollar	Replacement cost
Focus	Replace assets (service potential) presently owned	Replace existing productive capacity
Assets covered	Inventories and properties (net), generally	Inventories and properties (gross and net), generally
Exceptions	Current cost—unprocessed natural resources and income-producing real estate	Land, oil and gas reserves, long-term construction contracts, productive capacity not to be replaced, and miscellaneous others
	Constant dollar—none	
Value ceiling	Use net realizable value or value in use when lower than amounts under dual measurement approach	None—but disclose net realizable value when lower than replacement cost
Income measurement?	Yes, for both measurement methods	No—users cautioned against computing revised income
Depreciation	Same methods used in primary financial statements (generally)	Straight line

Source: *Financial Reporting Developments*, Ernst and Whinney, "Inflation Accounting: Implementing FASB Statement No. 33" (December 1979), pp. 44–45.

both amounts would be stated in 1985-size dollars. In that case, the adjustment would appear as follows:

	Unadjusted	Adjustment Factor (%)	Adjusted
1985	$10	100	$10.00
1995	10	66⅔	6.67
	$20		$16.67

This adjustment also expresses all amounts in the same-size dollars, but they are dollars of some previous period. The position of the FASB, and virtually all advocates of price-level adjustments, is that it is more meaningful to express items in terms of current dollars. Consequently, the first illustration reflects the preferred treatment.

Whichever approach is followed, the rationale is the same: all amounts are measured in the same-size monetary unit. For example, in measuring the fixed assets of a firm at the end of 1995, assets purchased in 1985 or any other year would be restated in terms of 1995 dollars; the total amount of fixed assets would be reflected in a common measuring unit.

The adjusted amount of fixed assets does not, and is not intended to, reflect the value of the assets, just as the unadjusted amount does not indicate value. The purpose of the adjustment is to measure all the amounts with a common measuring unit so that the mathematical processes of addition, subtraction, multiplication, and division can be legitimately accomplished. Therefore, these adjustments are not a departure from generally accepted accounting principles. The current concepts of revenue and expense recognition, depreciation methods, inventory valuation, and so forth are still applied.

Since 1940, the movement of prices has been generally upward, and to maintain that the dollar is a stable measuring unit no longer appears to be valid. Consequently, historical costs should be adjusted for changes in purchasing power. Purchasing power adjustments require an agreement on the proper index. Some believe the consumer price index should be used, others believe a manufacturing type index should be used, and *Accounting Research Study No. 6* and the exposure draft issued by the FASB recommended a general index based on the gross national product—the GNP implicit price deflator index. The rationale for using the GNP deflator is that it reflects a broad segment of the economy and it takes into consideration more variables than any of the other indexes. However, *SFAS No. 33* required the use of the Consumer Price Index for all Urban Consumers (CPIUC). This index was chosen mainly because it is available on a monthly basis.

The use of the consumer price index is criticized because it is a general index and because it does not apply to the total economy. Therefore, it may have little relevance to a particular business. This argument can be related to personal situations as well as to businesses. In a given year, suppose the cost of living, in general, increased by 10 percent. Depending on their consumption patterns, some individuals would suffer more than a 10 percent decrease in purchasing power while others might suffer less or might even gain. For example, a person owning a home with fixed monthly mortgage payments would not have lost purchasing power on the dollars paid on the debt. The person renting on a month-to-month basis would probably have had a rent increase. Therefore, each dollar spent on housing would have less purchasing power this year than in the previous year.

Statements of Financial Accounting Standards Nos. 33, 82, and 89

The unpredicted level of inflation experienced in the United States during the late 1970s caused additional concern that financial statements were being distorted. This concern ultimately resulted in the release of *Statement of Financial Accounting Standards No. 33*, "Financial Reporting and Changing Prices" in 1980. This pronouncement required certain companies to experiment with the disclosure of information on the effects of changing prices on business enterprises. In general, *SFAS No. 33* established a size test to determine if a company must comply with its provision (public companies with over $1 billion of assets or $125 million of inventories and property and equipment) and described the method for restating information on a constant-dollar and current-cost basis.

Later, after inflation had subsided, in 1984 and 1986, the FASB amended *SFAS No. 33*. These amendments, published as *SFAS No. 82*, "Financial Reporting and Changing Prices: Elimination of Certain Disclosures," and *SFAS No. 89*, "Financial Reporting and Changing Prices," were in response to an Exposure Draft issued by the board. A substantial majority of the comments received on this Exposure Draft supported the elimination of the requirement to disclose historical-cost/constant-dollar information. The reasons cited by the respondents for this position were (1) the elimination of confusion on the part of financial statement users, (2) the elimination of complexity, (3) the reduction of the cost of compliance, and (4) the greater usefulness of current-cost information.

Specifically, *SFAS No. 82* eliminated the requirement for supplementary disclosure of constant-dollar information for enterprises disclosing current-cost/constant-dollar information. And *SFAS No. 89* eliminated the requirement to disclose information on changing prices, although the disclosure of this information on a voluntary basis was encouraged.

Companies meeting the size test were required to disclose the following as supplementary information:

1. Income from continuing operations on a current-cost/constant-dollar basis.

2. Purchasing power gain or loss.

3. Increases or decreases in current-cost amounts of inventory and property, plant, and equipment.

4. Current-cost amounts of inventory, and property, plant, and equipment at year-end.

In the following sections we will review the specific current-value and constant-dollar provisions of *SFAS No. 33*. This review will focus on methods of preparing the required information and the necessary disclosures. It is important to remember that although many of the constant-dollar provisions of *SFAS No. 33* are no longer required, companies that disclose this information must continue to follow the established guidelines. Additionally, an enterprise may now substitute historical-cost/constant-dollar information for the required current-cost information if there is no material difference between the amount of income from continuing operations that would be disclosed by the two methods.

Current-Cost Accounting under *SFAS No. 33*

Current-cost accounting, as defined by the FASB, is an attempt to restate certain assets on the basis of their "value to the business." Comprehensive application of current-cost accounting is not required by *SFAS No. 33*. Current-cost measurements are required only for inventories, property, plant, and equipment, and the related expenses. Additionally, current-cost measurements of liabilities are not required.

The following reasons were cited by the FASB for requiring only partial application of current-cost accounting:

1. Inventories and property, plant, and equipment are normally the most significant assets of the companies affected by the *SFAS No. 33*. They also are most affected by specific price changes.
2. The FASB wished to restrict the costs of compliance with *SFAS No. 33*.
3. Current-cost measurements of some assets, such as goodwill and patents, may be too unreliable and subjective to serve any useful purpose.
4. The FASB did not wish to address the liability measurement issue at the time it was debating inflation accounting.

Under *SFAS No. 33*, current-cost accounting is used to determine the following supplemental disclosures each year:

1. Income from continuing operations.
2. Increases or decreases in the current-cost amounts of inventory and property, plant, and equipment. These amounts were to be disclosed both before and after the effects of general inflation.
3. Current cost of inventories and property, plant, and equipment (net) at the latest balance sheet date.

An important feature of the current-cost method is the separation of operating profit and holding gains (increases in the current cost of assets). For example, assume a company purchases inventory at $5,000 and subsequently sells it for $6,500 when the current cost of the inventory was $5,400. Historical-cost and current-cost incomes would be determined as follows.

	Historical Cost	Current Cost
Sales	$6,500	$6,500
Cost of goods sold	5,000	5,400
Income	$1,500	$1,100

The FASB maintains that the current-cost presentation is more likely to provide a basis for assessing future cash flows. That is, the relationship of cost of goods sold to sales will probably remain stable over time when selling prices are determined by current costs. Whether or not these holding gains should be disclosed as income has not been decided by the FASB. The decision is based on which capital maintenance theory is used. The two choices available are financial capital maintenance and physical capital maintenance.

Financial capital Capital is defined as the quantity of financial resources (dollars) invested in a business. Income is determined by the difference between revenues and the dollars (either nominal or constant dollars) invested in financial resources used to generate that revenue. In our preceding example the financial capital theory would say that total income was $1,500 even though it may be better to distinguish between operating profit ($1,100) and the results of holding activities ($400). The $400 increase in current cost would be described as a "holding gain," which connotes its status as income. It recognizes that a company could be better off as a result of wise (or fortunate) timing of its purchases, that is, before the price increases. Traditional historical-cost accounting generally reflects the financial capital theory.

Physical capital Capital is defined as the productive capacity (i.e., operating capability) of an enterprise. Income is not earned until an enterprise provides for maintenance (replacement) of its productive capacity, which is often represented by its inventories and properties. Essentially, the physical capital maintenance theory is concerned with providing an income figure that is a starting point in determining "distributable income." In our preceding example, the physical capital theory would say that only $1,100 of income has been earned rather than $1,500 because the $400 current-cost increase would be termed a "capital maintenance adjustment" and would not appear on the income statement, but would be shown as a direct adjustment to equity. While adoption of the physical capital maintenance theory would be a significant change over current GAAP, a similar concept is apparent in the LIFO inventory accounting method.

Until the FASB comes to a final decision on capital maintenance, it expects the disclosures required under *SFAS No. 33* to permit users to treat them as they see fit. That is, users may combine current-cost increases with income from continuing operations, or disregard them.

The disclosure of constant-dollar/current-cost information was also required by *SFAS No. 33*, in addition to current-cost increases measured before the effect of general inflation. For example, assume from the previous example that the increase in inflation between the time of the purchase of the inventory to the time of sale was 5 percent. The increase in current cost net of inflation would be determined as follows.

Increase in current costs	$400
Less: Effect of general inflation ($5,000 × 0.05)	250
Increase in current cost net of general inflation	$150

This disclosure is intended to inform users how the increase in the current cost of a firm's inventories and properties compares with the rate of general inflation. In the event the rate of inflation is in excess of current cost, a negative amount would be reported as a decrease in current cost net of general inflation.

Constant-Dollar Accounting under *SFAS No. 33*
The adjustment of financial statement elements via constant-dollar accounting was an attempt to report all financial statement elements in dollars of the same purchasing power. *SFAS No. 33* originally required constant-dollar accounting in three different areas:

1. As an adjustment to historical-cost figures to report in dollars of fixed purchasing power (historical cost/constant dollar).
2. As an adjustment to current cost to determine the effect of inflation on inventories and productive capacity (current cost/constant dollar).
3. As an adjustment to five-year summary information to remove the effect of inflation from trend data (five-year summary/constant dollar).

These constant-dollar measurements were to be stated in constant dollars represented by the *average level* over the fiscal year of the consumer price index for all urban consumers. The use of the fiscal-year average is a departure from previous proposals that employed an end-of-year index. However, the use of the fiscal-year average simplifies the computation of income from continuing operations in that revenues and expenses generally will already reflect constant dollars (except for cost of goods sold and depreciation) because revenues are usually earned and expenses usually incurred fairly evenly throughout the year. (A year-end index was allowed to be used if comprehensive constant-dollar financial statements were presented.)

Historical Cost/Constant Dollar
The requirements of *SFAS No. 33* resulted in only a partial application of constant-dollar accounting. The Board intended to simplify the adjustment process by requiring only the restatement of those items most frequently affected by inflation inventories: property, plant, and equipment; monetary assets; and monetary liabilities. However, a company could have elected to disclose comprehensive constant-dollar financial statements.

Historical-cost/constant-dollar measurement under the provisions of *SFAS No. 33* is a five-step process:

1. Determine the year of acquisition (or the year of historical-cost measurement) for each item. This is termed the base year.
2. Determine the average consumer price index corresponding to the base year.
3. Determine the average consumer price index for the current period.
4. Restate the historical cost to the current-year average constant dollars by multiplying it by the current-year index over the base-year index.
5. Determine that the adjusted amount does not exceed recoverable amounts (net realizable value or value in use.)[20]

For example, assume that an asset was acquired in 1980 for $20,000. The average consumer price index for 1980 was 116.3. The asset is being restated in 1990 when the average consumer price index is 217.6 and the adjusted amount does not exceed the recoverable amount. The asset would be restated as follows:

1. $20,000
2. 116.3
3. 217.6
4. $20,000 × 217.6/116.3 = $37,420.46
5. $37,420.46, since the adjusted amount does not exceed the recoverable amount.

SFAS No. 33 required two historical-cost/constant-dollar disclosures for the current year:

1. Income from continuing operations.
2. Purchasing power gain or loss on net monetary items.

Income from Continuing Operations   To meet the minimum requirements of *SFAS No. 33*, income from continuing operations is adjusted by converting cost of goods sold, depreciation, amortization, and depletion to average-for-the-year constant dollars. Additionally, if inventories or property, and plant and equipment were recorded at net realizable value or value in use, these write-downs were to be included in the computation of income from continuing operations and disclosed. *SFAS No. 33* goes on to state that these amounts

1. Need be used only for a group of assets when the amount is *materially* and *permanently* lower.
2. Need not be considered for individual assets unless they are used independently of other assets.

---

[20] Net realizable value is defined as the net amount of cash expected to be obtained from the sale of the asset. This amount would be used for all assets about to be sold. Value in use is the net present value of future cash flows expected to be derived from the use of an asset and is used when the asset is not expected to be sold.

Purchasing Power Gains or Losses Purchasing power gains and losses result from holding monetary assets and liabilities. Monetary items are those assets and liabilities that are fixed as to the dollar amount the firm has on hand, will receive, or will disburse. For example, if the firm has $1,000 receivable from a customer, $1,000 is the amount to be received, irrespective of the level of inflation or deflation. The same is true for monetary liabilities, such as bonds payable, where the amount to be paid is the face value of the bond, which is fixed. Among the items commonly identified as *monetary* are

Cash
Receivables (including allowances)
Accounts and notes payable
Accrued expenses payable
Bonds payable
Other long-term debt

The more common *nonmonetary* items are

Marketable securities
Inventories (except those produced under fixed-price contracts)
Prepaid expenses
Property, plant, and equipment and the related accumulated depreciation
Deferred income
Patents, goodwill, and other intangibles
Provision for guarantees
Minority interest
Preferred stock
Common stock
Additional paid-in capital

The reason for identifying and distinguishing between monetary and non-monetary items is that inflation and deflation have a different impact on each. For example, assume that a firm holds $100,000 of accounts receivable during a period of inflation. When the $100,000 is collected in the future, the cash received will not have as much purchasing power as it has today. (The amount of loss in purchasing power depends on both the time period and the rate of inflation.) Therefore, the firm will suffer a loss in purchasing power as a result of holding a monetary asset during an inflationary period. Just the opposite is true for holding monetary liabilities. If the firm owed $100,000, the dollars used to pay the debt in the future will not have as much purchasing power as when the dollars were borrowed. Thus, the firm will have a gain as a result of holding monetary liabilities during an inflationary period.

The effect of inflation on nonmonetary items is significantly different from the effect on monetary items because the nonmonetary items have the potential to keep pace with inflation, since their dollar amount is not fixed. For example, if the inflation rate is 10 percent during the year, property, plant, and equipment items similar to the ones owned by the firm would probably cost more dollars at the end of the year than at the beginning. Consequently, purchasing power gains and losses are *not* computed for nonmonetary items.

The gain or loss on net monetary items (monetary assets minus monetary liabilities) is disclosed separately and is not included in income from continuing operations. This requirement was intended to improve understanding by investors of the monetary components of working capital requirements and the amount of debt included in the capital structure of the company.

The purchase power gain or loss is determined by comparing the net monetary items at the beginning of the year and the end of the year and adjusting these amounts to fiscal-year averages. The result measures the average gain or loss in purchasing power experienced during the year. In a period of inflation, (1) a purchasing power gain will result from holding net monetary liabilities and (2) a purchasing power loss will result from holding net monetary assets. The following example illustrates the computation of purchasing power gains and losses:

Company A

	December 31	
	1996	1995
Monetary items		
Cash	$ 20,000	$ 15,000
Accounts Receivable	80,000	75,000
Notes Receivable	115,000	100,000
Monetary Assets	$215,000	$190,000
Notes Payable	30,000	30,000
Accounts Payable	50,000	70,000
Long-term Debt	150,000	140,000
Monetary Liabilities	$230,000	$240,000
Net Monetary Liabilities	$ 15,000	$ 50,000

		Purchasing Power Gain or Loss	
	Historical Dollar	Conversion Factor	Constant Dollars
1. Balance 1/1/96	$50,000	217.6 (1996 avg. index) / 202.4 (1995 year-end index)	$53,754.94
2. Net Change	(35,000)	A	(35,000.00)
3. Balance 12/31/96	15,000	217.6 (1996 avg. index) / 230.0 (1996 year-end index)	(14,191.30)
Purchasing Power Gain			$ 4,563.64B

A = assumed to be stated in average 1996 dollars.

B = 1 − 2 − 3.

In computing the price level gain or loss, the ending monetary position adjusted for inflation for the year, $18,754.94 ($53,754.94 − 35,000), is compared to the actual monetary liabilities adjusted to the average dollar level, $14,191.30, resulting in a price level gain of $4,563.64.

Five-Year Summary Information An additional requirement of *SFAS No. 33* was the disclosure of the following summary information in constant dollars for each of its five most recent fiscal years.

Net Sales and Other Operating Revenues
Historical-Cost/Constant-Dollar Information

1. Income from continuing operations
2. Income per common share from continuing operations
3. Net assets at fiscal year-end

Current-Cost Information

1. Income from continuing operations
2. Income per common share from continuing operations
3. Net assets at fiscal year-end
4. Increases or decreases in the current-cost amounts of inventories and property, plant, and equipment, net of inflation

Other Information

1. Purchasing power gain or loss on net monetary items
2. Cash dividends declared per common share
3. Market price per common share at fiscal year-end
4. Level of the consumer price index used to compute income from continuing operations. (Either the average-for-the-year index or the end-of-year index may be used if a company presents comprehensive supplementary constant-dollar financial statements. All other companies *must* use the average CPI.)

This information may be stated in one of two ways:

1. Average-for-the-year constant dollars or end-of-year constant dollars, whichever is used for the measurement of income from continuing operations for the current fiscal year.
2. Dollars having a purchasing power equal to that of dollars of the base period used by the Bureau of Labor Statistics in calculating the consumer price index.

Inasmuch as most business managers desire growth and expansion for their companies, the requirement to publish five-year summary information was expected to result in the following corporate policies:

1. The presentation of dividends on a real basis may cause dividend rates to rise with the rate of inflation so that equity capital sources are maintained.
2. The disclosure of net assets in real dollars may improve the internal analysis of return on investment by focusing on the real rates of return.

3. The disclosure of revenues on a real basis may indicate that real sales are declining and cause management to raise prices more frequently.

The prospect of continued inflation and the requirements of *SFAS No. 33* were expected to encourage managers to evaluate their businesses in real-dollar items. Among the specific changes expected were an increase in the number of companies shifting to LIFO inventory costing, increased investments in more productive equipment, the retirement of inefficient productive capacity, an attempt to improve accounts receivable turnover, and a reduction of the amount of cash on hand. Additionally, the requirement to report financial operations on a real, inflation-adjusted basis was expected to prompt managers to measure internal operating performances and new investment proposals on this basis. Such evaluations could improve reported results on an inflation-adjusted basis if both the original evaluation of projects and financial reporting are made on the same basis. However, as noted earlier, the FASB found that much of the information disclosed in *SFAS No. 33* was not being used. As a result, the cost of providing this information exceeded the benefits provided and the disclosure of much of this information is no longer required.

Comparison of Valuation Methods

Historical cost measures are objective and verifiable, and balance sheet values reflect the unexpired portion of dollars spent to acquire the assets reported. Yet historical cost may lack decision relevance because it does not reflect the bases for current managerial decisions. Moreover, historical cost amounts that reflect purchases made in different periods when the dollars spent had varying amounts of purchasing power are not additive. When specific and/or general price level changes occur, historical cost cannot provide measures that reflect the ability of the firm to continue its present productive capacity. That is, in order to assess the ability of a firm to maintain its capital base, measurement must be based on current cost and/or general price level adjustments.

Replacement cost measures are said to provide a means of measuring the amount that can be distributed to stockholders without eroding productive capacity. This argument is strongest when considering long-lived plant assets. In the long run, plant assets will be replaced. Sufficient capital should be retained by the business enterprise to make these replacements. Measurement at current replacement cost matches the cost of replacement against revenue. The remaining differences between replacement cost and historical cost are holding gains and losses. This separation allows for the assessment of whether enough revenue is being generated to provide for replacement purposes. A drawback of this approach is that eventual replacement may be at prices that are considerably different from current replacement cost. Consequently, an approach that utilizes expected replacement cost may be preferable. At the same time, the measurement and reporting of holding gains and losses is difficult to interpret. The typical interpretation is that holding gains and losses reflect the results of prior decisions to purchase the asset at lower or higher historical prices, respectively. Yet replacement cost does not measure the cost of assets acquired; rather, it measures the cost of replacing owned assets by assets that have not yet been acquired. Replacement cost increases indicate that replacement will cost more, while replacement cost decreases indicate that replacement will cost less. One might ask: How can an increased cost be interpreted as a gain or a decreased cost be interpreted as a loss?

Replacement cost is criticized as not being relevant to evaluate current management decision making. In making decisions to reinvest in the asset by holding it, management forgoes the opportunity to sell the asset in the marketplace. The opportunity cost of forgoing the sale of an asset is the asset's selling price. Therefore, it is argued that current exit price has decision relevance. This is certainly true for investments in financial instruments. Holding gains and losses reflected in changes in current fair values provide objective market-based measures of the results of investment strategies. Similar measures would provide immediate feedback on expected cash flow results of investments in inventory.

Another approach to the measurement of current value is present value. Current period discounting of the cash flows expected to be generated by an asset would provide a measure of the asset's value in use. Yet this concept is difficult to apply to individual assets because a group of assets, not a single asset, normally provides a given revenue stream. Hence, discounted cash flow measures are generally most useful in evaluating a capital budgeting proposal, in determining the value of a receivable or payable, or even in attempting to determine the value of an enterprise, but are not particularly useful for financial accounting reporting purposes in general.

Regardless of the approach taken, current cost measures are purported to provide information on amounts needed to maintain existing needs for physical productive capacity, and in the case of financial instruments, to maintain capital invested in those instruments. However, neither approach provides information on the impact of changing prices on the purchasing power of monetary assets and liabilities. Yet general purchasing power adjustments alone cannot provide sufficient information on capital maintenance when the specific prices of particular items do not move in the same manner as the general price index used. Current-cost/constant-dollar adjustments allow for an analysis of the effects of inflation and specific prices on performance measures as well as providing information regarding the effects of changes in purchasing power on holding monetary items. To date, research that examines the information content of inflation-adjusted information provided under *SFAS No. 33* is mixed. Nevertheless, there is limited evidence that the market does react to the required inflation disclosures.[21]

---

[21] See for example, B. Bublitz, T. J. Frecka, and J. C. McKeown, "Market Association Tests and FASB Statement No. 33 Disclosures: A Reexamination," *Journal of Accounting Research* (Supplement 1985), pp. 1–27; G. J. Lobo, and I. M. Song, "The Incremental Information in SFAS No. 33 Income Disclosures over Historical Cost Income and its Cash and Accrual Components," *The Accounting Review* (April 1989), pp. 329–43; and Ramasamy Odiayappa and S. M. Khalid Nainar, "Economic Consequences of SFAS No. 33—An Insider-Trading Perspective," *The Accounting Review* (July 1992), pp. 599–609.

Summary

In recent years, continuing, though modest, inflation has caused dissatisfaction with historical-cost financial statements in units of money. A variety of adjustments have been proposed to increase the relevance of financial statements and their ability to express the actual value of the assets they are measuring. These adjustments may be categorized as current-value adjustments and price-level adjustment.

Current-value accounting may use entry or replacement costs, exit or selling price, or discounted present value. Each of these methods gives only an approximation of asset value because the actual value can be determined only by an exchange. Constant-dollar/current-cost accounting required by *SFAS No. 33* is a partial application of current-value accounting.

The adjustment of financial statements to units of general purchasing power (constant-dollar/historical-cost accounting) does not require any departure from present generally accepted accounting principles. Instead, its purpose is to present items on the financial statements in common-sized dollars. The adjustment process requires that a distinction be made between monetary and nonmonetary items because there are purchasing power gains and losses on the former but not on the latter.

In the following reading Jack Hanna examines the issue of accounting for changing prices in more detail.

Accounting for Changing Prices: Dead or Alive?

Jack R. Hanna

One of the profession's major goals over the past 15 years has been to incorporate the impact of changing prices into the financial statements of business enterprises with publicly traded debt or equity securities. In Canada, this led the CICA's Accounting Standards Committee to issue *Handbook* Section 4510, "Reporting the Effects of Changing Prices," in December 1982.

The supplementary information to be disclosed under the section, like that required in the United Kingdom in its Accounting Standards Committee's 1980 Statement of Standard Accounting Practice (SSAP) 16, "Current Cost Accounting," and the United States, in its Financial Accounting Standards Board's (FASB) 1979 Statement of Financial Accounting Standards No. 33, "Financial Reporting and Changing Prices," was comprehensive, complex, and controversial. In addition to current costs for inventory, fixed assets, cost of goods sold, and depreciation, companies were to disclose a much-debated financing adjustment, the gain or loss in general purchasing power resulting from holding net monetary items, and the changes in the current cost of inventory and fixed assets attributable to inflation.

Unlike the U.K. and U.S. proposals, Section 4510 was voluntary. In addition, Canadian companies were given

considerable flexibility in determining amounts, disclosing results, and explaining and interpreting those results.

When the proposals were first introduced, there was widespread concern about high inflation rates and the need to experiment with accounting for changing prices. Canadian and foreign tax laws began recognizing inflation's impact in various ways, securities commissions added new requirements, government committees were established, and an increasing minority of businesses began commenting and, in some cases, making voluntary disclosures.

The situation has changed dramatically since then—along with the rate of inflation—and now we're hearing comments like: "Current-cost accounting is dead—the funeral rites are being arranged" (Price Waterhouse, *Review and Perspective on Accounting Developments,* 1986–87). In Canada in 1986, only 4 percent of eligible companies voluntarily reported in accordance with Section 4510. Mandatory requirements were suspended in the United Kingdom in June 1985 and made voluntary in the United States in December 1986. Moreover, accounting researchers generally agree that, while the evidence to date is mixed, these new disclosures provide little extra information and don't affect investors' decision making.

Given this turn of events, many now suggest we focus on improving our traditional historical-cost-based financial statements and give up on new changing-prices accounting initiatives. Are those who insist the recent changing-prices experiments have failed correct? Or does the fact that accounting for changing prices keeps coming back under conditions of high inflation suggest the problem is real, needs to be solved, and will return as soon as high inflation does?

Unfortunately, it's far from clear what direction researchers and standard setters should take. To help us decide where to go from here, let's look at the possible reasons for the recent changing-prices experiment's poor reception, as well as three separate problem areas and some of the questions they raise.

Why the Experiment Failed

The changing-prices experiment was probably foiled both by being incomplete and by its own complexity. Several aspects made it difficult for many to swallow.

First, the fixation on manufacturing companies. Since these companies represent only a minority of commercial activity, the proposals, even if they worked for them, might not work for the nonmanufacturing sectors such as forestry, agriculture, mining, oil, and gas. For example, in its 1983 annual report, Great Lakes Forest Products Ltd. gave this as a major reason for not reporting price changing results: "The forest products industry is not able to address . . . the valuation of its most precious asset: its fibre resource."

Then there's the piecemeal approach taken to net asset valuation. Only inventory and fixed assets are shown at current cost; other assets and all liabilities are disclosed according to traditional generally accepted accounting principles (GAAP).

The inadequate guidance on preparing current-cost valuations was yet another major shortcoming; also, current-cost techniques were applied inappropriately. For example, companies found it difficult to cope with the use of current costs for technologically updated facilities. Great Lakes Forest Products, for instance, in electing not to report current cost values, indicated that, "At best it would be possible to estimate the current capital cost of new facilities having similar productive capacity, but these would likely employ different production and environmental technologies with operating costs and efficiencies the effects of which we are not able to measure."

A number of companies did present current-cost information, but as Hilton Hotels Corporation says in its 1982 annual report, this information did "not take into consideration any operating costs savings or additional revenues which may result from the replacement of existing properties with properties having improved technology and facilities."

Here's an example of inappropriate application: although under GAAP, fixed assets should be written off over their useful lives, there's some evidence that many companies have tended to write them off over a shorter period, perhaps to better reflect depreciation under changing-prices conditions in the traditional income statement. Where companies have been writing off assets over shorter than useful life and current-cost asset values are written off over the same period, the current-cost depreciation expense will tend to be overstated. In fact, for certain companies, the "historical-cost depreciation expense" might be a lot closer to properly calculated current-cost depreciation expense than the reported "current-cost depreciation expense."

Another possible reason for the experiment's poor reception is that it required nontraditional, supplementary-to-normal accounting system data disclosure. Since many preparers and users aren't familiar with alternative changing-prices approaches, they reacted negatively. In fact, the ability of management, auditors, and users to deal with such complex, ambiguous information may be limited—at least without the benefit of a major educational effort. Management may also have a low tolerance for this information because it must be gathered from outside the regular accounting system.

Lastly, the emphasis many countries placed on a productive capacity capital maintenance concept may have helped doom the experiment from the start because of the introduction of complicated gearing and net productive monetary asset adjustments.

Juggling Everything at Once

Attempts to account for the impact of changing prices have focused on three major issues—all at the same time:

1. Changes in the valuation of net assets—essentially the switch in emphasis to current cost from historical-cost-dominated amounts for inventories and fixed assets in the balance sheet, and for cost of goods sold and depreciation in the income statement.

2. Changes in the measurement unit used in preparing financial statements—the change from a mixture of dollars to dollars of constant purchasing power.

3. Changes concerning the appropriate concept of capital—a change from the traditional money capital maintenance concept to that of financial capital maintenance in terms of general purchasing power or to mainte-

nance of an enterprise's productive capacity.

Although separate, these issues are still related; thus, it's been a highly complex manner to tackle all three at once. Let's turn now to some specific problem areas related to them.

Approaches for Determining Income

One question causing a lot of controversy is whether income should be determined after maintaining a business enterprise's productive capacity or, rather, on the financial capital the owners invested. In capital budgeting theory, used by many businesses in making investment decisions, financial capital maintenance seems to be the preferred approach. [Alex Milburn offers a similar argument from a somewhat different perspective in *Maintenance of Capital: Financial versus Physical* (Clarkson Gordon Foundation Symposium, Scholars Book Co., 1982, pp. 97–100).]

Take this example: Individual A invests $100,000 in a taxicab business where cabs will be used for a year and then replaced by new ones for $105,000 at the beginning of year two. Assume, for simplicity, that cash flows from the business, including taxes and the cabs' disposal value, all occur on the last day of the year and amount to $110,000 in year one and $115,500 in year two. Assume also that the owners are satisfied with a 10 percent return on this risk class of investment and that either no change in general prices occurs during the year or amounts have been restated in constant dollars.

Exhibit 1, based on these assumptions, shows that financial capital maintenance income for the first year is $10,000, while productive capacity maintenance income is only $5,000, because of the need to replace the used cabs.

EXHIBIT 1 *Financial Capital vs. Productive Capacity Maintenance*

Data	Jan 1, 19y1	Dec 31, 19y1	Jan 1, 19y2	Dec 31, 19y2
Taxi cost	$100,000		$105,000	
Net cash inflows		$110,000		$115,500

A	Financial maintenance— Year 1	
	Net cash inflows	$110,000
	Less taxi cost	100,000
	Net income (10%)	$ 10,000

B	Productive capacity maintenance—Year 1	
	Net cash inflows	$110,000
	Less current taxi cost	105,000
	Net income (5%)	$ 5,000

C	Financial maintenance— Year 2	
	Net cash inflows	$115,500
	Less: Taxicab costs	105,000
	Net income (10%)	$ 10,500

Capital budgeting theory suggests undertaking projects after comparing cash invested to net cash flows generated during the project life, without charging the replacement costs of assets to be used in future years against income for the first year. Furthermore, if the $105,000 replacement cost for taxis at the end of year one is to be taken into account based on this theory, it will be necessary to complete the second-year cycle by considering the $115,500 net cash inflow at the end of that year. The resulting year two income under capital budgeting theory and the financial capital maintenance approach is $10,500.

Capital budgeting theory can be applied to both the first and second year cases or to the two combined. In each instance, given our assumptions, a real return of 10 percent is indicated. The productive capacity maintenance approach, in working from productive capacity to productive capacity instead of cash to cash, charges the first year with the cost of taxis to be used in the second year without recognizing the benefits accruing at the end of that year from their use.

Results under the productive capacity approach seem out of step with economic reality, in that income of only $5,000 (a 5 percent return) is reported for year one, when a return of 10 percent on the initial investment has been earned. Moreover, the business will be able to continue and earn 10 percent in the second year. If the owners don't have enough capital to buy $105,000 worth of cabs at the beginning of year two, they should be able to borrow from capital markets, assuming their prospects justify it.

If the owners decide not to borrow extra funds, however, they may want to reinvest their $100,000 in a smaller number of cabs that would continue to earn the desired 10 percent return. Since some cab companies would be willing to operate on a fare schedule generating a 10 percent return on capital, competition should prevent others from charging fares that would enable them to recover next year's, as opposed to this year's, taxi cost.

The financial maintenance concept seems to tie in better with these realities, including the need to return to capital markets with a convincing enough case to raise the necessary capital at the end of year one—a process that helps allocate resources efficiently within the economy.

Cash Flow Statement Capital Maintenance Disclosures

There are other problems involved in trying to apply the productive capacity maintenance approach to financial statement preparation: dealing with the debt-financed share of increases in replacement costs, separating and treating assets not to be replaced, and identifying methods of providing for maintenance of the productive capacity of monetary assets. Also, what happens

when changes take place—for example, when assets are switched from being productive to nonproductive, or decisions are made to change the debt-equity ratio? And what happens when an entire enterprise is wound up or sold?

Whatever happens, managers must take replacement costs into account in planning for asset replacement, and it may be desirable, once they've actually decided what to do, to inform financial statement readers of their plans. The information could be provided by using an expanded cash flow statement rather than the income statement. See Exhibit 2 for a format (which can be simplified for practical use) for disclosing the impact of replacement, redeployment, expansion, and related financing decisions on cash flows. It should be useful in this or a modified form for all business enterprises, including service, financial, real estate, and other nonmanufacturing entities.

The suggested cash flow statement

EXHIBIT 2 *Format for Reporting the Impact of Changing Prices on Cash Flow*

Cash generated from operations		xxx
Deduct		
• Cash required to finance the replacement of inventory and property, plant, and equipment at current cost	xx	
• Funds required to finance the cost of productive capacity that is not to be replaced but is being redeployed	xx	
• Funds required to increase net working capital or for net productive monetary items adjustment	xx	
	xxx	
Less funds available for these purposes via debt at present debt-equity ratio	xx	xxx
		xxx
Plus or minus cash required or available because of planned change in debt-equity ratio		xx
Funds available for expansion and dividends		xxx
• Funds required for planned expansion	xxx	
• Less portion of planned expansion that can be financed via debt and issue of new equity securities	xxx	xxx
Funds available for dividends		xxx

should be accompanied by notes indicating management's reasons for not maintaining productive capacity, for changing the planned debt-equity ratio, and so on. In effect, the subjectivity of changing-prices disclosures is transferred to this new statement, which emphasizes actual management planning.

Valuation

Although choosing a measurement unit and a capital maintenance concept isn't easy, what's really crying out for further study is the problem of selecting a valuation method. The possibilities are many, and it may well be that by focusing on one attribute—current cost—we've prevented ourselves from preparing more useful financial statements. In addition to current and historical cost, frequently suggested valuation alternatives include current exit (or selling) prices and the present value of estimated net future cash flows.

Some might argue it's all right to exclude such alternatives (except in certain cases where the resulting amount is less than current cost), because the values they produce are too subjective. Others maintain considerable subjectivity can be involved in determining both historical and current-cost values. They might point to the use of selling prices in the primary financial statements of mutual funds and many mining companies.

It's probably fair to say those who prefer the productive capacity capital maintenance approach have helped bring pressure to bear in favor of using current cost in valuing net assets, since it's the value used to determine whether productive capacity has been maintained in going-concern situations. With productive capacity information moved to the cash flow statement, as

suggested earlier, it may be possible to look at the choice of attribute in a fresh light.

In addressing the valuation problem, remember that, given a stable measuring unit, income over the life of a transaction, venture, or business is fixed—selling price, less cost. The attribute choice affects only the *timing* of value changes and related income effects.

There's also the question of whether holding gains and losses should be disclosed separately from operating gains on a realizable or realized basis, or both. To date, a convincing case hasn't been made for separate disclosure, though it seems to be the preference—perhaps after the effect of inflation is eliminated. It is to be hoped that if separate disclosures are considered in future, it won't turn into a debate over whether holdings gains for a particular enterprise should be based on changes in either entry (buying) or exit (selling) prices.

After all, for those who want information on how successful management has been at holding items during periods of price change, changes in entry and exit prices might both be useful, depending on the circumstances. For example, the first might best reflect its success in holding raw material inventories; the second, its decisions to hold finished-goods inventories.

The Measurement Unit

Perhaps the worst result of the recent changing-prices experiment is its failure to identify a stable measuring unit for financial reporting. Even if accountants want to stick to the traditional historical-cost basis, a stable measurement unit should be used to do so. After all, economists have prepared and used real as well as nominal-dollar information for decades.

If accountants want to produce information for better decision making, doesn't our present rubber measurement unit impair that objective? Let's say Investor X invested $100,000 in real estate in 1970. Assume the investment is sold for $200,000, and $100,000 in net before-tax income is reported in the financial statements. If Investor X needs $300,000 to command the same purchasing power held in 1970 with $100,000, there's actually been a $100,000 loss in purchasing power before taxes. From an equity perspective, the tax contract with the government shouldn't require that taxes be paid on a supposed $100,000 amount accountants call income when, in fact, an economic loss of $100,000 has been incurred.

Neither decision makers trying to establish a fairer taxation system based on income, nor taxpayers who want such a system, are served by accounting rules that can lead to real losses being called income. If accountants would only start labeling economic losses for what they are and would deflate traditional accounting gains for inflation, taxation policymakers just might stop taxing capital. (This wouldn't mean taxes would go down. Assuming governments require a given level of tax revenues, new income definitions would lead to a redistribution of the tax burden and certain individuals and companies would face more or fewer taxes, depending on their situation after restatement in relation to others.)

Sometimes ad hoc tax rules are introduced to compensate for the lack of an inflation adjustment in accounting statements. It's difficult, however, to write rules that apply equitably in all circumstances. For example, as Charles W. Swenson points out in "An Analysis of ACRS [Accelerated Cost-Recovery System] During Inflationary Periods" (*Accounting Review,* 1987), a rule that provides a fast tax writeoff for fixed assets may be appropriate at a 10 percent inflation rate but not at one higher than 12 percent or below 8 percent. Constant-dollar historical-cost statements would automatically adjust for differing inflation rates, thus avoiding the resource misallocation that can otherwise occur.

It's likely that constant-dollar accounting would be useful in a variety of other decision-making situations as well. A stable measuring unit should also help accounting information users who want to make cross-sectional or longitudinal comparisons. In addition, constant-dollar information could help in other internal and external decision-making situations.

But before we consider moving to any form of constant-dollar accounting, we should remember that academics can point to a substantial body of research suggesting that constant-dollar historical-cost statements add little information beyond that already contained in traditional financial statements. Something may well be wrong, not only with our financial statements but also with our research. That's not to say the research is faulty; rather, it may need to be restructured to better address our accounting-for-changing-prices problems.

Consider the investment case mentioned earlier from a research perspective. If we accept that constant-dollar historical-cost statements add little to explain market price movements, it doesn't mean constant-dollar accounting isn't worthwhile. If it helps influence taxation policy decisions, the redistributional effects across the tax-paying population would have a direct effect not only on taxpayers but on market prices as well.

Precisely Wrong or Approximately Right?

If accounting adjusted for changing prices is more useful in predicting cash flows, assessing stewardship, and decision making, as many claimed when double-digit inflation raged, why has this enthusiasm faded to a mere murmur and almost disappeared?

If we just do more accounting research without directing it properly, we'll never find out but will simply remain caught in our present mire. We need more research on how the decision-making process is affected by changing prices rather than just on how to account for them. We need to know:

- Why the recent experiment went wrong. Was it merely bad timing, given the severe drop in inflation rates? Or was it a well-designed experiment that proved, once and for all, that changing-prices accounting isn't an important issue? Or are there other reasons?

- How many changes to the traditional accounting system can be proposed at one time? Did the Section 4510 requirements go too far—or not far enough?

- What impact do proposed changes affecting valuation, the measurement unit, and the capital maintenance concept have on decisions?

- Can the changing-prices issue be resolved before financial statement objectives are clarified?

- How much time is needed for a proper study of changing-prices disclosures? Five years? Longer?

- Is there a learning curve as users, preparers, and regulators of changing-prices disclosures come to better understand their impact on decision making?

- Are decision makers concerned about the comparability of current-cost information across companies and over time? Does this concern help explain their wide rejection of the Section 4510 information?

- Is there evidence that data reliability and comparability improved or deteriorated over the period of the experiment? Did preparers strive to improve disclosures as they gained experience with the requirements?

- Should future changing-prices disclosures, if any, be made mandatory or voluntary? To be useful, do they have to be in the primary financial statements rather than supplementary to them?

- Is it possible to have simpler disclosures and overcome the present concerns about complexity, flexibility, lack of comparability, and high cost, while still yielding more useful financial statements?

Of course, in answering those questions, we can't rewrite history; the recent experiment does seem to have fallen flat on its face. Some wish we had just moved to constant-dollar historical-cost financial accounting in the mid-'70s. They've suggested that, if we had only tackled the problem of achieving a stable measuring unit even for historical cost statements, we might now be pleased with our progress and in a better position to tackle the problems of valuing net assets and selecting a capital maintenance concept.

But none of this means the issue is unworthy of future study: most accounting and regulatory bodies still acknowledge the need for further efforts. Moreover, a recent U.K. survey (reported in *Accountancy Age,* December 10, 1987) indicates that inflation concerns still exist and users "would be concerned by the reliability and accuracy of historic cost accounts if inflation reached 10%."

What is certain is that if the profession is to be prepared, either with a satisfactory defense of the status quo or a more successful changing-prices proposal, the planning must be done now, while inflation is still low. We have to find out once and for all if changing-prices accounting is indeed dead or simply in need of resuscitation—in one form or another.

It might help to know that current cost has some fairly vocal proponents who don't mince words. *The Economist,* for one, takes a rather dim view of those who say there is no going back: "While SSAP 16's replacement costs are sometimes irrelevant, historical costs always are. Historic cost accounts show auditors at their worst: content to be precisely wrong rather than approximately right, and deaf to people interested more in the future than in the past" (February 4, 1984).

Cases

• Case 15-1

Merimac Manufacturing Corp. has been in business since 1950. Over the years the company has grown, expanding sales and productive capacity. This year, management is discussing providing additional data because it is felt that the present historical-cost financial statements do not provide information that meets the needs for investor decisions.

Required:
a. Describe how the historical-cost statements might be deficient for user decision making.
b. Compare the advantages and disadvantages of the following alternatives as supplementary information that might be useful to Merimac investors:
   i. Replacement cost
   ii. Exit prices
   iii. Discounted cash flows
   iv. Historical cost/constant dollar (HC/CD)
   v. Current cost/constant dollar (CC/CD)

• Case 15-2

Referring to the Merimac Manufacturing Corp. case above, assume that management decided to provide HC/CD supplementary information.

Required:
a. Distinguish between monetary and nonmonetary assets and liabilities. Give examples of each.
b. Outline the procedures that Merimac would follow in preparing the supplemental data.

c. How would the procedures to prepare the supplemental data differ if management decided instead to present CC/CD supplemental information?
d. Assume that prices in general have risen, but that the prices of property, plant, and equipment have risen more slowly than the general price level. Explain which method, CC/CD or HC/CD, would provide better information and how.

• Case 15-3

Financial reporting should provide information to help investors, creditors, and other users of financial statements. *Statement of Financial Accounting Standards No. 33* required large public enterprises to disclose certain supplementary information.

Required:
a. Describe the historical-cost/constant-dollar method of accounting. Include in your discussion how historical-cost amounts are used to make historical-cost/constant-dollar measurements.
b. Describe the principal advantage of the historical-cost/constant-dollar method of accounting over the historical-cost method of accounting.
c. Describe the current-cost method of accounting.
d. Why would depreciation expense for a given year differ using the current-cost method of accounting instead of the historical-cost method of accounting? Include in your discussion whether depreciation expense is likely to be higher or lower using the current-cost method of accounting instead of the historical-cost method of accounting in a period of rising prices, and why.

• Case 15-4

There has been a good deal of criticism of the traditional historical-cost records and the data they reflect, especially during times of inflation or deflation. In order to assist in the interpretation of accounting reports as normally prepared, many accountants have suggested that conventional financial statements first be prepared with recorded cost data, and then, as a supplementary technique, these statements be converted into dollars having a uniform purchasing power through applying price indices to the recorded dollar amounts. These accountants have had considerable difference of opinion as to whether to use a "general" price index, such as the wholesale commodity price index or the cost-of-living index, or a more "specific" price index that is more applicable to the industry involved or to the particular items being converted (for instance, using a construction index for the conversion of plant and equipment items, or a special price index constructed for a specific industry).

Required:
Give arguments in favor of and against each of these two types of indices.

● Case 15-5

Advocates of current-value accounting propose several methods for determining the valuation of assets to approximate current values. Two of the methods proposed are replacement cost and the discounted present value of future cash flows.

Required:
Describe each of the two methods cited and discuss the pros and cons of the various procedures used to arrive at the valuation for each method.

● Case 15-6

The financial statements of a business entity could be prepared by using historical cost or current value as a basis. In addition, the basis could be stated in terms of unadjusted dollars or dollars restated for changes in purchasing power. The various permutations of these two separate and distinct areas are shown in the following matrix.

	Unadjusted Dollars	Dollars Restated for Changes in Purchasing Power
Historical cost	1	2
Current value	3	4

Block 1 of the matrix represents the traditional method of accounting for transactions in accounting today, wherein the absolute (unadjusted) amount of dollars given up or received is recorded for the asset or liability obtained (relationship between resources). Amounts recorded in the method described in block 1 reflect the original cost of the asset or liability and do not give effect to any change in value of the unit of measure (standard of comparison). This method assumes the validity of the accounting concepts of going concern and stable monetary unit. Any gain or loss (including holding and purchasing power gains or losses) resulting from the sale or satisfaction of amounts recorded under this method is deferred in its entirety until sale or satisfaction.

Required:
For each of the remaining matrix blocks (2, 3, and 4), respond to the following questions. Limit your discussion to nonmonetary assets only. Complete your discussion for each matrix block before proceeding to the discussion of the next matrix block.
a. How will this method of recording assets affect the relationship between resources and the standard of comparison?
b. What is the theoretical justification for using each method?
c. How will each method of asset valuation affect the recognition of gain or loss during the life of the asset and ultimately from the sale or abandonment of the asset? Your response should include a discussion of the timing

and magnitude of the gain or loss and conceptual reasons for any difference from the gain or loss computed using the traditional method.

● **Case 15-7**

A common objective of accountants is to prepare meaningful financial statements. To attain this objective, many accountants maintain that the financial statements must be adjusted for changes in price level. Other accountants believe that financial statements should continue to be prepared on the basis of unadjusted historical cost.

Required:

a. List the arguments for adjusting financial statements for changes in price level.
b. List the arguments for preparing financial statements only on the basis of unadjusted historical cost.
c. In their discussions about accounting for changes in price levels and the methods of measuring them, uninformed individuals have frequently failed to distinguish between adjustments for changes in the price levels of specific goods and services and adjustments for changes in the general purchasing power of the dollar. What is the distinction? What are "price-level adjustments"? Discuss.

Recommended Additional Readings

Chambers, R. J. "NOD, COG, and PuPu: See How Inflation Teases." *Journal of Accountancy* (September 1975), pp. 56–62.

Ijiri, Y. "The Price Level Restatement and Its Dual Interpretation." *The Accounting Review* (April 1976), pp. 227–243.

Resvine, L., and J. J. Weygandt. "Accounting for Inflation: The Controversy." *Journal of Accountancy* (October 1974), pp. 72–78.

Schwartzback, H., and R. Vangermeersch. "The Current Value Experiences of The Rouse Company, 1973–1989." *Accounting Horizons* (June 1991), pp. 45–54.

Swanson, E. P. "Accounting for Changing Prices: Some Mid Course Corrections." *Journal of Accountancy* (April 1984), pp. 78–93.

Swanson, E. P., and K. A. Shriver. "The Accounting-for-Changing-Prices Experiment: A Valid Test of Usefulness?" *Accounting Horizons* (September 1987), pp. 69–78.

Bibliography

Anthony, Robert N. "A Case for Historical Costs." *Harvard Business Review* (November–December 1976), pp. 69–79.

Backer, Morton, and Richard Simpson. *Current Value Accounting.* New York: Financial Executive Research Foundation, 1973.

Bartlett, Ralph T., and Thomas H. Kelly. "Will FAS No. 33 Solve Inflation Accounting Problems?" *Management Accounting* (April 1980), pp. 11–14.

Baxter, W. T. *Accounting Values and Inflation.* Maidenhead, Berkshire, England: McGraw-Hill Book Company (U.K.) Limited, 1975.

Bedford, Norton M., and James C. McKeown. "Comparative Analysis of Net Realizable Value and Replacement Costing." *The Accounting Review* (April 1972), pp. 333–338.

Bradford, William D. "Price-Level Restated Accounting and the Measurement of Inflation Gains and Losses." *The Accounting Review* (April 1974), pp. 296–305.

Casler, Darwin J., and Thomas W. Hall. "Firm-Specific Valuation Accuracy Using a Composite Price Index." *Journal of Accounting Research* (Spring 1985), pp. 110–122.

Chippindale, Walter, and Philip L. Defliess, eds. *Current Value Accounting. A Practical Guide for Business.* New York: Amacom, 1977.

Davidson, Sidney, and Roman L. Weil. "Inflation Accounting: What Will General Price-Level Adjusted Income Statements Show?" *Financial Analysts Journal* (January–February 1975), pp. 27–31, 70–84.

Devon, Philip C. "Price-Level Reporting and Its Value to Investors." *Accounting and Business Research* (Winter 1978), pp. 19–24.

Dyckman, T. R. "Investment Analysis and General Price-Level Adjustments—A Behavioral Study." *Studies in Accounting Research No. 1.* Evanston, Ill.: American Accounting Association, 1969.

Edwards, Edgar O. "The State of Current Value Accounting." *The Accounting Review* (April 1975), pp. 235–245.

Freeman, Robert N. "Alternative Measures of Profit Margin: An Empirical Study of the Potential Information Content of Current Cost Accounting." *Journal of Accounting Research* (Spring 1983), pp. 42–64.

Friedman, Lawrence A. "An Exit-Price Income Statement." *The Accounting Review* (January 1978), pp. 18–30.

Gay, William C., Jr. "Inflation, Indexation and Violation of Human Rights." *Price Waterhouse Review* (1978, Vol. 23, No. 2), pp. 20–29.

Gill, Charles W., and S. Thomas Moser. "Inflation Accounting at the Crossroads." *Journal of Accountancy* (January 1979), pp. 70–78.

Giroux, Gary A., Steven D. Grossman, and Stanley H. Kratchman. "Accounting for the Impact of Inflation: The Experience of the Oil Companies." *Oil & Gas Tax Quarterly* (December 1980), pp. 331–348.

Giroux, Gary A., Steven D. Grossman, and Stanley H. Kratchman. "What FAS No. 33 Does to Bank Financial Statements." *Management Accounting* (January 1981), pp. 42–47.

Griffin, Paul, ed. *Financial Reporting and Changing Prices: The Conference.* Stamford, Conn.: FASB, 1979.

Gynther, R. S. *Accounting for Price-Level Changes: Theory and Procedures.* Oxford, England: Pergamon Press, 1966.

Hakansson, Nils H. "On the Relevance of Price-Level Accounting." *Journal of Accounting Research* (Spring 1969), pp. 22–31.

Heath, Loyd C. "Distinguishing Between Monetary and Nonmonetary Assets and Liabilities in General Price-Level Accounting." *The Accounting Review* (July 1972), pp. 458–468.

Heintz, James A. "Price-Level Restated Financial Statements and Investment Decision Making." *The Accounting Review* (October 1973), pp. 679–689.

Ijiri, Yuji. "A Defense for Historical Cost Accounting." In *Asset Valuation and Income Determination*, Robert R. Sterling, ed. Houston: Scholars Book Co., 1971, pp. 1–14.

King, Alfred M. "Price-Level Restatement: Solution or Problem?" *Management Accounting* (November 1976), pp. 16–18.

Kohler, Eric L. "Why Not Retain Historical Cost?" *Journal of Accountancy* (October 1963), pp. 35–41.

Largay, James A., III, and John Leslie Livingstone. *Accounting for Changing Prices.* New York: John Wiley & Sons, 1976.

Matolcsy, Z. P. "Evidence on the Joint and Marginal Information Content of Inflation—Adjusted Accounting Income Numbers." *Journal of Accounting Research* (Autumn 1984), pp. 555–569.

Mautz, Robert K. "A Few Words for Historical Cost." *Financial Executive* (January 1973), pp. 23–27, 64.

McDonald, Bill, and Michael H. Morris. "The Relevance of SFAS 33 Inflation Accounting Disclosures in the Adjustment of Stock Prices to Inflation." *The Accounting Review* (July 1984), pp. 432–446.

Moonitz, Maurice. "Restating the Price-Level Problem." *CA Magazine* (July 1974), pp. 27–31.

Morris, R. C. "Evidence of the Impact of Inflation Accounting on Share Prices." *Accounting and Business Research* (Spring 1975), pp. 82–90.

Paton, William A. "Cost and Value in Accounting." *Journal of Accountancy* (March 1946), pp. 192–199.

Paton, William A. "Measuring Profits under Inflation Conditions: A Serious Problem for Accountants." *Journal of Accountancy* (January 1950), pp. 16–27.

Perrin, John R. "Illusory Holding Gains on Long-Term Debt." *Accounting and Business Research* (Summer 1974), pp. 234–236.

Revsine, Laurence. "On the Correspondence between Replacement Cost Income and Economic Income." *The Accounting Review* (July 1970), pp. 513–523.

Revsine, Laurence. *Replacement Cost Accounting*. Englewood Cliffs, N.J.: Prentice-Hall, 1973.

Roehm, Harper A., and Joseph F. Castellano. "Inflation Accounting: A Compromise." *The CPA Journal* (September 1978), pp. 38–47.

Rosen, L. S. *Current Value Accounting and Price-Level Restatements*. Toronto: Canadian Institute of Chartered Accountants, 1972.

Rosenfield, Paul. "The Confusion Between General Price-Level Restatement and Current Value Accounting." *Journal of Accountancy* (October 1972), pp. 63–68.

Rosenfield, Paul. "Current Replacement Value Accounting—A Dead End." *Journal of Accountancy* (September 1975), pp. 63–73.

Samuelson, Richard A. "Should Replacement Cost Changes Be Included in Income?" *The Accounting Review* (April 1980), pp. 254–287.

Schaefer, T. F. "The Information Content of Current Cost Income Relative to Dividends and Historical Cost Income." *Journal of Accounting Research* (Autumn 1984), pp. 647–656.

Scott, George M. *Research Study in Current-Value Accounting Measurement and Utility*. New York: Touche Ross Foundation, 1978.

Seed, Allen H., III. *Inflation: Its Impact on Financial Reporting and Decision Making*. New York: Financial Executives Research Foundation, 1978.

Staubus, George J. "The Effects of Price-Level Restatements on Earnings." *The Accounting Review* (July 1976), pp. 574–589.

Sterling, Robert R. "Relevant Financial Reporting in an Age of Price Changes." *Journal of Accountancy* (February 1975), pp. 42–51.

Stickney, Clyde P., and David O. Green. "No Price Level Adjusted Statements, Please." *The CPA Journal* (January 1974), pp. 25–31.

Sweeney, Henry W. *Stabilized Accounting*. New York: Harper & Brothers, 1936.

Tierney, Cecelia. "Price-Level Adjustments—Problem in Perspective." *Journal of Accountancy* (November 1963), pp. 56–60.

Touche Ross & Co. *Current Value Accounting: Economic Reality in Financial Reporting*. New York: Touche Ross & Co. 1975.

Trienens, Howard J., and Daniel U. Smith. "Legal Implications of Current Value Accounting." *Financial Executive* (September 1972), pp. 44–77.

Vickrey, Don W. "General Price-Level Adjusted Historical Cost Statements and the Ration-Scale View." *The Accounting Review* (January 1976), pp. 31–40.

Wilcox, Edward B., and Howard C. Greer, "The Case against Price-Level Adjustments in Income Determination." *Journal of Accountancy* (December 1950), pp. 492–504.

Whittington, Geoffrey. "Pioneers of Income Measurement and Price-Level Accounting: a Review Article." *Accounting and Business Research* (Spring 1980), pp. 232–240.

Financial Reporting Disclosure Requirements and Ethical Responsibilities

In the preceding chapters of this text we have attempted to give a concise yet comprehensive explanation of current generally accepted accounting principles. We have given primary attention to those principles promulgated by the Financial Accounting Standards Board and its predecessors in their roles as the bodies of the accounting profession authorized to issue financial accounting standards. The discussion, therefore, has frequently been directed toward the identification of transactions to be treated as accounting information, the appropriate measurement of those transactions, criteria for the classification of the data in the financial statements, and the reporting and disclosure requirements of the various Accounting Research Bulletins, APB Opinions, and Statements of Financial Accounting Standards. In this chapter we will look more closely at the concept of disclosure and also examine accountants' ethical responsibility to society.

Disclosure Requirements

As indicated in Chapter 1, current standards are impacted by the conceptual framework of accounting and involve the concept of disclosure. However, various disclosure techniques are available and the selection of the best method of disclosure depends on the nature of the information and its relative importance. The most common types of disclosure are:

1. The financial statements.
2. Footnotes to the financial statements.
3. Supplementary statements and schedules.
4. The auditor's certificate.

The *financial statements* should contain the most relevant and significant information about the corporation expressed in quantitative terms. The form and arrangement of the financial statements should ensure that the most vital information is readily apparent and understandable to the financial statement users.

The *footnotes* should present information that cannot be easily incorporated into the financial statements themselves. However, footnotes should never be used to substitute for the proper valuation of a financial statement element nor should they be used to contradict information contained in the financial statements. The most common examples of footnotes are

1. Schedules and exhibits such as long-term debt.
2. Explanations of financial statement items such as pensions.
3. General information about the company such as subsequent events or contingencies.

Supplementary statements and schedules are intended to improve the understandability of the financial statements. They may be used to highlight trends such as five-year summaries or be required by FASB pronouncements such as information on current costs.

The *auditor's certificate* is a form of disclosure in that it informs users of the reliability of the financial statements. That is, an unqualified opinion should indicate more reliable financial statements than does a qualified or adverse opinion.

The presentation of financial statement information also involves a decision by the preparer on the level of sophistication of the financial statements users. That is, preparers should decide whether the information provided is to be understandable to the relatively uninformed investor or to individuals working with the information on a day-to-day basis such as security analysts. The FASB addressed this issue when it stated in *Statement of Financial Accounting Concepts No. 1* that financial information should be comprehensible to those who have a reasonable understanding of business and economic activities and are willing to study the information with reasonable diligence.

The purpose of this chapter is to draw additional attention to the special importance of disclosure in financial reporting. Specifically, we will review the disclosure requirements issued by

1. Private-sector authoritative bodies in various publications.
2. The Securities and Exchange Commission.

Private-Sector Authoritative Bodies

A casual perusal of the Accounting Research Bulletins, Opinions of the Accounting Principles Board, and Statements of the Financial Accounting Standards Board provides unmistakable evidence of the increased attention given to disclosure by the groups authorized to issue accounting pronouncements over the years. The Accounting Research Bulletins contain only three disclosure requirements. One of these pertains to income taxes, another to long-term leases, and the third to contingencies, and in each case the discussion is rather brief. Of course, there are several references to disclosure contained in the text of the ARBs, but the primary attention is directed toward recording and reporting procedures.

The increased concern with disclosure becomes apparent in *APB Opinion No. 5*, "Reporting of Leases in Financial Statements of Lessees," issued in September 1964. This release contains three paragraphs under the disclosure caption. From that point forward approximately one-half of the APB Opinions contain such captions, frequently with several paragraphs devoted to the topic, and almost every one includes a reference to disclosure. Similarly, virtually every FASB Statement includes a section devoted to disclosure.

APB Opinion No. 22, "Disclosure of Accounting Policies," provides another example of the increased concern for disclosure by the Accounting Principles Board. In *Opinion No. 22* the APB reviewed the issue of the impact of various alternative accounting policies on net income, and noted that these policies could have a significant effect on the usefulness of financial statements in making economic decisions. The APB concluded that the disclosure of information on the accounting policies selected is essential for financial statement users.

Accordingly, the Board stated that the accounting policies followed by the reporting entity and the methods used in applying these policies should be disclosed as a "Summary of Significant Accounting Policies" preceding the footnotes or as the first footnote. In particular, it was stated that accounting methods and procedures that involved the following cases should be disclosed:

1. A selection from existing acceptable alternatives.

2. Principles and methods peculiar to the industry in which the reporting entity operates.

3. Unusual or innovative applications of generally accepted accounting principles.

The Board's principle objective in issuing *APB Opinion No. 22* was to provide information that allows investors to utilize existing data in comparing firms across and between industries. Nevertheless, *APB Opinion No. 22* has been criticized as not going far enough. That is, simply saying that one company uses a 10-year straight-line depreciation method whereas another uses an 8-year double-declining balance depreciation method adds little to the information content of financial statements. A more important question is the effect on income of using one accounting procedure instead of another. Those who criticize *APB Opinion No. 22* on this basis would prefer industry-by-industry standards or additional information that would allow more exact comparisons to be made.

Securities and Exchange Commission

The Securities and Exchange Commission (SEC) is the agency charged with administering the Securities Act of 1933, the Securities Exchange Act of 1934, and the Foreign Corrupt Practices Act of 1977. These acts stress the need to provide prospective investors with full and fair disclosure of the activities of a company offering and selling securities to the public.

The Securities Act of 1933 regulates the initial public distribution of a corporation's securities. The disclosure issue addressed by the 1933 Act is the protection of the public from fraud when a company is initially issuing securities to the general public (*going public*). The disclosure system necessary under this legislation has developed over the years and emphasizes the disclosure of "relevant information." The disclosure requirements under the 1933 Act include the filing of a registration statement and a prospectus for review by the SEC. Once a registration statement is filed, it becomes effective on the 20th day after filing unless the SEC requires amendments. This 20-day period is termed the *waiting period*, and it is unlawful for a company to offer to sell securities during this period. The registration of securities under the provisions of the 1933 Act is designed to provide adequate disclosures of material facts to allow investors to assess the degree of potential risk. It should be emphasized that the registration of securities with the SEC does not protect investors from loss, and it is unlawful for anyone to suggest that registration prevents possible losses.

The Securities Exchange Act of 1934 regulates the trading of securities of publicly held companies. The disclosure issue addressed by the 1934 Act are the personal duties of corporate officers and owners (*insiders*) and the corporate reporting requirements. Periodic reporting for publicly held companies is termed *being public*. The disclosure system developed under this Act deals primarily with the formal content of the information contained in the corporate annual reports and interim reports issued to shareholders. One of the major goals of this legislation is to ensure that any *corporate insider* (broadly defined as any corporate officer, director, or 10-percent-or-more shareholder) does not achieve an advantage in the purchase or sale of securities because of a relationship with the corporation. Thus, the 1934 Act established civil and criminal liabilities for insiders making false or misleading statements when trading corporate securities. The specific SEC reporting requirements for going public and being public are beyond the scope of this text. In the following paragraphs we will focus on some of the major disclosure issues adopted by the SEC.

The SEC's Integrated Disclosure System

The dual reporting system generated by the 1933 and 1934 Acts frequently resulted in reporting much of the same information several times in slightly different forms. Additionally, the audited financial statements included in the annual report to shareholders were not explicitly covered by either piece of legislation.

In 1980, the SEC adopted a new integrated disclosure system for virtually all the reports covered by the 1933 and 1934 Acts. The new system was accomplished by revamping the two basic regulations of the SEC. These are Regulation S-X, which establishes the requirement for audited financial statements, and Regulation S-K, which covers other types of disclosure. The major change in Regulation S-X was that the audited financial statements included in the annual reports must conform and be identical to those required in the prospectus and all other reports filed with the SEC.

The major changes in Regulation S-K were (1) a requirement to include five years of selected data to highlight trends and (2) a revision of the requirements for management's discussion and analysis of financial condition and results of operations. The main items now required to be analyzed and discussed by management are

1. Unusual or infrequent events that materially affect the reported amount of income.
2. Trends or uncertainties having or expected to have a significant impact on reported income.
3. Changes in volume or price and the introduction of new products that materially affect income.
4. Factors that might have an impact on the company's liquidity or ability to generate enough cash to maintain operations.
5. Commitments for capital projects and anticipated sources of funds to finance these projects.
6. The impact of inflation on the company's operations (narrative presentation for companies not covered by *SFAS No. 33*).
7. That companies are encouraged but not required to provide financial forecasts.

The Securities Act of 1933 is primarily implemented through the requirement that a nonexempt firm that desires to offer securities for public sale must file a registration statement with the SEC and provide potential investors with a prospectus. The prospectus contains most of the information provided to the SEC in the registration statement; therefore, we will review only the registration statement. Furthermore, the review will be limited to SEC Form S-1, the general form to be used by all security issuers that are not required to use any of the many other S series forms.

The disclosure requirements of Form S-1 are listed in two parts as shown in Table 16.1. Part I information must be included in the prospectus, while Part II lists additional information that may be required.

The Securities Exchange Act of 1934 established extensive reporting requirements to provide continuous full and fair disclosure. Again, there are numerous forms, and the corporation must select those that are appropriate for presenting the desired disclosure. The most common forms are

1. Form 10, for registration of a class of security for which no other form is specified.
2. Form 10-K, the annual report to be used when no other form is specified. This form is the annual report counterpart of Form 10, which is used for registration.
3. Form 10-Q, a quarterly report of operations used by all firms.

TABLE 16.1 *Requirements of SEC Form S-1*

Part I	Part II
1. Distribution spread	22. Marketing arrangements
2. Plan of distribution	23. Other expenses of issuance
3. Use of proceeds	24. Relationship with registrants of experts named in statements
4. Sales other than for cash	
5. Capital structure	25. Sales to special parties
6. Summary of earnings	26. Recent sales of unregistered securities
7. Organization of registrant	
8. Parents of registrant	27. Subsidiaries of registrant
9. Description of business	28. Franchises and concessions
10. Description of property	29. Indemnification of directors and officers
11. Organization within five years	
12. Pending legal proceedings	30. Treatment of proceeds from stock being registered
13. Capital stocks being registered	
14. Long-term debt being registered	31. Financial statements
15. Other securities being registered	
16. Directors and executive officers	
17. Remuneration of directors and officers	
18. Options to purchase securities	
19. Principal holders of securities	
20. Interest of management in certain transactions	
21. Certified financial statements	

4. Proxy statement, which is used when the firm makes a proxy solicitation for stockholder meetings.

Of these, Form 10-K is usually considered to be the most important because it is the annual report, which must be filed within 90 days after the end of the firm's fiscal year. The new disclosure rules adopted by the SEC restructured Form 10-K. This restructuring was intended to encourage companies to combine Form 10-K with the annual shareholders' report, thereby satisfying the purposes of both reports. The major disclosure items of Form 10-K are shown in Table 16.2.

Additionally, the chief executive officer, the chief financial officer, the chief accounting officer, and a majority of the board of directors must sign Form 10-K. This requirement is intended to encourage the directors to devote the needed attention to reviewing the form and to obtain professional help whenever it is necessary.

The fact that much of the information provided to the SEC must be certified by an independent certified public accountant has been a significant factor in the growth and importance of the public accounting profession. Accumulat-

TABLE 16.2 *Requirements of SEC Form 10-K*

Part I	Part II	Part III	Part IV
1. Business 2. Properties 3. Pending legal proceedings 4. Security ownership of certain beneficial owners and management	5. Market for the registrant's common stock and related security holder matters 6. Selected financial data 7. Management's discussion and analysis of financial condition and results of operations 8. Financial statements and supplemental data	9. Directors and executive officers of the registrant 10. Management remuneration and transactions	11. Exhibits, financial statements, and reports

ing information for the various reports, as well as assisting in their preparation, also requires a substantial internal accounting effort, which has contributed to the growth and prestige of that segment of accounting.

Both internal and independent accountants, however, probably consider the SEC a mixed blessing at best, because of the detailed information required and the legal liability involved. The 1933 Act makes clear that anyone connected with the registration statement is liable to investors for the accuracy of the statements. The external accountant's liability under this Act has been summarized as follows:

1. *Any person acquiring securities described in the Registration Statement may sue the accountant, regardless of the fact that he is not the client of the accountant.*

2. *[The plaintiff's] claim may be based upon an alleged false statement or misleading omission in the financial statements, which constitutes his prima facie case. The plaintiff does not have the further burden of proving that the accountants were negligent or fraudulent in certifying to the financial statement involved.*

3. *The plaintiff does not have to prove that he relied upon the statement or that the loss which he suffered was the proximate result of the falsity or misleading character of the financial statement.*

4. *The accountant has thrust upon him the burden of establishing his freedom from negligence and fraud by proving that he had, after reasonable investiga-*

tion, reasonable ground to believe and did believe that the financial statements to which he certified were true not only as of the date of the financial statements, but beyond that, as of the time when the Registration Statement became effective.

5. *The accountant has the burden of establishing by way of defense or in reduction of alleged damages, that the loss of the plaintiff resulted in whole or part from causes other than the false statements or the misleading omissions in the financial statements. Under the common law it would have been the plaintiff's affirmative case to prove that the damages which he claims he sustained were proximately caused by the negligence or fraud of the accountant.* [1]

The magnitude of this liability has almost certainly been a factor in the continual increase in both voluntary and required financial statement disclosures. In addition, the SEC is constantly expanding and asserting its role in providing the investor with full and fair disclosure.

Organization Structure of the SEC

The Securities and Exchange Commission is directed by four commissioners appointed by the President with the approval of the U.S. Senate. Each commissioner is appointed for a five-year term and one member is designated by the President as the chairman of the SEC.

The SEC is administered from its Washington, D.C., headquarters but has regional and branch offices in the major financial centers of the United States. The commission is assisted by a professional staff of accountants, engineers, lawyers, and securities analysts. These individuals are assigned to the various offices throughout the United States.

The SEC is organized into the following five divisions:

1. **Market Regulation**   Responsible for the regulation of national securities exchanges and security brokers and dealers.

2. **Corporate Regulation**   Responsible for the regulation of public utilities and serves in an advisory function to federal courts in corporate reorganization or bankruptcy cases.

3. **Investment Management**   Responsible for regulating investment companies (companies engaged in trading corporate securities).

4. **Corporation Finance**   Responsible for reviewing all registration statements, prospectuses, quarterly and annual reports, proxy statements, and sales literature for corporations offering securities for sale to the public.

5. **Division of Enforcement**   Responsible for determining whether the available evidence supports allegations or complaints filed against publicly held companies.

---

[1] Saul Levy, *C.P.A. Handbook* (New York: AICPA, 1952), p. 39.

Duties of Public Accountants

Public accountants engaged in practicing before the Securities and Exchange Commission must conform to both SEC requirements and the AICPA Code of Professional Ethics (discussed later in the chapter). A public accountant is considered to be practicing before the SEC if he or she prepares any portion of a registration statement, application, or report and allows his or her name to be associated with the filing. The SEC is particularly sensitive to the *independence* of public accountants, which is defined in the Code of Professional Ethics as complete separation from the financial and business interests of the client.

Regulation S-X contains the SEC's independence requirements. That rule states two conditions that will cause the public accountant to be considered not independent:

1. Any direct financial interest or any material indirect financial interest in the issuer.

2. Any connection with the issuer of the securities as a promoter, underwriter, director, officer, or employee.

The 1933 Act establishes the liability of public accountants to third parties when the accountant makes an untrue statement of a material fact (or omits a material fact) in a registration statement. The accountant's main defense in such cases is *due diligence*. That is, after reasonable investigation, he or she had reasonable grounds to believe that the facts as presented by the client were true.

Under the 1934 Act, the accountant has the responsibility of acting in good faith. If an investor acted on false and misleading financial statements filed with the SEC, the accountant must prove that he or she had no knowledge that the financial statements were false or misleading. That is, the test is *gross negligence*, which means that the accountant acted with less care than would be exercised by a reasonable person under the circumstances.

Foreign Corrupt Practices Act of 1977

The Foreign Corrupt Practices Act (FCPA) enacted by Congress in 1977 has been viewed as the culmination of a trend toward upgrading the ethical behavior of American firms engaged in international trade. The FCPA has two main elements. The first makes it a criminal offense to offer bribes to political or governmental officials outside the United States and imposes fines on offending firms. It also provides for fines and imprisonment of officers, directors, or stockholders of offending firms.

The second element of the FCPA is the requirement that all public companies must (1) keep reasonably detailed records that accurately and fairly reflect company financial activity and (2) devise and maintain a system of internal control that provides reasonable assurance that transactions were properly authorized, recorded, and accounted for. This element is an amendment to the Securities and Exchange Act of 1934 and therefore applies to all corporations that are subject to the 1934 Act's provisions. This disclosure issues involved in this legislation are the prevention of bribery of foreign officials and the maintenance of adequate financial records.

Ethical Responsibilities

The study of ethics from a philosophical perspective explores and analyzes moral judgments, choices, and standards, and asks the question: How should I act? Consequently, society's moral value judgments and the bases for choices of moral beliefs and standards require more comprehensive analysis than is attainable from the data of other disciplines. For example, consider the distinction between science and philosophy. While acting in a professional capacity, the scientist does not find it necessary to pass value judgments on his or her work. In fact, the scientist may disclaim responsibility for the uses of his or her findings, as in the case of nuclear weapons. However, philosophers do evaluate and pass moral judgments on the work of scientists, since the goal of philosophy is to evaluate all aspects of human character, conduct, and experience. Similarly, the scientist (and also the accountant), as a thinking person, is required to make value judgments concerning his or her own work and its consequences.

The terms *ethics* and *morals* are not used interchangeably. In general, ethics (derived from the Greek *elhikē*—the science of character) is the study of moral issues, whereas morals (derived from the Greek *mores*—customs and manners) are standards that individuals observe in their daily conduct. The professions, including accounting, provide an exception to this general rule. Professional Codes of Conduct delineate minimum standards for the practice of a profession. Violation of these standards makes a professional unethical. For a layperson, the violation of his or her personal code of ethics makes the individual immoral.

The ethical philosophy of western civilization is largely based on the concept of *utilitarianism,* the greatest happiness of the greatest number, as refined by John Stuart Mill.[2] Professional ethics by accountants prescribes a duty that goes beyond that of an ordinary citizen. The special responsibility accountants have to society was summarized by Chief Justice Warren Burger as discussed in Chapter 1 (see page 25). Meeting this responsibility requires accountants to maintain high ethical standards of professional conduct. Society has granted many of the professions autonomy, including self-regulation, as a privilege; in return, these professions must assume the obligation to promote ethical conduct among their members, or public policy makers may react by reducing or removing self-regulation and autonomy. Ethical conduct by accountants, based on the concept of utilitarianism, should include consideration of all possible consequences of professional decisions for all individuals or groups affected by a decision. Among these individuals or groups are actual and potential stockholders, creditors, suppliers, customers, employees, and society as a whole.

---

[2] See, for example, *Mill's Ethical Writings,* J. B. Schneewind (New York: Collier, 1965).

The practice of professional accounting is characterized by uncertainties that can create ethical dilemmas. Loeb[3] has identified several major ethical issues or dilemmas that may confront individual accountants and accounting firms.

1. *Independence* The concept of independence requires the complete separation of the business and financial interests of the public accountant from the client corporation. Consequently, the auditor must maintain the role of an impartial observer maintaining the public watchdog function. How do firms develop policies to ensure that this duty is maintained?

2. *Scope of services* What other services (e.g., consulting, tax return preparation, tax advice) are compatible with financial auditing? At what point does the auditor lose independence by providing nonaudit services to a client?

3. *Confidentiality* When does the auditor's public watchdog function conflict with his or her duty to keep client activities confidential?

4. *Practice development* The removal of the rule prohibiting advertising (discussed later in the chapter) allows a great deal of latitude; however, an advertisement cannot be misleading or untrue. How do firms develop policies to delineate the nature and extent of professional development activities?

5. *Differences on accounting issues* How do public accounting firms develop policies to deal with situations in which a company wishes to account for a transaction in a manner not believed to be acceptable to the firm? (In these situations the company may threaten to fire the auditor and seek a public accounting firm that will agree with management's position on the accounting issue. This is termed *opinion shopping*).

The resolution of ethical dilemmas can be assisted by using a framework of analysis. The purpose of such frameworks is to help in identifying the ethical issues and to decide on an appropriate course of action. For example, the following six-step approach may be used:

1. Obtain the relevant facts.
2. Identify the ethical issues.
3. Determine the individuals or groups affected by the dilemma.
4. Identify the possible alternative solutions.
5. Determine how the individuals or groups are affected by the alternative solutions.
6. Decide on the appropriate action.

Another aspect of the ethics issue is the legal-ethical question. That is, if a particular action is legal, does that automatically make it ethical? The obvious

---

[3] Stephen S. Loeb, "Ethical Committees and Consultants in Public Accounting," *Accounting Horizons* (December 1989), pp. 1–10.

answer to this question is no, given that slavary was once legal in the United States. In fact, there is a general presumption in our society that ethical behavior should be at a higher level than legal behavior. Consequently, acts that are consistent with current ethical standards but inconsistent with current legal standards may be necessary to change unethical legal standards. For example, consider the issues of sexual and racial discrimination. Not many years ago public accounting firms did not hire either women or racial minorities. Various actions throughout society, some illegal under the then-current legal statutes, helped to eliminate these practices to the point that today over 50 percent of new hires by large public accounting firms are women; and the profession and public accounting firms are currently engaging in a variety of activities to encourage racial minorities to choose accounting as a career.

The Professional Code of Conduct

Accountants, as professionals, are expected to maintain a level of ethical conduct that goes beyond society's laws. The reason for this high level of ethical conduct is the need for public confidence in the quality of services provided by the profession, regardless of the individual providing the service. Public confidence in the quality of professional service is enhanced when the profession encourages high standards of performance and ethical conduct by its members.

Over the years, the American Institute of Certified Public Accountants (AICPA) has represented itself as an ethical professional body engaged in practicing an art rather than a science. Accounting was to be viewed by society, in a manner similar to the medical and legal professions, as more influenced by a service motive than entirely by a profit motive. As an art, the judgmental nature of accounting precludes a uniform set of rules to cover all situations; consequently, the foundation of the profession rests not on standardization and regulation but on ethical conduct.

In attempting to solidify this view by society, the accounting profession in the United States has had some form of a Code of Professional Conduct since early in the 20th century. The original code, which was a part of the bylaws of the American Association of Professional Accountants (AAPA), a predecessor of the AICPA, was first published in 1905, and contained only two rules. One prohibited members from allowing nonmembers to practice in the member's name, thereby requiring all members of the firm to join the AAPA, not just the managing partner. The second rule prohibited the payment of referral fees now commonly known as "kickbacks." This limited scope of the earliest version of the code was based on a belief that a written code could not and should not be taken as a complete representation of the moral obligations of accounting's responsibility to society.

Later, in 1917 and through subsequent adopted rules, the renamed organization, the American Institute of Accountants, amended the Code of Professional Conduct to include rules prohibiting various actions such as contingency fees, competitive bidding, advertising, the formation of partnerships, forecasts, and a substantial financial interest in a public corporation client.

Additionally, in response to the Securities Acts of 1933 and 1934, a rule on independence was adopted in 1934. Later, in 1941, the rules were codified into a new code that included a section on technical standards.

As discussed in Chapter 1, during the period following the collapse of the stock market in 1929, accountants were viewed very favorably by society. Consequently, it was not necessary for the profession to undertake any drastic measures to attain the public's confidence. The main concerns of the profession up to 1941 were with the concepts of confidentiality, competence, and independence. The main emphasis of the profession's disciplinary actions during this period, and even somewhat later, were directed toward restrictions on unprofessional competitive practices such as competitive bidding, advertising, encroachment on the practice of other CPAs, and the pirating of other firms' employees. The rules prohibiting such actions were based on the belief that they would erode independence and destroy harmony among practitioners.[4]

In 1962 the Code of Professional Conduct was again amended. Although this amended code contained essentially the same rules as did the 1941 code, they were classified into five separate articles. Article 1, "Relations with Clients and Public," contained a more explicit description of independence. Article 2 defined "Technical Standards." Article 3 covered advertising, promotional practices, and competitive bidding and was titled "Promotional Practices." Article 4 discussed the rules of membership and was termed "Operating Practices." Finally, Article 5, "Relations with Fellow Members," defined unacceptable client and employee acquisition practices.

The subsequent social upheaval of the 1960s, and the impact of the Watergate Investigation of 1974, also affected the accounting profession. For example, it was found that many of the largest corporations had made illegal contributions to the Republican Party, and investigations discovered secret bank accounts that were used to hide illegal bribes and kickbacks. The profession argued that it was difficult, if not impossible, to discover such transactions in a normal audit. Additionally, it was maintained that, even if detected, such illegal transactions would not have a material effect on companies' financial statements and, therefore, did not require disclosure. Nevertheless, the failure to uncover these illegal activities by normal audits served to erode confidence in the ethical conduct of the accounting profession. As a result of these issues, and due to the fact that public accounting firms had failed to detect imminent bankruptcies for several large audit clients such as National Student Marketing, Penn Central, and Equity Funding, in 1977 the United States Congress published a study that asserted an alarming lack of independence and a lack of dedication to public protection by the largest public accounting firms.[5]

During this period, the House Subcommittee on Oversight and Investigations (the congressional body that oversees the SEC) was also engaging in an inquiry of accounting practices in the oil and gas industry that culminated

[4] Olson, W. E., *The Accounting Profession: Years of Trial: 1969–1980* (New York: AICPA, 1982).

[5] U.S. Congress, *The Accounting Establishment: 95th Congress*, 1st session (Washington, D.C.: GPO, 1977).

into a much larger investigation. In a report issued in 1978,[6] the Committee's Chair, John Moss, summarized Congress' concern over the incidents that had occurred. Especially troubling were events such as bankruptcies with no prior warnings from auditors to investors that anything was amiss, the demise of over 100 brokerage firms in the late 1960s because of inconsistent methods of determining capital ratios, lack of uniform accounting procedures in the energy industry, and the incidents discovered in relation to the Watergate incident.

Subsequently, in the mid-1980s Congressional interest in the accounting profession arose again in the form of more hearings before the House Subcommittee on Oversight and Investigations now Chaired by Representative John Dingell. The committee's primary concern was the role of auditors in the detection of fraud. Representative Dingell questioned whether the public's perception of accountants' responsibility was the same as was the profession's. He also wondered: Were the rules deficient? Were the qualifications to be a CPA sufficient? Was self-policing of the accounting profession sufficient?[7] In other words, he was questioning the maintenance of ethical standards by the profession and suggesting that the profession did not have the ability to regulate itself.

Public policy makers were not the only ones voicing concerns. During the 1970s some accountants were joining the critics of the accounting profession. For example, Abraham Briloff, an accounting professor at Baruch College, City University of New York, in a series of books, articles, and testimony before Congress,[8] maintained that many published financial statements were not "prepared fairly" in accordance with generally accepted accounting principles; the FASB had not fulfilled its responsibility to develop accounting standards; and public accounting firms had not adequately resolved the differences in accounting issues dilemmas discussed above, resulting in several cases of successful "opinion shopping."

The events of the 1970s and 1980s served to question the ability of accountants to detect fraud, uncover illegal contributions, and predict bankruptcy; consequently, their competence as professionals was being questioned. As a result, the profession was facing legislation that threatened to regulate the practice of accounting.

Partially in response to these issues, the AICPA engaged in several activi-

---

[6] U.S. Congress, *Accounting and Auditing Practices and Procedures: 95th Congress,* 1st session (Washington, D.C.: GPO, 1978).

[7] J. Dingell, "Accountants Must Clean Up Their Act: Rep. John Dingell Speaks Out," *Management Accounting* (May 1985) pp. 52–55.

[8] See, for example, *Unaccountable Accounting* (Harper & Row, 1972); *More Debits Than Credits* (Harper & Row, 1976); *The Truth About Corporate Accounting* (Harper & Row, 1981); "Standards Without Standards/Principles Without Principles/Fairness Without Fairness," *Advances in Accounting* (1986), pp. 25–50; "Accounting and Society: A Covenant Desecrated," *Critical Perspectives on Accounting* (March 1990), pp. 5–30.

ties in an attempt to neutralize criticism of the accounting profession. In 1973 the Code of Professional Conduct was again amended. A major feature of this amended Code was the requirement to comply with auditing standards and the prohibition from expressing an opinion that financial statements are prepared in conformity with generally accepted accounting standards if such statements depart from an accounting principle. As discussed earlier in the text, the inclusion of this rule made Accounting Research Bulletins, Accounting Principles Board Opinions, and Statement of Financial Accounting Standards enforceable under the Code of Professional Conduct. The 1973 Code also included a discussion of the philosophical fashion by which the rules flow from the concepts, and why these concepts were of importance to the profession.

Next, in 1974 the AICPA formed a commission on auditors' responsibilities. The final report of this commission, known as the Cohen Report, called upon the Auditing Standards Executive Committee to consider developing an improved auditor's report. Additionally, the report recommended the development of criteria for the evaluation of internal accounting controls and the establishment of independent audit committees. Later the AICPA established a new division for CPA firms with two sections, one for firms with clients registered with the SEC and one for firms that had private practice clients. Membership in the SEC Practice Section requires self-regulation including external peer review of its practice procedures. Additionally, the activities of the SEC Practice Section are monitored by a Public Oversight Board.

As noted by Representative Dingell, some of the criticism of the professional practice of accounting can be attributed to an *expectations gap.* That is, there is a difference between what financial statement users and society as a whole perceive as the responsibility of public accountants versus what accountants and the profession perceive as their responsibility. As a result, the AICPA's Auditing Standards Board issued nine new Standards in 1988 in an attempt to narrow this expectations gap. Specifically, with respect to addressing some of the problem areas identified by critics, the effect of these new standards was to (1) broaden auditors' responsibility to consider the reliability of a company's internal control system when planning an audit, (2) delineate auditors' responsibility for reporting errors, irregularities, and illegal acts by clients, and (3) require auditors to evaluate a company's ability to continue as a going concern.

At about this same time, the Code of Professional Conduct was undergoing a review. In 1983 the AICPA appointed a Special Committee to study the relevance and effectiveness of the Code in the then-current environment. The report of this committee, commonly known as the Anderson Report, indicated that effective performance should meet six criteria:

1. Safeguard the public's interest.
2. Recognize the CPA's paramount role in the financial reporting process.
3. Help assure quality performance and eliminate substandard performance.

4. Help assure objectivity and integrity in public service.

5. Enhance CPA's prestige and credibility.

6. Provide guidance as to proper conduct.[9]

The members of the AICPA accepted the recommendations of the Anderson Report and amended the Code of Professional Conduct in 1988. The Code now consists of four sections as follows:

Principles   The standards of ethical conduct stated in philosophical terms.

Rules of conduct   Minimum standards of ethical conduct.

Interpretations   Interpretations of the rules by the AICPA Division of Professional Ethics.

Ethical rulings   Published explanations and answers to questions about the rules submitted to the AICPA by practicing accountants and others interested in ethical requirements.

The first two sections of the Code of Professional Conduct consist of general statements emphasizing positive activities that encourage a high level of performance (principles), and minimum levels of performance that must be maintained (rules). Consequently, implicit in the Code of Professional Conduct is the expectation that the CPAs will abide by the rules at the minimum and strive to achieve the principles at the maximum. The following six ethical principles, which are not enforceable, are contained in the Code of Professional Conduct:

1. *Responsibilities*   In carrying out their responsibilities as professionals, members should exercise sensitive professional and moral judgments in all their activities.

2. *The public interest*   Members should accept the obligation to act in a way that will serve the public interest, honor the public trust, and demonstrate commitment to professionalism.

3. *Integrity*   To maintain and broaden public confidence, members should perform all professional responsibilities with the highest level of integrity.

4. *Objectivity and independence*   A member should maintain objectivity and be free of conflict of interest in discharging professional responsibilities. A member in public practice should be independent in fact and appearance when providing auditing and other attestation services.

5. *Due care*   A member should observe the profession's technical and ethical standards, strive continually to improve competence and the quality of services, and discharge professional responsibility to the best of the member's ability.

6. *Scope and nature of services*   A member in public practice should observe the Principles of the Code of Professional Conduct in determining the scope and nature of services to be provided.

[9] AICPA, *Recruiting Professional Standards to Achieve Professional Excellence in a Changing Environment* (New York: AICPA, 1986) p. 11.

The principles, which are goal-oriented, also provide the framework for the rules, which represent the enforceable provisions of the Code. The rules deal with issues such as independence, integrity, and objectivity; compliance with standards of practice; confidentiality of client information; advertising; contingent fees and commissions. Later some of these rules were required to be liberalized because of a consent decree between the AICPA and the Federal Trade Commission that arose from a claim of restraint of fair trade. For example, contingent fees may now be accepted by CPA firms from nonattest clients, and advertising by CPA firms is now an acceptable practice.

The need for interpretations of the Code of Professional Conduct arises when there are questions from individuals or firms about a particular rule. Ethical rulings are explanations concerning specific factual situations. They have been published in the form of questions and answers. A detailed review of the interpretations and ethical rulings is beyond the scope of this book.

The goal of the Anderson Report and the revised Code of Professional Conduct was to be more responsive to the public's concern by providing

1. Ethical guidance.
2. Broad positive statements.
3. Specific behavioral rules.
4. Proactive monitoring.
5. Broader rules application.
6. Guidance on dealing with the changing environment.[10]

In summary, the past two decades have brought forward questions from some critics concerning the ethical conduct of professional accountants. The profession has responded by further delineations of its responsibilities and by attempting to narrow the expectations gap. However, in spite of its critics, the accounting profession continues to be viewed in a favorable manner. A recent Harris poll found that the public views accountants in high esteem and above other professions.[11] This favorable view may be partially due to the fact that the accounting profession has proven to be responsive to the external environment over the years. However, the accounting profession must strive to maintain this perception and the Code of Professional Conduct should be viewed as a starting point in the determination of the ethical behavior of professional accountants. Additionally, it may be necessary to revisit the scope of services issue, because this same Harris poll detected some concerns over the variety of services offered by CPA firms to the same client. This and other issues that trouble the public must be resolved in order for accounting to continue to serve its public watchdog function in a manner that is accepted by society.

---

[10] Michael K. Shaub, "Restructuring the Code of Professional Ethics: A Review of the Anderson Committee Report and its Implications," *Accounting Horizons* (December 1988), pp. 89–97.

[11] Louis Harris, *A Survey of Perceptions, Knowledge and Attitudes Toward CPAs and the Accounting Profession* (New York, 1986).

Summary

Fair and full disclosure has become increasingly important in financial reporting. In response to changing societal needs, the AICPA, the SEC, the APB, and the FASB have all addressed the question of disclosure. Additionally, maintaining ethical conduct has become increasingly important for the accounting profession. As professionals, accountants are required to maintain the highest ethical standards. In the readings for the chapter, John M. Fedders and L. Glenn Perry take the position that the SEC's top priority should be policing financial disclosure fraud. Additionally, Robert G. Ruland and Cristi K. Lindblom analyze the potential conflict between ethics and adequate disclosure.

Policing Financial Disclosure Fraud: The SEC's Top Priority

John M. Fedders and L. Glenn Perry*

Central to the disclosure system are financial statements and the disclosure of financial information. No other aspect of the disclosure process has a greater impact on the judgment of investors. No other disclosure has a greater impact on market prices.

Financial information is of the utmost relevance in 1984. The United States is recovering from a recession, and business enterprises continue to experience economic uncertainties and difficulties. History tells us that periods of fiscal turmoil and economic difficulties spawn abuses and deceptions. During periods of economic stress and business stagnation, some managements have engaged in acts designed to create an appearance of financial stability and prosperity. The reasons are obvious—to maintain the market price of a company's stock; to create the appearance of profitability in order to obtain financing or to prevent a default on bank loans; or to satisfy management greed and ego.

There are substantial pressures on managements to minimize financial

Copyright by the American Institute of Certified Public Accountants, *Journal of Accountancy*, July 1984. Reprinted by permission.

*The Securities and Exchange Commission, as a matter of policy, disclaims responsibility for any private statement by any of its employees. The views expressed here are those of Messrs. Fedders and Perry and do not necessarily reflect the views of the commission or of their colleagues on the staff of the commission.

problems. This environment has led to the collective efforts of the Securities and Exchange Commission's Divisions of Enforcement and Corporation Finance and the Office of the Chief Accountant to identify fiscal trends and related disclosure problems which require close surveillance and may lead to the need for enforcement actions.

The Enforcement Program

No matter what the composition of the commission or who manages the various offices and divisions, the enforcement program against financial fraud will remain at the forefront. We are focusing our enforcement actions against financial fraud, including "cooking the books," accounting irregularities, reckless application of GAAP and GAAS, and improprieties arising from "shopping" for auditors' opinions. We have initiated a score of these cases, and a greater number are in investigation. The longest and most significant chapter in the enforcement legacy of John S. R. Shad, the current chairman of the commission, will be the financial fraud program—longer and more significant than the much publicized "insider trading" prosecutions chapter.

A principal focus when "prospecting" for financial fraud is management's discussion and analysis (MD&A) of financial condition and results of operations. Since the MD&A was first required in 1974, its importance has dramatically increased. It provides information to enhance an understanding of historical financial statements. Also, it provides information to improve an understanding of the enterprise itself, including its future prospects. For example, the MD&A requires a description of known trends or uncertainties that are reasonably expected to have a material favorable or unfavorable impact on future operations.

Although the financial disclosure fraud enforcement program is designed to include a broad variety of misconduct, several areas have been particularly emphasized. They are as follows:

1. Liquidity problems, such as (a) decreased flow of collections from sales to customers, (b) the lack of availability of credit from suppliers, banks, and others, and (c) the inability to meet maturing obligations when they fall due. Corporate disclosure must not minimize or fail fully to explain liquidity problems.

2. Operating trends and factors affecting profits and losses, such as (a) curtailment of operations, (b) decline of orders, (c) increased competition, or (d) cost overruns on major contracts. Disclosure must include early notice of a significant reversal of previously reported sales trends. There must be an objective discussion of poor financial results.

   Not only must material facts affecting a company's operations be reported, they must be reported promptly. Corporate releases which disclose favorable developments but do not describe material adverse developments do not serve investors' needs and may violate the antifraud provisions. In the case of an issuer making an offering or a continuous offering of its shares, the failure to disclose such material adverse devel-

opments also may violate the Securities Act of 1933 if there is not an appropriate updating of information.

Unless adequate and accurate information is publicly available, a company may not purchase its own securities or make acquisitions using its securities. Furthermore, insiders who trade in the securities of their companies in these circumstances violate the antifraud provisions of the Securities Exchange Act of 1934.

3. Material increases in problem loans must be reported by financial institutions. Increased financial pressure on certain industries has caused a sharp increase in uncollectible and nonperforming loans. Disclosure must be made when there is a material increase in (a) interest that has not been paid, (b) interest that is reduced or deferred, or (c) doubtful collections. When necessary, an increase in provisions for losses must be timely reported.

4. Corporations cannot avoid their disclosure obligations when they approach business decline or failure. Economists report that the business failure rate is the highest since the trough of the Depression in 1932.

The principal method of projecting seeming economic well-being in the face of business decline and possible failure is through deceptive and fraudulent accounting practices. In order to hide fiscal difficulties and to deceive investors, declining and failing companies have (a) prematurely recognized income, (b) improperly treated operating leases as sales, (c) inflated inventory by improper application of the LIFO inventory method, (d) included fictitious amounts in inventories, (e) failed to recognize losses through write-offs and allowances, (f) improperly capitalized or deferred costs and expenses, (g) included unusual gains in operating income, (h) overvalued marketable securities, (i) created "sham" year-end transactions to boost reported earnings, and (j) changed their accounting practices to increase earnings without disclosing the changes.

These are not the universe of the trends and disclosure areas we have under scrutiny. The commission staff is looking for emerging problems. Although our focus is not entirely on financial information, the crucial choices for America's future are economic. Consequently, accurate reporting of material financial information is essential.

Prosecutorial Discretion

By prosecutorial discretion, the commission applies the available enforcement sanctions and remedies to the fraud or misconduct involved. Each fraud or misconduct does not require the most severe sanction. Although the commission's enforcement remedies are limited to (a) civil injunctions, (b) section 15(c)(4) and rule 2(e) administrative proceedings, and (c) section 21(a) reports of investigation, and do not include the ability to levy fines, the remedial purposes of the federal securities laws have been satisfied by the application of these remedies. Indeed, there are situations in which misconduct has occurred and prosecutorial discretion dictates that no enforcement action be initiated. Certain situations are best resolved by the company's voluntarily taking action such as a restatement of financial statements.

After the discovery of all facts regarding a financial fraud or an accounting irregularity, the difficult task is the application of prosecutorial discretion.

The commission possesses wide discretion in ways that help the disclosure system function effectively. Because certain conduct violates the federal securities laws does not mean that the commission must file charges and seek to impose sanctions on the malefactor. The task is not merely action which places sanctions on the malefactors and deters potential wrongdoers, but has as its principal focus the protection of investors and the maintenance of the integrity of the U.S. securities markets.

A difficult aspect of prosecutorial discretion regarding financial disclosure fraud relates to whether directors, officers, or employees of the entity also should be charged and, if so, whether as (a) participants, (b) control persons, or (c) aiders and abettors. Our objective is to identify the corporate officials responsible and to impose sanctions on them for their misconduct.

There also is the question whether the underwriters, lawyers, and accountants participated in the fraud or misconduct and, if so, should be charged (a) in injunctive actions as participants or aiders and abettors or (b) in administrative proceedings. The commission has not shied away from charging professionals, including accountants, in rule 2(e) administrative proceedings.

If a professional's conduct amounts to a violation of, or aiding and abetting a violation of, the federal securities laws, the commission should as a general matter sue to enjoin the professional from repetition of such conduct—not bring a rule 2(e) administrative proceeding. However, even if there is a violation of law, in appropriate circumstances, prosecutorial discretion may lead to a decision that an injunction would be improper and an administrative proceeding under rule 2(e) would be appropriate.

Accounting firms are the major key to sustaining high-quality work by the accounting profession. In our view, it is therefore imperative that the commission maintain its ability to influence the activities of such firms through its enforcement-related programs, while at the same time striving to use its enforcement and regulatory tools fairly and carefully within the legal constraints which the courts and others have construed or are likely to construe.

The fact that an accounting firm permits its name to be attached to a report on, or certification of, financial statements is a factor, but in our view not itself a sufficient factor, to support the appropriateness of naming the firm, instead of or in addition to individual firm members, in any rule 2(e) proceeding that might be instituted because of deficiencies in the audit. In determining whether proceedings should be instituted against an accounting firm under rule 2(e), it is important to the commission's deliberations to have information regarding the relationship of the alleged audit deficiencies, violations of the federal securities laws, or improper professional conduct to (a) the adequacy of applicable firm audit engagement and review practices or procedures and the extent to which those procedures were adhered to in the audit under inquiry; (b) the selection, training, supervision, and conduct of members or employees of the accounting firm involved in the engagement; (c) the role played by top-level managers in the firm; and (d) the audit work performed on other engagements in which deficiencies have been uncovered.

The SEC's Track Record

Enough talk about policy and objectives. What has the commission done?

The track record permits an evaluation of whether it has met its objectives.

The following is a description of 12 actions in this area.

1. In July 1982 the commission published a section 21(a) report of investigation regarding Fidelity Financial Corporation, a savings and loan holding company, and Fidelity Savings and Loan Association, its principal subsidiary. This report emphasizes the commission's concern with respect to the disclosure issues raised in connection with (a) offerings and sales of retail repurchase agreements and (b) a press release announcing fiscal year-end operational and financial results.

   The commission alleged that Fidelity and the Association violated the anti-fraud provisions of the securities laws by (a) making false and misleading statements and omitting to state material facts concerning the security interest in the collateral backing the "retail repos," the existence of a trust, and the financial condition of its subsidiary and (b) failing to disclose material information concerning its financial condition in a 1981 year-end press release in January 1982.

   The commission emphasized that issuers of retail repos should be mindful of the need to comply with the disclosure requirements of the securities laws as well as disclosure guidelines of other federal and state regulatory agencies. It also said it is incumbent on companies, when issuing press statements announcing year-end results prior to their release, to inform the public not only of the extent of losses suffered but also of the adverse impact that the continuation of losses may have on operations in the pending year if it is reasonably anticipated that such losses will continue.

2. In September 1982 the commission initiated an injunctive action against Saxon Industries and certain senior officers. The commission alleged that, from as early as 1968, Saxon and its officers knowingly and willfully falsified books and records to inflate earnings.

   It was alleged that the scheme was carried out by the creation of nonexistent inventories on the records of various divisions of Saxon. This allegedly was done by (a) creating and maintaining false records, (b) Saxon's computer being programmed automatically to add false inventory, and (c) transferring nonexistent inventory from one division to another to avoid detection. By 1981 the nonexistent inventory was approximately $75 million.

3. In December 1982 the commission initiated an injunctive action against McCormick & Company, Incorporated, and the general manager of its Grocery Products Division. It was alleged that from at least 1976 the company engaged in a scheme to inflate earnings to meet profit objectives mandated by corporate management by improperly deferring certain promotional and advertising expenses and by prematurely recognizing revenues for goods that were not shipped until a later fiscal period.

   In order to conceal these improper accounting practices from its independent accountants, it was alleged that McCormick personnel (a) intentionally made false statements to auditors, (b) maintained two sets of records, and (c) altered various documents, including shipping invoices and advertising bills.

4. In February 1983 a section 15(c)(4) administrative proceeding was initiated against Clabir Corporation. It used a method to price its marketable equity securities other than what is required by GAAP.

   The commission concluded that the use of a price other than the quoted market price for determining the market value of marketable equity securities is provided for neither by GAAP nor by commission pronouncements.

5. In March 1983 an injunctive action was initiated against the president and vice-president for operations of Security America Corporations, a holding company whose sole operating subsidiary was a multiple-line casualty and property insurance company. It was alleged that Security America overstated its earnings by understating loss reserves both for assumed workers' compensation claims and for direct insurance business.

   It was alleged that the defendants overstated the reserves by (a) using an outdated mortality table, (b) reducing estimated annual medical costs, (c) failing to factor in an inflation rate when estimating future claims, (d) failing to consider some unpaid claims in establishing reserves, and (e) arbitrarily reducing reserves. The commission also alleged deficiencies in disclosures of cash flow problems and false statements to the company's auditors.

6. In May 1983 the commission initiated an injunctive action against

A.M. International, Inc. It was alleged that throughout its 1980 fiscal year and continuing in its 1981 fiscal year, A.M. misrepresented its financial condition and results of operations by (a) making improper adjustments to its allowance and accrual accounts and its gross profit, (b) attributing certain expenses and charges to periods other than those to which the expenses and charges belonged, and (c) inflating revenues and results of operations. Moreover, it was alleged that A.M. failed to record on its books and records material amounts of adjustments relating to its results of operations.

This investigation uncovered examples of extreme management pressure on subordinates to meet performance goals. In response to such pressure, various divisions of A.M. engaged in widespread and pervasive accounting irregularities in order to present results of operations which conformed to budgeted performance objectives.

7. In July 1983 the commission issued a section 21(a) report of investigation regarding Aetna Life and Casualty Company. In 1981 it began recognizing currently in its financial statements anticipated future tax benefits of net operating loss (NOL) carry-forwards. The commission's position was that Aetna did not meet the "assurance beyond any reasonable doubt" standard imposed by GAAP.

GAAP states that tax benefits of NOLs should not be recognized until they are actually realized, except in unusual circumstances in which realization is assured beyond any reasonable doubt at the time the loss carry-forwards arise. Without admitting or denying the validity of the commission's position, Aetna restated its 1982 year-end and quarterly financial statements.

8. In August 1983 the commission initiated the second of two cases against Ronson Corporation in less than a year. In a civil action for an order directing compliance with the commission's order issued in the first case, it was alleged that Ronson failed to describe in its MD&A and business description that its largest customer (a) had shut down its operations, (b) had suspended all purchases from Ronson, and (c) was unlikely to resume such purchases until some future period. It also was alleged that Ronson failed to state that when sales to its largest customer resumed, such sales would most likely be reduced by 30 percent to 50 percent below previous levels.

9. In October 1983 the commission initiated a section 15(c)(4) proceeding against Southeastern Savings & Loan Company and Scottish Savings and Loan Association. The commission alleged that losses on the sale of securities hedged by future contracts must be recognized at the time of sale unless the sale qualified as a "wash sale." The SEC believed in this case that the sale of 15 percent and 16 percent "Ginnie Mae" certificates and the purchase of 8 percent through 12.5 percent Ginnie Mae certificates did not qualify as a wash sale because the certificates purchased and sold were not the same or substantially the same as contemplated by GAAP.

The commission ordered the two savings and loan associations to restate previously issued financial statements because they both improperly deferred net losses on these transactions when GAAP required the recognition of the losses in the period in which the transaction occurred.

10. In February 1984 the commission filed an injunctive action against United States Surgical Corporation and various senior corporate officials. It was alleged that from 1979 through 1981 they had engaged in various improper practices in which pretax earnings were overstated by more than $18 million. It was further alleged that certain of these practices continued during 1982 and 1983.

The commission alleged that these practices included (a) the falsification of corporate records, (b) the recording as sales of unordered products, (c) the improper capitalization of costs as fixed assets, (d) the improper capitalization of legal expenses, (e) the improper capitalization of various expenses as assets, and (f) the failure to write off assets which could not be located.

As part of its relief, the commission required that bonuses paid to certain officers which were based on the improperly reported earnings be repaid to the corporation.

11. In February 1984 the commission initiated an injunctive action against IntraWest Financial Corporation, a bank holding company, and two of its officers. The commission alleged that the allowance for possible loan and lease losses was understated for the first three-quarters of fiscal year 1982, causing IntraWest's reported income to be overstated materially.

The commission alleged that, despite material adverse information about their own loan portfolio, IntraWest's officers used an improper method to calculate the allowance for possible loan and lease losses that were based on average allowance percentages of a peer group.

12. In February 1984 the commission brought a section 15(c)(4) administrative proceeding against Utica Bankshares Corporation, a bank holding company. The commission alleged that UBC understated its allowance for possible loan losses for the third quarter of 1982 and, thus, materially overstated its reported income.

It was alleged that the former management of the bank, in establishing its allowances for possible loan losses, failed to give adequate consideration to the adverse impact on the quality of its loan portfolio of significant developments and trends, including a severe decline in the energy segment of the regional economy and the failure of a major bank in its operating area.

These are not the universe of the cases initiated in the past several years. They are representative of the types of financial disclosure investigations and enforcement actions on which the commission will continue to focus.

The commission will remain vigorous in the enforcement of the antifraud and reporting provisions of the federal securities laws. Whether investment decisions will be correct depends directly on the accuracy, quality, and timeliness of the financial information on which they are based. The commission will not temporize with financial disclosure fraud.

Public confidence in the commission is on the shoulders of its enforcement program. As custodian of this important responsibility, we are dedicated to protecting the interests of investors and the integrity of the capital markets.

Ethics and Disclosure: An Analysis of Conflicting Duties

Robert G. Ruland and Cristi K. Lindblom

Introduction

The ethics of accounting professionals[1] have come under increasing scrutiny and have been frequently challenged by segments of the public. Fairness of disclosure is one of the key issues of concern. Frequently referred to as "the expectation gap," there is a difference between what the public and accounting professionals perceive as constituting fair disclosure. In short, the public expects more of accountants in terms of ensuring against misleading accounting information than accountants accept as their duty.[2]

[1] This paper is about the duties of accountants and auditors in general. The terms *accountants* or *accounting professionals* are sometimes used for expository purposes when referring to both accountants and auditors.

[2] The duties of auditors at times are different than the duties of other accounting professionals. Auditor behaviour is governed by the AICPA Code of Professional Conduct which in turn designates the Statements on Auditing Standards issued by the Auditing Standards Board as authoritative. Since these standards are only applicable to auditors, they can be seen as distinguishing auditor

The accounting profession has attempted to reduce the difference in expectations through a variety of efforts. Among them are attempts within the profession to raise ethical awareness through revision of existing, or adoption of new, statements of ethics.[3] Most closely related to the expectation gap issue, the American Institute of Certified Public Accountants (AICPA), following the recommendations contained in the Anderson Report,[4] submitted to its

duties regarding disclosure from those of other accounting professionals. However, it is assumed here that the distinction relates to the rigor of review procedures, not to the objectives of disclosure. For example, the audit report states "presents fairly" but this does not mean that non-audited statements do not present fairly. The audit report simply makes a more explicit statement of what is implied for all accounting reports.

[3] Other efforts include the issuance of Statement of Auditing Standards numbers 53 through 59 by the Auditing Standards Board of the American Institute of Certified Public Accountants. These are commonly referred to as the "expectation gap standards." Efforts to improve ethics education in accounting can also be seen as addressing the expectations gap.

[4] The report was issued in 1986 and is commonly named after George D. Anderson,

membership a revision of the Institute's code of ethics which went into effect in 1988 as *The Code of Professional Conduct* (AICPA, 1988) (the Code). While the Code addresses the issue of disclosure, it does not resolve the issue of the accountant's responsibility for misleading information in a manner which leads to resolution of the expectation gap. Indeed, it will be illustrated that the Code reflects rather than resolves the controversy and contains a contradiction which may leave the accountant in a position of unresolvable conflict.

This paper is an attempt to clarify the ethical duties of accountants in the area of disclosure. Duties to disclose will be shown to be at times in conflict with one another and/or with other professional duties. The method for analysis will be to bring to bear the extensive research on conflicting ethical duties which appears in the philosophy literature. While the discussion in the paper will mainly concern the duties facing individual accountants, the primary implication of the paper is that the rules which establish expectations for professional behaviour are a source of ethical conflict.

The paper will focus on the duties facing members of the AICPA, whether they be in public practice or employed by industry or government. In spite of the discussion being limited to AICPA members, the analysis and conclusions will be general enough to be of interest to all accountants.

In the sections that follow, relevant and mandated disclosures are first dis-

cussed. This is followed by a discussion of professional duties in accounting, particularly for AICPA members. Next, a review of the philosophy literature pertaining to conflicting duties is introduced and the duties facing the accounting profession are discussed in the philosophical framework. Finally, the paper is summarized and its limitations are discussed.

Background—Relevant Versus Mandated Accounting Disclosures

Accounting disclosures provide information to users about conditions and events. In turn, accounting information may be used to make assessments and predictions which support decision making. Relevant disclosures are those which satisfy the decision-making needs of users. Depending upon their needs, the subset of information which is relevant may vary across users. Likewise, what is relevant may change over time as user needs change.

Required disclosures are those mandated as generally accepted accounting principles. If mandated accounting information were perfect, all relevant information would be disclosed and the required and relevant information subsets would be identical. In fact, accounting information is less than perfect; some relevant information is not required and some required information is not relevant. The difference between relevant and required disclosures develops from several sources, including changing socioeconomic conditions, insufficient measurement techniques, and an accounting policy-making process which is influenced by politics.

The existence of non-overlapping portions of the required and relevant information subsets may create a di-

---

who was chair of the AICPA's Special Committee on Standards of Professional Conduct for Certified Public Accountants. The actual title of the report is *Restructuring Professional Standards to Achieve Professional Excellence in a Changing Environment* (AICPA, 1986).

lemma for accounts. Presumably, accountants will better fulfill their role as providers of information and will benefit society if they act to disclose some non-mandated, relevant information and refrain from disclosing some mandated, irrelevant information. However, such behaviour may be seen as in conflict with other professional duties.

Professional Duties in Accounting

Professional duties may be explicit or they may be implicit. Explicit duties are specified in professional codes and standards. Implicit duties may be implied in professional codes and standards, or they may be derived from other sources such as the role of the profession in society.[5]

The AICPA's *Code of Professional Conduct* contains both Principles and Rules which constitute a source of professional duties for AICPA members.[6] According to the Code, the Principles "provide a framework for the rules" and "guide members in the performance of their professional responsibilities," while the Rules "govern the performance of professional services by members." Adherence to the Rules, but not the Principles, is required under the by-laws of the AICPA. Thus, the Principles are merely for guidance. They are a source which implies duties. Other sources which imply duties include the history and public image of the accounting profession, legal opinions, the

auditor's report and the FASB's Conceptual Framework.

The Rules of the Code, on the other hand, are a source of explicit duties. They make clear what is right and wrong behaviour and are enforceable by the AICPA. Other sources of explicit duties like accounting and auditing standards are empowered by the Rules in the Code.[7] Given the overarching authority of the Code, the discussion of explicit duties below will be limited to those specified in the Rules as opposed to standards authorized by the Rules.

Explicit Duties

The Rules section of the Code makes explicit two duties with regard to disclosure. First, Rule 203 addresses the issue of duty with regard to accounting principles. Second, Rule 301 addresses the issue of confidential client information.

Rule 301,[8] which specifies that confidential information should not be disclosed without the specified consent of the client,[9] has been discussed elsewhere in the literature. Beach (1984) describes Rule 301 as the "Professional Catch 22." Beach cites *Wagenheim, J. S.*

---

[5] W. D. Ross (1930), a Kantian scholar, calls these duties *prima facie*. For a discussion on Ross and the duties which face accounting policy-makers see Ruland (1984).

[6] The Code is applicable to all members of the AICPA whether they be in public practice, in industry, in government, or in academe. Certain parts of the Code are only applicable to members in public practice.

[7] Rule 202 of the Code establishes that members must comply with the standards promulgated by bodies designated by the Council of the AICPA. In turn, the Council has designated bodies, including the FASB and the Auditing Standards Board, as authoritative.

[8] Rule 301 is applicable only to AICPA members in public practice. The issue under discussion is applicable to a wider range of accountants, however, because the rule has a parallel in the codes of other professional accounting groups (e.g., The Institute of Management Accountants).

[9] The code makes exception only for subpoena and summons, authorized practice review, and inquiries by recognized investigative or disciplinary bodies.

(Consolidata Services Inc.) vs. Alexander Grant & Co. as a case in which substantial compensatory and punitive damages were awarded to Consolidata Services because Alexander Grant had made an unauthorized disclosure of client information. As a contrast Beach cites the case of *Fund of Funds vs. Arthur Andersen & Co.* in which the jury found that Arthur Andersen had a contractual duty to disclose information, confidential or not. In summarizing the dilemma Beach concludes:

> The clear implication is that there is conflict regarding duties. The disclosure of confidential information to the detriment of a client is an actionable wrong, but so too is the failure to disclose confidential information to the detriment of a third party. The accountant is damned if he does and damned if he doesn't! (p. 314).

Rule 203 states that when financial statements or data contain any departure from generally accepted accounting principles (GAAP) which has a material effect on the statements or data as a whole, members shall not express an opinion or state affirmatively that the statements or data are in conformity with GAAP. An exception may be made, however, in cases where, "due to unusual circumstances," statements or data in compliance with GAAP would be misleading and an explanation is given of any departure from GAAP, its effects, and the reason why GAAP would be misleading.

Thus, compliance with GAAP is mandated under Rule 203 with exceptions allowed only under "unusual circumstances." Exceptions are not mandated when GAAP is misleading.[10] This could

lead to two types of situations in which the public interest is not served. When confronting circumstances which are misleading but *are not* "unusual," Rule 203 requires an accountant to provide the misleading information and Rule 301 effectively forbids the disclosure of nonmandated information which is more revealing. When confronted with circumstances which *are* "unusual," Rule 203 does not forbid the disclosure of additional information. However, since the Rule does not require departures from GAAP, an accountant could use the Rule to justify providing misleading information without disclosing its dubious nature. In other words, if the misleading information is consistent with GAAP and, additional, more revealing disclosures are not required, the more revealing information could be concealed without there being a rules violation.

Congressional testimony about the failure of Lincoln Savings & Loan Association serves to illustrate the implications of Rule 203. A regional director for Ernst & Young is cited in *The Wall Street Journal* (Thomas, 1989) as saying that "accounting firms aren't auditing to determine the safety and soundness of the firm . . . 'we audited the statements to see if they complied with generally accepted accounting principles.' She said that all of them did." Meanwhile, several members of the House Banking Committee were described as "appalled that the accounting principles appeared to be adhered to in form only."

The two disclosure-related duties which are made explicit in the Rules section of the AICPA's Code of Professional Conduct appear to at times foster conflict about the duties of members of the accounting profession. However, these explicit duties may have more than a potential internal conflict; they

---

[10] Furthermore, Rule 203 is limited in scope to compliance with accounting principles and does not address situations which are simply not covered by GAAP (e.g., improper handling of hazardous waste).

may also conflict with the accountant's implicit duties.

Implicit Duties

As was discussed earlier in this paper, required accounting disclosures are not perfect information. This means that accountants may be able to provide more relevant information than that which is required and/or withhold misleading information which is required. Accountants are implicitly duty-bound to provide more relevant information or withhold misleading information only if:

1. it can be shown to be in the public interest to do so;

2. it is their implicit duty to act in the public interest; and

3. the duty supersedes other duties which obligate accountants.

Barring the impact of violating a conflicting duty, the public interest would at least sometimes be best served through the provision of all relevant, and the withholding of all misleading, information. Even without the caveat "at least sometimes," this seems consistent with economic models which rely on perfect information to facilitate resource allocations. With the caveat, the statement requires for validity only a single instance where the public interest would be served through a departure from disclosure requirements.

There also appears to be a duty to act in the public interest. In the Principles section of the Code the issue of the public interest is specifically addressed. The accounting profession's public is said to consist of:

clients, credit grantors, governments, employers, investors, the business and financial community, and others who rely on the objectivity and integrity of certified

public accountants to maintain the orderly functioning of commerce. This reliance imposes a public interest responsibility. . . . The public interest is defined as the collective well-being of the community of people and institutions the profession serves (p. 4).

Furthermore, there is an acknowledgement of the potential for conflict:

In discharging their professional responsibilities, members may encounter conflicting pressures from among each of those groups. In resolving those conflicts, members should act with integrity, guided by the precept that when members fulfill their responsibility to the public, clients' and employers' interests are best served (p. 4).

Other sources which provide an indication of the duties facing accountants in the area of disclosure include, specifically, the auditor's report and, generally, the public image of the accounting profession and public expectations of its role in society. The auditor's report clearly states that the financial statements are the responsibility of the Company's management. However, audit procedures are described as adequate to have obtained reasonable assurance that the statements are free from material misstatement and the procedures include an assessment of the accounting principles and estimates used by management. Furthermore, the report states that the financial statements present fairly, in all material respects, the financial position of the Company. This can be read as a clear indication that relevant information is not being withheld, and that misleading information is not being disclosed in financial statements.

The public image of accountants is that they are trustworthy professionals.[11] The public's trust in accounting professionals results in an expectation that accounting disclosure is complete and free from bias. While the accounting profession makes it clear that the financial statements are the responsibility of management, the public does not view management as free from bias. The duties implied by this public perception are less clear than the duties implied by the stated Principles, but it is clear that at least some people expect accounting professionals to act in the public interest. This general expectation seems to underlie much of the expectation gap.

While it seems clear that accountants have the ability and the duty to disclose information in the public interest, it is not clear whether this duty supersedes duties made explicit in Rules 203 and 301.[12] The balance of this paper (and its key analysis) will address the issue of conflicting duties.

Positive and Negative Duties

The above discussion was intended to indicate the nature of professional duties in accounting. The professional duties may be explicit or implicit and the duties may conflict. Extensive research

---

[11] Several surveys have shown that accountants are perceived to be among the most ethical of all professionals. For example, a survey of 795 business people ranked accountants on the top of the list of 16 professions in regard to business ethics (AICPA, 1989).

[12] Disclosing in the public interest also may place the accountant in conflict with personal duties, like providing for family, since it could put an accountant in conflict with a client and/or employer. In other words, accountants may be vulnerable when acting in the public interest because the rules do not necessarily support such behaviour.

---

on conflicting ethical duties has been reported in the philosophy literature and that research will now be reviewed and utilized to gain insight into the possible resolution of the conflict in the area of accounting disclosure.

The nature and relative importance of positive duties and negative duties[13] has been discussed at great length by contemporary ethical theorists. Positive duties are obligations to bring about good, to be meritorious. Consequently, positive duties require action. In contrast, negative duties are duties not to do bad, not to harm. Negative duties often require inaction or compliance with rules defining one's role. Many ethical theorists feel that negative duties are more obligatory than positive duties.

Duties to comply with professional standards are seen here as negative duties. Duties beyond the duty to comply with the rules of professional conduct are seen here as positive duties. Such

---

[13] The positive and negative duty debate has also been termed a conflict between acts and omissions (e.g., Glover, 1977), and doing and letting happen (e.g., Abelson, 1982). The debate is also similar to that between positive and negative responsibility (see Williams, 1973), though responsibility is a concept which pertains to consequences where duty may refer to intent without regard to consequences. It is worth noting that the terms positive and negative have opposite meanings when applied to duties and responsibilities. In other words, a positive duty gives rise to a negative responsibility and a negative duty gives rise to a positive responsibility. Since such terminology might be confusing, Ruland (1984) used the terms acting and refraining to describe the two types of duty. This has caused some confusion itself (e.g., see Ingram & Rayburn, 1989; Ruland, 1989), so the more commonly used terms in the philosophy literature, positive and negative duty, are used in this paper.

duties require action for their fulfillment, but they are most fundamentally distinguished from negative duties by the result of failures to fulfill. The failure to fulfill a positive duty does not necessarily constitute an ethical violation. Positive duties are duties of beneficence, duties to do good or prevent bad. The failure to fulfill a positive duty generally does not cause harm. Rather, it only fails to prevent harm.

In contrast, the failure to fulfill a negative duty is an ethical violation. Negative duties are duties not to act unethically; thus the failure to fulfill them results in an ethical violation. This direct unethical action is what leads to the view that, all other things being equal, negative duties are stronger than positive duties. It also may explain why the possibility of violating professional standards in the interest of ethics is in some ways counter-intuitive.

The philosophy literature contains much debate concerning the ethical validity of the positive/negative duty dichotomy. While those who argue against the significance of the distinction (e.g., Bennet, 1966; Tooley, 1972; Rachels, 1975) have successfully raised doubts about the universality of any significance, others, (e.g., Foot, 1967; Trammell, 1975; Blumfield, 1981; Abelson, 1982) seem to have successfully argued that negative duties are stronger in at least some circumstances.

Ruland (1984) argues that the positive/negative duty distinction is not only valid ethically in the accounting policy-making context, but is the basis of a strict ordering of duties. Three criteria for evaluating duties are applied to the positive/negative duty debate. The three criteria are relentlessness, the uncertainty of outcomes, and nature of responsibility for positive duties. These same criteria will be applied here in the context of disclosure issues facing accounting professionals. In addition, a fourth criterion, magnitude of the consequences, will be applied. This criterion is also used in Ruland (1984), but is there included as a characteristic of the responsibility criterion.

Relentlessness

Several philosophers (e.g., Blumfield, 1981; Trammell, 1975) have concluded that positive duties are not obligatory because they can never be discharged (because they are relentless). In other words, positive duties can only be satisfied when all possible acts of beneficence have been performed. In the general social context this would require that good deeds be performed until all social ills such as injustice have been alleviated. Clearly, this would be relentless and beyond the scope of what can be expected of persons. Positive duties can only be discharged and thus can only be obligatory if they can be limited by some criterion.[14]

The duty to disclose all relevant information is clearly relentless. Relevant information could range in impact from billions of dollars (e.g., savings and loan insolvency) or life and death (e.g., toxic waste) to matters of minor importance concerning a single user. It is obviously

[14] Smith (1990) provides additional criteria for determining if a positive duty is obligatory. Among them is "minimal action," which means little effort is required to fulfill the duty in a given circumstance. In the accounting context minimal action may mean that the information in question is easily available to the accountant and, thus, can be easily disclosed. In many circumstances an accountant would already have or easily could have relevant information available for disclosure. For example, market value information pertaining to loans made by banks is often available or readily determinable by accountants through present value techniques.

not possible to satisfy all these preferences. The implication of this finding is that, even if accountants are obligated to fulfill positive duties, the obligation does not extend to all circumstances where someone would benefit from action. Positive duties can only be obligatory under circumstances that can be defined as less than relentless.

Certainty of Outcomes

Some philosophers (e.g., Trammell, 1975) have established that the strictness of a positive duty is related to the probability that something bad will occur or that something good will not occur if the duty is not fulfilled. If a negative duty is violated there is generally little or no chance that a bad will be avoided or that a good will be realized. For example, if Gwen violates a negative duty not to kill Sam, there is no chance that Sam will not be dead. However, if a positive duty is violated, in most circumstances there are other means by which any bad can be avoided or good realized. The failure of John to save a drowning man at a crowded beach does not prevent others from saving the man.

There are circumstances, however, in which the failure to act on a positive duty will have an almost certain outcome. If John were the only person on the beach and a man was drowning, it would be a near certainty that the man would die if John did not act. Likewise, drowning would be a near certainty if many people were at the beach but no one else was making an effort to save the man.[15] Circumstances such as this exist, but are relatively uncommon.

[15] Smith (1990), when discussing the problem of defeasibility of duties, claims that, if no one acts, the number of persons who could take action does not alleviate each person of the duty to bring aid.

When the circumstances do occur they could (depending on the specifics) change the relative strictness of a positive duty to act.

In the case of accounting practice *vis a vis* disclosure, a violation of a rule such as the one regarding compliance with GAAP leaves no chance that a bad (violation of GAAP) will be avoided. This is, by definition, a characteristic of negative duties. The positive duty to make disclosures in the public interest, on the other hand, appears to have excepting cases which distinguish it from many other positive duties. Unlike many other positive duties, the duty to disclose will at times have a near certain outcome. Because of his/her expertise and unique relationship with the client, the accountant could be the only person with sufficient knowledge, ability, and motivation to make a disclosure which is in the public interest.

Consider, for example, the case of problem loans that have been made by banks. Accounting rules do not require revaluation of loans to market value and thereby result in accounting reports which serve to keep relevant information from the public. it is not at all certain that this information could be effectively disclosed by another source since other sources may lack expertise, credibility, or motivation to assess the situation and/or make the disclosure. Therefore, accountants could be in a unique position to identify institutions in risk of financial collapse. But to do so would require acceptance of a positive duty to act and a violation of a negative duty.

The fact that acts on the part of accountants may sometimes be necessary to ensure complete and unbiased disclosure strengthens positive duties. This finding furthers the possibility that there are circumstances in which accountants are obligated to fulfill positive duties and disclose information in the public interest.

Responsibility

Philosophers both favouring (e.g., Green, 1980; Trammell, 1975) and opposing (e.g., Morillo, 1977) the moral significance of the positive/negative duty distinction seem to agree that responsibility is a contributing factor in determining the strictness of a duty. Important to the distinction is a difference in the responsibility of persons for the good or bad that results from violations of negative duties as opposed to failures to fulfill positive duties.

A person is clearly responsible for violations of negative duties. If Gwen kills Sam she is clearly responsible for Sam's death. However, when a person fails to fulfill a positive duty he/she is not always so clearly (or deeply) responsible for the results. The extent of responsibility is dependent on the circumstances both in general and as they pertain to the person in particular. In many cases, John can be said to be more responsible for the fate of a drowning man on a deserted beach than he would be on a crowded beach.

John's responsibility depends on his role and the role of others. His responsibility would be greatly higher if he were a champion swimmer who held a lifesaving certificate or, even more, if he were a lifeguard. It would be greatly lower if he were a weak swimmer or if he had other duties such as caring for a toddler who, if left unattended, could be swept away by the waves. Likewise, the level of responsibility would vary depending on who else was in the area. If a lifeguard were at the beach, and John himself was not a lifeguard, John's duty and thus his responsibility for any bad outcome would be greatly diminished.

The reason for this changing level

of responsibility is that some circumstances create special duties for particular persons. Accountants are clearly responsible for the results when they violate their duty to adhere to explicit rules. They also can be seen as having special duties and thus responsibilities relative to disclosure in the public interest. The duties emanate somewhat from accountants' role as citizens given the sometimes relative certainty that acts are necessary for bad to be avoided or good to be realized. Moreover, the duties and resulting responsibilities are grounded both in the professional standing of accountants and the role of accountants in society. This makes the duties special and results in accountants being seen by the public as responsible for failures to disclose relevant information.

The strength of this responsibility is affected by who, if anyone, is also responsible and the nature of any responsibility shared by others. Other parties, in addition to accountants, share responsibility for disclosure. As was discussed previously, management has the primary duty to act in the public interest *vis a vis* disclosures. In the case of management, though, there is a recognized conflict of interest and a lack of expectation on the part of the public. Indeed, accountants are expected to monitor management and to fulfill a duty to the public when management fails to meet its duty to disclose.

In some circumstances (e.g., depository institutions) it can be argued that regulators have the primary responsibility to protect the public. However, accountants can be seen as primarily responsible when regulators do not fulfill their role. Like management, regulators may have a conflict of interest, in their case due to the political nature of their positions.

In short, the duty of accountants to

disclose is not "defeased"[16] when management or regulators shirk their responsibilities to the public. This explains why accountants are viewed as responsible for the failure to disclose in the public interest.[17]

Magnitude

Philosophers generally recognize that the strictness of positive duties is at least somewhat related to the consequences of inaction. For example, while Smith finds moral significance in the positive/negative duty distinction, she states that "(a) trivial negative duty does not override a significant positive duty" (Smith, 1990, p. 22). Abelson (1982) refers to the "gravity of foreseeable consequences" as the "most conspicuous factor" which should affect the strictness of duties (1982, p. 223).

The strictness of a duty to disclose is affected by the magnitude of any resulting consequences.[18] For example, the strictness of the duty to disclose the market value of a bank's loan portfolio varies with the consequences of failing to disclose. If the consequence is some

investors paying a 10% premium over the economic value for the bank's stock, the duty is less strict than it would be if the consequence was concealed insolvency which led investors to pay 100% more than the stock value and perhaps an increase by millions of dollars in the cost of a government bailout.

A difficulty with a consequences criterion for disclosure is that consequences may not be foreseeable. However, while it can be argued that the consequences of failing to disclose relevant information are often not foreseeable, the magnitude of the "disclosure gap" itself certainly is foreseeable by accountants. The disclosure gap is the difference between what is disclosed about an attribute and the relevant measurement of that attribute. It is likely that magnitude of the consequences of failing to disclose is correlated with the size of the disclosure gap. Thus, accountants can absolve themselves of responsibility for adverse consequences by disclosing, particularly in circumstances where the disclosure gap is significant.[19] In short, disclosure addresses the problem of foreseeability.

Codification

The analysis above established that for accountants positive duties *vis a vis* disclosure in the public interest are more strict under some circumstances than under others. It is yet to be established under what conditions, if any, the duty is so strict that an accountant is obligated to act beyond and/or in violation of professional rules. Any conclusion drawn must be based on the weight of

---

[16] For a discussion of the defeasibility of duties see Smith (1990).

[17] Due to their professional standing and clearly special duties in the area of disclosure, accountants are seen as more responsible than management for disclosure. For a discussion of the relative responsibility of accountants (auditors) for deception in financial statements see Gaa and Smith (1985).

[18] The conclusion that the economic consequences are the responsibility of accountants is not made on consequentialist grounds. Accountants are seen here as responsible for the consequences of failures to disclose relevant information. A consequentialist would claim that adverse consequences of disclosing relevant measurements would also be the responsibility of accountants. That claim is not being made here.

[19] Given that there may be multiple attributes which are relevant, there may be multiple disclosure gaps. Accountants can remedy the gaps by disclosing information about multiple attributes.

the evidence in light of the four criteria applied in the preceding section.

When the application of the four criteria, relentlessness, certainty, responsibility, and magnitude, is considered in total, the duty to disclose appears to be very strict in at least some circumstances. While the positive duty to act in this context is relentless, the results of a failure to fulfill the duty could at times have certain consequences, the responsibility for failing to disclose ultimately lies with the accountant, and the consequences of failing to disclose vary in magnitude. These last three characteristics serve to define and therefore limit the circumstances under which there is a duty to disclose. Limiting the circumstances under which there are duties mitigates the relentlessness of the duties. Thus, all four criteria are met. This means that there are circumstances under which the ethical duty of the accountant is to act beyond and possibly even in violation of professional rules. At times accountants are obligated to violate rules requiring confidentiality of client information and/or compliance with GAAP in order to disclose information which is in the public interest.

Accountants are only so obligated when they are responsible for the consequences of failing to disclose. When accountants are responsible, the circumstances where positive duties to disclose are obligatory have two dimensions which together create a strict duty. They are the probability of the desirable outcome occurring (or undesirable outcome not occurring) if no action is taken, and the magnitude of the good or bad that potentially would occur.[20]

The current savings and loan crisis in the United States is an example where, at some point, the outcome of failing to disclose was relatively certain and accountants at least share responsibility. The consequences from not acting on a positive duty to disclose the financial instability of these institutions are enormous. However, as described earlier, accountants who have been implicated for failing to disclose the problem have cited GAAP in their defense. The analysis in this paper indicates that compliance with GAAP does not always absolve accountants of their ethical duty to disclose information which is important to the public interest.

Conclusions and Limitations

Practicing accountants sometimes have a genuine conflict between duties to refrain from rules violations and duties to disclose information in the public interest. When the consequences of failing to disclose might be extreme, accountants seem to be ethically compelled to act beyond rules requiring compliance with GAAP even if it means violating client confidentiality.

This conclusion calls into question the AICPA's *Code of Professional Conduct,* which requires a public interest orientation in principle but neither considers the public interest in its Rules nor requires violation of the Rules when the Rules do not serve the public interest. The conclusion provides support, on the other hand, for the positions of legislators and judges who consider accoun-

---

[20] If it is assumed that the acceptable measure of consequences is expected utility, the absolute value of the expected utility multiplied times the probability of occurrence without action by the accountant would be a measure of compulsion to disclose. The higher the measure, the more compelling is the duty to disclose. Without an acceptance of expected utility additional judgments would need to be made.

tants responsible beyond compliance with professional rules.

There are several limitations to this study which should be acknowledged. First, the legal environment of accounting has not been considered. Practicing accountants may feel constrained in their behaviour due to their liability for client injury resulting from a rules violation. The reader should bear in mind, though, that this paper is not a prescription for practicing accountants, but is forwarded to enlighten policy-makers to the ethical dimension of disclosure issues in practice. Policy-makers could change the rules and provide better legal protection to accountants who act ethically *vis a vis* disclosure.

A second possible limitation of this paper is the use of the positive/negative duty dichotomy to analyze accountants' conflicting duties. Some readers may wish to criticize the appropriateness of the dichotomy to professional duties. However, the conclusions in this paper would be little different if the positive/negative duty distinction were dropped. Use of the dichotomy put the burden of proof on the concept that duties to disclose could override duties to refrain from rules violations. This burden of proof seemed appropriate given the propensity of accountants to view compliance with GAAP as a satisfactory execution of their ethical duties.

A third limitation of this paper is the focus on AICPA members and the AICPA Code of Professional Conduct. It is assumed that the duties discussed here in fact extend to all professional accountants whether or not they are AICPA members. The analysis is fundamentally about professionalism and the requisite duties of professionals to the public. The extent to which the conclusions of this analysis can be generalized to all practicing accountants will be lim-

ited to the extent that differing roles create differing strict duties. In any case, the analysis is at least applicable to AICPA members, and they represent a large and prominent group of practicing accountants.

Finally, the conclusions of this study were drawn from the weight of the evidence, and the evidence consisted of our analysis of the ethics literature in the accounting context. Consequently, our conclusions are not above debate. Hopefully, this study will encourage others to investigate the ethical issues facing accountants. We invite their analysis and interpretation. As important as ethics is in accounting, the accounting profession and society as a whole can only benefit from more research in this area.

Acknowledgements

The authors wish to thank Norm Bowie, Jim Gaa, Chris Humphrey, Leo Moerson, Joanne Rockness, Tony Tinker, Paul Williams, and the participants at the Critical Perspectives on Accounting Conference for their helpful comments on the paper.

References

Abelson, R., "To Do or to Let Happen," *American Philosophical Quarterly*, Vol. 19, July, 1982, pp. 219–228.

American Institute of Certified Public Accountants (AICPA), *Code of Professional Conduct* (New York: AICPA, 1988).

American Institute of Certified Public Accountants (AICPA), "Ethics Survey Ranks Accountants First," *Journal of Accountancy*, Vol. 168, No. 4, October, 1989, p. 110.

American Institute of Certified Public Accountants (AICPA), *Restructuring Professional Standards to Achieve Professional Excellence in a Changing Environment* (New York: AICPA, 1986).

Beach, J. E., "Code of Ethics: the Professional Catch 22," *Journal of Accounting and Public Policy,* Vol. 3, No. 4, 1984, pp. 311–323.

Bennet, J., "Whatever the Consequences," in J. Rachels (ed.), *Moral Problems,* pp. 42–46 (New York: Harper and Row, 1966).

Blumfield, J. B., "Causing Harm and Bringing Aid," *American Philosophical Quarterly,* Vol. 18, 1984, pp. 323–329.

Foot, P., "The Problem of Abortion and the Doctrine of Double Effect," *The Oxford Review,* Vol. 5, 1967, pp. 5–15.

Gaa, J. C., & Smith, C. H., "Auditors and Deceptive Financial Statements: Assigning Responsibility and Blame," *Contemporary Accounting Research,* Vol. 1, 1985, pp. 219–241.

Glover, J., *Causing Death and Saving Lives* (New York: Penguin, 1977).

Green, O. H., "Killing and Letting Die," *American Philosophical Quarterly,* Vol. 17, 1980, pp. 195–204.

Ingram, R. W., & Rayburn, F. R., "Representational Faithfulness and Economic Consequences: Their Roles in Accounting Policy," *Journal of Accounting and Public Policy,* Vol. 8, 1989, pp. 57–68.

Morillo, C. R., "Doing, Refraining and the Strenuousness of Morality," *American Philosophical Quarterly,* Vol. 14, 1977, pp. 29–39.

Rachels, J., "Active and Passive Euthanasia," *The New England Journal of Medicine,* Vol. 292, No. 1, January, 1975, pp. 78–80.

Ross, W. D., *The Right and the Good* (Oxford: Clarendon Press, 1930).

Ruland, R. G., "Duty, Obligation and Responsibility in Accounting Policy Making." *Journal of Accounting and Public Policy,* Vol. 3, 1984, pp. 223–237.

Ruland, R. G., "The Pragmatic and Ethical Distinction Between Two Approaches to Accounting Policy Making," *Journal of Accounting and Public Policy,* Vol. 8, 1989, pp. 69–80.

Smith, P., "The Duty to Rescue and the Slippery Slope Problem," *Social Practice and Theory,* Vol. 16, No. 1, 1990, pp. 19–41.

Thomas, P., "Auditors Say Lincoln S&L 'Sham' Deals Were Approved by Arthur Young & Co.," *The Wall Street Journal,* 15 November 1989, p. A3.

Tooley, M., "Abortion and Infanticide," *Philosophy and Public Affairs,* Vol. 2, 1972, pp. 58–65.

Trammell, R. L., "Saving a Life and Taking a Life," *The Journal of Philosophy,* Vol. 72, 1975, pp. 131–137.

Williams, B., "A Critique of Utilitarianism," In J. J. C. Smart and B. Williams (eds), *Utilitarianism For and Against,* pp. 77–150 (New York: Cambridge University Press, 1973).

Cases

• Case 16-1

The proponents of neoclassical, marginal economics (see Chapter 2) maintain that mandatory accounting and auditing standards inhibit contracting arrangements and the ability to report on company operations. Opponents of this view argue that market forces alone cannot be relied on to produce quality information that can be relied on by society.

Required:
Present arguments to support both viewpoints. What is your opinion? [*Hint:* You may wish to consult Richard Leftwich, "Market Failure Fallacies and Accounting Information," *Journal of Accounting and Economics* (December 1980), pp. 193–221; Steven Johnson, "A Perspective on Solomon's Quest for Credibility in Financial Reporting," *Journal of Accounting and Public Policy* (1988), pp. 137–154; as well as the Solomon and Tinker articles contained in Chapter 2 of this text.]

- ### Case 16-2

Barbara Montgomery is a first-year auditor for Coppers and Rose, a large public accounting firm. She has been assigned to the audit of Lakes Brothers, a large clothing retailer with retail outlets throughout the United States. This audit has proved troublesome in the past, and during a staff meeting preceding the audit, Robert Cooley, the supervisor on the audit indicates: "We are going to be required to work several hours 'off-the-clock' each week until this audit is completed." He also indicated that the client is giving the firm a great deal of pressure to maintain an acceptable level of fees.

Barbara has just been to staff training school, where it was emphasized that not charging a client for hours actually worked is a violation of Copper and Rose's employment policy, a violation that could cause her to be dismissed. She also knows that only staff personnel are paid overtime and that supervisors are evaluated on successfully completing audits within allowable budgets. Barbara discusses the issue with John Reed, a second-year staff accountant. John says: "Don't worry, if you go along nobody will find out and Robert will give you a good evaluation." John also indicates his opinion that Robert is very highly thought of by the senior members of the firm and likely to be promoted to manager in the near future.

Required:
a. Is it ethical for Barbara to work hours and not charge them to the client?
b. Use the six-step approach outlined in this chapter to resolve this ethical dilemma.

- ### Case 16-3

Lancaster Electronics produces electronic components for sale to manufacturers of radios, television sets, and phonographic systems. In connection with his examination of Lancaster's financial statements for the year ended December 31, 1995, Don Olds, CPA, completed fieldwork two weeks ago. Mr. Olds now is evaluating the significance of the following items prior to preparing his auditor's report. Except as noted, none of these items has been disclosed in the financial statements or footnotes.

Item 1   Recently Lancaster interrupted its policy of paying cash dividends quarterly to its stockholders. Dividends were paid regularly through 1989, discontinued for all of 1994 to finance equipment for the company's new plant, and resumed in the first quarter of 1996. In the annual report, dividend policy is to be discussed in the president's letter to stockholders.

Item 2   A 10-year loan agreement, which the company entered into three years ago, provides that dividend payments may not exceed net income earned after taxes subsequent to the date of the agreement. The balance of retained earnings at the date of the loan agreement was $298,000. From that date through December 31, 1995, net income after taxes has totaled $360,000 and cash dividends have totaled $130,000. Based on these data, the staff auditor assigned to this review concluded that there was no retained earnings restriction at December 31, 1995.

Item 3 The company's new manufacturing plant building, which cost $600,000 and has an estimated life of 25 years, is leased from the Sixth National Bank at an annual rental of $100,000. The company is obligated to pay property taxes, insurance, and maintenance. At the conclusion of its 10-year noncancelable lease, the company has the option of purchasing the property for $1. In Lancaster's income statement the rental payment is reported on a separate line.

Item 4 A major electronics firm has introduced a line of products that will compete directly with Lancaster's primary line, now being produced in the specially designed new plant. Because of manufacturing innovations, a competitor's line will be of comparable quality but priced 50 percent below Lancaster's line. The competitor announced its new line during the week following completion of fieldwork. Mr. Olds read the announcement in the newspaper and discussed the situation by telephone with Lancaster executives. Lancaster will meet the lower prices that are high enough to cover variable manufacturing and selling expenses but will permit recovery of only a portion of fixed costs.

Required:
For each of the preceding items, discuss any additional disclosures in the financial statements and footnotes that the auditor should recommend to his client. (The cumulative effect of the four items should not be considered.)

• Case 16-4

You have completed your audit of Carter Corporation and its consolidated subsidiaries for the year ended December 31, 1995, and are satisfied with the results of your examination. You have examined the financial statements of Carter Corporation for the past three years. The corporation is now preparing its annual report to shareholders. The report will include the consolidated financial statements of Carter Corporation and its subsidiaries and your short-form auditor's report. During your audit the following matters came to your attention.

1. The Internal Revenue Service is currently examining the corporation's 1992 federal income tax return and is questioning the amount of a deduction claimed by the corporation's domestic subsidiary for a loss sustained in 1991. The examination is still in process and any additional tax liability is indeterminable at this time. The corporation's tax counsel believes that there will be no substantial additional tax liability.

2. A vice-president who is also a stockholder resigned on December 31, 1995, after an argument with the president. The vice-president is soliciting proxies from stockholders and expects to obtain sufficient proxies to gain control of the board of directors so that a new president will be appointed. The president plans to have a footnote prepared that would include information

of the pending proxy fight, management's accomplishments over the years, and an appeal by management for the support of stockholders.

Required:
a. Prepare the footnotes, if any, that you would suggest for the foregoing listed items.
b. State your reasons for not making disclosure by footnote for each of the listed items for which you did not prepare a footnote.

• Case 16-5

The concept of adequate disclosure continues to be one of the most important issues facing accountants, and disclosure may take various forms.

Required:
a. Discuss the various forms of disclosure available in published financial statements.
b. Discuss the disclosure issues addressed by each of the following sources:
    i. The AICPA's Code of Professional Ethics
    ii. The Securities Act of 1933
    iii. The Securities Exchange Act of 1934
    iv. The Foreign Corrupt Practices Act of 1977

• Case 16-6

The Securities Act of 1933 and the Securities Exchange Act of 1934 established guidelines for the disclosures necessary and the protection from fraud when securities are offered to the public for sale.

Required:
a. Discuss the terms *going public* and *being public* as they relate to these pieces of legislation.
b. Regulation S-X requires management to discuss and analyze certain financial conditions and results of operations. What are these items?

• Case 16-7

Certified Public Accountants have imposed upon themselves a rigorous code of professional conduct.

Required:
a. Discuss the reasons for the accounting profession's adopting a code of professional conduct.
b. A rule of professional ethics adopted by CPAs is that a CPA cannot be an officer, director, stockholder, representative, or agent of any corporation engaged in the practice of public accounting, except for the professional corporation form expressly permitted by the AICPA. List the arguments supporting the rule that a CPA's firm cannot be a corporation.

Recommended Additional Readings

Anderson, G. D., and R. C. Ellison. "Restructuring Professional Standards: The Anderson Report." *Journal of Accountancy* (September 1986), pp. 92–104.

Briloff, A. M. "Standards Without Standards/Principles Without Principles/Fairness Without Fairness." *Advances in Accounting* (1986), pp. 25–50.

Brownlee, I. R., and S. D. Young. "The SEC and Mandated Disclosure: At the Crossroads." *Accounting Horizons* (September 1987), pp. 17–24.

Collins, S. H. "The SEC on Full and Fair Disclosure." *Journal of Accountancy* (January 1989), pp. 79–85.

Reimers, J. L. "Additional Evidence on the Need for Disclosure Reform." *Accounting Horizons* (March 1992), pp. 36–41.

Shaub, M. K. "Restructuring the Code of Professional Ethics: A Review of the Anderson Committee Report and Its Implications." *Accounting Horizons* (December 1988), pp. 89–97.

Bibliography

Adelberg, Arthur H., and Richard A. Lewis. "Financial Reports Can Be Made More Understandable." *Journal of Accountancy* (June 1980), pp. 44–50.

AICPA. *Restructuring Professional Standards to Achieve Professional Excellence in a Changing Environment.* New York: AICPA, 1986, p. 11.

Anderson, George D. "A Fresh Look at Standards of Professional Conduct." *Journal of Accountancy* (September 1985), pp. 91–92, 95–96, 98, 102, 104–106.

Atiase, Rowland K., Linda S. Bamber, and Robert N. Freeman. "Accounting Disclosures Based on Company Size: Regulations and Capital Market Evidence." *Accounting Horizons* (March 1988), pp. 18–26.

Baker, H. Kent, and John A. Haslem, "Information Needs of Individual Investors." *Journal of Accountancy* (November 1973), pp. 64–69.

Beaver, William H. "Current Trends in Corporate Disclosure." *Journal of Accountancy* (January 1978), pp. 44–52.

Bedford, Norton M. *Extension in Accounting Disclosure.* Englewood Cliffs, N.J.: Prentice-Hall, 1973.

Benjamin, James J., and Keith G. Stanga. "Differences in Disclosure Needs of Major Users of Financial Statements." *Accounting and Business Research* (Summer 1977), pp. 187–192.

Benston, George J. "The Value of the SEC's Accounting Disclosure Requirements." *The Accounting Review* (July 1969), pp. 515–532.

Benston, George J. "Evaluation of the Securities Exchange Act of 1934." *Financial Executive* (May 1974), pp. 28–36, 40–42.

Briloff, Abraham M. *Unaccountable Accounting.* New York: Harper & Row, 1972.

Briloff, Abraham M. *More Debits Than Credits.* New York: Harper & Row, 1976.

Briloff, Abraham M. *The Truth About Corporate Accounting.* New York: Harper & Row, 1981.

Briloff, Abraham M. "Accounting and Society: A Covenant Desecrated." *Critical Perspectives on Accounting* (March 1990), pp. 5–30.

Burton, John C. "Ethics in Corporate Financial Disclosure." *Financial Analysts Journal* (January–February 1972), pp. 49–53.

Carey, John L. "Professional Ethics and the Public Interest." *Journal of Accountancy* (November 1956), pp. 38–41.

Carey, John L. *Professional Ethics of Certified Public Accountants.* New York: AICPA, 1965.

Carmichael, D. R. *The Auditor's Reporting Obligation.* New York: AICPA, 1972.

Carmichael, D. R. "Standards for Financial Reporting." *Journal of Accountancy* (May 1979), pp. 76–84.

Casler, Darwin J. *The Evolution of CPA Ethics: A Profile of Professionalism.* Occasional Paper No. 12, Michigan State University: Bureau of Business and Economic Research, 1964.

Chandra, Gyan. "Study of the Consensus on Disclosure among Public Accountants and Security Analysis." *The Accounting Review* (October 1974), pp. 733–742.

Dingell, John. "Accountants Must Clean Up Their Act: Rep. John Dingell Speaks Out." *Management Accounting* (May 1985), pp. 52–55.

Stephen E. Loeb (ed.). *Ethics in the Accounting Profession.* New York: John Wiley & Sons, 1978.

Gibbins, M., A. Richardson, and J. Waterhouse. "The Management of Corporate Financial Disclosures: Opportunism, Ritualism, Policies and Processes." *Journal of Accounting Research* (Spring 1990), pp. 121–143.

Groves, Ray J. "Corporate Disclosure in the 1980's." *Financial Executive* (June 1980), pp. 14–19.

Kripke, Homer. "A Search for a Meaningful Securities Disclosure Policy." *The Arthur Andersen Chronicle* (July 1976), pp. 14–32.

Loeb, Stephen S. "A Behavioral Study of CPA Ethics." Ph.D. dissertation, University of Wisconsin, 1970.

Loeb, Stephen S. "Enforcement of the Code of Ethics." *The Accounting Review* (January 1972), pp. 1–9.

Loeb, Stephen S. "Ethical Committees and Consultants in Public Accounting." *Accounting Horizons* (December 1989), pp. 1–10.

Loeb, Stephen S. "Teaching Accounting Students Ethics: Some Crucial Issues." *Issues in Accounting Education* (Fall 1988), pp. 316–329.

Longstreth, B. "The SEC's Role in Financial Disclosure." *Journal of Accounting Auditing and Finance* (Winter 1984), pp. 110–122.

Merino, Barbara D., and Marilyn D. Neimark. "Disclosure Regulation and Public Policy: A Sociohistorical Reappraisal." *Journal of Accounting and Public Policy* (1982), pp. 32–57.

Mueller, Willard F. "Corporate Disclosure: The Public's Right to Know." In *Corporate Financial Reporting*, Alfred Rappaport, ed. Chicago: Commerce Clearing House, 1971, pp. 67–93.

Olson, W. E. *The Accounting Profession: Years of Trial: 1969–1980.* New York: AICPA, 1982.

Pastena, Victor. "Some Evidence on the SEC's System of Continuous Disclosure." *The Accounting Review* (October 1979), pp. 776–783.

Pointer, Larry G., and Richard G. Schroeder. *An Introduction to the Securities and Exchange Commission.* Plano, Tex.: Business Publications, 1986.

Ruhnka, J., and J. W. Bagby. "Disclosure: Damned If You Do, Damned If You Don't." *Harvard Business Review* (September–October 1986), pp. 35–45.

Singhvi, Surendra S. "Corporate Management's Inclination to Disclose Financial Information." *Financial Analysts Journal* (July–August 1972), pp. 66–73.

Skekel, Ted D. "Management Reports of Financial Statements." *The CPA Journal* (July 1979), pp. 32–37.

Skousen, K. Fred. *An Introduction to the SEC*, 5th ed. Cincinnati: South-Western Publishing Co., 1991.

U.S. Congress. *Accounting and Auditing Practices and Procedures: 95th Congress*, 1st session. Washington, D.C.: GPO, 1978.

U.S. Congress. *The Accounting Establishment: 95th Congress*, 1st session. Washington, D.C.: GPO, 1977.

Wallace, R. S. O., and T. E. Cooke. "The Diagnosis and Resolution of Emerging Issues in Corporate Disclosure Practices." *Accounting and Business Research* (Spring 1990), pp. 143–152.

International

Accounting

International Accounting Standards

Financial accounting is influenced by the environment in which it operates. Nations have different histories, values, cultures, and political and economic systems. Additionally, different nations are in various stages of economic development. These national influences interact with each other and, in turn, influence the development and application of financial accounting practices and reporting procedures. During the past several years, multinational corporations operating in many different countries have emerged. Because of the above-mentioned national differences, the financial accounting standards that are applied to the accounting data reported by these multinational companies often vary significantly from one country to another.

Companies prepare financial reports that are directed toward their primary users. In the past, most users were residents of the same country as the corporation issuing the financial statements. However, events such as the emergence of multinational corporations and the organization of the European Union (EU), the General Agreement on Trade and Tariffs (GATT), and the North American Free Trade Agreement (NAFTA) have made transnational financial reporting more commonplace. Transnational financial reporting requires users to understand the accounting practices employed by the company, the language of the country in which the company resides, and the currency used by the corporation to prepare its financial statements. If investors and creditors cannot obtain understandable financial information about companies that operate in foreign countries, they are not likely to invest in or lend money to these companies. As a result, there is a move to harmonize accounting standards among countries.

One of the major issues currently facing United States corporations is their ability to compete in a global economy with transnational financial reporting. This issue is complicated by the facts that (1) accounting standards differ between countries and (2) the value of foreign currencies fluctuates against the dollar.

The Development of Accounting Systems

The level of development of a country's accounting system is impacted by environmental forces such as the overall level of education, the type of political system, the type of legal system, and the extent of economic development. For example, the development of accounting standards in the United States was affected by the Industrial Revolution and the need to obtain private sources of capital. Consequently, financial accounting information was necessary to provide investors and creditors with information on profitability and stewardship. On the other hand, accounting standards in Russia are not well developed. Originally, the Russian economy was centrally planned and as a result required uniform accounting standards. As an emerging market economy country, these accounting standards are no longer useful and new standards must be developed. The impact of various environmental factors on the development of accounting standards is discussed in the following paragraphs.

Level of Education

In general, there is a direct correlation between the level of education obtained by a country's citizens and the development of the financial accounting reporting practices in that country. The characteristics composing these environmental factors include (1) the degree of literacy in a country; (2) the percentage of the population that have completed grade school, high school, and college; (3) the orientation of the educational system (vocational, professional, etc.); and (4) the appropriateness of the educational system to the country's economic and social needs. Countries with better educated populations are associated with more advanced financial accounting systems.

Political System

The type of political system (socialist, democratic, totalitarian, etc.) can influence the development of accounting standards and procedures. Accounting systems in a country with a centrally controlled economy will be different from an accounting system in a market-oriented economy. For example, companies in a socialist country may be required to provide information on social impact and cost–benefit analysis in addition to information on profitability and financial position.

Legal System

The extent to which a country's laws determine accounting practice has impact on the strengths of that country's accounting profession. When governments prescribe accounting rules, the authority of the accounting profession is usually weak, whereas the nonlegalistic establishment of accounting policies by professional organizations is a characteristic of common-law countries.

EXHIBIT 17.1 *Influences on the Development of Financial Reporting*

Type of economy	Agricultural
	Resource based
	Tourist based
	Manufacturing
Legal system	Codified
	Common law
Political system	Democratic
	Totalitarian
Nature of business ownership	Private enterprise
	Socialist
	Communist
Size and complexity of business firms	Conglomerates
	Sole traders
Social climate	Consumerism
	Laissez-faire
Stability of currency	
Sophistication of management	
Sophistication of financial community	
Existence of accounting legislation	
Growth pattern of the economy	Growing
	Stable
	Declining
Education system	

Economic Development

The level of a country's economic development influences both the development and application of its accounting reporting practices. Countries with low levels of economic development will have relatively less need for a sophisticated accounting system than countries with high levels of economic development.

Exhibit 17.1 lists some potential social, cultural, political, and legal influences on the development of national financial reporting standards and practices.

Current Accounting Practice

The classification of accounting practices into groupings has been attempted since the late 1960s. The initial grouping scheme was developed by Gerhard Mueller.[1] He grouped country accounting practices based on the impact of differing business environments as follows:

[1] Gerhard G. Mueller, "Accounting Principles Generally Accepted in the United States versus Those Generally Accepted Elsewhere," *International Journal of Accounting* (Spring 1968), pp. 91–103.

1. United States/Canada/The Netherlands
2. British Commonwealth (excluding Canada)
3. Germany/Japan
4. Continental Europe (excluding Germany, the Netherlands, and Scandinavia)
5. Scandinavia
6. Israel/Mexico
7. South America
8. Developing nations of the Near and Far East
9. Africa (excluding South Africa)
10. Communistic

Later, a committee of the American Accounting Association asserted that accounting practices throughout the world could be categorized according to spheres of influence.[2] This committee indicated that the following five zones of influence were discernible:

1. British
2. Franco-Spanish-Portuguese
3. Germanic-Dutch
4. United States
5. Communistic

Recent agreements such as the EU, GATT, NAFTA, and the changing economic systems in Eastern Europe have modified spheres of influence and resulted in the following groupings:

United States Financial accounting standards for this grouping have been developed primarily in the private sector, and the result has been a relatively restrictive set of accounting standards. The United States' sphere of influence includes Canada, Mexico, Venezuela, and Central America. The passage of NAFTA will undoubtedly result in greater standardization of accounting principles among these countries.

United Kingdom/The Netherlands This grouping closely resembles the United States group; however, it is characterized by relatively less restrictive accounting standards. In addition to the United Kingdom and The Netherlands, the countries included under this grouping are Ireland, Israel, and the former English colonies of India, Australia, New Zealand, South Africa, and Hong Kong. (Hong Kong is scheduled to become a part of China in the year 2000).

---

[2]American Accounting Association, "Report of the American Accounting Association Committee on International Operations and Education 1975−1976," *Accounting Review* (Supplement), (1977), pp. 65−101.

Continental/Japan The companies in this grouping rely on banks to supply most of their capital needs; consequently, conservative accounting practices have been developed. The countries in this group include most of Western Europe and Japan.

South American These countries share a common language (except for Brazil) and cultural heritage. Additionally, financial reporting within this group generally incorporates information on the impact of inflation. All South American countries except Venezuela are included in this group.

Third World This is a very loose grouping of countries that share a need to develop accounting standards for emerging economies. Many of these countries were formerly colonies of European countries and are now developing accounting standards to meet the needs of their economic systems. The countries included in this group are most of Africa (except South Africa) and many Far Eastern countries.

Changing Economies The political upheaval in Eastern Europe in 1989 and 1990 has resulted in the need to develop different accounting standards and practices to meet the needs of changing economic systems. These countries are in the process of changing their accounting practices from centralized planning to market economies. This group includes almost all of the Eastern European countries that were under the USSR's sphere of influence prior to the disintegration of the Warsaw Pact.

Communist The remaining communist countries use an accounting system that is designed to assist in central planning. The countries in this group are China, North Korea, and Cuba.

Specific accounting practices differ between countries as well as between groups. Exhibit 17.2 illustrates some of the areas of difference among selected countries.

Preparation of Financial Statements for Foreign Users

A company issuing financial reports to users in foreign countries may take one of several different approaches in the preparation of its financial statements:

1. Send the same set of financial statements to all users (domestic or foreign).
2. Translate the financial statements sent to foreign users into the language of the foreign nation's users.
3. Translate the financial statements sent to foreign users into the foreign nation's language and currency.
4. Prepare two sets of financial statements, one using the home country language, currency, and accounting principles, the second using the language, currency, and accounting principles of the foreign country's users.
5. Prepare one set of financial statements based on worldwide accepted accounting principles.

Option five is being increasingly advocated for transnational financial reporting, and the International Accounting Standards Committee (IASC) was

EXHIBIT 17.2 *Differences in Accounting Practice Between Selected Countries*

	Australia	Brazil	Britain	Canada	France	Germany	Japan	Netherlands
Requirements that make up GAAP	Company law and professional	Company law and professional	Company law and professional	Professional requirements	Primarily company law	Company law and professional	Company law and professional	Company law and professional
Companies required to have an audit	All	Public only	All large private	Public and large private	Public and large private	Public and large private	Public and large private	Public and large private
GAAP concerning leases	Similar to U.S.	None	Similar to U.S.	Similar to U.S.	Capitalization not allowed	Similar to U.S.	Similar to U.S.	Similar to U.S.
LIFO inventory	Not allowed	Not allowed	Not allowed	Permitted	Not allowed	Permitted	Permitted	Permitted
Research and development expenditures	May be capitalized	May be capitalized	Research capitalized, development expensed	May be capitalized	May be capitalized	Similar to U.S.	No GAAP	May be capitalized
Consolidated financial statements	Required	Required	Required	Required	Required for public companies	Required information for public companies	Supplemental	Required
Accounting for changing prices	No GAAP	No GAAP	Supplemental information permitted	Supplemental information required	No GAAP	Supplemental information permitted	No GAAP	No GAAP
Accounting for deferred taxes	Similar to U.S. (*APB Opinion No. 11*)	Not accounted for	Partial allocation	Similar to U.S. (*APB Opinion No. 11*)	Not accounted for	Similar to U.S. (*APB Opinion No. 11*)	Not accounted for	Similar to U.S. (*APB Opinion No. 11*)

Source: Adapted from Charles S. Dewhurst, "Accounting for International Operations," *CPA Journal* (January 1988), p. 81.

formed in 1973 to develop worldwide accounting standards. The original board members of the IASC were the accounting bodies of nine countries: Australia, Canada, France, Japan, Mexico, The Netherlands, the United Kingdom, the United States, and West Germany. Currently there are over 90 member accounting bodies from about 70 countries.

The IASC's *Agreement and Constitution* gives it the authority to promulgate standards for the presentation of financial statements that are audited by its member organizations. The constitution of the IASC also establishes its role in promoting worldwide acceptance of IASC standards. This need had arisen because many countries did not have a program of developing accounting standards and because of the need to harmonize differences among national standards.[3] Harmonization is seen by many as desirable because of the perceived need to increase the reliability of foreign financial statements. Improved decision making would occur because it would no longer be necessary to interpret foreign financial statements and because comparability would be improved.

Although many differences in worldwide financial reporting practices can be explained by environmental differences between countries, some cannot. The IASC is attempting to harmonize the differences that cannot be explained by environmental differences. The aim of the IASC is to formulate and publish accounting standards to be observed in the presentation of financial statements and to promote their worldwide acceptance and observance. The members of the IASC agree to support the standards and to use their best endeavors to ensure that published financial statements comply with the standards, to ensure that auditors enforce the standards, and to persuade governments, stock exchanges, and other bodies to back the standards.

The original intention of the IASC was to avoid complex details and concentrate on basic standards. IASC standards also allow a range of practices. The standard-setting process of the IASC is similar to that followed by the FASB. Exposure drafts are prepared by subcommittees of the board. An exposure draft must be approved by a two-thirds majority to be released, and by a three-fourths majority to become a standard.

The IASC has no enforcement authority and must rely on the "best endeavors" of its members. However, the influence of professional accounting bodies in the formation of accounting rules varies from country to country. In some countries, such as France and Germany, the strength and detail of company law leave little room for influence by accounting bodies. On the other hand, accounting standards are actually set by the professional bodies that belong to the IASC in the United Kingdom, Canada, and Australia. In the United States, the two bodies directly concerned with standard setting, the FASB and the SEC, are not members of the IASC.

The IASC's charter and actions do not accommodate national differences. That is, each nation has its own group of financial information users (owners, lenders, borrowers, employees, government, etc.) that all operate within the

---

[3] J. A. Hepworth, "International Accounting Standards," *The Chartered Accountant in Australia* (August 1977).

cultural, social, legal, political, and economic environment. The users may also have different relative importance from nation to nation, creating variations in the role of financial accounting from nation to nation.

Several authors have reviewed the difficulty of achieving effective international harmonization. They have generally focused on the extent to which various IASC standards reflect a compromise between differing national requirements. Compromises may be significant for achieving effectiveness in enforcing standards because they reduce a standard's ability to narrow variation in national practices. Additionally, compromises are generally made to accommodate these variations. As a result, the standards that form the reporting framework that results from compromises are likely to result in the adoption of the lowest common denominator of differing national practices. Such standards are likely to have very little effect on practices in those countries that already have comprehensive systems of accounting standards.

To date the IASC has issued 31 International Standards (IASs) covering a variety of issues such as disclosure of accounting policies; depreciation; information to be disclosed; the statement of changes in financial position, unusual items, prior period items and changes in accounting policies; research and development; income taxes; foreign exchange; business combinations; and related party disclosures. Additionally, the IASC has embarked on a comparability project aimed at eliminating most of the choices between various accounting methods currently allowed by the 31 IASs. This project may help to alleviate the compromise criticism discussed earlier.

Until recently, international accounting standards promulgated by the IASC have been little more than a curiosity in the United States.[4] This perspective is likely to change because of such factors as the increasing emphasis on transnational reporting and the growth of the global stock market. Therefore, the following issues will need to be addressed by standard-setting bodies:

1. Can international accounting standards be set voluntarily by organizations representing a broad set of sovereign nations?

2. What is the impact on standard setting of differing economies and social settings in various countries?

3. Can lessons be learned from other international world bodies with sovereign members having experience in bringing conflicting national laws into harmony?

4. Have the major political and economic questions involved in standard setting been examined sufficiently?

5. How can the roadblock of national restrictions be eliminated so that international accounting standards can be enforced?

An argument advanced to support the harmonization of international accounting standards is the growth of multinational corporations and the global stock market. Although U.S. companies seeking listings on foreign stock

---

[4]A. Wyatt, "Commentary: Arthur Wyatt on International Accounting Standards: A New Perspective," *Accounting Horizons* (September 1989) p. 105.

markets may use U.S. GAAP, many have decided to use the appropriate foreign GAAP or to use a dual presentation. The growth of international standards will go a long way toward alleviating this problem.

The harmonization of international accounting standards is not a universally accepted goal. Some individuals have criticized the goal of the harmonization of international accounting standards. These critics maintain that financial reporting must consider the extent to which existing practices reflect specific national environmental characteristics. For example, Zeff contends that the accounting principles peculiar to individual nations develop from the interaction of accounting practice and theory with various social, political, and economic factors that are nation-specific.[5]

Additionally, others maintain that global capital markets are developing without global GAAP and that global GAAP is not likely to come about because (1) too many national groups have vested interests in maintaining their own standards that have developed from widely different perspectives and histories, and (2) no international body has the authority to issue harmonized accounting principles.[6]

Foreign Currency Translation

There has been a substantial increase in foreign operations by United States corporations in recent years. At the same time, devaluation of the dollar, allowing it to float on world currency markets, has accentuated the impact of foreign currency fluctuation on the accounting information and reporting systems of multinational companies. As a result, foreign currency translation has become an important and widely debated accounting and reporting issue. More specifically, the issue is, How does a United States–based corporation measure monetary unit differences and changes in those differences in its foreign branches and subsidiaries?[7]

The problem arises in the following manner: The foreign subsidiary handles its transactions in foreign currency, which may include anything from long-term borrowing agreements for assets acquired, to credit sales carried as accounts receivable. When management or outside investors wish to evaluate the company's operations as a whole, it becomes necessary to express all activities, foreign and domestic, in common financial terms. Useful comparisons and calculations can be made only if measures of a company's profitabil-

---

[5] S. A. Zeff, *Forging Accounting Principles in Five Countries: A History and Analysis of Trends* (Champaign, Ill.: Stripes, 1972).

[6] Richard K. Goeltz, "International Accounting Harmonization: The Impossible (and Unnecessary?) Dream," *Accounting Horizons* (March 1991), pp. 85–88.

[7] It has been argued that in reality it is impossible to isolate the translation process from general price-level adjustments, since foreign exchange rates do to some extent reflect changes in the price level. But even though inflationary relationships between countries may be indirectly reflected in official exchange rates, translation is still considered to be an independent process.

ity and financial position are expressed in a common unit of measurement (usually the domestic currency); foreign monetary measures must be converted to domestic units. This process is known as translation.

In translating foreign currency, the foreign exchange rate defines the relationship between two monetary scales. The foreign currency is stated as a ratio to the U.S. dollar, and this ratio becomes the multiplying factor to determine the equivalent amount of domestic currency. For example, if the British pound (£) is quoted as $1.20 and an American subsidiary acquired an asset valued at £10,000, the translation into dollars will be $12,000 (10,000 × $1.20). Foreign exchange rates change over time in response to the forces of supply and demand and to the relative degree of inflation between countries. These changes are classified into three types—fluctuation, devaluation, and revaluation. *Fluctuation* denotes a rate change within the narrow margin allowed by the International Monetary Fund (IMF) (a deviation of 2¼ percent above or below that country's official exchange rate). If an entirely new support level of the foreign currency is allowed by the IMF and the dollar rate falls, it is called *devaluation. Revaluation* occurs when the dollar rate of the foreign currency rises to a new support level.

It is important to note that the translation process in no way changes the inherent characteristics of the assets or liabilities measured. That is, translation is a single process that merely restates an asset or liability initially valued in foreign currency in terms of a common currency measurement by applying the rate of exchange factor; it does not restate historical cost. Translation is a completely separate process just as adjusting for general price level changes is a separate process. The translation process is analogous to price-level adjustments in that neither changes any accounting principles; they merely change the unit of measurement.

If the exchange rate remained constant between a particular foreign country and the United States, translation would be a relatively simple process involving a constant exchange rate. However, recent history indicates that this is unlikely, and a method of translation must be established that adequately discloses the effect of changes in exchange rates on financial statements. There has been considerable debate among accountants on how to achieve this objective. In the following sections we will review the proposals advocated by several individuals and groups.

Historically, four methods of translation were proposed by various authors prior to the release of any official pronouncements by the APB or FASB: the current–noncurrent method, the monetary–nonmonetary method, the current rate method, and the temporal method.[8]

Current–Noncurrent Method

The current–noncurrent method is based on the distinction between current and noncurrent assets and liabilities. It was initially recommended by the

---

[8] See Leonard Lorensen, "Reporting Foreign Operations of U.S. Companies in U.S. Dollars," *Accounting Research Study No. 12* (New York: AICPA, 1972).

American Institute of Certified Public Accountants (AICPA) in 1931 and updated in *Accounting Research Bulletin No. 43* in 1953.[9] This method requires all current items (cash, receivables, inventory, and short-term liabilities) to be translated at the foreign exchange rate existing at the balance sheet date. The noncurrent items (plant, equipment, property, and long-term liabilities) are translated using the rate in effect when the items were acquired or incurred (the historical rate). The rationale for the dichotomy between current and noncurrent items is that those items that will not be converted into cash in the upcoming period (noncurrent) are not affected by changes in current rates. Thus, in using this method, the assumption is made that items translated at the historical exchange rate are not exposed to gains and losses caused by changes in the relative value of currencies. In 1965, *ARB No. 43* (Chapter 12) was modified by *Accounting Principles Board Opinion No. 6* to allow long-term payables and receivables to be translated at the current rather than historical rate if this treatment resulted in a better representation of a company's position.[10] With respect to the income statement, *ARB No. 43* required revenues and expenses to be translated at the average exchange rate applicable to each month, except for depreciation, which was translated at the historical rate.

Monetary–Nonmonetary Method

The monetary–nonmonetary method was first advocated by Samuel Hepworth,[11] and the National Association of Accountants' support of Hepworth's method in 1960 resulted in more widespread acceptance of its provisions.[12]

The monetary–nonmonetary method requires that a distinction be made between monetary items (accounts representing cash or claims on cash, such as receivables, notes payable, and bonds payable) and nonmonetary items (accounts not representing claims on a specific amount of cash such as land, inventory, plant, equipment, and capital stock). Monetary items are translated at the exchange rate in effect at the balance sheet date, whereas nonmonetary items retain the historical exchange rate. Exhibit 17.3 summarizes the results of the application of these two methods for a corporation that has experienced a devaluation. Prior to the devaluation one unit of foreign currency was worth $0.50, whereas after devaluation it was worth $0.25.

As illustrated in Exhibit 17.3 the only difference between the two methods for the reporting of assets is in the translation of inventories. If the current–noncurrent method is used, inventories are considered to be current assets (sensitive to foreign exchange gains and losses) and are translated at the cur-

---

[9] *Accounting Research Bulletin No. 43* (New York: AICPA, 1953), Chapter 12.

[10] *Accounting Principles Board Opinion No. 6*, "Status of Accounting Research Bulletins" (New York: AICPA, 1965), par. 18.

[11] Samuel Hepworth, "Reporting Foreign Operations," *Michigan Business Studies* (University of Michigan, 1956).

[12] National Association of Accountants, "Management Accounting Problems in Foreign Operations," *NAA Research Report No. 36* (New York, 1960).

EXHIBIT 17.3 *Currency Translation by Current–Noncurrent and Monetary–Nonmonetary Methods*

	Balance Sheet in FC*	Current–Noncurrent		Monetary–Nonmonetary	
		Translation Rate	Balance Sheet in DC⁺	Translation Rate	Balance Sheet in DC⁺
Assets:					
Cash	$120	0.25	$ 30	0.25	$ 30
Receivables	80	0.25	20	0.25	20
Inventories	80	0.25	20	0.50	40
Property, plant, land, and equipment	120	0.50	60	0.50	60
Total assets	$400		$130		$150
Liabilities and Owners' Equity:					
Payables	$ 40	0.25	$ 10	0.25	$ 10
Bank note (long-term)	200	0.50	100	0.25	50
Capital	160	0.50	80	0.50	80
Foreign exchange gain (loss)			(60)		10
Total liabilities and owners' equity	$400		$130		$150

*FC = foreign currency.

⁺DC = domestic currency.

Rate before devaluation = 0.50

Rate after devaluation = 0.25

rent rate, whereas the monetary–nonmonetary method classifies inventories as nonmonetary assets that are subsequently translated at the historical or preexisting rate. A difference also arises in translating long-term debt. The current–noncurrent approach uses the historical translation rate, whereas the monetary–nonmonetary method considers long-term debt to be monetary and uses the current rate. This difference between the two methods disappears, however, if the current–noncurrent approach is modified as was required by *APB Opinion No. 6.* Both approaches result in a foreign exchange gain or loss in order to balance the assets with the liabilities and equities, thereby creating a reporting problem. That is, how should a gain or loss on foreign currency translation be reported on the financial statements? (We will discuss this issue later in the chapter.)

While these two translation methods dominated accounting practices for approximately 40 years, the late 1960s and the early 1970s produced a proliferation of new proposals for dealing with foreign exchange problems. After 1971, when the dollar was devalued and allowed to float on the world monetary market, the dissatisfaction with the traditional methods came to the forefront. Most authors advocating new approaches contend that new problems surfaced in 1971 because foreign currencies were appreciating rather than depreciating in relation to the dollar, and that these problems could not be resolved by the traditional approaches. Two other methods, the current rate method and the temporal method, have been advocated as alleviating this problem.

Current Rate Method

The current rate method requires the translation of *all* assets and liabilities at the exchange rate in effect on the balance sheet date (current rate). It is, therefore, the only method that translates fixed assets at current rather than historical rates. Proponents of the current rate method claim that it most clearly represents the true economic facts, because stating all items currently presents the true earnings of a foreign operation at that time—particularly since from the investor's point of view the only real earnings are those that can actually be distributed.

While the current rate method has drawn some support, it is not without critics. Proponents argue that it presents true economic facts by stating all items at the current rate thus retaining operating relationships intact. However, critics attack the use of the current rate for fixed assets, stating that the resulting figure on the translated consolidated balance sheet does not represent the historical cost. They maintain that until the entire reporting system is changed, the current rate method will not be acceptable.

Temporal Method

In 1972, Lorensen advocated another approach, termed the temporal principle of translation.[13] Monetary measurements under this method depend on the temporal characteristics of assets and liabilities. That is, the time of measurement of the elements depends on certain characteristics. Lorensen summarized this process as follows:

> *Money and receivables and payables measured at the amounts promised should be translated at the foreign exchange rate in effect at the balance sheet date. Assets and liabilities measured at money prices should be translated at the foreign exchange rate in effect at the dates to which the money prices pertain.*[14]

This principle is simply an application of the fair value principle in the area of foreign translation. By stating foreign money receivables and payables at

[13] Leonard Lorensen, op. cit.

[14] Ibid., p. 19.

the balance sheet rate, the foreign currency's command over U.S. dollars is measured. (Lorensen believes this attribute, command over U.S. dollars, to be of paramount importance.) Nevertheless, the results from the use of this method are generally identical to the monetary–nonmonetary method except when the inventory valuation is based on the lower of cost or market rule.

Lorensen's main concern was that the generally accepted accounting principles being followed should not be changed by the translation process. Consequently, he strongly opposed any translation method that ultimately changed the attributes of a balance sheet account (e.g., historical cost being transformed into replacement cost or selling price). Unfortunately, the temporal method does not provide any solution to the problem of reporting change gains and losses that plague the traditional methods. Moreover, using the historical rate to translate fixed assets, while translating the long-term debt incurred to finance those assets at the current rate, may be inappropriate and may result in large gains and losses that will not be realized in the near future. Further, it is argued that because subsidiary assets are acquired with foreign, not the parent's, currency, use of the historic exchange rate is simply not relevant.

It must be stressed that none of these methods of translation provides a perfect representation of value because of the nature of the world's monetary systems. A country's currency is basically a one-dimensional scale that measures and compares economic values within that one political entity. Thus, even the best translation method attempting to restate a foreign asset or liability in terms of domestic currency will inevitably be limited in its representation of economic reality.

The FASB and Foreign Currency Translation

The Financial Accounting Standards Board took this issue under advisement and originally issued *SFAS No. 8,* "Accounting for the Translation of Foreign Currency Transactions and Foreign Currency Financial Statements."[15] The significant provisions of this pronouncement are summarized.

1. The overall objective of foreign currency translation is to measure and express, in dollars and in conformity with U.S. generally accepted accounting principles, the assets, liabilities, revenue, and expenses initially measured in foreign currency.
2. The following translation principles are to apply.
   a. Record each transaction at the exchange rate in effect at the transaction date.
   b. Adjust all cash and amounts owed to or by the enterprise by the current rate at the balance sheet date.
   c. Adjust assets carried at market price into an equivalent dollar price on the balance sheet date.

---

[15] Financial Accounting Standards Board *Statement of Financial Accounting Standards No. 8,* "Accounting for the Translation of Foreign Currency Transactions and Foreign Currency Financial Statements" (Stamford, Conn.: FASB, 1975).

3. For all other assets the particular measurement basis (e.g., historical cost, replacement cost, market, etc.) should be used to determine the translation rate.

   a. Accounts carried at prices in past exchanges should be translated at the historical rate.

   b. Accounts carried at current prices should be translated at the current rate.

4. Revenue and expenses should be translated in a manner that produces approximately the same dollar amount that would have resulted had the underlying transactions been translated into dollars on the dates they occurred. (An average rate may be used except for expenses that relate to specific assets and liabilities. In such cases, the same rate used to translate the assets and liabilities must also be used for related revenues and expenses.)

5. Exchange gains or losses can occur because of (a) changes in the relationship between currencies during the year, (b) conversion of foreign currency during the year, or (c) the settlement of receivables or payables at rates different from those at which the items were recorded. Such gains and losses should be included in the determination of net income for the period in which the rate changes.

6. Forward exchange contracts are agreements to exchange currencies at a predetermined rate on a specific date in the future. The purpose of such contracts may be to hedge either a foreign currency commitment, or a foreign currency exposed net asset position, or exposed net liability position, or to speculate. In general, gains and losses from forward exchange contracts should be included in the determination of net income for the period in which the rate changes. Gains or losses intended to be a hedge of an identifiable foreign currency commitment should be deferred subject to the following criteria:

   a. The life of the forward contract entered into extends at least to the anticipated transaction date.

   b. The forward contract is denominated in the same currency as the commitment and the amount is the same as or less than the amount of the commitment.

   c. The commitment is firm and uncancelable.[16]

It should be noted that this statement did not specifically advocate any one of the translation methods previously discussed, and none was adopted intact. Nevertheless, the general objectives of translation originally advocated by the FASB are most closely satisfied by the temporal method.

Statement of Financial Accounting Standards No. 52

The requirements of *SFAS No. 8* produced some perceived distortions in financial reporting that resulted in questions by many accountants and financial

---

[16] Ibid., par. 27.

statement users as to the relevance, reliability, and predictive value of the information presented. Among these perceived distortions were as follows:

1. The results of the application of *SFAS No. 8* were economically incompatible with reality. That is, since nonmonetary items such as inventory were translated at the historical rate, a loss could be reported during a period in which a foreign currency actually strengthened in relation to the dollar.

2. Matching of costs and revenues was inappropriate. For example, sales were measured and translated at current prices, whereas inventory was measured and translated at historical rates.

3. The volatility of earnings. *SFAS No. 8* required all translation gains and losses to be included in income. However, exchange rate changes are unrealized and frequently short-term in nature. This produced a so-called yo-yo effect upon earnings. Critics contended that this reporting requirement tended to obscure long-term trends.

The FASB took these criticisms under advisement and later replaced *SFAS No. 8* with *SFAS No. 52*, "Foreign Currency Translation."[17] The following translation objectives were adopted in this release:

1. To provide information that is generally compatible with the expected economic effects of a rate change on an enterprise's cash flow and equity.

2. To reflect in consolidated statements the financial results and relationships of the individual consolidated entities in conformity with U.S. generally accepted accounting principles.

SFAS No. 52 adopts the *functional currency* approach to translation. An entity's functional currency is defined as the currency of the *primary economic environment* in which it operates, which will normally be the environment in which it expends cash. Most frequently the functional currency will be the local currency, and four general procedures are involved in the translation process when the local currency is defined as the functional currency:

1. The financial statements of each individual foreign entity are initially recorded in that entity's functional currency. For example, a Japanese subsidiary would initially prepare its financial statements in terms of yen, as that would be the currency it generally uses to carry out cash transactions.

2. The foreign entity's statements must be adjusted (if necessary) to comply with generally accepted accounting principles in the United States.

3. The financial statements of the foreign entity are translated into the reporting currency of the parent company (usually the U.S. dollar). Assets and liabilities are translated at the current exchange rate at the balance sheet date. Revenues, expenses, gains, and losses are translated at the rate in effect at the date they were first recognized, or alternatively, at the average rate for the period.

---

[17] Financial Accounting Standards Board *Statement of Financial Accounting Standards No. 52,* "Foreign Currency Translation" (Stamford, Conn.: FASB, 1981).

4. Translation gains and losses are accumulated and reported as a separate component of stockholders' equity in the unrealized capital section.

SFAS No. 52 went on to define two situations in which the local currency would not be the functional currency:

1. The foreign country's economic environment is highly inflationary (over 100 percent cumulative inflation over the past three years such as recently experienced by Argentina and Brazil).

2. The company's investment is not considered long-term.

In these cases the foreign company's functional currency is defined by the U.S. dollar and the financial statements are translated using the *SFAS No. 8* approach. That is, exchange gains and losses are reported as a component of income.

Proponents feel that the situational approach adopted by the SFAS gives a true picture of economic reality. When the functional currency is the local currency, the translated accounting numbers parallel the local perspective of foreign operations. Moreover, the major criticism leveled against *SFAS No. 8* is eliminated. Because translation gains and losses are now included in stockholders' equity, rather than in income, the bottom line will no longer be adversely affected by the volatility of foreign exchange rates.

Nevertheless, critics maintain that the functional currency approach may afford management too much leeway in the selection of the functional currency. As a result, a given subsidiary's functional currency may be chosen to manipulate reported net income. Furthermore, when the current rate is applied to historical costs, the result in an accounting model that at best is a hybrid of historical cost. Moreover, when these numbers are aggregated with the parent company's historical costs, the resulting consolidated financial statements are a mixed bag and may not provide useful information.

Translation versus Remeasurement
Under the provisions of *SFAS No. 52, translation* is the process of expressing in the reporting currency of the enterprise those amounts that are demonstrated or measured in a different currency. The translation process is performed for the purpose of preparing financial statements and assumes that the foreign accounts *will not* be liquidated into U.S. dollars. Therefore, translation adjustments are disclosed as a part of stockholders' equity rather than as adjustments to income.

Remeasurement is significantly different from translation. It is the process of measuring transactions originally denominated in a different unit of currency (e.g., purchases of a German subsidiary of a U.S. company payable in French francs). Remeasurement is required when

1. A foreign entity operates in a highly inflationary economy.

2. The accounts of an entity are maintained in a currency other than its functional currency.

3. A foreign entity is a party to a transaction that produces a monetary asset or liability denominated in a currency other than its functional currency.

Remeasurement is accomplished by the same procedures as described earlier under the temporal method. That is, the financial statement elements are restated according to their original measurement bases. Remeasurement assumes that an exchange of currencies will occur at the exchange rate prevailing on the date of remeasurement. This produces a foreign exchange gain or loss if the exchange rate fluctuates between the date of the original transaction and the date of the assumed exchange. Therefore, any exchange gain or loss is included in income in the period in which it occurs.

Forward Exchange Contracts

As noted earlier, *forward exchange contracts* are agreements to exchange currencies at a predetermined rate on a specific date in the future. These agreements are frequently used to protect a company from experiencing exchange gains or losses when a transaction with a foreign entity is settled at an amount different from the amount at which it was initially recorded. Two viewpoints have been advocated to account for foreign exchange contracts.

1. *One transaction* All aspects are viewed as part of a single transaction. That is, commitments to buy or sell currency necessary to settle a foreign payable or receivable are viewed as a part of the purchase or sale transaction.

2. *Two transactions* The purchase or sale of goods is viewed as separate from any commitment to buy or sell foreign currency to settle the foreign payable or receivable.

Forward exchange contracts may be associated with four types of situations, each of which is viewed somewhat differently under the provisions of *SFAS No. 52:*

1. A hedge of a recorded but unsettled foreign currency transaction.

2. A hedge of an identifiable foreign currency commitment.

3. Speculating in foreign currency.

4. Hedging a net investment.

A recorded but unsettled foreign currency transaction arises when a company has an exposed liability position (a liability in a foreign currency) or an exposed asset position (a receivable in a foreign currency). These situations are similar, so only the liability position will be discussed. A U.S. company purchases inventory and agrees to pay a French company 100,000 francs in 30 days. The U.S. company is in an exposed liability position. To avoid the risk of an exchange rate increase, the U.S. company enters into a forward exchange contract whereby it agrees to purchase 100,000 francs at the exchange rate in effect on the date the inventory was purchased (this contract is defined as a *hedge* because it protects the company from experiencing an exchange rate loss). In the event the exchange rate between the dollar and the franc changes prior to the settlement of the liability, an exchange gain or loss is recorded as a component of net income. This treatment is an application of the two-transactions approach by the FASB. The rationale for this treatment is that cost or revenue was determined by the initial purchase or sale transaction and not by any subsequent agreement to exchange currencies.

A hedge of an identifiable foreign currency commitment occurs when a U.S. company purchases goods from a foreign entity to be delivered and paid for in the foreign company's currency in the future. The U.S. company, wishing to protect itself from the risks of exchange rate fluctuation, contracts with a currency dealer to purchase a specified amount of the foreign currency on the date of the purchase. In these situations any exchange gain or loss is deferred until the actual date the goods are acquired. This is an example of the one-transaction approach and is supported because both the purchase or sale and the forward exchange contract are future commitments.

Speculating in a foreign currency occurs when a company enters into an agreement to buy or sell a foreign currency that does not relate to the purchase or sale of goods. Any exchange gains or losses from speculating in foreign currency are recognized currently in income.

Hedging a net investment involves dealing in a foreign currency to offset the effects of changes on exchange rates on the company's total investment in a foreign operation. For example, several U.S. companies recently borrowed pesos to hedge against the effect of the possible devaluation of that currency on their investments in Mexico. Accounting for any gains or losses depends on whether the dollar or the foreign currency is the functional currency. If the dollar is the functional currency (which should be normal because devaluation normally takes place in highly inflationary economies), remeasurement is required and any gain or loss is reported on the income statement. If the foreign currency is the functional currency, any gain or loss is reported as a separate component of stockholders' equity as unrealized capital.

In analyzing foreign currency translation information, investors should keep in mind that it is a mixture of exceptional complexity. That is, foreign currency exchange reporting is inextricably intertwined with accounting for business combinations. The question of what constitutes the net income of a consolidated corporation with foreign subsidiaries may never be fully answerable.

Summary

Financial accounting is influenced by the environment in which it operates. The financial accounting policies of a country are determined by the interaction of many variables relating to its history, values, and political and economic systems.

United States companies increasingly must be able to compete in a global economy. This factor is complicated by the facts that accounting standards differ between countries, and the value of foreign currencies fluctuates against the dollar.

In the following readings, S. E. C. Purvis, Helen Gernon, and Michael Diamond discuss the IASC's comparability project in more depth, and Carol Olson Houston and Gerhard Mueller discuss the relationship of *SFAS No. 52* and hedging.

The IASC and Its Comparability Project: Prerequisites for Success

S. E. C. Purvis, Helen Gernon, and Michael A. Diamond

Introduction

As the volume of international financial operations and cross-border investments continues to surge, the need for a common language of business in financial statements is increasing in urgency. It has long been argued that different national accounting standards militate against the efficiency of international capital markets and may even impair the ability of corporations to compete effectively for capital in those markets. Barthes observed that the:

> business community is tired of differences in accounting. These differences lead to increased costs for those companies that operate and raise capital abroad and to an unlevel playing field for those international companies that are competing with one another for business opportunities.[1]

In the last three decades, standard-setters[2] and regulators[3] in different

countries have grappled with the problems posed by different national standards. Several international institutions have risen to the challenge presented by the development of international accounting standards. These include the United Nations (UN), the European Community (EC), the Organisation for Economic Cooperation and Development (OECD), all governmental or quasi-governmental institutions, and

[1] Georges Barthes, "Meeting the Expectations of Global Capital Markets." *IASC News,* Vol. 18, No. 3 (July 1989): 1–2.

[2] *Standard-setters* are institutions or groups responsible for setting national accounting and reporting standards. These groups may be in the private sector, e.g., the Financial Accounting Standards Board (FASB) and the current Accounting Standards Committees in Canada and the United Kingdom. In some countries, these national standard-setters may be government agencies, related to government agencies, or even the government

itself. For example, in Japan, the Business Accounting Deliberations Council, affiliated with the Ministry of Finance, is involved in setting accounting standards, whereas in Germany, accounting standards are set by Parliament through the Ministry of Justice. In the Netherlands, Parliament has primary responsibility (again through the Ministry of Justice), but there is also an independent, private sector Council for Annual Reporting.

[3] *Regulators* are groups or institutions with statutory authority to regulate stock exchanges, and which, in so doing, may prescribe accounting standards and disclosure requirements. These groups also have enforcement to ensure compliance. In many countries, the regulatory function is separated from the standard-setting function. For example, in the U.S., the Securities and Exchange Commission (SEC), while having statutory authority to set standards, has generally looked to the private sector (presently, the FASB) for the development of accounting standards. The SEC, however, has mandated disclosure requirements which apply to listed companies through regulations S-X and S-K. In other countries, the regulating body may be the same as the standard-setting body. The Swedish Accounting Standards Board is such an example.

the International Accounting Standards Committee (IASC), the only private standard-setter in the international arena. Two years ago, the IASC released Exposure Draft 32 (ED32), "Comparability of Financial Statements," proposing an improved set of international standards.[4] ED32 represents the culmination of a two-year project which had been encouraged by the International Organisation of Securities Commissions (IOSCO), and stakes the IASC's claim to be the preeminent provider of international financial accounting and reporting standards.

The purpose of this article is to assess the likely compliance with ED32 and to debate the prerequisites for the success of the IASC's proposal for international accounting comparability. The next section analyzes national compliance with existing IAS, and identifies several factors which may hinder this comparability attempt. The third section briefly reviews ED32 and discusses the likely compliance of five major countries with ED32. In the fourth section, possible responses from different groups of countries to the IASC's move are considered. In the fifth section, prerequisites for success of the Comparability Project are reviewed. In the sixth section, the desirability of harmonization is debated. Finally, it is concluded that the IASC

needs the cooperation and endorsement of standard-setters and regulators in the major markets in order to realize the aims of the Comparability Project.

Review of Compliance with Existing IAS

In 1988, the IASC published a major survey[5] of compliance with international accounting standards (IAS) in force at that time. Member institutions were asked to indicate the extent to which national standards or practices conformed with the 25 IAS.[6] Responses received from 54 member countries were reported in tabular form, but were not subjected to examination by the IASC. This study analyzes the IASC data from several different perspectives, including compliance by standard and by country.

Compliance by Standard

Table 1 shows the current level of compliance with existing IAS on a standard-by-standard basis. The numbered columns record the presence or absence of substantial conformity, as defined in the table.

The categories employed by the IASC in its questionnaire may be distinguished into conforming versus non-conforming responses (columns 1–4 and 5–6, respectively). In order to evaluate the degree of compliance with the 25 existing standards, two conformity indices were constructed. In each percentage-based index, the numerator

---

[4] International Accounting Standards Committee (a). "Comparability of Financial Statements: Proposed Amendments to International Accounting Standards 2, 5, 8, 9, 11, 16, 17, 18, 19, 21, 22, 23, and 25." *Exposure Draft 32* (London: IASC, 1989).

International Accounting Standards Committee (b). "Towards the International Harmonisation of Financial Statements: An Invitation to Comment on an Exposure Draft on the Comparability of Financial Statements." (London: IASC, 1989).

[5] International Accounting Standards Committee. *Survey of the Use and Application of International Accounting Standards.* (London: IASC, July 1988).

[6] A complete list of international accounting standards, titles, and release dates may be found in the inside back cover of ED32.

Table 1 *Conformity with Existing Standards: Analysis by Standard*

	Response Category[a]							Conformity Index A	Conformity Index B
	1	2	3	4	5	6	7[b]		
Standard									
IAS 1	7	7	25	9	3	2	1	90.6%	88.9%
IAS 2	7	4	30	7	5	1		88.9%	88.9%
IAS 3	7	4	21	13	4	4	1	84.9%	83.3%
IAS 4	7	7	29	10	1			98.2%	98.2%
IAS 5	7	6	28	11	2			96.3%	96.3%
IAS 7	7	4	24	15	1	3		92.6%	92.6%
IAS 8	7	3	30	8	4	2		88.9%	88.9%
IAS 9	7	4	18	12	7	2	4	82.0%	75.9%
IAS 10	7	6	28	11	1	1		96.3%	96.3%
IAS 11	7	6	21	15	2	2	1	92.5%	90.7%
IAS 12	7	3	16	8	9	6	5	69.4%	63.0%
IAS 13	7	5	26	13	2	1		94.4%	94.4%
IAS 14	7	2	6	10	7	19	3	49.0%	49.3%
IAS 15	4	5	11	5	22		7	42.6%	37.0%
IAS 16	7	3	26	14	2		2	96.2%	92.6%
IAS 17	7	3	15	10	6	11	2	67.3%	64.8%
IAS 18	7	4	18	18	2	1	4	94.0%	87.0%
IAS 19	6	4	13	9	3	11	8	69.6%	59.3%
IAS 20	6	1	17	14	4	7	5	77.6%	70.4%
IAS 21	7	6	17	11	6	4	3	80.4%	75.9%
IAS 22	6	2	15	14	5	8	4	74.0%	68.5%
IAS 23	7	4	15	17	2	5	4	86.0%	79.6%
IAS 24	4	1	15	12	2	14	6	66.7%	59.3%
IAS 25	4	3	16	14	5	4	8	80.4%	68.5%
IAS 26	4	3	6	9	3	15	14	55.0%	40.7%
Total	160	95	480	295	93	145	82	80.5%	76.3%

Notes: The response categories are defined as follows:

1. "IAS adopted as national standard."
2. "IAS used as the basis for a national requirement."
3. National requirements conform "in all material respects with IAS."
4. National practice "generally conforms with IAS."
5. National requirements do "not conform with IAS."
6. "National practice does not generally conform with IAS."
7. Not applicable.

[a] The values represent the number of countries (out of 54) that selected each response category.

[b] Some countries were not assigned a response in the IASC survey results. Recent correspondence with the IASC indicates that these should be coded "Not applicable," and therefore they have been assigned to category 7.

represents the sum of all *conforming* responses (in columns 1–4). There are two possible choices for the denominator: (A) the sum of conforming and nonconforming responses (in columns 1–6), or (B) 54, the number of countries surveyed.[7] The difference between the two denominators is column 7, which represents the number of countries omitting a response, or otherwise indicating that a particular standard was not applicable. The two indices are highly correlated (Spearman's correlation coefficient, rho = .849), and strongly statistically significant (p = .0001). Note that the number of countries in column 7 increases directly with the recency of the standard. Indeed, Spearman's correlation (rho) of the standard number (as a proxy for issue date) with column 7 is .746, a very high degree of association, which explains more than half of the observed variance (r^2 = .558).

Some of the missing responses surely reflect a lack of compliance with the standards rather than the standards' lack of relevance to the country. It is difficult to imagine that a country could argue that IAS1 "Disclosure of Accounting Policies" is "not applicable"! Consequently, Index B is used in subsequent analyses because it more accurately reflects *active* compliance.

Conformity by Standard

An examination of Table 1 shows a high level of conformity with the first group of standards issued, but much lower levels for standards issued more recently. Both conformity indices show a strong negative correlation with the date on which each standard came into effect (Index A, rho = −.534, p = .006; and Index B, rho = −.640, p = .0006). There are (at least) two explanations for this negative relationship. First, the early standards tended to address more fundamental issues at a high level of generality, which enabled many countries to conform with a minimum of effort. As noted by Stronge,[8] "compliance with International Accounting Standards means little because of the range of permitted alternative treatments." Second, the passage of time has perhaps permitted other countries with initially nonconforming standards or practices to adopt new approaches that are in line with IAS.

To test this suggestion, cluster analysis of the country responses by standard was performed. Clustering techniques essentially sort observations (raw data) into groups (or clusters) based on the degree of similarity that an observation bears to existing members of a cluster. The results suggest that the IASC has issued three types of standards: (1) standards issued early in the IASC's life and with which conformity was easily achieved; (2) standards issued more recently, perhaps requiring additional procedures for some countries to achieve conformity; and (3) some stan-

---

[7] It is recognized that this coding scheme is rather generous in that it weights each category of conformity equally. It could be argued that category 4 should be assigned a lower weight than categories 1–3. Similarly, one could argue that a national standard conflicting with IAS should receive greater weight than a nonconforming national practice. Different weights were used in a sensitivity analysis (not reported here). While the absolute scores changed according to the weights used, the relative rankings of each standard in the table were not significantly affected.

[8] Chris Stronge, "Financial Reporting: Disturbing Lack of a Common Language," *Accountant* (July 1988): 22–23.

dards which have not been adopted by the majority of the IASC's member countries. The first group contains 12 standards (IAS1–5, IAS7–8, IAS10–11, IAS13, IAS16, and IAS18), which have been in effect for an average of 11.0 years and have achieved an average conformity of 92 percent. The second group contains 10 standards (IAS9, IAS12, IAS17, and IAS19–25), which have been in effect for an average of 5.7 years. Only 69 percent of the member countries have demonstrated some form of conformity with these standards. The third group contains only three standards (IAS14–15) and IAS26), achieving conformity in only 41 percent of the member countries. IAS14 (segment disclosure) and IAS15 (price-level changes), which became effective in 1983, are apparently unwelcomed by the international accounting community. IAS26 (retirement benefits) came into effect in 1988, the year in which the data were collected.

Conformity by Country

Conformity Index B was calculated for each of the 54 countries responding to the IASC survey. The score represents the percentage of the 25 IAS with which each country complied (i.e., the country response to the questionnaire was one of columns 1–4). While the mean conformity score was 76.3 percent, there was substantial intercountry variation. Fifteen countries have scores of 90 percent or more and five have scores lower than 50 percent, meaning that they comply with fewer than half of the existing IAS.

There are, of course, many reasons why a country has or has not adopted an accounting treatment which conforms with IAS. One contributing factor is the strength of the national accounting institutions, which affects the way

in which standards are developed (see Table 2). Countries with weak or newly established accounting professions may lack a formalized system for developing, issuing, and enforcing accounting and reporting standards. These countries were identified from IASC questionnaire categories 4 and 6, conforming and nonconforming national *practices.* For example, Trinidad and Tobago and Bahrain have no national requirements at all in the areas covered by the 25 IAS in the survey. Other countries, such as India and Hong Kong, have national practices, but no standards, in 11 and 13 areas, respectively. Altogether, a total of 18 countries have not codified or otherwise standardized the majority of their accounting treatments (abbreviated as "unstandardized," see Table 2 column 1). On average, this group has issued standards corresponding to 5.5 of the 25 IAS.

The other 36 countries have a formalized system for promulgating and enforcing the majority of their accounting treatments, either via national laws, via the accounting profession, or a combination of both. This group may be further subdivided into two groups, one of which includes 11 countries which rely upon the IASC for the development of standards (abbreviated as "dependent," see Table 2 column 2) and a group of 25 countries which have a strong tradition of accounting or powerful accounting institutions and typically issue standards independently of the IASC (abbreviated as "independent," see Table 2 column 3).

In developing countries, the tendency is for local accounting institutions to adopt or adapt IAS for their own standards (IASC questionnaire categories 1 and 2, respectively). Illustrative of the dependent category are Botswana and Cyprus (both 100 percent), which have

TABLE 2 Development of Accounting Standards

Practice not yet Standardized		Dependent on IASC		Independent of IASC	
Country	%	Country	%	Country	%
Abu Dhabi	96	Botswana	100	Belgium	84
Bahrain	100	Cyprus	100	Brazil	92
Dubai	100	Fiji	44	Canada	84
Greece	80	Jamaica	76	Finland	100
Kuwait	88	Malawi	88	France	76
Lesotho	72	Malaysia	72	Germany	96
Malta	100	Oman	96	Ireland	84
Saudi Arabia	96	Pakistan	92	Japan	88
Switzerland	96	Singapore	96	Mexico	76
Trinidad and		Sri Lanka	44	Netherlands	88
Tobago	100	Zimbabwe	92	Spain	84
				Sweden	88
				United Kingdom	84
				United States	100
Ghana	64			Australia	64
Hong Kong	52			Austria	68
India	44			Denmark	60
Kenya	52			Iceland	60
Morocco	56			Indonesia	72
Nigeria	52			Italy	64
South Africa	36			New Zealand	64
Taiwan	60			Norway	60
				Swaziland	52
				Tanzania	60
				Yugoslavia	68
Total 18	Av. 74.7	Total 11	Av. 81.8	Total 25	Av. 76.6

Note: The figures indicate the percentage of the 25 standards which were developed in that mode for each country. Only the predominant mode is reported.

adopted the IAS as their own. Other countries, such as Jamaica and Singapore, use the IAS as a basis for developing their own standards. It is interesting to note that all the countries in column 2 of Table 2 are (or have been) members of the British Commonwealth. On average, these countries have adopted or followed 20.5 of the 25 IAS.

The independent category comprises countries which have national accounting requirements that were not developed from IAS (i.e., IASC questionnaire categories 3 and 5). On average, these 25 countries developed requirements corresponding to the IAS for 18.6 standards out of 25. The leading examples in this category are the United States (100 percent) and Germany (96 percent) (see Table 2, column 3). The authority underlying national accounting treatments in these countries typically predated the creation of IASC. For example, in the U.S.A., the Securities Acts of 1933 and 1934, the Committee on Accounting Procedure, and the Accounting Principles Board paved the way for the Financial Accounting Standards Board (FASB), which came into being in 1973. In Germany, the Commercial Code is the major source of accounting regulation. Both countries have created national guidelines or issued standards on topics well before the IASC pronounced on these issues.

In order to test the similarity of the three country grouping (IASC-dependent, independent, and unstandardized with respect to accounting treatments), the 54 country responses (level and type of conformity with the 25 existing IAS) were further analyzed by group. The intergroup correlations suggest that they are capturing significantly different behavior. The conformity indices of those countries which may be classified as independent of the IASC show a strong negative correlation (rho = $-.597$, $p \leq .001$) when compared to the conformity indices of the dependent group. The indices of the unstandardized group show similar negative correlations when compared to the independent group (rho = $-.409$, $p \leq .002$) and with the dependent group (rho = $-.488$, $p < .001$). Each group is distinctly different from the others, as is shown by the negative correlations, all highly significant, statistically. In particular, the strong negative Spearman correlation (rho = $-.597$) between the dependent and independent groups evidences the wide gulf that the IASC must bridge if the Comparability Project is to be realized.

The development of accounting standards in each country (Table 2) is associated with the level of conformity with existing IAS standards (Table 1). The mean Conformity Index for the "dependent" category is 89.1 percent, with a standard deviation of 12.7 percent. By way of contrast, the mean Conformity Index for the "independent" group is substantially lower, 74.2 percent, and has a larger standard deviation, 20.3 percent, and the mean for the "unstandardized" group is 71.3 percent, with a standard deviation of 19.5 percent. The dependency scores from Table 2 were correlated with the Conformity Index B scores from Table 1 for each country, using Spearman's rho. The IASC-dependent group scores were positively associated with the Conformity Index score (rho = $.382$), at a high level of statistical significance ($p = .001$). In other words, the statistical analysis suggests that the greater the degree of dependence on the IASC, the greater the country's score on the Conformity Index. Also, as expected, the "unstandardized" group scores were negatively associated with the Conformity Index (rho = $-.227$) but at a marginal level of statistical significance ($p = .107$).

The weak and negative correlation (rho = $-.170$) of the "independent" group with Conformity Index B reflects the bipolar distribution of countries on this dimension. Several countries with well-established accounting professions have issued standards or passed laws at variance with existing IAS, while others with their own standard-setting function have produced standards that are largely comparable with IAS. Typical of the latter are Canada, France, the United Kingdom, and the United States, with Conformity Index scores ranging from 84 percent to 96 percent. Remarkably, the former includes some of the founding members of the IASC, with comparatively low scores on Conformity Index B, notably Germany (28 percent) and Mexico (48 percent).

An examination of the individual country responses to the IASC survey shows that, as a group, the IASC founders demonstrate an average compliance that is fractionally worse than nonfounders (75.7 percent and 76.4 percent, respectively). The IASC survey respondents included 10 of the EC's 12 members. (Luxembourg and Portugal were omitted). These countries, all in the "independent" category (except for Greece, which was "unstandardized"), obtained a mean score of 71.6 percent on Index B, which is consistent with Doupnik and Taylor's[9] observation of lower levels of conformity with IAS within the EC. These findings pinpoint a major obstacle to the IASC's comparability quest. The cooperation of the major "independent" standard-setting groups must be obtained in order to progress.

Country Patterns of Conformity

Choi[10] observed a correlation between financial disclosure and the development and efficiency of capital markets. More recently, Pratt and Behr[11] sug-

gested that, in the case of the United States and Switzerland, differences in the standard-setting process and the types of standards promulgated may be explained in terms of differences in the "size, complexity, and diversity of capital transactions, the wide distribution of ownership and the opportunistic nature of the market participants." These contentions were examined in the context of the IASC survey data.

The country responses were subjected to two cluster analysis procedures available on SAS to ascertain whether discernible patterns of conformity existed. These two clustering techniques differ in two important ways: (1) the method used to structure initial clusters, and (2) the method of calculating similarity. When the SAS[12] CLUSTER procedure was used with the average link metric of similarity, the 54 countries were allocated to five clusters. The results are shown in Table 3. The first cluster includes all the countries that have not

[9] S. Doupnik and M. E. Taylor, "An Empirical Investigation of the Observance of IASC Standards in Western Europe." *Management International Review*, Vol. 25, No. 1 (1985): 27–33.

[10] Frederick D. S. Choi, "Financial Disclosure and Entry to the European Capital Market." *Journal of Accounting Research*, Vol. 11, No. 2 (Autumn 1973): 159–175.

[11] Jamie Pratt and Giorgio Behr, "Environmental Factors, Transaction Costs, and External Reporting: A Cross-National Comparison," *International Journal of Accounting, Education and Research*, Vol. 22, No. 2 (Spring 1987): 1–24.

TABLE 3 *Cluster Analysis of Responses to Standards*

Cluster 1: Unstandardized		
	B	U	r^2
Abu Dhabi	80	96	.99
Bahrain	80	100	.99
Dubai	68	100	.99
Greece	24	80	.78
Kuwait	72	88	.98
Lesotho	68	72	.91
Malta	68	100	.99
Saudi Arabia	68	96	.99
Switzerland	36	96	.91
Trinidad and Tobago	100	100	.95
Mean	66.4	92.8	.95

[12] SAS Institute. "SAS Users' Guide," Version 6, (Cary, NC: SAS Institute Inc., 1989).

TABLE 3 (*Continued*)

Cluster 2: Independent				Cluster 4: Unstandardized		
	B	I	r^2		B	U	r^2
Belgium	76	84	.99	Ghana	84	64	.92
Brazil	76	92	.99	Hong Kong	80	52	.98
Canada	96	84	.96	India	56	44	.94
Finland	12	100	.61	Kenya	52	52	.84
France	84	76	.96	Morocco	96	56	.96
Germany	28	96	.78	Nigeria	100	52	.85
Ireland	88	84	.98	South Africa	76	36	.82
Japan	68	88	.99	Taiwan	76	60	.95
Mexico	48	76	.95				
Netherlands	84	88	.96				
Spain	96	84	.96				
Sweden	84	88	.99				
United Kingdom	88	84	.98				
United States	92	100	.98				
Mean	72.9	87.4	.94	Mean	77.5	52.0	.91

Cluster 3: IASC-Dependent				Cluster 5: Independent		
	B	D	r^2		B	I	r^2
Botswana	100	100	.96	Australia	92	64	.97
Cyprus	100	100	.96	Austria	80	68	.95
Fiji	60	44	.77	Denmark	80	60	.99
Jamaica	88	76	.97	Iceland	76	60	.98
Malawi	88	88	.98	Indonesia	100	72	.93
Malaysia	100	72	.97	Italy	68	64	.94
Oman	96	96	.97	New Zealand	80	64	.97
Pakistan	92	92	.98	Norway	72	60	.98
Singapore	96	96	.95	Swaziland	72	52	.99
Sri Lanka	68	44	.80	Tanzania	60	60	.93
Zimbabwe	92	92	.98	Yugoslavia	56	68	.93
Mean	89.1	81.8	.94	Mean	76.0	62.9	.95

Notes: 1. The B column denotes the country's percentage compliance with IAS, as captured by Conformity Index B.
2. The columns headed I (Independent), D (Dependent), and U (Unstandardized) indicate each country's dominant mode of developing standards (see Table 2).
3. The r^2 column measures each country's degree of association with its own cluster.

yet standardized their accounting practice, which may explain the low average Index B score of 66.4 percent for this cluster. Cluster 3 comprises countries which are highly dependent on the IASC and, in general, have high scores on Conformity Index B, with an average of 89.1 percent. Cluster 2 contains the countries which set standards independently of the IASC, and which have a lower level of conformity, 72.9 percent, largely attributable to the nonconforming standards of Finland, Germany, and Mexico. Countries which had medium scores on the Unstandardized Index (ranging from 36 percent to 64 percent) were in cluster 4, and those with similar scores on the Independence Index (ranging from 52 percent to 72 percent) were grouped in cluster 5. As the results of the second cluster procedure were very similar,[13] there is evidence that these clusters represent different groupings on a meaningful dimension.

The clusters confirm the deep difference in country attitudes to the IASC, the IAS, and standard-setting that was highlighted by Table 2. The importance of the country differences in standard-setting is compounded by the presence of major stock exchanges (refer to Table 5). The latter are usually supervised by regulatory bodies that are independent of the accounting profession, and which may stipulate accounting treatments and specify disclosures as a condition of listing. Cluster 3 (IASC-dependent) and

[13] Because cluster analysis can yield unstable results, the data were subjected to a very different cluster procedure, VARCLUS, also available on SAS. VARCLUS, which utilizes an oblique principal component methodology, generated four clusters. Three clusters formed under this procedure were identical to the first three clusters shown in Table 3, with the sole exception of Yugoslavia, which was placed in cluster 2. The fourth cluster combined clusters 4 and 5 (again with the exception of Yugoslavia). The cluster summary for this procedure is shown below:

Oblique Principal Component Cluster Analysis

Cluster	Members	Cluster Variation	Variation Explained	Proportion Explained	Second Eigenvalue
1	10	10.00	9.49	0.940	0.415
2	15	15.00	14.06	0.937	0.798
3	11	11.00	10.30	0.936	0.579
4	18	18.00	16.88	0.937	0.649

Total variation explained = 50.72 Proportion = 0.939

cluster 1 (unstandardized) each contain only one major stock exchange country (Singapore and Switzerland, respectively). Eight of the world's major stock markets are located in countries appearing in cluster 2, which exhibits high IASC-independence. Three major markets operate in countries in cluster 5, which represents medium to high levels of IASC-independence. (The remaining exchange is in Luxembourg, which was not included in the IASC survey.) These findings are consistent with Choi (1973) and Pratt and Behr (1987), who noted the association between accounting disclosure and the development of capital markets.

If the IASC is to make real progress with its comparability initiative, the preceding analysis of conformity with IAS suggests that the IASC must win the support not only of the standard-setters but also of the regulators in the countries hosting the world's major stock exchanges. At the very minimum, ED32 requires the active endorsement of the United States, Japan, and the United Kingdom, which are the three largest markets and together have 50.8 percent of the total listings on major exchanges.

Country Conformity with ED32

The existing accounting requirements of five major countries were reviewed for conformity with ED32. Canada, France, Japan, the United Kingdom, and the United States were chosen for three reasons: (1) they were founder members of the IASC; (2) they are economically significant; and (3) they each host major stock exchanges, which together accounted for 91.1 percent of the annual turnover on major exchanges in 1986. Table 4 indicates the potential areas of conflict if ED32 in its present form were to be issued as a standard.

Revised IAS11 eliminates the completed contract method of accounting for construction contracts, whereas the five countries currently permit this treatment. Likely to be of greater economic significance are the changes that would ensue from the adoption of revised IAS22, which requires that positive goodwill be amortized over 5 and certainly no more than 20 years. Canada follows the American practice of a 40-year amortization period. The preferred (at the time of writing) British treatment, the immediate write-off of goodwill, would also be unacceptable.

The number of "No discussion" entries in the table is quite compelling. Some reflect an absence of a standard on a particular topic while there may be an understood practice which is not documented in country GAAP. However, a number have arisen because ED32 is breaking new ground, particularly in the areas of foreign currency and long-term investments. The IASC has also undertaken a major project on financial instruments, which were therefore excluded from the Comparability Project.

Canada and the United Kingdom would continue to exhibit a high degree of conformity with revised IAS, as each has only four areas of conflict. The United States has five, Japan six, and France nine potential departures from revised IAS. There will doubtless be opposition from countries whose accounting treatments are to be eliminated by ED32. While many countries are in compliance with either required, preferred, or allowed treatments, there are a number of instances where prevailing domestic practice would not conform. Even in those countries whose standards are in complete agreement with existing IAS, major adjustments may have to be made by companies that had selected any of the 23 treatments now prohibited, and minor adjustments would be necessary to provide a reconciliation from any allowed alternative selected to the benchmark provided by the preferred treatment. If each country chooses to ignore IAS in the area of noncompliance, little progress will be made in the quest for comparability. Perhaps the only practical way is for each country to "suffer" to some extent in the interest of achieving standards that are more comparable internationally.

The IASC Comparability Project: What Next?

Significant accounting policies in individual countries are likely to be at variance with revised IAS as prescribed by ED32. This raises the question of how national policy-setters and regulators will react to the Comparability Project. The responses from these groups will largely determine the future for comparable international standards. The spectrum of responses ranges from adoption of the revised IAS, through lobbying to change the less attractive features of the proposed standards, to maintaining the status quo. Potential responses to the Comparability Project, from the most optimistic to the most pessimistic, include:

(A) IASC standards as amended by Exposure Draft 32 are adopted or incorporated in national standards by both national policy-setters and regulators.

(B) Regulators and/or national policy-setters *require* reconciliation to the IASC required or preferred standards in the primary financial statements.

TABLE 4 *Current Country Compliance with Revised IAS*

Standard	Canada	France	Japan	UK	USA
IAS 2 Inventory	FIFO-Preferred LIFO-Allowed	Preferred	Possibly NIC	Preferred	FIFO-Preferred LIFO-Allowed
IAS 8 Prior Period Adjustments	Preferred	Statement disclosure may be acceptable. Footnote disclosure may not be in compliance.	Statement disclosure may be acceptable. Footnote disclosure may not be in compliance.	Preferred	Preferred
IAS 9 R & D	Preferred	Preferred	Preferred	Preferred	Preferred
IAS 11 Contracts	Capitalization-Allowed Percentage-Required Completion-NIC	Capitalization-Allowed Percentage-Required Completion-NIC	Capitalization-Allowed Percentage-Required Completion-NIC	Percentage-Required Completion-NIC	Percentage-Required Completion-NIC
IAS 16, p. 36 Fixed assets	Cost-Preferred Valuation-Allowed	Preferred	Preferred	Cost-Preferred Valuation-Allowed	Preferred
p. 47	ND[a]	NIC[b]	N/A[c]	ND	ND
IAS 17 Leases	ND	ND	ND	Required	Required
IAS 18 Revenue recognition	ND	ND	ND	ND	ND
IAS 19, p. 45a Retirement Benefits	Accrued-Preferred Projected-Allowed	NIC	NIC	NIC	Preferred
p. 5	Required	ND	ND	NIC	Required
p. 45c	Required	NIC	NIC	NIC	Required
IAS 21, p.28–30 Foreign Currency	Required	NIC	Required	Required	Required
p. 31	ND	ND	ND	ND	ND

p. 32c	Required Closing-NIC	Average-Required	NIC	Required	Required
p. 33	ND	Possibly NIC Losses-Preferred	ND	Required	Required
p. 34	ND Gains-NIC		ND	ND	ND
IAS 22 Business combinations					
p. 36–38	Required Pooling-NIC	Purchase-Required	Required	Required Pooling-Possibly NIC	Purchase-Required
Positive goodwill p. 40–42	Asset-Required Life 40-NIC	Required	Required	NIC	Asset-Required Life 40-NIC
Negative goodwill	Preferred	NIC	ND	NIC	Required
Minority interests p. 45	ND	ND	ND	ND	ND
IAS 23	Preferred Asset-Allowed	Expense-Preferred Asset-Allowed	Expense-Preferred Asset-Allowed	Expense-Preferred Asset-Allowed	Expense-Preferred
Capital. interest	Preferred		Preferred	Preferred	Preferred
IAS 25 Long term investments					
p. 47 Individual	Preferred	ND	Preferred	Preferred	NIC
p. 45	ND	ND	ND	NIC	ND
p. 46	Possibly NIC	ND	ND	ND	NIC
p. 48, 49	ND	ND	ND	ND	Required
p. 50	ND	ND	ND	ND	ND

[a]ND = Not discussed in standards
[b]NIC = Not in compliance
[c]N/A = not applicable

(C) Regulators and/or national policy-setters encourage adoption of or reconciliation to the IASC's benchmark in supplementary financial statements or notes to the primary financial statements.

(D) There is no international movement toward adoption of the new IASC standards.

This section debates the potential responses from two groups of countries: (1) those that are dependent on the IASC for setting standards; and (2) those that set standards independently of the IASC. The third group, countries that have not yet fully standardized their accounting treatments, may move closer to the IASC or may follow the leading independent countries in their economic sphere of influence.

IASC-dependent Countries

ED32 eliminates some 23 presently acceptable accounting policies. Immediate adoption of the revisions could have adverse economic consequences for companies required to comply with the revised standards. The stock market reaction to the new presentation (or new information) is unpredictable. However, if compliance with revised IAS alters accounting income, there may be an impact on tax flows. The dependent group, which in the past required primary financial statements prepared in accordance with international generally accepted accounting principles (I-GAAP), may be reluctant to endorse full adoption of ED32. Instead, they may encourage, rather than require, conformity with IAS, at least in the near-term, to permit companies to phase in the new standards. The creation of the transitional period also allows the accounting profession and the corporate CFOs time to debate

the tax impact of these changes with national revenue authorities. Alternatively, these countries may require the preparation of secondary financial statements in accordance with I-GAAP. This approach is without tax consequences and may promote greater domestic comparability than presently obtains. However, companies are then burdened with the additional reporting requirements. A hybrid alternative would give companies the option of preparing either primary or secondary financial statements in accordance with revised IAS. This may be a viable option in the short-run for countries like Singapore that have adopted IAS in the past.

IASC-independent Countries

As noted earlier, these countries have strong accounting institutions and, as hosts to most of the world's major stock-markets, have well-developed regulatory functions. The response of the standard-setters and regulators in these countries is critical for the Comparability Project. If IASC standards, as revised, are adopted by many countries as their national standards, international comparability in practice would be greatly enhanced. This is especially true if countries with large capital markets adopt these standards. However, for IASC standards permitting a preferred and/or alternative treatment, domestic comparability may be somewhat inhibited, despite the reconciliation that is required for the allowed alternative in countries that currently permit only one accounting treatment. National standard-setters, if unwilling to relax their standards in such cases, may adopt the IASC's proposals piecemeal.

If IASC standards are widely adopted, it would be appropriate for the current composition of the IASC to change. National standard-setting groups, such as the FASB, and other groups currently recognized on a consultative basis, such as the UN, the OECD, or the EC, might be invited to become full members of the IASC. There arises an interesting question of the relationship between the IASC and the national standard-setting groups. If the IASC emerges as a forum for consultation, a cooperative relationship may develop. On the other hand, if the IASC becomes the primary originator of new financial accounting and reporting standards, the role of the national standard-setting groups may diminish. Daley and Mueller have argued that national standard-setters might find that they were "relegated" to "lobbying for the interests of their local constituencies at the international level."[14] The current behavior of European Community members lends support to this view. The resolution of this issue may hinge on the locus of enforcement powers.

In theory, existing IAS apply to all public and private companies in the member countries. However, as there is no enforcement mechanism, current conformity varies greatly within this group (see cluster 2, Table 3). In our opinion, it is highly unlikely that this situation will improve with ED32. If these countries support ED32 at all, they may choose to restrict required conformity to a subset of firms in their jurisdiction. For example, in declining order of size of domain, IAS conformity may be required of (1) only listed domestic public companies; or (2) listed public companies whose securities are registered on foreign exchanges; or (3)

foreign companies seeking a listing on a domestic exchange. The first case has obvious implications for national standards. The second and third cases create the possibility of dual standards if countries were to accept I-GAAP in lieu of domestic GAAP for foreign registrants. Alternatively, countries may require that foreign financial statements be supplemented by a reconciliation to I-GAAP.

A. IASC Standards Adopted as the National Standards

It could be argued that all listed public companies should use international standards. No company is purely domestic if individuals or institutions from other countries can purchase its shares. The needs of a German, Japanese, or Australian investor for adequate and accurate information, coupled with investor protection, when purchasing shares of a U.S. company on the New York Stock Exchange, should be given as much consideration as the needs of a domestic investor.

It is possible that IASC standards could be adopted as the national standards in those countries which have in the past partially or fully adopted IASC pronouncements. However, the likelihood that both national standard-setters and regulators would adopt or revise national standards to conform with IASC standards is remote in countries with strong national policy-setting groups. For example, consider the posture of the EC regulators. The Fourth Directive permits a variety of accounting treatments, whereas ED32 permits at most a choice of two. In the Brussels Conference, the Commission concluded:

> *The time is not ripe for future accounting directives . . . for the foreseeable future, there will be no reduction of options and*

[14]Lane A. Daley and Gerhard G. Mueller, "Accounting in the Arena of World Politics." *Journal of Accountancy*, Vol. 153, No. 2 (February 1982): 40–46, 48, 50.

no extension of the directives to cover subject areas not previously addressed.[15]

More than a decade ago, the International Federation of Stock Exchanges "recommended to its member exchanges situated in IASC countries to require as part of the listing requirements reference to the adherence to international standards of accounting."[16] No country has yet undertaken this step. Canada, a prominent exception in this regard, currently encourages companies to follow IAS, and to disclose that fact in their annual report (Turner, 1983).[17] For example, GE Canada's 1988 annual report indicated in the Summary of Significant Accounting Policies: "These principles also conform in all material respects with International Accounting Standards on a historical cost basis." Some 100 Canadian companies, barely 9 percent of the listed companies, make such disclosures.[18] Even fewer companies in other countries disclose conformity with IAS. A rare exception is the French company Lafarge Coppée (see its English language annual report for 1988).

---

[15] Federation des Experts Comptables Europeens (FEE). "The Future of Harmonisation of Accounting Standards within the European Communities." Memorandum on Commission Conference 17/18 January, 1990, dated January 19, 1990.

[16] Seymour M. Bohrer, "Harmonization of Accounting." Pp. 198–205 in *Accounting for Multinational Enterprises.* Edited by Dhia D. AlHashim and James W. Robertson (Indianapolis: Bobbs-Merrill Inc., 1978).

[17] John N. Turner, "International Harmonization: A Professional Goal." *Journal of Accountancy,* Vol. 155, No. 1 (January 1983): 58–64, 66.

[18] John Kirkpatrick, "The Case for Visible Conformity." *Accountancy,* Vol. 99, No. 1121 (January 1987): 17–18.

B. Regulators Require Use of or Reconciliation to IASC Standards (in effect dual standards are promulgated)

Here, the regulators would require compliance with IASC standards only by foreign filers. For example, the SEC may require Mexican or Thai companies to use IASC standards if they wish to list on U.S. exchanges.

If a country does restrict the range of companies required to conform with IAS, two tiers of financial reporting are erected. Dual standards on a single exchange pose the question of preferential treatment for international filers vis-à-vis domestic filers. (Foreign international filers on the London Stock Exchange have been permitted to file statements prepared in accordance with I-GAAP for some years.) This problem is particularly salient in countries where domestic standards may be considered more complete or more rigorous than comparable IASC standards. The dual standards issue also creates a problem for international filers in the preparation of their domestic statements. This happens to a certain extent today, and some believe that it clouds rather than clears the comparability issue, and raises questions about the "fair presentation" of any given set of financial statements.

From a preparer's point of view, this approach might result in extra costs to prepare and disseminate dual sets of financial statements, designed for the domestic and international marketplaces. Whether this cost is great enough to offset the benefits of being able to file on various exchanges that recognize IAS is an empirical question. At the OECD forum in 1985, representatives of Shell International and Du Pont spoke in favor of international harmonization. In their view, it "would save costs, help understanding of accounting numbers of overseas subsidiaries, open up capital markets, etc."[19] There is little concrete evidence for these beliefs. However, Eiteman and Stonehill suggest that the "recent trend for European and Japanese firms to request bond ratings by Moody's and Standard and Poor's (supports) the idea that executives may believe further disclosure may reduce the cost of debt."[20] However, it is expected that using one set of financial statements to access several exchanges at the very least would provide considerable cost savings.

This scenario raises problems of attestation. Are the revised IASC standards set forth in such a complete and detailed manner that two different preparers would arrive at the same treatment? If not, it may be difficult for auditors to issue an opinion that states the financial statements "fairly present" or present "a true and fair view."[21] Further, would the regulators accept unaudited I-GAAP financial statements? Would domestic auditors extend the domestic opinion to the international financial statements, or would a separate opinion be required?

C. Regulators Encourage the Use of or Reconciliation to IASC Standards

Countries which are in the independent group and display low levels of confor-

mity with current IAS, such as Germany and Mexico, are likely to do nothing, or at the most, encourage some form of reconciliation. Members of the unstandardized group may do likewise. Optimistically, some of these may encourage the preparation of secondary financial statements, as may high conformity members of the independent group. A lower cost, and a less useful alternative, would be the preparation of a statement reconciling the reported income number to the one which would have resulted if revised IAS has been applied.

A reconciliation requirement for all filers would place a burden on preparers in countries with significant differences between domestic and I-GAAP. For example, Table 2 shows that eight of the 54 countries in the IASC survey currently do not comply with IAS3 (consolidations), 27 are not in compliance with IAS15 (inflation accounting), and 18 countries do not comply with IAS26 (postretirement benefits). Clearly, the costs of preparing a reconciliation in these countries would be significant. The legal ramifications of reporting under two standards must also be resolved. A reconciliation requirement, whether imposed on domestic or on international filers, also raises the attestation issues discussed earlier. Thus, standard-setting groups might be pressured by preparers and international audit firms to adopt at least some IASC standards in order to reduce financial statement preparation time and expense. Alternatively, the IASC might face continual pressure to permit more options, which would defeat the purpose of the Comparability Project.

The (British) Accounting Standards Committee, chaired by Mr. Renshall, has already opposed ED32's reconciliation requirement on two grounds.

---

[19] Rolf Rundfelt, "Views From Abroad: Europe." *Journal of Accounting, Auditing & Finance,* Vol. 9, No. 1 (Fall 1985): 85–88.

[20] David K. Eiteman and Arthur I. Stonehill, *Multinational Business Finance* (5th ed.). (Reading, Mass.: Addison-Wesley, 1989).

[21] The recent issue of Statement on Auditing Standards No. 51, "Reporting on Financial Statements Prepared for Use in Other Countries," by the (US) Auditing Standards Board has heightened the U.S. auditing profession's awareness of the difficulties.

There was concern that the IASC would seek:

> to override the requirements of national securities exchanges. There was a danger that there would be two reconciliation statements, one from the relevant securities exchange and one from the IASC and that would not be particularly useful (quoted by Spink).[22]

Doubtless, there will be support for the ASC's position from other policymakers. The disclosure of two sets of income and shareholders' equity amounts might prove confusing to users of the financial statements, thrusting the issue of dual standards into prominence. Whether the benefits of this reconciliation process outweigh the problems related to dual standards is an unsettled issue. However, even with the extra preparation time required for a reconciliation, international filers would most certainly benefit if IOSCO members accept a single reconciliation to I-GAAP income for access to their exchanges.

The Comparability Project: Prerequisites for Success

It would seem that there are three major obstacles which must be overcome in order for the Comparability Project to be successful. First, the member countries must be willing to cooperate with the IASC, rather than fight to promote their national interests. Second, regional efforts at harmonization must be restrained or otherwise subordinated to the IASC's endeavors. Third, the IASC must vigorously pursue its aims, and must be sufficiently funded to enable it

to achieve them. These points are developed further below.

The level of cooperation among IASC members appears to be the most critical concern. If, for example, each IASC member vehemently opposes the parts of the ED32 having the greatest effect on its national standards, the IASC may be unable to go forward with the project. Alternatively, the project may be so diluted as a result of lobbying that it garners little support from bodies such as IOSCO. Such a scenario would weaken the position of the IASC and reduce its influence over the development of international standards. Some fear that the "do nothing" alternative might lead to the de facto international adoption of American standards.[19,23] Simmonds considered that:

> there are only two credible pretenders to the crown of international standards setter—US GAAP and the IASC. The case in support of US GAAP is that it is already in a commanding lead over other national alternatives. . . . its standards show the natural signs of domestic influence—including unavoidable fiscal implications that are not applicable elsewhere. . . . I question whether US standards could adequately reflect the needs of groups operating in non-US international environment.[24]

Following Simmonds' reasoning, there may be a corps of countries that prefer the IASC to the alternative.

There are two different, but perhaps overlapping, approaches to harmonization, the first focusing on accounting

---

[22] Hazel Spink, "ASC Refuses to Yield on World Standards." (Newspaper, 1989).

[23] Paul Rutteman, "Demands of a Different Environment." *Accountancy* (October 1987): 17–18.

[24] Andy Simmonds, "Bridging the European Gap." *Accountancy* (August 1989): 29.

practices and the second on disclosure.[25] The IASC Comparability Project has addressed measurement issues, and has not broadened the disclosure requirements. The SEC Policy Statement[26] suggests that the ultimate goal should be the development of an integrated international disclosure system and would like to see more detail in IAS standards and greater coverage of topics. IOSCO has hinted that international accounting standards might eventually be used in prospectuses of MNE offerings, provided several problems can be overcome: the elimination of most accounting choices, and increased detailed guidance contained in each statement and increased breadth of coverage of the standards as a whole. The SEC has made similar statements. FASB's current chairman indicated in a presentation to the IASC that:

FASB would support an objective that seeks to create superior international standards that would gradually supplant national standards as the superior standards become universally accepted.[27]

As to the question of restraining regional efforts at harmonization, Choi argued that "harmonization efforts within clusters may be a more fruitful

and feasible development strategy that attempts to harmonize accounting standards on a worldwide basis."[28] Others have warned that the present efforts[29] of the EC to harmonize accounting standards within that community "pose a serious obstacle to development of worldwide standards."[30] Similar observations have been made by McComb[31] and Choi and Mueller.[32] Damant commented, "it is bad enough having so many different national standards. The last thing which is needed is a complication of international harmonization by the establishment of regional standards."[33]

Despite the comments expressed ear-

[25] Philip M. Reckers and D. J. Stagliano, "International Accounting Standards: Progress and Prospects." *Survey of Business*, Vol. 16, No. 4 (Spring 1981): 28–31.

[26] Securities and Exchange Commission (SEC). "Regulation of International Securities Markets." Policy Statement (November 1988).

[27] Dennis R. Beresford, "Internationalization of Accounting Standards: The Role of the Financial Accounting Standards Board." *Financial Accounting Standards Board Status Report*, Series 065, No. 195 (June 1988): 3–6.

[28] Frederick D. S. Choi, "A Cluster Approach to Accounting Harmonization." *Management Accounting*, Vol. LXIII, No. 2 (August 1981): 17–31.

[29] For a more detailed discussion of the progress of harmonization within the European Community, see the following articles by Van Hulle: Karel Van Hulle, (a). "The EC Experience of Harmonisation—Part I." *Accountancy* (September 1989): 76–77. (b). "The EC Experience of Harmonisation—Part II." *Accountancy* (October 1989): 96–99.

[30] Richard D. Fitzgerald, "International Harmonization of Accounting and Reporting." *International Journal of Accounting, Education and Research*, Vol. 17, No. 1 (Fall 1981): 21–32.

[31] Desmond McComb, "International Accounting Standards and the EEC Harmonization Program: A Conflict of Disparate Objectives." *International Journal of Accounting, Education and Research*, Vol. 17, No. 2 (Spring 1982): 35–48.

[32] Frederick D. S. Choi and Gerhard G. Mueller, *International Accounting* (2nd ed.). (Englewood Cliffs: Prentice-Hall Inc., 1984).

[33] David Damant, "Accounting Standards: Europe and the World." *European Accounting Focus* (May 1989): 14–15.

lier, members of the EC Commission in Brussels, such as Van Hulle,[34] see their efforts as consistent with international harmonization. Clearly, the IASC and the EC must work together to develop international standards. The current president of the Federation of European Accountants (FEE) also espoused this view.[35] Mr. Carey of the Accounting Standards Committee (ASC) said, "the UK profession's view is very clear. We believe harmonization should be through international standards and the IASC."[36] These views apparently prevailed, for the Commission Conference on accounting standards, held in Brussels in January 1990, recognized the IASC as "the appropriate forum for worldwide work in this field, and it was decided that the community would strengthen its input to IASC."[15]

Sir Henry Benson, a former IASC chairman, noted the key prerequisites of harmonization: focused leadership; reconciliation to a single set of international standards; compliance with international standards to be a requirement for stock exchange listing; national standard-setters to be on the IASC standard-setting board; greater industry involvement in standard-setting; and national accounting bodies to use disciplinary action to enforce IAS.[37] During

the last decade, the IASC has worked diligently on Benson's program for harmonization, perhaps spurred by the fear that the accounting profession might lose control of setting international standards,[38] and is now poised to meet several of Benson's prerequisites if the major funding problems of the IASC can be overcome: funding structure and level of financial support.

Currently, the IASC's budget is funded by IFAC, which, in turn collects membership fees from the member institutions. The IASC's effectiveness as a supplier of international accounting standards would doubtless be enhanced by restructuring the funding procedures to include direct contributions and increasing the membership fees. Without significant increases in the budget, there is little hope that the IASC can meet the challenge of providing detailed and complete international standards, without excessive reliance upon its previous pillars of support, the United Kingdom and the United States.

Is Harmonization Desirable?

Many professionals have questioned whether harmonization is feasible or even desirable.[39] They acknowledge that individual and institutional investors are not deterred by country boundaries in the selection of investment portfolios. Total transactions in U.S. corporate securities for foreigners in 1988 totaled US$452.7 billion. Total transactions in U.S. securities (includ-

[34] Karel Van Hulle, "Harmonisation of Accounting Standards Throughout the EC." *European Accounting Focus* (Spring 1989): 11–13.

[35] IASC, "FEE address to the IASC, April 1989." *IASC News*, Vol. 18, No. 2 (June 1989).

[36] Carey, quoted in *Accountancy Age* (August 31, 1989).

[37] J. C. Burton (ed.), *The International World of Accounting. Challenges and Opportunities.* (Reston, VA: Council of Arthur Young Professors, 1981).

[38] J. A. Burggraaff, "IASC developments: an Update." *Journal of Accountancy*, Vol. 154 (September 1982): 104, 106–110.

[39] Richard Karl Goeltz, "International Accounting Harmonization: The Impossible (and Unnecessary?) Dream." *Accounting Horizons*, Vol. 5, No. 1 (March 1991): 85–88.

ing treasury and government securities) amounted to US$3,579.3 billion, an increase of US$263.9 billion over 1987. U.S. investors purchased or sold a total of US$594.5 billion worth of foreign stocks and bonds in 1988.[40] Foreign direct investments into the United States increased by US$58.4 billion in 1988.[41] Similarly, institutions in search of capital are addressing the global marketplace. For example, funds raised in international capital markets totalled US$225 billion in 1986, but amounted to US$347 billion in 1989.[42] Many companies have already obtained listings on stock exchanges outside their own country.

Table 5 summarizes the relative size of the stock markets in 14 countries and their annual turnover and activity levels. While the United Kingdom has the most listings, the United States is the largest market in terms of size and turnover. However, the Tokyo Stock Exchange is a very strong second on both dimensions.

The table also indicates the percentage of listings that are "foreign." The huge variation in the foreign percentage is readily discerned, with the smaller exchanges heavily dependent on foreign registrants. (For example, 61.5 percent of Singapore's and 59.2 percent of the Netherlands' listings are foreign.) However, the percentage of foreign listings on the world's busiest exchanges

is still rather small (NYSE and AMEX combined, 4.6 percent; Tokyo, 3.4 percent). This lends support to the argument advanced by the Technical Committee of IOSCO that a "primary impediment to international offerings of securities is that different countries have different accounting standards."[43]

As the table confirms, there is a significant volume of foreign registrations. However, the countries with stringent listing requirements (for example, the U.S.A. and Japan) are capturing little of this market (4.6 percent and 3.4 percent respectively of their total listings are foreign). By way of contrast, foreign registration in Singapore comprises 61.5 percent of the total. This table is significant evidence that companies seek to avoid rigorous accounting and disclosure requirements. (Saudagaran[44] has recently confirmed this finding.)

The economic consequences of this maneuvering are profound. First, the paternalistic notion, so dear to the regulators, of investor protection is completely undermined where investors can (and do) purchase securities in jurisdictions with relatively fewer requirements. Second, the financial services industry (from stockbrokers to analysts and beyond) is separated from market transactions that take place in Belgium or Luxembourg, for example, rather than at home, with significant loss of revenue to that sector. Third, it has been suggested that the costs of raising debt and equity in different markets is affected by the perceived rigor of the ac-

[40] U.S. Bureau of the Census. "Statistical Abstract of the United States, 110th edition." (Washington, DC: 1990): Tables 840 and 841.

[41] Federal Reserve Bulletin. "Monetary Policy Report to the Congress." (August 1989): A55.

[42] Organisation for Economic Cooperation and Development (OECD). "Financial Statistics." (December 1990).

[43] Quoted in *IASC News*, Vol. 18, No. 1 (January 1989): 2.

[44] Shahrokh M. Saudagaran, "An Empirical Study of Selected Factors Influencing the Decision to List on Foreign Stock Exchanges." *Journal of International Business Studies*, Vol. 19, No. 1 (Spring 1988): 101–127.

TABLE 5 *Major Stock Exchanges in 1986*

	Total Listings	Foreign Percentage	Market Size US$B	Av. size per listing US$M	Annual Turnover US$B	Activity %
Australia	1,193	2.6	78	65.4	27.0	34.6
Belgium	331	42.3	36	108.8	7.0	19.4
Canada	1,085	4.7	166	153.0	57.0	34.3
Denmark	281	2.5	*	NC	1.9	NC
France	1,100	20.5	150	136.4	56.0	37.3
Germany	673	26.9	246	365.5	136.0	55.3
Italy	184	0.0	141	766.3	45.0	31.9
Japan	1,551	3.4	1,746	1,125.7	954.0	54.6
Luxembourg	421	39.9	*	NC	*	NC
Netherlands	409	59.2	73	178.5	30.0	41.1
Singapore	317	61.5	33	104.1	5.0	15.2
Switzerland	339	57.2	132	389.4	*	NC
United Kingdom	2,613	19.6	440	168.4	133.0	30.2
United States	2,373a	4.6	2,203	928.4	1,374.0b	62.4
Total	12,870		5,444		2,825.9	
Mean	919.29	24.63	388.86	299.32	201.85	29.74
Std. dev.	759.65	22.43	662.25	345.14	403.01	19.90

Notes: US$B = US$ billions
US$M = US$ millions
* = Not given in data source
NC = Not calculable
a = New York and American Stock Exchanges combined
b = NYSE only

Activity is defined as Turnover/Market size and may be viewed as a measure of market breadth.

Market size and turnover data are taken from Exhibits 10.8 and 10.9 in Eiteman and Stonehill, 1989.[20] Total listings are taken from, and the foreign percentages are derived from, data presented in the report of the Staff of the U.S. Securities and Exchange Commission to the Senate Committee on Banking, Housing and Urban Affairs and the House Committee on Energy and Commerce on the Internationalization of the Securities Market, July 29, 1987. p. II-66.

counting policies and disclosure requirements. Fourth, there is anecdotal evidence from analysts, and others, suggesting that funds are misallocated (see Damant in Gernon, Purvis, & Diamond[45]) because economic differences between investment vehicles in different jurisdictions are obscured by different financial accounting treatments and disclosure practices. Trade negotiators representing the United States, in response to initiatives from FEE, have recently acknowledged that the use of I-GAAP "would facilitate expansion of trade in services by removing barriers caused by different national accounting requirements." Accordingly, they "have proposed that the General Agreement on Trade and Services (GATS) agreement should recognize the importance of International Accounting Standards."[46] In view of these factors, we share IOSCO's view that increased comparability is an important objective, and that the IASC is the best vehicle to realize this goal.

Conclusion

Moulin,[47] among others, identified prerequisites for improved IAS: sufficient detail to guide interpretation; increased

scope to cover key areas, including earnings per share, discontinued operations, and accounting for specialized industries; additional disclosure requirements; and standards developed with the needs of users in mind. It seems clear that ED32 does not meet all of these preconditions, yet that does not mean that the IASC's venture is a failure. The Comparability Project has narrowed the range of choices, a major criticism in the past, and has provided a forum for debate of comparability issues. The IASC offers an institutional means of addressing (and implementing) subsequent steps in the quest for comparability.

If global comparability of accounting standards is ever to be achieved, significant effort will have to be expended to alter the direction of accounting evolution, to emphasize international, rather than national, interests. It is important to recognize that whatever scenarios evolve, progress toward international comparability of accounting standards is likely to be slow and will not proceed in the same direction nor at the same pace in the various IASC-member countries. Changing domestic standards is a slow process; the economic, legal, and professional differences among countries provide additional complexity in the international arena.

The pace of a planned evolution to comparable international accounting standards will be affected by several important factors: the responses of the national standard-setters and regulators to the Comparability Project and the extent to which the intent of the Steering Committee survives the exposure draft phase; the reaction of IOSCO and national regulators to the final version, and the extent of their subsequent support for the IASC's international stan-

[45] Helen Gernon, S.E.C. Purvis, and Michael A. Diamond, "An Analysis of the Implications of the IASC's Comparability Project." *Topical Issues Study No. 3* (Los Angeles: SEC and Financial Reporting Institute, School of Accounting, University of Southern California, 1990).

[46] IASC, "Board Supports Commitment to International Accounting Standards." *IASC News*, Vol. 19, No. 4 (December 1990): 1.

[47] Donald J. Moulin, "Practical Means of Promoting Common Accounting and Auditing Standards." Paper presented at the 13th Annual Conference of IOSCO, Melbourne, 1988.

dards; and the way in which future IASC standards are developed. It is essential that they be drafted with a breadth of coverage and sufficient detail to provide implementation guidance, thus promoting the comparability envisioned by the IASC and to allay the concerns of certain regulatory bodies. Even standards that require one treatment or have a preferred and allowed alternative with a reconciliation will not result in comparability if they do not provide adequate implementation guidance. The IASC Board has accepted this criticism. In its updated five-year plan, the Board has pledged to revise existing IAS "to ensure that they are sufficiently detailed and complete and contain adequate disclosure requirements to meet the needs of capital markets and the international business community."[48]

To realize the intent of the Comparability Project will require a long-term sustained effort on the part of the IASC, which will need to increase its staff. Member countries must provide greater support, not merely in terms of financial contributions, but also in active promotion of IAS. As Kanaga observed, "if the IASC fails in its mission, the UN or regional governmental bodies will step in as the clamor grows to improve transnational reporting" (cited in Burton).[37] Finally, the IASC must win the commitment of standard-setters and regulators in at least three major markets—the United Kingdom, the United States, and Japan—for comparability to proceed.

[48] IASC, "IASC's Five Year Plan—Update." *IASC News,* Vol. 19, No. 4 (December 1990): 3.

Foreign Exchange Rate Hedging and SFAS No. 52—Relatives or Strangers?

Carol Olson Houston and Gerhard G. Mueller

Business newspapers, newsletters, and professional accounting newslines make frequent references to the growing importance of foreign exchange transactions and policies. Increasing numbers of U.S. companies are adopting foreign exchange and interest rate hedging programs.[1] Concurrently, there has been rapid growth in the foreign exchange markets in the U.S. Some observers

[1] Price Waterhouse, *Hedging: Foreign Exchange and Interest Rate Risk Management Implementation Guide* (U.S.A.: Price Waterhouse, 1986), p. 1.

have pointed to the demands of corporate clients to help explain the rise in hedging and changes in the foreign exchange market. Kubarych[2] suggested that:

> . . . [M]ultinational companies have had to absorb two major overhauls of accounting rules [for foreign exchange] in the space of six or seven years. These rule changes have had complex and often confusing implications for a company's foreign currency exposures and how to handle them . . .

[2] Roger M. Kubarych, *Foreign Exchange Markets in the United States,* revised edition (New York: Federal Reserve Bank of New York, 1983), p. 6.

Other evidence suggests that there have been changes in the market proportions of various instruments, markets, and participants. According to the 1983 Federal Reserve Bank of New York survey, while total foreign exchange trade by banks rose about 44 percent from March 1980 to April 1983, outright forward transactions reported by U.S. banking institutions with non-financial customers *declined* 16 percent. One explanation for this decrease is that corporate activity in the forward exchange market—and possibly in the foreign exchange market—*dropped* following adoption of the new accounting pronouncement on foreign exchange, SFAS No. 52.[3] Such a decline has been explained by the statement that "many U.S. multinational companies felt less need to hedge accounting exposure [after changing to the new accounting rule]."[4] This argument implies that exposures which firms felt impelled to hedge as long as the previous accounting standard, SFAS No. 8, was in effect, may no longer need to be hedged. Moreover, these exposures may no longer concern management in the same manner as they did earlier.

The recent changes in U.S. foreign currency markets and related market volume trigger questions about the continued adequacy of applicable financial accounting standards. A better understanding of "economic consequences"—if any—generated by the last round of FASB action in this area is essential to asking appropriate questions now. Our paper addresses several

[3] Michael D. Andrews, *Federal Reserve Bank of New York Quarterly Review* (Winter 1983–84), p. 70.

[4] Michael D. Andrews, *Federal Reserve Bank of New York Quarterly Review* (Summer 1984), p. 38.

aspects of the possible relationship between a financial accounting standard and its economic effects. We explore the impact of SFAS No. 52 on U.S. corporate foreign currency hedging activities. A measurable impact is found. Qualitative feedback on our survey questionnaire also revealed a number of financial management practice changes apparently related to the adoption of SFAS No. 52. Thus we conclude, on the basis of earlier evidence as well as our own, that FASB action, in the forms of SFAS Nos. 8 and 52, triggered observable "economic consequences." The limits of our data do not permit a judgment on whether SFAS No. 52 "consequences" merely succeeded in reversing the "consequences" of SFAS No. 8 for at least some firms.

Do Accounting Standards Affect Foreign Exchange Rate Hedging?

Two types of foreign currency gains and losses are recognized in the accounting standards governing financial statement preparation for companies with foreign activities. The first type results from entering into *transactions* involving one or more foreign currencies. Since exchange rates are not generally constant, transactions are often settled at different amounts than originally expected. The amount at risk when settlement occurs at a different rate is called transaction exposure. Foreign currency transaction gains (losses) reflect the effects on the firm of such changes in exchange rates.

Translation gains and losses, on the other hand, arise when firms translate financial statements of their foreign operations from a foreign currency to the U.S. dollar. No economic exchange per se underlies the translation process: gains and losses arise due to changes in exchange rates which have occurred since the previous financial statement measurement (translation) date. Translation exposure can be defined as those amounts which are at risk of producing translation gains or losses.

SFAS No. 8, the predecessor to the current foreign exchange pronouncement, gathered some strong advocates and many (vocal) foes, primarily as a result of its treatment of translation gains and losses. Under SFAS No. 8, all translation gains and losses were included in income. This accounting requirement often led to wide swings in a company's reported net income. Early critics predicted that firms would begin hedging translation exposure in order to protect reported net income from such volatility subsequent to SFAS No. 8's 1976 implementation date. Critics also predicted that firms would turn to forward exchange contracts, an instrument commonly used to hedge foreign currency risk, in order to mitigate income volatility. Hedging of translation exposure was criticized as uneconomic, as firms would incur real costs by purchasing forward exchange contracts and other hedging instruments in order to protect net income from paper losses. Business International Corporation, for example, reported that:[5]

The elimination of currency-translation reserves, and the inclusion of translation adjustments in earnings as they occur, are also forcing some companies to consider covering their potential translation losses via a forward exchange contract, incurring a real cost to protect what is essentially a bookkeeping adjustment, a policy frowned upon until now.

In 1981 SFAS No. 52 was issued to replace SFAS No. 8. Under this standard, translation gains (losses) may be excluded from income. Exclusion depends on the determination of the "functional currency" of a firm's foreign operations. Foreign subsidiaries whose functional currencies are designated to be those of the countries where the foreign operations are located do not include translation gains (losses) on the income statement. Instead, firms report the translation gains (losses) of these subsidiaries as a separate element of owners' equity on the balance sheet. Subsidiaries designated to have the U.S. dollar as their functional currency, however, must continue to include translation gains and losses in the determination of income.

As a result of this change, adoption of SFAS No. 52 could impact translation exposure hedging by firms. Specifically, the replacement of the much criticized SFAS No. 8 should induce managers to change previous foreign currency hedging activities. For firms whose subsidiaries have been designated to have local foreign functional currencies, we would expect to find a shift away from translation exposure hedging subsequent to adoption of the new standard.[6] For firms still required to report translation gains and losses as they did under SFAS No. 8, however, no change is expected in the level of translation exposure hedging undertaken. Income of those firms with U.S. dollar functional currency subsidiaries is still subject to volatility due to continuing inclusion of translation gains (losses).

---

[5] Business International Corporation, *Solving International Financial & Currency Problems* (New York: Business International Corporation, 1976), p. 42.

[6] This type of shift in hedging by firms does not imply that the total amount of hedging would decrease. Consequently, such a change would be consistent with growth in the foreign exchange markets.

EXHIBIT 1 *Assets and Sales Characteristics of Responding Firms[+] (in 000s)*

	Total Assets	Foreign/Total Assets	Total Sales	Foreign/Total Sales
Mean	$ 8,166,642	.2739	$ 9,232,695	.3265
Standard deviation	8,866,681	.1419	10,529,807	.1541
Median	4,762,350	.2571	5,361,250	.3150
Minimum observation	98,035	.0000	140,849	.0741
Maximum observation	32,541,000	.6384	46,986,000	.6515

[+] Excludes Datagraphix Inc., Maremont, and one firm which responded anonymously.

Firms Surveyed and Nature of Questionnaire

Previous research on related topics was examined in order to identify U.S. firms with foreign operations and those which hedged translation exposure while applying SFAS No. 8. Doukas identified 75 firms which reportedly hedged some proportion of their financial statement (translation) exposure. Rodriguez identified 70 firms which had foreign operations, many of them identical to those identified by Doukas. Rodriguez's firms were not categorized by hedging activities. The firms identified by Rodriguez and Doukas, augmented by the 35 member firms of the Financial Executive Institute's Committee on Corporate Reporting, provided a total of 123 firms to which questionnaires were sent.

The questionnaire was designed to collect data regarding changes in policy as well as changes in levels of actual hedging. Questions about hedging activities were explicitly limited to those hedges undertaken via financial instruments.[7] Topics included not only trans-

lation exposure hedging but also related foreign exchange risk management issues, e.g., transaction exposure hedging and policies and actions which could have been pursued in lieu of translation exposure hedging.

Responses Obtained

Questionnaires were mailed to 123 firms. Three questionnaires were returned as undeliverable and an additional firm without foreign operations was deleted from the sample. Of the remaining 119 firms, 65 firms responded (55 percent), resulting in 48 usable responses (40 percent). Data from two letter responses and 46 questionnaires are included in the analysis.[8]

Profile of Firms

Exhibit 1 presents information regarding the size and relative importance of foreign operations of responding firms. Two measures of size are reported: sales and assets. The relative importance of foreign operations to each firm was measured by the proportion of foreign assets to total assets and the proportion of foreign sales to total firm sales. From the information in Exhibit 1, respondent firms vary not only in size, but also

---

[7] Other hedges, specifically "natural" hedges where assets and liabilities of a subsidiary are matched to reduce exposure, are not considered. The purpose of this study was to evaluate the effect of a change in accounting requirements on hedging activities with positive economic costs.

[8] Since not all firms responded to all questions, there were sometimes less than 48 responses to a specific question.

EXHIBIT 2 *Industry Membership and Recent Hedging Practices of Responding Firms**

		Firm By Hedging Behavior				
SIC	Industry	NH/NH	NH/CH	H/CH	H/H	Total
	Unclassified	1			1	2
20	Food and kindred products				4	4
21	Tobacco			1		1
26	Paper and allied products				1	1
27	Printing, publishing, and allied industries		1			1
28	Chemicals and allied products	3	1	3	3	10
29	Petroleum refining	1		1		2
30	Rubber and miscellaneous plastics			1		1
32	Stone, clay, glass, and concrete products			1		1
33	Primary metal industries				1	1
35	Machinery, except electrical	2		1	3	6
36	Electrical and electronic machinery, equipment, and supplies	1	1	2	2	6
37	Transportation equipment	1			1	2
38	Instruments	1		2	1	4
45	Transportation by air		1			1
61	Credit agencies other than banks			1		1
63	Insurance				1	1
79	Amusement and recreation services except motion pictures	1				1
		11	4	13	18	46

*Excludes two letter responses from firms in the petroleum refining industry (Standard Industry Code 29). The "unclassified" category includes Maremont and one firm which responded anonymously to the questionnaire.

in relation to the proportion of firm operations conducted outside of the United States.

Industry Representation of Firms

Exhibit 2 provides information about the industries and the hedging practices of each responding firm before and after adoption of SFAS No. 52. Industries were identified based on the two-digit standard industry classification (SIC) codes. Four possible combinations of hedging practices in firms were identified. Firms which did not hedge transla-

tion exposure under either SFAS No. 8 or SFAS No. 52 were identified as nonhedgers, abbreviated as "NH/NH." Those firms which did not hedge translation exposure under SFAS No. 8 but have hedged translation exposure since adopting SFAS No. 52 were identified as nonhedgers which changed, or "NH/CH." Firms which hedged under SFAS No. 8 and either reduced the level of translation exposure hedging or ceased hedging translation exposure hedging after adopting SFAS No. 52 are identified as hedgers that changed, or

"H/CH." Finally, firms which hedged translation exposure while SFAS No. 8 was in effect and continue to hedge translation exposure under SFAS No. 52 are identified as hedgers, abbreviated "H/H."

Exhibit 2 shows that the 48 respondent firms represent 17 different U.S. industries. With the exception of the Food and Kindred Products code (20), for those industries where more than one firm responded, Exhibit 2 indicates that hedging practices were fairly diverse among firms in a given industry. Thus, no evidence of industry effects on the hedging practices is apparent for sample firms.

SFAS No. 8/SFAS No. 52
Hedging Changes

Questionnaires from 31 firms, or 67 percent, indicated that the firms hedged translation exposure under SFAS No. 8. Of those firms which hedged while SFAS No. 8 was in effect, 13 (42 percent) decreased or ceased translation exposure hedging after adoption of SFAS No. 52. Eighteen firms, or 58 percent of pre-SFAS No. 52 hedgers, continued hedging at the same level as before adoption of the new standard. The remaining 15 respondent firms indicated that they did not hedge foreign currency translation exposure while the previous standard was in effect. Of those 15, four began hedging subsequent to adoption of SFAS No. 52.

In other words, under SFAS No. 8, 67 percent of the firms surveyed hedged accounting (translation) exposure. Under SFAS No. 52, the proportion of sample firms hedging translation exposure decreased to 48 percent. A total of 17 firms, 37 percent of the sample, reported a change in translation exposure hedging activities subsequent to adopting SFAS No. 52.

Factors Relating to Hedging Activities

The sample was evaluated to determine whether any systematic differences could be identified between firms which hedged translation exposure and firms which did not hedge translation exposure. Two variables of interest were identified: size of the firm, and proportion of overseas operations of the firm. One sided t-tests were used to determine whether the data gathered supported conclusions drawn about factors relating to the hedging decision.[9]

The larger a firm, the more likely it is to have multiple foreign operations. As the number of foreign operations increases, the geographical diversity should also increase. The more geographically diverse a firm is, the more likely it is to have offsetting translation

---

[9] A t-test is a statistical procedure used to provide a measure of the likelihood of observing results found in data by chance. Based on the number of observations and the size of the difference between two identified groups in the data, one can conclude how frequently random chance would lead to observation of the result actually found. The t-test uses the sample standard deviation to standardize the difference between the arithmetic means of two groups. Small values of the t-statistic indicate that little difference between the two groups has been found; as the statistic increases, the likelihood that observation of the difference would result due to random chance decreases. Results of a t-test are usually thought to support a premise if the likelihood or frequency of chance occurrence is less than 5 or 10 percent. For example, a value of a "t" statistic which is "significant at the .028 level" indicates that the results observed in the data would only be observed 2.8 times out of 100 by random chance. A "one-sided" t-test is used in situations where the direction of the difference between the two groups found in the population can be predicted.

EXHIBIT 3 *Size of Firms in Relation to Hedging Policy Choices (in 000s)*

	Mean	Standard Deviation
Size defined by Assets:		
Pre-SFAS No. 52 Hedgers	$5,609,020	$5,822,995
Pre-SFAS No. 52 Nonhedgers	6,523,526	6,948,909
one sided t-test t = −0.43		
Post-SFAS No. 52 Hedgers	6,621,990	7,003,323
Post-SFAS No. 52 Nonhedgers	5,067,004	4,992,394
one sided t-test t = 0.81		
Size defined by Sales:		
Pre-SFAS No. 52 Hedgers	6,821,261	7,639,395
Pre-SFAS No. 52 Nonhedgers	6,923,501	8,294,145
one sided t-test t = −0.04		
Post-SFAS No. 52 Hedgers	7,292,150	8,290,981
Post-SFAS No. 52 Nonhedgers	6,365,376	7,261,635
one sided t-test t = 0.37		

exposure in its various subsidiaries. Thus, larger firms were expected to have less need for translation exposure hedging. Exhibit 3 presents the results of partitioning the sample by size and hedging policies. Size was evaluated both with respect to pre-SFAS No. 52 hedging activities and the hedging activities subsequent to adopting SFAS No. 52.

Exhibit 3 shows that the posited size difference between hedgers and nonhedgers is not supported. No significant difference in size between firms that hedged translation exposure before SFAS No. 52 was issued and firms that did not hedge was found. Similarly, no significant difference in size was found between firms which chose to hedge translation exposure and firms which did not hedge subsequent to adoption of the new standard.

Since the importance of foreign operations may not be well described by the absolute size of a firm, a relative measure of size of the foreign operations was also investigated. Our general premise was that the greater the propor-

tion of foreign operations, the more impact those foreign operations could have on the financial statements. As a result, firms with larger relative proportions of foreign operations would be more likely to hedge translation exposure. Exhibit 4 provides the results of comparing nonhedgers and hedgers based on relative proportions of assets (foreign assets/total assets) and sales (foreign sales/total sales). Results using sales as a measure of relative importance showed insignificant differences between hedgers and nonhedgers. Since translation exposure occurs as a function of a firm's exposed assets and liabilities, it is reasonable that sales would not explain a difference in hedging policies. The measure of size using relative proportions of foreign assets led to detection of a weakly supported difference between the two groups. Based on the results reported in Exhibit 4, firms with larger proportions of foreign operations are more likely to hedge translation exposure than firms with smaller proportions of foreign operations.

EXHIBIT 4 *Proportion of Foreign Operations in Relation to Hedging Policy Choices*

	Mean	Standard Deviation
Foreign Assets/Total Assets:		
Hedgers	0.306	0.149
Nonhedgers	0.237	0.141
one sided t-test t = − 1.37*		
Foreign Sales/Total Sales:		
Hedgers	0.328	0.148
Nonhedgers	0.331	0.141
one sided t-test t = − 0.06		

*significant at the .092 level

Timing of Adopting a New Financial Accounting Standard

Financial accounting standards compel firms to adopt, i.e., implement, the new requirements during the current year or within a certain number of months after issuance of the standard. SFAS No. 52 was unique from that perspective since the FASB allowed firms to adopt the standard in 1981, 1982, or 1983. Firms which adopted it before the standard became mandatory are called "early adopters." With regard to SFAS No. 52, two different interpretations of "early adopter" have been made. In the first, only firms applying the standard in the first year are considered to be "early adopters." Another interpretation would be that firms adopting the standard in either 1981 or 1982 were acting prior to the point in time at which the standard became mandatory, and hence are "early adopters." In either case, one might argue that firms which changed their hedging policies might be more inclined to adopt the standard earlier rather than later. As a result, we expected to see a greater proportion of firms which changed hedging activities among the companies adopting the standard in 1981, or even 1982. As Exhibit 5 shows, this is not supported by the data. Mandatory adopters and firms adopting in 1981 showed roughly the same proportion of firms which changed hedging activities. Adopters in 1982, on the other hand, showed a much smaller proportion of firms that changed their translation exposure hedging activities.

EXHIBIT 5 *Year of SFAS No. 52 Adoption in Relation to Observed Hedging Activities*

	Year of Adoption					
	1981		1982		1983	
Firms that changed hedging activities	8	44%	5	24%	4	44%
Firms that did not change hedging activities	10	56%	16	76%	5	56%
	18	100%	21	100%	9	100%

EXHIBIT 6   *Proportion of U.S. Dollar Functional Currency Foreign Operations in Relation to Observed Hedging Activities*

	Mean	Standard Deviation
Firms which changed hedging activities	22.3%	29.6%
Firms which did not change hedging activities	49.9%	45.6%
one sided t-test value t = − 2.00**		

**significant at the .028 level

Why Didn't All Firms Stop Hedging?

For the most part, nonhedging firms reacted to the new standard as predicted: 73 percent of nonhedgers under SFAS No. 8 were also nonhedgers under SFAS No. 52. Ten of the 31 hedgers, or 32 percent, ceased hedging after adopting SFAS No. 52. An additional three firms, or 10 percent, reduced translation exposure hedging. The remainder, 18 firms (58 percent), continued hedging translation exposure at the same level as under the previous standard. Various factors might explain why 13 firms changed translation exposure hedging practices but 18 firms did not.

As we proposed earlier, a change in hedging activities was expected to be related to the functional currency choices of each firm's foreign subsidiaries. Since firms with greater proportions of U.S. dollar functional currency foreign operations must continue to include translation gains (losses) in income, they may be less likely to change translation exposure hedging activities after adopting SFAS No. 52. This hypothesis is supported by statistical tests reported in Exhibit 6. Based on the results of those tests, we conclude that firms with higher proportions of foreign operations having U.S. dollar functional currencies were less likely to change hedging activities than those with lower proportions

of U.S. dollar functional currency operations. Firms showing less translation gains (losses) in their income statements were reducing translation exposure hedging activities—and firms which still have to report a larger proportion of those gains (losses) in their income statements did not. This finding supports the belief that translation exposure hedging activities were undertaken during the time that SFAS No. 8 was in effect in order to protect net income from wide swings.

Other Corporate Financial Management Policy Changes

Among ancillary financial management policy changes reported on our questionnaires, we found that centralized hedging functions are very prevalent among all firms observed, regardless of the individual firm hedging policies. Thus, a parent company perspective prevails when corporate hedging decisions are made. This suggests a linkage between functional currency choices and hedging decisions. It strengthens further the statistical relationship reported in Exhibit 6.

Some firms reported changing other policies and activities as a result of adopting the new standard. The most common change was in the denomination of loans. Fully 25 percent of our sample stated that they had shifted the denomination of corporate debt from U.S. dollars to foreign currencies as a result of adopting SFAS No. 52. Two firms reported changes in intercompany billing practices. One firm reported changing invoice currencies from U.S. dollars to local foreign currencies, and another firm reported establishment of a reinvoicing center as a result of adopting the new standard.

Five firms, or 11 percent of the respondents, indicated that they changed the firm's management evaluation system as a result of adopting SFAS No. 52. The major element which appears to have changed for those firms was the currency in which foreign managers were evaluated, i.e., the U.S. dollar or the local foreign currency. The U.S. dollar is the major currency used for evaluation of foreign managers for foreign operations regardless of the functional currency of the foreign operations.

Conclusions

We have presented evidence that translation exposure hedging undertaken with financial instruments did not cease upon implementation of SFAS No. 52. However, it appears that translation exposure hedging was reduced subsequent to adoption of the new financial accounting standard. In particular, firms which must no longer include all translation gains (losses) arising from their foreign operations in their income statements are more likely to have stopped or reduced hedging translation exposure. As one unidentified executive

stated, "There's less need to play around [hedge] under FAS 52 because the P & L isn't getting hammered."[10] Thus, our title question is answered to the effect that foreign exchange rate hedging and SFAS No. 52 are related— they are not "strangers."

Our evidence further permits the observation that in some firms SFAS No. 52 implementation triggered a number of changes in financial management practices. Foreign loans were redenominated, billing practices changed, and performance of foreign managers evaluated differently. Hence, our evidence shows that "economic consequences" appeared in the wake of the SFAS No. 52 mandate.

Our statistical analysis explained only a modest portion of the reasons why firms hedge foreign exchange translation exposure. We were unable to make statistical assessments of larger foreign exchange markets operating in the U.S. and of a plethora of new market instruments. Similarly, world market conditions and exchange rate prospects for the U.S. dollar or any other national currency were not analyzed. Each of these might, individually or jointly, have some effect on the hedging practices of U.S. corporations. As attention to the subject of foreign exchange hedging grows, inclusion of these factors may help to further explain corporate decisions relating to foreign currency hedging practices.

[10] Business International Corporation, *BIMR Handbook on Global Treasury Management* (New York: Business International Corporation, 1984), p. 68.

Cases

● **Case 17-1**

The advantages and disadvantages of the harmonization of accounting standards were summarized in this chapter.

Required:
Expand on these advantages and disadvantages. [*Hint:* You may wish to consult John N. Turner, "International Harmonization: A Professional Goal," *Journal of Accountancy* (January 1983), pp. 58–59; and Richard K. Goeltz, "International Accounting Harmonization: The Impossible (and Unnecessary?) Dream," *Accounting Horizons* (March 1991), pp. 85–88.]

● **Case 17-2**

Five approaches to transnational financial reporting were identified in the chapter.

Required:
a. List some of the advantages and disadvantages of using each approach.
b. Which approach do you favor? Why?

● **Case 17-3**

The Financial Accounting Standards Board has discussed certain terminology essential to both the translation of foreign currency transactions and foreign currency financial statements. Included in the discussion is a definition of and distinction between the terms *measure* and *denominate*.

Required:
Define the terms *measure* and *denominate* as discussed by the Financial Accounting Standards Board and give a brief example that demonstrates the distinction between accounts measured in a particular currency and accounts denominated in a particular currency.

● **Case 17-4**

There are several methods of translating foreign currency transactions or accounts reflected in foreign currency financial statements. Among these methods are current–noncurrent, monetary–nonmonetary, current rate, and the temporal method.

Required:
Define the temporal method of translating foreign currency financial statements. Specifically include in your answer the treatment of the following four accounts.
a. Long-term accounts receivable.
b. Deferred income.
c. Inventory valued at cost.
d. Long-term debt.

● **Case 17-5**

Reporting forward exchange contracts continues to be a significant issue in accounting for foreign currency translation adjustments.

Required:
a. Discuss the one-transaction and two-transaction approaches to reporting forward exchange contracts.
b. Discuss the proper accounting treatment for each of the following types of forward exchange contracts.
   i. Hedge of a recorded but unsettled foreign currency transaction.
   ii. Hedge of an identifiable foreign currency commitment.
   iii. Speculating in foreign currency.
   iv. Hedging a net investment.

● **Case 17-6**

In *SFAS No. 52,* the Financial Accounting Standards Board adopted standards for financial reporting of foreign currency exchanges. This release adopts the functional currency approach to foreign currency translation.

Required.
a. Discuss the functional currency approach to foreign currency translation.
b. Discuss the terms *translation* and *remeasurement* as they relate to foreign currency translation.

● **Case 17-7**

The level of development of a country's accounting system is impacted by several environmental forces.

Required:
Discuss some of the environmental forces that may influence the development of accounting standards and procedures in a particular country.

● **Case 17-8**

The International Accounting Standards Committee (IASC) was formed in 1973.

Required:
a. What is the purpose of the IASC?
b. How does the IASC attempt to achieve its objectives?

Recommended Additional Readings

Daley, L. A., and G. G. Mueller. "Accounting in the Arena of World Politics." *Journal of Accountancy* (February 1982), pp. 40–46, 48, 50.

Goeltz, R. K. "International Accounting Harmonization: The Impossible (and Unnecessary?) Dream," *Accounting Horizons* (March 1991), pp. 85–88.

Pratt, J., and G. Behr. "Environmental Factors, Transaction Costs and External Reporting: A Cross National Comparison." *International Journal of Accounting, Education and Research* (Spring 1987), pp. 159–175.

Turner, J. N. "International Harmonization: A Professional Goal." *Journal of Accountancy* (January 1983), pp. 58–64, 66.

Van Hulle, K. "The EC Experience of Harmonization: Part I." *Accountancy* (September 1989), pp. 76–77.

Van Hulle, K. "The EC Experience of Harmonization: Part II." *Accountancy* (October 1989), pp. 96–99.

Bibliography

AlHashim, Dhia D., and Jeffrey S. Arpan. *International Dimensions of Accounting.* Mass.: PWS-Kent Publishing Company, 1993.

Benjamin, James J., and Steven D. Grossman. "Foreign Currency Translation: An Update." *The CPA Journal* (February 1981), pp. 38–42.

Benson, Sir Henry. "International Accounting—The Challenges of the Future." *Journal of Accountancy* (November 1977), pp. 93–96.

Berton, Lee. "Arthur Young Professors' Roundtable: The International World of Accounting." *Journal of Accountancy* (August 1980), pp. 74–79.

Brown, Jan G. "The Development of International Accounting Standards." *Woman CPA* (October 1977), pp. 9–11.

Cairns, David. "A New Thrust for International Standards." *The Accountant's Magazine* (July 1987), pp. 24–25.

Choi, F. D. S., and V. B. Bavishi. "International Accounting Standards: Issues Needing Attention." *The Journal of Accountancy* (March 1983), pp. 62–68.

Choi, Frederick D. S., and Gerhard G. Mueller. *International Accounting.* Englewood Cliffs, N.J.: Prentice-Hall, Inc., 1984.

Dewhurst, Charles S. "Accounting for International Operations." *The CPA Journal* (January 1988), pp. 78–81.

Evans, T. G., and M. E. Taylor. "Bottom Line Compliance With the IASC: A Comparative Analysis." *International Journal of Accounting* (Fall 1982), pp. 115–128.

Evans, Thomas G. "Some Concerns About Exposure After the FASB's Statement No. 8." *Financial Executive* (November 1976), pp. 28–30.

Fantl, Irving L. "Problems with Currency Translation—A Report on FASB No. 8." *Financial Executive* (December 1979), pp. 33–37.

Hayes, Donald. "The International Accounting Standards Committee—Recent Developments and Current Problems." *International Journal of Accounting* (Fall 1980), pp. 1–10.

Hayes, Donald J. "Translating Foreign Currencies." *Harvard Business Review* (January–February 1972), pp. 6–18.

Kanaga, William S. "International Accounting: The Challenge and the Changes." *Journal of Accountancy* (November 1980), pp. 55–60.

Kirkpatrick, John L. "The Gaps in International GAAP." *Corporate Accounting* (Fall 1985), pp. 3–10.

Mueller, Gerhard G., Helen Gernon, and Gary Meek. *Accounting, An International Perspective,* 3rd ed. Illinois: Richard D. Irwin, Inc., 1994.

Nobes, Christopher. "Is the IASC Successful?" *The Accountant* (August 21–28, 1985), pp. 20–21.

Noble, Christopher, and Robert Parker, eds. *Comparative International Accounting.* Homewood, Ill.: Richard D. Irwin, Inc., 1981.

Norr, David. "Improved Foreign Exchange Disclosure for the Investor." *Financial Analysts Journal* (March–April 1977), pp. 17–20.

Rodriguez, Rita M. "FASB No. 8: What Has It Done For Us?" *Financial Analysts Journal* (March–April 1977), pp. 40–47.

Rule, John E. "The Practical Business Effect of Exchange-Rate Fluctuations." *The Arthur Andersen Chronicle* (September 1977), pp. 63–75.

Seidler, Lee J. "An Income Approach to the Translation of Foreign Currency Financial Statements." *The CPA Journal* (January 1972), pp. 26–35.

Shank, John K., Jesse F. Dillard, and Richard J. Murdock. *Assessing the Economic Impact of FASB No. 8.* New York: Financial Executives Research Foundation, 1979.

Shank, John K., Jesse F. Dillard, and Richard J. Murdock. "FASB No. 8 and the Decision Makers." *Financial Executive* (February 1980), pp. 18–23.

Shank, John K. "FASB Statement No. 8 Resolved Foreign Currency Accounting—or Did It?" *Financial Analysts Journal* (July–August 1976), pp. 55–61.

Shwayder, Keith R. "Accounting for Exchange Rate Fluctuations." *The Accounting Review* (October 1972), pp. 747–760.

Taylor, Stephen L. "International Accounting Standards: An Alternative Rationale." *Abacus* (September 1987), pp. 157–171.

Violet, William J. "A Philosophical Perspective on the Development of International Accounting Standards." *International Journal of Accounting Education and Research* (Fall 1983), pp. 1–13.

Watt, George C., Richard M. Hammer, and Marianne Burge. *Accounting for the Multinational Corporation.* New York: Financial Executives Research Foundation, 1978.

Wesberry, James P., Jr. "The United States Constitution and International Accounting Standards." *The Government Accountants Journal* (Winter 1987), pp. 32–37.

Willey, Russell W. "In Defense of FASB No. 8." *Management Accounting* (December 1979), pp. 36–40.

Author Index

Subject Index